E9-11 Interest Revenue, $160
E9-12 (1) Cash received from bank, $8,034
E9-13 Cash received from bank, $14,307.50
E9-16 (1a) Office Supplies Expense, $190,000
E9-17 (5) Cash paid, $16,050
E9-19 (1) Accrued Salaries Payable credit, $47,120
E9-21 (1b) Current ratio, 2.02
E9-22 (1) Credit to Salaries Payable, $91,702.70
E9-23 (1) Credit to Salaries Payable, $94,786.10
P9-1 No key figure
P9-2 No key figure
P9-3 (3) Adjusted balance, $33,730
P9-4 (1) Adjusted balance, $42,125
P9-5 (1c) Cash received, $5,057.81
P9-6 (1) April 11 cash received, $2,002.17
P9-7 No key figure
P9-8 (1c) Entry amount, $22,750
P9-9 (2) Corrected net income, $56,900
P9-10 (2) Total assets, $236,820
P9-11 (1a) Credit to Salaries Payable, $7,316.50

E10-1 Total cost, $58,700
E10-2 Land, $66,667
E10-3 (1) Drilling equipment, $115,000
E10-4 (1b) Depreciation expense, $9,500
E10-5 (5) Gain on trade-in, $100
E10-6 (2) SYD depreciation, $3,500
E10-7 (1) Straight-line depreciation, $13,000
E10-8 DDB depreciation, $1,000
E10-9 (3) SYD depreciation, year 2, $4,877
E10-10 (3) Gain, $7,000
E10-11 (4) Book value, $130,000
E10-12 (5) Loss on trade-in, $2,000
E10-13 (2) Book value, $2,000
E10-14 (1) Loss on exchange, $3,070
E10-15 (2) Loss on trade-in, $600
E10-16 (2) Loss on sale, $4,000
E10-17 (2) Depletion Expense, $200,000
E10-18 (2) Depletion Expense, $70,000
E10-19 (2) Total intangible assets, $243,600
E10-20 (2) Amortization Expense, $751
P10-1 (1c) Depreciation Expense, $760
P10-2 (3b) Loss on trade-in, $1,500
P10-3 (2) DDB depreciation, 1984, $2,625
P10-4 (1) Depreciation Expense, $8,219
P10-5 (2c) Loss on trade-in, $13,000
P10-6 12/31/86 Depreciation Expense, $17,255
P10-7 (4) Gain on sale, $100
P10-8 (5) Gain on trade-in, $5,667
P10-9 (3) Book value, Uranium, $24,000
P10-10 (3) Book value, Goodwill, $19,000

E11-1 (3) Gain on sale, $100
E11-2 August 31 loss, $28,000
E11-3 (2) December 31 unrealized loss, $30,000
E11-5 (1c) Debit to Cash, $15,000
E11-6 (4) $2,083
E11-7 (3) $77,217
E11-8 (1) Alternative 1, $26,544.80
E11-9 (1) 16%
E11-10 Present value of an annuity, $189,540
E11-11 (2) $34,464
E11-12 (5) $220
E11-14 Interest earned each period, $629.40
P11-1 (3) $1,600 loss
P11-2 (1) December 31 loss, $1,900
P11-3 No key figure
P11-4 (1) July 1, 1984 gain, $10,000
P11-5 (2b) Present value, $3,523,905
P11-6 June 1, 1985 loss, $1,171.51
P11-7 No key figure
P11-8 (1) $217,061.60
P11-9 (1) $21,493.50
P11-10 No key figure
P11-11 No key figure

E12-1 (4) Credit to Cash, $5,440
E12-2 July 1, 1985 credit to Cash, $8,640
E12-3 (4) Credit to Cash, $7,620
E12-4 Debit to Trucks, $19,497
E12-5 (2) Unamortized discount, $3,700
E12-6 June 30, 1984 debit to Interest Expense, $24,583.33
E12-7 (4) Income Summary, $63
E12-8 Effective rate, Case B, 12.7%
E12-10 (2) Premium of $63
E12-11 Effective rate, 8.125%
E12-12 (2) $11,000 credit balance
E12-13 Deferred Income Taxes Payable, 1985, $3,840
E12-14 (2) Interest Expense, $9,600
E12-15 (9) Lease Obligation, $35,118
P12-1 (4) Effective rate, 20 percent
P12-2 (2) Debit to Cash, $1,078
P12-3 (2) Credit to Cash, $108,000
P12-4 (3c) Liability, $78,562.50
P12-5 (1) $93,373
P12-6 (2) Long-term liability, $1,038,572
P12-7 (2) Credit to Cash, $200,000
P12-8 (2) Loss on retirement, $12,600
P12-9 Income tax, 1981, $6,900
P12-10 (1) $33,901

E13-3 (5) Dividends on common stock, $30,200
E13-4 (5) Debit to Dividends, $95,200
E13-5 (2) Debit to Machine, $3,100
E13-6 (6) Debit to Cash, $12,600
E13-7 (3) Total stockholders' equity, $2,560,000
E13-8 (6) $52,600
E13-9 (5) $1,400,000
E13-10 (1) Retained earnings, $49,500
E13-11 (3) $2.85 per share
E13-12 (1) Credit to Dividends Payable, $45,000
E13-13 (Case C) preferred stock, $16,000
E13-14 (2) Dividends paid, $172,485
E13-15 (4) Debit to Retained Earnings, $197,220
E13-16 (4) No journal entry
E13-17 (3) Debit to Retained Earnings, $19,500
P13-1 (5b) $151,000
P13-2 (1d) Credit to Cash, $100
P13-3 (4) Preferred stock, $6,400
P13-4 (2) Common stock, $100,984
P13-5 (1c) Credit to Cash, $100,000
P13-6 (1b) Total stockholders' equity, $277,000
P13-7 (2) Total stockholders' equity, $268,100
P13-8 (1) Total retained earnings, $334,000
P13-9 (2) Total stockholders' equity, $782,750
P13-10 (2) Total stockholders' equity, $395,800

E14-1 (2) Ending capital, $18,250
E14-2 (2) Garcia, Capital, $89,500
E14-3 (2) Total capital, $246,200
E14-4 Credit to Dr. Meek, Capital, $95,150
E14-5 (6) Armstrong's share, $23,425
E14-6 (5) Evan's share, $8,450
E14-7 (3) Total capital, $106,000
E14-8 (3) Total capital, $130,000
E14-9 (1) Credit to Skinner, Capital, $1,200
E14-10 (1) Credit to Zobell, Capital, $29,200
E14-11 (2) Debit to Abbott, Capital, $40,000
E14-12 (4) Debit to Johnson, Capital, $55,000
E14-13 (1) Debit to Freeman, Capital, $65,000
E14-14 Gain on sale of business, $12,000
E14-15 (2) Credit to Cash, $55,000
P14-1 (2) Joe Young, Capital, $22,000
P14-2 (3) Total capital, $89,200
P14-3 (2) Ellis, Capital, $15,400
P14-4 (1f) 1984 to Kearl, $25,495
P14-5 (3) Miller, Capital, $15,216.67
P14-6 (3) Gray, Capital, $18,000
P14-7 (6) Debit to Coyne, Capital, $30,000
P14-8 (1d) Debit to Roberts, Capital, $45,000
P14-9 (4) Loss on sale, $140,000
P14-10 (2) Olsen's share, $200

E15-4 (3) Net working capital provided, $3,340
E15-5 (2) Net cash provided, $2,400
E15-6 Total working capital from operations, $31,700
E15-9 Decrease in working capital, $90,000
E15-11 Cash from operations, $211,600
E15-12 Net income, $7,400
E15-13 Net increase in working capital, $140,000
E15-14 Total sources of working capital, $35,400
E15-15 Total uses of cash, $49

(Continued on back endpaper)

PRINCIPLES OF ACCOUNTING

Principles of Accounting SECOND EDITION

K. Fred Skousen
Brigham Young University

Harold Q. Langenderfer
University of North Carolina, Chapel Hill

W. Steve Albrecht
Brigham Young University

WORTH PUBLISHERS, INC.

Principles of Accounting, Second Edition

Manufactured in the United States of America

Library of Congress Catalog Card Number 82-61997

ISBN: 0-87901-219-6

Second printing, August 1983

Editor: Betty Jane Shapiro

Production: Kenneth R. Ekkens

Design: Malcolm Grear Designers

Cover design: Aki Nowroozi

Composition: New England Typographic Services, Inc.

Printing and binding: Rand McNally & Company

Worth Publishers, Inc.

444 Park Avenue South

New York, New York 10016

To Julie, Joan, and LeAnn

PREFACE

Accounting can be an exciting course. It provides an access to the dynamic world of business and the basis upon which all financial decision making rests. It can also be a difficult course. Not only is there a lot to learn, but we teachers of introductory accounting are sometimes inclined to emphasize accounting procedures before giving students a sufficient sense of their logic or even their usefulness.

In writing this book, one of our main objectives has been to convey to students the logic and usefulness of what they are being asked to do, to show them clearly how concepts and procedures fit together. To accomplish this, to help students understand the "whys" of accounting as they come to learn its "hows," we introduce subjects in a general manner before covering the details. The Prologue and Chapter 1, for example, set the stage for the study of accounting; Chapter 2 provides an overview of the financial statements before we carefully explain the mechanics of the accounting process in Chapters 3–5. Similarly, Chapter 8, which is an overview of the balance sheet, is followed by chapters covering specific balance sheet items and issues. The result is greater student comprehension of both the concepts and the procedures.

Creating just the right mix of conceptual and procedural coverage, shortchanging neither the basic procedures nor their underlying rationale, is also an objective within chapters. For example, a logical three-step method for determining and recording adjusting entries is described in Chapter 4. Using this approach, students can easily see and perform the mechanics of adjusting entries, and appreciate the reasons for them as well.

In a like manner, we have chosen to integrate the explanation of present value into Chapter 11 because it plays such a basic role in accounting for investments and long-term liabilities. This discussion, while elementary and nonmathematical, enables students to grasp the concepts readily and to use the present value tables in a wide variety of applications.

As an extension of this philosophy, seven of the chapters are followed by supplements. The basic concepts and essential procedures are presented in the chapters; the supplements expand upon procedural aspects, describe alternative or more complex techniques, or simply provide additional coverage. This use of chapter supplements allows instructors greater flexibility in choosing the amount of detail appropriate to their course.

A second objective in writing this book has been to streamline the coverage of certain topics, without sacrificing clarity or completeness. All important subjects are covered thoroughly, but the number of chapters (in comparison to other texts) has been reduced by eliminating redundancies. Chapter 10, on long-term operational assets, illustrates this point: Many texts have a chapter on property, plant, and equipment, another on intangible assets, and sometimes one on natural resources. Each of these chapters deals primarily with the accounting for the same four basic events: acquisition of assets, expiration of asset costs, maintenance and repair of assets, and the disposal of assets. In this text, we clearly distinguish between the three classes of assets and then discuss and illustrate the accounting procedures in one chapter. Students have no trouble understanding that the same concepts and procedures apply to all three classes of assets.

By eliminating some duplications in this way, we were free to treat more fully subjects that we consider to be of growing importance to contemporary accounting. For example, we provide chapters on nonprofit accounting and internal control because we believe that introductory students should be exposed to both topics.

Another objective has been to organize the book so that learning is reinforced. Each chapter is carefully structured to help students focus on important ideas and remember them. First, an outline of major topics to be covered gives students a sense of the chapter's objectives. Second, the definitions of key terms in the margins make it easier to learn terminology and later to review for exams. Third, several concise summaries within the chapter help students to assimilate the important terms and ideas just discussed. Finally, the end-of-chapter review and the list of key terms (with page references) serve as additional reinforcement.

Each chapter contains numerous and various kinds of questions, exercises, and problems. Each type is designed to test student understanding in a different way.

The comprehensive *review problem,* new to the second edition, covers each chapter's major concepts and procedures. The step-by-step solution provides students with a review of the chapter's major ideas from a different perspective than that offered in the chapter summary. In Chapter 5, for example, the review problem takes students through the entire accounting cycle.

The *discussion questions* test the student's understanding of terms and concepts. They can also be used to stimulate class discussion.

The *exercises* are brief, usually dealing with single concepts and procedures. They also provide useful classroom examples.

The *problems* generally take longer to complete and probe for a deeper level of understanding than the exercises. Several of the problems are identified as *unifying problems;* these require students to integrate several concepts. Some problems include *interpretive questions* that require students to analyze the computed results.

The questions, exercises, and problems are graded in difficulty so that students gain confidence as they review and test their understanding. Instructors can assign material that will challenge students up to the level appropriate to their course goals.

ADDITIONAL FEATURES OF THE SECOND EDITION

The text and end-of-chapter materials have been reviewed carefully by instructors and students who used the first edition, as well as by many other specialists and professors teaching the course. Thanks in large part to their suggestions, several major improvements have been made.

1. The accounting cycle is now covered in three chapters instead of two. The mechanics of double-entry accounting are explained more fully and at a more appropriate pace.
2. Other topics have also been expanded. A complete chapter on proprietorships and partnerships (Chapter 14) and a supplement on consolidated financial statements (following Chapter 15) have been added.
3. Some reorganization has resulted in better pedagogy. Chapter 2 has been shortened and simplified; it is now limited to presenting a general overview of the financial statements. Long-term investments (Chapter 11) are discussed just prior to long-term liabilities (Chapter 12) so that bonds as investments and bonds as obligations can be taught in tandem, and students can see the similarities and differences in the accounting for each.
4. The presentation of the funds statement has been simplified by use of the work sheet approach. The T-account approach is described in a supplement to the chapter.
5. Inflation accounting is given more attention, particularly in Chapter 6 (on income measurement) and Chapter 8 (on the balance sheet).
6. A complete chapter is now devoted to C–V–P analysis. It follows the chapter on cost behavior patterns and so provides immediate reinforcement of the rationale for distinguishing between fixed, variable, and semivariable costs.
7. In Chapter 25 on standard cost systems, two-variance analysis is used (instead of three) for evaluating performance in terms of variable manufacturing overhead costs. The variable costing approach is emphasized, since it is more appropriate for decision-making purposes.
8. Chapter 29 includes a section on tax considerations in capital budgeting. The chapter reflects the 1981 and 1982 changes in the tax laws.
9. The complete set of annotated financial statements of IBM Corporation are included at the end of the book for student reference throughout the course.

LEARNING AND TEACHING AIDS THAT ACCOMPANY THE TEXTBOOK

We have personally written all supplements that accompany the text to ensure that they were well coordinated with the text and with each other. We think the result is an integrated package that is unmatched in usefulness to students and instructors.

The *Study Guide* includes chapter outlines with textbook page references; detailed chapter reviews, tests for self-appraisal, including matching, true-false, and multiple-choice questions, and computational exercises; and solutions to the tests. In effect, use of the *Study Guide* will enhance comprehension by providing reviews of the main concepts and procedures, chapter by chapter, from several different angles, each of which tends to reinforce the others.

There are two *Practice Sets* that cover the accounting cycle and financial statement analysis. In a sense they are "mini" practice sets because they each require only 6 to 12 hours to complete. In addition, there are two sets of *Working Papers*—one for the financial accounting chapters and one for managerial accounting—for student use in solving the problems in the book.

A complete set of pedagogical aids is available to instructors. The new *Instructor's Resource Guide* is a significant addition to the second edition. It begins with a number of recommendations and alternatives for planning the course, and provides some useful data derived from our experience at Brigham Young University. The main body of the *Guide* contains chapter outlines, teaching suggestions, alternative examples for classroom use, and sample quizzes. The *Guide* should be very helpful to new instructors or graduate teaching assistants who wish to use the teaching notes and examples. The *Solutions Manual* includes answers to all discussion questions, detailed solutions to every exercise and problem, and solutions to the practice sets. These solutions are printed in oversize type for easy reading and for use in making additional transparencies. A set of *Transparencies* includes solutions to all problems and selected exercises. The Test Bank (1,600 questions) and a Computerized Test Generating System provide tailor-made exams. The Test Bank also provides two exams for every group of five chapters.

ACKNOWLEDGMENTS

We are deeply indebted to many people for their support and help with this book, most notably our families, our colleagues, our students, and our publisher. We are especially grateful to the accounting educators listed below who critiqued the manuscript for content and accuracy during its development. Our reviewers' comments have been candid, demanding, and extremely helpful.

Wilton T. Anderson, *University of Hawaii, Honolulu*
John Beegle, *Western Carolina University*
Robert Bracken, *Rhode Island College*
Polly L. Corn, *Virginia Polytechnic Institute and State University*
Joseph Green, *Fairleigh Dickinson University, Teaneck*
Susan S. Hamlen, *State University of New York, Buffalo*
Richard Hodges, *Western Michigan University*
Harold Holen, *Montana State University*
Keith R. Howe, *Brigham Young University*

Philip Jagolinzer, *University of Southern Maine*
Joseph Kaderabek, *Baldwin-Wallace College*
Richard F. Kochanek, *University of Connecticut, Storrs*
David L. Rozelle, *Western Michigan University*
Fred S. Schaeberle, *Western Michigan University*
Paul W. Schreiner, *Miami University, Miami, Ohio*
David Shields, *University of Florida*
Karl M. Skousen, *Brigham Young University*
Gaylord N. Smith, *Albion College*
David Stout, *Rider College*
Larry Sundby, *St. Cloud State College*

Special thanks are due to John Beegle for reviewing and working all new exercises and problems and to Karl Skousen for his assistance and advice on the manuscript. We also wish to thank our typists, Diann Porter and Pat Penland.

Finally, we have enjoyed an extraordinary working relationship with our publisher. Special recognition goes to Betty Jane Shapiro, whose editorial support and guidance have been invaluable, and to Ken Ekkens, for the care and attention he has given to the production of this text. We sincerely appreciate the efforts of all our friends at Worth Publishers.

K. Fred Skousen
Harold Q. Langenderfer
W. Steve Albrecht

January 1983

TO THE STUDENT

Welcome to the study of accounting! Many of you are seeking only a general understanding of accounting and have no intention of becoming accountants; others intend to have careers in this field and need a strong foundation upon which to build a knowledge of its principles and procedures. Regardless of your objective, if you will follow the suggestions here, you will be more successful in this course.

First, you should realize that accounting is as essential to commerce as language is to civilization. In fact, accounting is often called the language of business. Without it, we couldn't judge the success of economic activities. We wouldn't be able to plan our personal finances or our country's economic policies. Thus, accounting affects each of us. It provides the information upon which almost every financial decision is based. Recognizing its importance and far-reaching effects should motivate you to study hard, which is the key to your success in this course.

Second, accounting is best learned by doing. That is why so much homework is assigned and why it is essential that you do the homework regularly. Those students who learn most are the ones who do not fall behind. Accounting concepts build upon each other, so it is difficult to understand concepts and applications in later chapters if the material in earlier chapters is not fully understood. Answering the discussion questions at the end of each chapter is a good way to review the chapter and to test your understanding of the topics covered. If you are not able to answer some of the questions, you probably do not understand the concepts and procedures well enough, which means you should restudy the appropriate sections of the chapter. A *Study Guide* is available that highlights the major points of each chapter and provides questions and exercises (with solutions) to help you test your understanding.

Finally, we have found that many students attempt to do well in this course by memorizing details, including the solutions to specific problems. However, accounting problems tend to be unique, each with a slightly different twist; so a better approach is to try to understand the concepts and the reasoning underlying accounting procedures, and then to apply this understanding to specific situations. Your emphasis should be on understanding and reasoning rather than on memorization.

Good luck!

CONTENTS IN BRIEF

CONTENTS

SECTION 7
Managerial Accounting for Decision Making 881

CHAPTER 27
Nonroutine Operating Decisions 882

CHAPTER 28
Capital Budgeting 911

CHAPTER 29
The Impact of Income Taxes on Business Decisions 941

PROLOGUE

Whatever your motivation—career interest, university requirement, or parental suggestion—you are about to begin the study of accounting. At the outset you may have several questions: What is accounting and why is it important? How is it related to other areas of business? Why should you study accounting? This Prologue provides answers to these questions and offers a perspective of the accounting profession, its nature and purposes. This background should make it easier for you to understand the concepts and techniques that will be examined in later chapters.

The Decision-Making Process

Every day you are required to make many decisions. For example, each morning you decide when to get up, what to wear, and whether or not to have breakfast. You make decisions like these routinely, without much thought, and sometimes by default (when, for example, you fail to wake up because there has been a power failure and your alarm did not go off). On the other hand, you may now be involved in selecting a college major and in determining the sort of contribution you want to make to society through your career. In making these and other important decisions throughout your life, you will need to consider carefully all available information and to use a rational decision-making process.

Even though some decisions are more crucial and complex than others, the *decision-making process* is essentially the same. The problem or question is identified, the facts surrounding the situation are gathered and analyzed, several courses of action are considered, and a decision or judgment is reached. Making decisions that result in the wise use of resources—money or time, for example—is critical because individuals and businesses have only a limited amount of resources to be allocated among alternative uses.

The Role of Accounting

Accounting contributes to the decision-making process by providing some of the information needed in determining how to allocate limited resources as efficiently as possible. The information supplied by accounting is in the form of quantitative data, primarily financial in nature, and is concerned with organizational units called *economic entities*. An economic entity may be an individual; a business, such as a grocery store, a steel plant, or a car dealership; a government agency; a school; a hospital; or the total economy of a nation. Whether large or small, the economic entity is the unit for which we account. Through the accounting process, economic data are identified, measured, recorded, summarized, and communicated to decision makers, some of whom (management) work within the economic entity and some of whom (investors and creditors, for example) do not.

Accounting information is used in making a wide variety of decisions. Investors use it to help them decide where to invest their money and how otherwise to meet their financial objectives. Bankers use it to determine whether a loan should be approved. Corporate managers use accounting information to keep track of and control costs, to price products, and to prepare budgets for use in achieving long-term goals. And government officials use accounting information to establish tax rates, set trade restrictions, and determine priorities for economic and social programs. Although these examples represent only a few of the many uses of accounting data, they illustrate the types of economic, social, and political decisions that make accounting necessary. When accounting information is used effectively as a basis for making decisions, limited resources are utilized efficiently. This results in an improved economy and a higher standard of living.

The Evolution of Accounting

Accounting is a service activity. It is not an end in itself but an integral part of the decision-making process, and it has evolved to meet the needs of those who use the information it provides. It can be argued that as a profession accounting is very young; however, as a service activity it dates back several thousand years. Among the earliest known records are those of the Egyptians and Babylonians (from approximately 3000 B.C.), who recorded on clay tablets such transactions as the payment of wages and taxes. During the Roman period (which lasted from approximately 500 B.C. to A.D. 500), detailed tax records were maintained. In England under Henry I (around 1100), investigations of financial records similar to contemporary audits were conducted. And as early as 1494, an Italian Franciscan monk, Luca Pacioli, published a treatise containing the essential elements of the double-entry accounting system that is still in use today.

Early business activity centered around a barter economy. Instead of using cash (or credit cards) as a medium of exchange, people traded goods and services. The emphasis of accounting was on the receipt and disposition of these goods and services. As the means of transacting business changed, accounting also changed. The essential elements of the accounting process were maintained, but certain concepts and procedures were modified in order to serve the users of accounting information better.

The Industrial Revolution brought about changes in business, and therefore in accounting. Beginning in England in the mid-1800s, manufacturing processes started to evolve from individualized, handicraft systems to mass-production, factory systems. Technological advances not only provided new machinery, but required new types of expenditures as well. Cost accounting systems had to be developed to analyze and control the financial operations of these increasingly complex manufacturing processes.

Also important to the evolution of accounting was the development of the corporate form of business. In a corporation, the owners of the business (the shareholders) often are not the managers of the business. This type of organization creates a need for accurate reporting of financial information to investors, creditors, security analysts, and the other external parties who have a direct interest in the company but who are not involved in its day-to-day management.

Governmental laws and requirements also have caused changes in the business environment and have stimulated the growth of accounting services. For example, the Companies Act in England in the 1850s established compulsory independent audits by chartered accountants. In the United States, the 1913 Revenue Act instituted the personal federal income tax, which created a need for income tax accounting. The 1934 Securities Exchange Act established the Securities and Exchange Commission (SEC), which monitors the reporting procedures of companies that sell stock publicly.

These and other factors have produced changes in the types of accounting services needed and, in many instances, have affected the accounting procedures themselves. Thus, the profession of accounting has evolved to meet the needs of the people it serves in an ever-changing and increasingly complex business environment.

The Relationship of Accounting to Business

Business is the general term applied to the production and distribution of goods and services. Some of the specific functions of business are the manufacturing and marketing of goods, and the raising of capital by organizations that produce and sell those goods. Accounting is related to these functions because it is used to communicate financial information within a business and between businesses. As a result, accounting is often called the language of business; it provides the means of recognizing and recording the financial successes and failures of organizations.

All organizations, whether profit-oriented or not, have certain objectives. The term *business entity* is used to describe an organization that has as its primary objective the making of a profit—that is, the selling of goods or services at a price sufficient to more than cover all production, marketing, and operating costs. In a *nonprofit organization,* such as a school, a hospital, or a government agency, the primary objective is to make sure the organization achieves its goals within its budgetary constraints and operates in an efficient and effective manner. A university, for example, tries to provide students with the best education at the least cost possible.

Regardless of their type, size, or complexity, all organizations have some activities in common. As depicted in Exhibit P–1, one common activity is the accumulation of money resources. These resources come from investors and creditors, and from the business itself in the form of earnings that have been retained. For many nonprofit organizations, the resources come from tax appropriations. Once resources are obtained, they are used to buy land, buildings, and equipment; to purchase materials and supplies; to hire employees; and to meet any other expenses involved in the production and marketing of goods or services. When the product or service is sold, revenues are earned. If revenues exceed expenses, "income" results; if expenses exceed revenues, a "loss" is incurred. The income generated by a business is converted to money resources that can be used to provide dividends to owners, pay off loans, and pay taxes; in addition, some resources may be retained in the business and used to buy new materials, pay wages, and otherwise continue business activity. The results of these activities are measured and communicated by accountants, who thus provide a basis for judging whether the entity has attained its financial objectives.

In order to measure these results as accurately as possible, accountants follow a standard set of procedures, usually referred to as the *accounting process,* or the *accounting cycle.* The cycle includes several steps, which involve the recording, classifying, summarizing, reporting, and interpreting of accounting data.

At the end of the accounting process, various reports are supplied to the users of accounting information. As depicted in Exhibit P–2, there are at least four major categories of reports. The general-purpose financial statements are prepared for those individuals, basically investors and creditors, who are involved financially with an enterprise but are not a part of its management. This area of accounting is referred to as financial accounting. In addition, income tax returns and other tax data are supplied to the Internal Revenue Service (IRS) and state and local governments. Special reports are provided to the government through various regulatory agencies, one of the most notable being the Securities and Exchange Commission (SEC). Detailed discussion of these last two categories—involving taxes and governmental reports, which are also considered financial accounting—are outside the scope of this text.

The accounting process also generates a number of internal reports for use by those who administer the daily affairs of an enterprise. These individuals are referred to collectively as management, and this area of accounting is called managerial accounting. All of this information is generated for the same basic purpose: to assist individuals in making decisions that maximize the use of limited resources.

EXHIBIT P-1 **Activities Common to All Organizations**

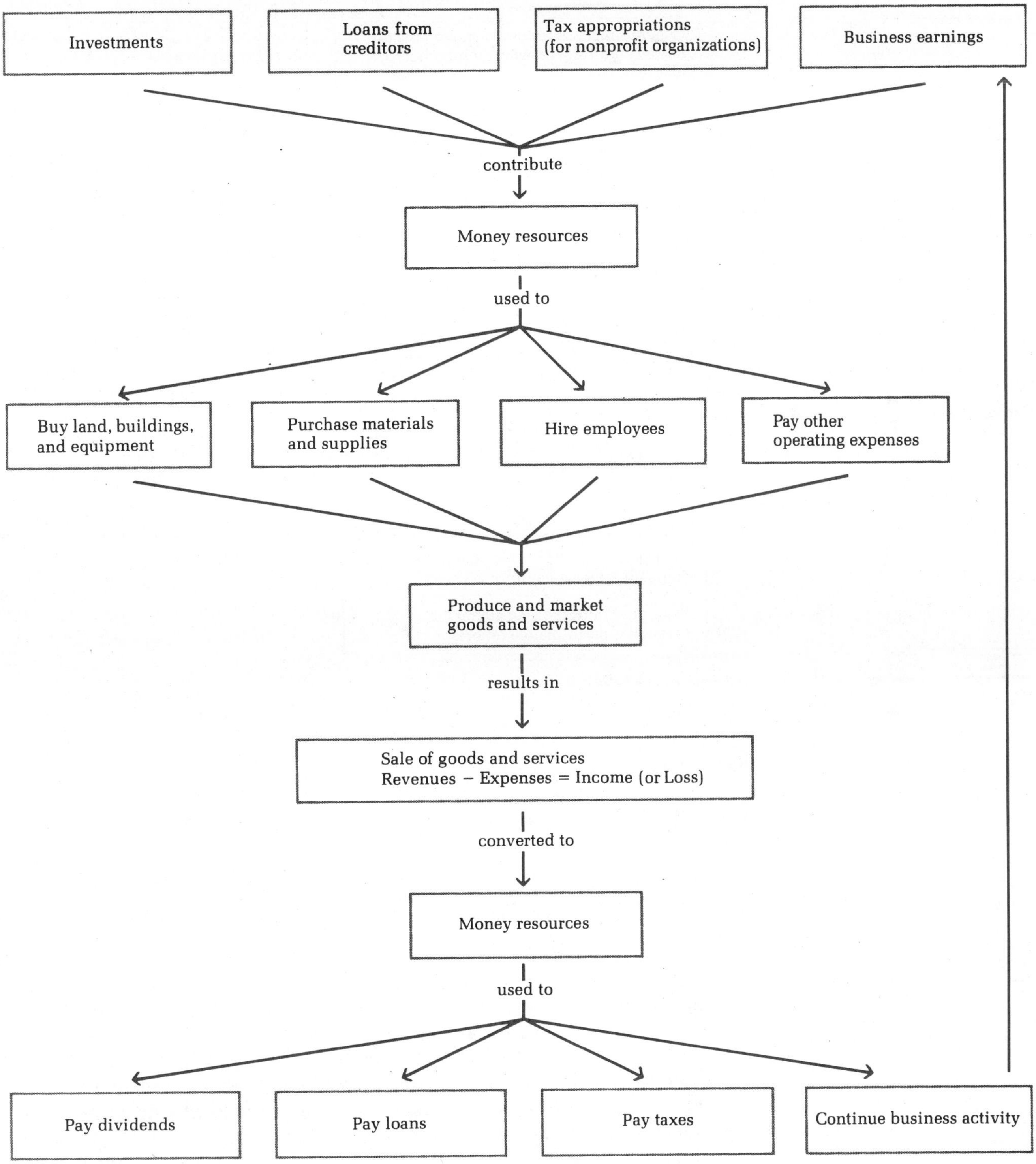

EXHIBIT P-2 **Outputs of the Accounting Process**

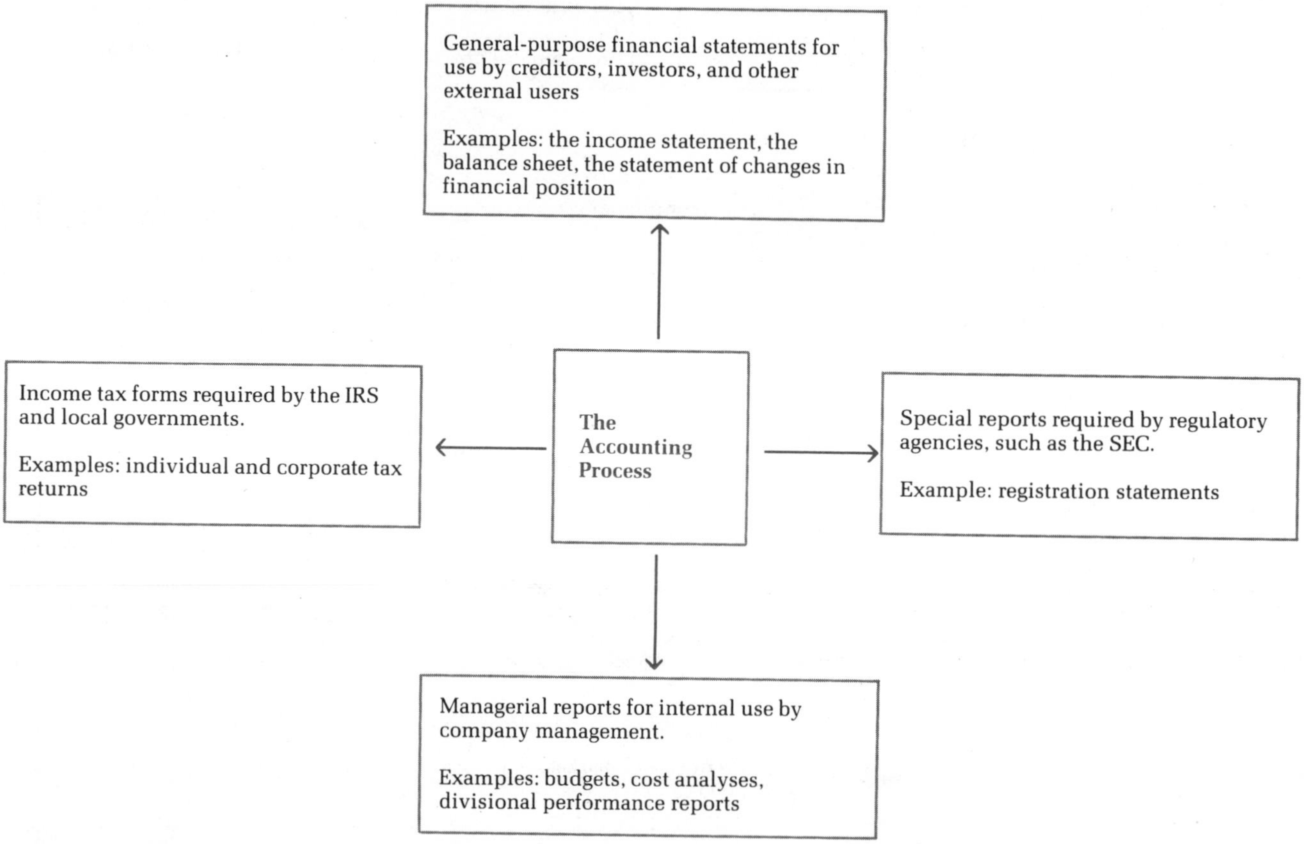

Career Opportunities in Accounting

Accounting is not only a field of study—an academic discipline—it is also one of the fastest growing professions in the United States and throughout the world, and it is playing an increasingly vital role in our economy. Accounting offers many attractive career opportunities. In addition, it provides an excellent educational background for anyone going into business.

Students who choose accounting as their major field of study in college may select from among at least four career paths. These include working for a certified public accounting (CPA) firm, a business, or a nonprofit organization, including the government, or using accounting as a background for other careers. These alternatives are shown in Exhibit P-3.

EXHIBIT P-3 **Career Opportunities in Accounting**

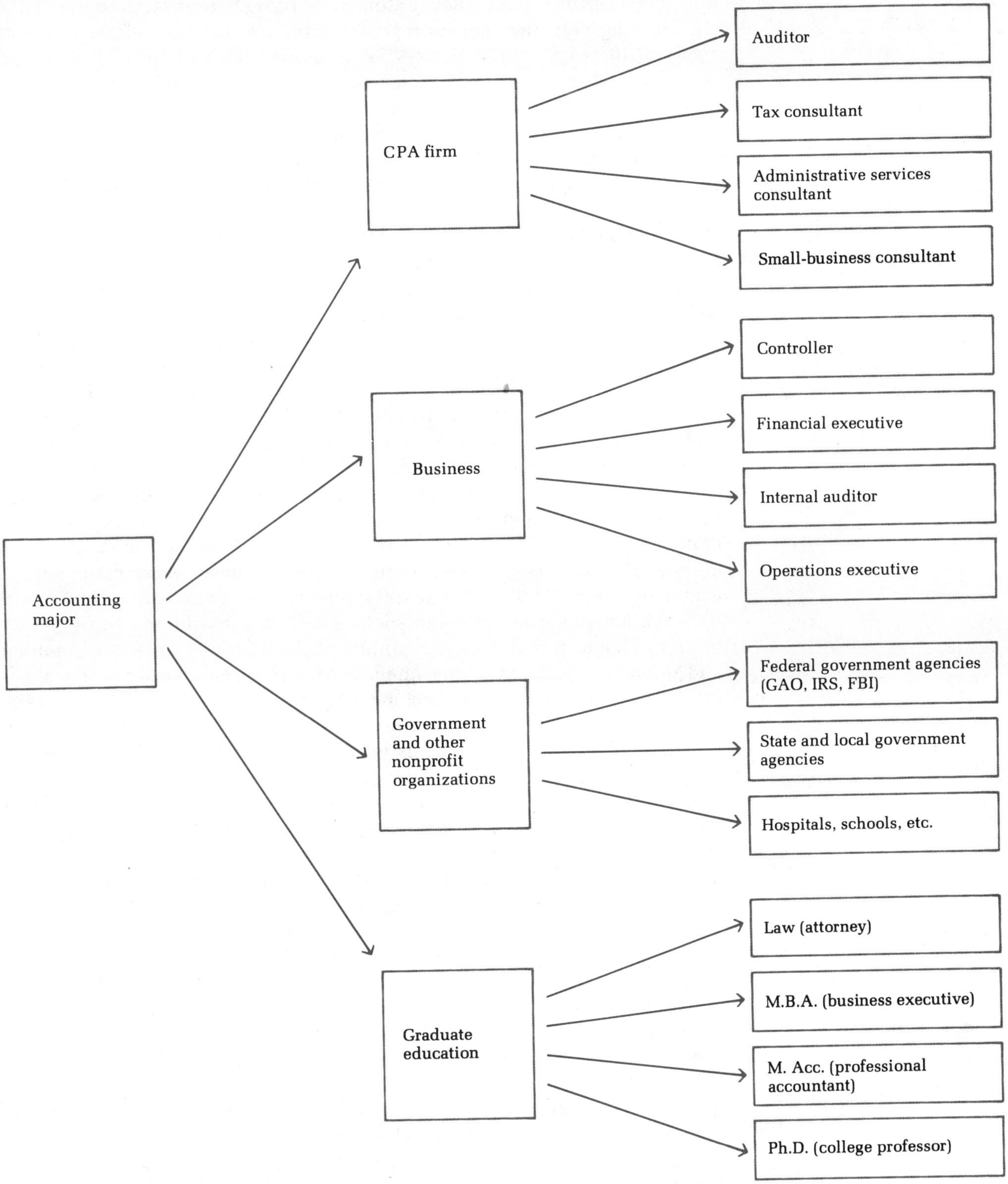

WORKING FOR A CPA FIRM

Most large certified public accounting firms provide four services to clients: (1) auditing, (2) tax consulting, (3) administrative services, and (4) small-business consulting. Small CPA firms also generally provide write-up services; that is, they handle some or all of their clients' bookkeeping in addition to preparing their financial statements.

Auditing is the term generally used to describe the verification of a company's general-purpose financial statements and accounting procedures. This review provides the basis for the auditor to issue a professional opinion as to the reliability of the information presented. After accountants employed by the company have assisted management in preparing financial statements for external use, public accountants carefully examine the company records. Thus, independent audits add credibility to the financial statements prepared by management.

The audit function, then, is not one of generating data but of investigating, inspecting, analyzing, testing, and checking as a basis for a professional opinion. Auditing deals with evidence and with judgments relating to the validity and reliability of that evidence. It is an essential accounting service that provides about 60 percent of the total business of large CPA firms. It offers an attractive career opportunity in public accounting.

Tax accountants do much more than just prepare tax returns. A highly complex and technical field, *tax accounting* involves the use of data generated from the accounting process in the preparation of financial reports according to tax laws. These reports provide the basis for assessing an organization's tax liability. The tax revenues produced are used to maintain the government's economic and social programs. In addition to preparing tax returns and reports, tax accountants become involved in tax planning and in analyzing the tax consequences of managerial decisions. Thus, another career possibility is to become a tax consultant, either within a CPA firm or as an independent practitioner.

A third main area of emphasis within CPA firms is *administrative services,* which is a consulting activity, generally provided on a project-by-project basis. For example, independent accountants may be asked by a client to analyze and make recommendations for improving a company's information system or its internal control procedures. Similarly, accountants performing administrative services may assist in installing a computer system, or they may conduct a study to determine the most efficient procedures for maintaining an inventory of essential materials. As these examples suggest, consultants in this field render a wide variety of services to clients. This career alternative may be especially appealing to those who would like to combine accounting expertise with computer and mathematical skills.

Small-business consulting is another activity in which an accountant with a CPA firm might specialize. The accounting services provided may include some or all of the activities just described. However, small-business consulting usually involves analysis of a company's entire operation, whereas administrative services generally are performed on a project-by-project basis. In many ways, small-business consulting is similar to working as a general practitioner in medicine; that is, the accountant in this area must know something about all aspects of accounting and be able to perform a variety of jobs.

WORKING FOR A BUSINESS

Managerial accounting is concerned with the planning, budgeting, and controlling of activities and with performance evaluation. The reports generated are those needed by management. Increasingly, the managerial accountant performs a variety of information-generating and information-interpreting functions as a member of the managerial team.

In a business, there are four positions that offer major accounting career opportunities: (1) controller, (2) chief financial executive, (3) internal auditor, and (4) operations executive. Of course, no one begins at a top management position. Entry-level jobs in accounting are plentiful and accounting majors are much in demand.

As the title indicates, a *controller* is an accountant who assists management in the planning and control functions of a business. The controller is usually responsible for determining the costs of operating the business and for making sure that those costs are not excessive. Specifically, he or she projects future costs and revenues, compares actual results with the projections, and determines whether and where the company needs better cost-control procedures. The controller also normally assumes at least some of the responsibility for preparing the external financial reports.

Employment as an accountant within a business may eventually lead to becoming the company's president or its *chief financial executive.* In the latter position, one is responsible for a broad range of activities, generally including all financial aspects of the company. More chief financial officers have backgrounds in accounting than in any other discipline.

Accountants employed by businesses also work as *internal auditors.* Generally, only larger firms have internal audit staffs to examine and test the reliability of the accounting information generated, and to see that procedures are being followed. Smaller firms usually must rely on annual audits by independent CPAs for this review function. Internal auditing includes some of the same types of audit activity and the same kinds of challenges that exist in external auditing. However, internal auditing usually involves a more detailed investigation of the operations of a company, a function called operational auditing.

Another aspect of working as an accountant in a business firm is the opportunity to become an *operations executive,* such as a divisional or regional manager. As accountants progress and are given greater responsibilities, they become knowledgeable about almost every aspect of a business and its operations. Consequently, accountants often become operations managers. The ability to understand and use accounting and other pertinent information in the decision-making process has projected many accountants into top administrative positions.

WORKING FOR THE GOVERNMENT AND OTHER NONPROFIT ORGANIZATIONS

There are numerous career opportunities for accountants in government. In the federal government, for example, many agencies and units—such as the military, the Environmental Protection Agency, and the Federal Power Commission—need audit staffs. Additional employers are the General Accounting Office (GAO), the Internal Revenue Service (IRS), and the Federal Bureau of Investigation (FBI). The GAO employs auditors to perform both internal operations audits and external financial audits of the various government agencies under its jurisdiction. The IRS hires accountants as agents to assist in determining appropriate tax revenues. For a number of years the FBI has sought individuals with accounting backgrounds, primarily to investigate financial frauds.

In addition, many accounting jobs are available in state and local government agencies and in nonprofit organizations such as schools, hospitals, and universities. All the financial and managerial accounting activities discussed earlier are applicable to nonprofit organizations. The reporting emphasis, however, is not on measuring income (or loss), but on determining how efficiently the organization is accomplishing its objectives. Consequently, different accounting concepts may be used. Accounting for nonprofit organizations is one of the fastest-growing segments of accounting practice.

EDUCATIONAL PREPARATION

Some college students decide to earn an undergraduate degree in accounting, even though they have no intention of working as an accountant. This is particularly true for those who want to obtain a degree in law (J.D.) or a graduate degree in business administration (M.B.A.). Accounting is considered by many educators to be one of the two or three best prelaw majors. A person with an undergraduate major in accounting combined with an M.B.A. degree is much sought after by business firms.

Another alternative that should receive careful consideration is graduate study in accountancy. For those who would seek careers as professional accountants, a master's degree in accountancy (M.Acc.) is likely to provide an advantage. The expanding role of accounting and the increasing complexity of business require additional formal education and training in the field. To meet this need, professional schools of accountancy have been established at more than a dozen universities in the United States. These schools offer 5-year professional programs leading to the M.Acc. degree.

Some students may want to consider a teaching career in accounting. To teach at the university level generally requires a Ph.D. degree and an interest in conducting research. The shortage of qualified accounting professors, combined with increased enrollments in accounting, has resulted in excellent job opportunities for accounting teachers.

CONCLUDING COMMENT

Each of the career opportunities described offers significant benefits, but none is without disadvantages. The practice of accounting is rigorous and often requires long hours, sometimes under adverse circumstances as a result of financial and legal pressures. (Accounting is not usually considered the easiest major in school, either.) However, the financial rewards are attractive, the work is challenging, and accountants can feel a sense of accomplishment in belonging to a profession that provides useful services to society.

PART I

FINANCIAL ACCOUNTING

SECTION 1

The Accounting Process

CHAPTER 1

Accounting and Its Environment

THIS CHAPTER EXPLAINS:

The differences between financial and managerial accounting.

Some of the basic assumptions and concepts that underlie financial accounting.

The structure and role of accounting theory, including the development of accounting principles.

The role of the Financial Accounting Standards Board and its Conceptual Framework Study.

business enterprise *an organization with a profit objective that derives its earnings by providing goods or services*

nonprofit organization *an entity without a profit objective, oriented toward accomplishing nonprofit goals in an efficient and effective manner*

Each member of society belongs to and interacts with organizations. These organizations, or entities, are defined by their objectives. That is, a business enterprise, such as a grocery store or a movie theater, strives to make a profit. A nonprofit organization, such as a city or a hospital, has a goal of providing service in an effective and efficient manner. And, on an informal basis, a social organization, such as a family, also has certain goals—for example, to save enough money to enable the children to attend college.

Every organization, regardless of its size or purpose, should have a means of keeping track of its activities and measuring how well it is accomplishing its objectives. Accounting provides such a mechanism. It therefore has a major role to play in business and in each of our personal economic lives. For this reason, a basic knowledge of accounting is useful to everyone.[1]

Financial and Managerial Accounting

Economic organizations, like individuals, have limited resources that must be allocated among alternative uses. Accounting helps these organizations to determine the optimal use of their resources and thereby accomplish

[1] The first few pages of Chapter 1 restate some information from the Prologue. The purpose of this repetition is to reinforce and broaden your understanding of certain key terms and concepts.

their objectives. It does so by providing information, primarily financial in nature, about the organization's activities and goals. For example, suppose that you own an auto parts store. You may need to decide whether to purchase only new parts for resale or whether, in addition, to maintain a machine shop where certain used parts can be rebuilt and then resold. Accounting information about the costs of operating the machine shop compared with the expected sales of used parts would help you make that decision. Indeed, it would be virtually impossible to make a rational decision without such information.

accounting *a service activity designed to accumulate, measure, and communicate financial information about organizations for decision-making purposes*

Thus, accounting is a service activity designed to accumulate, measure, and communicate economic information about organizations. Such information helps individuals make better economic decisions.

MANAGERIAL ACCOUNTING

management *individuals who are responsible for overseeing the day-to-day operations of a business and who are the "internal" users of accounting information*

managerial accounting *the area of accounting concerned with assisting managers in decision making, specifically with planning, budgeting, controlling costs, evaluating performance, and generating revenues*

Accounting information is useful to a number of different groups. The primary "internal" user group is management, individuals who make the day-to-day operating decisions in an organization. These people use accounting information in deciding which products to produce, what prices to charge, how to market the products, which costs seem excessive, and what cost controls need to be tightened. Thus, managerial accounting focuses on the specific functions of planning, budgeting, cost determination, performance evaluation, and the control of expenses—and, in general, on the accounting information used by management in making decisions.

FINANCIAL ACCOUNTING

The primary "external" users of accounting information are the individuals who have an interest, financial or otherwise, in an organization but who are not involved in its day-to-day management. Creditors and investors are considered the most important external users. They need accounting information to help them answer such questions as: Should a loan be made to a company and for how much? What company in an industry is likely to provide the best investment opportunity? Should a company's stock be held or sold? Is a particular return on an investment reasonable? The accounting concepts and financial information used by investors, creditors, and other external parties in making decisions about an organization belong to the area referred to as financial accounting. This area is concerned with measuring and reporting the financial status and operating results of organizations.

financial accounting *the area of accounting concerned with measuring and reporting, on a periodic basis, the financial status and operating results of organizations to interested external parties*

Managers, investors, and creditors are but three groups of users of accounting information. There are others: for example, individuals in government agencies, labor union officials, economists, attorneys, and financial analysts. There are also other types of business decisions for which accounting information may be used. Many of these will be described and illustrated in this book. The main point to remember is that accounting is not an end in itself but a service activity designed to provide the financial information needed by various decision makers.

Accounting is not an exact science. It has evolved over several centuries, changing to meet the needs of users and adapting itself to the economic environment in which it operates. The balance of this chapter examines the basic accounting assumptions, concepts, and principles that form a theoretical foundation for current accounting practice. Do not be concerned if you do not fully understand all of the terms and concepts at this first encounter. Accounting is often called the language of business, and it takes time to learn a new language. The terms and concepts will become much more familiar to you as you study later chapters.

Basic Assumptions and Concepts Underlying Financial Accounting

accounting model *the basic accounting concepts and assumptions that determine the manner of recording, measuring, and reporting an entity's transactions*

The basic assumptions of accounting are ideas that are accepted as valid, although they are not necessarily proven facts. These assumptions, along with certain basic concepts, set the boundaries of accounting practice, indicating which events will be accounted for and in what manner. In total, they provide the essential characteristics of the traditional accounting model.

This section will describe several basic concepts and assumptions: the entity concept, the assumption of arm's-length transactions, the concept of money measurement, the going-concern assumption, and the double-entry concept of accounting. A few additional concepts and assumptions will be introduced in later chapters.

THE ENTITY CONCEPT

entity *an organizational unit (a person, partnership, or corporation) for which accounting records are kept and about which accounting reports are prepared*

For accounting purposes, an entity is the organizational unit for which accounting records are maintained—for example, the XYZ Corporation. It is the focal point for identifying, measuring, and communicating accounting data.

An accountant records only the financial activities that occur between the entity being accounted for and other parties. The accountant for XYZ Corporation, for example, would record all sales of XYZ products to Companies A and B, but not sales of Company A products to Company B. Accountants for these other firms would keep track of their own companies' activities. In addition, XYZ's accountants would not be concerned with the personal activities and transactions of the owners (the shareholders) of XYZ Corporation.

There are three major types of business entities: a proprietorship, a partnership, and a corporation. Although the emphasis in this book will be on accounting for corporations and other business entities, note that most of the same principles are applicable to nonprofit organizations, which are discussed in Chapter 17.

Proprietorship

proprietorship *an unincorporated business owned by one person*

A proprietorship is an unincorporated business enterprise owned by one person. Usually, the owner of the business is also the manager. For example, most farmers supervise the planting and harvesting of their crops and then receive the benefits that accrue from the sale of those crops. Similarly, many owners of small businesses—especially those that provide personal services—manage the day-to-day activities of, and receive the profits from, those businesses.

Because accountants view the business unit as a separate entity, care must be exercised to distinguish between the resources and records of the owner, or proprietor, and those of the accounting entity, the business. If the resources of the reporting entity (the entity for which the records are being maintained) are not separately accounted for, the financial success of the entity cannot be measured accurately. Although business records must be kept separate from the proprietor's personal records, the owner is ultimately responsible for all obligations of the business.

Partnership

partnership *an unincorporated business owned by two or more individuals or entities*

A partnership is an unincorporated business owned by two or more individuals or entities. As in a proprietorship, the partners generally manage the business as well as own it. Sometimes, one partner takes the lead in managing the business and is considered the "general partner," while the other owners provide only financial support and are known as "limited partners."

A partnership agreement determines the ownership rights of the partners and specifies when and how the earnings of the business are to be distributed. Also, like a proprietorship, most partnerships are not separate legal entities, and the partners are ultimately responsible for any partnership obligations. For accounting purposes, however, the activities and records of the partnership are kept separate from the activities and records of the owners.

Corporation

corporation *a legal entity chartered by a state, with ownership represented by transferable shares of stock*

stockholders (shareholders) *individuals or organizations that own a portion (shares of stock) of a corporation*

A corporation is a business that is chartered (incorporated) as a separate legal entity under the laws of a particular state. The by-laws of a corporation describe its scope of activity and specify the amount and type of ownership interests it can sell. These ownership interests are in the form of stock certificates, and the owners of a corporation are called stockholders or shareholders. Within the constraints of the by-laws, shareholders can freely buy and sell their interests, thus allowing the corporate ownership to change without dissolution of the business.

The shareholders elect a board of directors, which, in turn, hires executives to manage the corporation. The management, as employees of the corporation, may or may not be shareholders. This separation of ownership from management illustrates the need for two kinds of accounting information. As noted earlier, the internal users, management, need managerial accounting information; the external users, investors as well as creditors, need financial accounting information.

In contrast to a proprietor and most partners, stockholders have only a "limited liability" for the obligations of the corporation. That is, they may lose their investment if the stock becomes worthless, but they cannot be held responsible for amounts in excess of their investment. Thus, the creditors of a corporation cannot recover monies owed them by the corporation from the personal resources of the individual shareholders.

Corporations have become very popular in modern business. The limited liability feature, the opportunity to invest in a business without becoming involved in managing its daily affairs, and the potential for a reasonable return on investment make the corporate form of business attractive to shareholders. The corporate form also enables businesses to raise large amounts of capital through the sale of stock to many shareholders.

Because of its widespread use in the business world, and because it involves most major accounting concepts, the corporate form of business will be emphasized in this book. Except in the area of owners' equity, most of the basic concepts that apply to corporations also apply to proprietorships and partnerships. To explain the differences, we have a separate chapter on owners' equity for proprietorships and partnerships (14).

TO SUMMARIZE Accounting information identifies, measures, and communicates the transactions of a specific entity that is considered separate from its individual owners. The entity may be small or large; a business or nonprofit organization; a proprietorship, a partnership, or a corporation; but it is the organizational unit about which accounting records are kept and financial reports prepared.

THE ASSUMPTION OF ARM'S-LENGTH TRANSACTIONS

transactions *exchanges of goods or services between entities (whether individuals, businesses, or other organizations), as well as other events having an economic impact on a business*

Viewed broadly, transactions include not only exchanges of economic resources between separate entities but also events that have an economic impact on a business but do not involve other entities. The borrowing and lending of money and the sale and purchase of goods or services are examples of the former type. A fire loss and the deterioration of a piece of equipment are examples of the latter. Collectively, transactions provide the data that are included in accounting records and reports.

arm's-length transactions *business dealings between independent and rational parties who are looking out for their own interests*

Accounting for economic transactions enables us to measure the success of an entity. The data for a transaction will not, however, accurately represent that transaction if any favoritism or irregularity is involved. Therefore, unless there is evidence to the contrary, accountants assume arm's-length transactions. That is, they make the assumption that both parties—for example, a buyer and a seller—are rational and free to act independently, each trying to make the best deal possible in establishing the terms of the transaction. For example, suppose that you are willing to pay $2,000 for a certain used car but the owner wants to sell the car for $3,000. You haggle over the price and reach a compromise market, or exchange, price of $2,500. The $2,500 is considered the accounting measurement of the transaction because it has been established through negotiation by independent parties acting in their own self-interest. Arm's-length transactions provide the basis for valid accounting measurements because they produce objective evidence of economic activities.

THE MONEY MEASUREMENT CONCEPT

money measurement *the idea that money, as the common medium of exchange, is the accounting unit of measurement, and that only economic activities measurable in monetary terms are included in the accounting model*

Accountants do not record all the activities of economic entities. They record only those that can be measured in monetary terms. Thus, the concept of money measurement becomes another important characteristic of the accounting model. For example, employee morale cannot be directly measured in monetary terms and is not reported in the accounting records. Wages paid or owed, however, are quantifiable in money terms and are reported. In accounting, all transactions are stated in monetary amounts, whether or not cash is involved.

In the United States the dollar is the unit of exchange and is thus the measuring unit for accounting purposes. For consistency, multinational U.S. companies must restate the results of overseas operations in terms of equivalent U.S. dollars.

In using the dollar as the measuring unit to account for transactions, accountants ignore the fact that its value is not stable. In other words, accountants record the dollar amount of a transaction, using the number of dollars exchanged in the transaction; they do not consider the amount of goods or services that a dollar would have purchased last year or that it may purchase next year. Traditionally, therefore, accountants have not reported the effects of inflation or deflation. However, current inflationary conditions in the United States—indeed, the rapid deterioration in the value of the U.S. dollar—have forced the accounting profession to question this concept. As a result, most large companies are now required to provide selected supplemental information on the impact of changing prices in addition to the financial statements that are based on historical costs—that is, the exchange prices on the date of the original transaction.

THE GOING-CONCERN ASSUMPTION

going concern *the idea that an accounting entity will have a continuing existence for the foreseeable future*

Another characteristic of accounting is the assumption that the entity being accounted for—whether it be a household, business, or governmental unit—is a going concern. This means that in the absence of evidence to the contrary, the entity is expected to continue in operation, at least for the foreseeable future. If accountants made the opposite assumption, that an entity was about to go out of business, they would record liquidation values (the generally lower prices that would be obtained if the entity were forced to sell all goods and resources) rather than the original exchange prices of transactions.

THE DOUBLE-ENTRY CONCEPT

accounting equation *an algebraic equation that expresses the relationship between assets (resources), liabilities (obligations), and owners' equity (net equity, or the residual interest in a business after all liabilities have been met): Assets = Liabilities + Owners' Equity*

The accounting model is built upon a basic equation. Known as the accounting equation, it is

Assets	=	**Liabilities**	+	**Owners' Equity**
Resources		Obligations		Net Equity
[*Property rights of an entity*]		[*Creditors' claims against assets*]		[*Resources less obligations; owners' claims against assets*]

Since the accounting equation is an algebraic equation, both sides must always be equal. This is a very important point. An increase on one side of the equation must be exactly matched by an increase on the other side of the equation, or by a decrease on the same side of the equation. To maintain this balance, accountants record all transactions with a double entry; that is, they balance the effect of any entry by making an offsetting entry. To illustrate, if a company borrows money from a bank, the transaction will be recorded on the company's books as an increase in cash (an asset) and a corresponding increase in the company's obligation (a liability) to the bank.

double-entry accounting *a system of recording transactions in a way that maintains the equality of the accounting equation*

The accounting equation is presented here merely to give you a first glimpse of double-entry accounting. An in-depth discussion of the elements of the equation is reserved for Chapter 2. The mechanics of double-entry accounting are explained in detail in Chapters 3, 4, and 5.

TO SUMMARIZE In conducting economic activities, entities enter into transactions that form the basis of accounting records. An accounting model has been developed for recording, measuring, and reporting an entity's transactions. This model is founded on certain basic concepts and several important assumptions. First, the organizational unit being accounted for is a separate entity. Second, the transactions are assumed to be arm's-length. Third, transactions must be measurable in monetary amounts. Fourth, the accounting entity is assumed to be a going concern. Fifth, the accounting model uses a double-entry system that is based on the fundamental accounting equation: Assets = Liabilities + Owners' Equity.

The Structure and Role of Accounting Theory

As noted in the Prologue, the history of accounting can be traced back several thousand years. Although the needs of early users were simple, their systems elementary, and their means of recording primitive (for example, the number of sheep was inscribed with a stylus on a soft clay tablet), the cornerstone for accounting theory had been laid. Today is an age of electronic data processing and microcomputers. However, the basic requirement that prompted the first forms of accounting is still present: a need for reliable economic data. As business practices and user needs continue to change, accounting theory and practice will be modified to satisfy those needs.

THE STRUCTURE OF ACCOUNTING THEORY

Accounting has two broad functions: (1) measurement, or the accumulation of reliable economic data reflecting the financial progress and status of an enterprise, and (2) communication, or the reporting and interpreting of these data in order to facilitate decision making. Accounting theory provides the framework for these two functions of accounting.

accounting concepts and assumptions *fundamental ideas that provide the foundation upon which the principles and procedures of accounting theory rest*

The structure of accounting theory is depicted in Exhibit 1-1. The foundation is formed by certain accounting concepts and assumptions, such as the five we have introduced in this chapter.

EXHIBIT 1-1 A Structure of Accounting Theory

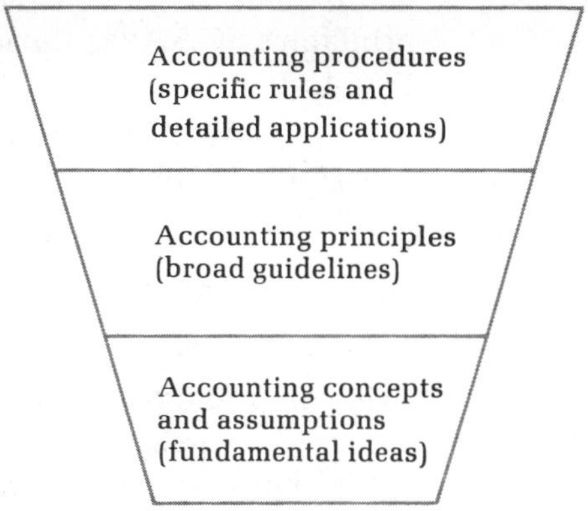

Accounting concepts and assumptions are not natural laws; rather, they are man-made and are derived from the general business environment. Although they are subject to change as the overall environment in which they operate evolves, such changes will be slow and infrequent.

accounting principles *broad guidelines that identify the procedures to be used in specific accounting situations*

Built upon the base of concepts and assumptions are accounting principles, broad guidelines or directives to action. Because they are directly related to specific accounting problems, principles are more numerous than concepts and are affected more by changes in technology and in other business activities. Principles find support in the concepts, but, more important, they find support in their acceptance by accountants and by users of economic information.

accounting procedures *specific rules or methods for applying accounting principles*

Accounting procedures are the specific methods and means of applying accounting principles—for example, the method a company uses to record the sale of merchandise. They are the "rules" of accounting. Accounting procedures are pragmatic, more numerous than principles, and more susceptible to change. They often represent alternative ways of applying the same principle.

THE ROLE OF ACCOUNTING THEORY

Accounting theory provides an explanation of or justification for accounting practices. It is the rationale for action. Further, it provides a guide for developing new accounting practices and procedures. Such a frame of reference is indispensable if accounting is to respond effectively to new business conditions. Indeed, this frame of reference is the essence of professionalism in the field of accounting. Without it, the professional accountant would be little more than a robot, mechanically handling prescribed accounting situations and unable to adjust to circumstances that do not coincide precisely with predetermined criteria. Thus, despite some inherent weaknesses, accounting theory forms the basis for the critical judgments required in the practice of accounting.

generally accepted accounting principles (GAAP) *authoritative guidelines that define accounting practice at a particular time*

Although business activity has changed and accounting principles have been modified accordingly, accounting practice is not subject to frequent and haphazard change. Accountants follow generally accepted accounting principles (GAAP), those principles that are based upon fundamental, time-tested accounting concepts. Only as concepts and principles prove useful are they incorporated into the body of knowledge referred to as generally accepted accounting principles.

HISTORICAL DEVELOPMENT OF GAAP

Since the 1930s, concerted efforts have been made to develop an authoritative, comprehensive code of generally accepted accounting principles. Significant progress has been made, but the task is a difficult one and additional work is required.

There are several reasons for this continuing interest in a statement of GAAP. Many accountants feel that more carefully specified GAAP would reduce the number of alternative accounting procedures and thus improve financial reporting. Others contend that a framework of GAAP is essential if accountants are to perform an ever-expanding role without undue legal risk. Still others see a formalized statement of GAAP as a natural conclusion to the evolution of a mature accounting profession.

The Early Period (1930–1959)

Securities and Exchange Commission (SEC) *the government body responsible for regulating the financial reporting practices of most publicly owned corporations in connection with the buying and selling of stocks and bonds*

American Accounting Association (AAA) *the national organization representing accounting educators and practitioners; it serves as a forum for the expression of accounting ideas and encourages research*

American Institute of CPAs (AICPA) *the national organization representing certified public accountants in the United States*

Accounting Principles Board (APB) *the organization established by AICPA in 1959 to set standards for financial accounting and reporting*

The first real period of interest in specifying GAAP began in the early 1930s. It was sparked by several events: (1) the passage of the 1933 and 1934 Securities Acts and the establishment of the Securities and Exchange Commission (SEC), (2) the reorganization of the American Accounting Association (AAA) and the renewed interest it took in accounting theory, and (3) the publication of several articles that attempted to set forth generally accepted accounting principles. As part of this activity, the American Institute of CPAs (AICPA), through its Committee on Accounting Procedures, began publishing Accounting Research Bulletins (ARBs), each of which identified and explained specific accounting principles and rules. During the next 20 years, the AICPA published 51 ARBs and, in an independent effort, the AAA revised its statement on accounting principles three times.

The APB Period (1959–1973)

The Accounting Principles Board (APB) was established in 1959 by the AICPA. It replaced the Committee on Accounting Procedures and attempted to increase its research effort and to reduce the number of alternative reporting practices being followed at the time.

The APB consisted of 18 to 21 members, each of whom served on a part-time, nonsalaried basis. During its life, the APB issued 31 Opinions and 4 interpretive Statements. (The Opinions were authoritative and considered GAAP; the Statements were not considered GAAP but were expressions of the committee's position on an issue.) Also during this period, the AICPA published 15 Research Studies and the AAA published one major statement of accounting theory; again, these publications focused attention on the need for more uniform financial reporting.

During the late 1960s and early 1970s, the APB was criticized severely, both within and outside the profession. Much of the criticism had to do with the APB's lack of independence and its inability to respond quickly enough to the demands of the profession. In response to these criticisms, a committee of the AICPA recommended the establishment of the Financial Accounting Standards Board (FASB).

The FASB Period (1973–present)

Financial Accounting Standards Board (FASB) *the private organization responsible for establishing the standards for financial accounting and reporting in the United States*

In March 1973, the Financial Accounting Standards Board replaced the APB as the primary standard-setting body for accounting principles in the private sector. It is important to note that the FASB is not a part of the AICPA, as the APB was. It is an independent body, and its members are appointed by the Financial Accounting Foundation (nine trustees representing a broad spectrum of the financial community). Furthermore, the seven members of the FASB are well paid, work full time on the Board, and must have severed all connections with their previous employers. The FASB is assisted by a large staff and by the Financial Accounting Standards Advisory Council (FASAC). Members of the Advisory Council serve on a part-time, voluntary basis for a period of one year, though this agreement can be renewed. A more complete description of the FASB—its background and operating procedures—is provided in the Supplement to this chapter.

There are several advantages inherent in the organizational structure of the FASB. The standard-setting process now resides in the private sector. The Board is independent of the AICPA and the influence of individual companies. And it is a small board of highly qualified professionals who devote their full time and energy to the difficult task of developing a complete and authoritative set of accounting standards.

The FASB is currently recognized as the primary source of generally accepted accounting principles. Since its organization, it has issued more than 60 Statements, over 15 Interpretations of those Statements, and 4 Statements of Concepts.

Although the Board has a broad base of support, there are those who maintain that it is not moving fast enough. The development of GAAP is a challenging assignment, and it remains to be seen if the FASB is up to the task. The SEC and Congress are now playing a more active role in the development of accounting principles; in fact, they periodically have threatened to take over that assignment should the FASB fail.

The FASB Conceptual Framework Study

Recognizing the importance of developing a framework of accounting principles, the FASB has undertaken a "Conceptual Framework Study." Completion of this project is viewed by many accountants as the most pressing task of the FASB and of the accounting profession. Until such a "constitution" is established, they maintain, the resolution of many individual accounting problems, such as how to account for leases or inflation, will not be possible except on a stopgap, temporary basis.

The FASB Conceptual Framework Study covers a broad range of issues. It is intended to build upon work already completed (past Opinions, Statements, and Research Studies) and to reach conclusions about such fundamental questions as: What are the objectives of financial statements? To whom are they directed and for what purposes? What type of information should be reported? What are the trade-offs between relevancy, objectivity, and comparability? What are the basic elements of accounting? What is an asset? A liability? Should the measuring unit be adjusted for inflation?

To accomplish the enormous task of answering these questions and resolving other difficult issues, the project was divided into stages. During the first stage, which took over three years to complete, the FASB identified the objectives of financial statements and specified the elements of those statements. In this process, it reached tentative conclusions, issued a proposed "Statement of Concepts," and then, after a discussion period, issued in December 1978 a final pronouncement, its first Statement of Concepts. The FASB is now studying such matters as the form and content of financial statements and how to measure a company's operating results.

Although a conceptual framework for accounting practice is necessary, it will not solve all accounting problems. Judgments will still be required, and improvements will still have to be made. Such is the nature of accounting. It is a dynamic, service-oriented discipline that is continually evolving to meet the needs of the people it serves.

This discussion of accounting theory, GAAP, and the FASB has been brief because you need not have a full understanding of these matters yet. However, these elements are basic parts of the accounting language and it is important for you to begin familiarizing yourself with them now.

CHAPTER REVIEW

Accounting is a service activity designed to accumulate, measure, and communicate economic data about organizations. The information is supplied to managers, creditors, investors, and other users to assist in the decision-making process. Managerial accounting deals primarily with the internal accounting functions of cost determination, planning, control, and performance evaluation. Financial accounting is concerned with reporting to external parties an organization's financial position, changes in that position, and results of the organization's operations. The objectives of both divisions of accounting are measurement and communication.

The boundaries of accounting are established by basic concepts and assumptions. These concepts and assumptions include the entity concept, the assumption of arm's-length transactions, the concept of money measurement, the going-concern assumption, and the concept of double-entry accounting, which is built upon the fundamental accounting equation: Assets = Liabilities + Owners' Equity. Collectively, they determine the essential characteristics of the accounting model.

Accounting theory provides the rationale or justification for accounting practice. It also assists policy makers in developing new accounting procedures, and provides a frame of reference for the critical judgments required of accountants.

The structure of accounting theory rests on a foundation of basic concepts and assumptions that are very broad, few in number, and derived from business practice. The accounting principles based upon this foundation provide guidelines or directives to action. Accounting procedures are applications of principles in specific circumstances.

Accounting principles have evolved over time to meet the changing demands of the business environment. They are therefore not absolute. Only if they prove useful do they become generally accepted. Accounting principles need to be applied with judgment.

The enormous range and the diverse nature of generally accepted accounting principles have prevented accountants from setting down an authoritative statement of GAAP that is agreeable to all preparers and users. Some view this as a significant problem within the accounting profession. Others do not; they see the need for continually striving to improve accounting principles but are not sure that a statement of principles that covers all situations is possible, or even desirable. However, almost all accountants agree that financial reporting would be improved if the number of alternative accounting practices were reduced.

Since the 1930s, several organizations have been involved in the development of accounting principles. The American Institute of CPAs (AICPA), the American Accounting Association (AAA), the Securities and Exchange Commission (SEC), and the Financial Accounting Standards Board (FASB) are among the most prominent. The FASB is currently the primary standard-setting body for accounting principles in the private sector.

One of the most important FASB projects is the Conceptual Framework Study. It is hoped that this project will provide a basic framework for accounting and reporting practices for many years to come. However, given the complexities of business and the judgments required in accounting, no single statement of principles can be expected to provide conclusive solutions to all accounting problems.

KEY TERMS AND CONCEPTS

accounting (17)
accounting concepts and assumptions (22)
accounting equation (21)
accounting model (18)
accounting principles (23)
Accounting Principles Board (APB) (24)
accounting procedures (23)
American Accounting Association (AAA) (24)
American Institute of CPAs (AICPA) (24)
arm's-length transactions (20)
business enterprise (16)
corporation (19)
double-entry accounting (22)
entity (18)
financial accounting (17)
Financial Accounting Standards Board (FASB) (25)
generally accepted accounting principles (GAAP) (24)
going concern (21)
management (17)
managerial accounting (17)
money measurement (21)
nonprofit organization (16)
partnership (19)
proprietorship (19)
Securities and Exchange Commission (SEC) (24)
stockholders (shareholders) (19)
transactions (20)

DISCUSSION QUESTIONS

(Note that some of the questions for this chapter also relate to material introduced in the Prologue.)

1 What is the nature of accounting?

2 What are the essential elements in decision making, and where does accounting fit into the process?

3 What types of personal decisions have required you to use accounting information?

4 What does the term "business" mean to you?

5 As you begin the study of accounting, what ideas do you have about its role and importance in the business world? Be specific by discussing your views of accounting in relation to marketing, finance, economics, and management.

6 Who are the primary users of accounting data?

7 Distinguish between financial accounting and managerial accounting.

8 List some of the basic concepts and assumptions that provide the foundation of accounting.

9 Explain why each of the following concepts or assumptions is important in accounting.
(a) The entity concept.
(b) The assumption of arm's-length transactions.
(c) The money measurement concept.
(d) The going-concern assumption.

10 What are the distinguishing features of a proprietorship, a partnership, and a corporation?

11 What is the purpose of accounting theory?

12 Why does the application of accounting principles require accountants to use professional judgment?

13 Define GAAP.

14 What is expected of the Conceptual Framework Study of the FASB?

15 Would you describe the practice of accounting more as a science or an art? Explain.

EXERCISES

NOTE: Because Chapter 1 is fairly general and is intended to be a brief introduction to important accounting concepts, these exercises can be used most effectively to initiate class discussions.

E1–1 The Role and Importance of Accounting

Assume that you are applying for a part-time job as an accounting clerk in a retail clothing establishment. During the interview, the store manager asks how you expect to contribute to her business. How would you respond?

E1–2 Accounting Information and Decision Making

You are the owner of Accounting Systems Inc., which sells Apple computers and related data processing equipment. You are currently trying to decide whether to continue selling the Apple computer line or distribute the IBM personal computer instead. What information do you need to consider in order to determine how successful your business is or will be? What information would help you decide whether to sell the Apple or the IBM personal computer line? Use your imagination and general knowledge of business activity.

E1–3 The Benefits of Studying Accounting

Assume that one of the following describes your future occupation. How would knowledge of accounting benefit you?

1. Financial executive.
2. City manager.
3. Financial analyst.
4. Proprietor of a small business.
5. Politician planning to become a representative in Congress.

E1–4 The Entity Concept

Delbert James lives in a small community where he is involved in a number of different business activities. He works for a real estate agency, is the mayor of the town, and prepares tax returns during the tax season. In accounting for the business activities of Delbert James, which of the following items of information would be considered in determining how successful his businesses are?

1. Real estate commissions paid to James.
2. The amounts paid for rent and utilities by the real estate agency.

3. Tax revenues for the town.
4. Salary paid to the mayor.
5. Fees paid for licenses to operate businesses in the town.
6. Parking tickets paid by citizens, including one by James.
7. The amount of interest received by a client and reported on her tax return.
8. Supplies used in preparing tax returns.
9. Gas, oil, and related costs of operating the family car.
10. Fees received from tax clients.
11. City council expenditures.
12. Receipts from the sale of houses owned by the real estate agency.

E1-5 The Characteristics of Accounting Entities

Several characteristics of business entities are listed below.

1. Organized with the objective of providing goods or services at prices that exceed their costs, that is, for the purpose of making a profit.
2. Generally has a large number of owners.
3. Engages in arm's-length transactions.
4. Created by charter after complying with state regulations.
5. Usually has an agreement that determines the distribution of earnings.
6. Owned by one person.
7. Owned by two or more people or entities.
8. Offers limited liability to its owners.
9. Is assumed to have continuity of existence.
10. Accounts only for the results of its financial affairs, not for those of its owners.
11. Has the ability to raise large amounts of money through the sale of ownership interests.

Using the following column headings, indicate with a check (✓) which form or forms of business organization the characteristic applies to.

Characteristic	Proprietorship	Partnership	Corporation
1	✓	✓	✓

E1-6 The Assumption of Arm's-Length Transactions

Susan Hamilton owns and manages a reception center. She has decided to build another reception center in a medium-sized town 50 miles away. Because of the short distance, she can manage both centers, and the new reception center can be built on some land she already owns. The land was purchased 10 years ago for $12,000 for personal use. Would $12,000 be the appropriate value at which to record the land if it is used for the new reception center? Discuss.

E1-7 The Going-Concern Assumption

Assume that you open an auto repair business. You purchase a building and buy new equipment. What difference does the going-concern assumption make with regard to how you would account for these assets?

E1-8 The Role of Accounting Theory

In a discussion with a friend, you explain that accounting is more like an art than a science and that accounting principles are not like the natural laws of science but are man-made and changeable. In reply, your friend asks why accountants are so concerned with accounting theory and with establishing accounting principles if they are so changeable. Briefly explain the role of accounting theory and the importance of developing a theoretical structure for accounting.

E1-9 The FASB

Soon after beginning a career with a large, international accounting firm, you are approached by a client who does not understand the objectives of the Financial Accounting Standards Board (FASB). Briefly explain the purpose of the FASB. (See the Supplement for additional information in answering this question.)

E1-10 The FASB Conceptual Framework Study

At a training seminar for new staff accountants in your firm, a debate arises over the Conceptual Framework Study of the FASB. Some argue that it will solve all of the profession's problems and others say that it is a waste of time. Briefly describe what the Conceptual Framework Study can be expected to accomplish, as well as its limitations.

SUPPLEMENT

The Financial Accounting Standards Board

This supplement, adapted from an FASB letter dated January 1982, provides additional information concerning the FASB and explains the process used in establishing financial accounting standards.

DESCRIPTION AND BACKGROUND OF THE FASB

Since 1973, the Financial Accounting Standards Board has been the organization in the private sector with the responsibility for establishing standards of financial accounting and reporting. The FASB is comprised of seven members who serve full time and who have severed all connections with their former firms or institutions. FASB standards are officially recognized as authoritative by the Securities and Exchange Commission (SEC) and the American Institute of Certified Public Accountants.

The SEC has statutory authority to establish financial accounting and reporting standards under the Securities Acts of 1933 and 1934. Throughout its history, however, the Commission's policy has been to rely on the private sector for this function, to the extent that the private sector demonstrates the ability to fulfill this responsibility in the public interest. The FASB was conceived by a special study group headed by a former SEC commissioner and was carefully designed to carry out this responsibility.

The FASB's sponsoring organizations, which also provide financial support, are:

American Accounting Association (educators)
American Institute of Certified Public Accountants (public accountants)
Financial Analysts Federation (investors and investment advisors)
Financial Executives Institute (corporate executives)
National Association of Accountants (primarily management accountants)
Securities Industry Association (investment bankers, brokers)

There also is a trustee-at-large whose election is endorsed by the principal national associations in the banking industry.

The Financial Accounting Standards Advisory Council has responsibility for consulting with the Standards Board about major technical issues, the Board's agenda and the assigning of priorities to projects, the matters likely to require the attention of the FASB, the selection and organization of task forces, and other issues that may be introduced by its chairman or the FASB chairman. The Council has 38 members who are broadly representative of the relevant constituencies, including government, law, education, large and small businesses, large and small accounting firms, investors, creditors, and other users of financial information.

DUE PROCESS OF THE FASB

The FASB issues Statements of Financial Accounting Standards, Statements of Concepts, and Interpretations. The former, usually referred to as Statements, establish new standards or amend those previously issued. Statements of Concepts, or just Concepts, provide guidelines in solving problems and enable those who use financial reports to understand the context in which financial accounting standards are formulated. The Concepts do not establish new standards or require any change in existing accounting principles. The Interpretations clarify, explain, or elaborate on existing standards. The FASB staff issues Technical Bulletins to provide guidance on applying existing standards to certain financial accounting and reporting problems on a timely basis.

Before it issues a Statement, the FASB is required by its rules to follow extensive "due process" procedures. In connection with each of its major projects, the Board takes the following steps:

Appoints a task force of technical experts representing a broad spectrum of preparers, auditors, and users of financial information to advise on the project.

Studies existing literature on the subject and conducts any additional research that may be necessary.

Publishes a comprehensive discussion of issues and possible solutions (a discussion memorandum) as the basis for public comment.

Conducts a public hearing.

Gives broad distribution to a draft of the proposed Statement for public comment.

Considers comments received and issues a Statement of Financial Accounting Standards.

The Board's deliberations are open to the public, and a complete public record is maintained.

CHAPTER 2

An Overview of Financial Reporting

THIS CHAPTER EXPLAINS:

The objectives of financial reporting.

The basic elements of general-purpose financial statements.

The purpose, general format, and relationships of the primary financial statements.

The notes to financial statements and the independent auditor's report.

We have described accounting as a means of accumulating, measuring, and communicating financial information that is useful in making economic decisions. It follows that the objective of the accounting process is to gather accounting data, organize them, and put them in a usable form. The financial statements prepared for external users are among the most important outputs of the accounting process. The purpose of this chapter is to provide an initial overview of these statements and of financial reporting in general. This should help you understand the related concepts and the mechanical aspects of accounting that will be explained in later chapters. Do not be concerned if you are not familiar with all the items illustrated on the financial statements. The income statement will be covered in depth in Chapter 6, the balance sheet in Chapter 8, and the funds statement in Chapter 16.

Objectives of Financial Reporting

Financial reports are designed to provide useful information about specific entities. As such, they must serve many purposes for a wide variety of users, including present and potential stockholders, creditors, financial analysts, and regulatory officials. Though each of these users has different needs, there is a common body of financial information about an entity that suits a large number of their purposes. This information is contained in the company's financial statements.[1]

THE GENERAL-PURPOSE FINANCIAL STATEMENTS

general-purpose (or primary) financial statements *the financial statements intended for general use by a variety of external groups; include the income statement, the balance sheet, and the funds statement*

Because financial statements are used by so many different groups, they are called general-purpose (or primary) financial statements.[2] Before we discuss the contents of these statements, it will be useful to examine the kinds of information needed by external users.

Cash Flow and Earnings Potential

cash flow *the receipt of cash in the form of dividends or interest, and from the proceeds upon liquidation of an investment or repayment of a loan principal*

dividends *the periodic distribution of earnings in the form of cash, stock, or other property to the owners (stockholders) of a corporation*

earnings potential *the ability of a company to generate positive future net cash flows from operations*

Investors in corporations want to know how much cash they eventually will receive as a result of an investment, that is, whether they will recover their original investment as well as earn a return, or profit, on that investment. For stockholders (owners), this cash flow is derived from one of two sources: (1) periodic payments from a company, called dividends, and (2) proceeds from the sale of stock to another party. In the first instance, cash is received but the investment remains intact; in the second situation, the investment itself is liquidated by the stockholder. For creditors, cash flow consists of periodic payments made to them for the use of money (interest) and the final payment of the principal amount at maturity.

A company's earnings potential stems from its ability to generate from operations positive cash flows, that is, future cash inflows that will exceed future cash outflows. This concept relates both to current earnings and to the expectations of future earnings. Current earnings provide the primary source of cash for dividend and interest payments; anticipated earnings influence the market price of stock, and therefore the amount of cash investors will receive when they sell the stock. Anticipated earnings also become a factor in whether creditors will receive their repayments of principal amounts.

Liquidity, Solvency, and Profitability

liquidity *a company's ability to meet current obligations with cash or with other assets that can be quickly converted to cash*

In assessing the adequacy of a company's expected cash flows and earnings potential, investors and creditors need to consider three related concepts: liquidity, solvency, and profitability. Liquidity generally refers to the ability of an enterprise to meet its current obligations. The basic question is whether an organization (or individual) has enough cash, or other assets that can be quickly converted to cash, to pay current bills. If a company cannot meet its short-term obligations, it may be forced to quit business and thus may never have a chance to prove its potential for long-term profitability.

[1] Our discussion of the objectives of financial reporting is based on the *Statement of Financial Accounting Concepts No. 1* (Stamford: Financial Accounting Standards Board, November 1978). The elements of the statements, discussed in the next section, are as described in the *Statement of Financial Accounting Concepts No. 3* (Stamford: Financial Accounting Standards Board, December 1980).

[2] The financial statements for International Business Machines (IBM) for 1981 are presented at the back of the book.

solvency *a company's long-run ability to meet all financial obligations*

Solvency usually relates to the enterprise's long-term ability to meet its obligations. The question here is not only how much cash is readily available to pay current bills, but whether the future cash inflows will be sufficient to meet all obligations as they come due over the lifetime of the enterprise.

profitability *a company's ability to generate revenues in excess of the costs incurred in producing those revenues*

Profitability has to do with the generation of revenues in excess of the costs incurred in producing those revenues. The excess is income, or earnings. Profitability is therefore directly related to an enterprise's ability to generate earnings and positive cash flows.

THE CONCEPT OF FULL DISCLOSURE

For financial reporting to be most effective, all relevant information must be presented in an unbiased, understandable, and timely manner. This is sometimes referred to as the "full and fair disclosure standard." Achieving such a standard is not an easy task. Too much information can confuse; too little information can mislead. Even selecting the most appropriate format for presentation is a challenge.

To the extent that full disclosure is achieved, external decision makers are better able to evaluate alternative courses of action and the expected returns, costs, and risks associated with those alternatives. This should result in a better allocation of resources, and therefore a more efficient economy.

TO SUMMARIZE External users of financial information, particularly potential investors and creditors, need to assess the size, timing, and degree of certainty of an entity's prospective cash flows and earnings potential. This information, much of which is found in the general-purpose financial statements, is related to a company's liquidity, solvency, and profitability. Full and fair disclosure is the overall standard sought in financial reporting.

The Basic Elements of the General-Purpose Financial Statements

The overall purpose of financial statements, and of financial reporting in general, is to provide information about an enterprise's economic resources, obligations, and results of operations. To introduce you to the distinctions and relationships among resources, obligations, and earnings, we will briefly describe the basic, interrelated elements of general-purpose financial statements: assets; liabilities; owners' equity, including investments by owners and distributions to owners; revenues; expenses; gains; losses; and net income (or loss). The relationships of these elements are reflected in the basic accounting equation—Assets = Liabilities + Owners' Equity—which will be discussed in Chapter 3.

ASSETS

assets *economic resources that are owned or controlled by an enterprise as a result of past transactions or events, and that are expected to have future economic benefits (service potential)*

In general terms, assets may be defined as economic resources that are owned or controlled by an enterprise as a result of past transactions or events, and that are expected to provide future economic benefits (have service potential) for that entity. Assets are financial representations and so are measured or estimated in monetary amounts. Thus, assets have four essential characteristics: (1) they represent potential future benefits; (2) the benefits have been secured to the entity, usually through ownership; (3) they can be measured in monetary terms; and (4) they result from past transactions. Assets include cash, accounts receivable (amounts owed from customers), inventory (goods held for sale), land, buildings, equipment, and even intangible items, such as copyrights and patents. Some of these assets are considered to be current or short-term assets; that is, they are expected to be converted to cash during the normal business cycle or at least within a year. Other assets, such as land and equipment, are long-term because they are not readily converted to cash and are usually held for more than one year.

LIABILITIES

liabilities *obligations of an enterprise to pay cash or other economic resources in return for past or current benefits; they represent claims against assets*

The term liabilities is used to describe an enterprise's obligations to pay cash or other economic resources to other people or organizations. Liabilities represent claims against assets and are measured in monetary amounts. They generally indicate that cash, goods, or services (economic resources) will be transferred in the future to settle an obligation that has resulted from a past transaction. In summary, four conditions must be met if an item is to qualify as a liability: (1) it must involve a future sacrifice of resources; (2) it must be measurable in monetary terms; (3) the sacrifice must be an obligation of the enterprise; and (4) the obligation must have arisen from a past transaction. Some common liabilities are accounts payable (amounts owed to suppliers), notes payable, and mortgage payable (an amount owed for purchased property, such as land or buildings). As with assets, the liabilities that are expected to be paid in cash within a year are considered current liabilities; others, such as a mortgage payable, which generally will not be paid within the current year, are classified as long-term liabilities.

OWNERS' EQUITY

owners' equity (stockholders' equity) *the ownership interest in the assets of an enterprise; equals net assets*

net assets *total assets minus total liabilities*

As can be observed if the basic accounting equation is restated in the form Assets − Liabilities = Owners' Equity, the ownership interest remaining in the assets of a business enterprise after the liabilities are deducted is owners' equity (also called stockholders' equity for corporations). It does not represent a specific asset, such as cash; instead it represents the "net equity" of the business, which is the amount of net assets (total assets minus total liabilities) available after all obligations are satisfied. Obviously, if there are no liabilities (an unlikely situation, except at the start of a business), then the total assets are exactly equal to the owners' claims against those assets—the owners' equity. Thus, owners' equity shows the amount of the owner's interest in a firm.

Another distinguishing feature of owners' equity is that it changes in response to the profitability of the entity and the amount of dividends paid. In contrast, liability amounts are determined by contractual agreement and will not change unless a particular agreement is modified, the liability is paid, or a new liability is incurred. Therefore, the total amount of liabilities will not automatically fluctuate with the enterprise's overall profitability, but instead will vary with the degree of indebtedness of the enterprise.

When viewed in terms of where assets came from, owners' equity and liabilities show the sources of assets committed to or invested in a business. Once resources are committed, those who made the commitment have claims against the business entity. This can be clearly seen by again referring to the accounting equation: Assets = Liabilities + Owners' Equity. Liabilities represent the amount of assets provided by creditors, and owners' equity represents the amount of assets owned by stockholders.

Investments by Owners

investments by owners *increases in a company's net assets, resulting from the transfer of resources from an investor to the enterprise in return for part ownership in the entity*

Companies acquire resources from three main sources: by borrowing, which increases liabilities; through investments by owners; and by profitable operations. Investments by owners (equity investments) involve the transfer of resources, usually cash, from the investor to the entity in return for part ownership in the company. The sale of stock to shareholders and capital contributions by the owner of a proprietorship or the partners in a partnership are examples of equity investments.

Distributions to Owners

distributions to owners *decreases in a company's net assets, resulting from the transfer of assets to owners, or the transfer of liabilities from the owners to the entity*

Distributions to owners result in a decrease in the net assets of an entity. The distribution may take the form of a company transferring assets (for example, paying cash dividends) or incurring liabilities. The net effect is to decrease the owners' equity in the entity. Corporate dividends and the withdrawal of funds by the owner of a proprietorship or a partner in a partnership are examples of distributions to owners.

REVENUES

revenues *resource increases from the sale of goods or services derived primarily from the normal operations of an enterprise*

The term revenues refers to the resource increases of an enterprise from its sale of goods or services. The increases are derived primarily from the normal operations of the enterprise. It is important to note the differences between revenues and income (or loss). Revenues represent total resource increases; expenses are subtracted from revenues to derive income or loss. Thus, whereas revenue is a "gross" concept, income (or loss) is a "net" concept. The major revenue item for a manufacturing or merchandising entity is sales. A service enterprise (for example, a CPA firm) generates revenues from the fees it charges for the services it renders. Companies might also earn revenues from other activities, for example, from charging interest or collecting royalties.

EXPENSES

expenses *costs of assets used up or additional liabilities incurred in the normal course of business to generate revenues*

The term expenses refers to the costs incurred in normal business operations to generate revenues. The costs of merchandise sold and of utilities used during a period are two common examples of expenses. Thus, expenses represent the costs of benefits derived from the use of a company's resources (assets), or in some instances by incurring additional liabilities (for example, when salaries and wages are recognized as expenses prior to payment). Expenses, like revenues, represent flows of resources during a period of time; but expenses are outflows instead of inflows.

In considering revenues and expenses, you should note that not all inflows of cash are revenues nor are all outflows of cash expenses of the current period. For example, cash may be received by borrowing from a bank, which is an increase in a liability, not a revenue. Similarly, cash may be paid to purchase land, which is an exchange of one asset for another asset, not an expense of the current period. This concept will be discussed further in Chapter 4.

GAINS AND LOSSES

gains (or losses) *net increases (or decreases) in an entity's resources derived from peripheral activities or associated with nonrecurring, unusual events and circumstances*

A fine and sometimes arbitrary distinction is made between gains and losses on the one hand, and revenues and expenses on the other. Revenues and expenses are associated with the normal operating activities of an enterprise: producing, buying, selling, rendering services, and so on. Gains and losses are associated with peripheral, nonoperating activities of an enterprise and also with nonrecurring and uncontrollable events affecting the enterprise. An example of a gain from a nonoperating activity might be the sale of land or a building for more than its cost by a company that is not in the real estate business. An example of a loss from a nonrecurring and uncontrollable event might be the loss of inventory as the result of a flooded warehouse or an earthquake.

Another distinction is made between gains and losses and revenues and expenses. Gains and losses are generally reported on a "net" basis. For example, referring again to the sale of land, the gain or loss to be reported is the excess or deficiency of receipts from its sale over its cost. Revenues and expenses, on the other hand, are accounted for on a "gross" basis and must be compared (matched) with each other to determine if there is income or loss.

NET INCOME (OR NET LOSS)

net income *a measure of the overall performance of a business entity; equal to revenues plus gains minus expenses and losses for the period*

Net income, sometimes called earnings or profit, is an overall measure of the performance of a business entity. As such, net income is a concept reflecting the business's accomplishments (revenues and gains) in excess of its efforts (expenses and losses)—from normal operating activities as well as from peripheral or nonrecurring activities during a particular period of time. If the difference is positive, it is generally called net income; if the difference is negative, it is called net loss.

operating income *a measure of the profitability of a business from normal operations; equals revenues minus operating expenses*

A distinction is usually made between operating income, which is regular business income before gains or losses, and net income. Thus, net income is equal to

	Revenues
−	Expenses
	Operating Income
+	Gains
−	Losses
	Net Income

Because it represents the net results of an enterprise's activities, the income measurement is considered by many to be the single most important indicator for predicting future cash flows.

TO SUMMARIZE General-purpose financial statements provide information for a variety of users about an enterprise's economic resources, obligations, and results of operations. The basic elements of the financial statements are assets; liabilities; owners' equity, including investments by owners and distributions to owners; revenues; expenses; gains; losses; and net income (or net loss).

The Primary Financial Statements

As noted earlier, the accounting process generates a number of different reports. However, most of the financial information needed by external users is contained in just three reports, the primary financial statements: (1) the balance sheet (or statement of financial position), (2) the income statement (or statement of earnings), and (3) the statement of changes in financial position (or funds statement). The names of these statements are used interchangeably with those following in parentheses. A fourth report, the statement of retained earnings, may be presented as a separate, major statement or may be combined with the income statement. However, an increasing number of companies substitute a more comprehensive statement of changes in owners' (or stockholders') equity for the statement of retained earnings.

THE STATEMENT OF FINANCIAL POSITION

balance sheet (statement of financial position) *the primary financial statement that shows the financial resources of an enterprise at a particular date and the claims against those resources, and therefore the relationships of assets, liabilities, and owners' equity*

The statement of financial position, commonly called a balance sheet, provides a financial picture of an enterprise at a particular date. It shows a company's financial resources (assets) and the sources of, or claims against, those resources (liabilities and owners' equity). It is referred to as a balance sheet because assets always equal the total of liabilities and owners' equity. This, you will recall, is in keeping with the basic accounting equation: Assets = Liabilities + Owners' Equity.

A typical format for a balance sheet is shown in Exhibit 2-1. (Another example, from the 1981 annual report of IBM, is provided at the back of the

EXHIBIT 2-1

Fashion Fabrics, Inc.
Comparative Balance Sheets as of December 31, 1984 and 1983

Assets	1984	1983	Liabilities and Stockholders' Equity	1984	1983
Current Assets:			*Current Liabilities:*		
Cash	$ 1,150	$ 1,200	Accounts Payable	$ 4,100	$ 4,500
Accounts Receivable	2,500	2,100	*Long-Term Liabilities:*		
Inventory	12,000	8,000	Bonds Payable	30,000	30,000
Total Current Assets	$15,650	$11,300	Total Liabilities	$34,100	$34,500
Long-Term Assets:			*Stockholders' Equity:*		
Land	$10,000	$ 3,000	Capital Stock (1,500 and 1,000 shares @ $15)	$22,500	$15,000
Buildings	40,000	42,000	Retained Earnings	9,050	6,800
Total Long-Term Assets	$50,000	$45,000	Total Stockholders' Equity	$31,550	$21,800
Total Assets	$65,650	$56,300	Total Liabilities and Stockholders' Equity	$65,650	$56,300

book.) The heading of the statement includes the name of the company and the title and date of the statement. All assets are then listed on the statement, generally by category and in decreasing order of their ability to be converted to cash. For example, cash and certain other assets are classified as current assets because they usually will be converted to cash within a year. Other assets are reported as long-term assets. When a balance sheet is categorized in this way, it is referred to as a classified balance sheet. A classified balance sheet is described in detail in Chapter 8.

classified balance sheet *a balance sheet on which assets, liabilities, and owners' equity are subdivided by age, use, and source*

To reinforce the idea that total assets always equal total liabilities and owners' equity, some companies list the liabilities and owners' equity items to the right of the assets. Liabilities and owners' equity are shown separately because they represent different claims against assets; liabilities are creditors' claims and owners' equity shows the owners' claims. Like assets, liabilities usually are classified as current (obligations expected to be paid within a year) or long-term. For a corporation, the owners' equity section is referred to as stockholders' equity; it reports the proceeds from the issuance of capital stock, and also the retained earnings of an enterprise. This is to distinguish the amounts invested by owners from the amounts earned and retained from profitable operations of the business. For a proprietorship, the owners' equity is called proprietorship equity; for a partnership, it is called partnership equity.

capital stock *the portion of owners' equity contributed by investors (the owners) through the issuance of stock*

retained earnings *the accumulated portion of owners' equity that has been earned and retained from profitable operations and not paid out in dividends or restricted for some other use; equal to owners' equity less contributed capital*

You will notice that Exhibit 2-1 includes financial information not only for the current year but also for the preceding year. Most companies prepare such comparative balance sheets, showing the current period and one or more preceding periods. This format allows readers to view the company's current financial picture in relation to that of the previous period or periods and to note any significant changes in assets, liabilities, and owners' equity. For example, Fashion Fabrics has increased its inventory significantly this past year, and has sold 500 more shares of stock.

TO SUMMARIZE The balance sheet provides a capsule view of the financial status of an enterprise at a particular date. It helps external users assess the financial relationships of the assets, liabilities, and owners' equity of a business. Chapters 8 through 14 analyze the balance sheet in detail.

THE STATEMENT OF EARNINGS

income statement (statement of earnings) *the primary financial statement that summarizes the revenues generated, the expenses incurred, and any gains or losses of an entity during a period of time*

The statement of earnings, or income statement, shows the results of an entity's operations for a period of time (a month, a quarter, or a year). It is a summary of the revenues generated and costs incurred (expenses) by an entity, as well as its gains or losses.

A simple but typical income statement is presented in Exhibit 2-2. (The 1981 statement of earnings for IBM is provided at the back of the book.) Like the balance sheet, the income statement begins with the name of the company and the title of the report. Note also that the income statement designates the period of time covered; here it refers to "the years ended," in contrast to the balance sheet, which is "as of" a particular date. The income statement covers a *period* of time; the balance sheet is a record at a *point* in time.

For most manufacturing and merchandising enterprises the first item on the income statement is sales revenue. The cost of goods sold—that is, the

EXHIBIT 2-2

Fashion Fabrics, Inc.
Comparative Income Statements
for the Years Ended December 31, 1984 and 1983

	1984	1983
Sales Revenue	$53,890	$48,820
Less Cost of Goods Sold	31,027	28,652
Gross Margin	$22,863	$20,168
Less Selling and Administrative Expenses:		
Advertising Expense	$ 1,060	$ 965
Salaries Expense	10,700	9,700
Rent Expense	3,600	3,360
Utilities Expense	1,800	1,780
Other Expenses	1,103	363
Total Expenses	$18,263	$16,168
Operating Income	$ 4,600	$ 4,000
Less Loss Due to Flood-Damaged Merchandise	-0-	1,000
Income Before Taxes	$ 4,600	$ 3,000
Income Taxes	1,840	1,200
Net Income	$ 2,760	$ 1,800

Earnings per Share: 1984: $2,760 ÷ 1,500 shares = $1.84 per share
1983: $1,800 ÷ 1,000 shares = $1.80 per share

gross margin *the excess of net sales revenues over the cost of goods sold*

cost of inventory sold—is subtracted from sales to derive a gross margin (gross profit) measurement. Gross margin is a measure of how much a company "marks up" its merchandise over cost for resale to its customers. For example, if a shoe store has sales revenues of $35,000 and pays $20,000 to purchase its inventory, the gross margin is $15,000—a markup of 43 percent of sales revenue.

Other expenses, such as advertising, employee salaries, utilities, and rent, are subtracted from the gross margin. After all operating expenses are subtracted, the result is operating income (or loss). Other revenues and expenses, any gains or losses, and the provision for income taxes are then added or subtracted. The "bottom line" is net income or net loss. Net income (or loss) is added to (or a loss is subtracted from) any past retained earnings to report the updated retained earnings figure on the balance sheet. It is also used to compute earnings (or loss) per share (EPS) of stock (net income ÷ number of shares outstanding).

earnings (or loss) per share (EPS) *the amount of net income (earnings) related to each share of stock; computed by dividing net income by the number of shares of common stock outstanding during the period*

NI / # shares

The income statement tells investors and creditors how profitable an enterprise has been for the period. Comparative income statements indicate trends and provide some basis for predicting future cash flows. Such relationships as the ratio of expenses to sales revenues and of net income to stockholders' equity also provide useful information in interpreting the operating results of a company. These relationships are identified through financial statement analysis, which is covered in Chapter 16.

TO SUMMARIZE The income statement provides a measure of the success of an enterprise over a specific period of time. It shows the major sources of revenues generated and the expenses associated with those revenues. It matches efforts against accomplishments over a period of operating activity and helps external users evaluate the earnings potential of a company. Chapters 6 and 7 examine the income statement in detail.

THE STATEMENT OF CHANGES IN FINANCIAL POSITION

statement of changes in financial position (funds statement) *the primary financial statement that shows an entity's major sources and uses of financial resources (funds) during a period of time*

The statement of changes in financial position, also called the funds statement, shows the origin and disposition of an enterprise's financial resources. For this reason, the statement is also referred to as a sources and uses of funds statement.

As mentioned earlier, companies obtain funds from three primary sources: from operations, from borrowing, and from investments by owners. For most companies the primary uses of funds are for current operating purposes (such as to pay salaries or utility bills), to pay dividends, to purchase additional equipment or to buy more land and buildings, to pay taxes, and so forth. Thus, a funds statement has two major sections: one that identifies the "funds provided" (or simply sources of funds) and one that shows "funds applied" (or uses of funds). Like the other two primary statements, the funds statement begins with a heading that states the company name, the title of the statement, and the period of time covered, which is the same time period as for the income statement.

Because the funds statement involves concepts and analytical procedures that have not yet been introduced, we will not illustrate a funds statement or discuss its preparation at this point. The preparation and interpretation of a funds statement will be explained in Chapter 15, when you are better able to see its importance and understand its complexities. For now, recognize that the statement of changes in financial position is one of the three primary financial statements and that it shows the major resource inflows and the major uses of resources by a company during a period of time.

ARTICULATION OF FINANCIAL STATEMENTS

articulation *the idea that financial statements tie together, that operating statement items (for example, net income) explain or reconcile changes in major balance sheet categories (for example, retained earnings)*

Although each of the three primary financial statements has been discussed separately, we should point out that they tie together, that is, they "articulate." In accounting language, articulation refers to the relationship between an operating statement (the income statement or the funds statement) and comparative balance sheets, whereby an item on the operating statement helps explain the change in an item on the balance sheet from one year to the next. For example, the net income figure on the income statement is added to the beginning retained earnings balance; then dividends are subtracted to obtain the ending retained earnings figure that is reported on the balance sheet (Beginning Retained Earnings + Net Income − Dividends = Ending Retained Earnings). Any other items that affect retained earnings would, of course, also be added or subtracted as appropriate. For example, distributions to owners would be subtracted from retained earnings. For Fashion Fabrics, retained earnings at December 31, 1983, was $6,800 (Exhibit 2–1). The net income reported on the income statement for 1984 was $2,760 (Exhibit 2–2). Assuming that dividends of $510 were declared and paid during that year, the retained earnings balance is $9,050 at December 31, 1984 ($6,800 + $2,760 − $510 = $9,050). As you study the primary financial statements, these relationships will become clearer and you will understand the concept of articulation better.

THE STATEMENTS OF RETAINED EARNINGS AND CHANGES IN OWNERS' EQUITY

Two other statements are sometimes included in the annual report to shareholders, although neither is considered one of the three primary financial statements. Because these two statements are commonly found in practice, each will be discussed.

statement of retained earnings *a report that shows the changes in retained earnings during a period of time*

The statement of retained earnings identifies changes in retained earnings. It contains a beginning balance, the net income for the period, a deduction for any cash dividends declared, and an ending balance. Generally, then, the ending retained earnings balance is a cumulative figure that equals the total amount of undistributed earnings since the business began operations. Assuming the data in the preceding section for Fashion Fabrics—a beginning retained earnings amount of $6,800, a net income of $2,760, and the declaration and payment of $510 in dividends—the statement of retained earnings would be as follows:

Fashion Fabrics, Inc.
Statement of Retained Earnings
for the Year Ended December 31, 1984

Retained Earnings, January 1, 1984	$6,800
Add Net Income for the Year	2,760
	$9,560
Less Dividends	510
Retained Earnings, December 31, 1984	$9,050

The statement of retained earnings may be combined with the income statement, as illustrated in Exhibit 2-3. This gives the reader a complete picture of current earnings and dividends, as well as the total earnings retained by the business over a period of years.

EXHIBIT 2-3

Fashion Fabrics, Inc.
Combined Statement of Income and Retained Earnings
for the Year Ended December 31, 1984

Sales Revenue		$53,890
Less Cost of Goods Sold		31,027
Gross Margin		$22,863
Less Selling and Administrative Expenses:		
Advertising Expense	$ 1,060	
Salaries Expense	10,700	
Rent Expense	3,600	
Utilities Expense	1,800	
Other Expenses	1,103	18,263
Income Before Taxes		$ 4,600
Income Taxes		1,840
Net Income		$ 2,760
Add Retained Earnings at Beginning of Year		6,800
		$ 9,560
Less Dividends		510
Retained Earnings at End of Year		$ 9,050

Earnings per Share: $2,760 ÷ 1,500 shares = $1.84 per share
Dividends per Share: $510 ÷ 1,500 shares = $0.34 per share

statement of changes in owners' equity *a report that shows the total changes in owners' equity (including retained earnings) during a period of time*

There may have been changes in owners' equity accounts during the period in addition to the change in retained earnings. For example, additional stock may have been issued. When all changes in owners' equity accounts are to be shown, the statement of changes in owners' equity replaces the statement of retained earnings. A simple example is presented in Exhibit 2-4.

EXHIBIT 2-4

Fashion Fabrics, Inc.
Statement of Changes in Owners' Equity
for the Year Ended December 31, 1984

	Capital Stock	Retained Earnings	Total Owners' Equity
Beginning Balances, January 1, 1984	$15,000	$6,800	$21,800
Add: Net Income for the Year		2,760	2,760
Issuance of Capital Stock	7,500		7,500
	$22,500	$9,560	$32,060
Less Dividends		510	510
Ending Balances, December 31, 1984 ...	$22,500	$9,050	$31,550

TO SUMMARIZE The statement of changes in financial position (the funds statement) shows the major resource inflows (from operations, from external borrowing, and from equity financing) and the major uses of resources (for current operating purposes or to declare dividends, purchase furniture and fixtures, and so forth). Chapter 15 contains a discussion of the funds statement. The statement of retained earnings identifies changes in the Retained Earnings account. It may be combined with the income statement. If there are also changes in the owners' equity accounts, a statement of owners' equity is prepared. Financial statements articulate; that is, they tie together.

Notes to Financial Statements

notes to financial statements *explanatory information considered an integral part of the primary financial statements*

The notes to financial statements are considered an integral part of those statements because they provide vital information that cannot be captured solely by the descriptions and dollar amounts of statement items. For example, inventories are listed on the balance sheet at a certain amount, but a note is usually necessary to describe the contents of the inventory, how it was valued, and any special circumstances. Thus, explanatory notes are necessary to provide a better understanding of the information in the statements.

The notes generally follow a standard sequence. The first note describes the accounting policies and principles followed by the business. Other notes refer to specific items in the statements, and are usually cross-referenced to those items and presented in the order in which the items appear in the statements. Generally, as illustrated by the IBM statements at the back of the book, a company will present the notes in a special section of the annual report adjacent to the statements themselves.

The Audit Report

certified public accountant (CPA) *a special designation given to an accountant who has passed a national uniform examination and has met other certifying requirements; CPA certificates are issued and monitored by state boards of accountancy or similar agencies*

audit report *a statement issued by an independent certified public accountant that expresses an opinion about the company's adherence to generally accepted accounting principles*

A company's financial statements are usually audited by an independent certified public accountant (CPA). The CPA firm will issue an audit report that expresses an opinion about the company's adherence to generally accepted accounting principles. Note that the financial statements are the representations of a company's management, and not of the CPA. Although not all company records have to be audited, audits are required for many purposes. For example, a banker generally will not make a commercial loan without first receiving audited financial statements from a prospective borrower. As another example, most securities cannot be sold to the general public until they are registered with the Securities and Exchange Commission, and the registration process requires inclusion of audited financial statements.

An audit report does not guarantee accuracy but it does provide added assurance that the financial statements are not misleading, since they have been examined by an unbiased and independent professional. However, the CPA cannot examine every transaction upon which the summary figures in the financial statements are based, so the accuracy of the statements must remain the responsibility of the company's management. An audit report is shown in Exhibit 2–5, as well as with the IBM statements at the back of the book.

EXHIBIT 2–5 Audit Report

Shareholders and Board of Directors
Bancorp Hawaii, Inc.
Honolulu, Hawaii

We have examined the consolidated statements of condition of Bancorp Hawaii, Inc. and subsidiaries as of December 31, 1981, 1980 and 1979, and the related consolidated statements of income, shareholders' equity and changes in financial position for each of the three years in the period ended December 31, 1981, the statements of condition of Bancorp Hawaii, Inc. (parent company) as of December 31, 1981, 1980 and 1979, and the related statements of income and changes in financial position for each of the three years in the period ended December 31, 1981, and the consolidated statements of condition of Bank of Hawaii (a subsidiary) as of December 31, 1981, 1980 and 1979. Our examinations were made in accordance with generally accepted auditing standards and, accordingly, included such tests of the accounting records and such other auditing procedures as we considered necessary in the circumstances.

In our opinion, the financial statements referred to above present fairly the consolidated financial position of Bancorp Hawaii, Inc. and subsidiaries as of December 31, 1981, 1980 and 1979, and the consolidated results of their operations and changes in their financial position for each of the three years in the period ended December 31, 1981, and the financial position of Bancorp Hawaii, Inc. (parent company) as of December 31, 1981, 1980 and 1979, and the related statements of income, and changes in financial position for each of the three years in the period ended December 31, 1981, and the consolidated financial position of Bank of Hawaii at December 31, 1981, 1980 and 1979, in conformity with generally accepted accounting principles applied on a consistent basis.

Ernst & Whinney

Honolulu, Hawaii
January 22, 1982

CHAPTER REVIEW

The primary financial statements are designed to satisfy the needs of a variety of users of financial information: managers, creditors, stockholders, potential investors, financial analysts, and others. The information supplied for external users, primarily investors and creditors, is intended to help them assess the size, timing, and degree of certainty of an entity's prospective cash flows and earnings potential. In analyzing a company, investors and creditors should consider its liquidity, solvency, and profitability. Information relating to these concepts is found in the primary general-purpose financial statements: the balance sheet, the income statement, and the funds statement.

The basic elements of the balance sheet are the economic resources of an entity (assets) and the sources of, or claims against, those resources (creditor claims are called liabilities and ownership claims are referred to as owners' equity). On the income statement, revenues reflect resource increases from the sale of goods or services derived from normal operations during a period of time. Expenses refer to the costs of using resources (assets) or incurring additional liabilities during normal operations to generate revenues. Gains also represent net increases in resources but are derived from peripheral and nonrecurring activities. Similarly, net decreases in resources from peripheral and nonrecurring activities are known as losses. Net income, or earnings, is a measure of the overall performance of a business. This measure includes all changes in equity during a period except those resulting from investments by owners or distributions to owners. Revenues less expenses is called operating income (or loss); operating income plus gains minus losses results in net income (or loss).

The balance sheet shows an entity's financial position at a particular date. It discloses the relations between the firm's assets, liabilities, and owners' equity. The income statement reports the results of a company's operations in terms of its overall income or loss for a period of time. The income statement itemizes revenues, expenses, and net gains or losses, and shows the resulting net income (or net loss) and the amount of earnings per share of stock. The funds statement reports the major sources and uses of financial resources during a period. It helps explain the significant financing and investing activities of an entity. Although not considered a primary financial statement, a statement of retained earnings or a more comprehensive statement of all changes in owners' equity is sometimes included in the set of financial statements reported to external users. The idea that the financial statements tie together is referred to as articulation.

In analyzing financial statements, it is important to consider the accompanying notes. These explanatory notes provide additional information about certain items and dollar amounts in the statements. They are considered an integral part of the financial statements and should be given special care and attention in terms of the full-disclosure standard.

Another key item associated with financial statements is the independent audit report. This report contains the opinion of an independent CPA about the company's adherence to generally accepted accounting principles. This professional opinion adds credence to management's representations.

KEY TERMS AND CONCEPTS

articulation (42)
assets (35)
audit report (45)
balance sheet (statement of financial position) (38)
capital stock (39)
cash flow (33)
certified public accountant (CPA) (45)
classified balance sheet (39)
distributions to owners (36)
dividends (33)
earnings (or loss) per share (EPS) (41)
earnings potential (33)
expenses (37)
gains (or losses) (37)
general-purpose (or primary) financial statements (33)
gross margin (41)
income statement (statement of earnings) (40)
investments by owners (36)
liabilities (35)
liquidity (33)
net assets (35)
net income (37)
notes to financial statements (44)
operating income (38)
owners' equity (stockholders' equity) (35)
profitability (34)
retained earnings (39)
revenues (36)
solvency (34)
statement of changes in financial position (funds statement) (41)
statement of changes in owners' equity (43)
statement of retained earnings (42)

REVIEW PROBLEM

The Income Statement and the Balance Sheet

J. P. Hughes, owner of Hughes Hardware, Inc., has come to you for help in preparing an income statement and a balance sheet for the year ending December 31, 1983. Hughes does not know the amount of accounts receivable or net income. Several account balances as of December 31, 1983, are presented below.

Retained Earnings (Ending Balance)	$ 35,000
Advertising Expense	2,000
Cash	27,000
Rent Expense	2,400
Building	100,000
Capital Stock	106,000
Interest Expense	700
Provision for Income Taxes	9,000
Mortgage Payable	72,000
Cost of Goods Sold	56,000
Accounts Payable	36,000
Land	64,000
Inventory	32,000
Salary Expense	10,000
Sales Revenue	92,000
Other Expenses	1,300
Accounts Receivable	X
Total Shares of Capital Stock Outstanding	2,650

Required:

1. Prepare an income statement for the year ended December 31, 1983.
2. Prepare a balance sheet as of December 31, 1983.
3. Determine the correct amount of accounts receivable at year-end.
4. Calculate the earnings per share (net income ÷ number of shares of outstanding stock).

Solution

1 and 2. Income Statement and Balance Sheet
The first step in solving this problem is to separate the income statement accounts from the balance sheet accounts. Revenue and expense accounts are reported on the income statement; accounts that show the company's financial position appear on the balance sheet.

Income Statement Accounts	Balance Sheet Accounts
Advertising Expense	Retained Earnings
Rent Expense	Cash
Interest Expense	Building
Income Taxes	Capital Stock
Cost of Goods Sold	Mortgage Payable
Salary Expense	Accounts Payable
Sales Revenue	Land
Other Expenses	Inventory
	Accounts Receivable

After the accounts are separated, the income statement and the balance sheet may be prepared using a proper format.

Hughes Hardware, Inc.
Income Statement
for the Year Ended December 31, 1983

Sales Revenue		$92,000
Less Cost of Goods Sold		56,000
Gross Margin		$36,000
Selling and Administrative Expenses:		
Advertising Expense	$ 2,000	
Rent Expense	2,400	
Interest Expense	700	
Salary Expense	10,000	
Other Expenses	1,300	16,400
Income Before Taxes		$19,600
Income Taxes		9,000
Net Income		$10,600

Earnings per share = $4.00

Net income is computed as above once the accounts have been put into proper income statement form. The earnings-per-share computation is explained later.

Hughes Hardware, Inc.
Balance Sheet as of December 31, 1983

Assets		
Current Assets:		
Cash	$ 27,000	
Accounts Receivable	26,000*	
Inventory	32,000	$ 85,000
Long-Term Assets:		
Land	$ 64,000	
Building	100,000	164,000
Total Assets		$249,000

* See item 3 for calculation.

Liabilities and Owners' Equity		
Current Liabilities:		
Accounts Payable	$ 36,000	
Long-Term Liabilities:		
Mortgage Payable	72,000	
Total Liabilities		$108,000
Owners' Equity:		
Capital Stock	$106,000	
Retained Earnings	35,000	
Total Owners' Equity		141,000
Total Liabilities and Owners' Equity		$249,000

3. Accounts Receivable
Since total assets must always equal total liabilities and owners' equity, accounts receivable may be computed by subtracting, as shown below.

Total Assets (total liabilities and owners' equity)		$249,000
Less: Cash	$ 27,000	
Inventory	32,000	
Land	64,000	
Building	100,000	223,000
Equals Accounts Receivable		$ 26,000

4. Earnings per Share
The only item left to be computed is earnings per share. This is done by dividing net income by the number of shares of capital stock outstanding, as shown below.

$$\frac{\text{net income}}{\text{shares outstanding}} = \frac{\$10{,}600}{2{,}650} = \$4.00 \text{ per share}$$

This earnings-per-share figure is disclosed on the income statement.

DISCUSSION QUESTIONS

1 What is the basic objective of financial reporting?

2 What factors determine the types of accounting reports generated?

3 Who are the primary users of general-purpose financial statements?

4 Why are investors and creditors interested in a company's earnings potential?

5 Distinguish between the concepts of liquidity, solvency, and profitability.

6 What are the primary characteristics of assets?

7 Distinguish between:
(a) Assets and expenses.
(b) Expenses and losses.
(c) Revenues and gains.

8 What are the primary characteristics of a liability?

9 Why is the measurement of earnings of a business considered useful information?

10 What is the major purpose of the:
(a) Balance sheet.
(b) Income statement.
(c) Statement of changes in financial position.

11 Where does the name "balance sheet" come from?

12 What are the two main components of owners' equity in a corporation? Why are they reported separately?

13 Some people feel that the income statement is more important than the balance sheet. Do you agree? Why or why not?

14 What are the main components of an income statement? Why is it important to list these major components separately?

15 What are the major sources and uses of funds reported on a funds statement?

16 What is the purpose of the notes to the financial statements?

17 You are thinking of investing in one of two companies. In one annual report, the auditor's opinion states that the financial statements were prepared in accordance with generally accepted accounting principles. The other makes no such claim. How important is that to you? Explain.

18 Why is an audit report required in many instances?

19 Some people think that auditors are responsible for assuring the accuracy of financial statements. Are they correct? Why or why not?

EXERCISES

E2–1 General-Purpose Financial Statements

Eakins Company's year-end is December 31. Company management is currently preparing the annual report to shareholders. Identify each major financial statement that should be included in the annual report and describe each statement's basic purpose.

E2–2 Classification of Balance Sheet Items

Indicate for each of the following whether it is: an asset (A), liability (L), or an owners' equity item (OE).

1. Accounts Payable
2. Accounts Receivable
3. Cash
4. Inventory
5. Land
6. Capital Stock
7. Equipment
8. Interest Receivable
9. Mortgage Payable
10. Notes Payable
11. Buildings
12. Retained Earnings

E2–3 Accounting Equation—Simple Computations

Balance the following accounting equations.

	Assets	=	Liabilities	+	Owners' Equity
1.	$40,000		$?		$25,000
2.	10,000		5,000		?
3.	?		10,000		20,000

E2–4 Accounting Equation

Compute the missing figures for firms A–D.

	A	B	C	D
Cash	$25,000	$ 9,000	$12,000	$?
Accounts Receivable	20,000	15,000	7,000	8,000
Plant and Equipment	50,000	?	40,000	26,000
Accounts Payable	?	6,000	12,000	5,000
Notes Payable	30,000	10,000	15,000	10,000
Owners' Equity	50,000	30,000	?	24,000

E2–5 Profitability Measures

Quick-Stop Gas Company determined the following for the year ended December 31, 1983: sales revenue, $120,000; cost of goods sold, $65,000; selling and administrative expenses, $32,000; unusual fire loss, $7,500. Calculate the gross margin, operating income, and net income for the year (ignore taxes).

E2–6 Comprehensive Accounting Equation

Assuming that no additional stock was issued or dividends declared, compute the missing figures for these companies.

	Roberts Company	Tolbert Company	Asay Company
Assets: January 1, 1984	$90	$?	$230
Liabilities: January 1, 1984	70	230	?
Owners' Equity: January 1, 1984	?	310	150
Assets: December 31, 1984	95	?	310
Liabilities: December 31, 1984	?	260	90
Owners' Equity: December 31, 1984	?	360	?
Revenues in 1984	20	?	400
Expenses in 1984	25	58	?

E2–7 Retained Earnings Computations

During 1984, Z-Bar Company had revenues of $90,000 and expenses of $50,000. On December 31, 1983, Z-Bar had assets of $400,000, liabilities of $100,000, and capital stock of $250,000. Z-Bar declared and paid a cash dividend of $20,000 in 1984. No additional stock was issued. Compute the Retained Earnings amounts on December 31, 1983, and December 31, 1984.

E2–8 Income and Retained Earnings Relationships

Assume that Retained Earnings increased by $60,000 from December 31, 1983, to December 31, 1984, for Jones Manufacturing Company. During the year, a cash dividend of $10,000 was declared and paid.

1. Compute the net income for the year.
2. Assume that the revenues for the year were $360,000. Compute the expenses incurred for the year.

E2–9 Balance Sheet Relationships

Correct the following balance sheet.

Mountain View Company
Balance Sheet as of December 31, 1983

Assets		Liabilities and Owners' Equity	
Cash	$ 7,000	Land	$ 5,000
Accounts Payable	8,000	Accounts Receivable	3,000
Inventory	2,000	Capital Stock	10,000
Equipment	10,000		
Retained Earnings	9,000		
	$36,000		$18,000

E2–10 Income Statement Computations

Given below are the operating data for Sporting Goods, Inc. for the year ended December 31, 1984.

Sales Revenue	$175,000
Cost of Merchandise Sold	150,000
Salary Expense	12,000
Rent Expense	1,500
Administrative Expense	6,000
Gain on Sale of Land	2,300
Inventory Loss Due to Flood Damage	4,800
Average Number of Shares Outstanding–1,500	

Determine:

1. The operating income and the net income for the year. (Ignore income taxes.)
2. The earnings per share.

E2–11 Income Statement Preparation

The following selected information is taken from the records of Allen Corporation. Prepare an income statement for the year ended December 31, 1983.

Accounts Receivable	$ 49,000
Advertising Expense	7,500
Capital Stock (10,000 shares outstanding)	50,000
Cash	15,500
Cost of Goods Sold	63,000
Dividends	5,000
Loss from Fire in Warehouse	9,500
Miscellaneous Operating Expenses	2,200
Income Taxes	17,320
Retained Earnings	75,000
Salaries Expense	24,000
Sales Revenue	142,000

E2–12 Balance Sheet Preparation

From the following selected data, prepare a balance sheet for Jolly Time Toys, Inc. at December 31, 1983.

Accounts Payable	$ 31,000
Accounts Receivable	66,000
Buildings	300,000
Capital Stock (1,000 shares outstanding)	100,000
Cash	77,500
Dividends (paid during 1983)	12,500
Inventory	91,500
Land	110,000
Mortgage Payable	275,000
Net Income	78,500
Retained Earnings, 1/1/83	173,000

E2–13 Preparation of a Statement of Retained Earnings

Prepare a statement of retained earnings for Super Ski Shop for the year ended June 30, 1984, based upon the following information:

Capital Stock (1,500 shares @ $100)	$150,000
Retained Earnings, July 1, 1983	76,800
Dividends	16,700
Ski Rental Revenue	155,800
Operating Expenses	128,300

PROBLEMS

P2–1 Balance Sheet Relationships

Holley Company sells greeting cards. As of December 31, 1984, its financial status is as follows:

Cash	$30,000
Accounts Receivable	25,000
Accounts Payable	21,000
Inventory	18,000
Land, Buildings, and Equipment	80,000
Notes Receivable	6,000
Notes Payable	12,000
Interest Receivable	3,000
Retained Earnings	47,000
Capital Stock	?

Required:

1. Compute the total amount of assets.
2. Compute the total amount of liabilities.
3. Compute the total amount of stockholders' equity.
4. Determine the amount of capital stock of Holley Company.

P2–2 Balance Sheet Preparation

The information presented below is taken from the records of Hansen Cookie Company.

Building	$50,000
Accounts Payable	15,000
Retained Earnings	26,000
Cash	15,000
Capital Stock	80,000
Inventory	65,000
Accounts Receivable	10,000
Notes Payable	30,000
Temporary Investments	5,000
Land	6,000

Required:

Prepare a balance sheet for Hansen Cookie Company as of March 31, 1983.

P2–3 Balance Sheet Preparation with a Missing Element

The following data are available for Julie's Smart Shop as of December 31, 1984.

Cash	$10,000
Accounts Payable	14,000
Capital Stock	?
Accounts Receivable	20,000
Building	28,000
Inventory	12,000
Retained Earnings	20,000
Land	10,000

Required:

1. Prepare a balance sheet for Julie's Smart Shop.
2. Determine the amount of capital stock at December 31, 1984.

P2–4 Income Statement Preparation

Use the following information for Tanaka Camera, Inc. for the month of December 1983.

Salary Expense	$ 7,200
Sales Revenue	46,800
Income Taxes	2,400
Miscellaneous Expenses	1,200
Rent Expense	10,800
Cost of Goods Sold	18,600
Gain from Sale of Investments	3,200
Advertising Expense	2,000

Required:

1. Prepare an income statement for Tanaka Camera, Inc., for the month ending December 31, 1983.
2. **Interpretive Question** Of what significance is the gross margin amount?
3. **Interpretive Question** Why is the gain from sale of investments shown separately from regular sales revenue?

P2–5 Unifying Problem: Net Income and a Statement of Retained Earnings

A summary of the operations of Construction Supply Company for the year ended May 31, 1984, is shown below:

Selling Expense	$ 2,760
Cost of Goods Sold	37,820
Loss Due to Flood Damage	4,900
Rent Expense	1,500
Salary Expense	18,150
Miscellaneous Expenses	4,170
Dividends	12,400
Retained Earnings (6/1/83)	156,540
Gain on Sale of Land	5,100
Income Taxes	21,180
Sales Revenue	115,100
Administrative Expense	7,250

Required:

1. Determine net income for the year by preparing an income statement.
2. Prepare a statement of retained earnings for the year ended May 31, 1984.

P2-6 Unifying Problem: Comprehensive Financial Statement Preparation

The following information was obtained from the records of Photo Supply Company as of December 31, 1983.

Land	$ 25,000
Buildings	96,700
Salary Expense	26,700
Utilities Expense	6,500
Accounts Payable	17,100
Sales Revenue	265,200
Inventory	46,300
Retained Earnings (1/1/83)	181,700
Capital Stock	30,000
Accounts Receivable	31,000
Cost of Goods Sold	138,600
Cash	38,900
Notes Payable	17,200
Gain on Sale of Land	2,300
Rent Expense	17,100
Dividends in 1983	42,800
Other Expenses	8,700
Income Taxes	35,200

Required:

1. Prepare an income statement for the year ended December 31, 1983.
2. Prepare a statement of retained earnings for the year ended December 31, 1983.
3. Prepare a balance sheet as of December 31, 1983.
4. **Interpretive Question** Why is the balance in Retained Earnings so large as compared with the balance in Capital Stock?

P2-7 Income Statement Preparation—Proprietorship

Jack Jones, a CPA, has worked for five years for a national CPA firm. On January 1, 1983, he began business as a single practitioner in his hometown. During the first year of operations he received professional fees of $68,500 for his services, and incurred the following expenses:

Secretarial Help	$20,000
Office Rent	6,000
Heat and Electricity	3,500
Telephone	750
Duplicating Services	500
Office Supplies	380
Professional Dues	220
Accounting and Tax Services	350
Travel and Entertainment	1,800
Total Expenses	$33,500

Required:

Prepare an income statement for the year ended December 31, 1983. (Ignore income taxes.)

P2-8 Unifying Problem: Elements of Comparative Financial Statements

The following report is supplied by Steins Sales Specialty Company.

Steins Sales Specialty Company
Comparative Balance Sheets
as of December 31, 1984 and December 31, 1983

Assets	**December 31, 1984**	**December 31, 1983**
Cash	$ 3,000	$ 5,000
Accounts Receivable	18,000	11,000
Temporary Investments	11,000	10,000
Land	38,000	38,000
Total Assets	$70,000	$64,000
Liabilities and Stockholders' Equity		
Accounts Payable	$ 5,000	$ 4,000
Commissions Payable	1,000	3,000
Salaries Payable	7,000	5,000
Notes Payable	25,000	27,000
Capital Stock	20,000	20,000
Retained Earnings	12,000	5,000
Total Liabilities and Stockholders' Equity	$70,000	$64,000

The company paid utilities of $4,500, salaries and commissions of $44,800, taxes of $3,000, and miscellaneous expenses of $1,500, and declared and paid dividends of $5,000.

Required:

1. Compute the total expenses incurred in 1984. (Assume that the Accounts Payable increase was offset by the increase in Temporary Investments.)
2. Compute the net income or net loss for 1984.
3. Compute the total revenue for 1984.
4. **Interpretive Question** Why are comparative financial statements generally of more value to users than statements for a single period?

P2-9 Basic Accounting Equation

You are furnished only the following information for RACO, Inc. for the year 1984.

a. Except for net income and a $15,000 dividend payment deducted from retained earnings, no other additions or deductions have been made to retained earnings.

b. The only other accounts that were changed were those listed on page 53; the amount of change for each account is shown as a net increase or decrease.

	Increase (Decrease)
Cash	$ 9,500
Accounts Receivable	(3,000)
Inventory	13,500
Accounts Payable	(11,500)
Mortgage Payable	20,000
Capital Stock	5,000

Required:

Using the accounting equation, compute net income for 1984.

P2–10 Unifying Problem: Preparation of Financial Statements

The Valley View Drive-In Theatre had the following operating figures for August 1984.

Sale of Tickets	$37,500
Equipment Rental Expense	3,500
Utilities, Taxes, and Licenses Expense	5,700
Film Rental Expenses	7,300
Advertising Expense	2,000
Wages and Salaries Expense	6,500
Dividends Paid	5,000

End-of-the-month balance sheet figures were as follows:

Cash	$28,300
Supplies	1,800
Land	20,000
Buildings and Screen	30,000
Accounts Payable	12,200
Other Assets	6,000
Capital Stock	40,000
Retained Earnings (August 1, 1984)	26,400

Required:

1. Prepare an income statement for August 1984.
2. Prepare a statement of retained earnings for August 1984.
3. Prepare a balance sheet as of August 31, 1984.

CHAPTER 3

An Introduction to Transaction Analysis

THIS CHAPTER EXPLAINS:

The process of transforming transaction data into useful accounting information.

The basic accounting equation.

The first four steps in the accounting cycle.

transaction analysis *the procedures for analyzing, recording, summarizing, and reporting transactions of an entity*

In the first two chapters we provided an overview of financial accounting. The environment of accounting and its objectives, the basic concepts and principles underlying accounting practice, and the outputs of the accounting process were discussed. With this chapter, we begin our study of transaction analysis. This simply means that we will examine the procedures for analyzing, recording, classifying, summarizing, and reporting the transactions of an entity. In this chapter we describe the first four steps in what is commonly called the accounting cycle, the nine specific procedures in the basic accounting process. In Chapters 4 and 5, we explain the remaining steps in the accounting cycle. An extended illustration is provided after Chapter 5 to show how transaction analysis is used in ordering the financial activities of the three major types of businesses: proprietorship, partnership, and corporation.

The Process of Transforming Transaction Data into Useful Accounting Information

accounting process *the means of transforming economic data into accounting reports that can be interpreted and used in decision making*

Business entities buy and sell goods or services; borrow and invest money; pay wages to employees; purchase land, buildings, and equipment; distribute earnings to their owners; and pay taxes to the government. In order to determine how well an entity is managing its resources, the results of these and similar types of transactions must be analyzed. The accounting process makes that analysis possible by recording, classifying, and summarizing an entity's transactions and preparing reports that present the summary results. Exhibit 3-1 is a diagram of the sequence, showing how accounting monitors the results of an entity's transactions. To fully understand how the inputs (transaction data) are transformed through the accounting process into the outputs (financial statements and reports), you should first learn the distinctions between certain key concepts.

EXHIBIT 3-1 **The Accounting Process**

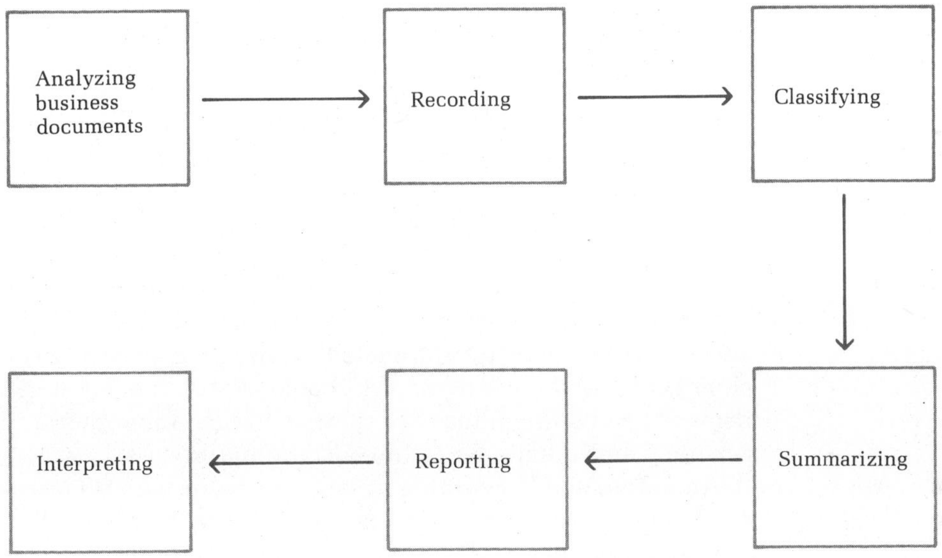

DATA VERSUS INFORMATION

data *inputs to the accounting process that are derived from transactions*

information *data organized by the accounting process*

Although the terms "data" and "information" are sometimes used interchangeably, they are distinguished here to show that the purpose of the accounting process is to transform financial data into useful information. The inputs to the accounting process are raw data, which are taken from documents reporting the various transactions of a business entity. These facts (data) are arranged chronologically and topically into useful formats through the accounting process. They are then summarized on various reports as information. For example, a sales invoice provides data concerning a specific transaction, whereas an income statement reports sales information for the accounting period. Thus, accounting information may be viewed as organized data directed toward a specific objective; in this form, the data have increased communicative value to the person receiving them.

ACCOUNTING VERSUS MANAGERIAL INFORMATION SYSTEMS

accounting information system *a subset of the managerial information system; the system whereby the financial data derived from recorded transactions are collected, processed, and reported*

managerial information system *the system whereby all information used by management is collected, processed, and reported*

A second important distinction can be made, between accounting and managerial information systems. The accounting information system is generally a highly formalized system within an organization. A relatively small but important part of the total managerial information system, the accounting system provides the financial information derived from transaction data. The managerial information system is the broader of the two systems; it encompasses all information related to the organization. For example, in addition to accounting information, it includes general market trends, economic indicators, and product-research reports.

MANUAL VERSUS AUTOMATED ACCOUNTING SYSTEMS

Because of the importance of computers in today's business world, a third distinction should be made, between a manually operated accounting system and an automated one. Historically, of course, all accounting systems had to be maintained by hand. The image of the accountant with green eyeshade and quill pen, sitting on a high stool and meticulously maintaining the accounting records, reflects those early manual systems. Today, few accounting systems are completely manual. Even small companies generally use some type of automated equipment—cash registers, adding machines, typewriters, calculators, bookkeeping machines. Such equipment helps to reduce the number of routine clerical functions and to improve the accuracy and timeliness of the accounting process.

automated accounting system *a system in which most of the data processing is performed by machines instead of people*

computerized accounting system *a system in which most of the data processing is performed by computers*

An automated accounting system is one in which most of the data processing is performed by machines. Depending on the needs of the organization, the system may be as simple as an essentially manual system with several special-purpose business machines or as complex as an electronic data processing (EDP) system that utilizes the latest developments in computer technology. In a computerized accounting system, the accounting records are kept on tapes or discs, and displayed on computer printouts or cathode-ray-tube terminals (see Exhibit 3-2). Although the accounting records and reports generated by a computerized system will usually look somewhat different from those of a manual system, the underlying accounting principles are the same. There is no difference in the accounting theory involved, only in the mechanical aspect of the bookkeeping process. Because a manual accounting system is easier to understand, we will use a manual system for our examples in this text.

The extent of automation depends not only on an organization's needs, but also on the costs of the system in relation to its benefits. Large complex organizations require a lot of information and need to review it often. For these companies, a high degree of automation is practical because the costs of automated equipment are outweighed by the benefits of more timely reports and more efficient performance of routine clerical functions. For smaller companies with relatively few transactions each month and little need for frequent accounting reports, large computer systems might be too expensive. However, many small- to medium-sized companies use large

EXHIBIT 3-2a **Computer Equipment**

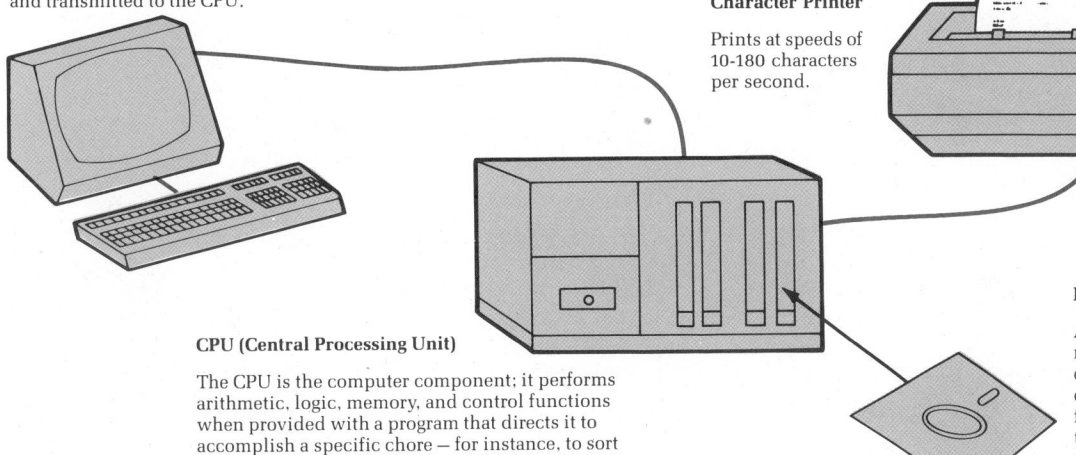

SMALL MICROCOMPUTER SYSTEM

Shown here are the least number of components that are likely to be useful for a small business

CRT (Cathode-Ray Tube) with Keyboard

Data and commands are entered via the keyboard, displayed on the CRT, and transmitted to the CPU.

Character Printer

Prints at speeds of 10-180 characters per second.

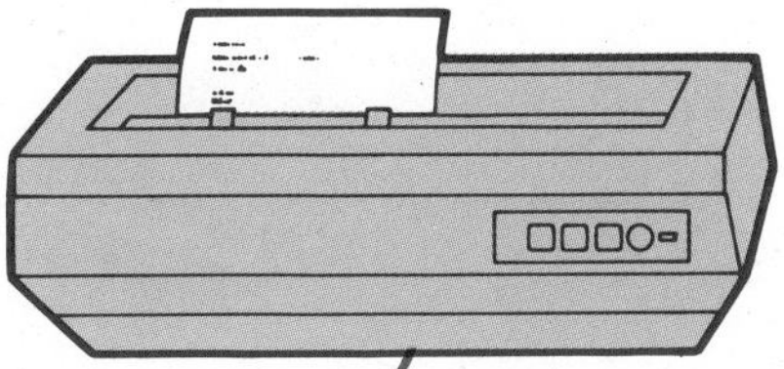

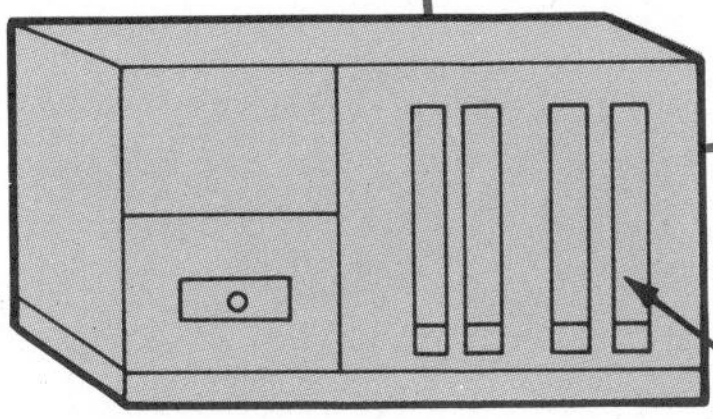

CPU (Central Processing Unit)

The CPU is the computer component; it performs arithmetic, logic, memory, and control functions when provided with a program that directs it to accomplish a specific chore – for instance, to sort the data (customer's names and addresses) in accordance with zip code.

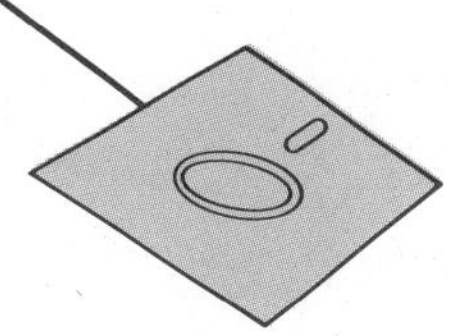

Floppy disk (diskette)

A recordlike disk of magnetically coated Mylar enclosed in a protective envelope. Capacity ranges from 30 to 200 pages of text per diskette. Used to store data or programs. Inexpensive.

ADDITIONAL COMPONENTS FOR USE WITH A COMPUTER OF GREATER CAPACITY, SUCH AS A MINICOMPUTER OR A MAIN FRAME

Minicomputer

Tape drive

Stores a vast amount of information that can be fed into the computer in a predetermined sequence.

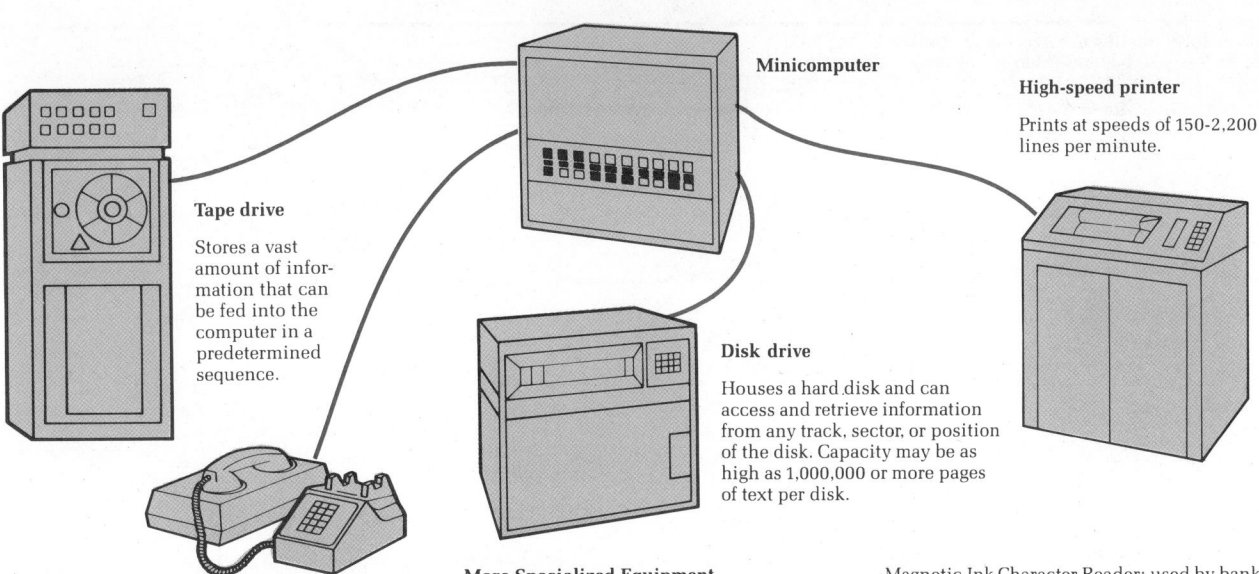

High-speed printer

Prints at speeds of 150-2,200 lines per minute.

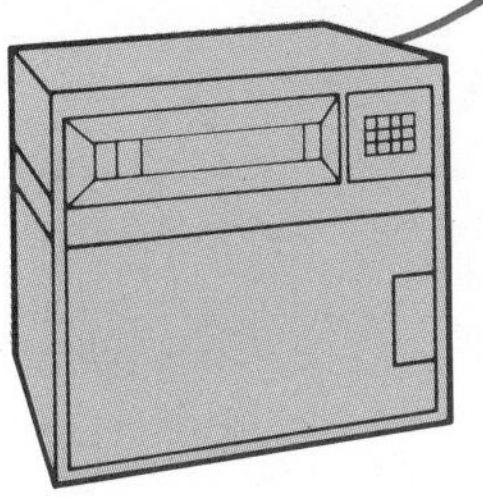

Disk drive

Houses a hard disk and can access and retrieve information from any track, sector, or position of the disk. Capacity may be as high as 1,000,000 or more pages of text per disk.

Modem (MOdulator, DEModulator) and acoustic coupler

Converts signals from the computer so that they can be carried over the telephone line. At the other end of the line, another modem reconverts the signals to digital form for printer or display by CRT.

More Specialized Equipment

Laser printer: prints at speeds of hundreds of pages per minute (both sides of the sheet).

OCR (Optical Character Reader): reads typed or printed documents directly – invoices or credit card charge slips, for example – and converts them to digital signals for use by the computer.

Magnetic Ink Character Reader: used by banks, for example, to cash and cancel checks by direct reading of the account number.

Microfiche: a sheet of microfilm, usually the size of a file card, containing photographically reproduced documents greatly reduced in size. Documents are indexed so that the computer can retrieve them for display on a CRT. Useful in the preservation of records.

(continued on the next page)

EXHIBIT 3-2b Computer Communications

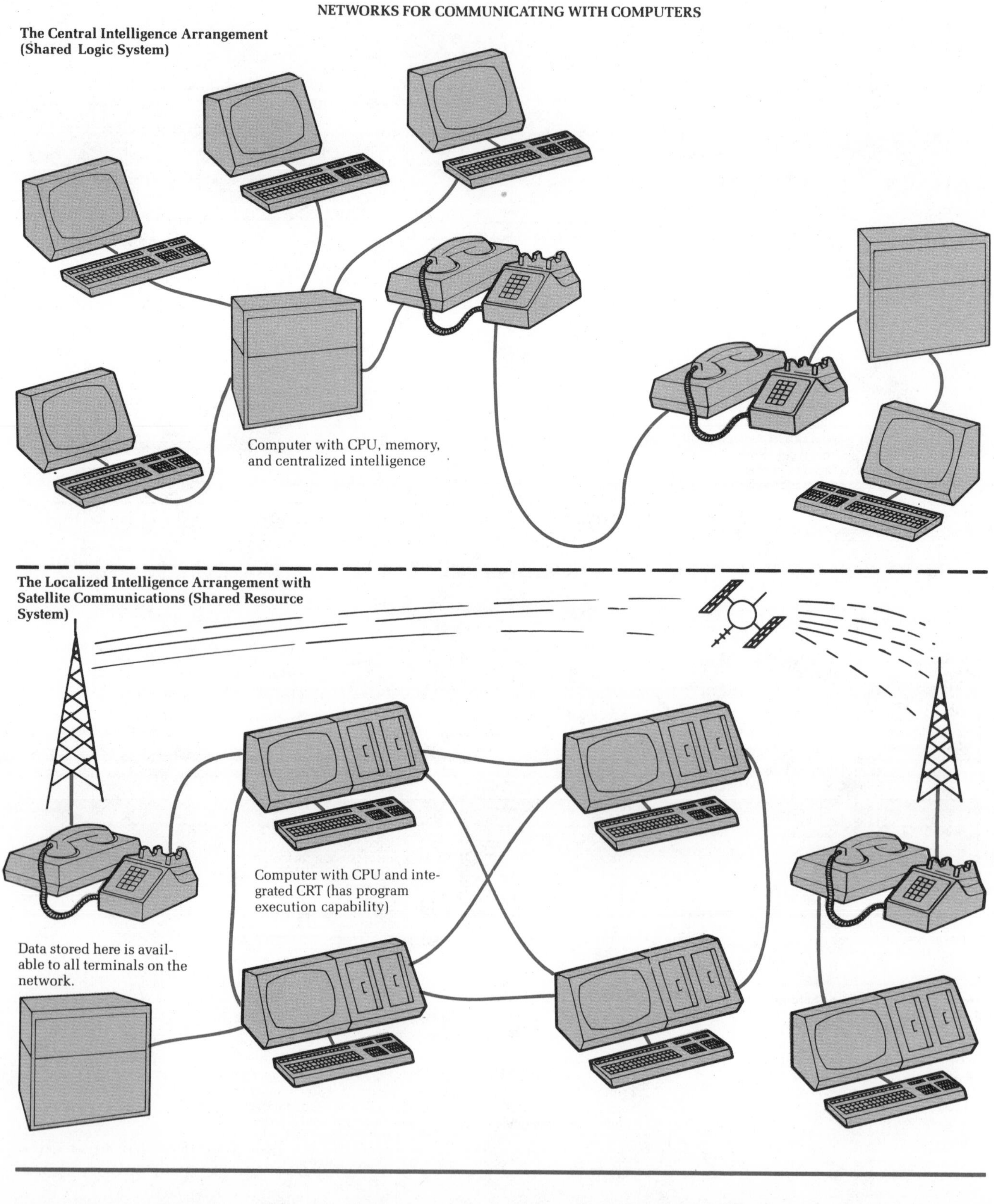
NETWORKS FOR COMMUNICATING WITH COMPUTERS
The Central Intelligence Arrangement (Shared Logic System)
Computer with CPU, memory, and centralized intelligence
The Localized Intelligence Arrangement with Satellite Communications (Shared Resource System)
Computer with CPU and integrated CRT (has program execution capability)
Data stored here is available to all terminals on the network.

computers on a rental basis, sharing the costs with several companies, or purchase their own mini- or microcomputers; in this way they enjoy the advantages of automation while keeping costs at a reasonable level.

The Increasing Role of the Computer

A computer is a high-speed electronic device that, among other things, is capable of performing many of the routine recording and summarizing functions of the accounting process. Computers can be programmed to perform designated operations without human intervention, and can also store and retrieve large amounts of data quickly. Because of their speed and accuracy, computers can significantly reduce the accountant's clerical workload.

Computers are also being used to "massage" data (that is, to reorder the figures in ways that will reveal certain comparisons and trends) and to predict the outcome of decision alternatives. Thus, computers are becoming a powerful tool for decision making. Accountants who are trained to use computers are better able to assist management in interpreting information and making decisions.

Internal Controls

internal control *an organization's methods and procedures for safeguarding assets, checking on the accuracy and reliability of accounting data, and promoting operational efficiency and adherence to managerial policy*

Internal control refers to a company's methods of safeguarding its assets, checking the reliability of the accounting data it produces, and promoting operational efficiency and adherence to managerial policies. Chapter 18 discusses internal controls in detail. The point to be made here is that internal controls are needed for automated accounting systems just as much as for manual systems. In fact, automation may increase the need for controls. In an EDP system, many of the records exist on tapes or disks stored in a computer, and are not available for physical inspection. One of the challenges facing the accounting profession is to learn how to take advantage of the benefits of computerized accounting systems and still maintain the strong internal controls that are characteristic of manual systems.

TO SUMMARIZE Accounting data are financial in nature and are taken from documents indicating an entity's transactions. The accounting process is designed to accumulate and report in summary form the results of these transactions, to transform financial data into useful information. A company's need for financial information is generally satisfied by its accounting system, which is a subset of its managerial information system. The extent to which the accounting system ought to be automated depends on a number of factors, particularly on the cost of the type of automation being considered in relation to its benefits for the enterprise.

General Business Activity

As explained in the Prologue, most businesses follow a basic pattern of activity whereby cash and other resources are converted to supplies, to inventory, and to other operational assets, such as land and buildings, in order to produce a product or service that can be sold at a profit. Although modifications are required for different types of businesses, the general pattern of business activity is essentially a cash-to-cash cycle involving the investing, purchasing, selling, and collecting functions.

Exhibit 3-3 illustrates the patterns of activity for three kinds of businesses: service, manufacturing, and merchandising. Note that the manufacturer's cycle has an element that other businesses do not—making a product. For example, a clothing manufacturer must produce the shirts and pants it sells. Merchandising firms, such as clothing and department stores and boutiques, buy the finished products from manufacturers and sell them to the public. CPA, law, engineering, or other service businesses sell services rather than physical products.

accounting cycle *in the accounting process, the sequence of procedures that includes analyzing business documents, journalizing, posting, determining account balances and preparing a trial balance and work sheet, journalizing and posting adjusting entries, preparing financial statements, closing nominal accounts, balancing the accounts, and preparing a post-closing trial balance*

Keeping track of the many financial activities of an organization requires an accounting system tailor-made to the needs of a particular enterprise. Obviously, the accounting system in a large multinational corporation (a company with operations in several countries) with tens of thousands of business transactions each month will be much more complex than the system needed by a small drugstore. Regardless of the type or complexity of the business, however, all accounting systems include certain basic steps, referred to collectively as the accounting cycle.

Before you study the specific steps in the cycle, it is important that you understand double-entry accounting more fully. This concept was introduced briefly in Chapter 1. You will recall that the accounting model is built upon a basic equation. You now need to learn how to use this equation in accounting for business activities.

EXHIBIT 3-3 **The General Pattern of Business Activity**

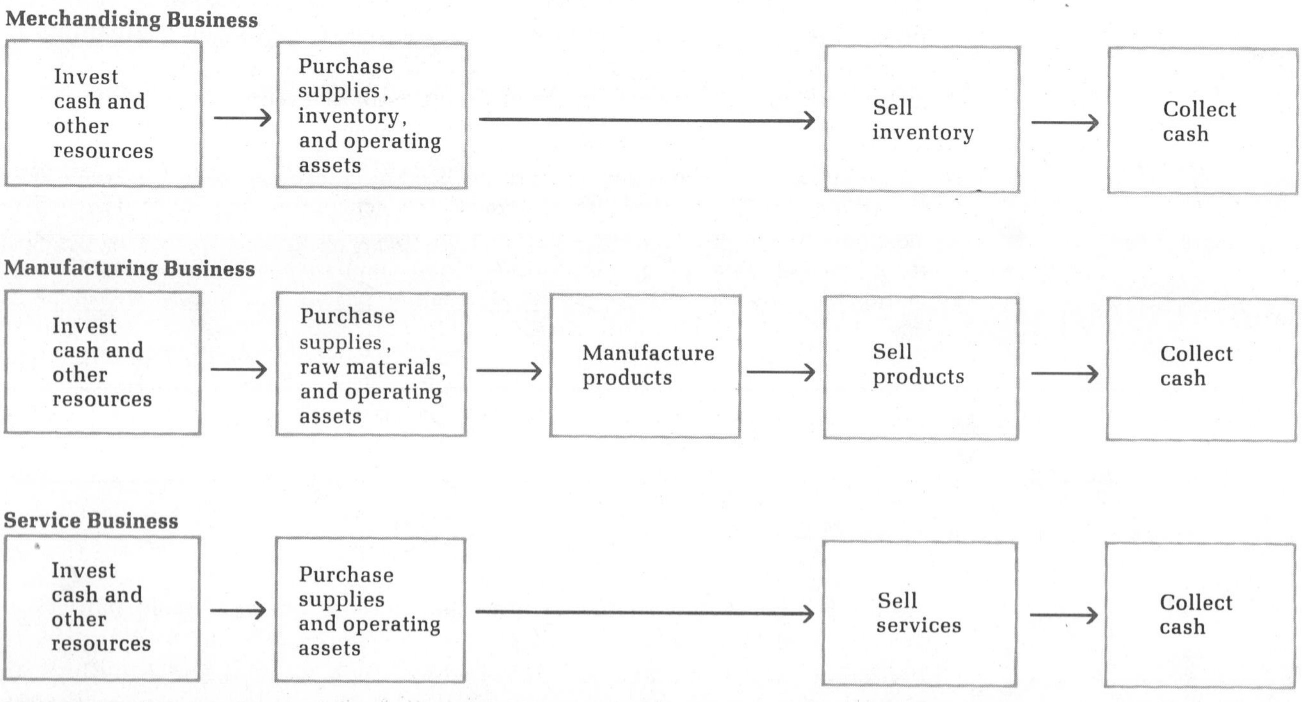

The Basic Accounting Equation

As you will recall, the fundamental accounting equation is

Assets	=	Liabilities	+	Owners' Equity
[*Resources*]		[*Creditors' claims against resources*]		[*Owners' claims against resources*]

net assets *total assets minus total liabilities; equal to owners' equity*

The resources of a company are provided by creditors and owners. Since creditors and owners have provided the resources, they have claims against them, either creditor (lender) claims or owner (investor) claims. To determine the amount of ownership equity at any one time, the amount of creditor claims can be subtracted from the assets. The difference is called net assets, or owners' equity. Thus, the equation also can be written:

Assets − Liabilities = Owners' Equity

Since the accounting equation is an equality, it must always remain in balance. To see how this balance is maintained when accounting for business transactions, consider the following activities.

Business Activity	Effect in Terms of the Accounting Equation
1. Borrow money from bank	Increase asset (cash), increase liability (notes payable): A↑ = L↑
2. Investment by owners	Increase asset (cash), increase owners' equity (capital stock): A↑ = OE↑
3. Pay off note	Decrease asset (cash), decrease liability (notes payable): A↓ = L↓
4. Purchase equipment for cash	Decrease asset (cash), increase asset (equipment): A↓ = A↑
5. Collect cash from customers	Increase asset (cash), decrease asset (accounts or notes receivable): A↑ = A↓
6. Give note to settle long-term debt	Increase liability (note payable), decrease liability (bond payable): L↑ = L↓

In each case the equation remains in balance because an identical amount is added to both sides, or subtracted from both sides, or added to and subtracted from the same side of the equation. The terms in parentheses are the appropriate *accounts* for the transactions, as we will now explain.

USING ACCOUNTS TO CATEGORIZE TRANSACTIONS

account *an accounting record in which the results of similar transactions are accumulated; shows increases, decreases, and a balance*

An account is a specific accounting record that provides an efficient way of categorizing transactions. Thus, we may designate asset accounts, liability accounts, and owners' equity accounts. Examples of asset accounts are Cash, Inventory, and Equipment. Examples of liability accounts are Accounts Payable and Notes Payable, and examples of equity accounts are Capital Stock and Retained Earnings.

debit *an entry on the left side of an account*

credit *an entry on the right side of an account*

Exhibit 3-4 illustrates a typical account. Note that each account has a title and usually an account number (in the illustration, Cash is account 101). Account formats may vary. However, most accounts have columns for the date of a transaction, its explanation, and a posting reference (a cross-reference to other records), as well as columns for debits, credits, and balances. A debit is defined as an entry on the left side of an account; a credit is defined as an entry on the right side of an account.

EXHIBIT 3-4 **Cash Account**

Cash — Account No. 101

Date	Explanation	Post Ref.	Debits	Credits	Balance

T-account *a simplified depiction of an account in the form of a letter T, showing the debits on the left and credits on the right*

A T-account is a simplified version of the account format illustrated in Exhibit 3-4. If a heavy line is drawn above the two columns for debits and credits and another heavy line is drawn to separate them, a T is formed, as shown below for the Cash account.

Cash — Account No. 101

Date	Explanation	Post Ref.	Debits	Credits	Balance

The following are examples of T-accounts.

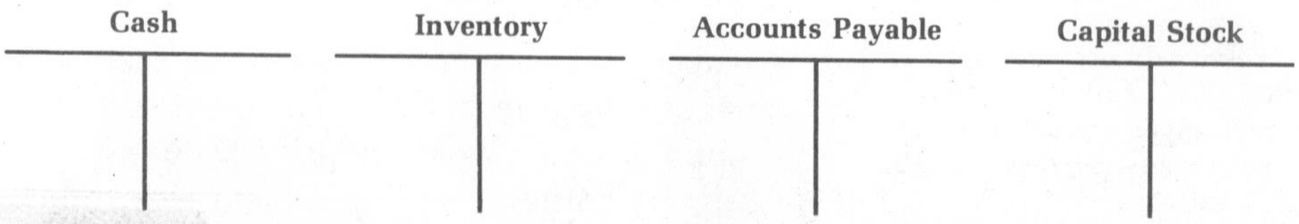

Since T-accounts are brief forms of formal accounts, they also have two sides, with debits representing entries on the left side and credits representing entries on the right side. Thus, the appropriate debit (DR) and credit (CR) notations for the above accounts would be

Cash		Inventory		Accounts Payable		Capital Stock	
DR	CR	DR	CR	DR	CR	DR	CR

In representing the left and right sides of an account, debits and credits refer to increases or decreases that result from each transaction, depending on the type of account. For asset accounts, debits refer to increases, and credits to decreases. For example, to increase the Cash account, we debit it; to decrease the Cash account, we credit it. This debit-credit, increase-decrease relationship holds true for any asset account. The opposite relationship is true of liability and owners' equity accounts; they are increased by credits and decreased by debits. For example, the Accounts Payable account is increased by a credit; it is decreased by a debit. The effect of this system is shown below, with an increase indicated by (+) and a decrease by (−).

Assets		=	Liabilities		+	Owners' Equity	
DR	CR		DR	CR		DR	CR
(+)	(−)		(−)	(+)		(−)	(+)

Why in accounting do the meanings of the terms debit and credit switch from an increase to a decrease, and vice versa, in going from one side of the accounting equation to the other? To understand this, keep three basic facts in mind: (1) For every transaction there must be a debit and a credit; (2) debits must always equal credits for each transaction; and (3) debits are always entered on the left side of an account and credits on the right side. Now, notice what this means for the first example of a business transaction in the table on page 61: borrowing money from the bank. An asset account (Cash) is increased; in other words, it is debited. A liability account (Notes Payable) is also increased; in other words, it is credited. There is both a debit and a credit for the transaction, and we have increased accounts on both sides of the equation by an equal amount, thus keeping the equation in balance.

Be careful not to let the general, nonaccounting meanings of the words "credit" and "debit" confuse you. In general conversation, credit has an association with plus and debit with minus. But on the asset side of the accounting equation, this association can lead you astray. To make sure you understand the relationship between debits and credits, the various accounts, and the accounting equation, let us reexamine the business activities listed on page 61.

Business Activity	Effect in Terms of the Accounting Equation: Assets (Debit side)	Assets (Credit side)	=	Liabilities (Debit side)	Liabilities (Credit side)	+	Owners' Equity (Debit side)	Owners' Equity (Credit side)
1. Borrow money from bank	Cash DR(+)				Notes Payable CR(+)			
2. Investment by owners	Cash DR(+)							Capital Stock CR(+)
3. Pay off note		Cash CR(−)		Notes Payable DR(−)				
4. Purchase equipment for cash	Equipment DR(+)	Cash CR(−)						
5. Collect cash from customers	Cash DR(+)	Accounts Receivable CR(−)						
6. Give note to settle long-term debt				Bonds Payable DR(−)	Notes Payable CR(+)			

Note that every time an account is debited, other accounts have to be credited for the same amount. This is a major characteristic of the double-entry accounting system: The debits must always equal the credits. This important characteristic of double-entry accounting creates a practical advantage: the opportunity for "self-checking." If debits do not equal credits, an error has been made in recording the entity's activities.

EXPANDING THE ACCOUNTING EQUATION TO INCLUDE REVENUES AND EXPENSES

revenues *resource increases from the sale of goods or services derived primarily from the normal operations of an enterprise*

expenses *costs of assets used up or additional liabilities incurred in the normal course of business to generate revenues*

At this point, we must bring revenues and expenses into the picture. Obviously, they are part of every ongoing business. Revenues provide resource inflows; they are increases in resources from the sale of goods or services during the normal operations of a business. Expenses represent resource outflows; they are costs of assets used up or additional liabilities incurred in the normal course of business to generate revenues.

The net result of revenues less expenses is income, and is reflected in owners' equity. Revenues increase owners' equity; consequently, they must be treated in the same way as owners' equity accounts and be increased by credits. Expense accounts, which are in effect the opposite of revenue accounts, reduce owners' equity and are increased by debits. Recall that owners' equity is made up of the amount of capital contributed by owners (capital stock) plus the amount of earnings retained in the business (retained earnings). Revenues and expenses, in turn, determine the amount of periodic income and have a direct impact on retained earnings.

Revenues and expenses may be thought of as subdivisions of owners' equity; that is, these two types of accounts are but temporary accumulation and storage compartments for operating transactions affecting Retained

Earnings, a permanent owners' equity account. The accounting equation may be expanded to include revenues and expenses as follows:

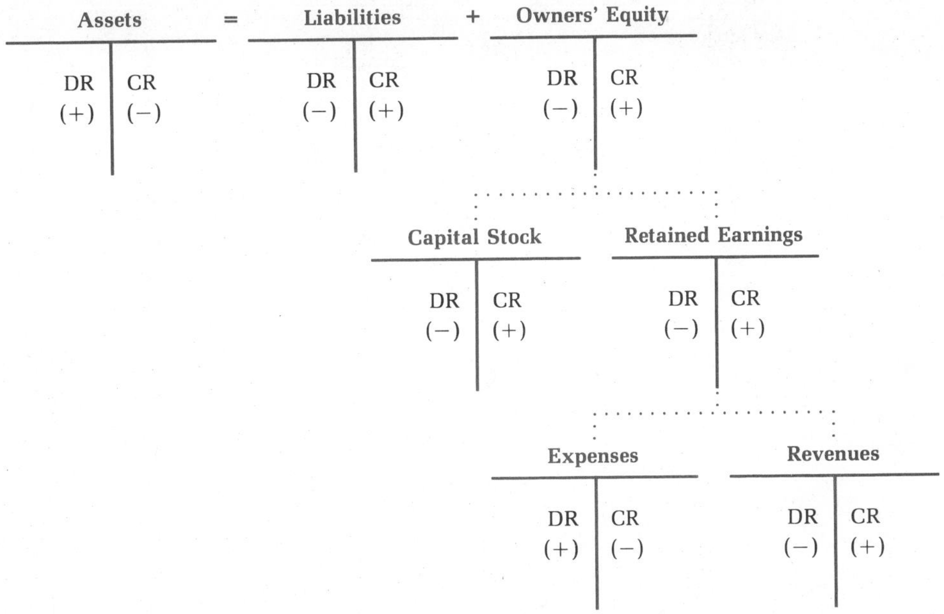

TO SUMMARIZE Debits are always entered on the left side of an account and credits are always entered on the right side. Debits increase asset and expense accounts and decrease liability, owners' equity, and revenue accounts. Credits decrease asset and expense accounts and increase liability, owners' equity, and revenue accounts. Revenues increase and expenses decrease owners' equity. Therefore, at any one time under a double-entry system of accounting, it is possible to check the accounting records to see that Assets = Liabilities + Owners' Equity, and that Debits equal Credits.

The First Steps in the Accounting Cycle

Although some of the procedures may be modified or combined, the accounting cycle generally consists of the specific steps shown in Exhibit 3–5. As each step in the cycle is introduced, you should try to understand the general concepts and terms. The first four steps are discussed in the remaining sections of this chapter; the other steps are covered in Chapters 4 and 5.

business documents *records of transactions used as the basis for recording accounting entries; includes invoices, check stubs, receipts, and similar business papers*

STEP 1. ANALYZE BUSINESS DOCUMENTS

The first step in the accounting cycle is to analyze the business documents—the sales invoices, check stubs, and other records that are evidence of business transactions. Business documents confirm that a transaction has

EXHIBIT 3-5 The Accounting Cycle

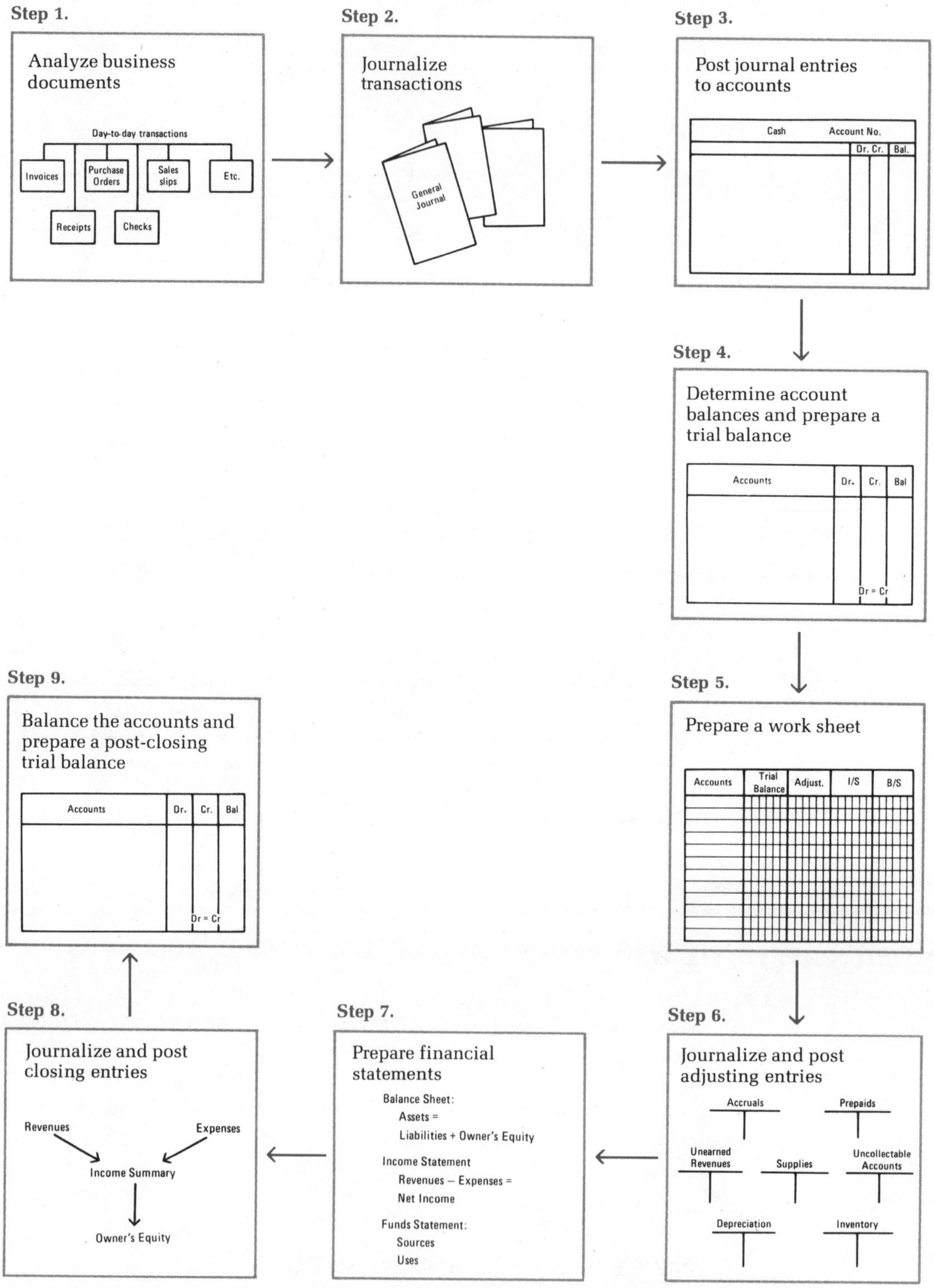

EXHIBIT 3-6 **Sales Invoice**

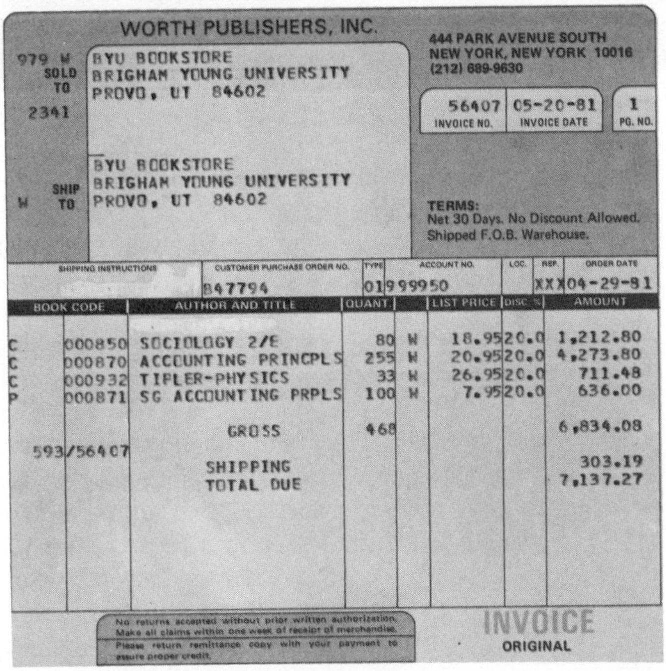

WORTH PUBLISHERS, INC.

444 PARK AVENUE SOUTH
NEW YORK, NEW YORK 10016
(212) 689-9630

979 W SOLD TO 2341
BYU BOOKSTORE
BRIGHAM YOUNG UNIVERSITY
PROVO, UT 84602

INVOICE NO.	INVOICE DATE	PG. NO.
56407	05-20-81	1

W SHIP TO
BYU BOOKSTORE
BRIGHAM YOUNG UNIVERSITY
PROVO, UT 84602

TERMS:
Net 30 Days. No Discount Allowed.
Shipped F.O.B. Warehouse.

SHIPPING INSTRUCTIONS	CUSTOMER PURCHASE ORDER NO.	TYPE	ACCOUNT NO.	LOC.	REP.	ORDER DATE
	847794	01	999950		XXX	04-29-81

	BOOK CODE	AUTHOR AND TITLE	QUANT.		LIST PRICE	DISC. %	AMOUNT
C	000850	SOCIOLOGY 2/E	80	W	18.95	20.0	1,212.80
C	000870	ACCOUNTING PRINCPLS	255	W	20.95	20.0	4,273.80
C	000932	TIPLER-PHYSICS	33	W	26.95	20.0	711.48
P	000871	SG ACCOUNTING PRPLS	100	W	7.95	20.0	636.00
		GROSS	468				6,834.08
	593/56407						
		SHIPPING					303.19
		TOTAL DUE					7,137.27

No returns accepted without prior written authorization. Make all claims within one week of receipt of merchandise.
Please return remittance copy with your payment to assure proper credit.

INVOICE
ORIGINAL

occurred and establish the amounts to be recorded. Exhibit 3–6 shows an example of a business document: a sales invoice. This exhibit shows that sales of $7,137.27 were made to the BYU Bookstore by Worth Publishers, Inc. The invoice also indicates the terms of the sale and shows that the purchase price is due to be paid within 30 days of the invoice date.

STEP 2. JOURNALIZE TRANSACTIONS

journal *an accounting record in which transactions are first entered; provides a chronological record of all business activities*

The second step in the accounting cycle is to record the results of transactions in a journal. Known as "books of original entry," journals provide a chronological record of all entity transactions. They show the dates of the transactions, the amounts involved, and the particular accounts affected by the transactions. Usually, an explanation of the transaction is also included.

Smaller companies, such as a locally owned drugstore, may use only one book of original entry, called a General Journal, to record all transactions. Larger companies having thousands of transactions each year may use specialized journals (for example, a cash receipts journal) as well as a General Journal. Special journals are described in the Supplement to this chapter.

journal entry *a recording of a transaction where debits equal credits; usually includes a date and an explanation of the transaction*

A specific format is used in journalizing (recording) transactions in a General Journal. The debit entry is listed first; the credit entry is listed second and is indented to the right, as shown on the next page. Normally, the date and a brief explanation of the transaction are considered essential parts of the journal entry. Dollar signs usually are omitted. Unless otherwise noted, this format is to be used whenever journal entries are presented.

General Journal Entry Format

Date	Debit Entry	XX	
	Credit Entry		XX
	Explanation		

Exhibit 3-7 is a partial page from a General Journal, showing typical journal entries. Study this exhibit carefully, because the entire accounting cycle is based on journal entries. If journal entries are incorrect, the resulting financial information will not be accurate.

To give you additional exposure to transaction analysis and journal entries, we now discuss the entries used to record the most common transactions of a business enterprise. These transactions fit into the following four general categories: acquisition of cash, acquisition of other assets, utilization of assets to manufacture and sell a product or provide a service, and the collection of cash and payment of obligations and dividends. Obviously, we cannot present all possible transactions in this chapter. In studying the illustrations, strive to understand the conceptual basis of transaction analysis rather than to memorize particular journal entries. Pay particular attention to the dual effect of each transaction on the entity in terms of the basic accounting equation, that is, in terms of its impact on assets and on liabilities and owners' equity. Remember that business activity naturally involves

EXHIBIT 3-7 **General Journal**

GENERAL JOURNAL — Page 1

Date		Account Titles and Explanation	Post Ref.	Debits	Credits
19	83				
Jan.	1	Cash		5000	
		Notes Payable			5000
		Borrowed $5,000 from bank, securing			
		loan with 1-year promissory note			
		at 15% interest.			
	4	Inventory		1500	
		Accounts Payable			1500
		Purchased inventory on account.			
	10	Accounts Payable		1500	
		Cash			1500
		Paid amount owed on inventory			
		purchase.			

revenues and expenses as well, and that these accounts eventually increase or decrease an owners' equity account (Retained Earnings for a corporation and Proprietorship or Partnership Capital for proprietorships and partnerships).

Acquiring Cash

One of the first tasks of any business is to acquire cash, either through owners' investments or by borrowing. Once a business is established, it normally generates cash from operations—by selling goods or services.

Example 1 The following transactions for two types of organizations—a proprietorship and a corporation—illustrate contributions by owners.

assets (+)	Cash	10,000	
owner's equity (+)	J. Smith, Capital		10,000
	Received $10,000 cash contribution from J. Smith, proprietor.		
assets (+)	Cash	50,000	
owners' equity (+)	Capital Stock		50,000
	Issued 5,000 shares of capital stock at $10 per share.		

These two transactions are similar in that each increased cash as a result of owners' contributions. In the first case, a proprietor contributed the cash (in a proprietorship, the owner's equity account is called a capital account). In the second case, capital stock of a corporation was issued, probably to several individuals. In both instances, the investment, and hence the ownership interest, was increased. The economic impact of these situations may be summarized as

Assets	= Liabilities	+ Owners' Equity
(increase $10,000 or $50,000)	(no change)	(increase $10,000 or $50,000)

Example 2 In this example, cash is obtained by borrowing.

assets (+)	Cash	25,000	
liabilities (+)	Notes Payable		25,000
	Borrowed $25,000 from First National Bank, securing the loan with a 6-month note at 12% interest. (The interest is entered into the accounting records later—in this case, when the note is paid; see Example 3, page 74.)		

The accounting model would capture the economic impact of borrowing the money as follows:

Assets	= Liabilities	+ Owners' Equity
(increase $25,000)	(increase $25,000)	(no change)

Example 3 In this example, cash is increased by the sale of merchandise.

assets (+)
revenues (+) [equity (+)]

Cash	15,300	
Sales Revenue		15,300
Sold merchandise for cash.		

The accounting equation remains in balance because sales represents a revenue item, which increases owners' equity. Therefore,

Assets	= Liabilities	+ Owners' Equity (Revenues)
(increase $15,300)	(no change)	(increase $15,300)

Acquiring Other Assets

Cash obtained from owners' contributions, borrowings, or sales can be used to acquire other assets needed to run the business. Such assets include supplies, inventory, buildings, and equipment. They may be obtained directly from investors or, as is more common, purchased with cash or on credit. Credit purchases require payment after a period of time, for example, 30 days. Normally, interest expense is incurred when assets are bought on a time-payment plan that extends beyond two or three months. (To keep our examples simple here, we will not include interest expense. We will show how to account for interest on page 74, where we discuss the payment of obligations.) Examples of transactions involving the acquisition of noncash assets follow.

Example 1 Inventory costing $4,500 has been purchased "on account," which means that the buyer has used credit instead of cash to make the purchase and has an obligation (liability) to pay for the inventory at some future date.

assets (+)
liabilities (+)

Inventory	4,500	
Accounts Payable		4,500
Purchased inventory on account.		

The accounting equation shows

Assets	= Liabilities	+ Owners' Equity
(increase $4,500)	(increase $4,500)	(no change)

When the company pays for its inventory, cash will be reduced and the liability, Accounts Payable, will also be reduced, thus keeping the equation in balance. Inventory and similar items purchased on account are generally paid for within 30–90 days and normally do not require an interest charge.

Example 2 An asset (for example, a building) has been acquired, a cash down-payment has been made, and a long-term obligation has been incurred for the balance of the asset's cost. As the journal entry illustrates, more than two accounts can be involved in recording a transaction. This type of entry is called a compound journal entry. Notice how the explanation clarifies the entry.

compound journal entry *a journal entry that involves more than one debit or more than one credit, or both*

assets (+)	Building	63,000	
liabilities (+)	Mortgage Payable		53,000
assets (−)	Cash		10,000

Purchased building for $63,000, making a $10,000 down payment and receiving a 10-year, 16% mortgage for the balance.

The accounting equation is

Assets	= Liabilities	+ Owners' Equity
(increase $63,000; decrease $10,000)	(increase $53,000)	(no change)

Example 3 An asset (for example, a machine) is given to a company by one of its owners. This is a valid transaction, but care must be exercised in determining a fair value for the asset. Since no arm's-length transaction is involved, the company must set a value based on the current market value of a similar asset. This concept is discussed further in Chapter 8.

asset (+)	Equipment	5,500	
owner's equity (+)	J. Smith, Capital		5,500

Acquired equipment valued at $5,500, contributed to the business by J. Smith, proprietor.

In the example given, the economic impact would be reflected in the equation as follows:

Assets	= Liabilities	+ Owners' Equity
(increase $5,500)	(no change)	(increase $5,500)

Example 4 When supplies are purchased for cash, an increase in one asset (supplies) is accompanied by a decrease in another asset (cash).

assets (+)	Supplies	1,250	
assets (−)	Cash		1,250

Purchased supplies for cash.

The accounting equation is

Assets	= Liabilities	+ Owners' Equity
(increase $1,250; decrease $1,250)	(no change)	(no change)

Selling Goods or Providing Services

The next category of common transactions involves the use of a company's assets to sell merchandise, to render services, or to produce goods that can be sold to customers. Revenues are generated and expenses incurred during this process. Sometimes products or services are sold for cash; at other times, a receivable is established and must be collected. Similarly, expenses may be incurred and paid for immediately by cash or they may be incurred on credit—that is, they may be "charged," with a cash payment to be made at a later date. Illustrative transactions follow.

Example 1 Cash has been received for services rendered.

assets (+)	Cash	17,000	
revenues (+) [equity (+)]	Consulting Fee Revenue		17,000
	Received cash for consulting services.		

Because revenues increase owners' equity, the accounting equation is

Assets	= Liabilities	+ Owners' Equity (Revenues)
(increase $17,000)	(no change)	(increase $17,000)

Example 2 Merchandise is sold to customers on account, establishing a receivable. In this case, the company is allowing a customer 30 days to make payment. Normally, no interest is charged on short-term credit sales or short-term credit purchases. At the time payment is received, Accounts Receivable is reduced or eliminated and Cash is increased by the same amount.

cost of goods sold *the expense incurred to purchase raw materials and manufacture the products sold during a period, or to purchase the merchandise sold during a period*

Sales, whether made on account or for cash, involve entries that reflect not only the sales but also the cost of the inventory sold. The cost of goods sold is an expense and, as such, is offset against the sales revenue to determine the profitability of sales transactions. The special procedures for handling inventory are described in Chapter 7. It is sufficient here to show an example of the impact of the transactions on the accounting equation.

assets (+)	Accounts Receivable	75,000	
revenues (+) [equity (+)]	Sales Revenue		75,000
	Sold merchandise on account.		
expenses (+) [equity (−)]	Cost of Goods Sold	60,000	
assets (−)	Inventory		60,000
	To record the cost of merchandise sold and to reduce inventory for its cost.		

The effect on the accounting equation for each transaction would be

Sales on Account

Assets	= Liabilities	+ Owners' Equity (Revenues)
(increase $75,000)	(no change)	(increase $75,000)

Cost of Goods Sold

Assets	= Liabilities	+ Owners' Equity (Expenses)
(decrease $60,000)	(no change)	(decrease $60,000)

Example 3 Expenses other than cost of goods sold are also incurred in operating a business, as the following entries for expenses for advertising and wages illustrate.

expenses (+) [equity (−)]	Advertising Expense	500	
assets (−)	Cash		500
	Paid advertising expense.		
expenses (+) [equity (−)]	Wages Expense	22,500	
assets (−)	Cash		22,500
	Paid wages expense.		

Collecting Cash and Paying Obligations

Obviously, once a product or service is sold on account, the receivable must be collected. The cash received generally is used to meet daily operating expenses and to pay other obligations. Excess cash can be reinvested in the business or distributed to the owners (in the form of dividends) as a return on their investment.

Example 1 The collection of accounts receivable is an important aspect of most businesses. Customers are allowed to purchase goods on charge accounts or with credit cards on the assumption that the availability of credit will increase total sales. If collections are not made, however, the seller may lose not only the cash but the merchandise as well. Even when the merchandise can be repossessed, it often cannot be resold at a price high enough to cover its cost. When receivables are collected, that asset is reduced and cash is increased, as is shown below.

assets (+)	Cash	75,000	
assets (−)	Accounts Receivable		75,000
	Collected $75,000 of receivables.		

The effect of collecting the receivables on the accounting equation is

Assets	= Liabilities	+ Owners' Equity
(increase $75,000, decrease $75,000)	(no change)	(no change)

Example 2 The entry to record the payment of obligations with cash is

liabilities (−)	Accounts Payable	4,500	
assets (−)	Cash		4,500
	Paid $4,500 of obligations.		

After payment of accounts payable, the accounting equation shows

Assets	= Liabilities	+ Owners' Equity
(decrease $4,500)	(decrease $4,500)	(no change)

To help bring these two examples into clearer focus, remember that two parties are always involved in exchange transactions. What one buys, the other sells. When sales are on credit, on one set of books (the seller's) a receivable will be recorded; on the books of the buyer a payable will be recorded. The two accounts are in a sense inversely related. The seller of goods records a receivable and a sale, and simultaneously records an expense for the cost of goods sold and a reduction of inventory, as in Example 2 on page 72. The buyer records receipt of the merchandise as inventory and at the same time records an obligation to pay the seller at some future time, as in Example 1 on page 70. When payment is made, the buyer reduces Accounts Payable and Cash while the seller increases Cash and reduces Accounts Receivable.

Example 3 As the following compound journal entry shows, certain obligations require an additional cash payment for interest.

liabilities (−)	Notes Payable	25,000	
expenses (+) [equity (−)]	Interest Expense	1,500	
assets (−)	Cash		26,500
	Paid $25,000 note with interest ($25,000 × 0.12 × 6/12 = $1,500).		

Analysis of this transaction reveals that assets have decreased for two reasons. First, a liability has been paid with cash; second, the interest expense associated with the note payable has been paid. This relationship will generally be present in most long-term and some short-term liability transactions. Since the interest charge is an expense and decreases owners' equity, the impact of the entry on the accounting equation is

Assets	= Liabilities	+ Owners' Equity (Expense)
(decrease $26,500)	(decrease $25,000)	(decrease $1,500)

Example 4 Corporations that are profitable generally pay dividends to their shareholders. Put simply, dividends represent a distribution to the shareholders of part of the earnings of a company. Dividends are generally paid in cash, but can also be a distribution of stock. Note that cash dividends are required to be paid (that is, they become a liability) only after they are declared payable by the board of directors. The following entries illustrate the declaration and payment of a cash dividend.

owners' equity (−)	Dividends	12,000	
liabilities (+)	Dividends Payable		12,000
	Declared a cash dividend of $12,000.		
liabilities (−)	Dividends Payable	12,000	
assets (−)	Cash		12,000
	Paid a $12,000 cash dividend.		

Dividends, like revenues and expenses, affect owners' equity. Unlike revenues and expenses, dividends are a distribution of profits and therefore are not considered in determining net income. Because dividends reduce the retained earnings accumulated by the business enterprise, they decrease owners' equity. Thus, the declaration and payment of a $12,000 dividend affects the accounting equation as follows:

Assets	= Liabilities	+ Owners' Equity
(decrease $12,000)	(no change)	(decrease $12,000)

The above entries have to do with corporations. When the owner(s) of proprietorships or partnerships withdraw cash, the entry would be

owners' equity (−)
assets (−)

Proprietorship (or Partnership) Drawings	12,000	
Cash		12,000
Withdrew cash from proprietorship (or partnership).		

The net effect on the accounting equation is the same. Drawings reduce the equity in proprietorships and partnerships, just as dividends reduce the equity in corporations.

STEP 3. POST JOURNAL ENTRIES TO ACCOUNTS

posting *the process of classifying and grouping similar transactions in common accounts by transferring amounts from the journal to the ledger*

Once transactions have been recorded in either the General Journal or various specialized journals, it is necessary to classify and group all similar items. This is accomplished by the bookkeeping procedure of posting all the journal entries to appropriate accounts. As indicated earlier, accounts are records of like items. They show transaction dates, increases and decreases, and account balances. For example, all items of cash, whether related to cash receipts or to cash disbursements (payments), are accumulated in one account called "Cash" and all sales transactions are grouped together in the "Sales Revenue" account. Exhibit 3-8 shows how the January 1 transaction from the General Journal (Exhibit 3-7, page 68) would be posted to the Cash account.

EXHIBIT 3-8 **Cash Account**

GENERAL LEDGER — Cash — Account No. 101

Date		Explanation	Post Ref.	Debits	Credits	Balance
1/1	83	Balance				10100
Jan	1	Note issued to bank		5000		15100

ledger *a book of accounts in which data from transactions recorded in journals are posted and thereby classified and summarized*

All accounts are maintained in an accounting record called the General Ledger. A ledger, then, is a "book" of accounts. Exhibit 3-9 shows how the two cash transactions in the General Journal would be posted to the Cash account in the General Ledger, with arrows depicting the posting procedures. Observe that a number has been inserted in the "posting reference" column (also called the "folio" column) in both books. This number serves

EXHIBIT 3-9 Posting to the General Ledger

GENERAL JOURNAL — Page 1

Date		Account Titles and Explanation	Post Ref.	Debits	Credits
19	83				
Jan	1	Cash	101	5000	
		Notes Payable			5000
		Borrowed $5,000 from bank, securing loan with 1-year promissory note at 10% interest.			
	4	Inventory		1500	
		Accounts Payable			1500
		Purchased inventory on account.			
	10	Accounts Payable		1500	
		Cash	101		1500
		Paid amount owed on inventory purchase.			

GENERAL LEDGER — Cash — Account No. 101

Date		Explanation	Post Ref.	Debits	Credits	Balance
1/1	83	Balance				10100
Jan	1	Note issued to bank	GJ1	5000		15100
	10	Payment for inventory purchase	GJ1		1500	13600

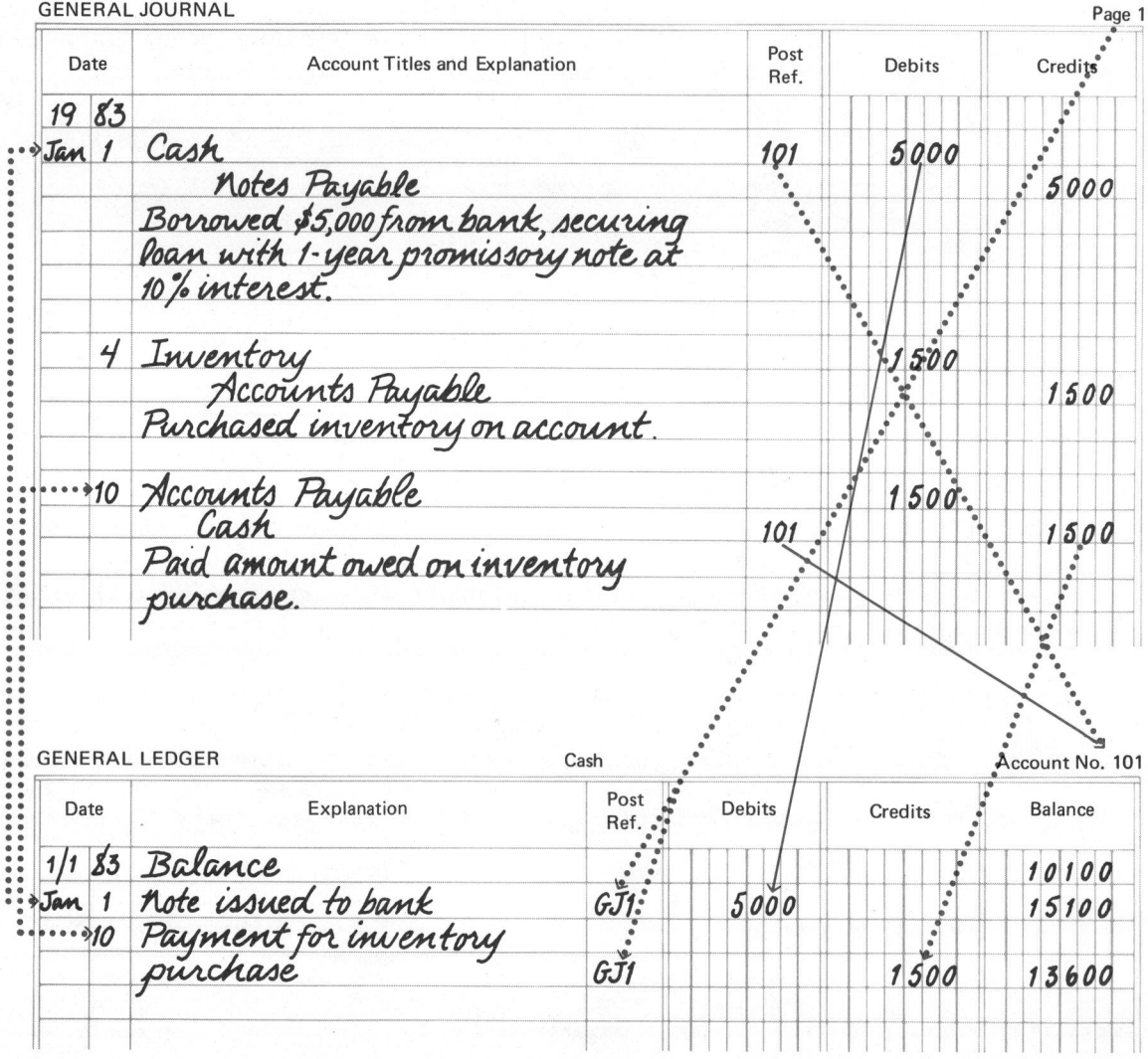

as a cross-reference between the General Journal and the accounts in the General Ledger. In the journal, it identifies the account to which the journal entry has been posted. In the ledger, it identifies the page on which the entry appears in the General Journal. For example, the GJ1 notation in the Cash account for the January 1 entry means that the $5,000 has been posted from page 1 of the General Journal.

chart of accounts *a systematic listing of all accounts used by a company*

Each organizational unit will have as many or as few accounts as it needs to provide a reasonable classification of its transactions. The list of accounts used by a company is known as its chart of accounts. Exhibit 3-10 shows some accounts that might appear in a typical merchandising company's chart of accounts.[1]

[1] To make Exhibit 3-10 realistic, several accounts that have not yet been explained have been listed. They will be defined and discussed in subsequent chapters.

EXHIBIT 3-10 Chart of Accounts for a Merchandising Business

Assets (100–199)

Current Assets (100–120):
101 Cash
102 Marketable Securities
103 Notes Receivable
105 Accounts Receivable
106 Allowance for Doubtful Accounts
107 Inventory
108 Supplies
109 Prepaid Rent
110 Prepaid Taxes
111 Prepaid Insurance

Investments (121–140):
131 Investment in Stock of X Co.

Long-Term Operational Assets (141–160):
141 Land
142 Buildings
143 Accumulated Depreciation—Buildings
144 Store Equipment
145 Accumulated Depreciation—Store Equipment
148 Office Furniture
149 Accumulated Depreciation—Office Furniture

Intangible Assets (161–180):
161 Patents
164 Goodwill

Other Assets (181–199)

Liabilities (200–299)

Current Liabilities (200–219):
201 Notes Payable
202 Accounts Payable
203 Salaries Payable
204 Interest Payable
205 Payroll Taxes Payable
206 Income Taxes Payable
219 Other Current Liabilities

Long-Term Liabilities (220–239):
222 Bonds Payable
223 Mortgage Payable

Stockholders' Equity (300–399)

301 Capital Stock
302 Paid-in Capital in Excess of Par
330 Retained Earnings

Sales (400–499)

400 Sales Revenue
402 Sales Returns and Allowances
404 Sales Discounts

Cost of Goods Sold (500)

Operating Expenses (501–599)

Selling Expenses (501–549):
501 Sales Salaries and Commissions
510 Freight-Out
520 Payroll Taxes
523 Utility Expense
524 Postage Expense
525 Travel Expense
528 Advertising Expense

General and Administrative Expenses (550–599):
551 Officers' Salaries
552 Office Salaries
553 Administrative Salaries
570 Payroll Taxes
571 Office Supplies Expense
573 Utility Expense
574 Postage Expense
575 Travel Expense
576 Depreciation Expense—Buildings
577 Depreciation Expense—Office Furniture
578 Office Equipment Rent Expense
579 Accounting and Legal Fees
581 Building Repair and Maintenance Expense
583 Doubtful Accounts Expense
584 Amortization of Goodwill
585 Amortization of Patents

Other Expenses (600–699)

601 Interest on Notes
602 Interest on Bonds
603 Interest on Mortgage

Other Income (700–799)

701 Interest Revenue
702 Revenue from Investments
704 Miscellaneous Income

STEP 4. DETERMINE ACCOUNT BALANCES AND PREPARE A TRIAL BALANCE

At the end of an accounting period, the accounts in the General Ledger are reviewed to determine each account's balance. Generally, the difference between debits and credits in each account has already been extended into the balance column. Asset and expense accounts usually have debit balances; liability, owners' equity, and revenue accounts have credit balances. In other words, the balance is usually on the side that increases the account.

trial balance *a listing of all account balances; provides a means of testing whether debits equal credits for all accounts*

After the account balances are determined, and as a means of checking the accuracy of the recording and posting functions (steps 2 and 3), a trial balance is usually prepared. A trial balance lists each account with its debit or credit balance. If total debits equal total credits, there is some assurance that the recording and posting functions have been performed correctly. Even if the trial balance appears to be correct, there may be errors. A transaction may be omitted completely, or it may have been recorded incorrectly or posted to the wrong account. These types of errors will not be discovered by preparing a trial balance; additional analysis would be required. A trial balance is illustrated in Exhibit 3-11.

EXHIBIT 3-11

Alfred Corporation

Trial Balance as of December 31, 1983

	Debits	Credits
Cash	$ 79,050	
Accounts Receivable	1,250	
Inventory	4,500	
Land	28,000	
Accounts Payable		$ 10,500
Notes Payable		25,000
Capital Stock		50,000
Sales Revenue		96,100
Cost of Goods Sold	60,000	
Advertising Expense	500	
Selling Expense	8,300	
Totals	$181,600	$181,600

TO SUMMARIZE The accounting cycle consists of nine steps, as shown in Exhibit 3-5 on page 66. Transactions between entities and related events provide the basis for all accounting records. For every transaction, a source document such as an invoice, a bank note, or a check is prepared; it provides the essential data of the transaction. The data must be analyzed carefully to determine the proper entries in the General Journal or special journals. If the entries are not properly recorded, the entire accounting system will break down because the rest of the steps in the cycle are based on the journal entries. After transactions are journalized, they can be classified and summarized by posting to the ledger accounts. At the end of the accounting period, the account balances are determined. Assets and expenses usually have debit balances (that is, debits exceed credits); liabilities, owners' equity, and revenues generally have credit balances (that is, credits exceed debits). A trial balance is then prepared as a check on the accuracy of the recording and posting functions, that is, to see that debits equal credits.

A Simple Illustration of the First Steps in the Accounting Cycle

We have briefly explained the first four steps in the accounting cycle. A simple illustration will help reinforce what you have learned about the relationship of assets, liabilities, and owners' equity, including revenues and expenses, and the mechanics of double-entry accounting. Rick Jones set up R. J. Corporation in 1983 with an initial capital contribution of $20,000, for which he received capital stock. R. J. Corporation paid $10,000 cash for inventory. It also borrowed $20,000 from a bank to buy some land, signing a long-term note with the bank. Land was then purchased for $25,000 cash. During the accounting period, R. J. Corporation sold 20 percent, or $2,000, of the inventory purchased. The company sold that inventory for $3,200, but in doing so incurred $200 in selling expenses and $100 in miscellaneous expenses. The sale of inventory was originally made on credit; the company later collected the full amount in cash.

The inventory purchases are verified by invoices showing the actual items purchased, dates, amounts, and so forth. There is a $20,000 note payable to the seller of the land. Other business documents indicate the sale of inventory and the expenses incurred. By analyzing these documents (step 1), the pertinent facts are obtained and the transactions recorded in a journal (step 2).

In keeping with the entity concept, the transactions of R. J. Corporation are accounted for separately from those of Rick Jones. The journal entries to record the transactions of R. J. Corporation are as follows (note that letters are used in places of dates):

		Debits	Credits
asset (+)	**a** Cash	20,000	
owners' equity (+)	Capital Stock		20,000
	Issued $20,000 of capital stock.		
asset (+)	**b** Inventory	10,000	
asset (−)	Cash		10,000
	Purchased $10,000 of inventory for cash.		
asset (+)	**c** Cash	20,000	
liability (+)	Notes Payable		20,000
	Borrowed $20,000 from a bank.		

			Debits	Credits
asset (+)	d	Land	25,000	
asset (−)		Cash		25,000
		Purchased land for cash.		
asset (+)	e	Accounts Receivable	3,200	
revenues (+) [equity (+)]		Sales Revenue		3,200
		Sold $3,200 of merchandise on account.		
expense (+) [equity (−)]		Cost of Goods Sold	2,000	
asset (−)		Inventory		2,000
		To record the cost of merchandise sold.		
expense (+) [equity (−)]	f	Selling Expenses	200	
expense (+) [equity (−)]		Miscellaneous Expenses	100	
asset (−)		Cash		300
		Paid selling and miscellaneous expenses.		
asset (+)	g	Cash	3,200	
asset (−)		Accounts Receivable		3,200
		Collected accounts receivable.		

Next, the transactions are posted to the ledger accounts (step 3). T-accounts are used to illustrate this process, with the letters **a** through **g** showing the cross-references to the journal entries. A balance is shown for the end of the period (where only one transaction is involved, the amount of the transaction is also the account balance).

Cash

a .. 20,000	10,000 ... b
c .. 20,000	25,000 ... d
g .. 3,200	300 ... f
Bal. ... 7,900	

Accounts Receivable

e .. 3,200	3,200 .... g

Inventory

b .. 10,000	2,000 ... e
Bal. ... 8,000	

Land

d .. 25,000	

Notes Payable

	20,000 ... c

Capital Stock

	20,000 ... a

Sales Revenue

	3,200 ... e

Cost of Goods Sold

e .. 2,000	

Selling Expenses

f 200	

Miscellaneous Expenses

f 100	

As a check on the accuracy of the journalizing and posting procedures, a trial balance may be prepared (step 4), as shown below. The balances are taken from each ledger account.

R. J. Corporation
Trial Balance as of December 31, 1983

	Debits	Credits
Cash	$ 7,900	
Inventory	8,000	
Land	25,000	
Notes Payable		$20,000
Capital Stock		20,000
Sales Revenue		3,200
Cost of Goods Sold	2,000	
Selling Expenses	200	
Miscellaneous Expenses	100	
Totals	$43,200	$43,200

An income statement and a balance sheet could be prepared directly from the ledger accounts. (We will explain this process in more detail in the following chapters.) The statements would appear as shown in Exhibit 3-12.

EXHIBIT 3-12

R. J. Corporation
Income Statement
for the Year Ended December 31, 1983

Sales Revenue		$3,200
Less Cost of Goods Sold		2,000
Gross Margin		$1,200
Less: Selling Expenses	$200	
Miscellaneous Expenses	100	300
Net Income		$ 900

R. J. Corporation
Balance Sheet as of December 31, 1983

Assets		Liabilities and Stockholders' Equity	
Cash	$ 7,900	Notes Payable	$20,000
Inventory	8,000	Capital Stock	20,000
Land	25,000	Retained Earnings	900
Total Assets	$40,900	Total Liabilities and Stockholders' Equity	$40,900

Note that since R. J. Corporation began operations in 1983 and paid no dividends during the year, the net income reported on the income statement ($3,200 revenues − $2,300 expenses = $900) becomes the ending retained earnings balance on the balance sheet. This situation is possible only during the first year of a company's operations, since retained earnings is an accumulation of earnings from past years adjusted for dividends and other special items affecting retained earnings.

The retained earnings balance plus the $20,000 original stock investment is the total owners' equity. When owners' equity is added to liabilities of $20,000, the sum equals total assets ($40,900). Thus, the accounting equation is in balance.

CHAPTER REVIEW

The objective of the accounting process is to gather and transform raw data into useful information that measures and communicates the results of business activity. Financial data needed by individuals and external parties are obtained primarily from the accounting information system. Managers need additional information that is supplied by a broader managerial information system. An accounting system may be manual or automated, depending on the organization's requirements. In designing and implementing an accounting system, a company should consider the system's efficiency, the timeliness of the reports it produces, and its overall costs and benefits.

The accounting process is based on double-entry accounting and the fundamental accounting equation: Assets = Liabilities + Owners' Equity. Revenues and expenses respectively increase and decrease retained earnings and therefore have a direct impact on the amount of owners' equity. The double-entry system of accounting assures that the accounting equation will always balance because debit entries require equal credit entries; that is, debits must always equal credits when transactions are properly recorded.

In conducting economic activities, businesses and other types of entities enter into exchange transactions. These transactions form the basis of accounting records. The procedures used in accounting for such transactions are known as the accounting cycle and include the following steps:

1. Analyze business documents.
2. Journalize transactions.
3. Post journal entries to accounts.
4. Determine account balances and prepare a trial balance.
5. Prepare a work sheet.
6. Journalize and post adjusting entries.
7. Prepare financial statements.
8. Journalize and post closing entries.
9. Balance the accounts and prepare a post-closing trial balance.

This chapter has discussed the first four steps in the cycle; the remaining steps will be explained in the next two chapters.

KEY TERMS AND CONCEPTS

account (61)
accounting cycle (60)
accounting information system (56)
accounting process (54)
automated accounting system (56)
business documents (65)
chart of accounts (76)
compound journal entry (70)
computerized accounting system (56)
control account (93)
cost of goods sold (72)
credit (62)
data (55)
debit (62)
expenses (64)
information (55)
internal control (59)
journal (67)
journal entry (67)
ledger (75)
managerial information system (56)
net assets (61)
posting (75)
revenues (64)
special journals (92)
subsidiary ledger (93)
T-account (62)
transaction analysis (54)
trial balance (78)

REVIEW PROBLEM

The First Steps in the Accounting Cycle

Journal entries are given below for October 1983, the first month of operation for Tyler Tool and Repair Service, Inc.

1983		Debits	Credits
Oct. 1	Cash	40,000	
	Capital Stock		40,000
	Issued capital stock for cash.		
1	Insurance Expense	500	
	Cash		500
	Purchased a 1-year insurance policy.		
2	Rent Expense	750	
	Cash		750
	Paid the rent for the month of October.		
3	Shop Equipment	8,000	
	Cash		8,000
	Purchased shop equipment for cash.		
4	Supplies	3,000	
	Accounts Payable		3,000
	Purchased shop supplies on account.		
5	Automotive Equipment	11,500	
	Cash		3,500
	Notes Payable		8,000
	Purchased a truck. Paid $3,500 cash and issued a 30-day note for the balance.		
8	Cash	1,750	
	Service and Repair Revenue		1,750
	Received cash for tool repairs.		
9	Advertising Expense	300	
	Cash		300
	Paid cash for radio spot announcements.		
12	Automotive Expense	200	
	Cash		200
	Paid gas, oil, and service costs on the truck.		
14	Accounts Payable	3,000	
	Cash		3,000
	Paid $3,000 of obligations.		
16	Accounts Receivable	1,200	
	Service and Repair Revenue		1,200
	Repaired tools on account for Acme Drilling Company.		
18	Telephone Expense	75	
	Cash		75
	Paid for installation and servicing of telephone for 1 month.		
19	Automotive Expense	180	
	Cash		180
	Paid for minor repairs on the truck.		
20	Cash	1,000	
	Notes Receivable	1,450	
	Service and Repair Revenue		2,450
	Collected $1,000 cash from Jones for tool repairs; accepted a 60-day note for the balance.		
24	Repairs and Maintenance Expense	150	
	Cash		150
	Paid cleaning and painting expenses on the building.		

25	Cash	1,500	
	Service and Repair Revenue		1,500
	Received cash for tool repairs and services from Hamilton, Inc.		
27	Supplies	2,500	
	Cash		2,500
	Purchased shop supplies.		
29	Office Equipment	1,250	
	Cash		1,250
	Purchased a calculator and a typewriter.		
30	Cash	1,200	
	Accounts Receivable		1,200
	Collected receivables from Acme Drilling Company.		
31	Utilities Expense	900	
	Cash		900
	Paid the monthly utility bill.		
31	Automotive Expense	350	
	Cash		350
	Paid for gas, oil, and servicing of the truck.		

Required:
Set up T-accounts, post all journal entries to the accounts, balance the accounts, and prepare a trial balance.

Solution

The first step in solving this problem is to set up T-accounts for each item; then post all journal entries to the appropriate ledger accounts, as shown. Once the amounts are properly posted, account balances can be determined. (The boldface numbers refer to the dates of the journal entries.)

Cash

Debit	Credit
1 40,000	500 .... **1**
8 1,750	750 .... **2**
20 1,000	8,000 .... **3**
25 1,500	3,500 .... **5**
30 1,200	300 .... **9**
	200 .... **12**
	3,000 .... **14**
	75 .... **18**
	180 .... **19**
	150 .... **24**
	2,500 .... **27**
	1,250 .... **29**
	900 .... **31**
	350 .... **31**
Bal. .. 23,795	

Notes Receivable

Debit	Credit
20 1,450	

Accounts Receivable

Debit	Credit
16 1,200	1,200 .... **30**
Bal. ... 0	

Supplies

Debit	Credit
4 3,000	
27 2,500	
Bal. ... 5,500	

Shop Equipment

Debit	Credit
3 8,000	

Automotive Equipment

Debit	Credit
5 11,500	

Office Equipment

Debit	Credit
29 1,250	

Notes Payable

Debit	Credit
	8,000 .... **5**

Accounts Payable

Debit	Credit
14 3,000	3,000 .... **4**
	0 ... **Bal.**

Capital Stock

Debit	Credit
	40,000 ... **1**

Service and Repair Revenue

Debit	Credit
	1,750 .... **8**
	1,200 .... **16**
	2,450 .... **20**
	1,500 .... **25**
	6,900 ... **Bal.**

Insurance Expense

Debit	Credit
1 500	

Rent Expense

Debit	Credit
2 750	

Advertising Expense

Debit	Credit
9 300	

Automotive Expense

Debit	Credit
12 200	
19 180	
31 350	
Bal. 730	

Telephone Expense

Debit	Credit
18 75	

Repairs and Maintenance Expense

Debit	Credit
24 150	

Utilities Expense

Debit	Credit
31 900	

The final step is to prepare a trial balance to see that the posting procedure has been performed correctly. List all the accounts with balances in financial statement order, then enter the balance in each account.

Tyler Tool and Repair Service, Inc.
Trial Balance as of October 31, 1983

	Debits	Credits
Cash	$23,795	
Notes Receivable	1,450	
Supplies	5,500	
Shop Equipment	8,000	
Automotive Equipment	11,500	
Office Equipment	1,250	
Notes Payable		$ 8,000
Capital Stock		40,000
Service and Repair Revenue		6,900
Insurance Expense	500	
Rent Expense	750	
Advertising Expense	300	
Automotive Expense	730	
Telephone Expense	75	
Repairs and Maintenance Expense	150	
Utilities Expense	900	
Totals	$54,900	$54,900

DISCUSSION QUESTIONS

1 What is the basic objective of the accounting process?

2 Distinguish between the terms "data" and "information."

3 Distinguish between a managerial information system and an accounting information system.

4 What are the characteristics of a manual accounting system as compared with an automated accounting system?

5 Are internal controls needed in a computerized accounting system? Explain.

6 How does the general pattern of activity in a merchandising business differ from that in a manufacturing business? How does a service business differ in its pattern of activity?

7 In a double-entry system of accounting, why must debits always equal credits?

8 Define a T-account and explain when and how it is used.

9 What is the relationship of revenues and expenses to the basic accounting equation?

10 What types of accounts are increased by credits? What types of accounts are increased by debits?

11 List and briefly explain the first four steps in the accounting cycle.

12 What purposes do business documents serve?

13 Distinguish between a journal and a ledger.

14 Assume an exchange transaction between a buyer and a seller of $1,500 of merchandise. What entries should the buyer and seller make, and what is the relationship of the accounts for this transaction?

15 Indicate how each of the following transactions affects the accounting equation.

(a) Purchase of supplies on account.
(b) Payment of wages.
(c) Cash sales.
(d) Payment of monthly utility bills.
(e) Purchase of a building.
(f) Cash investment by a shareholder.
(g) Payment of a cash dividend.
(h) Sale of goods for more than their cost.
(i) Sale of land at less than its cost.

16 What are dividends? What effect does a $1,000 dividend declaration and payment have on net income? Explain.

17 Distinguish between a Drawings account and a Dividends account.

18 What is a chart of accounts? What is its purpose?

19 If a trial balance appears to be correct, does that guarantee complete accuracy in the accounting records? Explain.

EXERCISES

E3-1 General Business Pattern

South African Diamond Store is an exclusive downtown operation that sells only high-quality cut diamonds on a retail basis. To encourage sales, generous credit terms are offered. Outline the pattern of activity that is likely to be used in this business.

E3-2 Basic Accounting Equation

For each of the following transactions show how the fundamental accounting equation is kept in balance. Example: Borrowed money (increase asset, increase liability).

1. Purchased merchandise for resale by paying cash.
2. Paid off a note.
3. Collected a customer's account balance.
4. Sold merchandise on credit at a profit.
5. Paid the month's rent.

E3-3 Expanded Accounting Equation

Sofa City, a furniture store, had the following transactions during the year.

1. Purchased inventory on account.
2. Sold merchandise for cash, assuming a profit on the sale.
3. Borrowed money from a bank.
4. Purchased land, making a cash down payment and issuing a note for the balance.
5. Issued stock for cash.
6. Paid salaries for the year.
7. Paid a vendor for inventory purchased on account.
8. Sold a building for cash and notes receivable at no gain or loss.
9. Paid cash dividends to stockholders.

Using the following column headings, indicate the net effect of each transaction on the accounting equation (+ increase; − decrease; 0 no effect). Transaction 1 above has been completed as an example.

Transaction	Assets	=	Liabilities	+	Owners' Equity
1	+ (inventory)		+ (accounts payable)		0

E3-4 Classification of Accounts

For each of the accounts listed below indicate whether it is an asset (A), a liability (L), or owners' equity (OE) account. If it is an account that affects retained earnings, indicate whether it is a revenue (R) or an expense (E) account.

1. Cash
2. Sales
3. Accounts Receivable
4. Cost of Goods Sold
5. Prepaid Insurance
6. Capital Stock
7. Mortgage Payable
8. Salaries and Wages Expense
9. Retained Earnings
10. Salaries Payable
11. Accounts Payable
12. Interest Revenue
13. Inventory
14. Interest Receivable
15. Notes Payable
16. Equipment
17. Office Supplies on Hand
18. Utilities Expense
19. Interest Payable
20. Rent Expense

E3-5 Normal Account Balances

For each account listed in E3-4, indicate whether it would normally have a debit balance or a credit balance.

E3-6 Journalizing Transactions

Record each of the following transactions in Joliet Company's General Journal. (Omit explanations.)

1. Issued capital stock for $50,000 cash.
2. Borrowed $10,000 from a bank. Signed a note to secure the debt.
3. Purchased inventory from a supplier on credit for $8,000.
4. Paid the supplier for the inventory received.
5. Sold inventory that cost $1,200 for $1,500 on credit.
6. Collected $1,500 from customers.

E3-7 Journalizing Transactions

Carol's Cookie Company had the following transactions during 1983.

1. Purchased a new building, paying $20,000 cash and issuing a note of $50,000.
2. Purchased $15,000 of inventory on account.
3. Sold inventory costing $5,000 for $6,000 on account.
4. Paid for inventory purchased on account (item 2).
5. Issued capital stock for $25,000.
6. Collected $4,500 of accounts receivable.
7. Paid utility bills totaling $360.
8. Sold old building for $27,000, receiving $10,000 cash and a $17,000 note (no gain or loss on the sale).
9. Paid $2,000 cash dividends to stockholders (use a Dividends account).

Record the above transactions in General Journal format (omit explanations).

E3–8 Journalizing Transactions

Sam Jones, owner of Sam's Food Supply, completed the following business transactions during March 1983. For each transaction, give the entry that Sam would make to record it in the company's General Journal (omit explanations).

March 1	Purchased $53,000 of inventory on credit.
4	Collected $10,000 from customers as payments on their accounts.
5	Paid a 3-year insurance premium for $3,000 (record as an asset).
6	Sold inventory that cost $30,000 to customers on account for $40,000.
10	Paid rent for March, $1,050.
15	Paid utilities for March, $100.
17	Paid a $300 monthly salary to the part-time helper.
20	Collected $33,000 from customers as payments on their accounts.
22	Paid $53,000 cash on inventory account payable (see March 1 entry).
25	Paid property taxes of $1,200.
28	Sold inventory that cost $20,000 to customers for $30,000 cash.

E3–9 Posting Journal Entries

For each of the transactions outlined in E3–6, draw T-accounts and post the journal entries to the T-accounts.

E3–10 Trial Balance

The account balances in SM Company's ledger as of July 31, 1983, are listed below in alphabetical order. The balance for the Capital Stock account has been omitted. Prepare a trial balance, listing the accounts in proper sequence, and insert the missing amount for Capital Stock.

Accounts Payable	$ 8,600	Land	$19,000
Accounts Receivable	2,000	Miscellaneous Expenses	1,400
Buildings	20,000	Mortgage Payable (due 1988)	24,000
Capital Stock	?	Retained Earnings	9,000
Cash	15,600	Salary Expense	10,000
Dividends	3,000	Supplies on Hand	600
Equipment	16,000	Utilities Expense	400
Fees Earned	22,000		
Insurance Expense	3,600		

E3–11 Correcting a Trial Balance

The following trial balance was prepared by a new employee unfamiliar with accounting. It appears that some debit and credit balances are mixed up. Prepare a corrected trial balance for the company. (Assume that all accounts have "normal" balances and that the recorded amounts are correct.)

Jake's Jogging Supplies Company
Trial Balance as of June 30, 1983

	Debits	Credits
Cash	$ 8,500	
Accounts Receivable	6,000	
Accounts Payable	10,000	
Inventory		$ 22,500
Supplies on Hand		1,000
Supplies Expense	1,500	
Notes Receivable		10,500
Notes Payable	5,500	
Insurance Expense		3,000
Utilities Expense	800	
Advertising Expense	4,500	
Sales Revenue	148,900	
Cost of Goods Sold		105,200
Wages Payable	3,800	
Wages Expense	18,400	
Rent Expense		6,000
Land	15,000	
Buildings	75,000	
Equipment	10,000	
Capital Stock		50,000
Retained Earnings		69,700
Totals	$307,900	$267,900

E3–12 Compound Journal Entries

Martin Merchandise Company had the following transactions during 1983.

1. Fred Martin began business by investing the following assets, receiving capital stock in exchange.

Cash	$ 20,000
Inventory	37,000
Land	25,500
Building	160,000
Equipment	12,500*
Total	$255,000

* A note of $5,000 on the equipment was assumed by the company.

2. Sold merchandise that cost $30,000 for $45,000; $15,000 cash was received immediately and the other $30,000 will be collected in 30 days.
3. Paid off the note of $5,000 plus $300 interest.
4. Purchased merchandise costing $12,000, paying $2,000 cash and issuing a note for $10,000.
5. Exchanged $2,000 cash and $8,000 in capital stock for office equipment costing $10,000.
6. Purchased a truck for $15,000 with $3,000 down and a 1-year note for the balance.

Journalize the above transactions (omit explanations).

E3–13 Posting to Ledger Accounts and Preparing a Trial Balance

Refer to your solution in E3–12.

1. Post the journal entries to a General Ledger, using T-accounts for each account listed.
2. Prepare a trial balance as of December 31, 1983.

E3–14 Journal Entries from Ledger Analysis

T-accounts for Cougar Ranch, Inc. are shown below. Analyze the accounts and prepare the appropriate journal entries that must have been made by the company (omit explanations).

Cash	
a 6,000	4,500 c
b 8,000	3,700 .... f
d 9,000	1,700 .... g
i 1,000	2,000 .... h

Accounts Receivable	
d 2,000	1,000 i

Inventory	
c 9,000	7,500 .... e

Accounts Payable	
f 3,700	4,500 c

Notes Payable	
	6,000 .... a

Capital Stock	
	8,000 .... b

Sales Revenue	
	11,000 ... d

Cost of Goods Sold	
e 7,500	

Salary Expense	
g 1,700	

Rent Expense	
h 2,000	

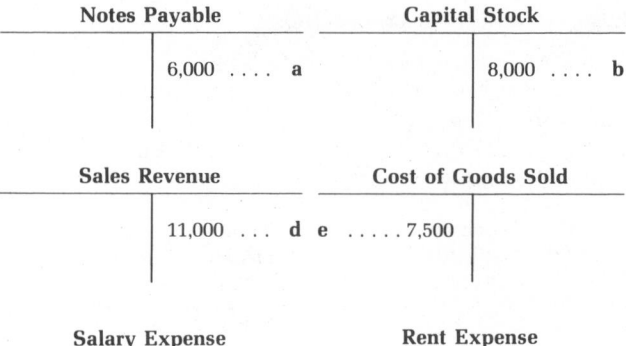

E3–15 Accounting for Dividends

The board of directors of Pro Enterprises declared a $40,000 cash dividend on March 8, 1983. The dividends will be paid on March 20. Give the entries to record both the declaration and the payment of the dividends to the stockholders. (Use a Dividends account.)

PROBLEMS

P3–1 Manual Versus Automated Accounting Systems

Alfred Holmes plans to open Holmes Sport Shop. The shop will be a medium-sized operation, specializing primarily in the sale of bicycle and ski equipment. Alfred also plans to service the types of equipment he sells. Although Alfred wants his accounting department to function smoothly and efficiently, he would like to keep expenditures to a minimum. He is considering the following accounting systems.

a. A system in which journal entries are recorded manually, but adding machines and calculators are provided to assist in making calculations.

b. A system in which a microcomputer is used to store accounting records and make calculations.

c. A system in which a computer journalizes and posts all transactions. Results of individual transactions are recorded as input into the computer by a clerk.

Required:

List the advantages and disadvantages of each of the proposed accounting systems, keeping in mind the costs and benefits of each. Consider the following: personnel, accuracy, speed, initial purchase price, efficiency.

P3–2 General Pattern of Business Activity

Three businesses that are members of the Midtown Chamber of Commerce are described below.

Sam's Fix-it Shop is a medium-sized business that has a reputation for being able to fix any kind of appliance. Sam maintains an inventory of parts for various household appliances, such as toasters and washing machines. No credit terms are offered.

Dandy Department Store is a large store that has operated in Midtown for many years. In order to encourage sales, management has decided to extend credit terms to customers who have satisfactory credit ratings.

Maxwell Manufacturing Company makes high-quality waffle irons. These products are sold on credit to retail outlets.

Required:

1. For each business, outline the basic pattern of activity.
2. Point out any similarities and differences between the activity patterns of service, merchandising, and manufacturing businesses.

P3-3 Journal Entries and Trial Balance

The balances in the Jan Jennings Company General Ledger as of January 1, 1984, were

	Debits	Credits
Cash	$18,000	
Accounts Receivable	200	
Inventory	26,000	
Equipment	3,000	
Salaries Payable		$ 4,000
Accounts Payable		2,500
Notes Payable		20,000
J. Jennings, Capital		20,700
Totals	$47,200	$47,200

Jan Jennings Company had the following transactions in 1984. All expenses were paid in cash, unless otherwise stated.

a. Purchased inventory for $17,500 cash. Accounts Payable as of January 1, 1984 (see above), were also paid.

b. Sold $98,000 of merchandise, 90 percent for cash and 10 percent on credit.

c. The cost of goods sold was $32,000.

d. Paid electricity and other utilities of $12,000.

e. Paid three high-school students $250 a month each to help out on a part-time basis.

f. Paid $25,000 in wages earned in 1984 by full-time employees.

g. Jan Jennings withdrew $1,500 a month for 12 months for living expenses.

h. Collected receivables of $9,500.

Required:

1. Prepare journal entries to record each of the above transactions (omit explanations).

2. Prepare a trial balance for Jan Jennings Company at December 31, 1984.

3. **Interpretive Question** If the debit and credit columns of the trial balance are equal, does this mean that no errors have been made in journalizing the transactions? Explain.

P3-4 Journal Entries from Ledger Analysis

Given below are a number of T-accounts. Transactions have been posted to the accounts and given a letter to indicate each transaction.

Cash

Debit	Credit
a ... 100,000	40,000 ... b
d ... 15,000	6,000 ... c
i ... 12,400	13,000 ... g
	10,000 ... k
	3,350 ... l

Accounts Payable

Debit	Credit
k 10,000	1,850 ... f
l 3,350	10,000 ... h
	6,500 .... j

Accounts Receivable

Debit	Credit
e 15,700	12,400 ... i

Capital Stock

Debit	Credit
	100,000 .. a

Delivery Equipment

Debit	Credit
b 40,000	
h 10,000	

Salaries Expense

Debit	Credit
g 13,000	

Delivery Revenues

Debit	Credit
	15,000 ... d
	15,700 ... e

Delivery Expenses

Debit	Credit
f 1,850	

Rent Expense

Debit	Credit
c 6,000	

Heating Expense

Debit	Credit
j 3,000	

Utilities Expense

Debit	Credit
j 2,000	

Telephone Expense

Debit	Credit
j 1,500	

Required:

Describe the event that is probably being recorded with each entry.

P3-5 Unifying Problem: Journalizing, Posting, and Preparing a Trial Balance and Balance Sheet

The following transactions of Alexander Company (a proprietorship) occurred during May 1983.

May 1 Received $100,000 cash from the owner, John Alexander, as an investment in the company.

10 Purchased land and a building for $20,000 cash and a 10-year $40,000 mortgage. The land was appraised at $15,000 and the building at $45,000.

15 Purchased supplies from Baltzer Company for $5,000 on account.

31 Sold half the land purchased on May 10 for $7,500, receiving $2,500 cash and a 60-day note in the amount of $5,000.

Required:

1. Journalize the above transactions.
2. Post to T-accounts.
3. Prepare a trial balance.
4. Prepare a balance sheet.

P3–6 T-Accounts, Trial Balance, and Income Statement

The following list is a selection of transactions from Duarte Corporation's business activities during 1983.

a. Received $50,000 cash for capital stock.

b. Paid $5,000 cash for equipment.

c. Purchased inventory costing $18,000 on account.

d. Sold $25,000 of merchandise to customers on account. Cost of goods sold was $15,000.

e. Signed a note with a bank for a $10,000 loan.

f. Collected $9,500 cash from customers who had purchased merchandise on account.

g. Purchased land, $10,000, and a building, $60,000, for $15,000 cash and a 30-year mortgage of $55,000.

h. Made a first payment of $2,750 on the mortgage principal plus another $2,750 in interest.

i. Paid $12,000 of accounts payable by giving cash of $3,000 and issuing a note for the balance of $9,000.

j. Purchased $1,500 of supplies on account.

k. Paid $2,500 of accounts payable.

l. Declared a cash dividend of $2,000.

m. Paid $7,500 in wages earned during the year.

n. Received $10,000 cash and $3,000 of notes in settlement of customers' accounts.

o. Paid the cash dividend previously declared in (l).

p. Received $3,000 in payment of a note receivable plus interest of $250.

q. Paid $600 cash for a utilities bill.

r. Sold excess land for its cost of $3,000.

s. Received $1,500 in rent for an unused part of a building.

t. Paid off a $19,000 note, plus interest of $1,200.

Required:

1. Set up T-accounts and appropriately record the debits and credits for each transaction. (Ignore any beginning balances in the accounts.) Leave room for a number of entries in the Cash account.
2. Prepare a trial balance.
3. Prepare an income statement for the period. (Ignore income taxes.)

P3–7 Analysis of Transactions

The following selected journal entries appear on the August 1983 books of Mott Motors, Inc.

1. Supplies on Hand	2,250	
Accounts Payable		2,250

Purchased supplies on account from Shure Supply Company.

2. Utilities Expense	1,200	
Cash		1,200

Paid monthly utility bill with cash.

3. Cash	6,900	
Accounts Receivable	10,000	
Sales Revenue		16,900

Sold a delivery truck to Wright Delivery Company for $6,900 cash, with the balance to be paid in 60 days.

Cost of Goods Sold	14,500	
Inventory		14,500

To record the cost of a delivery truck sold to Wright Delivery Company and to reduce inventory for its cost.

4. Inventory	112,500	
Cash		12,500
Accounts Payable		100,000

Purchased 9 new cars and trucks from Duro Motors, Inc., for $12,500 cash, with the balance to be paid as each car and truck is sold.

5. Repairs Expense	7,850	
Cash		7,850

Paid Sandy's Machine Shop for machine shop work for the month of August.

6. Cash	9,500	
Sales		9,500

Sold a car to A-1 Realty Company for use by its sales force.

Required:

From the journal entries above and the information given, record the journal entries for each of the other parties to the transactions. Give an explanation with each entry. Since you do not have cost data for merchandise sold, you may ignore any entries debiting Cost of Goods Sold and crediting Inventory for sales made to Mott Motors, Inc.

P3–8 Journalizing and Posting

Tricia's Tennis Ball Company had the following transactions during July 1983.

July 1 Issued capital stock for $35,000 cash.

3 Paid a note of $10,000 owed since January 1, 1983, together with interest of $600.

5 Paid $15,000 to employees for their July 1983 wages.

9 Paid yearly property taxes of $1,800.

17 Purchased $15,000 worth of tennis balls and racquets on account for resale.

21 Sold all the tennis balls and racquets purchased on July 17 for $22,500, with $7,500 received in cash and the balance on credit.

25 Paid $14,500 of obligations.

29 Received $10,300 from customers as payments on their accounts.

Required:

1. Journalize each of the transactions for July. (Omit explanations.)

2. Set up T-accounts and post each of the journal entries that you made in (1).

3. **Interpretive Question** If the owner of a business wanted to know at any given moment how much cash or inventory the company had on hand, where would the owner look? Why?

P3–9 Unifying Problem: Journal Entries; T-accounts; Trial Balance

Paperpro Company, a retailer of paper products, had the following account balances as of April 30, 1983.

	Debits	Credits
Cash	$ 7,100	
Accounts Receivable	4,900	
Inventory	16,000	
Land	26,000	
Building	24,000	
Furniture	4,000	
Accounts Payable		$12,000
Notes Payable		25,000
Capital Stock		30,000
Retained Earnings		15,000
Totals	$82,000	$82,000

During May the company had the following transactions.

May 3	Paid one-half of 4/30/83 accounts payable.
6	Collected all of 4/30/83 accounts receivable.
7	Sold $7,700 of inventory for $6,000 cash and $4,000 on account.
8	Sold one-half the land for $13,000, receiving $8,000 cash plus a note for $5,000.
10	Purchased inventory on account, $10,000.
15	Paid installment of $5,000 on note payable.
21	Issued additional capital stock for $2,000 cash.
23	Sold $4,000 of inventory for $7,500 cash.
25	Paid salaries of $2,000.
26	Paid rent of $500.
29	Purchased desk for $500 cash.

Required:

1. Prepare the journal entry for each transaction.
2. Post the entries to T-accounts.
3. Prepare a trial balance as of May 31, 1983.

P3–10 Unifying Problem: First Steps in the Accounting Cycle

The following balances were taken from the General Ledger of Stevens Company on January 1, 1984.

	Debits	Credits
Cash	$ 7,500	
Short-Term Investments	10,000	
Accounts Receivable	12,500	
Inventory	15,000	
Land	25,000	
Buildings	75,000	
Equipment	20,000	
Notes Payable		$ 17,500
Accounts Payable		12,500
Salaries and Wages Payable		2,500
Mortgage Payable		37,500
Capital Stock (7,000 shares outstanding)		70,000
Retained Earnings		25,000
Totals	$165,000	$165,000

During 1984, the company had the following transactions.

a. Purchased inventory for $110,000 on credit.

b. Issued an additional $25,000 of capital stock (2,500 shares) for cash.

c. Paid property taxes of $4,500 for the year 1984.

d. Paid advertising and other selling costs of $8,000.

e. Paid utility expenses of $6,500 for 1984.

f. Paid the salaries and wages for 1983. Paid an additional salaries and wages expense of $18,000 during 1984.

g. Sold merchandise costing $105,000 for $175,000. Of total sales, $45,000 were cash sales and $130,000 were credit sales.

h. Paid off notes of $17,500 plus interest of $1,600.

i. On November 1, 1984, received a loan of $10,000 from the bank.

j. On December 30, 1984, made annual mortgage payment of $2,500 and paid interest of $3,700.

k. Collected receivables for the year of $140,000.

l. Paid off accounts payable of $112,500.

m. Received dividends and interest of $1,400 on short-term investments during 1984 (record as Miscellaneous Revenue).

n. Purchased additional short-term investments of $15,000 during 1984.

o. Paid 1984 corporate income taxes of $11,600.

p. Declared and paid cash dividends of $7,600 (use a Dividends account).

Required:

1. Journalize the 1984 transactions (omit explanations).
2. Set up T-accounts with the proper balance at January 1, 1984, and post the journal entries to the T-accounts.
3. Determine the account balances and prepare a trial balance as of December 31, 1984.
4. Prepare an income statement and a balance sheet. (Remember that the Dividends account and all revenue and expense accounts are but temporary Retained Earnings accounts.)

SUPPLEMENT

Special Journals

special journals *books of original entry for recording similar transactions that occur frequently*

So far, we have shown all journal entries in General Journal format. In practice, however, most firms use special journals to record common transactions, such as sales, purchases, cash receipts, and cash disbursements. The use of such journals reduces the amount of posting and other clerical work necessary to account for these activities.

The Sales Journal

A typical page from a sales journal and the posting of that journal, in T-account form, are illustrated in Exhibit 3–13 on pages 96 and 97. You will note that there are columns to record the various aspects of sales transactions: Sales Returns and Allowances (DR), Sales Tax Payable (DR), Accounts Receivable (DR), Accounts Receivable (CR), Sales Revenue (CR), and Sales Tax Payable (CR).

The sales journal shows eleven transactions during January, each with terms 2/10, n/30 (the buyer receives a 2 percent discount if payment is made within 10 days of the purchase, but the total amount must be paid within 30 days or it will be considered past due). Ten of the transactions are regular sales transactions and one (January 8) is a sales return. For each transaction, the sales tax is assumed to be 5 percent of gross sales.

At the end of the accounting period, each column is added and the total of the debit columns is compared with the total of the credit columns to make sure that total debits equal total credits. The totals are then posted to the proper accounts in the General Ledger. The numbers in parentheses below the total in each column indicate the accounts to which the totals have been posted. For example, the (105) at the bottom of the Accounts Receivable column means the total has been posted to account 105 in the General Ledger: Accounts Receivable. In the General Ledger, the underscored reference is to the number of the sales journal page from which the entries came (in this case, page 1). The use of a sales journal saves consid-

subsidiary ledger *a grouping of individual accounts that in total equal the balance of a control account in the General Ledger*

control account *a summary account in the General Ledger that is supported by detailed individual accounts in a subsidiary ledger*

erable time and effort because each individual entry does not have to be separately posted to the General Ledger.

Exhibit 3-13 also gives, in T-account form, the entries in the accounts receivable subsidiary ledger. This subsidiary ledger is needed by a business to help monitor customers' balances. At all times, the cumulative total of all subsidiary ledger accounts must equal the Accounts Receivable balance in the General Ledger. Therefore, Accounts Receivable is called the control account for the subsidiary ledger. When the individual sales are posted to the accounts receivable subsidiary ledger, the account numbers (in this case, 105.1 to 105.10) are entered in the sales journal. Similarly, in the subsidiary accounts, the number of the sales journal page and the date of the transaction are referenced. Many companies will also reference the invoice number (or check number in the accounts payable subsidiary ledger). We have omitted that reference to simplify the illustration. This system of cross-referencing helps accountants check their work and minimizes the chances of their making a mistake.

The Purchases Journal

When a firm purchases merchandise for resale, it usually records the cost of those purchases in a separate purchases journal. Like the sales journal, the purchases journal saves considerable time and effort by minimizing the posting effort required. A typical page from a purchases journal and the posting of that journal, in T-account form, are illustrated in Exhibit 3-14 on pages 98 and 99.

The relationships between the purchases journal, the General Ledger, and the accounts payable subsidiary ledgers are similar to those between the sales journal, the General Ledger, and the subsidiary accounts receivable ledger. Thus, as shown in Exhibit 3-14, the seven purchases and the one purchase return made during January are recorded chronologically in the purchases journal. The amounts that represent purchases of goods to be sold are also recorded in a Purchases (DR) column, while items purchased for internal use are recorded in a Store Supplies (DR) column. The purchase return is recorded in an Other Accounts column, which covers all "irregular" transactions.

Then, the totals of each column—the Accounts Payable (CR), Accounts Payable (DR), Purchases (DR), and Store Supplies (DR) columns—are added and total debits and credits are compared to make sure they are equal. The total from each column is posted to its General Ledger account.

Finally, the individual purchases are posted to the separate creditor accounts in the subsidiary ledger. Again, as with the sales journal, the purchases journal is cross-referenced to the General Ledger and subsidiary ledgers, and the cumulative total of all balances in the accounts payable subsidiary ledger equals the balance in the Accounts Payable control account.

The Cash Receipts Journal

The third special journal is the one in which all cash receipts are recorded. A typical page from a cash receipts journal and the postings from that journal are displayed in Exhibit 3-15 on pages 100 and 101. The cash receipts journal includes columns for Cash (DR), Sales Discounts (DR), Accounts Receivable (CR), Sales Revenue (CR), and Sales Tax Payable (CR), which are used to record all cash receipts. In addition, an Other Accounts (CR) column is used to record all "irregular" cash transactions—that is, all items that do not fall naturally into a special column, such as cash, accounts receivable, and so forth. Examples of irregular transactions are collections of interest, rents, or notes receivable. The Other Accounts column is added for cross-checking purposes and a check mark (✓) is placed below the total to indicate that the individual items have been posted.

In reading Exhibit 3-15, notice that on June 1, Lewallyn and Sons made a cash payment of $686 to satisfy a $700 bill (debit Cash; credit Accounts Receivable). Because they paid promptly, they received a 2 percent cash discount (debit Sales Discounts for $14). The $125 cash sale on June 13 was credited to Sales Revenue and the interest revenue collected on June 18 was credited to Other Accounts.

In posting the entries from the cash receipts journal to the General Ledger, only those amounts in the Other Accounts (CR) column are handled individually, with the number of each ledger account appearing in the Post Reference column. For example, when the $150 payment was collected on July 2 and posted to Notes Receivable, the account number 103 was entered in the Post Reference column. All other columns are posted to the General Ledger as totals at the end of each accounting period. The total of the debit columns is compared with the total of the credit columns to make sure that total debits equal total credits. As the totals are posted, their account numbers are entered just below the column totals. The individual entries in the Accounts Receivable (CR) column are posted to the customers' accounts in the accounts receivable ledger. Check marks are placed in the Post Reference column to indicate that these subsidiary postings have been made.

The Cash Disbursements Journal

The cash payments of a business are usually recorded in a separate cash disbursements journal. A typical page from a cash disbursements journal and the postings from that journal are shown in Exhibit 3-16 on pages 102 and 103. The cash disbursements journal contains Other Accounts (CR and DR), Cash (CR), Purchase Discounts (CR), Accounts Payable (DR), Sales Salaries Expense and General and Administrative Salaries Expense (DR) columns. The Other Accounts (DR) column is used to record cash purchases of merchandise and other payments for which there are no special columns. The Sales and General and Administrative Salaries Expense (DR) columns are used to record the payment of salaries. The Purchase Discounts (CR) and Accounts Payable (DR) columns are used to account for payments for merchandise purchased.

EXHIBIT 3-13 Sales Journal

Sales Returns & Allowances DR	Sales Tax Payable DR	Accounts Receivable DR	Post Ref.	Date	Invoice No.
				1983	
		630 00	105.5	Jan. 2	125
		262 50	105.7	3	126
		330 75	105.8	6	127
200 00	10 00			8	X
		226 80	105.1	9	128
		863 10	105.4	10	129
		640 50	105.9	16	130
		532 35	105.3	23	131
		131 25	105.2	27	132
		367 50	105.6	29	133
		856 80	105.10	31	134
200 00	10 00	4841 55			
(402)	(403)	(105)			

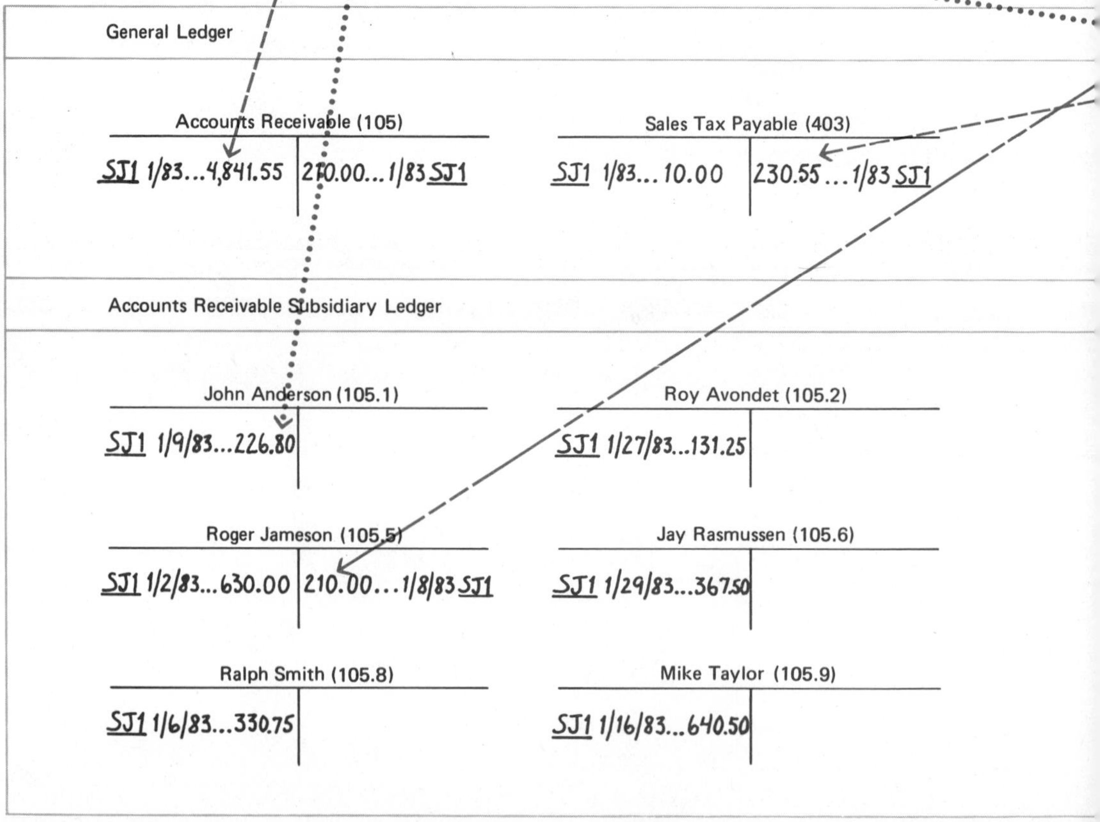

Account Name	Terms	Accounts Receivable CR	Post Ref.	Sales Revenue CR	Sales Tax Payable CR
Roger Jameson	2/10, EOM			600 00	30 00
Lee Smith	2/10, EOM			250 00	12 50
Ralph Smith	2/10, EOM			315 00	15 75
Roger Jameson		210 00	105.5		
John Anderson	2/10, EOM			216 00	10 80
Carl Hartford	2/10, EOM			822 00	41 10
Mike Taylor	2/10, EOM			610 00	30 50
Marvin Brinkerhoff	2/10, EOM			507 00	25 35
Roy Avondet	2/10, EOM			125 00	6 25
Jay Rasmussen	2/10, EOM			350 00	17 50
Jerry Woolsey	2/10, EOM			816 00	40 80
		210 00		4611 00	230 55
		(105)		(400)	(403)

Sales Revenue (400)	
	4,611.00...1/83 SJ1

Sales Returns and Allowances (402)	
SJ1 1/83...200.00	

Marvin Brinkerhoff (105.3)	
SJ1 1/23/83...532.35	

Carl Hartford (105.4)	
SJ1 1/10/83...863.10	

Lee Smith (105.7)	
SJ1 1/3/83...262.50	

Jerry Woolsey (105.10)	
SJ1 1/31/83...856.80	

EXHIBIT 3-14 Purchases Journal

Other Accounts Post Ref.	Other Accounts Amount CR	Accounts Payable CR	Post Ref.	Date		Invoice No.	Terms	Account Name
				1983				
		222	202.4	Jan.	1	125	2/10,n/30	Johnson Mfg. Co.
		616	202.6		2	732	1/10,n/60	Palmer Supply Co.
		485	202.2		6	81	2/10,EOM	Dudley Supply Co.
		690	202.1		12	629	n/30	Davies Wholesale, Inc.
451	150				14	1600R		Palmer Supply Co.
		810	202.3		15	841	n/60	Jackson Wholesale Co.
		700	202.7		22	1025	1/10,EOM	White Incorporated
		525	202.5		29	521	2/10,n/30	Mission Supply, Inc.
		400	202.8		30	1040	n/30	Tool Design Co.
	150	4448						
		(202)						

General Ledger

Accounts Payable (202)

Debit	Credit
PJ1 1/83...150	4,448... 1/83 PJ1

Store Supplies (125)

Debit	Credit
PJ1 1/83...222	

Purchase Returns and Allowances (451)

Debit	Credit
	150... 1/83 PJ1

Accounts Payable Subsidiary Ledger

Davies Wholesale, Inc. (202.1)

Debit	Credit
	690...1/12/83 PJ1

Dudley Supply Co. (202.2)

Debit	Credit
	485...1/6/83 PJ1

Mission Supply, Inc. (202.5)

Debit	Credit
	525...1/29/83 PJ1

Palmer Supply Co. (202.6)

Debit	Credit
PJ1 1/83...150	616...1/2/83 PJ1

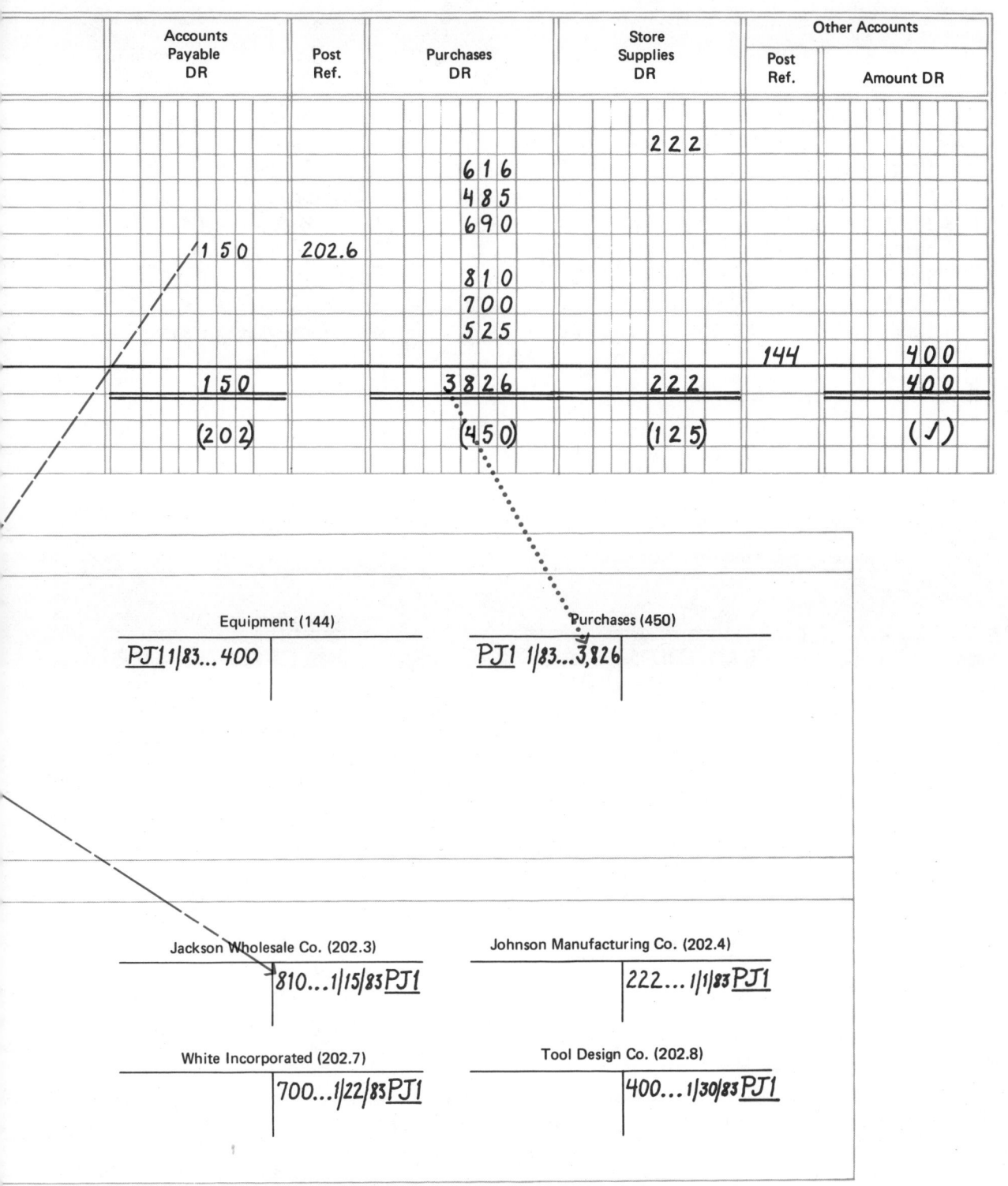

Accounts Payable DR	Post Ref.	Purchases DR	Store Supplies DR	Other Accounts Post Ref.	Other Accounts Amount DR
			222		
		616			
		485			
		690			
150	202.6				
		810			
		700			
		525			
				144	400
150		3826	222		400
(202)		(450)	(125)		(✓)

Equipment (144)

PJ1 1/83...400	

Purchases (450)

PJ1 1/83...3,826	

Jackson Wholesale Co. (202.3)

	810...1/15/83 PJ1

Johnson Manufacturing Co. (202.4)

	222...1/1/83 PJ1

White Incorporated (202.7)

	700...1/22/83 PJ1

Tool Design Co. (202.8)

	400...1/30/83 PJ1

EXHIBIT 3-15 **Cash Receipts Journal**

Cash DR	Sales Discounts DR	Date		Receipt No.	Account Title (Name)
		1983			
686 00	14 00	June	1	621	Lewallyn and Sons
150 00			5	622	Notes Receivable
131 25			13	623	Cash Sales
882 00	18 00		15	624	James Mann and Co.
50 00			18	625	Interest Revenue
31 50			21	626	Cash Sales
392 00	8 00		25	627	EmCo Trucking
588 00	12 00		28	628	Morrison Associates
2910 75	52 00				
(101)	(404)				

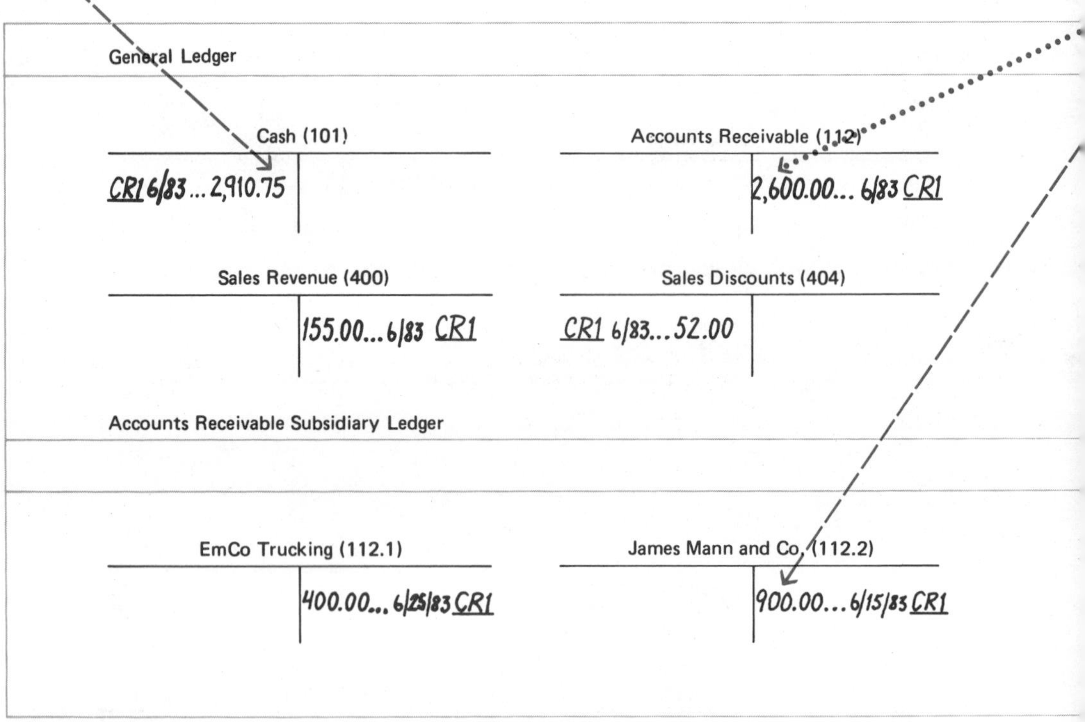

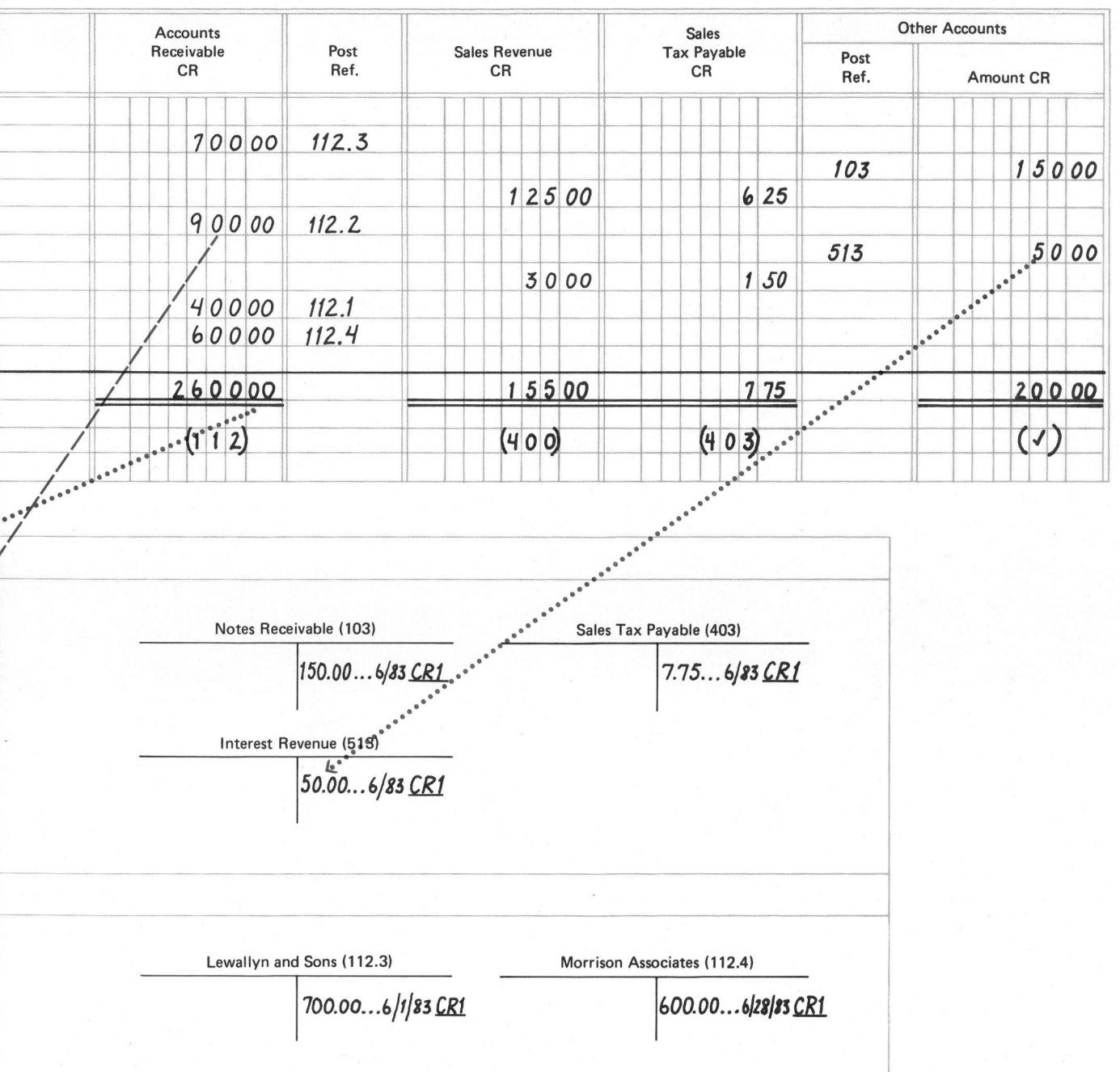

Accounts Receivable CR	Post Ref.	Sales Revenue CR	Sales Tax Payable CR	Other Accounts Post Ref.	Other Accounts Amount CR
700 00	112.3				
				103	150 00
		125 00	6 25		
900 00	112.2				
				513	50 00
		30 00	1 50		
400 00	112.1				
600 00	112.4				
2600 00		155 00	7 75		200 00
(112)		(400)	(403)		(✓)

Notes Receivable (103)

Credit: 150.00...6/83 CR1

Sales Tax Payable (403)

Credit: 7.75...6/83 CR1

Interest Revenue (513)

Credit: 50.00...6/83 CR1

Lewallyn and Sons (112.3)

Credit: 700.00...6/1/83 CR1

Morrison Associates (112.4)

Credit: 600.00...6/28/83 CR1

EXHIBIT 3-16 Cash Disbursements Journal

Other Accounts						
Post Ref.	Amount CR	Cash CR	Purchase Discounts CR	Date		Check No.
				1983		
		588	12	July	1	176
		3000			4	177
		225			8	178
		792	8		17	179
		2100			24	180
		297	3		29	181
		7002	23			
		(101)	(452)			

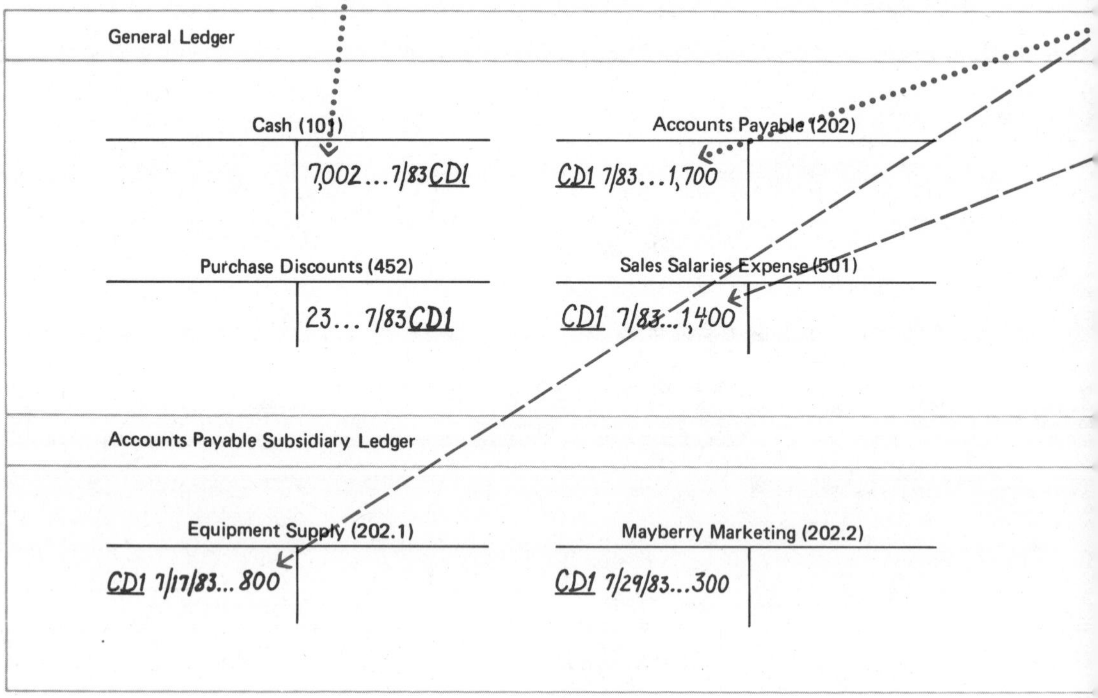

Account Title (Name)	Accounts Payable DR	Post Ref.	Salaries Expense Sales DR	Salaries Expense Gen. & Admin. DR	Other Accounts Post Ref.	Other Accounts Amount DR
United Co.	600	202.3				
First Federal Co.					201	225
Bell Telephone					569	3000
Equip. Supply	800	202.1				
Payroll			1400	700		
Mayberry Mktg.	300	202.1				
	1700		1400	700		3225
	(202)		(501)	(550)		(✓)

Notes Payable (201)

CD1 7/83...225	

Telephone Expense (569)

CD1 7/83...3,000	

General and Administrative Salaries Expense (550)

CD1 1/83...700	

United Company (202.3)

CD1 7/1/83...600	

EXERCISE AND PROBLEM

Exercise

E3-16 Special Journals

Brinkerhoff Implement Company uses five journals: cash receipts, cash disbursements, sales, purchases, and a General Journal. Indicate in which of the five journals each of the following transactions would be recorded.

1. Accrual of salaries payable (recognized by an adjusting entry).
2. Payment of property taxes.
3. Payment of salaries and other expenses.
4. Purchase of merchandise on account.
5. Purchase of merchandise for cash.
6. Sale of merchandise on credit.
7. Sale of merchandise for cash.
8. Purchase of supplies on account.
9. Purchase of a delivery truck for cash.
10. Cash refund to a customer who returned defective merchandise.
11. Return of merchandise purchased on account for credit.
12. Return of merchandise by a customer for credit.
13. Payment of a note payable.
14. Collection of a note receivable.
15. Expiration of a portion of prepaid insurance (recognized by an adjusting entry).

Problem

P3-11 Special Journals

Taylor Corporation began operations on January 1, 1983. Taylor's chart of accounts includes the following, among others.

Cash	101	Purchases	450
Marketable Securities	102	Purchase Returns and Allowances	451
Notes Receivable	103	Purchase Discounts	452
Supplies	112	Sales Salaries Expense	501
Notes Payable	201	General and Administrative Salaries Expense	550
Accounts Payable	202	Telephone Expense	569
Interest Payable	204	Interest Expense	601
Sales Tax Payable	208	Interest Revenue	701
Sales Revenue	400		
Sales Returns and Allowances	402		

Taylor used four special journals: purchases, sales, cash receipts, and cash disbursements.

Required:

Record the following July 1983 transactions in the four special journals. Assume a 5 percent sales tax on all sales transactions. Invoice, receipt, and check numbers have been omitted to simplify the problem. (Note: Sales tax is not paid on merchandise purchases that are to be resold.)

July 1	Purchased merchandise from Garn Company for $2,000, terms 2/10, n/30.
2	Purchased merchandise from Jacobs Company for $1,000, terms 2/10, n/30.
5	Sold $4,000 of merchandise to Bob Handy, terms 2/10, n/30. (Hint: Add sales tax to sales and accounts receivable on all sales transactions.)
6	Sold $3,000 of merchandise to Dave Harmon, terms 2/10, n/30.
7	Purchased $300 of office supplies on account from Utah Office Supply, terms n/30. (Add sales tax. Supplies are to be used, not resold.)
7	Returned merchandise costing $150 to Garn Company.
8	Paid Garn Company amount owed for July 1 purchase (net of July 7 return). Discounts are only given on the net amount.
13	Paid Jacobs Company amount owed for July 2 purchase.
13	Collected full amount owed by Bob Handy for July 5 sale.
14	Collected full amount owed by Dave Harmon for July 6 sale.
15	Paid June's salaries that were accrued on June 30. Sales Salaries Expense, $700; General and Administrative Salaries Expense, $1,400.
17	Paid a $2,000 note plus $200 interest on the note to First Security Corporation. Interest has not previously been recognized.
19	Collected a note of $1,800 plus $180 interest from Greg Steinkopf.
25	Had cash sales of $300.
28	Paid telephone bill of $80 to Mountain Bell Telephone.
30	Sold merchandise costing $1,500 to Hillway Company, terms 2/10, n/30.

CHAPTER 4

Adjusting Entries

THIS CHAPTER EXPLAINS:

The need for periodic reporting.

The concept of accrual accounting.

The adjustments required before the financial statements can be prepared, including those for unrecorded revenues, unrecorded expenses, unearned revenues, and prepaid expenses.

Transaction analysis was introduced in Chapter 3 as the process of analyzing, recording, classifying, summarizing, and reporting financial information. That chapter explained the first four steps of the accounting cycle: (1) analyzing business documents, (2) journalizing transactions, especially normal operating transactions, (3) posting journal entries, and (4) determining account balances and preparing a trial balance.

At the conclusion of Chapter 3, we presented a simple example (R. J. Corporation) involving only a few business transactions, none of which required adjustment at year-end. This made it possible for us to prepare financial statements directly from the account balances shown on the trial balance. Generally, the transactions of a business are much more numerous and complex, and require year-end adjustments for the individual account balances to be correctly reported on the financial statements. The nature of these adjustments and how they are calculated are explained in this chapter.

You must understand adjusting entries (step 6 in the accounting cycle) before you can prepare a work sheet (step 5), so we will discuss these steps in reverse order, leaving the work sheet until the next chapter. To see why adjusting entries are necessary, you must understand two additional characteristics of the accounting model: periodic reporting and accrual accounting.

Additional Characteristics of the Accounting Model

In Chapter 1 we described several characteristics of the accounting model. These include the assumptions that an accounting entity is a separate economic unit and a going concern, that entities enter into arm's-length transactions which become the basis for accounting entries, and that the dollar is the common unit used in the United States to measure and communicate the results of business transactions.

PERIODIC REPORTING

Another characteristic of the accounting model is that it requires accounting information to be reported regularly, usually at least annually. To be useful, information must be received in time to be taken into consideration before decisions are made. Thus, the financial statements of a business entity need to be issued periodically so that interested parties can review the company's status and progress on a continuing, timely basis. This accounting assumption is called the time-period assumption, or the periodicity concept. It says that an accounting entity's life can be divided into distinct and regular reporting periods, such as a year or a quarter or a month.

time-period assumption (periodicity concept) *the idea that the life of a business is divided into distinct and relatively short time periods so that accounting information can be timely*

Obviously, current owners, prospective investors, bankers, and others need to know periodically what economic events have taken place in a company and whether those events have had a positive or a negative impact. In brief, they need to know the financial position of the entity (from the balance sheet), significant changes in that financial position (from the statement of changes in financial position), and the relative success or failure of current operations (from the income statement).

The financial picture of an entity—its success or failure in meeting its economic objectives—cannot really be complete until the "life" of a business is over. However, managers, owners, and creditors cannot wait 10, 20, or 100 years to receive an exact accounting of a business. They must have timely information in order to make ongoing economic judgments. Accordingly, the life of an enterprise is divided into distinct accounting periods, each generally covering 12 months or less. The 12-month accounting period is referred to as the fiscal year. When an entity closes its books on December 31, it is said to be reporting on a calendar year basis.

fiscal year *an entity's reporting year, covering a 12-month accounting period*

calendar year *an entity's reporting year, covering 12 months and ending on December 31*

Most corporations, and even many small companies, issue a report to shareholders as of a fiscal year-end. This annual report includes the primary financial statements (the balance sheet, income statement, and statement of changes in financial position) and other financial data, such as a 5-year summary of operations. Other financial reports are prepared more frequently, perhaps quarterly or monthly. Indeed, some reports, such as sales reports for use by management, may be prepared on a daily basis.

Although periodic reporting is vital to a firm's success, the frequency of reporting forces accountants to use tentative data that are based on judgments and estimates. As you will see, the shorter the reporting period (for example, a month instead of a year), the less exact are the measurements of assets and liabilities and the recognition of revenues and expenses. Ideally, accounting judgments are carefully made and estimates are based on reliable evidence, but the limitations of accounting reports should be understood and kept in mind.

ACCRUAL ACCOUNTING

In some small businesses, entries are recorded and revenues and expenses are recognized only when cash is received or paid. This is referred to as cash-basis accounting. Most people prepare their income tax returns on a cash basis.

cash-basis accounting *a system of accounting in which transactions are recorded, and revenues and expenses are recognized, only when cash is received or paid*

accrual-basis accounting *a system of accounting in which revenues and expenses are recorded as they are earned and incurred, not necessarily when cash is received or paid*

On a cash basis, income is what is left when cash disbursements of a period are subtracted from cash receipts during the period. For most accounting purposes, however, accrual-basis accounting is more appropriate. This important characteristic of the traditional accounting model simply means that revenues are recognized when earned without regard to when cash is received, and that expenses are recorded as incurred without regard to when they are paid. For example, under accrual accounting, if XYZ Company sold $80,000 of goods in 1983, but did not receive the cash proceeds until 1984, the $80,000 would still be recognized as revenue in 1983, when it was earned. The same is true of expenses; they are recognized when incurred, not when paid. Therefore, net income under accrual accounting is equal to earned revenues minus related expenses, and not revenues minus expenses in the sense of cash receipts less cash disbursements.

The concept of accrual accounting is closely related to the time-period assumption. That is, not until the life of a business has been divided into time periods does it become necessary for revenues and expenses to be properly assigned to each period. In determining income on an accrual basis, only those revenues that have actually been earned during a period are reported. This is sometimes referred to as the revenue recognition principle, or realization principle. Similarly, all expenses incurred to generate those revenues should be associated with that same period. This is called the matching principle. It is this matching process that determines income when accrual-basis accounting is used.

revenue recognition principle *the idea that revenues should be recorded when (1) the earnings process has been substantially completed, and (2) an exchange has taken place*

matching principle *the idea that all costs and expenses incurred in generating revenues must be recognized in the same reporting period as the related revenues*

For revenues to be recognized in the accounting records, two main criteria have to be met.

1. The earnings process must be substantially complete, which generally means that a sale has been made or services have been performed.
2. An exchange must have taken place.

The first criterion ensures that the parties to the transaction have fulfilled their commitment, or are formally obligated to do so. For example, a company generally records sales revenues when goods are shipped or when services are performed. If a buyer pays in advance for goods not yet received, the seller does not record those payments as revenues until the goods are made available to the buyer. The second criterion ensures that there is objective evidence (documentation) by which to measure the amount of revenue involved. The subject of revenue recognition is an important one and is discussed more completely in later chapters.

Once a company determines which revenues should be recognized during a period, all expenses incurred to generate those revenues should also be associated, or matched, with that period. Sometimes, however, expenses cannot be associated with particular revenues, so they have to be assigned according to particular periods of time. As an example, the exact amount of electricity used to produce a particular product generally cannot be determined, but the amount used for a month or a year is known and can be matched to the revenues earned during that same period. This recognition and matching process, as shown in Exhibit 4-1, determines the amount of net income reported on the income statement.

EXHIBIT 4-1 **Determining Accrual Income**

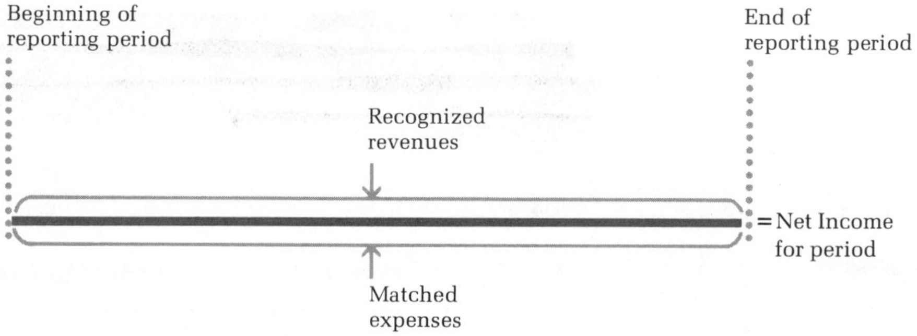

Recognized Revenues − Matched Expenses = Net Income for the Period

TO SUMMARIZE Users of accounting information need timely, periodic financial reports in order to make appropriate decisions. The revenue recognition and matching principles provide guidelines for assigning the appropriate amounts of revenues and expenses to each accounting period. At the end of each period, some accounts must be adjusted so that the balance sheet will reflect appropriate account balances and the income statement will show a proper measurement of earnings.

Step 6. Adjusting Entries

Not only is accrual-basis accounting important for proper income determination, it is also needed for the assignment of appropriate balance sheet values at a particular date. This concept is illustrated by the time line in Exhibit 4-2. As the time line shows, and as we discussed in Chapter 2, at the end of each accounting period a balance sheet is prepared *as of* that date and an income statement is prepared for the period ending *on* that date. Before any data can be reported in the financial statements, however, it is necessary to make sure that all accounts have appropriate balances and that all revenues and expenses have been properly recognized. This is accom-

EXHIBIT 4-2 **Relationship Between Income Statements and Balance Sheets**

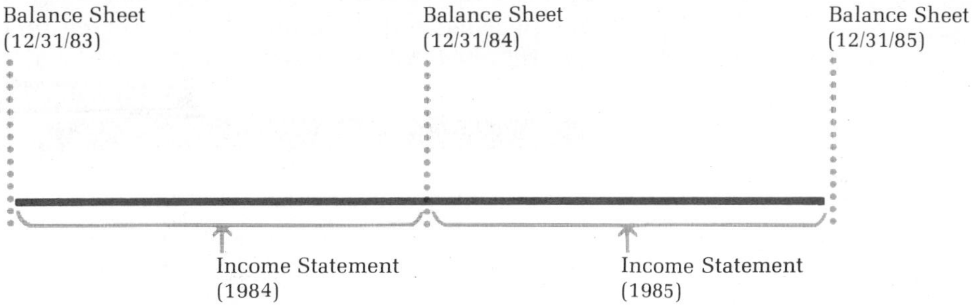

adjusting entries *entries required at the end of each accounting period to recognize, on an accrual basis, revenues and expenses for the period and to report proper amounts for asset, liability, and owners' equity accounts*

plished by making adjusting entries. For example, accounts that involve estimates of future amounts may need adjustment at the end of a period on the basis of existing facts or more current estimates. Similarly, earned revenues and incurred expenses for which no journal entries have been made must be recognized prior to the preparation of the financial reports. Thus, in order to report all asset, liability, and owners' equity amounts properly, and to recognize all revenues and expenses for the period on an accrual basis, adjustments generally are required at the end of each accounting period.

Adjusting entries are recorded in the General Journal and are posted to the accounts in the General Ledger in the same manner as other journal entries. However, unlike other journal entries, adjusting entries have no transactions or underlying documents to signal a need for their recording. Rather, they are recorded on the basis of analysis of the accounts at the close of each accounting period.

The accounts that usually need adjustments may be classified under four headings.

1. Unrecorded revenues.
2. Unrecorded expenses.
3. Unearned revenues.
4. Prepaid expenses.

As we illustrate and discuss these four categories of accounts, remember that the basic purpose of adjustments is to bring account balances to their correct amounts. This is done so that the income statement and the balance sheet will reflect the proper operating results and financial status at the end of the period.

Because adjusting entries are made to correct or update account balances and not to record transactions, the adjustment process is one of analysis rather than mere recording. Analyzing how to adjust the accounts involves three steps: (1) determine what entries, if any, were originally made to the accounts, (2) determine what the account balances should be, and (3) make the adjusting entries that are needed to bring existing balances to their appropriate amounts. T-accounts are helpful in analyzing adjusting entries and will be used in the illustrations that follow.

UNRECORDED REVENUES

unrecorded revenues and accrued assets *revenues not previously recognized, and companion receivable accounts, that are earned during a period but have not been received by the end of that period*

At the end of each accounting period, there are usually revenues that have been earned but have not been collected or recorded. Such revenue items are referred to as unrecorded revenues; their companion receivable accounts are accrued assets. Even though cash has not been received, the revenues are earned and should be reported as such. In order to recognize the total revenues earned and to report the corresponding receivables as assets, adjustments to the accounts are required.

To illustrate, we will assume that Alfie's, Inc. reports on a calendar year basis and has determined the following on December 31, 1983.

1. Rent revenues of $500 earned in 1983 will not be received until January 10, 1984.
2. Interest revenue of $600 has been earned on a 36-month $24,000 note issued to Alfie's on November 1. The interest rate is 15 percent with interest receipts due April 30 and October 31 of each year.

Following the three-step analysis, we observe that no original entry has been made; that is, there are no current balances in the appropriate revenue and receivable accounts. This will always be the case for both unrecorded revenues and unrecorded expenses. However, remember that under accrual-basis accounting, revenue is recorded when it is *earned*, not when the cash is received. Thus, the rent revenue must be recognized in 1983 (when earned) and not in 1984 (when received). The accounts involved and the correct balances as of December 31, 1983, are shown below in T-account form.

	Accrued Rent Receivable (Dr.)	Accrued Rent Receivable (Cr.)	Rent Revenue (Dr.)	Rent Revenue (Cr.)
Original Entry	none			none
Correct Balances (12/31/83) .	500			500

Once the original balances and the desired ending balances are known, you can determine what adjusting entry is needed. For this transaction, the entry required at December 31 is one that increases Accrued Rent Receivable (an asset account) from $0 to $500 and Rent Revenue (a revenue account) from $0 to $500. The adjusting entry is

Accrued Rent Receivable	500	
Rent Revenue		500
To record accrual of rent not yet received.		

Item 2 (interest revenue) is another example of an unrecorded revenue. In this case, interest is received semiannually, on April 30 and October 31 of each year. At the end of the year, therefore, the interest due for 2 months, November and December, has been earned but not yet received or recorded.

Accrual accounting dictates that unless an adjusting entry is made, the applicable revenue and asset accounts will be understated and the resulting financial statements will not be accurate. In this case, the 2 months' interest revenue should be recognized and the related interest receivable set up. The appropriate adjusting entry may be determined by following the same process used for the rent revenue example, as follows:

	Accrued Interest Receivable (Debit)	Accrued Interest Receivable (Credit)	Interest Revenue (Debit)	Interest Revenue (Credit)
Original Entry	none			none
Correct Balances (12/31/83)	600			600

The proper adjusting entry is

Accrued Interest Receivable	600	
Interest Revenue		600

To record accrual of interest[1] *on a $24,000 note at 15%, payments due April 30 and October 31: $24,000 × 0.15 = $3,600; $3,600 ÷ 12 = $300; $300 × 2 months (November, December) = $600.*

After the adjusting entries are journalized and posted, the receivables appear as assets on the balance sheet, and the rent and interest revenues are reported on the income statement. Through the adjusting entries, the accounts are properly stated and revenues are appropriately reported.

UNRECORDED EXPENSES

unrecorded expenses and accrued liabilities *expenses not previously recognized, and companion payable accounts, that are incurred during a period but have not been paid for by the end of that period*

Just as revenues can be earned before they are collected or recorded, expenses can be incurred prior to being paid or recorded. Expenses incurred in a particular period but not recorded during that time are referred to as unrecorded expenses, and their companion payable accounts are called accrued liabilities. When goods or services are received and used, even though they have not yet been paid for, valid expenses have been incurred. These expenses should be recorded in the period of incurrence, along with the corresponding liabilities, or obligations to pay for the goods or services. Thus, adjusting entries are required at the end of an accounting period to recognize any unrecorded expenses in the proper period of incurrence and to accrue the corresponding liabilities. If such adjustments are not made, the income for the period will be overstated and the corresponding liabilities on the balance sheet will be understated.

[1] As you know, *interest* is the cost of using money. The amount borrowed or lent is the *principal*. The *interest rate* is an annual rate stated as a percentage. The *period of time* involved may be stated in terms of a year. For example, if interest is to be paid for 3 months, time is 3/12, or 1/4 of a year. If interest is to be paid for 90 days, time is 90/360, or 1/4 of a year (often a 360-day year is used for interest computations). Thus, the formula for computing interest is *Interest = Principal × Interest Rate × Time.*

Again to illustrate, we will assume that on December 31, 1983, Alfie's, Inc. has determined the following.

1. Property taxes of $1,500 for this year will not be paid until January 3, 1984.
2. Interest expense of $420 is owed on a 2-year, $12,000 bank note issued by Alfie's. The interest rate is 14 percent and payments are due twice a year, March 31 and September 30.

To represent its financial position and earnings accurately, Alfie's must record the impact of these events in the accounts, even though cash transactions have not yet occurred. In the case of the property taxes, they will not be paid until 1984. However, under accrual-basis accounting, the property taxes are expenses of 1983 and should be recognized on this year's income statement, with the corresponding liability shown on the balance sheet as of the end of the year. The analysis and resulting adjusting journal entries required at year-end for the unrecorded property taxes would be

	Property Taxes Expense		Accrued Property Taxes Payable	
Original Entry	none			none
Correct Balances (12/31/83) .	1,500			1,500

Property Taxes Expense	1,500	
Accrued Property Taxes Payable		1,500
To record accrual of property taxes not yet paid.		

Regarding the interest on the note, it was last paid September 30 and will not be paid again until next March 31. However, at December 31 Alfie's has incurred 3 months' interest expense (for October, November, and December) that should be recognized in the accounts for this period. Accounting for this interest is illustrated with T-accounts followed by the appropriate adjusting entry.

	Interest Expense		Accrued Interest Payable	
Original Entry	none			none
Correct Balances (12/31/83) .	420			420

Interest Expense	420	
Accrued Interest Payable		420
To record interest accrual on a 2-year bank note of $12,000 at 14%; $12,000 × 0.14 = $1,680; $1,680 ÷ 12 = $140; $140 × 3 months (October, November, December) = $420.		

The property taxes and interest expense would be reflected on the income statement for the year ended December 31, and the accrued payables—property taxes and interest—would be shown as liabilities on the balance sheet as of December 31. Because of the adjusting entries, both statements would more accurately reflect the financial situation of Alfie's, Inc.

UNEARNED REVENUES

unearned revenues *amounts received before they have been earned*

Amounts received before the actual earning of revenue are known as unearned revenues. They arise when customers pay in advance of the receipt of goods or services. Since the company has received cash but has not yet given the customer the purchased goods or services, the unearned revenues are in fact liabilities. That is, the company must provide something in return for the amounts received. For example, a building contractor may require a deposit before proceeding to construct a house. Upon receipt of the deposit, the contractor has unearned revenue, a liability; that is, the contractor must construct the house to earn the revenue. If the house is not built, the contractor will be obligated to repay the deposit.

The three-step analysis we have used for unrecorded revenues and expenses applies equally well to the adjustments for unearned revenues (and prepaid expenses, to be discussed next). The objective is the same: to ensure that the proper amounts of revenues and expenses are recognized during the period and that the appropriate liability and asset account balances are shown on the balance sheet. There is one difference which is sometimes confusing. For unrecorded items there is no original entry, so when the adjustments are determined, the correct year-end balance becomes the amount of the adjusting entry. For unearned revenues and prepaid expenses, this is not the case. Since cash has already been received (in the case of unearned revenues) or paid (in the case of prepaid expenses), an original entry has been made to record the cash transaction. Therefore, the amount of the adjusting entry is the difference between what the correct balance should be and the amount resulting from the original entry.

To illustrate the adjustments for unearned revenues, we will assume the following about Alfie's, Inc.

1. On June 1, a tenant pays Alfie's $3,600 for 1 year's rent in advance, covering the period from June 1 of the current year to May 31 of the next year.
2. On October 1, a client pays a consulting fee of $1,800 for regular monthly services to be rendered by Alfie's during the next 9 months.
3. As before, Alfie's accounting year ends on December 31.

revenue approach *an accounting procedure whereby unearned revenues are originally credited to a revenue account, even though the amount is not yet earned; a year-end adjustment is required to reduce the revenue to that actually earned during the period and to establish a corresponding liability for the amount not earned at year-end*

In considering the $3,600 of rent received in advance, we need to make one further assumption concerning how the original entry was recorded. It could have been recorded as a debit to Cash and a credit to Rent Revenue, showing the total amount of revenue that will eventually be earned. This is sometimes called the revenue approach, since the original entry involved crediting a revenue account. On the other hand, the original entry could have been made as a debit to Cash and a credit to Unearned Rent, or Rent

Received in Advance (liability accounts), showing the actual liability that existed then. This is technically correct because until the revenue is earned by allowing the tenant to use the facility, the amount of rent received in advance is a liability. This approach is referred to as the liability approach, since the original entry involves a liability account. Both approaches are commonly used. The amount of the adjusting entry will differ, depending on which approach is taken in recording the original entry. However, the end result—the correct balances—will be the same with either approach after the adjusting entry is journalized and posted. We will illustrate both the revenue and liability approaches, so you can see that the final results are identical.

liability approach *an accounting procedure whereby unearned revenues are originally credited to a liability account; a year-end adjustment is required to record the revenue earned during that period and to reduce the companion liability account*

Original Entries to Revenue Accounts (Revenue Approach)

In analyzing adjusting entries for unearned revenues, two accounts must be considered: the appropriate revenue account and the corresponding unearned revenue (liability) account. Step 1 of the analysis, determining what entries were originally made to the accounts, shows that Cash was debited and Rent Revenue was credited for $3,600, as follows:

June 1	Cash	3,600	
	Rent Revenue		3,600
	Received 12 months' rent in advance: $300 × 12 = $3,600.		

At this point, no entry has been made to Unearned Rent and it has a zero balance. Step 2 in the analysis requires that the correct account balances be determined. Since the total year's rent is $3,600, rent of $300 is earned each month ($3,600 ÷ 12 = $300). During 1983, Alfie's should recognize 7 months' rent (June 1 through December 31), or $2,100 (7 × $300 = $2,100), as being earned. The balance of $1,500 ($3,600 − $2,100) is unearned. That is, on December 31, 1983, 5 months' rent (5 × $300 = $1,500) that will not be earned until 1984 has been received. Thus, the correct balances in the accounts are $2,100 for Rent Revenue, to be shown on the income statement, and $1,500 for Unearned Rent, to be reported as a liability on the balance sheet. Since the money was indeed received, the Cash account is correct. Incidentally, Cash is seldom one of the accounts adjusted when adjusting entries are made. The Cash account needs to be corrected only when it is wrong due to actual errors. The results from the rent transaction are shown in the following T-accounts.

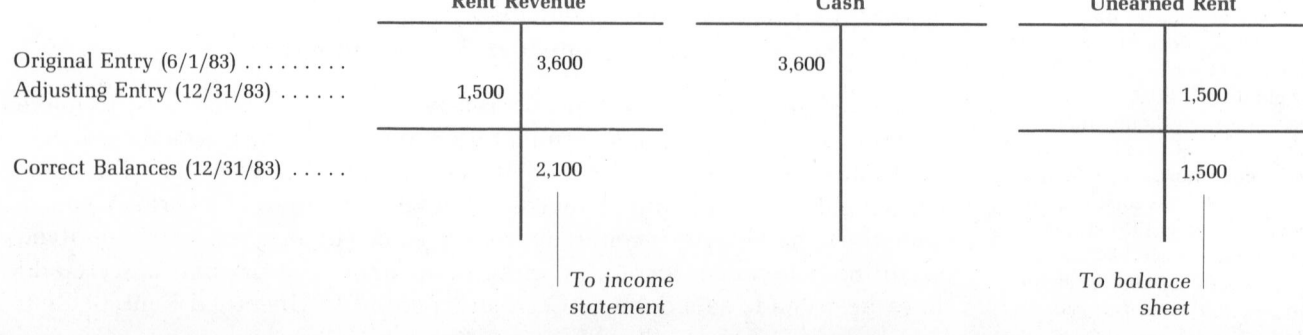

	Rent Revenue		Cash		Unearned Rent	
Original Entry (6/1/83)		3,600	3,600			
Adjusting Entry (12/31/83)	1,500					1,500
Correct Balances (12/31/83)		2,100				1,500
		To income statement				*To balance sheet*

Given the above analysis, the correct adjusting entry (step 3) can be made by debiting Rent Revenue for an amount ($1,500) that will decrease it from $3,600 to $2,100, and crediting Unearned Rent for an amount ($1,500) that will increase it from $0 to $1,500. The required adjusting entry at year-end would be

Rent Revenue	1,500	
Unearned Rent		1,500

To adjust for proper rent revenue earned for 7 months and to record the remaining obligation due: $300 × 5 months = $1,500.

Again assuming that the original entry was to a revenue account, the analysis of the transaction for consulting services (item 2 on page 113) would be the same as for the rent revenue transaction. The original entry on October 1 to record the receipt of cash for 9 months' consulting services would be

October 1	Cash	1,800	
	Consulting Revenue		1,800

Received 9 months' consulting revenue in advance: $200 × 9 = $1,800.

Note that no entry has been made to Unearned Consulting Fees (a liability account). On December 31, only 3 months' consulting fees have been earned (3 × $200 = $600). The balance of $1,200 ($1,800 − $600) should be recognized as unearned. It will be earned during the first 6 months of next year (6 × $200 = $1,200). Therefore, an adjusting entry is required to reduce the $1,800 originally credited to Consulting Revenue to $600, the amount actually earned, and increase the Unearned Revenue account from $0 to $1,200, which is the amount of the liability at December 31. The entries may be summarized in T-accounts as follows:

	Consulting Revenue (Dr)	**Consulting Revenue** (Cr)	**Cash** (Dr)	**Cash** (Cr)	**Unearned Consulting Fees** (Dr)	**Unearned Consulting Fees** (Cr)
Original Entry (10/1/83)		1,800	1,800			
Adjusting Entry (12/31/83)	1,200					1,200
Correct Balances (12/31/83)		600				1,200
		To income statement				*To balance sheet*

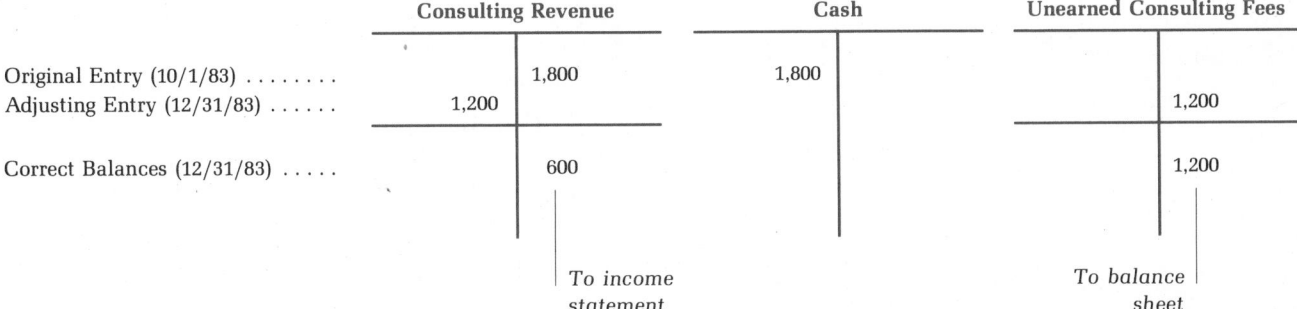

As the above analysis shows, $600 should be reported on the income statement as consulting revenue, and $1,200 should be reported on the balance sheet as a liability (Unearned Consulting Fees). The actual adjusting entry, then, would be

Consulting Revenue	1,200	
Unearned Consulting Fees		1,200

To adjust for proper consulting revenue earned for 3 months and to record the remaining obligation due: $1,800 ÷ 9 = $200; $200 × 6 months = $1,200.

A common mistake made by students new to accounting is to compute the correct balances and then use those amounts in making the adjusting entries. Remember that the *correct amounts* are what you want to show on the financial statements (step 2 in our three-step analysis). What must be done is to make appropriate adjusting entries to obtain those balances.

Original Entries to Liability Accounts (Liability Approach)

If the entries for the two previous transactions had originally been made to liability accounts rather than to revenue accounts, the amounts required for the year-end adjustments would be different. However, the process of analysis and the end result would be exactly the same.

The first step in the analysis is to determine that the original entry was made to Unearned Rent, a liability account, as follows:

June 1	Cash	3,600	
	Unearned Rent		3,600

Received 12 months' rent in advance: $300 × 12 = $3,600.

The second step is to determine the correct balances on December 31. At that date, $2,100, or 7 months' rent, has been earned (7 × $300 = $2,100), and should be shown on the income statement. Five months' rent (5 × $300 = $1,500) is still unearned, and should be reported as a liability on the balance sheet. These results may be shown in the following T-accounts.

	Rent Revenue (Dr)	Rent Revenue (Cr)	Cash (Dr)	Cash (Cr)	Unearned Rent (Dr)	Unearned Rent (Cr)
Original Entry (6/1/83)			3,600			3,600
Adjusting Entry (12/31/83)		2,100			2,100	
Correct Balances (12/31/83)		2,100				1,500
		To income statement				*To balance sheet*

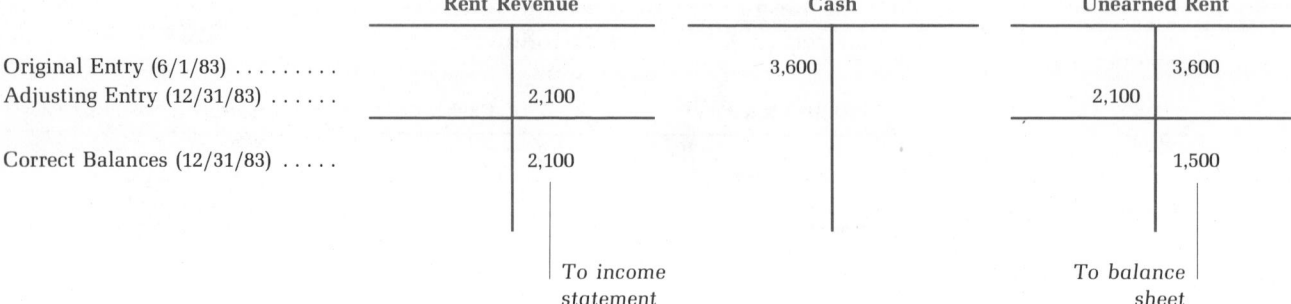

The adjusting entry to be journalized and posted would be

Unearned Rent	2,100	
Rent Revenue		2,100

To reduce the liability amount and to establish rent revenue for 7 months: $300 × 7 months = $2,100.

Note that after posting this entry, the balances in the Unearned Rent ($1,500) and the Rent Revenue ($2,100) accounts are *identical* to those derived using the revenue approach.

The same process of analysis can be used for the consulting transaction. The entries are summarized in T-account form as follows:

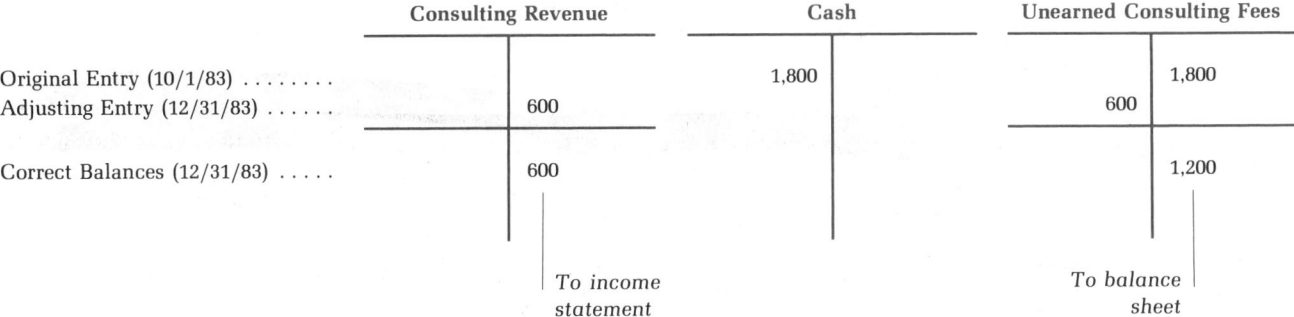

	Consulting Revenue (Dr.)	Consulting Revenue (Cr.)	Cash (Dr.)	Cash (Cr.)	Unearned Consulting Fees (Dr.)	Unearned Consulting Fees (Cr.)
Original Entry (10/1/83)			1,800			1,800
Adjusting Entry (12/31/83)		600			600	
Correct Balances (12/31/83)		600				1,200
		To income statement				*To balance sheet*

The adjusting entry—debiting Unearned Consulting Fees and crediting Consulting Revenue—is needed to bring the account balances current. After the adjusting entry is journalized and posted, the proper amount of consulting revenue ($200 × 3 months, or $600) will be shown on the income statement. The liability, Unearned Consulting Fees or Consulting Fees Received in Advance, will also be reported at its correct amount ($1,800 ÷ 9 = $200; $200 × 6 months' fees yet to be earned = $1,200). Note again that the balances are identical to those produced by the revenue approach.

Liability Approach Versus Revenue Approach

The liability approach recognizes that the seller is obligated either to return the asset received (usually cash) or deliver the goods or services promised. It has theoretical merit because, until the revenue is earned, the amount of revenue received in advance is technically a liability and should be accounted for as such. The revenue approach is justified on the grounds of expediency and on the assumption that the revenue will be earned during the coming period. Both approaches are used in practice, depending on the preference of the company's accountants.

Regardless of which approach is used, the final result will be the same. Therefore, the important concept to master is the analysis process for adjusting entries. First, determine what original entries have been made, if any. Second, analyze the accounts to determine the correct end-of-period balances. Third, make the adjusting entries needed to bring the accounts up-to-date, that is, from the original entry amounts to the correct balances as of the end of the period.

PREPAID EXPENSES

prepaid expenses *payments made in advance for items normally charged to expense*

Payments that a company makes in advance for items normally charged to expense are known as prepaid expenses. An example would be the payment of an insurance premium for three years. Theoretically, every resource acquisition is an asset, at least temporarily. Thus, the entry to record an advance payment should be a debit to an asset (Prepaid Expense) account and a credit to Cash, showing the exchange of cash for another asset.

Business enterprises do not acquire expenses. Expenses emerge as benefits are received from the assets acquired and the values of the assets decline. Therefore, an expense is a "used-up" asset, a resource whose service potential has been at least partly realized. For example, when supplies are purchased, they are recorded as assets; when they are used, they are treated as expenses. When it is apparent that the benefits of an expenditure will all be received within the current accounting period, the expenditure is usually recorded as an expense. Thus, a payment in advance, as a matter of expediency, may be initially recorded as an expense instead of as an asset.

expense approach *an accounting procedure whereby prepaid expenses are originally debited to an expense account, even though future benefits exist; a year-end adjustment is required to bring the expense account to its proper balance and to establish a companion asset account equal to the remaining future benefits*

asset approach *an accounting procedure whereby prepaid expenses are originally debited to an asset account; a year-end adjustment is required to record the asset value used up as an expense of the period, and to adjust the related asset account to its proper balance*

As with unearned revenues, the nature of the adjusting entries for prepaid expenses at the end of a period will depend on how the original prepayment was recorded—as an expense (the expense approach) or as an asset (the asset approach). If adjusting entries are analyzed and recorded correctly, regardless of which approach is used, the final result will be the same—that is, accurate recognition of expenses on the income statement and proper reporting of assets on the balance sheet.

If the expense approach is used for the original entry, the adjusting entry will reduce the expense to a proper amount and establish a companion asset account, a prepaid expense, which reflects the amount of expense that is postponed until future accounting periods. If the original entry is to an asset account, the adjusting entry reduces the asset to an amount that reflects its remaining future benefit, and at the same time recognizes the actual expense for the period. The objective of these adjustments is to show the complete or partial expiration of an asset's ability to help generate future revenues.

To illustrate, we will assume that on September 1, 1983, Alfie's, Inc. rents office space in a building. The rent is $150 a month, and Alfie's is required to pay 6 months' rent in advance. Then, on November 1, Alfie's purchases a 2-year insurance policy, paying a $2,400 premium. These items can be recorded as expenses or as assets (prepaid expenses). The amount of the adjusting entry required will depend on whether the asset or expense approach is used for the original entry. However, the process of analysis is the same. Assuming a calendar year-end, the entries for both alternatives are illustrated below.

Original Entries to Expense Accounts (Expense Approach)

In applying the expense approach, the original entry to record the $900 advance payment of rent expense would be

September 1	Rent Expense	900	
	Cash		900
	Paid 6 months' rent in advance: 6 × $150 = $900.		

At December 31, Alfie's must recognize that not all of the $900 is an expense of this accounting period. A portion of the 6-month advance payment—2 months' worth to be exact—will benefit the company during the next accounting period and should be reported on December 31 as an asset: Prepaid Rent or Rent Paid in Advance. The benefit of 4 months' worth of the $900 prepayment has been received and this portion of the rent is properly recognized as an expense of the current period. The T-accounts shown below reflect this information and identify the proper adjusting entry to be made.

	Rent Expense		Cash		Prepaid Rent	
Original Entry (9/1/83)	900			900		
Adjusting Entry (12/31/83)		300			300	
Correct Balances (12/31/83)	600				300	
	To income statement				*To balance sheet*	

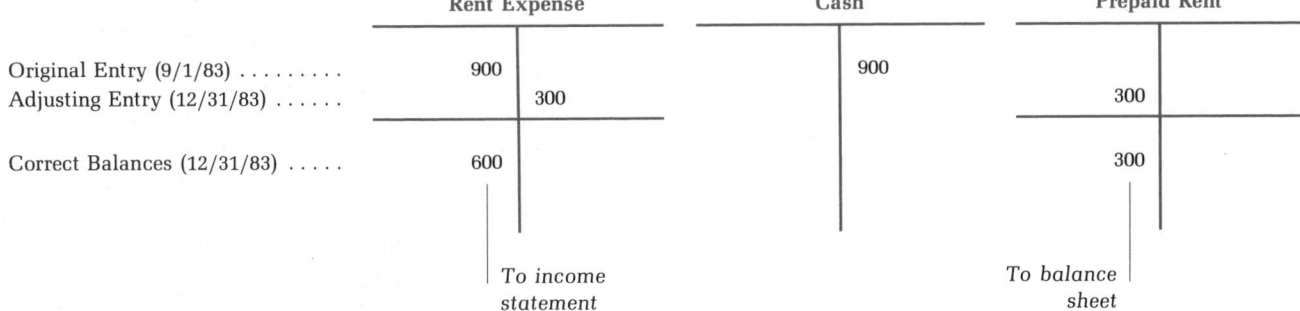

As journalized, the adjusting entry would be

Prepaid Rent	300	
Rent Expense		300

To adjust for proper rent expense for 4 months and record the remaining asset amount: 2 × $150 = $300.

After the adjustment, $600 would be properly shown as an expense on the income statement and $300 would be carried forward to the next period as an asset on the balance sheet.

The entries and analysis for the insurance transaction are similar. The original prepayment entry is debited to Insurance Expense. At year-end, an adjustment must be made to reflect the proper insurance expense for the period and the amount of prepaid insurance to be shown on the balance sheet as an asset. The entries, in T-account form, are

	Insurance Expense		Cash		Prepaid Insurance	
Original Entry (11/1/83)	2,400			2,400		
Adjusting Entry (12/31/83)		2,200			2,200	
Correct Balances (12/31/83)	200				2,200	
	To income statement				*To balance sheet*	

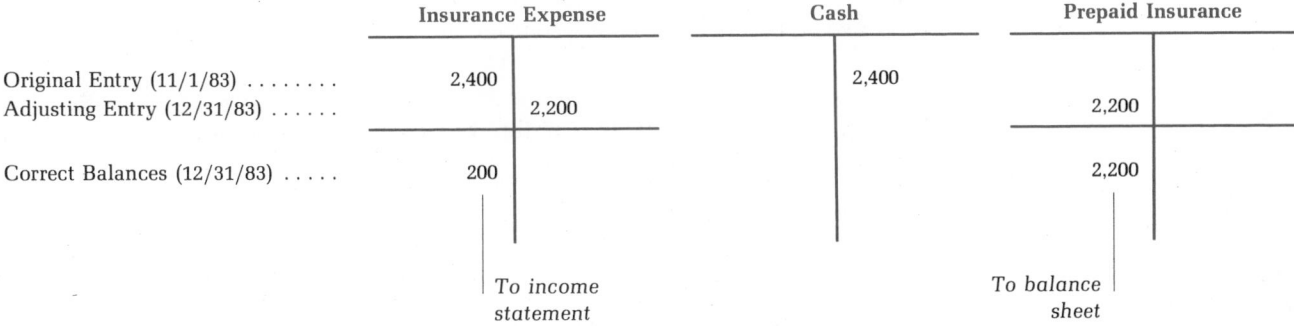

The adjusting entry updates the account so that 2 months' worth of insurance expense ($200) will be reported on the income statement. The remaining 22 months' of insurance benefits ($2,400 ÷ 24 months = $100; $100 × 22 = $2,200) will be shown as an asset, Prepaid Insurance or Unexpired Insurance, on the balance sheet.

Original Entries to Asset Accounts (Asset Approach)

In using the asset approach, the prepayment of rent would be recorded originally as

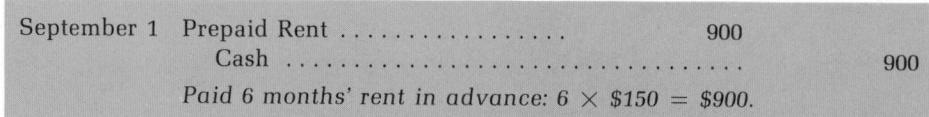

September 1	Prepaid Rent	900	
	Cash		900
	Paid 6 months' rent in advance: 6 × $150 = $900.		

At year-end, only those assets that still offer future benefits to the company should be reported on the balance sheet. Thus, an adjustment is required to reduce the Prepaid Rent account and to establish the amount of rent expense for the period. In this example, 4 months' rent has been used, so the rent expense should be $600 (4 months at $150 a month) and the balance in the asset account should be $300 (2 months' rent at $150 per month). As shown in the T-accounts, the adjusting entries would be

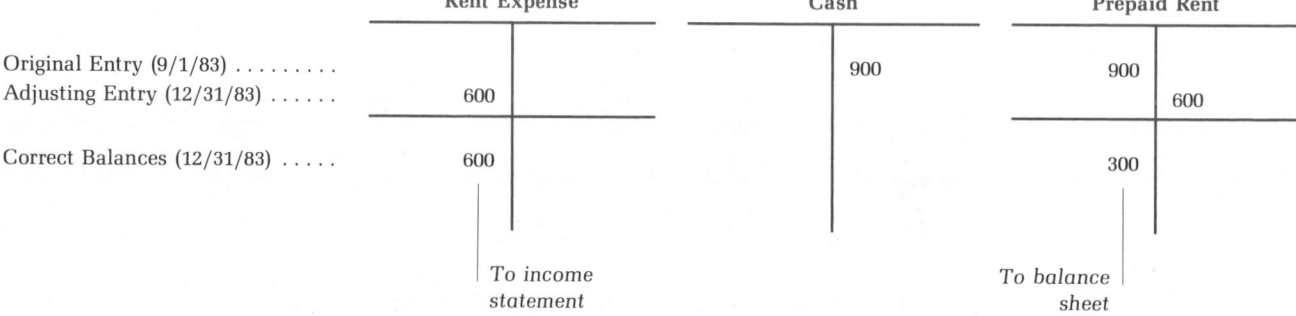

	Rent Expense		Cash		Prepaid Rent	
Original Entry (9/1/83)				900	900	
Adjusting Entry (12/31/83)	600					600
Correct Balances (12/31/83)	600				300	
	To income statement				*To balance sheet*	

The adjusting journal entry would be

Rent Expense	600	
Prepaid Rent		600
To adjust the proper asset amount and to record rent expense for 4 months: 4 × $150 = $600.		

Again, note that the resulting balances for Prepaid Rent ($300) and Rent Expense ($600) are the same whether this method or the expense method is used.

The analysis of the insurance transaction under the asset approach is the same as for prepaid rent, so it will not be explained in detail. The entries are summarized in T-account form as follows:

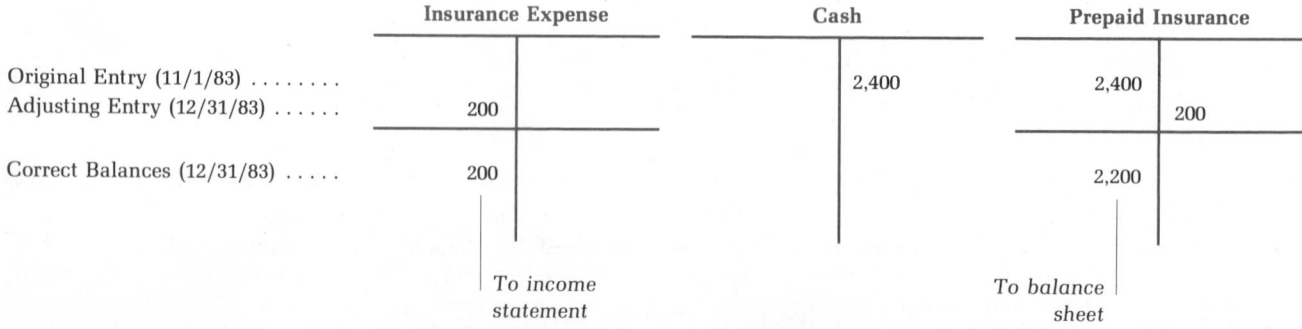

	Insurance Expense		Cash		Prepaid Insurance	
Original Entry (11/1/83)				2,400	2,400	
Adjusting Entry (12/31/83)	200					200
Correct Balances (12/31/83)	200				2,200	
	To income statement				*To balance sheet*	

Whether the asset or the expense approach is used depends on the accounting philosophy of the company, just as does the choice of the liability or revenue approach. A company will often use different approaches for different transactions, depending on the nature of the asset or expense item. Under either the asset or the expense approach, the objective is to report the proper amount of expense on the income statement and to show the appropriate balance in the asset account on the balance sheet.

TO SUMMARIZE In order to present financial statements that accurately report the financial position and the results of operations on an accrual basis and for specific periods of time, adjusting entries must be made. The four main categories of adjustments are unrecorded revenues, unrecorded expenses, unearned revenues, and prepaid expenses. In analyzing accounts at the end of an accounting cycle, adjusting entries are made in order to recognize all earned revenues and all incurred expenses, and to report the proper balances in the asset, liability, and owners' equity accounts. This requires a three-step analysis: (1) identifying the original entries, (2) determining the correct end-of-period balances, and (3) preparing adjusting entries to bring the original account balances to their proper end-of-period amounts. Exhibit 4–3 summarizes these adjustments.

EXHIBIT 4–3 **Summary of Adjustments**

Type of Adjusting Entry	Result of Adjusting Entry	Where Item Is Included on Financial Statements
Unrecorded revenue/accrued asset	Increases asset (DR) Increases revenue (CR)	Asset on balance sheet Revenue on income statement
Unrecorded expense/accrued liability	Increases expense (DR) Increases liability (CR)	Expense on income statement Liability on balance sheet
Unearned revenue		The adjusted balance appears as:
Initially recorded as a revenue	Reduces revenue (DR) Increases liability (CR)	Revenue on income statement Liability on balance sheet
Initially recorded as a liability	Reduces liability (DR) Increases revenue (CR)	Liability on balance sheet Revenue on income statement
Prepaid expense		The adjusted balance appears as:
Initially recorded as an expense	Increases asset (DR) Reduces expense (CR)	Asset on balance sheet Expense on income statement
Initially recorded as an asset	Increases expense (DR) Reduces asset (CR)	Expense on income statement Asset on balance sheet

CHAPTER REVIEW

In conducting economic activities, businesses and other types of entities enter into exchange transactions. These transactions form the basis of accounting records and must be analyzed, classified, recorded, summarized, and reported.

To facilitate the accounting process, an accounting model has been established. This model has several important characteristics, including the notion of a separate accounting entity that is a going concern and that enters into arm's-length transactions. In the United States these transactions are measured in money amounts using the U.S. dollar as the unit of measurement.

The model further assumes that accounting information is needed on a timely basis for decision-making purposes. This requires that the total life of a business be divided into accounting periods, generally a year or less, for which reports are prepared. Some of the data presented in the periodic reports must be tentative because allocations and estimates are involved in dividing an entity's life into relatively short reporting periods.

The necessity for periodic reporting further requires that accrual accounting be used to provide accurate statements of financial position and results of operations for an accounting period. Accrual-basis accounting means that revenues are recognized as they are earned, not necessarily when cash is received, and that expenses are recognized as they are incurred, not necessarily when cash is paid.

One of the most important functions accountants perform is the proper matching of the revenues recognized during a reporting period with the expenses incurred to generate those revenues. This requires that adjusting entries be made at the end of each accounting period. Adjusting entries are the means of increasing or decreasing accounts so as to report proper end-of-period revenue and expense amounts on the income statement and appropriate balances for balance sheet accounts. The accounts that generally require adjustments may be classified under four headings: unrecorded revenues, unrecorded expenses, unearned revenues, and prepaid expenses. A three-step analysis is used to determine the correct adjusting entries.

KEY TERMS AND CONCEPTS

accrual-basis accounting (107)
adjusting entries (109)
asset approach (118)
calendar year (106)
cash-basis accounting (107)
expense approach (118)
fiscal year (106)
liability approach (114)
matching principle (107)
prepaid expenses (117)
revenue approach (113)
revenue recognition principle (107)
time-period assumption (periodicity concept) (106)
unearned revenues (113)
unrecorded expenses and accrued liabilities (111)
unrecorded revenues and accrued assets (110)

REVIEW PROBLEM

Adjusting Entries: Unrecorded Revenues and Expenses, Unearned Revenues, and Prepaid Expenses

Travco, Inc., a service-oriented company, has completed operations for 1983. All regular transaction entries have been journalized and posted, a trial balance has been prepared, and an analysis has been made of the accounts to determine the required adjustments. The analysis reveals the following.

1. At the close of the year, two notes were uncollected. Interest of $370 had been earned by Travco on these notes, as computed below, but had not yet been recorded.
   (a) Note 1: $10,000, 60-day, 12 percent note dated December 1, 1983. Interest revenue earned from December 1 to December 31 was $100 ($10,000 × 0.12 × 30/360 = $100).
   (b) Note 2: $7,200, 180-day, 15 percent note dated October 2, 1983. Interest revenue earned from October 2 to December 31 was $270 ($7,200 × 0.15 × 90/360 = $270).

2. Unbilled but earned service fees on an incomplete contract amounted to $875. The total amount to be received on the contract is $4,380.

3. At the close of the year, three short-term notes issued by Travco were outstanding. (Assume a 360-day year.)

Note Date	Face Amount	Note Period	Interest Rate	Unrecorded Interest Expense at December 31
10/17/83	$16,000	90 days	12%	$400[a]
11/1/83	12,000	75 days	10%	200[b]
12/16/83	7,200	120 days	15%	45[c]
				$645

[a]$16,000 × 0.12 × 75/360 = $400 (14 days in October + 30 days in November + 31 days in December = 75 days)
[b]$12,000 × 0.10 × 60/360 = $200 (29 days in November + 31 days in December = 60 days)
[c]$7,200 × 0.15 × 15/360 = $45 (15 days in December)

4. Unrecorded property taxes at year-end were $4,550; the property taxes are for 1983 and are due January 10, 1984.

5. Earned but unpaid employee salaries and wages totaled $9,600 at December 31, 1984. The next payroll will be made on January 15, 1984 (ignore payroll taxes).

6. Service fees on two contracts were received in full, but the contracts were incomplete as of December 31. When the fees were received, a liability account was credited for the total amount. The status of the two contracts is as follows:
   (a) Contract 1: $8,500; 80 percent complete.
   (b) Contract 2: $6,800; 40 percent complete.

7. Malibu Company paid Travco $10,800 on August 1, 1983, to lease some of the company's equipment. The 1-year lease period began August 1; receipt of the $10,800 was credited to Equipment Rent Revenue.

8. All advertising costs had been charged to expense as incurred. The Prepaid Advertising account had a zero balance on December 31. Advertising services paid for in 1983 to be received in 1984 amount to $5,400.

9. The company issued a long-term note for $36,000 on October 1, 1983. The note is to be paid at the end of 6 years; interest at 12 percent (a total of $4,320) is due annually each October 1 until the note is paid.

10. Estimated income taxes for the year were $28,200.

Required:

Prepare appropriate adjusting journal entries for Travco, Inc. at December 31, 1983.

Solution

To solve this problem you must analyze each item and prepare the appropriate adjusting journal entry. The explanations for each entry help in understanding the entries made and why they are needed.

1. Accrued Interest Receivable	370	
Interest Revenue		370

To record previously unrecorded interest revenue and accrued interest receivable.

(The entry records interest earned to December 31, 1983, on notes 1 and 2, even though the interest has not been received. This is an example of an unrecorded revenue.)

2. Accrued Service Fees Receivable ...	875	
Service Fees Revenue		875

To record previously unrecorded service fees revenue and accrued service fees receivable to December 31, 1983.

(The service fees have been earned and should be recognized in 1983, even though they will not be received until 1984.)

3. Interest Expense	645	
Accrued Interest Payable		645

To record previously unrecorded interest expense and accrued interest payable to December 31, 1983, on three short-term notes.

(Interest will be paid when the notes mature in 1984. This is an example of an unrecorded expense.)

4. Property Tax Expense	4,550	
Accrued Property Taxes Payable		4,550

To record accrued property taxes payable and the related property tax expense for the period ending December 31, 1983.

(The property taxes must be recognized as expenses in 1983, even though they will not be paid until 1984.)

5. Salaries and Wages Expense	9,600	
Accrued Salaries and Wages Payable		9,600

To record employees' salary and wage expense applicable to the year 1983, and the related liability at December 31, 1983.

(This entry is necessary to recognize the salary and wage expense in 1983 and the obligation that exists at December 31. The wages will be paid in 1984.)

6. Unearned Service Fees Revenue ...	9,520	
Service Fees Revenue		9,520

(Contract 1: $8,500 × 0.80 = $6,800; contract 2: $6,800 × 0.40 = $2,720)

To recognize service fees revenue earned in 1983 on contracts 1 and 2, and to reduce unearned service fees revenue recorded as a liability when fees were received.

[This is an example of an unearned revenue that was originally recorded as a liability (liability approach). The adjusting entry is needed to recognize partial satisfaction of the obligation (liability) by services provided on the contracts in 1983.]

7. Equipment Rent Revenue	6,300	
Unearned Equipment Rent Revenue		6,300

($10,800 × 7/12 = $6,300)

To reduce equipment rent revenue previously recorded and to recognize the obligation (liability) on the equipment lease to Malibu Company.

[This is an example of an unearned revenue that was originally recorded as a revenue (revenue approach). Since all the revenue has not been earned by December 31, 1983, the amount not earned (7 months' rent) must be transferred from the revenue account, Equipment Rent Revenue, to the liability account, Unearned Equipment Rent Revenue.]

8. Prepaid Advertising	5,400	
Advertising Expense		5,400

To adjust the Advertising Expense and Prepaid Advertising accounts at December 31, 1983.

[This is an example of a prepaid expense that was originally recorded as an expense (expense approach). This entry recognizes that part of the recorded expenses should be shown as an asset, Prepaid Advertising, at December 31, 1983, since some of the advertising will benefit 1984.]

9. Interest Expense	1,080	
Accrued Interest Payable		1,080

($4,320 × 3/12 = $1,080)

To record interest expense and accrued interest payable to December 31, 1983, on a long-term note.

(Since no entry has been previously recorded, this adjustment is necessary to correctly report interest expense for 1983 and the obligation to pay the interest that has accrued. Obligation and interest will be paid in 1984.)

10. Income Tax Expense	28,200	
Income Tax Payable		28,200

To record income tax expense on income earned during 1983, and the related liability (income tax payable) that will be paid in 1984.

(This adjustment recognizes a previously unrecorded expense that is applicable to 1983 and that is to be paid in 1984.)

DISCUSSION QUESTIONS

1 What are the objectives of periodic financial reporting?

2 Distinguish between reporting on a calendar year and on a fiscal year basis.

3 Explain the importance of the time-period assumption in financial reporting.

4 Explain why accrual-basis accounting is more appropriate than cash-basis accounting for most businesses.

5 What is a significant disadvantage of accrual-basis accounting?

6 Why are accrual-based financial statements considered somewhat tentative?

7 When are revenues generally recognized?

8 What is the matching principle?

9 Why are adjusting entries necessary?

10 Identify four categories of transactions for which adjusting entries are commonly required prior to the preparation of financial statements.

11 Describe the three-step process used in determining the appropriate amounts of adjusting entries.

12 Explain the importance of step 2—determining the appropriate account balances—in the three-step process of analyzing adjusting entries.

13 Distinguish between the revenue approach and the liability approach in accounting for unearned revenues. Which do you think is the better approach? Why?

14 Whether the asset or the expense approach is used in making adjusting entries for prepaid expenses, the result is the same. Explain.

15 Explain why there are alternative ways of recording certain transactions, either as revenues or liabilities, or as expenses or assets.

16 The Cash account is generally not one of the accounts adjusted in an adjusting entry. Why?

EXERCISES

E4–1 Cash-Basis Accounting

In which year would John Johnson recognize the revenue or expense from each transaction below if Johnson's accounting records are kept on a cash basis?

1. On January 5, 1984, Johnson received and paid the December 1983 electricity bill.
2. On December 30, 1983, Johnson paid an insurance premium for the year 1984.
3. Johnson received $100 interest on January 3, 1984, on a note dated December 1, 1983. The principal on the note will be paid on December 1, 1984.
4. Johnson paid state property taxes on January 10, 1984. The taxes were assessed on his property for the year 1983.

E4–2 Accrual-Basis Accounting

Refer to the preceding problem. Assume that Mr. Johnson keeps his records on an accrual basis. For each situation, in which year would he recognize the revenue or expense?

E4–3 Cash- and Accrual-Basis Accounting

Westover Company had the following transactions during the first month of its operations in 1984.

January	1	Purchased $500 of supplies on account.
	9	Billed Hawkins Company $1,500 for services performed during this month.
	15	Received $1,200 from Hawkins for services performed.
	20	Paid $400 for supplies purchased on account on January 1.

1. Prepare journal entries using accrual-basis accounting.
2. Prepare journal entries using cash-basis accounting.
3. Which basis of accounting is generally more appropriate, and why?

E4–4 Classifications of Accounts Requiring Adjusting Entries

For each type of adjustment listed, indicate whether it is an unrecorded revenue, an unrecorded expense, an unearned revenue, or a prepaid expense at December 31, 1983.

1. Property taxes that are for the year 1983 but are not to be paid until 1984.
2. Rent revenue earned during 1983 but not collected until 1984.
3. Salaries earned by employees in December 1983, but not to be paid until January 5, 1984.
4. A payment received from a customer in December 1983 for services that will not be performed until February 1984.
5. An insurance premium paid on December 29, 1983, for the period January 1, 1984, to December 31, 1986.
6. Gasoline charged on a credit card during December 1983. The bill will not be received until January 15, 1984.
7. Interest on a certificate of deposit held during 1983. The interest will not be received until January 7, 1984.

E4–5 Balances in Expense Accounts

Assuming accrual-basis accounting for each of the following situations, state how much expense should be reported by BSI Inc. for 1984.

1. On January 1, 1984, BSI borrowed $1,000 from a bank. The note is due, with annual interest of $160 ($\$1{,}000 \times 0.16 = \$160$), on January 1, 1986.
2. BSI paid a car insurance premium of $120 in advance on October 1, 1984. The premium is for a 6-month period of insurance coverage.
3. BSI paid salaries of $3,000 on December 1, 1984. This amount represents salaries for December and January.
4. BSI signed an advertising contract for weekly radio spot announcements on August 1, 1984, paying $2,400 on that date for a 2-year advertising program.
5. BSI rented a storage shed, paying $1,200 on November 1, 1984, for a year's rent.

E4–6 Balances in Revenue Accounts

Johnson Company, a proprietorship, receives income from many sources. In preparing year-end financial statements at December 31, 1984, Johnson had trouble deciding how much revenue to report on the 1984 proprietorship income statement. Assuming accrual-basis accounting, for each revenue item listed below indicate how much Johnson should include as revenue for 1984.

1. Will receive interest revenue of $12,000 on short-term investments on February 1, 1985, for the 3-month period ending January 31, 1985.
2. Rented an office building to the McCord Corporation. On July 1, 1984, McCord paid Johnson $100,000 rent for the year ended June 30, 1985.
3. Will receive a dividend check from Locke Company on January 22, 1985. Johnson owns 20,000 shares of Locke Company stock. On December 30, 1984, Locke company declared a cash dividend of $2 per share payable to those who owned its stock on that date.

4. Received a check from a client on December 1, 1984, for $36,000. The payment is for professional advice and counseling for the 12-month period ending November 30, 1985.

E4–7 Year-End Analysis of Account Balances

Correct account balances for City Electric Supply at the beginning and end of 1983 are shown below.

	1/1/83	12/31/83
1. Prepaid Insurance	$3,200	$4,600
2. Accrued Wages Payable	1,700	1,200
3. Prepaid Rent	700	500

Expense accounts associated with the above accounts for 1983 are listed below.

1. Insurance Expense	$ 4,400
2. Wages Expense	26,000
3. Rent Expense	2,100

Determine the amount of cash paid out during the year for each type of expense, (1) through (3).

(**Note:** Unless otherwise indicated, assume accrual-basis accounting for all exercises and problems from this point on.)

E4–8 Adjusting Entries: Unrecorded Revenues

Sloan Brown is a professional investor. During 1983, she had the following economic transactions. For each transaction, give the entry that Sloan would make on December 31, 1983, to record the proper balance at year-end.

1. Sloan leased the Goodnight Hotel to Frank Goodwin on July 1, 1983, for $18,000 per year. Frank will pay the first year's rent on July 1, 1984.

2. Martha Higbee, Sloan's aunt, borrowed $20,000 from Sloan on September 1, 1983. Martha will repay the $20,000 with interest at 12 percent on March 1, 1984.

3. Sloan's certificates of deposit earn 18 percent interest per year. Her bank will pay her the interest for the year November 1, 1983, to November 1, 1984, on November 1, 1984. Sloan has $20,000 in certificates of deposit.

4. Sloan owns 10,000 shares of Oklahoma Drilling Company common stock. On November 15, 1983, the company declared a dividend of $5 per share to stockholders of record on that date. Sloan will receive her dividend check on January 15, 1984.

E4–9 Adjusting Entries: Unrecorded Expenses

Gary Blaylock owns Blaylock Safety Pin Company. In 1983, the company had the following economic transactions. For each transaction, give the adjusting entry that would be made to record the account balances properly at December 31, 1983.

1. The November and December utility bills have not yet been paid. Blaylock will pay $450 on January 15 ($150 a month for November, December, and January).

2. The company borrowed $10,000 from a bank on July 1, 1983. The loan will be repaid, together with interest at 15 percent, on July 1, 1984.

3. Employees will be paid their December salaries on January 5, 1984. The monthly salary expense is $10,000. (Ignore payroll taxes.)

4. Blaylock charged $500 per month in work-related gasoline expenses on a credit card in 1983. The company has not yet received the bill for charges made in December.

5. December rent will be paid on January 5, 1984. The rent is $2,500 per month.

E4–10 Adjusting Entries: Unearned Revenues Using the Revenue Approach

Gail Rubin is the owner/operator of Rubin Consulting Company. Gail uses the revenue approach in recording all unearned revenues. Give the entry that Rubin would make to record each of the following transactions on the date of occurrence, and assuming accrual-basis accounting, give the adjusting entries needed at December 31, 1983.

1. Rubin received $1,800 on September 15, 1983, in return for which the company agreed to provide consulting services for 18 months beginning immediately.

2. Rubin rented part of its office space to Bristle Brush Company. Bristle paid $1,200 on November 1, 1983, for the next 6 months' rent.

3. Rubin received $12,000 on November 1, 1983, in return for which the company agreed to provide consulting for the next 18 months to a client who wants to install a new computer system.

4. On September 1, 1983, $10,000 was received from a client who wants advice on investing in certain securities. In return for this sum, Rubin agreed to provide consulting services for the next 10 months, including September.

5. Rubin loaned $100,000 to a client. On November 1, the client paid $24,000, which represents 2 years' interest in advance (November 1, 1983, through October 31, 1985).

E4–11 Adjusting Entries: Unearned Revenues Using the Liability Approach

Refer to the transactions outlined in E4–10. Assume now that Rubin Consulting Company uses the liability approach in recording all unearned revenues. Give the entry that Rubin would make to record each of the transactions on the date it occurred, as well as the adjusting entries needed on December 31, 1983.

E4-12 Adjusting Entries: Prepaid Expenses Using the Expense Approach

Steve Simson owns and operates Simson Signs, Inc. Simson Signs uses the expense approach in recording all prepaid expenses. Give the entry that Steve would make to record each of the following transactions on the date it occurred, and prepare the adjusting entries needed on December 31, 1984.

1. On July 1, 1984, the company paid a 3-year premium of $7,200 on an insurance policy that is effective July 1, 1984, and expires June 30, 1987.
2. On February 1, 1984, Simson Signs paid its property taxes for the year February 1, 1984, to January 31, 1985. The tax bill was $1,800.
3. On May 1, 1984, the company paid $180 for a 3-year subscription to an advertising journal. The subscription starts May 1, 1984, and expires April 30, 1987.
4. On August 1, 1984, the company paid $36,000 rent for the year August 1, 1984, to July 31, 1985.
5. On December 1, 1984, Simson Signs paid utility bills totaling $300 for December 1984 and January 1985. The amount for each month was $150.

E4-13 Adjusting Entries: Prepaid Expenses Using the Asset Approach

Refer to the transactions outlined in E4-12. Assume now that Simson Signs uses the asset approach in recording all prepaid expenses. Give the entry the company would make on the date of each transaction's occurrence, as well as the adjusting entries it would make December 31, 1984.

E4-14 Adjusting Entries

The information presented below is from Becker Company. Prepare the adjusting entries that should be made on December 31, 1983. (Omit explanations.)

1. Accrued salaries for the period 12/26/83 through 12/31/83 amounted to $7,120. (Ignore payroll taxes.)
2. Interest of $3,000 is payable for 3 months on a 15 percent $80,000 loan.
3. Rent of $12,000 was paid for 6 months in advance on December 1 and charged to expense.
4. Rent of $41,000 was credited to a revenue account when received. Of this amount $16,700 is unearned at year-end.
5. The unexpired portion of an insurance policy is $500. The Insurance Expense account was originally debited.
6. Interest revenue of $150 from a $1,000 note has been earned, but has not been collected or recorded.

E4-15 Adjusting Entry Analysis

Apex Printers follows the revenue and expense approaches when recording cash receipts and payments. The company also leaves the balance sheet account balances resulting from year-end adjusting entries unchanged until the end of the next year when the accounts are again adjusted. Four accounts, with their balances before and after adjustment at December 31, 1983, are as follows:

	Before Adjustment	After Adjustment
Unearned Magazine Subscriptions	$3,900	$3,500
Property Taxes Payable	2,450	2,700
Printing Fees Receivable	4,600	5,200
Prepaid Advertising	1,200	900

Give the adjusting entries that should be made at December 31, 1983, by Apex Printers. (Omit explanations.)

PROBLEMS

P4–1 Cash- and Accrual-Basis Accounting

In the course of your examination of the books and records of Flexo Rubber Company, you find the following data.

Salaries Earned by Employees	$ 53,000
Salaries Paid	55,000
Total Sales Revenue	838,000
Cash Collected from Sales	900,000
Utilities Expense Incurred	5,000
Utility Bills Paid	4,800
Cost of Goods Sold	532,000
Cash Paid on Purchases in 1984	411,000
Inventory at December 31, 1984	320,000
Tax Assessment for 1984	5,000
Taxes Paid in 1984	4,900
Rent Expense for 1984	30,000
Rent Paid in 1984	25,000

Required:

1. Compute Flexo's net income for 1984 using cash-basis accounting.

2. Compute Flexo's net income for 1984 using accrual-basis accounting.

3. **Interpretive Question** Why is accrual-basis accounting usually used? Can you see any opportunities for improperly reporting income under cash-basis accounting? Explain.

P4–2 Calendar Year Versus Fiscal Year

Beason Company reports its income on a quarterly basis. Quarterly revenues and expenses for the years 1983 and 1984 are shown below.

	First Quarter	Second Quarter	Third Quarter	Fourth Quarter
		1983		
Total revenues	$50,000	$100,000	$76,000	$89,000
Total expenses	60,000	75,000	73,000	77,000
		1984		
Total revenues	$60,000	$110,000	$91,000	$81,000
Total expenses	68,000	82,000	86,000	72,000

Required:

1. Determine Beason Company's annual net income if it uses as its fiscal year the 12 months ended March 31, 1984.

2. Determine Beason Company's net income if it uses as its fiscal year the 12 months ended September 30, 1984.

3. Determine Beason Company's net income if it uses as its fiscal year the calendar year ended December 31, 1984.

P4–3 Determining Adjusting Entries from General Journal Entries

George Wilson, the bookkeeper of Meaders, Inc., thinks that the following journal entries may lead to adjusting entries at December 31, 1983.

February 1	Prepaid Insurance	1,200	
	Cash		1,200
March 31	Cash	18,000	
	Rent Revenue		18,000
May 1	Legal Service Expense	1,800	
	Cash		1,800
August 1	Property Tax Expense	12,000	
	Cash		12,000
October 31	Prepaid Interest	600	
	Cash		600

George has discovered the following additional information.

a. The insurance premium is for the 12-month period ending February 1, 1984.

b. The rent revenue represents rent received from a tenant for the period March 31, 1983, to September 30, 1983.

c. The legal service expense is for the services of Angus M. Carter, attorney-at-law, for the 12-month period ending April 30, 1984.

d. The property tax expense is for the state's fiscal year, which ends June 30, 1984.

e. The prepaid interest represents interest on a loan for the last 3 months of 1983.

Required:

Make adjusting entries required at December 31, 1983.

P4–4 Examination of Accounts and Adjusting Entries

During the course of your review of Gatenby Company at December 31, 1983, you find that the company owes the following notes to its bank.

a. A 2-year, $20,000, 10 percent note dated January 1, 1983, due December 31, 1984. Gatenby Company is required to make semiannual interest payments of $1,000 to the bank on June 30 and December 31 of each year.

b. A 6-month, 12 percent note dated November 1, 1983, due April 30, 1984. The face value of the note, $3,000, is payable on April 30, together with the interest.

Required:

1. For the first note, give the entries necessary to record the interest payments on June 30 and December 31, 1983; any adjusting entry that may be required on December 31; the interest payments on June 30, 1984, and December 31, 1984; and the payment of the note in full on December 31, 1984.

2. For the second note, give the entries necessary to record the receipt of the proceeds of the note on November 1, 1983, any adjusting entry that may be required on December 31, 1983, and the payment of the note in full on April 30, 1984.

3. What is Gatenby Company's total interest expense for the calendar year 1983?

P4-5 Unifying Problem: Adjusting Entries and Financial Statements

The 1984 year-end financial statements of Allen Company, a service business, are shown below. The company's accountants prepared the statements before making the necessary adjustments.

Allen Company
Income Statement
for the Year Ended December 31, 1984

Revenue from Services		$151,920
Operating Expenses:		
Insurance Expense	$ 5,480	
Rent Expense	500	
Office Supplies Expense	2,960	
Salaries Expense	55,000	63,940
Net Income		$ 87,980

Allen Company
Balance Sheet as of December 31, 1984

Assets	
Cash	$ 22,000
Accounts Receivable	40,000
Notes Receivable	12,800
Machinery	180,000
Total Assets	$254,800
Liabilities and Owner's Equity	
Accounts Payable	54,800
Mark Allen, Capital	200,000
Total Liabilities and Owner's Equity	$254,800

The following items are not reflected in the above financial statements.

a. Salaries earned but not recorded or paid were $5,000. (Ignore payroll taxes.)

b. Prepaid Insurance premiums amounted to $1,950. Insurance Expense was originally debited for all insurance expenditures.

c. Interest earned but not received or recorded was $700.

d. Service revenue collected but not earned was $4,180.

Required:

1. Give the required adjusting entries. (Omit explanations.)

2. Prepare a revised income statement and balance sheet.

3. Prepare a schedule reconciling the revised amount of owner's equity with the amount shown on the original statement.

P4-6 Adjusting Entries

You have just completed a trial balance and an analysis of the accounts of Vallo, Inc., at December 31, 1983. Your analysis reveals the following information.

a. The Prepaid Rent account shows a zero balance. Included in the Rent Expense account is an amount of $9,000, a payment of one year's rent for the period October 1, 1983, to September 30, 1984.

b. The Prepaid Insurance account was debited as the following insurance was bought.

Policy No.	Purchase and Effective Date of Policy	Life of Policy	Premiums
1AX	Jan. 1, 1982	3 years	$2,400
2BX	June 1, 1982	2 years	960
3CX	Sept. 1, 1982	1 year	480
4DX	Sept. 1, 1983	1 year	600

c. The balance in the Prepaid Advertising account is $3,600. This amount is for a series of radio spot announcements to be run for a 6-month period, beginning November 1, 1983.

d. At the close of the year, the company had two notes receivable. The first, a 90-day, 12 percent note for $7,200, was dated December 16, 1983. The second, a 60-day, 9 percent note for $6,000, was dated December 1, 1983. Accrued interest on these two notes at December 31 is $81 ($36 + $45).

e. At the close of the year, three short-term notes were outstanding.

Date of Note	Face Amount	Note Period	Interest Rate	Interest Expense Accrued
10/17	$ 8,100	90 days	8%	$135
11/1	12,000	4 months	10%	200
12/16	6,600	120 days	12%	33

f. Property taxes not yet recorded at December 31, 1983, amount to $2,275.

g. $21,600 was received on a 1-year equipment lease, effective August 1, 1983. The receipt was credited to Equipment Rent Revenue.

h. Salaries and wages incurred but not yet recorded at December 31, 1983, total $3,500.

Required:

Prepare the adjusting journal entries required at December 31, 1983.

P4–7 Adjustment of Accounts to Reflect Yearly Expenses

Several of the account balances at January 1, 1984, for Don's Dry Cleaners are listed below.

Accrued Rent Payable	$1,000
Accrued Salaries Payable	600
Accrued Interest Payable	300
Accrued Utilities Payable	100

The following information is pertinent.

a. For the year 1984, the rent was $800 per month. At December 31, 1984, the December 1984 rent had not yet been paid. Rent payments are debited to Rent Expense.

b. The company's monthly salaries expense in 1984 is $1,100. Workers are paid each month's wages on the fifth day of the next month. Salaries paid are debited to Salaries Expense.

c. The company paid off a bank loan during the year 1984. The interest paid on the loan was debited to Interest Expense. No loans were outstanding on December 31, 1984.

d. Utility expense in 1984 was $100 per month. The December 1984 utility bill amounting to $100 was paid on January 10, 1985. During 1984, all utility payments were debited to Utility Expense.

Required:

1. For each transaction, give the entry that would be made on December 31, 1984, to properly record the expenses for the calendar year 1984.

2. **Interpretive Question** Why is it important to know both the amount of an expense and the method used to record its payment in order to properly make an adjusting entry?

P4–8 Adjustments to Correct Ending Balances

During the year, Ross Company records all cash receipts from revenues and all cash payments of expenses in appropriate income statement accounts. At year-end, required adjustments are made to correct the revenue, unearned revenue, expense, and prepaid expense account balances. The following balances, taken from the accounts, have not been changed since January 1, 1984.

Unearned Rent Revenue	$ 575
Prepaid Property Taxes	750
Accrued Interest Receivable	800
Accrued Salaries Payable	1,900

An analysis of the accounts indicates that the following are the correct balances at December 31, 1984.

1. Unearned Rent Revenues	$1,050
2. Prepaid Property Taxes	750
3. Accrued Interest Receivable	260
4. Accrued Salaries Payable	2,750

Required:

In General Journal form, give the adjusting entries required to reflect the correct balances in the accounts at December 31, 1984.

P4–9 Unifying Problem: Analysis of Accounts

The summary totals below were taken from the accounting records of Game Products Company for the year ended December 31, 1983.

Assets	$62,700
Liabilities	26,500
Equity	36,200
Income	26,900

The controller overlooked the following information and did not make the necessary adjustments as of 12/31/83.

1. On July 1, 1983, the company loaned $12,000 to the president. The president gave the company a 1-year note with a 15 percent interest rate. The loan was recorded properly on July 1. The president has not paid anything in 1983. (Interest on the note is $1,800 a year.)

2. An insurance policy was purchased on November 1, 1983. The premium of $1,200 for the first year was prepaid and charged to Prepaid Insurance.

3. On June 1, 1983, the company received 1 year's advance rent of $2,100 and credited Rent Revenue.

4. Interest on a 12 percent, $10,000 note payable to the bank is due every July 1. (The interest was last paid on July 1, 1983.) Yearly interest on the note is $1,200.

5. Accrued salaries for the period 12/29/83 to 12/31/83 were $2,524.

6. Income taxes were 30 percent.

Required:

Determine the proper balances of assets, liabilities, owners' equity, and income as of December 31, 1983. Use the following format in working this problem.

Item	Assets	=	Liabilities	+	Owners' Equity	Income
Beg. Bal.	$62,700		$26,500		$36,200	$26,900
1.						
2.						
3.						
4.						
5.						
Subtotal						
6.						
Correct Balances	$		$		$	$

P4-10 Adjusting Entry Analysis

An analysis of cash records and account balances of Wells, Inc. included the following for 1984.

	Account Balances January 1, 1984	Account Balances December 31, 1984	Cash Received or Paid in 1984
Accrued Wages Payable	$2,600	$3,000	
Unearned Rent	4,500	5,000	
Prepaid Insurance	100	120	
For Wages			$29,600
For Rent			12,000
For Insurance			720

Required:

Determine the amounts that should be included on the 1984 income statement for (1) wages expense, (2) rent revenue, and (3) insurance expense.

CHAPTER 5

Completing the Accounting Cycle

THIS CHAPTER EXPLAINS:

How to use a work sheet.
The closing process in the accounting cycle.
How to prepare a post-closing trial balance.

As you have learned, the accounting cycle typically has nine steps. The first four steps include analyzing business documents, journalizing transactions, posting journal entries to ledger accounts, and determining account balances and preparing a trial balance. If all transactions were complete and involved only cash payments or receipts, the financial statements could be prepared directly from the trial balance. However, generally there are unrecorded revenues and expenses, unearned revenues, prepaid expenses, or other items that require year-end adjustments. Adjusting entries to account for these items often are made on a work sheet, which is then used as the basis for preparing the financial statements. In Chapter 4, we explained adjusting entries. Here we will describe how to set up a work sheet, as well as how to complete the accounting cycle.

Step 5. Preparing a Work Sheet

work sheet *columnar schedule used to summarize accounting data*

As noted in Chapters 3 and 4, preparing a work sheet is usually the fifth step in the accounting cycle. We have discussed adjusting entries (step 6) first since you need to understand adjustments before you can do a work sheet. As you will see, preparing a work sheet actually combines steps 4 through 7. That is, a work sheet lists a trial balance, adds adjusting entries, and extends the combined amounts into appropriate financial statement columns. The figures in these columns are then used in preparing the income statement, the balance sheet, and other financial reports. Note that work sheets are developed and used by the company's accountants and are not distributed to "outsiders," as are the financial statements of the company. Preparation of a work sheet is optional. It is most useful for organizing large quantities of data.

trial balance *a listing of all account balances; provides a means of testing whether debits equal credits for the total of all accounts*

A work sheet will usually have a minimum of eight columns. The accounts are listed on the left side, and columns 1 and 2 indicate the account balances prior to adjustments. That is, this set of columns contains the unadjusted trial balance. Columns 3 and 4 are for adjusting entries, such as those explained in Chapter 4. (Even when a work sheet is used, it should be noted, the adjusting entries must still be journalized and posted to the ledger accounts.) The last four columns are used for extending the unadjusted trial balance figures, plus or minus adjustments, into the appropriate set of financial statement columns. Revenue and expense accounts are extended into the income statement columns; asset, liability, and owners' equity accounts into the balance sheet columns. There are no columns for the statement of changes in financial position because this statement is a summary of elements taken from the balance sheet and income statement. However, other columns may be added; for example, a set of columns for the adjusted trial balance can be included as shown in Exhibit 5-1. It is also quite common to include a set of columns for the statement of retained earnings. This useful addition makes it possible to determine ending retained earnings and facilitates the preparation of a statement of retained earnings. The exact form of a work sheet is flexible and its content should reflect the needs of a particular business.

To illustrate the use of a work sheet, we will examine the operating activities of Yang Company for one month. To make the example realistic, we have included some transactions and adjustments that will be explained more fully in later chapters. Our present purpose is to show you how a work sheet is used. Do not be concerned if you do not understand every adjustment. The work sheet for Yang Company, Exhibit 5-1, is based on the following transactions (note that the company was organized on January 1, 1983).

January 1	Issued capital stock for $20,000 cash.
2	Bought a truck for $4,800 cash.
3	Received $600 from a tenant for 6 months' rent.
4	Paid $480 for a 1-year insurance policy.
8	Purchased $250 of supplies for cash.
10	Purchased inventory for $10,000 on account.
14	Sold $8,000 of inventory for $15,000 on account.
18	Collected $12,000 cash from customers' accounts receivable.
20	Paid $7,000 cash for inventories bought on January 10.
23	Paid $1,500 for sales representatives' salaries.
27	Purchased $14,000 of inventory for cash.
31	Sold $13,000 of inventory for $19,700 cash.

After all transactions have been journalized and posted, the balances in the accounts can be listed in the first two columns of the work sheet as the unadjusted trial balance (see Exhibit 5-1). The columns are then added to make sure that debits equal credits. Assuming an accounting period of one month, the following data are applicable to the necessary adjusting entries at January 31.

(a) Accrued sales salaries, $700. On January 23rd, $1,500 was paid to sales representatives. By the end of the month, an additional $700 in sales salaries had been earned but not yet paid.

(b) Expired insurance, $40. On January 4th, $480 was paid for insurance. At the end of the month, only one-twelfth of this annual fee can be expensed ($480 ÷ 12 = $40).

EXHIBIT 5-1

Yang Company

Work Sheet for the Month Ended January 31, 1983

Account Titles	Trial Balance Debits	Trial Balance Credits	Adjustments Debits	Adjustments Credits
Cash	24270			
Accounts Receivable	3000			
Inventory	3000			
Supplies on Hand	250			(d) 140
Prepaid Insurance	480			(b) 40
Truck	4800			
Accounts Payable		3000		
Rent Received in Advance		600	(c) 100	
Capital Stock		20000		
Sales		34700		
Cost of Goods Sold	21000			
Salaries Expense	1500		(a) 700	
	58300	58300		
Accrued Salaries Payable				(a) 700
Insurance Expense			(b) 40	
Rent Revenue				(c) 100
Supplies Expense			(d) 140	
Depreciation Expense			(e) 80	
Accumulated Depreciation-Truck				(e) 80
			1060	1060
Net Income (to balance)				

Adjustments:
(a) Accrued Salaries, $700
(b) Insurance Expense, $40 ($480 ÷ 12 = $40 a month)
(c) Rent Revenue Earned, $100

(c) Monthly rent revenue earned, $100. See January 3rd transaction.

(d) Supplies on hand, $110. This has to do with the supplies purchased on January 8th that remain on hand at the end of the month. A more complete explanation of this adjustment is given on page 137.

(e) Depreciation, $80. The truck purchased on January 2nd has an estimated service life of 5 years, which means that 20 percent of its purchase cost can be depreciated each year. This comes to $80 a month ($4,800 $\times$ 0.20 $\div$ 12 $=$ $80). This adjustment will also be explained more fully later in the chapter.

Adjusted Trial Balance		Income Statement		Balance Sheet	
Debits	Credits	Debits	Credits	Debits	Credits
24270				24270	
3000				3000	
3000				3000	
110				110	
440				440	
4800				4800	
	3000				3000
	500				500
	20000				20000
	34700		34700		
21000		21000			
2200		2200			
	700				700
40		40			
	100		100		
140		140			
80		80			
	80				80
59080	59080	23460	34800	35620	24280
		11340			11340
		34800	34800	35620	35620

(d) Supplies Used, $140 ($250 − $110)
(e) Depreciation of Truck, $80 (20% × $4,800 = $960; $960 ÷ 12 = $80 a month)

The adjustments appear in the adjustments columns of Exhibit 5-1 and are identified as entries (a) through (e). A key for the adjustments is usually included on the work sheet, as illustrated at the bottom of Exhibit 5-1. When the adjustments are entered on the work sheet, additional account titles must generally be added below those listed on the trial balance, as shown. The adjustments are added to or subtracted from the original trial balance debit and credit amounts to arrive at the adjusted trial balance. Then, the adjusted trial balance amounts are extended to the appropriate income statement or balance sheet columns as debits or credits, respectively. The totals for each set of columns must show the equality of debits and credits.

The financial statements are generally prepared directly from the work sheet (step 7 in the cycle); the statements for Yang Company are presented in Exhibits 5-2 and 5-3. (Taxes have been ignored to simplify the example.)

Note in Exhibit 5-1 that net income ($11,340 in this illustration) is added as the balancing figure when the income statement and balance sheet debit

EXHIBIT 5-2

Yang Company
Income Statement
for the Month Ended January 31, 1983

Sales Revenue		$34,700
Cost of Goods Sold		21,000
Gross Margin		$13,700
Operating Expenses:		
Insurance Expense	$ 40	
Salaries Expense	2,200	
Supplies Expense	140	
Depreciation Expense	80	
Total Operating Expenses		2,460
Operating Income		$11,240
Rent Revenue		100
Net Income		$11,340

EXHIBIT 5-3

Yang Company
Balance Sheet as of January 31, 1983

Assets			**Liabilities and Owners' Equity**		
Cash		$24,270	*Liabilities:*		
Accounts Receivable		3,000	Accounts Payable	$3,000	
Inventory		3,000	Accrued Salaries Payable	700	
Supplies on Hand		110	Rent Received in Advance	500	
Prepaid Insurance		440	Total Liabilities		$ 4,200
Truck	$4,800				
Less Accumulated Depreciation	80	4,720	*Owners' Equity:*		
			Capital Stock	$20,000	
Total Assets		$35,540	Retained Earnings	11,340	
			Total Owners' Equity		31,340
			Total Liabilities and Owners' Equity		$35,540

contra asset (on asset side but reduces assets)

and credit columns are totaled. A balancing debit figure in the income statement columns shows that revenues have exceeded expenses, and the resulting net income amount is included as a balancing credit figure (an increase to Retained Earnings) in the balance sheet columns.

ADDITIONAL ADJUSTING ENTRIES

The adjustments for items such as (a) through (c) in the Yang Company illustration were examined in Chapter 4. The adjustments for supplies and depreciation [items (d) and (e)] require additional explanation.

Adjusting for Supplies

supplies *materials used in a business that do not generally become part of the sales product and were not purchased to be resold to customers*

inventory *goods held for sale*

Students sometimes confuse supplies with inventory. Supplies include such items as paper, pencils, and paper clips, which are used in an office, as well as cleaning soap, paper towels, and lubricants, which might be used in a warehouse. These items are *not* classified as inventory; they have not been purchased with the intent to resell them to customers (as is inventory in a merchandising firm) or for direct use in the manufacture of products (as are raw materials in a manufacturing firm).

When supplies are consumed in the normal course of business, the asset account (Supplies or Supplies on Hand) must be adjusted and the used-up portion charged as an operating expense (Supplies Expense) on the income statement [see adjustment (d) in Exhibit 5-1 and the Supplies Expense account in Exhibit 5-2]. To determine the amount of the adjustment, the same three-step analysis described in Chapter 4 may be used. In the Yang Company illustration, for example, supplies were purchased for $250 and recorded as an asset. At the end of the period, only $110 of supplies remained on hand, indicating that $140 of supplies expense should be recognized for that period. If $110 of supplies is all that should be reported as an asset on the balance sheet at January 31 and the current balance is $250, then the adjusting entry must be

Supplies Expense	140	
Supplies on Hand		140

To reduce the Supplies on Hand account to the amount remaining for use in the next period and to recognize the amount of supplies used during the current period.

The analysis is summarized with the following T-accounts.

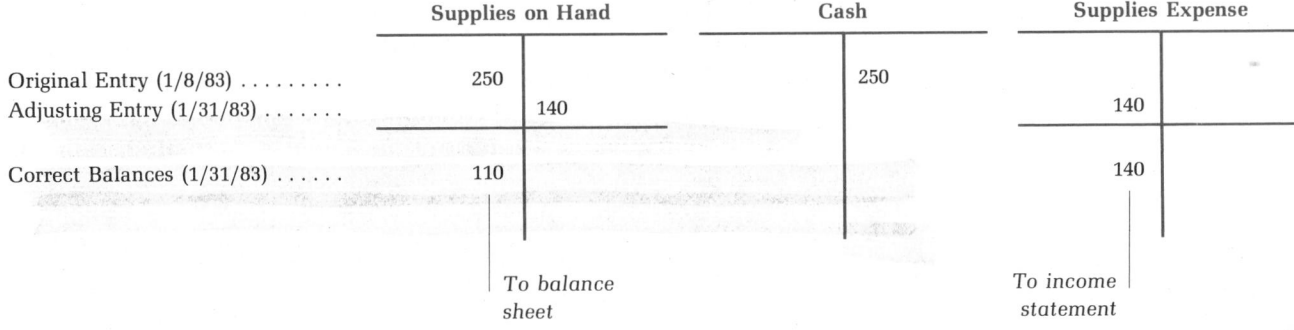

	Supplies on Hand		Cash		Supplies Expense	
Original Entry (1/8/83)	250			250		
Adjusting Entry (1/31/83)		140			140	
Correct Balances (1/31/83)	110				140	

To balance sheet (Supplies on Hand, 110) *To income statement* (Supplies Expense, 140)

As illustrated on the work sheet for Yang Company, the portion of supplies that are not used during an accounting period is extended to the balance sheet debit column and reported on the balance sheet as an asset (see Exhibit 5-3). Unlike supplies, inventory is sold to customers; when it is sold, it is recorded as Cost of Goods Sold and subtracted from Sales Revenue on the income statement (Exhibit 5-2). Like supplies that are not used, inventory that is not sold is extended to the balance sheet debit column and is shown as an asset on the balance sheet (Exhibit 5-3).

Adjusting for Depreciation

When operational assets, such as trucks or machinery, are purchased by a company, it is not appropriate to record the entire purchase price as an expense in the current year. These types of assets generally provide benefits to a company for several years. Accordingly, the cost of such an asset is allocated over the number of periods of expected future benefit. For example, if a machine that is expected to last five years is purchased, its total cost will be allocated over five annual accounting periods, with one-fifth the cost being assigned as an expense and reported on the income statement in each year of use. The unallocated portion will be reported as an asset on the balance sheet. This process is called depreciation; it is explained fully in Chapter 10.

depreciation *the process of cost allocation that assigns the original cost of plant and equipment to the periods benefited*

In the Yang Company illustration, a truck was purchased on January 2, 1983, at a cost of $4,800. From adjustment (e), we can see that the truck's cost is being allocated (depreciated) evenly over 5 years (20 percent per year). Thus, the appropriate amount of depreciation expense for January is $80 (20% × $4,800 = $960 per year; $960 ÷ 12 months = $80 per month). The entry to record the depreciation is a debit to Depreciation Expense and a credit to Accumulated Depreciation–Truck. The depreciation expense is shown on the income statement and the amount of accumulated depreciation is subtracted from the truck's cost in reporting the unallocated portion ($4,800 original cost less $80 accumulated depreciation for one month = $4,720) as an asset on Yang's balance sheet.

accumulated depreciation *the total amount of depreciation expense that has been recorded for a particular asset since it was originally purchased*

The Accumulated Depreciation–Truck account is used to record all amounts of depreciation on the truck over the period of its use by the company. At the end of January, only 1 month's depreciation has been recognized on Yang Company's truck, so the Accumulated Depreciation–Truck account balance is $80. Each month another $80 will be recognized as depreciation expense and added to the accumulated depreciation account. Over the years, the accumulated depreciation account will show how much total depreciation has been taken on the truck. At the end of each accounting period, the balance in the Accumulated Depreciation–Truck account can be subtracted from the balance in the Truck account to determine how much of the original cost of the truck remains to be assigned to depreciation expense. The difference between the truck's original recorded cost and its accumulated depreciation is the "net book value" of the truck ($4,800 − $80), and is the net amount reported as an asset on the balance sheet. For Yang Company at the end of January, the truck has a net book value of $4,720 (see Exhibit 5-3).

SPECIAL CONSIDERATIONS IN USING A WORK SHEET

A work sheet is an accounting tool. Its content depends on the type of business and the way a company handles certain transactions. Two items require additional explanation at this point: (1) accounting for inventory on a work sheet, and (2) the work sheet adjustment for income taxes.

Adjusting for Inventory

Due to its importance, inventory will be discussed in considerable detail in Chapters 6 and 7. At this point, we merely note that there are alternative ways in which inventory can be handled on a work sheet. Exhibit 5-1 shows one method, but you are likely to encounter others.

In Exhibit 5-1, we assumed that on January 1 Yang Company had no inventory because the business had just been established. On January 10 Yang purchased $10,000 of inventory; on January 14 the company sold $8,000 of inventory, reducing the Inventory account to $2,000 and increasing Cost of Goods Sold to $8,000. On January 27 Yang bought more inventory for $14,000, showing a total of $16,000 in its Inventory account. On January 31, however, Yang sold $13,000 of inventory, reducing its Inventory account by $13,000 to $3,000 and increasing its Cost of Goods Sold account from $8,000 to $21,000. The resulting T-accounts appeared as follows:

	Inventory	
Beginning Balance ..	-0-	
Jan. 10 Purchase ...	10,000	
Jan. 14 Sale		8,000
Jan. 27 Purchase ...	14,000	
Jan. 31 Sale		13,000
Ending Balance	3,000	

	Cost of Goods Sold	
Beginning Balance ..	-0-	
Jan. 14 Sale	8,000	
Jan. 31 Sale	13,000	
Ending Balance	21,000	

Because of the way Yang Company handled its inventory—increasing or decreasing its Inventory and Cost of Goods Sold accounts after each purchase or sale—the account balances are correct at month-end and no adjustments are required on the work sheet. (This is called the perpetual inventory method.)

Assume now that Yang makes no entries to its Inventory and Cost of Goods Sold accounts during the month, but instead records all inventory purchases in a Purchases account. For example, on January 10 and 27 Yang made the following entries:

January 10	Purchases	10,000	
	Accounts Payable		10,000
January 27	Purchases	14,000	
	Cash		14,000
	To record purchases of inventory.		

Then, at the end of January Yang physically counts its inventory to determine the amount of purchased inventory that has not yet been sold. (This is called the periodic inventory method.) If the count reveals that $3,000 of inventory is on hand, adjustments such as those illustrated in Exhibit 5-4 are required on the work sheet to show that not all purchased inventory has been sold. First, the Inventory account balance must be adjusted. The trial balance shows no beginning balance in Inventory, but from the count of inventory at the end of January, we know there is $3,000 on hand. This must be established in the inventory account by a debit in the adjustments col-

EXHIBIT 5-4

Yang Company
Work Sheet for the Month Ended January 31, 1983

Account Titles	Trial Balance Debits	Trial Balance Credits	Adjustments Debits	Adjustments Credits
Cash	24270			
Accounts Receivable	3000			
Inventory			(f) 3000	
Supplies on Hand	250			(d) 140
Prepaid Insurance	480			(b) 40
Truck	4800			
Accounts Payable		3000		
Rent Received in Advance		600	(c) 100	
Capital Stock		20000		
Sales Revenue		34700		
Purchases	24000			(f) 24000
Salaries Expense	1500		(a) 700	
	58300	58300		
Cost of Goods Sold			(f) 21000	
Accrued Salaries Payable				(a) 700
Insurance Expense			(b) 40	
Rent Revenue				(c) 100
Supplies Expense			(d) 140	
Depreciation Expense			(e) 80	
Accumulated Depreciation-Truck				(e) 80
			25060	25060
Net Income (to balance)				

Adjustments:
(a) Accrued Salaries, $700
(b) Insurance Expense, $40 ($480 ÷ 12 = $40 a month)
(c) Rent Revenue Earned, $100

umn [item (f)]. This $3,000 Inventory balance is extended to the balance sheet debit column and is reported as an asset on the balance sheet.

Second, the Purchases account must be transferred to Cost of Goods Sold. At the end of the month, the Purchases account, as shown by the unadjusted trial balance, contains a balance of $24,000 from the January 10 and January 27 purchases. However, Purchases is a temporary account used to accumulate the cost of all purchases and must be reduced to a zero balance at the end of the accounting period—by a credit in the adjustments column [item (f)]. Third, Cost of Goods Sold must be calculated. This is

Adjusted Trial Balance		Income Statement		Balance Sheet	
Debits	Credits	Debits	Credits	Debits	Credits
24270				24270	
3000				3000	
3000				3000	
110				110	
440				440	
4800				4800	
	3000				3000
	500				500
	20000				20000
	34700		34700		
2200		2200			
21000		21000			
	700				700
40		40			
	100		100		
140		140			
80		80			
	80				80
59080	59080	23460	34800	35620	24280
		11340			11340
		34800	34800	35620	35620

(d) Supplies Used, \$140 (\$250 − \$110)
(e) Depreciation of Truck, \$80 (20% × \$4,800 = \$960; \$960 ÷ 12 = \$80 a month)
(f) Physical Count of Ending Inventory, \$3,000

done by subtracting the inventory on hand at the end of the period ($3,000) from the beginning inventory (in this case zero) plus purchases ($24,000). The Cost of Goods Sold ($21,000) is established by a debit in the adjustments column [item (f)], and is then extended as an expense in the income statement debit column in the work sheet. The complete, compound adjusting entry (f) is

January 31	Inventory	3,000	
	Cost of Goods Sold	21,000	
	Purchases		24,000
	To record an end-of-period adjustment reflecting the periodic count of inventory.		

The above adjustment does three things. It establishes the inventory amount to be reported on the balance sheet, it determines the cost of goods sold amount to be deducted from sales revenue on the income statement, and it reduces the Purchases account to a zero balance, since all items purchased have either been sold or are on hand and reported as inventory. As with most compound entries, the same net effect could be achieved with two or more entries. For example, the entry to establish the inventory would be a debit to Inventory and a credit to Cost of Goods Sold for $3,000. The entry to close the Purchases account would be a debit to Cost of Goods Sold and a credit to Purchases for $24,000. The net amount in Cost of Goods Sold is $21,000, the same as shown in the compound entry. The financial statements taken from the work sheet would be the same as those illustrated in Exhibits 5-2 and 5-3.

Adjusting for Income Taxes

To keep the Yang Company illustration simple, we ignored income taxes. However, when a corporation earns income, it must pay income taxes. A year-end adjustment is required, debiting Income Tax Expense[1] and crediting Income Taxes Payable for the appropriate amount. Then when the taxes are actually paid, usually during the following year, Income Taxes Payable is debited and Cash is credited.

The adjustment for income taxes presents a minor problem on the work sheet because the amount of income taxes to be paid cannot be determined until the net income amount is computed. One way to solve this problem is to subtotal the work sheet columns, determine the balancing figure for income, multiply the balancing figure by the tax rate to determine the amount of the tax, and then make the adjusting entry for Income Tax Expense and Income Taxes Payable in the same way as the other adjustments.

With this approach, both of the income tax account titles and the amounts are shown on the work sheet following the column subtotals. To illustrate, we assume that Yang Company is a corporation and that the appropriate tax rate is 25 percent. The work sheet shown in Exhibit 5-1 would be completed as follows:

[1] Income Tax Expense is the proper account title. However, income statements often use the shorter form, Income Taxes.

	Adjustments		Adjusted Trial Balance		Income Statement		Balance Sheet	
	Debits	Credits	Debits	Credits	Debits	Credits	Debits	Credits
Subtotals	1,060	1,060	59,080	59,080	23,460	34,800	35,620	24,280
Income Tax Expense	2,835		2,835		2,835*			
Income Taxes Payable		2,835		2,835				2,835
Totals	3,895	3,895	61,915	61,915	26,295	34,800	35,620	27,115
After-Tax Net Income (to balance)					8,505*			8,505
Totals					34,800	34,800	35,620	35,620

* [$34,800 − $23,460 = $11,340 to balance the income statement columns; $11,340 × 0.25 = $2,835 Income Tax Expense and Income Taxes Payable; the balance ($11,340 − $2,835 = $8,505) is after-tax net income.]

TO SUMMARIZE A work sheet is often used to analyze end-of-period adjustments and to facilitate the preparation of financial statements. A work sheet will usually have columns for the unadjusted trial balance, the adjusting entries, the income statement, and the balance sheet. The exact format and content of the work sheet will be determined by the special needs of a particular business. Work sheet adjustments for supplies, depreciation, inventory, and income taxes require special attention.

Step 6. Adjusting Entries

Several types of adjusting entries were introduced in Chapter 4. In this chapter, we have explained four additional items that commonly require adjustment: supplies, depreciation, income taxes, and inventory (if the periodic method is used). We have also shown how these adjustments are included on a work sheet. Usually, the work sheet is completed before the adjusting entries are journalized and posted. By including the adjustments on a work sheet, an accountant is better able to see the total result of the accounting process. That is, the accountant uses a work sheet to determine the proper amount of net income and the appropriate asset, liability, and owners' equity account balances prior to preparing the financial statements.

Step 7. Preparing Financial Statements

Once all transactions have been analyzed, journalized, and posted and all adjusting entries have been made, the accounts can be summarized and presented as the general-purpose financial statements. The information for the income statement and the balance sheet is taken directly from the work sheet, when one is used. All that is needed is to organize the data into appropriate sections and categories so as to present it as simply and clearly as possible (as in Exhibits 5-2 and 5-3). Use of a work sheet permits the preparation of more timely statements since they can be completed prior to journalizing and posting adjusting and closing entries.

At this point, we suggest that you refer again to the financial statements for IBM at the back of the book in order to see the applicability of this knowledge to a real company.

Step 8. Closing Entries

We have almost reached the end of the accounting cycle. Thus far, the cycle has included journalizing transactions, posting to the ledger accounts, determining account balances and preparing a trial balance, setting up a work sheet, making adjusting entries, and producing the financial statements. Just two final steps must be taken: journalizing and posting closing entries and preparing a post-closing trial balance.

REAL AND NOMINAL ACCOUNTS

real accounts *accounts that are not closed to a zero balance at the end of each accounting period; permanent accounts appearing on the balance sheet*

To explain the closing process, we must first define two new terms. Certain accounts are referred to as real accounts. They report the cumulative additions and reductions in amounts from the date the company was organized. These accounts appear on the balance sheet and are permanent, in that they are not closed to a zero balance at the end of each accounting period. Balances existing in real accounts at the end of a period are carried forward to the next period.

nominal accounts *accounts that are closed to a zero balance at the end of each accounting period; temporary accounts generally appearing on the income statement*

Other accounts are known as nominal accounts. These accounts are temporary, in that they are reduced to a zero balance through the closing process at the end of each accounting period. Thus, nominal accounts begin with a zero balance at the start of each accounting cycle. Transactions throughout the period, generally a year, are journalized and posted to the nominal accounts, which are used to accumulate and classify all revenue and expense items for that period. At the end of the period, adjustments are made, the income statement is prepared, and the balances in the temporary accounts are then closed to an owners' equity (permanent) account. The closing entries bring the income statement accounts back to a zero balance, which makes the accounting records ready for a new cycle of transactions. In addition, the closing entries transfer the net profit or loss for the accounting period to Retained Earnings and reduce Retained Earnings for any dividends declared.

THE CLOSING PROCESS

closing entries *entries that reduce all nominal, or temporary, accounts to a zero balance at the end of each accounting period, transferring their pre-closing balances to a permanent balance sheet account*

The journal entries to close the nominal accounts, referred to as closing entries, must also be posted to the appropriate ledger accounts. Without closing entries, revenue and expense balances would extend from period to period, making it difficult to isolate the operating results of each accounting period.

The actual mechanics of the closing process are not complicated. Revenue accounts normally have credit balances, so they are closed by being debited; expense accounts generally have debit balances and are closed by being credited. For a corporation, the difference between total revenues and total expenses is debited or credited to Retained Earnings.

To illustrate the closing process, we refer again to Yang Company. If the data for the closing journal entry were taken from the income statement in Exhibit 5-2, the closing entry would be

January 31	Sales Revenue	34,700	
	Rent Revenue	100	
	Cost of Goods Sold		21,000
	Insurance Expense		40
	Salaries Expense		2,200
	Supplies Expense		140
	Depreciation Expense		80
	Retained Earnings		11,340
	To close revenues and expenses to Retained Earnings.		

We need to explain a number of points related to the above entry. First, because Yang Company began operations on January 1, the total closed to Retained Earnings as net income for the period ($11,340) is also the amount of Retained Earnings reported on the balance sheet (see Exhibit 5-3). This means that Yang Company had a beginning Retained Earnings balance of zero and paid no dividends during January. Usually, the amounts reported for retained earnings and net income will differ. The ending retained earnings balance is an accumulation of earnings retained by an entity since it started business. To illustrate, if Yang Company reported $15,000 of net income for February and also declared a $2,000 dividend during that month, its ending retained earnings balance at the end of February would be $24,340 ($11,340 beginning Retained Earnings, accumulated from January operations, + $15,000 net income − $2,000 dividends = $24,340 ending Retained Earnings).

Second, books normally are closed at the end of an accounting year, not at the end of each month, as in our example. A shorter period is used here to simplify the illustration.

Third, closing entries are generally made from data in the income statement columns of a work sheet rather than from the income statement itself. The income statement may not report each item of revenue or expense separately, but may combine or summarize some of the items. In the closing process, it is not sufficient to close the balance in a combined or summarized income statement category, such as total expenses or total revenues. Each individual revenue and expense account balance must be reduced to a zero balance. Since the work sheet lists each individual revenue and expense account, the closing entries are more appropriately made from it.

Finally, the Cost of Goods Sold account is an expense account. Like other expense accounts, Cost of Goods Sold must be closed. If the cost of merchandise sold is not recorded after each sale, as it is in the perpetual inventory method illustrated earlier in this chapter, then cost of goods sold becomes a computed amount determined at the end of the accounting period, as discussed on pages 139–142. That is, it results from a calculation involving purchases of merchandise, adjusted for beginning and ending inventory balances. When we used the periodic inventory method and a Purchases account in the Yang Company example, the cost of goods sold was computed to be $21,000.

Beginning Inventory	$ -0-
Add Purchases	24,000
Cost of Goods Available for Sale	$24,000
Less Ending Inventory	3,000
Cost of Goods Sold	$21,000

Since the Purchases account was used, its balance must be transferred to Cost of Goods Sold. Also, the Inventory account balance must be adjusted as was previously illustrated on the work sheet [item (f)], page 140. Once these adjustments are made, the Cost of Goods Sold account will have a $21,000 debit balance and will be closed to Retained Earnings.

USING AN INCOME SUMMARY ACCOUNT

Income Summary *a clearing account used to close all revenues and expenses at the end of an accounting period; the preclosing balance of the Income Summary account represents the operating results (income or loss) of an accounting period*

clearing account *a temporary account, such as Income Summary, used to collect a group of costs and/or revenues so as to simplify the transfer of the balance to another account (or accounts)*

In the example on page 145, the revenue and expense accounts were closed directly to Retained Earnings. An alternative approach involves using a special account called Income Summary. This account is a temporary clearing account; its function is to facilitate the process of combining all revenue and expense amounts into one figure—the net income or loss for the period. An Income Summary account is used in the following manner. Revenue accounts usually have credit balances, so they are closed by being debited, with the total credited to Income Summary. Expenses generally have debit balances, so they are closed by being credited, with the total debited to Income Summary. The balance in the Income Summary account, which now represents the income or loss for the period (the difference between revenues and expenses), is in turn closed to the appropriate permanent owners' equity account.

Although the Income Summary account facilitates the closing process, it is not required and many companies close revenues and expenses directly to Retained Earnings, as illustrated earlier. However, use of an Income Summary account keeps the Retained Earnings account from becoming cluttered; only the net income (or loss) and dividend closing entries are transferred to Retained Earnings.

The closing journal entries for Yang Company when an Income Summary account is used would be

January 31	Sales Revenue	34,700	
	Rent Revenue	100	
	Income Summary		34,800
	To close revenues to Income Summary.		

January 31	Income Summary	23,460	
	Cost of Goods Sold		21,000
	Salaries Expense		2,200
	Insurance Expense		40
	Supplies Expense		140
	Depreciation Expense		80
	To close expenses to Income Summary.		
January 31	Income Summary	11,340	
	Retained Earnings		11,340
	To close Income Summary to Retained Earnings ($34,800 − $23,460).		

The closing procedure above requires three entries. The first two could be combined as a compound entry.

January 31	Sales Revenue	34,700	
	Rent Revenue	100	
	Cost of Goods Sold		21,000
	Salaries Expense		2,200
	Insurance Expense		40
	Supplies Expense		140
	Depreciation Expense		80
	Income Summary		11,340
	To close revenues and expenses to Income Summary.		

The final step again would be to close the Income Summary account to Retained Earnings. No matter how many entries are made, and whether or not an Income Summary account is used, the effect is the same. All nominal accounts will have a zero balance. Correspondingly, all real accounts, including the owners' equity accounts, will be stated at their appropriate balances. The books are now ready for a new accounting cycle. The closing process for the revenues and expenses of a corporation is shown schematically in Exhibit 5-5.

EXHIBIT 5-5 The Closing Process

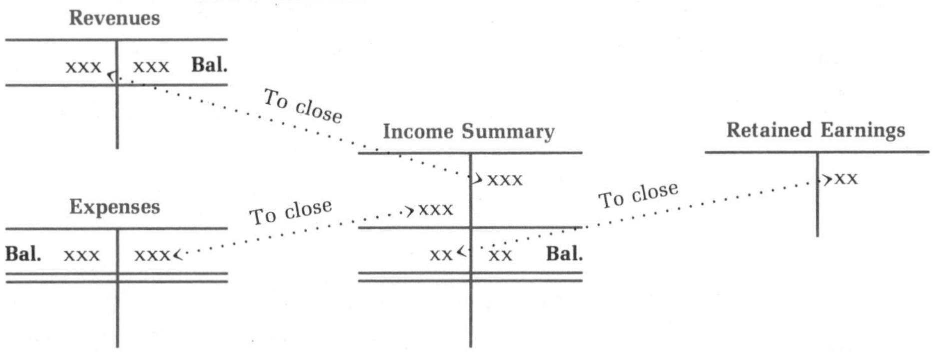

CLOSING DIVIDENDS

Recall from Chapter 3 that dividends are distributions to shareholders of part of a corporation's earnings. When dividends are declared, the amount that will be paid is debited to a temporary Dividends account and credited to a liability account, Dividends Payable, or to Cash if paid immediately. Since Dividends is a temporary account, it must be closed to Retained Earnings at the end of the accounting period. The Dividends account is closed by crediting it and by debiting Retained Earnings, thereby reducing owners' equity.

We omitted dividends from the Yang Company example because they generally are not declared or paid on a monthly basis. However, if Yang had declared dividends during January, the Dividends account would have to be closed on January 31 by crediting Dividends and debiting Retained Earnings for the declared amount. Note that dividends are not closed to Income Summary because dividends are not an expense but a distribution of earnings that directly reduces Retained Earnings. The Income Summary account is only a clearing account for closing all revenues and expenses.

THE CLOSING PROCESS FOR PROPRIETORSHIPS AND PARTNERSHIPS

We have illustrated the closing process for a corporation by debiting or crediting the difference between revenues and expenses directly to Retained Earnings, or indirectly through an Income Summary account. If a business is a proprietorship or a partnership, the balancing portion of the closing entry will be made to a Proprietorship or Partnership Capital account. For example, if Yang Company were a proprietorship, the entry to close Income Summary to the permanent capital account would be

January 31	Income Summary	11,340	
	M. L. Yang, Capital		11,340
	To close Income Summary to the Capital account of M. L. Yang.		

drawings *distributions to the owner(s) of a proprietorship or partnership; similar to dividends for a corporation*

Neither a proprietorship nor a partnership pays dividends. Instead, funds are withdrawn by owners in anticipation of earnings or for living expenses and are called drawings or withdrawals. The closing process for a proprietorship or partnership Drawings account is the same as for a corporate Dividends account. Each such account is closed to a permanent proprietorship or partnership capital account by crediting the Drawings account and debiting the respective proprietorship or partnership equity account. The owners' equity section of the balance sheet for proprietorships, partnerships, and corporations is explained fully in Chapters 13 and 14.

TO SUMMARIZE Step 6 in the accounting cycle is to make adjusting entries. Step 7 involves the preparation of the financial statements, generally from the work sheet. Step 8 requires the closing of all nominal, or temporary, accounts to a zero balance.

All real, or permanent, accounts are carried forward to the new reporting period. Revenue accounts are closed by being debited; expense accounts are closed by being credited. If Income Summary is used as a clearing account, the total amount debited by closing all revenue accounts is credited to Income Summary, and the total amount credited by closing expense accounts is debited to Income Summary. The balance in Income Summary is then closed directly to Retained Earnings. Alternatively, revenues and expenses may be closed directly to Retained Earnings. Dividends is also a nominal account and must be closed to Retained Earnings. Although the account titles are different, the closing process is the same for proprietorships, partnerships, and corporations.

Step 9. Preparing a Post-Closing Trial Balance

post-closing trial balance *a listing of all real account balances after the closing process has been completed; provides a means of testing whether debits equal credits for all real accounts prior to beginning a new accounting cycle*

The last step in the accounting cycle is to balance the accounts and to prepare a post-closing trial balance. The accounts are to be balanced—that is, the debits and credits added and a balance determined—only after the closing entries have been recorded and posted in the General Ledger. The information for the post-closing trial balance is then taken from the ledger. The nominal accounts will not be shown since they have been closed, and thus have zero balances. Only the real accounts will have current balances. This step is designed to provide some assurance that the previous steps in the cycle have been performed properly, prior to the start of a new accounting period. Exhibit 5-6 illustrates a post-closing trial balance for Yang Company.

EXHIBIT 5-6

Yang Company

Post-Closing Trial Balance as of January 31, 1983

	Debits	Credits
Cash	$24,270	
Accounts Receivable	3,000	
Inventory	3,000	
Supplies on Hand	110	
Prepaid Insurance	440	
Truck	4,800	
Accumulated Depreciation—Truck		$ 80
Accounts Payable		3,000
Accrued Salaries Payable		700
Rent Received in Advance		500
Capital Stock		20,000
Retained Earnings		11,340
Totals	$35,620	$35,620

Interpretation of Accounting Data

Although not usually considered one of the routine steps in the accounting cycle, interpretation of the products of the cycle—the accounting reports—is of the utmost importance. Interpretation refers to the explanations, verbal or written, that accountants give to managers and external users to help them understand the information in accounting reports. For example, it would be useful not only to report an increase in total expenses but also to explain which individual expenses have increased, which have decreased, and why. Thus, interpretation is related to the full-disclosure standard mentioned in Chapter 2, and provides an opportunity for service by accountants. The procedures in the accounting cycle are meaningful only if the accounting information is relevant and is presented in a manner that assists users in making better decisions. The interpretation and analysis of accounting data are treated in detail in Chapter 16.

CHAPTER REVIEW

A work sheet is often used to facilitate the preparation of financial statements. The accounts and their balances are listed on the work sheet, adjustments are made, and the adjusted balances are transferred to the appropriate financial statement columns. When a work sheet is used, the accountant can prepare the financial statements without having to refer to individual accounts in the ledger.

Once the financial statements have been prepared and the adjusting entries have been journalized and posted to the accounts, the accounting records should be made ready for the next accounting cycle. This is accomplished by journalizing and posting closing entries for all nominal accounts. Revenue accounts are closed by being debited; expense accounts are closed by being credited. An Income Summary account may be used or revenues and expenses may be closed directly to a permanent owners' equity account. This is true for proprietorships, partnerships, and corporations. For a corporation, dividends are closed by being credited, and are closed directly to Retained Earnings. Drawings for a proprietorship or partnership are similar to dividends and are handled in the same way.

The final step in the accounting cycle is to balance the accounts and prepare a post-closing trial balance. This provides some assurance that previous steps have been performed correctly and that the records are in order prior to the start of a new accounting cycle.

While not usually considered a routine step in the accounting cycle, the interpretation of accounting data and reports is an important responsibility of accountants.

The Supplement to this chapter explains alternative methods of clearing the balance sheet accounts of the adjusting entries made at the end of an accounting period, including the reversing-entry approach.

A case study is presented on pages 174 to 195 as a review of the first five chapters of the text. It is intended to help solidify your understanding of the accounting cycle.

KEY TERMS AND CONCEPTS

accumulated depreciation (138)
clearing account (146)
closing entries (144)
depreciation (138)
drawings (148)
Income Summary (146)
inventory (137)
nominal accounts (144)
post-closing trial balance (149)
real accounts (144)
reversing entry (170)
supplies (137)
trial balance (133)
work sheet (132)

REVIEW PROBLEM

The Accounting Cycle

The post-closing trial balance for Warren's Waterbeds as of December 31, 1983, is presented below. (This Review Problem is longer than most. However, it provides a useful summary of the entire accounting cycle.)

Warren's Waterbeds
Post-Closing Trial Balance
as of December 31, 1983

	Debits	Credits
Cash	$ 13,500	
Accounts Receivable	17,000	
Inventory	28,800	
Furniture and Fixtures	22,000	
Accumulated Depreciation—Furniture and Fixtures		$ 8,800
Building	65,000	
Accumulated Depreciation—Building		13,000
Accounts Payable		18,000
Mortgage Payable		36,000
Capital Stock		54,000
Retained Earnings		16,500
Totals	$146,300	$146,300

As Warren Jensen, the owner, analyzes the business documents for the year ended December 31, 1984, he finds the following information.

a. Total purchases of inventory were $49,500; all purchases were made on credit and are recorded in an Inventory account (perpetual inventory method).

b. Total sales were $85,000; of this amount, $62,900 were on credit, and the rest were cash sales. The cost of goods sold was $47,500; the Inventory account is to be reduced after each sale.

c. New office furniture was purchased in November for $9,200 cash.

d. The company paid $17,000 of its beginning accounts payable, which was $18,000.

e. The company issued 1,500 new shares of capital stock at $20 per share.

f. The year's rent was $1,500, all of which was paid in cash.

g. The company collected $62,000 of its accounts receivable during the year.

h. The company made a $15,000 payment on the mortgage; of this amount, $7,000 was interest.

i. The company paid for all the inventory purchased during the year (item a, above).

j. Warren Jensen's salary for the year was $9,000, which the company paid in cash.

k. Advertising and utilities expenses for the year were $800 and $650, respectively. These were paid in cash.

Adjusting entries to account for the following must also be made.

l. Additional interest of $500 on the mortgage has been incurred. No entry has been made to record the interest.

m. The advertising expense that was paid during 1984 is for a two-year advertising campaign in 1984 and 1985. The expense approach was used.

n. The rent expense paid by the company during 1984 includes $100 of rent for January 1985. The expense approach was used.

o. The company did not pay its entire utilities expense for 1984. The company should have paid $800; the deficiency will be paid in January 1985.

p. The building is being depreciated at 10 percent per year, and the furniture and fixtures at 20 percent, with no depreciation charged on acquisitions made during the last 6 months of the year.

Required:

1. Make entries in the General Journal to record each of the transactions (a through k).
2. Set up T-accounts with beginning balances as shown in the post-closing trial balance as of December 31, 1983, and post the journal entries to these T-accounts.
3. Prepare a trial balance as of December 31, 1984, as the first columns in a work sheet for the company.

4. Make any necessary adjusting entries on the work sheet (l through p).
5. Complete the work sheet and use it to prepare an income statement and a balance sheet (ignore taxes).
6. Journalize the adjusting entries in the company's General Journal and then post them to the General Ledger.
7. Journalize and post the closing entries.
8. Prepare a post-closing trial balance.

Solution

1. Journal Entries

Following are General Journal entries to record the transactions.

a	Inventory	49,500	
	Accounts Payable		49,500

The company purchased $49,500 of goods on credit. We must increase the Inventory account for this amount by debiting it. We must also increase the Accounts Payable account to show that the goods have not yet been paid for. We increase a liability account by crediting it.

b	Accounts Receivable	62,900	
	Cash	22,100	
	Sales Revenue		85,000

Total sales were $85,000, and so we increase the Sales Revenue account $85,000 by crediting it. Of this amount, $62,900 were on credit, and $22,100 were cash sales. We increase the Accounts Receivable and Cash accounts by debiting them.

	Cost of Goods Sold	47,500	
	Inventory		47,500

The cost of the goods sold was $47,500. We increase this expense account by debiting it. Since the goods have been sold, we must reduce the Inventory account by crediting it.

c	Furniture and Fixtures	9,200	
	Cash		9,200

This entry increases the Furniture and Fixtures account for the new office furniture. Since cash was paid, the Cash account must be decreased.

d	Accounts Payable	17,000	
	Cash		17,000

The company paid part of the accounts payable. Therefore, the Accounts Payable account must be reduced to show that the company's obligation has been reduced. Since cash was paid, the Cash account must also be reduced.

e	Cash	30,000	
	Capital Stock		30,000

The company issued more of its capital stock, and so the Capital Stock account must be credited. Since the company received cash, the Cash account is also increased.

f	Rent Expense	1,500	
	Cash		1,500

Since the company has incurred an expense, the Rent Expense account must be increased by being debited. Since cash was paid, the Cash account is decreased by being credited.

g	Cash	62,000	
	Accounts Receivable		62,000

Since the company has collected some of its accounts receivable, that account must be credited to show a reduction. Since cash was received, the Cash account must be debited.

h	Mortgage Payable	8,000	
	Interest Expense	7,000	
	Cash		15,000

Since the company paid $15,000 cash on its mortgage, the Cash account is credited for $15,000 to decrease its balance. Of this amount, $7,000 was interest, and so the Interest Expense account is increased by being debited for $7,000. The remainder reduces the mortgage liability, and so the Mortgage Payable account is debited for $8,000.

i	Accounts Payable	49,500	
	Cash		49,500

The company paid for the inventory it purchased in entry (a). The Accounts Payable and the Cash accounts must be reduced by being debited and credited, respectively.

j	Salary Expense	9,000	
	Cash		9,000

The Salary Expense account must be debited to show that an expense has been incurred. Since cash was paid, the Cash account must be credited to be reduced.

k	Advertising Expense	800	
	Utilities Expense	650	
	Cash		1,450

The Advertising Expense and Utilities Expense accounts must be debited to show that the company has incurred these expenses. Since cash was paid, the Cash account must be decreased by a credit.

2. T-accounts

T-accounts with the beginning balance and journal entries posted are shown below.

Cash

Debit	Credit
Beg. Bal. . . 13,500	9,200 . . . **c**
b 22,100	17,000 . . . **d**
e 30,000	1,500 . . . **f**
g 62,000	15,000 . . . **h**
	49,500 . . . **i**
	9,000 . . . **j**
	1,450 . . . **k**
24,950	

Accounts Receivable

Debit	Credit
Beg. Bal. . . 17,000	62,000 . . . **g**
b 62,900	
17,900	

Inventory

Debit	Credit
Beg. Bal. . . 28,800	47,500 . . . **b**
a 49,500	
30,800	

Furniture and Fixtures

Debit	Credit
Beg. Bal. . . 22,000	
c 9,200	
31,200	

Accumulated Depreciation— Furniture and Fixtures

	Beg. Bal. . . . 8,800

Building

Beg. Bal. . . 65,000	

Accumulated Depreciation— Building

	Beg. Bal. . . 13,000

Accounts Payable

d 17,000	18,000 . . Beg. Bal.
i 49,500	49,500 . . . a
	1,000

Mortgage Payable

h 8,000	36,000 . . Beg. Bal.
	28,000

Capital Stock

	54,000 . . Beg. Bal.
	30,000 . . . e
	84,000

Retained Earnings

	16,500 . . Beg. Bal.

Sales Revenue

	85,000 . . . b

Cost of Goods Sold

b 47,500	

Rent Expense

f 1,500	

Interest Expense

h 7,000	

Salary Expense

j 9,000	

Advertising Expense

k 800	

Utilities Expense

k 650	

3, 4, and 5. Work sheet (see pages 154 and 155).

4. Adjusting Entries

The adjusting entries for the company at the end of 1984 are

l. Step 1 No entry has been made to record this $500 interest expense.

Step 2 The Interest Expense account should be increased by $500. An Accrued Interest Payable account should be used to show that interest has not been paid.

Step 3 The correct adjusting entry is a debit to Interest Expense and a credit to Accrued Interest Payable.

Interest Expense	500	
Accrued Interest Payable		500

m. Step 1 The advertising expense for 1984 has been recorded using the expense approach.

Step 2 The Advertising Expense account should have a year-end balance of $400 since only half the recorded amount applies to 1984. The other $400 is applicable to 1985 and should be shown in a Prepaid Advertising account, since this amount has already been paid.

Step 3 The correct adjusting entry is a credit to Advertising Expense (to decrease the recorded expense for 1984) and a debit to Prepaid Advertising.

Prepaid Advertising	400	
Advertising Expense		400

n. Step 1 The rent paid during 1984 for January 1985 has been recorded using the expense approach.

Step 2 The correct balance in the Rent Expense account for 1984 is $1,400, since $100 of the original amount does not apply to 1984. A Prepaid Rent account should be used to show that the rent has already been paid.

Step 3 The correct adjusting entry is a credit to Rent Expense (to decrease the recorded expense) and a debit to Prepaid Rent.

Prepaid Rent	100	
Rent Expense		100

o. Step 1 A utilities expense of $650 has been recorded on the company's books.

Step 2 The debit to Utilities Expense should have been for $800. An Accrued Utilities Payable account should be used to show that the company has a liability to pay an additional $150 utilities expense.

Step 3 The correct adjusting entry is a debit to Utilities Expense and a credit to Accrued Utilities Payable.

Utilities Expense	150	
Accrued Utilities Payable		150

p. Step 1 No entry has been made to record depreciation expense for 1984.

Step 2 Depreciation on furniture and fixtures at 20 percent per year and on the building at 10 percent per year must be recorded and the respective accumulated depreciation accounts increased. According to company policy, no depreciation is charged on acquisitions during the last 6 months of the year; therefore, no depreciation expense is required for the $9,200 of furniture purchased in November 1984.

Warren's Waterbeds

Work Sheet for the Year Ended December 31, 1984

	Trial Balance		Adjustments	
	Debits	Credits	Debits	Credits
Cash	24950			
Accounts Receivable	17900			
Inventory	30800			
Furniture and Fixtures	31200			
Accumulated Depreciation—Furniture and Fixtures		8800		(p) 4400
Building	65000			
Accumulated Depreciation—Building		13000		(p) 6500
Accounts Payable		1000		
Mortgage Payable		28000		
Capital Stock		84000		
Retained Earnings		16500		
Sales Revenue		85000		
Cost of Goods Sold	47500			
Rent Expense	1500			(n) 100
Interest Expense	7000		(l) 500	
Salary Expense	9000			
Advertising Expense	800			(m) 400
Utilities Expense	650		(o) 150	
Interest Payable				(l) 500
Prepaid Advertising			(m) 400	
Prepaid Rent			(n) 100	
Utilities Payable				(o) 150
Depreciation Expense			(p) 10900	
Totals	236300	236300	12050	12050
Net Income (to balance)				
Totals				

Adjustments Key:

l. Accrued Interest, $500

m. Prepaid Advertising, $400 ($800 ÷ 2)

n. Prepaid Rent, $100

o. Additional Utilities, $150 ($800 − $650)

$\int$ (A) × momentaum

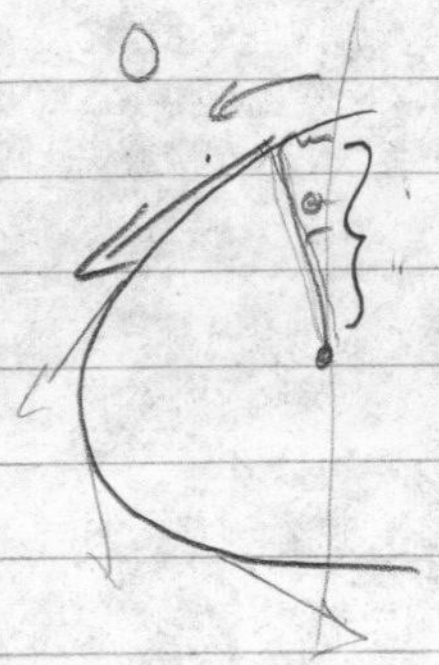

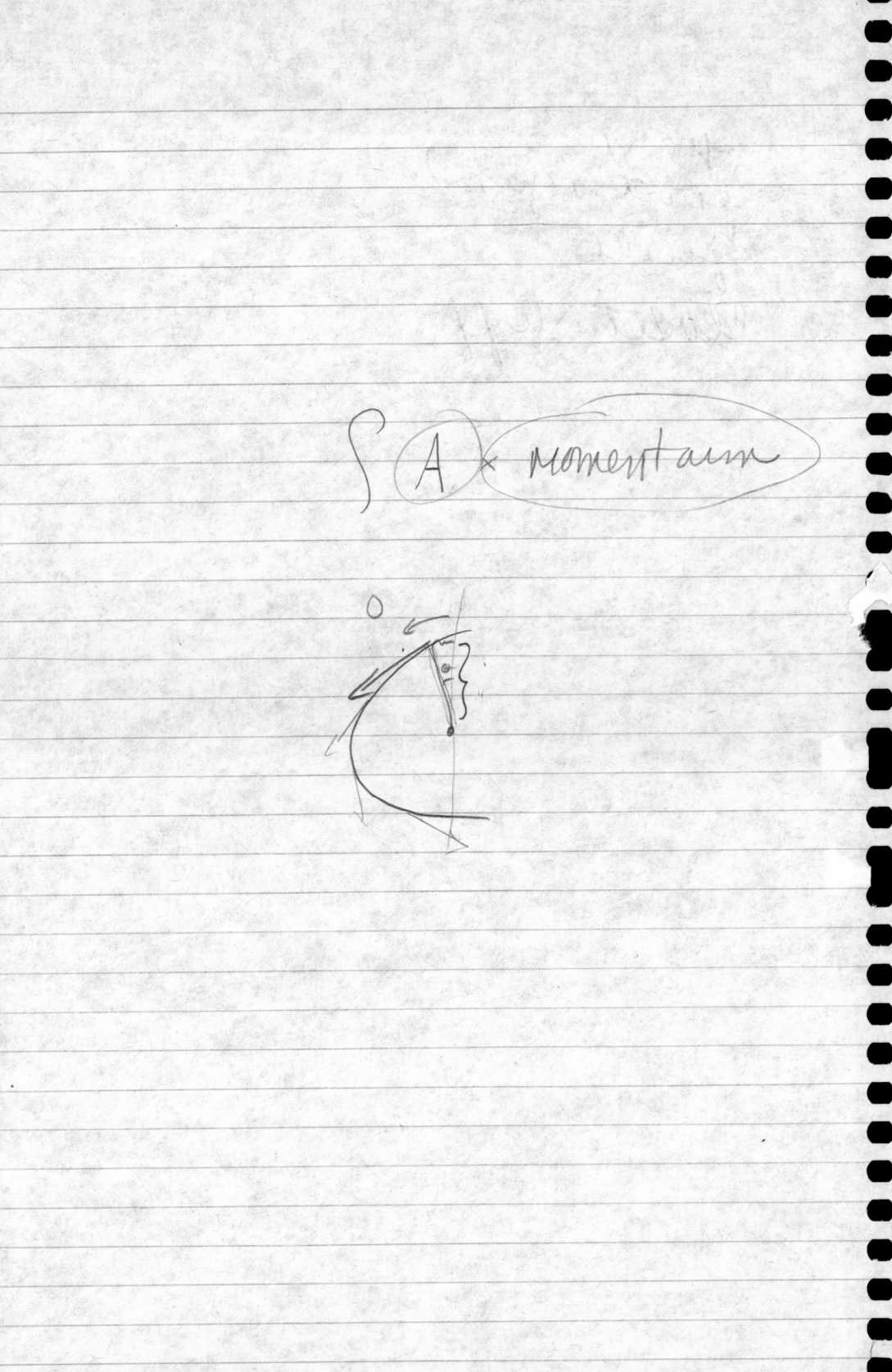

jeans
food (gum
quilt
closet stuff.

20: 6, 8, 10

1, 5, 10

Income Statement		Balance Sheet	
Debits	Credits	Debits	Credits
		24950	
		17900	
		30800	
		31200	
			13200
		65000	
			19500
			1000
			28000
			84000
			16500
	85000		
47500			
1400			
7500			
9000			
400			
800			
			500
		400	
		100	
			150
10900			
77500	85000	170350	162850
7500			7500
85000	85000	170350	170350

p. Depreciation for years, ($4,400 + $6,500)
-(Furniture and Fixtures = $22,000×.20=$4,400)
-(Building = $65,000×.10 = $6,500)

Step 3 The correct adjusting entry is a debit to Depreciation Expense and credits to Accumulated Depreciation–Furniture and Fixtures and Accumulated Depreciation–Building.

Depreciation Expense	10,900	
Accumulated Depreciation–Furniture and Fixtures		4,400[1]
Accumulated Depreciation–Building		6,500[2]

[1] $22,000 × 0.20 = $4,400

[2] $65,000 × 0.10 = $6,500

5. Income Statement and Balance Sheet

After entering the adjusting entries on the work sheet, transfer the income statement and balance sheet account balances to their respective columns on the work sheet. The income statement and balance sheet may be prepared directly from the work sheet.

Warren's Waterbeds
Income Statement
for the Year Ended December 31, 1984

Sales Revenue		$85,000
Less Cost of Goods Sold		47,500
Gross Margin		$37,500
Operating Expenses:		
Rent Expense	$ 1,400	
Interest Expense	7,500	
Salary Expense	9,000	
Advertising Expense	400	
Utilities Expense	800	
Depreciation Expense	10,900	
Total Operating Expenses		30,000
Net Income		$ 7,500

Warren's Waterbeds
Balance Sheet as of December 31, 1984

Assets

Current Assets:		
Cash	$24,950	
Accounts Receivable	17,900	
Inventory	30,800	
Prepaid Advertising	400	
Prepaid Rent	100	
Total Current Assets		$ 74,150
Long-Term Assets:		
Furniture and Fixtures	$31,200	
Less Accumulated Depreciation–Furniture and Fixtures	13,200	18,000
Building	$65,000	
Less Accumulated Depreciation–Building	19,500	45,500
Total Assets		$137,650

Liabilities and Stockholders' Equity

Current Liabilities:		
Accounts Payable	$ 1,000	
Accrued Interest Payable	500	
Accrued Utilities Payable	150	
Total Current Liabilities		$ 1,650
Long-Term Liabilities:		
Mortgage Payable		28,000
Total Liabilities		$ 29,650
Stockholders' Equity:		
Capital Stock	$84,000	
Retained Earnings*	24,000	
Total Stockholders' Equity		108,000
Total Liabilities and Stockholders' Equity		$137,650

* Note that in preparing the balance sheet, net income must be added to the beginning balance in Retained Earnings. If dividends had been declared, that amount would have been subtracted from Retained Earnings.

6. Posting Adjusting and Closing Entries

Journal entries for the adjustments have been given and explained under requirement 4. The next step is to post the adjusting entries to the General Ledger. (The entries labeled **q**, **r**, and **s** were posted from the closing entries made for requirement 7.)

Warren's Waterbeds
General Ledger
for the Year Ended December 31, 1984

Cash

Bal. . . 13,500	9,200 . . . c
b 22,100	17,000 . . . d
e 30,000	1,500 . . . f
g 62,000	15,000 . . . h
	49,500 . . . i
	9,000 . . . j
	1,450 . . . k
24,950	

Accounts Receivable

Bal. . . 17,000	62,000 . . . g
b 62,900	
17,900	

Inventory

Bal. . . 28,800	47,500 . . . b
a 49,500	
30,800	

Prepaid Advertising

m 400	

Prepaid Rent

n 100	

Furniture and Fixtures

Bal. . . 22,000	
c 9,200	
31,200	

Accumulated Depreciation—Furniture and Fixtures

	8,800 . . . Bal.
	4,400 . . . . p
	13,200

Building

Bal. . . 65,000	

Accumulated Depreciation—Building

	13,000 . . Bal.
	6,500 . . . p
	19,500

Accounts Payable

d 17,000	18,000 . . Bal.
i 49,500	49,500 . . . a
	1,000

Accrued Interest Payable

	500 l

Mortgage Payable

h 8,000	36,000 . . Bal.
	28,000

Accrued Utilities Payable

	150 . . . . . . o

Capital Stock

	54,000 . . Bal.
	30,000 . . . e
	84,000

Retained Earnings

	16,500 . . Bal.
	7,500 . . . s
	24,000

Sales Revenue

q 85,000	85,000 . . . b

Cost of Goods Sold

b 47,500	47,500 . . . r

Rent Expense

f 1,500	100 . . . . n
	1,400 . . . . r
1,500	1,500

Interest Expense

h 7,000	
l 500	
7,500	7,500 .... r

Salary Expense

j 9,000	9,000 .... r

Advertising Expense

k 800	400 ...... m
	400 ...... r
800	800

Utilities Expense

k 650	
o 150	
800	800 ...... r

Depreciation Expense

p 10,900	10,900 ... r

Income Summary

r 77,500	85,000 ... q
s 7,500	

7. Closing Entries

The next step is to journalize and post closing entries for all income statement accounts. Although it is optional, an Income Summary account will be used here.

The first entry is to close the only revenue account, Sales Revenue. Since Sales Revenue has a credit balance, it is debited.

q.	Sales Revenue	85,000	
	Income Summary		85,000

Next, we close out the expense accounts by crediting them.

r.	Income Summary	77,500	
	Cost of Goods Sold		47,500
	Rent Expense		1,400
	Interest Expense		7,500
	Salary Expense		9,000
	Advertising Expense		400
	Utilities Expense		800
	Depreciation Expense		10,900

The balance in the Income Summary account, the company's net income, is next transferred to Retained Earnings. When the company has earned a profit, the Income Summary account will have a credit balance. It is closed to a zero balance by being debited.

s.	Income Summary	7,500	
	Retained Earnings		7,500

These journal entries (**q**, **r**, and **s**) have already been posted to the ledger as shown under requirement 6.

8. Post-Closing Trial Balance

The final step in the accounting cycle is to prepare a post-closing trial balance. This procedure is a check on the accuracy of the closing process. It is a listing of all ledger account balances at year-end. Note that only real accounts appear because all nominal accounts have been closed to a zero balance in preparation for the next accounting cycle.

Warren's Waterbeds
Post-Closing Trial Balance
as of December 31, 1984

	Debits	Credits
Cash	$ 24,950	
Accounts Receivable	17,900	
Inventory	30,800	
Prepaid Advertising	400	
Prepaid Rent	100	
Furniture and Fixtures	31,200	
Accumulated Depreciation—Furniture and Fixtures		$ 13,200
Building	65,000	
Accumulated Depreciation—Building		19,500
Accounts Payable		1,000
Accrued Interest Payable		500
Utilities Payable		150
Mortgage Payable		28,000
Capital Stock		84,000
Retained Earnings		24,000
Totals	$170,350	$170,350

DISCUSSION QUESTIONS

1 What is the purpose of a work sheet?

2 Why is preparing a work sheet a useful but not a required step in the accounting cycle?

3 List in appropriate order the steps that are normally taken in preparing and completing a work sheet.

4 The first two columns in a work sheet are referred to as the unadjusted trial balance. What is meant by unadjusted? Explain.

5 Why are columns not included in a work sheet for the statement of changes in financial position?

6 What is the purpose of the work sheet adjustment columns?

7 When would adjusted trial balance columns be included in a work sheet? What is their purpose?

8 After making the adjustments and preparing an adjusted trial balance on a ten-column work sheet, the income statement and balance sheet columns are completed. Explain the procedure used when adjusted trial balance columns are not included on a work sheet.

9 When a work sheet is completed, each pair of columns should balance; that is, each pair should have equal total debits and total credits. Explain the balancing procedure for the financial statement columns.

10 Why are supplies not considered inventory? What type of account is Supplies? What type of account is Inventory?

11 In completing a work sheet, why does the adjustment for income taxes present a minor problem? How might this problem be solved?

12 Explain how a work sheet helps in preparing a company's end-of-year financial statements.

13 Which are prepared first, the year-end financial statements or the General Journal adjusting entries? Explain.

14 Distinguish between real and nominal accounts.

15 What purpose do closing entries serve?

16 Which types of accounts remain "open" after the closing process?

17 Why must nominal accounts be closed at the end of each accounting period?

18 What is the purpose of the Income Summary account? Is its use required? Explain.

19 How would a corporation's closing process differ from that of a proprietorship or partnership?

20 Why is interpretation of the information presented in the financial statements considered an important part of the accounting cycle?

EXERCISES

E5-1 Unadjusted Trial Balance

The following list of accounts was taken from the General Ledger of Pearl's Print Shop, as of December 31, 1984.

Cash	$34,200
Notes Receivable	24,000
Accounts Receivable	26,800
Office Supplies	3,500
Printing Supplies	4,000
Prepaid Rent	6,800
Printing Equipment	50,000
Accumulated Depreciation–Equipment	5,000
Accounts Payable	27,200
Notes Payable	24,400
Property Taxes Payable	4,800
Pearl Dawson, Capital	54,000
Pearl Dawson, Drawings	3,000
Printing Revenue	53,270
Salaries and Wages Expense	10,000
Depreciation Expense	5,000
Maintenance Expense	720
Heat, Light, and Power Expense	650

Prepare the unadjusted trial balance columns of a work sheet for Pearl's Print Shop.

E5-2 Partial Work Sheet

The adjusted trial balance at December 31, 1983, of Nunn Tool Company is presented below. Use the trial balance to prepare a partial work sheet. Place the accounts in the order they would normally appear on a balance sheet and on an income statement, beginning with Cash.

	Debits	Credits
Sales Revenue		$150,000
Cash	$ 34,500	
Accounts Payable		65,000
Salary Expense	30,000	
Cost of Goods Sold	99,000	
Equipment	30,000	
Accumulated Depreciation–Equipment		10,000
Prepaid Insurance	2,500	
Accounts Receivable	25,000	
C. C. Nunn, Capital		43,000
Salaries Payable		5,000
Rent Expense	12,000	
Ending Inventory	35,000	
Depreciation Expense	5,000	
Totals	$273,000	$273,000

E5-3 Preparation of Financial Statements from a Work Sheet

Use the work sheet from E5-2 to prepare an income statement for the year ended December 31, 1983, and a balance sheet at December 31, 1983. Ignore income taxes.

E5-4 Ten-Column Work Sheet

The following unadjusted trial balance is taken from the records of Marden Company.

Marden Company
Unadjusted Trial Balance
as of December 31, 1983

	Debits	Credits
Cash	$ 6,345	
Accounts Receivable	9,735	
Notes Receivable	7,200	
Office Supplies on Hand	480	
Land	11,100	
Notes Payable		$ 4,620
Capital Stock		22,500
Dividends	90	
Retained Earnings, December 31, 1982		6,030
Fees Earned		7,311
Rent Earned		429
Advertising Expense	438	
Office Expense	402	
Wages Expense	5,100	
Totals	$40,890	$40,890

Data for adjustments:

a. Earned fees not yet recorded, $222.
b. Interest on notes receivable not yet recorded, $72.
c. Liability for office expense, $90.
d. Interest on notes payable not yet recorded, $54.

Using a 10-column work sheet, make any necessary adjustments and extend the adjusted trial balance figures to the income statement and balance sheet columns.

E5-5 Reconstruction of a Work Sheet

Given below are the December 31, 1984, unadjusted and adjusted account balances taken from the work sheet of Long Company.

	Unadjusted Account Balances	Adjusted Account Balances
Cash	$ 5,600	$ 5,600
Accounts Receivable	8,460	8,460
Store Supplies	800	1,200
Prepaid Insurance	3,600	1,800
Prepaid Rent	$ -0-	$ 3,000
Equipment	86,000	86,000
Accumulated Depreciation–Equipment	8,600	17,200
Accounts Payable	16,000	16,000
Accrued Wages Payable	1,500	1,700
Accrued Interest Payable	250	100
Notes Payable	5,000	5,000
Capital Stock	30,000	30,000
Retained Earnings	10,100	10,100
Dividends	6,000	6,000
Service Fees Revenue	95,210	95,210
Wages Expense	42,700	42,900
Store Supplies Expense	4,000	3,600
Insurance Expense	-0-	1,800
Rent Expense	9,000	6,000
Depreciation Expense–Equipment	-0-	8,600
Interest Expense	500	350

Using the above data, prepare a partial work sheet with trial balance, adjustments, and adjusted trial balance columns.

E5-6 Work Sheet to Correct a Trial Balance

The following trial balance was prepared for Jex Company as of December 31, 1984.

Jex Company
Trial Balance
as of December 31, 1984

	Debits	Credits
Cash	$ 3,875	
Notes Receivable	5,600	
Accounts Receivable	14,610	
Inventory	28,500	
Prepaid Insurance	1,260	
Land	18,000	
Building	52,000	
Accumulated Depreciation–Building		$ 5,200
Equipment	6,400	
Accumulated Depreciation–Equipment		3,200
Accounts Payable		12,430
Notes Payable		8,740
Mortgage Payable		16,000
Capital Stock		35,000
Retained Earnings		10,820
Sales Revenue		217,850
Interest Revenue		560
Cost of Goods Sold	132,890	
Wages Expense	36,150	
Selling Expense	4,865	
Insurance Expense	2,420	
Supplies Expense	480	
Interest Expense	2,750	
Totals	$309,800	$309,800

Although the trial balance is in balance, a review and analysis of the accounts reveals the following.

a. Jex Company records Cost of Goods Sold and reduces Inventory each time a sale is made. On one sale the cost and inventory reduction entry was not made. The merchandise sold cost $2,250.

b. A payment on the mortgage of $2,000 was incorrectly recorded as a payment on the note.

c. A policy to provide fire insurance for the year 1985 was purchased at the end of December 1984, at a cost of $480. It was charged to Insurance Expense.

d. A note of $1,000 was collected in late 1984. The collection was incorrectly credited to Accounts Receivable.

e. Interest of $300 on a note was received in advance and recorded as Interest Revenue; the $300 was unearned at December 31, 1984.

f. Depreciation of $5,200 on the building and $1,280 on the equipment has not been recorded for 1984.

Given the information above, complete the following:

1. Prepare and complete a six-column work sheet with columns for the unadjusted trial balance, adjustments, and the adjusted trial balance.

2. Since both debits and credits total $309,800, why make any adjustments? Explain.

E5–7 Classifying Account Balances

For each of the following accounts, indicate whether it would be found in the income statement or the balance sheet columns of a company's work sheet.

1. Cash
2. Inventory
3. Salary Expense
4. Prepaid Salaries
5. Retained Earnings
6. Office Supplies Expense
7. Accounts Receivable
8. Cost of Goods Sold
9. Maintenance Expense
10. Interest Receivable
11. Capital Stock
12. Accounts Payable
13. Buildings
14. Accumulated Depreciation–Machinery
15. Interest Expense
16. Accounts Payable
17. Notes Receivable
18. Office Supplies on Hand
19. Sales Revenue
20. Insurance Expense
21. Machinery
22. Land
23. Salaries Payable
24. Prepaid Insurance
25. Notes Payable
26. Depreciation Expense
27. Accumulated Depreciation–Buildings

E5–8 Real and Nominal Accounts

Classify each of the following accounts as either a real account (R) or a nominal account (N).

1. Cash
2. Sales Revenue
3. Accounts Receivable
4. Cost of Goods Sold
5. Prepaid Insurance
6. Capital Stock
7. Retained Earnings
8. Insurance Expense
9. Salaries Payable
10. Depreciation Expense
11. Insurance Premiums Payable
12. Salary Expense
13. Accounts Payable
14. Prepaid Salaries
15. Utility Expense
16. Notes Payable
17. Inventory
18. Property Tax Expense
19. Rent Expense
20. Equipment
21. Interest Payable
22. Income Taxes Payable
23. Land
24. Buildings
25. Office Supplies on Hand
26. Income Tax Expense

E5–9 Closing Entries

Given below is the income statement for Margo Enterprises for the year ended June 30, 1984.

Margo Enterprises
Income Statement
for the Year Ended June 30, 1984

Sales Revenue	$187,000
Cost of Goods Sold	122,000
Gross Margin	$ 65,000
Selling and General Expenses	20,500
Income Before Taxes	$ 44,500
Income Taxes	17,800
Net Income	$ 26,700

1. Prepare a compound journal entry to close the accounts directly to Retained Earnings.

2. What problem may arise in closing the accounts if the information from the income statement is used?

E5–10 Closing Entries–Income Summary

Snow's Ski Shop reported the following revenue and expense items on its 1984 income statement. Prepare all necessary entries to close the account balances, using an Income Summary account.

Revenues:	
Ski Sales Revenue	$200,000
Accessory Sales Revenue	75,000
Total Revenues	$275,000
Expenses:	
Rent Expense	$ 24,000
Utilities Expense	9,500
Salaries Expense	58,000
Depreciation Expense	5,000
Property Tax Expense	2,000
Wax and Supplies Expense	800
Cost of Goods Sold	151,250
Total Expenses	$250,550

E5-11 Closing Entries

Income and expense accounts of Hair Supply Company for September 1983 are presented below. Prepare the entries required to close the income and expense accounts to the Retained Earnings account.

	DR	CR
Sales Revenue		$55,000
Cost of Goods Sold	$26,000	
Salary Expense	6,400	
Rent Expense	1,000	
Supplies Expense	200	
Depreciation Expense	1,400	
Interest Expense	800	

E5-12 Closing Entries—Income Summary

The balances in some of the accounts of Quality Foods, Inc. are given below. Make all necessary journal entries to close the accounts on December 31, 1984. Use an Income Summary account in the closing process.

Sales Revenue	$192,640
Cost of Goods Sold	115,584
Salary Expense	25,000
Interest Expense	2,200
Utility Expense	2,750
Insurance Expense	3,600
Miscellaneous Expenses	126
Office Supplies Expense	1,500

E5-13 Closing Entries—Proprietorship, Partnership, and Corporation

Gary Garbo & Company shows a credit balance in the Income Summary account of $20,510 after closing all revenue and expense items to this account. Give the remaining entries to close the books, assuming that:

1. The business is a proprietorship and that Gary Garbo has withdrawn $10,000 during the year; the amount is recorded in an account called Drawings.

2. The business is a partnership with two partners, Gary Garbo and Grace Garbo, who share profits equally. Gary has withdrawn $9,500 and Grace has withdrawn $8,000 during the year. These amounts are recorded in individual Drawings accounts.

3. The business is a corporation and the Dividends account shows that dividends of $16,000 have been paid during the year.

E5-14 Post-Closing Trial Balance

Before the final closing entries were made at December 31, 1983, a listing of account balances taken from the work sheet of B. A. Hill Enterprises showed the following.

Cash	$12,890
Accounts Receivable	28,240
Inventory	39,180
Prepaid Insurance	3,260
Land	18,000
Buildings	55,000
Accumulated Depreciation—Buildings	15,000
Machinery	14,000
Accumulated Depreciation—Machinery	5,600
Accounts Payable	14,320
Notes Payable	20,000
Salaries Payable	4,500
Taxes Payable	12,200
Unearned Rent	7,600
Mortgage Payable	45,000
B. A. Hill, Capital	50,000
B. A. Hill, Drawings	24,000
Income Summary (credit balance)	20,350

Prepare: (1) the closing entry or entries and (2) a post-closing trial balance.

E5-15 Completing a Work Sheet (with Retained Earnings Statement Columns)

The accountant for Justin, Inc. was in the process of completing a work sheet prior to preparing the company's 1984 end-of-year financial statements when he was unexpectedly called out of town. Part of the work sheet is given below. Complete the work sheet, assuming a 25 percent income tax rate.

	Adjustments		Income Statement	
	Debits	Credits	Debits	Credits
Subtotals	62,800	62,800	70,940	90,260

	Retained Earnings Statement		Balance Sheet	
	Debits	Credits	Debits	Credits
Subtotals	5,000	14,320	109,315	80,675

PROBLEMS

P5-1 Work Sheet and Financial Statements

The year-end trial balance of Karen's Calculators, Inc., is presented below.

Karen's Calculators, Inc.
Trial Balance
as of December 31, 1984

	Debits	Credits
Cash	$ 25,000	
Accounts Receivable	7,500	
Inventory	38,500	
Prepaid Insurance	500	
Prepaid Rent	1,100	
Equipment	26,000	
Accumulated Depreciation—Equipment		$ 8,000
Land	85,000	
Notes Payable		25,000
Accounts Payable		12,500
Salaries Payable		1,500
Capital Stock		50,000
Retained Earnings		61,600
Sales Revenue		320,000
Cost of Goods Sold	210,000	
Salary Expense	48,000	
Rent Expense	12,000	
Insurance Expense	3,000	
Property Tax Expense	2,500	
Office Supplies Expense	1,500	
Income Tax Expense	18,000	
Totals	$478,600	$478,600

Required:

1. Prepare a work sheet using the trial balance data. Assume that there are no adjusting entries.

2. Use the work sheet to prepare an income statement for the year ended December 31, 1984, and a balance sheet as of December 31, 1984.

3. **Interpretive Question** In what ways does a work sheet facilitate the preparation of financial statements?

P5-2 Work Sheet, Adjustments, and Financial Statements

An inexperienced bookkeeper for Brown Supply Company has prepared a list of account balances at the end of 1984. The following information is also provided for your use.

a. An insurance premium of $1,200 was paid on July 1, 1984, for the period July 1, 1984, to June 30, 1985.

b. No entry has been made to record the interest expense on a $5,000 note. The note was signed on October 1, 1984, and is due with interest at 12 percent ($150) on March 31, 1985.

c. The salaries earned by company personnel in December have not yet been recorded. These salaries, totaling $5,000, will be paid on January 5, 1985.

	Debits	Credits
Cash	$ 51,000	
Accounts Receivable	22,500	
Accounts Payable		$ 12,500
Inventory	63,250	
Salary Expense	50,000	
Depreciation Expense	2,500	
Sales Revenue		300,000
Cost of Goods Sold	150,000	
Office Supplies Expense	2,500	
Interest Expense	1,000	
Retained Earnings		36,450
Accrued Interest Payable		-0-
Accrued Salaries Payable		-0-
Insurance Expense	-0-	
Rent Expense	45,000	
Property Tax Expense	3,000	
Prepaid Insurance	1,200	
Accumulated Depreciation—Fixtures		12,500
Capital Stock		80,000
Rent Payable		500
Fixtures	55,000	
Notes Payable		5,000
Totals	$446,950	$446,950

Required:

1. Prepare an eight-column work sheet with properly ordered accounts. (Omit adjusted trial balance columns.)

2. Make any necessary adjusting entries.

3. Prepare a year-end income statement and balance sheet at December 31, 1984.

P5-3 Classification and Analysis of Accounts

For each of the following accounts, indicate: (1) whether it is a real or a nominal account, (2) whether it will appear on an income statement or a balance sheet, (3) whether it will be "closed" or remain "open" at the end of the accounting period, and (4) if closed, whether it is normally closed by a debit or a credit. Use the format below. (Two items have been completed as examples.)

Account Title	Real or Nominal	Income Statement or Balance Sheet	Closed or Open	Closed by Debit or Credit
Accounts Receivable	Real	B/S	Open	—
Advertising Expense	Nominal	I/S	Closed	Credit

1. Cash
2. Sales Revenue
3. Depreciation Expense
4. Office Supplies on Hand
5. Retained Earnings
6. Salaries Expense
7. Machinery
8. Income Taxes Payable
9. Accounts Payable
10. Interest Revenue
11. Prepaid Insurance
12. Accrued Salaries Payable
13. Dividends
14. Accumulated Depreciation—Machinery
15. Office Supplies Expense
16. Cost of Goods Sold
17. Dividends Payable
18. Inventory
19. Capital Stock
20. Income Tax Expense

P5-4 Closing Entries

Astro Company's trial balances as of August 31, 1984 and 1983 are shown below.

Astro Company
Trial Balances
as of August 31, 1984 and 1983

	1984		1983	
Cash	$33,400		$12,500	
Accounts Receivable	6,400		7,500	
Inventory	2,800		8,600	
Accounts Payable		$ 1,400		
Land			14,800	
Capital Stock		36,600		$36,600
Dividends			500	
Retained Earnings		6,800		-0-
Sales Revenue		22,000		34,000
Cost of Goods Sold	12,000		16,400	
Rent Expense	1,400		1,400	
Advertising Expense	800		500	
Salaries Expense	10,000		8,400	
Totals	$66,800	$66,800	$70,600	$70,600

Required:

1. Prepare journal entries to close the books as of August 31, 1983. Close nominal accounts directly to Retained Earnings.

2. In 1984, the company suffered a net loss, which reduced Retained Earnings accordingly. Prepare closing entries as of August 31, 1984. How much was the loss?

P5-5 Closing Entries and Accounting for Dividends

The income statement for Edwards Eraser Company for the year ended December 31, 1984, is as follows:

Edwards Eraser Company
Income Statement for the Year Ended December 31, 1984

Sales Revenue		$512,000
Less Cost of Goods Sold		363,000
Gross Margin		$149,000
Operating Expenses:		
Salary Expense	$72,000	
Interest Expense	5,250	
Office Supplies Expense	3,820	
Insurance Expense	4,930	
Property Tax Expense	11,200	
Total Operating Expenses		97,200
Net Income		$ 51,800

Dividends of $40,000 were declared by the board of directors on December 30, 1984.

Required:

1. Give the entries required on December 31, 1984, to properly close the income statement accounts using an Income Summary account.

2. Give the entry required to record the declaration of dividends by the board of directors.

P5-6 Closing Entries—Income Summary

Electronic Specialty Company's income statement is given below.

Electronic Specialty Company
Income Statement for the Year Ended December 31, 1984

Sales Revenue		$400,000
Less Cost of Goods Sold		250,000
Gross Margin		$150,000
Operating Expenses:		
Selling Expenses:		
Sales Salaries Expense	$25,000	
Sales Supplies Expense	500	
Depreciation Expense—Sales Vehicles	1,000	
Total Selling Expenses	$26,500	
General and Administrative Expenses:		
Officers' Salaries	$50,000	
Office Supplies Expense	1,000	
Postage Expense	50	
Total General and Administrative Expenses	$51,050	
Total Operating Expenses		77,550
Income from Operations		$ 72,450
Other Revenues and Expenses:		
Interest Revenue	$ 2,250	
Rent Revenue	3,000	
Total Other Revenues and Expenses		5,250
Income Before Taxes		$ 77,700
Income Taxes		23,310
Net Income		$ 54,390

Required:

1. Give the journal entries to close the revenue and expense accounts to an Income Summary account.
2. Give the entries required to close the Income Summary account to Retained Earnings.
3. **Interpretive Question** Some companies prepare a post-closing trial balance after the accounts have been closed at year-end. What are the advantages of doing this?

P5-7 Unifying Problem: Adjusting and Closing Entries

Two trial balances of Bailey Company as of December 31, 1983, are presented below. One is before adjustments and the other is after adjustments.

Bailey Company
Trial Balances as of December 31, 1983

	Unadjusted		Adjusted	
	DR	CR	DR	CR
Cash	$ 1,820		$ 1,820	
Supplies	585		600	
Prepaid Rent	1,350		745	
Prepaid Insurance	380		148	
Building	12,500		12,500	
Accumulated Depreciation—Building		$ 2,500		$ 2,500
Equipment	8,700		8,700	
Accumulated Depreciation—Equipment		3,000		3,000
Accrued Utilities Payable		750		865
Accrued Salaries Payable		-0-		250
Accrued Taxes Payable		-0-		148
Capital Stock		16,245		16,245
Service Fees Earned		11,750		11,750
Salaries Expense	2,750		3,000	
Rent Expense	-0-		605	
Supplies Expense	1,880		1,865	
Depreciation Expense—Equipment	1,000		1,000	
Depreciation Expense—Building	1,250		1,250	
Utilities Expense	470		585	
Taxes Expense	1,000		1,148	
Insurance Expense	-0-		232	
Miscellaneous Expenses	560		560	
Totals	$34,245	$34,245	$34,758	$34,758

Required:

1. Prepare the entries that were required to adjust the accounts at December 31, 1983.
2. Prepare the journal entries that are required to close the accounts at December 31, 1983.

P5-8 Comprehensive Work Sheet—Corporation

Account balances taken from the General Ledger of Stacey Supply Company on December 31, 1983, follow.

Cash	$ 10,030
Accounts Receivable	33,600
Inventory, January 1, 1983	30,400
Land	28,700
Buildings	34,000
Accumulated Depreciation—Buildings	9,800
Accounts Payable	18,000
Notes Payable—Short-Term	12,000
Mortgage Payable	26,000
Capital Stock	50,000
Retained Earnings, January 1, 1983	6,470
Dividends	6,000
Sales Revenue	124,000
Selling Expense	21,220
Purchases	67,260
Insurance Expense	1,140
Supplies Expense	1,750
Property Tax Expense	3,320
Office Expense	8,100
Interest Revenue	480
Interest Expense	1,230

Adjustments required on December 31, 1983, are:

a. Inventory, December 31, 1983, $34,760.
b. Accrued wages payable, $2,500.
c. Buildings are depreciated at the rate of 5 percent a year.
d. Supplies on hand total $350.
e. Accrued property taxes are $150.
f. Accrued selling expenses are $1,640.
g. Prepaid insurance to be deferred to future years is $470.
h. Accrued interest on the mortgage is $1,820.
i. The company estimates that income taxes will be 40 percent of income before taxes.

Required:

1. Prepare an eight-column work sheet.
2. Prepare adjusting and closing entries.
3. Prepare a post-closing trial balance.

P5-9 Comprehensive Work Sheet—Proprietorship

The following account balances were taken from the General Ledger of Jan Jones, a proprietorship, at the end of the first year of business operations. The proprietorship has a fiscal year ending September 30, 1984.

Cash	$12,250
Notes Receivable	3,000
Accounts Receivable	5,300
Store Supplies	500
Furniture and Fixtures	4,200
Accumulated Depreciation–Furniture and Fixtures	-0-
Accounts Payable	6,600
Notes Payable	5,000
Jan Jones, Capital	19,300
Jan Jones, Drawings	3,000
Sales Revenue	95,000
Interest Revenue	200
Purchases	78,000
Sales Salaries Expense	7,500
General Expenses	10,900
Property Tax Expense	750
Interest Expense	700

Data for adjustments to be made at year-end are:

a. Inventory at September 30, 1984, $20,100.

b. Store supplies on hand, $310.

c. Furniture and fixtures depreciate at 10 percent a year. Furniture was purchased April 1, 1984, at a cost of $1,000, increasing the account total to $4,200. (Assume that depreciation is $370 per month.)

d. Accrued advertising, $105.

e. Property taxes paid in advance, $300.

f. Accrued interest on notes payable, $145.

g. Accrued interest on notes receivable, $212.

h. Ignore income taxes.

Required:

1. Prepare an eight-column work sheet.
2. Prepare adjusting and closing entries.

P5-10 Unifying Problem: The Accounting Cycle

The post-closing trial balance of Segal Company at December 31, 1983, is presented below.

Segal Company
Post-Closing Trial Balance
at December 31, 1983

	Debits	Credits
Cash	$ 15,000	
Accounts Receivable	20,000	
Inventory	30,000	
Land	25,000	
Buildings	75,000	
Accumulated Depreciation–Buildings		$ 10,000
Equipment	50,000	
Accumulated Depreciation–Equipment		15,000
Accounts Payable		25,000
Notes Payable		35,000
Capital Stock		100,000
Retained Earnings		30,000
Totals	$215,000	$215,000

During 1984, Segal Company had the following transactions.

a. Inventory purchases were $80,000, all on credit (debit Inventory).

b. An additional $10,000 of capital stock was issued.

c. Merchandise that cost $100,000 was sold for $180,000. Of the $180,000, $100,000 were credit sales; the balance were cash sales.

d. The notes were paid, including $7,000 interest.

e. $105,000 was collected from customers.

f. $95,000 was paid to reduce accounts payable.

g. Salary expenses were $30,000, all paid in cash.

h. A $10,000 cash dividend was declared and paid (use a Dividends account).

i. Depreciation expense for the year was: Buildings, $5,000; Equipment, $10,000.

Required:

1. Prepare journal entries to record each of the 1984 transactions.
2. Set up T-accounts with the proper balances at January 1, 1984, and post the journal entries to the T-accounts.
3. Prepare a work sheet beginning with a trial balance as of December 31, 1984. Assume no adjusting entries.
4. Using your work sheet, prepare an income statement for the year ended December 31, 1984, and a balance sheet as of that date.
5. Prepare the entries necessary to close the nominal and Dividend accounts.
6. Post the closing entries to the ledger accounts and prepare a post-closing trial balance at 12/31/84.

P5-11 Unifying Problem: Trial Balance, Financial Statements, Closing Entries, Post-Closing Trial Balance

The following account balances were taken from the General Ledger of Central Sales, Inc., at December 31, 1983, before closing the books.

Cash	$14,500
Supplies	4,250
Prepaid Insurance	3,750
Prepaid Rent	3,400
Equipment	30,000
Accumulated Depreciation–Equipment	6,000
Note Payable–Long-Term	15,500
Capital Stock	12,500
Retained Earnings	4,640
Dividends	2,500
Service Revenue	27,500
Concession Revenue	3,250
Salaries Expense	7,250
Repair Expense	1,600
Heat and Light Expense	1,450
Telephone Expense	180
Miscellaneous Expenses	510

Additional Data:

a. A physical count and pricing of supplies showed $325 on hand.

b. The Prepaid Insurance account is for a 2-year insurance policy premium. The policy covers 1983 and 1984, and became effective January 1, 1983.

c. Rent expense for 1983 is $2,400.

d. Equipment of $30,000 is to be depreciated at the rate of 20 percent a year.

e. Employee salaries that were earned but unpaid at December 31 were $350.

Required:

1. Enter the account balances in the trial balance columns of an eight-column work sheet.
2. Record work sheet adjustments from the additional data (ignore income taxes).
3. Complete the work sheet.
4. Prepare an income statement from the work sheet.
5. Prepare a balance sheet from the work sheet.
6. Make the closing entries. Use an Income Summary account.
7. Prepare a post-closing trial balance.

P5-12 Unifying Problem: Analysis and Correction of Errors

At the end of November 1984, the General Ledger of Poole Supply Company showed the following amounts.

Assets	$64,250
Liabilities	28,800
Owners' Equity	62,000

The company's bookkeeper is new on the job and does not have a lot of accounting experience. Because he has made numerous errors, total assets do not equal liabilities plus owners' equity. The following is a list of errors made.

a. Inventory that cost $21,000 was sold, but the entry to record cost of goods sold was not made.

b. Credit sales of $12,100 were posted to the General Ledger as $21,100. The accounts receivable were posted correctly.

c. $12,500 of inventory was purchased on account and received before the end of November, but no entry to record the purchase was made until December.

d. November salaries payable of $2,500 were not recorded until paid in December.

e. Common stock was issued for $18,500 and credited to Accounts Payable.

f. Inventory purchased for $31,050 was incorrectly posted to the asset account as $13,500. No error was made in the liability account.

Required:

Determine the correct balances of assets, liabilities, and owners' equity.

SUPPLEMENT

Disposal of Amounts from Adjusting Entries

Adjusting entries at the end of an accounting period affect both the income statement and the balance sheet. All income statement accounts are reduced to a zero balance through the closing process. However, the balance sheet accounts are not closed. So what happens to the adjustment amounts posted to balance sheet accounts? When and how are these amounts cleared from the accounts? This Supplement is intended to answer these questions, and to explain where reversing entries, which are sometimes considered a part of the accounting cycle, fit in.

Accounting for Adjustments to Balance Sheet Items

Any one of four methods can be used to account for the year-end adjustments to balance sheet accounts. First, leave the amount as it is; do nothing. The amount remains in the account as a "permanent" adjustment. Second, remove the amount as part of a "split" entry in the ensuing accounting period. Third, readjust to a new balance as part of the adjusting entry process at the *end* of the next accounting period. Fourth, readjust at the *beginning* of the next accounting period by reversing the adjusting entry made. Examples of each of the four methods follow. All four methods accomplish the same thing, but each has advantages that recommend it in certain situations.

LEAVE AS IS

Assume that the following salary arrangement was made by Jerry's Garage with an employee, Dan Jones. Dan is to receive $2,000 on the fifteenth of each month for work performed during the month-long period ending on that day. Jerry's Garage closes its books on December 31 each year. The normal journal entry to record Dan's last salary payment for 1983 (ignoring payroll taxes) would be as shown on the next page.

December 15	Salary Expense	2,000	
	Cash		2,000
	Paid monthly salary to Dan Jones for the period ending December 15, 1983.		

At the end of December, an adjusting entry would be needed to record the actual salary expense for the period and to accrue the liability as of December 31. The adjusting entry would be

December 31	Salary Expense	1,000	
	Accrued Salaries Payable		1,000
	To record the accrual of salaries payable to Dan Jones for one-half month.		

At the end of 1983, the Salary Expense account would be closed. On January 15, 1984, when the regular payroll is paid, the entry would be the same as that made on December 15, 1983: a debit to Salary Expense and a credit to Cash for $2,000. This same entry would be made for each month of the year, resulting in a Salary Expense account balance of $24,000, the correct amount.

As of December 31, 1984, the liability account, Accrued Salaries Payable, is also correctly stated as $1,000—the amount accrued at December 31, 1983, and left in the account throughout 1984. Furthermore, as long as Dan Jones' salary arrangement and pay period remain unchanged, the accounts will be properly maintained by recording the monthly salary expense when cash is paid on the fifteenth of each month.

Some of the most common adjusting entries that use this method are for the depreciation of tangible operational assets (machinery, for example), the write-off of intangible operational assets (a patent, for example), and bond interest accrual on long-term bonds in instances where the interest period and accounting period do not coincide. Adjustments for these types of transactions are covered in later chapters. It is sufficient at this point for you to understand that for some types of adjusting entries, balance sheet amounts may not require readjustment until years later, if at all.

SPLIT ENTRY

Again take the example of Dan Jones and Jerry's Garage. In using the split-entry approach, the adjusting entry on December 31 would be unchanged. When payment to Dan is made on January 15, 1984, however, the entry would be

Salary Expense	1,000	
Accrued Salaries Payable	1,000	
Cash		2,000
Paid monthly salary to Dan Jones for the period ending January 15, 1984; a portion of the salary expense was previously recorded.		

This entry splits the payment into two parts—one part to account for the expense for the 15-day period since December 31, and the other to pay the accrual for the last half of December.

READJUST AT THE END OF THE NEXT YEAR

We have explained that with the "leave as is" method, $1,000 remains in the Jerry's Garage account called Accrued Salaries Payable and is correctly stated at the end of the following year. Since salary expense is also correctly stated, no adjusting entry is required. However, some accounts need readjustment at the end of the next year, particularly those in which the adjustments vary in amount from year to year. One such account is office supplies.

Assume that office supplies of $940 were on hand at the end of 1983, but that the Supplies on Hand account showed a balance before adjustment of $480. A total of $1,290 was spent for supplies during 1983 and $1,430 during 1984, all charged to Supplies Expense, an income statement account. Furthermore, after a physical count and pricing, Supplies on Hand is determined to be $750 at the end of 1984. Entries based upon these assumptions and T-accounts reflecting the effect of these entries on the two companion accounts would be

1983	Supplies Expense	1,290	
	Cash		1,290
	Purchased office supplies, 1983.		
December 31	Supplies on Hand	460	
	Supplies Expense		460
	To adjust office supplies to the balance remaining at December 31, 1983 ($940 − $480).		
December 31	Income Summary	830	
	Supplies Expense		830
	To close Supplies Expense to Income Summary ($1,290 − $460).		
1984	Supplies Expense	1,430	
	Cash		1,430
	Purchased office supplies, 1984.		
December 31	Supplies Expense	190	
	Supplies on Hand		190
	To adjust office supplies to balance remaining at December 31, 1984 ($940 − $750).		
December 31	Income Summary	1,620	
	Supplies Expense		1,620
	To close Supplies Expense to Income Summary ($1,430 + $190).		

Office Supplies on Hand

Debit	Credit
Balance (12/30/83) 480	
Adjusting Entry (12/31/83) 460	
Balance (12/31/83) 940	Adjusting Entry 190 .... (12/31/84)
Balance (12/31/84) 750	

Office Supplies Expense

Debit	Credit
Purchases (1983) 1,290	Adjusting Entry 460 .... (12/31/83)
	830 .... To close (12/31/83)
Balance (12/31/83) 0	
Purchases (1984) 1,430	
Adjusting Entry (12/31/84) 190	
	1,620 .... To close (12/31/84)
Balance (12/31/84) 0	

REVERSING ENTRIES (READJUSTMENT AT THE BEGINNING OF THE NEXT YEAR)

reversing entry *a journal entry made at the beginning of a year that exactly reverses an adjusting entry made at the end of the previous year*

A reversing entry is a journal entry made at the beginning of a year that exactly reverses an adjusting entry made at the end of the previous year. Reversing entries are never required; they are always optional. In some instances, they facilitate the recording of expenses and revenues with routine entries. Thus, they may reduce the need for account analysis to determine how much of a payment is expense, how much is settlement of a liability, and how much is revenue or asset collection.

To illustrate reversing entries, we will again assume that Dan Jones receives a $2,000 salary payment on the fifteenth of each month. As previously shown, the monthly salary entry for December and the adjusting and closing entries at December 31, 1983, would be

December 15	Salary Expense	2,000	
	Cash		2,000
	Paid monthly salary to Dan Jones for the period ending December 15, 1983.		
December 31	Salary Expense	1,000	
	Accrued Salaries Payable		1,000
	To record the accrual of salaries payable for Dan Jones for one-half month.		
December 31	Income Summary	24,000	
	Salary Expense		24,000
	To close Salary Expense to Income Summary (assuming $2,000 a month × 12).		

The following reversing entry could be made as of January 1, 1984, after Salary Expense has been closed:

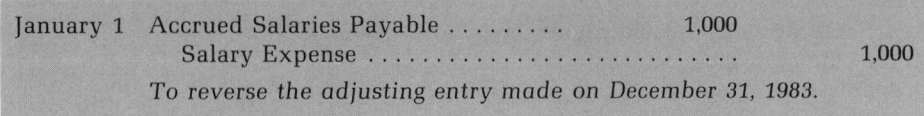

January 1	Accrued Salaries Payable	1,000	
	Salary Expense		1,000
	To reverse the adjusting entry made on December 31, 1983.		

Note the effect on the companion accounts from these entries. The balance sheet account, Accrued Salaries Payable, set up to show the liability as of December 31, 1983, has now been canceled. The Salary Expense account shows a credit balance of $1,000. This amount will be deducted from the 12 monthly payments of $2,000. The addition of the $1,000 accrual at December 31, 1984, will then result in the correct amount in the Salary Expense account for 1984 [(12 × $2,000) − $1,000 + $1,000 = $24,000]. Here are the T-accounts for 1983, with reversing entries shown.

Salary Expense

Debit	Credit
Payments (Jan.–Nov. 1983) 22,000	Reversing Entry (1/1/83, from previous period) 1,000 . . . .
Payment (12/15/83) . . . 2,000	
Adjusting Entry (12/31/83) 1,000	
	Closing Entry 24,000 . . . . (12/31/83)
Balance (12/31/83) 0	Reversing Entry 1,000 . . . . (1/1/84)

Accrued Salaries Payable

Debit	Credit
	Adjusting Entry 1,000 . . . . (12/31/83)
	1,000 . . . . . Balance (12/31/83)
1,000	
	0 . . . . . . Balance (1/1/84)

Reversing entries are appropriate for transactions that involve unrecorded revenues, unrecorded expenses (such as our example), unearned revenues that are originally credited to a revenue account, and prepaid expenses that are originally debited to an expense account. Stated more simply, as a general guideline, if an adjusting entry increases a balance sheet account, then a reversing entry may be made. (In our example, note that the adjusting entry on December 31, 1983, increased Accrued Salaries Payable.) If a reversing entry is not used, the adjusting entry must be accounted for by one of the other methods described in this Supplement.

DISCUSSION QUESTIONS AND EXERCISES

Discussion Questions

21 Once year-end adjustments are made and financial statements are prepared, what accounting methods are available for removing: (1) the adjustments to income statement accounts? (2) the adjustments to balance sheet accounts?

22 Since reversing entries are optional, when and why would the reversing entry method be used?

23 Give the reasoning that underlies the "general guideline" for possible use of the reversing entry method.

Exercises

E5-16 Adjusting and Reversing Entries

Paul's Publishing Company, in preparation for issuing its annual report for fiscal year 1983, obtained the data listed below. Paul's does not reverse adjusting entries and records current transactions in income statement accounts. The company's fiscal year ends September 30.

a. The Unearned Subscriptions Revenue account has an unadjusted balance of $18,750 at September 30, 1983. An analysis of collections received is as follows:

Date Received	Amount Received	Term of Subscription
July 1, 1982	$12,000	2 years
Sept. 1, 1982	9,000	1 year
Mar. 1, 1983	18,000	2 years
July 1, 1983	15,000	1 year

b. At September 30, 1983, the Prepaid Insurance account showed a balance of $5,000. Paul's has the following policies in force.

Policy	Date	Term	Cost	Coverage
A	1/1/81	3 years	$7,200	Building
B	2/1/81	2 years	3,000	Printing equipment
C	4/1/83	1 year	2,400	Autos and trucks

c. The balance in the Salaries Payable account is $9,500. Paul's Publishing Company pays its employees on the 5th and 20th of each month, based on salaries and wages earned through the 15th and last day of each month. Accrued salaries and wages since September 15 total $6,750.

d. Interest Payable has a balance of $400. Paul's owes two notes as follows:

	Unrecorded Interest
12%, 60-day note for $10,000 dated August 16 . . .	$150
15%, 90-day note for $24,000 dated September 10	200
	$350

e. A physical count and pricing of supplies on hand reveals a total of $490. The Supplies account shows a balance of $940.

Given the above, complete the following:

1. Prepare adjusting entries as required.
2. Indicate which of the five adjusting entries, if any, could be reversed (following the general guidelines for reversing entries).

E5-17 Adjusting, Reversing, and Split Entries

The trial balance of Cox Company shows the following balances, among others, on December 31, 1983, the end of its first fiscal year.

Buildings	$170,000
Accumulated Depreciation—Buildings	-0-
Rent Revenue	36,800
Office Supplies Expense	2,700
12% First-Mortgage Bonds Payable	130,000

Inspection of the company's records reveals that:

a. Rent revenue of $2,800 is unearned at December 31, 1983.

b. Interest of $7,800 on the first-mortgage bonds is payable semiannually on March 1 and September 1.

c. Buildings are depreciated at 6 percent a year; however, included in the Buildings account are new acquisitions of $30,000 made during the year. The company follows a practice of taking depreciation on acquisitions during the year at one-half the annual rate.

d. Office supplies of $500 are on hand on December 31. When purchases of office supplies were made during the year, they were charged to the Office Supplies Expense account.

Given the information above, complete the following:

1. Prepare journal entries to adjust the books as of December 31, 1983.
2. Give the reversing entries that may be appropriately made at the beginning of 1984.

3. Assume that reversing entries are not made and that split entries are made in 1984.

   (a) Give the entry to record the interest payment on the first-mortgage bonds on March 1, 1984.

   (b) Which of the remaining adjusting entries could use the split-entry approach? Comment.

4. Assuming that the first-mortgage bonds are to be paid at the end of ten years, which of the adjusting entries made in part (1) could be "left as is"? Explain.

SUPPLEMENT
(Chapters 1–5)

A Case Study

In the first five chapters of the text, we have laid a foundation for the study of accounting. The purpose of this Supplement is to help you solidify your understanding of the basic accounting cycle by providing a case study of the recording process. The three major types of businesses are highlighted: the company depicted here begins as a proprietorship, changes to a partnership, and finally becomes a corporation.

As you follow the evolution of a small business through the proprietorship, partnership, and corporate stages, you should be able to recognize the accounting similarities and differences. The main differences arise in accounting for the equity of the owners (proprietors, partners, or stockholders).

Obviously, our example has to be a simple one, with many details summarized or omitted. Taxes, for example, are introduced in simplified form. In brief, a corporation pays taxes on its profits, whereas a proprietorship and a partnership do not. The profits of a proprietorship and a partnership are taxed as income to the owners and not as income of the business entity.

In the "real world," as opposed to our simplified case study, transactions are more numerous and complex, and, for a large business, require an automated accounting system that includes high-speed data processing equipment, specialized journals, and a well-designed internal control system. Nonetheless, the basic steps in the accounting cycle and the essential record-keeping procedures will be similar to those illustrated, and need only be adapted to specific business environments.

The setting for the case study is a relatively small university town of 70,000 people, 20,000 of whom are students. Other than the university, the local economy in Mountain View is supported by small industry, tourism (there are excellent facilities in the area for skiing in the winter and for a variety of recreational activities in the summer), and a fairly large steel plant located nearby.

Dixon Able was a junior in college, majoring in business management. An enterprising young man with a desire to run his own business, Dixon observed a need for "homelike" housing for parents who came to Mountain View to bring entering students to the university, for friends and relatives who wanted to visit students enrolled in the university, and for some of the students themselves. There also appeared to be a market among vacationers for this type of housing.

In checking with professors, other students, and his father (who is in the real estate and home construction business), and after conducting a market survey, Dixon decided that a one-bedroom unit with a small living room, a dining room–kitchen combination, and a bath would be most popular (see layout in Exhibit 5A–1). There also appeared to be some demand for two- and three-bedroom units. The construction costs for a 20-foot by 20-foot one-bedroom unit ran between $35 and $40 per square foot. Common walls for multiple units kept those costs to a minimum. Land costs near the university were high, but this area was considered most desirable because of the favorable location.

EXHIBIT 5A–1 **Layout for One-Bedroom Apartment**

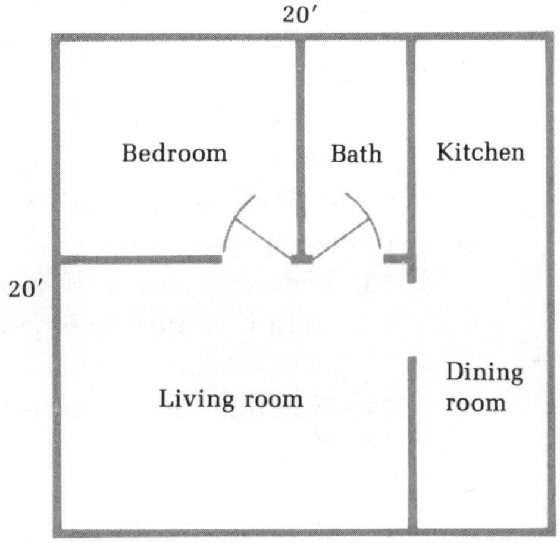

On the basis of the information above, and with the encouragement of his father, Dixon decided to start his business with a four-unit complex (three one-bedroom units and a two-bedroom unit). He began business July 1, 1983. During the first six months, Dixon had the following transactions.

1. Invested $8,000 of personal savings in the business.
2. Borrowed $15,000 from his father, Charles Able, on a 2-year note at 12 percent interest.
3. On July 1, purchased a lot near the university for $9,500 down and a 10-year contract for the $30,000 balance of the purchase price. The interest rate was 14 percent. Payments are made semiannually.
4. Constructed a building containing 2,000 square feet at a cost of $36.25 per square foot. Landscaping and other exterior building improvements cost an additional $7,300. The construction and landscaping were financed by a loan dated July 1, 1983, from First National Bank on a 20-year

mortgage at 15 percent interest, with semiannual payments. Dixon's father cosigned the mortgage; no down-payment was required.

5. Purchased furnishings for the rental units at a cost of $5,300. Paid half in cash on July 1, with the balance due in 60 days at no interest.
6. Paid advertising and promotion expenses of $475.
7. Paid two friends a total of $840 for helping with the clean-up work.
8. Paid $1,205 for utility hook-ups and nonrefundable deposits.
9. Withdrew $500 from the business for school-related expenses.
10. Paid accounts payable on furnishings, $2,650.

The demand for Dixon's "home-style" rental units was impressive. During the first few months the units were available, the occupancy rate increased from 60 percent to 90 percent. Dixon rented the one-bedroom units for $55 a day, or $350 a week, and the two-bedroom unit for $75 a day, or $500 a week. Additional transactions for the remainder of this 6-month period were

11. Received cash revenues of $8,400. The balance of the $24,920 total revenues were credit card sales. Of the $16,520 total receivables, three-fourths had been remitted by year-end, less the 3 percent service charge retained by the credit card companies.
12. Paid an average of $325 per month for utilities. Maintenance costs were $460 for 3 months. Advertising amounted to $900. (Accrual accounting is assumed.)
13. Recorded one-half year's depreciation on the building, furnishings, and building improvements in the amounts of $1,813, $265, and $182, respectively.
14. Paid 6 months' interest of $8,985 on notes ($900 + $2,100 + $5,985 = $8,985 interest expense).
15. Made semiannual principal payments of $1,500 on the land note and $1,995 on the building note.
16. Withdrew $1,000 for additional school expenses. Any remaining profits were closed to Dixon's Proprietor's Capital account.

Dixon's accounting records consisted of a General Journal and a General Ledger. Anxious to know the results of his first 6 months in business, Dixon journalized the above transactions; posted them to the ledger accounts; and prepared a trial balance, an income statement, and a balance sheet (see Exhibits 5A–2 through 5A–6).

As you review Dixon's records, remember that for a proprietor the owner's equity account is simply Dixon Able, Capital. This account shows the amount remaining after all liabilities (creditor claims) are subtracted from the assets. It represents the original investment of the proprietor less any withdrawals plus any additions to capital from further investments and from earnings of the business. Also note the cross-referencing between the ledger accounts and the journal. The Post Reference column is designed for this purpose. Note also that all figures have been rounded to the nearest dollar. Finally, observe that instead of using dates, the transactions are identified by the numbers in parentheses—for example, transactions (1), (2), and so forth.

EXHIBIT 5A-2 General Journal—Dixon Able, Proprietor

Page 1

Date	Account Titles and Explanation	Post Ref.	Debits	Credits
(1)	Cash	100	8000	
	Dixon Able, Capital	220		8000
	Invested $8,000 in company.			
(2)	Cash	100	15000	
	Notes Payable	211		15000
	Issued note to Charles Able			
	(terms: 2 years, 12 %).			
(3)	Land	112	39500	
	Cash	100		9500
	Notes Payable	211		30000
	Purchased land for $9,500 cash			
	and issued note of $30,000			
	(terms: 10 years, 14 %).			
(4)	Building	113	72500	
	Building Improvements	114	7300	
	Notes Payable	211		79800
	Constructed building financed			
	by 20-year note at 15%.			
(5)	Furnishings	115	5300	
	Cash	100		2650
	Accounts Payable	200		2650
	Purchased furnishings, ½ down			
	and balance in 60 days at			
	no interest.			
(6)	Advertising Expense	501	475	
	Cash	100		475
	Paid advertising and promotion			
	expenses.			
(7)	Cleaning Expense	502	840	
	Cash	100		840
	Paid clean-up expenses.			

(continued on the next page)

Page 2

Date	Account Titles and Explanation	Post Ref.	Debits	Credits
(8)	Utility Expense	503	1205	
	Cash	100		1205
	Paid utility hook-up charge.			
(9)	Dixon Able, Drawings	220	500	
	Cash	100		500
	Withdrew cash from the business.			
(10)	Accounts Payable	200	2650	
	Cash	100		2650
	Paid accounts payable on furnishings.			
(11)	Cash	100	8400	
	Accounts Receivable	101	16520	
	Revenues	401		24920
	Received service revenues earned.			
	Cash	100	12018	
	Financing Expense	504	372	
	Accounts Receivable	101		12390
	Collected accounts receivable, less finance expense ($16,520 × 3/4 = $12,390 × 3% = $371.70).			
(12)	Utility Expense	503	975	
	Cash	100		975
	Paid utilities expense for 3 months ($325 × 3 = $975)			
	Maintenance Expense	505	460	
	Cash	100		460
	Paid for maintenance for 3 months.			
	Advertising Expense	501	900	
	Cash	100		900
	Paid advertising expenses.			

Page 3

Date	Account Titles and Explanation	Post Ref.	Debits	Credits
(13)	Depreciation Expense	506	2260	
	Accumulated Depreciation-Building	113A		1813
	Accumulated Depreciation-Improvements	114A		182
	Accumulated Depreciation-Furnishings	115A		265
	To record depreciation for 6 months.			
(14)	Interest Expense	507	8985	
	Cash	100		8985
	Paid 6 months' interest on notes.			
(15)	Notes Payable	211	3495	
	Cash	100		3495
	Paid principal on notes ($1,500 on land note and $1,975 on building note).			
(16)	Dixon Able, Drawings	220A	1000	
	Cash	100		1000
	Withdrew cash from the business			
	Revenues	401	24920	
	Income Summary	305		24920
	To close Revenues to Income Summary.			
	Income Summary	305	16472	
	Advertising Expense	501		1375
	Cleaning Expense	502		840
	Utility Expense	503		2180
	Financing Expense	504		372
	Maintenance Expense	505		460
	Depreciation Expense	506		2260
	Interest Expense	507		8985
	To close expense accounts to Income Summary.			

(continued on the next page)

Page 4

Date	Account Titles and Explanation	Post Ref.	Debits	Credits
	Income Summary	305	8498	
	Dixon Able, Capital	220		8448
	To close Income Summary to Dixon Able, Capital.			
	Dixon Able, Capital	220	1500	
	Dixon Able, Drawings	220A		1500
	To close Drawings to Dixon Able, Capital.			

EXHIBIT 5A-3 General Ledger—Dixon Able, Proprietor

Cash — Account No. 100

Date	Explanation	Post Ref.	Debits	Credits	Balance
	Beginning Balance				-0-
(1)		GJ1	8000		8000
(2)		GJ1	15000		23000
(3)		GJ1		9500	13500
(5)		GJ1		2650	10850
(6)		GJ1		475	10375
(7)		GJ1		840	9535
(8)		GJ2		1205	8330
(9)		GJ2		500	7830
(10)		GJ2		2650	5180
(11)		GJ2	8400		13580
(11)		GJ2	12018		25598
(12)		GJ2		975	24623
(12)		GJ2		460	24163
(12)		GJ2		900	23263
(14)		GJ3		8985	14278
(15)		GJ3		3495	10783
(16)		GJ3		1000	9783

Accounts Receivable — Account No. 101

Date	Explanation	Post Ref.	Debits	Credits	Balance
	Beginning Balance				-0-
(11)		GJ2	16520		16520
(11)		GJ2		12390	4130

Land — Account No. 112

Date	Explanation	Post Ref.	Debits	Credits	Balance
	Beginning Balance				-0-
(3)		GJ1	39500		39500

(continued on the next page)

Building — Account No. 113

Date		Explanation	Post Ref.	Debits	Credits	Balance
		Beginning Balance				-0-
(4)			GJ1	72500		72500

Accumulated Depreciation—Building — Account No. 113A

Date		Explanation	Post Ref.	Debits	Credits	Balance
		Beginning Balance				-0-
(13)			GJ3		1813	< 1813 >

Building Improvements — Account No. 114

Date		Explanation	Post Ref.	Debits	Credits	Balance
		Beginning Balance				-0-
(4)			GJ1	7300		7300

Accumulated Depreciation—Building Improvements — Account No. 114A

Date		Explanation	Post Ref.	Debits	Credits	Balance
		Beginning Balance				-0-
(13)			GJ3		182	< 182 >

Furnishings — Account No. 115

Date	Explanation	Post Ref.	Debits	Credits	Balance
	Beginning Balance				-0-
(5)		GJ1	5300		5300

Accumulated Depreciation—Furnishings — Account No. 115A

Date	Explanation	Post Ref.	Debits	Credits	Balance
	Beginning Balance				-0-
(13)		GJ3		265	<265>

Accounts Payable — Account No. 200

Date	Explanation	Post Ref.	Debits	Credits	Balance
	Beginning Balance				-0-
(5)		GJ1		2650	<2650>
(10)		GJ2	2650		-0-

Notes Payable — Account No. 211

Date	Explanation	Post Ref.	Debits	Credits	Balance
	Beginning Balance				-0-
(2)		GJ1		15000	<15000>
(3)		GJ1		30000	<45000>
(4)		GJ1		79800	<124800>
(15)		GJ3	3495		<121305>

(continued on the next page)

Dixon Able, Capital — Account No. 220

Date	Explanation	Post Ref.	Debits	Credits	Balance
	Beginning Balance				-0-
(1)		GJ1		8000	⟨8000⟩
(16)		GJ4		8448	⟨16448⟩
(16)		GJ4	1500		⟨14948⟩

Dixon Able, Drawings — Account No. 220A

Date	Explanation	Post Ref.	Debits	Credits	Balance
(9)		GJ2	500		500
(16)		GJ3	1000		1500
(16)		GJ4		1500	-0-

Income Summary — Account No. 305

Date	Explanation	Post Ref.	Debits	Credits	Balance
(16)		GJ3		24920	⟨24920⟩
(16)		GJ3	16472		⟨8448⟩
(16)		GJ4	8448		-0-

Revenues — Account No. 401

Date	Explanation	Post Ref.	Debits	Credits	Balance
(11)		GJ2		24920	⟨24920⟩
(16)		GJ3	24920		-0-

Advertising Expense — Account No. 501

Date	Explanation	Post Ref.	Debits	Credits	Balance
(6)		GJ1	475		475
(12)		GJ2	900		1375
(16)		GJ3		1375	-0-

Cleaning Expense — Account No. 502

Date	Explanation	Post Ref.	Debits	Credits	Balance
(7)		GJ1	840		840
(16)		GJ3		840	-0-

Utility Expense — Account No. 503

Date	Explanation	Post Ref.	Debits	Credits	Balance
(8)		GJ2	1205		1205
(12)		GJ2	975		2180
(16)		GJ3		2180	-0-

Financing Expense — Account No. 504

Date	Explanation	Post Ref.	Debits	Credits	Balance
(11)		GJ2	372		372
(16)		GJ3		372	-0-

(continued on the next page)

Maintenance Expense — Account No. 505

Date	Explanation	Post Ref.	Debits	Credits	Balance
(12)		GJ2	460		460
(16)		GJ3		460	-0-

Depreciation Expense — Account No. 506

Date	Explanation	Post Ref.	Debits	Credits	Balance
(13)		GJ3	2260		2260
(16)		GJ3		2260	-0-

Interest Expense — Account No. 507

Date	Explanation	Post Ref.	Debits	Credits	Balance
(14)		GJ3	8985		8985
(16)		GJ3		8985	-0-

EXHIBIT 5A-4

Dixon Able, Proprietor

Trial Balance

as of December 31, 1983 (Before Closing Entries)

Number	Account	Debits	Credits
100	Cash	$ 9,783	
101	Accounts Receivable	4,130	
112	Land	39,500	
113	Building	72,500	
113A	Accumulated Depreciation–Building		$ 1,813
114	Building Improvements	7,300	
114A	Accumulated Depreciation–Building Improvements		182
115	Furnishings	5,300	
115A	Accumulated Depreciation–Furnishings		265
200	Accounts Payable		-0-
211	Notes Payable		121,305
220	Dixon Able, Capital		8,000
220A	Dixon Able, Drawings	1,500	
401	Rent Revenue		24,920
501	Advertising Expense	1,375	
502	Cleaning Expense	840	
503	Utility Expense	2,180	
504	Financing Expense	372	
505	Maintenance Expense	460	
506	Depreciation Expense	2,260	
507	Interest Expense	8,985	
	Totals	$156,485	$156,485

EXHIBIT 5A-5

Dixon Able, Proprietor

Income Statement

for the Six Months Ended December 31, 1983

Rent Revenue		$24,920
Less Expenses:		
Advertising Expense	$1,375	
Cleaning Expense	840	
Utility Expense	2,180	
Financing Expense	372	
Maintenance Expense	460	
Depreciation Expense	2,260	
Interest Expense	8,985	
Total Expenses		16,472
Net Income		$ 8,448

EXHIBIT 5A-6

Dixon Able, Proprietor

Balance Sheet as of December 31, 1983

Assets		
Cash		$ 9,783
Accounts Receivable		4,130
Land		39,500
Building	$72,500	
Less Accumulated Depreciation—Building	1,813	70,687
Building Improvements	$ 7,300	
Less Accumulated Depreciation—Building Improvements	182	7,118
Furnishings	$ 5,300	
Less Accumulated Depreciation—Furnishings	265	5,035
Total Assets		$136,253
Liabilities and Proprietor's Capital		
Notes Payable		$121,305
Dixon Able, Capital		14,948
Total Liabilities and Proprietor's Capital		$136,253

The financial statements were impressive, especially as the units were available for occupancy only in the final few months of the year. Dixon was excited about future prospects. In fact, he was convinced that expansion held the key to even greater earnings. Specifically, he wanted to construct more four-unit buildings. This would require additional outside capital, as well as extra help in managing the units. Dixon convinced his close friend, John Graden, who was a graduate student in accounting, to enter into a partnership with him. John agreed to invest $10,000. Dixon's father and John's uncle, Sam Graden, were also brought in as partners, with Sam Graden contributing $15,000 and Charles Able investing the principal amount on the note owed him as his share of the partnership interest. Since only Dixon and John contributed to the management of the business, profits were to be distributed 30 percent each to Dixon and John and 20 percent each to Charles and Sam.

The partnership agreement was signed on January 1, 1984. Dixon and John then arranged for the purchase of additional land and the construction of two new four-unit complexes. The following transactions took place during the next year, 1984.

1. Collected the balance of accounts receivable, $4,130 less a 3 percent finance charge.
2. Purchased two adjacent building lots for $10,000 down plus a 5-year note for $65,000 at an interest rate of 13 percent. The note is payable in five annual installments of $13,000, plus interest, beginning December 31, 1984.

3. Constructed two building complexes of 2,000 square feet each at a cost of $38 per square foot. Building improvements were an additional $12,000. Construction of the building and the improvements were financed by a 10-year loan of $164,000 from City Bank at an interest rate of 14 percent. The buildings were completed and placed in service September 1, 1984. The loan requires ten annual payments of $16,400, plus interest, with the first payment due September 1, 1985. Again, no downpayment was required.

4. Purchased furnishings for the new units at a cost of $9,200. $6,000 was paid in cash with the balance due in 6 months with no interest.

5. Paid clean-up expenses of $700.

6. Paid utility hook-up expenses of $1,200.

7. Earned revenues of $92,600. Of this amount, $32,600 was received in cash and the balance was credit card sales. Of the $60,000 total receivables, 80 percent were collected by the end of the year, less the 3 percent service charge retained by the credit card companies.

8. Paid an average of $425 per month for utilities for the year. Maintenance costs amounted to $1,200. Cleaning costs, in addition to the $700 already incurred, amounted to $1,600. Advertising and promotion costs were $200 a month throughout the year.

9. Paid interest and principal on notes. The amount of interest expense incurred was $23,856 and the amount of principal paid was $19,990.

10. Accrued interest of $7,654 on City Bank loan.

11. Recorded depreciation for the year: buildings, $6,158; building improvements, $565; and furnishings, $837.

12. Paid the bill for furnishings in full.

13. Dixon and John withdrew $12,000 each during the year for college and living expenses.

Dixon and John journalized the transactions for 1984, posted them to the ledger accounts, and prepared a trial balance and selected financial statements (see Exhibits 5A-7 through 5A-9).

EXHIBIT 5A-7

Able & Graden Partnership

Trial Balance as of December 31, 1984

Number	Account	Debits	Credits
100	Cash	$ 18,703	
101	Accounts Receivable	12,000	
112	Land	114,500	
113	Buildings	224,500	
113A	Accumulated Depreciation—Buildings		$ 7,971
114	Building Improvements	19,300	
114A	Accumulated Depreciation—Building Improvements		747
115	Furnishings	14,500	
115A	Accumulated Depreciation—Furnishings		1,102
211	Notes Payable		315,315
212	Accrued Interest Payable		7,654
220	Dixon Able, Capital		14,948
220A	Dixon Able, Drawings	12,000	
221	Charles Able, Capital		15,000
222	John Graden, Capital		10,000
222A	John Graden, Drawings	12,000	
223	Sam Graden, Capital		15,000
401	Rent Revenue		92,600
501	Advertising Expense	2,400	
502	Cleaning Expense	2,300	
503	Utility Expense	6,300	
504	Financing Expense	1,564	
505	Maintenance Expense	1,200	
506	Depreciation Expense	7,560	
507	Interest Expense	31,510	
	Totals	$480,337	$480,337

EXHIBIT 5A-8

Able & Graden, Partnership

Income Statement

for the Year Ended December 31, 1984

Rent Revenue		$92,600
Less Expenses:		
Advertising Expense	$ 2,400	
Cleaning Expense	2,300	
Utility Expense	6,300	
Financing Expense	1,564	
Maintenance Expense	1,200	
Depreciation Expense	7,560	
Interest Expense	31,510	
Total Expenses		52,834
Net Income		$39,766

EXHIBIT 5A-9

Able & Graden, Partnership

Balance Sheet as of December 31, 1984

Assets

Cash		$ 18,703
Accounts Receivable		12,000
Land		114,500
Buildings	$224,500	
Less Accumulated Depreciation–Buildings	7,971	216,529
Building Improvements	$ 19,300	
Less Accumulated Depreciation–Building Improvements	747	18,553
Furnishings	$ 14,500	
Less Accumulated Depreciation–Furnishings	1,102	13,398
Total Assets		$393,683

Liabilities and Partners' Capital

Liabilities:		
Accrued Interest Payable	$ 7,654	
Notes Payable	315,315	
Total Liabilities		$322,969
Partners' Capital:		
Dixon Able, Capital	$ 14,878	
Charles Able, Capital	22,953	
John Graden, Capital	9,930	
Sam Graden, Capital	22,953	
Total Partners' Capital		70,714
Total Liabilities and Partners' Capital		$393,683

The partners were pleased with the results of the first year of the partnership. Dixon and John decided to continue to manage the partnership, but on a part-time basis because both had been graduated from college and had accepted full-time positions with a consulting firm and a CPA firm, respectively. The demand for temporary housing in Mountain View continued to increase, however, and the business became substantially more profitable over the next two years (1985 and 1986). As a result, Dixon and John decided that they would have to run the business on a full-time basis. The partners further decided to incorporate the business and to raise $200,000 of additional capital by issuing stock.

On January 1, 1987, the partnership was converted into the Valley Housing Corporation, and the partners accepted shares in the new corporation at the rate of $10 per share in lieu of their capital accounts. In addition, 20,000 shares were issued privately to a few friends at $10 per share.

Dixon Able, Capital	50,500	
Charles Able, Capital	46,000	
John Graden, Capital	47,500	
Sam Graden, Capital	46,000	
Capital Stock		190,000
Converted partners' capital to capital stock; 19,000 shares of stock were issued.		
Cash	200,000	
Capital Stock		200,000
Issued 20,000 shares of capital stock at $10 per share.		

During 1987 and 1988, additional buildings were constructed, several full-time and part-time employees were hired, and expansion into nearby markets proceeded smoothly. At the end of the second year of operation as a corporation, the company's accountant journalized the transactions for that year, including the adjustments listed below, posted them to the ledger accounts, and prepared an adjusted trial balance, an income statement, and a balance sheet (see Exhibits 5A-10 through 5A-12). (Assume that financial statements were prepared during the first year, so the numbers used here cannot be tied back to the partnership.)

1. Salaries unpaid for the last 4 days of the year amounted to $1,000.
2. Supplies on hand totaled $2,600. (Supplies are charged to expense when purchased.)
3. Rent received in advance as of the end of the year amounted to $1,100. (A revenue account is credited when cash is received.)
4. Taxes of $7,000 for the next 6 months have already been paid and charged to Income Tax Expense.

Note that the capital accounts of the corporation include Capital Stock and Retained Earnings. Retained Earnings shows the amount of net income accumulated in a business since incorporation after dividends are distributed to the stockholders.

EXHIBIT 5A-10

Valley Housing Corporation

Adjusted Trial Balance as of December 31, 1988

Number	Account	Debits	Credits
100	Cash	$ 78,780	
101	Accounts Receivable	75,600	
102	Supplies	2,600	
103	Prepaid Taxes	7,000	
112	Land	215,000	
113	Buildings	317,000	
113A	Accumulated Depreciation—Buildings		$ 27,950
114	Building Improvements	42,100	
114A	Accumulated Depreciation—Building Improvements		8,210
115	Furnishings	22,600	
115A	Accumulated Depreciation—Furnishings		6,300
200	Accounts Payable		2,500
201	Salary Payable		1,000
202	Rent Received in Advance		1,100
211	Notes Payable		190,000
220	Capital Stock		390,000
221	Retained Earnings		37,600
401	Rent Revenue		314,180
501	Advertising Expense	2,300	
503	Utility Expense	24,600	
504	Financing Expense	7,560	
505	Maintenance Expense	8,600	
506	Depreciation Expense	24,200	
507	Interest Expense	45,700	
508	Salary Expense	93,000	
509	Income Tax Expense	7,000	
510	Supplies Expense	5,200	
	Totals	$978,840	$978,840

EXHIBIT 5A-11

Valley Housing Corporation
Income Statement
for the Year Ended December 31, 1988

Rent Revenue		$314,180
Less Expenses:		
Advertising Expense	$ 2,300	
Utility Expense	24,600	
Financing Expense	7,560	
Maintenance Expense	8,600	
Depreciation Expense	24,200	
Interest Expense	45,700	
Salary Expense	93,000	
Supplies	5,200	
Total Expenses		211,160
Income Before Taxes		$103,020
Income Taxes		7,000
Net Income		$ 96,020
EPS ($96,020 ÷ 39,000 shares outstanding)		$2.46

EXHIBIT 5A-12

Valley Housing Corporation
Balance Sheet as of December 31, 1988

Assets	
Cash	$ 78,780
Accounts Receivable	75,600
Supplies	2,600
Prepaid Taxes	7,000
Land	215,000
Buildings (net of accumulated depreciation of $27,950)	289,050
Building Improvements (net of accumulated depreciation of $8,210)	33,890
Furnishings (net of accumulated depreciation of $6,300)	16,300
Total Assets	$718,220
Liabilities and Stockholders' Equity	
Accounts Payable	$ 2,500
Salary Payable	1,000
Rent Received in Advance	1,100
Notes Payable	190,000
Capital Stock	390,000
Retained Earnings	123,107
Total Liabilities and Stockholders' Equity	$718,220

EXERCISES

E5A–1 Journalizing and Posting

Dixon's proprietorship was changed to a partnership. Several transactions for the Able & Graden partnership are identified on pages 188 and 189. Journalize these transactions and post to appropriate ledger accounts. (If you account for the transactions properly, you should end up with the trial balance amounts on page 190.) Make all closing entries required. (When this is done, a post-closing trial balance should contain the account balances shown on the balance sheet, Exhibit 5A–9, page 191.)

E5A–2 Work Sheet and Closing Entries

From the information presented on page 192 and in Exhibits 5A–10 through 5A–12, prepare a work sheet that shows the adjustments required at the end of the year. Also prepare the closing journal entries for Valley Housing Corporation at year-end.

SECTION 2

Income Determination

CHAPTER 6

Income Measurement and Reporting

THIS CHAPTER EXPLAINS:

What income is.
Alternative ways of measuring income.
The recognition of revenues.
How cost of goods sold and other expenses are measured.
The income statement.

In Chapter 2 we introduced the income statement and the balance sheet as end products, or outputs, of the accounting process. Each of these statements plays a significant role in informing interested investors and others about the results of operations and the financial condition of a firm. The next nine chapters will help you understand these primary financial statements. Specifically, this and the next chapter analyze the income statement, and Chapters 8 through 14 cover the balance sheet.

This chapter will first describe different ways of measuring income and then will explain the currently used measurement method in some detail. The explanation will include discussions of the recognition and nature of (1) revenues, (2) cost of goods sold, and (3) other expenses, as well as a description of the income statement.

Although only one method of reporting income is currently used in the primary financial statements, an understanding of alternative income concepts is important because supplementary disclosures using other methods are required of some firms. In addition, there is considerable controversy about the adequacy of the currently accepted method. Many experts believe that it is only a matter of time until one of the alternatives is selected as the required method for reporting purposes.

A Definition of Income

In an economic sense, income can be thought of as the increase in wealth experienced during a period. Economic income has been defined as the

economic income *the maximum amount a person or a firm can consume during an accounting period and still be as well off at the end of the period as at the beginning*

maximum amount a person or firm can consume during an accounting period and still be as well off at the end of the period as at the beginning. In other words, if a firm has $1,000 of purchasing power at the beginning of an accounting period, its income would be the amount it could spend during the period and still have $1,000 of purchasing power at the end of the period (assuming no investments or withdrawals). Conceptually, this definition of income is excellent; in practice, economic income is difficult to measure.

To illustrate the complexity of measuring economic income, we will assume that three individuals decide to open a clothing store and that each contributes $17,000 to the business. We will also assume that they use the $51,000 (3 × $17,000) of invested funds to purchase a building for $50,000 and an inventory of ten coats for a total cost of $1,000, or $100 each. If during their first month of business they sell all ten coats at a price of $200 each and have no other operating expenses, how much income did they earn? Your first reaction may be to say that their income is $1,000 (10 coats × $100 profit on each coat). This answer, while logical, may or may not be correct. If the building is still worth exactly $50,000, their economic income is indeed $1,000. If, however, the building's value has increased or decreased, economic income may be something more or less than $1,000. How much more or less cannot be exactly determined unless the owners choose to sell the building or have it appraised at the end of the month.

Some accounting theorists would argue that income could be determined by valuing the building at either its replacement cost (the amount it would cost to purchase a similar building) or the amount at which it could be sold. In reality, the only sure measure of the building's value is its sales price when it is actually sold.

When this single complication is considered in relation to an actual business with numerous assets and transactions, the problems of measuring income multiply considerably. In fact, the income of a business can only be accurately and objectively determined at the end of the firm's life, after it has sold or otherwise disposed of all its operating and other assets and when cash is the only remaining asset. At that time cash can be counted, and the increase over the beginning amount, adjusted for all owner withdrawals and investments since the firm was established, is income.

Since stockholders and others are unwilling to wait until the end of a firm's life to find out how well it has performed, firms compute and report estimates of net income at regular intervals (at least annually, and often monthly or quarterly). These periodic estimates are reported on the income statement. Although the income statement reports a precise net income amount, you should realize that there are usually several estimates included in the calculation of this number.

Traditional Methods of Measuring Income

Various methods may be used to measure income. Four of these will be considered in this chapter: (1) the cash-basis method, (2) the currently used accrual-basis historical cost method, (3) the constant-dollar (or general price-level-adjusted historical cost) method, and (4) the current-value method. The first two methods are the traditional ones; they ignore inflation (increases in the general costs of goods and services). The last two methods, which will be discussed in the following sections, attempt to adjust income for the effects of inflation. In reading about these methods, you should note that this discussion is at an elementary level and that each method involves complexities and has variations not mentioned here.

CASH-BASIS INCOME

cash-basis method *an income measurement method in which income is defined as cash receipts less cash disbursements during an accounting period*

Probably the simplest and most objective measure of income results from using the cash-basis method. With this approach, income is the difference between a business's cash receipts and its cash disbursements during an accounting period. Cash receipts and disbursements can be measured with a high degree of objectivity. In fact, it is only after we have determined our cash-basis income that most of us make such personal decisions as whether or not we can afford to buy a new or used car. Most individuals also pay taxes on the amount of their cash-basis income.

To illustrate the cash-basis method of measuring income, we will assume that Fox Sporting Goods had the following transactions.

inventory *goods held for sale*

1. Started business on January 1, 1983. On that day Fox purchased a building for $100,000, as well as $50,000 of sporting goods inventory. The building is expected to have a useful life of 20 years.
2. During 1983, Fox sold one-half the inventory for $60,000.
3. The only other expense incurred during 1983 was $20,000 paid for salaries.

Given these data, the cash-basis loss might be computed as follows:

Cash Receipts		$ 60,000
Cash Disbursements:		
Purchase of Sporting Goods Inventory	$ 50,000	
Purchase of Building	100,000	
Payment of Salaries	20,000	
Total Cash Disbursements		170,000
Net Loss		($110,000)

As you can see, there are some serious problems when income is computed on a cash basis. First, did Fox really lose $110,000? Certainly, cash outflows exceeded cash inflows by $110,000. However, the major reason for the excess outflows was a $100,000 expenditure for a building that will benefit the company for many years and is more of an investment (asset) than an expense. Wouldn't it be better to allocate or assign a portion of the cost of the building to each of the periods in which it is used by the company? For example, if the building can be used effectively for 20 years, wouldn't it be preferable to charge only one-twentieth of the cost against income in the current year?

expenses *costs of assets used up or additional liabilities incurred in the normal course of business to generate revenues*

Also, only half the inventory was actually sold. Shouldn't only the cost of the portion that was sold be an expense? And, what if additional sporting goods had been sold on credit, with payment yet to be received? Shouldn't such sales be recognized currently as revenues? And what if additional sporting goods inventory had been bought on credit near the fiscal year-end, with payment to be made 60 days later? Shouldn't such purchases be recognized currently as an asset? The answers to these and other questions indicate that the cash-basis income measurement method is not the most useful for determining income in many companies. However, some government and other nonprofit organizations, as well as many small businesses, rely heavily on this method of accounting measurement.

ACCRUAL-BASIS HISTORICAL COST INCOME

accrual-basis historical cost method *an income measurement method in which income is defined as revenues earned minus expenses incurred during a period, without regard to changes in the values of assets or liabilities or in the general price level*

A second income measurement method, and the one currently used for the primary financial statements, is the accrual-basis historical cost method. With this approach, the historical costs of operational assets (buildings, machines, and so forth) are allocated (depreciated) over their useful lives and only the cost of inventory actually sold is charged as an expense. Net income is equal to revenues *earned* minus expenses *incurred*. To illustrate the accrual-basis historical cost method, we again calculate the net income of Fox Sporting Goods for 1983.

Sales Revenue		$60,000
Expenses:		
Cost of Inventory Sold (1/2 × $50,000 cost)	$25,000	
Salary Expense	20,000	
Depreciation Expense ($100,000 cost ÷ 20 years)	5,000	
Total Expenses		50,000
Net Income		$10,000

The accrual-basis historical cost method will be explained in greater detail later in the chapter and used throughout the text, since it is the method currently required for the primary financial statements.

Inflation-Adjusted Methods of Measuring Income

inflation *an increase in the general price level of goods and services; alternatively, a decrease in the purchasing power of the dollar*

For the past 15 or 20 years, Americans have been faced with a high rate of inflation, in some years amounting to double digits (10 percent or more). No one needs to tell you that it now costs more to buy the same amount of goods than it did a few years ago. The groceries that cost $100 ten years ago now cost $200 or more. And the automobile that cost $4,000 five years ago would probably cost $10,000 or $12,000 today. This increase in price, or decrease in the purchasing power of the dollar, is called inflation. It means that a dollar today isn't the same in terms of purchasing power as a dollar you had last year or, in all probability, one you will have next year. Although the monetary units (dollar bills) look identical, when they are spent at different times they buy different amounts of goods and services.

In our inflationary economy, however, goods and services have increased in price by varying amounts and a few prices have even decreased. So, how can it be said that the purchasing power of the dollar itself has declined? The answer is that inflation is an index of *average* changes in prices, not of changes in the prices of specific goods and services. The prices of specific goods and services change in response to fluctuations in demand, supply, competition, or other factors, as well as to general inflation.

Both the cash-basis and the accrual-basis historical cost methods of measuring income ignore the impact of inflation. There are, however, two other methods of measuring income that take into consideration these changes in prices as they affect purchasing power. The constant-dollar income method accounts only for changes in general price levels; the current-value method measures changes in *specific* prices.

general price level *an index of the overall market value of a group of goods or services at a point in time*

CONSTANT-DOLLAR INCOME

constant-dollar method *an income measurement method in which income is defined as revenues less expenses as adjusted by a general (economy-wide) price index, plus any purchasing power gains or losses due to changes in the general price level; also called the general price-level-adjusted historical cost method*

The first inflation-adjusted method we will discuss is the constant-dollar income method. With this approach, which can get complicated, the original costs of nonmonetary assets, certain liabilities, and owners' equity are adjusted upward or downward according to some economy-wide price index (such as the Consumer Price Index).[1] Because this method merely adjusts historical costs, it does not report assets at their current market value. Rather, it attempts to measure financial statement information of different periods in constant dollars—that is, dollars of equivalent purchasing power.

To illustrate, we will again use the Fox Sporting Goods example. To remind you:

1. Fox started business on January 1, 1983. On that date, the company purchased a building for $100,000 and bought $50,000 of sporting goods inventory. The building is expected to have a useful life of 20 years.
2. During 1983, Fox sold one-half the inventory for $60,000.
3. The only other expense during 1983 was $20,000 paid for salaries.

We will also assume that on December 31, 1983, an economy-wide index (such as the Consumer Price Index) indicated that, on the average, prices had risen 20 percent during the year. In addition, to simplify the example

[1] The consumer price index (CPI) is a general inflation index published each month by the U.S. Bureau of Labor Statistics. It is determined by sampling the prices of a broad selection of goods and services (transportation, housing, food, clothing, and so on) in approximately 50 cities each month to determine how much general prices have changed. Using 1967 as the base year (100 percent), the consumer price index for selected years has been:

1960	88.7	1975	161.2	1980	246.8
1967	100	1978	195.3		

According to the CPI, general prices almost tripled between 1960 and 1980. That is, goods that cost $88.70 in 1960 cost $246.80 in 1980.

we will assume that sales revenue and salary expense were stated at year-end according to the value of the dollar then, and thus require no adjustment.

Given these data, the amount of constant-dollar income could be computed as follows:

Sales Revenue		$60,000
Cost of Inventory Sold ($25,000 × 1.20)	$30,000	
Salary Expense	20,000	
Depreciation Expense [($100,000 × 1.20) ÷ 20 years]	6,000	56,000
Net Income		$ 4,000

In this example, the cost of inventory sold and the depreciation expense were adjusted by 1.20 because both the inventory and the building were purchased on January 1, and since that time there has been 20 percent inflation. These assumptions were made to keep the example simple—otherwise these figures would have had to be adjusted at varying rates depending on the specific dates the assets were purchased and the amount of inflation that occurred between those dates and the end of the year. Remember also that this approach does not include in income any changes in the *values* of the assets. Rather, it adjusts *historical* costs to constant dollars.

Several other technical adjustments have been eliminated here, again to keep the illustration as simple as possible. For example, gains and losses would be computed on monetary assets and liabilities held by a company, such as accounts receivable and notes payable. Since these types of assets and liabilities are fixed in total dollars, inflation, which reduces the purchasing power of the dollar, reduces their value. Thus, during a period of inflation, someone who owes money gains (because the debt will be paid with dollars that are worth less), whereas a holder of cash loses purchasing power. These types of monetary gains and losses must also be included in the calculation of net income.

The constant-dollar alternative has received significant support in the profession. Its advantage is that inflation indexes are readily available from the government and can be mechanically applied to any set of numbers. Its major disadvantage is that specific assets and liabilities often do not increase or decrease in value at the same rate as economy-wide inflation. In fact, inflation is only one factor that affects price. Other factors are increases or decreases in productivity and technology, and changes in supply or demand. An example of an asset whose reported value would be distorted by this method is a computer. With constant-dollar income measurement, the historical cost of a computer would be adjusted upward because of inflation, whereas in fact, due to technological advances, prices of computers have dropped significantly in recent years. Nevertheless, in most cases this alternative works quite well. In fact, supplementary disclosure of the impact of general price changes on assets, liabilities, owners' equity, and income is currently required of many large companies by the Financial Accounting Standards Board (FASB Statement No. 33).

CURRENT-VALUE INCOME

current-value method *the income measurement method in which income is defined as the excess of revenues over expenses plus the net increases or decreases in the values of specific assets and liabilities during a period*

The second inflation-adjusted method of income measurement is the current-value income method. With this approach, which considers specific price changes, all elements of the financial statements (assets, liabilities, revenues, expenses, and so forth) are recorded at their current values. The net income for a period, then, is the increase in net assets (assets minus liabilities) adjusted for any contributions or withdrawals by the owners of the business. For example, suppose that a company's total assets and total liabilities at the beginning and the end of a year were

	Current Values at Beginning of Year	Current Values at End of Year
Total Assets	$60,000	$80,000
Total Liabilities	30,000	34,000
Net Assets	$30,000	$46,000

If no additional investments or withdrawals were made during the year, current-value net income would be $16,000 ($46,000 − $30,000).

To further illustrate, we will refer to the data for Fox Sporting Goods. In addition, we will assume that on December 31, 1983, the values of the building and remaining inventory, as determined by appraisals, had increased to $125,000 and $35,000, respectively.

Given these data, current-value net income might be computed as follows:

Sales Revenue	$60,000	
Increase in Value of Building*	25,000	
Increase in Value of Inventory*	10,000	$95,000
Current Cost of Inventory Sold	$35,000	
Salary Expense	20,000	
Current Cost of Depreciation—Building ($125,000 ÷ 20 years)	6,250	61,250
Net Income		$33,750

* Some accountants argue that these increases in value should be recognized as revenues. The FASB disagrees; it allows companies to increase the value of buildings only for depreciation purposes, and the cost of inventory only for computing the current cost of inventory sold. Their reasoning is that it is not a company's intention to sell its buildings, and that an increase in the value of inventory will be recognized as revenue when the inventory is sold at current market prices.

In this example, the building is allocated (depreciated) at its increased value over its useful life (20 years). Also, the cost of inventory sold is expensed at its replacement cost of $35,000. (Since the remaining half of the inventory has a current value of $35,000, it can be assumed that the replacement cost of the half that was sold is also $35,000.) Sales revenue and salary expense are already stated at their current costs and require no adjustment.

The current-value approach has received a significant amount of support in recent years because it is an attempt to measure the increase or decrease in the wealth of a business. Since 1979, the FASB has required that many of the largest companies in the United States provide both current-value and constant-dollar data[2] as supplementary information in their financial reports.

The major disadvantage of this method is the subjectivity of the current-value numbers. Unless the company's inventory and buildings, for example, are actually sold, it is difficult to know their exact current values. Nevertheless, this method is theoretically sound and may be the required reporting alternative of the future.

TO SUMMARIZE Four alternative methods of measuring income are (1) cash-basis, (2) accrual-basis historical cost, (3) constant-dollar, and (4) current-value. The first two methods ignore inflation; the third considers general price-level changes; and the fourth takes into account specific price changes. Each has advantages and disadvantages. The method that will be used throughout this text, the accrual-basis historical cost income method, is currently required for the primary financial statements. The constant-dollar and current-value methods are required as supplementary disclosures for some companies.

Accrual-Basis Historical Cost Income

Net income under the accrual-basis historical cost method is equal to revenues earned minus expenses incurred. We will first discuss and illustrate the issues relating to revenue recognition. Then we will describe how expenses are measured and recognized.

THE MEASUREMENT OF REVENUES

revenues *increases in resources from the sale of goods or services derived primarily from the normal operations of an enterprise*

revenue recognition principle *the idea that revenues should be recorded when (1) the earnings process has been substantially completed, and (2) an exchange has taken place*

Revenues, as you will recall from Chapter 2, are the increases in resources derived from the normal operating activities of an enterprise. According to the revenue recognition principle, revenues are usually recorded when two important criteria have been met: (1) the earnings process has been substantially completed, generally meaning that a sale has been made or a service has been performed, and (2) an exchange has taken place.[3] Thus, credit sales are recognized as revenues before cash is collected, and revenue

[2] The requirements of the FASB are far more complex than indicated by the simple examples used here. The illustrations are only intended to show the general nature of the various alternatives. (Incidentally, the SEC requirement to report replacement costs has been suspended.)

[3] There are cases in which revenue is recognized according to other criteria, such as upon production (when there is a ready market) or upon partial completion of the earnings process. However, these are exceptions to the rule.

from services performed is usually recognized when the service is performed and billed, not when cash is collected.

To illustrate this principle, we will assume that on a typical business day Gro Rite Products sells 30 sacks of fertilizer for cash and 20 sacks on credit, all at $10 per sack. Given these data, the $500 of revenue would be recorded as follows:

Cash	300	
Accounts Receivable	200	
Sales Revenue		500
Sold 30 sacks of fertilizer for cash and 20 sacks on credit.		

Although the debit entries are made to different accounts, the credit entry for the full amount is to a revenue account. Thus, accrual-basis accounting allows the recognition of $500 in revenue instead of the $300 that would be recognized with the cash-basis method.

The example given above is a simple illustration of how sales are recorded and revenue is recognized. In reality, sales transactions are usually more complex, involving such things as discounts for prompt payment, returns of merchandise sold, and losses from uncollectible credit sales. Before we discuss these complexities, one note is appropriate. In many companies, the most frequent types of journal entries are those to record sales, cash collections, purchases, and payments to suppliers. Because such transactions are so frequent, most firms maintain four separate special journals. As noted in the Supplement to Chapter 3, these are (1) the sales journal, (2) the cash receipts journal, (3) the purchases journal, and (4) the cash disbursements journal. However, in the following analysis of transactions, we will use only a few selected journal entries and so we will continue to use the General Journal format.

Recognizing Revenue on Credit Sales

Most sales do not involve cash. Instead, they are made on credit, with the buyer usually having from 10 days to 2 months in which to pay the seller for the merchandise purchased. The asset that arises from this kind of transaction is called an account receivable, meaning that the buyer owes the seller for the merchandise purchased. An entry to record such a transaction and to recognize the sales revenue might be

account receivable *money due from rendering services or selling merchandise on credit; a current asset*

Accounts Receivable—Adam Smith	1,000	
Sales Revenue		1,000
Sold $1,000 of merchandise to Adam Smith.		

This entry shows that a customer, Adam Smith, purchased $1,000 of merchandise on credit. When Adam Smith pays the full amount, the entry to record the receipt of cash and the canceling of the receivable will be

Cash	1,000	
Accounts Receivable—Adam Smith		1,000
Received payment in full from Adam Smith for merchandise purchased.		

Complexities of Revenue Recognition

The two entries above are typical of those used to recognize sales revenue and record and cancel accounts receivable when the sales or collections transactions are simple. In many cases, however, there are complexities, such as sales discounts, returns of merchandise, or nonpayment by customers, that need to be considered.

sales discount *a reduction in the sales price, allowed if payment is received within a specified period*

Sales Discounts In many sales transactions the buyer is given a cash discount if the bill is paid promptly. Such incentives to pay quickly are called sales discounts, or cash discounts, and are typically expressed in abbreviated form. For example, 2/10, n/30 means that a buyer will receive a 2 percent discount from the purchase price if payment is made within 10 days of the date of purchase, but that the full amount must be paid within 30 days or it will be considered past due. (Other common terms are 1/10, n/30 and 2/10, EOM. The latter means that a 2 percent discount is granted if payment is made within 10 days after the end of the month.) A 2 percent discount is a strong incentive to pay within 10 days because it is equal to an annual interest rate of about 36 percent.[4] In fact, if the amount owed is substantial, most firms will borrow money, if necessary, to take advantage of the sales discount. This is because the interest rate they will have to pay a lending institution to borrow the money is considerably less than the effective interest rate of the sales discount.

If an account receivable is paid within a specified discount period, the entry to record the receipt of cash is different from the cash receipt entry shown earlier. Thus, if Adam Smith had purchased the $1,000 of merchandise on credit with terms 2/10, EOM and had paid within the discount period, the entry to record the receipt of cash would have been

contra-rev

Cash	980	
Sales Discounts	20	
Accounts Receivable—Adam Smith		1,000
Received payment from Adam Smith within the discount period.		

contra account *an account that is offset or deducted from another account*

Sales Discounts is a contra account, specifically a contra-revenue account, which means that it is deducted from Sales Revenue on the income statement. This account is included with other revenue accounts in the General Ledger but, unlike other revenues, it has a debit balance. Exhibit 6-1 summarizes the entries for sales discounts, using the Adam Smith example.

[4] This is calculated by computing an annual interest rate for the period that the money is "sacrificed." With terms 2/10, n/30, a buyer who pays on the 10th day instead of the 30th sacrifices the money for 20 days. Since 2 percent is earned in 20 days and there are just over 18 periods of 20 days in a year, earnings would be 18 times 2 percent, or approximately 36 percent annual interest.

EXHIBIT 6-1 **Accounting for Sales Discounts**

Transaction	Journal Entry		
Sale	Accounts Receivable	1,000	
	Sales Revenue		1,000
Payment (if within discount period)	Cash	980	
	Sales Discounts ($1,000 × 0.02)	20	
	Accounts Receivable		1,000
Payment (if not within discount period)	Cash	1,000	
	Accounts Receivable		1,000

Sales Returns and Allowances A customer often returns merchandise, either because the item is defective or for more personal reasons, such as a change of heart. Whatever the reason, most companies generally accept returned merchandise in order to maintain good customer relations. When merchandise is returned, the company must make additional entries to correct both the Accounts Receivable and the Sales Revenue accounts. A similar adjustment is required when the sales price is reduced because the merchandise was defective or damaged during shipment to the customer.

To illustrate the type of adjustment that is needed, we will assume that Adam Smith has returned $200 of the $1,000 of merchandise he purchased. The entry to record the return of merchandise would be

Sales Returns and Allowances	200	
Accounts Receivable–Adam Smith		200
Received $200 of merchandise back from Adam Smith.		

Adam Smith would be sent a "credit memorandum" for the return, stating that credit has been granted and that the balance of his account is now $800. The Sales Returns and Allowances account is a contra account similar to Sales Discounts.

Sales Returns and Allowances *a contra-revenue account in which the return of or allowance for the reduction in the price of merchandise previously sold is recorded*

It might seem that the use of offsetting contra accounts (Sales Discounts and Sales Returns and Allowances) involves extra steps that would not be necessary if returns of merchandise were deducted directly from the Sales Revenue account. Although such deductions would have the same final effect on net income, the separation of initial sales from all returns and allowances and discounts permits a company's management to analyze the extent to which customers are returning merchandise and taking advantage of discounts. If they find that excessive amounts of merchandise are being returned, they may decide that the company's sales returns policy is too liberal or that the quality of its merchandise needs improvement.

Losses from Uncollectible Accounts The third kind of complication that can arise in the sales and collections cycle is the nonpayment of accounts. When companies sell goods and services on credit (as most do), there are usually some customers who do not pay for the merchandise they purchase.

In fact, most businesses expect a certain percentage of their sales to be uncollectible. If a firm tries too hard to eliminate all losses from nonpaying customers, it usually makes its credit policy so restrictive that valuable sales are lost. On the other hand, if a firm extends credit too easily or to everyone, it may have so many uncollectible sales that it goes bankrupt. Because of this dilemma, most firms carefully monitor their credit sales to ensure that their policies are neither too restrictive nor too liberal.

bad debt *an uncollectible account receivable*

When an account receivable becomes uncollectible, a firm incurs a bad-debt loss. This loss must be recognized as a cost of doing business, so it is classified as an operating expense. There are two ways to account for losses from uncollectible accounts: the direct write-off method and the allowance method.

direct write-off method *the recording of actual losses from uncollectible accounts as expenses during the period in which accounts receivable are determined to be uncollectible*

With the direct write-off method, an uncollectible account is recognized as an expense at the time it is deemed to be uncollectible. For example, assume that during the month of July, a certain store had credit sales of $30,000. These sales would be recorded as a debit to Accounts Receivable and a credit to Sales Revenue. If payments for all the sales except one for $150 to R. Reynolds are received in August, the total of the entries to record collections is $29,850 in debits to Cash and credits to Accounts Receivable. If after receiving several past-due notices Reynolds still does not pay, the company will probably turn the account over to an attorney or an agency for collection. Then, if collection attempts fail, the company may decide that the R. Reynolds account will not be collected and write it off as a loss. The entry to record the loss under the direct write-off method would be

Doubtful Accounts Expense	150	
Accounts Receivable—R. Reynolds		150
To write off the uncollectible account of R. Reynolds.		

matching principle *the idea that all costs and expenses incurred in generating revenues must be recognized in the same reporting period as the related revenues*

Although the direct write-off method is objective, in that the account is written off at the time it proves to be uncollectible, it often violates the matching principle, which requires that all costs and expenses incurred in generating revenues be identified with those revenues, period by period. Thus, with the direct write-off method, sales made near the end of one accounting period may not be recognized as uncollectible until the next period. As a result, expenses are understated and net income is overstated in the current period, and expenses are overstated in the following period. This makes the direct write-off method unacceptable (from a theoretical point of view) unless bad debts involve only small amounts.

allowance method *the recording of estimated losses due to uncollectible accounts as expenses during the period in which the sales occurred*

The allowance method, on the other hand, satisfies the matching principle since it accounts for uncollectibles during the period in which the sale takes place. With this method, a firm uses its experience or industry averages to estimate the amount of receivables that will become uncollectible. That estimate is recorded as a doubtful accounts expense in the period of sale. Although the use of estimates may result in a rather imprecise expense figure, this is generally thought to be a less serious problem than the understatement of expenses created by the direct write-off method. In addition, with experience, these estimates tend to be quite accurate.

To illustrate the allowance method, we will assume that during 1983 total credit sales for a small appliance store were $200,000. If management estimates that one-half of 1 percent (0.005) of these sales will be uncollectible, the entry to record the doubtful accounts expense will be

Doubtful Accounts Expense	1,000	
Allowance for Doubtful Accounts		1,000
Estimated 1983 uncollectible accounts based on one-half of 1 percent of credit sales.		

Doubtful Accounts Expense *an account that represents the portion of the current period's receivables that are estimated to become uncollectible.*

Allowance for Doubtful Accounts *a contra account, deducted from Accounts Receivable, that shows the estimated losses from uncollectible accounts*

The Doubtful Accounts Expense is an account on the income statement, and Allowance for Doubtful Accounts (sometimes called Allowance for Bad Debts) is a contra account that is offset against Accounts Receivable on the balance sheet. In 1984, as actual losses are recognized, the balance in Allowance for Doubtful Accounts is written off. For example, if in 1984 a receivable of $150 could not be collected, the entry would be

Allowance for Doubtful Accounts	150	
Accounts Receivable		150
To write off an uncollectible account.		

Because both Allowance for Doubtful Accounts and Accounts Receivable are balance sheet accounts, the entry to write off accounts as uncollectible does not affect net income in 1984. Instead, the net income in 1983 (when the sale was actually made) already reflected the doubtful accounts expense. The net amount in Accounts Receivable after the $150 write-off is exactly the same as it was before the entry, as shown below.

Before Write-off Entry		**After Write-off Entry**	
Accounts Receivable	$200,000	Accounts Receivable	$199,850
Less Allowance for Doubtful Accounts	1,000	Less Allowance for Doubtful Accounts	850
Net Balance	$199,000	Net Balance	$199,000

book value of accounts receivable *the net amount that would be received if all receivables considered collectible were collected; equal to total accounts receivable less the allowance for doubtful accounts; also called net realizable value*

This net balance of $199,000 is sometimes called the book value of accounts receivable (the amount of receivables that are expected to be collected).

Occasionally, a customer whose account has been written off as uncollectible pays the outstanding balance. When this happens, the company reverses the entry that was used to write off the account and then recognizes the payment. For example, if the $150 were collected, the entries to correct the accounting records would be

Accounts Receivable	150	
Allowance for Doubtful Accounts		150
To reinstate the balance previously written off as uncollectible.		

Cash	150	
Accounts Receivable		150
Received payment in full of previously written-off accounts receivable.		

In situations of this kind, it is extremely important to have good control over both the cash-collection procedures and the accounting for accounts receivable. Otherwise, such payments as the previously written off $150 could be pocketed by the person who receives the cash and would never be missed. For this reason, most companies separate the handling of cash from the recording of cash transactions in the accounts. This separation is an example of internal control of cash (which is discussed in Chapter 9).

Estimating the Allowance for Doubtful Accounts Because the amount recorded in Doubtful Accounts Expense affects net income directly, it is important that good estimation procedures be used. There are several methods of estimating uncollectible receivables.

1. As a percentage of total sales (usually credit sales.)
2. As a percentage of total accounts receivable.
3. As an amount based on an "aging" of accounts receivable.

To use these methods, a company must estimate the aggregate amount of the loss on the basis of experience and/or industry averages. Obviously, a company that has been in business for several years should be able to make more accurate estimates than a new company. Many established companies will use a 3- or 5-year average as the basis for estimating current losses from uncollectible accounts.

If a company were to use credit sales as a basis for its estimate, the amount of uncollectibles would be a straight percentage of the current year's credit sales. That percentage would be a projection based on experience and modified for the current period. For example, if credit sales for the year were $300,000 and if experience indicated that 1 percent of all credit sales would be uncollectible, the entry to record the estimate would be

Estimate as a Percentage of Sales

Doubtful Accounts Expense ($300,000 × 0.01)	3,000	
Allowance for Doubtful Accounts		3,000
To record the doubtful accounts expense for the current year.		

Allowance for Doubtful Accounts

	500 Existing Balance
	3,000 Percentage of this year's sales estimated to be uncollectible
	3,500 New Balance

When this method is used, the existing balance, if there is one, in Allowance for Doubtful Accounts is ignored. The 1 percent of the current year's sales that is estimated to be uncollectible is calculated separately and then added to that balance. For example, as shown in the margin, if the existing balance was $500, the $3,000 would be added, making the new balance $3,500. The rationale for not considering the existing balance in Allowance for Doubtful Accounts is that it relates to previous periods' sales and, as a strict interpretation of the matching principle suggests, should not affect the estimate for the current period.

If a company bases its estimate of losses on total accounts receivable, the amount of uncollectibles is a percentage of the total balance. Thus, if

Estimate as a Percentage of Receivables

Allowance for Doubtful Accounts	
	500 Existing Balance
	2,200 Adjustment Needed
	2,700 Desired Balance

Meyers and Company has a balance of $90,000 in Accounts Receivable and its management determines that 3 percent of the receivables will be uncollectible, the balance in Allowance for Doubtful Accounts should be $2,700. However, if the account has an existing balance, only the net amount needed to bring the balance to $2,700 would be added. For example, as shown in the margin, a credit balance of $500 in Allowance for Doubtful Accounts would require the following entry.

Doubtful Accounts Expense	2,200	
Allowance for Doubtful Accounts		2,200
To adjust allowance to desired balance.		

When uncollectible accounts are estimated as a percentage of accounts receivable, the matching principle is not a consideration because, theoretically, the balance in the receivables could relate to any period.

The third method of estimating bad-debt losses requires that a company base it calculations on how long its receivables have been outstanding. With this procedure, called aging accounts receivable, each receivable is categorized according to age, such as current, 1–30 days past due, 31–60 days past due, 61–90 days past due, 91–120 days past due, and over 120 days past due. Once the receivables in each age classification are totaled, each total is multiplied by the appropriate uncollectible rate (as determined by experience). Exhibit 6–2 shows how a company with $90,000 in Accounts Receivable typically would determine that $3,600 of its current receivables are likely to be uncollectible.

aging accounts receivable *the process of categorizing each account receivable by the number of days it has been outstanding*

If the existing credit balance in Allowance for Doubtful Accounts is $500, the entry would be

Estimate as an Amount Based on Aging of Accounts Receivable

Allowance for Doubtful Accounts	
	500 Existing Balance
	3,100 Adjustment Needed
	3,600 Desired Balance

Doubtful Accounts Expense	3,100	
Allowance for Doubtful Accounts		3,100
To adjust allowance to desired balance.		

The aging of accounts receivable is probably the most accurate method of estimating uncollectible accounts. It is also a means whereby a company can quickly identify its problem customers. And because the method can identify such customers, even those companies that base their estimate of bad debts on total credit sales or outstanding receivables often also age their receivables as a way of monitoring the individual accounts receivable balances.

TO SUMMARIZE Revenue is generally accounted for according to the revenue recognition principle. That is, revenue is recognized when earned, which is at the time the earnings process has been substantially completed and an exchange has taken place. The entries to record revenue from the sale of merchandise or the performance of a service involve debits to Cash or Accounts Receivable and credits to Sales or Service Revenue. Revenue transactions can be complicated by (1) sales discounts, (2) sales returns, or (3) the uncollectibility of receivables that result from credit sales. There are two ways of accounting for losses from uncollectible receivables:

EXHIBIT 6-2 **Aging of Accounts Receivable**

			Days Past Due				
Customer	*Balance*	*Current*	*1–30*	*31–60*	*61–90*	*91–120*	*Over 120*
A. Abel	$ 1,000	$ 1,000					
R. Beatty	150						$150
F. Brock	625	500	$ 125				
G. Dick	726			$ 726			
M. Edwin	400	400					
G. Ely	225				$ 225		
R. Farmer	100					$ 100	
T. Fisher	200		200				
E. Williams ..	400	400					
Totals	$90,000	$70,000	$15,000	$1,500	$2,000	$1,000	$500

NOTE: Wavy lines through a listing indicate that items have been omitted.

Estimate of Losses from Uncollectible Accounts

Age	**Balance**	**Percentage Estimated to Be Uncollectible**	**Amount**
Current	$70,000	1.5	$1,050
1–30 days past due	15,000	3.0	450
31–60 days past due	1,500	20.0	300
61–90 days past due	2,000	40.0	800
91–120 days past due	1,000	60.0	600
Over 120 days past due ..	500	80.0	400
Totals	$90,000		$3,600

the direct write-off method and the allowance method. The allowance method is generally accepted practice because it is consistent with the matching principle. The three ways of estimating losses from uncollectible receivables are: (1) as a percentage of sales, (2) as a percentage of total outstanding receivables, and (3) as an amount based on an aging of accounts receivable.

THE MEASUREMENT OF EXPENSES

Thus far, our focus has been on the importance of carefully and correctly measuring revenues. Expenses are equally important and should also be carefully accounted for. Expenses are often referred to as revenue deductions, which means that they are subtracted from revenues in computing net income. As a general rule, revenue deductions are recognized according to the matching principle; that is, they are recorded during the same time period that the revenues they make possible are recognized.

cost of goods sold *the expenses incurred to purchase or manufacture the merchandise sold during a period; equal to beginning inventory plus cost of goods purchased or manufactured less ending inventory*

While most revenue deductions can be classified as expenses, the format of an income statement usually separates the cost of inventory sold from other operating expenses. The amount expended for inventory sold is usually called cost of goods sold and it appears as a separate calculation on the income statement immediately following the revenue section. As an example, consider a typical retail grocery store. The cost of goods sold would be the costs incurred in purchasing all vegetables, meat, canned goods, and other merchandise sold during the period. The other expenses would be the amounts incurred for rent, utilities, telephone, salaries, property taxes, and other operating items.

The Cost of Goods Sold Expense

The measurement of cost of goods sold differs according to the type of business. In a retail business, such as a clothing store, the cost of goods sold is simply the expenses incurred in purchasing the clothing sold during that period. In a manufacturing firm, however, goods are produced, so cost of goods sold must include all manufacturing costs of the products sold. Because the differences between accounting for purchased versus produced goods are significant, and because it is much easier to understand the concept of cost of goods sold in the context of a retail firm, manufacturing firms will not be considered here.

Even in retail and wholesale firms, the measurement of cost of goods sold is complicated by the fact that not all inventory on hand is sold before new inventory is purchased. Indeed, a company's management would be foolish to deplete all inventory before ordering new merchandise. Such a practice would result in frequent out-of-stock situations, thus drastically reducing income because of lost sales.

In any given accounting period, a firm may purchase more inventory than it sells, sell more inventory than it purchases, or buy and sell exactly the same amount of inventory. No matter which situation occurs, a company records inventory as an expense only when it is sold. Until it is sold, inventory is classified as an asset on the balance sheet. Thus, it is possible for the cost of goods sold to be higher, lower, or the same as the amount of inventory purchased during an accounting period.

As we discussed briefly in Chapter 5, there are two principal methods of accounting for inventory and cost of goods sold: (1) the perpetual method and (2) the periodic method. We will now discuss them in more detail.

The Perpetual Inventory Method

perpetual inventory method *a system of recording inventory in which detailed records of the number of units and the cost of each purchase and sales transaction are prepared throughout the accounting period*

The perpetual inventory method requires a company to maintain inventory records that identify the number and cost of all units purchased and sold each day. Accounting for inventory with the perpetual method is similar to accounting for cash. Because every inventory transaction is recorded in detail, the balance in the inventory account should at all times represent the amount of inventory actually on hand.

To illustrate the perpetual inventory method, we will consider the case of Rainy Day Lawn Mower Company, which sells lawn mowers, snowblowers, and garden tillers, and maintains a separate inventory record for each product. The inventory record for the snowblower line for 1983 is shown in Exhibit 6–3.

EXHIBIT 6-3 **Perpetual Inventory Record—Snowblowers, 1983**

		Purchased			Sold			Balance in Inventory		
Date	*Explanation*	*No. of Units*	*Cost per Unit*	*Total Cost*	*No. of Units*	*Cost per Unit*	*Total Cost*	*No. of Units*	*Cost per Unit*	*Total Cost*
Jan. 1	Beginning inventory							32	$200	$ 6,400
Jan. 28	Sold				20	$200	$ 4,000	12	$200	$ 2,400
Mar. 3	Sold				8	$200	$ 1,600	4	$200	$ 800
Aug. 2	Purchased	100	$250	$25,000				104	4 at $200 100 at $250	$25,800
Aug. 8	Purchased	30	$250	$ 7,500				134	4 at $200 130 at $250	$33,300
Sept. 4	Purchased	10	$250	$ 2,500				144	4 at $200 140 at $250	$35,800
Sept. 6	Returned to manufacturer	(5)	$250	$(1,250)				139	4 at $200 135 at $250	$34,550
Sept. 20	Sold				15	4 at $200* 11 at $250	$ 3,550	124	$250	$31,000
Sept. 30	Returned from customer				(1)	$250	$ (250)	125	$250	$31,250
Nov. 20	Sold				81	$250	$20,250	44	$250	$11,000
Dec. 15	Sold				24	$250	$ 6,000	20	$250	$ 5,000
Dec. 31	Ending inventory							20	$250	$ 5,000
Totals		135		$33,750	147		$35,150			

* In this example, the oldest units on hand are assumed to be sold first. Inventory flow alternatives are discussed in the next chapter.

The mechanics of the perpetual method can be illustrated by examining the September transactions. The first transaction, on September 4, involved the purchase of 10 snowblowers for $250 each and would be accounted for as follows:

Inventory	2,500	
Accounts Payable		2,500
Purchased 10 snowblowers at $250 each.		

Rainy Day Lawn Mower Company then decided to return five defective snowblowers to the manufacturer. If the snowblowers had not yet been paid for, the entry would be

Accounts Payable	1,250	
Inventory		1,250
Returned 5 defective snowblowers to the manufacturer.		

When a company is using the perpetual inventory method, the entries to record sales transactions are slightly more complicated than those for purchase transactions. Since a sales transaction involves both the recognition of a sale and a reduction of inventory, two entries are needed. The two entries that would be made to account for the September 20 sale of 15 snowblowers at a price of $350 each would be

Accounts Receivable (or Cash)	5,250	
Sales Revenue		5,250
Cost of Goods Sold (4 at $200, 11 at $250)	3,550	
Inventory		3,550
Sold 15 snowblowers.		

This entry illustrates that cost of goods sold expense is incurred only when merchandise is sold. In this case, the merchandise that was sold for $5,250 cost the company $3,550. The difference between the revenue of $5,250 and the cost of goods sold of $3,550 is $1,700 gross margin, which is the amount the company can use to cover its operating expenses and to provide profit to its owners.

Finally, the entry to account for the return of one snowblower from a customer on September 30 would be

Sales Returns and Allowances	350	
Accounts Receivable (or Cash)		350
Inventory	250	
Cost of Goods Sold		250
Received 1 snowblower back from a customer.		

When using the perpetual method, at year-end a company can quickly determine its cost of goods sold as well as the amount of its ending inventory by examining the Inventory and Cost of Goods Sold accounts. In theory, the perpetual inventory method should eliminate the need to physically count the inventory. However, because of the possibility of clerical errors, spoilage, and theft, even firms that maintain perpetual inventory records usually count their inventory at least once a year. After the inventory is counted, the perpetual inventory records are adjusted to correct the balance in Inventory.

If a count were to reveal two snowblowers missing from inventory, the entry needed to account for the shortage would be

Inventory Shrinkage	500	
Inventory		500
To adjust the inventory balance to the physical count, 18 snowblowers.		

At the end of the period, the Inventory Shrinkage account would be closed to Income Summary as an expense.

For many companies, the perpetual method involves too much clerical work. Imagine keeping track of every item of inventory on a perpetual basis for General Motors Corporation. However, with the advent of computers to handle these repetitive transactions, use of the perpetual inventory method has become feasible for department stores and other businesses with large inventories. They can often maintain perpetual records by coding each inventory item and programming the cash register to adjust the records as an item is sold.

The Periodic Inventory Method

Although the perpetual inventory method provides excellent control over merchandise and allows for a quick determination of the amount of inventory on hand at all times, many businesses do not use this system because it is too time-consuming or does not fit their needs. For these firms, there is an alternative known as the periodic inventory method. It allows a company to determine Inventory and Cost of Goods Sold balances without keeping detailed records of the inventory effects of every sale and purchase transaction. Because a firm that uses the periodic inventory method does not record the effect on inventory of each transaction, it can only find out how much inventory it has remaining at the end of the period by physically counting and pricing its entire stock.

periodic inventory method *a system of recording inventory in which cost of goods sold is determined and inventory is adjusted at the end of the accounting period, not when merchandise is purchased or sold*

When using the periodic inventory method, a company initially records all purchases of inventory in a Purchases account. During the period, the effects of sales are not reflected in either the Inventory or Purchases account. At the end of the period, the company takes a physical count of all inventory on hand and determines the cost of goods sold for the period by making the following calculation.

Purchases *an account in which all inventory purchases are recorded; used with the periodic inventory method*

Beginning Inventory, January 1, 1983	$ 800
+ Purchases for the Year	2,200
= Cost of Goods Available for Sale During 1983	$3,000
− Ending Inventory, December 31, 1983	700
= Cost of Goods Sold for 1983	$2,300

The first item in this calculation is the dollar cost of the beginning inventory, which is the ending inventory balance of the previous year as determined by a physical count. The second item is the total amount of inventory purchased during the year. This is added to the beginning inventory and the total is the third item, the cost of goods available for sale during the period. The label "cost of goods available for sale" is a useful one since all the inventory a firm sells must come either from units it had on hand at the beginning of the period or from units it purchased during the period. Fourth is the ending inventory, which is determined by a physical count. This amount is subtracted from the cost of goods available for sale and the result is the cost of goods sold expense. Since inventory available for sale has to be either included in the ending inventory or sold during the period, the ending inventory and cost of goods sold are complementary amounts and their sum must always equal the total cost of goods available for sale.

Although the simple periodic inventory method outlined here is correct, it is not complete. Several other items—for example, purchase discounts, returns of merchandise purchased, and the cost of transporting merchandise into the firm—require that adjustments be made to purchases.

purchase discount *a reduction in the purchase price, allowed if payment is made within a specified period*

Purchase Discounts Purchases are simply sales viewed from the other side of the transaction. That is, many purchase transactions include terms (such as 2/10, n/30) to encourage prompt payment. And, just as sales discounts reduce the net amount of sales, so purchase discounts reduce the net cost of purchases. When a company uses the periodic inventory method, it subtracts purchase discounts from purchases in the cost of goods sold calculation. The Purchase Discounts account is a contra account: it is deducted from Purchases and has a credit balance.

Purchase Returns and Allowances *a contra-Purchases account in which the return of or allowances for previously purchased merchandise are recorded*

Freight-In *an account used to record the costs of transporting into a firm all purchased merchandise or materials intended for sale; added to Purchases in calculating cost of goods sold*

Purchase Returns and Allowances A firm may purchase merchandise for resale and find out that it is defective, does not meet specifications, or is otherwise unacceptable. This merchandise will be returned to the supplier, either for credit or for a cash refund. The company will then account for the return by crediting a contra account in the General Ledger called Purchase Returns and Allowances, which reduces the amount of purchases in the calculation of cost of goods sold on an income statement.

Freight-In The third adjustment to purchases is the cost of transporting merchandise into a firm (freight-in). Because merchandise cannot usually be sold by a firm until it is on hand, the cost of transporting it into the firm is considered an addition to the net amount of the purchase. If, for example, an appliance dealer in Salt Lake City purchases dishwashers from a firm in Chicago for $200 each, with transportation costs of $30 per unit, the cost of the dishwashers is $230, not $200. (When the appliance dealer later sells the dishwashers, if it pays the cost of delivering them to customers, this cost will not be added to Purchases but will be a delivery expense that will be separately recognized on the income statement as Freight-Out.)

Now that you are familiar with these three adjustments, we can expand the cost of goods sold calculation. But first you must determine the amount of ending inventory. As you will recall, Exhibit 6–3 showed perpetual inventory records for the snowblowers purchased and sold by Rainy Day Lawn Mower Company. The calculation of ending inventory is the same using the periodic inventory method, except that it is prepared in the following format.

Beginning Inventory, January 1, 1983		32 units
Purchases	140 units	
Less Purchase Returns (to manufacturers)	5 units	135 units
Goods Available for Sale		167 units
Units Sold	148 units	
Less Sales Returns (from customers)	1 unit	147 units
Ending Inventory, December 31, 1983		20 units
		at $250 = $5,000

Given an ending inventory of $5,000, we can calculate the cost of goods sold as follows. (Note that for this computation only we have included a 2/10, n/30 purchase discount and an arbitrary figure for freight-in.)

Beginning Inventory, January 1, 1983			$ 6,400
Purchases	$35,000		
Add Freight-In	500	$35,500	
Less: Purchase Discounts (2/10, n/30)		(700)	
Purchase Returns and Allowances		(1,250)	
Net Purchases			33,550
Cost of Goods Available for Sale During 1983			$39,950
Less Ending Inventory, December 31, 1983			5,000
Cost of Goods Sold for 1983			$34,950

The above computations, which appear in the cost of goods sold section of the income statement, must also be journalized so that the accounts are accurate. Although individual entries usually would be made for each transaction, in summary form the General Journal entries to account for these data would be as follows (assuming that each snowblower is sold for $350):

Purchases	35,000	
Accounts Payable (or Cash)		35,000
Purchased 140 snowblowers for $250 each.		
Accounts Payable (or Cash)	1,250	
Purchase Returns and Allowances		1,250
Returned 5 defective snowblowers.		
Accounts Receivable (or Cash)	51,800	
Sales Revenue		51,800
Sold 148 snowblowers at $350 each.		
Sales Returns and Allowances	350	
Accounts Receivable (or Cash)		350
Received 1 snowblower back from a dissatisfied customer.		

If, as shown in the cost of goods sold calculation, there had been either a cost for transporting the goods into the firm or discounts when the snowblowers were purchased, entries to record these items would also have to be made.

Freight-In	500	
Cash		500
Transported into company 140 snowblowers.		
Accounts Payable (Cash)	700	
Purchase Discounts		700
Received purchase discounts from suppliers.		

As you can see, several accounts have been affected by these transactions. However, no adjustments have been made to the Inventory account. In fact, the balance in the Inventory account at any time during the year is the same as it was at the beginning of the year. Adjustments are made to that account only when a physical count is taken at the end of an accounting period. At that time, the adjusting entries are made as a debit to Inventory to set up the new amount and a credit to eliminate the old, now incorrect, balance. The offsetting debits and credits are made to Cost of Goods Sold. In the case of Rainy Day Lawn Mower, the entries to adjust Inventory at the end of 1983 would be

Cost of Goods Sold	6,400	
Inventory (amount of beginning inventory, 32 units at $200)		6,400
To close beginning inventory to Cost of Goods Sold.		
Inventory (amount of ending inventory, 20 units at $250)	5,000	
Cost of Goods Sold		5,000
To adjust the balance in the Inventory account to the 12/31/83 physical count.		

Closing Entries for Cost of Goods Sold In Chapter 5, we discussed the closing entries for several revenue and expense accounts. Since cost of goods sold is also an income statement account, it must be closed at the end of each accounting period. If the perpetual inventory method is being used, the amount is already summarized in a Cost of Goods Sold account, which can be closed simply by crediting the account for its balance and debiting Retained Earnings directly or by debiting Income Summary, which is later closed to Retained Earnings for the same amount. Thus, if in 1983 Rainy Day Lawn Mower Company had used the perpetual inventory method as shown in Exhibit 6-3 on page 215, the closing entry would be

Income Summary (Retained Earnings)	35,150	
Cost of Goods Sold		35,150
To close the Cost of Goods Sold account for 1983.		

This amount represents the sale of 32 snowblowers that cost $200 each, and 115 snowblowers (116 less 1 returned) that cost $250 each. Note that the amount in this entry assumes no shortage of snowblowers when the physical inventory count was made.

With the periodic inventory method, the closing entries for Cost of Goods Sold are somewhat more complex. You will recall that, with the periodic method, when sales or purchases are recorded, no adjustment is made to the Inventory account. Instead, purchases of merchandise are recorded in an account called Purchases and the entries to record sales of merchandise include only entries for Accounts Receivable and Sales Revenue.

Therefore, the net amount of purchases (gross purchases minus returns and discounts) must be added to Cost of Goods Sold. This account, which was created when the inventory balance was adjusted (see entry above), will then reflect the correct amount of cost of goods sold and can be closed to Income Summary. The closing entries for the snowblower line of Rainy Day Lawn Mower Company would be

Cost of Goods Sold	35,000	
Purchases		35,000
To close the Purchases account for 1983.		
Purchase Returns and Allowances	1,250	
Cost of Goods Sold		1,250
To close the Purchase Returns and Allowances account for 1983.		

An examination of the Cost of Goods Sold account now shows that the balance is $35,150, or the same as when the perpetual inventory method was used.

Snowblowers
Cost of Goods Sold (1983)

Purchases; see entry above	35,000	1,250	Purchase Returns and Allowances; see entry above
Beginning Inventory; see entry on page 220	6,400	5,000	Ending Inventory; see entry on page 220
	$35,150		

The final entry, which is the same as that used with the perpetual inventory method, is the one that closes the Cost of Goods Sold account.

Income Summary (Retained Earnings)	35,150	
Cost of Goods Sold		35,150
To close the Cost of Goods Sold account for 1983.		

Note that we have not included the cost of transporting merchandise into the firm or discounts on purchases. That is because these factors were not considered under the perpetual method. However, under the periodic method, when there are balances in Freight-In and Purchase Discounts, these accounts have to be closed to Cost of Goods Sold. The entries to close these accounts would be

Cost of Goods Sold	500	
Freight-In		500
Purchase Discounts	700	
Cost of Goods Sold		700
To close the Freight-In and Purchase Discounts accounts in 1983.		

From the snowblower example, you can see that at the end of an accounting period both the perpetual and periodic inventory methods produce equal amounts of cost of goods sold and inventory. With both methods, inventory is recognized as an expense only when it is sold, and the ending inventory balances should be the same. The difference between the two methods is in the timing of the adjustments to inventory. With the perpetual method, adjustments are made with each purchase and sales transaction; with the periodic method, they are made only at the end of the period.

The importance of properly accounting for all purchases and sales transactions cannot be emphasized too strongly. Both directly affect cost of goods sold and an error in accounting for these transactions affects net income by the same amount. To make sure that the amounts in the Inventory and Cost of Goods Sold accounts are proper, most firms close their warehouses while they take a physical count of inventory. By not allowing any merchandise to enter or leave the warehouse during this period, they attempt to ensure that all inventory counted is actually recorded in the accounting records and that all inventory recorded is actually in the warehouse.

Other Operating Expenses

You now know how to account for revenues, which are recognized when earned, and inventory, which becomes an expense only when it is sold. Other operating expenses—such as payments for salaries, advertising, rent, and insurance—must also be accounted for.

As we have already noted, expenses are recognized in accordance with the matching principle; that is, all expenses incurred in producing revenues should be identified with the revenues generated, period by period. Obviously, the matching principle is easier to apply to some expenses than to others. For example, sales commissions are easily associated with sales revenue, but the allocation of a building's cost over its useful life is not so closely tied to sales revenue. To solve this problem and still apply the matching principle, companies usually record portions of such costs as expenses as the asset values of the items are used up. For example, interest paid would be classified as an expense over the period of time for which the money was borrowed. Similarly, the cost of supplies would be recognized as an expense as the supplies are used up. To consider another example, if Century Metal rented a building for the month of December at a monthly rental fee of $500, the rent expense would be incurred and should be recognized in December, no matter when Century Metal pays the December rent.

Monies that are paid before expenses are incurred are called prepaid expenses (sometimes prepaid assets or prepayments) and are classified as assets until used. Expenses that are incurred before they are paid for result in accrued liabilities until paid. Thus, in any given accounting period, a firm can pay for expenses not yet incurred (prepaid expenses), incur expenses not yet paid for (accrued liabilities), and of course both incur and pay for expenses. The important point is that only expenses actually incurred should be reflected on the income statement. Both prepaid expenses and accrued liabilities have been discussed in detail in Chapter 4 and will be mentioned again in Chapter 9.

TO SUMMARIZE Expenses are recognized according to the matching principle; that is, they are recorded at the same time the associated revenues are recognized. Operating expenses are separated into cost of goods sold expense and other operating expenses. There are two common methods of accounting for inventory and cost of goods sold: periodic and perpetual. With the perpetual method, a running account of actual inventory is maintained; with the periodic method, inventory adjustments are made only at the end of the period. Other entries are required for purchase discounts, purchase returns, and the cost of transporting goods. The entries made under the two methods are summarized in Exhibit 6-4. (Note that the numbers do not relate to prior examples, and that freight-in and purchase discounts are not included.) In addition to cost of goods sold, a firm has many other operating expenses. Monies expended prior to the incurrence of an expense are called prepaid expenses and are classified as assets. Expenses incurred before they are paid for result in accrued liabilities until they are paid.

EXHIBIT 6-4 Comparison of the Periodic and Perpetual Inventory Methods

Event	Periodic Inventory Method			Perpetual Inventory Method		
Purchased merchandise on credit (terms 2/10, n/30)	Purchases	2,000		Inventory	2,000	
	Accounts Payable		2,000	Accounts Payable		2,000
Returned merchandise to supplier	Accounts Payable	100		Accounts Payable	100	
	Purchase Returns and Allowances		100	Inventory		100
Paid for merchandise (not within discount period)	Accounts Payable	1,900		Accounts Payable	1,900	
	Cash		1,900	Cash		1,900
Sold merchandise on credit (terms 2/10, n/30)	Accounts Receivable	4,000		Accounts Receivable	4,000	
	Sales Revenue		4,000	Sales Revenue		4,000
				Cost of Goods Sold	2,400	
				Inventory		2,400
Received merchandise back from customer	Sales Returns and Allowances	200		Sales Returns and Allowances	200	
	Accounts Receivable		200	Accounts Receivable		200
				Inventory	120	
				Cost of Goods Sold		120
Adjusted for inventory (assumes a beginning inventory of $8,000). The ending inventory ($7,620) would be determined by a physical count.	Cost of Goods Sold	8,000		No entry		
	Inventory		8,000			
	Inventory	7,620				
	Cost of Goods Sold		7,620			
To close Cost of Goods Sold account	Cost of Goods Sold	2,000		Income Summary	2,280	
	Purchases		2,000	Cost of Goods Sold		2,280
	Purchase Returns and Allowances	100				
	Cost of Goods Sold		100			
	Income Summary	2,280				
	Cost of Goods Sold		2,280			

The Income Statement

Having separately reviewed the accounting for revenues and expenses, you are now ready to examine an accrual-basis historical cost income statement, such as the one in Exhibit 6–5.

Revenues, cost of goods sold, and operating expenses (which are separated into selling and general and administrative expenses on the income statement) have already been explained. The other revenues and expenses, extraordinary items, and earnings per share need some clarification. Other revenues and expenses (sometimes called financial revenues and expenses) are those items incurred or earned from activities that are outside of, or peripheral to, the normal operations of a firm. The most common entries in this section are interest and investment revenues and expenses.

EXTRAORDINARY ITEMS

extraordinary items *special nonoperating gains and losses that are unusual in nature, infrequent in occurrence, and material in amount*

The extraordinary items section of an income statement is reserved for reporting special nonoperating gains and losses. This category is restrictive and includes only those items that are (1) unusual in nature, (2) infrequent in occurrence, and (3) material in amount. They are separated from other revenues and expenses so that readers can identify them as one-time, or nonrecurring, events. The most common types of extraordinary items are losses or gains from floods, fires, earthquakes, and so on. For example, in 1980 when Mount St. Helens erupted, much of the Weyerhaeuser Company's timberlands were adversely affected by the mud slides and flooding. Weyerhaeuser reported an extraordinary loss of $66,700,000 in 1980 to cover standing timber, buildings and equipment, and other damages.

If a firm has an extraordinary loss, the amount of taxes it pays is less than it would have paid on the basis of ordinary operations. On the other hand, if a firm has an extraordinary gain, its taxes are increased. So that the full effect of the gain or loss can be presented, extraordinary items are always shown together with their tax effects, so that a net-of-tax amount can be seen. Thus, an income tax expense may appear in two places on the income statement: below operating income before taxes and in the extraordinary items section.

EARNINGS PER SHARE

earnings per share *net income divided by the average number of shares of stock outstanding during the period*

A company is required to show earnings per share (EPS) on the income statement. Usually, a firm will report EPS figures on income before extraordinary items, on extraordinary items, and on net income. Earnings per share is calculated by dividing a firm's income by the average number of shares of stock outstanding during the period. In Exhibit 6–5 it has been assumed that 100,000 shares of stock are outstanding. Earnings-per-share numbers are important because they allow potential investors to compare the profitability of all firms, whether large or small. Thus, the performance of a company earning $200,000 and having 200,000 shares of stock outstanding can be compared with the performance of a company that earns $60,000 and has 30,000 shares outstanding.

EXHIBIT 6-5

Aslaw Company
Income Statement
for the Year Ended December 31, 1983

Gross Sales Revenue		$2,500,000	
Less: Sales Returns and Allowances		(12,000)	
Sales Discounts		(13,000)	
Net Sales Revenue			$2,475,000
Cost of Goods Sold:			
Beginning Inventory		$ 800,000	
Purchases	$1,200,000		
Add Freight-In	36,000		
Less: Purchase Returns and Allowances	(26,000)		
Purchase Discounts	(24,000)		
Net Purchases		1,186,000	
Cost of Goods Available for Sale		$1,986,000	
Less Ending Inventory		(900,000)	
Cost of Goods Sold			1,086,000
Gross Margin			$1,389,000
Operating Expenses:			
Selling Expenses:			
Sales Salaries Expense	$ 200,000		
Advertising Expense	45,000		
Depreciation Expense—Stores	78,000		
Warranty Expense	14,000		
Total Selling Expenses		$ 337,000	
General and Administrative Expenses:			
Administrative Salaries Expense	$ 278,000		
Depreciation Expense—Office Equipment	18,000		
Property Tax Expense	22,000		
Miscellaneous Expenses	8,000		
Total General and Administrative Expenses		326,000	
Total Operating Expenses			663,000
Income from Operations			$ 726,000
Other Revenues and Expenses:			
Interest Expense		$ 81,000	
Interest Revenue		(5,000)	
Net Other Expenses			76,000
Income Before Taxes			$ 650,000
Income Taxes on Operations (46%)			299,000
Net Income Before Extraordinary Items			$ 351,000
Extraordinary Items:			
Flood Loss	$ 100,000		
Less Income Tax Effect	(50,000)		50,000
Net Income			$ 301,000
Earnings per Share:			
Income Before Extraordinary Items			$3.51
Extraordinary Loss			(0.50)
Net Income			$3.01

CHAPTER REVIEW

The four major ways of measuring income are: cash-basis, accrual-basis historical cost, constant-dollar, and current-value. The first two ignore the effects of inflation; the third accounts only for general price-level changes; and the fourth considers specific price changes. Each has its advantages and disadvantages, but the accrual-basis historical cost method is the one currently used for preparing the primary financial statements.

The income statement is the means of reporting net income. Its major sections are revenues, cost of goods sold, operating expenses, other revenues and expenses, extraordinary items, net income, and earnings per share.

In general, revenues are recognized when the earnings process has been substantially completed and when an exchange has taken place. Revenue transactions can be straightforward or can involve complications, such as sales discounts, sales returns and allowances, or bad debts.

The cost of goods sold section of an income statement reports the cost of the merchandise sold during a period. Inventory and cost of goods sold can be accounted for using either of two methods: perpetual or periodic. While the accounting for each method is different, both produce the same ending balances for inventory and cost of goods sold. The differences between the two methods are in the control they provide over inventory and the amount of clerical effort required to maintain the inventory records. No adjustments are made to the inventory records during the year when the periodic inventory method is used, but inventory is adjusted for every sales or purchase transaction with a perpetual inventory method. Both methods take into consideration such things as discounts on purchases, returns of merchandise purchased, and the cost of transporting goods intended for resale into the firm.

In addition to cost of goods sold expense, businesses incur many other expenses. With accrual accounting, these are recognized as they are incurred, not when they are paid for. Monies paid prior to the incurrence of an expense are called prepaid expenses. Expenses incurred before they are paid for give rise to accrued liabilities. On the income statement, financial and other nonoperating revenues and expenses are classified separately. The income statement is not complete until all extraordinary items and earnings-per-share amounts have been included.

KEY TERMS AND CONCEPTS

account receivable (206)
accrual-basis historical cost method (201)
aging accounts receivable (212)
Allowance for Doubtful Accounts (210)
allowance method (209)
bad debt (209)
book value of accounts receivable (210)
cash-basis method (200)
constant-dollar method (202)
contra account (207)
cost of goods sold (214)
current-value method (204)
direct write-off method (209)
Doubtful Accounts Expense (210)
earnings per share (224)
economic income (199)
expenses (200)
extraordinary items (224)
Freight-In (218)
general price level (202)
inflation (201)

inventory (200)
matching principle (209)
periodic inventory method (217)
perpetual inventory method (214)
purchase discount (218)
Purchase Returns and Allowances (218)
Purchases (217)
revenue recognition principle (205)
revenues (205)
sales discount (207)
Sales Returns and Allowances (208)

REVIEW PROBLEM

The Income Statement

From the following information prepare, in good form, an income statement for Jacobs Corporation for the year ended December 31, 1983. Assume that there are 200,000 shares of stock outstanding.

Sales Returns and Allowances	$ 50,000
Sales Discounts	70,000
Gross Sales Revenue	9,000,000
Flood Loss	80,000
Income Taxes on Operations	500,000
Administrative Salaries Expense	360,000
Sales Salaries Expense	800,000
Depreciation Expense–Building (General and Administrative)	32,000
Depreciation Expense–Equipment (General and Administrative)	4,000
Supplies Expense (General and Administrative)	16,000
Warranty Expense (Selling)	6,300
Payroll Tax Expense (Selling)	6,000
Amortization of Patents (General and Administrative)	3,800
Insurance Expense (General and Administrative)	34,000
Advertising Expense	398,000
Interest Revenue	6,000
Interest Expense	92,000
Insurance Expense (Selling)	7,000
Doubtful Accounts Expense (Selling)	7,200
Miscellaneous Selling Expenses	15,000
Miscellaneous General and Administrative Expenses	10,800
Purchases	6,000,000
Purchase Discounts	30,000
Beginning Inventory	200,000
Ending Inventory	210,000
Purchase Returns and Allowances	20,000
Freight-In	10,000
Tax Rate Applicable to Flood Loss	30%

Solution

1. The first step in preparing a comprehensive income statement is classifying items. In this case, we have the following.

Revenue Accounts

Sales Discounts	$ 70,000
Sales Returns and Allowances	50,000
Gross Sales Revenue	9,000,000

General and Administrative Expense Accounts

Administrative Salaries Expense	$ 360,000
Depreciation Expense–Building	32,000
Depreciation Expense–Equipment	4,000
Supplies Expense	16,000
Amortization of Patents	3,800
Insurance Expense	34,000
Miscellaneous General and Administrative Expenses	10,800

Miscellaneous Accounts

Income Taxes on Operations	$ 500,000

Extraordinary Item Accounts

Flood Loss	$ 80,000
Tax Rate	30%

Cost of Goods Sold Accounts

Purchases	$6,000,000
Purchase Discounts	30,000
Beginning Inventory	200,000
Ending Inventory	210,000
Purchase Returns and Allowances	20,000
Freight-In	10,000

Selling Expense Accounts

Sales Salaries Expense	$ 800,000
Warranty Expense	6,300
Payroll Tax Expense	6,000
Advertising Expense	398,000
Insurance Expense	7,000
Doubtful Accounts Expense	7,200
Miscellaneous Selling Expenses	15,000

Other Revenue and Expense Accounts

Interest Expense	$ 92,000
Interest Revenue	6,000

2. Once the accounts are classified, the income statement is prepared by including the accounts in the following format (see page 229).

Revenues (Gross Sales Revenue − Sales Returns and Allowances − Sales Discounts = Net Sales)
− Cost of Goods Sold [Beginning Inventory + Net Purchases (Gross Purchases + Freight-In − Purchase Returns and Allowances − Purchase Discounts) − Ending Inventory]
= Gross Margin
− Selling Expenses
− General and Administrative Expenses
= Income from Operations
+/− Other Revenues and Expenses (add Net Revenues, subtract Net Expenses)
= Income Before Taxes
− Income Taxes on Operations
= Net Income Before Extraordinary Items
+/− Extraordinary Items (add Extraordinary Gains, subtract Extraordinary Losses, net of applicable taxes)
= Net Income

3. After net income is computed, earnings per share is calculated and added to the bottom of the statement. It is important that the proper heading be included.

DISCUSSION QUESTIONS

1 Why is economic income so difficult to measure?

2 When is it theoretically possible to precisely determine the income of a firm?

3 What are the major problems in measuring income on a cash basis?

4 Assume that the price of college textbooks has doubled since 1960; this means that there has been 100 percent inflation since that time. Is this a valid conclusion? Discuss, with reference to the difference between general and specific price changes.

5 When should revenues be recognized?

6 When should expenses be recognized?

7 Why is it usually important to take advantage of purchase discounts?

8 Why is it important to have separate accounts for Sales Returns and Allowances and Sales Discounts? Wouldn't it be much easier to directly reduce the Sales Revenue account for these adjustments?

9 Why do most companies tolerate a small percentage of their accounts receivable becoming uncollectible?

10 Why does the accounting profession require use of the allowance method of accounting for losses due to uncollectible accounts rather than the direct write-off method?

11 What type of an account is Inventory?

12 Under what conditions will the dollar amount of cost of goods sold for a period be equal to the dollar purchases made during that period?

13 Why is it necessary to physically count inventory when the perpetual inventory method is being used?

14 Which inventory method (perpetual or periodic) provides the best control over a firm's inventory?

15 Is the accounting for purchase discounts and purchase returns the same with both the perpetual and periodic inventory methods? If not, what are the differences?

16 Are the costs of transporting inventory in and out of a firm treated the same way under the periodic and perpetual methods? If not, what are the differences?

17 What adjusting entries to the Inventory account are required when the perpetual inventory method is used?

18 What is the difference between a prepaid expense and an expense?

EXERCISES

E6-1 Recording Sales Transactions—Periodic Inventory Method

On May 24, 1983, N and N Company sold $20,000 of merchandise to Fred Jones with terms of 2/10, n/30. Assuming that N and N Company uses the periodic inventory method, prepare journal entries to record the following:

1. The initial sale.

2. The payment of $9,800 by Jones on May 30 on his account.

3. The payment of $6,000 by Jones on June 20 on his account. Also, on June 20, Jones returned merchandise which he paid $4,000 for, claiming that it malfunctioned and did not meet contract terms.

Jacobs Corporation

Income Statement for the Year Ended December 31, 1983

Revenues:				
Gross Sales Revenue			$9,000,000	
Less: Sales Returns and Allowances			(50,000)	
Sales Discounts			(70,000)	
Net Sales Revenue				$8,880,000
Cost of Goods Sold:				
Beginning Inventory		$ 200,000		
Purchases	$6,000,000			
Less: Purchase Returns and Allowances	(20,000)			
Purchase Discounts	(30,000)			
Plus Freight-In	10,000	5,960,000		
Cost of Goods Available for Sale		$6,160,000		
Less Ending Inventory		(210,000)		
Cost of Goods Sold				5,950,000
Gross Margin				$2,930,000
Operating Expenses:				
Selling Expenses:				
Sales Salaries Expense		$ 800,000		
Warranty Expense		6,300		
Payroll Tax Expense		6,000		
Advertising Expense		398,000		
Insurance Expense		7,000		
Doubtful Accounts Expense		7,200		
Miscellaneous Expenses		15,000		
Total Selling Expenses			$1,239,500	
General and Administrative Expenses:				
Administrative Salaries Expense		$ 360,000		
Depreciation Expense—Building		32,000		
Depreciation Expense—Equipment		4,000		
Supplies Expense		16,000		
Amortization of Patents		3,800		
Insurance Expense		34,000		
Miscellaneous Expenses		10,800		
Total General and Administrative Expenses			460,600	
Total Operating Expenses				1,700,100
Income from Operations				$1,229,900
Other Revenues and Expenses:				
Interest Expense			$ 92,000	
Interest Revenue			(6,000)	
Total Other Expenses and Revenues				86,000
Income Before Taxes				$1,143,900
Income Taxes on Operations				500,000
Net Income Before Extraordinary Items				$ 643,900
Extraordinary Items:				
Flood Loss			$ 80,000	
Less Income Tax Effect (30%)			24,000	56,000
Net Income				$ 587,900
Earnings per Share:				
Before Extraordinary Items	$3.22 ($643,900 ÷ 200,000 shares)			
Extraordinary Loss	0.28 ($56,000 ÷ 200,000 shares)			
Net Income	$2.94 ($587,900 ÷ 200,000 shares)			

E6-2 Recording Sales Transactions—Perpetual Inventory Method

Record the events in E6-1, except now assume that N and N Company uses the perpetual inventory method and that the cost of merchandise is 70 percent of its selling price.

E6-3 Recording Sales Transactions—Periodic Inventory Method

Sunshine Company sold $2,000 of merchandise on account to Atlantic Company on June 3, 1983, with terms 2/10, n/30. On June 7, 1983, Sunshine Company received $100 of merchandise back from Atlantic Company and issued a credit memorandum for the appropriate amount. Sunshine Company received payment for the balance of the bill on June 21, 1983. Record these events on Sunshine Company's books, assuming that the company uses the periodic inventory method.

E6-4 Recording Sales Transactions—Perpetual Inventory Method

Record the events in E6-3, except now assume that Sunshine Company uses the perpetual inventory method and that the cost of the merchandise is 60 percent of the selling price.

E6-5 Computing and Recording a Doubtful Accounts Expense

During 1983, Abco Corporation has had a total of $2,500,000 in sales, of which 80 percent were on credit. Also, $30,000 of accounts receivable are to be written off as uncollectible at year-end. At year-end the Accounts Receivable balance shows a total of $1,150,000, which has been aged as follows:

Age	Amount
Current	$ 950,000
1–30 days past due	100,000
31–60 days past due	50,000
61–90 days past due	35,000
Over 90 days past due	15,000
	$1,150,000

Prepare the journal entry required at year-end to properly record the doubtful accounts expense under each of the following conditions. Assume, where applicable, that Allowance for Doubtful Accounts has a credit balance of $2,750 immediately before these adjustments.

1. Use the direct write-off method. [Assume that all accounts determined to be uncollectible ($30,000) are written off in a single year-end entry.]

2. Based on experience, annual uncollectible accounts are estimated to be approximately 1.4 percent of total credit sales for the year.

3. Based on experience, uncollectible accounts for the year are estimated to be approximately 3 percent of total accounts receivable.

4. Based on experience, uncollectible accounts are estimated to be the sum of:

1 percent of current accounts receivable
6 percent of accounts 1–30 days past due
10 percent of accounts 31–60 days past due
20 percent of accounts 61–90 days past due
30 percent of accounts over 90 days past due

E6-6 Aging of Accounts Receivable and Uncollectible Accounts

XYZ Company has found that, historically, ½ percent of its current accounts receivable, 1 percent of accounts 1 to 30 days past due, 1½ percent of accounts 31 to 60 days past due, 3 percent of accounts 61 to 90 days past due, and 10 percent of accounts over 90 days past due are uncollectible. The following schedule shows an aging of the accounts receivable as of December 31, 1983.

		Days Past Due			
	Current	*1 to 30*	*31 to 60*	*61 to 90*	*Over 90*
Balance	$45,600	$9,850	$4,100	$850	$195

The balances at December 31, 1983, in certain selected accounts are as follows (assume that the allowance method is used):

Sales Revenue	$120,096
Sales Returns	1,209
Allowance for Doubtful Accounts	113 (credit balance)

1. Given the data above, make the necessary adjusting entry (or entries) for uncollectible accounts on December 31, 1983.

2. On February 14, 1984, Jason Marks, a customer, informed XYZ Company that he was going bankrupt and would not be able to pay his account of $46. Make the appropriate entry (or entries).

3. On June 29, 1984, Jason Marks was able to pay the amount he owed in full. Make the appropriate entry (or entries).

4. Assume that Allowance for Doubtful Accounts at December 31, 1983, had a debit balance of $113 instead of a credit balance of $113. Make the necessary adjusting journal entry that would be needed on December 31, 1983. [The entry should be similar to that called for in part (1), except for the amount.]

E6-7 Income Statement Calculations

Complete the following cost of goods sold calculations by filling in all missing numbers.

	Company A	Company B	Company C	Company D
Sales Revenue	$2,000	(4) $___	$480	$1,310
Beginning Inventory	200	76	0	600
Purchases	(1) ___	423	480	249
Purchase Returns and Allowances	20	19	0	(8) ___
Ending Inventory	300	110	(6) ___	195
Cost of Goods Sold	1,200	370	(7) ___	(9) ___
Gross Margin	(2) ___	(5) ___	155	(10) ___
Expenses	108	22	34	129
Income (or Loss)	(3) ___	107	121	546

E6-8 Estimating Cost of Goods Sold

PDQ Company is located in Los Angeles, California. During 1983, an earthquake demolished its building and most of the accounting records. The president of the company has requested that you reconstruct an income statement for the year ended December 31, 1983. In doing so, you have been able to gather the following information. (Ignore income taxes.)

Inventory Balance, January 1, 1983	$ 28,600
Purchases Made During 1983	62,400
Sales Made During 1983	100,000
Operating Expenses Incurred During 1983 (other than Cost of Goods Sold)	10,000

PDQ Company's cost of goods sold is normally 75 percent of sales; 1983 was a normal year.

E6-9 Cost of Goods Sold Calculations

ABC Company has provided the following information for the calendar year 1983.

Inventory Balance, January 1, 1983	$ 50,000
Total Cost of Goods Available for Sale	150,000
Sales Returns and Allowances	6,500
Purchase Returns and Allowances	2,500
Freight-In	1,000
Sales (net of Returns and Allowances)	153,500
Operating Expenses	13,500

The gross sales of ABC Company are 160 percent of cost of goods sold. Using the available information, compute the following (ignore income taxes).

1. Gross sales for 1983.
2. Net purchases for 1983.
3. Cost of goods sold for 1983.
4. Inventory balance at December 31, 1983.
5. Gross margin for 1983.
6. Net income for 1983.

E6-10 Preparation of a Partial Income Statement

The following account balances were included in the ledger of John R. Emerson Company on December 31, 1983.

Name of Account	Balance
Cash	$ 800
Freight-In	1,920
Beginning Inventory, Balance Carried from January 1, 1983	13,000
Purchases	164,000
Purchase Discounts	400
Purchase Returns and Allowances	2,240
Sales Revenue	186,000
Sales Discounts	600
Sales Returns and Allowances	2,800

The amount of inventory on hand on December 31, 1983, was $29,000. Prepare a partial income statement (through gross margin) from the available data for Emerson Company for the year ended December 31, 1983.

E6-11 Cost of Goods Sold Calculation

The accounts of Aquarius Company had the following balances for 1983.

Purchases	$130,000
Inventory, January 1, 1983	20,000
Purchase Returns and Allowances	3,820
Purchase Discounts	440
Freight-In	6,200
Freight-Out (Selling Expense)	1,200
Cash	2,000

The inventory balance on December 31, 1983, is $24,000. Using the information above, construct the cost of goods sold section of the income statement for Aquarius Company for 1983.

E6-12 The Effect of Inventory Errors

The following are the abbreviated income statements for Blue Sky Corporation for the last two periods.

	Period 1	Period 2
Net Sales	$20,000	$25,000
Cost of Goods Sold:		
Beginning Inventory	$ 5,000	$ 4,000
Net Purchases	13,000	15,000
Cost of Goods Available for Sale	$18,000	$19,000
Ending Inventory	4,000	5,000
Cost of Goods Sold	$14,000	$14,000
Gross Margin	$ 6,000	$11,000
Operating Expenses	7,000	7,000
Net Income (or Loss)	$ (1,000)	$ 4,000

Answer each of the following *unrelated* questions.

1. If the beginning inventory in period 1 ($5,000) is overstated by $2,000 (it should be $3,000), what is the correct net income (or loss) for that period?
2. If the beginning inventory in period 2 ($4,000) is understated by $2,000 (it should be $6,000), what is the correct amount of net income for period 2?
3. If the ending inventory in period 1 ($4,000) is overstated by $2,000 (it should be $2,000), what is the correct cost of goods sold for the two periods combined?
4. If the cost of goods sold in period 2 ($14,000) is understated by $1,000 (ending inventory in period 2 was overstated), what is the correct net income for period 2?
5. If the ending inventory in period 2 ($5,000) is understated by $2,000 (it should be $7,000), what is the total correct cost of goods sold for the two periods combined?

E6–13 Inventory: Adjusting and Closing Entries

In 1983, Bjorn Company had the following account balances.

Inventory, January 1, 1983	$ 60,000
Purchases	110,000
Cost of Goods Sold	120,000
Purchase Returns and Allowances	2,000

Assuming that a physical count of inventory on December 31, 1983, showed $46,000 of ending inventory, complete the following. (Note that this problem involves $2,000 of inventory shrinkage.)

1. Adjust the inventory records and close the related purchases accounts, assuming that the periodic inventory method is used.
2. Adjust the inventory records and close the appropriate accounts, assuming that the perpetual inventory method is used.

E6–14 The Effect of Errors in Recording Expenses

An examination of the records of Treadwell Company early in 1984 revealed that the following errors and omissions had occurred during 1983 and 1984.

a. Wages of $600 owed to employees at December 31, 1983, were not recognized as an expense in 1983 and were recorded as an expense when paid in 1984.

b. All office supplies were charged to expense when purchased. Supplies on hand of $300 were overlooked when the appropriate December 31, 1983, adjusting entries were made.

c. A customer's payment of $400 in December 1983 for merchandise to be delivered in 1984 was recorded as a sale in 1983. No entry was made in 1984 when the goods were actually sold.

d. Rent for January 1984 of $450 was paid in advance during 1983 and was charged to expense when paid.

Given the information above, complete the following two requirements:

1. For each of the above four errors state (a) whether 1983 net income would be under- or overstated and by how much; and (b) whether 1984 net income would be under- or overstated and by how much.
2. If the reported net incomes for 1983 and 1984 were $20,000 and $30,000, respectively (before adjustments for the above items), what should the amount of net income have been for each of the two years?

E6–15 Completing an Income Statement

Randy Forgetful, the accountant for Swenson Supplies Company, forgot where he put the accounting records. After searching the premises, he did manage to find the following information for 1983 and 1984. The president of the company has requested comparative financial statements and Randy needs your help in determining the missing numbers before he turns in his report to Mr. Swenson.

	1983	1984
Sales Revenue	$276,00	(5)$ ___
Beginning Inventory	65,000	(6) ___
Purchases	(1) ___	214,000
Cost of Goods Available for Sale	273,000	(7) ___
Ending Inventory	(2) ___	57,000
Cost of Goods Sold	224,000	(8) ___
Gross Margin	(3) ___	61,000
Expenses	30,000	(9) ___
Income Before Taxes	(4) ___	24,000

E6–16 Income Statement Analysis

The following table represents portions of the income statements of Atlas Company for the years 1983–1985. Fill in the missing numbers. Assume that gross margin is 40 percent of net sales revenue.

	1983	1984	1985
Gross Sales Revenue	$25,800	(9)$ ___	$42,000
Sales Discounts	100	100	-0-
Sales Returns and Allowances	700	200	-0-
Net Sales Revenue	(1) ___	(10) ___	42,000
Beginning Inventory	(2) ___	8,000	(15) ___
Purchases	15,000	(11) ___	24,800
Purchase Discounts	500	300	700
Freight-In	500	-0-	(16) ___
Cost of Goods Available for Sale	(3) ___	25,000	29,000
Ending Inventory	(4) ___	(12) ___	3,800
Cost of Goods Sold	(5) ___	(13) ___	(17) ___
Gross Margin	(6) ___	14,000	(18) ___
Selling Expenses	(7) ___	(14) ___	4,000
General and Administrative Expenses	3,000	3,200	(19) ___
Income Before Taxes	4,000	8,000	9,000
Income Taxes	(8) ___	4,000	4,500
Net Income	2,000	4,000	(20) ___

E6–17 Preparing an Income Statement

Big Company is preparing financial statements for the calendar year 1983. The totals given below for each account have been verified as correct.

Office Supplies on Hand	$ 150
Insurance Expense	60
Gross Sales Revenue	3,000
Cost of Goods Sold	1,610
Sales Returns and Allowances	100
Interest Expense	50
Accounts Payable	60
Accounts Receivable	130
Extraordinary Loss	540
Selling Expenses	180
Office Supplies Used	40
Cash	150
Revenue from Investments	140
Number of shares of Capital Stock	90

Prepare an income statement. Assume a 20 percent income tax rate on both income from operations and extraordinary items. Your solution should include earnings-per-share numbers.

PROBLEMS

P6–1 Different Concepts of Income

Maryland Retail Association is a new store in Cambridge, Md., that sells hardware and other merchandise. During 1983, the store had the following information in its records.

a. Started business on January 2, 1983. On that date, the company purchased a store building at a cost of $80,000. The building is expected to have a 20-year life.

b. On January 3, 1983, inventory was purchased for $50,000. No other inventory purchases were made during the year.

c. During the year, the store had the following transactions:

(1) Sold merchandise that cost $30,000 for $70,000.

(2) Paid $22,000 in salaries and other expenses.

d. All the above were cash transactions.

e. On December 31, 1983, it was determined that the current values of the store building and remaining inventory were $100,000 and $26,000, respectively.

Required:

1. Compute the following:
   (a) Cash-basis income (or loss).
   (b) Accrual-basis historical cost income (or loss).
2. **Interpretive Question** Which of these net income numbers provides better information regarding the performance of the store during 1983? Why?
3. **Interpretive Question** Do either of these alternatives reflect the effects of increases or decreases in the values of assets and liabilities caused by inflation, technological advances, and so forth? If not, what methods could be used to account for these factors?
4. **Interpretive Question** Briefly, what are the major differences between the constant-dollar and current-value approaches to measuring income?

P6–2 Different Concepts of Income

RPA Corporation is a retail firm that sells video discs in the new and emerging home movie market. The company was formed on January 3, 1983, and during 1983 had the following cash transactions:

a. On January 3, purchased a new building at a cost of $100,000, some furniture at a cost of $40,000, and inventory at a cost of $20,000. The building has a 50-year life and the furniture a 10-year life.

b. During the year, sold $10,000 (one-half) of its inventory for $25,000, and paid salaries of $10,000. (No other expenses were recorded during the year.)

Required:

1. Given the above data, compute the following.
   (a) Cash-basis income (or loss).
   (b) Accrual-basis historical cost income (or loss).

2. **Interpretive Question** Other than at the time of an exchange (sale or other arm's-length transaction), do either of these methods recognize changes in the values of assets and liabilities?

3. **Interpretive Question** Explain why constant-dollar accounting does not recognize all changes in the values of assets and liabilities.

P6–3 Concepts of Income—Cash and Accrual Accounting

During its initial year of operation in 1983, Johnson Company had the following transactions.

Sales Revenue	$80,000	($60,000 of which has been collected and $20,000 of which is still in receivables)
Purchases of Merchandise	$40,000	($36,000 of which has been paid for, and the remainder of which is still owed at year-end)
Expenses:		
Salaries Expense	$32,000	($30,000 of which has been paid)
Utilities Expense	$ 2,000	(all of which has been paid)
Rent Expense	$10,000	(all of which has been paid)
Other Purchases (on December 31, 1983):		
Building	$22,000	($5,000 of which has been paid)
Land	$ 6,000	($2,000 of which has been paid)

Required:

1. Assuming that the amount of ending inventory is $4,000 and that there was no beginning inventory, compute the following.
   (a) Net income (using the currently required method) for 1983 (ignore income taxes, depreciation, and interest expense).
   (b) Net cash inflow (or outflow) for 1983.

2. **Interpretive Question** Which of the statements required in part (1) better indicates the performance of the company during 1983?

P6–4 Net Income and Cash Flows

As the controller for Sherwood Enterprises, you have just completed the annual report for 1983 and determined that net income for the year was $20,000. Notwithstanding the company's profitable operations, it is being plagued by a severe cash shortage. Helen Sherwood, the company president, has asked you to find the reasons for the company's cash problems. In preparing your report, you discover the following with respect to the year's operation.

a. Clock Corporation, a customer, was unable to pay for merchandise purchased during 1983. As a result, on November 1, 1983, Sherwood accepted a 90-day, 15 percent note from Clock in the amount of $8,000.

b. Accounts receivable were $24,000 on January 1, 1983, and $32,000 on December 31, 1983.

c. Accounts payable were $18,000 on January 1, 1983, and $12,000 on December 31, 1983.

d. During 1983, the company purchased a new building costing $200,000. Twenty percent of the purchase price was paid in cash and the balance was borrowed from a local bank. (Ignore interest.) The building has a 40-year life.

e. Inventory on hand totaled $42,000 on January 1, 1983, and $48,000 on December 31, 1983.

f. Other payables totaled $2,000 on January 1, 1983, and $0 on December 31, 1983.

g. Prepaid expenses increased $12,000 during 1983.

h. Depreciation expense for 1983 was $7,000.

i. Dividends paid during 1983 totaled $3,000.

Required:

1. Using the above information, compute the net amount of cash inflow or outflow for 1983.

2. **Interpretive Question** Does the company have a critical cash shortage or does it appear that its negative cash position is only a temporary problem?

P6–5 Selling and Purchasing Transactions

Hopkins Bicycle Shop had the following transactions during the first nine days of March 1983.

March 1	Purchased 10 bicycles at $100 each, terms 2/10, n/30.
2	Returned 1 bicycle to supplier because the frame was bent; received credit memorandum for $100.
5	Sold 5 bicycles for $200 each to a local cycling club for cash.
8	One of the bicycles sold on March 5 was returned because of a defective tire; refunded for cash.
9	Paid supplier the net amount owed for the bicycles purchased on March 1.

Required:

1. Journalize the above transactions using:
   (a) The periodic inventory method.
   (b) The perpetual inventory method.

2. **Interpretive Question** What types of companies are more likely to use the perpetual inventory method?

P6-6 Inventory Adjustment and Closing Entries

During 1983, Birch Company had the following transactions.

a. Sold merchandise costing $25,000 for $60,000.

b. Purchased merchandise costing $22,000.

c. Returned merchandise costing $2,000 to the supplier.

d. Received merchandise that was sold for $3,000 (cost $1,300) back from dissatisfied customer.

Required:

Assuming that all the above are cash transactions and that inventory on hand at January 1, 1983, cost $29,000:

1. Journalize the above transactions using:
   (a) The periodic inventory method.
   (b) The perpetual inventory method.

2. Make all needed adjusting and closing entries related to the inventory and sales at December 31, 1983. (The ending inventory balance can be calculated by posting the perpetual inventory accounts.)

P6-7 Income Statement Analysis

The following information is available for Yellow Jacket Corporation for the year 1983.

	First Quarter	Second Quarter	Third Quarter	Fourth Quarter	Annual Statement
Revenues	$3,000	$4,000	$4,000	(13)$____	$15,000
Beginning Inventory	(1)____	(5)____	300	(14)____	(24)____
Purchases	1,000	1,500	2,000	(15)____	6,500
Purchase Discounts	15	(6)____	(10)____	(16)____	100
Purchase Returns and Allowances	(2)____	25	15	(17)____	100
Net Purchases	960	1,450	(11)____	(18)____	6,300
Cost of Goods Available for Sale	(3)____	(7)____	2,250	(19)____	6,600
Ending Inventory	(4)____	300	250	(20)____	(25)____
Cost of Goods Sold	1,110	(8)____	2,000	(21)____	6,200
Gross Margin	1,890	2,700	2,000	2,210	8,800
Other Expenses	1,500	1,500	(12)____	(22)____	5,200
Net Income	390	(9)____	1,000	(23)____	3,600

Required:

1. Complete the income statement entries given above by filling in all missing numbers in each quarter and in the annual statement.

2. **Interpretive Question** Ignoring the numbers above and in general terms, if the beginning inventory of the first quarter were overstated by $100, what would be the amount and direction of the over- or understatement of net income in the second quarter?

3. **Interpretive Question** Again, in general terms, if the ending inventory of the second quarter were understated by $200, what would be the amount and direction of the over- or understatement of net income in the third quarter?

P6-8 Estimating Uncollectible Accounts

Jason Corporation makes and sells athletic equipment to sporting goods stores throughout the country. On December 31, 1983, before adjusting entries were made, it had the following account balances on its books.

Accounts Receivable	$1,160,000	
Sales Revenue—1983 (60% were credit sales)	8,000,000	
Allowance for Doubtful Accounts	2,000	(credit balance)
Doubtful Accounts Expense	64,000	

Required:

1. Make the appropriate adjusting entry on December 31, 1983, to record the allowance for doubtful accounts if uncollectible accounts are estimated to be 1 percent of credit sales.

2. Make the appropriate adjusting entry on December 31, 1983, to record the allowance for doubtful accounts if uncollectible accounts are estimated to be 3 percent of accounts receivable.

3. Make the appropriate adjusting entry on December 31, 1983, to record the allowance for doubtful accounts if uncollectible accounts are estimated on the basis of an aging of accounts receivable and the aging schedule reveals the following.

Balance of Accounts Receivable		Percent Estimated to Become Uncollectible
Not yet due	$600,000	½ of 1 percent
1–30 days past due	$400,000	1 percent
31–60 days past due	$100,000	4 percent
61–90 days past due	$ 40,000	20 percent
Over 90 days past due	$ 20,000	30 percent

4. Now assume that on March 3, 1984, it was determined that a $32,000 account receivable from Outdoors Unlimited is uncollectible. Record the bad debt, assuming that:
   (a) The direct write-off method is used.
   (b) The allowance method is used.

5. Further assume that on June 4, 1984, Outdoors Unlimited paid this previously written-off debt of $32,000. Record the payment, assuming that:
   (a) The direct write-off method had been used on March 3 to record the bad debt.
   (b) The allowance method had been used on March 3 to record the bad debt.

6. **Interpretive Question** Which method of accounting for uncollectible accounts, direct write-off or allowance, is generally used? Why?

P6-9 Unifying Problem: The Income Statement

Use the following information to prepare an income statement for General Electronics Corporation for the year ending December 31, 1983. You should show separate classifications for revenues, cost of goods sold, gross margin, selling expenses, general and administrative expenses, income from operations, other revenue and expenses, income before taxes, income taxes, and net income. (Hint: Net income is $27,276.)

Sales Returns and Allowances	$ 4,280
Income Tax Expense	26,000
Interest Revenue	2,400
Office Supplies Expense (General and Administrative)	400
Depreciation Expense–Building (General and Administrative)	3,980
Office Salaries Expense (General and Administrative)	12,064
Miscellaneous Selling Expenses	460
Insurance Expense (Selling)	1,160
Advertising Expense	6,922
Sales Salaries Expense	40,088
Inventory, December 31, 1983	44,300
Purchases	230,560
Sales Discounts	3,644
Interest Expense	1,170
Miscellaneous General and Administrative Expenses	620
Insurance Expense (General and Administrative)	600
Payroll Tax Expense (General and Administrative)	3,600
Store Supplies Expense (Selling)	800
Depreciation Expense–Store Equipment (Selling)	2,198
Purchase Discounts	3,050
Inventory, January 1, 1983	79,400
Sales Revenue	395,472
Average Number of Shares of Stock Outstanding	10,000

P6-10 Unifying Problem: The Income Statement

From the following information prepare an income statement for Reynolds Incorporated for the year ended December 31, 1983. (Hint: Net income is $119,100.) Assume that there are 10,000 shares of capital stock outstanding.

Gross Sales Revenue	$3,625,000
Income Tax Expense	140,000
Cost of Goods Sold	2,415,000
Sales Salaries Expense	410,000
Depreciation Expense–Store Equipment (Selling)	16,000
Payroll Tax Expense (Selling)	3,100
Amortization of Trademarks (Selling)	2,000
Miscellaneous Selling Expenses	7,800
Miscellaneous General and Administrative Expenses	5,400
Doubtful Accounts Expense (Selling)	3,500
Insurance Expense (General and Administrative)	1,900
Interest Expense	46,000
Interest Revenue	3,000
Sales Returns and Allowances	10,000
Advertising and Promotion Expense	199,000
Insurance Expense (Selling)	17,000
Warranty Expense (Selling)	3,100
Office Supplies Used (General and Administrative)	8,000
Depreciation–Office Equipment (General and Administrative)	1,100
Administrative Salaries Expense	180,000
Fire Loss (net of tax)	40,000

CHAPTER 7

Inventory and Cost of Goods Sold

THIS CHAPTER EXPLAINS:

What items should be included in inventory.
The effects of errors in accounting for inventory.
Four inventory cost flow alternatives.
How inventories are valued.
Methods of estimating inventories.

Chapter 6 was an introduction to the income statement. It focused on the major elements of net income, including revenues, cost of goods sold (using the periodic and the perpetual inventory methods), and other expenses. Here, inventories and cost of goods sold will be examined in more detail. We will discuss: (1) what items belong in inventory, (2) the effects of errors in accounting for inventory, (3) inventory costing alternatives, (4) the valuation of inventories, and (5) methods of estimating inventories and cost of goods sold.

The Proper Measurement of Inventory

A typical company's inventories are constantly in flux; at any given time they are being bought, sold, and returned. As a result, it is sometimes difficult to keep track of which inventories on hand are owned, which are owned but not in stock, which have been sold but have not yet been shipped, and which have been purchased but have not yet arrived. Indeed, for many companies the key problem in computing net income is the proper measurement of inventory and cost of goods sold.

INVENTORY CUTOFF

inventory cutoff *the determination of which items should be included in the year-end inventory balance*

Although inventory is physically counted at the end of each accounting period, determining how much inventory is on hand is similar in many ways to measuring the amount of water in a sink that has the drain open and the tap on. The determination of which inventory should be included in the account balance for a period is called inventory cutoff. This is shown in Exhibit 7-1.

EXHIBIT 7-1 **Inventory Cutoff**

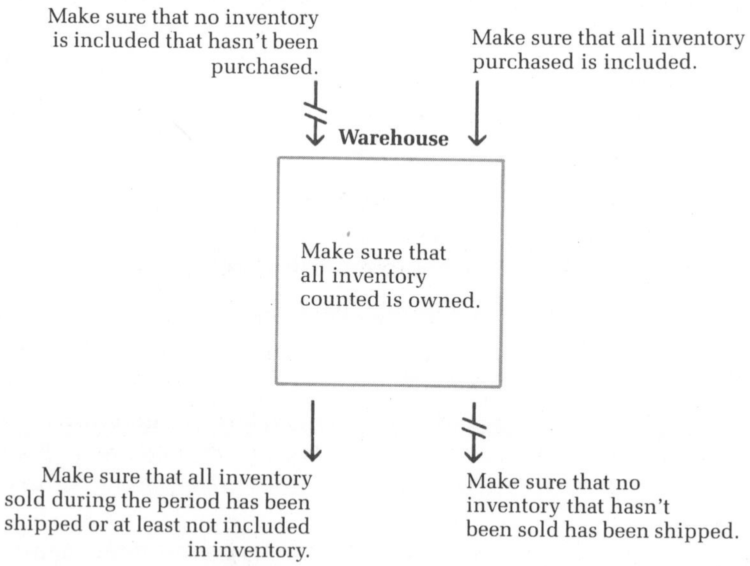

When inventory is purchased, the entry to record the purchase (assuming the periodic inventory method) is

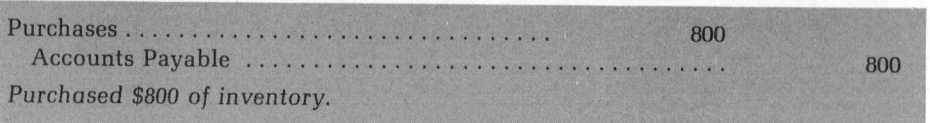

Purchases	800	
Accounts Payable		800
Purchased $800 of inventory.		

Since cost of goods sold is equal to beginning inventory plus purchases minus ending inventory, purchases have the effect of increasing total cost of goods sold. If a purchase has been entered in the accounting records but has not been physically counted and thus has been omitted from the ending inventory balance, cost of goods sold will be overstated and net income will be understated. On the other hand, if a purchased item has been counted and included in the inventory balance but has not yet been recorded as a purchase, cost of goods sold is understated and net income is overstated. To examine the effects of these types of inventory errors, we will assume that J. C. Sears Company had the following inventory records for 1983.

Inventory balance, January 1, 1983	$ 8,000
Purchases through December 30, 1983	20,000
Inventory balance, December 30, 1983	12,000

We will further assume that on December 31 the company purchased and received another $1,000 of inventory. The following comparison shows the kinds of inventory situations that might result.

	Incorrect*	**Incorrect**	**Incorrect**	**Correct**
The $1,000 of merchandise was	*not recorded as a purchase and not counted as inventory*	*recorded as a purchase but not counted as inventory*	*not recorded as a purchase but counted as inventory*	*recorded as a purchase and counted as inventory*
Beginning Inventory	$ 8,000 (OK)†	$ 8,000 (OK)	$ 8,000 (OK)	$ 8,000 (OK)
Net Purchases	20,000 (↓)	21,000 (OK)	20,000 (↓)	21,000 (OK)
Cost of Goods Available for Sale	$28,000 (↓)	$29,000 (OK)	$28,000 (↓)	$29,000 (OK)
Ending Inventory	12,000 (↓)	12,000 (↓)	13,000 (OK)	13,000 (OK)
Cost of Goods Sold	$16,000 (OK)	$17,000 (↑)	$15,000 (↓)	$16,000 (OK)

* This calculation produces the correct cost of goods sold but by an incorrect route—the errors in purchases and ending inventory counterbalance each other.

† ↓ indicates that the balance is too low; ↑ means it is too high; and OK means it is correct.

From this example you can see the extent to which cost of goods sold (and net income) can be misstated by the improper recording or counting of inventory.

A similar situation can occur when inventory is sold. If a sale is recorded but the merchandise remains in the warehouse and is counted in the ending inventory, gross margin and net income will be overstated. If a sale is not recorded but inventory is shipped and not counted in the ending inventory, gross margin and net income will be understated.

gross margin *the excess of net sales revenues over the cost of goods sold*

net income *a measure of the overall performance of a business entity; equal to revenues plus gains minus expenses and losses for the period*

To illustrate these potential inventory errors, we will again consider the data of J. C. Sears Company. Note that sales figures have been added and that the ending inventory and 1983 purchases now include the $1,000 purchase of merchandise made on December 31, 1983.

Sales Revenue through December 30, 1983	$32,000 (200% of cost)
Inventory Balance (January 1, 1983)	8,000
Net Purchases During 1983	21,000
Inventory Balance (December 31, 1983)	13,000

In addition, assume that on December 31, inventory that cost $1,000 was sold for $2,000. The merchandise was delivered to the buyer on December 31. The following comparison shows the kinds of situations that might result.

	Incorrect	Incorrect	Incorrect	Correct
The $2,000 sale was	*not recorded and the merchandise was counted as inventory*	*recorded and the merchandise was counted as inventory*	*not recorded but the merchandise was excluded from inventory*	*recorded and the merchandise was excluded from inventory*
Sales Revenue	$32,000 (↓)*	$34,000 (OK)	$32,000 (↓)	$34,000 (OK)
Cost of Goods Sold:				
Beginning Inventory	$ 8,000 (OK)	$ 8,000 (OK)	$ 8,000 (OK)	$ 8,000 (OK)
Net Purchases	21,000 (OK)	21,000 (OK)	21,000 (OK)	21,000 (OK)
Cost of Goods Available for Sale	$29,000 (OK)	$29,000 (OK)	$29,000 (OK)	$29,000 (OK)
Ending Inventory	13,000 (↑)	13,000 (↑)	12,000 (OK)	12,000 (OK)
Cost of Goods Sold	$16,000 (↓)	$16,000 (↓)	$17,000 (OK)	$17,000 (OK)
Gross Margin	$16,000 (↓)	$18,000 (↑)	$15,000 (↓)	$17,000 (OK)

* ↓ indicates that the balance is too low, ↑ means it is too high, and OK means it is correct.

Because inventory cutoff errors cause such severe problems, most businesses close their warehouses for one or two days at year-end while they count inventory. During this period they do not accept or ship merchandise, nor do they enter purchase or sales transactions in their accounting records.

ANALYZING THE EFFECTS OF INVENTORY ERRORS

As explained, an error in inventory results in cost of goods sold being overstated or understated. This error has the same effect on gross margin, and hence on net income. For example, if at the end of the accounting period $2,000 of inventory is not counted, cost of goods sold will be $2,000 higher than it should be, and gross margin and net income will be understated by $2,000. Such inventory errors affect gross margin and net income not only in the current year, but in the following year as well. An understatement in one year results in an overstatement in the next year, and vice versa.

To illustrate how inventory errors affect gross margin and net income, let us first assume the following correct data for Quality Corporation.

	1983		1984	
Sales Revenue		$50,000		$40,000
Cost of Goods Sold:				
Beginning Inventory	$10,000		$ 5,000	
Net Purchases	20,000		25,000	
Cost of Goods Available for Sale	$30,000		$30,000	
Ending Inventory	5,000		10,000	
Cost of Goods Sold		25,000		20,000
Gross Margin		$25,000		$20,000
Expenses		10,000		10,000
Net Income		$15,000		$10,000

Now, suppose that ending inventory in 1983 was overstated. That is, instead of the correct amount of $5,000, the count erroneously showed $7,000 of inventory on hand. The following analysis shows the effect of the error on net income in both 1983 and 1984.

	1983		1984	
Sales Revenue		$50,000		$40,000
Cost of Goods Sold:				
Beginning Inventory	$10,000		$ 7,000 (↑)	
Net Purchases	20,000		25,000	
Cost of Goods Available for Sale	$30,000		$32,000 (↑)	
Ending Inventory	7,000 (↑)*		10,000	
Cost of Goods Sold		23,000 (↓)		22,000 (↑)
Gross Margin		$27,000 (↑)		$18,000 (↓)
Expenses		10,000		10,000
Net Income		$17,000 (↑)		$ 8,000 (↓)

* ↑ means the balance is too high; ↓ means it is too low.

As you can see, when the amount of ending inventory is overstated (as it was in 1983), both gross margin and net income are overstated by the same amount ($2,000 in 1983). If the ending inventory amount had been understated, net income and gross margin would also have been understated, again by the same amount.

Since the ending inventory in 1983 becomes the beginning inventory in 1984, the net income and gross margin for 1984 are also misstated. In 1984, however, beginning inventory is overstated, so gross margin and net income are understated, again by $2,000. Thus, the errors in the two years offset each other, and if the count taken at the end of 1984 is correct, income in subsequent years should be properly stated.

OTHER FACTORS IN ACCOUNTING FOR INVENTORY

consignment *an arrangement whereby merchandise owned by one party (the consignor) is sold by another party (the consignee), usually on a commission basis*

consignor *the owner of merchandise to be sold by someone else, known as the consignee*

consignee *a vendor who sells merchandise owned by another party, known as the consignor, usually on a commission basis*

In addition to inventory cutoff and resulting errors, at least two other factors complicate a company's attempt to determine the proper amount of inventory. One factor involves the issuing of goods on consignment. Often, the inventory a firm stocks in its warehouse has not actually been purchased from suppliers. With this arrangement, suppliers, known as the consignors, retain ownership of the inventory until it is sold, and the firm selling the merchandise, known as the consignee, merely stocks and sells the merchandise for the consignor, and receives a commission on any sales as payment for services rendered. Some farm implement dealers, for example, do not actually own the tractors and other equipment they stock and sell.

It is extremely important that goods being held on consignment not be included in the inventory of the consignee, even though they are physically on the consignee's premises. It is equally important that consignors properly include all such inventory in their records, even though it is not on their premises.

Another factor that complicates the accounting for inventory has to do with shipping. The question is: Who owns the inventory that is on a truck or railroad car, the seller or the buyer? If the seller is bearing the shipping costs, the arrangement is known as FOB (free-on-board) destination, and the seller owns the merchandise from the time it is shipped until it is delivered to the buyer. If the buyer is bearing the shipping costs, the arrangement is known as FOB shipping point, and the buyer owns the merchandise during transit. Thus, in determining which inventory should be counted and included in the inventory balance for a period, a company must note the amount of inventory in transit and the terms under which it is being shipped.

FOB (free-on-board) destination *business term meaning that the seller of merchandise bears the shipping costs and maintains ownership until the merchandise is delivered to the buyer*

FOB (free-on-board) shipping point *business term meaning that the buyer of merchandise bears the shipping costs and acquires ownership at the point of shipment*

INVENTORY IN MANUFACTURING VERSUS NONMANUFACTURING FIRMS

Inventory cutoff, consignment shipments, and shipping costs are factors that affect inventory accounting in *all* types of businesses. Accounting for inventory in a *manufacturing* company, however, is quite different from accounting for inventory in a retail or wholesale firm. In the latter types of firms, inventory consists only of merchandise purchased from suppliers. In manufacturing companies, three types of inventory must be accounted for: (1) raw materials, (2) work-in-process, and (3) finished goods.

raw materials *goods purchased for use in manufacturing products*

work-in-process *partially completed units in production*

finished goods *manufactured products ready for sale*

Raw material inventories are goods purchased from suppliers for use in the manufacturing process. In a tire manufacturing firm, for example, raw materials would include rubber, steel, and other items used in making a tire. Work-in-process inventories are those production units that are in the process of being manufactured, together with their related manufacturing costs. For the tire manufacturer, the work-in-process inventory would include raw materials, factory labor (called direct labor), and other production costs (called overhead). Finally, finished goods inventories represent those units that are completed and ready for sale. At this point you need not be concerned about these different types of inventories. The specific techniques of accounting for inventory in a manufacturing firm will be covered when you learn about managerial accounting.

TO SUMMARIZE It is important to account for inventory properly because inventory errors can have a significant effect on cost of goods sold, gross margin, and net income. First, inventory errors affect cost of goods sold, gross margin, and net income on a dollar-for-dollar basis. That is, a $1 error in inventory results in a $1 error in the cost of goods sold, gross margin, and net income. Second, the misstatement of an ending inventory balance affects net income, both in the current year and in the next year. Third, errors in beginning and ending inventory have the opposite effect on cost of goods sold, gross margin, and net income. Finally, errors in inventory correct themselves after two years because the physical count at the end of the second year should reveal the correct amount of ending inventory for that period, which means that the records for the following year should show the correct amount of beginning inventory.

Besides inventory cutoff, the measurement of inventory is affected by consignments and shipping costs. In addition, manufacturing companies have three different types of inventory to account for.

Inventory Cost Flows

Merchandise is purchased or manufactured, stocked, and then sold. In most companies, the inventory purchased first is sold first to avoid problems of spoilage, obsolescence, or changing consumer demands. However, the specific physical flow of inventory depends on the nature of a firm's business.

To illustrate why it is so important to understand the flow of inventory, we will consider the September 1983 records of McDermitt Company (which sells one type of lawn mower).

Beginning inventory		10 lawn mowers, cost $200 each
September	3	Purchased 8 lawn mowers, cost $250 each
	5	Sold 12 lawn mowers at $400 each
	18	Purchased 16 lawn mowers, cost $300 each
	20	Purchased 10 lawn mowers, cost $320 each
	25	Sold 16 lawn mowers at $400 each

These inventory records show that during September the company had 44 lawn mowers (10 from beginning inventory and 34 that were purchased) that it could have sold. However, only 28 lawn mowers were sold, leaving a balance of 16 on hand at the end of September. Since the lawn mowers were purchased on different dates and cost different amounts (as would happen with a very high inflation rate), the company, in order to correctly calculate the cost of goods sold and ending inventory, must know which lawn mowers were sold and which are still in inventory.

Actually, there are four patterns in which the lawn mowers could have flowed through the firm: (1) The oldest units could have been sold first, (2) the most recently purchased units could have been sold first, (3) the units could have been sold in a random sequence and an average cost could have been used, or (4) specifically identified units could have been sold.

Each of these inventory flows is appropriate for certain businesses. For example, a grocery store usually tries to sell the oldest units first so that spoilage will not occur, whereas a company that stockpiles coal must first sell the coal purchased last, as it is on the top of the pile. In another type of company, say one that mixes chocolate in large vats and then sells it as candy bars, the units sold are a mixture of all ingredients purchased, and so some kind of average flow is used. Finally, automobile dealers usually specifically identify the cars sold.

PERIODIC INVENTORY COST FLOW ALTERNATIVES

As the actual merchandise flows through a firm, the costs of that merchandise must flow from the Inventory account to Cost of Goods Sold. The four patterns previously identified provide the basis for this cost flow accounting. The names of these inventory costing alternatives are: FIFO (first-in, first-out), LIFO (last-in, first-out), weighted average, and specific identification.

Before explaining each of these alternatives, we should note that firms can, and do, use an inventory costing procedure that may not represent the actual physical flow of their merchandise. For example, a coal company could decide to use FIFO as an inventory costing method, even though the physical flow of its coal more correctly matches the LIFO alternative. Similarly, a grocery store could use LIFO as an inventory costing alternative, even though most of its merchandise generally flows on a FIFO basis. When the cost of each inventory item is the same, all methods of inventory costing result in the same amounts for cost of goods sold and ending inventory. On the other hand, if inventory costs are rising, falling, or fluctuating during the year, each of the four cost flow alternatives will generally produce different numbers for ending inventory and cost of goods sold. Consequently, in a period of nonstable prices (which has been the case in most countries in recent years), firms can, to some extent, influence the amount of cost of goods sold, gross margin, and net income they will report—as well as the amount of taxes they will pay—by choosing a particular inventory costing procedure. The only current requirement is that firms be reasonably consistent and not change cost flow alternatives from year to year.

In the next few sections, we will use each of the four inventory costing procedures to calculate inventory. Each alternative will be analyzed first in the context of the *periodic inventory method* and then in the context of the *perpetual inventory method.* Data for McDermitt Company will again be used in illustrating the different inventory cost flows.

McDermitt Company
Inventory Data as of September 30, 1983

Beginning Inventory	10 lawn mowers, cost $200 each
Purchases:	
September 3	8 lawn mowers, cost $250 each
18	16 lawn mowers, cost $300 each
20	10 lawn mowers, cost $320 each
Sales:	
September 5	12 lawn mowers at $400 each
25	16 lawn mowers at $400 each

FIFO Periodic Inventory Costing

FIFO (first-in, first-out) *an inventory cost flow whereby the first goods purchased are assumed to be the first goods sold, so that the ending inventory consists of the most recently purchased goods*

The FIFO inventory costing alternative assumes that the units purchased first are sold first; the periodic inventory method requires that all calculations be made at the end of the period. Thus, the FIFO periodic inventory and cost of goods sold amounts for McDermitt Company would be computed as follows:

	Lawn Mowers	Costs
Beginning Inventory	10	$ 2,000
Net Purchases (8 at $250, 16 at $300, 10 at $320)	34	10,000
Goods Available for Sale	44	$12,000
Ending Inventory	16	5,000 (a)
Cost of Goods Sold	28	$ 7,000 (b)

The 16 units on hand at the end of the period must be the last ones purchased, since FIFO assumes that the first units purchased were the first ones sold. In order to determine which 16 units are on hand at the end of the period, McDermitt Company will simply identify the last 16 lawn mowers purchased during the month. These were

10 lawn mowers purchased on September 20 at $320 each	=	$3,200
6 lawn mowers purchased on September 18 at $300 each	=	1,800
Total ending inventory cost	=	$5,000 (a)

Accordingly, the 28 lawn mowers sold were the first ones purchased, or

10 lawn mowers of beginning inventory at $200 each	=	$2,000
8 lawn mowers purchased on September 3 at $250 each	=	2,000
10 lawn mowers purchased on September 18 at $300 each	=	3,000
Total cost of goods sold	=	$7,000 (b)

LIFO Periodic Inventory Costing

LIFO (last-in, first-out) *an inventory cost flow whereby the last goods purchased are assumed to be the first goods sold, so that the ending inventory consists of the first goods purchased*

The LIFO inventory costing alternative is the opposite of FIFO. Instead of assuming that the first units purchased are the first ones sold, LIFO assumes that the last units purchased during a period are the first ones sold. If prices are rising, as they have in recent years, the LIFO alternative tends to leave the oldest inventory costs on the balance sheet. Often, these costs are quite different from the current cost of replacing the inventory. The income statement, however, is generally more realistic with LIFO. Since the most recent inventory costs are charged against sales as cost of goods sold, the LIFO method is better than FIFO in matching current costs with current revenues.

With the LIFO periodic inventory costing alternative, the cost of goods sold and ending inventory for the McDermitt Company would be computed as follows:

	Lawn Mowers	Costs
Beginning Inventory	10	$ 2,000
Net Purchases	34	10,000
Goods Available for Sale	44	$12,000
Ending Inventory	16	3,500 (c)
Cost of Goods Sold	28	$ 8,500 (d)

The 16 lawn mowers remaining on hand at the end of the period must be from the beginning inventory and the first lawn mowers purchased.

10 lawn mowers of beginning inventory at $200 each	=	$2,000
6 lawn mowers purchased on September 3 at $250 each	=	1,500
Total ending inventory cost	=	$3,500 (c)

Accordingly, the 28 lawn mowers sold were the last ones purchased, or

10 lawn mowers purchased on September 20 at $320 each =	$3,200
16 lawn mowers purchased on September 18 at $300 each =	4,800
2 lawn mowers purchased on September 3 at $250 each =	500
Total cost of goods sold =	$8,500 (d)

Weighted-Average Periodic Inventory Costing

weighted average *a periodic inventory cost flow alternative whereby the cost of goods sold and the cost of ending inventory are determined by using a weighted-average cost of all merchandise available for sale during the period*

A third inventory costing alternative is weighted average. This alternative uses the costs of neither the first nor the last inventory units purchased to determine cost of goods sold. Instead, a weighted-average cost of all units on hand is charged against revenues each time a unit is sold. This alternative probably points up most clearly the difference between the flow of costs and the flow of goods through the firm. Although it may not be possible to mix the actual inventory items being sold (for instance, lawn mowers), it is perfectly acceptable to mix their costs to find the weighted-average cost of each item. The total cost of goods sold and ending inventory for McDermitt Company would then be computed as follows:

	Lawn Mowers	Costs
Beginning Inventory	10	$ 2,000
Net Purchases	34	10,000
Goods Available for Sale	44	$12,000
Ending Inventory	16	4,364*
Cost of Goods Sold	28	$ 7,636

* Rounded.

In this case, a weighted-average cost per lawn mower of $272.73 was used in computing both ending inventory and cost of goods sold. This weighted-average cost per unit is the total cost of goods available for sale divided by the total number of units available for sale, or

$$\frac{\text{cost of goods available for sale}}{\text{total number of units available for sale}} = \frac{\$12{,}000}{44} = \begin{array}{l}\$272.73\\ \text{per lawn mower}\end{array}$$

The cost of the ending inventory is the weighted-average cost per unit multiplied by the number of units on hand at the end of a period, or 16 units × $272.73 = $4,364. And the cost of goods sold is the weighted-average cost per unit multiplied by the number of units sold, or $272.73 × 28 units = $7,636.

Specific-Identification Inventory Costing

specific identification *a method of valuing inventory and determining cost of goods sold, whereby the actual costs of specific inventory items are assigned to them*

The LIFO, FIFO, and weighted-average inventory costing alternatives involve cost flow assumptions. Specific identification is not an assumption; it requires that the individual costs of the actual units sold be charged against revenue as cost of goods sold. In order to compute cost of goods sold and ending inventory amounts with this alternative, a company must know which units were actually sold and what the unit cost of each was.

Suppose that of the 12 lawn mowers sold by McDermitt on September 5, 8 came from the beginning inventory and 4 from the September 3 purchase, and that all of the 16 units sold on September 25 came from the September 18 purchase. With this information, cost of goods sold and ending inventory would be computed as follows:

	Lawn Mowers	Costs
Beginning Inventory	10	$ 2,000
Net Purchases	34	10,000
Goods Available for Sale	44	$12,000
Ending Inventory	16	4,600 (f)
Cost of Goods Sold	28	$ 7,400 (e)

The cost of goods sold is the total of the costs of the specific lawn mowers sold, or

8 lawn mowers from beginning inventory at $200 each	=	$1,600
4 lawn mowers purchased on September 3 at $250 each	=	1,000
16 lawn mowers purchased on September 18 at $300 each	=	4,800
Total cost of goods sold	=	$7,400 (e)

Similarly, the cost of ending inventory is the total of the individual costs of the lawn mowers still on hand at the end of the month, or

2 lawn mowers from beginning inventory at $200 each	=	$ 400
4 lawn mowers purchased on September 3 at $250 each	=	1,000
10 lawn mowers purchased on September 20 at $320 each	=	3,200
Total ending inventory	=	$4,600 (f)

A Comparison of Costing Alternatives Using the Periodic Inventory Method

The cost of goods sold and gross margin under each of the four periodic cost flow alternatives are

	FIFO	LIFO	Weighted Average	Specific Identification
Sales Revenue (28 lawn mowers @ $400 each)	$11,200	$11,200	$11,200	$11,200
Cost of Goods Sold	7,000	8,500	7,636	7,400
Gross Margin	$ 4,200	$ 2,700	$ 3,564	$ 3,800

This comparison shows that the two extremes are FIFO and LIFO. This is always the case when the cost of inventory items is either continually increasing (as in the example) or decreasing. Since in times of increasing prices FIFO assumes the highest value of ending inventory, a firm that wishes to report the highest possible net income (in order to attract investors) would employ that alternative. Many firms, however, choose to report the lowest possible net income since a higher net income results in paying higher income taxes. Accordingly, they elect to use LIFO in a period of rising prices in order to minimize tax payments in the current year. You should recognize, however, that over the life of a firm (as all inventory is eventually sold), total net income will be the same regardless of the inventory costing alternative used.

Although in most instances where alternatives exist firms are allowed to use one accounting method for tax purposes and another for financial reporting, such is not the case in accounting for inventory costs. The Internal Revenue Service (IRS) has ruled that firms may use LIFO for tax purposes, but that if they do so, they must also use LIFO for financial reporting purposes. Therefore, companies must choose between reporting high profits and paying high taxes or reporting low profits and paying low taxes.

In recent years, many organizations have switched from FIFO to LIFO, a trend that has been accelerated by the high rate of inflation. While FIFO and LIFO are the two most common procedures for accounting for inventory, specific identification is often used by companies with high-value inventory items, such as airplanes or diamonds, and weighted average is used by firms that have numerous small-value inventory items.

PERPETUAL INVENTORY COST FLOW ALTERNATIVES

So far, the four inventory cost flow alternatives have been illustrated only in the context of the periodic inventory method. A choice must also be made from among these same cost flows when the perpetual inventory method is used. Recall that the basic difference between these two inventory methods is that under the periodic approach all calculations are made at the end of a period, while with the perpetual method inventory costs are calculated continuously throughout the period as inventory is purchased or sold. (Specific identification will not be analyzed again because it is identical under both the periodic and the perpetual methods.)

FIFO Perpetual Inventory Costing

The ending inventory and cost of goods sold for McDermitt Company using the FIFO perpetual inventory alternative would be

	Lawn Mowers	Costs
Beginning Inventory	10	$ 2,000
Net Purchases	34	10,000
Goods Available for Sale	44	$12,000
Ending Inventory	16	5,000
Cost of Goods Sold	28	$ 7,000

The ending inventory of 16 lawn mowers at a cost of $5,000 is calculated as shown at the top of the next page. Note that these same amounts were obtained with the FIFO periodic method. This is not a coincidence. Whereas the analytic process is different, the amount of ending inventory, and thus the cost of goods sold, will always be the same under the FIFO costing alternative, no matter which inventory method (periodic or perpetual) is used. This is not true of the LIFO or averaging cost flow alternatives.

	Purchased			Sold			Remaining		
Date	*Number of Units*	*Unit Cost*	*Total Cost*	*Number of Units*	*Unit Cost*	*Total Cost*	*Units*	*Unit Cost*	*Total Cost*
Beginning inventory							10	$200	$2,000
Sept. 3	8	$250	$ 2,000				18	10 at $200 8 at $250	$4,000
5				12	10 at $200 2 at $250	$2,500	6	$250	$1,500
18	16	$300	$ 4,800				22	6 at $250 16 at $300	$6,300
20	10	$320	$ 3,200				32	6 at $250 16 at $300 10 at $320	$9,500
25				16	6 at $250 10 at $300	$4,500	16	6 at $300 10 at $320	$5,000
Totals	34		$10,000	28		$7,000			

LIFO Perpetual Inventory Costing

LIFO perpetual (like LIFO periodic) provides ending inventory and net income figures that are lower than those of FIFO when prices are rising. The difference between LIFO and FIFO perpetual is usually not so large as with the periodic method, however. The amount of ending inventory for McDermitt Company using a LIFO perpetual inventory costing method would be determined as follows:

	Purchased			Sold			Remaining		
Date	*Number of Units*	*Unit Cost*	*Total Cost*	*Number of Units*	*Unit Cost*	*Total Cost*	*Units*	*Unit Cost*	*Total Cost*
Beginning inventory							10	$200	$2,000
Sept. 3	8	$250	$ 2,000				18	10 at $200 8 at $250	$4,000
5				12	8 at $250 4 at $200	$2,800	6	$200	$1,200
18	16	$300	$ 4,800				22	6 at $200 16 at $300	$6,000
20	10	$320	$ 3,200				32	6 at $200 16 at $300 10 at $320	$9,200
25				16	10 at $320 6 at $300	$5,000	16	6 at $200 10 at $300	$4,200
Totals	34		$10,000	28		$7,800			

The ending inventory amount of $4,200 is different from the $3,500 computed with the LIFO periodic costing method, as shown below.

LIFO Periodic	$2,000 (10 at $200) + $1,500 (6 at $250) = $3,500
LIFO Perpetual	$1,200 (6 at $200) + $3,000 (10 at $300) = $4,200

Since the LIFO perpetual method requires that computations be made as lawn mowers are sold or purchased, only the costs of the lawn mowers actually on hand can be recognized. Consider, for example, the September 5 sale of 12 units. On that date, only the units from beginning inventory and the September 3 purchase were available, so all the September 3 units purchased at $250 each were sold (because they were the last ones in). Under the LIFO periodic method, no calculations are made until the end of the period, so the unit costs that remain in inventory are the oldest ones, no matter which units were actually available for sale on which dates.

With the LIFO perpetual method, the calculation for cost of goods sold would be

	Lawn Mowers	Costs
Beginning Inventory	10	$ 2,000
Net Purchases	34	10,000
Goods Available for Sale	44	$12,000
Ending Inventory	16	4,200
Cost of Goods Sold	28	$ 7,800

Moving-Average Inventory Costing

moving average *a perpetual inventory cost flow alternative whereby the cost of goods sold and the cost of ending inventory are determined by using a weighted-average cost of all merchandise on hand after each purchase*

Weighted-average perpetual costing involves the computation of weighted averages at different times throughout the period. It is, therefore, referred to as the moving-average alternative. (With the periodic method, the average is taken only once, at the end of the period.) A company using the moving-average alternative would compute a new average after each purchase transaction and would derive its ending inventory as follows:

	Purchased			Sold			Remaining		
Date	*Units*	*Unit Cost*	*Total Cost*	*Units*	*Unit Cost*	*Total Cost*	*Units*	*Unit Cost*	*Total Cost*
Beginning inventory							10	$200.00	$2,000
Sept. 3	8	$250.00	$ 2,000				18	$222.22	$4,000
5				12	$222.22	$2,667	6	$222.22	$1,333
18	16	$300.00	$ 4,800				22	$278.77	$6,133
20	10	$320.00	$ 3,200				32	$291.67	$9,333
25				16	$291.67	$4,667	16	$291.67	$4,667
Totals	34		$10,000	28		$7,333*			

* Rounding error.

The moving-average cost of $222.22 on September 3, for example, is the total cost of all units available on that date divided by the total number of units available, or $4,000/18 units = $222.22.

With the moving-average alternative, cost of goods sold is calculated as follows:

	Units	Costs
Beginning Inventory	10	$ 2,000
Net Purchases	34	10,000
Goods Available for Sale	44	$12,000
Ending Inventory	16	4,667
Cost of Goods Sold	28	$ 7,333

A COMPARISON OF ALL INVENTORY COSTING ALTERNATIVES

The cost of goods sold amounts we have calculated in the chapter are summarized along with their resultant gross margins as follows:

	FIFO		LIFO		Weighted Average (Periodic)	Moving Average (Perpetual)	Specific Identification
	Periodic	*Perpetual*	*Periodic*	*Perpetual*			
Sales Revenue	$11,200	$11,200	$11,200	$11,200	$11,200	$11,200	$11,200
Cost of Goods Sold	7,000	7,000	8,500	7,800	7,636	7,333	7,400
Gross Margin	$ 4,200	$ 4,200	$ 2,700	$ 3,400	$ 3,564	$ 3,867	$ 3,800

This comparison points up several interesting facts. First, no matter which inventory costing alternative a company uses, during a period of rising prices, cost of goods sold is highest (and net income lowest) with LIFO and lowest with FIFO. Second, the difference between the FIFO and LIFO cost of goods sold is usually greater with the periodic method than with the perpetual method. Third, perpetual and periodic cost of goods sold amounts are always the same when FIFO is used.

It is impossible to conclude that any one of these alternatives is best, even though in most circumstances there will be one method that is theoretically most appropriate, given a company's physical flow of goods. In practice, however, many smaller owner-operated businesses are interested in paying lower taxes and will choose LIFO in periods of rising prices; larger, publicly owned firms want to impress current and potential stockholders, so they have more incentive to show high profits. As the inflationary economy continues, however, more and more firms are tending to switch to LIFO in order to reduce their taxes.

TO SUMMARIZE There are four principal inventory costing alternatives: FIFO, LIFO, weighted (or moving) average, and specific identification. These alternatives can be used with either the perpetual or the periodic inventory method. During periods of inflation, LIFO periodic inventory results in the lowest net income, and FIFO (either periodic or perpetual) results in the highest net income.

Reporting Inventory at Amounts Below Cost

All the inventory costing alternatives we have discussed have one thing in common—they report inventory at cost. Occasionally, however, it becomes necessary to report inventory at an amount that is less than cost. This happens when inventory items are damaged or obsolete, or when inventory can be replaced new at a price that is less than its original cost.

INVENTORY VALUED AT NET REALIZABLE VALUE

net realizable value *the selling price of an item less reasonable selling costs*

When inventory is damaged or becomes obsolete, it should be reported at no more than its net realizable value. This is the amount the inventory can be sold for minus any selling costs. Suppose, for example, that an automobile dealer has a demonstrator car that originally cost $6,000, and now can be sold for only $5,000. The car should be reported at its net realizable value. If a commission of $500 must be paid to sell the car, then the net realizable value is $4,500, or $1,500 less than cost. This loss is calculated as follows:

Cost		$6,000
Estimated Selling Price	$5,000	
Less Selling Commission	500	4,500
Loss		$1,500

In order to achieve a good matching of revenues and expenses, a company must recognize this estimated loss as soon as it is known that a loss will be realized (even before the car is sold). The journal entry required to recognize the loss and reduce the inventory amount of the car would be

Loss on Write-Down of Inventory (Expense)	1,500	
Inventory		1,500
To write down demonstrator car to a net realizable value of $4,500.		

By writing down inventory to its net realizable value, a company recognizes a loss when it happens and is thus able to break even when the inventory is finally sold. Using net realizable values means that assets are not being reported at amounts that exceed their future economic benefits.

INVENTORY VALUED AT LOWER OF COST OR MARKET

Inventory also must be written down to an amount below cost if it can be replaced new at a price that is less than its original cost. Although the replacement cost of inventory seldom falls below original cost in an inflationary environment, this has happened in certain industries. In the electronics industry, for instance, the costs of computers and electronic calculators have fallen dramatically in recent years.

lower-of-cost-or-market rule (LCM) *a basis for valuing certain assets at the lower of original cost or market value (current replacement cost), provided that the replacement cost is not higher than net realizable value or lower than net realizable value minus normal profit*

To illustrate the accounting for inventories using the lower-of-cost-or-market rule, we will consider the following situation. You own an office supply store; 10 calculators that cost you $200 each six months ago were to be sold for $250 each. However, these same calculators would now cost you only $125 each. Since the competition is selling the $125 calculators for $175, you drop your price to the market price of $175 and your reported inventory cost to $125. You have experienced a loss of $75 ($200 − $125) per calculator, which must be recognized immediately. In this way you have preserved the $50 normal profit margin that will be recognized when the calculators are actually sold, and at the same time you have written off the expired portion ($75) of the assets. The journal entry to recognize this loss would be

Loss on Write-Down of Inventory (Expense) . . .	750	
Inventory		750
To write down inventory of calculators to lower of cost or market (10 × $75).		

Note that market in this context means the price that would have to be paid to purchase or replace the item in inventory. The lower-of-cost-or-market rule specifies that in no case should inventory be carried at an amount greater than the net realizable value (the selling price less reasonable selling costs) or at an amount less than net realizable value minus a normal profit.

Both the lower-of-cost-or-market and the net-realizable-value rules have gained wide acceptance because they place inventory on the balance sheet at amounts that are in keeping with future economic benefits. With both methods, losses are recognized when they occur, not necessarily when a sale is made.

TO SUMMARIZE There are two cases in which the recorded amount of inventory should be written down: (1) when it is damaged or obsolete, and (2) when it can be replaced (purchased new) at an amount that is less than its original cost. In the first case, inventory is reported at no more than net realizable value, an amount that allows a company to break even when the inventory is sold. In the second case, inventory is written down to the lower of cost or market, an amount that may restore a normal profit margin for the firm when the item is sold. In no case, however, should inventory be reported at an amount that exceeds the net realizable value. Both reporting alternatives are attempts to show assets at amounts that reflect realistic future economic benefits.

Methods of Estimating Inventories

We have assumed thus far that the number of inventory units on hand is known, generally by a physical count that takes place at the end of each accounting period. As we indicated, for the periodic inventory method this physical count is the only way to determine how much inventory is on hand at the end of a period. For the perpetual inventory method, the physical count provides a verification of the quantity on hand. There are times, however, when a company needs to know the dollar amount of ending inventory, but a physical count is either impossible or impractical. For example, many firms prepare quarterly, or even monthly, financial statements, but it is too expensive and time-consuming to count the inventory at the end of each period. In such cases, if the perpetual inventory method is being used, the balance in the Inventory account is usually assumed to be correct. With the periodic inventory method, however, some estimate of the Inventory balance must be made.

There are two common methods of estimating the dollar amount of ending inventory. The first, the gross margin method, is used by all types of firms; the second, the retail inventory method, is used primarily by department stores and other retail businesses.

THE GROSS MARGIN METHOD

gross margin method *a procedure for estimating the amount of ending inventory; the historical relationship of cost of goods sold to sales revenue is used in computing ending inventory*

With the gross margin method, a firm uses its knowledge of the dollar amounts of beginning inventory and purchases and its historical gross margin percentage to estimate the dollar amounts of cost of goods sold and ending inventory.

To illustrate, we will assume the following data for Jason Brick Company.

Net Sales Revenue (January 1 to March 31)	$100,000
Inventory Balance (January 1)	15,000
Net Purchases (January 1 to March 31)	65,000
Gross Margin Percentage (historically determined percentage of net sales price)	40%

With this information, the dollar amount of inventory on hand on March 31 can be estimated as follows:

		Dollars	Percentage of Sales
Net Sales Revenue		$100,000	100%
Cost of Goods Sold:			
Beginning Inventory	$15,000		
Net Purchases	65,000		
Total Goods Available for Sale	$80,000		
Ending Inventory	20,000 (3)*		
Cost of Goods Sold		60,000 (2)*	60%
Gross Margin		$ 40,000 (1)*	40%

* The numbers indicate the order of calculation.

In this example, the gross margin was first determined by calculating 40 percent of sales (step 1). Next, the cost of goods sold was found by subtracting gross margin from sales (step 2). Finally, the dollar amount of ending inventory was obtained by subtracting cost of goods sold from total goods available for sale (step 3). Obviously, the gross margin method of estimating cost of goods sold and ending inventory assumes that the historical gross margin percentage is appropriate for the current period. This assumption is a realistic one in many fields of business. In cases where the gross margin percentage has changed, either because of higher selling prices, higher inventory costs, or for other reasons, this method should be used with caution.

The gross margin method of estimating ending inventories is also useful when a fire or other calamity destroys a company's inventory. In these cases, the dollar amount of inventory lost must be determined before insurance claims can be made. The dollar amounts of sales, purchases, and beginning inventory can be obtained from prior years' financial statements, and from customers, suppliers, and other sources. Then the gross margin method can be used to estimate the dollar amount of inventory lost.

THE RETAIL INVENTORY METHOD

retail inventory method *a procedure for estimating the dollar amount of ending inventory; the ending inventory at retail prices is converted to a cost basis by using a ratio of the cost and the retail prices of goods available for sale*

The retail method of estimating the dollar amount of ending inventory is similar to the gross margin method. It is widely used by department stores, chain stores, and other retail businesses. In these types of organizations, all items are marked, when they are put into inventory, at the prices for which they will be sold. When a physical count of inventory is taken, these retail, or selling, prices are applied to all inventory items. Inventory at retail prices is then converted to inventory at cost by applying the appropriate ratio between costs and sales. For example, if a store's markup is 100 percent of cost, and if the retail inventory records showed a balance of $40,000, the cost of the inventory would be $20,000.

The retail method may also be used to estimate the dollar cost of inventory on hand when a physical count is not taken. When used, it requires that beginning inventory and purchases be recorded on both a cost and a selling price basis. Then, total goods available for sale can be calculated at both cost and selling price. By deducting sales revenue for the period from the goods available for sale at selling price, the ending inventory at selling price is derived. This number is converted to ending inventory at cost by using the appropriate markup ratio.

To illustrate, we will consider the following data for Macey's Hardware Store.

	Cost	Selling Price
Beginning Inventory	$ 42,000	$ 63,000
Net Purchases During the Month	105,900	154,500
Total Goods Available for Sale	$147,900	$217,500
Less Net Sales Revenue for the Month		160,000
Ending Inventory at Selling Price		$ 57,500
Cost-to-Selling-Price Ratio ($147,900 ÷ $217,500)		68%
Ending Inventory at Cost (0.68 × $57,500)	$ 39,100	

In this case, the cost-to-selling-price ratio of goods available for sale is 68 percent. This percentage is applied to the ending inventory at selling price to determine the cost of the ending inventory.

The major difference between the gross margin and the retail inventory methods is that the latter uses the percentage markup—that is, the cost-to-selling-price ratio for goods available for sale—*from the current period* (by keeping current records at both cost and retail), whereas the former uses the *historical* gross margin rates. To the extent that the gross margin percentages change over time, inventory estimates based on the retail method should be more accurate.

TO SUMMARIZE There are two common methods of estimating the dollar amounts of inventory: (1) the gross margin method, and (2) the retail inventory method. The former uses a historical gross margin percentage to estimate the cost of ending inventory; the latter uses the current cost-to-selling-price ratio to estimate inventory levels in retail firms.

CHAPTER REVIEW

The three major factors affecting inventory measurement are inventory cutoff, consignments, and shipping costs. When inventory is not correctly accounted for, both cost of goods sold and net income will be reported incorrectly. Inventory errors affect net income on a dollar-for-dollar basis and usually correct themselves after two periods.

The four major cost flow alternatives used in accounting for inventories are: FIFO, LIFO, weighted (or moving) average, and specific identification. Each of these may result in different dollar amounts of ending inventory, cost of goods sold, gross margin, and net income. A firm may choose any costing alternative without regard for the way goods physically flow through that firm. Often, the costing alternative selected will depend on tax considerations. During an inflationary period, LIFO provides the lowest net income and therefore lower taxes. Because of this tax advantage, LIFO is currently very popular. These inventory cost flows may be used with either the periodic or the perpetual inventory method.

Sometimes inventory must be reported at amounts below cost. This occurs (1) when inventory is damaged or obsolete, and (2) when the replacement price drops below inventory cost. In the first case, inventory is valued at net realizable value, and in the second, it is valued at the lower of cost or market. When the second approach is used, market is taken to mean the replacement cost of the inventory, but in no case can it be greater than the item's net realizable value, or less than net realizable value minus a normal profit.

Although most firms take a physical count of inventory at the end of each year, there may be other times when the dollar amount of inventory must be estimated. There are two common methods of estimating ending inventories: the gross margin method, which can be used in almost any situation, and the retail inventory method, which is limited to retail firms, such as chain or department stores. The gross margin method estimates the amount of inventory on the basis of historical gross margin percentages; the retail method uses the cost-to-selling-price ratio from the current period.

KEY TERMS AND CONCEPTS

consignee (241)
consignment (241)
consignor (241)
FIFO (244)
finished goods (242)
FOB destination (242)
FOB shipping point (242)
gross margin (239)
gross margin method (254)
inventory cutoff (238)
LIFO (245)
lower-of-cost-or-market rule (253)
moving average (250)
net income (239)
net realizable value (252)
raw materials (242)
retail inventory method (255)
specific identification (246)
weighted average (246)
work-in-process (242)

REVIEW PROBLEM

Inventory Cost Flow Alternatives

Armanda Wholesale Distributors buys typewriters from manufacturers and sells them to office supply stores. During January 1983, its inventory records showed the following.

Beginning Inventory	26 typewriters at $200 each
January 10	Purchased 10 typewriters at $220 each
12	Sold 15 typewriters
15	Purchased 20 typewriters at $250 each
17	Sold 14 typewriters
19	Sold 8 typewriters
28	Purchased 9 typewriters at $270 each

Required:
Calculate ending inventory and cost of goods sold, using:

1. FIFO perpetual inventory.
2. FIFO periodic inventory.
3. LIFO perpetual inventory.
4. LIFO periodic inventory.
5. Moving-average inventory.
6. Weighted-average inventory.

Solution

When computing ending inventory and cost of goods sold, it is usually easiest to get an overview first. The following calculations are helpful.

Beginning inventory:	26 units at $200 each =		$ 5,200
Purchases:	10 units at $220 =	$2,200	
	20 units at 250 =	5,000	
	9 units at 270 =	2,430	
			9,630
Cost of Goods Available for Sale (65 units)			$14,830
Less Ending Inventory (28 units)			?
Cost of Goods Sold (37 units)			?

Given a beginning inventory, only ending inventory and cost of goods sold will vary with the different inventory costing alternatives. Because ending inventory and cost of goods sold are complementary numbers whose sum must equal total goods available for sale, you can calculate only one of the two missing numbers in each case, and then compute the other by subtracting the first number from goods available for sale. Thus, in the calculations that follow, we will always calculate ending inventory first.

1. FIFO perpetual inventory

With this alternative, records must be maintained throughout the period, as shown on page 258. The final calculation is

Cost of Goods Available for Sale	$14,830
Ending Inventory [($250 × 19) + $2,430]	7,180
Cost of Goods Sold	$ 7,650

FIFO Perpetual Calculations

Date	Purchased Units	Purchased Unit Cost	Purchased Total Cost	Sold Units	Sold Unit Cost	Sold Total Cost	Remaining Units	Remaining Unit Cost	Remaining Total Cost
Beginning inventory							26	$200	$5,200
January 10	10	$220	$2,200				36	26 at $200 10 at $220	$7,400
12				15	$200	$3,000	21	11 at $200 10 at $220	$4,400
15	20	$250	$5,000				41	11 at $200 10 at $220 20 at $250	$9,400
17				14	11 at $200 3 at $220	$2,860	27	7 at $220 20 at $250	$6,540
19				8	7 at $200 1 at $250	$1,790	19	$250	$4,750
28	9	$270	$2,430				28	19 at $250 9 at $270	$7,180
Totals	39		$9,630	37		$7,650			

2. FIFO periodic inventory

With this alternative, calculations can be made at the end of the period. Since we know that 28 units are left in ending inventory, we look for the last 28 units purchased, because the first units purchased would all be sold. The last 28 units purchased were

9 units at $270 each on January 28 =	$2,430
19 units at $250 each on January 15 =	4,750
	$7,180

Note that the FIFO periodic inventory amount is the same as that calculated with FIFO perpetual. This is always the case. In this example, ending inventory is $7,180, and cost of goods sold is $7,650.

3. LIFO perpetual inventory

With this alternative, as shown in the table on page 259, the calculation is

Cost of Goods Available for Sale	$14,830
Ending Inventory	6,230
Cost of Goods Sold	$ 8,600

4. LIFO periodic inventory

With this alternative, calculations can again be made at the end of the period, and so the first 28 units available would be considered the ending inventory (since the last ones purchased are the first ones sold). The first 28 units available were

Beginning inventory:	26 units at $200 =	$5,200
January 10 purchase:	2 units at $220 =	440
		$5,640

Thus,

Cost of Goods Available for Sale	$14,830
Ending Inventory	5,640
Cost of Goods Sold	$ 9,190

LIFO Perpetual Calculations

Date	Purchased Units	Purchased Unit Cost	Purchased Total Cost	Sold Units	Sold Unit Cost	Sold Total Costs	Remaining Units	Remaining Unit Cost	Remaining Total Cost
Beginning inventory							26	$200	$5,200
January 10	10	$220	$2,200				36	26 at $200; 10 at $220	$7,400
12				15	10 at $220; 5 at $200	$3,200	21	$200	$4,200
15	20	$250	$5,000				41	21 at $200; 20 at $250	$9,200
17				14	$250	$3,500	27	21 at $200; 6 at $250	$5,700
19				8	6 at $250; 2 at $200	$1,900	19	$200	$3,800
28	9	$270	$2,430				28	19 at $200; 9 at $270	$6,230
Totals	39		$9,630	37		$8,600			

5. Moving-average inventory

With this alternative, a new average cost of inventory items must be calculated each time a purchase is made.

Cost of Goods Available for Sale	$14,830
Ending Inventory	6,748
Cost of Goods Sold	$ 8,082

6. Weighted-average inventory

With this alternative, the calculation again can be made at the end of the period. Thus, total units available for sale is divided into total cost of goods available for sale to get a weighted-average cost.

$$\frac{\text{Cost of Goods Available for Sale} \ \$14{,}830}{\text{Units Available for Sale} \ 65} = \$228.15 \text{ per unit}$$

Cost of Goods Available for Sale	$14,830
Less Ending Inventory (28 units at $228.15)	6,388
Cost of Goods Sold (37 units at $228.15)	$ 8,442

Moving-Average Calculations

Date	Purchased	Sold	Remaining	Computations
Beginning inventory			26 units at $200 = $5,200	
January 10	10 units at $220 = $2,200		36 units at $205.56 = $7,400	$5,200 + $2,200 = $7,400; $7,400 ÷ 36 = $205.56
12		15 units at $205.56 = $3,083	21 units at $205.56 = $4,317	
15	20 units at $250 = $5,000		41 units at $227.24 = $9,317	$4,317 + $5,000 = $9,317; $9,317 ÷ 41 = $227.24
17		14 units at $227.24 = $3,181	27 units at $227.24 = $6,136	
19		8 units at $227.24 = $1,818	19 units at $227.24 = $4,318	
28	9 units at $270 = $2,430		28 units at $241 = $6,748	$4,318 + $2,430 = $6,748; $6,748 ÷ 28 = $241

DISCUSSION QUESTIONS

1 When is the cost of inventory transferred from an asset to an expense?

2 Is net income under- or overstated when purchased merchandise is counted and included in the inventory balance but not recorded as a purchase?

3 Is net income under- or overstated if inventory is sold and shipped but not recorded as a sale?

4 If an ending inventory amount in period 1 were understated by $200, what would be the effect on reported net income in period 2?

5 What is the effect on net income when goods held on consignment are included in the ending inventory balance?

6 Who owns merchandise during shipment under the terms FOB shipping point?

7 Why is it more difficult to account for the inventory of a manufacturing firm than for that of a merchandising firm?

8 Explain the difference between cost flows and the movement of goods.

9 Why have many firms switched to LIFO inventory costing in recent years?

10 Which inventory cost flow alternative results in paying the least amount of taxes when prices are falling?

11 Why is the weighted-average perpetual inventory cost flow alternative referred to as moving average?

12 Why might you expect to see a different inventory costing alternative used in smaller, owner-operated firms than in larger, publicly owned companies?

13 Would a firm ever be prohibited from using one inventory costing alternative for tax purposes and another for financial reporting purposes?

14 When should inventory be valued at its net realizable value?

15 When should inventory be valued at the lower of cost or market?

16 Why is the gross margin method of estimating dollar amounts of inventory more useful when the periodic inventory method is used than when the perpetual inventory method is used?

17 Why is it necessary to know which inventory cost flow alternative is being used before the financial performances of different firms can be compared?

EXERCISES

E7–1 The Effect of Inventory Errors

As the accountant for Misty Enterprises, you are in the process of preparing its income statement for the year ended December 31, 1983. In doing so, you have noticed that a shipment of merchandise that cost $4,000 was received on December 29, 1983.

Before the effects of the $4,000 transaction were taken into account, the relevant income statement figures were

Sales Revenue	$80,000
Beginning Inventory	18,000
Purchases	44,000
Ending Inventory	13,000

1. Prepare a partial income statement through gross margin under each of the following four assumptions.
   (a) The shipment is recorded as a purchase in the accounting records and is also counted in the ending physical inventory.
   (b) The shipment is recorded as a purchase but is not counted in ending inventory.
   (c) The shipment is not recorded as a purchase in the accounting records but is counted in ending inventory.
   (d) The shipment is not recorded as a purchase in the accounting records and is not counted in the ending inventory.
2. Under the given circumstances, which of the four assumptions is correct?
3. Which assumption overstates gross margin (and therefore net income)?
4. Which assumption understates gross margin (and therefore net income)?

E7–2 The Effect of Inventory Errors

Mildred, the accountant for Cimba Company, reported the following accounting treatments for several purchase transactions that took place near December 31, 1983, the company's year-end.

Date Inventory Was Received	Was the purchase recorded in the company's books on or before December 31, 1983?	Amount	Was the inventory counted and included in the inventory balance at December 31, 1983?
1983:			
Dec. 26	Yes	$1,300	Yes
29	Yes	900	No
31	No	1,900	Yes
1984:			
Jan. 1	No	200	Yes
1	Yes	2,900	No
2	No	700	No

1. If Cimba Company's records reported purchases and ending inventory balances of $40,400 and $14,900, respectively, for 1983, what should the proper amounts in these accounts have been?

2. What would the correct amount of cost of goods sold be for 1983 if the beginning inventory balance on January 1, 1983, was $10,100?

3. By how much would the cost of goods sold be over- or understated if the corrections in question (1) were not made?

E7-3 The Effect of Inventory Errors

1. If the current year's accounting records of EMCO Manufacturing Company included an overstatement of purchases of $1,900, an understatement of beginning inventory of $2,400, and an understatement of ending inventory of $300, by how much would the cost of goods sold be misstated and would the misstatement be an overstatement or an understatement?

2. Given these same errors, what will the amount and direction (overstatement or understatement) of the misstatement in the current year's net income be?

3. What effect will these errors have on net income of the next period, assuming that purchases and ending inventory are stated correctly in the next period?

E7-4 What Should Be Included in Inventory?

Pierre is trying to compute the inventory balance for the December 31, 1983, financial statements of his cutlery shop. He has computed a tentative balance of $26,300 but suspects that several adjustments still need to be made. In particular, he believes that the following could affect his inventory balance.

a. A shipment of goods that cost $1,700 was received on December 28, 1983. It was properly recorded as a purchase in 1983 but not counted with the ending inventory.

b. Another shipment of goods (FOB destination) was received on January 2, 1984, and cost $400. It was properly recorded as a purchase in 1984 but was counted with 1983's ending inventory.

c. A $1,400 shipment of goods to a customer on January 3 was recorded as a sale in 1984 but was deducted from the December 31, 1983, ending inventory balance. The goods cost $900.

d. The company had $3,000 of goods on consignment with a customer, and $2,500 of merchandise was on consignment from a vendor. Neither amount was included in the $26,300 figure.

e. The following amounts represent merchandise that was in transit on December 31, 1983, and was recorded as purchases and sales in 1983 but not included in the December 31 inventory.

(1) Ordered by Pierre, $900, FOB destination.
(2) Ordered by Pierre, $300, FOB shipping point.
(3) Sold by Pierre, $2,000, FOB shipping point.
(4) Sold by Pierre, $2,300, FOB destination.

Given the above information, answer the following for Pierre.

1. What is the proper amount of ending inventory at December 31, 1983?

2. If purchases (before any adjustment from above, if any) totaled $43,200 and beginning inventory (January 1, 1983) totaled $15,800, what is the cost of goods sold in 1983?

E7-5 Goods on Consignment

Company A has consignment arrangements with Supplier B and also with Customer C. In particular, Supplier B ships some of its goods to Company A on consignment while Company A ships some of its goods to Customer C on a consignment basis. At the end of 1983, Company A's accounting records showed:

Goods on Consignment from Supplier B	$6,000
Goods on Consignment to Customer C	$8,000

1. If a physical count of all inventory revealed that $30,000 of goods were on hand, what amount of ending inventory should be reported?

2. If the amount of the beginning inventory for the year was $27,000 and purchases during the year were $59,000, what is the cost of goods sold for the year? [Assume the ending inventory from question (1).]

3. If, instead of the above facts, Company A had only $4,000 of the goods on consignment with Customer C and $10,000 of consigned goods from Supplier B, and if physical goods on hand totaled $36,000, what would the correct amount of the ending inventory be?

4. With respect to question (3), if beginning inventory totaled $24,000 and the cost of goods sold was $47,500, what were the purchases?

E7-6 Transportation Terms (FOB)—Ownership of Inventory

1. In the following four cases, who would pay the freight charges?

The ABC Company buys goods from Supplier X with terms:

(a) FOB shipping point
(b) FOB destination

The ABC Company sells goods to Customer Y with terms:

(c) FOB shipping point
(d) FOB destination

2. ABC Company has $30,600 of goods on hand, with a shipment of $4,600 in transit from Supplier X (FOB destination), and a shipment of $6,000 in transit to Customer Y (FOB shipping point). What is the proper amount of inventory of the ABC Company?

3. If the shipment from Supplier X described in question (2) was FOB shipping point and the shipment to Customer Y was FOB destination, what would the proper amount of inventory be?

E7-7 FIFO, LIFO, and Weighted-Average Calculations (Periodic Inventory Method)

The following transactions took place in Wolfe's Sporting Goods Store during April 1983.

April 1	Beginning Inventory	24 suits at	$12.00
5	Purchase of Jogging Suits	15 suits at	13.00
11	Purchase of Jogging Suits	16 suits at	13.50
19	Sale of Jogging Suits	20 suits at	30.00
24	Purchase of Jogging Suits	10 suits at	14.00
30	Sale of Jogging Suits	12 suits at	30.00

Assuming the periodic inventory method, compute the cost of goods sold and ending inventory balances using the following inventory costing alternatives.

1. Weighted average
2. FIFO
3. LIFO

E7-8 Specific-Identification Inventory Costing

Loosee's Diamond Shop is computing its inventory and cost of goods sold for November 1983. At the beginning of the month, the following jewelry items were in stock.

Ring A	8 at $600 =	$ 4,800
Ring A	10 at 650 =	6,500
Ring B	5 at 300 =	1,500
Ring B	6 at 350 =	2,100
Ring B	3 at 450 =	1,350
Ring C	7 at 200 =	1,400
Ring C	8 at 250 =	2,000
		$19,650

During the month, the following rings were purchased: 4 type A rings at $600, 2 type B rings at $450, and 5 type C rings at $300. Also during the month, the following sales were made.

Ring Type	Quantity Sold	Sales Price	Cost
A	2	$1,000	$600
A	3	1,050	600
A	1	1,200	650
B	2	850	450
B	2	800	350
C	4	450	200
C	3	500	250
C	1	550	250

Because of the high cost per item, Loosee uses specific-identification inventory costing.

1. Calculate cost of goods sold and ending inventory balances for November.
2. Calculate gross margin for the month.

E7-9 FIFO, LIFO, and Weighted-Average Calculations (Periodic Inventory Method)

Marjo's Bookstore has just closed its operations on the last day of July 1983. On that date, the inventory records showed the following.

July 1	Beginning Inventory	14,000 at $4.00 =	$56,000
5	Sold	2,000	
13	Purchased	3,000 at 4.50 =	13,500
17	Sold	1,500	
25	Purchased	4,000 at 5.00 =	20,000
27	Sold	2,500	
			$89,500

Assuming the periodic inventory method, compute Marjo's cost of goods sold and ending inventory balances for July using the following cost flows. (Round to the nearest tenth of a cent.)

1. FIFO
2. LIFO
3. Weighted average

E7-10 FIFO, LIFO, and Moving-Average Calculations (Perpetual Inventory Method)

1. Using the figures in E7-9, compute the ending inventory and cost of goods sold balances with (1) FIFO, (2) LIFO, and (3) moving average, using the perpetual inventory method. Compute unit costs to the nearest tenth of a cent.

2. Why are the LIFO periodic and LIFO perpetual cost of goods sold amounts different?

3. Which of the three alternatives is best? Why?

E7-11 Tax Effects of FIFO, LIFO, and Weighted Average (Periodic Inventory Method)

James Corporation shows the following transactions in its 1983 books.

Beginning Inventory	700 units at	$3	=	$2,100
Purchase	300 units at	4	=	1,200
Sale	400 units at	8 (sales price)		
Purchase	200 units at	5	=	1,000
Sale	300 units at	9 (sales price)		
				$4,300

1. If James Corporation is taxed at 22 percent, what is its 1983 tax liability under each of the following three inventory alternatives (also assume that the only expense during 1983, other than cost of goods sold, was a $2,500 administrative expense)? Round income statement numbers to the nearest dollar.
   (a) FIFO (periodic)
   (b) LIFO (periodic)
   (c) Weighted average (periodic)
2. Which alternative results in the lowest tax liability? Why?

E7-12 Various Inventory Costing Alternatives

The records of Trim & Slim Company showed the following with regard to one of the major inventory items being sold. Assume the transactions occurred in the order given.

	Units	Unit Cost
Beginning Inventory	50	$1.00
Purchase No. 1	50	2.00
Sale No. 1	20	
Purchase No. 2	100	3.00
Sale No. 2	110	

Compute the value of the *ending inventory* under each of the following alternatives (round to the nearest dollar).
1. Weighted-average cost with the periodic inventory method.
2. Weighted-average cost with the perpetual inventory method (moving average).
3. FIFO cost with the periodic inventory method.

E7-13 Cost of Goods Sold Calculations

The management of Huey's Discount Store wants to minimize its income taxes and intends to use the inventory costing procedure that best meets this objective. Prices in the economy are currently falling and Huey's tax rate is 40 percent.
1. Which alternative should Huey use to minimize income taxes?
2. Concerning inventory and purchases, the following information is available.
   (a) Beginning inventory consisted of 100 units at $23.
   (b) The last purchase of 150 units cost $3,000 in total.
   (c) There was only one additional purchase (besides the 150 units) during the period.
   (d) 370 units were sold during the period.
   (e) The ending inventory is 80 units.
   (f) The total cost of goods available for sale for the period is $9,500.

   Given this information, what were the number of units purchased and the price per unit of the one additional purchase?
3. Assuming the periodic inventory method, what are the dollar amounts of the ending inventory and cost of goods sold under the FIFO and LIFO alternatives?
4. How much tax is saved by using the alternative you suggested in answer to question (1) instead of the less favorable one?

E7-14 Cost of Goods Sold Calculations

Complete the Cost of Goods Sold section for the income statements of the following five companies.

	Company M	Company N	Company O	Company P	Company Q
Beginning Inventory	$16,000	$24,800	(5)$ ____	(7)$ ____	$19,200
Purchases	26,500	(3) ____	43,000	89,500	(9) ____
Purchase Returns and Allowances	(1) ____	1,000	1,800	200	2,200
Goods Available for Sale	42,100	(4) ____	58,300	(8) ____	81,500
Ending Inventory	(2) ____	22,200	15,200	28,800	(10) ____
Cost of Goods Sold	33,400	67,200	(6) ____	93,400	68,400

E7-15 Lower of Cost or Market

Prepare the necessary General Journal entries to account for the purchases and year-end adjustments of the inventory of T & D Manufacturing Company (periodic inventory method). All purchases are made on account.
1. Purchased 50 standard widgets for $4.00 each to sell at $7 per unit.
2. Purchased 15 deluxe widgets at $9.00 per unit to sell for $15 per unit.
3. At the end of the year, the standard widgets could be purchased for $4.50 and are selling for $7.50.
4. At the end of the year, the deluxe widgets could be purchased for $5.00 and are selling for $8.00 per unit.

5. At the end of the second year, standard widgets could be purchased for $3.00 and are selling for $4.00.

6. At the end of the second year, the deluxe widgets could be purchased for $4.50 and are selling for $10.00.

E7–16 Valuation of Inventory

A flood recently damaged a warehouse of Clark Company. After the flood, an examination and valuation of the inventory showed the following.

Item No.	Quantity	Original Unit Cost	Current Replacement Cost	Net Realizable Value
1062	50	$14	$14	$12
3095	40	16	17	10
4348	86	8	7	7
5326	24	32	25	21

1. By what amount, if any, should each item be written down?
2. Make the appropriate journal entry (or entries).

E7–17 Gross Margin Method of Estimating Inventory

Chris Corporation is interested in estimating the inventory balance for its quarterly financial statements. The periodic inventory method is used. Records show that quarterly sales totaled $200,000, beginning inventory was $45,000, and purchases totaled $140,000; the historical gross margin percentage has averaged approximately 50 percent.

1. What is the approximate amount of ending inventory?
2. If a physical count shows only $80,000 in inventory, what could the explanation for the difference be?

E7–18 Retail Inventory Estimation Method

Red-D Department Store uses the retail inventory method. During the first three months of 1983, the store had the following balances.

	At Cost	At Selling Price
Beginning Inventory	$45,000	$ 65,000
Purchases	75,000	112,000
Sales Revenue		118,000

Given these data, what is the cost of the inventory that Red-D should report on its March 31 quarterly financial statements? (Round percentage in the calculation to the nearest percent.)

PROBLEMS

P7–1 The Effect of Inventory Errors

You have been hired as the accountant for Farmers Seed Company, which uses the periodic inventory method. In reviewing the firm's records, you have noted what you think are several accounting errors made during the current year, 1983. These potential mistakes are listed below.

a. A $3,000 purchase of merchandise was properly recorded in the Purchases account but the related Accounts Payable account was credited for only $2,000.

b. A $3,300 shipment of merchandise received just before the end of the year was properly recorded in the Purchases account but was not physically counted in the inventory and hence was excluded from the ending inventory balance.

c. A $6,700 purchase of merchandise was erroneously recorded as a $7,600 purchase.

d. A $500 purchase of merchandise was not recorded either as a purchase or an account payable.

e. During the year, $1,200 of defective merchandise was sent back to a supplier. The original purchase entry had been recorded but the merchandise return entry was not recorded.

f. During the physical inventory count, inventory that cost $400 was counted twice.

Required:

1. If the previous accountant had tentatively computed the 1983 gross margin to be $10,000, what would be the correct gross margin for the year?
2. If the company is taxed at 40 percent, how much additional tax will it have to pay when these errors are corrected?
3. If these mistakes are not corrected, how much will the 1984 net income be in error?

P7-2 Analysis of Inventory Costing Alternatives

For the years 1983 through 1985, Mantle Company reported the following ending inventories and net incomes. Mantle Company uses the LIFO inventory costing alternative.

December 31	LIFO Ending Inventory	Net Income
1983	$132,000	$562,000
1984	198,000	548,000
1985	258,000	600,000

Required:

1. Ignoring the effects of income taxes, determine the amount of net income the company would have reported in 1984 and 1985 if it had used FIFO instead of LIFO. Assume FIFO ending inventories of $150,000 in 1983, $210,000 in 1984, and $280,000 in 1985.
2. If the company's tax rate is 45 percent, how much additional tax would it have to pay in 1985 if it uses FIFO instead of LIFO?

P7-3 The Perpetual and Periodic Inventory Methods

Required:

1. Journalize the following transactions of Handy Ice Cream Company, assuming the periodic inventory method.
   (a) Purchased 40 units of product X at $18/unit.
   (b) Purchased 50 units of product Y at $46/unit.
   (c) Sold 15 units of product Z at $8/unit (cost = $5/unit).
   (d) Sold 25 units of product X at $30/unit (cost = $16/unit).
   (e) Purchased 40 units of product Y at $48/unit.
   (f) Closed the nominal accounts relating to inventory.

Beginning inventory consisted of: 30 units of X at $16; 40 units of Z at $5.

2. Journalize the above transactions, assuming the perpetual inventory method.
3. **Interpretive Question** Which inventory cost flow alternative is being used by Handy Company?

P7-4 Inventory Cost Flow Alternatives

The sales and inventory records of Jensen Golf Sales, Inc., were as follows for January through March 1983.

	Clubs	Unit Cost	Total Cost
Beginning Inventory, January 1, 1983	460	$15	$6,900
Purchase, January 16, 1983	110	16	1,760
Sale, January 25 ($22.50/unit)	216		
Purchase, February 16	105	18	1,890
Sale, February 27 ($20.00/unit)	307		
Purchase, March 10	150	14	2,100
Sale, March 30 ($25.00/unit)	190		

Required:

1. Find the amounts for the ending inventory, cost of goods sold, and gross margin under the following costing alternatives: (a) FIFO, (b) LIFO, and (c) weighted average, all with the periodic inventory method. Round amounts to the nearest dollar.
2. **Interpretive Question** Which alternative results in the highest gross margin? Why?

P7-5 Inventory Cost Flow Alternatives

Ernst Garden Company sells two products: fertilizer and weed killer. Beginning inventory for March 1, 1983, is as follows:

Item	No. of Bags	Unit Cost
Fertilizer	100	$8.00
Weed Killer	300	7.00

Purchases during March were as follows:

Date	Item	No. of Bags	Unit Cost
March 5	Fertilizer	100	$8.30
5	Weed Killer	200	7.10
16	Fertilizer	100	7.90
28	Weed Killer	100	6.80

During March, the firm sold 150 bags of fertilizer at $11 each and 350 bags of weed killer at $10 each.

Required:

1. Assuming the periodic inventory method, calculate separately for fertilizer and weed killer the sales revenue, cost of goods sold, ending inventory, and gross margin as of March 31, 1983, using the following cost flow alternatives.
   (a) FIFO
   (b) LIFO
   (c) Weighted average
2. **Interpretive Question** Which alternative would result in paying the lowest taxes? Why?

P7–6 Effects of Different Inventory Cost Flows

Taylor Company uses the periodic inventory method. The following data are available for 1983.

	Date	No. of Units	Cost/ Unit	Total
Beginning Inventory ..	Jan. 1	20	$11	$ 220
Purchases	Jan. 10	7	11	$ 77
	Feb. 24	18	12	216
	June 12	9	13	117
	Aug. 30	25	14	350
	Sept. 20	14	15	210
	Dec. 30	8	15	120
Total Purchases ...		81		$1,090
Sales	Jan. 5	20		
	Mar. 10	10		
	Sept. 13	35		
	Sept. 21	10		
	Nov. 15	5		
Total Sales		80		

Required:

1. Compute the ending inventory at December 31, 1983, using LIFO.
2. Assume that your answer to question (1) was $231 and that the gross margin using this figure for ending inventory was $700. What would the ending inventory be using FIFO? What would the gross margin be using FIFO?
3. Again assume that ending inventory was $231 using LIFO and that the resulting net income was $500. What would the amount of net income be using weighted average? (Ignore taxes and round to the nearest dollar.)
4. **Interpretive Question** Which alternative would a company use if it wanted to report the highest possible net income?

P7–7 The Gross Margin Method of Estimating Inventory

On December 20, 1984, a major fire destroyed the contents of Fuller Paint Company's warehouse. In order to file a claim for an insurance reimbursement, the company needs to estimate the amount of inventory lost in the fire. In an attempt to estimate the fire loss, the following information has been gathered.

a. By consulting with vendors, it was found that total purchases to the date of the fire amounted to $605,000.

b. The December 31, 1983, balance sheet noted an inventory balance of $125,000.

c. Sales commissions for the year (for the sales staff) totaled $80,000. Of the $80,000 in commissions, 40 percent was paid at a commission rate of 5 percent, and the balance was paid at a rate of 10 percent. Gross margin rates during the past several years have averaged about 45 percent.

Required:

1. What is the estimated amount of the inventory destroyed in the fire?
2. **Interpretive Question** If the insurance company thought the claim was too high, on what basis might it argue that your calculations are not valid?
3. What would the estimate of the loss be if the appropriate gross margin rate were 35 percent instead of 45 percent?

P7–8 Cost of Goods Sold Calculations

On July 1, 1984, the main warehouse of Mercury Company, a producer of outboard engines for boats, was destroyed by fire. Almost all the inventory was unsalvageable. However, the company carried insurance on the warehouse and its contents and will be reimbursed for its loss by the insurance company. Your job is to estimate the amount of inventory destroyed so that the insurance proceeds can be collected. In attempting to estimate the inventory destroyed, you have gathered the following data from the financial statements as of December 31, 1983.

Net Sales Revenue	$500,000
Gross Margin	175,000
Inventory Balance	40,000
Net Income, 1983	12,500

From customers:

Sales from January 1, 1984, to June 30, 1984	$300,000
Accounts Receivable on June 30, 1984	37,500

From suppliers:

Net Purchases for the first six months of 1984	$240,000
Amount owed on June 30, 1984	32,500

Required:

1. Assuming that the 1983 results were typical of those in 1984, determine the cost of the inventory lost in the fire.
2. **Interpretive Question** What is the major assumption of this type of estimate? What would cause this assumption to be violated?

P7–9 Unifying Problem: Inventory Cost Flow Alternatives

Salem's Wholesale buys canned peaches from canneries and sells them to retail markets. During August 1983 Salem's inventory records showed the following.

Aug. 1	Beginning Inventory	4,100 cases at $10.50
4	Purchase	1,500 cases at 11.00
9	Sale	950 cases at 19.95
13	Purchase	1,000 cases at 11.00

Aug. 19	Sale	1,450 cases at $19.95
26	Purchase	1,700 cases at 11.50
30	Sale	1,900 cases at 19.95

Even though it requires more computational effort, Salem's uses the perpetual inventory method because management feels the extra cost is justified by the advantage of always having current knowledge of inventory levels.

Required:

1. Calculate the cost of goods sold and ending inventory using the following cost flow alternatives (calculate unit costs to the nearest tenth of a cent).
   (a) FIFO
   (b) LIFO
   (c) Moving average

2. **Interpretive Question** Why are the cost of goods sold amounts the same under the FIFO perpetual and FIFO periodic costing methods?

3. Calculate the ending inventory and cost of goods sold using the LIFO periodic method.

4. **Interpretive Question** In this particular case, why does LIFO result in the same amounts under both periodic and perpetual inventory methods?

P7–10 Unifying Problem: Inventory Estimation Methods

Monterey Department Store has the following information available.

	At Cost	At Selling Price	Other
Purchases during January 1983	$60,000	$85,000	
Inventory balance, January 1, 1983	24,000	31,000	
Sales during January 1983		90,000	
Average gross margin rate for the last three years			20%

Required:

1. On the basis of this information, estimate the cost of inventory on hand at January 31, 1983, using:
   (a) The gross margin method.
   (b) The retail inventory method. (Round to the nearest whole percent.)

2. **Interpretive Question** Which method is probably the most accurate? Why?

SECTION 3

Reporting Assets, Liabilities, and Owners' Equity

CHAPTER 8

An Overview of the Balance Sheet

THIS CHAPTER EXPLAINS:

The historical cost approach of the balance sheet and its resulting limitations in terms of measuring the worth of a firm.
What's in a balance sheet.
The classification of balance sheet accounts by age, use, and source.
Some limitations of the balance sheet.

Every day thousands of real estate investors shop for apartment buildings and other rental property. Almost without exception they ask the following two questions: (1) How much income will there be from this investment? (2) How much is this building worth? In answering the first question, realtors consider such things as rent revenues and the likely expenses for interest, property taxes, repairs, maintenance, and utilities. In answering the second question, they consider the square footage of the building, number of rooms, location, repairs needed, and similar factors.

Although a business is usually much more complex than an apartment building, it too can be considered a salable asset; and every day thousands of people invest in businesses. In contrast to rental properties, where a single investor may buy an entire building complex, investors in corporations usually buy only a relatively small percentage of ownership through the purchase of stock. Despite this difference, investors in corporate stocks are basically interested in the same two items of information: (1) how much income the firm makes (and is likely to make in the future), and (2) how much the firm is worth.

balance sheet (statement of financial position) *the primary financial statement that shows the financial resources of an enterprise at a particular date and the claims against those resources, and therefore the relationships of assets, liabilities, and owners' equity*

Historically, two basic financial statements have been used to answer these questions. As discussed in Chapters 6 and 7, the income statement reports the results of operations, that is, the revenues and expenses and the income produced. The statement of financial position, or balance sheet,[1] is the report that comes closest to answering the second question: How much is a firm worth?

[1] The official literature now calls this report the statement of financial position. Because "balance sheet" is more concise, however, that term will be used in this text.

This chapter is an overview of the balance sheet. It focuses on (1) valuation problems of the balance sheet—that is, the degree to which it presents a realistic and current assessment of the worth of a firm, (2) the elements of the balance sheet, (3) the classification of balance sheet accounts, and (4) some limitations of the balance sheet.

Valuation Problems of the Balance Sheet

operating cycle *the general pattern of business activity whereby cash and other resources are converted to inventory and operational assets and eventually to products or services that can be sold for cash and other resources*

In Chapter 3, we described the general pattern of activity for all businesses. The pattern for a typical merchandising business is summarized by the flow chart in Exhibit 8-1. Despite the orderly and sequential appearance of the flow chart, the normal operating cycle of a business is often a fairly complicated process. At any particular time, most businesses are involved in all the operating-cycle activities. For example, a firm will have purchased but not yet paid for inventory; it will have sold inventory but not yet collected the proceeds; and it will have purchased but not yet completely used up equipment and furniture.

If a firm's inventory and all its other assets were sold and the money collected at the end of each period, the cash could be counted and the worth of the firm could be determined. However, the dynamic nature of the operating cycle makes it difficult to get an accurate picture of how much a firm is worth at any single point in time. Changing prices also make it difficult to evaluate a firm. For example, in an inflationary period, what is the current value of inventory purchased during a prior period, or buildings

EXHIBIT 8-1 **Operations of a Business**

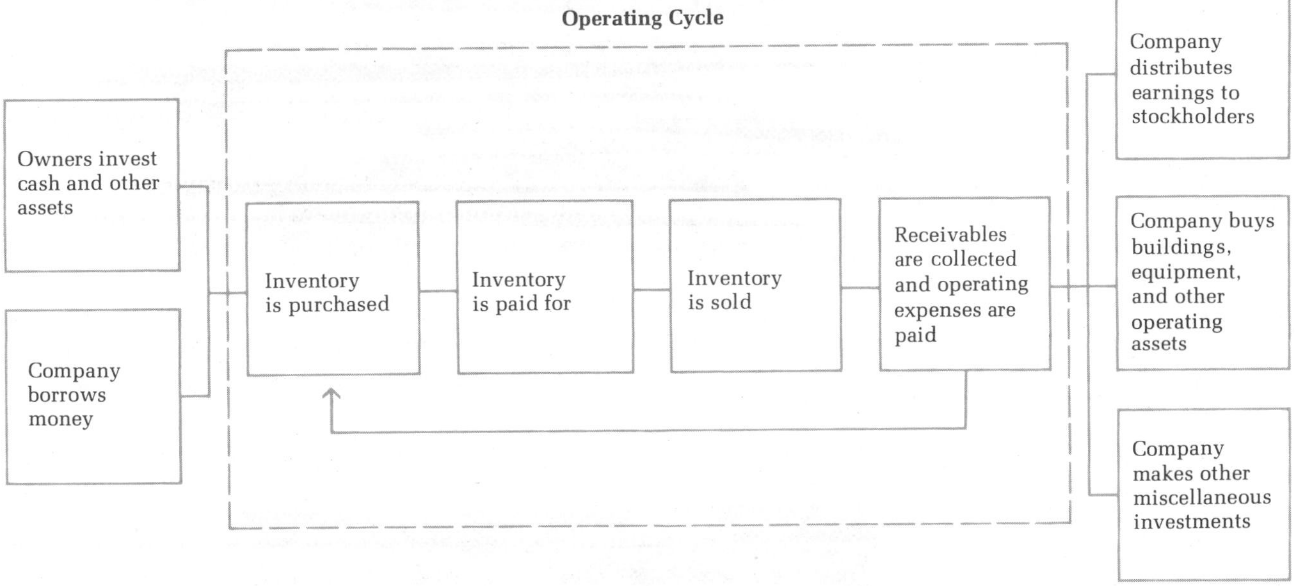

purchased 10 periods ago? Should they be reported on the balance sheet at their original cost, at some measure of their current value, or at some other amount?

Current practice is to report all assets at their historical (original) costs, so a balance sheet cannot be said to indicate the worth or value of a company. For instance, if land originally cost $10,000 in 1975 but has a current value of $20,000, it would be reported on the balance sheet at $10,000 (perhaps with the current value shown in parentheses). With the historical cost approach, then, balance sheet amounts are stated at their current values only in the period when they were originally acquired and placed on the balance sheet. Subsequently, the amounts reported can be quite close to or very different from current values, depending on many factors—one of which is the length of time the item has been carried on the balance sheet.

The historical cost approach means that the balance sheet discloses a mixture of items: short-term assets and liabilities closely approximating current values, and older assets representing only historical costs. Specifically, since the costs of buildings, equipment, and similar assets are usually depreciated over their estimated useful lives, the reported amounts for these items represent only undepreciated original costs, which may be far different from the current values of these assets.

Accountants who support the historical cost balance sheet maintain that even though it is not a current-value statement, it is still very useful. Their arguments usually include the following points. First, the statement provides accountability for all the dollars invested by the owners. That is, the actual dollars invested can be traced through operations or to residual valuations. With this accountability, fraud and embezzlement can be detected more readily than if historical costs were abandoned and current values were substituted. Second, the process of determining current values is too subjective and only the historical cost method provides a reliable summary of the operations and assets of a business. Third, the historical cost balance sheet provides a necessary bridge between two income statements by indicating which asset values will be carried forward to future periods. Fourth, although it does not accurately measure current worth or value, an historical cost balance sheet identifies the assets owned by a firm, and gives readers a good idea of how a company is financed—by borrowings, by earnings, or by owner contributions.

Finally, the balance sheet traditionally has reported historical costs because of accounting's insistence upon linking it to the income statement—that is, Retained Earnings is the account into which net income is closed. If a balance sheet were to report current values and still be tied to an income statement, net income would have to reflect changes in net asset values, a procedure many accountants believe would seriously jeopardize the value of the statement by lessening its objectivity.

THE EFFECT OF INFLATION ON MONETARY AND NONMONETARY ITEMS

One of the largest single factors causing the current values of assets to differ from their historical costs is inflation. The extent to which inflation affects assets, liabilities, and owners' equity can best be understood by considering

monetary items *those assets and liabilities that command a fixed amount of future dollars (determined by nature or contract) in the marketplace*

nonmonetary items *those assets and equities that are not fixed in the amount of future dollars they can command and hence fluctuate in value according to their demand in the marketplace*

the monetary and nonmonetary nature of these accounts. Monetary items are those assets or liabilities, such as cash, receivables, and payables, that involve dollar amounts that are fixed in the future either by contract or by nature. That is, these items are always equal to a specific number of dollars no matter what happens to the inflation rate or the purchasing power of the dollar. In contrast, nonmonetary items, such as inventories, buildings, equipment, and capital stock, fluctuate in value according to the changing purchasing power of the dollar, the demand for these items in the marketplace, and other factors.

Since the absolute dollar amounts of monetary assets (and liabilities) are fixed, companies having these items generally lose (or gain) purchasing power during periods of inflation. For example, a 1983 note payable (a liability) due in 1990 will be satisfied with the payment of 1990 dollars, regardless of whether a 1990 dollar is equivalent in purchasing power to a 1983 dollar. Similarly, cash (an asset) held for several years during a period of inflation loses purchasing power. Although the cash involved always represents the same number of dollars, cash spent later will buy less. Thus, during a period of inflation, companies holding monetary assets such as cash or receivables lose purchasing power, and companies with monetary liabilities such as accounts or notes payable gain purchasing power.

This phenomenon does not occur with nonmonetary assets and liabilities. Whereas the future dollar amount of monetary items is fixed, the value of nonmonetary items increases or decreases in response to demand in the marketplace. Thus, the price of such items as inventories, buildings, and equipment will generally rise in inflationary periods and fall during deflationary periods. In most countries inflation has been substantial over the last several years, so inventories, buildings, land, and other assets are often worth considerably more than their reported historical costs. The result has been that the older an asset is, the greater the difference between historical costs and current values.

ALTERNATIVE VALUATION AND REPORTING METHODS

Because historical cost reporting does not reflect either current values or the inflation-adjusted historical costs (constant dollars), critics argue that some other method of valuation and measurement should be used. The two most popular alternatives are constant-dollar statements and current-value statements. Both of these were considered in the context of income measurement in Chapter 6; here we will discuss their effect on the balance sheet.

constant-dollar method *an income measurement method in which income is defined as revenues less expenses as adjusted by a general (economy-wide) price index, plus any purchasing power gains or losses due to changes in the general price level; also called the general price-level-adjusted historical cost method*

As indicated in Chapter 6, the constant-dollar method of measuring income suggests that historical costs should be adjusted upward or downward by some general economy-wide price index. This index, which would measure the rate of inflation (or deflation), would adjust historical costs from nominal dollars to constant dollars. Thus, if an adding machine or other asset were purchased for $100 at a time when the general price index was 100 percent and a year later the general price index had increased to 110 percent, the asset's historical cost would be adjusted to $110. This method has the advantage of converting the dollar costs of transactions entered into at different times into comparable measurements that reflect units of equivalent purchasing power.

One of the major disadvantages of this approach is that it considers only changes caused by inflation and not changes in value that result from increases or decreases in such factors as supply, demand, and productivity. Clearly, some assets increase in value faster than others, and in some cases, assets actually decline in value during inflationary periods. Thus, using a general index to adjust historical costs may result in reporting assets at figures that are further from their current values than would be the case if unadjusted historical costs had been used. The constant-dollar approach can also become quite complicated, perhaps even to the extent that many people would find it difficult to understand.

current values *the amounts that assets or liabilities are presently worth in the marketplace*

The second approach is to abandon historical cost valuation completely and adopt current-value accounting. Using the current-value approach, assets, liabilities, and stockholders' equity are reported at their values as of the dates of the financial statements. These values are reported on the balance sheet and the difference between the valuations at successive reporting dates is considered income (or loss) to the business. Conceptually, this approach is very appealing, but implementing it presents many problems. The major difficulty is in obtaining accurate valuations that can be verified objectively. For example, the current values of many stocks and bonds can be readily obtained because their prices are quoted daily on national stock exchanges. But how do you determine the current value of a plant that is 30 years old and still servicing the needs of a particular firm? To replace that facility would cost the company much more money; however, the advantage of being able to install modern machinery in a new building or the chance to move to a different location might outweigh the cost. Many accountants are concerned that the valuations required in order to use this approach would not always be objective because it is difficult to assess the ongoing value of such a facility; therefore, the balance sheet might present misleading information to the public.

It is difficult to decide which method—historical cost, constant dollar, or current value—is preferable. Because there are significant advantages and disadvantages to each, in 1979 the FASB issued Statement No. 33. This Statement requires that certain large companies report, as supplementary information to their primary historical cost financial statements, inventories and most plant assets on both a constant-dollar and a current-value basis. In requiring all three types of disclosures, the FASB concluded that experimentation is necessary before the most effective reporting method can be selected.

TO SUMMARIZE Currently, the primary financial statements are prepared on an historical cost basis. However, because inflation and other factors cause these historical costs to be significantly different from current values, two reporting alternatives have been proposed. The constant-dollar alternative modifies historical costs by restating all costs in terms of equivalent purchasing power. The current-value method abandons historical costs completely and measures assets and liabilities at their present worth. Supplementary disclosures incorporating both methods are required of many large firms by the FASB.

What's in a Balance Sheet?

As explained in Chapter 2, the balance sheet is divided into three major sections: assets, liabilities, and owners' equity. The first section identifies the types of assets owned by a firm and the amounts paid for those assets. Further, it categorizes the assets as current, or short-term, and noncurrent, or long-term, and thus discloses the composition of assets and their liquidity.

The liability section informs readers of the extent and nature of a firm's borrowings, and provides a measure of its financial stability. This section, together with owners' equity, indicates how an entity is financed (whether by borrowings or by owner contributions).

Finally, the owners' equity section completes the balance sheet by identifying the portion of a firm's resources that were contributed by owners and the amount of undistributed earnings (retained earnings) a firm has had since inception. People often think that since this section represents the residual portion of the balance sheet equation—the remainder after liabilities have been subtracted from assets—it refers to the net worth of a firm. If the assets and liabilities were stated at current market values, this would be the case. As it now stands, however, owners' equity merely shows two of the ways in which resources are brought into a firm (owner contributions and retained earnings). The only other source of resources is borrowings, which are included in the liabilities section.

The Classified Balance Sheet

classified balance sheet *a balance sheet on which assets, liabilities, and owners' equity are subdivided by age, use, and source*

In Chapter 2, we briefly discussed the classified balance sheet and the reasons for classification. Here is a review of the most common subcategories of assets, liabilities, and owners' equity.

In the following sections we will describe each of these subcategories. (Note, however, that this is still an overview; in-depth discussions will be provided in Chapters 9 through 14.)

Balance Sheet

Assets	Liabilities	Owners' Equity
Current Assets	Current Liabilities	Contributed Capital
Long-Term Investments	Long-Term Liabilities	Retained Earnings
Property, Plant, and Equipment		
Intangible Assets		

You will find it helpful as you read on to refer to the detailed balance sheet of Radio Tune-Up Company, shown in Exhibit 8-2.

EXHIBIT 8-2

Radio Tune-Up Company

Balance Sheet as of December 31, 1983

Assets			
Current Assets:			
Cash		$ 300,000	
Short-Term Investments		50,000	
Notes Receivable		15,000	
Accounts Receivable	$ 675,000		
Less Allowance for Doubtful Accounts	20,000	655,000	
Inventory		300,000	
Prepaid Expenses		6,000	
Total Current Assets			$1,326,000
Long-Term Investments:			
Stock of Y Company		$ 20,000	
Bonds of Z Company		30,000	
Total Long-Term Investments			50,000
Property, Plant, and Equipment:			
Land		$ 100,000	
Store Equipment and Furniture	$ 300,000		
Less Accumulated Depreciation	50,000	250,000	
Buildings	$2,600,000		
Less Accumulated Depreciation	125,000	2,475,000	
Total Property, Plant, and Equipment			2,825,000
Intangible Assets:			
Patents		$ 20,000	
Franchises		25,000	
Total Intangible Assets			45,000
Total Assets			$4,246,000

CURRENT ASSETS

current assets *cash and other assets that may reasonably be expected to be converted to cash within one year or during the normal operating cycle*

Current assets include cash and other short-term assets that may reasonably be expected to be converted to cash, sold, or consumed either within one year of the balance sheet date or during the normal operating cycle of a business, if the cycle is longer than one year. As shown in Exhibit 8-1, the operating cycle of most businesses involves three types of current assets: cash, inventory, and accounts receivable.

short-term investments *expenditures for nonoperational assets that a business intends to hold only for a short period of time, usually less than a year*

note receivable *a claim against a debtor, evidenced by an unconditional written promise to pay a certain sum of money on or before a specified future date*

In addition, current assets include such nonoperational items as short-term investments, notes receivable, and prepaid expenses. Short-term investments are marketable securities (stocks or bonds of other companies or government agencies) that a business plans to hold for a period shorter than the normal operating cycle. A company will make such investments when there is a temporary surplus of cash. Investments that are to be held for periods longer than one year or the normal operating cycle are reported as long-term investments.

Notes receivable are claims against debtors, evidenced by unconditional written promises to pay amounts of money on or before specified future

Liabilities and Stockholders' Equity

Current Liabilities:		
Accounts Payable	$ 200,000	
Notes Payable	70,000	
Wages Payable	7,000	
Current Portion of Mortgage Payable	26,000	
Income Taxes Payable	29,000	
Estimated Warranty Obligation	14,000	
Total Current Liabilities		$ 346,000
Long-Term Liabilities:		
Mortgage Payable (final payment due in 1988)	$ 300,000	
Bonds Payable (8%, maturity in 1992)	600,000	
Total Long-Term Liabilities		900,000
Total Liabilities		$1,246,000
Stockholders' Equity:		
Contributed Capital:		
Preferred Stock, 6%, 20,000 shares authorized, 10,000 shares outstanding, $70 par	$ 700,000	
Common Stock, 200,000 shares authorized, 160,000 shares outstanding, $10 par	1,600,000	
Paid-in Capital in Excess of Par—Common Stock	160,000	
Total Contributed Capital	$2,460,000	
Retained Earnings	540,000	
Total Stockholders' Equity		3,000,000
Total Liabilities and Stockholders' Equity		$4,246,000

dates. They are either interest-bearing or non-interest-bearing, although the former is more common, and they are usually written when money is lent or when customers are allowed extended periods to pay for merchandise. Like short-term investments, these notes must be collectible within one year in order to be classified as current assets.

prepaid expenses *payments made in advance for items normally charged to expense*

As you will recall from Chapters 4 and 6, prepaid expenses are payments made in advance for the use of goods and services, such as insurance, property taxes, and interest. For example, the cost of a one-year insurance policy paid in advance is a prepaid expense. Office supplies are also often classified as prepaid expenses until they are used.

Current assets are usually presented in the order of their liquidity; that is, those that are most easily and quickly converted to cash are listed first and those most difficult and/or requiring the most time to convert are listed last. In Exhibit 8–2, current assets total $1,326,000 and are listed in the following order: cash, short-term investments, notes receivable, accounts receivable, inventory, and prepaid expenses.

LONG-TERM INVESTMENTS

long-term investments *expenditures for nonoperational assets that a business intends to hold for more than a year or the normal operating cycle*

All nonoperating investments that a company intends to hold for more than a year (or the normal operating cycle) are considered long-term investments. The most common types are stocks and bonds of other companies, real estate, and government bonds. Also included in this category are monies set aside for special purposes, such as to purchase land for a new plant site or pay off a loan in the future. Exhibit 8-2 indicates that Radio Tune-Up Company has two long-term investments: stock of Y Company and bonds of Z Company.

PROPERTY, PLANT, AND EQUIPMENT

property, plant, and equipment *tangible, long-lived assets acquired for use in the business rather than for sale*

Property, plant, and equipment is a group of assets that are tangible and permanent, or at least long-term, and that were acquired for use by the business rather than for sale. These are sometimes called long-term assets. The most common long-term assets are land, buildings, furniture, and equipment.

depreciation *the process of cost allocation that assigns the original cost of plant and equipment to the periods benefited*

With the exception of land, which is not consumed or used up, these assets gradually wear out or become obsolete and must be depreciated; that is, their cost must be written off as an expense over their useful lives. The amount an asset is to be depreciated each year is difficult to determine because it is impossible to know exactly how long an asset will benefit a company or how much, if anything, it can be sold for at the end of its useful life. Indeed, most companies merely estimate how long an asset will last and expense a percentage of the cost each year.

accumulated depreciation *the total depreciation charged against an asset since acquisition; a contra account deducted from the original cost of an asset on the balance sheet*

book value (or carrying value) *the net amount shown in the accounts for an asset, liability, or owners' equity item*

The fact that costs are assigned in such an arbitrary way means that depreciation is merely an allocation scheme, not a method of valuing assets. In most cases, the undepreciated cost of an asset is far different from the asset's current value. The amount of depreciation assigned to a given year is reported as an expense for that year on the income statement, and the cumulative amount of depreciation since the acquistion of an asset is reported on the balance sheet in an account called Accumulated Depreciation. Accumulated Depreciation is a contra account that is deducted from the asset account to produce the book value (or carrying value) of the asset. As shown in Exhibit 8-2, land, store equipment and furniture, and buildings are the only property, plant, and equipment items owned by Radio Tune-Up Company.

INTANGIBLE ASSETS

intangible assets *long-lived assets that do not have physical substance and are not held for sale*

This classification includes long-lived assets that are useful in the operation of a business, are not held for sale, and do not have physical substance. Intangible assets are patents, copyrights, franchises, trademarks, and other such assets that provide competitive advantages to a company. Intangible assets can only be reported when they have been purchased or when cash has been expended for their development. The belief that one of these assets exists is not sufficient reason to include it as an asset.

The accounting for intangible assets is very similar to that for property, plant, and equipment. For both, the cost of the asset is apportioned over its estimated life and charged as an expense on the income statement. For intangible assets, this process is called amortization and is similar to the depreciation process for tangible assets. The two intangible assets held by Radio Tune-Up (in Exhibit 8-2) are patents and franchises. A patent is an exclusive protection of an invention granted by the government and a franchise is the right, granted by a company (such as McDonald's), to sell a product or offer a service in a certain geographical area.

amortization *the process of cost allocation that assigns the original cost of an intangible asset to the periods benefited*

patent *an exclusive right granted for up to 17 years by the federal government to an inventor to manufacture and sell an invention*

franchise *an exclusive right to sell a product or offer a service in a certain geographical area*

CURRENT LIABILITIES

This category includes those obligations or debts of a company that will be paid within a short time (one year or the normal operating cycle) and that are expected to be paid with current assets. The most common current liabilities are short-term cash obligations, such as accounts payable (amounts owed for the purchase of inventory and other items), short-term notes payable (obligations to pay certain amounts on or before a specified future date), wages payable, interest payable, rent payable, and income taxes payable. However, not all current liabilities are obligations to pay cash. Obligations to perform future services, such as providing rental space (because rent has been prepaid) or servicing a warranty, are also liabilities. If services are to be performed within one year, the warranty or unearned rent is recorded as a current liability at the time it is issued.

current liabilities *debts or other obligations that will be paid with current assets or otherwise discharged within one year or the normal operating cycle*

The difference between total current assets and total current liabilities is called working capital and the ratio of current assets to current liabilities is the current ratio (or the working capital ratio). This ratio is a measure of the short-term liquidity of a firm. For example, the total working capital of Radio Tune-Up Company is $980,000 ($1,326,000 − $346,000) and the current ratio is approximately 3.83 to 1 ($1,326,000 ÷ $346,000). Certainly, with 3.83 times as much in current assets as in current liabilities, Radio Tune-Up Company should have no problem paying its current liabilities. How good this current ratio is can be determined by comparing it with the ratios of other firms in the same industry.

working capital *the funds available to finance current operations; equal to current assets minus current liabilities*

current ratio (or working capital ratio) *current assets divided by current liabilities*

LONG-TERM LIABILITIES

Debts or other obligations that will not be paid within one year are called long-term liabilities. As these liabilities come within one year of payment, they are reclassified as current liabilities. Typical accounts in this section are long-term notes payable, mortgages payable, and bonds payable. Bonds are long-term, interest-bearing liabilities that are commonly used by businesses and other organizations such as cities, school districts, and public utilities to raise capital.

long-term liabilities *debts or other obligations that will not be paid within one year or the normal operating cycle*

Exhibit 8-2 shows that Radio Tune-Up has $900,000 of long-term liabilities, which include a mortgage payable (probably on a building) and bonds payable.

OWNERS' EQUITY

Because Radio Tune-Up is a corporation, its owners' equity section is called stockholders' equity. If it were a partnership it would be called partners' equity, and if it were a proprietorship it would be called proprietor's equity. Stockholders' equity represents the owners' interests in and claims to net assets and is usually subdivided into contributed capital and retained earnings. Contributed capital is that portion of the equity provided from investments by the owners (usually through the purchase of stock). Retained earnings is the amount of undistributed earnings (earnings not paid out to the owners) accumulated since the business was organized. Retained earnings is not the same as cash. In fact, in most companies, cash coming into the firm through operations is used to purchase other current and noncurrent assets, such as land, buildings, and inventories. The use of cash to purchase such assets does not reduce retained earnings. Retained earnings is reduced by the payment of these earnings to owners, usually in the form of cash dividends, or by the company having sustained losses during a year. Thus, when a firm has income, both cash and retained earnings are usually increased, but seldom in identical amounts.

stockholders' equity *the ownership interest in an enterprise's assets; equals net assets (total assets minus total liabilities)*

contributed capital *that portion of stockholders' equity contributed by investors (the owners) through the issuance of stock*

retained earnings *the accumulated portion of owners' equity that has been earned and retained from profitable operations and not paid out in dividends or restricted for some other use; equal to owners' equity less contributed capital*

An examination of the stockholders' equity section of Radio Tune-Up shows that two types of stock have been issued by the company: preferred and common. These types of stock are discussed in Chapter 13. For now, all you need to know is that common and preferred stock offer different dividend payments and ownership rights. When dividends are paid, for example, preferred stockholders usually receive a predetermined percentage of the stated value of the preferred stock. (Preferred stockholders of Radio Tune-Up, who own 10,000 shares of stock valued at $70 per share, receive 6 percent of $700,000.) In addition, the payment of preferred stock dividends has priority over the payment of common stock dividends. The board of directors of a company determines whether to pay dividends and the size of the common stock dividend. It is the common stockholders, on the other hand, who usually elect the board of directors and vote on other important matters concerning the corporation.

In addition to the two stock accounts, Radio Tune-Up has another equity account, Paid-in Capital in Excess of Par, which has a balance of $160,000. This means that when the common stock was issued, although it had a par value (or face value) of $10 per share, it was actually issued for an average price of $11 per share (160,000 shares × $10 par = $1,600,000; $160,000 ÷ 160,000 shares = $1 in excess of par). The par value of a stock does not represent the market value or current sales price of the stock; rather, it is a nominal amount specified in the corporate charter and printed on the face of each stock certificate. Its purpose is chiefly a legal one—when stock is issued, the proceeds received are divided into a par value amount and the amount that was paid in excess of par value. The total par value of a firm's outstanding stock is often referred to as its legal capital, which is the amount of contributed capital not available for dividends.

par value (or face value) *the nominal value printed on the face of a share of stock*

Finally, Radio Tune-Up has a retained earnings balance of $540,000. In other words, since incorporation this company has retained in the business $540,000 of its earnings. Taking into account the probability that cash dividends were distributed to stockholders over the period, total earnings would have been more than $540,000.

TO SUMMARIZE The most common format for balance sheet classifications separates assets into current assets, long-term investments, property, plant, and equipment, and intangible assets; divides liabilities into current and long-term liabilities; and divides owners' equity into contributed capital and retained earnings. The categorization of accounts by age (such as long-term and short-term), by use (such as investments and property, plant, and equipment), and by source (such as retained earnings and contributed capital) helps make the balance sheet easy to read and understand.

Limitations of the Balance Sheet

The valuation problems discussed earlier present one limitation of the balance sheet; that is, the balance sheet generally does not reflect the current value of a company. Two other limitations should also be noted: (1) The balance sheet only reports resources that can be expressed in monetary (dollar) terms, which means that some items commonly considered to be assets or liabilities are not included on the balance sheet, and (2) two similar companies may use different accounting methods for the same types of transactions or events, making comparisons between companies difficult.

Regarding the first limitation, consider the value of an efficient management team to a business organization. Certainly, most people would agree that sound management is as much an asset as a piece of machinery. Yet, because it is difficult to quantify the value of the management team, no appropriate asset is reported on the balance sheet. Other unreported nonmoney items include major discoveries of new products or new sources of materials, strategic locations, and loyal and valued employees. Likewise, an event such as the emission of pollutants into the air or water is not recorded on the statements but could be considered a liability.

As another example, if a company purchases another business for more than the value of its reported assets, the excess cost is called goodwill and is classified as an intangible asset. On the other hand, if a company develops goodwill through good customer relations, a quality product, or some other means, the goodwill is not reported as an asset on the balance sheet. This is because it was not purchased in an arm's-length transaction and its value cannot be objectively determined.

With respect to the second limitation, firms are allowed to use alternative methods of accounting for several assets (for example, a firm may choose among the various inventory cost flow alternatives discussed in Chapter 7). When companies use different reporting methods, comparisons are difficult and sometimes meaningless.

CHAPTER REVIEW

Historically, the primary purpose of the balance sheet was to report the financial position and worth of a business enterprise. However, because balance sheet items are not adjusted for inflation and other factors affecting their current values, the statement does not really show the worth of a firm. Instead, it reports assets, liabilities, and owners' equity at their original costs (less depreciation or amortization, where appropriate). This lack of valuation information has caused many accountants to suggest alternative measurement methods, including constant-dollar and current-value.

Notwithstanding this deficiency, the balance sheet aids readers in understanding the financial position of a business. In fact, when balance sheet accounts are classified by age, by use, and by source, the statement provides a relatively clear picture of a business's financial position. The most common classification scheme divides assets into current assets, long-term investments, property, plant, and equipment, and intangible assets; liabilities into current and long-term liabilities; and owners' equity into contributed capital and retained earnings.

In addition to the valuation question, the balance sheet has two other limitations: (1) It only reports resources that can be expressed in monetary terms, omitting items often considered to be assets or liabilities, and (2) companies may use different accounting methods, making comparisons difficult.

KEY TERMS AND CONCEPTS

accumulated depreciation (278)
amortization (279)
balance sheet (statement of financial position) (270)
book value (or carrying value) (278)
classified balance sheet (275)
constant-dollar method (273)
contributed capital (280)
current assets (276)
current liabilities (279)
current ratio (or working capital ratio) (279)
current values (274)
depreciation (278)
franchise (279)
intangible assets (278)
long-term investments (278)
long-term liabilities (279)
monetary items (273)
nonmonetary items (273)
note receivable (276)
operating cycle (271)
par value (or face value) (280)
patent (279)
prepaid expenses (277)
property, plant, and equipment (278)
retained earnings (280)
short-term investments (276)
stockholders' equity (280)
working capital (279)

REVIEW PROBLEM

The Balance Sheet

McGregory Company has the following accounts as of December 31, 1983.

Common Stock	$400,000
Patent	20,000
Bonds Payable (maturity in 1990)	640,000
Accounts Receivable	18,000
Notes Payable (due in 30 days)	36,000
Prepaid Expenses	47,800
Income Taxes Payable	11,000
Cash	75,000
Inventory	65,800
Retained Earnings	20,000
Mortgage Payable (due in 1989)	121,000
Building	372,800
Land	50,000
Accumulated Depreciation–Building	98,000
Accumulated Depreciation–Equipment	40,000
Accounts Payable	19,400
Allowance for Doubtful Accounts	2,000
Equipment	738,000

Required:
Use the above accounts to prepare, in good form, a balance sheet as of December 31, 1983, for McGregory Company.

Solution
1. The first step in preparing the balance sheet is to classify various accounts into current assets; property, plant, and equipment; intangible assets; current liabilities; long-term liabilities; and owners' equity.

Current Assets

Accounts Receivable	$ 18,000
Prepaid Expenses	47,800
Cash	75,000
Inventory	65,800
Allowance for Doubtful Accounts	(2,000)

Property, Plant, and Equipment

Building	$372,800
Accumulated Depreciation–Building	(98,000)
Land	50,000
Equipment	738,000
Accumulated Depreciation–Equipment	(40,000)

Intangible Assets

Patent	$ 20,000

Current Liabilities

Notes Payable (due in 30 days)	$ 36,000
Income Taxes Payable	11,000
Accounts Payable	19,400

Long-Term Liabilities

Bonds Payable (maturity in 1990)	$640,000
Mortgage Payable (due in 1989)	121,000

Owner's Equity

Common Stock	$400,000
Retained Earnings	20,000

2. When the accounts are classified, the balance sheet can be prepared. Since the balance sheet is a formal financial statement, proper format, including the heading, is important. Also, current assets and current liabilities should be listed in order of liquidity.

McGregory Company
Balance Sheet as of December 31, 1983

Assets		
Current Assets:		
Cash		$ 75,000
Accounts Receivable	$ 18,000	
Less Allowance for Doubtful Accounts	2,000	16,000
Inventory		65,800
Prepaid Expenses		47,800
Total Current Assets		$ 204,600
Property, Plant, and Equipment:		
Land		$ 50,000
Equipment	$738,000	
Less Accumulated Depreciation	40,000	698,000
Building	$372,800	
Less Accumulated Depreciation	98,000	274,800
Total Property, Plant, and Equipment		$1,022,800
Intangible Assets:		
Patent		$ 20,000
Total Assets		$1,247,400
Liabilities and Owners' Equity		
Current Liabilities:		
Notes Payable (due in 30 days)	$ 36,000	
Accounts Payable	19,400	
Income Taxes Payable	11,000	
Total Current Liabilities		$ 66,400
Long-Term Liabilities:		
Bonds Payable (maturity in 1990)	$640,000	
Mortgage Payable (due in 1989)	121,000	
Total Long-Term Liabilities		761,000
Total Liabilities		$ 827,400
Owners' Equity:		
Common Stock		$ 400,000
Retained Earnings		20,000
Total Owners' Equity		$ 420,000
Total Liabilities and Owners' Equity		$1,247,400

DISCUSSION QUESTIONS

1 What can be learned about a company by studying its balance sheet?

2 Why are balance sheet accounts separated into current, long-term, and other categories?

3 What characteristics differentiate depreciation from most other expenses?

4 Why is the periodic depreciation expense only an estimate?

5 What is the difference between the book value and the market value of an asset?

6 What is the basis for including as assets items that have no physical substance (intangible assets)?

7 What types of obligations other than those requiring cash payments are liabilities?

8 Why are stockholders' equity and liabilities considered the "sources" of assets?

9 Distinguish between retained earnings and cash.

10 Why is it important to understand the monetary and nonmonetary nature of balance sheet accounts? Does inflation affect both monetary and nonmonetary items in the same way? Explain.

11 What is the effect on purchasing power of holding cash during a period of inflation?

12 Why do critics argue that financial statements adjusted by a general price-level index do not necessarily represent current market values?

13 What is a major practical problem involved in adopting the current-value method of preparing financial statements? Are current-value statements as objective as historical-cost statements?

14 When can a patent, goodwill, or another intangible asset be reported as an asset on the balance sheet?

EXERCISES

E8-1 The Balance Sheet Equation

Complete the financial statements of Johnson and McDermitt Companies by filling in the blanks. (Note: No stock was sold by either company during 1983.)

	Johnson Company	McDermitt Company
Assets, January 1, 1983	$ 980	(4) $____
Liabilities, January 1, 1983	420	640
Owners' Equity, January 1, 1983	(1) ____	340
Assets, December 31, 1983	1,000	(5) ____
Liabilities, December 31, 1983	(2) ____	600
Owners' Equity, December 31, 1983	(3) ____	400
Revenues in 1983	140	(6) ____
Operating Expenses in 1983	120	120

E8-2 Balance Sheet Classifications

For each of the following accounts, identify whether it normally has a debit or a credit balance and how it would be classified on the balance sheet. The first two have been completed as examples for you to follow.

Account	Debit or Credit Balance	Balance Sheet Classification
Cash	Debit	Current Assets
Capital Stock	Credit	Contributed Capital

Wages Payable
Mortgage Payable (due in 10 years)
Allowance for Doubtful Accounts
Building
Short-Term Investments
Inventory
Accumulated Depreciation
Accounts Receivable
Income Taxes Payable
Notes Payable (due in 90 days)
Stock of X Company
Land
Bonds Payable (maturity in 1990)
Retained Earnings
Estimated Warranty Obligation
Accounts Payable
Patents

E8-3 The Effect of Transactions on the Balance Sheet

Capital Reef Company had the following transactions.

1. Issued stock for $500.
2. Purchased supplies on account for $750.
3. Paid a secretary's salary of $800.
4. Paid the current month's rent of $350.
5. Collected $325 for services performed this period.
6. Paid dividends of $600.
7. Paid a $300 note owed to a bank.

Using the column heads below, indicate the effect on total assets, total liabilities, and total stockholders' equity for each transaction. Your solutions should indicate both amount and direction (increase or decrease). Transaction (1) has been completed as an example.

Transaction	Total Assets	=	Total Liabilities	+	Total Stockholders' Equity
Issued stock for $500	+500				+500

E8–4 The Effect of Transactions on the Balance Sheet

Thousand Lakes Corporation had the following transactions.

1. Paid an account payable.
2. Billed a customer for services performed.
3. Declared a cash dividend that is payable 15 days after the close of the current accounting period.
4. A customer paid in advance for repair work to be completed while he is on vacation next month. The advance was accounted for using the liability approach.
5. Purchased a new service truck. Paid 10 percent down and issued a note for the balance.
6. Purchased supplies for cash.
7. Paid a loan in full.

Indicate the effect of each of the above transactions on total assets, total liabilities, and total stockholders' equity. Transaction (1) has been completed for you.

Transaction	Total Assets	=	Total Liabilities	+	Total Stockholders' Equity
1	Decrease		Decrease		No effect

E8–5 Monetary and Nonmonetary Items

Selected accounts and balances from Jackson Company's balance sheet appear as follows.

Cash	$ 1,600
Accounts Receivable	2,400
Inventory	4,000
Property, Plant, and Equipment (Net)	20,000
Accounts Payable	3,000
Notes Payable	4,400

1. What is the total amount of the monetary assets?
2. What is the total amount of the monetary liabilities?
3. Compare the effect of inflation on this company's financial position with that on a company whose monetary liabilities were less than its monetary assets.

E8–6 Balance Sheet Analysis and the Effects of Inflation on Monetary and Nonmonetary Items

Lopes Company has an extremely conservative management and has the following balance sheet as of December 31, 1983.

Lopes Company
Balance Sheet as of December 31, 1983

Cash	$ 40,000
Accounts Receivable	80,000
Notes Receivable	50,000
Inventory	120,000
Property, Plant, and Equipment (net)	200,000
Total Assets	$490,000
Accounts Payable	$ 4,000
Notes Payable	8,000
Total Liabilities	$ 12,000
Common Stock	$160,000
Retained Earnings	318,000
Total Stockholders' Equity	$478,000
Total Liabilities and Stockholders' Equity	$490,000

1. Why do you think this company is described as a conservative company?
2. How has this company primarily financed its operations?
3. What are the company's total monetary assets and total monetary liabilities?
4. Is this company's financial position one that will be adversely or positively affected by inflation? Why?

E8–7 Working Capital and Current Ratios

Scott and Tyler Companies both operate in the same industry. At December 31, 1983, their respective balance sheets contained the following data.

	Scott Company	Tyler Company
Cash	$ 1,600	$ 2,400
Accounts Receivable	2,400	4,800
Inventory	4,000	6,000
Property, Plant, and Equipment (Net)	12,000	10,000
Accounts Payable	1,000	1,200
Notes Payable (due in 6 months)	3,000	2,400
Notes Payable (due in 4 years)	8,000	8,000
Stockholders' Equity	8,000	11,600

1. Determine the amount of working capital for each firm.
2. Compute the current ratio for each company.

E8–8 Working Capital and Current Ratios

Summarized balance sheet information for Mayberry and Roseberry Companies is as follows:

	Mayberry Company	Roseberry Company
Current Assets	$400	$1,050
Property, Plant, and Equipment (Net)	600	3,000
Current Liabilities	200	700
Long-Term Liabilities	200	1,500
Stockholders' Equity	600	1,350

1. Determine the amount of working capital for each company.
2. Compute the current ratios of each company.

E8–9 Balance Sheet Classification—Matching

Selected balance sheet classifications for MBA Company as of December 31, 1983, are given on the right. Match each of the accounts on the left with the proper balance sheet classification.

MBA Company
Balance Sheet Accounts as of December 31, 1983

1. Equipment	a. Current Assets
2. Goodwill	b. Long-Term Investments
3. Prepaid Rent	c. Property, Plant, and Equipment
4. Accrued Wages Payable	d. Intangible Assets
5. Building	e. Current Liabilities
6. Accumulated Depreciation—Building	f. Long-Term Liabilities
7. Patents	g. Contributed Capital
8. Advances from Customers	h. Retained Earnings
9. Retained Earnings	
10. Common Stock	
11. Accounts Receivable	
12. Income Taxes Payable	
13. Cash	
14. Notes Payable, due in 1987	
15. Mortgage Payable, due in 2003	
16. Land	

E8–10 Classified Balance Sheet Preparation

Using the accounts listed below, prepare, in good form, a classified balance sheet for Dixie Company as of December 31, 1983. The company was established January 1, 1983.

Account	Amount
Depreciation Expense	$ 400
Prepaid Insurance	400
Estimated Utilities Payable	100
Office Equipment	2,000
Common Stock	8,000
Miscellaneous Expenses	300
Rent Receivable	200
Note Payable (due on 12/31/85)	4,000
Dividends	200
Unearned Rent	200
Cash	1,000
Accumulated Depreciation—Furniture and Fixtures	300
Utilities Expense	200
Rent Revenue	2,000
Accounts Payable	300
Furniture and Fixtures	10,000
Insurance Expense	300
Accumulated Depreciation—Office Equipment	100

E8–11 Balance Sheet and Income Statement Classification—Matching

Some of the balance sheet and income statement accounts from Door Manufacturing Company are given below. For each numbered item, identify the classification to which it belongs.

Accounts	Classifications
1. Accounts Receivable	a. Current Assets
2. Patents	b. Long-Term Investments
3. Dividends Payable	c. Property, Plant, and Equipment
4. Cash	d. Intangible Assets
5. Sales Revenue	e. Current Liabilities
6. Short-Term Investments	f. Long-Term Liabilities
7. Depreciation Expense	g. Stockholders' Equity
8. Franchises	h. Revenue
9. Office Supplies on Hand	i. Cost of Goods Sold
10. Purchases	j. Operating Expenses
11. Note Payable (5-year maturity)	
12. Estimated Warranty Obligation	
13. Capital Stock	
14. Income Taxes Payable	
15. Salary Expense	

E8–12 Balance Sheet Classification

Milato Corporation had the following balance sheet accounts on December 31, 1983.

Short-Term Investments	$ 6,000
Accounts Payable	2,000
Accounts Receivable	4,000
Wages Payable	3,000
Cash	1,500
Retained Earnings	12,000
Stock of Z Company	4,500
Accumulated Depreciation—Building	2,000
Land	9,000
Building	26,200
Inventory	9,000
Common Stock	30,000
Income Taxes Payable	1,800
Prepaid Expenses	600
Bonds Payable (maturity in 1992)	10,000

Given this information, determine:

1. Current assets.
2. Long-term investments.
3. Property, plant, and equipment.
4. Current liabilities.
5. Long-term liabilities.
6. Stockholders' equity.

E8-13 Relationships Between a Balance Sheet and an Income Statement

The total amount of assets and liabilities of Village Green Company at January 1, 1983, and December 31, 1983, are presented below.

	January 1	Post-Closing Trial Balance, December 31
Assets	$38,000	$56,000
Liabilities	13,000	14,400

Determine the amount of net income or loss for 1983, applying each of the following assumptions concerning the additional issuance of stock and dividend declarations by the firm. Each case is independent of the others.

1. Dividends of $5,400 were declared (no additional stock was issued) during the year.
2. Additional stock of $2,400 was issued (no dividends were declared) during the year.
3. Additional stock of $31,000 was issued and dividends of $7,800 were declared during the year.

E8-14 Interpreting Balance Sheet Items—Property, Plant, and Equipment

Garvey Pharmaceutical Company was established on January 1, 1983. Russell Pharmaceutical Company was established in 1912. At the end of 1984, selected items from the financial statements of the two companies were as follows:

	Garvey Company	Russell Company
Property, Plant, and Equipment (net of accumulated depreciation)	$800,000	$100,000
Patents	160,000	12,000

1. From this information, can you conclude that Garvey is a much larger company than Russell? What could account for the reported differences in the amounts of property, plant, and equipment?
2. What could account for the low amount in the Patents account of Russell Company? Does this information indicate that Garvey has more patents?

E8-15 Balance Sheet Analysis

The balance sheet of Hafen's Auto Supply at March 31, 1983, is shown below in a format that matches the accounting equation.

Assets									=
Cash	+	Accounts Receivable	+	Inventory	+	Delivery Truck	+	Office Equipment	
$7,050	+	$21,560	+	$23,000	+	$8,400	+	$5,400	=

Liabilities					+	Owners' Equity
Accounts Payable	+	Notes Payable	+	Interest Payable	+	P. Hafen, Capital
$8,200	+	$16,400	+	0	+	$40,900

During the month of April, Hafen's had the following transactions:

April 1 Paid $1,500 of accounts payable.
3 Purchased inventory on account for $2,300 (perpetual inventory method).
7 Sold inventory costing $3,200 for $3,650 on account.
10 Purchased office equipment costing $4,500. Paid $900 down and signed a 6-month note at 14 percent interest for the balance.
15 Collected accounts receivable of $3,250.

April 20 P. Hafen used $350 of company funds to pay his daughter's doctor bill.
24 P. Hafen contributed a $250 typewriter to the company.
26 Sold inventory costing $500 for $750 cash.
30 The truck has a remaining useful life of 3 years and 5 months at April 30. The cost of the truck is being depreciated evenly over 42 months.

Given this information:

1. Prepare a schedule similar to that above and show the effect of each transaction. The April 1 transaction has been completed as an example.
2. Compute the account balances at April 30.
3. Compute the current ratios at April 30.

	Assets					=	Liabilities			+	Owners' Equity
Beg. Bal.	$7,050	+ $21,650	+ $23,000	+ $8,400	+ $5,400	=	$8,200	+ $16,400	+ 0	+	$40,900
4/1	($1,500)						($1,500)				

PROBLEMS

P8-1 Balance Sheet Preparation

Davis Knight opened an office supply store on October 1, 1983. During October he had the following transactions.

October	1	Invested $20,000 cash and a building worth $60,000 in the business. The building is expected to last 20 years with no resale value.
	1	Purchased office equipment (for use in the business) costing $7,500, paying $1,500 down and signing a 5-year note at 10 percent for the balance. The office equipment is expected to have a 5-year life with no scrap value.
	3	Purchased inventory costing $30,000 on account. (Use the perpetual inventory method.)
	10	Sold one-half the inventory (costing $15,000) for $20,000 on account.
	15	Purchased inventory costing $17,000 on account.
	20	Sold inventory costing $16,000 for $22,000 cash.
	25	Collected $12,500 of the accounts receivable.
	27	Paid accounts payable of $15,000.
	31	Davis recorded depreciation on the building and the office equipment.
	31	Davis recorded the interest expense on the 5-year 10 percent note.

Required:

1. Record the October transactions in General Journal form.
2. Prepare T-accounts and post the journal entries.
3. Prepare an income statement for the month ended October 31, 1983.
4. Prepare a balance sheet as of October 31, 1983.

P8-2 Classification of Balance Sheet Accounts

Maestro Corporation has the following balance sheet accounts as of December 31, 1983.

Land	$ 69,000
Cash	26,000
Short-Term Investments	12,000
Building	178,000
Accounts Payable	100,000
Common Stock	335,000
Accounts Receivable	88,000
Notes Payable (Short-Term)	105,000
Equipment	350,000
Patent	30,000
Bonds Payable (due in 1992)	300,000
Retained Earnings	58,000
Franchise	10,000
Inventory	170,000
Prepaid Expenses	15,000
Accumulated Depreciation–Building	20,000
Accumulated Depreciation–Equipment	30,000

Required:

1. Compute the total amount of:
   (a) Current assets.
   (b) Property, plant, and equipment.
   (c) Intangible assets.
   (d) Current liabilities.
   (e) Long-term liabilities.
   (f) Stockholders' equity.
2. What is Maestro's current ratio?

P8-3 Current-Ratio and Balance Sheet Interpretation

Zog Company had the following unclassified balance sheet as of December 31, 1983.

Zog Company
Balance Sheet as of December 31, 1983

Assets		
Cash		$ 8,500
Accounts Receivable		4,000
Inventory		16,000
Prepaid Expenses		1,500
Land		15,000
Building (net of depreciation)		40,000
Equipment (net of depreciation)		50,000
Patent		3,000
Total Assets		$138,000
Liabilities and Stockholders' Equity		
Liabilities:		
Notes Payable (Short-Term)	$ 8,000	
Accounts Payable	4,500	
Wages Payable	2,500	
Income Taxes Payable	3,000	
Bonds Payable (due in 1985)	25,000	
Total Liabilities		$43,000
Stockholders' Equity:		
Common Stock	$80,000	
Retained Earnings	15,000	
Total Stockholders' Equity		95,000
Total Liabilities and Stockholders' Equity		$138,000

Required:

1. Compute Zog's current ratio.
2. **Interpretive Question** Zog is presently applying for a 4-year bank loan of $30,000. The bank is willing to loan the money only if Zog can achieve and maintain a current ratio of 2 to 1. Which of the following actions would give Zog the needed ratio?
   (a) Payment of all wages payable.
   (b) Payment of all accounts payable.
   (c) Payment of all income taxes and accounts payable.

3. **Interpretive Question** Will anything happen in the next couple of years that will probably put Zog in violation of the debt requirement? Explain.

P8-4 Interpreting the Balance Sheet

The balance sheet for RTV Corporation as of December 31, 1983, is as follows:

RTV Corporation
Balance Sheet as of December 31, 1983

Assets		
Cash		$13,600
Accounts Receivable		13,000
Land		20,000
Office Equipment	$ 6,000	
Less Accumulated Depreciation	600	5,400
Total Assets		$52,000
Liabilities and Stockholders' Equity		
Liabilities:		
Accounts Payable	$ 900	
Income Taxes Payable	1,100	
Interest Payable	200	
Notes Payable (payable in 1 year)	2,000	
Total Liabilities		$ 4,200
Stockholders' Equity:		
Common Stock (par value $10)	$30,000	
Paid-in Capital in Excess of Par	3,000	
Retained Earnings	14,800	
Total Stockholders' Equity		47,800
Total Liabilities and Stockholders' Equity		$52,000

Required:

1. When was the office equipment purchased if it is expected to have a useful life of 10 years and no scrap value?
2. What is the annual interest rate on the note if it has been outstanding for six months and no interest has yet been paid?
3. If the company has been in existence since January 1, 1983, and if $3,000 of dividends were declared during 1983, what was 1983's net income?
4. How many shares of common stock are outstanding at December 31, 1983?
5. At what price was the stock issued if it was all issued at one time at the same price?
6. What is RTV's current ratio? (Round to the nearest tenth of a percent.)

P8-5 Analysis of a Balance Sheet

Parker Corporation had the following balance sheet as of December 31, 1984.

Parker Corporation
Balance Sheet as of December 31, 1984

Assets		
Cash		$ 5,000
Accounts Receivable	$28,000	
Less Allowance for Doubtful Accounts	560	27,440
Land		20,000
Building	$50,000	
Less Accumulated Depreciation	5,000	45,000
Total Assets		$97,440
Liabilities and Stockholders' Equity		
Liabilities:		
Accounts Payable	$20,000	
Income Taxes Payable	12,840	
Interest Payable	1,600	
Notes Payable	20,000	
Total Liabilities		$54,440
Stockholders' Equity:		
Common Stock (par value $20)	$20,000	
Paid-in Capital in Excess of Par	2,000	
Retained Earnings	21,000	
Total Stockholders' Equity		43,000
Total Liabilities and Stockholders' Equity		$97,440

Required:

1. If Parker Company estimates its bad debts on the basis of total receivables and has just made its adjusting entry, what percentage of accounts receivable has it estimated to be uncollectible?
2. If the company was started on January 1, 1983, and the building was purchased on that date, what is the useful life of the building? (The estimated scrap value of the building is zero.)
3. If the note has been outstanding for eight months and no interest has yet been paid, what is the interest rate of the loan?
4. What was the market price of the stock when it was issued to shareholders?
5. How many shares of common stock are outstanding?

P8-6 Preparation of a Classified Balance Sheet

Following are the December 31, 1984, account balances for E-Z Rental Company. The inventory balance on December 31, 1984, was $1,500.

Cash	$ 2,700
Accounts Receivable	2,500
Supplies on Hand	1,800
Prepaid Insurance	1,000
Equipment	11,275
Accounts Payable	3,450
Accrued Wages Payable	250

Dividends Payable	$ 1,750
Common Stock	6,225
Retained Earnings, January 1, 1984	12,000
Sales Revenue	15,000
Purchases	11,000
Freight-In	200
Dividends Declared	1,750
Other Operating Expenses	1,550
Inventory, January 1, 1984	3,700
Wages Expense	2,200
Accumulated Depreciation–Equipment	1,000

Required:

1. Prepare a classified balance sheet as of December 31, 1984.

2. **Intepretive Question** On the basis of its 1984 earnings, was this company's decision to pay dividends of $1,750 a sound one?

P8–7 Preparation of a Classified Balance Sheet

Following are the account balances as of December 31, 1984, for McGee Manufacturing Corporation.

Retained Earnings	$ 91,468
Mortgage Payable (current portion)	1,200
Mortgage Payable (noncurrent portion)	15,000
Accounts Receivable	15,760
Cash	15,180
Building	100,000
Accumulated Depreciation–Building	21,800
Office Equipment	9,140
Accumulated Depreciation–Office Equipment	5,440
Store Equipment	24,400
Accumulated Depreciation–Store Equipment	11,400
Salaries Payable	392
Land	12,000
Common Stock	60,000
Accounts Payable	16,840
Office Supplies on Hand	1,660
Prepaid Insurance	1,400
Inventory	44,000

Required:

1. Prepare a classified balance sheet as of December 31, 1984.

2. **Interpretive Question** Does it appear that McGee is a financially sound company?

P8–8 Balance Sheet Analysis

Jay Coughlin, a casket vendor, is sole proprietor of Coughlin's Coffins. Jay started his business by investing $50,000 on July 1, 1983. Below is a series of balance sheets that were prepared after each transaction.

a. **Coughlin's Coffins**
Balance Sheet as of July 1, 1983

Assets	
Cash	$50,000
Total	$50,000
Liabilities and Owner's Equity	
J. Coughlin, Capital	$50,000
Total	$50,000

b. **Coughlin's Coffins**
Balance Sheet as of July 20, 1983

Assets	
Cash	$30,000
Inventory	50,000
Total	$80,000
Liabilities and Owner's Equity	
Accounts Payable	$30,000
J. Coughlin, Capital	50,000
Total	$80,000

c. **Coughlin's Coffins**
Balance Sheet as of August 1, 1983

Assets	
Cash	$ 19,600
Inventory	50,000
Land	30,000
Building (20-year life)	90,400
Total	$190,000
Liabilities and Owner's Equity	
Accounts Payable	$ 30,000
Mortgage Payable (12% interest)	110,000
J. Coughlin, Capital	50,000
Total	$190,000

d. **Coughlin's Coffins**
Balance Sheet as of August 31, 1983

Assets	
Cash	$ 62,100
Accounts Receivable	37,500
Inventory	10,000
Land	30,000
Building (20-year life)	90,400
Total	$230,000
Liabilities and Owner's Equity	
Accounts Payable	$ 30,000
Mortgage Payable (12% interest)	110,000
J. Coughlin, Capital	90,000
Total	$230,000

e.

Coughlin's Coffins
Balance Sheet as of September 30, 1983

Assets	
Cash	$ 56,500
Accounts Receivable	28,100
Inventory	10,000
Land	30,000
Building (20-year life)	90,400
Total	$215,000
Liabilities and Owner's Equity	
Accounts Payable	$ 15,000
Mortgage Payable (12% interest)	110,000
J. Coughlin, Capital	90,000
Total	$215,000

Required:

1. Given the above balance sheets, record in General Journal form the transaction(s) that resulted in each of the balance sheets.

2. Now assume that between September 20 and December 31, 1983, Jay sells the remaining inventory on account for $14,000, collects $15,000 of the accounts receivable balance, and pays $7,000 of accounts payable. Prepare the balance sheet at December 31, 1983, after accounting for these transactions and recording adjustments for 5 months' interest and depreciation expense. T-accounts may simplify your solution.

P8-9 Unifying Problem: A Classified Balance Sheet

Marco Company has the following balance sheet accounts as of December 31, 1984.

Notes Payable (short-term)	$ 20,000
Accounts Payable	170,000
Land	40,000
Cash	58,000
Prepaid Expenses	27,000
Bonds Payable (maturity in 1990)	250,000
Common Stock	150,000
Retained Earnings	50,000
Inventory	155,000
Building	110,000
Accumulated Depreciation—Equipment	$ 30,000
Accumulated Depreciation—Building	10,000
Equipment	330,000
Mortgage Payable (due in 1988)	40,000

Required:

1. Prepare a classified balance sheet for Marco Company as of December 31, 1984.

2. Compute Marco Company's current ratio.

3. Compute Marco Company's total monetary assets and monetary liabilities.

4. **Interpretive Question** Is Marco's financial position one that will be eased or made more difficult by inflation?

P8-10 Unifying Problem: The Balance Sheet

Lynette Company has the following balance sheet accounts at December 31, 1983.

Common Stock	$200,000
Bonds Payable (maturity in 2000)	230,000
Notes Payable (due in 6 months)	18,000
Cash	32,900
Inventory	37,000
Land	28,000
Building	102,000
Accumulated Depreciation—Building	52,000
Equipment	369,000
Accumulated Depreciation—Equipment	20,000
Accounts Payable	9,700
Mortgage Payable (due in 1992)	60,000
Retained Earnings	10,000
Income Taxes Payable	12,000
Prepaid Expenses	24,800
Accounts Receivable	8,000
Patent	10,000

Required:

1. Prepare a classified balance sheet as of December 31, 1983.

2. Compute Lynette's current ratio.

3. Compute Lynette's total monetary assets and total monetary liabilities.

4. **Interpretive Question** How has this company acquired most of its financial resources?

CHAPTER 9

Current Assets and Current Liabilities

THIS CHAPTER EXPLAINS:

Accounting for cash, including cash control, petty-cash funds, and the reconciliation of bank accounts.

Accounting for receivables, including the discounting of notes receivable.

Accounting for current liabilities, including accounts payable, notes payable, accrued liabilities, payroll-related liabilities, and noncash liabilities.

The relationship between current assets and current liabilities.

working capital *the funds available to finance current operations; equal to current assets minus current liabilities*

With this chapter, we begin a detailed examination of the balance sheet. Current assets and current liabilities are covered together because they involve similar accounting procedures and because they are generally considered as a unit for planning and evaluation purposes. Most of the funding for day-to-day business operations must come from working capital (the excess of total current assets over total current liabilities). For this reason, business managers and those who monitor business reports (security analysts, investors, bankers, and others) tend to pay special attention to the ratio of current assets to current liabilities.

The current assets discussed here include cash, accounts receivable, notes receivable, and prepaid expenses. Inventories were examined in Chapter 7 and short-term investments will be discussed in Chapter 11. Current liabilities include accounts payable, notes payable, accrued liabilities (such as payroll liabilities), and noncash liabilities. Contingent liabilities are also touched upon briefly.

Current Assets

current assets *cash and other assets that may reasonably be expected to be converted to cash within one year or during the normal operating cycle*

liquidity *a company's ability to meet current obligations with cash or with other assets that can be quickly converted to cash*

Current assets are cash and other assets that can reasonably be expected to be converted to cash or used within one year or during the normal operating cycle. Since current assets are listed on the balance sheet in order of liquidity, we will follow that sequence in describing the individual accounts.

Accounting for Cash

Cash is obviously the most liquid of all assets. It includes coins, currency, money orders and checks (made payable or endorsed to the company), and money on deposit with banks or savings institutions. All of the various transactions involving these forms of cash are summarized and reported under a single balance sheet caption, Cash. This category does not, however, include postage stamps (prepaid expenses), IOUs (receivables), or postdated checks. Also, cash that is restricted for special purposes (such as the repayment of a long-term liability) or restricted by law is excluded from the cash balance and reported elsewhere.

The major elements of accounting for cash are (1) recording and processing cash transactions, (2) accounting for petty cash, and (3) preparing bank reconciliations.

In many companies, cash transactions are journalized, posted, and summarized by a computer. Accountants merely "input" the original data; the computer performs most of the accounting functions, including the preparation of special journals and the financial statements. In relatively small businesses, cash transactions are more likely to be entered manually, often in separate cash receipts and cash disbursements journals. These journals were discussed in the Supplement to Chapter 3.

CONTROL OF CASH

Because of its value, and because it is the most liquid asset, cash must be carefully safeguarded. In particular, management must attempt to

1. Prevent losses of cash by theft or fraud.
2. Provide accurate accounting of all inflows, outflows, and balances of cash.
3. Maintain a sufficient balance of cash on hand to provide for day-to-day requirements, finance current operations, and satisfy maturing liabilities.
4. Prevent large amounts of excess or idle cash from accumulating on hand or in checking accounts.

Several control procedures have been developed to help management meet these objectives. One of the most important is that the handling of cash should be separated from the accounting for cash. The purpose of this separation of duties is to make it difficult for theft to occur unless at least two people are involved. Without such collusion (two or more people working together), the theft of a cash payment by a mailroom employee, for example, will probably be discovered by an accounting clerk, either because the total of the invoices will not match the cash total or because a customer will complain when he or she receives a second invoice for an amount already paid.

As an example of what can happen without this safeguard, consider the case of an employee who both opens the mail and keeps the books. He or she could pocket a portion of the cash payment from one customer and not record that portion until payment is received from a second customer. The recording of a portion of a second customer's payment could then be delayed until a third customer pays, and so on. This type of lagged recording of payments is called lapping and allows an employee to use company money for extended periods of time.

lapping *a procedure used to conceal the theft of cash by crediting the payment from one customer to another customer's account on a delayed basis*

Separation of duties actually involves three procedures: (1) the separation of cash receiving from cash disbursing, (2) the clear identification and use of specific routines for cash receiving and cash disbursing, and (3) the assignment of each aspect of cash handling and accounting to different individuals.

A second cash-control practice is to require that all cash receipts be deposited daily in bank accounts. Most cash comes from over-the-counter sales or accounts receivable collected through the mail. To ensure that all such sales are properly accounted for, businesses use cash registers that provide a tape of the day's sales. At the end of the day, all cash is counted, compared with the amount on the tape, and deposited in the bank. Payments received through the mail are controlled by separating the receiving, recording, and depositing functions. The person who receives the cash and checks makes a list, then forwards the cash and checks to the cashier for deposit in the bank. The list is also sent to the accounting department to be compared with the actual receipted deposit slip from the bank, and entered into the cash receipts journal. If all cash receipts are deposited on the day they are received, the likelihood of cash being lost or misused is minimized.

A third cash-control practice is to require that all cash expenditures (except those paid out of petty cash) be made with prenumbered checks. In addition, the person or persons who approve payment should be different from those who actually sign the checks. In companies where this system is used, no checks can be signed unless they are accompanied by an approved invoice, which gives the purpose of the check and the justification and verification for the expenditure. Any check not actually used should be clearly marked "void," mutilated, and filed in sequence in the checkbook so all checks can be accounted for.

In addition to safeguarding and protecting cash, a business must ensure that cash is wisely managed. In fact, many businesses establish elaborate control and budgeting procedures for monitoring cash balances, working capital ratios, and estimated future cash needs.

ACCOUNTING FOR PETTY CASH

petty-cash fund *a small amount of cash kept on hand for making miscellaneous payments*

For control purposes, it makes sense to pay all bills by check, since a check provides a permanent record of each transaction. However, most businesses find it too expensive and inconvenient to write checks for all small miscellaneous cash expenditures. Instead, they usually pay for items such as minor delivery charges, stamps, and inexpensive supplies out of cash kept on hand in what is called a petty-cash fund. The size of a petty-cash fund depends on the number, magnitude, and frequency of these miscellaneous expenditures. Obviously, the petty-cash funds of a multinational corporation will be much larger than those of a small business. Businesses want the fund to be large enough so that it does not have to be replenished too often but not so large that it tempts theft or misuse. Most firms keep enough cash on hand to cover about one month's miscellaneous expenditures. It is also common for firms to limit the amount that can be taken from the petty-cash fund for a single expenditure.

imprest petty-cash fund *a petty-cash fund in which all expenditures are documented by vouchers or vendors' receipts or invoices; the total of the vouchers and cash in the fund should equal the established balance*

Although a petty-cash fund is more difficult to control than checks, potential losses can be minimized by handling the petty-cash fund on an imprest basis. That is, any cash removed from the fund must be replaced by a prenumbered petty-cash voucher accompanied by a receipt or invoice from the supplier of the item or service purchased. The receipt or invoice validates the type and amount of the expenditure. Thus, with an imprest petty-cash fund, the balance can easily be checked. The total of unused cash and vouchers should always equal the imprest balance. Exhibit 9-1 is a voucher showing that a $42 delivery bill from EmCo Trucking Company was paid from petty cash.

EXHIBIT 9-1 **Petty-Cash Voucher**

No. 22

Payment made to: *EmCo Trucking* Date *July 17*

Description	Account to be charged	Amount
Delivery Bill	*616 (Freight-In)*	*$42.00*

Signature of person using funds *John Doe*

To illustrate the accounting for an imprest petty-cash fund, we will assume that on July 1, Miller Company decided to establish a petty-cash fund of $200. A check was made out to petty cash and cashed at the bank. The $200 cash was placed in a convenient but safe place. The entry in the cash disbursements journal would be as shown on the next page.

July 1	Petty Cash	200	
	Cash		200
	Established a $200 petty-cash fund.		

For each expenditure, a voucher (accompanied by a receipt) is prepared to account for the money spent. For example, if Miller paid $40 for office supplies, $42 for freight, and $30 for postage, three vouchers would be placed in the fund. Petty-cash expenditures are not accounted for as they occur; instead, a single entry is made when the petty-cash fund is replenished. The entry to replenish Miller's petty-cash fund would be

August 1	Office Supplies	40	
	Freight-In	42	
	Postage	30	
	Cash		112
	Replenished the petty-cash fund.		

As this entry indicates, when the petty-cash fund is replenished, a check is written for the total amount of all expenditures, Cash is credited, and the affected expense accounts are debited individually. The items in this entry are then posted to their respective accounts. At no time is the petty-cash fund replenished by debiting or crediting the Petty Cash account. The only entries ever made to that account are those that permanently increase or decrease it.

For control purposes, one person should have complete responsibility for the petty-cash fund. A different person should be authorized to write the checks that replenish the fund. The custodian of the petty-cash fund should be responsible for maintaining the fund's balance and should make sure that all petty-cash vouchers are prenumbered and used only once.

Cash Over and Short *an account used to record overages and shortages in petty cash*

If the actual balance is ever different from the amount that should be in the fund (usually because of an error in making change), the discrepancy should be noted in an account called Cash Over and Short. This account, which is used only to correct small errors, is debited when there is a shortage and credited when there is an excess of cash. For example, if Miller Company had found on August 1 that the petty-cash fund had only $82 in cash (instead of the correct amount of $88) and $112 in validated expenditures, the entry to replenish the petty-cash fund would have been

August 1	Office Supplies	40	
	Freight-In	42	
	Postage	30	
	Cash Over and Short	6	
	Cash		118
	Replenished the petty-cash fund and recognized a shortage of $6.		

Cash Over and Short is an expense account (Other Expenses) when it has a debit balance and a revenue account (Other Revenues) when it has a credit balance. Entries to replenish a petty-cash fund are recorded in the cash disbursements journal. At the end of an accounting period, an entry must be made to debit expenses and credit cash, so that income will not be overstated. The result is that the petty-cash fund will be replenished at the end of each accounting period.

RECONCILING THE BANK ACCOUNT

With the exception of petty cash, most cash is kept in checking accounts at one or more banks. Generally, only a few employees are authorized to sign checks and they must have their signatures on file with the bank.

Every month, the bank sends the business a statement that shows the cash balance at the beginning of the period, the deposits, the amounts of the checks processed, and the cash balance at the end of the period. With the statement, the bank includes all of that month's canceled checks, as well as debit and credit memos (for example, an explanation of charges for NSF checks and service fees). Keep in mind that a bank considers customers' deposits as a liability; hence, debit memos reduce the company's cash balance and credit memos increase it.

NSF (Not Sufficient Funds) check *a check that is not honored by a bank because of insufficient cash in the customer's account*

Miller Company's bank statement for July is presented in Exhibit 9–2. This statement includes three bank adjustments to Miller's balance—a bank service charge of $7 (the bank's monthly fee), $60 of interest paid by First Security Bank on Miller's average balance, and a $3,200 direct deposit apparently made by a customer who regularly deposits payments directly to Miller's bank account. Other adjustments that are commonly made to a company's bank account include

EC (Error Correction): Bank arithmetic and other errors and their corrections.

NSF (Not Sufficient Funds): The cancellation of a prior deposit that could not be collected because of insufficient funds in the check writer's account.

MS (Miscellaneous): Other adjustments made by a bank.

It is unusual for the ending balance on the bank statement to equal the amount of cash recorded in a company's Cash account. The most common reasons for differences are

1. *Time period differences:* The time period of the bank statement does not coincide with the timing of the company's postings to the Cash account.
2. *Deposits in transit:* These are deposits that have not yet reached the bank for processing, usually because they were made during the last days of the month.
3. *Outstanding checks:* These are checks that have been written and deducted from a company's Cash account but have not yet reached the bank for processing.
4. *Bank charges:* These are bank fees and other bank charges that have not yet been recorded by the company. The most common are monthly service charges and NSF checks.

EXHIBIT 9-2 Bank Statement

First Security Bank
Provo, Utah 84602

Statement of Account

MILLER COMPANY
1900 S. PARK LANE
PROVO, UT 84602

Account Number 325-78126

Date of Statement JULY 31, 1983

CHECK NUMBER	CHECKS AND WITHDRAWALS	DEPOSITS AND ADDITIONS	DATE	BALANCE
			6/30	13,000
620	140		7/01	12,860
621	250	1,500	7/03	14,110
622	860		7/05	13,250
623	210		7/08	13,040
		2,140	7/09	15,180
624	205		7/10	14,975
626	310		7/14	14,665
627	425		7/15	14,240
		3,200 D	7/18	17,440
628	765		7/19	16,675
629	4,825		7/22	11,850
630	420		7/24	11,430
632	326	1,600	7/25	12,704
		2,100	7/26	14,804
633	210		7/29	14,594
635	225		7/31	14,369
	7 SC	60 I	7/31	14,422
	9,171 TOTAL CHECKS AND WITHDRAWALS	10,600 TOTAL DEPOSITS AND ADDITIONS	7 SERVICE CHARGE	14,422 BALANCE

EC = Error Correction D = Direct Deposit I = Interest
NSF = Not Sufficient Funds SC = Service Charge MS = Miscellaneous

5. *Bank credits:* These are credits that are made by a bank to a company's account before they are recorded by the company. The most common sources are notes that have been collected for the company by the bank, direct deposits made by the company's customers, and interest paid on the account.

6. *Accounting errors:* These are numerical errors made by either the company or the bank. The most common are transpositions of numbers.

bank reconciliation *the process of systematically comparing the cash balance as reported by the bank with the cash balance on the company's books, and explaining any differences*

The process of determining the reasons for the differences between the bank balance and the company's Cash account balance is called reconciling the bank account. This usually results in adjusting both the bank statement and the book (Cash account) balances.

We will use Miller Company's bank account to illustrate a bank reconciliation. The statement shown in Exhibit 9-2 indicates an ending balance of $14,422 for the month of July. After arranging the month's checks in numerical order and examining the bank statement, Miller's accountant notes the following.

1. A deposit of $3,100 on July 31 was not shown on the bank statement.
2. Checks #625 for $326, #631 for $426, and #634 for $185 are outstanding.
3. The bank's service charge for the month is $7.
4. A direct deposit of $3,200 was made by Joy Company, a regular customer.
5. The bank paid interest of $60 on Miller's average balance.
6. Check #630 for John Jones' wages was recorded in the accounting records as $240 instead of the correct amount, $420.
7. The Cash account in the General Ledger shows an ending balance of $13,512.

Given these data, the bank reconciliation would be as shown in Exhibit 9-3.

EXHIBIT 9-3

Miller Company Bank Reconciliation
July 31, 1983

Ending Balance on Bank Statement		$14,422	Balance per Books		$13,512
Reconciling Items			**Reconciling Items**		
Additions to Bank Balance:			*Additions to Book Balance:*		
Deposits in Transit		3,100	Direct Deposit	$3,200	
Total		$17,522	Interest	60	3,260
			Total		$16,772
Deductions from Bank Balance:			*Deductions from Book Balance:*		
Outstanding Checks: 625	$326		Service Charge	$ 7	
631	426		Error in Recording Check (for Jones'		
634	185	(937)	wages) #630	180	(187)
Adjusted Bank Balance		$16,585	Adjusted Book Balance		$16,585

If adjusted book and bank balances do not agree the first time a reconciliation is attempted, the accountant will look for errors in bookkeeping, in back-up calculations, or in the bank's figures. When the balances finally agree, any necessary adjustments are made to the Cash account to bring it to the correct balance. The entries to correct the balance include debits to

Cash for all reconciling additions to the book balance and credits to Cash for all reconciling deductions from the book balance. Additions and deductions from the bank balance do not require adjustments to the company's books, since the deposits in transit and the outstanding checks have already been recorded by the company, and of course bank errors are corrected by notifying the bank. The adjustments required to correct Miller's Cash account would be

Cash	3,260	
Accounts Receivable		3,200
Interest Revenue		60
To record the additions due to the July bank reconciliation (a $3,200 deposit made by Joy Company and $60 interest).		
Miscellaneous Expenses	7	
Wages Expense	180	
Cash		187
To record the deductions due to the July bank reconciliation (service charge of $7 and a $180 error in recording check #630).		

TO SUMMARIZE Cash is a company's most liquid asset and is the first asset listed on its balance sheet. Companies must carefully monitor and control the way cash is handled and accounted for. Common controls include: (1) separation of duties in the handling of and accounting for cash, (2) daily deposits of all cash receipts, and (3) payment of all expenditures by prenumbered checks, except for the small miscellaneous ones paid from petty-cash funds. The petty-cash fund is usually maintained on an imprest basis.

Because most payments are made by check, companies need to reconcile monthly bank statements with the cash balance reported on the company's books. This reconciliation process involves determining reasons for the differences and bringing the book and bank balances into agreement. Adjusting entries are then made for additions to and deductions from the book balance.

Receivables

receivables *claims for money, goods, or services*

The term receivables refers to all claims for money, goods, or services by a company. Receivables are created through various kinds of transactions, the two most common being the sale of inventory on credit and the lending of money. A company may have several other kinds of receivables: from officers or employees of the company (a loan to an employee, for example), from interest, and from affiliated companies. In order to identify and maintain the distinctions between these receivables, businesses establish a separate General Ledger account for each classification. If the amount of a receivable is material, it is separately identified on the balance sheet. When receivables are to be converted to cash in a relatively short period of time, they are classified as current assets and listed on the balance sheet just below cash and short-term investments.

ACCOUNTS RECEIVABLE

account receivable *money due from rendering services or selling merchandise on credit*

Many sales involve credit, with the buyer typically having from 10 to 60 days to pay the seller for merchandise purchased. The receivable that arises from the sale of merchandise or services is called an account receivable (also often called a trade account receivable). Since we discussed accounts receivable in Chapter 6 in connection with the measurement and reporting of revenues, we now focus on other types of receivables.

NOTES RECEIVABLE

note receivable *a claim against a debtor, evidenced by an unconditional written promise to pay a certain sum of money on or before a specified future date*

A note receivable is an unconditional written promise to pay a sum of money on or before a specified future date. Depending on the length of time until the due date, the note may be classified as a current or a long-term asset. In addition, it may be either a trade note receivable (that is, one due from a customer who purchased merchandise) or a nontrade note receivable. Exhibit 9-4 shows a typical note receivable.

EXHIBIT 9-4 **Note Receivable**

July 15, 1983 (DATE) Provo, Utah (CITY) $ 2,000 xx/00

PAY TO THE ORDER OF Miller Company

Two thousand and xx/00 DOLLARS

VALUE RECEIVED AND DEBIT THE SAME TO THE ACCOUNT OF SHERWOOD COMPANY. INTEREST RATE IS 12 PERCENT PER ANNUM.

TO: FIRST SECURITY BANK
Provo, UT 84602

George Solomon

maker *a person (entity) who signs a note to borrow money and who assumes responsibility to pay the note at maturity*

payee *the person (entity) to whom payment on a note is to be made*

principal on a note *the face amount of a note; the amount (excluding interest) that the maker agrees to pay the payee*

maturity date *the date on which a note or other obligation becomes due*

interest rate *the cost of using money, expressed as an annual percentage*

interest *the amount charged for using money*

There are several key terms associated with a note receivable. The maker of a note is the person who signs the note and who must make payment on or before the due date. The payee is the person to whom payment will be made. The principal is the face amount of the note. The maturity date is the date the note becomes due. Notes can either be interest- or non-interest-bearing. For example, a bank note to borrow money for the purchase of an automobile or furniture is usually interest-bearing. The interest rate is the percentage of the principal that the payee annually charges the maker for the loan, and the interest is the dollar amount paid by the maker in accordance with this rate. Interest can also be thought of as the service charges, or rent, for the use of money. The formula for computing the interest on a note is shown on the next page.

principal × interest rate × time (in terms of a year) = interest

For example, if Miller Company accepted from Sherwood Company a 12 percent, 60-day, $2,000 note receivable, the interest would be calculated as follows:

$2,000 × 0.12 × 60/360 = $40

In calculating the time, we will use 360 days (rather than 365) to represent a business year.

If the $2,000 note were accepted in settlement of an account because Sherwood Company could not pay its account receivable with Miller Company on time, the journal entry to record the note in Miller's books would be

Notes Receivable–Sherwood Company	2,000	
Accounts Receivable–Sherwood Company		2,000
Accepted 60-day, 12% note from Sherwood Company in lieu of payment of its account receivable.		

When the collection is made on the maturity date of the note (60 days later), the entry to record the receipt of cash is

Cash	2,040	
Notes Receivable–Sherwood Company		2,000
Interest Revenue		40
Received payment from Sherwood Company for $2,000 note plus interest.		

maturity value *the amount of an obligation to be collected or paid at maturity date; equal to principal plus any interest*

Principal plus interest ($2,040 in this example) is known as the maturity value of the note. If the note is not paid by the maturity date, negotiations with the maker usually result in the company's extending the grace period for payment, issuing a new note, or retaining an attorney or collection agency to collect the money. If the note eventually proves to be worthless, it is written off as a loss of the current period.

Often, notes receivable are classified on the balance sheet as special receivables when an agency or attorney is attempting to make collection.

Non-Interest-Bearing Notes

Occasionally, a company will accept a non-interest-bearing note. The advantage of this type of note over an account receivable is that it is a written promise to pay. The accounting for a short-term non-interest-bearing note is similar to that for an interest-bearing one—except, of course, there is no stated interest. If the note is long-term—that is, for more than one year—generally accepted accounting principles require that the principal be reduced in amount, so that it will reflect the real interest that is probably already included in the face amount. The accounting profession argues that no rational person or business would accept a non-interest-bearing, long-term note that does not have some interest built into the principal amount.

The concept that underlies this position—the fact that money has a time value—is discussed in Chapter 11, as are the techniques needed to account for long-term non-interest-bearing notes.

Discounting Notes Receivable

discounting a note receivable *the process of the payee's selling notes to a financial institution for less than the maturity value*

Because notes receivable are promises to pay money in the future, they are negotiable. They can be sold, or discounted, to banks and other financial institutions. This means that a holder of a note who needs cash before a note matures can sell the note (simply by endorsing it) to a financial institution. The maker of the note, therefore, owes the money to the financial institution or other endorsee.

To financial institutions, the purchase of a note for cash is just like making a loan; that is, cash is given out now in return for repayment of principal with interest in the future. To a company selling a note, discounting is a way of receiving cash earlier than otherwise would be possible.

discount rate *the interest rate charged by a financial institution for buying a note receivable*

discount *the amount charged by a bank when a note receivable is discounted; calculated as maturity value times discount rate times discount period*

discount period *the time between the date a note is sold to a financial institution and its maturity date*

Several key terms are associated with the discounting of notes. The discount rate is the annual rate (percentage of maturity value) charged by the financial institution for buying the note; the discount is the actual amount the bank will earn (in terms of interest) on the transaction; and the discount period is the length of time for which the note is discounted. The formula for computing discount is

$$\text{maturity value} \times \text{discount rate} \times \text{discount period} = \text{discount}$$

To illustrate the discounting of a note, we refer to the 60-day, 12 percent note for $2,000 that Miller accepted from Sherwood Company. After holding the note for 15 days, Miller decides to discount it at 16 percent at First Security Bank. The discount would be $40.80, which is computed as follows:

$$\underset{\text{maturity value}}{\$2{,}040} \times \underset{\text{discount rate}}{0.16} \times \underset{\text{discount period}}{45/360} = \underset{\text{discount}}{\$40.80}$$

net proceeds *the difference between maturity value and discount when a note receivable is discounted*

Face of Note	$2,000.00
Interest the Note earns ($2,000 × 0.12 × 60/360)	40.00
Maturity Value	$2,040.00
Discount ($2,040 × 0.16 × 45/360)	(40.80)
Net Proceeds	$1,999.20

Since the note that Sherwood Company will now pay to the bank is worth $2,040 at maturity, Miller will receive $1,999.20 ($2,040.00 − $40.80), called net proceeds, from the bank for the note. The calculations for these net proceeds are summarized in the margin. The entry to record the discounting of the note would be

Cash	1,999.20	
Interest Expense	.80	
Notes Receivable—Sherwood Company		2,000.00

To record the discounting of the 60-day, 12%, $2,000 note from Sherwood Company at 16% for 45 days.

The net effect of this transaction of Miller Company is a cost of $0.80. Since the bank's 16 percent discount rate is higher than the note's 12 percent interest rate, Miller Company has no interest revenue on the note, even though the note was held for 15 days. If Miller had held the note for 45 days and then discounted it, the amount of discount would have been $13.60 ($2,040 × 0.16 × 15/360), leaving $26.40 interest revenue ($40.00 − $13.60).

The entry to record the transaction would have been

Cash	2,026.40	
Interest Revenue		26.40
Notes Receivable—Sherwood Company		2,000.00

To record the discounting of the 60-day, 12%, $2,000 note from Sherwood Company at 16% for 45 days.

In this case, Miller would have had $26.40 of interest revenue, which would have been earned by holding the Sherwood Company note for 45 days.

recourse *the right to seek payment on a discounted note from the payee if the maker defaults*

In most cases, notes are discounted with recourse. That is, if the maker of a note does not pay the bank on the maturity date, the firm discounting the note is responsible for payment. Thus, if Sherwood Company does not pay its note, Miller has to reimburse First Security Bank. The amount due is usually the maturity value of the note plus a handling fee charged by the bank. For example, if Sherwood defaults and Miller pays the bank the maturity value plus a $10 handling fee, the entry would be

Accounts Receivable	2,050	
Cash		2,050

To restore receivable from Sherwood Company, and to record reimbursement to First Security Bank for a discounted note defaulted on by Sherwood ($2,000 + $40 interest + $10 handling fee).

Because Miller expects to collect both the maturity value ($2,040) and the handling fee ($10) from Sherwood, it debits the entire amount to Accounts Receivable. In some cases, a "special receivable" is debited so the company can be reminded that this is a problem account.

OTHER RECEIVABLES

Besides accounts and notes receivable, a firm may have other kinds of receivables. The most common are receivables from employees, interest receivables, and receivables from affiliates (subsidiary or parent companies). The accounting for these receivables presents no new problems. If short-term, they are included with the accounts and notes receivable under current assets on the balance sheet. If long-term, they are usually included as other long-term assets on the balance sheet. Whatever their nature, these other receivables, if material, should be kept separate from accounts and notes receivable and should bear appropriate descriptive titles when shown on the balance sheet.

TO SUMMARIZE A company can have several types of receivables. Accounts receivable, which arise from credit sales, are the most common. Notes receivable, which are unconditional written promises to pay specific amounts in the future, may also be included. Notes receivable that result from sales or loans are negotiable, and so can be discounted with banks. Any other receivables that are material should be carefully labeled and separately accounted for.

Prepaid Expenses

prepaid expenses *payments made in advance for items normally charged to expense*

Prepaid expenses (sometimes called prepayments or prepaid assets) are payments made for goods and services in advance of their use. Because they represent a company's claim to the future use of goods or services, they are classified as assets until they are consumed or used. The most common prepaid expenses include insurance premiums, rent, and interest paid in advance. Office supplies purchased prior to their use are sometimes included in this category. Prepaid expenses are classified as current assets, since they usually will be consumed within the next year.

Although prepaid expenses were discussed in Chapter 4, a short review is presented here. Most prepaid expenses are recorded initially as assets and then expensed as they are used, but the accounting can be accomplished in either of two different ways. These methods, you will recall, are the asset and expense approaches.

To illustrate, we will assume that on April 1, Miller paid a $360 premium for a 1-year (April 1 to March 31) fire insurance policy. Since coverage includes a portion of the coming year, the $360 is a prepaid expense. Assuming an accounting year-end of December 31, this payment could be handled in either of the two ways shown in Exhibit 9-5.

EXHIBIT 9-5 **Two Ways of Accounting for Prepaid Expenses**

	Asset Approach	**Expense Approach**
	Assume that the $360 is originally classified as an asset.	*Assume that the $360 is originally classified as an expense.*
Entry when paid (April 1)	Prepaid Insurance ...... 360 Cash .... 360 *Purchased a 1-year insurance policy.*	Insurance Expense ...... 360 Cash .... 360 *Purchased a 1-year insurance policy.*
Entry to adjust the accounts on December 31 (year-end)	Insurance Expense ...... 270 Prepaid Insurance .... 270 *To adjust for proper insurance expense (9/12 × $360).*	Prepaid Insurance ...... 90 Insurance Expense ...... 90 *To adjust for proper prepaid insurance (3/12 × $360).*
Prepaid Insurance account after both entries	**Prepaid Insurance** (4/1) ...... 360 | 270 .... (12/31) **Bal.** 90	**Prepaid Insurance** **Bal.** 90
Insurance Expense account after both entries	**Insurance Expense** **Bal.** 270	**Insurance Expense** (4/1) ...... 360 | 90 ..... (12/31) **Bal.** 270

Under both methods, the amounts in Prepaid Insurance (a current asset) and Insurance Expense on December 31 are the same. Prepaid Insurance has an ending balance of $90, which represents that portion of the premium covering January, February, and March of the next year. Insurance Expense has a balance of $270, which represents the premiums for the first nine months.

The accounting procedures for supplies, prepaid rent, prepaid interest, and other prepaid expenses are essentially the same.

TO SUMMARIZE Prepaid expenses are payments made for goods and services in advance of their use. Because they represent a company's claims to the future use of goods or services, they are classified as assets until they are used. There are two ways to account for prepaid expenses: (1) the asset approach and (2) the expense approach. With each approach, the relevant asset and expense accounts have proper balances at year-end.

Current Liabilities

current liabilities *debts or other obligations that will be paid with current assets or otherwise discharged within one year or the normal operating cycle*

Current liabilities are obligations that can reasonably be expected to be paid or satisfied within one year or during the normal operating cycle. They can be obligations either to pay cash or to perform services. The most common cash obligations are accounts payable, short-term notes payable, and accrued liabilities (including payroll-related liabilities). The most common noncash obligations are those to deliver goods to customers (in return for advances received) or to perform a future service, such as the repair of an automobile or stereo under a warranty agreement.

Accounts Payable

account payable *money owed to creditors*

An account payable (sometimes called a trade payable) is an amount owed for a credit purchase. The accounting for accounts payable is fairly simple: Accounts Payable is increased, or credited, when inventory or other items are purchased on credit; and decreased, or debited, when cash is paid to vendors.

Notes Payable

note payable *a debt owed to a creditor, evidenced by an unconditional written promise to pay a sum of money on or before a specified future date and signed by the maker*

Notes payable differ from accounts payable in that they usually represent unconditional written promises to pay certain amounts of money on or before some future date. If a note is short-term, that is, if the business signs a note in order to borrow money from a bank or financial institution for less than a year, it is considered a current liability. If it has a term that extends beyond a year or the current operating cycle, it is classified as a long-term liability. As the maturity date of a long-term liability draws to within a year, the obligation is reclassified as short-term.

Notes payable are usually interest-bearing and interest is computed in the same way it is for notes receivable.

principal × interest rate × time (in terms of a year) = interest

For example, if Harvey Company borrows $2,000 from the First Security Bank for two months at 15 percent interest, the calculation would be

$2,000	×	0.15	×	60/360	=	$50.00
principal	×	interest rate	×	time (fraction of a year)	=	interest

The entries to record Harvey's borrowing of $2,000 and repayment of it two months later would be

Cash	2,000	
Notes Payable—First Security Bank		2,000
Borrowed $2,000 from First Security Bank at 15% for 60 days.		
Notes Payable—First Security Bank	2,000	
Interest Expense	50	
Cash		2,050
Repaid $2,000, 15% note to First Security Bank with interest.		

As we explained earlier, notes are negotiable and can be transferred to a third party by endorsement. Therefore, it is not uncommon to find that a note payable has been discounted or transferred by the original payee to a third party, usually a bank. (See pages 303 and 304 for a discussion of discounting notes.)

Accrued Liabilities

accrued liability *an obligation for benefits received but not yet paid for*

Accrued liabilities are obligations that have been incurred but not yet paid for. For example, taxes on property might be accrued during a period but not paid until the next period. At the end of the accounting period, adjusting entries must be made to recognize the amount of these liabilities. If they are not properly recorded, expenses and liabilities will be understated and net income will be overstated.

To illustrate the accounting for a typical accrued liability, we will assume that Miller Company pays its annual property taxes of $3,600 (for the period July 1, 1983, through June 30, 1984) on June 30, 1984. Although the company does not pay the property taxes until June 30, 1984, the estimated property tax expense and liability must be recorded at the end of each accounting period, beginning in July 1983. The entry would be as shown on the next page.

Property Tax Expense	1,800	
Accrued Property Taxes Payable		1,800
To record property tax expense and liability for 6 months.		

Because these types of liabilities usually accumulate on a day-to-day basis but are not recorded until the end of the period, the word "accrued" is often used in the liability account titles, thus distinguishing these liabilities from others that are created by economic transactions. The use of "accrued" is optional, however, and some companies prefer to omit it. Thus, the credit portion of Miller's allocation of $1,800 for property taxes could be labeled either Accrued Property Taxes Payable or just Property Taxes Payable. Similar labeling options exist for other accrued items.

Payroll Liabilities

The accounting for accrued rent, utilities, and interest is similar to that for property taxes. However, the accounting for salaries and related payroll taxes is somewhat more complex, primarily because every business is legally required to withhold certain taxes from employees' salaries.

social security (FICA) taxes *Federal Insurance Contributions Act taxes imposed on employee and employer; used mainly to provide retirement benefits*

Very few people receive their full salary as take-home pay. For example, an employee who earns $25,000 a year probably takes home between $16,000 and $20,000. The balance is withheld by the employer to pay the employee's federal and state income taxes, social security (FICA) taxes, and any voluntary or contractual withholdings that the employee has authorized (such as union dues, medical insurance premiums, and charitable contributions). Thus, the accounting entry to record the liability for an employee's monthly salary (computed as one-twelfth of $25,000) might be

Salary and Wages Expense	2,083.34	
FICA Taxes Payable—John Doe		125.00
State Withholding Taxes Payable		166.67
Federal Withholding Taxes Payable		375.00
Union Dues Payable		50.00
Salary and Wages Payable		1,366.67
To record John Doe's salary expense for July.		

All the credit amounts (which are arbitrary in this example) are liabilities that must be paid by the employer to the federal and state governments, the union, and the employee.

In addition to serving as agents for the government by paying employees' income and FICA taxes, companies must also pay certain payroll-related taxes, such as the employer's portion of the FICA tax (an amount equal to the employee's portion) and state and federal unemployment taxes. These taxes are included in the operating expenses of a business. An entry to record the payroll taxes relating to John Doe's employment would be

Payroll Tax Expense	195.65	
FICA Taxes Payable—Employer		125.00
Federal Unemployment Taxes Payable		14.41
State Unemployment Taxes Payable		56.24
To record employer payroll tax liabilities associated with John Doe for July.		

Again, the numbers in this entry are arbitrary and were chosen for illustrative purposes only. The eight different liabilities listed in the above two entries for payroll would be eliminated as payments are made. The entries to account for the payments would be

FICA Taxes Payable	250.00	
Federal Withholding Taxes Payable	375.00	
Cash		625.00
Paid July payroll withholdings on John Doe to the federal government.		
Federal Unemployment Taxes Payable	14.41	
Cash		14.41
Paid July unemployment taxes on John Doe to the federal government.		
State Withholding Taxes Payable	166.67	
Cash		166.67
Paid July payroll withholdings on John Doe to the state.		
State Unemployment Taxes Payable	56.24	
Cash		56.24
Paid July unemployment taxes on John Doe to the state.		
Union Dues Payable	50.00	
Cash		50.00
Paid July union dues for John Doe.		
Salary and Wages Payable	1,366.67	
Cash		1,366.67
Paid July salary to John Doe.		

If you are interested in learning more about payroll accounting, you should read the Supplement to this chapter.

Noncash Current Liabilities

unearned revenues (or advances from customers) *amounts received before they have been earned*

Noncash current liabilities are obligations to perform future services or to supply goods. The most common noncash performance obligations arise when customers pay in advance (the amounts are called advances from customers, or unearned revenues) and when warranties or guarantees are issued on a company's products. With advances from customers, the company has an obligation to ship a product or perform a service. With warranties, the company has to repair or replace defective parts of merchandise sold.

To illustrate advances, we assume that Jason Company pays Miller Company $300 for goods to be shipped in the future. Miller thus has a liability until the time of shipment. The entry to record this advance from Jason would be

Cash	300	
Advances from Customers		300
Received an advance payment from Jason Company.		

When the goods are shipped, revenue is earned and Miller's liability is eliminated. The entry to eliminate the liability would be

Advances from Customers	300	
Sales Revenue		300
To recognize revenue on the shipment of goods to Jason Company.		

The performance liability created when a firm offers a warranty or guarantee involves a similar recording process. For example, many major automobile manufacturers offer a 12,000-mile, 12-month warranty on new cars. Because warranties create obligations to perform repair services free of charge, they must be recognized as current liabilities at the time of sale. Obviously, the amount of a warranty liability can only be estimated since the actual repair expenditures will not be known until the services have been performed. Accounting principles require that a period's expenses be matched with its revenues, so it is better to make a timely but somewhat imprecise estimate than to record no expense at all. A typical warranty liability entry would be

Warranty Expense	15,000	
Provision for Warranties		15,000
Estimated warranty costs on 1983 sales.		

The credit entry, Provision for Warranties, is a current liability. When actual expenses are incurred in servicing the warranties, the liability is eliminated with the following type of entry.

Provision for Warranties	15,000	
Wages Payable (to service employees)		4,000
Supplies		11,000
Paid service costs of the warranties.		

This entry shows that supplies and labor were required to honor the warranty agreements. Note that if the entire Provision for Warranties is not used, a lower estimate is made in a subsequent period; if the Provision for Warranties is inadequate, a higher estimate is made.

Contingent Liabilities

contingent liability *a potential obligation, dependent upon the occurrence of future events*

In addition to actual obligations to pay cash or perform services, a company often has potential obligations to do so. These contingent liabilities are usually tied to the occurrence of some future event, and so are paid only when that event takes place (if it does). Examples of liabilities that qualify as contingent liabilities are notes receivable that have been discounted with recourse (for which the payee is obligated to pay if the maker of the note defaults), lawsuits (in which the company is obligated to pay if the lawsuit is lost), and cosigned notes (for which the company is obligated to pay if the signer does not). Potential obligations that qualify as contingent liabilities can be recorded as actual liabilities, ignored, or disclosed in the notes to the financial statements, depending on the materiality of these obligations and their probability of occurrence.

TO SUMMARIZE Current liabilities are obligations that can reasonably be expected to be paid or satisfied within one year or during the normal operating cycle. The most common types of current liabilities are (1) accounts payable, (2) notes payable, (3) accrued liabilities, including payroll-related liabilities, and (4) obligations to perform future services. Contingent liabilities are potential obligations that will be paid only if specific future events occur.

Analyzing Current Assets and Current Liabilities

current ratio (or working capital ratio) *a measure of the liquidity of a business; equal to current assets divided by current liabilities*

Current assets and current liabilities have been discussed separately. However, it is important to consider these accounts together because that is how management and investors usually examine them when assessing a firm's liquidity and planning its short-term operations. The relationship between these accounts is best analyzed in terms of working capital, which, as defined earlier, is the excess of total current assets over total current liabilities. The current ratio (or working capital ratio) is total current assets divided by total current liabilities. (Both of these concepts were introduced in Chapter 8 and will be covered in more detail in Chapter 16.) For example, if total current assets are $500,000 and total current liabilities are $200,000, working capital is $300,000 and the current ratio is $500,000/$200,000, or 2.5 to 1.

The concepts of working capital and current ratio are extremely important because they probably provide the best single barometer of a company's liquidity, as well as of the efficiency with which current assets are being managed. If a current ratio is too low, investors and creditors may fear that a company will have difficulty meeting its current obligations. If a current ratio is too high, they may be concerned that management is not taking sufficient advantage of current assets that could be reinvested in the business and earn a higher return. Because the current ratio is closely monitored, there is great pressure on businesses to maintain ratios close to the average for their particular industry (newspaper publishing, retail shoe stores, and so forth). These averages vary from industry to industry and are usually indicative of an efficient level of operations.

acid-test ratio (or quick ratio) *a measure of the liquidity of a business; equal to cash plus short-term investments and receivables divided by current liabilities*

Another ratio often used to measure a firm's liquidity is the acid-test ratio (or quick ratio). It is defined as cash, accounts receivable, and short-term investments divided by total current liabilities. Since the numerator excludes inventory and prepaid expenses, the ratio measures a firm's ability to meet its current obligations with cash and near-cash items. In industries with large inventories that turn over slowly, the acid-test ratio is probably a better barometer of liquidity than the working capital ratio.

CHAPTER REVIEW

Current assets and current liabilities are accounts that are of a short-term nature. Common current assets are cash, short-term investments, accounts receivable, notes receivable, inventories, and prepaid expenses. Current liabilities include accounts payable, notes payable, accrued liabilities, payroll taxes, and obligations to perform future services.

Cash is the most liquid of all assets. Therefore, stringent procedures for controlling cash must be established and maintained. Most cash is kept in bank accounts, which are reconciled each month. One exception is a petty-cash fund, which is usually maintained on an imprest basis to cover small, miscellaneous expenditures.

A note receivable is an unconditional written promise to pay a sum of money on or before a specified future date. Notes receivable are usually interest-bearing. The amount of interest to be earned annually is equal to the principal times the interest rate times the time period (in terms of a year) of the note. Notes can be discounted at a bank or other financial institution. Discounting allows the original payee of a note to receive money prior to the maturity date.

Prepaid expenses are payments made for goods or services in advance of their use. Common prepaid expenses are insurance, rent, and interest. Office supplies purchased prior to their use are sometimes included as prepaid expenses. Prepaid expenses must be adjusted at year-end so that the related asset and expense accounts will be properly stated.

Accounting for current liabilities is similar to accounting for current assets. Notes payable are the reverse of notes receivable. Accrued liabilities are usually recorded as adjusting entries at the end of an accounting period. Payroll accounting is complicated by federal and state requirements to withhold employee taxes and to pay both employee and employer taxes. Contingent liabilities are potential obligations tied to the occurrence of some future event. They can be included with other liabilities on the balance sheet, ignored, or disclosed in the footnotes to the financial statements, depending on their materiality and probability of occurrence.

Current assets and current liabilities are considered together by managers, investors, and creditors in financial planning and analysis. Working capital, which is total current assets less total current liabilities, and the related current and acid-test ratios are measures of the liquidity of a firm.

KEY TERMS AND CONCEPTS

account payable (306)
account receivable (301)
accrued liability (307)
acid-test ratio (or quick ratio) (312)
bank reconciliation (299)
Cash Over and Short (296)
contingent liability (311)
current assets (293)
current liabilities (306)
current ratio (or working capital ratio) (311)
discount (303)
discount period (303)
discount rate (303)
discounting a note receivable (303)
imprest petty-cash fund (295)
interest (301)
interest rate (301)
lapping (294)
liquidity (293)
maker (301)
maturity date (301)
maturity value (302)
net proceeds (303)
note payable (306)
note receivable (301)
NSF (Not Sufficient Funds) check (297)
payee (301)
petty-cash fund (295)
prepaid expenses (305)
principal (301)
receivables (300)
recourse (304)
social security (FICA) taxes (308)
unearned revenues (or advances from customers) (309)
working capital (292)

REVIEW PROBLEM

Current Assets and Current Liabilities

Merriweather Corporation has applied to Second National Bank for a loan. As part of the application, Merriweather provided the following balance sheet.

Merriweather Corporation
Balance Sheet as of December 31, 1983

Assets		
Current Assets:		
Cash	$16,000	
Accounts Receivable	40,000	
Notes Receivable	22,000	
Inventory	80,000	
Prepaid Insurance	6,000	
Total Current Assets		$164,000
All Other Assets		100,000
Total Assets		$264,000

Liabilities and Stockholders' Equity		
Current Liabilities:		
Accounts Payable	$18,000	
Short-Term Notes Payable	22,000	
Income Taxes Payable	25,000	
Total Current Liabilities		$ 65,000
Long-Term Liabilities:		
Mortgage Payable		169,000
Stockholders' Equity:		
Capital Stock	$10,000	
Retained Earnings	20,000	
Total Stockholders' Equity		30,000
Total Liabilities and Stockholders' Equity		$264,000

In reviewing this balance sheet, Second National Bank computed Merriweather's current and quick ratios and agreed that the 2.52 current ratio ($164,000/$65,000) and 1.20 acid-test ratio ($78,000/$65,000) meet the minimum established criteria of 2.5 and 1.15 for this industry. However, to be safe, Second National decided to commission an audit to see if the books were accurate. During the audit, the following information was discovered.

a. The Cash account includes $8,000 in a bank in Mozachare, an unfriendly nation that will not allow the money to be withdrawn.

b. Accounts receivable of $12,000 are 310 days old and should be written off as uncollectible. In addition, an allowance for doubtful accounts of 1½ percent of remaining receivables should be established.

c. The note receivable of $22,000 is for one year and has been outstanding for one month. Interest revenue at 10 percent has not been recognized.

d. Half the inventory is obsolete and should be valued at its scrap value of $600.

e. No interest expense has been accrued on either the short-term note or long-term mortgage. The short-term note is for one year at 12 percent and has been outstanding for four months. One full year's interest on the 10 percent mortgage should be recognized.

f. Accrued property tax expenses of $3,000 should have been recorded.

g. The prepaid insurance was purchased on April 2 and is a 1-year policy; $6,000 represents the total cost of the insurance.

Required:

Prepare a revised balance sheet that takes into consideration the above information.

Solution

The easiest and most thorough way to revise the balance sheet is (1) to set up a T-account for each balance sheet item, (2) to journalize and post the transactions discovered in the audit, and (3) to revise the balance sheet based on the adjusted account balances. Note that all revenues and expenses have been extended directly into Retained Earnings rather than using an income statement.

1. T-accounts

Cash

Beg. Bal. . . 16,000	8,000 . . . a
8,000	

Accounts Receivable

Beg. Bal. . . 40,000	12,000 . . . b
28,000	

Allowance for Doubtful Accounts

	420 . . . . . b

Notes Receivable

Beg. Bal. . . 22,000	

Interest Receivable

c 183	

Inventory

Beg. Bal. . . 80,000	39,400 . . . d
40,600	

Prepaid Insurance

Beg. Bal. . . . 6,000	4,500 . . . . g
1,500	

All Other Assets

Beg. Bal. . . 100,000	
a . . 8,000	
108,000	

Accounts Payable

	18,000 . . Beg. Bal.

Short-Term Notes Payable

	22,000 . . Beg. Bal.

Interest Payable

	17,780 . . . e

Property Taxes Payable

	3,000 . . . . f

Income Taxes Payable

	25,000 . . Beg. Bal.

Mortgage Payable

	169,000 . . Beg. Bal.

Capital Stock

	10,000 . . Beg. Bal.

Retained Earnings

b 12,420	20,000 . . Beg. Bal.
d 39,400	183 . . . c
e 17,780	
f 3,000	
g 4,500	
56,917	

2. Journal Entries (The explanations are omitted.)

a	All Other Assets	8,000	
	Cash		8,000

When cash is restricted and not readily accessible, it must be classified as a long-term investment.

b	Retained Earnings	12,420	
	Allowance for Doubtful Accounts		420
	Accounts Receivable		12,000

The $12,000 must be written off as a loss (to Retained Earnings), and the allowance is 0.015 × $28,000.

c	Interest Receivable	183	
	Retained Earnings		183

The credit entry would normally be to Interest Revenue, which would be closed to Retained Earnings. Since an income statement is not prepared, the credit must be to Retained Earnings. Interest is $22,000 × 0.10 × 1/12 = $183 (rounded to nearest dollar).

d	Retained Earnings	39,400	
	Inventory		39,400

The write-off is a loss, which must be closed to Retained Earnings. The amount is ($80,000 × 1/2) − $600.

e	Retained Earnings	17,780	
	Interest Payable		17,780

The amount of interest expense is ($22,000 × 0.12 × 4/12 = $880) + ($169,000 × 0.10 = $16,900) = $17,780.

f	Retained Earnings	3,000	
	Property Taxes Payable		3,000

Property Tax Expense would normally be debited; because an income statement has not been prepared, the debit is to retained earnings.

g	Retained Earnings	4,500	
	Prepaid Insurance		4,500

The amount of prepaid insurance written off is $6,000 × 9/12 = $4,500.

3. The Balance Sheet

Once the transactions are posted, the next step is to balance the accounts and prepare the revised balance sheet. (See the T-accounts for balances.)

Merriweather Corporation

Balance Sheet (Revised) as of December 31, 1983

Assets		
Current Assets:		
Cash		$ 8,000
Accounts Receivable	$28,000	
Less Allowance for Doubtful Accounts	420	27,580
Notes Receivable		22,000
Interest Receivable		183
Inventory		40,600
Prepaid Insurance		1,500
Total Current Assets		$ 99,863
All Other Assets		108,000
Total Assets		$207,863
Liabilities and Stockholders' Equity		
Current Liabilities:		
Accounts Payable	$18,000	
Short-Term Notes Payable	22,000	
Interest Payable	17,780	
Property Taxes Payable	3,000	
Income Taxes Payable	25,000	
Total Current Liabilities		$ 85,780
Long-Term Liabilities:		
Mortgage Payable		169,000
Stockholders' Equity:		
Capital Stock	$10,000	
Retained Earnings	(56,917)	
Total Stockholders' Equity		(46,917)
Total Liabilities and Stockholders' Equity		$207,863

The balance sheet now shows a deficit in stockholders' equity and current and acid-test ratios as follows:

$$\text{current ratio} = \frac{\$99,863}{\$85,780} = 1.16$$

$$\text{acid-test ratio} = \frac{\$57,763}{\$85,780} = 0.67$$

Second National Bank should probably not make the loan.

DISCUSSION QUESTIONS

1 Why do companies usually have more controls for cash than over other assets?

2 What are three generally practiced controls for cash, and what are their purposes?

3 What is an impreset petty-cash fund, and why is it important that petty cash be handled this way?

4 What are the major reasons that the balance of a bank statement is usually different from the Cash book balance (Cash per the General Ledger)?

5 Why don't the additions and deductions from the bank balance on a bank reconciliation require adjustment by the company?

6 What is the difference between a note receivable and an account receivable?

7 Why would a company accept a non-interest-bearing note?

8 What is the difference between an asset and an expense?

9 What information is conveyed by the "current" and "quick" ratios?

10 Why are obligations to perform services considered liabilities?

11 What types of financial statement disclosures are required for contingent liabilities?

EXERCISES

E9–1 The Definition of Cash

For each of the following separate cases, compute the amount that would be reported as cash on the balance sheet.

1. Balance in general checking account at Bank A, $20,000; IOU from company employee, $200; balance in savings account at Bank C, $2,000; balance in fund to be used to repay a bond debt, $7,000; balance in bank account in South Korea, $5,000 (restricted).

2. Cash on hand, $1,850; petty-cash fund, $250; overdraft in special checking account at Bank A, $100; NSF check for $500; postage stamps, $85; undeposited checks, $1,025.

3. Money orders, $800; short-term certificates of deposit, $5,000; money advanced to company president, $2,000; note receivable left with bank for collection, $2,500.

E9–2 Control for Cash

Jack Kane is an employee of Grow Big Company, a small manufacturing concern. His responsibilities include opening the daily mail, depositing the cash and checks received in the bank, and making the accounting entries to record the receipt of cash and the reduction of receivables.

Explain briefly how Mr. Kane might be able to misuse some of Grow Big's cash receipts. As a consulting accountant, what control procedures would you recommend?

E9–3 Accounting for Petty Cash

The following transactions relating to petty cash were completed by Williams Corporation, a firm with a December 31 year-end.

Dec.	19	Established a petty-cash fund of $250 with check #1135.
	20	Paid a Great Southern Railroad delivery bill of $96 for freight on merchandise purchased—used petty-cash voucher #1.
	21	A count of cash in the petty-cash fund revealed $150. Replenished the fund with check #1240.
	23	Decided to increase the fund permanently to $500 with check #1290.
	27	Purchased stamps, $24 (petty-cash voucher #2); paid newspaper carrier, $8 (petty-cash voucher #3); purchased office supplies, $215 (petty-cash voucher #4).
	31	Replenished the fund with check #1335 for $247.

Where appropriate, prepare General Journal entries to account for these transactions.

E9–4 Accounting for Petty Cash

Patty McClintock is interested in setting up a petty-cash fund to handle the small cash transactions of her new company. She has heard that you have experience in accounting matters and asks you to handle the accounting for the fund. Prepare appropriate journal entries for the following January 1983 transactions.

Jan. 1 Transferred $250 from the checking account to a petty-cash fund.
10 Purchased $10 of postage stamps.
12 Purchased $25 of office supplies.
18 Patty was short of cash and borrowed $50 from the fund for personal use.
19 Replenished the petty-cash fund by depositing a check for $90. (The $90 includes a personal loan to McClintock and an amount sufficient to make up any discovered shortage.)
31 Permanently reduced the fund to $150.

E9–5 Bank Reconciliation Computations

Dudley Corporation has the following financial information (assume that all receipts and payments are by check).

March 31, 1983, Bank Reconciliation

Balance per Bank	$12,000
Add Deposits in Transit	2,550
	$14,550
Deduct Outstanding Checks	3,250
Balance per Books	$11,300

April Results	Per Bank	Per Books
Balance, April 30	$14,220	$17,230
April deposits	8,600	12,500
April checks	12,450	11,650
April note collected by bank	1,000	—
April bank charges	10	—

From the information provided, compute the amount of:
1. Deposits in transit on April 30, 1983.
2. Outstanding checks on April 30, 1983.

E9–6 Preparing a Bank Reconciliation

The July 1983 bank statement for Jonathan Corporation shows an ending cash balance of $8,642. The cash balance in Jonathan's books is $7,526 at the end of July. Based on the following items, prepare a bank reconciliation for Jonathan for the month of July.
1. A deposit of July 31 was not recorded on the bank statement—$52.
2. Checks outstanding as of July 31—$658.
3. A non-interest-bearing note was collected by the bank and not yet recorded in the books—$1,000.
4. A check written for $750 was improperly recorded as $75 in the books.
5. Bank service charges not recorded in the books—$15.
6. Direct deposit by Jason Caloma, a customer—$200.

E9–7 Preparing a Bank Reconciliation

From the following information for Cey Manufacturing Company, prepare a bank reconciliation and any journal entries needed to adjust the Cash account as of August 31, 1983.
1. August 1, 1983, cash balance per books—$5,246.
2. Net increase in cash balance per books for the month of August—$3,039.
3. Balance per bank statement as of August 31, 1983—$7,887.
4. Deposits in transit as of the end of August—$2,649.
5. Checks outstanding as of August 31, 1983—$2,355.
6. The bank improperly recorded a $650 deposit by Cey as $560.
7. A check of $45 payable to the Energy Express Company for delivery charges was mistakenly recorded in the books at $54.
8. Bank service charges—$23.

E9–8 Preparing a Bank Reconciliation

Using the following information, prepare a bank reconciliation for Roberto Company at September 30, 1983, and make any necessary adjusting journal entries.
1. At September 30, cash per books was $27,798; per bank statement, $16,427.
2. Deposits in transit totaled $12,122.
3. Service charges for the month were $38.
4. Checks outstanding: #284 for $548, #291 for $607, and #293 for $496.
5. NSF check—Jesse James, $378.
6. Among the checks returned by the bank was a check paid in error by the bank for $484 after Roberto Company had issued a stop payment and had voided the check in the cash disbursements journal.

E9–9 Reconciling Book and Bank Balances

McMan Company has just received the September 30, 1983, bank statement summarized in the following schedule.

	Charges	Deposits	Balance
Balance, September 1			$ 5,100
Deposits recorded during September		$27,000	32,100
Checks cleared during September	$27,300		4,800
NSF check—J. J. Jones	50		4,750
Bank service charges	10		4,760
Balance, September 30			4,760

Cash on hand (booked but not deposited) on September 1 and September 30 amounted to $200. There were no deposits in transit or checks outstanding at September 1, 1983. The Cash account for September reflected the following.

Cash			
Sept. 1 balance	5,300	28,000	Sept. checks
Sept. deposits	29,500		

Answer the following questions. (Hint: It may be helpful to prepare a complete bank reconciliation.)

1. What is the ending balance per the Cash account before adjustments?
2. What adjustments should be added to the depositor's books?
3. What is the total amount of the deductions from the depositor's books?
4. What is the total amount to be added to the bank's balance?
5. What is the total amount to be deducted from the bank's balance?

E9–10 Preparing a Bank Reconciliation

On the basis of the following information, prepare a bank reconciliation for Wilson Company.

1. The June 30, 1983, bank statement showed the following.

Balance, June 1	$21,000.00
Canceled Checks	13,904.20
Deposits	16,500.40
Balance, June 30	23,596.20

2. The Cash account showed the following for the month of June.

Balance, June 1	$21,000.00
Debits	22,700.40
Credits	22,886.34
Ending Balance, June 30	20,814.06

3. A service charge on the bank statement was $18.00.
4. Outstanding checks totaled $9,100.14.
5. Deposits in transit totaled $8,000.00.
6. The bank statement reveals that the company's account has been reduced by $100.00. The company had deposited a $100 check from one of its customers, which was subsequently returned to the company's bank and marked "Not Sufficient Funds."
7. The bank collected an $1,800 note for the company. The company was not aware of this collection until now.

E9–11 Journal Entries for a Note Receivable

As the accountant for Music Man Company, which uses the periodic inventory method, prepare General Journal entries for the following events.

Apr. 1	Professor Harold Hill purchased band uniforms costing $8,000 for a small-town band in Indiana on credit terms of 2/10, n/30.
May 1	A letter from Professor Hill included an explanation of his inability to pay immediately and a note promising payment in three months with interest at 12 percent compounded annually.
June 30	A check from Professor Hill was received, which included the total amount of principal and accrued interest.
July 5	The check from Professor Hill was returned by the bank because of insufficient funds.
Dec. 31	Professor Hill seems to have disappeared from the area. The debt was determined to be uncollectible. (Ignore interest from June 30 and assume that the allowance method of accounting for bad debts is being used.)

E9–12 Discounting a Note Receivable

Assume the same facts as in E9–11, except that on May 31 Music Man Company discounted the note at a local bank at a 15 percent discount rate (with recourse).

1. As the accountant for the company, prepare an appropriate journal entry to record the discounting of the note.
2. Prepare the appropriate entry assuming that at maturity (July 31) Hill defaulted on the note. The bank charges a penalty fee of 0.25 percent of maturity value for all defaulted notes discounted with recourse.

E9–13 Discounting a Note Receivable

You are the accountant for Lowe Finance Company. The following transactions and events occurred in June 1983 and 1984.

1983: June 1	Lowe made a $15,000 loan to Henry Leggs, who signed a note promising to pay the loan plus interest at 18 percent in one year.
June 16	Due to excessive loans made in the month of June, Lowe Finance discounted Mr. Leggs' note at a local bank at 20 percent (with recourse).
1984: June 1	The local bank notified Lowe of the default by Mr. Leggs and demanded immediate payment of the principal, accrued interest, and a $50 penalty fee.
July 1	Lowe collected the entire receivable from Mr. Leggs plus 18 percent interest on the amount paid to the bank on June 1, 1984.

1. Prepare journal entries for the above, assuming a 360-day year.

2. Should any disclosure of the discounted liability on the note have been made on Lowe Finance Company's financial statements for December 31, 1983? If so, what type of disclosure?

E9–14 Accounting for Prepaid Expenses

During 1983 Jagger Corporation had the following transactions.

Apr. 1	Purchased a 2-year fire insurance policy for $600; policy effective immediately.
June 30	Purchased on account (on credit) office supplies costing $150.
July 10	Paid the $150 due for the June 30 purchase of supplies.
Sept. 30	Paid the $15,000 annual rent for the warehouse and plant facilities. (The rental payment covers the period of October 1, 1983, to October 1, 1984.)

Assuming that Jagger Corporation's fiscal year ends March 31, prepare:

1. Journal entries for all the transactions.
2. The adjusting entries as of March 31, 1984.

Assume that Jagger Corporation originally classifies all prepaid expenses as assets. On March 31, 1984, there were $45 worth of office supplies on hand.

E9–15 Accounting for Prepaid Expenses

With the information and transactions described in E9–14, prepare original journal entries and adjusting entries for Jagger Corporation based upon the assumption that Jagger Corporation originally records all prepayments as expenses.

E9–16 Accounting for Prepaid Expenses

1. On December 31, 1984, the following information is available for Johanson Company.

Office supplies on hand, January 1, 1984	$ 15,000
1984 cash purchases of office supplies	50,000
1984 credit purchases of office supplies	150,000
Office supplies on hand, December 31, 1984	25,000

(a) What is the total office supplies expense for 1984?
(b) Give the adjusting entry on December 31, 1984, assuming that Office Supplies Expense was debited for all purchases.
(c) Give the adjusting entry on December 31, 1984, assuming that Office Supplies on Hand was debited for all purchases.

2. On September 1, 1983, a 2-year insurance premium of $1,080 was paid. At the time of payment, Prepaid Insurance was debited for the full amount. Give the December 31, 1984, adjusting entry.

E9–17 Accounts and Notes Payable

Jimbo Bubble Gum Company purchases raw materials on credit with terms of 2/10, n/30. Occasionally, a short-term note payable is executed to obtain cash for current operations. The following two transactions were selected from the many 1983 transactions for your analysis.

August 10, 1983	Purchased materials on credit, $7,000; terms, 2/10, n/30. (Assume that the company uses the periodic inventory method.)
August 31, 1983	Borrowed $15,000 cash from a local bank in return for a 6-month note with 14 percent annual interest payable at maturity.

1. Prepare the original journal entry for each of the foregoing transactions.
2. Prepare an entry to record the payment of the August 10 account payable within the discount period.
3. Prepare the same entry as in (2) but assume that the payment was not made within the discount period.
4. Prepare the entry to record the accrued interest on the $15,000 note as of December 31, 1983.
5. Prepare the entry to record the payment of the note in (4) plus interest at maturity.

E9–18 Accounting for Notes Payable

Black Corporation borrowed $4,000 on a 9 percent, 1-year note dated October 1, 1983. Its annual accounting period ends on December 31. Give entries on the following dates (assuming that all interest is paid on September 30, 1984): October 1, 1983, December 31, 1983, and September 30, 1984.

E9–19 Accrued Liabilities (Including Simple Payroll Entries)

Assume that December 31, 1983, is a Thursday. As the accountant for Mason Industries, you are to make all necessary adjusting journal entries on that date. The following information (assume a calendar year) is available.

1. Mason Industries pays salaries weekly, with the payroll for the five-day workweek distributed on the following Monday. The payroll is fairly consistent from week to week and usually includes the following items (ignore unemployment taxes).

Salaries Expense	$80,000
Income Taxes Withheld from Employees	16,000
FICA Taxes Withheld from Employees	4,800
Union Dues Withheld from Employees	300
Cash Distributed	58,900

2. On November 1, 1983, rent revenue of $5,000 was collected in advance. The payment was for the period November 1, 1983, to October 31, 1984, on an apartment held as an investment. The original entry included a credit to Unearned Rent Revenue for the full amount of the cash received.

3. Assume the same facts as in (2), except that the credit in the original entry was to Rent Revenue instead of Unearned Rent Revenue.

E9–20 Accounting for Warranties

Jim E. Carter, president of Reliable Television Stores, has been concerned recently with declining sales due to increased competition in the area. Jim has noticed that many of the national stores selling television sets and appliances have been placing heavy emphasis in their marketing programs on warranties. In an effort to revitalize his sales, Jim has decided to offer free service and repairs for one year as a warranty on his television sets. Based on past experience, Jim believes that first-year service and repair costs on the television sets will be approximately 5 percent of sales. The first month of operations following the initiation of Jim's new marketing plan showed significant increases in sales of TV sets. Total sales of TV sets for the first three months under the warranty plan were $10,000, $8,000, and $12,000, respectively.

1. Assuming that Jim prepares adjusting entries and financial statements for his own use at the end of each month, prepare the appropriate entry to recognize warranty expense for each of these first three months.

2. Prepare the appropriate entry to record services provided to repair sets under warranty in the second month, assuming that the following costs were incurred: labor (paid in cash), $550; supplies, $330.

E9–21 Current and Acid-Test Ratios

As a financial analyst, you are interested in the liquidity position of Orton Tool Company. The following balance sheet shows the financial position of Orton Tool Company as of December 31, 1983.

Orton Tool Company
Balance Sheet as of December 31, 1983

Assets			
Current Assets:			
Cash		$ 30,900	
Accounts Receivable		1,800	
Inventory		55,100	
Prepaid Insurance		2,000	
Total Current Assets			$ 89,800
Property, Plant, and Equipment:			
Land		$150,000	
Plant and Equipment	$559,700		
Less Accumulated Depreciation	100,000	459,700	
Total Property, Plant, and Equipment			609,700
Other Assets:			
Land Held as Investment			25,000
Total Assets			$724,500
Liabilities and Stockholders' Equity			
Current Liabilities:			
Accounts Payable		$ 34,000	
Property Taxes Payable		4,500	
Accrued Wages Payable		6,000	
Total Current Liabilities			$ 44,500
Long-Term Liabilities:			
Notes Payable			200,000
Total Liabilities			$244,500
Stockholders' Equity:			
Capital Stock, par $10 (40,000 shares)		$400,000	
Paid-in Capital in Excess of Par		50,000	
Retained Earnings		30,000	480,000
Total Liabilities and Stockholders' Equity			$724,500

1. Based on the information provided in this balance sheet, compute (a) working capital, (b) the current ratio, and (c) the acid-test ratio.

2. Assuming that the average current ratio in Orton's industry is approximately 1.5, evaluate the company's current position.

PROBLEMS

P9-1 The Definition of Cash

Required:

1. Determine which of the following items should be included in the cash balance of a company.
   (a) A check returned by a bank (NSF).
   (b) Postage stamps.
   (c) IOUs signed by employees.
   (d) Money orders on hand (made payable to the company).
   (e) Petty cash on hand.
   (f) A deposit made with a utility company.
   (g) A deposit in a foreign bank (unrestricted).
   (h) Postdated checks.
   (i) Money advanced to officers.
   (j) A note receivable left with a bank for collection.
   (k) The bank account balance at City Bank.
   (l) Cashier's checks payable to the company.
2. State how each of the noncash items would be accounted for.

P9-2 Accounting for Petty Cash

Harmon Company uses an imprest petty-cash fund to pay for small, miscellaneous expenditures.

Required:

1. Prepare the necessary journal entries to record the following events.
   (a) Establishment of a petty-cash fund of $1,000 on January 1, 1983.
   (b) On January 12, a disbursement of $65 is made to Coca-Cola to pay for office drinks.
   (c) On January 15, $30 is taken from the fund to pay for postage stamps.
   (d) On January 18, because the company is short of cash, $600 of the fund is used to meet payroll expenses.
   (e) On January 25, with the company cash position restored, the petty-cash fund is replenished.
   (f) On January 26, it is decided that only $500 is needed in the fund, and it is reduced accordingly.
2. **Interpretive Question** Explain why a petty-cash fund should be handled on an imprest basis.
3. **Interpretive Question** Explain why one person is usually given complete responsibility for handling a petty-cash fund. Doesn't that make it easy for that person to steal from the fund?

P9-3 Preparing a Bank Reconciliation

Ellett Company has just received the following monthly bank statement for June.

Date	Debits	Credits	Balance
June 1			$25,000
2	$ 150		24,850
3		$ 6,000	30,850
4	750		30,100
5	1,500		28,600
7	8,050		20,550
9		8,000	28,550
10	3,660		24,890
11	2,690		22,200
12		9,000	31,200
13	550		30,650
17	7,500		23,150
20		5,500	28,650
21	650		28,000
22	700		27,300
23		4,140†	31,440
25	1,000		30,440
31	50*		30,390
Total	$27,250	$32,640	

* Bank service charge.
† Note collected, including $140 interest.

Data from the Cash account of Ellett Company for June are as follows:

June 1 balance	$20,440
Deposits:	
June 2	$ 6,000
5	8,000
10	9,000
18	5,500
30	6,000
	$34,500
Checks written:	
June 1	$ 1,500
4	8,500
6	2,690
8	550
9	7,500
12	650
19	700
22	1,000
26	1,300
27	1,360
	$25,750

At the end of May, Ellett had three checks outstanding for a total of $4,560. All three checks were processed by the bank during June. There were no deposits outstanding at the end of May. It was discovered during the reconciliation process that a check for $8,050 written on June 4 for supplies was improperly recorded on the books at $8,500.

Required:

1. Determine the amount of deposits in transit at the end of June.
2. Determine the amount of outstanding checks at the end of June.
3. Prepare a June bank reconciliation.
4. Prepare the journal entries to correct the Cash account.
5. **Interpretive Question** Why is it important that the Cash account be reconciled on a timely basis?

P9–4 Preparing a Bank Reconciliation

The records of Perry Corporation show the following information for December.

Bank Statement Information

a. Bank balance, December 31	$43,700
b. Service charges for December	25
c. Rent collected by bank	500
d. Note receivable collected by bank (including $150 interest)	1,150
e. December check returned marked NSF (check was a payment of an account receivable)	100
f. Bank erroneously reduced Perry's account for a check written by Pert Company	500
g. Cash account balance, December 31	40,600
h. Outstanding checks	4,600
i. Deposits in transit	2,500

Required:

1. Prepare a bank reconciliation for December. Other than the error identified in (f) above, the bank statement has been verified to be correct.
2. Prepare the entry to correct the Cash account as of December 31.
3. **Interpretive Question** Why is it important for you to know that the bank statement was verified as correct?

P9–5 Discounting a Note Receivable

On May 1, 1983, Hanks Company sold $5,000 of merchandise to Jim Radebaugh on credit terms of 2/10, n/30. On June 1, 1983, Radebaugh was unable to pay the $5,000. Instead, Hanks Company agreed to accept a 90-day note for $5,000 at 15 percent. On July 15, Hanks needed cash and decided to discount the note at 20 percent at a local bank. Upon maturity of the note, Radebaugh defaulted and the bank subsequently collected from Hanks the amount due plus a $10 handling fee. A month later, Hanks decided that the debt was uncollectible and wrote it off.

Required:

1. Prepare journal entries to record in Hanks Company's books the following.
   (a) Sale of the merchandise (assume the periodic inventory method).
   (b) Acceptance of the note.
   (c) Discounting of the note.
   (d) Payment to the bank upon default.
   (e) Write-off of the Jim Radebaugh account (assume that Hanks uses the allowance method of recording bad debts).
2. How would you account for the transaction if Jim Radebaugh six months later paid $5,197.50?
3. How would Hanks Company account for the note during the period July 15 to the maturity date?

P9–6 Discounting a Note Receivable

Required:

1. Record the following transactions in General Journal form in the books of Lyman Drilling Company. Assume that Lyman Drilling closes its books monthly.

March 1	Sold 100 barrels of oil to Shellaco Oil for $2,000, terms 2/10, n/30 (periodic inventory method).
March 12	Accepted a $2,000, 90-day, 10 percent note from Shellaco Oil in payment of its account.
April 11	Discounted the note with recourse at the bank at a 14 percent discount rate.
June 10	On the maturity date of the note, Shellaco Oil paid the amount due.
June 15	Notified by the bank that Shellaco Oil defaulted; the check was returned marked NSF. (Give the necessary entries in Lyman's books to record its payment of the note to the bank.)
June 30	Write off the Shellaco note as uncollectible.

2. **Interpretive Question** Why did Lyman have to pay off Shellaco's note?
3. How would the note receivable have been accounted for on Lyman's April 30 financial statements?
4. How would Lyman account for the note if on July 7, Shellaco paid the amount in full?

P9–7 Accounting for Payables and Prepaid Expenses

Required:

1. Prepare journal entries to record the following events in the books of Loa Drug Store.
   (a) On January 17, 1984, Loa purchased $500 of drugs for resale. The terms of payment were 2/10, n/30. The perpetual inventory method is used.
   (b) On March 1, 1984, Loa paid the semiannual interest on a $1,000, 9 percent, 2-year note. The note had been outstanding since September 1, 1983, and an adjusting entry for the 1983 interest expense had been made on December 31, 1983.
   (c) On March 16, 1984, Loa paid the full $500 due on the January drug purchase.

(d) On April 1, 1984, Loa paid $2,000 of insurance premiums, effective immediately, to cover its delivery truck for a full year. (Any prepayments are generally recorded as assets by Loa.)
(e) On September 1, 1984, Loa paid semiannual interest on the 9 percent $1,000 note.
(f) On December 31, 1984, properly record:
(1) Accrual of interest expense on the note payable.
(2) Accrual of salary expense, assuming that salaried employees are paid every Monday for the previous week's work. This year, December 31 is a Wednesday. The weekly payroll totals $5,000. (Assume that $400 and $300 are withheld for federal and state income taxes, respectively, that no other withholdings are made, and that employees work a 5-day workweek starting Monday.)
(3) The appropriate insurance expense on the delivery truck.
(4) Accrual of annual property taxes of $4,000 for the period ending June 30, 1985. (Assume that no other accrual entries have been made for property taxes during 1984.)

2. The insurance paid for in item (d) could have been recorded in one other way. Show this other possible entry.

P9–8 Analyzing Prepaid Expenses

Halstrom Company had the following cash expenditures during 1984:

a. Insurance Coverage	$ 2,900
b. Rent	8,200
c. Advertising	12,750
d. Property Taxes	3,980
e. Supplies	11,115

Halstrom's accountant has determined that the correct balances for the related prepaid expenses on December 31, 1983, and December 31, 1984, are as follows:

	1983	1984
Prepaid Insurance	$ 2,500	$2,200
Prepaid Rent	950	1,000
Prepaid Advertising	10,000	-0-
Prepaid Property Taxes	1,450	1,250
Supplies on Hand	1,100	1,375

Required:

1. Prepare the adjusting entries that would be needed on December 31, 1984, if Halstrom uses the asset approach in accounting for its prepaid assets.
2. Prepare the adjusting entries that would be needed on December 31, 1984, if Halstrom uses the expense approach in accounting for its prepaid assets.

P9–9 Unifying Problem: Payables, Prepaid Expenses, and Their Effect on Net Income, Total Liabilities, and Total Assets

Dodge Bookkeeping Agency is making adjusting entries on December 31.

Required:

1. Prepare the necessary December 31 adjusting entries in General Journal form to account for the following transactions.
(a) Weekly salaries total $1,500 for a 5-day workweek and are payable on Fridays. December 31 of the current year is a Thursday. (Ignore payroll taxes.)
(b) The firm paid $3,600 for a 2-year insurance policy on September 1 of the current year, effective the same date. The entire amount of the premium was debited to Prepaid Insurance and no subsequent adjustments have been made.
(c) During December, Dodge provided $2,000 worth of bookkeeping services to clients whom it will bill on January 2.
(d) The prior year's property tax expense was $2,000. The tax assessment for the current year (January 1 through December 31) has not yet been received, and no amount had been recorded for this year's expense. It is estimated that the assessment will be 30 percent higher this year.
(e) In December, Dodge received $500 to complete a tax return for Art Jacobs. At the time the money was received, Cash was debited and Service Fees Revenue was credited. The tax work will be performed in January.
(f) The Supplies on Hand account has a balance of $960 on December 31. However, $200 of supplies purchased on December 21 were debited to Supplies Expense, which now has a balance of $200 for the year. A count of supplies on December 31 indicates that $970 of supplies are still on hand.
(g) On September 1, Dodge borrowed $3,000 from the City National Bank at 12 percent for one year. Record the accrued interest as of December 31.
(h) Dodge's lease calls for rent at $200 per month to be paid in advance on the first of each month. The next payment is due on January 1 of the following year.
(i) The agency estimates that its utility expense for December will be $90.
2. If, before considering these adjustments, Dodge had a reported net income of $60,000, what would the agency's correct income be for the year?
3. How much would Dodge's liabilities have been understated if the foregoing adjusting entries had not been made?
4. **Interpretive Question** How do you explain the fact that the understatement of liabilities is greater than the resulting decrease in net income?

P9–10 Unifying Problem: Current Assets and Current Liabilities

Torrey Corporation is applying to the First National Bank for a loan. As part of the application, Torrey provided the following balance sheet.

Torrey Corporation
Balance Sheets as of December 31, 1983

Assets		
Current Assets:		
Cash	$ 6,000	
Accounts Receivable	14,000	
Inventory	45,000	
Prepaid Insurance	9,000	
Total Current Assets		$ 74,000
All Other Assets		193,000
Total Assets		$267,000
Liabilities and Stockholders' Equity		
Current Liabilities:		
Accounts Payable	$13,000	
Short-Term Note Payable	8,000	
Income Taxes Payable	6,000	
Total Current Liabilities		$ 27,000
Long-Term Bonds Payable		100,000
Stockholders' Equity		140,000
Total Liabilities and Stockholders' Equity		$267,000

In reviewing the balance sheet and computing Torrey's current ratio, the First National Bank has agreed that it meets the bank's minimum established criterion of 2 to 1 for making loans. However, to be safe, the bank decides to audit Torrey's books to see if they are accurate. During the audit, the following information is discovered.

a. The Cash account includes $3,000 that was restricted for the purpose of retiring the bonds in six years.

b. $5,000 of the accounts receivable are over 200 days old and should be written off as uncollectible. Torrey also does not maintain an allowance for doubtful accounts. The auditor believes that 2 percent of the remaining receivables is a good estimate of the amount that will be uncollectible.

c. The inventory contains $22,000 of damaged or obsolete inventory that has no value.

d. No interest has been accrued on either the short-term note or the bonds payable. The short-term note is an 8 percent note that has been outstanding for six months, and three months' interest has accrued on the 10 percent bonds.

e. Accrued wages totaling $2,000 should have been recorded. (Ignore payroll taxes.)

f. Accrued property taxes totaling $2,500 should have been recorded.

g. The prepaid insurance was purchased on May 1 and is a 2-year policy on the office building. The $9,000 represents the total cost of the policy.

Required:

1. Make the necessary General Journal entries to account for the new information discovered by the auditor.

2. Prepare a new balance sheet (in the same format) for Torrey Corporation. (Hint: It may be helpful to use T-accounts.)

3. Compute Torey's old and new current ratios.

4. **Interpretive Question** State why you would or would not make the loan to Torrey.

SUPPLEMENT

Payroll Accounting

Salaries and the related payroll taxes are major expenses in most businesses. Many large corporations have tens of thousands of employees and labor costs are their largest single operating expense. Accounting for salaries and the related payroll taxes creates several types of current liabilities.

Payroll Taxes

Payroll accounting is constantly changing because, almost every year, state and federal governments pass new tax legislation. Although some payroll-related taxes are paid by employers and some by employees, the employer is responsible for reporting and remitting all payroll taxes to the government. Employers withhold taxes from employees' salaries and periodically make deposits of these withholdings to the government. Companies that fail to report and remit taxes are subject to severe fines and penalties, so it is important to have accurate and timely systems of accounting for payroll. We will first examine the various kinds of taxes and other withholdings that affect payroll accounting, then we will study the accounting for these transactions.

FICA (SOCIAL SECURITY) TAXES

The Federal Insurance Contributions Act (FICA), which became effective in 1937, established a national social security program through which older people would be provided with a continuing source of income during their retirement years. This act demanded only small taxes from employees (1 percent of the first $3,000 of wages), and payments to retired persons were correspondingly small. Subsequent acts have increased the payments and the taxes. For example, the 1965 Medicare law raised taxes in order to provide medical care to individuals 65 and over. The 1977 law again increased social security taxes for the following ten years, making it the single largest peacetime tax increase in the history of the United States. In addition to providing benefits to retirees, social security has added disabled persons and dependents of deceased workers to its rolls.

The current FICA tax rate schedule (established in December 1977), together with a sample of the schedules used in previous years, is shown in Exhibit 9–6. FICA taxes have increased dramatically in recent years. Approximately 31 percent of all federal receipts now come from FICA taxes.

EXHIBIT 9–6 Sample FICA Tax Rates and Amounts*

Year	Tax Rate	Salary Ceiling	Maximum Tax Withheld
1937	1.00%	$ 3,000	$ 30
1951	1.50	3,600	54
1959	2.50	4,800	120
1966	4.20	6,600	277
1972	5.20	9,000	468
1975	5.85	14,100	825
1977	5.85	16,500	965
1978	6.05	17,700	1,071
1980	6.13	25,900	1,588
1981	6.65	29,700	1,975
1982	6.70	32,400	2,171
1983	6.70	33,900	2,271
1984	6.70	36,000	2,412
1985	7.05	38,100	2,686
1986	7.15	40,200	2,874
1987	7.15	42,600	3,046

* FICA rates are subject to frequent change. In fact, the ceiling for 1983 may be raised to $35,000.

In computing FICA taxes, an employer multiplies the current rate by the salary earned, up to the current yearly ceiling. FICA taxes are not withheld and paid on any amount earned in excess of this ceiling. The product of the tax rate times the salary (up to the ceiling) is the amount of taxes to be paid by the employee and matched by the employer. For example, an employee who earned $35,000 in 1983 paid FICA taxes of $2,271 (0.067 × $33,900) and the employer paid an equal amount. Had the employee made only $20,000, the FICA tax payments would have been $1,340 (0.067 × $20,000) for both the employee and employer. In paying the FICA taxes, employers deduct the employees' portion of the tax from their paychecks and remit it, together with the company's share, to the federal government. Self-employed persons also pay FICA taxes, but at rates approximately $1\frac{1}{2}$ times as high as those of employed persons.

FEDERAL AND STATE INCOME TAXES

The amount of state and federal income tax withheld from each employee's paycheck depends on three factors: income level, marital status, and number of dependents. In general, the higher the income, the higher the percentage of salary that is withheld. Obviously, the lower the income level and the more dependents an employee has, the lower the tax. Presently, federal income tax rates range from 11 to 50 percent of a person's income.

States have no standard rates; in fact, a few states have no individual income tax. When a person starts a new job, he or she is required to fill out a W-4 form (Employee's Withholding Allowance Certificate). Along with income level, the information provided on this form—the number of exemptions (dependents), other withholding allowances, and marital status—determines the amount of income tax to be withheld from an employee's paycheck.

OTHER WITHHOLDINGS

In addition to withholding the FICA and federal and state income taxes from an employee's paycheck, employers may be authorized by an employee to withhold other amounts. The most common types of nontax withholdings are payments for life or medical insurance coverage, contributions to firm retirement plans, company credit union payments, purchases of savings bonds, union dues, and contributions to charitable organizations (such as United Way). Of course, once a firm withholds amounts from an employee's paycheck, it has an obligation to make prompt payment on behalf of the employee.

FEDERAL AND STATE UNEMPLOYMENT TAXES

Another kind of payroll tax is the unemployment tax levied on employers by both federal and state governments. Federal unemployment taxes (FUTA) are used by the federal government primarily to pay the administrative costs of unemployment programs. Only a small percentage of these taxes is paid out directly as unemployment compensation. The present FUTA rate is 0.7 percent of the first $6,000 of annual wages paid to each employee.

States use unemployment taxes (SUTA) to make payments to unemployed persons, usually for approximately one year after they become unemployed. Although each state sets its own unemployment tax rate, the rates tend to be similar: about 2.7 percent of the first $6,000 of annual wages paid to each employee. However, in most states, employers with a good employee-retention record are rewarded with a decrease from the standard 2.7 percent rate.

REPORTING AND REMITTING PAYROLL TAXES TO THE GOVERNMENT

Generally, every employer who is liable for social security tax or who is required to withhold income tax and social security tax from wages must file a quarterly return on Form 941. Employers are also required to make periodic deposits of taxes withheld and payable to a Federal Reserve Bank or authorized commercial bank. The timing and frequency of the deposits depend on the amounts payable. For example, cumulative undeposited taxes exceeding $3,000 by the 3rd, 7th, 11th, 15th, 19th, 22nd, 25th, or last day of a month must be deposited within 3 banking days. Cumulative undeposited taxes of $500 or more but less than $3,000 at the end of the first or second month of the calendar quarter must be deposited within 15 days after the end of the month. Smaller amounts can be deposited less frequently. The company is given a receipt for each deposit made (Federal Tax Deposit Form 501) and these receipts are remitted to the government with Form 941, along with any balance payable.

Federal unemployment taxes are reported annually on Form 940. State unemployment taxes are generally reported on a quarterly basis, although state requirements may differ.

Illustration of Payroll Accounting

To illustrate the accounting for payroll, we assume that, in 1983, three employees of Miller Company, Mr. X, Mr. Y, and Mr. Z, earned $20,000, $30,000, and $40,000, respectively. Table 9-1 summarizes their salary withholding information for the year.

Table 9-1 Earnings and Deductions of Three Employees in 1983

		Taxable Earnings		**Taxes**			**Other Deductions**		
Employee	*Salary*	*FICA Ceiling*	*Unemployment Tax Ceiling*	*FICA (6.70%)*	*Federal With-holding*	*State With-holding*	*Medical Insur-ance*	*United Way*	*Net Pay*
Mr. X	$20,000	$20,000	$ 6,000	$1,340	$ 3,200	$ 600	$ 360	$120	$14,380
Mr. Y	30,000	30,000	6,000	2,010	4,600	925	360	72	22,033
Mr. Z	40,000	33,900	6,000	2,271	7,100	1,330	360	144	28,795
Totals	$90,000			$5,621	$14,900	$2,855	$1,080	$336	$65,208

Although these three employees would probably be paid on a semimonthly basis, for simplicity it is assumed that they are paid only once a year. The debits and credits would be handled in exactly the same manner (though the amounts would be different, of course) no matter how often they were paid.

The entries to account for payroll can be divided into those that recognize the payroll expense and those that record the payments of the payroll tax liabilities. The entry to record the salary expense for Employees X, Y, and Z would be

Salary Expense	90,000	
FICA Taxes Payable—Employees		5,621
Federal Income Tax Withholding Payable		14,900
State Income Tax Withholding Payable		2,855
Medical Insurance Payable		1,080
United Way Payable		336
Salaries Payable		65,208

To record salary expense for Employees X, Y, and Z for 1983.

In addition to the salary expense, paid partly to the three employees directly and partly to others on their behalf, the employer must also pay the associated payroll tax expense, which includes the federal and state unemployment taxes and the employer's share of the FICA taxes. The entry to record these payroll-related taxes would be

Payroll Tax Expense	6,233	
Federal Unemployment Tax Payable ($6,000 × 3 × 0.007)		126
State Unemployment Tax Payable ($6,000 × 3 × 0.027)		486
FICA Taxes Payable—Employer		5,621

To record the payroll tax liabilities associated with Employees X, Y, and Z for 1983.

The entries to record the payment of the payroll and payroll-related taxes would be

Salaries Payable	65,208	
Cash		65,208
Paid wages to Employees X, Y, and Z in 1983.		
FICA Taxes Payable (2 × $5,621)	11,242	
Federal Income Tax Withholding Payable	14,900	
Cash		26,142
Paid federal payroll withholdings on Employees X, Y, and Z for 1983.		
Federal Unemployment Tax Payable	126	
Cash		126
Paid federal unemployment taxes on Employees X, Y, and Z for 1983.		
State Income Tax Withholding Payable	2,855	
Cash		2,855
Paid state payroll withholdings on Employees X, Y, and Z for 1983.		
State Unemployment Tax Payable	486	
Cash		486
Paid state unemployment taxes on Employees X, Y, and Z for 1983.		
Medical Insurance Payable	1,080	
Cash		1,080
Paid medical insurance withholdings on Employees X, Y, and Z for 1983.		
United Way Payable	336	
Cash		336
Paid contributions to the United Way for Employees X, Y, and Z for 1983.		

These payments are all shown as being made at year-end; however, each of the withholdings may have a different payment date depending, to a great extent, on the magnitude of the gross withholdings by the company. As mentioned earlier, companies in which the withholdings involve large amounts of money must make more frequent deposits than those whose withholdings are relatively small.

At the end of each year, the employer summarizes each employee's earnings and tax withholdings on a W-2 form, which is submitted to the government and to the employee (see Exhibit 9-7). Employees must attach a copy of their W-2 forms to their income tax returns as proof of earnings for the year.

EXHIBIT 9-7 W-2 Form

1 Control number
222

2 Employer's name, address, and ZIP code
Grayson Company
13 Main Street
Provo, UT 84601

3 Employer's identification number
13-2473504

4 Employer's State number

5 Stat em-ployee ☐ De-ceased ☐ Pension plan ☐ Legal rep ☐ 942 emp. ☐ Sub-total ☐ Cor-rection ☐ Void ☐

6 Group Term Life Ins. Included in Box 10

7 Advance EIC payment

8 Employee's social security number
152-64-5986

9 Federal income tax withheld
6250.03

10 Wages, tips, other compensation
25000.00

11 FICA tax withheld
1675.00

12 Employee's name, address, and ZIP code
George Rafferty
178 South Emerson
Orem, UT 84057

13 FICA wages
25000.00

14 FICA tips

16 State unemp/dis w/h
0

17 State income tax
845.00

18 State wages, tips, etc.
25000.00

19 Name of State
Utah

20 Local income tax
100.00

21 Local wages, tips, etc.
25000.00

22 Name of locality
UT-R

Form **W-2 Wage and Tax Statement** Copy D For Employer Department of the Treasury Internal Revenue Service

DISCUSSION QUESTION, EXERCISES, AND PROBLEM

Discussion Question

12 Which payroll-related taxes are usually paid by employers and which are usually paid by employees?

Exercises

E9-22 Payroll Accounting

IMB Corporation has four employees, W, X, Y, and Z. During 1983, these employees made $22,000, $30,000, $26,000, and $40,000, respectively. During 1983, the FICA tax rate is 6.7 percent of the first $33,900, federal and state unemployment taxes (FUTA and SUTA) are 0.7 and 2.7 percent of the first $6,000, respectively, and the employees paid federal and state income taxes as follows:

Employee	Federal Income Tax	State Income Tax
W	$ 3,500	$ 700
X	4,600	900
Y	2,500	500
Z	5,100	1,000
Totals	$15,700	$3,100

Given this information, record the following entries for the full year.

1. Salaries expense.
2. Employer's payroll taxes.
3. Payment of salaries to employees.
4. Payment of all payroll-related taxes and withholdings.

E9-23 Payroll Accounting

Johnson Electric Company has three employees, John Baker, Max Able, and Mary Johnson. Summaries of their 1983 salaries and withholdings are as follows:

Employee	Gross Salary	Federal Income Taxes Withheld	State Income Taxes Withheld
John Baker	$ 40,000	$ 4,200	$ 600
Max Able	36,000	2,800	500
Mary Johnson	39,000	4,600	700
Totals	$115,000	$11,600	$1,800

Also during 1983, the FICA and Unemployment Tax rates were

FICA tax rate	6.7 percent of first $33,900
FUTA tax rate	0.7 percent of first $ 6,000
SUTA tax rate	2.7 percent of first $ 6,000

Given this information, record for Johnson Electric the following summary entries for 1983.

1. Salaries expense.
2. Employer's payroll taxes.
3. Payment of salaries to employees.
4. Payment of all appropriate payroll liabilities to the state.
5. Payment of all appropriate payroll liabilities to the federal government.

Problem

P9-11 Payroll Accounting

Wayne County Bank has three employees, Ms. T, Mr. V, and Ms. W. During November 1983, these three employees made $2,500, $3,000, and $3,500, respectively. The following table summarizes their earnings and withholdings to date.

Employee	Annual Salary	Salary Received Through October 31, 1983	Federal Income Tax Withholdings	State Tax Withholdings
Ms. T	$30,000	$25,000	9%	3%
Mr. V	36,000	30,000	10%	4%
Ms. W ...	42,000	35,000	12%	5%

In addition, during 1983 FICA taxes are 6.7 percent of the first $33,900 and FUTA and SUTA tax rates are 0.7 percent and 2.7 percent, respectively, of the first $6,000.

Required:

1. Given these data, record the following for November 1983.
   (a) Salaries expense.
   (b) Employer's payroll tax expenses.
   (c) Payment of salaries.
   (d) Payment of withholdings and payroll taxes.
2. **Interpretive Question** Why were the November FICA taxes so low and why weren't any unemployment taxes paid?

CHAPTER 10

Property, Plant, and Equipment; Natural Resources; and Intangible Assets

THIS CHAPTER EXPLAINS:

Accounting for the acquisition of property, plant, and equipment.
Accounting for the allocation of the cost of plant and equipment over their useful lives (depreciation).
Accounting for repairs of, improvements to, and expenditures on property, plant, and equipment.
Accounting for the disposal of property, plant, and equipment.
Accounting for natural resources.
Accounting for intangible assets.

long-term operational assets *long-lived assets acquired for use in the business rather than for resale; includes property, plant, and equipment; natural resources; and intangible assets*

Current assets were discussed in Chapter 9. Here we describe the noncurrent assets that are used in operating a business. We refer to them collectively as long-term operational assets. They include (1) property, plant, and equipment, (2) natural resources, such as minerals, ores, and timber, and (3) intangible assets, such as patents, franchises, and goodwill. In Chapter 11 we conclude our discussion of assets by explaining how to account for short-term and long-term investments.

The theory underlying the accounting for all long-term operational assets is basically the same. That is, when an operational asset is purchased, its cost is recorded as an asset; then, as the benefits expire (or as the asset is used up), the cost is transferred from an asset to an expense account. Because the useful lives of operational assets usually extend over a number of years, the methods used in accounting for them can dramatically affect reported income over several accounting periods.

Types of Long-Term Operational Assets

As we have mentioned, long-term operational assets are generally identified as belonging to one of three major categories—property, plant, and equipment; natural resources; and intangible assets.

Property, plant, and equipment refers to long-term, tangible assets acquired for use in the operation of a business and not intended for resale. This category includes land, buildings, equipment, and furniture. The process of allocating the costs of these assets over their estimated useful lives is called depreciation. All of these assets, except land, are depreciated.

Natural resources, such as mineral deposits, oil wells, gravel deposits, and timber tracts, are assets that are physically consumed or that waste away. The process of allocating the costs of natural resources over their estimated useful lives is called depletion. All natural resources are depleted.

Intangible assets are long-lived assets that are used in the operation of a business but do not have tangible substance. In most cases, they provide their owners with competitive advantages over other firms. Typical intangible assets are patents, licenses, franchises, and goodwill. The process of allocating the costs of intangible assets over their estimated useful lives is called amortization. All intangible assets are eventually fully amortized, that is, written down to zero.

The major elements in accounting for a long-term operational asset, such as a piece of equipment, are

1. Accounting for its purchase.
2. Accounting for the allocation of its cost over its useful life.
3. Accounting for maintenance, repairs, and capital improvements (for example, overhauling the engine of a truck).
4. Accounting for its sale or disposal.

Accounting for the Initial Cost of Property, Plant, and Equipment

property, plant, and equipment *tangible, long-lived assets acquired for use in the business rather than for resale*

Like other assets, property, plant, and equipment are initially recorded at cost. This includes the purchase price, shipping, installation, sales taxes, and any other costs incurred to get the asset installed and in operating condition. A company can purchase these operational assets by paying cash, incurring a liability, or trading in another asset, or by a combination of these.

If a single asset is purchased for cash, the accounting is simple. To illustrate, we assume that Marianna Hotel Corporation paid $15,000 cash for a new delivery truck. The entry to record this purchase would be

Delivery Truck	15,000	
Cash		15,000
Purchased a delivery truck for $15,000 cash.		

In this instance, cash was paid for a single asset, the truck. An alternative would have been to borrow part of the purchase price. If the company had borrowed $12,000 of the $15,000 from a bank or other lending institution, the entry would have been as shown on the next page.

Delivery Truck	15,000	
Cash		3,000
Notes Payable		12,000

Purchased a delivery truck for $15,000; paid $3,000 cash and issued a note for $12,000 to Bankers' Trust.

The $12,000 represents the principal of the note; it does not include any interest charged by the lending institution. (The interest is recognized later as an interest expense.)

Another type of transaction, a basket purchase, involves two or more assets. A common basket purchase is land and the building on it. Since a single price is usually assigned to the purchase, it may be difficult to know how much of the total cost should be allocated to the individual assets.

To illustrate, we will assume that Marianna Hotel Corporation purchased a 40,000-square-foot building on 2.6 acres of land for $360,000. How much of the total cost should be assigned to the land and how much to the building? Their respective costs can be determined by using the relative fair market value method. If the fair market values of the land and the building are $100,000 and $300,000, respectively, the resulting individual costs would be $90,000 and $270,000, as calculated here.

fair market value *the amount that would be paid or received for an asset in an arm's-length transaction*

Asset	Fair Market Value	Percentage of Total Value	Apportionment of Lump-Sum Cost
Land	$100,000	25	0.25 × $360,000 = $ 90,000
Building	300,000	75	0.75 × 360,000 = 270,000
Total	$400,000	100	$360,000

The fair market values would probably have been determined by a real estate appraisal. The journal entry to record this basket purchase would be

Land	90,000	
Building	270,000	
Cash		360,000

Purchased 2.6 acres of land and a 40,000-square-foot building.

Again, if part of the purchase price were financed by a bank, an additional credit to Notes or Mortgage Payable would have been included in the entry.

An asset can also be purchased by trading a used asset plus cash for a new asset. This type of transaction is discussed on pages 349–351. In brief, the general rule for trade-ins is that a newly acquired asset should be recorded at the fair market value (that is, at the cash equivalent price) of the new asset or the asset(s) traded to obtain it, whichever can be determined more objectively.

TO SUMMARIZE There are three types of long-term operational assets: property, plant, and equipment; natural resources; and intangible assets. All are originally recorded at cost (which includes all associated costs, such as installation, sales tax, and shipping). The cost is then allocated over the estimated useful life of the asset. The annual amount assigned to an expense is called depreciation, depletion, or amortization, depending on the type of asset. When two or more assets are purchased together (a basket purchase), the relative fair market value method is used to determine their respective costs. When one asset is traded for another, the recorded cost of the new asset is usually its fair market value or the fair market value of the asset(s) given up, whichever can be determined more objectively.

Allocating the Cost of Plant and Equipment to Expense

depreciation *the process of cost allocation that assigns the original cost of plant and equipment to the periods benefited*

salvage value *estimated value or actual price of an asset at the conclusion of its useful life, net of disposal costs*

The second element in accounting for plant and equipment is the allocation of the assets' costs over their useful lives. The matching principle requires that these costs be allocated to expense in all periods benefited. The process of allocating the cost of plant and equipment over their useful lives is called depreciation. Because depreciation is an expense that is deducted from revenues in order to determine income, it directly affects the amount of taxes to be paid. The Internal Revenue Service (IRS) allows firms to use different methods of depreciation for financial reporting purposes and for the computing of taxes. In this discussion, we will consider the allocation methods commonly used in financial reporting; then we will discuss the newly established IRS alternatives for tax purposes.

To calculate depreciation expense on plant and equipment, you need to know the following about an asset: (1) its original cost, (2) its estimated useful life (number of periods benefited), and (3) its estimated salvage value, or residual value (the net portion of the asset's cost that will be recovered when it is sold or disposed of). Of course, when an asset is purchased, its actual useful life and salvage value are not known; they must be systematically and rationally estimated, usually on the basis of experience with similar assets.

We will discuss several common methods of depreciating the costs of assets in the next few sections. Each method is based on a different assumed pattern of benefits. For example, if an asset is purchased with the expectation that it will benefit all periods equally, a straight-line method of depreciation should probably be used. If, on the other hand, most of the benefits will be realized in the earlier periods of the asset's life, an accelerated method should be used, such as the sum-of-the-years'-digits method or one of the declining-balance methods. Exhibit 10–1 compares these three depreciation methods with regard to the relative amount of depreciation expense incurred in each year of a 5-year useful life.

If an asset's benefits are thought to be related to its productive output (miles driven, for example), the units-of-production depreciation method would be appropriate.

EXHIBIT 10-1 **Comparison of Depreciation Methods**

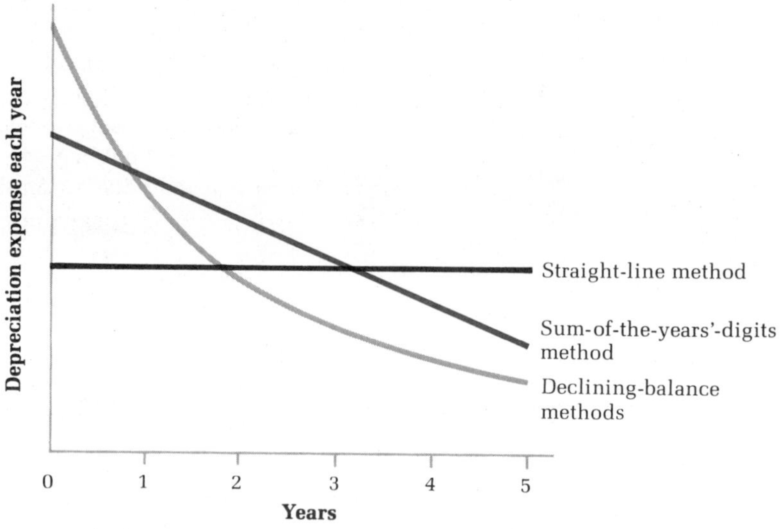

To illustrate the four common depreciation methods, we assume that Marianna purchased a dishwasher for use in one of its hotels. The following facts apply.

Acquisition cost	\$24,000
Estimated salvage value	\$ 4,000
Estimated service life:	
In years	4 years
In dishes washed	40,000 loads of dishes

THE STRAIGHT-LINE METHOD OF DEPRECIATION

straight-line depreciation method *the depreciation method in which the cost of an asset is allocated equally over the periods of the asset's estimated useful life*

The straight-line depreciation method is the simplest and one of the most commonly used depreciation methods. It assumes that an asset's cost should be assigned equally to all periods benefited. The formula for calculating annual straight-line depreciation is

$$\frac{\text{cost} - \text{salvage value}}{\text{estimated useful life (years)}} = \text{annual depreciation expense}$$

With this formula, the annual depreciation expense for the dishwasher would be calculated as follows:

$$\frac{\$24{,}000 - \$4{,}000}{4 \text{ years}} = \$5{,}000 \text{ depreciation expense per year}$$

accumulated depreciation *the total depreciation recorded on an asset since its acquisition; a contra account deducted from the original cost of an asset on the balance sheet*

book value *the net amount shown in the accounts for an asset, liability, or owners' equity item*

When the depreciation expense for an asset has been calculated, a schedule showing the annual depreciation expense, the total accumulated depreciation, and the asset's book value (undepreciated cost) for each year can be prepared. The depreciation schedule for the dishwasher is shown in Exhibit 10–2.

EXHIBIT 10–2 **Depreciation Schedule with Straight-Line Depreciation**

Year	Depreciation Expense	Accumulated Depreciation	Book Value at End of Year
Acquisition date	—	—	$24,000
1	$5,000	$ 5,000	19,000
2	5,000	10,000	14,000
3	5,000	15,000	9,000
4	5,000	20,000	4,000

The entry to record straight-line depreciation each year would be

Depreciation Expense	5,000	
Accumulated Depreciation—Dishwasher		5,000
To record the annual depreciation expense for the dishwasher.		

The debit entry, Depreciation Expense, appears on the income statement. The credit entry, Accumulated Depreciation—Dishwasher, is a contra-asset account that is offset against the cost of the dishwasher on the balance sheet. At the end of the first year, the acquisition cost, accumulated depreciation, and book value of the machine would be presented on the balance sheet as follows:

Property, Plant, and Equipment:		
Dishwasher	$24,000	
Less Accumulated Depreciation	5,000	$19,000 (book value)

THE UNITS-OF-PRODUCTION METHOD OF DEPRECIATION

units-of-production depreciation method *the depreciation method in which the cost of an asset is allocated to each period on the basis of the productive output of the asset during the period*

The units-of-production depreciation method (sometimes called the productive output method) is based on the assumption that an asset's cost should be allocated on the basis of use rather than time. Assets for which this method of depreciation may be appropriate are airplanes, where life is estimated in terms of number of hours flown; trucks, where life is estimated in terms of number of miles driven; and certain machines, where life is estimated in terms of number of units produced or processed. The formula for calculating the units-of-production depreciation for the year is

$$\frac{\text{(cost} - \text{salvage value)}}{\text{total estimated life in units}} \times \begin{matrix}\text{number of units}\\ \text{produced or processed}\\ \text{during the current year}\end{matrix} = \begin{matrix}\text{depreciation}\\ \text{expense}\end{matrix}$$

To illustrate, we again consider Marianna's dishwasher, which has an expected life of 40,000 loads of dishes. With the units-of-production method, if 8,000 loads were washed during the first year, the depreciation expense for that year would be calculated as follows:

$$\frac{(\$24{,}000 - \$4{,}000)}{40{,}000} \times 8{,}000 = \$4{,}000 \text{ depreciation expense}$$

The entry to record units-of-production depreciation during the first year of the machine's life would be

Depreciation Expense	4,000	
Accumulated Depreciation—Dishwasher		4,000
To record depreciation for the first year of the dishwasher's life.		

The depreciation schedule for the 4 years is shown in Exhibit 10–3. This exhibit assumes that 10,000 loads were washed the second year, 12,000 the third year, and 10,000 the fourth year.

EXHIBIT 10–3 **Depreciation Schedule with Units-of-Production Depreciation**

Year	Loads Washed	Depreciation Expense	Accumulated Depreciation	Book Value at End of Year
Acquisition date	—	—	—	$24,000
1	8,000	$4,000	$ 4,000	20,000
2	10,000	5,000	9,000	15,000
3	12,000	6,000	15,000	9,000
4	10,000	5,000	20,000	4,000

THE SUM-OF-THE-YEARS'-DIGITS METHOD OF DEPRECIATION

sum-of-the-years'-digits (SYD) depreciation method *the accelerated depreciation method in which a declining depreciation rate is multiplied by a constant balance (cost minus salvage value)*

The sum-of-the-years'-digits (SYD) method provides for a proportionately higher depreciation expense in the early years of an asset's life. It is therefore appropriate for assets that provide greater benefits in their earlier years as opposed to assets that benefit all years equally. The formula for calculating SYD is

$$\frac{\text{number of years of life remaining at the beginning of the year}}{\text{sum of the years' digits}} \times (\text{cost} - \text{salvage value}) = \text{depreciation expense}$$

The numerator is the number of years of estimated life remaining at the beginning of the current year. Therefore, an asset with a 10-year life would have 10 years remaining at the beginning of the first year, 9 at the beginning of the second, and so on.

The dishwasher, for example, would have 4 years of life remaining in the calculation for the first year, 3 years for the second year, 2 years for the third year, and 1 year for the fourth year. The sum of the years' digits is 10 (4 + 3 + 2 + 1). The depreciation on the machine for the first 2 years would be

$$\text{First year: } \frac{4}{10} \times (\$24{,}000 - \$4{,}000) = \$8{,}000$$

$$\text{Second year: } \frac{3}{10} \times (\$24{,}000 - \$4{,}000) = \$6{,}000$$

The depreciation schedule for 4 years is shown in Exhibit 10–4.

EXHIBIT 10–4 **Depreciation Schedule with Sum-of-the-Years'-Digits Depreciation**

Year	Depreciation Expense	Accumulated Depreciation	Book Value at End of Year
Acquisition date	–	–	$24,000
1	$8,000	$ 8,000	16,000
2	6,000	14,000	10,000
3	4,000	18,000	6,000
4	2,000	20,000	4,000

When an asset has a long life, the computation of the denominator (the sum of the years' digits) can become quite involved. There is, however, a simple formula for determining the denominator. It is

$$\frac{n(n+1)}{2}, \text{ where } n \text{ is the life (in years) of the asset}$$

Given that the dishwasher has a useful life of 4 years, the formula would work as follows:

$$\frac{4(5)}{2} = 10$$

As you can see, the answer is the same as if you had added the years' digits (4 + 3 + 2 + 1). If an asset has a 10-year life, the sum of the years' digits is

$$\frac{10(11)}{2} = 55$$

DECLINING-BALANCE METHODS OF DEPRECIATION

declining-balance depreciation methods *accelerated depreciation methods in which an asset's book value is multiplied by a constant depreciation rate (such as double the straight-line percentage, in the case of double-declining-balance)*

Declining-balance depreciation methods are similar to sum-of-the-years'-digits depreciation in that they provide for higher depreciation charges in the early years of an asset's life. Declining-balance methods involve multiplying a fixed percentage (usually 1.5 or 2 times the straight-line rate) by a decreasing book value. In past years, the double-declining-balance (DDB) method, in which the percentage is twice (200 percent of) the straight-line rate, was popular because it was the most accelerated depreciation method the IRS would allow for many assets. However, in 1981, Congress passed the Economic Tax Recovery Act, which provided for even more acceleration of depreciation. Double-declining-balance depreciation may still be theoretically appropriate for depreciating certain assets for financial reporting purposes, while a lesser declining-balance rate (150 or 175 percent) is now allowed for income tax purposes over lives that are shorter than the assets' economic lives.

Declining-balance depreciation is different in two respects from the other three methods discussed: (1) the initial computation ignores the asset's salvage value, and (2) a constant depreciation rate is multiplied by a decreasing undepreciated cost. The formula for calculating double-declining-balance depreciation is

$$\left(\frac{1}{\text{estimated life (years)}} \times 2\right) \times \left(\text{cost} - \begin{array}{c}\text{accumulated}\\ \text{depreciation}\end{array}\right) = \begin{array}{l}\text{annual}\\ \text{depreciation}\\ \text{expense}\end{array}$$

In the first part of this formula, the straight-line rate is converted to a percentage [1/estimated life (years)], which is doubled. The resulting percentage is then multiplied by the undepreciated cost (the book value) to arrive at the amount of annual depreciation expense. For example, the depreciation calculation for the dishwasher would be

Straight-line rate	4 years = 1 ÷ 4 = 25 percent
Double the straight-line rate	25 percent × 2 = 50 percent
Annual depreciation expense	50 percent × undepreciated cost

The double-declining-balance depreciation for the 4 years is shown in Exhibit 10–5.

It is important to emphasize that although the calculation for double-declining-balance depreciation ignores the salvage value of an asset, this method never allows an asset to be depreciated below that salvage value.

Although double-declining-balance depreciation (at 200 percent) was used in the example, other rates can also be used. For example, if 150 percent declining-balance depreciation were being used, the "2" in the formula would be replaced by "1.5," and so on.

EXHIBIT 10-5 **Depreciation Schedule with Double-Declining-Balance Depreciation**

Year	Computation	Depreciation Expense	Accumulated Depreciation	Book Value at End of Year
Acquisition date		—	—	$24,000
1	$24,000 × 0.50	$12,000	$12,000	12,000
2	12,000 × 0.50	6,000	18,000	6,000
3	6,000 × 0.50	2,000*	20,000	4,000
4			20,000	4,000

* Although the depreciation for the year was calculated to be $3,000 ($6,000 × 0.50), only $2,000 can be depreciated because you cannot depreciate below the salvage value of $4,000. Note that the 50 percent is being multiplied by the book value at the beginning of the year and not by the last year's depreciation expense (which happens to produce identical results when the useful life is 4 years).

A COMPARISON OF DEPRECIATION METHODS

The amount of depreciation expense will vary according to the depreciation method used by a company. Exhibit 10-6 compares the annual depreciation expense on Marianna's dishwasher under the straight-line, units-of-production, sum-of-the-years'-digits, and double-declining-balance depreciation methods.

EXHIBIT 10-6 **Comparison of Depreciation Expense Using Different Depreciation Methods**

Year	Straight-Line Depreciation	Units-of-Production Depreciation	SYD Depreciation	DDB Depreciation
1	$5,000	$4,000	$8,000	$12,000
2	5,000	5,000	6,000	6,000
3	5,000	6,000	4,000	2,000
4	5,000	5,000	2,000	-0-

This schedule makes it clear that the double-declining-balance method provides the highest amounts of depreciation in the early years of an asset's life, whereas the straight-line rate provides the lowest amounts of depreciation in these early years. (The units-of-production method cannot be compared for this particular feature, since units-of-production calculations do not depend on time periods.)

Note that depreciation is not a process of valuation. A company never claims that an asset's recorded book value is equal to its market value. In fact, market values of assets often increase at the same time that depreciation expense is being recorded. Depreciation expense is an allocation of cost and does not reflect market value changes.

PARTIAL-YEAR DEPRECIATION CALCULATIONS

Thus far, depreciation expense has been calculated on the basis of a full year. However, businesses purchase assets at all times during the year, so partial-year depreciation calculations are often required. To compute depreciation expense for less than a full year with any of the methods discussed, first calculate the depreciation expense for the year and then prorate it (distribute it evenly) over the number of months the asset is held during the year. This is equivalent to saying that any one of the depreciation methods can be used for calculating depreciation expense for full years, but a straight-line proportion (based on the number of months the expense applies out of the 12 months in a year) is always used when computing depreciation expense within a year.

To illustrate, we will assume that Marianna purchased its $24,000 dishwasher on July 1 instead of January 1. The depreciation calculations for the first 1½ years are shown in Exhibit 10–7. (You may find it helpful to refer also to Exhibit 10–6, which shows the full-year calculations.) The units-of-production method has been omitted from the exhibit; midyear purchases do not complicate the calculations with this method, since it involves numbers of miles driven, hours flown, and so on, rather than time periods.

EXHIBIT 10–7 **Partial-Year Depreciation**

Method	Full-Year Depreciation	Depreciation 1st Year (6 Months)	Depreciation 2nd Year (12 Months)
Straight-line	$ 5,000	$2,500 (5,000 × ½)	$5,000
Sum-of-the-years'-digits	8,000	4,000 (8,000 × ½)	7,000 {8,000 × ½ plus 6,000 × ½}
Double-declining-balance	12,000	6,000 (12,000 × ½)	9,000 {12,000 × ½* plus 6,000 × ½}

* An alternative calculation would be to apply the DDB rate to the beginning-of-the-year book value [($24,000 − $6,000) × 0.50].

Note that in Exhibit 10–7, the SYD and DDB depreciations for succeeding years are also affected by partial-year calculations. This is because a full year of depreciation is recorded at each rate before the rate changes. However, in actual practice, many companies simplify their depreciation computations by taking a full year of depreciation in the year an asset is purchased and none in the year the asset is sold, or vice versa.

CHANGES IN DEPRECIATION ESTIMATES

As mentioned earlier, useful lives and salvage values are only estimates. Marianna's dishwasher, for example, was assumed to have a useful life of 4 years and a salvage value of $4,000. In reality, the machine's life and salvage value may be different from the original estimates. Thus, if after 3 years Marianna realizes that the machine will last another 3 years and that the salvage value will be $3,000 instead of $4,000, the accountant would need to calculate a new depreciation expense for the remaining 3 years. Using straight-line depreciation, the calculations would be

	Formula	Calculation	Total Depreciation
Annual depreciation for the first 3 years	$\frac{\text{cost} - \text{salvage value}}{\text{estimated useful life}}$ = depreciation expense	$\frac{\$24,000 - \$4,000}{4 \text{ years}}$ = $5,000	$15,000
Book value after 3 years	cost − accumulated depreciation to date = book value	$24,000 − $15,000 = $9,000	
Annual depreciation for the last 3 years (based on a new life span of 6 years and a new salvage value of $3,000)	$\frac{\text{book value} - \text{salvage value}}{\text{remaining useful life}}$ = depreciation expense	$\frac{\$9,000 - \$3,000}{3 \text{ years}}$ = $2,000	6,000
Total depreciation			$21,000

This example shows that a change in the estimate of useful life or salvage value does not require a modification of the depreciation expense already taken. New information only affects depreciation in future years. Exhibit 10-8 shows the revised depreciation expense.

EXHIBIT 10-8 **Depreciation Schedule When There Is a Change in Estimate**

Year	Depreciation Expense	Accumulated Depreciation	Book Value at End of Year
Acquisition Date	—	—	$24,000
1	$5,000	$ 5,000	19,000
2	5,000	10,000	14,000
3	5,000	15,000	9,000
Change			
4	2,000	17,000	7,000
5	2,000	19,000	5,000
6	2,000	21,000	3,000

COST ALLOCATION METHODS USED FOR TAX PURPOSES

Good tax planning suggests that, whenever possible, the payment of taxes should be deferred into the future. Prior to the 1981 Economic Recovery Tax Act, a company that wanted to pay the least amount of taxes in the early years of an asset's life would usually choose an accelerated rate such as SYD or DDB depreciation. In fact, some companies were using these accelerated methods for tax purposes and the straight-line method for financial reporting purposes. However, the 1981 law introduced new alternatives for allocating costs for tax purposes. We will describe these new allocation alternatives briefly, but the laws contain complexities we will not consider here. (The methods previously discussed continue to be used for financial reporting.)

accelerated cost recovery system (ACRS) *IRS regulations that allocate the cost of an asset according to predefined recovery percentages*

The 1981 tax act replaced the concepts of depreciation involving the useful life of an asset with an accelerated cost recovery system (ACRS). For tax purposes, this system provides a faster write-off (expensing) of an asset's cost in three ways: (1) It abandons the concept of useful life and provides for each category of asset a cost recovery period that is usually shorter than the asset's useful life. For example, machinery can now be depreciated over 5 years, whereas in the past 10 or 15 years had to be used. (2) Salvage value is ignored; that is, at the end of the recovery period the asset is fully depreciated, including its salvage value. (3) A table giving the percentages of an asset's cost that can be expensed each year is provided for each of the five categories of productive assets: 3-year, 5-year, 10-year, and 15-year properties, and real estate (see Exhibit 10–9). For assets acquired after 1980, these percentages are based on the 150 percent declining-balance method, changing to the straight-line method at the optimal point (that is, when the straight-line method produces the greater amount of depreciation). Note that the percentage given in the table for the first year is actually for a half year only.

EXHIBIT 10–9 **The ACRS Categories of Assets**

	Percentage of Cost Allocated Each Year				
Year	**3-Year Property**	**5-Year Property**	**10-Year Property**	**15-Year Property**	**Real Estate***
1	25%	15%	8%	5%	12%
2	38	22	14	10	10
3	37	21	12	9	9
4		21	10	8	8
5		21	10	7	7
6			10	7	6
7–9			9	6	6
10			9	6	5
11–15				6	5

Some of the Assets Included in Each Category

3-Year Property: Automobiles, light trucks, research and development, equipment, and other personal property
5-Year Property: Most machinery and equipment
10-Year Property: Short-lived public utility assets
15-Year Real Property: Buildings

* Real estate and 15-year properties require different tables because the 15-year tables have a half-year depreciation built in for the first year of the asset's life, whereas the realty tables compute depreciation from the month of purchase. In this table, we assume that the real estate was acquired in the first month of the year.

To illustrate how cost allocation under ACRS differs from depreciation for financial reporting, we assume that a $30,000 machine with a 10-year life and $4,000 salvage value is purchased on January 1, 1983. Cost allocations using the straight-line, sum-of-the-years'-digits, and double-declining-balance depreciation methods and the 5-year ACRS category are shown in Exhibit 10–10.

EXHIBIT 10–10 A Comparison of Cost Allocations Using Financial Reporting Methods and ACRS

Year	Straight-Line Depreciation	SYD Depreciation	DDB Depreciation	ACRS
1983	$ 2,600	$ 4,727	$ 6,000	$ 4,500
1984	2,600	4,255	4,800	6,600
1985	2,600	3,782	3,840	6,300
1986	2,600	3,309	3,072	6,300
1987	2,600	2,836	2,458	6,300
1988	2,600	2,364	1,966	-0-
1989	2,600	1,891	1,573	-0-
1990	2,600	1,418	1,258	-0-
1991	2,600	945	1,007	-0-
1992	2,600	473	26	-0-
Total	$26,000	$26,000	$26,000	$30,000

In order to provide flexibility for depreciation deductions, ACRS also allows use of the straight-line method (with no salvage value) over a specified period of time depending on the type of asset. Note that the ACRS alternative applies only to assets placed in service after 1980.

Under the 1981 tax rules, a company can elect not to use ACRS. However, if such an election is made, the units-of-production method must be used.

As suggested earlier, companies can use one method of depreciation for tax purposes and another for financial reporting purposes. Accordingly, many firms use ACRS for taxes and standard straight-line depreciation for computing net income. This allows them to report the highest possible net income to stockholders and the lowest possible net income to the IRS.

TO SUMMARIZE There are four depreciation methods commonly used for financial reporting. The two alternatives that allow for accelerated cost allocations in the early years of an asset's life are the sum-of-the-years'-digits (SYD) and declining-balance methods. The straight-line and units-of-production methods allocate cost proportionately over an asset's life on the basis of time and use, respectively. Regardless of which method is used, depreciation is only an estimate and it may require modification as new information becomes available. In addition to the four methods that are used for financial reporting purposes, the IRS has provided its own cost allocation systems for tax purposes. These are the accelerated cost recovery system (ACRS) alternative and the units-of-production method.

Improving and Repairing Plant and Equipment

Sometime during its useful life, an asset will probably need to be repaired or improved. Two types of expenditures can be made on existing assets. The first is *ordinary* expenditures for repairs, maintenance, and other minor improvements. For example, a delivery truck requires oil changes and periodic maintenance. Since these types of expenditures typically benefit only the period in which they are made, they are expenses of the current period.

capital expenditure *an expenditure that is recorded as an asset because it is expected to benefit more than the current period*

The second type is capital expenditures that lengthen an asset's useful life, increase its capacity, or change its use. These expenditures are capitalized; that is, they are added to the asset's cost instead of being expensed in the current period. For example, overhauling the engine of a delivery truck would involve a major expenditure. In order to qualify for capitalization, an expenditure should meet three criteria: (1) it must be significant in amount; (2) it should benefit the company over several periods, not just during the current one; and (3) it should increase the productive life or capacity of the asset.

To illustrate the differences in accounting for capital and ordinary expenditures, we will assume that Marianna Hotel also purchased a delivery truck for $42,000. This truck had an estimated useful life of 8 years and a salvage value of $2,000. The straight-line depreciation on this delivery truck would be $5,000 per year [($42,000 − $2,000)/8 years]. Now, if the company spent $1,500 each year for new tires and other normal maintenance, it would record these expenditures as

Repairs and Maintenance Expense	1,500	
Cash		1,500
Spent $1,500 for maintenance of delivery truck.		

This entry has no effect on either the recorded cost or the depreciation expense of the truck. On the other hand, if at the end of the sixth year of the truck's useful life, Marianna spent $8,000 to overhaul the engine (an expenditure that increases the truck's remaining life from 2 to 4 years), the depreciation for the last 4 years would be $4,500 per year, calculated as follows:

Annual depreciation for first 6 years	$\frac{(\$42{,}000 - \$2{,}000)}{8 \text{ years}} = \frac{\$5{,}000}{\text{per year}}$
Total depreciation for first 6 years	$30,000
Book value at end of 6 years	$12,000 ($42,000 − $30,000)
Capital expenditures	$8,000
New balance to be depreciated	$20,000 ($12,000 + $8,000)
Less salvage value	−2,000
New depreciable amount	$18,000
Remaining life	4 years
Annual depreciation for last 4 years	$18,000/4 years = $4,500 per year

The journal entry to record the $8,000 capitalized expenditure would be

Delivery Truck[1]	8,000	
Cash		8,000
Spent $8,000 to overhaul the engine of the $42,000 delivery truck.		

It is often difficult to determine whether a given expenditure should be capitalized or expensed. However, because the two procedures produce a different net income, every expenditure should be properly classified. In practice, if there is any doubt, a firm usually expenses rather than capitalizes, primarily because this results in the paying of lower taxes in the immediate year.

TO SUMMARIZE There are two types of expenditures for existing long-term operational assets: ordinary and capital. In general, for an expenditure to be capitalized, it must (1) be significant in amount, (2) provide benefits for more than one period, and (3) increase the productive life or capacity of an asset. Ordinary expenditures merely maintain an asset's productive capacity at the level originally projected. Capital expenditures are added to the cost of an asset and thus affect future depreciation, whereas ordinary expenditures are expenses of the current period.

Disposal of Property, Plant, and Equipment

Plant and equipment eventually become worthless or are sold. When a company removes one of these assets from service, it has to eliminate the asset's cost and accumulated depreciation from the accounting records. There are basically three ways to dispose of an asset: (1) discard or scrap it, (2) sell it, or (3) trade it in for a new one.

DISCARDING PROPERTY, PLANT, AND EQUIPMENT

When an asset becomes worthless and must be scrapped, its cost and its accumulated depreciation balance should be removed from the accounting records. If the asset's total cost has been depreciated, there is no loss on the disposal. If, on the other hand, the cost is not completely depreciated, the undepreciated cost represents a loss on disposal.

To illustrate, we assume that Marianna Hotel purchased a transport bus for $15,000. The bus had a 5-year life and no estimated salvage value, and

[1] An alternative treatment would be to debit Accumulated Depreciation instead of Delivery Truck and recalculate the net book value on the remaining life of the truck. The effect would be the same, in that the book value would be $18,000 and the depreciation expense would still be $4,500 in each of the last 4 years.

was depreciated on a straight-line basis. If the bus were scrapped after 5 full years, the entry to record the disposal would be

Accumulated Depreciation—Transport Bus	15,000	
Transport Bus		15,000
Scrapped $15,000 transport bus.		

If it cost Marianna $300 to have the old bus towed away, the entry to record the disposal would be

Accumulated Depreciation—Transport Bus	15,000	
Loss on Disposal of Transport Bus	300	
Transport Bus		15,000
Cash		300
Scrapped $15,000 transport bus and paid disposal costs of $300.		

If the transport bus had been scrapped after only 4 years of service (and after $12,000 of the original cost had been depreciated), there would have been a loss on disposal of $3,000, and the entry would have been

Accumulated Depreciation—Transport Bus	12,000	
Loss on Disposal of Transport Bus	3,000	
Transport Bus		15,000
Scrapped $15,000 transport bus and recognized loss of $3,000.		

SELLING PROPERTY, PLANT, AND EQUIPMENT

A second way of disposing of property, plant, or equipment is to sell it. If the net sales price of the asset exceeds its book value (the original cost less accumulated depreciation), there is a gain on the sale. Conversely, if the sales price is less than the book value, there is a loss.

To illustrate, we refer again to Marianna Hotel's $15,000 transport bus. If the bus were sold for $600 after 5 full years of service, the entry to record the sale would be

Cash	600	
Accumulated Depreciation—Transport Bus	15,000	
Transport Bus		15,000
Gain on Sale of Transport Bus		600
Sold $15,000 transport bus at a gain of $600.		

Since the bus was fully depreciated, its book value was zero and the $600 was a gain. If the transport bus had been sold for $600 after only 4 years of service, there would have been a loss of $2,400 on the sale, and the entry to record the sale would have been

Cash	600	
Accumulated Depreciation—Transport Bus	12,000	
Loss on Sale of Transport Bus	2,400	
Transport Bus		15,000
Sold $15,000 transport bus at a loss of $2,400.		

The $2,400 loss is the difference between the sales price of $600 and the book value of $3,000 ($15,000 − $12,000). The amount of a gain or loss is thus a function of two factors: (1) the amount of cash received from the sale, and (2) the book value of the asset at the date of sale.

EXCHANGING PROPERTY, PLANT, AND EQUIPMENT

A third way of disposing of property, plant, or equipment is to trade it for another asset. Such exchanges occur regularly with cars, trucks, machines, and other types of large equipment.

When assets are exchanged in a regular arm's-length transaction between a buyer (customer) and a seller (dealer), the general rule is that the new asset should be recorded either at its fair market value (the cash-equivalent price) or at the fair market value of the assets given up, whichever amount may be more accurately determined. The difference between the total amount of assets given up (the additional cash paid plus the book value of the old asset) and the amount received (the fair market value of the new asset) should be recognized as a gain or loss on the exchange.[2]

The entry to record a trade-in includes a debit to the new asset at its fair market value (or at the fair market value of the assets given up), a debit to the old asset's accumulated depreciation account, a credit to cash, and a credit to the old asset for its original cost. The difference between total debits and total credits is the gain or loss on the transaction.

To illustrate the general situation in accounting for exchanges, assume that Marianna, Inc., is acquiring a new asset by exchanging an old asset and paying $11,000 in cash. If the old asset cost $10,000, accumulated depreciation is $8,000, and the fair market value of the new asset is $14,000, the entry to record the exchange would be

New Asset	14,000	
Accumulated Depreciation—Old Asset	8,000	
Old Asset		10,000
Cash		11,000
Gain on Exchange of Assets		1,000
Exchanged used asset plus $11,000 cash in return for new asset costing $14,000.		

[2] Some accountants (and textbooks) maintain that exchanges of similar assets should be treated differently from exchanges of dissimilar assets. That is, they do not believe that a gain from a trade of similar assets should be recognized. However, recent clarifications of APB Opinion No. 29 suggest that a gain from any arm's-length transaction should be recognized, whether the assets are similar or dissimilar.

In this case, the recorded amount of the new asset is its cash-equivalent price of $14,000. That is how much it would have cost to buy that asset if the entire amount had been paid in cash. Since the amount given up by Marianna (the $2,000 book value of its old asset plus the $11,000 cash) was less than the fair market value of the asset received, a gain was recognized on the exchange.

In accounting for trade-ins, you must be careful not to confuse the list price of a new asset, or the trade-in allowance offered by a dealer on an old asset, with the fair market values of the assets. The list price of a new asset may be higher than the amount of cash that would be required to purchase that asset. For example, if you pay cash for a new car, you can often buy it for less than the "sticker," or list, price. Similarly, a dealer may offer a trade-in allowance that is higher than the fair market value of the old asset. This higher trade-in allowance is usually accompanied by a higher sales price for the new car, because the dealer is protecting the profit margin. Thus, if you are offered $500 for your "clunker" when it is worth no more than $100 as scrap metal, the price of the new car has probably been increased above what you would have paid if you had used cash. For accounting purposes, the list price should not be considered the fair market value unless it *is* the amount you would pay if you paid in cash, and the trade-in allowance should likewise not be recorded as the fair market value of the old asset. However, the trade-in allowance does determine the amount of cash required to complete the transaction.

Returning to our example of Marianna's exchange of assets, let's assume that the fair market value of the new asset was not available information, but that Marianna determined that the old asset could be sold for $1,000. The new asset would be recorded at $12,000 ($11,000 cash plus the $1,000 cash-equivalent price of the old asset). Using this information, the entry to record the exchange would be

New Asset	12,000	
Accumulated Depreciation—Old Asset	8,000	
Loss on Exchange of Assets	1,000	
Old Asset		10,000
Cash		11,000
Exchanged used asset plus $11,000 cash in return for new asset costing $12,000.		

In both illustrations, fair market value was used to record the cost of the new asset. In the first case, the cash-equivalent price of the new asset was objectively determinable; in the second case, the fair market value of the old asset plus the cash paid became the cost of the new asset. When a fair market value cannot be determined for either the new asset or the old asset, then the book value of the old asset plus the cash paid becomes the recorded amount of the new asset, and no gain or loss is recognized. For financial reporting purposes, this is an exception to the general rule of recognizing a gain or a loss on an exchange. This "book value" method of accounting for exchanges applies when a highly specialized asset is exchanged for a new model and neither asset has a fair market value.

Whether or not an asset has a fair market value, for tax purposes gains and losses are generally not recognized on an exchange. The book value of the exchanged asset plus the amount of cash paid is assigned as the value of the new asset. However, unless otherwise noted, we will not use the tax method.

When Sellers Exchange Similar Assets

The rule that new assets acquired by exchanging old assets are to be recorded at their fair market values does not apply when *sellers* exchange *similar* assets. For example, two car dealers (sellers) may exchange a blue car for a white car so that a customer's color preference can be satisfied. This type of exchange is not an arm's-length transaction between a seller and a buyer, but rather an exchange of inventory between two sellers. In such cases, the book value of the asset received is recorded at the value of the exchanged asset plus any amount of cash that may have been required. In this text, however, we will limit our discussions to exchange transactions between buyers and sellers. We will therefore follow the general rule for recording property acquisitions (to use the most accurate fair market value obtainable), whether these acquisitions are by outright purchase or by exchange.

TO SUMMARIZE There are three ways of disposing of assets: (1) scrapping, (2) selling, and (3) exchanging. If a scrapped asset has not been fully depreciated, a loss equal to the undepreciated cost or book value is recognized. When an asset is sold, there is a gain if the sales price exceeds the book value, and a loss if the sales price is less than the book value. When assets are exchanged, there is a gain if the cash-equivalent price of the asset received exceeds the sum of the book value of the old asset and the cash paid, and a loss if the opposite is true. An asset acquired through an exchange should be valued at its fair market value or at the fair market value of the assets given up, whichever amount may be more accurately determined.

Accounting for Natural Resources

natural resources *assets, such as minerals, oil, timber, and gravel, that are extracted or otherwise depleted*

depletion *the process of cost allocation that assigns the original cost of a natural resource to the periods benefited*

As noted at the beginning of this chapter, natural resources include such things as oil, timber, coal, and gravel. Like all other assets, newly purchased or developed natural resources are recorded at cost. This cost must be written off as the assets are extracted or otherwise depleted. The process of writing off the cost of natural resources is called depletion and involves the calculation of a depletion rate for each unit of the natural resource.

To illustrate, we will assume that Marathon Company, which manufactures heavy tractor equipment, decides to diversify (invest in another type of business) and purchases a coal mine for $1,200,000 cash. The entry to record the purchase would be as shown on the next page.

Coal Mine	1,200,000	
Cash		1,200,000
Purchased a coal mine for $1,200,000.		

If the mine has an estimated 200,000 tons of coal deposits, the depletion expense for each ton of coal extracted will be $6 ($1,200,000/200,000 tons). Now, if 12,000 tons of coal were mined in the current year, the depletion entry would be

Depletion Expense	72,000	
Coal Mine		72,000
To record depletion for the year: 12,000 tons at $6.00 per ton.		

A contra-asset account, such as Accumulated Depletion, is not used in this example. Instead, the asset account, Coal Mine, is credited directly. Actually either approach would be appropriate. We have used the direct approach because it is more common in practice in accounting for natural resources, since the asset actually is physically depleted or used up.

After the first year's depletion expense has been recorded, the coal mine will be shown on the balance sheet as follows:

Natural Resources:	
Coal Mine (cost $1,200,000)	$1,128,000

But how do you determine the number of tons of coal in a mine? Since most natural resources cannot be counted, the amount of the resource owned is an estimate. The depletion calculation is therefore likely to be revised as new information becomes available. When an estimate is changed, a new depletion rate per unit is calculated and used to compute depletion during the remaining life of the natural resource, or until another new estimate is made.

Accounting for Intangible Assets

intangible assets *long-lived assets that do not have physical substance and that are not held for resale*

amortization *the process of cost allocation that assigns the original cost of an intangible asset to the periods benefited*

Intangible assets are assets that are long-lived, are not held for resale, have no physical substance, and usually provide their owner with competitive advantages over other firms. Familiar examples are patents, franchises, licenses, and goodwill. Although intangible assets have no physical substance, they are accounted for in the same way as other long-term operational assets. That is, they are originally recorded at cost and the cost is written off over the useful or legal life, whichever is shorter. The periodic charge made to write off an intangible asset's cost is called amortization. Straight-line amortization is generally used for intangible assets.

PATENTS

patent *an exclusive right granted for 17 years by the federal government to manufacture and sell an invention*

A patent is an exclusive right to produce and sell a commodity that has one or more unique features. Issued to inventors by the federal government, patents have a legal life of 17 years. They may be obtained on new products developed in a company's own research laboratories or they may be purchased from others. If a patent is purchased from others, its cost is simply the purchase price. The cost of a patent for a product developed within a firm, however, is difficult to determine. Should it include research and development costs as well as legal fees to obtain the patent? Should other company expenses be included? Prior to 1974, there were no real accounting guidelines specifying which expenditures should be capitalized as part of the cost of a patent. In 1974, however, the Financial Accounting Standards Board determined that, due to the high degree of uncertainty about their future benefits, research and development costs must be expensed in the period in which they are incurred. Therefore, the costs of most internally developed patents are expensed.

To illustrate the accounting for patents, we assume that Marianna Corporation acquires, for $200,000, a patent granted 7 years earlier to another firm. The entry to record the purchase of the patent would be

Patent	200,000	
Cash		200,000
Purchased patent for $200,000.		

Because 7 years of its 17-year legal life have already elapsed, the patent now has a legal life of only 10 years. If its useful life is at least 10 years, one-tenth of the $200,000 cost should be amortized each year for the next 10 years. The entry each year to record the patent amortization expense would be

Amortization Expense—Patent	20,000	
Patent		20,000
To amortize one-tenth of the cost of the patent.		

As was the case with natural resources, a contra-asset account, such as Accumulated Amortization, was not used in this example. Although crediting such an account would have been appropriate, the direct approach is again more common in practice.

FRANCHISES AND LICENSES

franchise *an exclusive right to sell a product or offer a service in a certain geographical area*

Issued either by companies or government agencies, franchises and licenses are exclusive rights to perform services in certain geographical areas. For example, McDonald's Corporation sells franchises to individuals to operate its hamburger outlets in specific locations. Similarly, the Interstate Commerce Commission issues licenses to trucking firms, allowing them to transport certain types of goods in specific geographical areas. The cost of a franchise or license is amortized over its useful or legal life, whichever is shorter.

GOODWILL

goodwill *an intangible asset showing that a business is worth more than the value of its net assets because of strategic location, reputation, good customer relations, or similar factors; equal to the excess of cost over the fair market value of the net assets purchased*

When businesses are purchased, the negotiated price often exceeds the total value of the specific assets minus the outstanding liabilities. This excess in purchase price that cannot be allocated to specific assets is called goodwill and is an intangible asset. The emergence of goodwill in such a transaction is considered an indication that the purchased business is worth more than its net assets, due to such favorable characteristics as a good reputation, a strategic location, product superiority, or management skill.

Goodwill should be recorded only if its value can be objectively determined by a transaction. Therefore, even though two businesses may enjoy the same favorable characteristics, goodwill will be recognized only in the accounts of the buyer of a firm. This disparity in accounting exists because the action of a buyer in paying a premium for a firm is objective evidence that goodwill exists and has a specific value.

Unlike other intangible assets that decrease in value with time, goodwill often increases in value. Nevertheless, in order to ensure that different firms account for goodwill in similar ways, accounting practice dictates that goodwill must be amortized over its expected life, not to exceed 40 years.

To illustrate the accounting for goodwill, we assume that Marianna Corporation purchased Ideal Drug Store for $400,000. At the time of purchase, the recorded assets and liabilities of Ideal Drug had the following fair market values. Note that fair market values (the current prices of items) will generally differ from book values (the historical costs paid for items less any depreciation, amortization, or depletion). The amount paid in excess of current market value is recorded as goodwill.

Inventory	$220,000
Long-Term Operational Assets	110,000
Other Assets (Prepaid Expenses, etc.)	10,000
Liabilities	(20,000)
Total Net Assets	$320,000

Because Marianna was willing to pay $400,000 for Ideal Drug, there must have been other favorable, intangible factors worth approximately $80,000. These factors are called goodwill and the entry to record the purchase of the drug store would be

Inventory	220,000	
Long-Term Operational Assets	110,000	
Other Assets	10,000	
Goodwill	80,000	
Liabilities		20,000
Cash		400,000
Purchased Ideal Drug Store for $400,000.		

If Marianna decides to use 40 years as the useful life of the goodwill, each year the amortization entry will be

Amortization Expense—Goodwill	2,000	
Goodwill		2,000
To record annual straight-line amortization of goodwill ($80,000 ÷ 40 years).		

TO SUMMARIZE Natural resources are assets, such as gravel or coal, that are consumed or that waste away. Intangible assets are long-term assets that have no physical substance but that provide competitive advantages to owners. Common intangible assets are patents, franchises, licenses, and goodwill. The costs of natural resources are depleted, whereas the costs of intangible assets are amortized.

CHAPTER REVIEW

There are three major types of long-term operational assets: (1) property, plant, and equipment; (2) natural resources; and (3) intangible assets. The four elements in accounting for these assets are (1) acquisition, (2) allocation of cost to expense over the life of the asset, (3) repairs and improvements, and (4) disposal. Long-term operational assets are always recorded at cost, which includes shipping, sales taxes, and other incidental expenses. In the case of basket purchases, costs are usually determined by using the relative fair market value method.

Allocating costs over the lives of plant and equipment is called depreciation. Four common techniques are used for depreciating the costs of these assets for financial reporting: the straight-line, units-of-production, sum-of-the-years'-digits (SYD), and declining-balance methods. Two of these, SYD and declining-balance, are accelerated depreciation methods; the other two assign cost proportionately over an asset's life, either as a function of time (straight-line) or of use (units-of-production). In addition, the IRS has provided other methods, such as the accelerated cost recovery system (ACRS), that can be used to depreciate assets for tax purposes. Changes in depreciation estimates affect depreciation amounts in current and subsequent years.

Repairs, maintenance, and improvement expenditures are either expensed or capitalized. Expenditures that provide benefits only in the current accounting period and do not increase productive capacity or useful life are charged against current income as expenses. Expenditures that are material in amount, that provide benefits extending beyond the current accounting period, and that increase productive capacity or useful life are capitalized.

Assets can be disposed of in three ways: they can be (1) scrapped, (2) sold, or (3) exchanged for new assets. There is usually no gain involved in scrapping an asset. Any loss to be recognized is equal to an asset's undepreciated cost, or book value. If the proceeds received from the sale of an asset exceed its book value, there is a gain on the sale. If the proceeds are less than the book value, a loss is experienced. As a general rule, assets acquired through exchanges are recorded at their fair market value or at the fair market value of the assets given up, whichever can be determined more objectively. Thus, gains and losses are recognized on arm's-length exchanges.

Accounting for natural resources is similar to that for property, plant, and equipment. Thus, natural resources are originally recorded at cost and the cost is subsequently depleted over an asset's useful life.

Intangible assets are long-term operational assets that do not have physical substance and that usually provide owners with advantages over competitors. Common examples are patents, franchises, licenses, and goodwill. The process of writing off the costs of intangible assets over their useful lives is called amortization.

KEY TERMS AND CONCEPTS

accelerated cost recovery system (ACRS) (344)
accumulated depreciation (337)
amortization (352)
book value (337)
capital expenditure (346)
declining-balance depreciation methods (340)
depletion (351)
depreciation (335)
fair market value (334)
franchise (353)
goodwill (354)
intangible assets (352)
long-term operational assets (332)
natural resources (351)
patent (353)
property, plant, and equipment (333)
salvage value (335)
straight-line depreciation method (336)
sum-of-the-years'-digits (SYD) depreciation method (338)
units-of-production depreciation method (337)

REVIEW PROBLEM

Property, Plant, and Equipment

Richland Transport is a trucking company that hauls crude oil in the Rocky Mountain states. It presently has 20 trucks. The following information relates to a single truck.

a. Date truck was purchased: July 1, 1981.

b. Cost of truck:

Truck	$125,000
Paint job	3,000
Sales tax	7,000

c. Estimated useful life of truck: 120,000 miles.

d. Estimated salvage value of truck: $27,000.

e. 1983 expenditures on truck:

(1) $6,000 on new tires and regular maintenance.

(2) $44,440 to completely rework the truck's engine; increased life by 80,000 miles but left expected salvage value unchanged.

f. Miles driven:

1981	11,000
1982	24,000
1983 (before reworking of engine)	13,000
1983 (after reworking of engine)	7,000
1984 (to date of trade-in)	14,000

g. During 1984, the truck was traded in for a new one with a list price of $142,000. Richland determined that the new truck could have been purchased for $130,000 cash. Cash of $50,000 was paid on the trade-in.

Required:

Record journal entries to account for the following. (Use the units-of-production depreciation method.)

1. The purchase of the truck.
2. Depreciation expense for
   (a) 1981.
   (b) 1982.
   (c) 1983.
   (d) 1984 (to date of sale).
3. The expenditures on the truck during 1983.
4. The exchange of the truck for the new one during 1984.

Solution

1. Truck Purchase

The cost of the truck includes both the amount paid for it and all costs incurred to get it in working condition. In this case, the cost includes both the paint job and the sales tax. Thus, the entry to record the purchase is

Truck	135,000	
Cash		135,000

2. Depreciation Expense

The formula for units-of-production depreciation on the truck is

$$\frac{\text{cost} - \text{salvage value}}{\text{total miles expected to be driven}} \times \text{number of miles driven in any given year} = \text{depreciation expense}$$

Depreciation for the 4 years is calculated as follows.

1981:

$$\frac{\$135{,}000 - \$27{,}000}{120{,}000 \text{ miles}} \times 11{,}000 \text{ miles} = \$9{,}900$$

or \$0.90 per mile × 11,000 miles

1982:

$$\frac{\$135{,}000 - \$27{,}000}{120{,}000 \text{ miles}} \times 24{,}000 \text{ miles} = \$21{,}600$$

or \$0.90 per mile × 24,000 miles

1983 (before reworking engine):

$$\frac{\$135{,}000 - \$27{,}000}{120{,}000 \text{ miles}} \times 13{,}000 \text{ miles} = \$11{,}700$$

or \$0.90 per mile × 13,000 miles

1983 (after reworking engine):

Depreciation already taken: \$43,200
Left to depreciate: \$64,800 (\$135,000 − \$43,200 − \$27,000)
New amount to depreciate: \$109,240 (\$64,800 + \$44,440)
Remaining life in miles: 152,000 (120,000 + 80,000 − 48,000)
New depreciation per mile: \$0.719 (\$109,240 ÷ 152,000 miles)

Depreciation for remainder of 1983:
\$0.719 per mile × 7,000 miles = \$5,033

1984 (to date of trade-in):
\$0.719 per mile x 14,000 miles = \$10,066

The depreciation entries are

(a) 1981	Depreciation Expense	9,900	
	Accumulated Depreciation		9,900
(b) 1982	Depreciation Expense	21,600	
	Accumulated Depreciation		21,600
(c) 1983	Depreciation Expense	16,733	
	Accumulated Depreciation (\$11,700 + \$5,033)		16,733
(d) 1984	Depreciation Expense	10,066	
	Accumulated Depreciation		10,066

3. Expenditures

The first expenditure is an ordinary expenditure and is expensed in the current year. The \$44,440 expenditure is capitalized because it lengthens the truck's life. The entries are

Repairs and Maintenance Expense	6,000	
Cash		6,000
Truck	44,440	
Cash		44,440

4. Exchange

This is an arm's-length transaction between a buyer and a seller, so the new asset is recorded at its fair market value (its cash-equivalent price of \$130,000). The gain or loss is the difference between the value received (\$130,000) and the amount given up (cash plus the book value of the old truck). The calculation of the gain or loss is as follows:

Cost of old truck		\$179,440 (\$135,000 + \$44,400)
Depreciation to date of trade:		
1981	\$ 9,900	
1982	21,600	
1983	16,733	
1984	10,066	58,299
Book value of old truck		\$121,141
Cash paid		50,000
Total assets given up		\$171,141
Cash price of new truck		130,000
Loss on trade-in		\$ 41,141

Given these calculations, the journal entry is

Truck (New)	130,000	
Accumulated Depreciation	58,299	
Loss on Trade-In	41,141	
Cash		50,000
Truck (Old)		179,440

DISCUSSION QUESTIONS

1 What is the difference between an asset and an expense?

2 What expenditures, other than the net purchase price, can be included in the cost of an asset?

3 When is it necessary to use the relative fair market value method to determine the cost of long-term operational assets?

4 Is depreciation a method of allocating the cost of an asset over its useful life, or is it a way of reflecting the annual reduction in market value as the asset ages? Discuss.

5 Which of the depreciation methods discussed in this chapter will usually result in the highest net income in the early years of an asset's life?

6 In which of the four traditional methods of depreciation (that is, not including ACRS) is the estimated salvage value ignored in the calculation?

7 What type of an account is Accumulated Depreciation? Where does it appear on the financial statements?

8 It is said that no matter which depreciation method is being used to allocate costs over a period of years, a straight-line method apportionment is always made when an asset is acquired or disposed of during a year. What does this statement mean?

9 When changing the estimate of the useful life of an asset, should depreciation expense for all of the previous years be recalculated? If not, how do you account for a change in this estimate?

10 What is the difference between an ordinary and a capital expenditure?

11 If it is uncertain whether an expenditure will benefit one or more than one accounting period, or whether it will increase the capacity or useful life of an operational asset, most firms will expense rather than capitalize the expenditure. Why?

12 Why is it common to have a gain or loss on the disposal of a long-term operational asset? Is it true that if the useful life and salvage value of an asset are known with certainty and are realized, there will never be such a gain or loss?

13 When recording the disposal of a long-term operational asset, why is it necessary to debit the accumulated depreciation of the old asset?

14 Why is the list price of a new asset often ignored in accounting for the purchase of long-term operational assets?

15 Why is it often necessary to recalculate the depletion rate for natural resources?

16 Is raw land depleted like other natural resources? Why or why not?

17 Why are intangible assets considered assets if they have no physical substance?

18 Why does accounting practice require that research and development costs be expensed as they are incurred?

19 When should goodwill be recorded? Why?

20 Goodwill can only be recorded when a business is purchased. Does this result in similar businesses having incomparable financial statements?

21 Why does the accounting profession require goodwill to be amortized over a period not exceeding 40 years?

EXERCISES

E10-1 Accounting for the Acquisition of Assets

Straw Furniture Company decided to purchase a new furniture-polishing machine for its store in New York City. After a long search, it found the appropriate polisher in Chicago. The machine cost $50,000, and had an estimated 10-year life and no salvage value. Straw Company had the following additional expenditures with respect to this purchase.

Sales tax	$2,500
Delivery costs (FOB shipping point)	3,000
Installation costs	1,200
Painting of machine to match the decor	2,000

1. What is the cost of the machine to Straw Furniture Company?

2. What is the amount of the first full year's depreciation if Straw Company uses the straight-line depreciation method?

E10-2 Accounting for the Acquisition of Assets (Basket Purchase)

Palmer Corporation purchased land and a building for a total cost of $200,000. After the purchase, the property was appraised. Fair market values were determined to be $60,000 for the land and $120,000 for the building.

Given these appraisals, record the purchase of the property by Palmer Corporation.

E10-3 The Acquisition and Depreciation of Assets

Big Oil Company purchased new drilling equipment on July 1, 1983, using checks #1015 and #1016 to do so. The check totals are shown below, along with a breakdown of the charges.

1015 (Payee—Oil Equipment, Inc.):	
Cost of drilling equipment	$ 75,000
Cost of cement platform	25,000
Installation charges	13,000
Total	$113,000
1016 (Payee—Red Ball Freight):	
Freight-in on drilling equipment	$ 2,000

Assuming that the estimated life of the drilling equipment is 10 years and its salvage value is $5,000:

1. Record the disbursements on 7/1/83, assuming that no entry had been recorded for the drilling equipment.
2. Disregarding the information given about the two checks, assume that the drilling equipment was capitalized at a total cost of $95,000. Calculate the depreciation expense for 1983 using the following methods.
   (a) Sum-of-the-years'-digits.
   (b) Double-declining-balance.
   (c) 150 percent declining-balance.
   (d) Straight-line.
3. Prepare the journal entry to record the depreciation for 1983 in accordance with part 2(a).

E10-4 The Acquisition, Depreciation, and Disposal of Assets

On January 1, 1983, Hybird Company purchased a building and land for $300,000. The most recent appraisals of the building and the land were $100,000 and $50,000, respectively. The building has an estimated useful life of 20 years and a salvage value of $10,000.

1. Assuming cash transactions and straight-line depreciation, prepare journal entries to record: (a) purchase of the building and land on January 1, 1983, and (b) depreciation expense on December 31, 1983.
2. Assume that after 3 years the property (land and building) was sold for $225,000. Prepare the journal entry to record the sale.

E10-5 The Acquisition and Trade-In of Assets

Prepare entries in the books of Wendy's Incorporated to reflect the following (assume cash transactions).

1. Purchased a lathing machine to be used by the firm in its production process.

Invoice price	$20,000
Cash discount taken	200
Installation costs	1,200
Sales tax on the machine	500

2. Added a waste-reducing gauge, which cost $2,000, to the lathing machine. This gauge is expected to increase the resale value of the machine.
3. Performed normal periodic maintenance on the lathing machine at a cost of $300.
4. Added to the lathing machine a governor costing $400, which is expected to increase the machine's life but not to increase its resale value.
5. On January 1, traded a $5,000 cleaning machine for a new cleaning machine with a cash purchase price of $6,000. At the time of the trade, the old machine had an accumulated depreciation balance of $3,000. The company received a trade-in allowance of $2,100 and paid $3,900 in cash.

E10-6 Depreciation Calculations

Kerry Company purchased a new car on July 1, 1983, for $12,000. The estimated life of the car was 4 years or 108,000 miles, and its salvage value was estimated to be $2,000. The car was driven 9,000 miles in 1983 and 27,000 miles in 1984.

Compute the amount of depreciation expense for both 1983 and 1984, using the following methods.

1. Straight-line.
2. Sum-of-the-years'-digits.
3. Double-declining-balance.
4. Units-of-production.

E10-7 Depreciation Calculations

On January 1, 1983, a machine was purchased for $70,000. Installation cost was $2,000. It was determined that the salvage value of the machine would be $7,000. The machine has a useful life of 5 years.

Compute the depreciation expense for 1983 and 1984, using the following methods.

1. Straight-line.
2. 150 percent declining-balance.
3. Sum-of-the-years'-digits.

E10-8 Depreciation Calculations

On October 1, 1983, Mays, Inc., bought a pitching machine to be used in its newly established Sports World Complex. The machine cost $10,000 and is estimated to have a useful life of 5 years or 450,000 pitches, after which it can be sold for $1,000.

Assuming that Mays, Inc., is a calendar year business, compute the amount of depreciation using the

1. Straight-line method for 1983.
2. Sum-of-the-years'-digits method for 1984.
3. Double-declining-balance method for 1983.

4. Units-of-production method for 1983, assuming there were 50,000 pitches.
5. Double-declining-balance method for 1984.

E10–9 Depreciation Calculations

Harker Hardware Company has a giant paint mixer that cost $42,500 plus $200 to install. The estimated salvage value of the paint mixer at the end of its useful life in 15 years is estimated to be $900. Harker estimates that the machine can mix 850,000 cans of paint during its lifetime.

Compute the second full year's depreciation expense, using the following methods.

1. Straight-line.
2. Double-declining-balance.
3. Sum-of-the-years'-digits.
4. Units-of-production, assuming that the machine mixes 56,000 cans of paint during the second year.

E10–10 Depreciation Calculations

On January 1, AT Company purchased a $19,000 machine. The estimated life of the machine was 5 years and the estimated salvage value was $4,000. The machine had an estimated useful life in productive output of 75,000 units. Actual output for the first 2 years was: year 1, 20,000 units; year 2, 15,000 units.

1. Compute the amount of depreciation expense for year 1, using each of the following methods.
   (a) Straight-line.
   (b) Units-of-production.
   (c) Sum-of-the-years'-digits.
   (d) Double-declining-balance.
2. What was the book value of the machine at the end of the first year, assuming that straight-line depreciation was used?
3. If the machine is sold at the end of the fourth year for $14,000, how much should the company report as a gain or loss (assume straight-line depreciation)?

E10–11 Changes in Depreciation Estimates

Schultz Brewing Company purchased a $400,000 vat for its brewery on January 1, 1983. The vat's estimated useful life is 20 years with no salvage value. Schultz uses straight-line depreciation on all its brewery equipment.

1. Compute the depreciation expense for year 1.
2. What will the book value of the vat be on December 31, 1994?
3. If, on January 1, 1995, Schultz determines that the vat will last another 16 years instead of 8 years, what will the depreciation expense be for 1995?
4. Given the information in (3), what will the book value of the vat be on December 31, 1997?

E10–12 Disposal of Long-Term Operational Assets

Rest Easy Mattress Company purchased a delivery truck 5 years ago for $30,000. Presently, accumulated depreciaton on the truck is $18,000.

Prepare journal entries to record the sale or exchange of the truck, assuming that:

1. The truck is sold for $14,000 cash.
2. The truck is exchanged for $8,000 of supplies.
3. The truck is exchanged for a new truck with a fair market value of $16,000. In addition to the old truck, $6,000 cash is paid in the exchange.
4. The truck is exchanged for a $10,000 note receivable.
5. The truck, plus a cash payment of $4,000, is exchanged for a new truck having a fair market value of $14,000.

E10–13 Accounting for the Exchange of Assets

On June 30, 1984, Bretwood Corporation exchanged a used $40,000 machine for a new one with a list price of $60,000. (The cash price of the new machine was determined to be $57,000.) The old machine was originally purchased on January 1, 1980, and had a 4-year life expectancy with no estimated salvage value. In making the exchange, the company received a trade-in allowance of $5,000 for the old machine. Bretwood Corporation uses SYD depreciation.

Assuming that Bretwood is a calendar year corporation, complete the following.

1. Update the depreciation on the old machine to the date of trade. (Depreciation was last recorded on December 31, 1983.)
2. Compute the book value of the old machine at the date of trade.
3. Record the exchange in General Journal form.

E10–14 Exchanges and Depreciation of Assets

Equipment belonging to Johnson Manufacturing Company was traded for new equipment that had a fair market value of $120,000 on March 31, 1984. A trade-in allowance of $90,000 was given and the balance was paid in cash. Accounts relating to the old equipment had the following balances on December 31, 1983.

Equipment	$100,000
Accumulated Depreciation—Equipment	4,950

Depreciation expense is calculated using the units-of-production method, with the machine's estimated useful life being 100,000 units. Salvage value is expected to be $1,000. Two thousand units were produced in the first quarter of 1984.

1. Provide the journal entries necessary on March 31, 1984, to update the depreciation expense and record the exchange.

2. Now assume that the March 31, 1984, exchange did not take place. If the cost of the old machine is still $100,000, record its depreciation expense for 1984 if a salvage value of $5,000 is now expected. Its remaining useful life is estimated to be 23,750 units, and 3,500 units were produced in 1984.

E10–15 Accounting for the Exchange of Assets

Knudsen Company decided to purchase a new vehicle that had a list price of $9,000 and a cash price without trade-in of $8,400. The dealer required a cash payment of $6,600 in addition to the trade-in of an old vehicle that had a $1,400 book value. (The cost of the old vehicle was $8,000.)

1. Give the entry to record the exchange.
2. Record the exchange, assuming now that $7,600 cash plus the old vehicle were given for the new one.

E10–16 Accounting for the Disposal of Assets

Gale Cement Company has a truck that it would like to either sell or trade. The truck had an original cost of $60,000, was purchased 3 years ago, and was expected to have a useful life of 5 years with no salvage value.

Using straight-line depreciation, and assuming that depreciation expense to the date of sale has been properly recorded, prepare journal entries to record the disposal of the truck under each of the following conditions.

1. Gale Company sells the truck for $25,000 cash.
2. Gale Company sells the truck for $20,000 cash.
3. Gale Company trades the truck for a new one with a fair market value of $80,000 and is given a trade-in allowance of $30,000 on the old truck.
4. Gale Company trades the truck for a piece of land that is valued at $60,000, and pays $32,000 in addition to the old truck.
5. The old truck is wrecked and Gale Company hauls it to the junkyard.

E10–17 Accounting for Natural Resources

On January 1, 1983, Donald Investment Corporation purchased a coal mine for cash, having taken into consideration the favorable tax consequences and the inevitable energy crunch in the future. Donald paid $800,000 for the mine. Shortly after the purchase, an engineer estimated that there were 80,000 tons of coal in the mine.

1. Record the purchase of the mine on January 1, 1983.
2. Record the depletion expense for 1983, assuming that 20,000 tons of coal were mined during the year.
3. Assume that on January 1, 1984, the company received a new estimate that the mine contained 120,000 tons of coal. Record the entry (if any) to show the change in estimate.
4. Record the depletion expense for 1984, assuming that another 20,000 tons of coal were mined.

E10–18 Accounting for Natural Resources

On April 30, 1983, Super Oil Company purchased an oil well, with reserves of an estimated 100,000 barrels of oil, for $1,000,000 cash.

Prepare journal entries to record the following.

1. The purchase of the oil well.
2. During 1983, 7,000 barrels of oil were extracted from the well.
3. During 1984, 15,000 barrels of oil were extracted from the well.
4. At the beginning of 1985, it was determined that only 60,000 barrels of oil remained in the well. During that year, 20,000 barrels of oil were extracted from the well. Record the appropriate depletion expense.

E10–19 Accounting for Intangible Assets

During 1983, Jeppson Research Institution had the following intangible assets.

Asset	Cost	Date Purchased	Expected Useful or Legal Life
Goodwill	$ 16,000	January 1, 1978	40 years
Patent	136,000	January 1, 1980	17 years
Franchise	180,000	January 1, 1981	10 years

1. Record the amortization expense for each of these intangible assets for 1983.
2. Prepare an intangible asset section of the balance sheet for Jeppson Research Institution as of December 31, 1983.

E10–20 Accounting for Intangible Assets (Goodwill)

On January 1, 1983, Wright Company purchased the following assets and liabilities of Brooke Company for $250,000.

	Book Value	Fair Market Value
Inventory	$40,000	$ 50,000
Building	80,000	100,000
Land	50,000	60,000
Accounts receivable	20,000	20,000
Accounts payable	(10,000)	(10,000)

1. Prepare a journal entry to record the purchase of Brooke by Wright Company.
2. Record any amortization of goodwill as of December 31, 1983. (Assume a 40-year amortization period for the goodwill.)

PROBLEMS

P10-1 The Acquisition, Depreciation, and Sale of an Asset

On July 1, 1983, George Meyer bought a used pickup truck at a cost of $2,300 for use in his business. On the same day, Mr. Meyer had the truck painted blue and white (his company's colors) at a cost of $330. Mr. Meyer estimates the life of the truck to be 3 years or 40,000 miles. He further estimates that the truck will have a $400 scrap value at the end of its life, but that it will also cost him $50 to transfer the truck to the junkyard.

Required:

1. Record the following in General Journal form.
   - (a) July 8, 1983 — Paid all bills pertaining to the truck. (No previous entries have been recorded concerning these bills.)
   - (b) Dec. 31, 1983 — The depreciation expense for the year, using the straight-line method.
   - (c) Dec. 31, 1984 — The depreciation expense for 1984, again using the straight-line method.
   - (d) Jan. 2, 1985 — Sold the truck for $2,000 cash.
2. What would the depreciation expense for 1983 have been if the truck had been driven 8,000 miles and the units-of-production method of depreciation had been used?
3. **Interpretive Question** In 1(d), there is a gain of $510. Why did this gain occur?

P10-2 The Acquisition, Depreciation, and Sale of an Asset

On January 2, 1983, Energy Express Oil Company purchased a new airplane. The following costs are related to the purchase.

Airplane—base price	$62,000
Cash discount (if paid prior to 1/31/83)	2,000
Sales tax	4,000
Delivery charges	3,000

Required:

1. In General Journal form, record the payment of these items on January 2, 1983.
2. Ignore your answer to (1) and assume that the airplane cost $50,000 and has an expected useful life of 5 years or 1,500 hours. The estimated salvage value is $5,000. Using each of the following methods, calculate the amount of depreciation expense to be recorded for the second year.
   - (a) Units-of-production (assume that 300 hours are flown in 1984).
   - (b) Sum-of-the-years'-digits.
   - (c) Double-declining-balance.
3. Ignore the information in (1) and (2) and assume that the airplane costs $50,000, that its expected useful life is 5 years, and that its estimated salvage value is $5,000. The company now uses the straight-line depreciation method. On July 1, 1986, the following balances are in the related accounts.

Airplane	$50,000
Accumulated Depreciation—Airplane	27,000

Prepare the necessary journal entries to record the trade-in of this airplane on July 1, 1986, for a smaller airplane with a list price of $20,000. (The cash price was determined to be $17,000.) No additional cash is paid for the new airplane.

4. **Interpretive Question** In (3), why is the new airplane not recorded at $20,000? What effect does the recording of the new airplane at a cost of less than $20,000 have on depreciation charges in subsequent years?

P10-3 Depreciation Calculations

Bigfoot, Inc., a firm that makes oversized boots, purchased a machine for its factory. The following data relate to the machine.

Price	$12,000
Delivery charges	100
Installation charges	500
Date purchased	May 1, 1983
Estimated useful life:	
In years	8 years
In hours of production	14,000 hours of operating time
Salvage value	$1,800

During 1983, the machine was used 1,400 hours. During 1984, the machine was used 2,100 hours.

Required:

Determine the depreciation expense and the year-end book values for the machine for the years 1983 and 1984, assuming that:

1. The straight-line method is used.
2. The double-declining-balance method is used.
3. The units-of-production method is used.
4. The sum-of-the-years'-digits method is used.
5. **Interpretive Question** Which method would you use in order to report the highest profits in 1983 and 1984?

P10–4 Depreciation Calculations

Meredith Manufacturing Corporation reports the following data on its assets at December 31, 1983.

Asset	Cost	Life: Years	Life: Hours	Purchase Date	Salvage Value
Forklift	$11,000	5		5/1/79	$1,000
Drill press	8,000		8,000	6/30/81	-0-
Power tool	5,000	6		12/31/78	800
Power saw	4,000	3		11/1/81	700
Fuel tank	4,000	5		7/1/82	-0-
Converter	7,000		9,000	6/30/80	500
Hydraulic lift	12,000	6		7/1/79	1,500

The company uses SYD depreciation for the forklift and the power tool, units-of-production for the drill press and the converter, straight-line for the power saw, DDB for the fuel tank, and 150 percent declining-balance for the hydraulic lift.

Required:

1. Record the depreciation expense on the assets for 1983. The drill press and the converter are used approximately 2,000 hours per year.
2. Determine the assets' book values at December 31, 1983.

P10–5 The Depreciation and Disposal of an Asset

A truck with an estimated life of 5 years was acquired on January 1, 1983, for $10,800. The estimated salvage value is $1,000 and the service life is estimated to be 140,000 miles. The company's accounting year ends December 31.

Required:

1. Compute the depreciation expense for 1983 and 1984, using the following four methods.
   (a) Straight-line.
   (b) Sum-of-the-years'-digits.
   (c) Double-declining-balance.
   (d) Units-of-production, given 20,000 miles in 1983 and 30,000 miles in 1984.
2. A machine that cost $54,000 has an estimated useful life of 7 years and a salvage value of $5,000. Journalize the disposal of the machine under each of the following conditions (assume straight-line depreciation).
   (a) Sold the machine for $42,000 cash after 2 years.
   (b) Sold the machine for $18,000 cash after 5 years.
   (c) After 3 years traded the machine for a similar new one that had a fair market value of $57,000. A trade-in allowance of $20,000 was received.
3. **Interpretive Question** Why is the loss on the trade-in in question 2(c) recognized? If only $5,000 cash had been paid, would a gain have been recognized?

P10–6 Changes in Depreciation Estimates, and Capitalized Expenditures

Gunther Metal Products, Inc. acquired a machine on January 2, 1981, for $96,680. The useful life of the machine was estimated to be 8 years with a residual value of $4,600. Depreciation was recorded each year on December 31 using the straight-line method.

In 1983, the company revised its estimate of the useful life of the machine from 8 to 6 years, and the scrap value from $4,600 to $2,600. On January 2, 1986, major repairs on the machine cost the company $34,000. The repairs added 2 years to the machine's useful life.

Required:
Give the necessary journal entries to record the purchase of the machine, the major expenditure in 1986, and the annual depreciation expense for the years 1981 to 1988. Record the journal entries in chronological sequence.

P10–7 Changes in Depreciation Estimates

On January 1, 1977, Woodfield Trucking Company purchased two new trucks at a total cost of $225,000. It was estimated that each truck would have a useful life of 8 years and a salvage value of $4,500. Woodfield uses the SYD method of depreciation for all of its equipment.

Required:

1. Record the purchase of the trucks on January 1, 1977.
2. Record the depreciation expense on the trucks for 1982.
3. Assume that during 1983 the company realized that the trucks would last 4 more years instead of 2 but that they would still have the same salvage value. Record the revised depreciation expense on the trucks for 1983.
4. Make the necessary entry to record the sale of one of the trucks on December 31, 1983, for $10,000. (Assume that the two trucks had an equal cost.)
5. **Interpretive Question** How much depreciation expense would be recorded on the second truck during 1989 if it were still being used and if its estimated salvage value was still $4,500? Why?

P10–8 Unifying Problem: Property, Plant, and Equipment

Sherwood Corporation owns and operates three sawmills that make lumber for building homes. The operations consist of cutting logs in the forest, hauling them to the various sawmills, sawing the lumber, and shipping it to building supply warehouses throughout the western part of the United States. To haul the logs, Sherwood has several trucks. Relevant data pertaining to one truck are:

a. Date of purchase: July 1, 1981

b. Cost:

Truck	$60,000
Trailer	20,000
Paint job (to match company colors)	1,500
Sales tax	3,500

c. Estimated useful life of the truck: 150,000 miles

d. Estimated salvage value: Zero

e. 1982 expenditures on the truck:

(1) Spent $5,000 on tires, oil changes, greasing, and other miscellaneous items.

(2) Spent $22,000 to overhaul the engine, replace the brakes, and replace the gears on January 1, 1982. This expenditure increased the life of the truck by 135,000 miles.

f. Exchanged the truck on April 1, 1983, for a new truck with a fair market value of $90,000. The old truck was driven 20,000 miles in 1983. A payment of $30,000 was made on the exchange.

Required:

Record journal entries to account for:

1. The purchase of the truck.
2. The 1981 depreciation expense using units-of-production depreciation and assuming the truck was driven 45,000 miles.
3. The expenditures relating to the truck during 1982.
4. The 1982 depreciation expense using the units-of-production method and assuming the truck was driven 60,000 miles.
5. The exchange of the truck on April 1, 1983.

P10–9 Unifying Problem: Accounting for Natural Resources

Wilderness Associates buys and develops natural resources for profit. Since 1982, it has had the following activities.

1/1/82	Purchased for $800,000 a tract of timber estimated to contain 1,600,000 board feet of lumber.
1/1/83	Purchased for $600,000 a silver mine estimated to contain 30,000 tons of silver.
7/1/83	Purchased for $60,000 a uranium mine estimated to contain 5,000 tons of uranium.
1/1/84	Purchased for $500,000 an oil well estimated to contain 100,000 barrels of oil.

Required:

1. Provide the necessary journal entries to account for the following.

(a) The purchase of these assets.

(b) The depletion expense for 1984 on all four assets, assuming that the following were extracted.

(1) 200,000 board feet of lumber

(2) 5,000 tons of silver

(3) 1,000 tons of uranium

(4) 10,000 barrels of oil

2. Assume that on January 1, 1985, after 20,000 tons of silver had been mined, engineers' estimates revealed that only 4,000 tons of silver remained. Record the depletion expense for 1985, assuming that 2,000 tons were mined.

3. Compute the book values of all four assets as of December 31, 1985, assuming that the total extracted to date is:

(a) Timber tract—800,000 board feet.

(b) Silver mine—22,000 tons [only 2,000 tons left per part (2)].

(c) Uranium mine—3,000 tons.

(d) Oil well—80,000 barrels.

P10–10 Unifying Problem: Accounting for Intangible Assets

R&D Nightclub owns several intangible assets:

a. A patent on a combination cash register–drink mixer that shows various mixed drinks instead of dollar amounts on its keys. When the key for a certain drink is pushed, that drink is automatically mixed and an amount equal to the cost of the drink must be deposited in the cash register. This patent, which cost $90,000 on July 1, 1982, is valuable because it makes it almost impossible for bartenders to steal. The patent had a remaining life of 15 years when purchased.

b. A franchise that provides R&D with the exclusive right to sell Highlight Beer in the eastern part of the United States. This franchise cost $10,000 on January 1, 1981, at which time it had a life of 10 years.

c. Goodwill was purchased with the nightclub on December 30, 1962, for $40,000 and is being amortized over 40 years.

d. A license to sell liquor, which originally cost $6,500 on January 1, 1980, and had a 13-year life.

Required:

1. Make the journal entries to record the acquisition of these four intangible assets. (Assume that the goodwill was paid for separately at the time the company was purchased.)
2. Record the amortization expense on the four intangible assets for 1983.
3. Compute the book values of the four intangibles at December 31, 1983.

CHAPTER 11

Short- and Long-Term Investments

THIS CHAPTER EXPLAINS:

The nature of investments.
Accounting for short-term investments.
Accounting for long-term investments in stocks.
Accounting for long-term investments in bonds.

In order to sell goods or services, a company must usually purchase operational assets, either current assets, like inventories, or long-term assets, such as land, buildings, and equipment. A business may also find it advantageous to invest a portion of its available resources in assets not directly related to its primary operations. These may be long-term investments in assets that are expected to contribute to the success of the firm—for example, purchasing the business of a key supplier. Or they may be long-term investments that independently contribute to earnings. And sometimes they are short-term investments that make use of temporarily idle funds.

investment *an expenditure to acquire assets that are expected to produce future earnings*

In general, the higher the potential return on an investment, the riskier the investment. Exhibit 11-1 on page 366 shows in a general way how this relationship applies to a few types of investments.

The investments shown in Exhibit 11-1 can be either short-term or long-term, depending on how long management intends to hold them. Certainly, a wise investment would be a relatively short-term one that provides both low risk and a high return. (In past years, real estate has often been such an investment.) In this chapter, both short- and long-term investments are discussed.

EXHIBIT 11-1 **A Classification of Investments by Risk and Potential Return**[1]

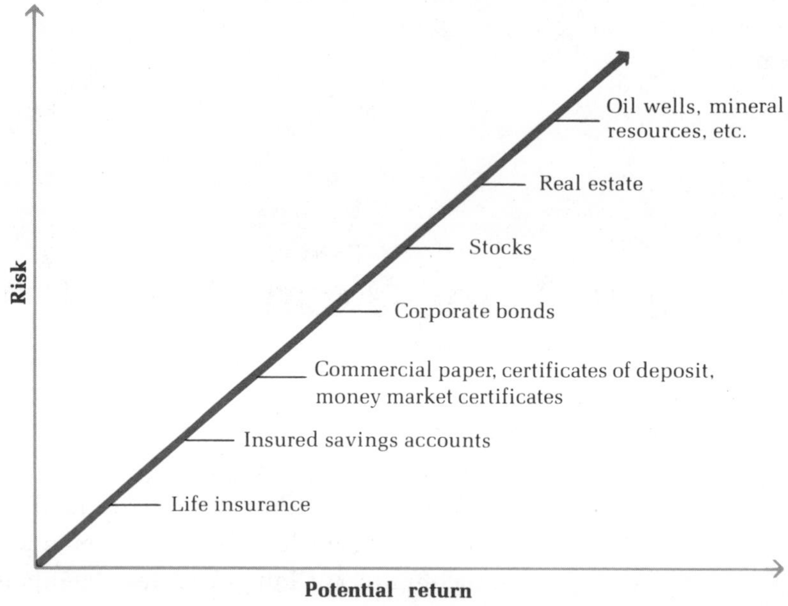

[1] The levels of risk and return of these investments are far less predictable than this graph might lead you to believe. In fact, the order shown here often changes. In the last few years, for example, money market certificates have paid higher earnings than many stocks and bonds.

Short-Term Investments

Most businesses are cyclical or seasonal; that is, their cash inflows and outflows vary significantly throughout the year. At certain times (particularly when inventories are being purchased), a company's cash supply is low. At other times (usually during or shortly after heavy selling seasons), there is excess cash on hand. An example of a cash flow pattern for a firm is shown in Exhibit 11-2.

line of credit *an arrangement whereby a bank agrees to loan an amount of money (up to a certain limit) on demand for short periods of time, usually less than a year*

To ensure that there is always cash available to meet current obligations, most firms have a line of credit with their bank. Such an arrangement allows a company to borrow on demand up to a certain amount of cash on a short-term basis—usually for less than a year. Having a line of credit allows companies to maintain only enough cash on hand to meet their average cash needs. A credit line thus enables firms to invest in long-term high-income-yielding investments when operations generate funds in excess of average cash needs.

Even though a profitable company will try to keep a minimum of cash on hand, it will usually have excess cash at least sometime during a year.

EXHIBIT 11-2 **A Cash Flow Pattern**

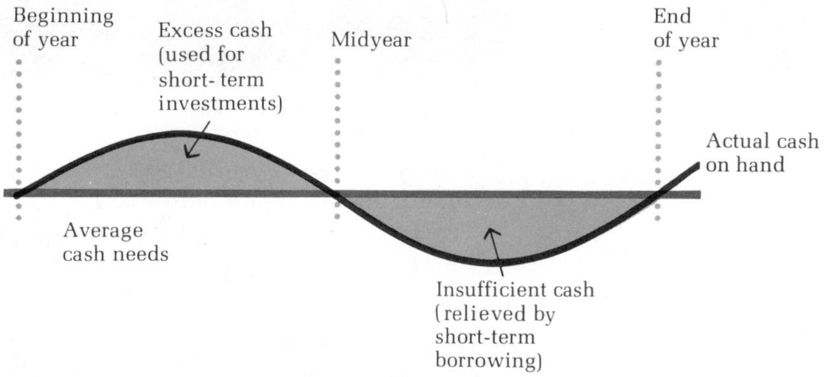

short-term investments *expenditures for nonoperational assets that a business intends to hold for a short period of time, usually less than a year*

Because money has a time value and can earn a return, these temporary excesses of cash are usually invested, in some cases for as short a time as three or four days. Typical short-term investments include stocks and bonds of other companies, commercial paper, certificates of deposit, money market funds, savings accounts, government bonds (long-term), and treasury bills (short-term). Both commercial paper and certificates of deposit are investment contracts at guaranteed interest rates for specific periods; the former are short-term and are issued by companies and the latter are long-term and are issued by financial institutions. Money market funds contain a variety of short-term securities; thus, their interest rates vary each week, depending on the market rate of interest and the investments purchased by the fund.

Also referred to as marketable securities, short-term investments are classified as current assets because of their extreme liquidity, which means that they can be readily sold for cash at any time (although an early withdrawal penalty may be assessed). Investments must be properly classified as either short-term or long-term because there are important differences in accounting for them. Note also that there are two categories of marketable securities: debt and equity. Debt refers primarily to bond investments and equity refers to stocks.

ACCOUNTING FOR SHORT-TERM INVESTMENTS

Short-term investments, like all other assets, are recorded at cost when purchased. For accounting purposes, cost includes the market price of the asset plus any extra expenditures required in making the purchase (such as a stockbroker's fee).

To illustrate, we will assume that during a period of excess cash, Bicknell Incorporated has purchased 100 shares of Mohawk stock at $171 per share and has paid a broker's commission of $500. The entry to record the investment would be as shown on the next page.

Short-Term Investments—Mohawk Stock	17,600	
Cash		17,600

Purchased 100 shares of Mohawk stock as a short-term investment at $171 per share plus $500 in commissions.

Obviously, Bicknell's managers invested in Mohawk because they thought the stock would earn a good return. Such returns are earned either from dividends or through a gain made on the sale of the stock.

The accounting entry for the receipt of a quarterly dividend of $1.40 per share of Mohawk's stock would be

Cash	140	
Dividend Revenue		140

Received dividends on the investment in Mohawk stock.

The entry to account for a gain on the sale of Mohawk stock for $185 per share, less a $300 commission, would be

Cash	18,200	
Short-Term Investment—Mohawk Stock		17,600
Gain on Sale of Short-Term Investments		600

Sold 100 shares of Mohawk stock at $185 per share, less a $300 sales commission.

In this case, the market price at the time of the sale is $185 per share but the company only receives $18,200 because a sales commission of $300 must be paid. Note that the increase in market price (to $185) above the cost of the stock ($171) is not recognized until the stock is actually sold.

The last entry, Gain on Sale of Short-Term Investments, would be included on the income statement with Other Revenues and Expenses. The investment has been written off and the proceeds are included in Cash on the balance sheet. Accounting for investments in bonds or commercial paper is the same as for stock.

VALUING SHORT-TERM INVESTMENTS AT LOWER OF COST OR MARKET

lower of cost or market (LCM) *a basis for valuing certain assets at the lower of original cost or market value (current replacement cost)*

Short-term investments are initially recorded at cost and are never written up to recognize increases in market prices until they are sold. On the other hand, when investments in marketable equity (stock) securities drop below their original costs, they must be written down to market value. This practice of recording short-term investments at the lower of cost or market (LCM) represents an important departure from the usual procedure of reporting assets at cost. Technically, only marketable equity securities must be reported at the lower of cost or market; however, this procedure is appropriate and followed by many companies for all marketable securities, whether equity or debt. In this book, we will apply the lower-of-cost-or-market rule to all marketable securities.

In deciding whether short-term investments should be written down, a company should consider all marketable securities (its entire portfolio) as a unit. When the selling price of one particular stock investment drops below its original cost, it is not written down if the market value of the company's total portfolio of all short-term marketable securities is still equal to or greater than the original cost.

To illustrate, we will assume that Bicknell's portfolio of short-term investments includes the following.

	Cost	Market	Unrealized Gain (or Loss)
Common stock of Mohawk Company	$17,600	$18,500	$ 900
U.S. Government bonds	21,000	19,000	(2,000)
Bonds of MMM Company	26,500	25,000	(1,500)
Other marketable securities	13,200	14,100	900
Total	$78,300	$76,600	($1,700)

Because the aggregate portfolio's market value is $1,700 less than its aggregate original cost, short-term investments should be written down to $76,600. The entry to recognize this loss is

Loss on Short-Term Investments	1,700	
Allowance to Reduce Short-Term Investments to LCM		1,700
To reduce short-term investments to lower of cost or market ($78,300 − $76,600).		

Loss on Short-Term Investments[2] appears on the income statement under Other Revenues and Expenses, and Allowance to Reduce Short-Term Investments to LCM is a contra-short-term investments account on the balance sheet.

If the market prices of previously written-down short-term investments subsequently rise above cost, such investments should be written back up to, but never to more than, their original cost. However, because these investments are usually held only for short periods of time, such subsequent adjustments are seldom necessary.

TO SUMMARIZE Short-term investments are extremely liquid, so they are listed just below Cash on the balance sheet. Revenue from short-term investments usually takes the form of dividends, interest, or gains when selling the investments and is included under Other Revenues and Expenses on the income statement. Short-term marketable securities should be written down to the lower of cost or market if the market value of the company's total portfolio drops below cost.

[2] Losses incurred in writing down short-term investments to a market price that is lower than cost are not deductible for tax purposes.

Long-Term Investments

long-term investments *expenditures to acquire nonoperational assets that are expected to be owned for longer than a year or the normal operating cycle*

There are many types of long-term investments, including real estate, life insurance, and corporate stocks and bonds. Real estate and life insurance investments are initially recorded at cost, and gains and losses are recognized upon sale or maturity. The accounting for long-term investments in stocks and bonds is more complex, and is therefore the focus of this section.

ACCOUNTING FOR LONG-TERM INVESTMENTS IN STOCKS

Like short-term investments, long-term investments in stocks (equity securities) are initially accounted for on a cost basis. That is, the total amount paid to acquire stock (market price plus commission) is recognized as the cost of the long-term investment.

To illustrate, we assume that Lyman Incorporated purchases 300 shares of Davis Company stock at $10 a share as a long-term investment. In addition, Lyman pays $200 in commissions. The entry to record the long-term investment would be

Long-Term Investment—Davis Stock	3,200	
Cash		3,200
Purchased 300 shares of Davis stock [(300 × $10) + $200 commission].		

There are several reasons for a company to purchase the stock of another company on a long-term basis. The two most common reasons are

1. To receive the dividends paid on the stock (and, ideally, to realize additional earnings when the stock is eventually sold).
2. To purchase a significant or controlling interest in another company.

subsidiary company *a company owned or controlled by another company, known as the parent company*

parent company *a company that owns or maintains control over other companies, known as subsidiaries, which are themselves separate legal entities*

consolidated financial statements *statements that show the operating results and financial position of two or more legally separate but affiliated companies as if they were one economic entity*

If a company owns over 50 percent of the outstanding stock of another company, a controlling interest obviously exists. The company that is owned and controlled is called the subsidiary company, or just the subsidiary, and the company exercising the ownership and control is called the parent company. In such cases, the companies' financial statements are usually combined as consolidated financial statements. (See the Supplement to Chapters 6 through 15 on pages 538–555 for a discussion of the accounting involved in preparing consolidated statements.)

If a company owns less than 50 percent of the outstanding stock of another company, a controlling interest does not exist. There are two alternative methods of accounting for such long-term investments: cost and equity. Exhibit 11-3 outlines the circumstances that determine when the cost and equity methods of accounting for long-term stock investments should be used.

EXHIBIT 11-3 **The Cost and Equity Methods of Accounting for Long-Term Investments in Stocks**

Accounting Method	Circumstances
Cost	The cost method is to be used when the number of shares of stock owned is so small that the investor can exercise *no significant influence on or control over* the company. The inability to exercise influence or control is presumed to exist if an investor owns less than 20 percent of the outstanding voting stock.
Equity	The equity method is to be used when one company's investment in the stock of another company is large enough that the investor can exercise a *significant influence* on the operations of that company. The ability to exercise significant influence is presumed to exist if an investor owns at least 20 percent but no more than 50 percent of the outstanding voting stock of another company. (A controlling interest exists if over 50 percent is owned; this generally requires the use of consolidated financial statements.)

The Cost Method

cost method of accounting for investments in stocks *accounting for an investment in another company where less than 20 percent of the outstanding voting stock is owned, by recording the initial acquisition at cost and recognizing dividends as revenue earned*

The cost method of accounting for long-term investments in the stock of other companies is essentially the same as the method used in accounting for short-term equity investments. That is, the original investment is recorded at cost; dividends received are recognized as earned revenue; and the investment is carried on a lower-of-cost-or-market basis. Generally, if the market value of a company's portfolio of long-term equity investments falls below its original cost, the long-term investments are written down to the market value. The entry to recognize the lower market price, however, is different from the one used to write down short-term investments. With arbitrary numbers, it would be

Unrealized Loss on Long-Term Investments	8,000	
Allowance to Reduce Long-Term Investments to Market		8,000
To recognize long-term investments at lower of cost or market.		

The debit entry Unrealized Loss on Long-Term Investments is a contra-owners' equity (balance sheet) account and the credit entry Allowance to Reduce Long-Term Investments to Market is a contra–long-term investment (balance sheet) account. Since neither account appears on the income statement (unlike Loss on Short-Term Investments), there is no loss recognized when the market price of long-term investments drops below cost.[3]

[3] However, if the decline in the market value of a long-term equity security is judged to be other than temporary, the cost basis should be written down and the write-down should be recorded as a loss on the income statement. In such cases, the new cost basis is not to be changed for subsequent increases in market value. As with short-term equity securities, such losses are not deductible for tax purposes.

The rationale for not taking these declines into current income is that the investments will be held for a long time and the price may rise and fall several times before the stock is sold.

As was the case with short-term investments, if the market price of a written-down portfolio of long-term investments subsequently rises, it should be written up to the new market price, as long as that price does not exceed the original cost. Under no circumstances are investments written up to a market price that exceeds cost. The entry to recognize a subsequent recovery in the market price of long-term investments that have previously been written down is the reverse of the previous entry. With arbitrary numbers, the entry would be

Allowance to Reduce Long-Term Investments to Market	4,000	
Unrealized Loss on Long-Term Investments		4,000
To recognize partial recovery in the market price of long-term investments.		

With the cost method, no adjustment is made by the investing company (investor) when the company invested in (investee) has earnings. The equity method does call for such an adjustment, as we shall see.

The Equity Method

When a stock investment involves significant influence (usually 20 to 50 percent ownership), it is presumed that the investor can affect the timing and extent of dividend payments by the investee. If the cost method were permitted, the investor would be allowed to report revenues when dividends were received and so could increase its income by putting pressure on the investee to pay larger and more frequent dividends. Because of this potential for abuse, where significant influence exists the equity method is required.

equity method of accounting for investments in stocks *accounting for an investment in another company where significant influence can be imposed (presumed to exist when 20 to 50 percent of the outstanding voting stock is owned), by recording the initial acquisition at cost and recognizing (1) dividends as a return of investment and (2) its share of earnings as revenue that increases the book value of the investment*

Under the equity method, dividend payments represent a return of investment; they do not represent revenue, as they do with the cost method. Revenue *is* recognized when the investee company has earnings. When earnings are announced, the book value of the investment is increased because the investor owns a fixed percentage of a company that is worth more now than it was when the investment was originally made.

In accounting for investments with the equity method, the original investment is first recorded on the books at cost and is subsequently modified to reflect the investor's share of the investee's reported incomes and losses. In this way, book value is increased to recognize the investor's share of earnings and decreased by the dividends received or to recognize the investor's share of losses. Unless a permanent decline in the value of an investment is considered to have occurred, the lower-of-cost-or-market rule is not applied under the equity method.

There is one exception to the rule that the equity method must be used when 20 to 50 percent of an investee's stock is owned. If the purchased stock does not carry with it voting rights in the company, the investment is accounted for with the cost method, no matter what the percentage of ownership. The reason the cost method is used in these circumstances is that a nonvoting investor has little or no influence on the operating and dividend policies of an investee.

When a stock investment is sold, any proceeds that exceed its book value (under either the cost or equity method) are recognized as a gain. With arbitrary numbers, the entry to record the sale of a stock held as a long-term investment would be

Cash	10,000	
Long-Term Investment		9,000
Gain on Sale of Investment		1,000
Sold long-term investments at more than book value.		

To illustrate the cost and equity methods of accounting for long-term investments in stock, we will assume that Loa Corporation plans to purchase some stock in Blue Ridge Company. Blue Ridge has 1,000 shares of outstanding stock, currently selling at $10 a share. The accounting for the purchase of shares of stock would be as shown in Exhibit 11-4 (assuming that no commissions are paid).

EXHIBIT 11-4 **Long-Term Investments in Stock**

	Cost Method			Equity Method		
Event:	*Loa purchases 150 shares of Blue Ridge Company stock (15% ownership):*			*Loa purchases 400 shares of Blue Ridge Company stock (40% ownership):*		
The initial purchase	Investment in Blue Ridge Stock . .	1,500		Investment in Blue Ridge Stock . .	4,000	
	Cash		1,500	Cash		4,000
	Purchased 150 shares of Blue Ridge Company stock (15% ownership).			*Purchased 400 shares of Blue Ridge Company stock (40% ownership).*		
Payment of an 80¢-per-share dividend by Blue Ridge Company	Cash	120		Cash	320	
	Dividend Revenue—Blue Ridge Stock		120	Investment in Blue Ridge Stock		320
	Received 80¢-per-share dividend from Blue Ridge Company.			*Received 80¢-per-share dividend from Blue Ridge Company.*		
Announcement by Blue Ridge Company of earnings of $6,000 for the year	No entry			Investment in Blue Ridge Stock . .	2,400	
				Revenue from Investments		2,400
				To recognize share of Blue Ridge Company earnings for the year (40% of $6,000).		

TO SUMMARIZE All long-term investments in stock are initially accounted for on a cost basis. However, because different levels of investment provide different degrees of influence over investee companies, two methods of accounting for long-term stock investments are used. If an investor company owns less than 20 percent of the voting stock of another company, the cost method is generally used. With the cost method, revenue is recognized when dividends are received, and the investment is accounted for at the lower of cost or market. (Note that when long-term investments are written down to the lower of cost or market, the adjustment reduces owners' equity and investments; it does not affect the income statement. This is not true of short-term investments.) When the percentage of outstanding voting stock owned is sufficient to exercise significant influence (as is usually true with ownership of 20 to 50 percent), the equity method is used. This method involves increasing the book value of the investment for earnings and decreasing it for losses and dividends.

LONG-TERM INVESTMENTS IN BONDS

bond *a certificate of debt issued by a company or government agency guaranteeing a stated rate of interest and payment of the original investment by a specified future date; usually issued in units of $1,000*

Another common type of long-term investment is a bond. Essentially, bonds are long-term borrowings by a company or government agency. For example, in order to raise money to build new schools, school districts often sell bonds to the public. Similarly, corporations issue bonds to finance plant expansions or for other reasons. A typical bond is shown in Exhibit 11-5.

EXHIBIT 11-5 **A Sample Bond with Coupons**

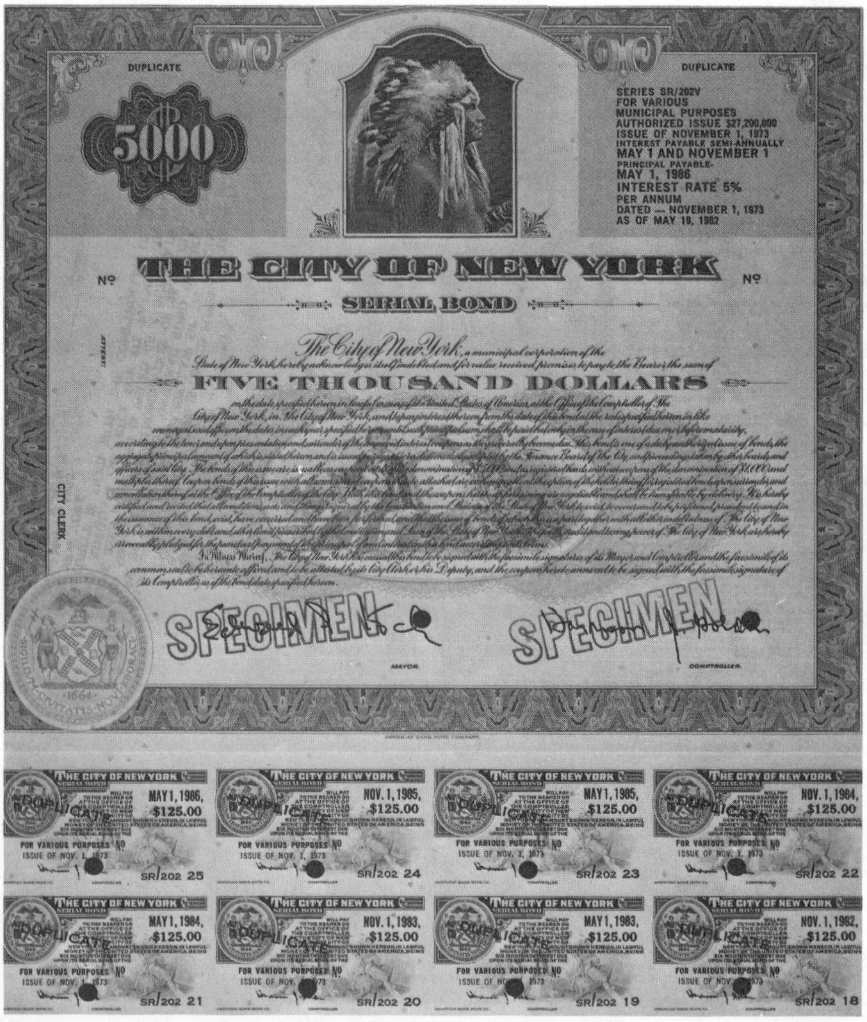

Types of Bonds

Bonds can be categorized on the basis of certain characteristics. A three-way classification system is

1. On the basis of whether the bonds are secured:
   (a) *Debentures or unsecured bonds.* Bonds that have no underlying security, such as a mortgage or pledge of assets, as a guarantee of their repayment.
   (b) *Secured bonds.* Bonds that have a pledge of assets as a guarantee of their repayment.
2. On the basis of how the bond interest is paid:
   (a) *Registered bonds.* Bonds for which the issuing company keeps a file of the names and addresses of all bondholders and pays interest only to those individuals whose names are on file.
   (b) *Coupon bonds.* Bonds for which the issuer has no record of current bondholders but instead pays interest to anyone who can show evidence of ownership. Usually, these bonds contain a printed coupon for each interest payment. When a payment is due, the bondholder clips the coupon from the certificate and sends it to the issuer as evidence of bond ownership. The issuer then sends an interest payment to the bondholder.
3. On the basis of how the bonds mature:
   (a) *Term bonds.* Bonds that mature in one lump sum on a specified future date.
   (b) *Serial bonds.* Bonds that mature in a series of installments.
   (c) *Callable bonds.* Term or serial bonds that the issuer can redeem at any time at a specified price.
   (d) *Convertible bonds.* Term or serial bonds that can be converted to other securities, such as stocks, after a specified period, at the option of the bondholder.

debentures *bonds for which no collateral has been pledged*

secured bonds *bonds for which assets have been pledged in order to guarantee repayment*

registered bonds *bonds for which the names and addresses of the bondholders are kept on file by the issuing company*

coupon bonds *bonds for which owners receive periodic interest payments by clipping a coupon from the bond and sending it to the issuer as evidence of ownership*

term bonds *bonds that mature in one lump sum at a specified future date*

serial bonds *bonds that mature in a series of installments at specified future dates*

callable bonds *bonds for which the issuer reserves the right to pay the obligation before its maturity date*

convertible bonds *bonds that can be traded for or converted to capital stock after a specified period of time*

Characteristics of Bonds

When an organization issues bonds, it usually sells them to underwriters (bondbrokers and investment bankers), who in turn sell them to various institutions and to the public. At the time of the original sale, the company issuing the bonds chooses a trustee to represent the bondholders. In most cases, the trustee is a large bank or trust company to which the company issuing bonds delivers a contract that provides security for the bonds. This contract, which is called a deed of trust, bond indenture, or trust indenture, specifies that in return for an investment of cash by investors, the company promises to pay a specific amount of interest each period the bonds are outstanding and to repay the principal (also called face, or maturity, value) of the bonds at a specified future date (the maturity date). It is the duty of the trustee to protect investors and to make sure that the bond issuer fulfills its responsibilities.

bond indenture *a contract between a bond issuer and a bond purchaser that specifies the terms of a bond*

interest *the amount charged for using money*

principal (face value or maturity value) *the amount that will be paid on a bond at the maturity date*

bond maturity date *the date at which a bond principal or face amount becomes payable*

The total value of a single "bond issue" often exceeds several million dollars. A bond issue is generally divided into a number of individual bonds, which may be of varying denominations. Usually, the principal of each bond is $1,000, or a multiple thereof. By issuing bonds in small denominations, a company increases the chances that a broad range of investors will be able to compete for the purchase of the bonds. This increased demand usually results in the bonds selling for higher prices.

Like stocks, bonds are traded on major exchanges and their prices fluctuate from day to day. Investors often find it profitable to sell bonds before their maturity dates. Thus, there are two ways of earning a return on an investment in bonds: (1) by receiving the periodic interest payments made on the bonds, and (2) by selling the bonds at a profit.

The market price of bonds in most cases is influenced by (1) the riskiness of the bonds and (2) the interest rate at which the bonds are issued. The first factor, riskiness of the bonds, is determined by general economic conditions and the financial status of the company selling the bonds, as measured by organizations (Moody's or Standard and Poor's, for instance) that regularly assign a rating, or a grade, to all corporate bonds.

Companies strive to earn as high a bond rating as possible because the higher the rating, the lower the interest rate they will have to pay to attract buyers. A high-risk bond, on the other hand, will have a low rating, which means the company will have to offer a higher rate of interest to attract buyers.

market rate of interest *the prevailing interest rate in the marketplace for certain categories and grades of securities*

bond premium *the difference between the face value and the sales price of a bond when it is sold above its face value*

bond discount *the difference between the face value and the sales price of a bond when it is sold below its face value*

Interest rates affect the market prices of bonds according to the following general rule: If the stated interest rate of a particular bond is higher than the current market interest rate for similar investments (bonds with identical ratings, for example), the bond will sell at a premium, which means that its market price will be above its face value. If the interest rate on the bond is lower than the prevailing market rate for equivalent investments, the bond will sell at a discount, and its market price will be less than its face value.

Once bonds have been issued and their stated interest rates (and interest payments) have been fixed, their prices usually increase when market interest rates fall and decrease when market interest rates rise. For example, a 10 percent, $1,000, 10-year bond may sell at a price of $887 while the market rate of interest for 10-year bonds at the same rating is 12 percent, but the price may increase to $1,134 if the market interest rate drops to 8 percent. To see why this happens, assume the following: You own a 10 percent bond but have an opportunity to buy a 12 percent bond with a similar risk rating. If you, along with many other investors, decide to sell the former and buy the latter, the price of the 10 percent bond is very likely to drop and the price of the 12 percent bond is likely to increase.

Incidentally, the price paid for a bond is usually expressed as a percentage of the face value. For example, if $980 is paid for a $1,000 bond, the bond is said to have been purchased "at 98." Likewise, if $1,020 is paid for a $1,000 bond, it was purchased at 102.

TO SUMMARIZE Bonds can be classified by their level of security (debentures versus secured bonds), by the way interest is paid (registered versus coupon bonds), and by the way they mature (term bonds, callable bonds, serial bonds, and convertible bonds).

When bonds are sold, a bond indenture is written. It specifies the amount of interest to be paid bondholders each period and the amount of principal to be paid at the maturity date. Depending on the market rate of interest for similar bonds, a bond may be sold at a premium or at a discount.

Components of a Bond Investment

When a company invests in bonds, it is essentially purchasing two elements: (1) the right to receive interest payments of a fixed amount at equal intervals over the life of the bond, and (2) the right to receive a fixed sum—the principal, or face value, of the bond—at the maturity date. For example, suppose that Torrey Company plans to purchase twenty $1,000 bonds of Sunglow Company. If the bonds mature in 5 years and pay annual interest of 12 percent with payments every 6 months, Torrey would be buying the right to receive two $1,200 interest payments each year ($20,000 × 0.12 × $\frac{1}{2}$ year) plus one payment of $20,000 when the bonds mature. The following diagram shows how this would work.

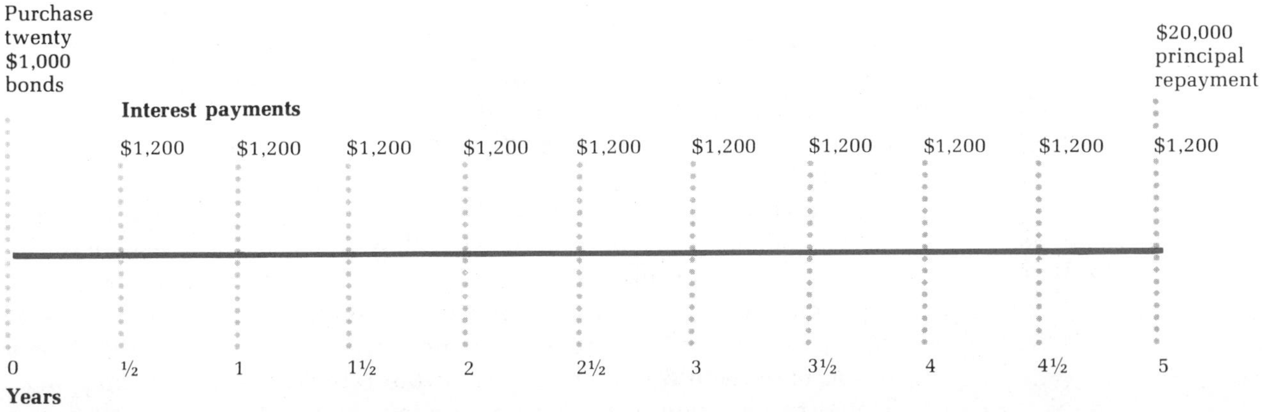

Assuming that Torrey paid $17,316 for the bonds, at the end of the 5 years the company would have earned $14,684, as calculated below.

Maturity Value	$20,000
10 Interest Payments	12,000
Total Amount Received	$32,000
Amount Paid	17,316
Total Revenue Earned	$14,684

Although $14,684 appears to be a good return on the investment, we must consider that the money will be received over a 5-year period. Since money paid today could, at no risk, be placed in a savings account where it would earn interest, an amount received in the future is not worth as much as the same amount received today. In order to determine the real return from the bond investment, money paid and received in different time periods must be equated. The concept of present value is used to measure the effect of time on the value of money.

The Present Value Concept

present value of $1 *the value today of $1 to be received at some future date, given a specified interest rate*

The present value of $1 is the value today of $1 to be received in the future, given a specified interest rate. Present value tells investors how much they should be willing to pay now for money to be received in the future. Obviously, money to be received in the future cannot earn interest between now and then, so it is worth less than money in hand, which can earn interest. To determine how much money received in the future is worth today, it must be discounted by an appropriate interest rate. We find, for example, that if money can earn 10 percent, \$100 to be received 1 year from now is approximately equal to \$90.91 paid today [\$90.91 + (\$90.91 × 0.10) = \$100]. Thus, we say that the present value of \$100 to be received in 1 year at a 10 percent interest rate is \$90.91.

The calculation for deriving the present value of \$100 for 1 year is fairly simple. However, if more than 1 year or 1 period is involved, the calculations become more complicated. Therefore, it is convenient to use a table that reports the present value of \$1 for varying periods and interest rates (see Table I, page 395). To find the present value of an amount other than \$1, you merely multiply the factor in the table by the amount to be received in the future.

To illustrate the use of the present value table, we will assume that an investment will pay \$10,000 in 4 years. If the prevailing interest rate is 14 percent, how much should be paid for the investment today? From the table, the present value factor of \$1 received in 4 periods at 14 percent interest is \$0.5921. Multiplying \$10,000 by this factor gives us a present value of \$5,921.

compounding period *the period of time for which interest is calculated*

A warning is in order here. The examples thus far have assumed an annual compounding period for interest, so the number of years has been in a 1-to-1 ratio with the number of periods. If the 14 percent for the 4-year investment had been compounded semiannually—that is, if the interest had been paid twice a year rather than once a year—the number of periods used in the table would have been 8, and the rate would have been 7 percent. Since interest may also be compounded quarterly, monthly, or for some other period, you should learn the relationship of interest to the compounding period. Semiannual interest means that you double the interest periods and halve the annual interest rate; with quarterly interest you quadruple the periods and take one-fourth of the annual interest rate. The formula for interest rate is

$$\frac{\text{yearly interest rate}}{\text{compounding periods per year}} = \begin{array}{c}\text{interest rate per}\\ \text{compounding period}\end{array}$$

The number of interest periods is simply the number of periods per year times the number of years.

The Present Value of an Annuity

annuity *a series of equal amounts to be received or paid at the ends of equal time intervals*

present value of an annuity of \$1 *the value today of a series of equally spaced payments of \$1 to be made or received in the future, given a specified interest, or discount, rate*

The discussion of present values has so far assumed only a single, or lump-sum, payment or receipt of money at a specified future date. However, as noted earlier, an investment in bonds provides two elements: a series of interest payments and the payment of the face value when the bond matures. The payment of the face value is a lump-sum payment, so the present value concept already discussed can be used to compute its value today. However, determining the value today of a series of equally spaced, equal-amount interest payments (called an annuity) is more complicated and requires a different type of calculation. If you were to try to calculate the present value of an annuity by hand, you would have to discount the first interest payment for one period, the second interest payment for two periods, and so on, and then add all the present values together.

Such calculations are obviously time-consuming. So, a table for determining the present value of an annuity has been developed (see page 395). Based on the present value of an annuity of $1, the table provides for varying interest rates and periods. To demonstrate how to use the table, we will assume that an investment will pay $10,000 at the end of each of 10 years. If the interest rate is 12 percent compounded annually, Table II on page 395 shows that the present value of the ten $10,000 payments is $56,502 (5.6502 × $10,000). Similarly, this table may be used to determine how much should be paid for an investment if the desired return is 16 percent. If an investment is to pay $10,000 per year for 5 years, how much should a company pay for it? Using the factor for 16 percent and 5 periods in Table II, the company determines that it should pay no more than $32,743 (3.2743 × $10,000) if it wants to earn 16 percent.

TO SUMMARIZE Present value concepts are used to equate the value of money received or paid in different periods. If a lump-sum payment is involved, Table I should be used. If a series of equal payments is involved, it is an annuity and Table II should be used. In calculating present values, you must consider the compounding period and the interest rate. For other than annual payments, the number of periods is the number of periods per year times the number of years; the interest rate is the annual rate divided by the number of periods in a year.

Determining the Price to Pay for Bonds

With a knowledge of present values, you can now determine how much a company should pay for bonds. Referring to the earlier example of the $20,000, 12 percent, 5-year bonds of Sunglow Company, Torrey would be purchasing 10 semiannual payments of $1,200 each ($20,000 × 0.12 × ½ year) and a lump-sum payment of $20,000 (the maturity value) at the end of the 5 years.

In calculating how much to pay for this investment, Torrey must decide what rate of return it wants to earn. For example, let's assume that Torrey needs 16 percent interest to justify the investment. The purchase price Torrey should pay may be obtained by adding the present value of $20,000 (received 10 periods in the future and discounted at 8 percent) to the present value of the annuity of the 10 interest payments of $1,200 each (discounted at 8 percent). The reason for the use of 8 percent is that interest is received semiannually; recall that in calculating present value you must halve the interest rate (16 percent ÷ 2) for semiannual compounding periods. Likewise, you must double the number of years to determine the number of periods (5 years × 2 periods per year = 10 periods). The calculations are

Semiannual interest payment →	$1,200	$20,000	← Maturity value of bonds
Present value of an annuity of 10 payments of $1 at 8%—Table II	→× 6.7101	× 0.4632	← Present value of $1 received 10 periods in the future and discounted at 8%—Table I
	$8,052	$9,264	
	$17,316		

effective (or yield) rate of interest *the actual interest rate earned or paid on a bond investment; takes into account the interest earned by buying at a discount or the interest lost by paying a premium*

stated (or nominal) rate of interest *the interest rate printed on a bond; used to determine how much cash will be paid or received each period as bond interest*

In this example, 16 percent is the effective, or yield, rate of interest because that is the amount of interest actually earned; 12 percent is the stated, or nominal, rate of interest of Sunglow Company's bonds. Note that the 12 percent stated rate determines the size of the annuity payments but not the purchase price of the bond; the purchase price varies according to market conditions. The 16 percent effective rate depends on three amounts: the purchase price, the interest payments, and the face value of the bonds.

The $17,316 bond price is the amount that earns Torrey exactly 16 percent; any lower price returns more than 16 percent and any higher price returns less than 16 percent. Assuming that a 16 percent rate of return is needed, if Torrey could purchase Sunglow's bonds for $17,316 or less, the investment would be worthwhile. If not, Torrey should probably look elsewhere for investment opportunities. The one exception, of course, would be if Torrey expected the market rate of interest to drop, which would result, as noted earlier, in an increase in the value of the bonds.

Accounting for Long-Term Investments in Bonds

Regardless of the price at which bonds are originally purchased, if they are held to maturity, the investor receives the principal, or face value, of the bonds from the issuing company. Because the difference between the principal and the cost represents earnings (or loss) that occur during the period the bonds are held, investments in bonds must be written up or down to their face value over the life of the bonds. This process is shown in Exhibit 11-6. Accounting for long-term investments in bonds involves four major steps:

1. Accounting for the acquisition of bonds.
2. Accounting for the interest received on bonds.

EXHIBIT 11-6 **Writing Bond Investments Up or Down**

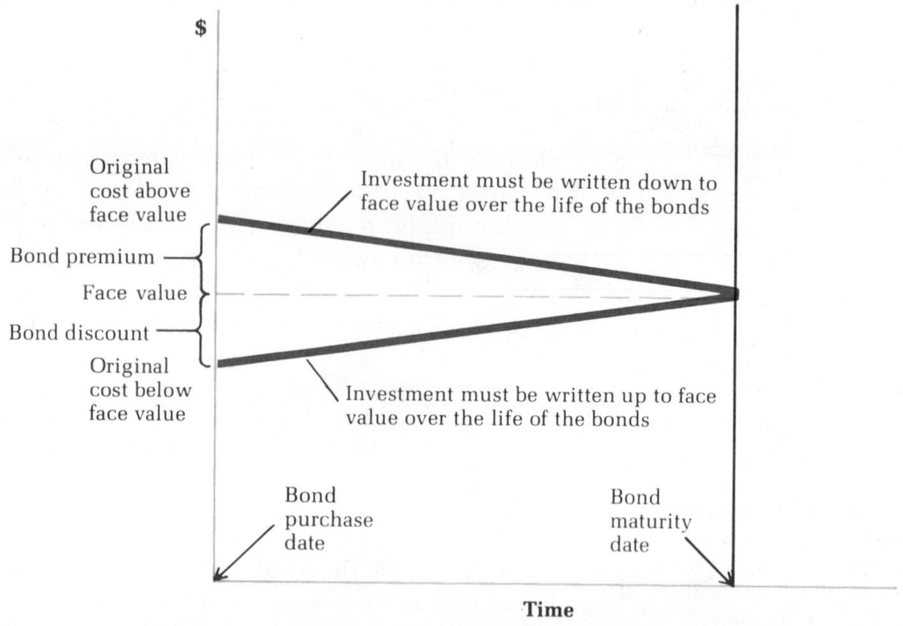

3. Accounting for the write-up or write-down of bonds from their original acquisition cost to their face value.

4. Accounting for the sale of bonds, if they are sold before their maturity date, or for the receipt of their face value.

Accounting for the Acquisition of Bonds Bonds can be purchased at amounts either above face value (at a premium), below face value (at a discount), or at face value (at par). Regardless of the purchase price, like all other assets, bonds are initially recorded at cost. The cost is the total amount paid to acquire the bonds, which includes the price of the bonds and any other purchasing expenditures, such as commissions or broker's fees. The entry to record Torrey Company's investment in Sunglow's bonds would be (assuming no sales commission)

Investment in Bonds–Sunglow Company	17,316	
Cash		17,316
Purchased $20,000 of Sunglow bonds at a discount.		

The only possible complication to this entry occurs when bonds are purchased between interest dates. Every 6 months (or however often the bonds pay interest), each bondholder is paid the full period's interest. Therefore, an investor purchasing bonds between interest dates must also pay the previous owner for the interest earned (called accrued interest) between the last interest payment date and the purchase date.

To illustrate this concept, we will assume that Torrey purchased the Sunglow bonds for $17,316 on May 1 and that the bonds ($20,000 at 12 percent) pay interest every January 1 and July 1. On July 1, Torrey will receive $1,200 ($20,000 × 0.12 × ½), even though the bonds were purchased only 2 months ago. Since the previous owner is entitled to 4 months' interest on May 1, Torrey will have to pay that individual or company—which could be the issuing corporation or some other intermediate investor—the interest for the period January 1 to May 1. This is illustrated in Exhibit 11-7.

EXHIBIT 11-7 **Investing Between Interest Dates**

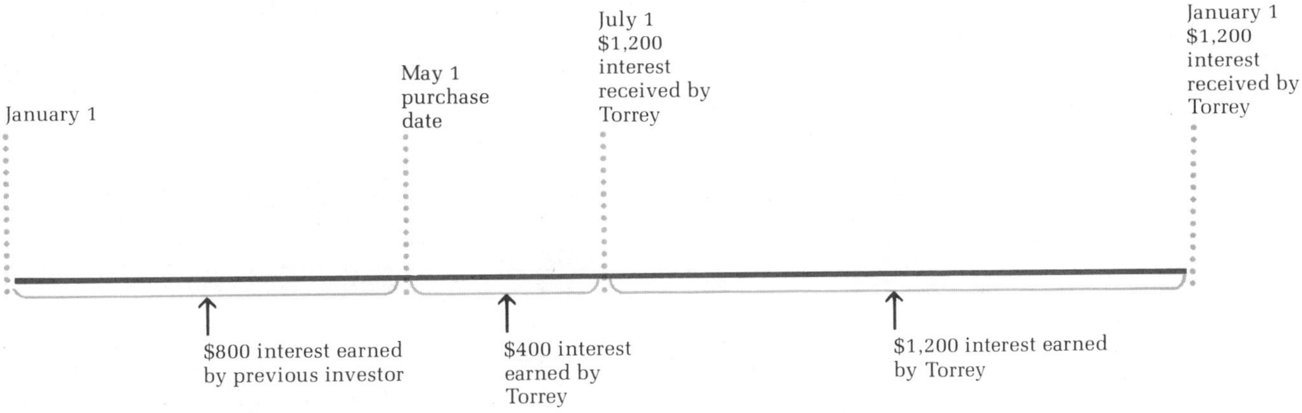

The entry to record the investment in bonds on May 1 (between interest dates) would be

Investment in Bonds—Sunglow Company	17,316	
Bond Interest Revenue	800	
Cash		18,116
Purchased $20,000 of Sunglow bonds at discount and paid accrued interest.		

Accounting for Interest Earned on Bond Investments When the $1,200 interest is received on July 1, the entry to record its receipt is

Cash	1,200	
Bond Interest Revenue		1,200
Received the first interest payment from Sunglow bonds.		

As shown here, on July 1, the Bond Interest Revenue account has a credit balance of $400, which represent Torrey's earnings for the 2 months.

Bond Interest Revenue

Amount paid with purchase on May 1. . . 800	1,200 .... Amount received on July 1
	400 .... Balance—amount earned

An alternative method of recording interest on bonds purchased between interest payment dates is to debit Bond Interest Receivable instead of Bond Interest Revenue. When this alternative is used, the entry on the interest payment date (in this case, July 1) will include two credits: one to Bond Interest Receivable ($800), and one to Bond Interest Revenue ($400). Both methods produce the same balance in the Bond Interest Revenue account after the interest payment date. The examples and problems in this book will use the previously outlined approach referred to as the revenue approach.

Whichever method is used, the entry to record subsequent receipts of interest will be

Cash	1,200	
Bond Interest Revenue		1,200
Received interest on Sunglow bonds.		

Bond Interest Revenue is a revenue account and, if material in amount, it is shown separately on the income statement under the caption Other Revenues and Expenses.

amortization of bonds *the systematic writing off of a bond discount or premium over the life of the bond*

straight-line interest amortization *a method of systematically writing off a bond discount or premium, in equal amounts each period until maturity*

Accounting for the Amortization of Bond Discounts and Premiums As indicated previously, bonds are not always purchased at their face value. In fact, only in those rare instances when the stated interest rate of a bond is exactly equivalent to the prevailing market, or yield, rate for similar investments is a bond purchased at par (at its face value). At all other times, bonds are purchased either at a discount (below face value) or at a premium (above face value). Because the face amount, or principal, of a bond is received at maturity, discounts and premiums must be written off over the period that a bond is held. This writing off of bond premiums and discounts is referred to as amortization.

There are two common methods of amortizing discounts and premiums on bonds; the simpler is straight-line interest amortization. With straight-line amortization, a company writes off the same amount of premium or discount each period the bonds are held.

To illustrate this method of amortizing a bond discount, we will assume again that Torrey purchased the Sunglow $20,000, 12 percent, 5-year bonds for $17,316, that is, at a discount. The entry to record this investment was given on page 381. If the bonds were purchased on the issuance date, Torrey would amortize the $2,684 discount ($20,000 face amount − $17,316 purchase price) at the rate of $536.80 a year ($2,684 ÷ 5 years). Each year for 5 years an amortization entry would be made. At the end of 5 years, the Investments in Bonds—Sunglow Company would have a balance of $20,000. These annual entries would be

Investment in Bonds—Sunglow Company	536.80	
Bond Interest Revenue		536.80
To record the annual straight-line amortization of Sunglow bonds.		

Note that with the straight-line amortization method, bond premiums and discounts can be amortized annually, as illustrated, or on each interest payment date.

The $536.80 in bond discount amortization is revenue earned on the bonds because, when the bonds mature, Torrey will receive $20,000, or the face value, in return for an original investment of $17,316. It is this additional revenue of $2,684 that increases the return the investor actually earns from the 12 percent stated interest rate to the effective interest rate of 16 percent. The following analysis shows how this works.

Maturity Value to Be Received	$20,000
Interest to Be Received ($1,200 × 10 payments)	12,000
Total Amount to Be Received	$32,000
Investment	17,316
Total Interest Revenue to Be Earned	$14,684

Interest Earned per Year:

Stated Amount of Interest ($20,000 × 0.12)	$2,400.00	12%
Additional Interest from Discount ($2,684 ÷ 5 years)	536.80	4%[4]
Total	$2,936.80	16%

[4] This is an approximation because with the straight-line method the actual interest earned each year changes.

When accounting for the amortization of a bond discount, a company must be careful to amortize the discount only over the period the bonds are actually held. For example, if Torrey had purchased the Sunglow bonds 4 months after the issuance date, the discount would have been amortized over a period of 56 months (4 full years plus 8 months of the first year). The amortization for the first year would then have been approximately $383.43 ($2,684 × 8/56) and the amortization for each of the succeeding 4 years would be approximately $575.14 ($2,684 × 12/56).

Accounting for the amortization of a premium on investments is essentially the opposite of accounting for a discount. Basically, amortization of a premium results in a decrease in revenue earned, and the effect of the amortization entry is to reduce Investments in Bonds to the face value of the bonds by maturity date.

To illustrate the accounting for amortization of a bond premium, we will assume that Grover Corporation purchased ABC Company's $20,000, 18 percent, 5-year bonds for $21,800 on the issuance date. The entries to record the purchase of bonds at a premium and receipt of interest on bonds are similar to those for bonds purchased at a discount. However, the annual entry to record amortization of the bond premium is different and results in a decrease both in revenues earned and in the investment balance, as shown here.

Bond Interest Revenue	360	
Investment in Bonds—ABC Company		360

To record the annual straight-line amortization of one-fifth of the $1,800 premium on ABC Company bonds ($1,800 ÷ 5 years).

Grover would be willing to pay such a premium only when the stated interest rate on bonds is higher than the prevailing market interest rate for similar investment opportunities. The effect of the amortization entries is to reduce the return earned on the bonds from the stated interest rate of 18 percent to the rate actually earned on the investment (approximately 16 percent).

effective-interest amortization *a method of systematically writing off a bond premium or discount that takes into consideration the time value of money and results in an equal rate of amortization for each period*

Effective-Interest Amortization Another common method of amortizing bond premiums and discounts is the effective-interest amortization method. This method is theoretically more correct than the straight-line method because it takes into consideration the time value of money. Rather than amortizing the same amount each period, as the straight-line method does, the effective-interest method amortizes a varying amount, which is the difference between the interest actually earned and the cash actually received. The amount actually earned is obtained by multiplying the changing investment balance (the original cost plus the amortization to date) by a constant rate, the effective rate of interest.

To illustrate the computations involved in using the effective-interest amortization method, we will again consider Torrey's purchase of 12 percent, 5-year, $20,000 bonds of Sunglow Company for $17,316. The amount of discount amortized in each of the 5 years using the effective-interest method would be

(1) Time Period	(2) Cash Received	(3) Interest Actually Earned (0.16 × ½ × Investment Balance)	(4) Amount of Amortization [(3) – (2)]	(5) Investment Balance
Acquisition date				$17,316
Year 1, first 6 months	$1,200	(0.08 × $17,316) = $1,385	$185	17,501
Year 1, second 6 months	1,200	(0.08 × 17,501) = 1,400	200	17,701
Year 2, first 6 months	1,200	(0.08 × 17,701) = 1,416	216	17,917
Year 2, second 6 months	1,200	(0.08 × 17,917) = 1,433	233	18,150
Year 3, first 6 months	1,200	(0.08 × 18,150) = 1,452	252	18,402
Year 3, second 6 months	1,200	(0.08 × 18,402) = 1,472	272	18,674
Year 4, first 6 months	1,200	(0.08 × 18,674) = 1,494	294	18,968
Year 4, second 6 months	1,200	(0.08 × 18,968) = 1,517	317	19,285
Year 5, first 6 months	1,200	(0.08 × 19,285) = 1,543	343	19,628
Year 5, second 6 months	1,200	(0.08 × 19,628) = 1,572	372	20,000
			$2,684	

In this computation, column (2) represents the cash received at the end of each interest period; column (3) shows the amount of effective interest earned, which is the amount that will be reported on the income statement each period; column (4) is the difference between columns (3) and (2) and so represents the amortization; and column (5) shows the investment balance that will be reported on the balance sheet at the end of each period. Note that the interest rate used to compute the actual interest earned is the effective rate of 8 percent (16 percent ÷ 2) and not the stated rate of 12 percent. Also note that the total discount is the same as it was when the straight-line method was used—$2,684.

When bonds are purchased at a discount, the amount of amortization increases each successive period. This is so because the investment balance of the bonds increases, and a constant interest rate times an increasing balance results in an increasing amount of interest income. If the bonds had been purchased at a premium, the effective-interest amortization method would involve a constant interest rate being multiplied by a declining investment balance each period. The result would be a decline in actual interest earned each period.

Since the effective-interest amortization method takes into account the time value of money and thus shows the true revenue earned each period (whereas the straight-line method represents only approximations), the accounting profession requires companies to use the effective-interest amortization method. As an exception to this rule, however, companies are allowed to use the straight-line method when the two methods produce amortization amounts that are not significantly different. Because that is often the case, both methods continue to be used.

Accounting for the Sale of Bonds or the Receipt of Their Maturity Value If bonds are held until their maturity date, the accounting for the proceeds at maturity includes a debit to Cash and a credit to the investment account for the principal amount. For example, if Torrey Company were to hold the

$20,000, 12 percent bonds from Sunglow until they mature, the entry to record the receipt of the bond principal on the maturity date would be

Cash	20,000	
Investment in Bonds–Sunglow Company		20,000
Received the principal of Sunglow bonds at maturity.		

This entry assumes, of course, that all previous receipts of interest and bond amortizations have been properly recorded.

Bonds are accounted for as though they will be held until maturity. However, because they are usually traded on major exchanges that provide a continuous and ready market, they are often sold to other investors prior to that time. When bonds are sold prior to their maturity, the difference between the sales price and the investment balance is recognized as a gain or loss on the sale of investments.

To illustrate, we will assume that Grover Company purchased ten $1,000, 8 percent, 5-year bonds of RTA Company. We will also assume that the bonds were originally purchased on January 1, 1980, at 101 percent of face value for $10,100, and that on January 1, 1983, Grover showed an unamortized balance of $10,040 for these bonds. If the bonds were sold on that day for $10,300 the entry to record the sale and recognize the gain would be (assuming no sales commission)

Cash	10,300	
Gain on Sale of Bonds		260
Investment in Bonds–RTA Company		10,040
Sold the RTA bonds for $10,300.		

When bonds are sold prior to their maturity date, it is important that the amortization of bond premiums or discounts be adjusted up to the date of sale. If the amortization of discounts or premiums is not updated, the gains or losses recognized on the sale will be incorrect.

TO SUMMARIZE Companies often make long-term investments in bonds issued by other companies or government agencies. The price paid for a bond usually depends on the risk involved (reflected in the bond's rating) and the bond interest rate. If the stated interest rate of a bond is less than the current market rate of similar investments, the bond usually sells at a discount. If the stated interest rate is higher than the market rate, a premium is usually paid. Companies investing in bonds purchase two elements: the right to receive interest payments at regular intervals over the life of the bond, and the right to receive the face amount of the bond at maturity.

Accounting for investments in bonds involves four steps: (1) accounting for the purchase of bonds, (2) accounting for interest received on bonds, (3) accounting for premium or discount amortization, and (4) accounting for the sale or maturity of the bonds. Amortization of premiums and discounts is usually accounted for by (1) the simple straight-line amortization method, or (2) the theoretically more correct effective-interest amortization method. The amortization adjusts the interest earned on bonds from the stated to the effective rate.

CHAPTER REVIEW

In addition to purchasing inventories, land, buildings, and equipment, firms often invest in other assets not directly related to their primary operations. These investments are classified as short-term assets if they are readily marketable and if management intends to hold them for one year or less, and as long-term assets if management does not intend to dispose of them within one year.

Short-term equity investments are accounted for on a lower-of-cost-or-market basis. That is, they are carried at cost unless the market price of a firm's total portfolio of short-term investments drops below cost, at which time the investments are written down to market. Gains and losses resulting from either the sale of short-term investments or their reduction to the lower of cost or market are included in a firm's net income.

Long-term investments in stocks can be accounted for by using either the cost or the equity method, depending on the degree of ownership in the investee company. If ownership of the outstanding stock of another company results in no significant influence over the investee's operating policies (as is usually the case with less than 20 percent ownership), the cost method is used. If the level of ownership results in significant influence (as generally happens with from 20 to 50 percent ownership), the equity method is used. With the cost method, dividends received from investee companies are recorded as revenue. With the equity method, the investment balance (its book value) is decreased by dividends or losses and increased by the investor's share of the investee company's earnings. If the ownership is more than 50 percent, consolidated financial statements are usually prepared.

In accounting for long-term investments in bonds, it is important to recognize that money has a time value: that is, money received or paid at different times does not have the same value. Two concepts are used to equate the value of money received or paid in different periods: the present value of $1, and the present value of an annuity of $1. These concepts discount money received in the future to its value today. The present value concepts are used in analyzing and accounting for long-term investments in bonds.

Long-term investments in bonds are initially recorded at cost. The cost is adjusted over the life of the bonds as discounts or premiums are amortized. The amortization of premiums and discounts adjusts the interest earned on bonds from the stated to the effective rate and writes the book value of bonds up or down to face value at maturity. Bond discounts and premiums can be amortized by using either the straight-line or the effective-interest method. The latter is theoretically more correct and is required by current accounting standards, but since the differences between the two are usually insignificant, both are widely used.

KEY TERMS AND CONCEPTS

amortization of bonds (383)
annuity (378)
bond (374)
bond discount (376)
bond indenture (375)
bond maturity date (375)
bond premium (376)
callable bonds (375)

compounding period (378)
consolidated financial statments (370)
convertible bonds (375)
cost method of accounting for investments in stocks (371)
coupon bonds (375)
debentures (375)
effective-interest amortization (384)
effective (or yield) rate of interest (379)
equity method of accounting for investments in stocks (372)
interest (375)
investment (365)
line of credit (366)
long-term investments (370)
lower of cost or market (LCM) (368)
market rate of interest (376)
parent company (370)
present value of an annuity of $1 (378)
present value of $1 (377)
principal (face value or maturity value) (375)
registered bonds (375)
secured bonds (375)
serial bonds (375)
short-term investments (367)
stated (or nominal) rate of interest (379)
straight-line interest amortization (383)
subsidiary company (370)
term bonds (375)

REVIEW PROBLEM

Long-Term Investments in Stocks and Bonds

On January 1, 1983, Jensen Manufacturing purchased $100,000 of 12 percent, 20-year bonds of McDonald Corporation as a long-term investment for $96,460 plus accrued interest. The bonds mature on September 1, 2002, and interest is payable semiannually on March 1 and September 1. Jensen Manufacturing uses the straight-line method of amortizing bond premiums and discounts.

On January 2, 1983, Jensen also purchased 35 percent of the 60,000 shares of outstanding stock of Taylor Company at $36 per share, plus broker's fees of $1,300. On December 31, 1983, Taylor announced that its net income for 1983 was $94,000, and it paid an annual dividend of $1 per share. Closing price of Taylor Company stock on December 31 was $34 per share.

Required:
Record all necessary transactions to account for these investments during 1983.

Solution

1. To account for the two investments, seven transactions must be recorded.

Investment in Bonds	Investment in Stock
1 Original Investment (Jan. 1)	5 Original Investment .... (Jan. 2)
2 Interest Receipt and Amortization of Discount .... (Mar. 1)	6 Recognition of Investee's Income .... (Dec. 31)
3 Interest Receipt and Amortization of Discount .... (Sept. 1)	7 Dividend Receipt .... (Dec. 31)
4 Interest Accrual and Amortization of Discount ..... (Dec. 31)	

The entries to record these events are

1	Investment in Bonds	96,460	
	Interest Revenue	4,000	
	Cash		100,460

Purchased $100,000 of McDonald Corporation's 12 percent bonds for $96,460 plus accrued interest.

The interest is $100,000 × 0.12 × 4/12 year = $4,000. Interest Revenue is debited so that when it is credited in step 2 below, the result is a net interest revenue of $2,000 ($6,000 − $4,000), which is the amount earned during January and February.

2	Cash	6,000	
	Investment in Bonds	30	
	Interest Revenue		6,030

Receipt of semiannual interest payment on McDonald Corporation's bonds and amortization of discount for 2 months.

The amortization of the discount is $100,000 − $96,460 = $3,540; $3,540 ÷ 236 months = $15 per month. The discount is amortized over 236 months instead of 20 years because only 236 months remains from the date of investment until the date of maturity.

3	Cash	6,000	
	Investment in Bonds	90	
	Interest in Revenue		6,090

To record receipt of semiannual interest payment on McDonald Corporation's bonds, and amortization of discount for 6 months.

The amortization is 6 months × $15.

4	Interest Receivable	4,000	
	Investment in Bonds	60	
	Interest Revenue		4,060

To record accrued interest for period September 1–December 31, and amortization of discount for 4 months.

The amortization in item (4) is 4 months × $15. Also, 4 months of interest have been earned, although payment will not be received until the following year.

5 Investment in Stock	757,300	
Cash		757,300

Purchased 35 percent of the outstanding stock of Taylor Company.

60,000 shares × 0.35 × $36 = $756,000; $756,000 + $1,300 = $757,300

6 Investment in Stock	32,900	
Revenue from Investments		32,900

To recognize 35 percent of Taylor's Company's 1983 earnings.

$94,000 × 0.35 = $32,900. (The equity method is used to account for this investment since more than 20 percent is owned. With the equity method, the Investments account increases when the investee has earnings.)

7 Cash	21,000	
Investment in Stock		21,000

Received $1 per share dividend on Taylor Company's stock.

60,000 shares × 0.35 × $1 = $21,000. (With the equity method, receipt of dividends is accounted for by reducing the Investments account. Under the equity method, declines in market price are ignored.)

DISCUSSION QUESTIONS

1 Why do firms invest in assets that are not directly related to their primary business operations?

2 Describe the risk and return trade-off of investments.

3 Why is a dollar received today generally worth more than a dollar received in the future?

4 What is the primary basis for classifying investments as short- or long-term?

5 Why are short-term investments in stocks written down if cost exceeds market price, but not written up if the market price exceeds cost?

6 What is meant by a portfolio of stocks?

7 Are losses resulting from the write-down of long- and short-term investments to market treated the same? If not, how does the accounting differ?

8 Define a subsidiary and a parent company.

9 Why is the equity method required when accounting for investments in which an investor has between 20 and 50 percent ownership of all outstanding voting stock?

10 Do you think that the "less than 20" and "20 to 50" percent classifications of stock ownership correctly identify situations of little or no control versus significant influence? Why?

11 What are bonds, and why are they issued?

12 What future cash inflows is a company buying when it purchases a bond?

13 When would a company be willing to pay more than the face amount (that is, a premium) for a bond?

14 What factors cause the prices of bonds to fluctuate in the marketplace?

15 Why does the discounting of future sums with higher interest rates result in lower present values than the discounting of future sums with lower interest rates?

16 Why does the amortization of a bond discount increase the amount of interest revenue earned on a bond?

17 Why is the effective-interest amortization method theoretically superior to the straight-line method?

18 Why must an investor purchasing bonds between interest payment dates pay the previous owner for accrued interest on those bonds?

19 In which direction would the market interest rate have to move in order for an investor in bonds to be able to sell the bonds at a price that is higher than the acquisition cost?

EXERCISES

E11–1 Short-Term Investments—Journal Entries

Prepare journal entries to record the following short-term investment transactions. (Assume that the cost method is used.)

1. Purchased 100 shares of Smith Corporation stock at $64 per share, and paid brokerage costs of $400.
2. Received a cash dividend of 75 cents per share on Smith Corporation stock.
3. Sold 50 shares of Smith Corporation stock at $70 per share.

E11–2 Short-Term Investments in Stock

In December 1983, the treasurer of Harmon Company discovered that the company had excess cash on hand and decided to invest in Stewart Corporation stock. The company intends to hold the stock for a period of 6 to 12 months. The following transactions took place.

January 1	Purchased 5,500 shares of Stewart Corporation stock for $82,500.
April 15	Received a cash dividend of 65 cents per share on the Stewart Corporation stock.
May 22	Sold 1,500 shares of the Stewart Corporation stock at $20 per share for cash.
July 15	Received a cash dividend of 45 cents per share on the Stewart Corporation stock.
August 31	Sold the balance of the Stewart Corporation stock at $8 per share for cash.

Give the appropriate journal entries to record each of these transactions, assuming that the cost method is used.

E11–3 Long-Term Investments in Stock

On March 15, 1983, Jackson Inc. acquired 10,000 shares of Carolina Mills common stock as a long-term investment. Carolina has 100,000 shares of outstanding voting common stock. The Carolina Mills shares are the only holdings in Jackson's portfolio of long-term stocks. The following events occurred during the fiscal year ending December 31, 1983.

Mar. 15	Jackson purchased 10,000 shares of Carolina Mills common stock at $45 per share.
Dec. 1	Jackson received a cash dividend of $2 per share from Carolina Mills.
31	Carolina announced earnings for the year of $150,000.
31	Carolina Mills common stock had a closing market price of $42 per share.

1. What accounting method should be used to account for this investment? Why?

2. Record the above events in General Journal form.

3. Prepare a partial income statement and balance sheet to show how the Investments and related accounts would be shown on the financial statements.

E11–4 Long-Term Investments in Stock

Assume the same facts as in E11–3, except that Jackson Inc. acquired 30,000 shares of Carolina Mills common stock.

1. What accounting method should be used? Why?

2. Record the listed transactions in General Journal form.

E11–5 Long-Term Investments in Stock—The Equity Method

During 1983, Jacob Company purchased 60,000 shares of Suker Corporation for $30 per share. Suker had a total of 240,000 shares of stock outstanding.

1. Record the following transactions.
   (a) January 1—Purchased 60,000 shares at $30 per share.
   (b) December 31—$175,000 of total net income reported by Suker Corporation.
   (c) December 31—$0.25 per share dividend declared and paid by Suker Corporation.

2. On December 31, the market price of Suker's stock was $27. Show how this investment would be reported on the balance sheet (assuming that this is the only stock owned by Jacob Company).

E11–6 Present Values—Simple Computations

Find the present value of:

1. $10,000 due in 10 years at 5 percent compounded annually.

2. $15,000 due in 8½ years at 10 percent compounded semiannually.

3. $7,500 due in 4 years at 12 percent compounded quarterly.

4. $10,000 due in 20 years at 8 percent compounded semiannually.

E11–7 The Present Value of an Annuity—Simple Computations

For each of the following annuities, determine the present value.

1. $1,000 per quarter for 5 years at 16 percent compounded quarterly.

2. $5,000 every 6 months for 15 years at 6 percent compounded semiannually.

3. $10,000 per year for 10 years at 5 percent compounded annually.

4. $2,000 every 6 months for 8½ years at 10 percent compounded semiannually.

E11–8 Investment Analysis—Present Value Concepts

Lamping Construction Company is deciding between two alternative investments. The first investment involves purchasing 1,000 shares of Handy Company stock at $25 per share. Lamping believes that if it holds the stock for 5 years the stock can be sold for $42 per share, and that the company will receive dividends of $2 per share each year. The second investment involves purchasing thirty $1,000, 10 percent bonds of Tracy Corporation. The bonds mature in 5 years, pay interest semiannually, and are currently selling at 98 (at 98 percent of face value).

1. If Lamping wants to earn 16 percent, should it make either investment?
2. Which of the two investments is the more attractive, assuming that they are equally risky?

E11–9 Present Values of an Annuity

1. An investment opportunity costing $96,664 will earn a return of $20,000 per year for 10 years. What is the annual rate of return on this investment?
2. If a company can earn 10 percent per year by investing its capital elsewhere, should it make the investment described in part (1)?
3. Suppose that the investment costs $147,202 and will earn $20,000 per year for 10 years. Should the company now make the investment? Why or why not?

E11–10 Present Values of an Annuity

Electric Power Company accumulated $500,000 of excess cash during a recent profitable year. Management has determined that it needs to invest enough of the excess cash in marketable securities to provide a cash flow of $50,000 a year for the next 5 years. The remainder will then be spent on research and development activities. How much cash must Electric Power Company invest in marketable securities in order to provide the necessary cash flow if investment opportunities are available at 6 percent? At 10 percent?

E11–11 Bond Price Determination

Action Incorporated has decided to purchase bonds of Rain Company as a long-term investment. The 10-year bonds have a stated interest rate of 8 percent, and interest payments are made semiannually. How much should Action be willing to pay for $30,000 of the bonds if

1. A rate of return of 10 percent is deemed necessary to justify the investment?
2. A rate of return of only 6 percent is considered adequate for the investment?

E11–12 Long-Term Investments in Bonds

On January 1, 1983, Company K purchased a $2,000, 10 percent bond at 97 as a long-term investment. The bond pays interest annually on each December 31, and matures on December 31, 1985. Assuming straight-line amortization, answer the following questions.

1. What will be the net amount of cash received (total inflows minus total outflows) from this investment over its life?
2. How much cash will be collected each year?
3. How much discount will be amortized each year (using straight-line amortization)?
4. By how much will the Long-Term Investments account increase each year?
5. How much investment revenue will be reported on the income statement each year?

E11–13 Long-Term Investments in Bonds

Barton Tools purchased twenty $1,000, 8 percent, 20-year bonds of Mr. Kleen Corporation on January 1, 1983, as a long-term investment. The bonds mature on January 1, 2003, and interest is payable every January 1 and July 1. Barton Tools' reporting year ends December 31 and the company uses the straight-line method of amortizing bond premiums and discounts. Amortization is recorded on December 31 of each year.

Make all necessary journal entries relating to the bonds for 1983, assuming that:

1. The purchase price is 105 percent of the face value.
2. The purchase price is 97 percent of the face value.

E11–14 Straight-Line Amortization of Bond Premium

Phillips Company purchased twenty $1,000, 8 percent, 5-year bonds of Quigley Company on their issuance date as a long-term investment for $21,706. Interest payments and amortization entries are made semiannually. Prepare a schedule showing the amortization of the bond premium over the 5-year life of the bonds. Use the straight-line method of amortization.

E11–15 Effective-Interest Amortization of Bond Premium

Assume the same facts as in E11–14. Prepare a schedule showing the amortization of the bond premium over the 5-year life of the bonds, using the effective-interest method of amortization. (Hint: The effective rate of interest earned on the bonds is 6 percent compounded semiannually.)

PROBLEMS

P11-1 Short-Term Investments—Analysis

The following data pertain to the marketable securities of Reed Company during 1983, the company's first year of operations.

a. Purchased 200 shares of A Corporation stock at $40 per share, plus brokerage fees of $100.

b. Purchased $3,000 of B Corporation bonds at face value, plus accrued interest of $90.

c. Received a cash dividend of 50 cents per share on the A Corporation stock.

d. Sold 50 shares of A Corporation stock for $46 per share.

e. Received interest of $120 on the B Corporation bonds.

f. Purchased 50 shares of C Corporation stock for $3,500.

g. Received interest of $120 on the B Corporation bonds.

h. Sold 150 shares of A Corporation stock for $28 per share.

i. Received a cash dividend of $1.40 per share on the C Corporation stock.

j. Interest receivable at year-end on the B Corporation bonds amounts to $30.

Required:

Enter the foregoing transactions in T-accounts and determine the amount of each of the following for the year.

1. Dividend revenue.
2. Bond interest revenue.
3. Net gain or loss from selling securities.

P11-2 Short-Term Investments in Stocks

Marshall Company often purchases common stocks of other companies as short-term investments. During 1983, the following events occurred.

July 1 Marshall purchased the common stocks listed below.

Corporation	Number of Shares	Total Price per Share
A	200	$ 72
B	300	46
C	150	156
D	100	84

Sept. 30 Marshall received a cash dividend of $2.50 per share on Corporation A stock.

Dec. 1 Marshall sold the stock in Corporation D for $74 per share.

Dec. 31 The market prices were quoted as follows: Corporation A stock, $64; Corporation B stock, $48; Corporation C stock, $150.

Required:

1. Record the events in General Journal entry form.
2. Illustrate how these investments would be reported on the balance sheet at December 31.
3. What items and amounts would be reported on the income statement for the year?
4. **Interpretive Question** Why are losses from the write-down of short-term investments in stock to the lower of cost or market included in the current year's income, whereas most similar losses for long-term investments in stock are not?

P11-3 Long-Term Investments in Stock—The Cost and Equity Methods

During January 1983, Handy, Inc. acquired 37,500 shares of Corporation A common stock for $22 per share. In addition, it purchased 5,000 shares of Corporation B preferred (nonvoting) stock for $120 per share. Corporation A has 150,000 shares of common stock outstanding and Corporation B has 12,000 shares of nonvoting stock outstanding.

The following data were obtained from operations during 1983.

	1983
Net Income:	
Corporation A	$170,000
Corporation B	75,000
Dividends Paid (per Share):	
Corporation A	$ 0.50
Corporation B	2.50
Market Value per Share at Dec. 31:	
Corporation A	$ 24
Corporation B	118

Required:

1. **Interpretive Question** What method should Handy, Inc. use in accounting for the investment of Corporation A stock? Why? What accounting method should be used in accounting for Corporation B nonvoting stock? Why?
2. Give the General Journal entries necessary to record the transactions for 1983.

P11-4 Long-Term Investments in Stock—The Cost and Equity Methods

The following activities relate to Martin Company during the years 1983 and 1984.

Feb. 15 Martin purchased 5,000 shares of Nelson Sporting Equipment stock for $35 per share.

Dec. 1 Martin received payment of $1.25 per share cash dividend from Nelson Sporting Equipment.

Dec. 31 Nelson Sporting Equipment announced earnings for the year of $60,000.

Dec. 31 Nelson Sporting Equipment common stock had a closing market price of $32 per share.

July 1 Martin sold 5,000 shares of Nelson Sporting Equipment stock for $37 per share.

Nelson Sporting Equipment had 25,000 shares of common stock outstanding on January 1, 1983.

Required:

1. Record the transactions in General Journal entry form, using (a) the cost method and (b) the equity method.
2. Show the amounts that would be reported on the financial statements of Martin Company at December 31, 1983, under each assumption.
3. **Interpretive Question** What is the minimum number of shares of stock that Nelson could have outstanding in order for Martin to use the cost method?

P11–5 Present Value Computations

Gulf Transit plans to acquire a large new computer for use in its accounting department. Cherry Town Computers, Inc., a distributor of Cherry Computers, has offered their computer under the following two alternative arrangements.

a. A 5-year purchase plan: Under this plan, Gulf Transit would pay $1,000,000 down, $500,000 at the end of each year for 4 years, and a final lump-sum payment of $1,250,000 at the end of the 5th year.

b. An 8-year purchase plan: With this plan, Gulf Transit would pay $820,000 down, $400,000 at the end of each year for 7 years, and a final lump-sum payment of $1,150,000 at the end of the 8th year.

Required:

1. Assuming that Gulf Transit must borrow the money to finance the project at 12 percent (compounded annually), which plan should Gulf accept?
2. Assuming that Gulf must borrow the money to finance the project at 8 percent (compounded annually), which terms should Gulf accept?

P11–6 Long-Term Investments in Bonds

Clampett Corporation purchased $25,000 of Becker Construction Company's $6\frac{1}{2}$ percent bonds at $102\frac{1}{2}$ plus accrued interest on February 1, 1983. The bonds mature on April 1, 1990, and interest is payable on April 1 and October 1.

On June 1, 1985, Clampett Corporation sold the Becker Construction Company bonds at 97 plus accrued interest. Clampett Corporation uses the straight-line method of amortizing bond premiums and discounts and makes amortization adjustments at year-end.

Required:

1. Record all journal entries to account for this investment during the years 1983, 1984, and 1985, assuming that Clampett closes its books annually on December 31.
2. **Interpretive Question** At the time these bonds were purchased (February 1, 1983), was the market rate of interest above or below $6\frac{1}{2}$ percent?

P11–7 Long-Term Investments in Bonds

Desert Equipment Company made the following purchases of bonds during 1983. All are long-term investments and all pay interest semiannually.

Purchase Date	Corp.	Face Amount	Cost	Interest Rate, %	Maturity Date	Last Interest Payment Date
10/15/83	A	$ 5,000	94	$7\frac{1}{2}$	1/1/90	7/1/83
12/1/83	B	10,000	$102\frac{1}{2}$	6	4/1/88	10/1/83
12/15/83	C	15,000	106	$8\frac{1}{4}$	6/1/89	12/1/83
12/31/83	D	12,000	$97\frac{3}{4}$	5	5/1/86	11/1/83

Required:

1. Record the purchases in General Journal entry form.
2. Show all adjusting entries relating to the bonds on December 31, 1983, assuming that Desert Equipment closes its books on that date and uses the straight-line amortization method.
3. **Interpretive Question** On the basis of these data, which of these four investments do you think has the highest rating—is the least risky?

P11–8 Determining the Purchase Price of Bonds and Effective-Interest Amortization

A total of $200,000 of 5-year, 8 percent bonds is being sold at a time when the market rate of interest for similar investments is 6 percent. These bonds pay semiannual interest.

Required:

1. Would these bonds be issued at a premium or at a discount?
2. Compute the total selling price of the bonds. (Hint: Determine the price that would result in an effective rate of interest of 6 percent.)

3. Ignore your solutions to (1) and (2), and assume that your calculations in (2) yielded a selling price of $220,000. Using this amount, compute the bond premium to be amortized the first year using the effective-interest method. Assume that all bonds were sold on the first day of the year in which they were authorized.

P11-9 Determining the Purchase Price of Bonds and Effective-Interest Amortization

Glenn Corporation decided to purchase twenty $1,000, $7\frac{1}{2}$ percent, 10-year bonds of Shelton Aviation as a long-term investment on February 1, 1983. The bonds mature on February 1, 1989, and interest payments are made semiannually on February 1 and August 1.

Required:

1. How much should Glenn Corporation be willing to pay for the bonds if the current interest rate on similar investments is 6 percent?

2. Prepare a schedule showing the amortization of the bond premium or discount over the remaining life of the bonds, assuming that Glenn Corporation uses the effective-interest method of amortization.

3. How much interest would be earned each year if the straight-line method of amortization were used? Show how these amounts differ from the annual interest earned using the effective-interest method.

4. **Interpretive Question** Which of the two amortization methods is preferable? Why?

P11-10 Unifying Problem: Short-Term Investments in Stocks and Bonds

On January 1, Inland Aviation Company had surplus cash. The management decided to invest in marketable securities. The following transactions occurred during the year.

Jan. 1	Purchased twenty $1,000, 6 percent bonds of Swift Corporation at par, plus accrued interest. Semiannual interest payment dates are November 1 and May 1 each year.
Feb. 15	Purchased 400 shares of Canton Corporation stock at $35 per share, plus brokerage fees of $500.
May 1	Received a semiannual interest payment on the Swift Corporation bonds.
Sept. 30	Received an annual cash dividend of $1.50 per share on Canton stock.
Oct. 15	Sold 250 shares of the Canton Corporation stock at $42 per share.
Nov. 1	Received a semiannual interest payment on the Swift Corporation bonds.
Dec. 31	Adjusted the accounts to accrue interest on the Swift Corporation bonds.

Required:

1. Record the transactions in General Journal entry form.

2. The market quote for Swift Corporation's bonds at closing on December 31 was 104. The Canton stock closed at $40 per share. Prepare a partial balance sheet showing all the necessary data for these securities. Assume that marketable securities are reported at cost and that market value is shown parenthetically.

P11-11 Unifying Problem: Long-Term Investments in Stocks and Bonds

On January 1, 1983, Custom Disco purchased $25,000 of 8 percent, 10-year bonds of Jefferson Trucking as a long-term investment at 96, plus accrued interest. The bonds mature on November 1, 1989, and interest is payable semiannually on May 1 and November 1. Custom Disco uses the straight-line method of amortizing bond premiums and discounts.

In addition, on January 2, 1983, Custom Disco purchased 30 percent of the 50,000 shares of outstanding common stock of Mayberry Company at $42 per share, plus brokers' fees of $450. On December 31, 1983, Mayberry announced that its net income for the year was $150,000 and paid an annual dividend of $2 per share. The closing market price of Mayberry common stock on that date was $38 per share.

Required:

1. Record all the 1983 transactions relating to these two investments in General Journal entry form.

2. Show how the long-term investments and the related revenues would be reported on the financial statements of Custom Disco at December 31, 1983.

Table I The Present Value of $1 Due in *n* Periods*

Period	1%	2%	3%	4%	5%	6%	7%	8%	9%	10%	12%	14%	15%	16%	18%	20%	24%	28%	32%	36%
1	.9901	.9804	.9709	.9615	.9524	.9434	.9346	.9259	.9174	.9091	.8929	.8772	.8696	.8621	.8475	.8333	.8065	.7813	.7576	.7353
2	.9803	.9612	.9426	.9246	.9070	.8900	.8734	.8573	.8417	.8264	.7972	.7695	.7561	.7432	.7182	.6944	.6504	.6104	.5739	.5407
3	.9706	.9423	.9151	.8890	.8638	.8396	.8163	.7938	.7722	.7513	.7118	.6750	.6575	.6407	.6086	.5787	.5245	.4768	.4348	.3975
4	.9610	.9238	.8885	.8548	.8227	.7921	.7629	.7350	.7084	.6830	.6355	.5921	.5718	.5523	.5158	.4823	.4230	.3725	.3294	.2923
5	.9515	.9057	.8626	.8219	.7835	.7473	.7130	.6806	.6499	.6209	.5574	.5194	.4972	.4761	.4371	.4019	.3411	.2910	.2495	.2149
6	.9420	.8880	.8375	.7903	.7462	.7050	.6663	.6302	.5963	.5645	.5066	.4556	.4323	.4104	.3704	.3349	.2751	.2274	.1890	.1580
7	.9327	.8706	.8131	.7599	.7107	.6651	.6227	.5835	.5470	.5132	.4523	.3996	.3759	.3538	.3139	.2791	.2218	.1776	.1432	.1162
8	.9235	.8535	.7894	.7307	.6768	.6274	.5820	.5403	.5019	.4665	.4039	.3506	.3269	.3050	.2660	.2326	.1789	.1388	.1085	.0854
9	.9143	.8368	.7664	.7026	.6446	.5919	.5439	.5002	.4604	.4241	.3606	.3075	.2843	.2630	.2255	.1938	.1443	.1084	.0822	.0628
10	.9053	.8203	.7441	.6756	.6139	.5584	.5083	.4632	.4224	.3855	.3220	.2697	.2472	.2267	.1911	.1615	.1164	.0847	.0623	.0462
11	.8963	.8043	.7224	.6496	.5847	.5268	.4751	.4289	.3875	.3505	.2875	.2366	.2149	.1954	.1619	.1346	.0938	.0662	.0472	.0340
12	.8874	.7885	.7014	.6246	.5568	.4970	.4440	.3971	.3555	.3186	.2567	.2076	.1869	.1685	.1372	.1122	.0757	.0517	.0357	.0250
13	.8787	.7730	.6810	.6006	.5303	.4688	.4150	.3677	.3262	.2897	.2292	.1821	.1625	.1452	.1163	.0935	.0610	.0404	.0271	.0184
14	.8700	.7579	.6611	.5775	.5051	.4423	.3878	.3405	.2992	.2633	.2046	.1597	.1413	.1252	.0985	.0779	.0492	.0316	.0205	.0135
15	.8613	.7430	.6419	.5553	.4810	.4173	.3624	.3152	.2745	.2394	.1827	.1401	.1229	.1079	.0835	.0649	.0397	.0247	.0155	.0099
16	.8528	.7284	.6232	.5339	.4581	.3936	.3387	.2919	.2519	.2176	.1631	.1229	.1069	.0930	.0708	.0541	.0320	.0193	.0118	.0073
17	.8444	.7142	.6050	.5134	.4363	.3714	.3166	.2703	.2311	.1978	.1456	.1078	.0929	.0802	.0600	.0451	.0258	.0150	.0089	.0054
18	.8360	.7002	.5874	.4936	.4155	.3503	.2959	.2502	.2120	.1799	.1300	.0946	.0808	.0691	.0508	.0376	.0208	.0118	.0068	.0039
19	.8277	.6864	.5703	.4746	.3957	.3305	.2765	.2317	.1945	.1635	.1161	.0829	.0703	.0596	.0431	.0313	.0168	.0092	.0051	.0029
20	.8195	.6730	.5537	.4564	.3769	.3118	.2584	.2145	.1784	.1486	.1037	.0728	.0611	.0514	.0365	.0261	.0135	.0072	.0039	.0021
25	.7798	.6095	.4476	.3751	.2953	.2330	.1842	.1460	.1160	.0923	.0588	.0378	.0304	.0245	.0160	.0105	.0046	.0021	.0010	.0005
30	.7419	.5521	.4120	.3083	.2314	.1741	.1314	.0994	.0754	.0573	.0334	.0196	.0151	.0116	.0070	.0042	.0016	.0006	.0002	.0001
40	.6717	.4529	.3066	.2083	.1420	.0972	.0668	.0460	.0318	.0221	.0107	.0053	.0037	.0026	.0013	.0007	.0002	.0001	†	†
50	.6080	.3715	.2281	.1407	.0872	.0543	.0339	.0213	.0134	.0085	.0035	.0014	.0009	.0006	.0003	.0001	†	†	†	†
60	.5504	.3048	.1697	.0951	.0535	.0303	.0173	.0099	.0057	.0033	.0011	.0004	.0002	.0001	†	†	†	†	†	†

* The formula used to derive the values in this table was $PV = F\frac{1}{(1+i)^n}$ where PV = present value, F = future amount to be discounted, i = interest rate, and n = number of periods.
† The value of 0 to four decimal places.

Table II The Present Value of an Annuity of $1 per Period*

Number of payments	1%	2%	3%	4%	5%	6%	7%	8%	9%	10%	12%	14%	15%	16%	18%	20%	24%	32%
1	0.9901	0.9804	0.9709	0.9615	0.9524	0.9434	0.9346	0.9259	0.9174	0.9091	0.8929	0.8772	0.8596	0.8621	0.8475	0.8333	0.8065	0.7576
2	1.9704	1.9416	1.9135	1.8861	1.8594	1.8334	1.8080	1.7833	1.7591	1.7355	1.6901	1.6467	1.6257	1.6052	1.5656	1.5278	1.4568	1.3315
3	2.9410	2.8839	2.8286	2.7751	2.7232	2.6730	2.6243	2.5771	2.5313	2.4869	2.4018	2.3216	2.2832	2.2459	2.1743	2.1065	1.9813	1.7663
4	3.9820	3.8077	3.7171	3.6299	3.5460	3.4651	3.3872	3.3121	3.2397	3.1699	3.0373	2.9137	2.8550	2.7982	2.6901	2.5887	2.4043	2.0957
5	4.8884	4.7135	4.5797	4.4518	4.3295	4.2124	4.1002	3.9927	3.8897	3.7908	3.6048	3.4331	3.3522	3.2743	3.1272	2.9906	2.7454	2.3452
6	5.7985	5.6014	5.4172	5.2421	5.0757	4.9173	4.7665	4.6229	4.4859	4.3553	4.1114	3.8887	3.7845	3.6847	3.4976	3.3255	3.0205	2.5342
7	6.7282	6.4720	6.2303	6.0021	5.7864	5.5824	5.3893	5.2064	5.0330	4.8684	4.5638	4.2883	4.1604	4.0386	3.8115	3.6046	3.2423	2.6775
8	7.6517	7.3255	7.0197	6.7327	6.4632	6.2098	5.9713	5.7466	5.5348	5.3349	4.9676	4.6389	4.4873	4.3436	4.0776	3.8372	3.4212	2.7860
9	8.5660	8.1622	7.7861	7.4353	7.1078	6.8017	6.5152	6.2469	5.9952	5.7590	5.3282	4.9464	4.7716	4.6065	4,3030	4.0310	3.5665	2.8651
10	9.4713	8.9826	8.5302	8.1109	7.7217	7.3601	7.0236	6.7101	6.4177	6.1446	5.6502	5.2161	5.0188	4.8332	4.4941	4.1925	3.6819	2.9304
11	10.3676	9.7868	9.2526	8.7605	8.3064	7.8869	7.4987	7.1390	6.8052	6.4951	5.9377	5.4527	5.2337	5.0286	4.6560	4.3271	3.7757	2.9776
12	11.2551	10.5733	9.9540	9.3851	8.8633	8.3838	7.9427	7.5361	7.1607	6.8137	6.1944	5.6603	5.4206	5.1971	4.7932	4.4392	3.8514	3.0133
13	12.1337	11.3484	10.6350	9.9856	9.3936	8.8527	8.3577	7.9038	7.4869	7.1034	6.4235	5.8424	5.5831	5.3423	4.9095	4.5327	3.9124	3.0404
14	13.0037	12.1062	11.2961	10.5631	9.8986	9.2950	8.7455	8.2442	7.7862	7.3667	6.6282	6.0021	5.7245	5.4675	5.0081	4.6106	3.3616	3.0609
15	13.8651	12.8493	11.9379	11.1184	10.3797	9.7122	9.1079	8.5595	8.0607	7.6061	6.8109	6.1422	5.8474	5.5755	5.0916	4.6755	4.0013	3.0764
16	14.7179	13.5777	12.5611	11.6523	10.8378	10.1059	9,4466	8.8514	8.3126	7.8237	6.9740	6.2651	5.9542	5.6685	5.1624	4.7296	4.0333	3.0882
17	15.5623	14.2919	13.1661	12.1657	11.2741	10.4773	9.7632	9.1216	8.5436	8.0216	7.1196	6.3729	6.0472	5.7487	5.2223	4.7746	4.0591	3.0971
18	16.3983	14.9920	13.7535	12.6593	11.6896	10.8276	10.0591	9.3719	8.7556	8.2014	7.2497	6.4674	6.1280	5.8178	5.2732	4.8122	4.0799	3.1039
19	17.2260	15.6785	14.3238	13.1339	12.0853	11.1581	10.3356	9.6036	8.9501	8.3649	7.3658	6.5504	6.1982	5.8775	5.3162	4.8435	4.0967	3.1090
20	18.0456	16.3514	14.8775	13.5903	12.4622	11.4699	10.5940	9.8181	9.1285	8.5136	7.4694	6.6231	6.2593	5.9288	5.3527	4.8696	4.1103	3.1129
25	22.0232	19.5235	17.4131	15.6221	14.0939	12.7834	11.6536	10.6748	9.8226	9.0770	7.8431	6.8729	6.4641	6.0971	5.4669	4.9476	4.1474	3.1200
30	25.8077	22.3965	19.6004	17.2920	15.3725	13.7648	12,4090	11.2578	10.2737	9.4269	8.0552	7.0027	6.5660	6.1772	5.5168	4.9789	4.1601	3.1242
40	32.8347	27.3555	23.1148	19.7928	17.1591	15.0463	13.3317	11.9246	10.7574	9.7791	8.2438	7.1050	6.6418	6.2335	5.5482	4.9966	4.1659	3.1250
50	39.1961	31.4236	25.7298	21.4822	18.2559	15.7619	13.8007	12.2335	10.9617	9.9148	8.3045	7.1327	6.6605	6.2463	5.5641	4.9995	4.1666	3.1250
60	44.9550	34.7609	27.6756	22.6235	18.9293	16.1614	14.0392	12.3766	11.0480	9.9672	8.3240	7.1401	6.6651	6.2482	5.5553	4.9999	4.1667	3.1250

* The formula used to derive the values in this table was $PV = R\left(\frac{1 - \frac{1}{(1+i)^n}}{i}\right)$ where PV = present value, R = periodic payment to be discounted, i = interest rate, and n = number of payments.

CHAPTER 12

Long-Term Liabilities

THIS CHAPTER EXPLAINS:

The advantages and disadvantages of debt financing.

Factors to be considered in measuring long-term liabilities, including notes payable.

Accounting for bond liabilities.

Accounting for mortgages, deferred income taxes, and leases.

equity financing *raising money, or capital, by issuing stock or otherwise receiving contributions from owners*

debt financing *raising money, or capital, by borrowing*

Financing a business often requires resources beyond those available from current earnings. Two common ways of generating additional financial resources are (1) equity financing: issuing stock (by a corporation) or making additional owner contributions (in a partnership or proprietorship); and (2) debt financing: borrowing money. Because both types of financing have their advantages and disadvantages, firms usually try to reach an appropriate balance between the two. Equity financing is covered in Chapters 13 and 14. Here we will concentrate on debt financing.

Advantages and Disadvantages of Debt Financing

The major advantages and disadvantages of obtaining additional financial resources through borrowing are outlined in Exhibit 12-1. Although most of these advantages and disadvantages are self-explanatory, two may need some clarification. As indicated in Exhibit 12-1, interest paid on debts is deductible for income tax purposes. This means that the real cost of borrowing is reduced. For example, if a company that is taxed at a 40 percent rate can borrow money at 10 percent, its real cost of borrowing is only 6 percent. Or, put another way, every dollar of interest paid reduces the amount of taxes owed by 40 cents. Thus, when this 40-cent reduction in

EXHIBIT 12-1 **Debt Financing**

Advantages	Disadvantages
Borrowing does not dilute the ownership of a firm, as does the selling of stock in a corporation.	Borrowed money must be repaid.
Interest paid on borrowed money is tax deductible, whereas dividends paid to stockholders of a corporation are not.	Interest on borrowed money must be paid, usually each year throughout the life of the debt.
Since the number of shares of stock in a corporation is not increased through borrowing, earnings per share usually will be higher than if stock were issued.	Interest payments generally reduce the absolute amount of net income.
If a firm can borrow at a net interest rate that is less than its rate of earnings, profits can be increased. This is called leveraging.	In the case of liquidation or bankruptcy of a corporation, debtholders rank ahead of stockholders in receiving the firm's assets. Thus, stockholders may lose a larger amount of their investment than would be the case if there were no debt.

taxes is combined with each $1 of interest, the net cost of borrowing is only 60 cents, or in this case 6 percent [(60/100) × 10 percent interest].[1]

leveraging *the use of borrowed money to finance a business when the net interest rate of the borrowed funds is less than the company's earnings rate*

A second advantage of borrowing that may need explanation is leveraging. If a company's annual profits are regularly 20 percent of total assets, it can increase its earnings significantly by borrowing (to purchase additional assets) at 10 percent. In this case, total earnings would be the original 20 percent plus a 10 percent net return on borrowed resources (or even more, if we take into account the tax deductibility of the interest on the loan). This use of outside money is a real advantage for a company with a good earnings rate. Leveraging becomes a disadvantage, however, if the earnings rate drops below the interest rate. And if a company has losses, not only are those losses usually greater than they would be if there were no borrowing, but also, since there are no income taxes on a loss, the real cost of borrowing is not reduced by the fact that interest is tax deductible.

Measuring Long-Term Liabilities

The obligations that result from borrowing money for periods longer than one year are classified on the balance sheet as long-term liabilities. There are many different types of long-term liabilities; the most common are notes

[1] This principle also holds true for individuals who borrow money to purchase a house or other asset. Since interest paid on home mortgages is tax deductible (if deductions are itemized), the net interest cost of a home loan is less than the stated amount of interest.

payable, bonds payable, mortgages payable, deferred income taxes payable, and lease obligations. Before discussing these individual liabilities, we should mention some factors that affect the measurement of all long-term liabilities.

present value *the value today of an amount to be received or paid in the future; the future amount must be discounted at a specified rate of interest*

Conceptually, the amount of a liability at any particular time is the present value of all future outflows of assets required to pay the liability in full. Obviously, if a liability is short-term, the present value of outflows needed to pay it is approximately equal to the stated amount of the liability. (Recall from Chapter 11 that the difference between stated amounts and present values increases as the number of discount periods increases.) Thus, the value of short-term liabilities is easily measured. In the case of long-term liabilities, however, the present value of future outflows of assets needed to settle an obligation is often significantly different from the stated amount of that liability.

NOTES PAYABLE: MEASURING A TYPICAL LONG-TERM LIABILITY

note payable *a debt owed to a creditor, evidenced by an unconditional written promise to pay a sum of money on or before a specified future date*

To illustrate the measurement of long-term liabilities, we will assume that Jacobs Automobile Company buys a car-washing machine. Jacobs purchased the machine by issuing a $100,000, 5-year, non-interest-bearing note payable. This means that $100,000 is due in one lump sum 5 years from now. Is the liability really $100,000? Certainly, in an economy where money has value over time, a loan with such favorable terms would never be extended. (That is, the manufacturer would never extend to Jacobs a 5-year interest-free loan, which is what the transaction would amount to if the current price of the machine actually were $100,000.) Therefore, the $100,000 must include a finance charge, and the real liability (the cash price for which the car-washing machine could have been purchased today) must be less than $100,000. If the market rate of interest is 15 percent, then the $100,000 should be discounted to a present value of $49,720 (see Table I, page 395). Given a cash-equivalent price of $49,720, the purchase would be recorded as follows:

Car-Washing Machine	49,720	
Discount on Note Payable	50,280	
Note Payable		100,000

Purchased car-washing machine by issuing a 5-year non-interest-bearing $100,000 note.

The discount represents the implicit finance charge and is a contra-liability account. As such, it must be subtracted from Notes Payable on the balance sheet and amortized, or written off, as interest expense over the life of the loan. Thus, in the car-washing machine example, the journal entry to recognize the interest expense and discount amortization for the first and second years of the note would be

Interest Expense	7,458	
Discount on Note Payable		7,458

To recognize the first year's implicit interest expense on the 5-year, $100,000 note ($49,720 × 0.15 = $7,458).

Interest Expense	8,576	
Discount on Note Payable		8,576

To recognize the second year's implicit interest expense on the 5-year, $100,000 note ($49,720 + $7,458 = $57,178; $57,178 × 0.15 = $8,576).

Each year the discount is amortized by the amount of that year's interest expense, until at the end of 5 years the Discount on Note Payable account has a zero balance. The interest expense is calculated by multiplying the effective rate of interest, 15 percent, by the growing loan balance (the total of the Note Payable and the Discount on Note Payable accounts). The amortization of the discount over the 5-year period is summarized as follows:

Year	Interest Expense and Discount Amortization (0.15 × Loan Balance)	Loan Balance
Beginning Balance		$ 49,720
Year 1	(0.15 × $49,720) = $ 7,458	57,178
Year 2	(0.15 × 57,178) = 8,576	65,754
Year 3	(0.15 × 65,754) = 9,863	75,617
Year 4	(0.15 × 75,617) = 11,342	86,959
Year 5	(0.15 × 86,959) = 13,041	100,000

The final journal entry will be to record the payment of the note, as follows:

Note Payable	100,000	
Cash		100,000

Paid 5-year non-interest-bearing $100,000 note for car-washing machine.

While this type of note is sometimes referred to as non-interest-bearing, it is really an interest-bearing note because the present value is less than the face value.

What about an interest-bearing, long-term note? Is its present value equal to its stated amount? If the stated rate of interest on a long-term liability is less than the market rate of interest, the present value is again less than the stated amount of the liability. On the other hand, if the stated rate of interest is approximately equal to the market rate of interest, the stated amount and its present value are equal and no discounting is necessary. These measurement alternatives are summarized in Exhibit 12–2.

EXHIBIT 12-2 Measurement of Liabilities

Type of Liability	Amount of Liability (as recorded in the accounting records)	Reason
Short-term	The stated amount of the liability, which is approximately equal to its present value	The time period involved is usually so short that the difference between the present value and the stated amount of the liability is immaterial.
Long-term interest-bearing—interest rate is equivalent to the market rate of interest	The stated amount of the liability, which is equivalent to its present value	The present value of the sum of the principal and interest payments is approximately equal to the stated amount of the liability.
Long-term non-interest-bearing	The present value of the liability, which is less than its stated amount	Part of the stated amount of the liability is really implicit interest being charged to the borrower.
Long-term interest-bearing—interest rate is lower than the market rate of interest	The present value of the liability, which is less than its stated amount	Part of the stated amount of the liability is really implicit interest (less than in the case of a non-interest-bearing note, but still an amount significant enough to warrant discounting).

Exhibit 12-3 shows how these general measurement principles would be applied to three different long-term notes payable.

TO SUMMARIZE Because debt financing offers several advantages over equity financing in certain situations, companies often borrow money to help finance their business. The amount of a liability (such as a note payable) is the present value of all future outflows of assets required to pay the liability in full. Liabilities with an interest rate approximately equal to the market rate of interest are recorded at full values; noninterest or lower-than-market-interest-rate liabilities are discounted.

Bonds Payable

In the last chapter, the nature of bonds and the accounting for bond investments were discussed. Here, we examine how a company issuing bonds accounts for the bond liability. Because accounting for bond liabilities is the reciprocal of accounting for bond investments, there are many similarities.

EXHIBIT 12-3 Accounting for Long-Term Notes

Type of note	Interest-bearing note with stated rate of interest equal to market rate of interest	Non-interest-bearing note	Interest-bearing note with stated rate of interest less than market rate of interest
Situation	On January 1, 1983, XYZ Company borrowed $10,000 from City Bank for 3 years at 10%. Interest is payable annually on December 31. The market rate of interest is 10%.	On January 1, 1983, XYZ Company purchased a machine from Alvin Company. There was no down-payment and $10,000 is to be paid in 3 years. There is no interest to be paid and the market rate of interest is 10%.	On January 1, 1983, XYZ Company purchased a machine from ABC Company. There was no down-payment and $10,000 is to be paid in 3 years. Interest of 6% must be paid annually every December 31. The market rate of interest is 10%.
Entry to record the note, rounded to the nearest dollar	Cash . . . . 10,000 Note Payable 10,000	Machine . . . . 7,513 Discount on Note Payable . . . . 2,487 Note Payable . . . . 10,000 *(The $10,000 is discounted at 10% for 3 years, rounded to the nearest dollar.)*	Machine . . . . 9,005 Discount on Note Payable . . . . 995 Note Payable . . . . 10,000 *(The $600 annuity and the $10,000 are discounted at 10% for 3 years.)*
Entry on December 31, 1983	Interest Expense . . . . . 1,000 Cash . . . . 1,000 *($10,000 × 0.10)*	Interest Expense . . . . 751 Discount on Note Payable . . . . 751 *(See amortization schedule A.)*	Interest Expense . . . . 901 Discount on Note Payable . . . . 301 Cash . . . . 600 *(See amortization schedule B.)*
Entry on December 31, 1984	Interest Expense . . . . . 1,000 Cash . . . . 1,000 *($10,000 × 0.10)*	Interest Expense . . . . 826 Discount on Note Payable . . . . 826 *(See amortization schedule A.)*	Interest Expense . . . . 931 Discount on Note Payable . . . . 331 Cash . . . . 600 *(See amortization schedule B.)*
Entries on December 31, 1985	Interest Expense . . . . . 1,000 Cash . . . . 1,000 *($10,000 × 0.10)* Note Payable . . . . 10,000 Cash 10,000	Interest Expense . . . . 909 Discount on Note Payable . . . . 909 *(See amortization schedule A.)* Note Payable . . . . 10,000 Cash 10,000	Interest Expense . . . . 964 Discount on Note Payable . . . . 364 Cash . . . . 600 *(See amortization schedule B.)* Note Payable . . . . 10,000 Cash 10,000

Amortization Schedule A

Date	Interest Expense and Discount Amortization	Loan Balance
Beginning Balance		$ 7,513
December 31, 1983	(0.10 × $7,513) = $751	8,264
December 31, 1984	(0.10 × 8,264) = 826	9,090
December 31, 1985	(0.10 × 9,090) = 909	10,000 (rounded)

Amortization Schedule B

Date	Interest Expense (0.10 × Loan Balance)	Cash Payment ($10,000 × 0.06)	Discount Amortization	Loan Balance
Beginning Balance				$ 9,005
December 31, 1983	(0.10 × $9,005) = $901	$600	$301	9,306
December 31, 1984	(0.10 × 9,306) = 931	600	331	9,637
December 31, 1985	(0.10 × 9,637) = 964	600	364	10,000 (rounded)

The four elements involved in accounting for bond liabilities, together with their corresponding counterparts from Chapter 11, are

Bond Liabilities	Investments in Bonds
1. Accounting for the issuance of bonds	1. Accounting for the purchase of bonds
2. Accounting for interest payments	2. Accounting for interest receipts
3. Amortizing bond premiums and discounts	3. Amortizing the difference between the investment cost and the face value of the bonds
4. Accounting for the retirement of bonds[2]	4. Accounting for bond investments at maturity or when sold

[2] Bonds are retired either at maturity or, in the case of callable bonds, when the issuer may pay the obligation before the maturity date.

In accounting for each of these four elements, the investor and the issuer record the same amounts but in a different way. With bond investments, the actual amount paid for the bonds, not the face value, is originally debited to the Investment account. The amortization of the bond premium or discount is then recorded directly in the Investment account. With bond liabilities, the face value of the bonds issued is recorded in the Bonds Payable account and a separate contra account is maintained for any discount or premium. Amortization of the discount or premium is then recorded in these contra accounts. We now examine the accounting for each of these four elements of bond liabilities.

ACCOUNTING FOR BONDS SOLD AT FACE VALUE

Two factors influence the accounting for bonds at the date of issuance: (1) the initial price of the bonds, and (2) the date on which the bonds were issued. If bonds are sold at their face value on an interest payment date, the accounting is relatively simple. However, if they are issued at a price above or below face value or between interest dates, the accounting can be quite complicated. In this and the following sections, we explain the accounting for bonds under each of these different circumstances, using the following basic data to illustrate our points.

On January 1, 1983, Jacobs Automobile Company issued 10-year bonds with a face value of $100,000, a stated interest rate of 8 percent, and interest payable semiannually on January 1 and July 1. If we assume that Jacobs Company is no more or less risky than other firms in its industry and that 8 percent is the market rate of interest for similar bonds, we can also assume that investors will be willing to pay approximately the face amount for the bonds. In such cases, the bonds are said to sell at par and the journal entry to record their sale on January 1, 1983, would be

par *the nominal amount printed on the face of a bond or share of stock*

Cash	100,000	
Bonds Payable		100,000
Sold $100,000, 8%, 10-year bonds at par.		

The entry to record the first payment of interest on July 1, 1983, would be

Bond Interest Expense	4,000	
Cash		4,000

Paid semiannual interest on the $100,000, 8%, 10-year bonds ($100,000 × 0.08 × ½ year).

If Jacobs Automobile Company operates on a calendar year basis, it would need to make the following adjusting entry on December 31, 1983, to account for the interest expense between July 1 and December 31, 1983.

Bond Interest Expense	4,000	
Accrued Bond Interest Payable		4,000

To recognize expense for the 6 months July 1 to December 31, 1983 ($100,000 × 0.08 × ½ year).

At the end of the accounting period (December 31, 1983), the financial statements would report the following.

Income Statement

Bond Interest Expense ($4,000 × 2)	$ 8,000

Balance Sheet

Current Liabilities:	
Accrued Bond Interest Payable	$ 4,000
Long-Term Liabilities:	
Bonds Payable (8%, due January 1, 1993)	100,000

Then, on January 1, 1984, when semiannual interest is paid, the Accrued Bond Interest Payable account is eliminated. The January 1 entry would be

Accrued Bond Interest Payable	4,000	
Cash		4,000

Made semiannual interest payment.

The entries to record the interest expense payments during the remaining nine years would be the same as those made during 1983 and on January 1, 1984. The only other entry required in accounting for these bonds is the recording of their retirement on January 1, 1993. That entry, assuming that all interest has been accounted for, would be

Bonds Payable	100,000	
Cash		100,000

Retired the $100,000, 10-year, 8% bonds.

ACCOUNTING FOR BONDS SOLD AT A DISCOUNT

bond discount *the difference between the face value and the sales price when bonds are sold below their face value*

Investors may be unwilling to pay the face amount of a bond because its stated interest rate is lower than the market rate. When bonds sell at a price below their face value, they are said to have been sold at a discount.

To illustrate the accounting for bonds sold at a discount, we will assume that the $100,000, 10-year, 8 percent bonds issued by Jacobs Automobile on January 1, 1983, were sold for $98,000. The entry to record the issuance of the bonds on January 1, 1983, would be

Cash	98,000	
Discount on Bonds	2,000	
Bonds Payable		100,000
Sold $100,000, 8%, 10-year bonds at 98.		

Discount on Bonds is a contra-liability account that is deducted from Bonds Payable on the balance sheet. Bonds Payable is recorded at the full $100,000 because, although the bonds were issued for only $98,000, $100,000 is the amount the company will have to repay investors in 10 years.

The $2,000 discount is not an immediate loss or expense to Jacobs Automobile; it represents an adjustment to the interest expense over the life of the bonds. This can be illustrated by comparing the proceeds received by Jacobs ($98,000) with the amounts it must pay its bondholders ($180,000) over the life of the bonds: $100,000 face value plus 20 interest payments of $4,000 each. The comparison shows the following.

Amount to Be Paid to Bondholders	$180,000
Proceeds Received from Sale of Bonds	98,000
Total Interest to Be Paid	$ 82,000
Average Interest Expense Each Year ($82,000/10 years)	$ 8,200

Although Jacobs pays only $8,000 in interest each year, its actual interest expense is $8,200 (assuming straight-line amortization of the discount). To show this larger interest expense, the discount on bonds must be amortized so that each year $200 is transferred from the contra account, Discount on Bonds, to Bond Interest Expense.

straight-line interest amortization *a method of systematically writing off a bond premium or discount, resulting in equal amounts being amortized each period*

effective-interest amortization *a method of systematically writing off a bond premium or discount, taking into consideration the time value of money and resulting in an equal rate of amortization for each period*

As we explained in Chapter 11, there are two ways of accounting for the amortization of bond discounts: (1) straight-line interest and (2) effective interest. Because of its simplicity, the straight-line method is used for this example; the effective-interest amortization method is illustrated later in the chapter.

With the straight-line amortization method, an equal amount of the discount is amortized each year of the bond's 10-year life. Thus, Jacobs would amortize $200 ($2,000/10 years) each year. The semiannual entry to record amortization of the bond discount would be made at the same time as the interest expense, so the July 1, 1983 entry would be

Bond Interest Expense	4,100	
Discount on Bonds		100
Cash		4,000

Paid semiannual interest on the $100,000, 8%, 10-year bonds ($100,000 × 0.08 × ½ year) and amortized the bond discount ($2,000 ÷ 10 years × ½ year).

As illustrated, amortization of a discount increases a bond's interest expense. In this case, the interest expense is $4,100, or the sum of the semiannual interest payments and the semiannual amortization of the bond discount. Over the 10-year life of the bonds, the interest expense will be increased by $2,000, the amount of the discount, and so will be higher than the 8 percent stated rate. Thus, these bonds pay an effective interest rate of approximately 8.37 percent[3] per year ($8,200 interest/$98,000 received on the bonds).

effective interest rate *the actual interest rate earned or paid on a bond investment*

The adjusting entry to record the accrual of the interest expense on December 31, 1983, would be

Bond Interest Expense	4,100	
Discount on Bonds		100
Accrued Bond Interest Payable		4,000

To recognize interest expense for the 6 months July 1 to December 31, 1983.

At the end of the accounting period (December 31, 1983), the financial statements would report the following.

Income Statement

Bond Interest Expense ($4,100 × 2)		$ 8,200

Balance Sheet

Current Liabilities:		
Accrued Bond Interest Payable		$ 4,000
Long-Term Liabilities:		
Bonds Payable (8%, due January 1, 1993)	$100,000	
Less Unamortized Discount ($2,000 − $200)	1,800	98,200

The entries to account for the interest expense and bond discount amortization during the remaining nine years would be the same as those made in 1983. And, since the bond discount would be completely amortized at the end of the 10 years, the entry to record the retirement of the bonds would be the same as that for bonds issued at face value. As previously shown, that entry would be as shown on page 406.

[3] Because straight-line amortization was used, this effective rate of 8.37 percent is only an approximation that will change slightly each period. An accurate effective rate can only be calculated if the effective-interest method of amortization is used.

Bonds Payable	100,000	
Cash		100,000
Retired the $100,000, 8%, 10-year bonds.		

Note that although amortization entries were made as part of each interest entry (semiannually in this example), one amortization entry for $200 at the end of the accounting period would have been sufficient. The critical factor is that the discount be properly amortized for the year-end financial statements.

ACCOUNTING FOR BONDS SOLD AT A PREMIUM

bond premium *the difference between the face value and the sales price when bonds are sold above their face value*

Just as bonds may be sold at a discount when the interest rates or risk factors are less favorable than those of competing bonds, bonds may sell at amounts above their face value when one or both of these factors are more favorable than those of similar bonds. Bonds that sell at amounts above face value are said to sell at a premium. Like discounts, premiums must be amortized over the life of the bonds.

To illustrate the accounting for bonds sold at a premium, we will assume that Jacobs Automobile Company was able to sell its $100,000, 8 percent, 10-year bonds at 103 (that is, at 103 percent of par). The entry to record the issuance of these bonds on January 1, 1983, would be

Cash	103,000	
Premium on Bonds		3,000
Bonds Payable		100,000
Sold $100,000, 8%, 10-year bonds at 103.		

Premium on Bonds is added to Bonds Payable on the balance sheet and, like Discount on Bonds, is amortized using either the straight-line or effective-interest method. Thus, if Jacobs were to use the straight-line method, the annual amortization of the premium would be $300 ($3,000/10 years), or $150 every 6 months. The entry to record the first semiannual interest payment and the premium amortization on July 1, 1983, would be

Bond Interest Expense	3,850	
Premium on Bonds	150	
Cash		4,000
Paid semiannual interest on the $100,000, 8%, 10-year bonds ($100,000 × 0.08 × ½ year) and amortized the bond premium ($3,000 ÷ 10 years × ½).		

The amortization of a premium on bonds has the opposite effect of the amortization of a discount; that is, it reduces the actual interest expense on the bonds. The following analysis shows why interest expense is reduced when bonds are sold at a premium.

Amount to Be Paid to Bondholders	$180,000
Proceeds Received from Sale of Bonds	103,000
Total Interest to Be Paid	$ 77,000
Average Interest Expense Each Year ($77,000/10 years)	$ 7,700

In this case, with the annual $8,000 in interest payments, the company is repaying one-tenth (1/10) of the bond premium. Since the amount of bond premium being repaid is not included in the interest expense, the effective rate is not the stated rate of 8 percent, but is approximately 7.48 percent ($7,700/$103,000).

The adjusting entry to record the accrual of the interest expense on December 31, 1983, would be

Bond Interest Expense	3,850	
Premium on Bonds	150	
Accrued Bond Interest Payable		4,000

To recognize interest expense on the bonds for the 6 months July 1 to December 31, 1983.

At the end of the accounting period (December 31, 1983), the financial statements would report the following.

Income Statement

Bond Interest Expense ($3,850 × 2)		$ 7,700

Balance Sheet

Current Liabilities:		
Accrued Bond Interest Payable		$ 4,000
Long-Term Liabilities:		
Bonds Payable (8%, due January 1, 1993)	$100,000	
Plus Unamortized Premium ($3,000 − $300)	2,700	102,700

Like discounts, premiums can be amortized once at year-end, instead of when the interest payments are made.

ACCOUNTING FOR BONDS SOLD BETWEEN INTEREST DATES

As noted in Chapter 11, when bonds are sold between interest dates, the accounting for interest payments and the amortization of the premium or discount becomes somewhat more complicated. With regard to the first interest payments, the complication arises because interest is usually paid for a full period regardless of how long the bonds have been held. Therefore, if interest is to be paid semiannually and the bonds are sold between interest dates, it is customary for the bond investor to pay the seller (the previous owner or the original issuer) for that portion of the 6 months' interest that will be received but not earned.

To illustrate, we will assume that on January 1, 1983, ReMae Corporation received authorization to issue \$200,000 of 12 percent, 7-year bonds with interest payments to be made on January 1 and July 1 of each year. Since the bonds mature in 7 years, they should have a life of 84 months and pay interest of \$12,000 (\$200,000 × 0.12 × $\frac{1}{2}$ year) every January 1 and July 1. However, if ReMae Corporation did not actually sell the bonds until May 1, 1983, then on July 1 the investors would have held the bonds for only 2 months and would have earned only \$4,000 in interest (\$200,000 × 0.12 × $\frac{1}{6}$ year). Since the investors would receive \$12,000 on July 1, ReMae Corporation would add the \$8,000 in unearned interest to the selling price of the bonds. This interest complication can be diagrammed as shown in Exhibit 12-4.

EXHIBIT 12-4 **Interest for Bonds Issued Between Periods**

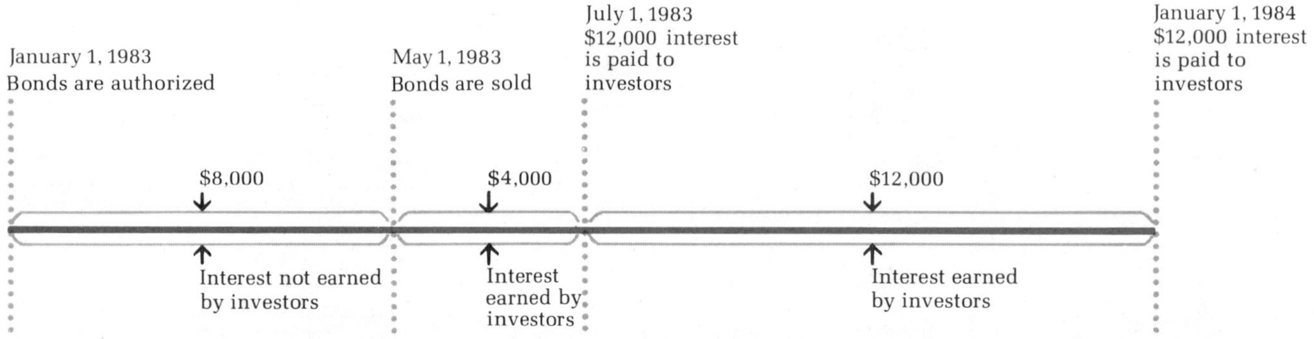

If the bonds were sold on May 1, 1983, at 104 (at a premium), the entry to account for the sale of the bonds and the payment of \$8,000 interest to investors would be

Cash	216,000	
Bonds Payable		200,000
Premium on Bonds Payable		8,000
Bond Interest Expense		8,000
Sold \$200,000, 12%, 7-year bonds at 104 plus accrued interest.		

The \$8,000 interest is credited to Bond Interest Expense so that on July 1, 1983, when the full \$12,000 of interest is debited to that account, there is a net interest expense of \$4,000 for the 2 months. This is shown in the following T-account.

Bond Interest Expense

July 1, 1983 12,000	8,000 . . . . May 1, 1983
4,000	

Alternatively, the $8,000 could have been credited to Bond Interest Payable instead of Bond Interest Expense. With this approach, the entry on the interest payment date would include two debits: $4,000 to Bond Interest Expense and $8,000 to Bond Interest Payable.

At this point you are probably wondering why the issuer does not simply keep track of bonds as they are sold, and pay only the net amount of interest due on that date instead of the full amount due for the period. Unfortunately, such a system would actually be more complicated than the one just outlined. There are two reasons for this: First, since many bonds are coupon bonds, each coupon is worth a certain amount of interest. Second, since bonds are traded daily, it would be an impossible task for bond issuers to keep track of which investors own how many bonds and on what dates the different bonds were purchased. Therefore, it is actually easier for issuers to pay specified amounts of interest every period and require investors who buy between interest dates to pay in advance for any unearned interest.

With regard to premium and discount amortizations, the complication arises because the bond premium or discount must be amortized over the actual time the bonds are outstanding, not over their entire authorized life. In this case, since the bonds were authorized on January 1, 1983, but were not issued until May 1, 1983, the amortization period would be 6 years and 8 months (80 months), not the full 7 years. The monthly amortization of the premium (assuming that the straight-line amortization method was used) would therefore be $100 per month ($8,000/80 months). On July 1, 1983, with the bonds outstanding for only 2 months, the entry to record the interest payment and premium amortization would be

Bond Interest Expense	11,800	
Premium on Bonds	200	
Cash		12,000

Made semiannual interest payment on the $200,000, 12%, 7-year bonds ($200,000 × 0.12 × ½ year) and amortized the bond premium ($8,000 ÷ 80 months × 2).

Note that on all succeeding interest payment dates, the amount of the premium amortization would be $600 ($100 per month × 6 months).

EFFECTIVE-INTEREST AMORTIZATION

Companies can often justify use of the straight-line method of amortizing bond premiums and discounts on the grounds that its results are not significantly different from those of the theoretically more accurate effective-interest method. However, as noted in Chapter 11, the effective-interest method is also widely used because it considers the time value of money, and is therefore required by the FASB if it leads to results that differ significantly from those obtained by the straight-line method.

To illustrate the effective-interest method, we assume that on January 1, 1983, Howe Baking Company sold $40,000 of 10 percent, 5-year bonds for $43,246. If the bonds pay interest semiannually on January 1 and July 1, their effective interest rate is approximately 8 percent a year, or 4 percent every 6 months. Since the actual interest expense for each period is equal to the effective rate of 8 percent multiplied by the bond balance, the amortization (rounded to the nearest $1) for the 5 years would be as follows:

Period	(1) Cash Paid for Interest	(2) Semiannual Interest Expense (0.04 × Bond Balance)	(3) Premium Amortization [(1) − (2)]	(4) Bond Balance
Issuance date:				$43,246
Year 1, first 6 months	$2,000	(0.04 × $43,246) = $1,730	$270	42,976
Year 1, second 6 months	2,000	(0.04 × 42,976) = $1,719	281	42,695
Year 2, first 6 months	2,000	(0.04 × 42,695) = $1,708	292	42,403
Year 2, second 6 months	2,000	(0.04 × 42,403) = $1,696	304	42,099
Year 3, first 6 months	2,000	(0.04 × 42,099) = $1,684	316	41,783
Year 3, second 6 months	2,000	(0.04 × 41,783) = $1,671	329	41,454
Year 4, first 6 months	2,000	(0.04 × 41,454) = $1,658	342	41,112
Year 4, second 6 months	2,000	(0.04 × 41,112) = $1,644	356	40,756
Year 5, first 6 months	2,000	(0.04 × 40,756) = $1,630	370	40,386
Year 5, second 6 months	2,000	(0.04 × 40,386) = $1,614	386	40,000

In this computation, the $2,000 in column (1) is the actual interest paid each 6 months; column (2) shows the interest expense for each 6 months, which is the amount that will be reported on the income statement; column (3), which is the difference between columns (1) and (2), represents the amortization of the premium; and column (4) shows the carrying, or book, value of the bond (that is, the total of the bond payable and the unamortized bond premium), which is the amount that will be reported on the balance sheet each period. Using the effective-interest method, the bond balance is always equal to the present value of the bond obligation. Note that as the bond balance decreases, the amount of money borrowed decreases, and, because the effective rate of interest is constant, the interest expense also decreases.

Because the straight-line method would show a constant interest expense ($3,246 ÷ 10 = $324.60 per 6-month period) on a decreasing bond balance, the straight-line interest rate cannot be constant. It is for this reason that, when the straight-line results differ significantly from the effective-interest results, FASB guidelines advise use of the effective-interest method.

The effective-interest method of amortizing a bond discount is essentially the same as amortizing a bond premium. The main difference is that the bond balance increases instead of decreases.

TO SUMMARIZE Bonds are long-term interest-bearing liabilities of businesses and government agencies. The accounting for bonds involves four steps: (1) accounting for their issuance, (2) accounting for the periodic interest payments over their lives, (3) accounting for the amortization of discounts and premiums, and (4) accounting for their retirement. The accounting for bonds sold between interest dates is more complicated, because investors pay in advance for the unearned interest they will receive in their first interest payment. When bonds are sold at a premium or at a discount, the effective-interest method of amortization reflects a constant effective interest rate, whereas the straight-line method only approximates an effective rate.

Mortgages Payable

mortgage payable *a written promise to pay a stated amount of money at one or more specified future dates; a mortgage is secured by the pledging of certain assets—usually, real estate—as collateral*

A mortgage payable is similar to a note payable in that it is a written promise to pay a stated sum of money at one or more specified future dates. It is different from a note in the way it is applied: Whereas money borrowed with a note can often be used for *any* business purpose, mortgage money is usually related to a specific asset, typically real estate. Assets purchased with a mortgage are usually pledged as security or collateral on the loan, and the liability involves a separate mortgage document, which is appended to the loan agreement. For individuals, home mortgages are common, and for companies, plant mortgages are frequent. In either case, mortgages generally require periodic (usually monthly) payments of the principal.

To illustrate the accounting for a mortgage, we will assume that Jacobs Automobile Company borrows $600,000 to purchase a new showroom and signs a mortgage agreement pledging the showroom as collateral on the loan. If the mortgage is at 15 percent for 30 years, and the monthly payment is $7,900, the entries to record the acquisition of the mortgage and the first monthly payment will be

Cash	600,000	
Mortgage Payable		600,000
Borrowed $600,000 to purchase the automobile showroom.		
Mortgage Payable	400	
Interest Expense	7,500	
Cash		7,900
Made first month's mortgage payment.		

mortgage amortization schedule *a schedule that shows the breakdown between interest and principal for each payment over the life of a mortgage*

As this entry shows, only $400 of the $7,900 payment is applied to reducing the mortgage; the remainder is interest ($600,000 × 0.15 × 1/12 = $7,500). In each successive month, the amount applied to reducing the mortgage will increase slightly until, toward the end of the 30-year mortgage, almost all of the payment will be for principal. A mortgage amortization schedule identifies how much of each mortgage payment is interest and how much is principal reduction.

At the end of each year, a mortgage is reported on the balance sheet in two places: (1) the principal to be paid during the next year is shown as a current liability, and (2) the balance of the mortgage payable is shown as a long-term liability. Also, any interest owed on the mortgage is reported as a current liability and the interest expense for the year is included with other expenses on the income statement. Note that since the 15 percent interest rate charged on this mortgage is assumed to be approximately equal to the market rate of interest, the stated value of $600,000 is not discounted.

Deferred Income Taxes Payable

Often, the income taxes a company pays to federal and local governments differ considerably from the income tax expense shown on the income statement. This happens because different methods are used for calculating these amounts. Whereas income tax expense is obtained by accounting for income on the basis of generally accepted accounting principles, income taxes payable to governments are calculated on the basis of taxable income as defined by the Internal Revenue Service and by state government codes. A full account of the many differences between generally accepted accounting principles and the Internal Revenue Service and other tax codes is beyond the scope of this book. However, it is important to mention that there are two types of differences: (1) permanent differences, which are never reversed; and (2) timing differences, which are temporary and may be reversed in the future. Because timing differences often create long-term liabilities, we will describe how they work with a common business element—depreciation.

Assume that Jacobs Automobile Company has been in business for 4 years and that abbreviated income statements for those years are as shown in the table below. On the first day of year 1, Jacobs purchased a $10,000 tune-up machine with a 4-year life and no salvage value.

Jacobs Automobile Company
Condensed Income Statements for Financial Reporting (Years 1–4)

	Year 1	Year 2	Year 3	Year 4	Total
Sales Revenue	$10,000	$10,000	$10,000	$10,000	$40,000
Expenses (Excluding Depreciation on Tune-Up Machine)	4,000	4,000	4,000	4,000	16,000
Income Before Depreciation and Taxes	$ 6,000	$ 6,000	$ 6,000	$ 6,000	$24,000
Depreciation Expense on Tune-Up Machine—Straight-Line Basis with No Salvage Value	2,500	2,500	2,500	2,500	10,000
Income Before Taxes	$ 3,500	$ 3,500	$ 3,500	$ 3,500	$14,000
Income Tax Expense (40% × $3,500)	1,400	1,400	1,400	1,400	5,600
Net Income	$ 2,100	$ 2,100	$ 2,100	$ 2,100	$ 8,400

As the statements show, net income and income tax expense are $2,100 and $1,400, respectively, in each of the 4 years. Because Jacobs chose to use the straight-line method, the depreciation expense on the tune-up machine is the same each year. Although the straight-line method may be appropriate for financial reporting purposes, the ACRS (Accelerated Cost Recovery System) is used for tax purposes. The ACRS method, as you will recall from Chapter 10, enables companies to delay payment of taxes because it specifies a cost recovery period that is usually shorter than the asset's estimated useful life, and it provides a table of cost recovery percentages that are based on an accelerated depreciation method. Even though the same total amount of taxes will be paid using any cost allocation method, under ACRS, cost allocation is accelerated and taxes are delayed. This is a distinct advantage to a business because the present value of tax payments made in later years is less than the present value of the same payments made sooner.

To illustrate the ACRS method of cost allocation, we will assume that under ACRS the tune-up machine qualifies for a 3-year write-off period. Thus, 25 percent will be expensed in year 1, 38 percent in year 2, and 37 percent in year 3. The write-off for years 1 through 3 would then be $2,500, $3,800, and $3,700. Using these amounts, the company's income tax payable and net income for its tax return in each of the four years would be

Jacobs Automobile Company
Condensed Income Statements for Tax Return (Years 1–4)

	Year 1	Year 2	Year 3	Year 4	Total
Sales Revenue	$10,000	$10,000	$10,000	$10,000	$40,000
Expenses (Excluding Depreciation on Tune-Up Machine)	4,000	4,000	4,000	4,000	16,000
Income Before Depreciation and Taxes	$ 6,000	$ 6,000	$ 6,000	$ 6,000	$24,000
Depreciation Expense on Tune-Up Machine—ACRS	2,500	3,800	3,700	-0-	10,000
Income Before Taxes	$ 3,500	$ 2,200	$ 2,300	$ 6,000	$14,000
Income Tax Payable (40%)	1,400	880	920	2,400	5,600
Net Income	$ 2,100	$ 1,320	$ 1,380	$ 3,600	$ 8,400

Although ACRS and straight-line depreciation result in the same total amount of income taxes over the four years, the timing of the payments is different, as shown in the following.

	Year 1	Year 2	Year 3	Year 4	Total
Taxes Using Straight-Line Depreciation (Financial Statements)	$1,400	$1,400	$1,400	$ 1,400	$5,600
Taxes Using ACRS (Tax Return)	1,400	880	920	2,400	5,600
Difference in Taxes	$ 0	$ 520	$ 480	$(1,000)	$ 0

deferred income taxes *the difference between income tax expense, calculated as a function of accounting income based on generally accepted accounting principles, and current taxes payable, calculated as a function of taxable income based on the Internal Revenue Service and other tax codes*

With the ACRS approach, Jacobs has the use of an extra $520 in year 2 and $480 in year 3. Although income taxes must eventually be paid, in the meantime the money can be invested to earn a return for the company. The differences between income tax expense per the financial statements and income taxes payable per the tax return are called deferred income taxes. Because deferred income taxes usually are not paid for several periods, they may be classified as long-term liabilities on the balance sheet.

The entries to record income taxes with the ACRS method in this example would be as shown on page 414.

	Year 1		Year 2		Year 3		Year 4	
	DR	*CR*	*DR*	*CR*	*DR*	*CR*	*DR*	*CR*
Income Tax Expense	1,400		1,400		1,400		1,400	
Deferred Income Taxes Payable		-0-		520		480	1,000	
Income Taxes Payable—Current		1,400		880		920		2,400

In practice, the credit balance in the deferred income taxes payable account seldom decreases. This is because as a business expands, it continues to buy new depreciable assets that are often more expensive than the old ones (as a result of inflation). The accelerated depreciation benefits derived from these new assets are usually large enough to offset the declining benefits of the old assets. Therefore, deferred income tax liabilities only diminish when a firm is not buying new assets. However, firms usually stop buying new assets only when they are losing money, and since there is no tax when there is no income, the deferred taxes may never be paid. As a result, many accountants argue that deferred income taxes should not be considered a liability. Others maintain that even if deferred income taxes are paid, the present value of the payments is so small that these taxes should not be reported with the other liabilities. So far, neither of these points of view has persuaded rule-makers to change the accounting for deferred income taxes. However, this topic has been placed on the agenda for consideration by the FASB.

TO SUMMARIZE In addition to notes and bonds payable, two common long-term liabilities are mortgages payable and deferred income taxes payable. Mortgages usually arise because companies borrow money to construct buildings or purchase additional operating assets. Deferred income taxes arise because the amount of income taxes a business actually pays is usually different from the income tax expense reported on the income statement. This occurs because the requirements specified by generally accepted accounting principles differ from the IRS and other tax requirements. (For example, straight-line depreciation is a GAAP practice, whereas ACRS cost allocation is an IRS requirement.)

Accounting for Leases

lease *a contract whereby the lessee (user) agrees to pay periodic payments (rents) to the lessor (owner) for the use of an asset*

lessee *an entity that agrees to pay periodic rents for the use of leased property*

lessor *renter or owner of leased property*

When a company needs a new asset, it can either buy it or lease it. Leasing an asset is like renting an apartment: Instead of a lump-sum payment or a large initial payment and the transfer of title, smaller periodic payments are involved with no initial transfer of ownership. Because leasing can be an attractive way of financing the use of assets, it has grown in popularity. With a lease, the entity acquiring the use of the asset and making the payments is known as the lessee and the owner or landlord is called the lessor.

Until recently, most periodic lease payments were considered expenses of the period in which they were payable, and future lease liabilities (lease

lease obligations *the net present value of all future lease payments discounted at an appropriate rate of interest*

capitalization *the recording of an expenditure expected to benefit more than the current period as an asset*

obligations) and leased assets were not shown on the financial statements. However, because some companies leased rather than purchased assets solely because of these favorable effects on the balance sheet (no long-term debt was reported), and because many leases are in fact equivalent to purchasing assets, accounting practice now requires in many cases that a lease be capitalized—that is, recorded as an asset and a liability, rather than as an expense. Under current accounting guidelines (FASB Statement No. 13), a lease containing at least one of the following features must be treated as a purchase and shown on the balance sheet as both an asset and a liability.

1. Ownership is to be transferred to the lessee at the end of the lease.
2. The lease contains a bargain (less than fair market value) purchase option. That is, at the end of the lease the asset can be purchased for a sum significantly lower than its fair market value.
3. The lease term is 75 percent or more of the leased property's estimated economic life.
4. The present value of the lease payments is 90 percent or more of the fair market value of the property.

If a lease meets any of these criteria, it must be capitalized at an amount equal to the present value of the lease payments discounted at the market interest rate. If a lease does not meet any of these criteria, it is expensed—that is, the periodic payments are recorded as lease expenses and no asset or liability accounts are established. If a lease requires capitalization under criterion 1 or 2, the leased asset is depreciated over its useful life because the lessee will receive the asset at the termination of the lease. If criterion 3 or 4 is applicable, the leased asset is amortized over the life of the lease.

To illustrate the accounting for a capitalized lease, we will assume that Jacobs Automobile Company leases a computer from the Macro Data Corporation for $10,000 a year for 10 years. The computer has an estimated useful life of 12 years; its fair market value is $55,000; and the current rate of interest is 14 percent. Because the life of the lease is at least 75 percent of the computer's life (10 ÷ 12 = 83 percent), or because the present value of the lease payments ($52,161) is more than 90 percent of the fair market value of the computer, the lease must be capitalized. (See Table II, page 395,[4] for the present value of an annuity of 10 payments of $10,000 discounted at 14 percent.) The entry to record the lease in Jacobs' books would be

Leased Asset—Computer	52,161	
Lease Obligation		52,161
Leased a Macro Data computer for $10,000 a year for 10 years discounted at 14%.		

At the end of the first year, the balance sheet would include the long-term accounts Leased Asset—Computer and Lease Obligation.

[4] Although most leases require payments at the beginning of each year, end-of-year payments are assumed here in order to simplify the calculations.

Although at first the asset and liability accounts have equal balances, they seldom remain the same during the lease period. The asset should be amortized (depreciated) over the life of the lease and the lease liability should be reduced in a way that produces a constant interest rate each period. In this case, the asset is amortized over 10 years using the straight-line method, and the interest expense each period is 14 percent of the lease balance. If we assume that the lease payments are due at the end of each year, the interest for each year would be as shown in Exhibit 12-5.

EXHIBIT 12-5 Payments on a Computer Lease

	Interest Expense	Lease Expense			
Year	*(0.14 × Lease Obligation)*	*Total Amount*	*Interest*	*Principal*	**Lease Obligation**
					$52,161
1	(0.14 × $52,161) = $7,303	$10,000	$7,303	$2,697	49,464
2	(0.14 × 49,464) = 6,925	10,000	6,925	3,075	46,389
3	(0.14 × 46,389) = 6,494	10,000	6,494	3,506	42,883
4	(0.14 × 42,883) = 6,004	10,000	6,004	3,996	38,887
5	(0.14 × 38,887) = 5,444	10,000	5,444	4,556	34,331
6	(0.14 × 34,331) = 4,806	10,000	4,806	5,194	29,137
7	(0.14 × 29,137) = 4,079	10,000	4,079	5,921	23,216
8	(0.14 × 23,216) = 3,250	10,000	3,250	6,750	16,466
9	(0.14 × 16,466) = 2,305	10,000	2,305	7,695	8,771
10	(0.14 × 8,771) = 1,229	10,000	1,229	8,771	-0-

The entries to account for the lease during the first year would be

Lease Obligation	2,697	
Interest Expense	7,303	
Cash		10,000
Paid first-year lease obligation for computer ($52,161 × 0.14 = $7,303).		
Amortization (Depreciation) Expense—Leased Computer	5,216	
Accumulated Amortization—Leased Computer		5,216
Amortized the leased computer for the first year ($52,161 ÷ 10 years).		

Similar entries would be made in each of the 10 years of the lease, except that the principal payment (Lease Obligation) would increase while the interest payment (Interest Expense) would decrease.

TO SUMMARIZE If a lease meets any one of four conditions, it must be capitalized, that is, recorded both as an asset and as a liability. The amount recorded is the present value of the total lease payments at the market rate of interest. The recorded asset is amortized (depreciated) and the lease obligation is written off as periodic payments are made. Part of the lease payment is interest expense and part is a reduction of the principal amount of the long-term liability.

CHAPTER REVIEW

The two most common nonoperating sources of funds are (1) debt financing (borrowing money) and (2) equity financing (primarily issuing stock). Although both have advantages and disadvantages, debt financing provides tax-deductible interest payments; often helps increase profits through leveraging; and, in a corporation, does not dilute the ownership of a firm, thus allowing for higher earnings per share.

Long-term liabilities are measured in the accounting records at the present value of all future outflows of assets required to pay for them. If the interest rate of a long-term liability is approximately equal to the market rate of interest, the present value is approximately equal to the stated amount of the liability. On the other hand, if there is no interest or if the interest rate is significantly below the market rate of interest, the long-term liability must be discounted to its present value.

The most common types of long-term liabilities are notes payable, bonds payable, mortgages payable, deferred income taxes payable, and lease obligations.

A note payable is an unconditional written promise to pay a stated sum of money on or before some specified future date. It can be interest-bearing or non-interest-bearing. If the latter, the note must be discounted to its present value using the market rate of interest.

Bonds are essentially long-term interest-bearing notes issued by businesses and other organizations through underwriters to institutions and to the public. Accounting for bonds includes four elements: accounting for their issuance, for interest payments, for the amortization of premiums and discounts, and for their retirement. If bonds are sold at par on an interest date, accounting for them is relatively simple. However, if they are sold at either a discount or a premium or between interest dates, the accounting becomes more complicated. Premiums and discounts on bonds may be amortized using either the straight-line or the effective-interest method.

A mortgage is similar to a note in that it is also a written promise to pay a stated sum of money in the future; however, a specific asset is pledged as collateral in the case of a mortgage. Most mortgage loans usually require monthly or other periodic payments over their lives.

Deferred income taxes arise when a firm is able to defer into the future a portion of the income taxes it would otherwise pay in the current year. Many items give rise to deferred taxes, but one of the most common is depreciation, whereby one method of depreciation is used for financial reporting purposes and another (ACRS) is used for tax purposes.

A firm can acquire new assets either by purchasing or leasing them. Leasing involves periodic payments over the life of the lease. A lease is treated as a purchase if it meets at least one of four characteristics; as such, it is recorded as both an asset and a long-term liability. The asset is amortized and the liability is reduced as payments are made.

KEY TERMS AND CONCEPTS

bond discount (404)
bond premium (406)
capitalization (415)
debt financing (396)
deferred income taxes (413)
effective-interest amortization (404)
effective interest rate (405)
equity financing (396)
lease (414)
lease obligations (415)
lessee (414)
lessor (414)
leveraging (397)
mortgage amortization schedule (411)
mortgage payable (411)
note payable (398)
par (402)
present value (398)
straight-line interest amortization (404)

REVIEW PROBLEM

Bonds Payable

Dudley Engineering Company received authorization on January 1, 1983, to issue $300,000 of 12 percent callable bonds. (Recall that these are bonds for which the issuer reserves the right to pay the obligation before its maturity date.) The maturity date of the bonds is January 1, 2003. Interest is payable on July 1 and January 1 of each year. The bonds were sold for $289,190 on November 1, 1983. Dudley Engineering uses straight-line amortization and records amortization only on December 31 of each year.

Required:

1. Record the journal entries needed on
   (a) January 1, 1983.
   (b) November 1, 1983.
   (c) December 31, 1983.
   (d) January 1, 1984.
   (e) July 1, 1984.
   (f) December 31, 1984.
2. Because the market rate of interest decreased, Dudley Engineering recalled (reacquired) all the bonds on the open market at 102 on April 1, 1985. Record all journal entries needed to account for this transaction.

Solution

1. Journal Entries
   (a) There is no entry for a bond authorization.
   (b) On the date the bonds are sold, Dudley will require investors to pay the interest that has accrued from July 1, 1983, to November 1, 1983, because on January 1, 1984, Dudley will pay a full 6 months' interest. Also, since bonds are always recorded at their face value, a discount of $10,810 must be recorded. Thus, the entry is

Cash	301,190	
Discount on Bonds	10,810	
Bonds Payable		300,000
Interest Expense ($300,000 × 0.12 × 4/12)		12,000

Sold $300,000 bonds for $289,190 plus accrued interest.

(c) On December 31, 1983, the unpaid interest expense for the year must be recognized, and 2 months' discount amortization must be recorded. The entries are

Bond Interest Expense	94	
Discount on Bonds		94

Amortized discount for 2 months on $300,000 bonds.

Bond Interest Expense	18,000	
Accrued Bond Interest Payable		18,000

Accrued interest on $300,000 bonds.

The first entry records the amortization of the bond discount for 2 months. Since the bonds are expected to be outstanding for 230 months (20 years less 10 months), the $10,810 discount is divided by 230 to arrive at a monthly amortization rate of $47.

The second entry records the interest expense for the 6 months (July 1, 1983–December 31, 1983). Since the entry on November 1 included a credit to Bond Interest Expense of $12,000, the balance in this account (ignoring, for the moment, the discount amortization) for 1983 is $6,000, as shown in the following T-account.

Bond Interest Expense

Dec. 31 18,000	12,000 .... Nov. 1
Balance 6,000	

This $6,000 represents the actual interest expense of the bonds for 2 months ($300,000 × 0.12 × 2/12 = $6,000). Note that the two December entries could have been combined as follows:

Bond Interest Expense	18,094	
Discount on Bonds		94
Accrued Bond Interest Payable		18,000

Amortized discount for 2 months and accrued interest on $300,000 bonds.

(d) The January 1, 1984, entry records the semiannual interest payment. Since $12,000 was collected from investors when the bonds were issued on November 1, 1983, the full 6 months' interest of $18,000 can be paid. The entry is

Accrued Bond Interest Payable	18,000	
Cash		18,000

Paid semiannual interest on $300,000 bonds.

(e) The July 1, 1984, entry records another interest payment.

Bond Interest Expense	18,000	
Cash		18,000

Paid semiannual interest on $300,000 bonds.

(f) The December 31, 1984, entries record the interest expense for the last 6 months of 1984 and the discount amortization for all of 1984. The entries are

Bond Interest Expense	18,000	
Accrued Bond Interest Payable		18,000

Accrued interest on $300,000 bonds.

Bond Interest Expense	564	
Discount on Bonds		564

Amortized discount for 12 months on $300,000 bonds.

The first entry records the interest expense for 6 months, and the second records the discount amortization for 12 months (12 × $47 = $564). Note that the balance in the Bond Interest Expense account for 1984 is $36,564. Since the bonds sold at a discount, the actual or effective interest expense is higher than the stated interest rate of 12 percent. The effective interest rate can be approximated as follows:

$$\frac{\$36,564}{\$289,190} \cong 12.64\%$$

2. Retirement of Bonds*

The first entry on April 1, 1985, updates the amortization to the call date.

Interest Expense	141	
Discount on Bonds		141

Updated discount amortization (3 months × $47).

The entry to recall the bonds is

Bonds Payable	300,000	
Bond Interest Expense	9,000	
Loss on Retirement of Bonds	16,011	
Discount on Bonds		10,011
Cash		315,000

Recalled $300,000 bonds at 102.

The $9,000 interest expense must be paid for the period January 1, 1985, through April 1, 1985. The unamortized discount ($10,810 - $94 - $564 - $141) must be written off when the bonds are retired. The cash paid is equal to 102 percent of $300,000 plus the $9,000 interest. The loss can be computed as the cash paid for retirement (exclusive of interest) less the book value of the bonds, as shown below.

Bond Principal	$300,000
Unamortized Discount	10,011
Book Value	$289,989
Cash Paid	$306,000
Book Value	289,989
Loss on Retirement	$ 16,011

* Because the market interest rate has dropped, the company finds it advantageous to recall the bonds so that it can issue new bonds at a lower interest rate. Although there is an immediate loss when the bonds are recalled, over the long run less cash will be paid for interest expense, thus decreasing the cost of the debt.

DISCUSSION QUESTIONS

1 What is the difference between debt and equity financing?

2 For a profitable company, why is the effective cost of borrowing usually lower than the stated interest rates on loans?

3 What are the advantages and disadvantages of debt financing?

4 When does the stated amount of a liability equal its present value?

5 To whom do companies usually sell bonds?

6 What two major factors affect the issuance price of bonds?

7 If a bond's stated interest rate is below the market interest rate, will the bond sell at a premium or at a discount?

8 If you think the market interest rate is going to drop in the near future, should you invest in bonds?

9 When do you think bonds would sell at or near face value?

10 What type of account is Discount on Bonds?

11 Why does the amortization of a bond discount increase the effective interest rate of bonds?

12 Why is the effective-interest amortization method more theoretically appropriate than the straight-line amortization method?

13 Why must investors pay for unearned interest when purchasing bonds between interest dates?

14 What is the difference between a note and a mortgage payable?

15 Why do you think the real monthly cost of a home mortgage is less than the monthly cash payment?

16 Why would a company defer the payment of taxes into the future?

17 On the basis of what you've read in the chapter, what do you think the term "off-balance-sheet financing" implies?

18 Under what conditions is it necessary to capitalize a lease?

EXERCISES

E12–1 Accounting for an Interest-Bearing Note

Shirley Company borrowed $4,000 on an 18 percent, 2-year interest-bearing note dated October 1, 1983. The annual accounting period ends on December 31. Give entries on the following dates (assume that all interest is paid on the maturity date).

1. October 1, 1983
2. December 31, 1983
3. December 31, 1984
4. October 1, 1985

E12–2 Accounting for an Interest-Bearing Note

On July 1, 1983, Xenia Corporation borrowed $8,000 for 2 years from a bank at 8 percent interest. Give all necessary journal entries to account for this note, assuming that the company's accounting year ends on December 31 and that interest is paid annually on July 1.

E12–3 Accounting for an Interest-Bearing Note

Toni Corporation borrowed $6,000 on a 9 percent, 3-year interest-bearing note dated October 1, 1983. The annual accounting period ends on December 31. Give entries on the following dates (assume that all interest is paid at maturity and that interest is accrued each year on December 31).

1. October 1, 1983
2. December 31, 1983
3. December 31, 1985
4. October 1, 1986

E12–4 Accounting for a Non-Interest-Bearing Note

On January 1, 1983, Delicious, Inc., makers of quality applesauce, purchased two new delivery trucks by issuing a non-interest-bearing note for $30,000, payable in full at the end of 5 years. The current market rate of interest is 9 percent.

Prepare journal entries to account for the purchase of the trucks on January 1, 1983, and related entries at December 31, 1983, and December 31, 1984, to account for the interest expense. You are not required to make any depreciation entries. Assume that the effective-interest method is used.

E12–5 Accounting for Bonds Sold at a Discount

Truman Corporation issued $200,000 of 10 percent, 10-year bonds at 98 on April 1, 1983. Interest is payable semiannually on April 1 and October 1.

1. Record the necessary entries to account for these bonds on the following three dates. (Use the straight-line method to amortize the bond discount and record discount amortization with each semiannual interest entry.)
   (a) April 1, 1983
   (b) October 1, 1983
   (c) December 31, 1983
2. Show how the bonds would be reported on the balance sheet of Truman Corporation on December 31, 1983.

E12–6 Accounting for Bonds Sold at a Premium

Mapleton Implement Corporation issued $500,000 of 12 percent, 10-year bonds at 102 on June 30, 1983. Interest is payable on June 30 and December 31. The corporation uses the straight-line method to amortize bond premiums and discounts. The corporation's fiscal year runs from February 1 through January 31.

Prepare all necessary entries to account for the bonds from the date of issuance through June 30, 1984. Also record the retirement of the bonds on June 30, 1993, assuming that all interest has been paid and that the premium has been amortized. Note that the bond premium should be amortized with each interest entry.

E12–7 Accounting for Bonds Sold at a Premium

On April 1, 1983, Rice Corporation issued a $1,000, 12 percent, 5-year bond for $1,177 plus accrued interest. The bond was dated March 1, 1983, and interest is payable each March 1 and September 1. Provide entries at each of the following dates.

1.	April 1, 1983	Issuance
2.	September 1, 1983	Interest payment (assume straight-line amortization of bond premium)
3.	December 31, 1983	Adjusting entry
4.	December 31, 1983	Closing entry for the interest expense

E12–8 Analysis of Bonds

A $200,000, 12 percent bond was sold on March 1, 1983. The bonds pay interest each February 28 and August 31 and mature 10 years from March 1, 1983. Using these data, complete the table below (show computations and assume straight-line amortization).

Case A: The bonds sold at par.

Case B: The bonds sold at 97.

Case C: The bonds sold at 103.

	Case A	Case B	Case C
Cash inflow at issuance date	______	______	______
Total cash outflow through maturity	______	______	______
Income Statement for 1983			
Bond Interest Expense	______	______	______
Balance Sheet at December 31, 1983			
Long-Term Liabilities:			
Bonds Payable, 12%	______	______	______
Unamortized Discount	______	______	______
Unamortized Premium	______	______	______
Net Liability	______	______	______
Approximate Effective Interest Rate*	______	______	______

* Round to the nearest tenth of a percent.

E12–9 Accounting for Bonds

Read Corporation, a calendar year firm, is authorized to issue $500,000 of 14 percent, 10-year bonds dated April 1, 1983, with interest payable semiannually on April 1 and October 1.

Provide General Journal entries to record the following events, assuming that the bonds sold at 104 on April 1, 1983. Amortization of bond premiums or discounts is recorded only at year-end and the straight-line amortization method is used.

1. The bond issuance on April 1, 1983.
2. Payment of interest on October 1, 1983.
3. Adjusting entries at December 31, 1983.

E12–10 Effective-Interest Amortization

Johnson Company issued a 12 percent, 4-year, $1,000 bond on January 1, 1983. The interest is payable each year on December 31. The bond was sold at an effective interest rate of 10 percent. With respect to these bonds, the following computations have been made.

Date	Cash	Interest	Principal	Balance
January 1, 1983				$1,063
End of year 1 . . .	$120	$106	$14	1,049
End of year 2 . . .	120	105	15	1,034
End of year 3 . . .	120	104	16	1,018
End of year 4 . . .	120	102	18	1,000

1. At what price was the bond issued?
2. Did the bond sell at a premium or a discount? How much?

3. How much interest expense would be shown on the income statement each year?
4. What long-term liability amount would be shown on the balance sheet at the end of year 3?
5. How were the following amounts calculated for year 3? (a) $120 (b) $104 (c) $16 (d) $1,018

E12–11 Effective-Interest Calculations

Determine the approximate effective rate of interest for $100,000, 7 percent, 5-year bonds issued at 96 (assume straight-line amortization).

E12–12 Deferred Income Taxes

Judson Corporation had pretax income of $20,000, $50,000, $10,000, zero, and $30,000 during the years 1981 to 1985. Judson Corporation pays taxes at a rate of 40 percent. During those same years, Judson determined that current taxes payable to the IRS were $5,000, $10,000, $8,000, $3,000, and $7,000, respectively. (Note that the amount of taxes payable is not necessarily equal to the tax expense due to differences between IRS and accounting rules.)

1. Record the 1983 income tax expense and income taxes payable in General Journal format.
2. Calculate the balance of deferred income taxes for these 5 years as of December 31, 1985.

E12–13 Deferred Income Taxes

In 1983, RCB Corporation purchased a computer at a cost of $80,000. The computer had a 4-year life, was depreciated on a straight-line basis for financial reporting, and had no expected salvage value. Using straight-line depreciation, RCB Corporation had pretax financial income of $20,000, $30,000, $40,000, and $30,000, respectively, in the 4 years 1983 to 1986. Assuming that RCB Corporation's tax rate is 40 percent and that its ACRS depreciation on the computer for the years 1983 to 1986 was $20,000, $30,400, $29,600, and zero, record the tax entries for each of the 4 years.

E12–14 Lease Accounting

Mead Corporation signed a noncancelable lease to use a machine for 10 years. The fair market value of the machine is $80,000, which is approximately equal to the present value of the lease payments. The annual lease payment is $14,159 payable at the end of each year.

1. Record the lease, assuming that the lease should be capitalized.
2. For the initial year only, record the annual payment of the lease and interest expense (assuming 12 percent interest). Also record amortization expense using the straight-line method and assuming no salvage value.
3. Now record the annual payment of the lease, assuming that the lease is not capitalized.

E12–15 Lease Accounting

On July 1, 1983, Taylor Farms, Inc. leased a grain harvester. The lease agreement called for payments of $5,000 a year (payable each July 1) for 10 years. The fair market value of the harvester is $37,500 and the market rate of interest is 7 percent. (Assume that Taylor Farms, Inc. uses straight-line depreciation and that its accounting year-end is December 31.)

1. Prepare journal entries for the following dates.
   (a) July 1, 1983, to record the capitalization of the lease.
   (b) December 31, 1983, to recognize interest.
   (c) July 1, 1984, to show the first payment on the lease.
2. Now assume that the fair market value of the harvester is $40,000 when purchased. Prepare journal entries for the same dates as in part (1).

PROBLEMS

P12–1 Accounting for Interest- and Non-Interest-Bearing Notes

Sweet's Candy Company needed cash for working capital. On March 1, 1983, the company secured a $5,000 interest-bearing note at 8.5 percent due in 2 years from Peterson Bank (interest payable at maturity). It also received $2,500 from Laurence National Bank in return for a non-interest-bearing note of $4,000 due in 3 years.

Required:

1. Give the journal entries to record the receipt of cash on March 1, 1983.
2. Give the entries to record the interest expense on the two notes for 1983 (assume straight-line amortization of the Laurence National Bank discount).
3. Give the entries that would be required on the payment dates of the two notes, assuming that adjusting entries had been made each year on December 31.
4. Compute the effective rate of the Laurence National Bank note.
5. **Interpretive Question** What would the Laurence Bank note's rate of interest have been if the amount of interest had remained the same—$1,500—but the non-interest-bearing note had been instead a $4,000 interest-bearing note. Explain why the interest rate is higher or lower than the rate calculated in part (4).

P12-2 Accounting for Bonds

Required:

1. On July 1, 1983, Wheeler Corporation issued $90,000, 10-year, 14 percent bonds at 96. The bonds were dated July 1, 1983, and pay interest each June 30 and December 31.

(a) Give the entry to record the issuance of the bonds.

(b) Give the December 31, 1983, interest payment entry. Assume straight-line amortization of bond discount.

2. On May 1, 1983, Merrimae Corporation sold a $1,000, 12 percent, 5-year bond for $1,058 plus accrued interest. The bond was dated March 1, 1983, and interest is payable each March 1 and September 1. Record the issuance of the bond.

3. **Interpretive Question** Why must investors who buy bonds between interest dates pay for accrued interest?

P12-3 Accounting for Bonds

W. R. Sheldon and W. O. Rentz incorporated their training school in 1983. On January 1, 1984, $100,000 of 12 percent callable bonds were authorized. The maturity date is January 1, 1991. Interest is payable on July 1 and January 1. The bonds were sold at 102 plus accrued interest on May 1, 1984. The company closes its books each year on December 31. (Note: Any bond premium or discount is amortized only on December 31, using the straight-line method.)

Required:

1. Make the appropriate General Journal entries on the following dates.

(a) May 1, 1984

(b) July 1, 1984

(c) December 31, 1984

2. Due to the cancellation of a previously planned school expansion and the lowering of market interest rates, the corporation reacquired all the bonds on the open market at 105, plus accrued interest, on April 1, 1985. Show these transactions in General Journal format.

P12-4 Accounting for Bonds

Martin Boat Company authorized and sold $75,000 of 8 percent, 15-year bonds on April 1, 1983. The bonds pay interest each April 1 and Martin's year-end is December 31.

Required:

1. Prepare journal entries to record the issuance of these bonds under each of the following three assumptions.

(a) Sold at 97.

(b) Sold at par.

(c) Sold at 105.

2. Prepare adjusting journal entries for the bonds on December 31, 1983, under all three assumptions (use the straight-line amortization method).

3. Show how the bond liabilities would appear on the December 31, 1983, balance sheet under each of the three assumptions.

4. **Interpretive Question** What situation would cause the bonds to sell at 97? At 105?

P12-5 Effective-Interest Amortization

Moose Trucking Company issued $100,000 of 6 percent bonds on January 1, 1983. The bonds pay interest on December 31 of each year and have a 4-year life.

Required:

Given that the bonds sold at a price that yielded an 8 percent return, complete the following.

1. At what price were the bonds issued?

2. Prepare a bond amortization schedule to amortize any premium or discount on the bonds using the effective-interest amortization method.

3. **Interpretive Question** When must this method of amortization be used? Why?

P12-6 Unifying Problem: Bonds

On January 1, 1983, Talbot Company decided to issue $1,000,000 of 8 percent, 10-year bonds with interest payable on January 1 and July 1 of each year. Due to several problems, Talbot was not able to sell the bonds until September 1, 1983, at which time the bonds were issued at 104. (Assume straight-line amortization of any discount or premium and record the amortization with each interest expense entry.)

Required:

1. Prepare all necessary journal entries to account for the bonds through December 31, 1984.

2. Determine the effective rate of interest on the bonds.

3. Show how all the bond-related items would appear on the December 31, 1983, balance sheet.

4. **Interpretive Question** Why isn't the bond premium amortized over 120 months?

P12-7 Unifying Problem: Callable Bonds

Patterson Construction Company decided to issue $200,000 of 12 percent callable bonds on January 1, 1983. The maturity date of the bonds is January 1, 1994. Interest is payable on July 1 and January 1. The bonds were sold at 96 plus accrued interest on August 1, 1983. The company uses the straight-line method of amortizing bond premiums and discounts and records such amortizations only at year-end, December 31.

Required:

1. Make the required journal entries for each of the following dates.
   (a) August 1, 1983
   (b) December 31, 1983
   (c) January 1, 1984
   (d) July 1, 1984

2. Because of economic considerations (the lowering of the market rate of interest), Patterson Company recalled all of the bonds on the open market at face value (100). The bonds were recalled on July 1, 1986. The following entry had just been made on that day.

Bond Interest Expense	12,000	
Cash		12,000

Made semiannual interest payment on the bonds.

Record the entry to reacquire the bond. (Hint: Your entry must include an updating of the discount amortization.)

P12-8 Unifying Problem: Callable Bonds with Partial Retirement

Boulder Mountain Corporation was authorized to issue $2,000,000 of 6 percent, 15-year callable bonds, dated January 1, 1983. However, because of an unusually tight money market, it could not sell the bonds until November 1, 1983, at which time they were sold at 91½ plus accrued interest. Interest is payable semiannually on January 1 and July 1.

Required:

1. Record, in General Journal form, entries on:
   (a) November 1, 1983
   (b) December 31, 1983
   (c) January 1, 1984

2. On February 1, 1986, the corporation retired $400,000 of the 15-year bonds at 96. Record all necessary journal entries.

3. **Interpretive Question** Why would the company call the bonds at 96 and suffer a loss on the retirement?

P12-9 Deferred Income Taxes

On January 1, 1979, Big Horn Mountain Association purchased a road grader for $100,000. Big Horn depreciates the road grader on a straight-line basis for financial reporting purposes but uses ACRS for tax purposes. The grader has an expected useful life of 5 years and no salvage value. Assuming that it qualifies for a 3-year write-off, ACRS depreciation for the first 3 years is $25,000, $38,000, and $37,000 respectively, and zero in the last 2 years of its life.

Required:

1. Given that the financial statements of Big Horn Mountain Association show income before taxes of $60,000, $50,000, $40,000, $60,000, and $70,000 in the years 1979 to 1983, prepare the journal entry in each of the 5 years to record the income tax expense. (Note: Big Horn Mountain Association is taxed at 30 percent.)

2. **Interpretive Question** Why is ACRS, which allows a company to defer income tax payments into the future, beneficial to the company?

P12-10 Lease Accounting

On January 1, 1983, Veiwig Trucking Company leased a truck from Peterbuilt, Inc. The lease terms call for payments of $6,000 per year for 10 years. The truck is expected to have a 10-year useful life, after which time it will have no value to either Veiwig or Peterbuilt.

Required:

Assuming that the payments are due at the end of each year, and that the market rate of interest is 12 percent, complete the following.

1. What is the present value of the lease payments?
2. Record the lease in the accounting records at January 1, 1983.
3. Complete a lease amortization schedule (rounded to the nearest dollar).
4. **Interpretive Question** Why should this lease be capitalized?

CHAPTER 13

Owners' Equity—The Corporation

THIS CHAPTER EXPLAINS:

The basic characteristics of a corporation.

Accounting for contributed capital, including common, preferred, and treasury stock.

Accounting for dividends.

Accounting for retained earnings.

Assets and liabilities were discussed in Chapters 8 through 12. In this chapter and the next, the focus is on owners' equity. This will complete our coverage of the balance sheet. Although accounting for the asset and liability accounts is generally the same in all businesses (corporations, partnerships, and proprietorships), accounting for equity is different for each of the three forms of business. Here owners' equity is discussed in the context of corporations; in Chapter 14, equity considerations for partnerships and proprietorships are covered.

There are certain basic characteristics common to all owners' equity accounts, no matter what the type of business. The first is that they represent the owners' interests in a firm, revealing how much the owners have contributed and how much of the firm's earnings have been retained for its owners. Owners' equity accounts can therefore be thought of as identifying some of the sources of a firm's assets. Second, if all three types of businesses entered into the same transactions over their lifetimes, the total amounts in their owners' equity sections would be approximately the same.[1] These totals are determined by the types of transactions entered into and the amounts involved, not by the form of organization. In other words, while owners' equity accounts differ in ways that will be illustrated for the three types of businesses, their purposes and functions are the same.

[1] There would probably be some differences due to differing tax treatments. If taxes were ignored, the totals would be equal.

Characteristics of a Corporation

corporation *a legal entity chartered by a state; ownership is represented by transferable shares of stock*

Corporations are the dominant form of business enterprise in the United States. Established as separate legal entities, corporations are legally distinct from the persons responsible for their creation. In many respects, they are accorded the same rights as individuals; they can conduct business, be sued, enter into contracts, and own property. Firms are incorporated by the state in which they are organized and are subject to its laws and requirements.

Suppose that you wanted to start a corporation. First, you would study your state's corporate laws (usually with the aid of an attorney). Then you would apply for a charter with the appropriate state official. In the application, you would give the intended name of your corporation, its purpose (that is, the type of activity it will engage in), the type and amount of stock you plan to have authorized for your corporation, and, in some cases, the names and addresses of the potential stockholders. Finally, if the state approves your application, you will be issued a charter (also called articles of incorporation), giving legal status to your corporation.

charter (articles of incorporation) *a document issued by a state that gives legal status to a corporation and details its specific rights, including the authority to issue a certain maximum number of shares of stock*

limited liability *the legal protection given stockholders whereby they are responsible for the debts and obligations of a corporation only to the extent of their capital contribution*

Corporations have several characteristics that distinguish them from other types of business entities. Probably the most significant is the limited liability of stockholders. This means that in the event of corporate bankruptcy the maximum financial loss any stockholder can sustain is his or her investment in the corporation (unless fraud can be proved). Since a corporation is a separate legal entity and is responsible for its own acts and obligations, creditors cannot usually look beyond the corporation's assets for satisfaction of their claims. This is not true of other forms of business. In a partnership, for example, the partners can usually be held liable for the debts of the partnership, even to the extent of their personal assets. This limited liability feature has probably been most responsible for the phenomenal growth of the corporate form of business.

A second characteristic of a corporation is the easy transferability of ownership interests. This means that shares of stock in a corporation can be bought, sold, passed from one generation to another, or otherwise transferred, without affecting the legal or economic status of the corporation. When you buy stock in a corporation, you become an owner and receive a stock certificate as evidence of ownership (see Exhibit 13-1). All of the owners are called stockholders and they govern the corporation through an elected board of directors. (In most corporations, the board of directors then chooses a management team to direct the daily affairs of the corporation.)

stock certificate *a document issued by a corporation to shareholders evidencing ownership in the corporation*

stockholders *individuals or organizations that own a portion (shares of stock) of a corporation*

board of directors *individuals elected by the shareholders to govern a corporation*

A third characteristic of corporations is that they are taxed independently. Because corporations are separate legal entities, they are taxed independently of their owners. This often results in a disadvantage, however, because the portion of corporate profits that is paid out in dividends is taxed twice. First, the profits are taxed to the corporation; second, assuming that dividends have been declared, the owners are taxed on their dividend income. (Small corporations can avoid this double taxation by forming a Subchapter S corporation.)

Subchapter S corporation *a corporation legally organized in such a way that income or loss is passed through to individual shareholders without being taxed at the corporate level*

A fourth characteristic of very large corporations is that they are relatively closely regulated by government. Because large corporations may have millions of shareholders, each with only small ownership interests,

EXHIBIT 13-1 A Typical Stock Certificate

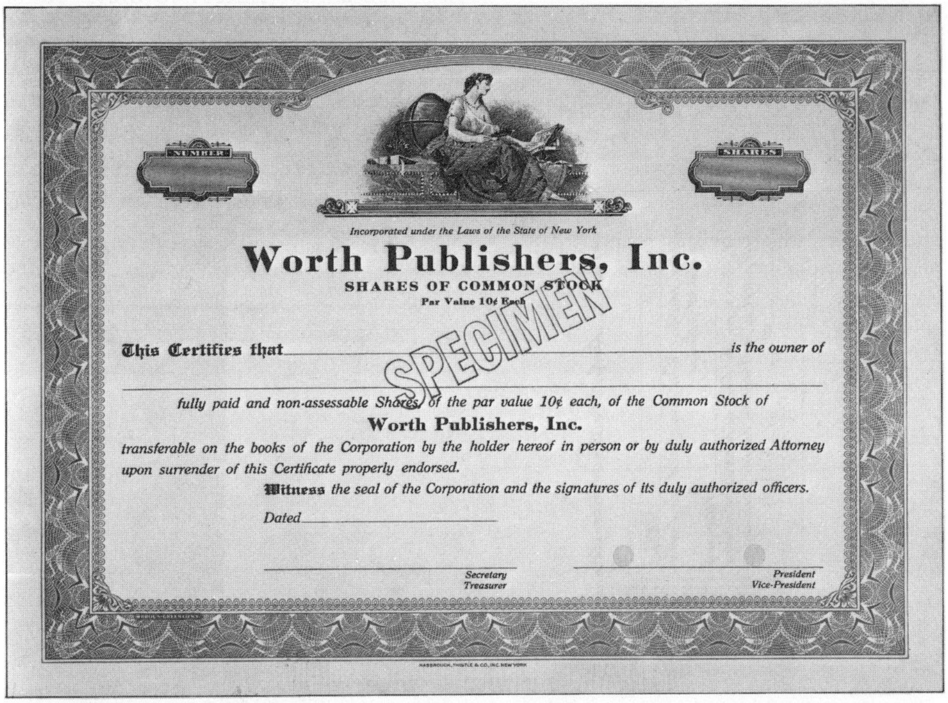
NUMBER

SHARES

Incorporated under the Laws of the State of New York

Worth Publishers, Inc.

SHARES OF COMMON STOCK

Par Value 10¢ Each

SPECIMEN

This Certifies that ______ *is the owner of*

fully paid and non-assessable Shares of the par value 10¢ each, of the Common Stock of

Worth Publishers, Inc.

transferable on the books of the Corporation by the holder hereof in person or by duly authorized Attorney upon surrender of this Certificate properly endorsed.

Witness *the seal of the Corporation and the signatures of its duly authorized officers.*

Dated ______

Secretary
Treasurer

President
Vice-President

government has assumed the task of monitoring certain corporate activities. Examples of government regulations are the requirements that all major corporations be audited and that they issue periodic financial statements. As a result, in certain respects major corporations often enjoy less freedom than do partnerships or proprietorships.

TO SUMMARIZE Unlike the asset and liability accounts, the owners' equity accounts vary depending on whether the business is a corporation, a partnership, or a proprietorship. A corporation is a business entity that has a legal existence separate from that of its owners; it can conduct business, own property, and enter into contracts. The four major features of a corporation are (1) limited liability for stockholders, (2) easy transferability of ownership, (3) separate taxation, and (4) (for major corporations) greater regulation by government.

The Stock of a Corporation

contributed capital *the portion of owners' equity contributed by investors (the owners) through the issuance of stock*

The owners' equity section of a corporate balance sheet is usually divided into two parts: (1) contributed capital, which identifies capital contributed by the owners of a firm, and (2) retained earnings, which shows the undistributed earnings of a firm since incorporation. In this section, we focus on the contributed capital accounts.

capital stock *the general term applied to all shares of ownership in a corporation*

authorized stock *the amount and type of stock that may be issued by a company, as specified in its articles of incorporation*

issued stock *authorized stock originally issued to stockholders; it may or may not still be outstanding*

outstanding stock *issued stock that is still being held by investors*

treasury stock *issued stock that has subsequently been reacquired by the corporation*

When a corporation is given its charter by a state, it can sell shares of stock to raise capital. These shares, which are generally referred to as capital stock, may be sold publicly to many individuals, or privately to only a few individuals.

Corporate stock that has been approved for sale by a state is known as authorized stock. When the stock is sold, it becomes issued stock. If it is issued and not bought back by the corporation, it is said to be issued and outstanding, but if it has been reacquired by the corporation, it is known as treasury stock. These stages in the status of stock are diagrammed in Exhibit 13–2.

EXHIBIT 13–2 **Stages in the Status of Stock**

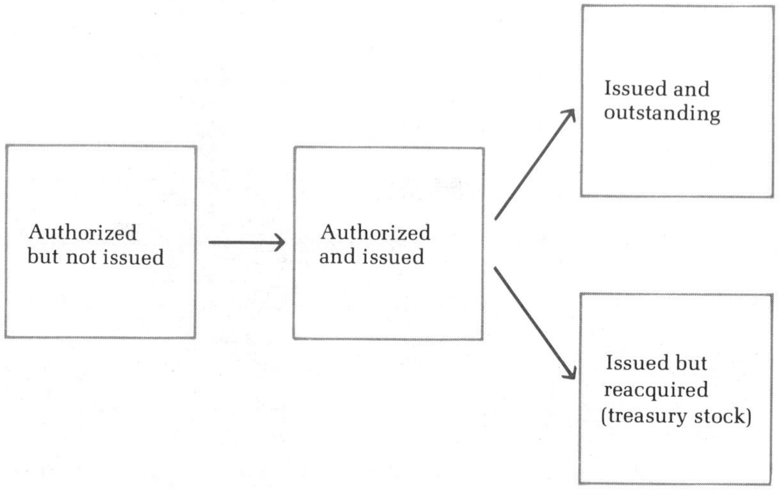

common stock *the class of stock most frequently issued by corporations; it usually confers a voting right in the corporation; its dividend and liquidation rights generally come second to those of preferred stock*

preferred stock *a class of stock issued by corporations; it usually confers dividend and liquidation rights that take precedence over those of common stock*

par-value stock *stock that has a nominal value assigned to it in the corporation's charter and printed on the face of each share of stock*

In addition, several types of stock can be authorized by the charter and issued by the corporation. The most familiar types are common stock and preferred stock, and the major difference between them concerns the degree to which their holders are allowed to participate in the rights of ownership of the corporation. The three basic rights inherent in the ownership of common stock are (1) the right to vote in corporate matters, (2) the right to share in distributed corporate earnings, and (3) the right to share in corporate assets upon liquidation. Usually, preferred stock takes precedence over common stock in rights (2) and (3), whereas common stock is often the only type of stock that provides voting rights. By issuing stocks with different rights and privileges, companies can appeal to a wider range of investors.

When only one type of stock is issued by a corporation, it is common stock. There are several different types of common stock, the most popular of which is par-value stock. Basically, this stock has a par, or nominal, value provided for in the corporate charter and printed on the face of each stock certificate. When par-value stock sells for a price above par, it is said to sell

premium on stock *the excess of the issuance (market) price of stock over its par or stated value*

legal capital *the amount of contributed capital not available for dividends, as restricted by state law for the protection of creditors; usually equal to the par or stated value of outstanding capital stock*

no-par stock *stock that does not have a par value printed on the face of the stock certificate*

stated value *a nominal value assigned to no-par stock by the board of directors of a corporation*

at a premium; by law, it generally cannot be issued for a price below par value. The par value multiplied by the total number of shares outstanding is usually equal to the legal capital and it represents the amount of contributed capital that is not available for dividends. This legal capital requirement was intended to provide a means of protecting a company's creditors; without it, excessive dividends could be paid, leaving nothing for creditors. Because the assignment of a par value to stock has proved to be an ineffective way of protecting creditors, most states now allow the sale of no-par stock. Many states require, however, that no-par stock have a stated value, which is designated by the board of directors of a corporation and has the same purpose as par value. For no-par stock without a stated value, the legal capital is usually the total amount for which the stock was initially issued.

A final note about par value: Stock often sells for a much higher price than its par value. Indeed, the trend has been for companies to establish a very low par value, say $1, or 10 cents, per share, and then sell the stock for a much higher amount, say $10 per share. This strategy usually eliminates the possibility of stock ever selling below par value. If stock were to be issued at a discount (below par), stockholders could be liable for legal capital in excess of their investments in the corporation.

TO SUMMARIZE The owners' equity section of a corporation's balance sheet is divided into two parts: (1) contributed capital and (2) retained earnings. A corporation's stock can be authorized but unsold, issued and outstanding, or repurchased by the company and held as treasury stock. Common stock confers three rights upon its owners: (1) the right to vote in corporate matters, (2) the right to share in company earnings, and (3) the right to share in the assets upon liquidation of a corporation. Preferred stock typically carries preferential claims to dividend and liquidation privileges, but no voting rights. Stock can be par value, no par with a stated value, or no par with no stated value. If par value, it usually sells above par (at a premium). The minimum amount of contributed capital a firm must maintain is called its legal capital.

ACCOUNTING FOR THE ISSUANCE OF PAR-VALUE STOCK AND NO-PAR STOCK WITH A STATED VALUE

When par-value stock is issued by a corporation, usually Cash is debited and the appropriate stockholder's equity accounts are credited. For par-value common stock, the equity accounts credited are Common Stock, for an amount equal to the par value, and Paid-in Capital in Excess of Par—Common Stock, for the premium on common stock.

To illustrate, we will assume that the Dallas Oilers Football Team (a corporation) issued 1,000 shares of $10 par common stock for $50 per share. (Note that an accounting entry is not required at the time the stock is authorized, only when it is issued.) The entry to record the stock issuance would be as shown on the next page.

Cash (1,000 shares × $50)	50,000	
Common Stock (1,000 shares × $10 par value)		10,000
Paid-in Capital in Excess of Par— Common Stock (1,000 shares × $40)		40,000
Issued 1,000 shares of $10 par-value stock at $50 per share.		

If the par-value stock being issued were preferred stock, the entry would be

Cash (1,000 shares × $50)	50,000	
Preferred Stock (1,000 shares × $10 par value)		10,000
Paid-in Capital in Excess of Par— Preferred Stock (1,000 shares × $40)		40,000
Issued 1,000 shares of $10 par-value preferred stock at $50 per share.		

This illustration points out two important elements in accounting for the issuance of stock: (1) the equity accounts identify the type of stock being issued (common or preferred), and (2) the proceeds from the sale of the stock are divided into the portion attributable to its par value and the portion paid in excess of par value. These distinctions are important because the owners' equity section of the balance sheet should correctly identify the specific sources of capital, so that the respective rights of the various shareholders can be known.

If issued stock is no-par with a stated value, the entries are virtually the same. To illustrate, we now assume that the Dallas Oilers' authorized stock was no-par stock with a stated value of $1 per share, and that 4,000 shares were issued for $5 per share. The entry would be

Cash (4,000 shares × $5)	20,000	
Common Stock (4,000 shares × $1 stated value)		4,000
Paid-in Capital in Excess of Stated Value— Common Stock (4,000 shares × $4)		16,000
Issued 4,000 shares of no-par stock with a $1 stated value at $5 per share.		

Again, if the stock being issued were preferred stock, the only change in this entry would be to identify the stock as preferred stock.

Although stock is usually issued for cash, other considerations may be involved. When a corporation is being organized, for example, attorneys and accountants may be paid with stock. The only difference between stock issued for noncash considerations and stock purchased for cash is in the debit entry. In the case of stock being given to an attorney for help in organizing a corporation, the debit entry is usually to Organization Costs, rather than to Legal Expense. The Organization Costs account is an intangible asset that is usually amortized over the first 5 years of a corporation's existence.

To illustrate the kinds of entries that are made when stock is issued for noncash considerations, we will assume that a prospective stockholder exchanged a piece of land with a fair market value of $25,000 for 5,000 shares of the Dallas Oilers' $1-per-share stated-value common stock. The entry would be as follows:

Land	25,000	
Common Stock (5,000 shares × $1)		5,000
Paid-in Capital in Excess of Stated Value—Common Stock		20,000
Issued 5,000 shares of no-par stock, $1 stated value, for land valued at $25,000.		

ACCOUNTING FOR THE ISSUANCE OF NO-PAR STOCK WITHOUT A STATED VALUE

If the stock being issued is no par without a stated value, only one credit is recorded in the entry. To illustrate, we assume that the Oilers' stock does not have a par or stated value and that the corporation issued 2,000 shares for $14 per share. The entry to record this issuance would be

Cash (2,000 shares × $14)	28,000	
Common Stock		28,000
Issued 2,000 shares of no-par stock at $14 per share.		

Since most stock issued is either par-value stock or no-par stock with a stated value, only these two categories will be discussed in the remainder of this chapter.

ACCOUNTING FOR TREASURY STOCK

As noted earlier, a corporation may acquire some of its own outstanding stock. This reacquired stock is called treasury stock and is much like unissued stock in that it has no voting, dividend, or other rights. Because the acquisition of treasury stock effectively reduces the amount of stock outstanding and thereby allows a corporation to reduce its legal capital, most states restrict the amount of treasury stock a firm can have.

There are many reasons for a firm to buy back its own stock. Five of the most common are that management (1) may want the stock for a profit-sharing, bonus, or stock-option plan for employees, (2) may feel that the stock is selling for an unusually low price and is a good buy, (3) may want to stimulate trading in the company's stock, (4) may want the stock for use in purchasing another company, and (5) may want to increase reported earnings per share by reducing the number of shares of stock outstanding.

When a firm purchases another company's stock, the investment is included as an asset on the balance sheet. However, a corporation cannot own part of itself, so treasury stock is not considered an asset. Instead, it is a contra-equity account and is included on the balance sheet as a deduction from stockholders' equity.

Most commonly, treasury stock is accounted for on a cost basis. (Although other methods exist, they will not be shown here.) That is, the stock is debited at its cost, not at its par or stated value. To illustrate, we assume that 100 shares of the $10 par common stock were reacquired by the Dallas Oilers for $60 per share. The entry to record the acquisition would be

Treasury Stock, Common (100 shares at $60) . . .	6,000	
Cash		6,000
Acquired 100 shares of treasury stock at $60 per share.		

The effect of this entry on the balance sheet is to reduce both total assets (cash) and total stockholders' equity by $6,000.

When treasury stock is reissued, the entry depends on its issuance price. If the stock's price exceeds its cost, there is an increase in total stockholders' equity; if its price is below cost, there is an overall decrease in stockholders' equity.

To illustrate, we assume that 40 of the 100 shares of treasury stock are reissued at $80 per share. The entry to record this reissuance would be

Cash (40 shares × $80)	3,200	
Treasury Stock, Common (40 shares × $60 cost)		2,400
Paid-in Capital—Treasury Stock		800
Reissued 40 shares of treasury stock at $80 per share.		

As indicated, when price exceeds cost, the excess is entered in a special account: Paid-in Capital—Treasury Stock. The $800 is thus the difference between the purchase price and the sales price ($80 − $60 = $20) multiplied by the number of shares reissued. After this transaction, the company retains a balance of $3,600 in treasury stock (60 shares held at $60 per share). Note that Retained Earnings is never credited for the excess. While Retained Earnings may be reduced by treasury stock transactions, as shown on the next page, it cannot be increased by such transactions.

If additional treasury stock is subsequently issued for less than the acquisition price, the entry depends on whether Paid-in Capital—Treasury Stock has a balance from previous transactions. If it has a balance, then it can be reduced to account for the difference between cost and selling price; if not, Retained Earnings is reduced to account for the difference. Alternatively, Retained Earnings can be reduced for the entire amount, even if Paid-in Capital—Treasury Stock exists. (In this book, we will always assume that if Paid-in Capital—Treasury Stock exists, it will be reduced first, with any balance going to Retained Earnings.)

To illustrate, we assume that another 50 shares of treasury stock are reissued for $50 per share, $10 less than their cost. Since Paid-in Capital—Treasury Stock has a balance of $800, the entry to record this subsequent transaction may be

Cash (50 shares × $50)	2,500	
Paid-in Capital—Treasury Stock	500	
Treasury Stock, Common (50 shares × $60 cost)		3,000
Issued 50 shares of treasury stock at $50 per share; original cost was $60 per share.		

If Paid-in Capital—Treasury Stock had not had a balance from previous transactions, the entry would have been

Cash (50 shares × $50)	2,500	
Retained Earnings	500	
Treasury Stock, Common (50 shares × $60 cost)		3,000
Issued 50 shares of treasury stock at $50 per share; cost was $60 per share.		

SUMMARIZING STOCKHOLDERS' EQUITY

Thus far, we have discussed the ways in which individual transactions affect owners' equity accounts. It is now appropriate to show how these accounts are summarized and presented on the balance sheet. The following data, which summarize the stockholders' equity transactions of the Dallas Oilers, will be used to illustrate our points.

1. $10 par-value preferred stock: issued 1,000 shares at $50 per share.
2. $10 par-value common stock: issued 1,000 shares at $50 per share.
3. No-par common stock with a $1 stated value: issued 4,000 shares at $5 per share.
4. No-par common stock with a $1 stated value: issued 5,000 shares for land with a fair market value of $25,000.
5. No-par, no-stated-value common stock: issued 2,000 shares at $14 per share.
6. Treasury stock, common: purchased 100 shares at $60; reissued 40 shares at $80; reissued 50 shares at $50.

With these data, the stockholders' equity section would be as shown on the next page.

Dallas Oilers Football Team
*Summarized Stockholders' Equity Section**

Preferred Stock ($10 par value, 1,000 shares issued)	$10,000	
Common Stock ($10 par value, 1,000 shares issued)	10,000	
Common Stock (no par, $1 stated value, 9,000 shares issued)	9,000	
Common Stock (no par, no stated value, 2,000 shares issued)	28,000	
Paid-in Capital in Excess of Par—Preferred Stock	40,000	
Paid-in Capital in Excess of Par—Common Stock	40,000	
Paid-in Capital in Excess of Stated Value—Common Stock	36,000	
Paid-in Capital—Treasury Stock	300	
Total Contributed Capital		$173,300
Retained Earnings (to be discussed)		-0-
Total Contributed Capital Plus Retained Earnings		$173,300
Less Cost of Treasury Stock on Hand (10 shares at $60)		(600)
Total Stockholders' Equity		$172,700

* Note: The number of shares authorized is deleted in this illustration.

Although this stockholders' equity section is not realistic (companies rarely issue more than one type of common stock), it does summarize the information discussed thus far, and it illustrates that the various types of stock, as well as their par or stated values, must be separately identified in the stockholders' equity section.

TO SUMMARIZE When a company issues stock, it debits Cash or a noncash account (property, for example) and credits various stockholders' equity accounts. The credit entries depend on the type of stock issued (common or preferred), its features (par value, no-par with stated value, or no-par without a stated value), and the per-share amounts the stock is issued for (above par and at par). A company's own stock that is reacquired in the marketplace is known as treasury stock and is included in the financial statements as a contra-stockholders' equity account. Treasury stock is usually accounted for on a cost basis. The stockholders' equity section of a balance sheet contains separate accounts for each type of stock issued, amounts paid in excess of par or stated values, treasury stock, and retained earnings.

Distributing the Earnings

If you had your own business and wanted to withdraw money for personal use, you would simply withdraw it from the company's checking account or cash register. In a corporation, a formal action by the board of directors is required before money can be distributed to the owners. In addition, such

pro rata *a term describing an allocation that is based on a proportionate distribution of the total*

dividends *periodic distributions of earnings in the form of cash, stock, or other property to the owners (stockholders) of a corporation*

payments must be made on a pro rata basis (that is, each owner must receive a proportionate amount based on percentage of ownership). These pro rata distributions to owners are called dividends and are usually paid on a per-share basis. Thus, the amount of dividends a shareholder receives depends on the number of shares owned and on the per-share amount of the dividend.

Note that a company does not have to pay dividends. Theoretically, a company that does not pay dividends should be able to reinvest its earnings in assets that will enable it to grow more rapidly than its dividend-paying competitors. This added growth will presumably be reflected in increases in the per-share price of the stock. In practice, most public companies pay regular cash dividends because investors expect them to.

ACCOUNTING FOR DIVIDENDS

cash dividend *a cash distribution of earnings to shareholders*

liquidating dividend *the distribution of a firm's assets to its shareholders when a corporation is permanently reducing its operations or going out of business*

stock dividend *a pro rata distribution of additional shares of stock to shareholders*

property dividend *the distribution to shareholders of assets other than cash or stock*

declaration date *the date on which a corporation's board of directors formally decides to pay a dividend to shareholders*

Corporations can pay any one of several types of dividends. The most common is a cash dividend, which is a payment of cash out of corporate earnings. Another type is a liquidating dividend, which is a cash dividend paid from previous owner contributions. Liquidating dividends are usually paid only when a corporation is permanently reducing its operations or winding down its affairs. A third type is a stock dividend, which is a distribution of additional shares of stock to shareholders. Stock dividends will be discussed later in the chapter. Finally, there is a property dividend, a distribution of corporate assets (for example, the stock of another firm) to shareholders. Property dividends are quite rare.

Three important dates are associated with dividends. The first is when the board of directors formally declares its intent to pay a dividend. On this declaration date, the company becomes legally obligated to pay the dividends. This liability may be recorded as follows:

Dividends—Common Stock	8,000	
Dividends Payable		8,000

Declared a 50-cent-per-share dividend to stockholders of record on December 15, 1983.

At the end of the year, the account Dividends—Common Stock is closed to Retained Earnings by the following entry.

Retained Earnings	8,000	
Dividends—Common Stock		8,000

To close Dividends to Retained Earnings.

From this entry you can see that a declaration of dividends reduces Retained Earnings, and, eventually, the amount of cash on hand. Thus, although not considered to be expenses, dividends do reduce the amount a company could otherwise invest in productive assets.

An alternative way of recording the declaration of dividends involves debiting Retained Earnings directly. However, using the Dividends account instead of Retained Earnings allows a company to keep separate records of dividends paid to preferred and common shareholders. Whichever method is used, the result is the same: a decrease in Retained Earnings.

date of record *the date selected by a corporation's board of directors on which the shareholders of record are identified as those who will receive dividends*

The second important dividend date is the date of record. Falling somewhere between the declaration date and the payment date, this is the date selected by the board of directors on which the shareholders of record are identified as those who will receive dividends. Since many corporate stocks are in flux—being bought and sold daily—it is important that the shareholders who will receive the dividends be identified. No journal entry is required on the date of record; the date of record is simply noted in the minutes of the directors meeting and in a letter to shareholders.

payment date *the date on which a corporation pays dividends to its shareholders*

As you might expect, the third important date is the dividend payment date. This is the date on which, by order of the board of directors, dividends will be paid. The entry to record a dividend payment would typically be

Dividends Payable	8,000	
Cash		8,000
Paid a 50-cent-per-share dividend.		

Once a dividend-paying pattern has been established, the expectation of dividends is built into the per-share price of the stock. A break in the pattern usually produces a sharp drop in the price. Similarly, an increased dividend is a sign of growth and usually triggers a stock price increase. Dividend increases are usually considered to set a precedent, indicating that future dividends will be at this per-share amount or more. With this in mind, boards of directors are careful about increasing or decreasing dividends.

Cash Dividends and Dividend Preferences

The declaration and payment of a cash dividend requires: (1) a sufficient amount of uncommitted retained earnings, (2) cash to pay the dividend, and (3) a formal written action (referred to as a dividend declaration) by the board of directors. Cash dividends are by far the most common types of dividends. They can be paid on any kind of stock, except, of course, unissued or treasury stock.

When cash dividends are declared, allocation of the dividends depends on the rights of the preferred stockholders. These rights are identified when the stock is approved by the state. Three "dividend preferences," as they are called, are (1) current-dividend preference, (2) cumulative-dividend preference, and (3) participating-dividend preference. Preferred stockholders often have current- and cumulative-dividend preferences, but the participating feature is rare.

Current-Dividend Preference Preferred stock has a dividend-paying percentage associated with it and is typically described as follows: "5 percent preferred (the percentage can be any amount, depending on the particular stock), par $10 per share, 6,000 shares outstanding." The "5 percent" in this example is a percentage of the par value, or $10. So, 50 cents per share (0.05 × $10 = $0.50) is the amount that will be paid in dividends to preferred stockholders each year that dividends are declared. The fact that preferred stock dividends are fixed at a specific percentage of their par value makes them somewhat similar to the interest paid to bondholders. The current-dividend preference requires that, when dividends are paid, this percentage of the preferred stock's par value will be paid to preferred shareholders before common shareholders receive any dividends.

current-dividend preference *the right of preferred shareholders to receive current dividends before common shareholders receive dividends*

To illustrate the payment of different types of dividends, the following data from the Dallas Oilers Football Team will be used throughout this section. (The various combinations of dividend preferences illustrated over the next few pages are summarized as Cases 1–6 in Exhibit 13–3.) Assume that outstanding stock includes

Preferred Stock (5%, $10 par value, 6,000 shares issued)	$ 60,000
Common Stock ($5 par value, 8,000 shares issued)	40,000
Total	$100,000

EXHIBIT 13–3 **Dividend Preferences: Summary of Cases 1–6**

Case	Preferred Dividend Feature	Years in Arrears	Total Dividend	Preferred Dividend	Common Dividend
1	5%, noncumulative, nonparticipating	Non-applicable	$ 2,000	$ 2,000	-0-
2	5%, noncumulative, nonparticipating	Non-applicable	4,000	3,000	$1,000
3	5%, cumulative, nonparticipating	2	7,000	7,000	-0-
4	5%, cumulative, nonparticipating	2	11,000	9,000	2,000
5	5%, noncumulative, participating	Non-applicable	20,000	12,000	8,000
6	5%, cumulative, participating	2	20,000	14,400	5,600

To begin, assume that the Oilers' 5 percent preferred stock has a current-dividend preference: Before any dividends can be paid to common shareholders, preferred shareholders must be paid a total of $3,000 ($60,000 × 0.05). Thus, if only $2,000 of dividends were declared (Case 1), preferred shareholders would receive the entire dividend payment. If $4,000 were declared (Case 2), preferred shareholders would receive $3,000 and common shareholders, $1,000.

cumulative-dividend preference *the right of preferred shareholders to receive current dividends plus all dividends in arrears before common shareholders receive any dividends*

Cumulative-Dividend Preference The cumulative-dividend preference can be quite costly for common shareholders, because it requires that preferred shareholders be paid current dividends plus all unpaid dividends from past years before common shareholders receive anything. If dividends have been paid in all previous years, then only the current 5 percent must be paid to preferred stockholders. But, if dividends on preferred stock were not paid in full in prior years, the cumulative deficiency must be paid before common shareholders receive a penny.

dividends in arrears *missed dividends for past years that preferred shareholders have a right to receive under the cumulative-dividend preference when dividends are declared*

With respect to the cumulative feature, it is important to repeat that companies are not required to pay dividends. Such past unpaid dividends are called dividends in arrears. Since they do not have to be paid unless dividends are declared in the future, dividends in arrears do not represent actual liabilities and thus are not recorded in the accounts. Instead, they are reported in the notes to the financial statements.

To illustrate the distribution of dividends for cumulative preferred stock, we will assume that the Dallas Oilers Football Team has not paid any dividends for the last 2 years but has declared a dividend in the current year. The Oilers must pay $9,000 in dividends to preferred shareholders before they can give anything to the common shareholders. The calculation is as follows:

Dividends in Arrears—2 Years (0.05 × $60,000 × 2)	$6,000
Current Dividend Preference (0.05 × $60,000)	3,000
Total	$9,000

Therefore, if the Oilers paid only $7,000 in dividends (Case 3), preferred shareholders would receive all of the dividends, common shareholders would receive nothing, and there would still be dividends in arrears of $2,000 the next year. If $11,000 in dividends were paid (Case 4), preferred shareholders would receive $9,000 and common shareholders would receive $2,000.

participating-dividend preference *the right of preferred shareholders to receive equal distributions of dividends on a proportionate basis with common shareholders*

Participating-Dividend Preference A third dividend preference that can be accorded preferred shareholders is that of participation. Basically, this feature describes the distribution of dividends *after* the current and cumulative preferences (if any) have been met. Thus, if preferred stock is fully participating, then after these other preferences are fulfilled, common shareholders first receive a pro rata share of the dividends (that is, a share based on the same percentage of par as preferred stock: in this case, the common shareholders get 5 percent of the outstanding par value of the common stock), and preferred shareholders participate in the remaining dividends on an equal percentage basis with common shareholders. If preferred stock is nonparticipating, after preferred shareholders have received their rightful dividends, common shareholders receive all remaining dividends.

To illustrate the accounting for this preference, we will assume that the preferred stock of the Dallas Oilers Football Team is fully participating and that the company pays $20,000 in dividends (Case 5). If the participating preferred stock were noncumulative or cumulative with no dividends in arrears, the dividend allocation would be

	Preferred	Common	Total Dividend
Current-dividend preference ($60,000 × 0.05)	$ 3,000		$ 3,000
Common's pro rata share ($40,000 × 0.05)		$2,000	2,000
Allocation of remainder (3/5, 2/5 basis)*	9,000	6,000	15,000
	$12,000	$8,000	$20,000

* Preferred, $60,000/$100,000 = 3/5; common, $40,000/$100,000 = 2/5; 3/5 × $15,000 = $9,000 and 2/5 × $15,000 = $6,000.

Note that after the preferred and common stockholders have each received their 5 percent, the remaining dividends are split on the basis of the par value of the outstanding stock in each category. In this case, the total outstanding par value of the preferred stock is $60,000 ($10 par × 6,000 shares) and the total outstanding par value of the common stock is $40,000 ($5 par × 8,000 shares). The sum of the total par values of all outstanding stock is $100,000 ($60,000 + $40,000); preferred stockholders receive 3/5 ($60,000/$100,000) of the remaining dividends, while common stockholders receive only 2/5 ($40,000/$100,000).

If the participating preferred stock were cumulative and if there were 2 years of dividends in arrears (Case 6), the dividend allocation would be

	Preferred	Common	Total Dividend
Cumulative-dividend preference ($60,000 × 0.05 × 2 years)	$ 6,000		$ 6,000
Current-dividend preference ($60,000 × 0.05)	3,000		3,000
Common's pro rata share ($40,000 × 0.05)		$2,000	2,000
Allocation of remainder (3/5, 2/5 basis):			
Preferred (3/5 × $9,000)	5,400		5,400
Common (2/5 × $9,000)		3,600	3,600
	$14,400	$5,600	$20,000

The entries to account for the transactions in Case 6 would be

Date of Declaration

Dividends—Preferred (or Retained Earnings)	14,400	
Dividends—Common (or Retained Earnings)	5,600	
Dividends Payable		20,000

Declared dividends on preferred and common stock.

Date of Payment

Dividends Payable	20,000	
Cash		20,000

Paid dividends on preferred and common stock.

Stock Dividends

Corporations sometimes issue a stock dividend instead of paying a cash dividend. Basically, a stock dividend is a distribution of additional stock to each owner in proportion to the number of shares held. For example, if a company issued a 10 percent stock dividend, each shareholder would receive 1 additional share for every 10 shares owned.

There is considerable disagreement as to whether stockholders receive anything of value from a stock dividend. Certainly, they do not receive corporate assets, as with a cash or property dividend. Nor does any stockholder own a larger percentage of the corporation after the stock dividend than before, since each shareholder receives a pro rata share of the stock issued. Those who argue that stock dividends have value to stockholders give two reasons for their view.

1. If a company maintains the same level of cash dividends per share after the stock dividend as before, then an investor's long-run cash dividends will be increased by a stock dividend. Clearly, the issuance of a stock dividend in such a case represents a firm's decision to increase the total amount of cash dividends it will pay in the future.
2. If the stock dividend is small, say 10 percent, it is commonly believed that the market will probably not discount the company's stock to a price that reflects the new total of shares outstanding. In other words, the stock's market price will usually not drop by a percentage equivalent to that of the stock dividend. The investor's increased number of shares would, if this view is correct, have an increased value. (In fact, if the price of the stock does not drop proportionately, the reason may be the anticipation of increased future dividends, as described above.)

Stock dividends play an important role for the corporation issuing them by maintaining dividend consistency. Corporations that issue dividends each year do not want to miss a year, so for them a stock dividend can be a useful substitute for cash. Because of the expectation of increased future dividends, most investors are satisfied with stock dividends.

To illustrate the accounting for a stock dividend, we will assume that stockholders' equity of the Dallas Oilers Football Team was

Common Stock ($10 par value, 1,000 shares issued)	$10,000	
Paid-in Capital in Excess of Par—Common Stock	40,000	
Retained Earnings	50,000	
Total Stockholders' Equity		$100,000

If a 10 percent stock dividend is issued when the current market price of the company's stock is $70, the entry to record the stock dividend would be

Retained Earnings (100 shares × $70)	7,000	
Common Stock (100 shares × $10 par)		1,000
Paid-in Capital—Stock Dividend		6,000
Declared and issued a 10% stock dividend.		

Since the dividend was 10 percent, and since there were previously 1,000 shares outstanding, 100 additional shares were issued for the dividend. The market value of the stock ($70) was used as the basis for converting retained earnings to contributed capital because this was a relatively small stock dividend and presumably would not have a significant effect on the existing market price of the stock. Debiting the Retained Earnings account only for the par value of $10 would not have been realistic since the market value of the stock was much greater than $10.

If a stock dividend is relatively large, the market price of the outstanding stock is greatly affected over the immediate future, so the market price at the time the dividend is issued becomes irrelevant. For this reason, the accounting profession has required that par value be used for reporting large stock dividends.

Where does one draw the line between a large and a small stock dividend? The range of 20 to 25 percent of total outstanding stock has been selected, somewhat arbitrarily, by accounting rule-makers. Thus, for a stock dividend of 20 percent or larger, retained earnings are generally debited at par value; for stock dividends smaller than 20 percent, the market value is normally used.

To illustrate the accounting for a large stock dividend, we assume the same stockholders' equity for the Dallas Oilers Football Team, except that the stock dividend is now 30 percent. The entry would be

Retained Earnings	3,000	
Common Stock (300 shares × $10 par)		3,000

Declared and issued a 30% stock dividend (1,000 shares × 0.30 = 300 shares; 300 shares × $10 = $3,000).

ACCOUNTING FOR STOCK SPLITS

stock split *a reduction in the par or stated value of stock and a proportionate increase in the number of shares outstanding*

A stock split increases the amount of outstanding stock more dramatically than a stock dividend does. With a stock split, a company reduces the par or stated value of its stock by a certain amount, say half, and at the same time increases the number of shares outstanding by the reciprocal amount; if par value is halved, the number of shares is doubled. Thus, the total par or stated value of stock outstanding is unchanged. For example, a firm with 20,000 shares of $10 par-value stock outstanding may reduce the par value to $5 and increase the number of shares outstanding to 40,000. In this case—involving a 2-for-1 stock split—an investor who had one share of stock will instead own two shares of the new $5 par-value stock. (Other ratio splits, such as 3-for-1 and 4-for-1, are also common.)

A company generally authorizes a stock split in order to reduce the market price of its stock. Presumably, more investors will be encouraged to enter the market for a given stock if its trading price is lowered.

In contrast to a stock dividend, a stock split does not require an accounting entry or involve a transfer of retained earnings to contributed capital. Rather, the company simply notes in the records that both the par value and the number of shares of stock outstanding have changed.

TO SUMMARIZE Four types of dividends are cash dividends, liquidating dividends, stock dividends, and property dividends, with cash and stock dividends being the most common. The important dividend dates are the date of declaration, the date of record, and the payment date. Preferred stockholders can be granted a current and a cumulative preference, and either type can be participating or nonparticipating. Stock dividends are distributions of additional stock to shareholders. Although a stock dividend does not increase percentage ownership in a corporation, the additional stock provides the expectation of increased future cash dividends. With small stock dividends, Retained Earnings is debited at the stock's market value; with large stock dividends (20 percent or more), Retained Earnings is debited at the stock's par value.

A stock split is an increase in the number of shares outstanding corresponding to a reduction in the par or stated value of the stock. Generally, stock splits are authorized so that companies can attract more investors with a lower market price per share.

ACCOUNTING FOR RETAINED EARNINGS

Retained Earnings is the account into which all of a company's earnings are closed. As such, it is increased each year by net income and decreased by losses and dividends declared. As was illustrated in Chapter 5, the entries to close net income and dividends to Retained Earnings, when an Income Summary account is used, are

Income Summary	XXX	
Retained Earnings		XXX
To close net income to retained earnings.		
Retained Earnings	XXX	
Dividends		XXX
To close the Dividends account to retained earnings.		

As we pointed out in Chapter 8, retained earnings are not the same as cash. In fact, a company can have a large retained earnings balance and be without cash, or it can have a lot of cash and a very small retained earnings balance. Although both cash and retained earnings are usually increased when a company has earnings, the amounts by which they are increased are usually different. This occurs for two reasons: (1) the company's net income, which increases retained earnings, is accrual-based, not cash-based; and (2) cash from earnings may be invested in productive assets, such as inventories, used to pay off loans, or spent in any number of ways, many of which do not affect net income or retained earnings.

Prior-Period Adjustments

Besides profits and losses, dividends, and certain treasury stock transactions, there is one other type of event that affects retained earnings directly. This category includes adjustments to correctly restate the net income of prior periods; these are called, appropriately, prior-period adjustments. Prior-period adjustments are rare. In addition to some technical prior-period adjustments involving taxes and bonds, which are beyond the scope

prior-period adjustments *adjustments made directly to Retained Earnings in order to correct errors in the financial statements of prior periods*

of this book, the main event that qualifies as a prior-period adjustment is the correction of a material error in the financial statements of a prior period. A prior-period adjustment may be made, for example, to correct an error in accounting for the inventory of a previous period. In accounting for prior-period adjustments, retained earnings is increased or decreased directly, because the net income for the years affected by the adjustments has already been closed to the Retained Earnings account.

The Statement of Retained Earnings

statement of retained earnings *a report that shows the changes in the Retained Earnings account during a period of time*

Prior-period adjustments (if there are any) and dividends are usually disclosed in a statement of retained earnings. While such a statement is not required, it is often provided by a corporation. Exhibit 13-4 shows how the Dallas Oilers Football Team might present a statement of retained earnings, using arbitrary numbers.

EXHIBIT 13-4

Dallas Oilers Football Team
Statement of Retained Earnings
for the Year Ended December 31, 1984

Retained Earnings Balance, January 1, 1984		$300,000
Prior-Period Adjustment:		
Deduct Adjustment for 1983 Inventory Correction		(25,000)
Balance as Restated		$275,000
Net Income for 1984		50,000
Total		$325,000
Less Dividends Declared in 1984:		
On Preferred Stock	$10,000	
On Common Stock	12,000	(22,000)
Retained Earnings Balance, December 31, 1984		$303,000

Retained Earnings Restrictions

Corporations frequently place restrictions on part of retained earnings. This means that the earnings are earmarked for special purposes, such as plant expansion or the purchase of treasury stock, and hence are removed from dividend-availability status.

Although restrictions on retained earnings do not actually create cash funds, they do serve to alert stockholders and others of management's intentions and requirements. Such restrictions are usually disclosed in the financial statements.

To illustrate, we will assume that Timpview Corporation has a $160,000 balance in Retained Earnings. If $40,000 of that amount had been appropriated to retire preferred stock, the entry would be

Retained Earnings	40,000	
Retained Earnings Appropriated for Retirement of Preferred Stock		40,000
Appropriated $40,000 of retained earnings for the retirement of preferred stock.		

Note that the same effect can be produced by a footnote disclosure, which is becoming a more common way of identifying the restriction of retained earnings.

Exhibit 13-5 is the owners' equity section of Timpview's balance sheet. (Note that the entries under Contributed Capital are arbitrary.) In the absence of any restrictions, the balance in Retained Earnings usually represents the maximum amount of dividends that can be declared and paid.

EXHIBIT 13-5

Timpview Corporation
Owners' Equity Section
of Balance Sheet as of December 31, 1983

Contributed Capital:		
Preferred Stock (10%, $30 par, 4,000 shares authorized, 2,000 shares issued and outstanding)	$ 60,000	
Common Stock ($10 par, 10,000 shares authorized, 5,000 shares issued and outstanding)	50,000	
Paid-in Capital in Excess of Par—Preferred Stock	10,000	
Paid-in Capital in Excess of Par—Common Stock	20,000	
Total Contributed Capital		$140,000
Retained Earnings:		
Retained Earnings Appropriated for the Retirement of Preferred Stock	$ 40,000	
Unappropriated Retained Earnings	120,000	
Total Retained Earnings		160,000
Total Owners' Equity		$300,000

TO SUMMARIZE The Retained Earnings account reflects the total undistributed earnings of a business since incorporation. It is increased by net income and prior-period adjustments, when they occur; it is decreased by dividends and losses, and by treasury stock transactions and prior-period adjustments, when they occur. Prior-period adjustments usually involve corrections of errors in prior years' financial statements. Retained earnings can be appropriated or restricted for special purposes, such as the retirement of preferred stock or debt. Such appropriations do not provide cash, but they do remove a portion of retained earnings from dividend-availability status and alert financial statement users to management's plans.

CHAPTER REVIEW

The accounting for all three types of business entities—corporations, proprietorships, and partnerships—is identical except for owners' equity.

A corporation is a business entity that is legally separate from its owners, and chartered by a state. It is independently taxed, and it can incur debts, conduct business, own property, and enter into contracts. The owners' equity section of a corporation's balance sheet is generally divided into two sections: contributed capital and retained earnings. Contributed capital identifies the resources contributed by owners and the stock that has been issued by the corporation.

The two major types of stock are common and preferred. Common stock is usually voting stock. Preferred stock may have current- and cumulative-dividend privileges as well as participating-dividend privileges, and it is usually nonvoting. Stock can be authorized but not yet issued; authorized, issued, and outstanding; or authorized, issued, and reacquired by the corporation. Reacquired stock is called treasury stock. Stock can have a par value, be no-par with a stated value, or be no-par with no stated value. The accounting is different for each case. When treasury stock is purchased by a corporation, it is usually accounted for at cost and deducted from total stockholders' equity as a contra-equity account.

Corporations usually pay dividends to their owners. These distributions to owners can be in the form of cash, additional stock, or property. The three important dates in accounting for dividends are the declaration date, the date of record, and the payment date. Dividends are not a liability until they are declared. If a company has common and preferred stock, the allocation of dividends between the two types depends on the dividend preferences of the preferred stock.

A company can also have a stock split, such as a 2-for-1 split, which increases the number of shares outstanding and decreases proportionately the par or stated value of the stock.

Owners' equity also includes retained earnings, which shows the cumulative undistributed earnings of a company since incorporation. Retained earnings is decreased by: (1) the declaration of dividends, (2) operating losses, (3) some treasury stock transactions, and (4) certain prior-period adjustments. Retained earnings is increased by net income and some prior-period adjustments. Retained earnings may be restricted or appropriated for specific uses.

KEY TERMS AND CONCEPTS

authorized stock (428)
board of directors (426)
capital stock (428)
cash dividend (435)
charter (articles of incorporation) (426)
common stock (428)
contributed capital (427)
corporation (426)
cumulative-dividend preference (438)
current-dividend preference (437)
date of record (436)
declaration date (435)
dividends (435)
dividends in arrears (438)
issued stock (428)
legal capital (429)
limited liability (426)
liquidating dividend (435)
no-par stock (429)
outstanding stock (428)
participating-dividend preference (438)
par-value stock (428)
payment date (436)
preferred stock (428)
premium on stock (429)
prior-period adjustments (442)
property dividend (435)
pro rata (435)
stated value (429)
statement of retained earnings (443)
stock certificate (426)
stock dividend (435)
stockholders (426)
stock split (441)
Subchapter S corporation (426)
treasury stock (428)

REVIEW PROBLEM

Owners' Equity

P & R Corporation was organized during 1964. At the end of 1983 the equity section of the balance sheet was as follows:

Contributed Capital:	
Preferred Stock (8%, $30 par, 6,000 shares authorized, 5,000 shares issued)	$150,000
Common Stock ($5 par, 50,000 shares authorized, 20,000 shares issued, 3,000 held as treasury stock)	100,000
Paid-in Capital in Excess of Par—Common Stock	80,000
Total Contributed Capital	$330,000
Retained Earnings	140,000
Total Contributed Capital Plus Retained Earnings	$470,000
Less Treasury Stock (at cost, $10 per share)	30,000
Total Stockholders' Equity	$440,000

During 1984 the following stockholders' equity transactions occurred in chronological sequence.

a. Issued 800 shares of common stock at $11 per share.
b. Resold 1,200 shares of treasury stock at $12 per share.
c. Issued 300 shares of preferred stock at $33 per share.
d. Resold 400 shares of treasury stock at $9 per share.
e. Declared and paid a dividend large enough to meet the current-dividend preference on the preferred stock and to pay the common shareholders $1.50 per share.
f. Appropriated $25,000 of retained earnings for the retirement of debt.
g. Declared a 2-for-1 stock split on common stock.
h. Net income for 1984 was $70,000.

Required:

1. Journalize the above transactions.
2. Set up T-accounts with beginning balances and post the journal entries to the T-accounts (adding any necessary new accounts).
3. Prepare the stockholders' equity section as of December 31, 1984.

Solution

1. Journalize the Transactions

a	Cash	8,800	
	Common Stock		4,000
	Paid-in Capital in Excess of Par—Common Stock		4,800
	Issued 800 shares of common stock at $11 per share.		

Cash received is $11 × 800 shares; common stock is par value times the number of shares ($5 × 800); and paid-in capital is the excess.

b	Cash	14,400	
	Treasury Stock		12,000
	Paid-in Capital—Treasury Stock		2,400
	Resold 1,200 shares of treasury stock at $12 per share.		

Cash is $12 × 1,200 shares; treasury stock is the cost times the number of shares sold ($10 × 1,200 shares); and paid-in capital is the excess.

c	Cash	9,900	
	Preferred Stock		9,000
	Paid-in Capital in Excess of Par—Preferred Stock		900
	Issued 300 shares of preferred stock at $33 per share.		

Cash is $33 × 300 shares; preferred stock is par value times the number of shares issued ($30 × 300); and paid-in capital is the excess.

d	Cash	3,600	
	Paid-in Capital—Treasury Stock	400	
	Treasury Stock		4,000
	Resold 400 shares of treasury stock at $9 per share.		

Cash is $9 × 400 shares; treasury stock is the cost times the number of shares sold ($10 × 400); and paid-in capital is decreased for the deficiency. If no Paid-in Capital—Treasury Stock had existed, Retained Earnings would have been debited.

e	Retained Earnings	41,820	
	Cash		41,820
	Declared and paid cash dividend.		

Calculations:

Preferred Stock	Number of Shares	Par-Value Amount
Original balance	5,000	$150,000
Entry c	300	9,000
Total	5,300	$159,000
		× 0.08
		$ 12,720

Common Stock	Number of Shares	
Original balance	17,000	(excludes treasury stock)
Entry a	800	
Entry b	1,200	
Entry d	400	
Total	19,400	shares
	×$1.50	
	$29,100	

Total Preferred Stock Dividend	$12,720
Total Common Stock Dividend	29,100
Total Dividend	$41,820

f	Retained Earnings	25,000	
	Retained Earnings Appropriated for Debt Retirement		25,000

Appropriated $25,000 of retained earnings for debt retirement.

g No entry.

There is no journal entry with a stock split. The accountant generally notes in the records that the par value of the common stock is divided in half, and so the number of shares is doubled.

h	Income Summary	70,000	
	Retained Earnings		70,000

To close net income to retained earnings.

2. Set Up T-Accounts and Post to the Accounts

Cash*

a 8,800	41,820 ... e
b 14,400	
c 9,900	
d 3,600	

Preferred Stock

	150,000 Beg. Bal.
	9,000 .. c
	159,000

Paid-in Capital in Excess of Par—Preferred Stock

	900 c

Common Stock

	100,000 Beg. Bal.
	4,000 .. a
	104,000

Paid-in Capital in Excess of Par—Common Stock

	80,000 Beg. Bal.
	4,800 ... a
	84,800

Treasury Stock

Beg. Bal. .. 30,000	12,000 ... b
	4,000 ... d
14,000	

Paid-in Capital—Treasury Stock

d 400	2,400 .... b
	2,000

Income Summary†

h 70,000	

* Non-stockholders' equity account.
† Temporary closing account.

Retained Earnings

e 41,820	140,000 Beg. Bal.
f 25,000	70,000 .. h
	143,180

Retained Earnings Appropriated for Debt Retirement

	25,000 ... f

3. Prepare Stockholders' Equity Section

P & R Corporation
Stockholders' Equity Section of Balance Sheet as of December 31, 1984

Contributed Capital:		
Preferred Stock (8%, $30 par, 6,000 shares authorized, 5,300 shares issued)		$159,000
Common Stock ($2.50 par, 100,000* shares authorized, 41,600* shares issued, 2,800* held as treasury stock)		104,000
Paid-in Capital in Excess of Par—Preferred Stock		900
Paid-in Capital in Excess of Par—Common Stock		84,800
Paid-in Capital—Treasury Stock		2,000
Total Contributed Capital		$350,700
Retained Earnings:		
Unrestricted Retained Earnings	$143,180	
Retained Earnings Appropriated for Debt Retirement	25,000	168,180
Total Contributed Capital Plus Retained Earnings		$518,880
Less Treasury Stock (2,800* shares)		14,000
Total Stockholders' Equity		$504,880

* The number of common shares and treasury stock has been doubled to account for the stock split. Also, the par value has been divided in half. The following table summarizes the calculations.

Transaction	Common Stock Issued	Common Stock Authorized	Treasury Stock
Number of shares originally issued	20,000	50,000	3,000
Entry **a**	800		
Entry **b**			(1,200)
Entry **d**			(400)
Total	20,800	50,000	1,400
Stock Split	× 2	× 2	× 2
Number of shares as of December 31, 1984	41,600	100,000	2,800

DISCUSSION QUESTIONS

1 In what way is the balance sheet of a corporation different from that of a partnership or proprietorship?

2 In what way does the owners' equity section of a balance sheet identify the sources of the assets?

3 In which type of business entity do owners have limited liability?

4 What is meant by the term "transferability of ownership"?

5 In what way is there a double taxation of corporate profits?

6 How are common and preferred stock different from each other?

7 How is treasury stock different from unissued stock?

8 Is treasury stock an asset? If not, why not?

9 What is the purpose of having a par or stated value for stock?

10 Does treasury stock possess the same voting, dividend, and other rights that outstanding stock does?

11 How is treasury stock usually accounted for?

12 When does a corporation have a legal obligation to pay dividends to its shareholders?

13 Based on what you've read in this chapter, what do you suppose is the difference between a "growth company" and a "dividend company"?

14 Why should a potential common stockholder carefully examine the dividend preferences of a company's preferred stock?

15 Are dividends in arrears a liability? If not, why not?

16 Does a stock dividend have value to stockholders? Explain.

17 What is the difference between a stock dividend and a stock split? Why would a company split its stock?

18 Is it possible for a firm to have a large Retained Earnings balance and no cash? Explain.

19 Why are prior-period adjustments entered directly into Retained Earnings instead of being reflected on the income statement?

EXERCISES

E13–1 Issuance of Stock

Reed Corporation was organized on July 15, 1983. Record the journal entries to account for the following.

1. The state authorized 25,000 shares of 6 percent preferred stock ($20 par) and 100,000 shares of no-par common stock.
2. Peter Reed gave 2,000 shares of common stock to his attorney in return for her help in incorporating the business. Fees for this type of work are normally about $6,000.
3. Reed gave 15,000 shares of common stock to a friend who contributed a building worth $30,000 to the business.
4. Reed issued 5,000 shares of preferred stock at $25 per share.
5. Reed paid $50,000 cash for 40,000 shares of common stock.
6. Another friend donated a $10,000 machine and received 3,000 shares of common stock.
7. The attorney sold all her shares to her brother-in-law for $7,000.

E13–2 No-Par Stock Transactions

Miller Maintenance Corporation was organized in early 1983 with 20,000 shares of no-par common stock authorized. During 1983, the following transactions occurred.

a. Issued 8,500 shares of stock at $36 per share.
b. Issued another 1,200 shares at $38 per share.
c. Issued 1,000 shares for a building appraised at $40,000.
d. Declared dividends of $1 per share.
e. Earned $49,500 during the year.

Given the above information:

1. Journalize the transactions.
2. Present the stockholders' equity section of the balance sheet as it would appear on December 31, 1983.

E13–3 Stock Transactions

On January 1, 1983, Mayfield Corporation was granted a charter authorizing the following capital stock: common stock, $20 par, 100,000 shares; preferred stock, $10 par, 6 percent, 30,000 shares.

Record the following 1983 transactions.

1. Issued 80,000 shares of common stock at $35 per share.
2. Issued 14,000 shares of preferred stock at $12 per share.
3. Bought back 5,000 shares of common stock at $40 per share.
4. Reissued 500 shares of treasury stock at $25 per share.
5. Paid dividends of $38,600. How much is the dividend per share on common stock? (The preferred stock,

which has a current-dividend preference, is noncumulative and nonparticipating.)

E13-4 Stockholders' Equity Transactions

On January 1, 1983, Morris Corporation was authorized to issue 100,000 shares of common stock, par value $10 per share, and 20,000 shares of 6 percent preferred stock, par value $50 per share.

Journalize the following transactions.

1. Issued 60,000 shares of common stock at $12 per share.
2. Issued 12,000 shares of preferred stock at $56 per share.
3. Reacquired 1,000 shares of common stock for the treasury at $14 per share.
4. Reissued 200 of the treasury shares for $2,600.
5. Declared a cash dividend sufficient to meet the current-dividend preference on preferred stock and pay common stockholders $1 per share.

E13-5 Trading Stock for Other Assets

If 200 shares of common stock with a par value of $5 and a market price of $16 are traded for a machine with a fair market value of $3,200, complete the following.

1. Provide the journal entry to record the transaction.
2. If the machine's appraised fair market value was $3,100, what would the correct journal entry be to record the transaction?
3. Make the necessary journal entry, assuming the same facts as in (2), except that the stock is not actively traded and therefore its market price is unknown.
4. Record the necessary journal entry, assuming that the stock's par is $10 and its market price is $15 per share.

E13-6 Treasury Stock Transactions

Provide the necessary journal entries to record the following:

1. Westchester Corporation was granted a charter authorizing the issuance of 50,000 shares of no-par common stock. Management established a stated value of $8 per share.
2. The company issued 40,000 shares of common stock at $10 per share.
3. The company reacquired 2,000 shares of its own stock at $11 per share, to be held in treasury.
4. Another 2,000 shares of stock were reacquired at $12 per share.
5. Eight hundred of the shares reacquired in part (3) were reissued for $13 per share.
6. Fourteen hundred of the shares reacquired in part (4) were reissued for $9 per share.
7. Given the preceding transactions, what is the balance in the Treasury Stock account?

E13-7 Preparing a Stockholders' Equity Section

The following account balances appear on the books of Ririe Corporation as of December 31, 1983.

Preferred Stock (7%, $40 par value, 30,000 shares authorized, 25,000 shares outstanding)	$1,000,000
Common Stock ($3 par value, 200,000 shares authorized, 150,000 shares outstanding)	450,000
Paid-in Capital in Excess of Par:	
Preferred Stock	155,000
Common Stock	245,000
Net Income for 1983	65,000
Dividends Paid During 1983	35,000
Retained Earnings, January 1, 1983	680,000

1. If the preferred stock is selling at $45 per share, what is the maximum cash that Ririe Corporation can obtain by issuing preferred stock, given the present number of authorized shares?
2. If common stock is selling for $12 per share, what is the maximum cash that can be obtained by issuing common stock, given the present number of authorized shares?
3. Given the above data, and ignoring parts (1) and (2), prepare the stockholders' equity section of the balance sheet.

E13-8 Analysis of Stockholders' Equity

The stockholders' equity section of Nielson Corporation at the end of the current year showed:

Preferred Stock (6%, $40 par value, 10,000 shares authorized, 6,000 shares outstanding)	$?
Common Stock ($6 par value, 80,000 shares authorized, 53,000 issued—including 350 shares of treasury stock)	318,000
Paid-in Capital in Excess of Par—Preferred Stock	?
Paid-in Capital in Excess of Par—Common Stock	129,000
Retained Earnings	86,000
Less Treasury Stock	(2,000)
Total Stockholders' Equity	?

1. What is the dollar amount to be entered under Preferred Stock?
2. What is the average price for which common stock was issued? (Round to the nearest penny.)
3. If preferred stock was issued at an average price of $43 per share, what amount should appear in the Paid-in Capital in Excess of Par—Preferred Stock account?
4. What is the average cost per share of treasury stock? (Round to the nearest penny.)

5. Assuming that the preferred stock was issued for an average price of $43 per share, what is total stockholders' equity?

6. If net income for the year were $67,000 and if only preferred dividends were paid, by how much would retained earnings increase?

E13-9 Analysis of Stockholders' Equity

The stockholders' equity section of the balance sheet of Cox Corporation as of December 31, 1983, is as follows:

Stockholders' Equity

Contributed Capital:		
Preferred Stock (6%, $10 par value, cumulative and nonparticipating, 100,000 shares authorized)		$ 500,000
Common Stock (no par, $10 stated value, 100,000 shares authorized)		900,000
Paid-in Capital in Excess of Stated Value—Common Stock		450,000
Total Contributed Capital		$1,850,000
Retained Earnings:		
Retained Earnings—Unrestricted	$600,000	
Retained Earnings—Appropriated	200,000	800,000
Total Contributed Capital Plus Retained Earnings		$2,650,000
Less Treasury Stock (Common) (5,000 shares at $15 per share)		(75,000)
Total Stockholders' Equity		$2,575,000

1. How many shares of preferred stock have been issued?
2. How many shares of common stock have been issued?
3. How many shares of preferred stock are outstanding?
4. How many shares of common stock are outstanding?
5. What is the total amount of legal capital?

E13-10 The Retained Earnings Statement and Stockholders' Equity

The following balances appear in the accounts of Kelling Corporation as of December 31, 1983.

Retained Earnings, January 1, 1983	$64,000
Prior-Period Adjustment (tax adjustment for 1981)	(28,500)
Net Income for 1983	19,000
Preferred Stock (7%, $12 par, 2,500 shares issued and outstanding)	30,000
Common Stock ($5 par, 8,000 shares issued, of which 200 shares are in the treasury)	40,000
Paid-in Capital in Excess of Par—Preferred Stock	6,700
Paid-in Capital in Excess of Par—Common Stock	21,400
Treasury Stock	1,800
Cash Dividends Paid During 1983	5,000

1. Prepare the retained earnings statement for Kelling Corporation as of December 31, 1983.
2. Prepare the stockholders' equity section of Kelling Corporation's balance sheet as of December 31, 1983.

E13-11 Dividend Calculations

On January 1, 1983, Mozly Corporation had 65,000 shares of common stock issued and outstanding (market price = $8/share). During 1983, the following transactions occurred (in chronological order).

a. 5,000 new shares of common stock were issued.
b. 1,000 shares of stock were reacquired for use in the company's stock option plan.
c. At the end of the option period, 600 shares had been purchased by corporate officials.

Given this information, compute the following.

1. After the foregoing three transactions occur, what amount of dividends must Mozly Corporation declare in order to pay 50 cents per share? To pay $1 per share?
2. What is the dividend per share if $199,752 is paid?
3. If all 1,000 treasury shares had been purchased by corporate officials through the stock-option plan, what would the dividends per share have been, again assuming $199,752 in dividends were paid? (Round to the nearest penny.)

E13-12 Dividend Calculations

Dee's stockholders' equity section shows:

Preferred Stock (6%, $50 par, 4,000 shares outstanding)	$200,000
Common Stock ($20 par, 20,000 shares outstanding)	400,000
Retained Earnings	250,000

The board of directors is considering the declaration of dividends. No dividends were declared last year. For each of the following situations, compute the amount of dividends that would be declared and paid to common and preferred stockholders, and make the journal entries that are necessary to record the declaration.

1. The preferred stock is noncumulative and nonparticipating, and dividends of $45,000 are declared.
2. The preferred stock is noncumulative and participating, and dividends of $54,000 are declared.
3. The preferred stock is cumulative and nonparticipating, and dividends of $35,000 are declared.
4. The preferred stock is cumulative and participating, and dividends of $60,000 are declared.

E13-13 Dividend Calculations

Moon Corporation has the following stock outstanding.

Preferred Stock (5%, $20 par, 5,000 shares)	$100,000
Common Stock ($5 par, 40,000 shares)	200,000

For each of the three cases below, compute the amount of dividends that would be paid to preferred and common shareholders. Assume that total dividends paid are $28,000. No dividends have been paid for the past 2 years.

Case A—Preferred is noncumulative and nonparticipating.
Case B—Preferred is cumulative and nonparticipating.
Case C—Preferred is cumulative and fully participating.

E13-14 Cash Dividends and Treasury Stock Transactions

During 1983, Siesta Corporation had the following transactions and related events.

Jan. 15	Issued 6,500 shares of common stock at par ($16 per share), bringing the total number of shares outstanding to 121,300.
Feb. 6	Declared a 50-cent-per-share dividend on common stock for shareholders of record on March 6.
Mar. 6	Date of record.
Mar. 8	John Jones, a prominent banker, purchased 20,000 shares of Siesta Corporation common stock from the company for $346,000.
Apr. 6	Paid dividends declared on February 6.
Jun. 19	Reacquired 800 shares of common stock as treasury stock at a total cost of $9,350.
Sept. 6	Declared dividends of 55 cents per share to be paid to common shareholders of record on October 15, 1983.
Oct. 6	The Dow Jones Industrial Average plummeted 24 points and Siesta's stock price fell $3 per share.
Oct. 15	Date of record.
Nov. 6	Paid dividends that were declared on September 6.
Dec. 15	Declared and paid a 6 percent cash dividend on 18,000 outstanding shares of preferred stock (par value $32).

Given this information:

1. Prepare the journal entries for these transactions.
2. What is the total amount of dividends paid to common and preferred shareholders during 1983?

E13-15 Accounting for Stock Dividends and Stock Splits

Loa Meat Packing Corporation would like to pay a cash dividend to its stockholders, but the company has a very low cash balance. In an attempt to partially satisfy stockholders, Loa decides to pay a stock dividend.

Record the following transactions.

1. Loa issues for cash 4,000 new shares of common stock at a price equal to the par value of $17 per share. This brings the number of common shares outstanding to 76,000.
2. A 30 percent stock dividend is declared and distributed. The market price of the stock at the time of the dividend is $20 per share.
3. An additional 5,000 shares of common stock are issued for cash at $21 per share.
4. A stock dividend of 10 percent is declared and distributed. The market price of the stock is now $19 per share.
5. A 3-for-1 stock split is declared. How would it affect the stockholders' equity accounts?

E13-16 Accounting for Stock Dividends and Stock Splits

Jackson Company's stockholders' equity section is shown below.

Preferred Stock (6%, $50 par, 8,000 shares outstanding)	$400,000
Common Stock ($20 par, 40,000 shares outstanding)	800,000
Retained Earnings	250,000

Given these data, complete the following four *independent* requirements.

1. Make the necessary journal entry to record a 10 percent common stock dividend. (The market value of the common stock at the time of the dividend is $30 per share.)
2. Make the necessary journal entry to record a 5 percent common stock dividend. (The market value of the common stock at the time of the dividend is $35 per share.)
3. Make the necessary journal entry to record a 50 percent common stock dividend. (The market value of the common stock at the time of the dividend is $40 per share.)
4. What entry would be made to record a 4-for-1 split of common stock? What difference would a 4-for-1 stock split make in the equity section of the balance sheet?

E13-17 Accounting for Stock Dividends

The following contributed capital balances appear in the accounts of Anderson Corporation as of December 31, 1983.

Preferred Stock (7%, $12 par, 2,500 shares issued and outstanding)	$30,000
Common Stock ($5 par, 8,000 shares issued, 200 of which are in the treasury)	40,000
Paid-in Capital in Excess of Par—Preferred Stock	6,700
Paid-in Capital in Excess of Par—Common Stock	21,400
Total Contributed Capital	$98,100

Given this information, make the necessary journal entries to record the following *independent* transactions.

1. A 2 percent stock dividend on common stock is declared and distributed. (The market price of common stock at the time of the dividend is $5.50 per share.)
2. A 5 percent stock dividend on common stock is declared and distributed. (The market price of common stock at the time of the dividend is $5.50 per share.)
3. A 50 percent stock dividend on common stock is declared. (The market price of common stock at the time of the dividend is $6.50 per share.)
4. A stock split (2-for-1) is declared.

PROBLEMS

P13–1 Stock Transactions and Analysis

The following selected accounts and amounts were taken from the balance sheet of Western Shipping Company as of December 31, 1983.

Cash	$ 93,000
Property, Plant, and Equipment	850,000
Accumulated Depreciation	150,000
Liabilities	50,000
Preferred Stock (7%, $100 par, noncumulative, nonparticipating, 10,000 shares authorized, 5,000 shares outstanding)	500,000
Common Stock ($10 par, 100,000 authorized)	800,000
Paid-in Capital in Excess of Par–Preferred Stock	1,000
Paid-in Capital in Excess of Par–Common Stock	125,000
Paid-in Capital–Treasury Stock	1,000
Retained Earnings:	
Appropriated for Plant Expansion	84,000
Unappropriated	226,000

Required:

For each part (1)–(7), (a) prepare the necessary journal entry (or entries) to record each transaction; and (b) calculate the amount that will appear on the December 31, 1984, balance sheet as a consequence of this transaction only. (Note: In your answer to each part of this problem, consider this to be the *only* transaction that took place during 1984.)

1. Two hundred shares of common stock are issued in exchange for a cash payment of $4,000.
   (a) Entry
   (b) Paid-in Capital in Excess of Par–Common Stock $ ______
2. Two hundred shares of preferred stock are issued at a price of $102 per share.
   (a) Entry
   (b) Paid-in Capital in Excess of Par–Preferred Stock $ ______
3. Five hundred shares of common stock are issued in exchange for a building. The common stock is not actively traded, but the building was recently appraised at $11,000.
   (a) Entry
   (b) Property, Plant, and Equipment $ ______
4. One thousand shares of common stock were reacquired from a stockholder for $23,000 and subsequently reissued for $21,500 to a different investor. (Note: Make two entries.)
   (a) Entries
   (b) Paid-in Capital–Treasury Stock $ ______
5. The board of directors *declared* (not paid) dividends of $75,000.
   (a) Entry
   (b) Retained Earnings–Unappropriated $ ______
6. The board of directors declared and the stockholders approved a 5-for-4 stock split on common stock.
   (a) Entry
   (b) Retained Earnings–Unappropriated $ ______
7. The planned plant expansion is now expected to cost $100,000, and the additional appropriation has been authorized.
   (a) Entry
   (b) Total Retained Earnings $ ______

P13–2 Stock Transactions and Preparation of the Stockholders' Equity Section

The balance sheet for Thompson Corporation as of December 31, 1983, is as follows:

Assets		$750,000
Liabilities		$410,000
Stockholders' Equity:		
Convertible Preferred Stock (5%, $20 par)	$ 50,000	
Common Stock ($10 par)	150,000	
Paid-in Capital in Excess of Par–Common Stock	30,000	
Retained Earnings	116,000	
	$346,000	
Less Treasury Stock, Common (500 shares at cost)	(6,000)	340,000
Total Liabilities and Stockholders' Equity		$750,000

During 1984, the following transactions were completed in the order given.

a. 750 shares of outstanding common stock were reacquired by the company at $7 per share. (Treasury stock is recorded at cost.)

b. 150 shares of common stock were reacquired in settlement of an account receivable of $1,500.

c. Semiannual cash dividends of 75 cents per share on common stock and 50 cents per share on preferred stock were declared and paid.

d. Each share of preferred stock is convertible into four shares of common stock. Five hundred shares of preferred stock were traded for common stock. Accrued dividends totaling $100 were paid to preferred stockholders exchanging their holdings. (Hint: Shares are traded at par value and any excess must come from Retained Earnings.)

e. The 900 shares of common treasury stock acquired during 1984 were sold at $13. The remaining treasury shares were exchanged for machinery with a fair market value of $6,300.

f. 3,000 shares of common stock were issued in exchange for land appraised at $39,000.

g. Semiannual cash dividends of 75 cents on common stock and 50 cents on preferred stock were declared and paid.

h. Net income was $35,000.

Required:

1. Give the necessary journal entries to record the transactions listed.
2. Prepare the stockholders' equity section of the balance sheet as of December 31, 1984.

P13–3 Dividend Calculations

Dye Corporation has authorization for 10,000 shares of 6 percent preferred stock, par value $10 per share, and 4,000 shares of common stock, par value $100 per share, all of which are issued and outstanding. During the years beginning in 1983, Dye Corporation maintained a policy of paying out 50 percent of net income in cash dividends. Net income for the 3 years beginning in 1983 was $8,000, $80,000, and $64,000. There are no dividends in arrears for years prior to 1983.

Required:

Compute the amount of dividends paid to each class of stock for each year under the following separate cases.

1. Preferred stock is noncumulative and nonparticipating.
2. Preferred stock is cumulative and nonparticipating.
3. Preferred stock is noncumulative and fully participating.
4. Preferred stock is cumulative and fully participating.
5. **Interpretive Question** Why is it important that a common shareholder know about the dividend privileges of the preferred stock?

P13–4 Dividend Transactions and Calculations

Kaye Corporation currently has 200,000 shares of $10 par-value common stock authorized, with 100,000 of these shares issued and outstanding.

Required:

1. Prepare journal entries to record the following 1983 transactions.

   (a) January 1. Received authorization for 100,000 shares of 7 percent fully participating, cumulative preferred stock with a par value of $10.

   (b) January 2. Issued 10,000 shares of the preferred stock at $15 per share.

   (c) February 1. Declared a 2-for-1 common stock split to be effective on February 15.

   (d) February 15. Common stock is split as announced at the beginning of the month.

   (e) June 1. Reacquired 20 percent of the common stock outstanding for $18 per share.

   (f) June 2. Declared a cash dividend of $10,000. The date of record is June 15.

   (g) June 30. Paid the previously declared cash dividend of $10,000.

   (h) October 10. A 40 percent common stock dividend was declared and issued to common shareholders. (The market price of common stock is $16 per share.)

2. Determine the proper allocation to preferred and common shareholders of a $100,000 cash dividend declared on December 31, 1983. (This dividend is in addition to the June 2 dividend.)
3. **Interpretive Question** Why didn't the preferred shareholders receive their current-dividend preference of $7,000 in part (2)?

P13–5 Treasury Stock and Dividend Transactions

The following is Tracey Company's stockholders' equity section as of December 31, 1983.

Preferred Stock (7%, $60 par, noncumulative, nonparticipating, 8,000 shares authorized, 4,000 shares issued and outstanding)	$240,000
Common Stock ($10 par, 60,000 shares authorized, 40,000 shares issued and outstanding)	400,000
Paid-in Capital in Excess of Par—Preferred Stock	65,000
Paid-in Capital in Excess of Par—Common Stock	126,000
Retained Earnings	165,000

Required:

1. Journalize the following 1984 transactions.

   (a) Issued 1,000 preferred shares at $70 per share.

   (b) Reacquired 500 of the common shares for the treasury at $13 per share.

(c) Declared and paid a $2-per-share dividend on common stock in addition to paying the required preferred dividends.

(d) Reissued 300 of the treasury shares at $14 per share.

(e) Reissued the remaining treasury shares at $12 per share.

(f) Earnings for the year were $46,000.

2. Prepare a stockholders' equity section for the company at December 31, 1984.

P13-6 Preparing Stockholders' Equity Sections and Recording Dividends

The two independent cases presented below each require preparation of the stockholders' equity section of a corporation's balance sheet.

a. In 1983, Myrna Smith and some old college buddies organized Kandi-Land, Inc., a gourmet candy company. In 1983, Kandi-Land issued 150,000 shares of common stock, par value $15, for $3,000,000, and 50,000 shares of 10 percent, $20 par, cumulative, participating preferred stock for $1,100,000. Combined earnings for 1983, 1984, 1985, and 1986 amounted to $1,250,000. Dividends paid in the 4 years were as follows: 1983—$100,000, 1984—$300,000, 1985— -0-, 1986—$150,000.

b. In 1983, Carol Devey and some friends formed Delta Corporation. The corporation issued 10,000 shares of common stock, par value $20, for $250,000. Combined earnings for 1983 and 1984 were $65,000. In 1985, Delta had a loss of $23,000. In 1984, Delta authorized and executed a 2-for-1 stock split. Dividends paid during the 3 years were as follows: 1983—$10,000 cash, 1984—$5,000 cash, 1985—5 percent stock (market value $20/share).

Required:

1. Prepare in good form the stockholders' equity section of the balance sheets for each of the above companies as of December 31, 1986, for Kandi-Land and as of December 31, 1985, for Delta.

2. Prepare the journal entries that would be necessary to record the dividends paid in 1986 for Kandi-Land and in 1985 for Delta.

3. **Interpretive Question** What is the effect on earnings per share when a company has a stock dividend or stock split?

P13-7 Stockholders' Equity, Dividends, and Treasury Stock

The stockholders' equity section of Forsyth Corporation's December 31, 1983, balance sheet is as follows:

Stockholders' Equity:	
Preferred Stock (10%, $50 par, 1,000 shares issued) .	$ 50,000
Common Stock ($15 par, 5,000 shares issued)	75,000
Paid-in Capital in Excess of Par— Preferred Stock	2,000
Paid-in Capital in Excess of Par— Common Stock	25,000
Total Contributed Capital	$152,000
Retained Earnings	102,000
Total Stockholders' Equity	$254,000

During 1984, Forsyth Corporation had the following transactions affecting stockholders' equity:

Jan. 20	Paid a cash dividend of $2 per share on common stock. The dividend was declared on December 15, 1983.
May 15	Declared a 10 percent common stock dividend. The market price on this date was $24 per share.
June 1	Issued the stock dividend declared on May 15.
Aug. 15	Reacquired 1,000 shares of common stock at $20 per share.
Sept. 30	Reissued 500 shares of the treasury stock at $21 per share.
Oct. 15	Declared and paid cash dividends of $3 per share on the common stock.
Nov. 1	Reissued 200 shares of treasury stock at $18 per share.
Dec. 15	Declared and paid the 10 percent preferred cash dividend.
Dec. 31	Closed the Income Summary account, reporting net income of $40,000, to Retained Earnings. Also closed the Dividends accounts to Retained Earnings.

Required:

1. Journalize the above transactions.

2. Prepare the stockholders' equity section of Forsyth Corporation's December 31, 1984, balance sheet.

3. **Interpretive Question** What is the effect on earnings per share when a company purchases treasury stock?

P13-8 The Statement of Retained Earnings

McKay Brothers Corporation records show the following at December 31, 1983.

a. Extraordinary loss (net of tax)	$ (25,000)
b. Current year retained earnings appropriation for bond retirement	10,000
c. January 1, 1983, retained earnings appropriation balance for bond retirement ..	90,000
d. Cash dividends paid during 1983	15,000
e. Stock dividends issued during 1983	7,000
f. January 1, 1983, unappropriated retained earnings balance	255,000
g. Prior-period adjustment (net of tax)	(12,000)
h. Net income before extraordinary items and taxes (assume a 40 percent tax rate)	80,000

Required:

1. Prepare a 1983 statement of retained earnings.
2. **Interpretive Question** Why would a firm appropriate retained earnings if such action does not provide any cash?

P13–9 Unifying Problem: Stock Transactions and the Preparation of the Stockholders' Equity Section

Arnold Corporation was founded on January 1, 1983, and is heavily involved in raising capital through the issuance of stock.

a. Received authorization for 100,000 shares of $20 par-value common stock, 50,000 shares of 6 percent preferred stock with a stated value of $5, and 50,000 shares of no-par common stock.

b. Issued 25,000 shares of the $20 par-value common stock at $24 per share.

c. Issued 10,000 shares of the preferred stock at $8 per share.

d. Issued 5,000 shares of the no-par common stock at $22 per share.

e. Reacquired 1,000 shares of the $20 par-value stock at $25 per share.

f. Reacquired 500 shares of no-par common stock at $20 per share.

g. Reissued 250 of the 1,000 reacquired shares of $20 par-value common stock at $23 per share.

h. Reissued all of the 500 reacquired shares of no-par stock at $23 per share.

i. Income for the year was $10,500.

Required:

1. Prepare journal entries to record the above 1983 transactions in Arnold Corporation's books.
2. Prepare the stockholders' equity section of Arnold Corporation's balance sheet at December 31, 1983. Assume that the above transactions represent all of the events involving equity accounts during 1983.

P13–10 Unifying Problem: Stockholders' Equity

Brandon Corporation was organized during 1983. At the end of 1984 the equity section of its balance sheet appeared as follows:

Contributed Capital:		
Preferred Stock (6%, $20 par, 10,000 shares authorized, 5,000 shares issued)	$100,000	
Common Stock ($10 par, 50,000 shares authorized, 11,000 shares issued, 1,000 held as treasury stock)	110,000	
Paid-in Capital in Excess of Par—Preferred Stock	20,000	
Total Contributed Capital		$230,000
Retained Earnings		100,000
Total Contributed Capital Plus Retained Earnings		$330,000
Less Treasury Stock (at cost)		(12,000)
Total Owners' Equity		$318,000

During 1985, the following stockholders' equity transactions occurred (in chronological sequence).

a. Issued 500 shares of common stock at $13 per share.

b. Reissued 500 shares of treasury stock at $13 per share.

c. Issued 1,000 shares of preferred stock at $25 per share.

d. Reissued 500 shares of treasury stock at $10 per share.

e. Declared a dividend large enough to meet the current-dividend preference of the preferred stock and to pay the common shareholders $2 per share.

f. Appropriated $15,000 of retained earnings for the retirement of debt.

g. Declared a 2-for-1 stock split on the common stock.

h. Net income is $65,000.

Required:

1. Journalize the transactions.
2. Prepare the stockholders' equity section at December 31, 1985.
3. **Interpretive Question** Does the appropriated retained earnings mean that $15,000 cash is available to retire the debt? If not, what is the purpose of such an account?

CHAPTER 14

Owners' Equity–Proprietorships and Partnerships

THIS CHAPTER EXPLAINS:

Characteristics of proprietorships and partnerships.

Basic accounting for proprietorships.

Basic accounting for partnerships, including admission and withdrawal of partners and the liquidation of a partnership.

Due to their size, corporations dominate economic activity in the United States. However, proprietorships and partnerships are by far the most common types of businesses. They are most numerous in the professions and businesses that stress personal services. For example, many doctors, lawyers, dentists, accountants, and small businesses (repair shops, real estate agencies, and other service businesses) operate as proprietorships or partnerships.

A partnership allows two or more people to combine their capital and skills in order to operate on a larger scale and perhaps more efficiently than they could individually, as proprietorships. For example, a realtor and a building contractor may combine their talents in a construction partnership. The flexibility of a partnership allows the partners to withdraw funds and make business decisions without having meetings or adhering to legal procedures. In this chapter, we discuss the principles and procedures used in accounting for proprietorships and partnerships. As noted in Chapter 13, accounting for assets and liabilities is the same in proprietorships, partnerships, and corporations; only the equity sections differ.

The discussion of owners' equity of proprietorships and partnerships will be divided into seven parts: (1) characteristics shared by proprietorships and partnerships, (2) accounting for proprietorships, (3) characteristics unique to partnerships, (4) basic accounting for partnerships, (5) accounting for partnership profits and losses, (6) accounting for changing partnership members, and (7) liquidating a partnership.

Characteristics Shared by Proprietorships and Partnerships

proprietorship *an unincorporated business owned by one person*

partnership *an unincorporated business owned by two or more persons or entities*

A proprietorship is an unincorporated business owned by one person. A partnership is an unincorporated business owned by two or more persons or entities. In most respects, proprietorships and partnerships are similar to each other but very different from corporations. Corporations are legal entities authorized by states; they are separately taxed and offer limited liability to their shareholders. Proprietorships and partnerships are unincorporated businesses that are not legally separate from their owners, nor are they taxed separately. Both types of businesses are less subject to government regulation than are corporations. Some of the common characteristics of proprietorships and partnerships are their ease of formation, limited life, and unlimited liability.

EASE OF FORMATION

Proprietorships and partnerships can be formed with few legal formalities. When a person decides to establish a proprietorship, he or she merely acquires the necessary cash, inventory, equipment, and other assets, and begins providing goods and/or services to customers. The same is true for a partnership, except that since two or more persons are involved, they must decide together which assets will be acquired and how business will be conducted.

partnership agreement *a legal agreement between partners; it usually specifies the capital contributions to be made by each partner, the ratios in which partnership earnings will be distributed, the management responsibilities of the partners, and the partners' rights to transfer or sell their individual interests*

When two or more persons voluntarily agree to be partners, the agreement between them becomes a contract. Partnership agreements can be oral or written, but because each partner is legally responsible for the actions of the other partner(s), the agreement should be written to avoid misunderstandings. A partnership agreement should specify the following:

1. The name, location, and purpose of the business.
2. The names of the partners and their respective duties, obligations, and rights.
3. The investments in the partnership to be made by each partner.
4. The arrangement agreed upon for sharing business profits and losses.
5. The amount of assets the partners are allowed to withdraw, and when.
6. The partners' rights to transfer or sell their interests and the procedures to be followed when new partners are admitted and when partners withdraw.
7. The procedures for dissolving the partnership.

LIMITED LIFE

Because proprietorships and partnerships are not legal entities that are separate and distinct from their owners, they are easily terminated. In the case of a proprietorship, the owner can decide to dissolve the business anytime he or she wants. For a partnership, anything that terminates or changes the contract between the partners legally dissolves the partnership. Events that dissolve a partnership are (1) the death or withdrawal of a partner, (2) the bankruptcy of a partner, (3) the admission of a new partner, (4) the retirement of a partner, or (5) the completion of a project for which the partnership was formed. The occurrence of any of these events does not necessarily mean that a partnership must cease business; rather, the existing partnership is legally terminated and a new partnership must be formed.

UNLIMITED LIABILITY

unlimited liability *the lack of a ceiling on the amount of liability a proprietor or partner must assume, meaning that if business assets are not sufficient to settle creditor claims, the personal assets of the proprietor or partners will be used to settle the claims*

Proprietorships and partnerships have unlimited liability, which means that the proprietor or partners are personally responsible for all the debts of the business. If a partnership is in poor financial condition, creditors first attempt to satisfy their claims from the assets of the partnership. After those assets are exhausted, creditors may seek payment from the personal assets of the partners. In addition, since partners are responsible for one another's actions (within the scope of the partnership), creditors can seek payment for claims authorized by a departed partner from the personal assets of the remaining partners.

There are two exceptions to this unlimited liability rule. First, a person joining an existing partnership does not have to assume liability for debts incurred prior to his or her admission. Second, if a partner decides to withdraw from a partnership and gives adequate public notice of withdrawal, then he or she cannot be held liable for debts incurred subsequent to his or her withdrawal.

This unlimited liability feature is probably the single most significant disadvantage of a proprietorship or partnership. It can deter a wealthy person from joining a partnership for fear of losing personal assets.

TO SUMMARIZE A proprietorship is an unincorporated business owned by one person. A partnership is an unincorporated business owned by two or more persons. Both types of businesses are easy to start and easy to terminate, and they are not separately taxed. Most partnerships are based on a partnership agreement that specifies how business will be conducted, how profits will be divided, and other important elements of the partnership. Anything that changes the partnership agreement, such as the death or retirement of a partner, legally terminates the partnership. A major disadvantage of proprietorships and partnerships is the unlimited liability of the owner or partners.

Proprietorship Accounting

As indicated earlier, the difference between accounting for a proprietorship and accounting for a corporation is in the owners' equity accounts. In a corporation, owners' equity is divided into contributed capital and retained earnings, with each of these categories possibly having several different

Capital account *an account in which a proprietor's or partner's interest in a firm is recorded; it is increased by owner investments and net income and decreased by owner withdrawals and net losses*

Drawings account *a temporary account in which the owners' withdrawals of cash or other assets from proprietorships or partnerships are recorded*

accounts. In a proprietorship, all owner's equity transactions are handled by only two accounts: Capital and Drawings accounts.

To illustrate the accounting for the owner's equity of a proprietorship, we will assume that Julie Shaw decides to become a real estate broker. On January 1, 1983, she deposits $40,000 into a bank account to finance the business. The entry to record the $40,000 deposit would be

Cash	40,000	
Julie Shaw, Capital		40,000
Invested $40,000 to start a real estate business.		

Once the business is established, the entries to account for the purchase of assets, the payment of business expenses, and the receipt of revenues are similar to those for corporations. There is one exception, however: whereas in a corporation salaries to management are accounted for as expenses, in a proprietorship the salary paid to the owner is a distribution of earnings. This is because the managers of a corporation are considered to be employees, even if they are also stockholders in the company. The owners of a corporation receive dividends, which are deducted directly from the Retained Earnings account. In a proprietorship, the owner receives no dividends, so any "drawing out" of funds is considered to be a distribution to the owner. Hence, the name "Drawings account." If Julie Shaw decided to withdraw $650 cash for personal use or as salary, the entry would be

Julie Shaw, Drawings	650	
Cash		650
Withdrew $650 for personal use.		

The account "Julie Shaw, Drawings" is similar to a dividends account in a corporation; at year-end it is closed to the owner's equity account, "Julie Shaw, Capital."

Assuming that Julie Shaw withdrew only $650 during the year, the closing entry to eliminate the balance in the Drawings account would be

Julie Shaw, Capital	650	
Julie Shaw, Drawings		650
To close the Drawings account for the year.		

If we also assume that an Income Summary account is used and that it has a $14,000 credit balance (profit) at the end of the year, Julie Shaw's closing entry for net income will be

Income Summary	14,000	
Julie Shaw, Capital		14,000
To close net income for the year to the owner's Capital account.		

From the above two entries, we see that Julie Shaw's capital account has increased by $13,350 since January 1. Adding this amount to her original contribution results in a $53,350 balance at year-end, as the following calculation shows.

Owner's Equity

Julie Shaw, Capital, January 1, 1983	$40,000
Add Net Income	14,000
Total	$54,000
Less Withdrawals	(650)
Julie Shaw, Capital, December 31, 1983	$53,350

The owner's equity section of Julie Shaw's balance sheet would have only one entry.

Julie Shaw, Capital	$53,350

TO SUMMARIZE The assets and liabilities of a proprietorship are accounted for in the same way as they are in a corporation. Equity is handled differently. Whereas corporate equity involves several accounts, proprietorship equity has only two accounts: Drawings and Capital. The Drawings account is used for recording withdrawals of funds by the owner. It is closed to the Capital account at year-end. The Capital account is increased when capital is invested in the business and when profits are earned; it is decreased when cash or other assets are withdrawn from the business or when losses occur.

Characteristics Unique to Partnerships

Earlier in the chapter we discussed the characteristics shared by proprietorships and partnerships: their ease of formation, limited life, and unlimited liability. We now discuss the characteristics that are unique to partnerships: (1) mutual agency, (2) co-ownership of all partnership property, and (3) sharing of partnership profits.

MUTUAL AGENCY

mutual agency *the right of all partners in a partnership to act as agents for the partnership, with the authority to bind it to business agreements*

Each partner is an agent of the partnership and can enter into contracts, incur debts, buy merchandise, or conduct other business on behalf of the partnership. This mutual agency feature allows any partner to bind the partnership to agreements that relate to normal business operations. For example, suppose Jim Jones and Harry Haley have a building construction company. If Jim Jones contracts to purchase lumber, bricks, or other building materials for the partnership, the partnership is obligated to pay for these items. Of course, if Jim Jones decides to buy himself a sports car or anything else not intended for the business, the partnership has no such obligation. The mutual agency aspect of partnerships makes it important to select partners who are responsible and honest.

CO-OWNERSHIP OF PARTNERSHIP PROPERTY

Property invested in a partnership becomes an asset of the business and is jointly owned by all partners, not just by the partner transferring the property. Thus, if a partner transfers a building, land, inventory, or other assets to a partnership, he or she gives up the right to separate use of the property. And, when the property is sold, all partners benefit from the gain, or share in the loss, from the sale.

SHARING OF PARTNERSHIP PROFITS

All members of a partnership have the right to share in the partnership's profits, and the obligation to share in its losses. The arrangement for dividing the profits and losses should be spelled out in the partnership agreement. If the partnership agreement only states how profits are to be distributed, losses must be shared in the same ratio. If the agreement does not specify how earnings are to be divided, or if no formal partnership agreement exists, the law requires that profits and losses be shared equally.

TO SUMMARIZE Three important characteristics of a partnership are mutual agency, co-ownership of partnership property, and the sharing of partnership profits and losses. Mutual agency means that each partner is an agent of the partnership and can bind it to business agreements that relate to normal operations. Co-ownership of property means that property transferred to a partnership is jointly owned by all partners.

Basic Partnership Accounting

Like a proprietorship, a partnership differs from a corporation primarily in accounting for owners' equity. That is, a partnership has only two types of owners' equity accounts: Capital and Drawings. Whereas a proprietorship has only one of each type of account, a partnership maintains a separate Capital and Drawings account for each partner.

FORMING A PARTNERSHIP

To illustrate the accounting for the formation of a partnership, we assume that Dr. Joan Allen and Dr. James Baker decide to form a partnership on January 1, 1983. Their partnership agreement specifies that Dr. Allen will contribute land valued at $20,000, a building valued at $30,000, and $10,000 cash to the business, and that Dr. Baker will contribute medical equipment valued at $40,000 plus $20,000 cash. The entry to record the capital contributions of the two partners would be

Cash	30,000	
Equipment	40,000	
Land	20,000	
Building	30,000	
Allen, Capital		60,000
Baker, Capital		60,000
To record the investments of Allen and Baker in the partnership.		

One of the most difficult aspects of accounting for the formation of a partnership is in assigning values to the noncash assets invested in the business. Generally, the fair market values on the date of transfer should be used, but these values must be agreed upon by all partners. For example, if the assets contributed by either Baker or Allen had been used in a business prior to the partnership, the values assigned to them for the partnership might be quite different from the amounts they were being carried at on the previous business's books. Although the equipment invested by Baker may have had a book value of only $30,000, or the land and building invested by Allen may have cost her only $15,000 several years ago, it is only fair to give each partner credit for the current market values of the assets at the time they are transferred to the partnership.

ADDITIONAL INVESTMENTS BY OWNERS

Additional investments are recorded in the same manner as original investments. That is, the assets contributed are recorded at their fair market values and the partners' respective Capital accounts are credited for the appropriate amounts. For example, if on September 1, 1983, Baker invested another $30,000 because the business had a cash shortage, the investment would be recorded as follows:

Cash	30,000	
Baker, Capital		30,000
To record investment of $30,000 cash by Dr. Baker.		

PARTNERS' DRAWINGS ACCOUNTS

As mentioned previously, in a corporation the managers are employees, so their salaries are accounted for as expenses; the shareholders are the owners and distributions to them are in the form of dividends. In a partnership, the managers are usually the owners, and any amounts they withdraw either as salary or as a distribution of profits are debited to a Drawings account, which eventually reduces the Capital account. Each partner has a Drawings account in which his or her withdrawals are recorded for the year. Any salaries paid to employees who are not partners are expenses of the business. For example, if Allen and Baker each withdrew $35,000 as salary for the year, the entry would be

Allen, Drawings	35,000	
Baker, Drawings	35,000	
Cash		70,000
To record cash taken from the partnership as salary.		

If Allen or Baker had withdrawn funds, say to repay a personal loan, that amount would also be debited to the Drawings account. At year-end the debits in the Drawings accounts would be totaled and the accounts would be closed to the partners' Capital accounts. Assuming that the total in each Drawings account was the $35,000 salary, the entry to close the Drawings accounts for the year would be

Allen, Capital	35,000	
Baker, Capital	35,000	
Allen, Drawings		35,000
Baker, Drawings		35,000
To close the Drawings accounts for the year.		

THE STATEMENT OF PARTNERS' CAPITAL

statement of partners' capital *a partnership report that reconciles the balances in the partners' equity accounts from year to year; similar to a statement of changes in retained earnings for a corporation*

Because most partners want an explanation of how their capital accounts change from year to year, a statement of partners' capital is usually prepared. This statement, which is analogous to a retained earnings statement for a corporation, lists the beginning capital balances, additional investments, profits or losses from operations, withdrawals, and a final balance for each partner's capital. For example, given the preceding information and assuming that the Allen and Baker Partnership had a 1983 profit of $90,000, which was shared equally, the statement of partners' capital as of December 31, 1983, would be as shown in Exhibit 14–1.

EXHIBIT 14–1

Allen and Baker Partnership
Statement of Partners' Capital
for the Year Ended December 31, 1983

	Dr. Allen	Dr. Baker	Total
Investments, January 1, 1983	$ 60,000	$ 60,000	$120,000
Add: Additional Investments During 1983		30,000	30,000
Net Income for 1983	45,000	45,000	90,000
Subtotal	$105,000	$135,000	$240,000
Less Withdrawals During 1983	(35,000)	(35,000)	(70,000)
Capital Balances, December 31, 1983	$ 70,000	$100,000	$170,000

In addition, a partnership will prepare a balance sheet and an income statement. The format of the income statement will be exactly the same as for a corporation, with one exception: the distribution of net income (or loss) will be noted at the bottom of the statement [see Exhibit 14-2(a)]. The balance sheet resembles that of a corporation, again with one exception: the owners' equity section [see Exhibit 14-2(b)].

EXHIBIT 14-2 Financial Statements of a Partnership*

(a)

Allen and Baker Partnership
Income Statement
for the Period Ending December 31, 1983

Fee Revenues		$190,000
Expenses:		
Salary Expense	$20,000	
Utilities Expense	10,000	
Other Expenses	70,000	
Total Expenses		100,000
Net Income		$ 90,000
Distribution to Partners:		
To Allen		$ 45,000
To Baker		45,000
Net Income Distributed		$ 90,000

(b)

Allen and Baker Partnership
Balance Sheet
as of December 31, 1983

Assets		
Cash	$ 30,000	
Accounts Receivable	20,000	
Inventory	6,000	
Land	20,000	
Equipment (net)	40,000	
Buildings (net)	114,000	
Total Assets		$230,000
Liabilities and Partners' Equity		
Accounts Payable	$ 20,000	
Notes Payable	40,000	
Allen, Capital	70,000	
Baker, Capital	100,000	
Total Liabilities and Partners' Equity		$230,000

* The figures are arbitrary, and we assume that the partners share the profits equally.

TO SUMMARIZE The basic elements in accounting for a partnership are (1) accounting for the initial investments by the partners, (2) accounting for any additional investments by the partners, (3) recording withdrawals of assets by partners, (4) closing the partners' Drawings accounts, and (5) preparing a statement of partners' capital. Both initial and subsequent investments by owners are credited to the owners' capital balances. Owners' withdrawals of cash, inventory, and other business assets are recorded in Drawings accounts, which are closed to the Capital accounts at year-end. There is one Capital and one Drawings account for each partner. A statement of partners' capital reconciles the beginning and the ending capital balance by adding profits and additional investments to the beginning capital balances and then subtracting withdrawals.

Accounting for Partnership Profits and Losses

In the preceding section, we assumed that Allen and Baker split the profits equally. Partnership profits (or losses) may be divided in any way the partners see fit—60%/40%, 70%/30%, and so forth. This profit-and-loss sharing ratio is usually specified in the partnership agreement. If it is not, the partners are legally bound to split the profits (or losses) equally.

In order to determine an equitable distribution of profits, partners normally consider three factors: (1) how much cash and other property each partner contributed, (2) how much time and energy each partner expends working in the business, and the value of the respective partner's talents, and (3) the risks each partner is taking (for example, by forgoing other opportunities or by tying his reputation to the other partners). For example, Dr. Allen and Dr. Baker each contributed $60,000 of assets to the partnership. Assuming that they also devote equal time to the business, a 50/50 division of profits would probably be equitable. If, however, Dr. Allen works five days each week and Dr. Baker spends only two days working, then Dr. Allen should probably receive a larger percentage of the profits. Note that their $35,000 salaries are paid in anticipation of profits, and are considered to be an advance distribution of those profits. If a partner whose share of net income is $40,000, for example, has already received $35,000 in salary, he or she would either receive another $5,000 or have it assigned to his or her Capital account, assuming that all profits are distributed.

Because profits and losses may be allocated in any manner agreed upon by the partners, there are many ways of sharing profits. We will discuss five of the most common types of profit-sharing arrangements.

STATED RATIO

Partnership profits are frequently distributed on the basis of a predetermined fixed ratio, such as an equal percentage to each partner, or 60 percent to one partner and 40 percent to the other. To illustrate the allocation of profits on a stated ratio, we will assume that although Allen and Baker invested equally in the business, Baker manages all the daily operations, whereas Allen spends considerably less time in the business. So they agree that Allen will receive only 40 percent of the profits and that Baker will get 60 percent. (Note that the total of all partner percentages must equal 100 percent.) The $90,000 of profits would then be divided as follows:

Allen ($90,000 × 0.40)	$36,000
Baker ($90,000 × 0.60)	54,000
Total	$90,000

The entry to close net income to the partners' Capital accounts would be

Income Summary	90,000	
Allen, Capital		36,000
Baker, Capital		54,000
To close 1983 earnings to the partners' Capital accounts.		

CAPITAL INVESTMENT RATIO

In the above example, Allen and Baker contributed the same amount of capital but different amounts of time. If they were to contribute equal time but different amounts of capital, they might decide to divide profits on the basis of their respective investments. With this approach, the profits may be allocated on the basis of capital balances at the beginning of the year or the average capital balances during the year.

To illustrate these two approaches, we assume that Allen and Baker had the following capital and drawings balances in 1983 (each withdrew $35,000 during the year).

Allen, Capital

Debit	Credit
	60,000 ...... 1/1/83

Allen, Drawings

Debit	Credit
35,000	

Baker, Capital

Debit	Credit
	60,000 ...... 1/1/83
	30,000 ...... 9/1/83

Baker, Drawings

Debit	Credit
35,000	

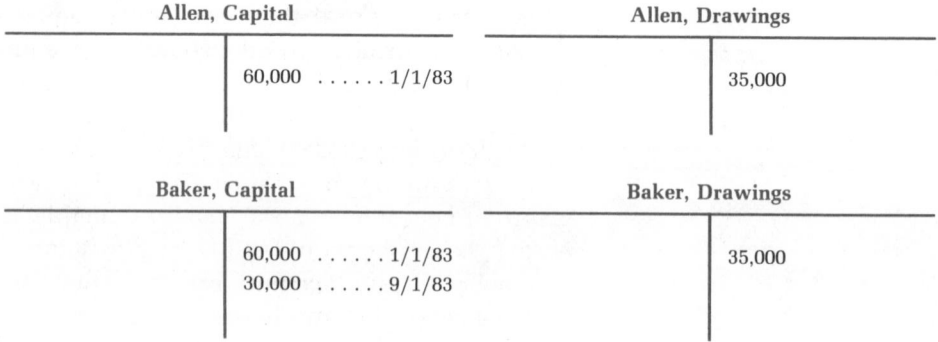

Because the beginning capital balances for Allen and Baker were $60,000 each, profits allocated on the basis of beginning capital balance ratios would be split equally, that is, $45,000 to each.

When the beginning capital balance ratio is used, withdrawals and additional investments made during the year are ignored. Because such withdrawals and subsequent investments can drastically alter investment ratios, many partnership agreements specify that average capital balances must be used.

To illustrate how profits are distributed using average capital balances, recall that Baker contributed an additional $30,000 on September 1. For the purposes of our calculations, we will assume that the $35,000 withdrawal by each partner consisted of a $15,000 withdrawal on May 1 and a $20,000 withdrawal on October 1. Using these data, the capital balances for Allen and Baker would be calculated as follows:

Partner	Date	Capital Balance	×	Months Unchanged	=	Total				Average Capital
Allen	1/1/83–4/30/83	$60,000	×	4	=	$240,000				
	5/1/83–9/30/83	45,000	×	5	=	225,000				
	10/1/83–12/31/83	25,000	×	3	=	75,000				
						$540,000	÷	12	=	$45,000
Baker	1/1/83–4/30/83	$60,000	×	4	=	$240,000				
	5/1/83–8/31/83	45,000	×	4	=	180,000				
	9/1/83–9/30/83	75,000	×	1	=	75,000				
	10/1/83–12/31/83	55,000	×	3	=	165,000				
						$660,000	÷	12	=	$55,000

Note that Allen and Baker both had capital balances of $60,000 from January 1 to April 30; on May 1 each partner withdrew $15,000. Their capital balances were then $45,000 until September 1, when Baker invested an additional $30,000; Allen's balance remained at $45,000 until October 1, when both partners' capital balances were decreased by the $20,000 withdrawals. The average capital balances are computed by multiplying each capital balance by the number of months it remained unchanged, adding the totals, and dividing by 12 months. The result is that Allen's average capital balance is $45,000 and Baker's is $55,000.

Using these average capital balances, the $90,000 of net income would be distributed as follows:

Allen ($90,000 × 45/100)	$40,500
Baker ($90,000 × 55/100)	49,500
Total	$90,000

The entry to close net income to the partners' Capital accounts would be

Income Summary	90,000	
Allen, Capital		40,500
Baker, Capital		49,500
To close 1983 earnings to the partners' Capital accounts.		

ALLOWANCE FOR SALARIES WITH THE REMAINDER AT STATED RATIO

Individual partners may take on greater responsibilities or, by their special initiative or talent, may contribute more to the partnership than others. In such cases, salaries that reflect the partners' different responsibilities can be made part of the profit-sharing arrangement.

To illustrate this method of allocating profits, assume that the Allen and Baker partnership agreement specifies that Allen is to be the full-time manager of the business. For this reason, she will receive a salary of $36,000. Baker will be paid a small salary of $12,000; the rest of the net income is to be divided equally. With this agreement, Allen and Baker will receive $57,000 and $33,000, respectively, in 1983, as calculated below.

	Allen	Baker	Net Income
Net Income			$90,000
Salaries to Partners	$36,000	$12,000	(48,000)
Remainder to Be Divided Equally:			$42,000
Allen (50%)	21,000		
Baker (50%)		21,000	(42,000)
Total to Each Partner	$57,000	$33,000	$ -0-

ALLOWANCE FOR INTEREST ON INVESTED CAPITAL WITH THE REMAINDER AT STATED RATIO

When two or more people decide to invest their capital in a partnership, they lose the opportunity to invest that money in certificates of deposit, treasury bills, or savings accounts that pay interest on a regular basis. In order to compensate partners for this lost interest, some partnership agreements specify that a portion of the profits will be allocated on the basis of interest that could have been earned on invested capital, with the remainder being allocated at some fixed ratio.

To illustrate this approach, we assume that Allen and Baker could have earned 15 percent interest on the amount they invested in the partnership. So, they are each due 15 percent interest on their investments; the remainder is to be divided equally. With this arrangement, the calculation for 1983 would be

	Allen	Baker	Net Income
Net Income			$90,000
Interest on Invested Capital:			
Allen ($60,000 × 0.15)	$ 9,000		
Baker ($60,000 × 0.15 × 8/12)		$ 6,000	
($90,000 × 0.15 × 4/12)		4,500	(19,500)
Remainder to Be Divided Equally:			$70,500
Allen (50%)	35,250		
Baker (50%)		$35,250	(70,500)
Total to Each Partner	$44,250	$45,750	$ -0-

ALLOWANCE FOR SALARIES AND INTEREST WITH THE REMAINDER AT STATED RATIO

Any of three factors we have mentioned—capital balance, salary, or interest—may be used alone in determining how partnership profits are to be divided, but they can also be used together. In this section we show how two of them, interest and salary, together with a stated ratio, might be combined to divide the 1983 net income in the Allen and Baker partnership. We now assume that Allen and Baker have agreed that Allen will receive a salary of $36,000 and Baker a salary of $12,000, that each will be paid 15 percent on invested capital, and that the remaining profits will be divided equally. Given these data, the calculation is

	Allen	Baker	Net Income
Net Income			$90,000
Salaries to Partners	$36,000	$12,000	(48,000)
Remaining Income After Salaries			$42,000
Interest on Invested Capital:			
Allen ($60,000 × 0.15)	9,000		
Baker ($60,000 × 0.15 × 8/12)		6,000	
($90,000 × 0.15 x 4/12)		4,500	(19,500)
Remaining Income After Salaries and Interest			$22,500
Remainder to Be Divided Equally:			
Allen (50%)	11,250		
Baker (50%)		11,250	(22,500)
Total to Each Partner	$56,250	$33,750	$ -0-

With this arrangement, if profits were insufficient to pay both salaries and interest, one of the profit-distribution factors would have to be given priority. For example, if net income were only $50,000, should the partners receive their salaries and split the remaining $2,000? Or, should they receive interest first and allocate the remaining $30,500 ($50,000 – $19,500) to salaries? The most common way to deal with insufficient profits is to allocate salaries and interest as originally planned, and then to prorate the loss in the agreed-upon ratio. For example, if profits had been $50,000 instead of $90,000, the calculation would have been

	Allen	Baker	Net Income
Net Income			$50,000
Salaries to Partners	$36,000	$12,000	(48,000)
Remaining Income After Salaries			$ 2,000
Interest on Invested Capital:			
Allen ($60,000 × 0.15)	9,000		
Baker ($60,000 × 0.15 × 8/12)		6,000	
($90,000 × 0.15 × 4/12)		4,500	(19,500)
Deficiency to Be Divided Equally:			($17,500)
Allen (50%)	(8,750)		
Baker (50%)		(8,750)	17,500
Total to Each Partner	$36,250	$13,750	$ -0-

One final note: Partnerships do not pay taxes on profits earned. Although they do file a tax return that shows how profits are divided among the partners, it is for information purposes only. Taxes are paid by the individual partners, who include their portion of the partnership's profits on their personal tax returns. The income tax rules pertaining to partnerships are too complex to discuss here; but you do need to know that all partnership income is taxable to the respective partners in the year it is earned, regardless of whether cash is distributed to them. In the Allen and Baker partnership, the partners would be taxed on their shares of the $90,000 net income, not on their withdrawals of $35,000. This principal is also true of proprietorships.

TO SUMMARIZE Partnership profits and losses can be shared in a variety of ways. Allocation arrangements are usually specified in the partnership agreement. If they are not, profits and losses must be shared equally. Losses must be shared in the same ratio as profits. Factors that are often considered in determining how to allocate profits are (1) the personal services provided by the partners, (2) the amounts of capital invested in the business by the partners, and (3) the risks being taken by the partners. Five common methods of distributing profits are (1) stated ratio, (2) capital investment ratio, (3) allowance for salaries with the remainder at stated ratio, (4) allowance for interest on invested capital with the remainder at stated ratio, and (5) allowance for salaries and interest with the remainder at stated ratio.

Accounting for Changing Partnership Members

Partnership agreements specify the names of the partners and their respective duties, obligations, and rights. If a new partner is admitted or an original partner withdraws, the agreement is legally terminated and a new one must be written. Note, however, that this does not necessarily end the business itself; it may continue to function, except under the direction of the new partners. In this section, we discuss the accounting for changes in partners' interests.

There are two alternatives that can be used to account for changes in partners: the book-value and the market-value approaches. Because the admission of a new partner or the withdrawal of an existing partner makes necessary the creation of a new legal entity, the assets of the old partnership can be transferred to the new entity at their recorded book values or at their current market values. Transferring assets at book value is straightforward; transferring them at market value usually involves revaluing each asset and often recognizing goodwill. Proponents of the market-value approach argue that market values should be used whenever a new partnership is formed, because they were used when the original partnership was created. If a new partner, for example, is willing to pay the withdrawing partner more than book value of the withdrawing partner's Capital account to join the business, then it can be argued that the assets of the partnership are understated and should be written up. Proponents of the book-value approach argue that although a change in partners legally creates a new entity, in substance the business is not changed.

goodwill *an intangible asset that exists when a business is valued at more than the fair market value of its net assets, usually due to strategic location, reputation, good customer relations, or similar factors; equal to the excess of the purchase price over the fair market value of the net assets purchased*

In practice, although both alternatives are used, the book-value approach is more common because it is usually more conservative. It is even required in many cases. Therefore, we will illustrate only the more commonly used book-value alternative.

ADMITTING A NEW PARTNER

Sometimes a partnership will need additional capital or a person who will bring in new skills. Alternatively, a partnership may be so successful that individuals will ask to be admitted. If the partners are unable to invest more of their own capital or borrow the necessary funds, or if they find the idea of a new partner attractive, they may decide to admit someone who will contribute assets or skills that are needed. Of course, the new partner must be someone approved by all the existing partners.

A new partner can be admitted to a partnership in either of two ways: (1) an ownership interest may be bought directly from one or more of the present partners, or (2) an interest may be bought by investing cash or other assets in the partnership. (Note that an ownership interest is simply a fraction or percentage of the total capital balance on the date the new partner is admitted; it does not determine the profit-sharing allocation.) In the first case, where the interest is bought outright, payment is made directly to the original partner or partners and the assets of the partnership are not affected. In the second case, where the interest is purchased through an investment in the partnership, the new partner's contribution increases the partnership's total assets and total partners' equity.

Purchasing Another Partner's Interest

To illustrate the accounting for purchasing another partner's interest, we will assume that at the end of 1983, Allen and Baker had capital balances of $70,000 and $100,000, respectively, as calculated below.

	Allen	Baker	Total
Initial Investments	$ 60,000	$ 60,000	$120,000
Additional Investments		30,000	30,000
Profits (shared equally)	45,000	45,000	90,000
Total	$105,000	$135,000	$240,000
Less Withdrawals	(35,000)	(35,000)	(70,000)
Balance at 12/31/81	$ 70,000	$100,000	$170,000

Now assume that Dr. Allen decides to sell her interest in the partnership to Dr. Scott Ririe for $90,000. Since the transaction is between Allen and Ririe, it does not matter how much Ririe actually pays Allen for her interest. Even if the new partner pays several times the book value, the amount recorded is always the book value of the withdrawing partner's equity. Dr. Allen keeps the extra $20,000 as a bonus. Thus, the entry to record the sale to Dr. Ririe would be

Allen, Capital	70,000	
Ririe, Capital		70,000
To record the sale of Dr. Allen's equity in the partnership to Dr. Ririe.		

In the above example, Ririe purchased Allen's entire interest in the partnership. Assume now that Allen wants to remain a partner, but both she and Baker feel that the partnership needs a younger person. They decide to admit Dr. Scott Ririe, who agrees to invest $75,000. Of that sum, $15,000 is to go for a one-seventh interest in Dr. Allen's equity, and $60,000 is to go to Dr. Baker for a two-fifth's interest in his equity. As the following calculations show, Allen and Baker now have capital balances of $60,000 while Ririe has a capital balance of $50,000.

			Sold			
Partner	**Beginning Balances**	×	**Percentage**	=	**Amount**	**Ending Balances**
Allen	$ 70,000	×	1/7	=	$10,000	$ 60,000
Baker	100,000	×	2/5	=	40,000	60,000
Ririe	-0-				(50,000)	50,000
Totals	$170,000					$170,000

Although Ririe paid a total of $75,000, the entry to record the transfer would be

Allen, Capital	10,000	
Baker, Capital	40,000	
Ririe, Capital		50,000

To record the transfer of 1/7 of Allen's interest and 2/5 of Baker's interest to a new partner, Dr. Ririe.

Since Ririe purchased an interest in the partnership for an amount greater than book value, there is excess cash and it goes to Allen and Baker. In this case, since Ririe paid $15,000 for a $10,000 (1/7 × $70,000) share of Allen's equity and $60,000 for a $40,000 (2/5 × $100,000) share of Baker's equity, Allen and Baker keep $5,000 and $20,000, respectively.

Investing an Amount Equal to Book Value

The second way a partner can gain admission is by buying an interest through investment in the firm. This investment can be for an amount that is equal to, greater than, or less than the book value of the amount to be credited to the new partner's capital account. For example, a new partner might invest $90,000 but have his capital account credited for only $70,000; the $20,000 above the book value of $70,000 is a bonus to the original partners. We will illustrate all three situations using independent examples.

To illustrate the investment of an amount equal to book value, we assume that on December 31, 1983, Allen and Baker decide to admit Dr. Nathaniel Brooks, a noted orthopedic surgeon, to the partnership. Dr. Brooks agrees to invest $85,000 for a one-third interest. Assuming that the Capital accounts of Drs. Allen and Baker are $70,000 and $100,000, respectively, on December 31, 1983, Dr. Brooks' payment of $85,000 is exactly one-third of the new total capital.

Allen's Capital	$ 70,000
Baker's Capital	100,000
Brooks' Investment	85,000
Total Capital of New Partnership	$255,000
One-Third Interest ($255,000/3)	$ 85,000

The entry to record the admission of Brooks would be

Cash	85,000	
Brooks, Capital		85,000
To record the admission of Brooks into the partnership at a one-third interest.		

You should note, however, that a one-third interest in the partnership does not automatically entitle Brooks to one-third of the profits. The profit-sharing arrangement, which would be specified in the new partnership agreement, might depend on other factors, such as the services Brooks will provide.

Investing an Amount Greater than Book Value

A partnership may be so attractive that a new partner is willing to pay an amount greater than the book value to join the partnership. Such a situation may exist because the business has exceptionally high earnings, a good location, an excellent clientele, or other attributes. Under the book-value approach, when a new partner invests an amount greater than book value, the excess is said to be a bonus to the existing partners and is credited to their Capital accounts.

To illustrate, we assume that Dr. Brooks is willing to pay $130,000 for a one-third interest in the partnership. To determine how much Brooks' Capital account should be, the calculation is

Allen's Capital	$ 70,000
Baker's Capital	100,000
Investment by Brooks	130,000
Total Capital of New Partnership	$300,000
One-Third Interest ($300,000/3)	$100,000

Based on these calculations, Brooks' Capital account should be $100,000. The excess $30,000 would then be allocated to Allen's and Baker's Capital accounts according to their original profit-sharing ratio. Assuming that they share profits equally, each gets $15,000. The entry to record the admission of Brooks at a $130,000 investment is

Cash	130,000	
Brooks, Capital		100,000
Allen, Capital		15,000
Baker, Capital		15,000
To record the admission of Brooks into the partnership at a one-third interest.		

Investing an Amount Less than Book Value

If a partnership is short of cash or needs someone with a special skill or other characteristic, a new partner might be admitted for an amount less than book value.

To illustrate, we assume that Drs. Allen and Baker are anxious to have Dr. Brooks join their partnership because they believe that his presence will enhance their reputations and increase their clientele. So, on December 31, 1983, they agree to allow Brooks to pay only $70,000 for a one-third interest in the partnership. As the following calculations show, Brooks is receiving an interest worth $80,000 for only $70,000.

Allen's Capital	$ 70,000
Baker's Capital	100,000
Brooks' Investment	70,000
Total Capital of New Partnership	$240,000
One-Third Interest ($240,000/3)	$ 80,000

With the book-value approach, the new partner is said to receive a bonus and the old partners' capital balances are reduced accordingly. The amount that each partner's capital balance is reduced depends on the profit-sharing arrangement. If we again assume that Allen and Baker split profits and losses equally, each partner's capital would be reduced by $5,000 and the entry to record the admission of Brooks for a $70,000 investment would be

Cash	70,000	
Allen, Capital	5,000	
Baker, Capital	5,000	
Brooks, Capital		80,000
To record the admission of Brooks to the partnership at a one-third interest.		

TO SUMMARIZE A new partner may gain admission into a partnership either by buying an interest directly from an existing partner (or partners) or by investing in the partnership. If the interest is purchased from another partner, the transaction is a personal one between the buyer and the seller, and regardless of the purchase price the only entry on the books of the partnership is the transfer of the capital from the old partner to the new partner at book value. Admission by investment in the partnership can result in a bonus to the old partners, no bonus to anyone, or a bonus to the new partner, depending on the amount of the investment.

Exhibit 14-3 summarizes the various ways a new partner can be admitted into a partnership and the effect each way has on partnership assets and the individual partners' Capital accounts, assuming that assets are transferred to the new partnership at book value rather than at market value.

THE WITHDRAWAL OF A PARTNER

A partner may withdraw from a partnership for a variety of reasons—a desire to start a new company, for example, or a difference of opinion among the partners. Because assets are divided upon the withdrawal of a partner, to avoid misunderstandings most partnership agreements specify whether or not an audit must be performed when a partner withdraws, how

EXHIBIT 14-3 **Admission of a New Partner**

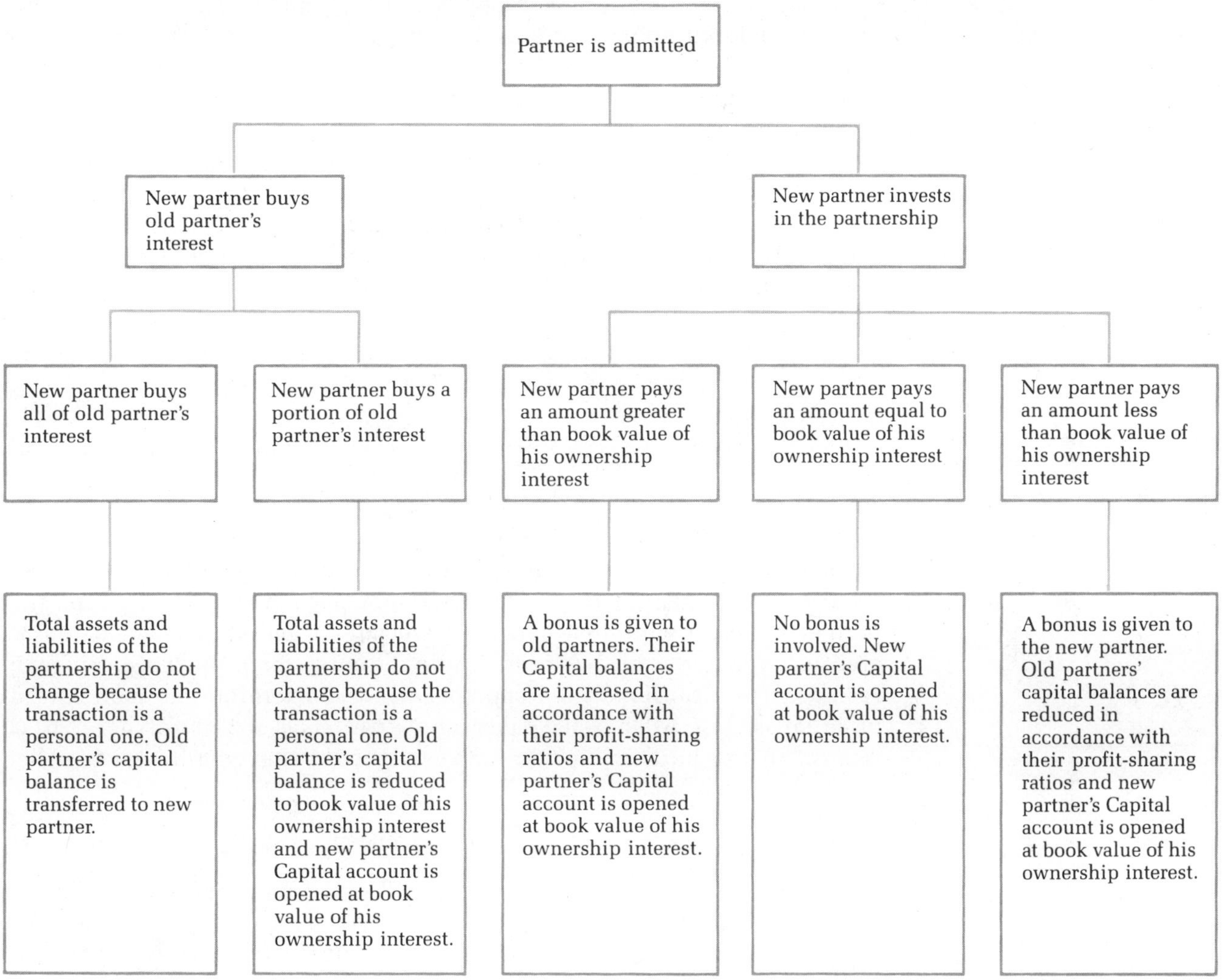

values will be assigned to company assets, whether a bonus will be given to the departing partner, how that partner will be paid, and other procedures to be followed.

Because the withdrawal of a partner is the reciprocal of admitting a partner, the transactions and accounting are quite similar. Just as there are several ways to admit a new partner, there are several ways a partner can withdraw from a partnership. Common alternatives are (1) selling his or her interest to an outsider, (2) selling his or her interest to the other partners, or (3) being paid with partnership assets. If the partner is paid with assets, the amount may be equal to, greater than, or less than the departing partner's capital balance, depending on the market values of the partnership's assets, the existing agreements, and other factors.

Selling an Interest to an Outsider

A partner can sell his or her interest to an outsider only with the consent of the other partner or partners. The price of the interest is a personal matter between the exiting partner and the new partner. Therefore, regardless of the amount paid to the departing partner, the entry made in the partnership records is simply to replace the old partner's capital balance with the new partner's capital balance for the same amount.

To illustrate the selling of an interest to an outsider, we will assume that Drs. Allen, Baker, and Ririe now work together in a partnership and have capital balances of $70,000, $100,000 and $60,000, respectively, on December 31, 1983. If, on that date, Allen sold her interest to Dr. Cummings for $90,000, the entry to record the transfer of capital balances in the company's books would be

Allen, Capital	70,000	
Cummings, Capital		70,000
To record the sale of Allen's interest in the partnership to Dr. Cummings.		

Selling an Interest to the Other Partners

A partner will sometimes withdraw from a partnership by selling his or her interest to the other partners. If the remaining partners pay for the departing partner's interest with their personal assets, the transaction is again considered to be outside the business. The only entry made in the partnership records is the transfer of the capital balances. Therefore, no matter what price is paid, if Allen sells Baker and Ririe each $35,000 of her $70,000 interest in the partnership, the entry to record the withdrawal of Allen would be

Allen, Capital	70,000	
Baker, Capital		35,000
Ririe, Capital		35,000
To record the purchase of Allen's partnership interest by Baker and Ririe.		

Payment to a Departing Partner from the Partnership's Assets

The partnership agreement may specify that the business's assets be used to pay the departing partner. In such cases, the agreement would probably also specify how assets are to be valued in order to determine how much the exiting partner is to be paid. Because of inflation, goodwill, and other factors, it is unlikely that the market value of the partnership's assets would be equal to their book value. Obviously, the partners would want to be fair, so they would probably agree to value the assets at the market price for purposes of determining how much to give the departing partner. As discussed earlier, these market values may or may not be recorded on the books of the new partnership. When book values are transferred, any excess paid to the departing partner over his or her book value results in a decrease in the remaining partners' capital balances. Likewise, if the amount paid the exiting partner is less than book value, the remaining partners' capital balances are increased.

To illustrate, we again assume that Allen, Baker, and Ririe have capital balances of $70,000, $100,000, and $60,000 on December 31, 1983. The following three entries show how Allen's withdrawal would be recorded if she were paid $50,000, $70,000, or $100,000, respectively, from partnership assets, and if Baker and Ririe split profits and losses equally.

Amount Less than Book Value: $50,000

Allen, Capital	70,000	
Cash		50,000
Baker, Capital		10,000
Ririe, Capital		10,000

To record the payment of $50,000 to Allen on her withdrawal from the partnership.

Amount Equal to Book Value: $70,000

Allen, Capital	70,000	
Cash		70,000

To record the payment of $70,000 to Allen on her withdrawal from the partnership.

Amount Greater than Book Value: $100,000

Allen, Capital	70,000	
Baker, Capital	15,000	
Ririe, Capital	15,000	
Cash		100,000

To record the payment of $100,000 to Allen on her withdrawal from the partnership.

Note that when the departing partner is paid more or less than book value, the remaining partners' capital balances are increased or decreased in accordance with their profit-sharing ratios, not their capital balance ratios.

Sometimes, the full amount of cash is not paid at the time of withdrawal. In such cases, the departing partner is usually given a note indicating that payments are to be made later—monthly, annually, or on any other schedule agreed upon by the partners or specified by the partnership agreement. To illustrate, we assume that in the above case, Allen is to receive the $100,000 in annual installments. She is given $20,000 down and a note for $80,000. The entry to record this transaction would be

Allen, Capital	70,000	
Baker, Capital	15,000	
Ririe, Capital	15,000	
Cash		20,000
Note Payable		80,000

To record the withdrawal of Allen from the partnership; paid $20,000 down, the balance to be paid at the rate of $10,000 a year for 8 years, with 15 percent interest to be paid annually on the unpaid balance.

THE DEATH OF A PARTNER

The death of a partner has basically the same effect on a partnership as the addition or withdrawal of a partner. In all cases, the partnership agreement is terminated and a new one must be written if the partnership is to continue. Because assets often have to be valued to determine how much to pay the partner's estate, an audit may be conducted. The original partnership agreement should specify how this and other matters are to be handled.

Two aspects of the accounting required upon the death of a partner are somewhat different from accounting for the withdrawal of a partner. First, as indicated above, the payment is made to an estate. Second, when a partner dies, interim financial statements are usually prepared so that the capital balances can be updated to the date of death.

Because the success of many partnerships is so dependent upon the contribution of the individual partners, partnerships often obtain life insurance on the partners, with the partnership named as the beneficiary. Then, upon the death of a partner, the proceeds are used to pay the estate of the deceased. Having life insurance policies ensures that sufficient cash will be available to pay the estate of the deceased partner.

TO SUMMARIZE A partner can withdraw from a partnership any time he or she chooses, provided that an agreement can be reached among the partners. To avoid misunderstandings, the partnership agreement should specify procedures to be followed if a partner exercises this right of withdrawal. Withdrawal can be handled in one of three ways: (1) the departing partner can sell his or her interest to an outsider, (2) to the remaining partners, or (3) to the partnership. If partnership assets are used, the remaining partners' capital balances increase, stay the same, or decrease, depending on the amount paid.

Exhibit 14-4 summarizes the various ways a member may withdraw from a partnership, and the effect each way has on the assets and liabilities of the partnership and the remaining partners' capital balances, assuming that assets are transferred to the new partnership at book value.

The Liquidation of a Partnership

Any time a new partner is admitted or an existing partner withdraws or dies, a partnership is legally terminated. This does not mean that the *business* has to be terminated. Usually, partnership agreements define admission and withdrawal procedures in such a way that there is no outward appearance that any change has taken place.

liquidation *the process of dissolving a partnership by selling the assets, paying the debts, and distributing the remaining equity to the owners*

Sometimes, however, a business is terminated. The process of dissolving a partnership is called liquidation. Liquidation means that all assets except cash are sold or disposed of, liabilities are paid, and the remaining cash is divided among the partners. Three steps are usually involved in a liquidation: (1) the business is sold; (2) the profit or loss from the sale of noncash

EXHIBIT 14-4 Withdrawal of a Partner

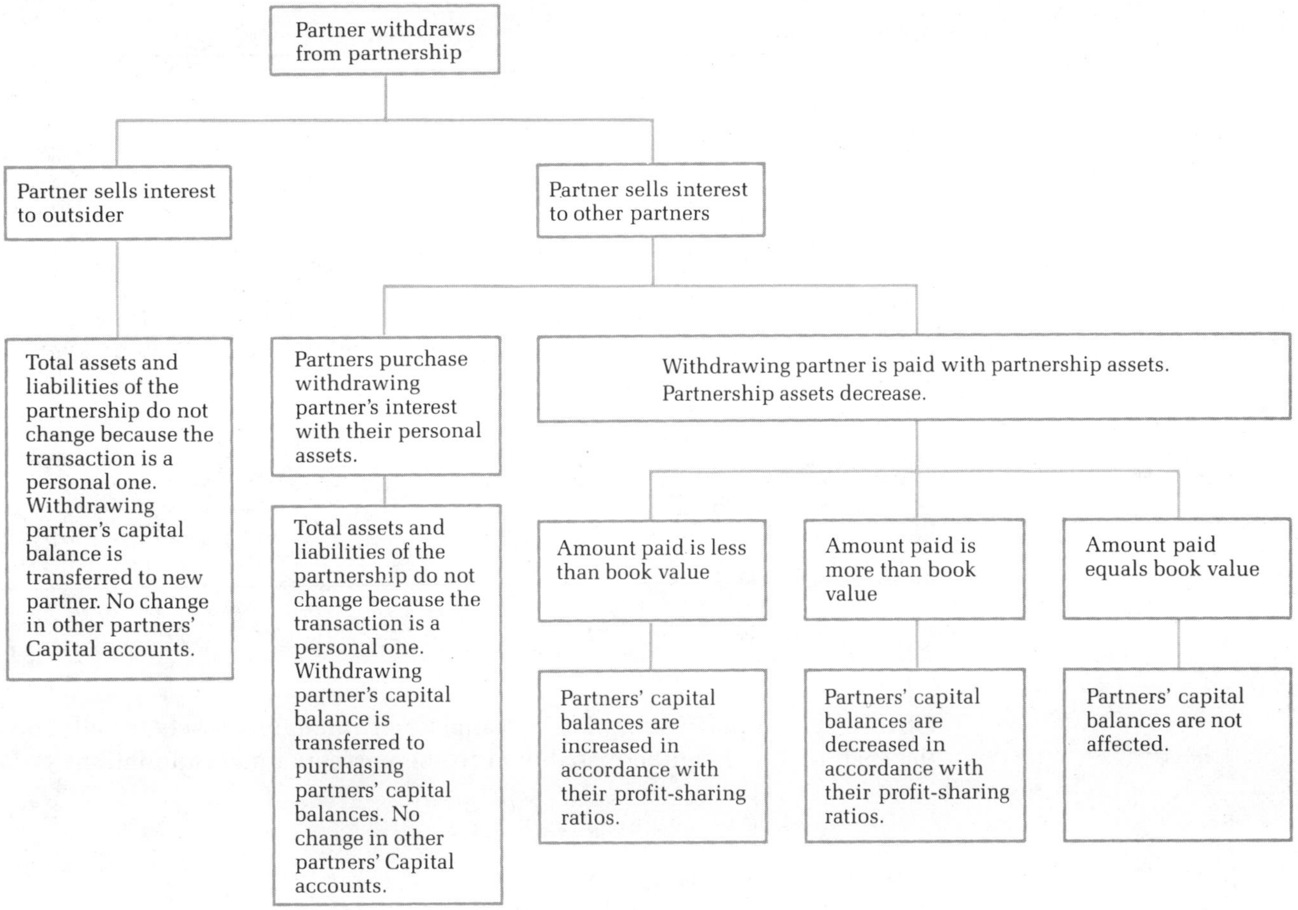

assets is allocated to the partners in accordance with their profit-sharing ratio; and (3) the liabilities are paid and the remaining cash is distributed to the partners.

THE SALE OF THE BUSINESS

A partnership being liquidated usually has assets that can be sold: tangible assets such as property, plant, and equipment, or intangible assets such as a large clientele, a good reputation, or a favorable location. To illustrate how such a sale would be handled, we will assume that Johnson, Jackson, and Jeffrey own a real estate business. Due to high mortgage rates and other factors, business is becoming sluggish; in fact, the sale of two expensive houses in a month is unusual. Since they cannot afford to run their business under current market conditions, they decide to liquidate and sell the business to Century 22 Corporation. On the date of the sale, the balance sheet of their partnership is as shown on the next page.

Johnson, Jackson, and Jeffrey
Balance Sheet as of July 1, 1983

Assets		Liabilities and Partners' Equity	
Cash	$100,000	Notes Payable	$120,000
Land	210,000	Jackson, Capital	130,000
Building	160,000	Johnson, Capital	80,000
Other Assets	40,000	Jeffrey, Capital	180,000
Total Assets	$510,000	Total Liabilities and Partners' Equity	$510,000

Terms of the sale are that all assets except cash will be sold for $290,000 and that Johnson, Jackson, and Jeffrey will pay off the $120,000 note payable. The entry to record the sale would be

Cash	290,000	
Loss on Sale of Business	120,000	
Land		210,000
Building		160,000
Other Assets		40,000
To record the sale of the business to Century 22 Corporation.		

Obviously, if a partnership has no tangible or intangible assets to sell, only the cash on hand can be distributed to the partners upon liquidation.

THE DIVISION OF GAINS AND LOSSES ON THE SALE OF A BUSINESS

In the above example the partners suffered a loss of $120,000 on the sale of the partnership because they sold assets with a book value of $410,000 for $290,000. Liquidation sales occasionally produce a gain, though this is unusual. In any event, the gain or loss must be divided among the partners in accordance with their agreed-upon profit-and-loss-sharing ratio. Only after each Capital account has been increased or decreased by the amount of the gain or the loss from the sale of the business can the amount of cash that goes to each partner be determined. If we assume that Johnson, Jackson, and Jeffrey share profits and losses equally, the entry to allocate the $120,000 loss would be

Johnson, Capital	40,000	
Jackson, Capital	40,000	
Jeffrey, Capital	40,000	
Loss on Sale of Business		120,000
To allocate the loss on the sale of the business to the partners in their agreed-upon profit-and-loss-sharing ratio.		

THE PAYMENT OF LIABILITIES AND DISTRIBUTION OF REMAINING CASH

The balance sheet of the Johnson, Jackson, and Jeffrey partnership after the sale of all assets except cash and the distribution of the loss appears as follows:

Johnson, Jackson, and Jeffrey
Balance Sheet as of July 1, 1983

Assets		Liabilities and Partners' Equity	
Cash	$390,000	Notes Payable	$120,000
		Johnson, Capital	90,000
		Jackson, Capital	40,000
		Jeffrey, Capital	140,000
Total Assets	$390,000	Total Liabilities and Partners' Equity	$390,000

Before the partners can receive the cash, the liabilities of the business must be paid in full. The entry to record the payment of the note would be

Notes Payable	120,000	
Cash		120,000
Paid obligations in full.		

After all liabilities are paid, the remaining cash can be divided among the partners according to their capital balances. The entry to record the distribution of cash would be

Johnson, Capital	90,000	
Jackson, Capital	40,000	
Jeffrey, Capital	140,000	
Cash		270,000
Completed liquidation of the partnership by distributing the remaining cash to the partners in amounts equal to their capital balances.		

It is important that you distinguish the method of distributing cash at liquidation from the method of sharing profits and losses. The profit-and-loss-sharing ratio is spelled out in the partnership agreement; the distribution of cash at liquidation is made in accordance with the capital balances of the respective partners.

Because the profit-and-loss-sharing ratio is often different from the capital contributions, it is conceivable that a partner could end up with a negative capital balance at liquidation. For example, assume that the partnership were sold to Century 22 for $140,000 instead of $290,000. The entry to record the sale would be as shown on the next page.

Cash	140,000	
Loss on Sale of Business	270,000	
Land		210,000
Building		160,000
Other Assets		40,000

To record the sale of the business to Century 22 Corporation.

Since profits and losses are shared equally, the entry to allocate the $270,000 loss would be

Johnson, Capital	90,000	
Jackson, Capital	90,000	
Jeffrey, Capital	90,000	
Loss on Sale of Business		270,000

To allocate the loss on the sale of business to the partners in their agreed-upon profit-and-loss-sharing ratio.

With this entry, the capital balances of the partners would be

Partner	Capital Balances Before Loss	Share of Loss	New Capital Balances
Johnson	$130,000	$ 90,000	$ 40,000
Jackson	80,000	90,000	(10,000)
Jeffrey	180,000	90,000	$ 90,000
Total	$390,000	$270,000	$120,000

The balance in the Cash account is now $240,000, which consists of the $100,000 that was on hand before the sale and the $140,000 that was received from the sale. However, before the cash can be distributed to the partners, the $120,000 note must be paid. The entry to record the payment of the liability is the same as the one illustrated earlier.

Notes Payable	120,000	
Cash		120,000

Paid obligations in full.

In order to eliminate the $10,000 debit balance in Jackson's Capital account, the partnership should collect $10,000 from Jackson. If Jackson pays the $10,000, Jackson's capital balance will be zero and the $130,000 in the Cash account [$120,000 on hand ($240,000 − $120,000 note paid) + $10,000 paid by Jackson] would be allocated $40,000 to Johnson and $90,000 to Jeffrey, which matches their capital balances. However, if Jackson cannot or does not pay, the $10,000 would be absorbed by Johnson and Jeffrey in accordance with their profit-and-loss-sharing arrangement. If they share profits and losses equally, they would each absorb $5,000. The $120,000 of cash on hand would then be divided with $35,000 going to Johnson and $85,000 going to Jeffrey. The entries to record the absorption of a $5,000 loss by each partner and the distribution of cash would be

Johnson, Capital	5,000	
Jeffrey, Capital	5,000	
Jackson, Capital		10,000
To eliminate the deficit in Jackson's capital balance.		
Johnson, Capital	35,000	
Jeffrey, Capital	85,000	
Cash		120,000
To distribute the remaining cash to the partners in accordance with their capital balances.		

TO SUMMARIZE A partnership liquidation usually proceeds in three steps: (1) the sale of the business, (2) the allocation of gains or losses among the partners' capital accounts, and (3) the payment of liabilities and the distribution of cash to the partners. Gains and losses are allocated to the partners in accordance with their profit-and-loss-sharing ratio. The cash remaining after all liabilities are paid is distributed to the partners in accordance with their capital balances.

CHAPTER REVIEW

Proprietorships and partnerships are unincorporated businesses. Proprietorships are owned by one person; partnerships are owned by two or more persons or entities. Partnerships and proprietorships share three characteristics: (1) ease of formation, (2) limited life, and (3) unlimited liability.

There are two owner's equity accounts in a proprietorship: a Capital and a Drawings account. The Capital account is increased by owner contributions and profits and decreased by owner withdrawals and losses.

Three additional characteristics unique to partnerships are: (1) mutual agency, which means that each partner is an agent and can bind the partnership to business agreements; (2) co-ownership of partnership property, which means that property transferred to the partnership is jointly owned by all partners; and (3) sharing of partnership profits, meaning that all partners have a right to share in partnership profits and an obligation to share in partnership losses.

There are several aspects of partnership accounting. Events that are accounted for are: investments by owners, withdrawals by partners, partnership profits and losses, admission of new partners, withdrawal of old partners, the death of a partner, and partnership liquidation. In addition, a statement of partners' capital is prepared at year-end.

Investments and withdrawals by partners are treated in the same way as they are in a proprietorship. That is, investments increase the partners' capital balances and withdrawals decrease the capital balances.

The statement of partners' capital reconciles the ending capital balances with the beginning capital balances by adding profits and additional investments and deducting losses and partner withdrawals.

Partnership profits and losses can be shared in any way the partners specify. Factors considered in determining the allocation of profits and losses include interest on invested capital, beginning or average capital balances, and services performed by the respective partners.

Partners can be admitted only with the consent of all existing partners. A new partner may gain admission by purchasing the interest of an existing partner (or partners) or by investing in the partnership. When a partner's interest is purchased by an outsider, the price paid in the transaction is extraneous to the partnership; only the book value of the departing partner's capital balance is transferred to the new partner. With regard to investing in the partnership, since there is a legal obligation to form a new partnership due to a change in partners, the partnership can choose to restate the assets of the old partnership at their market values or transfer them to the new partnership at their book values. With the book-value approach, if the amount invested is greater or less than the book value of the equity received, the investment is still recorded at book value. (If the investment is greater than the book value, the original partners receive bonuses; if the investment is less, the new partner receives a bonus.)

A partner can withdraw from a partnership any time he or she desires. If a partner withdraws, the departing partner's interest can be purchased by an outsider or by the other partners, either with their personal assets or with partnership assets. Purchase of one partner's equity by an outsider or by other partners does not involve a change in the partners' asset or liability accounts. The other alternative, payment of partnership assets, results in an increase, no change, or a decrease in the remaining partners' capital balances, depending on the amount paid.

Any time a partner is admitted, withdraws, or dies, the partnership is legally terminated. Since a new partnership agreement is easily written, such changes often go unnoticed by outsiders. However, sometimes a partnership's business is terminated. The process of dissolving a partnership is referred to as liquidation. The three steps typically taken in an orderly liquidation are (1) the sale of the business, (2) the allocation of profits and losses among the partners in accordance with their profit-and-loss-sharing ratio, and (3) the payment of all liabilities and the distribution of the remaining cash to the partners according to their capital balances.

KEY TERMS AND CONCEPTS

Capital account (459)
Drawings account (459)
goodwill (470)
liquidation (478)
mutual agency (460)
partnership (457)
partnership agreement (457)
proprietorship (457)
statement of partners' capital (463)
unlimited liability (458)

REVIEW PROBLEM

Distribution of Income and Admission of a Partner

On January 1, 1983, Steven Thomas and Brent Woolsey entered into a partnership agreement to open a drug store. In forming the partnership, Thomas and Woolsey contributed $40,000 and $60,000, respectively. Their partnership agreement specified the following: Thomas was to be the full-time manager of the business, and he would receive a salary of $18,000 per year. In addition, each partner would receive 10 percent annual interest on his original investment, with any remaining profits (or deficiencies) to be shared equally.

Required:

1. Compute the amount of profit that Thomas and Woolsey each received in 1983, 1984, and 1985, if profits during those 3 years were $24,000, $36,000, and $50,000, respectively. Make the necessary journal entries to close net income to the partners' respective Capital accounts in each year.

2. Assume that on January 1, 1986, Joe Silverstein offers to pay $50,000 to Thomas and Woolsey for a 20 percent interest in the partnership. Thomas and Woolsey agree to admit Silverstein on these terms because they need the additional $50,000 to expand into the crutch, wheelchair, and artificial brace business. The capital balances of Thomas and Woolsey on January 1, 1986, are $48,000 and $72,000, respectively. Record the admission of Silverstein to the partnership, assuming that his investment is to represent a 20 percent interest in the total partners' capital and that any bonus is to be divided equally between Thomas and Woolsey.

Solution

1. Distribution of Profits

	Thomas	Woolsey	Net Income
1983:			
Net Income			$24,000
Salaries to Partners	$18,000		(18,000)
Remaining Income After Salaries			$ 6,000
Interest on Invested Capital:			
Thomas ($40,000 × 0.10)	4,000		
Woolsey ($60,000 × 0.10)		$6,000	(10,000)
Deficiency After Salaries and Interest			($4,000)
Deficiency to Be Divided Equally	($ 2,000)	($2,000)	4,000
Total to Each Partner	$20,000	$4,000	$ -0-
1984:			
Net Income			$36,000
Salaries to Partners	$18,000		(18,000)
Remaining Income After Salaries			$18,000
Interest on Invested Capital:			
Thomas ($40,000 × 0.10)	4,000		
Woolsey ($60,000 × 0.10)		$ 6,000	(10,000)
Remaining Income After Salaries and Interest			$ 8,000
Remainder to Be Divided Equally	4,000	4,000	(8,000)
Total to Each Partner	$26,000	$10,000	$ -0-
1985:			
Net Income			$50,000
Salaries to Partners	$18,000		(18,000)
Remaining Income After Salaries			$32,000
Interest on Invested Capital:			
Thomas ($40,000 × 0.10)	4,000		
Woolsey ($60,000 × 0.10)		$ 6,000	(10,000)
Remaining Income After Salaries and Interest			$22,000
Remainder to Be Divided Equally	11,000	11,000	(22,000)
Total to Each Partner	$33,000	$17,000	$ -0-

1983 Entry:

Income Summary	24,000	
Thomas, Capital		20,000
Woolsey, Capital		4,000

To close 1983 earnings to the partners' Capital accounts.

1984 Entry:

Income Summary	36,000	
Thomas, Capital		26,000
Woolsey, Capital		10,000

To close 1984 earnings to the partners' Capital accounts.

1985 Entry:

Income Summary	50,000	
Thomas, Capital		33,000
Woolsey, Capital		17,000

To close 1985 earnings to the partners' Capital accounts.

2. Admission of Joe Silverstein

Capital Balance Before Investment	$120,000	($48,000 + $72,000)
Investment by Silverstein	50,000	
Total Capital of New Partnership	$170,000	
Silverstein's 20% Interest ($170,000 × 0.20)	$ 34,000	
Silverstein's Investment	$ 50,000	
Silverstein's Capital	34,000	
Bonus to Be Divided Equally	$ 16,000	

January 1, 1985

Cash	50,000	
Thomas, Capital		8,000
Woolsey, Capital		8,000
Silverstein, Capital		34,000

To record the admission of Joe Silverstein to the partnership at a one-fifth interest.

DISCUSSION QUESTIONS

1 What are the major differences between a partnership and a corporation?

2 How is a proprietorship or partnership established?

3 Identify some of the elements that should be spelled out in a partnership agreement.

4 Does the death of a partner legally terminate a partnership? If so, does it mean that the partnership must cease operating?

5 Are partners legally liable for the actions of other partners?

6 Is the payment of salary to a proprietor an expense that would be deducted on a proprietorship's income statement? Explain.

7 In a corporation, contributions by owners and accumulated earnings of the business are separated into Contributed Capital and Retained Earnings accounts. Are earnings and contributions separated into different accounts in a partnership? Explain.

8 If a partnership agreement does not specify how profits are to be shared by the partners, how much does each partner receive?

9 What is the purpose of a statement of partners' capital?

10 What factors are usually considered in determining how much profit each partner should receive?

11 What is the disadvantage of using the partners' beginning capital balance ratio as a basis for splitting profits between partners?

12 Assume that the XYZ Partnership Agreement specifies that salaries, interest on investments, and a stated ratio will serve as the basis for dividing profits between X, Y, and Z. If profits are insufficient to cover all three elements, how would profits be divided?

13 Are partnerships taxed on their profits?

14 When a new partner is admitted, can the partnership increase the recorded amounts of its assets up to their current market values?

15 What are the two ways a new partner can be admitted to a partnership?

16 What steps are usually involved in liquidating a partnership?

17 In a liquidation, is the remaining cash distributed to the partners in accordance with their profit-and-loss sharing ratio? Explain.

18 Is it possible for a partner to have a negative capital balance when a partnership is liquidated? Explain.

EXERCISES

E14-1 Accounting for a Proprietorship

Myrtle Johnson decided to go into the business of making and selling sweaters and socks. During the year, she had the following transactions.

a. Invested $12,000 in a company and immediately spent the entire amount to purchase needles and yarn.

b. Invested another $6,000 in the business.

c. Sold 50 sweaters at $60 each for cash.

d. Sold 100 pairs of socks and 60 more sweaters. The socks sold for $4 a pair and the sweaters for $60 each.

e. Paid $4,250 of expenses for the year (including $2,000 for needles and yarn that went into the sweaters that were sold).

f. Withdrew $2,500 for personal use.

Journalize these transactions and prepare a statement of owner's equity for Myrtle Johnson's proprietorship at year-end.

E14-2 Accounting for a Proprietorship

Juan Garcia is sole proprietor of a grocery store he opened on June 1, 1983. During the year, he had the following transactions.

a. Contributed a building worth $50,000, furniture and fixtures valued at $20,000, and $10,000 cash to establish the business.

b. Withdrew $6,000 for personal use from the interim earnings of the proprietorship.

c. Contributed a new set of shelves to the business. The cost of the shelves was $4,500.

d. Contributed another $3,000 in cash to the business.

e. During 1983, Garcia's income from the business was $14,300. (Show only the entry to close the Income Summary account.)

f. Withdrew all remaining earnings except $2,000, which he left in the business.

Given this information:

1. Prepare the journal entries (including closing entries) for the above transactions.

2. Prepare a statement of owner's equity for Garcia's Corner Grocery Store as of December 31, 1983.

E14–3 Partnership Accounting

On August 1, 1984, Mr. Garcia (see E14–2) accepted Albert Paolini as a partner. At that time, Garcia's Capital account showed a balance of $135,000. Paolini contributed $90,000 cash for a 40 percent share in both capital and earnings. During the rest of 1984, the following transactions took place.

a. Garcia withdrew $12,000 cash and Paolini withdrew $3,000 cash and $1,000 in groceries.

b. Garcia invested another $4,500 cash and Paolini invested a delivery truck valued at $6,000.

c. Net income from August 1, 1984, through December 31, 1984, was $26,700.

Given this information:

1. Prepare the journal entries (including closing entries) for the above three transactions.

2. Prepare a statement of partners' capital as of December 31, 1984, for the Garcia and Paolini partnership.

E14–4 Starting a Partnership

On July 1, 1983, Dr. Meek and Dr. Nelson decided to form a partnership by combining all the assets and liabilities of their respective dental practices. The partnership will have a new and separate set of books. Dr. Meek's balance sheet at June 30, 1983, was as follows:

Assets		
Cash		$ 13,500
Accounts Receivable	$58,000	
Less Allowance for Doubtful Accounts	3,300	54,700
Dental Equipment	$26,450	
Less Accumulated Depreciation	12,100	14,350
Building	$84,700	
Less Accumulated Depreciation	6,750	77,950
Total Assets		$160,500
Liabilities and Partners' Equity		
Accounts Payable		$ 11,350
Mortgage Payable		75,000
Dr. Meek, Capital		74,150
Total Liabilities and Partners' Equity		$160,500

The partners agreed that $2,800 of the accounts receivable were uncollectible, and that $1,200 was a reasonable allowance for the uncollectibility of the remaining receivables. They also agreed that the dental equipment and the building should be recorded at their respective fair market values of $23,000 and $91,000.

Prepare the journal entry to record Dr. Meek's investment in the partnership.

E14–5 Allocation of Partnership Income

On January 1, 1983, Ted Armstrong and Ronald Blackham formed a partnership by investing $50,000 and $15,000, respectively. For the year ended December 31, 1983, the partnership had net income of $53,000.

Compute each partner's share of the partnership's 1983 income under the following assumptions.

1. The partnership agreement makes no mention of the sharing of profits and losses.

2. Profits and losses are to be shared by Armstrong and Blackham in a ratio of 3:2.

3. Income is to be shared in the ratio of the original investments.

4. Profits and losses are to be divided equally after salary allowances of $19,000 to Armstrong and $29,000 to Blackham are provided.

5. Net income is to be divided in a ratio of 3:2 after interest of 13 percent is allowed on the partners' original investments.

6. Profits and losses are to be shared by allowing interest of 11 percent on the partners' original investments, providing salary allowances of $15,000 to Armstrong and $25,000 to Blackham, and dividing the balance equally.

E14–6 Allocation of Partnership Income

On June 1, 1983, Jane Evans and Bruce Francis formed a partnership by investing $35,000 and $45,000, respectively. Partnership net income for the first full year of operations was $18,000.

Compute each partner's share of the partnership's net income after the first year of operations under the following assumptions:

1. The partnership agreement makes no mention of the sharing of profits and losses.

2. Profits and losses are to be shared by Evans and Francis in a ratio of 3:5.

3. Income is to be shared in the ratio of the original investments.

4. Profits and losses are to be divided in a ratio of 3:2 after salary allowances of $15,000 to Evans and $12,000 to Francis are provided.

5. Net income is to be divided equally after 11 percent interest is allowed on the partners' original investments.

6. Profits and losses are to be shared by allowing 13 percent interest on the partners' original investments,

providing salary allowances of $14,000 to Evans and $18,000 to Francis, and dividing the balance equally. The agreement specifies that if net income isn't sufficient to cover both interest and salary, both will still be paid and the deficiency will be allocated on an equal basis.

E14-7 Sharing of Profits—the Capital Investment Ratio

On January 1, 1983, the capital balances of Olson and Partridge were $45,000 and $37,000, respectively. On June 30, Olson made an additional contribution of $5,000. Olson made withdrawals of $20,000 on April 1 and $10,000 on November 1. Partridge made withdrawals of $15,000 on April 1 and $5,000 on November 30. Partnership profits for 1983 were $69,000.

1. Compute each partner's share of the partnership's 1983 profits, assuming that profits are to be shared in the ratio of partners' average capital balances.
2. Prepare the journal entry to close net income for 1983.
3. Prepare a statement of partners' capital as of December 31, 1983.

E14-8 Preparation of Partnership Financial Statements and Admission of a Partner

On January 1, 1983, Brad Kelly, Frank Long, and Brian Miller formed the partnership of Kelly, Long, & Miller, with investments of $25,000, $15,000, and $10,000, respectively. They agreed to share profits in a ratio of 3:2:1. During 1983, the partnership had net income of $80,000. There were no withdrawals during 1983. On January 1, 1984, each agreed to sell a portion of his interest to Ken Nash. Nash purchased one-fifth of Kelly's interest, one-third of Long's interest, and one-third of Miller's interest for $55,000. The partnership agreement of Kelly, Long, Miller, & Nash called for the allocation of profits and losses in a ratio of 4:2:1:3.

1. Prepare a statement of partners' capital at December 31, 1983.
2. Prepare any required journal entries for the admission of Ken Nash to the partnership.
3. What is the capital balance of each partner on January 1, 1984?

E14-9 Admitting a New Partner

Frank Richmond and Eugene Skinner have agreed to admit Rich Templeton to their partnership on January 1, 1984. Templeton will be given a one-third interest in the partnership for an investment of $20,000 cash plus library assets costing $5,000. The fair market value of the library assets is $10,000.

The balance sheet of Richmond & Skinner on December 31, 1983, was as follows:

Richmond & Skinner
Balance Sheet as of December 31, 1983

Assets	
Cash	$ 5,000
Accounts Receivable	25,000
Equipment	51,000
Accumulated Depreciation	(9,000)
Total Assets	$72,000
Liabilities and Partners' Equity	
Accounts Payable	$ 6,000
Notes Payable	15,000
Richmond, Capital	28,500
Skinner, Capital	22,500
Total Liabilities and Partners' Equity	$72,000

Richmond and Skinner currently share profits and losses in a ratio of 3:2.

1. Prepare the journal entry to record the admission of Templeton to the partnership.
2. Compute the partners' capital balances as of January 1, 1984.

E14-10 Admitting a New Partner

Prior to the admission of Kathy Zobell to the partnership of Wheeler & Young, the capital accounts showed balances of $34,000 for Wheeler and $21,000 for Young. The partners have always shared partnership profits and losses in a ratio of 2:1. On July 1, 1983, Zobell, a well-known salesperson, was to be given a 40 percent share of the partnership for an investment of $15,000 cash and a home computer that cost $2,000 (fair market value, $3,000).

1. Prepare the journal entry to record Kathy Zobell's investment in the new partnership.
2. Compute the partners' capital balances as of July 1, 1983.

E14-11 Withdrawal of a Partner

On June 30, 1983, Dick Abbott decided to sell his interest in the partnership of Abbott, Baynes, & Crawford. The partners' Capital accounts at that date were $40,000, $45,000, and $50,000, respectively.

Given this information, do the following [items (1) and (2) involve independent assumptions].

1. Prepare the journal entry to record Abbott's sale of his partnership interest to Mark Denison for $52,000 cash, assuming that the partners approve the sale to Denison.
2. Prepare the journal entry to record Abbott's sale of half his partnership interest to Baynes and the other half of his partnership to Crawford for $18,000 each.
3. Would the journal entry in item (1) above differ if Abbott were to accept $12,000 cash and a $40,000 note from Denison? If so, how?

E14–12 Withdrawal of a Partner

On September 30, 1983, Jim Johnson retired from the partnership of Johnson, Kallis, & Lancaster. The partnership agreement calls for payments to retiring partners to be made from partnership assets. It also calls for the sharing of partnership profits and losses in a ratio of 3:2:3. The partners' capital balances on September 30 were $55,000, $35,000, and $45,000, respectively.

Prepare journal entries (you may omit explanations) to show the retirement of Johnson, assuming that

1. He was paid $55,000 cash.
2. He was paid $70,000 cash.
3. He was paid $45,000 cash.
4. He was paid $10,000 cash and given a $50,000 note, payable in five equal annual installments with interest at 10 percent on the remaining balance.
5. He was given equipment that had a book value of $30,000 and a fair market value of $50,000.

E14–13 The Death of a Partner

On February 15, 1983, Bud Freeman died unexpectedly in an automobile accident. In order to settle its affairs with Freeman's estate, the partnership of Freeman, Gibson, & Havens prepared interim financial statements as of the date of Freeman's death. The partners' capital balances on February 15 were $65,000, $80,000, and $75,000, respectively. The partnership agreement of Freeman, Gibson, & Havens stated that upon the death of a partner, the partners' share of partnership assets, based upon their fair market valuation, is paid to the deceased partner's estate. The agreement also called for the sharing of partnership profits and losses in the ratio 4:3:3. The remaining partners agreed that on February 15, equipment was undervalued by $16,000 and accounts receivable were overvalued by $1,000.

1. Prepare the journal entry to record the partnership's settlement with Freeman's estate. (Assume that Freeman's estate was given a note for $50,000, with the remainder of the claim being paid in cash.)
2. Compute the capital balances of Gibson and Havens after the settlement with Freeman's estate.

E14–14 Liquidation of a Partnership

In liquidating the partnership of Johnson, Knight, & Littlefield, all the assets of the partnership are sold for $125,000. The partnership had outstanding accounts payable of $13,000, and the partners had capital balances of $50,000, $35,000, and $15,000, respectively. Partnership profits and losses are shared in the ratio 2:1:1.

Prepare all the journal entries needed to complete the liquidation.

E14–15 Distribution of Cash After Liquidation

After the sale of all the assets and the payment of all the liabilities of Simmons, Turner, & Underwood, the partnership had a cash balance of $55,000. Upon allocating losses from the sale of assets, the partners' capital balances were $30,000, ($5,000), and $30,000, respectively. Partnership profits and losses are shared equally by the partners.

Prepare all the journal entries needed to complete the liquidation, assuming the following independent situations.

1. Turner pays the amount owed to the firm.
2. Turner cannot pay his partnership deficit.

PROBLEMS

P14–1 Accounting for a Proprietorship

In 1983, Joe Young decided to open the Fantastic Pizza Shop. Joe deposited $10,000 of his own money in a company bank account and obtained a $7,500 loan from a local bank. During its first year of operations, the shop had earnings of $21,000. Joe withdrew a lump sum of $9,000 from the business that year to cover personal living expenses.

Required:

1. Prepare journal entries to record:
   (a) Joe's original contribution to the firm.
   (b) The bank loan.
   (c) Joe's withdrawal for his living expenses.
   (d) Any closing entries required at year-end.
2. Prepare a statement of owner's equity for 1983.
3. **Interpretive Question** How would the accounting for the four journal entries in item (1) be different if Joe's business were a corporation?

P14–2 Partnership Accounting

Delta and Epsilon have established a partnership to sell Olympic wreaths.

a. Delta invested $42,000 cash in the partnership, and Epsilon invested $20,000 cash and a building valued at $25,000.

b. Delta invested another $6,000 cash. Epsilon donated a truck valued at $7,000.

c. Net income from operations for the year was $19,000.

d. Delta withdrew $11,000 cash and Epsilon withdrew $6,300 of inventory.

e. A fire destroyed half of the building donated by Epsilon. There was no insurance on the building.

f. Delta and Epsilon agree to admit a third partner on March 1 of the next year. This partner, Gamma, promises to invest $50,000 cash.

Required:

Assuming that the partners share profits equally:

1. Journalize the above transactions.
2. Journalize the closing entries.
3. Compute each partner's capital balance.
4. What is the relationship between the amount of capital contributed by each owner and the way profits are to be allocated?

P14–3 Unifying Problem: Partnership Financial Statements

On January 1, 1983, Carla Daines and Bonnie Ellis formed a partnership with investments of $18,000 and $14,000, respectively. Their partnership agreement called for annual salary allowances of $20,000 for Daines and $18,000 for Ellis. It also provided the partners with an interest allowance of 13 percent of their beginning-of-the-year capital balances, with the remainder of the profit or loss to be divided equally. During the year, Ellis made an additional investment of $3,000 of office equipment.

The adjusted trial balance of Daines & Ellis at December 31, 1983, was as follows:

	Debits	Credits
Cash	$ 5,650	
Accounts Receivable	19,800	
Allowance for Doubtful Accounts		$ 850
Office Furniture (new)	8,500	
Office Equipment	11,400	
Accumulated Depreciation–Office Equipment		1,980
Accounts Payable		2,650
Carla Daines, Capital		18,000
Carla Daines, Drawings	13,800	
Bonnie Ellis, Capital		17,000
Bonnie Ellis, Drawings	19,350	
Service Fees		69,850
Salary Expense	18,900*	
Rent Expense	3,960	
Office Supplies Expense	1,540	
Depreciation Expense	1,980	
Miscellaneous Expenses	5,450	
Totals	$110,330	$110,330

* Salary Expense does not include any payments to the partners.

Required:

1. Prepare an income statement, including a schedule showing the allocation of the partnership's net income, for the year ended December 31, 1983.
2. Prepare a statement of partners' capital as of December 31, 1983.
3. Prepare a balance sheet as of December 31, 1983.

P14–4 Allocation of Partnership Profits and Losses

Joe Jones and Kelly Kearl are in the process of forming a real estate partnership. In order to complete their partnership agreement, they need to determine an equitable method of allocating partnership profits and losses. Mr. Jones is investing $25,000 in the partnership; Mr. Kearl is investing $48,000. The partners have agreed that Jones' service is worth $25,000 annually, and that Kearl's service is worth $18,000 annually. Estimated net income for the partnership is $18,000 for 1983 and $55,000 for 1984.

Required:

1. Compute each partner's share of the partnership's net income for 1983 and 1984 under each of the following proposed allocation methods:

(a) The partners do not agree on any method.

(b) Jones and Kearl agree to share profits in a ratio of 3:2.

(c) The partners agree to share profits in the ratio of their original investments.

(d) The partners agree to share profits by making salary allowances to each partner according to the value of their services, with any balance (or deficiency) being shared equally by the partners.

(e) The partners agree to share profits by allowing interest at 13 percent on their original investments, with any balance being shared in a ratio of 3:2.

(f) The partners agree to share profits by making salary allowances to each partner according to the value of their services, allowing 13 percent interest on each partner's original investment, and sharing any balance (or deficiency) equally.

2. Prepare a schedule of your findings for presentation to Mr. Jones and Mr. Kearl, using the following format.

	1983		1984	
Plan	**Jones**	**Kearl**	**Jones**	**Kearl**

3. **Interpretive Question** Which allocation method is the fairest? Explain.

P14-5 Admitting a New Partner

On June 30, 1983, the adjusted trial balance of Mitchell & Monson, attorneys-at-law, was as follows:

	Debits	Credits
Cash	$ 8,550	
Accounts Receivable	15,800	
Allowance for Doubtful Accounts		$ 1,300
Office Equipment (new)	13,800	
Office Furniture	6,400	
Accumulated Depreciation—Office Furniture		4,800
Accounts Payable		2,300
Notes Payable		3,000
Mitchell, Capital		10,000
Monson, Capital		10,150
Mitchell, Drawings	18,000	
Monson, Drawings	19,500	
Professional Fees		78,500
Salary Expense	14,400	
Rent Expense	5,400	
Interest Expense	450	
Office Supplies Expense	1,250	
Depreciation Expense	2,200	
Miscellaneous Expenses	4,300	
Totals	$110,050	$110,050

On July 1, 1983, Ron Miller is to be admitted to the partnership by contributing $8,000 cash and library assets that cost $3,000 but have a fair market value of $4,500. Because Miller is considered an expert in the field of tax law, the other partners have agreed that Miller will receive a one-third interest in the partnership for his investment.

Required:

1. Prepare a balance sheet, income statement, and statement of partners' capital for Mitchell & Monson, attorneys-at-law, as of June 30, 1983. (Assume that profits and losses were shared equally in the old partnership.)

2. Give the necessary journal entry to record Ron Miller's admission to the partnership. (Assume that profits and losses are to be shared in the ratio 3:3:4 in the new partnership.)

3. Prepare the balance sheet of Mitchell, Monson, & Miller as of July 1, 1983.

P14-6 Unifying Problem: Preparing a Statement of Partners' Capital and Admitting a New Partner

On January 1, 1983, Evans and Fisher admitted Steve Gray into their partnership. Before the allocation of 1982 net income, the partners' capital balances were $39,000 and $15,000, respectively. Evans and Fisher, who share profits and losses equally, had net income of $30,000 in 1982. On January 1, 1983, Gray purchased one-third of Evans' interest for $20,000, and one-fifth of Fisher's interest for $9,000. The partnership of Evans, Fisher, & Gray had net income of $45,000 in 1983. The partners' Drawings accounts for 1983 showed balances of $12,000, $10,000, and $15,000, respectively.

On January 1, 1984, Robert Hall obtained a 25 percent interest in the partnership with an investment of $20,000.

Required:

1. Compute the capital balances of Evans and Fisher as of December 31, 1982.

2. Prepare the journal entry to record the admission of Steve Gray to the partnership.

3. Prepare a statement of partners' capital for the partnership of Evans, Fisher, & Gray as of December 31, 1983. (Assume that partnership profits and losses are allocated in the ratio 5:3:2.)

4. Prepare the journal entry to record the admission of Robert Hall to the partnership.

5. Compute the partners' capital balances as of January 1, 1984.

P14–7 Withdrawal of a Partner

On March 31, 1983, Jim Coyne retired from the partnership of Coyne, Duggan, & Edwards. After closing the books on March 31, the partners' capital balances were $30,000, $25,000, and $20,000, respectively. The partners share partnership profits and losses in the ratio 5:3:2.

Required:

Assuming that Duggan and Edwards plan to continue business under a new partnership agreement, prepare the journal entries to record the retirement of Coyne given the following independent situations.

1. Coyne sells his partnership interest to Bill Carman for $35,000 cash.
2. With the approval of the other partners, Coyne sells his partnership interest to Carman for $15,000 cash and a $25,000 personal note.
3. With the approval of the other partners, Coyne sells one-third of his partnership interest to Duggan for $15,000, and two-thirds of his interest to Edwards for $30,000.
4. Coyne's interest in the partnership is settled with a cash payment of $10,000 from the partnership assets and a note for $20,000.
5. Coyne is given $15,000 cash and equipment that cost $10,000 and that has accumulated depreciation of $3,000 for his equity in the partnership.
6. Coyne is given cash of $10,000, equipment that cost $20,000 and that has accumulated depreciation of $8,000, and a $20,000 note for his interest in the partnership. (All payments are made from partnership assets.)

P14–8 Withdrawal of a Partner

On June 30, 1983, Mike Roberts will retire from the partnership of Roberts, Smith, & Taylor. In planning for this retirement, the partners want to determine how various methods of handling the retirement would affect the partnership assets and financial statements. It is estimated that on June 30 the partners' Capital accounts will be $45,000, $50,000, and $55,000, respectively.

Required:

1. Prepare journal entries for each of the following independent proposals to handle the retirement of Mike Roberts.

   (a) Vance Roberts (Mike's son) purchases his father's interest in the partnership for $10,000 cash and a $50,000 note, payable to Mike in five equal annual installments with 10 percent interest on the unpaid balance.

   (b) Smith and Taylor agree to personally purchase Roberts' interest in the partnership. Smith will purchase one-third of his interest for $5,000 cash and a $20,000 non-interest-bearing note due in 3 years. Taylor will purchase two-thirds of Roberts' interest for $30,000 cash and a $12,000 note due in 1 year.

   (c) Smith, Taylor, and Vance Roberts each agree to purchase one-third of Mike Roberts' partnership interest for $20,000.

   (d) Smith and Taylor agree to make payments to Mike Roberts for his partnership interest from the partnership assets. The partners agree that Roberts' interest in the partnership, based on current market values, is $62,000. He will be paid $12,000 cash and be given a $50,000 note to be paid in five equal annual installments with 10 percent interest on the unpaid balance. Assume that profits are shared equally among the partners.

2. What effect will each of the proposals have on the partnership assets and the continuity of the business?
3. What effect will each of the proposals have on the sharing of future profits and losses by the partners?

P14–9 Liquidation of a Partnership

Frazier, Galbraith, and Hatfield, who share partnership profits and losses in the ratio 4:3:3, plan to liquidate their partnership. In accordance with the plan of liquidation, the following balance sheet was prepared as of September 1, 1983.

Frazier, Galbraith, and Hatfield
Balance Sheet as of September 1, 1983

Assets		
Cash		$ 25,000
Inventory		45,000
Land		40,000
Building	$100,000	
Accumulated Depreciation—Building	(30,000)	70,000
Equipment	$ 35,000	
Accumulated Depreciation—Equipment	(10,000)	25,000
Total Assets		$205,000
Liabilities and Partners' Equity		
Accounts Payable		$ 12,000
Notes Payable		48,000
Frazier, Capital		65,000
Galbraith, Capital		30,000
Hatfield, Capital		50,000
Total Liabilities and Partners' Equity		$205,000

Required:

Prepare the journal entries to record the sale of the business, the allocation of gains or losses among the partners, the payment of the liabilities, and the distribution of cash to the partners, under the following independent assumptions.

1. All noncash assets were sold to S&T Corporation for $200,000.

2. All noncash assets were sold to S&T Corporation for $140,000.

3. All noncash assets were sold to S&T Corporation for $50,000. The partner with the deficit balance pays the amount he owes the firm.

4. All noncash assets were sold to S&T Corporation for $40,000. The partner with the deficit balance is not able to pay his debt to the firm.

P14-10 Unifying Problem: Liquidation of a Partnership

Michaels, Norberg, and Olsen will discontinue business operations on March 31, 1983, according to a prearranged plan of liquidation. The partners, who share profits and losses in the ratio 3:1:2, have prepared the following balance sheet.

Michaels, Norberg, and Olsen
Balance Sheet as of March 31, 1983

Assets		
Cash		$ 15,000
Accounts Receivable		30,000
Inventory		45,000
Land		25,000
Building	$115,000	
Accumulated Depreciation—Building	(50,000)	65,000
Equipment (net)		40,000
Total Assets		$220,000
Liabilities and Partner's Equity		
Accounts Payable		$ 25,000
Mortgage Payable		75,000
Michaels, Capital		70,000
Norberg, Capital		15,000
Olsen, Capital		35,000
Total Liabilities and Partners' Equity		$220,000

Required:

1. Prepare the journal entries to record the receipt of cash from accounts receivable, the sale of the business, the allocation of gains and losses to the partners, the payment of the liabilities, and the distribution of cash to the partners, under the following independent assumptions.
   (a) Accounts receivable of $24,000 were collected. (The remainder were considered uncollectible and written off.) All noncash assets of the partnership were sold to XYZ Corporation for $205,000 cash.
   (b) Accounts receivable of $24,000 were collected. (The remainder were considered uncollectible and written off.) All noncash assets of the partnership were sold to XYZ Corporation for $79,000 cash. The partner with the deficit balance pays the amount he owes the firm.

2. Assuming the same facts as in item 1(b) above, prepare the journal entries to record the allocation of profits and losses and the distribution of cash to the partners, if the partner with the deficit balance refuses to pay his debt to the firm.

3. If sale of the partnership assets were to bring only $40,000, and there was not enough cash to pay the liabilities, how would the books be closed? How would the liabilities be settled?

SECTION 4

Other Dimensions of Financial Reporting

CHAPTER 15

Statement of Changes in Financial Position

THIS CHAPTER EXPLAINS:

The purpose and significance of a funds statement.

Various ways of defining funds, highlighting the all-financial-resources concept.

How to prepare a funds statement on both a working-capital and a cash basis.

Annual reports to stockholders must include three primary financial statements: the income statement, the balance sheet, and the statement of changes in financial position (traditionally called the funds statement). In earlier chapters the income statement and balance sheet were discussed in some detail. In this chapter we explain the statement of changes in financial position.

The Purpose and Significance of the Statement of Changes in Financial Position

The balance sheet, as you are aware, is formally known as the statement of financial position because it depicts the financial condition of a company at a particular point in time. In reporting to shareholders, a company includes comparative balance sheets for two consecutive periods in order to show how the company's financial status has changed during the period between the two balance sheet dates. The income statement ties two balance sheets together by measuring the results of operations for the intervening period (see Exhibit 15-1). To put this more explicitly, retained earnings on the prior balance sheet plus net income and minus dividends equals retained earnings on the next balance sheet.

EXHIBIT 15-1 **The Relationship Between Income Statements and Balance Sheets**

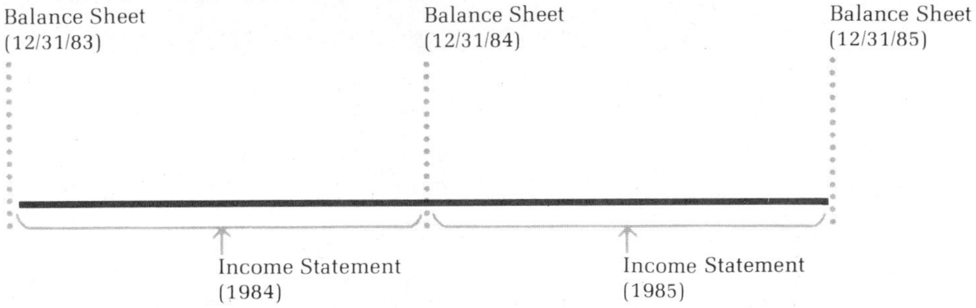

statement of changes in financial position (funds statement) *the primary financial report that shows an entity's major sources and uses of financial resources (funds) during a period*

Like the income statement, the statement of changes in financial position provides a connecting link between two balance sheets. But while the income statement helps to explain only the change in retained earnings, the statement of changes in financial position helps to justify the changes in the balances of *all* asset, liability, and owners' equity accounts, not just Retained Earnings. Thus, it reports all inflows and outflows of financial resources (funds): those generated from external financing and investing activities as well as those resulting from internal operations.

The purpose of a statement of changes in financial position, then, is to report all financial resources that have flowed into a business during an accounting period and to show how those resources have been used. This is why the statement is often called a statement of sources and uses of funds, or simply a funds statement. We will use these titles interchangeably, generally choosing the shorter title—funds statement—in the text discussion. The official title—statement of changes in financial position—will be used for all statement illustrations and problem solutions.

To illustrate the elements of a funds statement, Exhibit 15-2 on page 498 shows the major categories of resource flows during an accounting period. Companies obtain resources from three main sources: income from operations or from the sale of assets, such as equipment; proceeds from issuing stock (equity financing); and proceeds from borrowing money (debt financing). Companies use these resources primarily to finance normal operations, to pay dividends, to retire debt, to reacquire stock, to replace assets, and/or to acquire additional assets in order to maintain and expand operations.

Knowledge of the primary sources and uses of a company's funds helps investors, creditors, and others compare the firm's financial policies with those of competing firms in light of the current economic environment. Indeed, it enables an analyst to determine whether a firm is (1) retrenching (reducing) or expanding operations, (2) increasing or decreasing its reliance on operating income, equity capital, or borrowing, and (3) following financial policies that are in keeping with or in contrast to those of previous years and those of other firms in the industry.

Although the data for preparing a funds statement are derived from comparative balance sheets and the associated income statement, the funds statement highlights particular relationships that are not readily apparent

EXHIBIT 15-2 **The Flow of Funds**

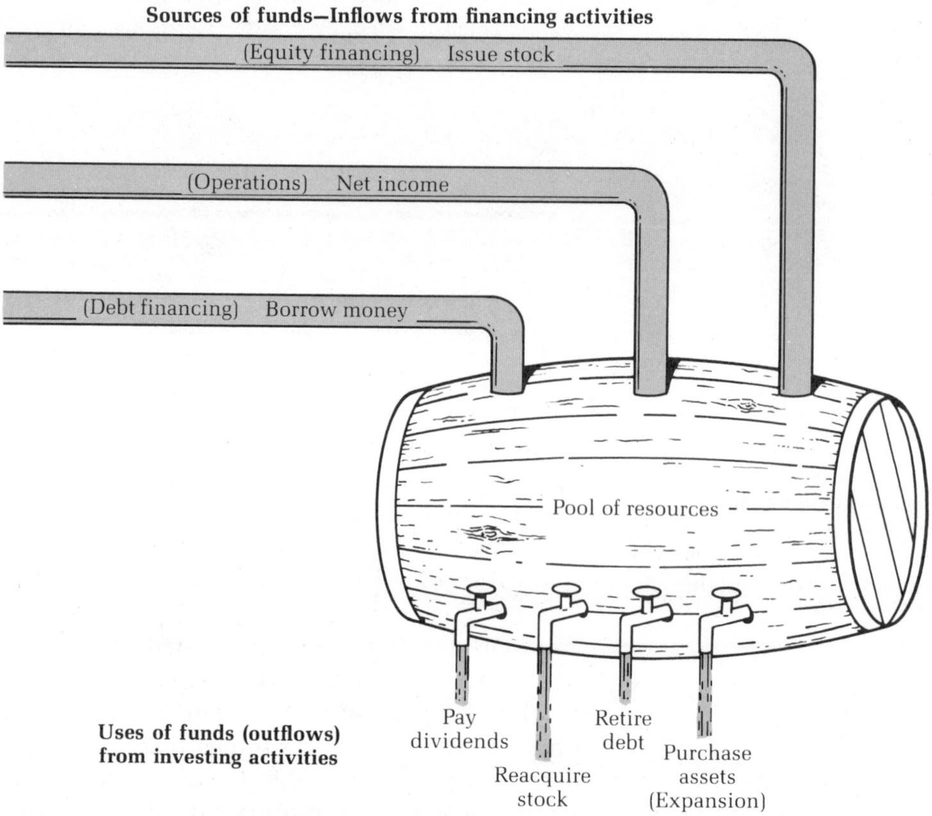

from a review of these other statements. It helps to answer such specific questions as: How is a company able to pay dividends when it has a net loss? Why might a company be short on cash despite increased earnings? How was a new office building financed? A funds statement may show, for example, that external borrowing or the issuance of capital stock provided the funds from which a dividend was paid, even though a net loss was reported for that year. Similarly, a company may be short on cash, even with increased earnings, due to plant expansion or debt retirement. Or, a new office building may have been financed by the sale of investments or by borrowing.

TO SUMMARIZE The statement of changes in financial position is one of the three primary financial statements. It shows the financial resources generated from external sources as well as from operations, and indicates how those funds have been used. The funds statement serves as a connecting link between two balance sheets because it helps to explain why the account balances have increased or decreased. This analysis of how funds have flowed through a firm highlights particular relationships that are useful in assessing a company's health and prospects.

Various Ways of Defining Funds

funds *the financial resources that flow into and out of a company; usually defined as working capital or cash*

cash concept of funds *a concept used in preparing a funds statement that reflects transactions in which cash is either received or paid*

working-capital concept of funds *a concept used in preparing a funds statement that reflects transactions in which current assets or current liabilities are either increased or decreased*

In the context of a funds statement, funds are the financial resources flowing into and out of a company. Most companies define funds either as cash or as working capital, applying these concepts on an "all-financial-resources" basis.

The cash concept of funds measures the inflows and outflows of cash that result from transactions in which cash is either received or paid. The working-capital concept of funds measures the inflows and outflows of working capital that occur from transactions that increase or decrease current assets or current liabilities.

THE ALL-FINANCIAL-RESOURCES CONCEPT OF FUNDS

A funds statement prepared *strictly* on a cash or a working-capital basis does not provide a complete picture of all changes in financial position. For example, a company may exchange some of its stock for a tract of land. Since neither cash nor other working-capital accounts are involved, this transaction would not be reported if a strict cash or working-capital concept of funds were applied. In such cases, the funds statement would not completely accomplish its objectives; that is, it would not help to explain all changes in account balances, nor would it report all significant inflows and outflows of resources from financing and investing activities.

Because many firms engage in transactions that significantly affect their financial position but do not affect cash or working capital, the cash and working-capital concepts of funds must always be applied on an all-financial-resources basis. Its use is required by generally accepted accounting principles.

all-financial-resources concept *a concept used in preparing a funds statement that reflects all financing and investing activities for a period as sources and uses of funds, whether or not they increase or decrease cash or working capital*

The all-financial-resources concept measures the funds flow from all financing and investing activities, even those that do not actually result in an increase or decrease in cash or working capital. The following types of financing and investing transactions are typical examples.

1. Exchanges of common stock or long-term liabilities for property, plant, and equipment.
2. Conversion of long-term liabilities into stockholders' equity; for example, conversion of a bond into stock.
3. Conversion of preferred stock into common stock.

Although these transactions do not affect cash or working capital, they represent changes in internal debt–equity relationships and should be called to the attention of financial statement readers.

With the all-financial-resources concept, transactions that involve investing and financing activities but that do not affect cash or working capital are reported as if cash or working capital were simultaneously increased and decreased. This is done by reporting both a *source* and a *use* of funds. In the example of exchanging stock for land, the source of funds is the stock issued and the use of funds is the purchase of the land. It is as though the company issued the stock for cash, then used the cash to purchase the land. When property, plant, or equipment is purchased by issuing a long-term liability, such as a bond, the debt that is created is the source of funds; the purchase of the operational asset is the use of funds. Thus, transactions of this type can be represented as shown below.

Source of Funds		Use of Funds
Issuance of a long-term bond	**for**	Purchase of property, plant, or equipment
Issuance of common stock	**for**	Retirement of long-term bonds
Issuance of common stock	**for**	Retirement of preferred stock

TO SUMMARIZE Funds are financial resources that flow into and out of a company. In preparing a statement of changes in financial position, most companies define funds as either cash or working capital. Regardless of how funds are defined, all significant financing and investing activities should be reported by applying the all-financial-resources concept.

Preparing a Funds Statement

Once a company determines how it wants to define funds—as cash, working capital, or some other concept such as cash plus short-term investments—the company is ready to prepare a statement of changes in financial position. A three-step procedure may be used.

1. Determine the change in the fund balance for the period. With the cash concept, this is simply the increase or decrease in the cash account. With the working-capital concept, this is the net change in working capital during the accounting period.
2. Identify the major sources and uses of funds during the period in order to explain the fund balance that was determined in step 1. This step requires that each account not considered in step 1 be analyzed to see if funds were provided by or used in transactions affecting that account.
3. Use the results of the analysis in step 2 to prepare a formal statement of changes in financial position. The statement reports all significant financing and investing activities and identifies the primary sources and uses of funds.

To illustrate the process of preparing a funds statement, we will assume that Mountain Land Resources, Inc. had the comparative balance sheets, income statement, and statement of retained earnings shown in Exhibits

15-3 and 15-4. Since funds have traditionally been defined as working capital, we will first use the working capital concept applied on an all-financial-resources basis. However, many companies have recently switched to a cash-basis funds statement to emphasize immediate liquidity and cash flows, so we will also explain how to prepare a funds statement using the cash concept applied on an all-financial-resources basis.

EXHIBIT 15-3

Mountain Land Resources, Inc.
Balance Sheets as of December 31, 1984 and 1983

Assets	**1984**	**1983**
Current Assets:		
Cash	$ 17,600	$ 7,900
Accounts Receivable (net of Allowance for Doubtful Accounts)	106,700	104,900
Inventory	187,300	197,500
Prepaid Expenses	7,000	9,200
Total Current Assets	$318,600	$319,500
Property, Plant, and Equipment:		
Land (Note 1)	$ 90,000	$ 10,000
Plant and Equipment (at cost)	623,200	577,200
Less Accumulated Depreciation	(243,900)	(223,600)
Total Property, Plant, and Equipment	$469,300	$363,600
Total Assets	$787,900	$683,100
Liabilities and Stockholders' Equity		
Current Liabilities:		
Accounts Payable	$ 72,200	$ 71,700
Income Taxes Payable	7,000	1,500
Total Current Liabilities	79,200	$ 73,200
Long-Term Liabilities:		
Notes Payable	$ 20,000	—
Mortgage Payable	72,100	$ 85,000
Total Long-Term Liabilities	$ 92,100	$ 85,000
Stockholders' Equity:		
Common Stock, $1 Par Value (Note 1)	$ 82,500	$ 42,500
Paid-in Capital in Excess of Par—Common Stock (Note 1)	186,900	146,900
Retained Earnings	347,200	335,500
Total Stockholders' Equity	$616,600	$524,900
Total Liabilities and Stockholders' Equity	$787,900	$683,100

Note 1 Land with a fair market value of $80,000 was acquired through the issuance of 40,000 shares of common stock.

EXHIBIT 15-4

Mountain Land Resources, Inc.
Income Statement
for the Year Ended December 31, 1984

Net Sales Revenue	$859,400
Other Revenues (Note 2)	7,800
Total Revenues	$867,200
Expenses:	
Cost of Goods Sold	$610,100
Selling and Administrative Expenses	147,000
Depreciation Expense	32,100
Interest Expense	14,200
Total Expenses	$803,400
Income Before Taxes	$ 63,800
Income Taxes	27,200
Net Income	$ 36,600

Note 2 Gain on the sale of equipment (cost, $12,300; book value, $500; sale price, $8,300 cash).

Mountain Land Resources
Statement of Retained Earnings
for the Year Ended December 31, 1984

Retained Earnings, January 1, 1984	$335,500
Add Net Income	36,600
	$372,100
Dividends Declared and Paid	24,900
Retained Earnings, December 31, 1984	$347,200

Preparing a Funds Statement on a Working-Capital Basis

working capital *the funds available to finance current operations; equal to current assets minus current liabilities*

When a funds statement is prepared on a working-capital basis, attention is focused on the sources and uses of working capital. Recall that working capital is a general measure of a firm's liquidity—that is, its ability to pay short-term liabilities (current liabilities) with short-term assets (current assets). Thus, working capital is equal to total current assets minus total current liabilities.

STEP 1: DETERMINE THE CHANGE IN WORKING CAPITAL

The first step in preparing a working-capital funds statement is to determine the change in working capital during the period. In effect, all current asset and current liability accounts are considered as though they were one account. Increases or decreases in any of the current accounts affect the amount of change in working capital. Thus, the change in working capital is the difference between current assets minus current liabilities at the beginning of the period and current assets minus current liabilities at the end of the period. A schedule of changes in working capital is included with each funds statement prepared on a working-capital basis so that readers can see how changes in the individual current accounts result in the overall change in working capital.

To illustrate, the working capital for Mountain Land Resources at the end of 1983 is $246,300 (current assets of $319,500 − current liabilities of $73,200). At the end of 1984, the working capital is $239,400 ($318,600 − $79,200). Since working capital was higher at the beginning of the period than it was at the end, the change in working capital is a decrease of $6,900 ($246,300 − $239,400). A schedule of changes in working capital for Mountain Land Resources is presented in Exhibit 15-5. The schedule shows which individual current accounts changed to produce the $6,900 net decrease in working capital. The most significant account changes were the increase in cash, the decrease in inventory, and the increase in income taxes payable. Notice that whereas an increase in a current asset increases working capital, an increase in a current liability decreases working capital. Thus, for current assets the change in working capital will be positive if the account increased and negative if it decreased; the reverse is true for current liabilities.

EXHIBIT 15-5

Mountain Land Resources, Inc.

*Schedule of Changes in Working Capital**

	Balances at December 31 1983	1984	Changes in Working Capital
Current Assets:			
Cash	$ 7,900	$ 17,600	$ 9,700
Accounts Receivable (net)	104,900	106,700	1,800
Inventory	197,500	187,300	(10,200)
Prepaid Expenses	9,200	7,000	(2,200)
Totals	$319,500	$318,600	$ (900)
Current Liabilities:			
Accounts Payable	$ 71,700	$ 72,200	$ (500)
Income Taxes Payable	1,500	7,000	(5,500)
Totals	$ 73,200	$ 79,200	$ (6,000)
Working Capital	$246,300	$239,400	$ (6,900)

* Note that the years are not presented here in the usual format of comparative statements—the current year first, then the preceding year. A chronological format has been used to make it easier for you to see the changes in working capital in terms of whether they are due to increases or decreases in the accounts. Also, this format matches that of the work sheet we will be using later.

STEP 2: EXPLAIN THE CHANGE IN WORKING CAPITAL

The second step in preparing a funds statement on a working-capital basis is to determine the sources and uses of working capital during the period that resulted in the change in working capital computed in step 1. This

noncurrent accounts *all operational asset, long-term investment, long-term liability, and owners' equity accounts; all accounts except for working-capital accounts*

requires that any transaction affecting both a working-capital account and a noncurrent (non-working-capital) account be analyzed. In addition, any transaction affecting *only* noncurrent accounts must be analyzed for sources and uses of funds under the all-financial-resources concept. Noncurrent accounts are all balance sheet accounts except for current assets and current liabilities. Transactions that involve only working-capital accounts do not need to be analyzed since they have contributed to the change in working capital and have therefore been included in the schedule of changes in working capital.

Noncurrent accounts may be analyzed in either of two ways: with T-accounts or with a columnar work sheet. When T-accounts are used, the transactions are recorded in a manner similar to their posting to the General Ledger. A work sheet, on the other hand, may be used to assemble and organize all appropriate information; it ties the entire funds statement together in one place. As shown later, the analysis is essentially the same with either approach. In this chapter, we will use a work sheet and the data for Mountain Land Resources, Inc.; the Supplement illustrates the T-account approach.

Set Up a Work Sheet

The format of the work sheet to be used is illustrated in Exhibit 15-6. The first and last columns on the upper portion of the work sheet list the entries on the comparative balance sheets. The middle columns, identified as the analysis of accounts section, are debit and credit adjustment columns that show how much each account has increased or decreased. Note that total working capital plus non-working-capital assets must equal total non-working-capital liabilities plus stockholders' equity for both the beginning and the ending balance sheets. If there are errors in any of the account balances, they must be corrected before an accurate funds statement can be prepared. Also remember that with the working-capital concept, all current accounts have already been lumped together in computing the change in working capital, as shown in Exhibit 15-5. The lower portion of the work sheet, which is referred to as the funds statement section, identifies the major sources and uses of funds. The formal statement of changes in financial position can be prepared directly from this part of the work sheet.

Analyze the Noncurrent Accounts

In analyzing the noncurrent accounts, the objective is to explain why each of them increased or decreased, and in the process to identify the major sources and uses of working capital during the period. One of the main sources, which according to generally accepted accounting principles must be separately identified, is the amount of working capital provided by operations. Therefore, we will start by analyzing the Retained Earnings account and establishing net income as a primary source of working capital.

As shown on the income statement (Exhibit 15-4), Mountain Land Resources reported $36,600 of net income for the year. This amount is credited in the analysis column of the work sheet in Exhibit 15-7 [entry (1)] on page 506, to explain the increase in retained earnings during the year. Since net

EXHIBIT 15-6

Mountain Land Resources, Inc.

Funds Statement Work Sheet (Working-Capital Basis)
for the Period Ended December 31, 1984

	Beginning Balances 12/31/83	Analysis of Accounts		Ending Balances 12/31/84
		Debits	Credits	
Working Capital	246300			239400
Non-Working-Capital Assets:				
Land	10000			90000
Plant and Equipment	577200			623200
Accumulated Depreciation	(223600)			(243900)
Total Working Capital and Non-Working-Capital Assets	609900			708700
Non-Working-Capital Liabilities and Stockholders' Equity:				
Notes Payable				20000
Mortgage Payable	85000			72100
Common Stock, $1 Par	42500			82500
Paid-in Capital in Excess of Par--Common Stock	146900			186900
Retained Earnings	335500			347200
Total Non-Working-Capital Liabilities and Stockholders' Equity	609900			708700
		Funds Statement		
Sources of Working Capital				
Uses of Working Capital				

EXHIBIT 15-7

Mountain Land Resources, Inc.

Funds Statement Work Sheet (Working-Capital Basis)
for the Period Ended December 31, 1984

	Beginning Balances 12/31/83	Analysis of Accounts		Ending Balances 12/31/84
		Debits	Credits	
Working Capital	246300			239400
Non-Working-Capital Assets:				
Land	10000			90000
Plant and Equipment	577200			623200
Accumulated Depreciation	(223600)			(243900)
Total Working Capital and Non-Working-Capital Assets	609900			708700
Non-Working-Capital Liabilities and Stockholders' Equity:				
Notes Payable				20000
Mortgage Payable	85000			72100
Common Stock, $1 Par	42500			82500
Paid-in Capital in Excess of Par--Common Stock	146900			186900
Retained Earnings	335500	(2) 24900	(1) 36600	347200
Total Non-Working-Capital Liabilities and Stockholders' Equity	609900			708700
		Funds Statement		
Sources of Working Capital				
Operations:				
Net Income		(1) 36600		
Uses of Working Capital				
Declaration and Payment of Dividends			(2) 24900	

income affects Retained Earnings, a non-working-capital account, it is considered a source of funds and is therefore reported as such below, under the heading "Operations."

However, net income alone does not explain the total change in retained earnings. As reported on the statement of retained earnings, $24,900 of dividends were declared and paid. This amount must be debited to retained earnings and entered as a use of funds on the work sheet [entry (2)]. The entire change in the Retained Earnings account has now been explained and a major source and a major use of working capital have been identified. Observe in Exhibit 15-7 that whenever an amount is entered as a credit in the analysis section of the work sheet, it becomes a source of funds in the lower portion of the work sheet; a debit entry in the analysis section becomes a use of funds in the funds statement section.

As the following illustrates, the same result can be obtained by T-account analysis. With either the work sheet or the T-account approach, net income is shown as providing a source of working capital and dividends as a use of working capital.

Retained Earnings

	335,500 . . . . 12/31/83 Balance
Use of Funds—Dividends 24,900	36,600 . . . . . . Source of Funds—Net Income
	347,200 . . . . 12/31/84 Balance

All other noncurrent accounts are analyzed in the same way as retained earnings. Generally, they are analyzed in the order listed on the comparative balance sheets, so we will begin with the Land account. As shown later, the change in working capital becomes the last item to be included on the work sheet, at which point it is the amount needed to balance the work sheet.

The Land account has increased $80,000 ($90,000 − $10,000). As Note 1 in Exhibit 15-3 explains, the change resulted from a purchase of land by issuing 40,000 shares of stock. Working capital was not affected. However, the all-financial-resources concept requires that all significant financing and investing activities be accounted for, so this transaction must be considered a source and a use of funds. The issuance of the stock represents an important financing activity and the purchase of the land represents a significant investing activity. Thus, we must report the $80,000 purchase of land as a use of funds and the issuance of the stock as a corresponding source of funds [entry (3) in Exhibit 15-8 on page 508]. Note that two equity accounts (Common Stock and Paid-in Capital in Excess of Par—Common Stock) must be credited to explain the stock issuance. (Note that in Exhibit 15-8 space is left between Net Income and Issuance of Stock to Acquire Land so that adjustments to income can be made, as will be explained later.)

The next two accounts, Plant and Equipment and the related Accumulated Depreciation, must be considered together. In analyzing the changes in these accounts, you must be certain to recognize all transactions affecting

EXHIBIT 15-8

Mountain Land Resources, Inc.
Funds Statement Work Sheet (Working-Capital Basis)
for the Period Ended December 31, 1984

	Beginning Balances 12/31/83	Analysis of Accounts		Ending Balances 12/31/84
		Debits	Credits	
Working Capital	246300			239400
Non-Working-Capital Assets:				
Land	10000	(3) 80000		90000
Plant and Equipment	577200			623200
Accumulated Depreciation	(223600)			(243900)
Total Working Capital and Non-Working-Capital Assets	609900			708700
Non-Working-Capital Liabilities and Stockholders' Equity:				
Notes Payable				20000
Mortgage Payable	85000			72100
Common Stock, $1 Par	42500		(3) 40000	82500
Paid-in Capital in Excess of Par--Common Stock	146900		(3) 40000	186900
Retained Earnings	335500	(2) 24900	(1) 36600	347200
Total Non-Working-Capital Liabilities and Stockholders' Equity	609900			708700
		Funds Statement		
Sources of Working Capital				
Operations:				
Net Income		(1) 36600		
Issuance of Stock to Acquire Land		(3) 80000		
Uses of Working Capital				
Declaration and Payment of Dividends			(2) 24900	
Acquisition of Land by Issuance of Stock			(3) 80000	

them. You cannot automatically assume that the difference in account balances is a source or a use of funds.

To illustrate, we know from Note 2 on the income statement (Exhibit 15-4) that equipment purchased for $12,300 in a previous year was sold for $8,300 in 1984 and a gain was recognized. This transaction reduces both the Plant and Equipment and Accumulated Depreciation accounts. (On the other hand, any equipment purchased during 1984 would have caused the Plant and Equipment account to increase.)

All these transactions must be analyzed to determine their effects on the sources and uses of working capital. First, consider the sale of the equipment. During 1984, the cost of the equipment ($12,300) was written off along with the related portion of the accumulated depreciation. Since the book value is $500 and the cost of the equipment is $12,300, the amount of accumulated depreciation written off was $11,800 ($12,300 − $500 book value). The cash proceeds from the sale were $8,300, which produced the gain of $7,800 ($8,300 proceeds − $500 book value = $7,800 gain), as shown in the following journal entry.

Cash	8,300	
Accumulated Depreciation	11,800	
Equipment		12,300
Gain on Sale of Equipment		7,800
Sold used equipment for $8,300.		

This transaction is different from those explained so far. The $12,300 credit to Plant and Equipment and the $11,800 debit to Accumulated Depreciation are required to close those accounts upon the sale of the asset, so they are included in the analysis section of the work sheet. However, these amounts relate to earlier accounting periods, dating from the time the equipment was first purchased. They are not sources or uses of working capital in the current period. Only the proceeds from the sale are a source of funds for the current period, so $8,300 should be shown as a source of working capital. However, the $36,600 of net income already includes the $7,800 gain. If net income is reported at $36,600 and the $8,300 is listed separately as a source of funds, the $7,800 gain would be counted twice. Therefore, to correctly show the total amount of the proceeds from the sale as a separate source of funds requires that we adjust the net income amount by subtracting the $7,800 gain. After this adjustment is made, the amount of funds provided by operations ($36,600 − $7,800) will be reported and the total proceeds from the sale of equipment ($8,300) will be shown as a separate source of funds [entry (4)], as illustrated in the partially completed work sheet in Exhibit 15-9 on page 510.

The remaining change in the Plant and Equipment account ($58,300) must have resulted from the use of funds to purchase equipment. That is, the beginning balance for plant and equipment was $577,200. The sale of equipment reduced this amount by $12,300. Therefore, $58,300 of equipment must have been purchased in order for the ending balance in plant and equipment to be $623,200, as shown on page 511.

EXHIBIT 15-9

Mountain Land Resources, Inc.

Funds Statement Work Sheet (Working-Capital Basis)
for the Period Ended December 31, 1984

	Beginning Balances 12/31/83	Analysis of Accounts: Debits	Analysis of Accounts: Credits	Ending Balances 12/31/84
Working Capital	246300			239400
Non-Working-Capital Assets:				
Land	10000	(3) 80000		90000
Plant and Equipment	577200		(4) 12300	623200
Accumulated Depreciation	(223600)	(4) 11800		(243900)
Total Working Capital and Non-Working-Capital Assets	609900			708700
Non-Working-Capital Liabilities and Stockholders' Equity:				
Notes Payable				20000
Mortgage Payable	85000			72100
Common Stock, $1 Par	42500		(3) 40000	82500
Paid-in Capital in Excess of Par--Common Stock	146900		(3) 40000	186900
Retained Earnings	335500	(2) 24900	(1) 36600	347200
Total Non-Working-Capital Liabilities Stockholders' Equity	609900			708700
		Funds Statement		
Sources of Working Capital				
Operations:				
Net Income		(1) 36600		
Adjustments to Net Income:				
Gain on Sale of Equipment			(4) 7800	
Issuance of Stock to Acquire Land		(3) 80000		
Proceeds from Sale of Equipment		(4) 8300		
Uses of Working Capital				
Declaration and Payment of Dividends			(2) 24900	
Acquisition of Land by Issuance of Stock			(3) 80000	

Plant and Equipment

12/31/83 Balance	577,200		
1984 Purchases	58,300	12,300	1984 Sale
12/31/84 Balance	623,200		

Similarly, after the write-off of accumulated depreciation on the sale of the equipment, the depreciation charge for the period ($32,100, as shown on the income statement in Exhibit 15-4) accounts for the remaining difference in the Accumulated Depreciation account ($223,600 beginning balance − $11,800 write-off + $32,100 accumulated depreciation = $243,900 ending balance). Depreciation, however, is only a bookkeeping entry; it does not involve cash or working capital. Although net income has been reduced by the amount of the depreciation expense, no working capital has actually flowed out of the company. Thus, the amount of depreciation expense must be added back to net income to correctly report the working capital generated from operations. These results are now shown on the work sheet in Exhibit 15-10 [entries (5) and (6)] on page 512.

It is important to note that other noncash expenses would be treated as adjustments to net income in the same way as depreciation. For example, the amortization expense for intangible assets such as patents or goodwill, the amortization of bond discounts or premiums, or any other expense that decreases (or increases) net income but not cash must be added to (or subtracted from) net income to arrive at the amount of funds from operations.

The total amount of working capital provided by operations has now been obtained ($36,600 + $32,100 − $7,800 = $60,900). This key element of the funds statement represents the amount of working capital that flowed into the company from normal operations. It is the equivalent of net income for the period plus non-working-capital deductions (the depreciation expense) and minus the gain on the sale of plant and equipment, which is shown as a separate source. Non-working-capital additions and deductions refer to bookkeeping items that do not reflect actual inflows and outflows of working capital. If these non-working-capital effects and nonoperating gains or losses were removed from the income statement, the total would be $60,900, as shown here.

Net Sales Revenue	$859,400
Expenses:	
Cost of Goods Sold	$610,100
Selling and Administrative Expenses	147,000
Interest Expense	14,200
Total Expenses	$771,300
Working Capital from Operations Before Income Taxes	$ 88,100
Less Income Taxes	27,200
Net Working Capital from Operations	$ 60,900

EXHIBIT 15-10

Mountain Land Resources, Inc.

Funds Statement Work Sheet (Working-Capital Basis)
for the Period Ended December 31, 1984

	Beginning Balances 12/31/83	Analysis of Accounts: Debits	Analysis of Accounts: Credits	Ending Balances 12/31/84
Working Capital	246300			239400
Non-Working-Capital Assets:				
Land	10000	(3) 80000		90000
Plant and Equipment	577200	(5) 58300	(4) 12300	623200
Accumulated Depreciation	(223600)	(4) 11800	(6) 32100	(243900)
Total Working Capital and Non-Working-Capital Assets	609900			708700
Non-Working-Capital Liabilities and Stockholders' Equity:				
Notes Payable				20000
Mortgage Payable	85000			72100
Common Stock, $1	42500		(3) 40000	82500
Paid-in Capital in Excess of Par--Common Stock	146900		(3) 40000	186900
Retained Earnings	335500	(2) 24900	(1) 36600	347200
Total Non-Working-Capital Liabilities Stockholders' Equity	609900			708700
		Funds Statement		
Sources of Working Capital				
Operations:				
Net Income		(1) 36600		
Adjustments to Net Income:				
Gain on Sale of Equipment			(4) 7800	
Depreciation		(6) 32100		
Total Working Capital from Operations		60900		
Issuance of Stock to Acquire Land		(3) 80000		
Proceeds from Sale of Equipment		(4) 8300		
Uses of Working Capital				
Declaration and Payment of Dividends			(2) 24900	
Acquisition of Land by Issuance of Stock			(3) 80000	
Purchase of Equipment			(5) 58300	

By comparing this modified version of the income statement with Exhibit 15-4, you will be able to see the differences. The modified statement excludes the gain on the sale of the equipment and the depreciation expense. By excluding these items, the flow of working capital from operations during the year is highlighted.

Only two additional accounts need to be analyzed. The Notes Payable account increased by $20,000, indicating that funds were provided by borrowing [entry (7)]. The Mortgage Payable account decreased by $12,900, indicating that funds were used to pay a portion of the mortgage [entry (8)]. Since the stockholders' equity accounts have already been analyzed [in entry (3)], all changes in financial position have now been explained and we are ready to complete the work sheet. If all accounts have been analyzed correctly, the difference in total sources and total uses of working capital will equal the net change in working capital as computed earlier in step 2. Thus, that amount can be used to balance the sources and uses columns. When it is added to the sources column [entry (9)]—because the change in working capital is a decrease—the sources and uses do balance, as shown on the completed work sheet in Exhibit 15-11 on page 514.

STEP 3: PREPARE A FORMAL STATEMENT OF CHANGES IN FINANCIAL POSITION

The formal statement of changes in financial position for Mountain Land Resources, Inc. can be taken directly from the work sheet. It is presented in Exhibit 15-12 on page 515. As noted earlier, this statement would be supported by a schedule of changes in working capital, like the one shown in Exhibit 15-5. Although the illustration in Exhibit 15-12 is for only one year, in most instances the funds statements for two consecutive years will be presented on a comparative basis.

The statement in Exhibit 15-12 is balanced; that is, total sources equal total uses. In some cases, however, the change in working capital is not shown as a use (when it increases) or as a source (when it decreases). Instead, total uses of funds are subtracted from total sources (both exclusive of the change in working capital) to produce a residual figure labeled Increase (or Decrease) in Working Capital.

The funds statement for Mountain Land Resources highlights the three primary sources of funds: internal operations (net income as adjusted), equity financing (issuance of stock), and debt financing (borrowing). It also provides an example of the major uses of funds and illustrates the application of the all-financial-resources concept.

TO SUMMARIZE The preparation of a funds statement involves three steps: (1) determining the change in the fund balance during the period, (2) explaining why the change occurred, by identifying the major sources and uses of funds, and (3) preparing the formal statement. A work sheet may be used to help organize appropriate information to be presented in the formal statement of changes in financial position.

EXHIBIT 15-11

Mountain Land Resources, Inc.

Funds Statement Work Sheet (Working-Capital Basis)
for the Period Ended December 31, 1984

	Beginning Balances 12/31/83	Analysis of Accounts: Debits	Analysis of Accounts: Credits	Ending Balances 12/31/84
Working Capital	246300		(9) 6900	239400
Non-Working-Capital Assets:				
Land	10000	(3) 80000		90000
Plant and Equipment	577200	(5) 58300	(4) 12300	623200
Accumulated Depreciation	(223600)	(4) 11800	(6) 32100	(243900)
Total Working Capital and Non-Working-Capital Assets	609900			708700
Non-Working-Capital Liabilities and Stockholders' Equity:				
Notes Payable			(7) 20000	20000
Mortgage Payable	85000	(8) 12900		72100
Common Stock, $1 Par	42500		(3) 40000	82500
Paid-in Capital in Excess of Par--Common Stock	146900		(3) 40000	186900
Retained Earnings	335500	(2) 24900	(1) 36600	347200
Total Non-Working-Capital Liabilities and Stockholders' Equity	609900	187900	187900	708700
		Funds Statement		
Sources of Working Capital				
Operations:				
Net Income		(1) 36600		
Adjustments to Net Income:				
Gain on Sale of Equipment			(4) 7800	
Depreciation		(6) 32100		
Total Working Capital from Operations		60900		
Issuance of Stock to Acquire Land		(3) 80000		
Proceeds from Sale of Equipment		(4) 8300		
Proceeds from Long-Term Note		(7) 20000		
Decrease in Working Capital		(9) 6900		
Total Sources of Working Capital		176100		
Uses of Working Capital				
Declaration and Payment of Dividends			(2) 24900	
Acquisition of Land by Issuance of Stock			(3) 80000	
Purchase of Equipment			(5) 58300	
Reduction in Mortgage			(8) 12900	
Total Uses of Working Capital			176100	

EXHIBIT 15-12 **Mountain Land Resources**

Statement of Changes in Financial Position (Working-Capital Basis) for the Period Ended December 31, 1984

Sources of Working Capital	
Operations:	
Net Income	$ 36,600
Add Depreciation	32,100
	$ 68,700
Subtract Gain on Sale of Equipment	(7,800)
Total Working Capital from Operations	$ 60,900
Issuance of Stock to Acquire Land	80,000
Proceeds from Sale of Equipment	8,300
Proceeds from Long-Term Note	20,000
Decrease in Working Capital*	6,900
Total Sources of Working Capital	$176,100
Uses of Working Capital	
Declaration and Payment of Dividends	$ 24,900
Acquisition of Land by Issuance of Stock	80,000
Purchase of Equipment	58,300
Reduction in Mortgage	12,900
Total Uses of Working Capital	$176,100

* See the Schedule of Changes in Working Capital (Exhibit 15-5).

Preparing a Funds Statement on a Cash Basis

We will now explain and illustrate how the all-financial-resources concept is applied in preparing a funds statement where funds are defined as cash. A cash-basis funds statement is prepared in the same way as a working-capital-basis statement, with two important and related differences.

First, on a working-capital basis only non-working-capital accounts must be analyzed. That is because the changes in all the current accounts become the increase or decrease in working capital. On a cash basis, in addition to the non-working-capital accounts, all changes in current asset accounts other than cash and all current liability accounts must also be analyzed. For Mountain Land Resources, this means that five additional accounts must be analyzed: Accounts Receivable, Inventory, Prepaid Expenses, Accounts Payable, and Income Taxes Payable.

Second, a major source of funds to be highlighted on a working-capital basis is the total working capital from operations. With the cash basis, this amount must be converted to total cash provided by operations. In other words, the amount of working capital generated from operations, which is based on accrual accounting, must be converted to a cash basis to show the amount of cash provided by normal operations. This is accomplished by analyzing the noncash current assets and current liabilities referred to above.

Like a working-capital-basis funds statement, a cash-basis funds statement may be prepared in three steps. The first step is to determine the change in the fund balance—the increase or decrease in the Cash account during the period. The second step is to analyze all noncash accounts and to identify the major sources and uses of cash during the period. If the analysis is performed correctly, the change in the Cash account will be the balancing figure that makes total sources and total uses of cash equal. The final step is to prepare a formal cash-basis funds statement. As before, one of the main sources to be highlighted is the total funds (in this case, cash) provided by operations, and the cash basis must be applied using the all-financial-resources concept. Since you are familiar with Mountain Land Resources, we will again use the data in Exhibits 15-3 and 15-4. We will also use the same work sheet format, as illustrated in Exhibit 15-13.

By comparing Exhibit 15-13 with Exhibit 15-11, you may observe the similarities and the two main differences in the cash and working capital concepts. First, under the cash basis, all noncash current accounts must be analyzed individually, whereas they were considered as one amount under the working-capital basis. Therefore, all the working-capital accounts are listed on the cash-basis work sheet and a separate schedule of changes in working capital is not needed. Second, the amount of working capital from operations must be further adjusted to a cash basis to show the total cash generated by operations. Exhibit 15-13 shows the amount of working capital from operations for illustrative purposes only, with additional space left below it to make the necessary adjustments to a cash basis. A more common practice in preparing a cash-basis funds statement is to list all adjustments to net income in one section and not show the amount of working capital from operations as an intermediate figure. In the future we will use this latter approach in preparing cash-basis funds statements.

To illustrate how to prepare a cash-basis work sheet, we will begin by explaining the change in Accounts Receivable. The change in the Cash account will be added as the last item to balance the work sheet.

Accounts Receivable has increased $1,800 during the period. As with most current asset and current liability accounts, this change affects net income. That is, as Accounts Receivable is increased, so is Sales Revenue, which increases net income. This is in accordance with accrual-basis accounting, whereby revenues are recognized when they are earned whether or not cash has been received, and expenses are reported when they are incurred whether or not cash has been paid. However, to determine the amount of cash generated from operations—a key element to be disclosed on a cash-basis funds statement—we must reverse the process. We must convert total working capital from operations to total cash from operations by removing from accrual-basis net income any noncash items. Since the increase in Accounts Receivable produced an increase in accrual-basis income, but not in cash-basis income, the $1,800 must be subtracted from the reported net income of $36,600. As shown in Exhibit 15-14 on page 518, the change in Accounts Receivable is explained and the appropriate adjustment made to convert accrual-basis income to a cash basis [entry (9)]. If Accounts Receivable had decreased, the amount of the change would have been added to net income since more cash would have been generated during the period than was reported as income on an accrual basis.

EXHIBIT 15-13

Mountain Land Resources, Inc.
Funds Statement Work Sheet (Cash Basis)
for the Period Ended December 31, 1984

	Beginning Balances 12/31/83	Analysis of Accounts		Ending Balances 12/31/84
		Debits	Credits	
Cash	7900			17600
Accounts Receivable (Net)	104900			106700
Inventory	197500			187300
Prepaid Expenses	9200			7000
Land	10000	(3) 80000		90000
Plant and Equipment	577200	(5) 58300	(4) 12300	623200
Accumulated Depreciation	(223600)	(4) 11800	(6) 32100	(243900)
Total Assets	683100			787900
Accounts Payable	71700			72200
Income Taxes Payable	1500			7000
Notes Payable			(7) 20000	20000
Mortgage Payable	85000	(8) 12900		72100
Common Stock, $1 Par	42500		(3) 40000	82500
Paid-in Capital in Excess of Par--Common Stock	146900		(3) 40000	186900
Retained Earnings	335500	(2) 24900	(1) 36600	347200
Total Liabilities and Stockholders' Equity	683100			787900
		Funds Statement		
Sources of Cash				
Operations:				
Net Income		(1) 36600		
Adjustments to Net Income:				
Gain on Sale of Equipment			(4) 7800	
Depreciation		(6) 32100		
Total Working Capital from Operations		60900		
Adjustments to Cash Basis:				
Issuance of Stock to Acquire Land		(3) 80000		
Proceeds from Sale of Equipment		(4) 8300		
Proceeds from Long-Term Note		(7) 20000		
Uses of Cash				
Payment of Dividends			(2) 24900	
Acquisition of Land by Issuance of Stock			(3) 80000	
Purchase of Equipment			(5) 58300	
Reduction of Mortgage			(8) 12900	

EXHIBIT 15-14

Mountain Land Resources, Inc.
Funds Statement Work Sheet (Cash Basis)
for the Period Ended December 31, 1984

	Beginning Balances 12/31/83	Analysis of Accounts		Ending Balances 12/31/84
		Debits	Credits	
Cash	7900	(14) 9700		17600
Accounts Receivable (net)	104900	(9) 1800		106700
Inventory	197500		(10) 10200	187300
Prepaid Expenses	9200		(11) 2200	7000
Land	10000	(3) 80000		90000
Plant and Equipment	577200	(5) 58300	(4) 12300	623200
Accumulated Depreciation	(223600)	(4) 11800	(6) 32100	(243900)
Total Assets	683100			787900
Accounts Payable	71700		(12) 500	72200
Income Taxes Payable	1500		(13) 5500	7000
Notes Payable			(7) 20000	20000
Mortgage Payable	85000	(8) 12900		72100
Common Stock, $1 Par	42500		(3) 40000	82500
Paid-in Capital in Excess of Par--Common Stock	146900		(3) 40000	186900
Retained Earnings	335500	(2) 24900	(1) 36600	347200
Total Liabilities and Stockholders' Equity	683100	199400	199400	787900

	Funds Statement	
Sources of Cash		
Operations:		
Net Income	(1) 36600	
Adjustments to Net Income:		
Gain on Sale of Equipment		(4) 7800
Depreciation	(6) 32100	
Total Working Capital from Operations	60900	
Adjustments to Cash Basis:		
Increase in Accounts Receivable		(9) 1800
Decrease in Inventory	(10) 10200	
Decrease in Prepaid Expenses	(11) 2200	
Increase in Accounts Payable	(12) 500	
Increase in Income Taxes Payable	(13) 5500	
Total Cash from Operations	77500	
Issuance of Stock to Acquire Land	(3) 80000	
Proceeds from Sale of Equipment	(4) 8300	
Proceeds from Long-Term Note	(7) 20000	
Total Sources of Cash	185800	
Uses of Cash		
Payment of Dividends		(2) 24900
Acquisition of Land by Issuance of Stock		(3) 80000
Purchase of Equipment		(5) 58300
Reduction of Mortgage		(8) 12900
Increase in Cash		(14) 9700
Total Uses of Cash		185800

Note that some current accounts do not affect operations, so they do not require adjustments to net income. For example, suppose a company has a decrease in its Short-Term Investment account. The change would involve an addition to cash—the proceeds from the sale of the securities—rather than an adjustment to net income, since this transaction does not involve cash from operations.

Continuing with the Mountain Land illustration, inventory decreased by $10,200. This amount would have to be credited in the work sheet analysis column to explain the change in the inventory account balance, and added as an adjustment to net income in the funds statement section, as shown in Exhibit 15-14 [entry (10)]. Instead of using cash to purchase new inventory, Mountain Land allowed inventory to decline. The cash-basis income, therefore, would be greater than the accrual-basis income by this amount, so the decrease in inventory should be added to the accrual-basis net income figure. Similar reasoning can be used to explain the changes in Prepaid Expenses, Accounts Payable, and Income Taxes Payable, and the corresponding adjustments to accrual-basis net income [entries (11), (12), and (13)]. The cash-basis work sheet is now complete.

You should especially note two items in Exhibit 15-14. First, the total cash from operations ($77,500) is now highlighted. That is, the amount of net income has been converted from an accrual basis to a cash basis. The $77,500 represents the cash that flowed into the company from normal operations during the period. This amount could have been computed directly by converting individual elements on the accrual-basis income statement to a cash basis, as shown in Exhibit 15-15.

EXHIBIT 15-15

Mountain Land Resources, Inc.
Analysis of Income for the Year Ended December 31, 1984

Key:
- (4) Gain on Sale of Equipment
- (6) Depreciation
- (9) Increase in Accounts Receivable (sales not yet collected)
- (10) Decrease in Inventory (inventory sold this period but purchased last period)
- (11) Decrease in Prepaid Expenses (prepaid expenses used this period but paid for last period)
- (12) Increase in Accounts Payable (purchases made this period but not yet paid)
- (13) Increase in Income Taxes Payable (income taxes of this period but not yet paid)

	Accrual Basis	Adjustments Debits	Adjustments Credits	Cash Basis
Net Sales Revenue . . .	$859,400	(9) $1,800		$857,600
Other Revenues	7,800	(4) 7,800		-0-
Total Revenues . . .	$867,200			$857,600
Expenses:				
Cost of Goods Sold . .	$610,100		(10) $10,200 (12) 500	$599,400
Selling and Administrative Expenses	147,000		(11) 2,200	144,800
Depreciation Expense	32,100		(6) 32,100	-0-
Interest Expense	14,200			14,200
Total Expenses . . .	$803,400			$758,400
Income Before Taxes .	$ 63,800			$ 99,200
Income Taxes	27,200		(13) 5,500	21,700
Net Income	$ 36,600			$ 77,500

The second point to be observed in Exhibit 15–15 is that the $9,700 increase in cash has been added as the balancing figure so that total sources of cash equal total uses of cash. In effect, a major use of cash was to increase the Cash account by $9,700. If the Cash account had decreased, the amount of change would have been shown as a source. The formal statement of changes in financial position on a cash basis can now be prepared, as shown in Exhibit 15–16.

EXHIBIT 15–16 **Mountain Land Resources, Inc.**
Statement of Changes in Financial Position (Cash Basis)
for the Year Ended December 31, 1984

Sources of Cash		
Operations:		
Net Income		$ 36,600
Add: Depreciation	$32,100	
Decrease in Inventory	10,200	
Decrease in Prepaid Expenses	2,200	
Increase in Accounts Payable	500	
Increase in Income Taxes Payable	5,500	50,500
		$ 87,100
Subtract: Gain on Sale of Equipment	$ 7,800	
Increase in Accounts Receivable	1,800	9,600
Total Cash from Operations		$ 77,500
Issuance of Stock to Acquire Land		80,000
Proceeds from Sale of Equipment		8,300
Proceeds from Long-Term Note		20,000
Total Sources of Cash		$185,800
Uses of Cash		
Payment of Dividends		$ 24,900
Acquisition of Land by Issuance of Stock		80,000
Purchase of Equipment		58,300
Reduction of Mortgage		12,900
Increase in Cash		9,700
Total Uses of Cash		$185,800

TO SUMMARIZE A cash-basis funds statement, as modified by the all-financial-resources concept, is prepared in basically the same way as a working-capital-basis funds statement. There are two major differences, however. First, with the cash basis, all changes in noncash accounts must be analyzed; with the working-capital basis, only non-working-capital (noncurrent) accounts must be explained because all current accounts are considered in total as working capital. Second, a cash-basis funds statement must highlight total cash generated from operations as one of the major sources of funds. This requires that the amount of net income be converted from an accrual basis to a cash basis. The formal statement of changes in financial position on a cash basis is similar in form and purpose to its counterpart on a working-capital basis. That is, it reports the major sources and uses of funds from internal and external financing and investing activities during an accounting period.

CHAPTER REVIEW

Together with the balance sheet and the income statement, the statement of changes in financial position (the funds statement) is one of the three primary financial statements. A careful analysis of the funds statement will indicate shifts in the operating, investing, and financing policies of a company. The funds statement explains changes in the balance sheet accounts, emphasizing the major sources and uses of funds during a period.

The most common definitions of funds are cash and working capital. However, neither of these concepts is used in its pure form. Rather, both are modified to include the all-financial-resources concept, so that all transactions that reflect significant financing and investing activities are included, whether or not working capital or cash is directly affected.

A statement of changes in financial position may be prepared by following three basic steps.

1. Determine the change in the fund balance for the period.
2. Explain why the change occurred by analyzing all accounts not included in the fund balance. This analysis identifies the major sources and uses of the funds.
3. Prepare a formal funds statement.

A work sheet helps to accumulate and organize the necessary information to be reported in the formal statement of changes in financial position.

The steps required to prepare a cash-basis funds statement are similar to those for a statement based on working capital, except that (1) changes in current asset accounts other than cash and in all current liability accounts must also be analyzed, and (2) the amount of working capital generated from operations must be converted from an accrual basis to a cash basis.

When a funds statement is prepared on a working-capital basis, a schedule similar to Exhibit 15-5 should be attached to show the changes in the individual working-capital accounts. When a cash basis is used, significant changes in the individual working-capital accounts are reflected in the body of the statement, so no such schedule is necessary.

KEY TERMS AND CONCEPTS

all-financial-resources concept (499)
cash concept of funds (499)
funds (499)
noncurrent accounts (504)
statement of changes in financial position (funds statement) (497)
working capital (502)
working-capital concept of funds (499)

REVIEW PROBLEM

Preparing Statements of Changes in Financial Position

Collins Corporation produces clock radios. Comparative income statements and balance sheets for Collins for the years ended December 31, 1984 and 1983, are presented on the next page.

Collins Corporation
Income Statements for the Years Ended December 31, 1984 and 1983

	1984	1983
Net Sales	$600,000	$575,000
Cost of Goods Sold	500,000	460,000
Gross Margin	$100,000	$115,000
Operating Expenses	66,000	60,000
Operating Income	$ 34,000	$ 55,000
Interest Expense	4,000	3,000
Income Before Taxes	$ 30,000	$ 52,000
Income Taxes	12,000	21,000
Net Income	$ 18,000	$ 31,000

Collins Corporation
Balance Sheets as of December 31, 1984 and 1983

Assets	1984	1983
Current Assets:		
Cash	$ 11,000	$ 13,000
Accounts Receivable (net)	92,000	77,000
Inventory	103,000	92,000
Prepaid Expenses	6,000	5,000
Total Current Assets	$212,000	$187,000
Property, Plant, and Equipment:		
Land	$ 61,000	$ 59,000
Machinery and Equipment	172,000	156,000
Less Accumulated Depreciation—Machinery and Equipment	(113,000)	(102,000)
Total Property, Plant, and Equipment	$120,000	$113,000
Other Assets	$ 8,000	$ 7,000
Total Assets	$340,000	$307,000
Liabilities and Stockholders' Equity		
Current Liabilities:		
Accounts Payable	$ 66,000	$ 55,000
Notes Payable	-0-	23,000
Dividends Payable	2,000	-0-
Income Taxes Payable	3,000	5,000
Total Current Liabilities	$ 71,000	$ 83,000
Long-Term Debt	75,000	42,000
Total Liabilities	$146,000	$125,000
Stockholders' Equity:		
Common Stock ($1 par)	$ 10,000	$ 10,000
Paid-in Capital in Excess of Par—Common Stock	16,000	16,000
Retained Earnings	168,000	156,000
Total Stockholders' Equity	$194,000	$182,000
Total Liabilities and Stockholders' Equity	$340,000	$307,000

Additional information:

1. Dividends declared in 1984 amounted to $6,000.
2. Market price per share of stock on December 31, 1984, was $14.50.
3. Machinery and equipment worth $10,000 were acquired through the issuance of a long-term note included in long-term debt.
4. Land was acquired for $2,000 cash.
5. Depreciation of $11,000 is included in operating expenses for 1984.

Required:

Prepare a work sheet and a statement of changes in financial position on a working-capital basis, reflecting the all-financial-resources concept.

Solution

Step 1. Determine the change in working capital—an increase of $37,000—as shown below.

Collins Corporation
Schedule of Changes in Working Capital for the Year Ended December 31, 1984

	Balances at 12/31/83	Balances at 12/31/84	Changes in Working Capital
Current Assets:			
Cash	$ 13,000	$ 11,000	$ (2,000)
Accounts Receivable (net)	77,000	92,000	15,000
Inventory	92,000	103,000	11,000
Prepaid Expenses	5,000	6,000	1,000
Totals	$187,000	$212,000	$ 25,000
Current Liabilities:			
Accounts Payable	$ 55,000	$ 66,000	$ (11,000)
Notes Payable	23,000	-0-	23,000
Dividends Payable	-0-	2,000	(2,000)
Income Taxes Payable	5,000	3,000	2,000
Totals	$ 83,000	$ 71,000	$ 12,000
Working Capital	$104,000	$141,000	$ 37,000

Step 2. Explain why working capital increased $37,000 by identifying the major sources and uses of funds. This requires an analysis of all noncurrent accounts. A work sheet is used.

Collins Corporation
Funds Statement Work Sheet (Working-Capital Basis)
for the Period Ended December 31, 1984

	Beginning Balances 12/31/83	Analysis of Accounts		Ending Balances 12/31/84
		Debits	Credits	
Working Capital	104000	(9) 37000		144000
Non-Working-Capital Assets:				
Land	59000	(3) 2000		61000
Machinery and Equipment	156000	(4) 10000		172000
		(5) 6000		
Accumulated Depreciation--Machinery and Equipment	(102000)		(6) 11000	(113000)
Other Assets	7000	(7) 1000		8000
Total Working Capital and Non-Working-Capital Assets	224000			269000
Non-Working-Capital Liabilities and Stockholders' Equity:				
Long-Term Debt	42000		(4) 10000	75000
			(8) 23000	
Common Stock ($1 Par)	10000			10000
Paid-in-Capital in Excess of Par--Common Stock	16000			16000
Retained Earnings	156000	(2) 6000	(1) 18000	168000
Total Non-Working-Capital Liabilities and Stockholders' Equity	224000	62000	62000	269000
		Funds Statement		
Sources of Working Capital				
Operations:				
Net Income		(1) 18000		
Adjustments to Income:				
Depreciation		(6) 11000		
Total Working Capital from Operations		29000		
Issued Long-Term Note to Purchase Land		(4) 10000		
Issued Additional Long-Term Debt		(8) 23000		
Total Sources of Working Capital		62000		
Uses of Working Capital				
Declared Dividends			(2) 6000	
Purchased Land			(3) 2000	
Purchased Machinery and Equipment by Issuing Long-Term Note			(4) 10000	
Purchased Additional Machinery and Equipment			(5) 6000	
Purchased other Assets			(7) 1000	
Increase in Working Capital			(9) 37000	
Total Uses of Working Capital			62000	

Explanation of entries on work sheet:

(1) Net income increased retained earnings, so it is shown as a source of funds from operations.
(2) The dividends declared reduced retained earnings, so they are reported as a use of funds.
(3) The purchase of land used funds.
(4), (5) The Machinery and Equipment account increased $16,000. Part of the purchase ($10,000) was financed by the issuance of a long-term note. The $10,000 portion is shown as both a source and a use of funds in keeping with the all-financial-resources concept.
(6) Depreciation of $11,000 was charged to expense during the year, accounting for the increase in the Accumulated Depreciation account. Since the depreciation entry does not affect working capital but has been subtracted in computing net income, the $11,000 must be added back to net income to show the total working capital provided by operations during 1984.
(7) Other assets were purchased, which used funds.
(8) Additional long-term debt provided funds.
(9) Funds were used to increase working capital during the year. The $37,000 is the balancing amount needed for total sources to equal total uses of funds. The $37,000 increase is supported by the schedule of changes in working capital.

Step 3. Prepare a formal statement of changes in financial position, as shown at the right.

Collins Corporation
Statement of Changes in Financial Position
(Working-Capital Basis)
for the Year Ended December 31, 1984

Sources of Working Capital		
Operations:		
Net Income	$18,000	
Add Depreciation Expense	11,000	
Total Working Capital from Operations		$29,000
Issuance of Long-Term Note to Purchase Machinery and Equipment		10,000
Issuance of Other Long-Term Debt		23,000
Total Sources of Working Capital		$62,000
Uses of Working Capital		
Declaration of Dividends		$ 6,000
Purchase of Land		2,000
Purchase of Machinery and Equipment Through Issuance of Long-Term Debt		10,000
Other Purchases of Machinery and Equipment		6,000
Purchase of Other Assets		1,000
Increase in Working Capital		37,000
Total Uses of Working Capital		$62,000

DISCUSSION QUESTIONS

1 What is the purpose of a statement of changes in financial position (a funds statement)?

2 Along with the balance sheet and the income statement, the statement of changes in financial position is one of the primary financial statements. Why?

3 What is the relationship between the statement of changes in financial position and the balance sheet? Between the funds statement and the income statement?

4 What are the major categories of sources and uses of funds?

5 What is the purpose of using the all-financial-resources concept of funds in preparing the statement of changes in financial position?

6 List three steps that may be followed in using a work sheet to prepare a funds statement.

7 Why are certain items added to or subtracted from net income in computing the amount of funds from operations?

8 Suppose that a company decides to shift from the straight-line method of depreciation to an accelerated method of depreciation. How does this decision affect the amount of working capital from operations in the early years?

9 In order to determine the total sources of funds from operations, depreciation must be added to net income. Does this mean that depreciation is a source of funds? Explain.

10 For each of the following transactions or events, determine whether it is a source of funds or a use of funds, or whether it has no effect on funds, when a statement of changes in financial position is prepared on a working-capital basis.

(a) Purchase of inventory for cash.
(b) Collection of an account receivable.
(c) Sale of an operational asset at a gain.
(d) Declaration of a cash dividend.
(e) Payment of a cash dividend.
(f) Acquisition of land by issuing a long-term note.
(g) Purchase of inventory on account.
(h) Payment of an account payable.
(i) Sale of an operational asset at a loss.

11 For each transaction or event listed in Question 10, determine whether it is a source of funds or a use of funds, or whether it has no effect on funds, when a statement of changes in financial position is prepared on a cash basis.

12 Describe the differences between a statement of changes in financial position prepared under the working-capital concept of funds and one prepared under the cash concept of funds.

13 Is it possible for a company to report an increase in working capital provided by operations even though a net loss is reported for the year? Explain.

14 Briefly, explain why a company's cash balance may have decreased during the year, even though the company reported a substantial net income.

15 In advising a company with respect to the preparation of a statement of changes in financial position, what factors would you consider in choosing between the working capital and cash concepts of funds?

EXERCISES

E15–1 Analysis of Changes in Account Balances

The treasurer of Adams Company provides you with the following information.

Adams Company
Partial Balance Sheets
as of December 31, 1984 and 1983

	1984	1983
Current Assets:		
Cash	$ 19,000	$ 30,000
Accounts Receivable	50,000	42,000
Inventory	100,000	80,000
Prepaid Insurance	6,000	5,000
Total Current Assets	$175,000	$157,000
Current Liabilities:		
Accounts Payable	$ 50,100	$ 72,000
Short-Term Notes Payable	30,000	22,000
Accrued Salaries Payable	1,400	1,500
Total Current Liabilities	$ 81,500	$ 95,500

Determine the change in each of the following from 1983 to 1984; indicate whether the change is an increase or a decrease in the account balance.

1. Current Assets.
2. Accounts Receivable.
3. Prepaid Insurance.
4. Short-Term Notes Payable.
5. Current Liabilities.

E15–2 The Change in Working Capital

On the basis of the data in E15–1, answer the following questions:

1. What was the amount of working capital on December 31, 1983?
2. What was the amount of working capital on December 31, 1984?
3. What was the change in working capital from 1983 to 1984?

E15–3 The Change in Working Capital

Romero Company, a manufacturer of burglar alarms, has provided you with the following information.

	1984	1983
Current Assets:		
Cash	$ 22,000	$ 19,000
Accounts Receivable	21,000	24,000
Marketable Securities	44,000	38,000
Inventory	67,000	73,000
Prepaid Insurance	4,000	3,000
Total Current Assets	$158,000	$157,000
Current Liabilities:		
Accounts Payable	$ 40,000	$ 46,000
Interest Payable	8,000	7,000
Dividends Payable	9,000	2,000
Notes Payable	71,000	85,000
Total Current Liabilities	$128,000	$140,000

Determine the change in working capital from 1983 to 1984.

E15–4 Working Capital Provided by Operations

Keeler Corporation had only five transactions during the year.

a. Sold merchandise costing $6,000 for $10,000 on account. The company uses the perpetual inventory method.

b. Paid $100 rent for office space.

c. Paid this month's wages of $500.

d. Received a bill of $60 for insurance for the year.

e. Depreciation on equipment used by the company was $2,000.

Complete the following:

1. Prepare the journal entry for each of these transactions.
2. Indicate whether each transaction provided working capital, used working capital, or had no effect on working capital.

3. Determine the net amount of working capital provided or used by these five transactions.
4. Prepare an income statement for Keeler Corporation.
5. Compare Keeler Corporation's net income from operations with the net working capital provided by operations, as calculated in (3).

E15–5 Cash Provided by Operations

In addition to the five transactions listed in E15–4, assume that $3,000 of accounts receivable were collected by Keeler Corporation and that $5,000 of additional merchandise was purchased on account.

1. Prepare the journal entries for these additional transactions.
2. What was the net cash provided or used during the year?
3. Compare Keeler Corporation's net income from operating the business with the net amount of cash provided by these transactions.

E15–6 Working Capital Provided by Operations

Consider the following information.

Net Income	$26,000
Depreciation:	
Machinery	5,000
Equipment	1,200
Gain on Sale of Investments	4,000
Loss on Sale of Plant	3,500

Prepare the Working Capital Provided by Operations portion of the statement of changes in financial position.

E15–7 Transaction Analysis

Following are transactions of High Crane Company.

a. Sold equipment for $1,000. The original cost was $15,700 with accumulated depreciation of $14,000.
b. Purchased plant and equipment costing $710,000 by issuing a 20-year note.
c. Received $5,000 of the principal and $100 interest on a long-term note.
d. Bondholders converted bonds with a $100,000 face value into 50,000 shares of $1 par common stock. The common stock was selling at $2 per share and the bonds were selling at par at the time of the conversion.

Complete the following.

1. Prepare journal entries for each of these transactions.
2. Indicate the amount of working capital provided or used by each transaction.

E15–8 Working Capital from Operations

For the year ended December 31, 1983, Hawkin, Inc. reported net income of $400,000. Additional information is as follows:

Depreciation Expense—Plant and Equipment	$350,000
Allowance for Doubtful Accounts	70,000

On the basis of this information, compute the working capital from operations for a 1983 statement of changes in financial position.

E15–9 The Change in Working Capital

The following information was taken from the 1984 accounting records of Caroline Corporation.

Purchase of Plant and Equipment	$280,000
Collection of Accounts Receivable	400,000
Payment of Accounts Payable	300,000
Proceeds from Long-Term Debt	150,000
Dividends Declared on Common Stock	90,000
Purchase of Treasury Stock	20,000
Payment on Long-Term Debt	50,000
Working Capital Provided from Operations	200,000
Working Capital at December 31, 1983	900,000

If funds are defined as working capital, what should be the change in working capital shown on the December 31, 1984, statement of changes in financial position for Caroline Corporation?

E15–10 Working Capital Provided by Operations

Fraizer Corporation had net income of $300,000 for 1983. The following additional information was taken from the 1983 financial statements.

Provision for Uncollectible Accounts Receivable	$ 91,000
Interest Expense on Long-Term Debt	273,000
Depreciation Expense on Plant and Equipment	320,000
Amortization of Goodwill	8,000

If funds are defined as working capital, what is the amount of working capital provided by operations for 1983?

E15–11 Cash Provided by Operations

The following information was taken from the comparative financial statements of the Pachinco Corporation for the years ended December 31, 1983 and 1984.

Net Income for 1984	$140,000
Depreciation Expense—Equipment for 1984	60,000
Amortization of Goodwill for 1984	10,000
Interest Expense on Short-Term Debt—1984	3,500
Dividends Declared and Paid in 1984	65,000

	Account Balances at December 31 1984	1983
Accounts Receivable (net)	$30,000	$43,000
Inventory	50,000	42,000
Accounts Payable	56,000	59,400

If funds are defined as cash, what is the amount of cash provided by operations for 1984?

E15-12 Analyzing Accounts

Comparative balance sheets for Benito Corporation for the years ending December 31, 1984 and 1983, are as follows:

Benito Corporation
Comparative Balance Sheets
as of December 31, 1984 and 1983

	December 31 1984	1983
Current Assets	$23,700	$16,000
Equipment	61,500	60,000
Accumulated Depreciation	(21,800)	(21,000)
Goodwill	24,000	25,000
Total Assets	$87,400	$80,000
Current Liabilities	$18,000	$ 8,000
Bonds Payable	20,000	30,000
Common Stock	55,000	55,000
Retained Earnings	(5,600)	(13,000)
Total Liabilities and Stockholders' Equity	$87,400	$80,000

Additional information:

a. During 1984 the corporation sold old equipment at its book value (no gain or loss) of $3,800 and purchased new equipment costing $7,500.

b. During 1984 bonds payable with a face value of $10,000 were retired.

c. Retained earnings was affected only by the 1984 net income or loss. There were no dividends paid during the year.

On the basis of the above:

1. What was the amount of net income or net loss for 1984?

2. How much working capital was provided by operations in 1984?

E15-13 The Change in Working Capital

The following information was taken from Rio Hondo Company's financial statements for 1983.

Proceeds from Short-Term Debt	$ 60,000
Proceeds from Long-Term Debt	200,000
Purchase of Operational Assets	160,000
Purchase of Inventory	400,000
Proceeds from the Sale of Rio Hondo Company Stock	100,000

If funds are defined as working capital, what is the increase or decrease in working capital for 1983 as a result of the foregoing information?

E15-14 Funds Statement Preparation: Working-Capital Basis

The following data are from the 1984 and 1983 balance sheets for Sleep-Easy Corporation.

Sleep-Easy Corporation
Comparative Balance Sheets
as of December 31, 1984 and 1983

Assets	1984	1983
Cash	$ 16,400	$ 8,000
Accounts Receivable	36,000	30,000
Inventory	34,000	40,000
Equipment	40,000	28,000
Accumulated Depreciation	(14,400)	(12,000)
Total Assets	$112,000	$94,000
Liabilities and Stockholders' Equity		
Accounts Payable	$ 20,000	$ 16,000
Long-Term Notes Payable	20,000	10,000
Capital Stock	50,000	50,000
Retained Earnings	22,000	18,000
Total Liabilities and Stockholders' Equity	$112,000	$ 94,000

Additional information:

a. Net income for the year as reported on the income statement was $17,000.

b. Equipment that cost $6,000 and had a book value of $400 was sold during the year for $1,400.

c. Dividends amounting to $13,000 were declared and paid.

Prepare a work sheet and a formal statement of changes in financial position on a working-capital basis, including a supporting schedule of changes in working capital.

E15-15 Funds Statement Preparation: Cash Basis

The following data (in thousands of dollars) are taken from the records of Wagstaff Company.

Wagstaff Company
Balance Sheets
as of December 31, 1984 and 1983

Assets	1984	1983
Cash	$ 30	$ 28
Marketable Securities	15	10
Accounts Receivable	40	32
Inventory	35	40
Equipment	140	130
Total Assets	$260	$240
Liabilities and Stockholders' Equity		
Current Accounts Payable	$ 47	$ 54
Long-Term Debt	53	46
Capital Stock	105	100
Retained Earnings	55	40
Total Liabilities and Stockholders' Equity	$260	$240

Wagstaff Company
Statement of Retained Earnings
for the Year Ended December 31, 1984

Balance, December 31, 1983	$40
Net Income for the Year	18
	$58
Less Dividends Paid on December 31, 1984	(3)
Balance, December 31, 1984	$55

Additional data:

a. Depreciation of $16 was charged against operations in 1984.

b. Long-term debt of $20 was issued for equipment in the same amount.

Prepare a work sheet and a statement of changes in financial position on a cash basis for Wagstaff Company for 1984.

PROBLEMS

P15–1 The Funds Statement: Working-Capital Basis

The 1984 and 1983 balance sheets of Plymouth Electric Company are as follows:

Plymouth Electric Company
Balance Sheets
as of December 31, 1984 and 1983

Assets	1984	1983
Cash	$ 9,000	$ 4,000
Accounts Receivable	14,000	6,000
Inventory	10,000	11,000
Plant and Equipment	59,000	34,000
Less Accumulated Depreciation	(17,000)	(12,000)
Goodwill	18,000	19,000
Total Assets	$93,000	$62,000
Liabilities and Stockholders' Equity		
Accounts Payable	$11,000	$ 9,000
Accrued Wages Payable	2,000	3,000
Bond Payable	30,000	10,000
Common Stock	29,000	26,000
Retained Earnings	21,000	14,000
Total Liabilities and Stockholders' Equity	$93,000	$62,000

Additional information:

a. Plymouth Electric Company's net income for 1984 was $11,000.

b. The company paid dividends of $4,000 to shareholders in 1984.

c. No equipment was sold during 1984.

Required:

1. Prepare a schedule of changes in working capital for Plymouth Electric for 1984.
2. Prepare a working-capital-basis statement of changes in financial position for Plymouth Electric for 1984. (A work sheet is not required but may be useful in solving this problem.)

P15–2 Reconstruction of a Balance Sheet

A flood recently destroyed the records of Kingline Manufacturing Company. Luckily, however, the president had taken home the 1983 balance sheet and the statement of changes in financial position for the year just past, 1984. Correspondence from creditors indicates that the current liabilities of Kingline at December 31, 1984, were $20,000.

Kingline Manufacturing Company
Balance Sheet as of December 31, 1983

Current Assets	$ 40,000
Property, Plant, and Equipment	120,000
Less Accumulated Depreciation	(24,000)
Goodwill	9,000
Total Assets	$145,000
Current Liabilities	$ 24,000
Bonds Payable	60,000
Capital Stock	40,000
Retained Earnings	21,000
Total Liabilities and Stockholders' Equity	$145,000

Kingline Manufacturing Company
Statement of Changes in Financial Position
(Working-Capital Basis)
for the Year Ended December 31, 1984

Sources of Working Capital		
Operations:		
Net Income		$18,000
Add:		
Depreciation	$6,000	
Amortization of Goodwill	1,000	7,000
Total Working Capital from Operations		$25,000
Issuance of Common Stock		22,000
Sale of Equipment (Original Cost $10,000)		6,000
Total Sources of Working Capital		$53,000
Uses of Working Capital		
Payment of Dividends		$ 4,000
Retirement of Bonds		25,000
Acquisition of a Patent		5,000
Increase in Working Capital		19,000
Total Uses of Working Capital		$53,000

Required:

The president of Kingline has hired you as a consultant. Prepare a work sheet that will show the amounts in the balance sheet accounts at December 31, 1984.

P15-3 The Funds Statement: Cash Basis

The treasurer of Rocky Mountain Trucking Company has received a request from a creditor for a cash-basis statement of changes in financial position. The treasurer has hired you to prepare the statement and has provided you with a working-capital-basis statement of changes in financial position and partial balance sheets for 1984 and 1983.

Rocky Mountain Trucking Company
(Partial) Balance Sheets
as of December 31, 1984 and 1983

	1984	1983
Current Assets:		
Cash	$15,000	$12,000
Accounts Receivable	4,000	6,000
Inventory	8,000	7,000
Prepaid Expenses	3,000	1,000
Total Current Assets	$30,000	$26,000
Current Liabilities:		
Accounts Payable	$ 8,000	$ 6,000
Accrued Wages	2,000	3,000
Income Taxes Payable	7,000	3,000
Total Current Liabilities	$17,000	$12,000

Rocky Mountain Trucking Company
Statement of Changes in Financial Position
(Working-Capital Basis)
for the Year Ended December 31, 1984

Sources of Working Capital		
Operations:		
Net Income	$36,000	
Add Depreciation	4,000	
Total Working Capital from Operations		$40,000
Issuance of Long-Term Note		3,000
Decrease in Working Capital		1,000
Total Sources of Working Capital		$44,000
Uses of Working Capital		
Purchase of Equipment		$30,000
Declaration and Payment of Dividends		9,000
Payment of Long-Term Debt		5,000
Total Uses of Working Capital		$44,000

Required:

Prepare a statement of changes in financial position based on the cash concept of funds for 1984. (A work sheet is not required but may be useful in solving this problem.)

P15-4 The Funds Statement: Working-Capital Basis

The following information was provided by the treasurer of R. U. Forit, Inc., a manufacturer of voting machine equipment, for the year 1983.

a. Net income for the year was $134,000.
b. Depreciation of equipment for the year was $27,000.
c. Doubtful accounts expense was $9,000.
d. Amortization of goodwill was $2,000.
e. Write-off of bad debts was $11,000.
f. Collection of accounts receivable was $38,000.
g. Payments on accounts payable were $39,000.
h. Rent expense was $11,000.
i. 20,000 shares of $10 par stock were issued for $240,000.
j. Land was acquired by issuance of a $100,000 bond that would have sold for $102,000.
k. Equipment was purchased at a cost of $84,000.
l. Dividends of $6,000 were declared.
m. $5,000 of dividends that had been declared the previous year were paid.
n. A machine used on the manufacturing assembly line was sold for $8,000. The machine had a book value of $7,000.
o. Another machine with a book value of $500 was scrapped and was reported as an ordinary loss.

Required:

Prepare a statement of changes in financial position for R. U. Forit, Inc., for the year ending December 31, 1983, using the working-capital concept of funds.

P15–5 The Funds Statement: Working-Capital Basis

Balance sheets and additional information for Bickel Company for 1984 and 1983 are presented here. (All numbers are shown rounded to the nearest thousand, with the final three zeros omitted.)

Bickel Company
Balance Sheets
as of December 31, 1984 and 1983

Assets	1984	1983
Cash	$ 159	$1,638
Inventory	2,449	1,634
Equipment	8,600	7,000
Less Accumulated Depreciation	(405)	(293)
Total Assets	$10,803	$9,979
Liabilities and Stockholders' Equity		
Accounts Payable	$ 853	$ 781
Bonds Payable	3,500	4,000
Common Stock	3,800	3,000
Retained Earnings	2,650	2,198
Total Liabilities and Stockholders' Equity	$10,803	$9,979

Additional information:

a. Net income for 1984 was $677.

b. A dividend of $225 was declared to shareholders of record on March 31, 1984.

c. Equipment was purchased for $1,600 during 1984. No equipment was disposed of during 1984.

d. Stock was issued for $800 to help finance the purchase of equipment.

e. Bonds were retired during 1984 at face value.

Required:

1. Using the working-capital basis, prepare a work sheet and a formal statement of changes in financial position, including a schedule of changes in working capital.

2. **Interpretive Question** How was Bickel able to finance its equipment purchases in 1984?

P15–6 Unifying Problem: The Working-Capital and Cash Concepts of Funds

Balance sheets and additional information for European Fashions, Inc. for the years 1984 and 1983 are presented below. (All numbers are shown rounded to the nearest thousand, with the final three zeros omitted.)

European Fashions, Inc.
Balance Sheets
as of December 31, 1984 and 1983

Assets	1984	1983
Cash	$ 549	$ 633
Accounts Receivable	354	211
Advances to Suppliers	245	105
Inventory	614	562
Long-Term Investments	620	807
Machinery and Equipment	812	344
Accumulated Depreciation	(441)	(224)
Land	344	400
Total Assets	$3,097	$2,838
Liabilities and Stockholders' Equity		
Accounts Payable	$ 583	$ 488
Short-Term Note Payable	-0-	200
Payroll Taxes Payable	147	233
Noncurrent Liabilities	657	767
Common Stock, Par $5	1,250	800
Paid-in Capital in Excess of Par	155	75
Retained Earnings	305	275
Total Liabilities and Stockholders' Equity	$3,097	$2,838

Additional information:

a. Net income during 1984 was $108 and dividends of $78 were declared.

b. Machinery with a book value of $85 (cost, $120; accumulated depreciation, $35) was sold for $92.

c. Long-term investments purchased for $187 were sold for $246.

d. A petition for a zoning change was unsuccessful and land was disposed of at a loss of $32.

e. Common stock was sold for $530.

f. Noncurrent liabilities were retired at face value.

Required:

1. Using a work sheet, prepare a statement of changes in financial position for 1984 on a working-capital basis.

2. Using a work sheet, prepare a statement of changes in financial position for 1984 on a cash basis.

P15–7 The Funds Statement: Working-Capital Basis

The president of Fast Food Company has received letters from stockholders inquiring about some financial aspects of the company's operations for the year 1984. One of the stockholders cannot understand how the firm could retire more debt than it earned in after-tax income. Another stockholder said that the firm made more money from depreciation than from selling food.

Required:

1. Using the following information, prepare a work sheet and a statement of changes in financial position on

a working-capital basis. (All numbers are rounded to the nearest thousand, with the final three zeros omitted.)

2. **Interpretive Question** Write a one-paragraph response to each of the stockholders.

Fast Food Corporation
Income Statement
for the Year Ended December 31, 1984

Revenues	$740
Cost of Goods Sold	351
Gross Margin	$389
Expenses:	
Advertising Expense	$ 86
Depreciation Expense	126
Rent Expense	68
Interest Expense	29
Utilities Expense	17
Loss on Sale of Equipment	3
General Administration Expenses	15
Total Expenses	$344
Income Before Taxes	$ 45
Income Taxes	21
Net Income	$ 24
Dividends	5
Increase in Retained Earnings	$ 19

Fast Food Corporation
Comparative Balance Sheets
as of December 31, 1984 and 1983

	1984	1983
Current Assets	$ 47	$ 30
Property, Plant, and Equipment	379	352
Accumulated Depreciation	(139)	(39)
Total Assets	$287	$343
Current Liabilities	$ 38	$ 29
Long-Term Debt	21	131
Total Liabilities	$ 59	$160
Common Stock	$204	$178
Retained Earnings	24	5
Total Stockholders' Equity	$228	$183
Total Liabilities and Stockholders' Equity	$287	$343

Additional information:

a. Equipment with a book value of $9 was sold for $6 (cost, $35; accumulated depreciation, $26).

b. Additional equipment was purchased and long-term debt was retired.

c. Common stock was sold for cash.

P15-8 The Funds Statement: Cash Basis

Comparative balance sheets for Mirror Lake Corporation as of December 31, 1984 and 1983, are shown here.

Mirror Lake Corporation
Balance Sheets
as of December 31, 1984 and 1983

Assets	**1984**	**1983**
Cash	$ 105,000	$ 115,000
Accounts Receivable (net)	267,000	273,000
Merchandise Inventory	685,000	642,000
Prepaid Expenses	13,000	8,000
Office Equipment	60,000	61,700
Accumulated Depreciation—Office Equipment	(20,000)	(19,000)
Store Equipment	400,000	375,000
Accumulated Depreciation—Store Equipment	(110,000)	(75,000)
Total Assets	$1,400,000	$1,380,700
Liabilities and Stockholders' Equity		
Notes Payable	$ 20,000	$ 25,000
Accounts Payable	173,000	176,000
Common Stock ($5 Par)	805,000	800,000
Paid-in Capital in Excess of Par—Common Stock	55,000	53,500
Retained Earnings	347,000	326,200
Total Liabilities and Stockholders' Equity	$1,400,000	$1,380,700

Additional information:

a. Net income for 1984 was $47,300.

b. Depreciation on office equipment was $3,000; depreciation on store equipment was $35,000.

c. Office equipment costing $300 was purchased during the year. Fully depreciated office equipment costing $2,000 was discarded and its cost and accumulated depreciation were removed from the accounts.

d. A stock dividend was declared and distributed during the year. The shares were selling for $6.50 per share when the dividend was declared. The total distribution amounted to 1,000 shares.

e. Cash dividends of $20,000 were paid during the year.

f. The only change in the Store Equipment account came from the purchase of additional equipment during 1984.

Required:

Prepare a work sheet and a statement of changes in financial position, assuming that funds are defined as cash.

P15-9 Unifying Problem: The Funds Statement, Preparation and Analysis

The financial statements of Consolidated Department Stores and Amalgamated Retail Corporation follow. Consolidated Stores and Amalgamated Corporation are competing firms within their marketing region. As an investment adviser, you have been asked to identify the financial policies of the two firms and explain the similarities and differences between them. (All numbers are shown rounded to the nearest thousand, with the final three zeros omitted.)

Consolidated Department Stores, Inc.
Income Statement
for the Year Ended December 31, 1984

Sales Revenue	$1,290
Cost of Goods Sold	978
Gross Margin	$ 312
Operating Expenses:	
Depreciation Expense	$ 14
Sales and Administration Expenses	105
Other Expenses	87
Total Operating Expenses	$ 206
Income Before Taxes	$ 106
Income Taxes	51
Net Income	$ 55
Dividends Paid	10
Increase in Retained Earnings	$ 45

Consolidated Department Stores, Inc.
Balance Sheets
as of December 31, 1984 and 1983

Assets	**1984**	**1983**
Cash	$ 852	$ 725
Accounts Receivable	461	448
Appliances Inventory	38	225
Housewares Inventory	101	301
Clothing Inventory	87	427
Land	1,240	1,240
Store Fixtures	369	369
Less Accumulated Depreciation—Store Fixtures	(51)	(37)
Total Assets	$3,097	$3,698
Liabilities and Stockholders' Equity		
Liabilities:		
Accounts Payable	$ 175	$ 378
Short-Term Notes Payable	525	768
Long-Term Debt	804	1,004
Total Liabilities	$1,504	$2,150
Stockholders' Equity:		
Common Stock	$ 448	$ 448
Paid-in Capital in Excess of Par	500	500
Retained Earnings	645	600
Total Stockholders' Equity	$1,593	$1,548
Total Liabilities and Stockholders' Equity	$3,097	$3,698

Amalgamated Retail Corporation
Income Statement
for the Year Ended December 31, 1984

Sales Revenue	$1,233
Cost of Goods Sold	1,018
Gross Margin	$ 215
Operating Expenses:	
Depreciation Expense	$ 6
Sales and Administration Expenses	110
Other Expenses	41
Total Operating Expenses	$ 157
Income from Operations	$ 58
Gain on Sale of Real Estate	110
Income Before Taxes	$ 168
Less Income Taxes	61
Net Income	$ 107
Dividends Paid	0
Increase in Retained Earnings	$ 107

Amalgamated Retail Corporation
Balance Sheets
as of December 31, 1984 and 1983

Assets	**1984**	**1983**
Cash	$ 149	$ 761
Accounts Receivable	163	151
Appliances Inventory	796	142
Housewares Inventory	618	253
Clothing Inventory	807	317
Land	1,159	1,639
Store Fixtures	281	255
Less Accumulated Depreciation—Store Fixtures	(31)	(25)
Total Assets	$3,942	$3,493
Liabilities and Stockholders' Equity		
Liabilities:		
Accounts Payable	$ 270	$ 300
Short-Term Notes Payable	601	491
Long-Term Debt	709	1,102
Total Liabilities	$1,580	$1,893
Stockholders' Equity:		
Common Stock ($1 Par)	$ 750	$ 500
Paid-in Capital in Excess of Par	840	435
Retained Earnings	772	665
Total Stockholders' Equity	$2,362	$1,600
Total Liabilities and Stockholders' Equity	$3,942	$3,493

Required:

1. Prepare a work sheet and a statement of changes in financial position for Consolidated Department Stores using the working-capital concept of funds.

2. **Interpretive Question** Does the working-capital concept reveal what changes are taking place in the firm's assets?

3. Prepare a work sheet and a statement of changes in financial position for Amalgamated Retail Corporation using the working-capital concept of funds.

4. **Interpretive Question** How has management changed Amalgamated's commercial strategy for 1984 in contrast to 1983?

5. **Interpretive Question** Contrast the postures of the two firms. Which firm would benefit most from increased consumer spending during 1985? Which firm would be more seriously affected if 1985 were a recession year?

P15-10 Unifying Problem: The Working-Capital and Cash Concepts of Funds

A stockholder of Alford Mining and Smelting Corporation has written to the president inquiring how the company was able to operate in 1984 and 1985 despite the fact that each year the income statement showed a substantial net loss. The president has sent the stockholder's letter to the controller, who has asked you to make an analysis that can be used as the basis for a response. The controller asks you to prepare a statement of changes in financial position for both 1984 and 1985. In order to assess the relative merits of the cash concept and the working-capital concept of funds, the controller asks you to prepare the statement for 1984 on a cash basis and for 1985 on a working-capital basis. Following are comparative balance sheets and income statements for 1984 and 1985 for Alford Mining. (All numbers are shown rounded to the nearest thousand, with the final three zeros omitted.)

Alford Mining and Smelting Corporation
Balance Sheets
as of December 31, 1985, 1984, and 1983

Assets	**1985**	**1984**	**1983**
Cash	$ 800	$ 987	$ 1,132
Accounts Receivable	422	271	328
Ore Stockpile—Bauxite	548	516	493
Galena	222	307	358
Metal Ingots—Aluminum	512	882	543
Lead	151	490	857
Tin	788	774	745
Land	6,390	6,974	5,491
Machinery and Equipment	4,635	3,839	3,564
Accumulated Depreciation	(1,500)	(1,391)	(1,132)
Total Assets	$12,968	$13,649	$12,379

Liabilities and Stockholders' Equity	**1985**	**1984**	**1983**
Liabilities:			
Accounts Payable	$ 1,724	$ 1,681	$ 1,951
Short-Term Notes Payable—Banks	578	373	352
Total Liabilities	$ 2,302	$ 2,054	$ 2,303
Stockholders' Equity:			
Common Stock	$ 7,000	$ 7,000	$ 5,000
Paid-in Capital in Excess of Par—Common Stock	2,000	2,000	1,000
Retained Earnings	1,666	2,595	4,076
Total Stockholders' Equity	$10,666	$11,595	$10,076
Total Liabilities and Stockholders' Equity	$12,968	$13,649	$12,379

Alford Mining and Smelting Corporation
Income Statements
for the Years Ended December 31, 1985 and 1984

	1985	**1984**
Revenues	$6,303	$ 7,408
Operating Expenses:		
Wages and Salaries Expense	$5,973	$ 6,421
Supplies Expense	934	1,637
Depreciation Expense	256	259
Interest Expense	58	37
Other Expenses	11	235
Total Operating Expenses	$7,232	$ 8,589
Net Loss	$ (929)	$(1,181)
Dividends Paid	—	300
Decrease in Retained Earnings	$ (929)	$(1,481)

Additional information:

a. Revenues included a gain of $23 on the sale of equipment during 1985 (cost, $240; accumulated depreciation, $147).

b. The land was sold at book value.

Required:

Using the foregoing financial statement information for 1984 and 1985, prepare the following.

1. A statement of changes in financial position for 1984, on a cash basis.

2. A statement of changes in financial position for 1985, on a working-capital basis.

3. **Interpretive Question** Comment on how the operating losses are being financed in this case.

P15–11 Unifying Problem: Funds Statement Analysis

The following statement of changes in financial position was prepared by Modicum Corporation's accountant.

Modicum Corporation
Statement of Changes in Financial Position
for the Year Ended December 31, 1984

Sources of Funds		
Net Income	$ 51,000	
Add: Depreciation	59,000	
Increase in Long-Term Debt	178,000	
Changes in Current Receivables and Inventories, Less Current Liabilities	11,000	$299,000
Subtract: Gain on Sale of Equipment		2,000
Total Sources of Funds		$297,000
Uses of Funds		
Net Expenditures for Property, Plant, and Equipment		$202,000
Cash Dividends		33,000
Investments Purchased		9,000
Increase in Cash		53,000
Total Uses of Funds		$297,000

Additional information:

a. A transaction only partially reflected in the above statement occurred on July 1, 1984, when 16,000 shares of Modicum stock (par value, $5; market value, $6) were issued to bondholders to cancel $100,000 of the face value of bonds payable that had a carrying value of $93,000 on that date (the market price per $1,000 bond on that date was 96).

b. Transactions in property, plant, and equipment were as follows:

Purchase of Property, Plant, and Equipment	$212,000
Sale of Equipment at a Gain of $2,000 (cost, $15,000; accumulated depreciation, $7,000)	10,000
Net Acquisitions of Property, Plant, and Equipment	$202,000

Required:

1. What concept of funds was used in preparing this statement?
2. How should the exchange of stock for bonds have been presented on the statement?
3. What was the amount of cash generated from the sale of the property, plant, and equipment?
4. What is the cash generated from operations?
5. **Interpretive Question** What factors should a company consider in choosing between the cash concept of funds and the working-capital concept in preparing a statement such as the one presented?

SUPPLEMENT

Using the T-Account Approach to Prepare a Statement of Changes in Financial Position

This supplement illustrates how to prepare a statement of changes in financial position using a T-account approach. The T-account approach produces the same results as the columnar work sheet approach, and follows the same three-step procedure. It differs only in the format used. So that you can see the similarities between the two approaches, we will use the data for Mountain Land Resources, Inc., as presented in Exhibits 15-3 and 15-4, on pages 501 and 502. For this supplement, we will define funds as working capital, applied on the all-financial-resources basis.

STEP 1: DETERMINE THE CHANGE IN WORKING CAPITAL

The first step is to determine the change in working capital. This is done by preparing a schedule like the one in Exhibit 15-5 on page 503. The beginning and ending balances of all current asset and current liability accounts are listed. Then, the beginning and ending working capital is determined. Since the beginning balance was $246,300 and the ending balance was $239,400, working capital decreased $6,900 during the period. This change in working capital is shown in a T-account as follows:

Working Capital

Beginning Balance 246,300	6,900 . . . . **Decrease in Working Capital**
Ending Balance 239,400	

STEP 2: EXPLAIN THE CHANGE IN WORKING CAPITAL

To explain why working capital decreased $6,900, we need to analyze all non-working-capital accounts. With the work sheet approach, we entered the change in each account in the analysis section of the work sheet, and the offsetting debits or credits in the funds statement section. With the T-account approach, we follow the General Ledger format. Thus, a T-account is prepared for each account that has changed, and a master T-account called Sources and Uses of Funds is established to receive the offsetting amounts. When the analysis is complete, the formal statement of changes in financial position can be prepared from this master T-account.

The T-accounts are provided below. Each entry is keyed to an explanation. As before, we analyze the Retained Earnings account first, then we continue in balance sheet order, beginning with the Land account.

Retained Earnings

	335,500 . . . . Beg. Bal.
	36,600 1
2 24,900	
	347,200 . . . . End. Bal.

Working Capital

Beg. Bal. 246,300	
	6,900 9
End. Bal. 239,400	

Land

Beg. Bal. 10,000	
3 80,000	
End. Bal. 90,000	

Plant and Equipment

Beg. Bal. 577,200	
5 58,300	12,300 4
End. Bal. 623,200	

Accumulated Depreciation

	223,600 . . . . Beg. Bal.
4 11,800	
	32,100 6
	243,900 . . . . End. Bal.

Notes Payable

	-0-
	20,000 7
	20,000 . . . . End. Bal.

Mortgage Payable

	85,000 . . . . Beg. Bal.
8 12,900	
	72,100 . . . . End. Bal.

Common Stock

	42,500 . . . . Beg. Bal.
	40,000 3
	82,500 . . . . End. Bal.

Paid-in Capital in Excess of Par

	Beg.
	146,900 . . . . Bal.
	40,000 3
	End.
	186,900 . . . . Bal.

Sources and Uses of Funds

Operations:	24,900 2
1 36,600	80,000 3
4 . . . . (7,800)	58,300 5
6 32,100	12,900 8
Working Capital from Operations	
. . . . 60,900	
3 80,000	
4 8,300	
7 20,000	
9 6,900	
176,100	176,100

Explanation of entries:

1. Net income, $36,600; a source of funds.
2. Dividends declared and paid, $24,900; a use of funds.
3. Land purchased by issuance of stock, $80,000; both a source and a use of funds under the all-financial-resources concept.
4. Proceeds from sale of equipment, $8,300, adjustment to funds from operations due to gain ($7,800); gain equals proceeds of $8,300 minus net book value of equipment sold (cost of $12,300 − accumulated depreciation of $11,800).
5. Purchases of equipment, $58,300; a use of funds.
6. Depreciation for the year, $32,100; an adjustment to funds from operations.
7. Proceeds from issuance of long-term notes, $20,000; a source of funds.
8. Reduction of mortgage, $12,900; a use of funds.
9. Decrease in working capital, $6,900; a source of funds.

For a more detailed explanation of each transaction, you might wish to refer to the chapter. However, to give you a sense of what is being done here, we will elaborate on the entries in the Retained Earnings account. Retained Earnings had a beginning balance of $335,500, which is entered as a credit. Net income for the period was $36,600, which is added to the beginning balance. Since net income is a source of funds, the $36,600 is entered as debit to Sources and Uses of Funds. However, Mountain Land Resources paid dividends of $24,900 during the year. This amount is debited to Retained Earnings and credited as a use of funds. A similiar analysis is performed for all non-working-capital accounts.

STEP 3: PREPARE A FORMAL STATEMENT OF CHANGES IN FINANCIAL POSITION

From the Sources and Uses of Funds T-account and the explanation of the entries, we can now prepare the formal funds statement. It would be identical to the one shown on page 515 as Exhibit 15–12.

SUPPLEMENT

(Chapters 6–15)

Consolidated Financial Statements

parent company *a company that owns or maintains control over other companies, known as subsidiaries, which are themselves separate legal entities; control generally refers to ownership of 50 percent or more of the stock of another company*

subsidiary company *a company owned or controlled by another company, known as the parent company*

consolidated financial statements *statements that show the operating results and financial position of two or more legally separate but affiliated companies as if they were one economic entity*

In Chapters 6 through 15, you learned how to account for the transactions of a single company, and how to prepare the financial statements based on that accounting. Many large corporations, however, are the owners or part-owners of other companies, and it is important to be aware of the accounting principles and procedures used in these situations. Generally, if a parent company has effective control over a subsidiary company, the statements of earnings and financial position of the subsidiaries should be combined with those of the parent company. In this way, the financial statements reflect the operating results and financial position of the total economic entity, which is what stockholders, creditors, and prospective investors are primarily interested in.

Consolidated financial statements are prepared by combining the individual statements of the entities, item by item, except for intercompany transactions—that is, transactions between the parent company and its subsidiaries, or between subsidiaries. Thus, if a parent company sells materials to its subsidiary, that transaction would not be included in the combined sales, purchases, or inventory figures in the consolidated financial statements for the two companies.

For certain purposes, separate accounting data for major segments of a company are also needed. This is especially important when a company is diversified, that is, operating in several different lines of business. Suppose that a company has two main divisions, one producing household appliances and the other, men's clothing. Users of financial statements would want to know more than the results of total company activity; they would want to know how well each segment of the business is doing. Supplement B, at the back of this text, illustrates the breakdown of sales by segments in the 1981 statements for IBM.

The Need for Consolidated Financial Statements

If a company acquires over 50 percent of the outstanding voting stock of another company, a controlling interest exists. When this happens, the two companies sometimes become one. Companies can legally combine

merger *the acquisition of one company by another company, whereby the companies combine as one legal entity, with the acquired company going out of existence*

consolidation *the combining of two or more companies into a new legal corporation, with the original companies going out of existence*

into one company by means of either a merger or a consolidation. A merger occurs when one company, A, acquires another company, B, and Company B goes out of existence. A consolidation occurs when Company A and Company B are combined into Company C, and both Companies A and B go out of existence. Alternatively, the combining companies may remain as separate legal entities, but may prepare consolidated financial statements as if they were one economic entity. Consolidated statements are necessary in such cases because they provide a more informative picture of the combined companies.

Note that consolidated financial statements are allowed only if the two companies have similar activities. This prerequisite is imposed in order to prevent the combining of assets and liabilities and revenues and expenses that are so dissimilar that the financial statements would be misleading. Generally accepted accounting principles do not allow, for example, a manufacturing company and a subsidiary insurance company to prepare consolidated financial statements.

In this supplement, we will assume that both the acquiring and the acquired companies stay in existence and that their activities are substantially similar.

Preparation of Consolidated Financial Statements

purchase *the acquisition of one company by another, whereby the acquiring company exchanges cash or other assets for more than 50 percent of the acquired company's outstanding voting stock*

pooling of interests *the acquisition of one company by another, whereby the acquiring company issues voting stock to the acquired company's stockholders in exchange for at least 90 percent of the acquired company's outstanding voting stock (and 11 other conditions are met)*

minority interest *the interest owned in a subsidiary by stockholders other than those of the parent company; occurs when the acquring company has less than a 100 percent ownership interest*

A parent company can acquire a controlling interest in a subsidiary by exchanging cash, other assets, or some of its own stock for over 50 percent of the subsidiary's outstanding voting stock. When control is achieved in this way, the acquisition is called a purchase. When a company acquires another company by exchanging its stock for at least 90 percent of the acquired company's outstanding voting stock (and when 11 other specific conditions are met), the acquisition is referred to as a pooling of interests. If the acquiring company does not acquire 100 percent of the outstanding voting shares of the subsidiary, the shares not acquired by the parent are referred to as the minority interest in the combined companies. Since we are concerned here with helping you understand the general concepts and procedures involved in preparing consolidated financial statements, we will limit our discussion to the situation where the parent company acquires 100 percent of the outstanding voting stock of the subsidiary. In addition, we will keep our examples of transactions between the parent company and its subsidiaries simple. First, we will discuss the purchase method, and then the pooling-of-interests method.

THE PURCHASE METHOD—CONSOLIDATED BALANCE SHEETS

When the stock of the acquired company is purchased with cash, other assets, or debt (such as bonds or notes), the purchase method is used to prepare the consolidated financial statements. To illustrate, we will assume

purchase method *a method used to prepare consolidated financial statements when one company has acquired a controlling interest in another company with similar activities by exchanging cash or other assets for more than 50 percent of the acquired company's outstanding voting stock*

that Pepper Corporation is acquiring Salt Corporation, and that the two companies had the balance sheets shown in Exhibit 15A-1 just prior to the acquisition. When the Salt stock is acquired, the investment in Salt is recorded on the books of Pepper Corporation by debiting an Investment in Subsidiary account and crediting Cash, Other Assets, or an account for the debt issued. If we assume that Pepper Corporation acquired all the common stock of Salt Corporation on December 31, 1983, by making a cash payment of $250,000 (which is equal to the book value of Salt's equity and likewise to the book value of its net assets: $700,000 − $450,000), the entry on the books of Pepper Corporation would be

Investment in Salt Corporation	250,000	
Cash		250,000

Acquired 100% (1,000 shares) of the stock of Salt Corporation at book value.

EXHIBIT 15A-1 **Pepper and Salt Corporations**

Condensed Balance Sheets as of December 31, 1983

Assets	**Pepper**	**Salt**
Cash	$ 450,000	$ 50,000
Accounts Receivable (net)	650,000	200,000
Note Receivable (owed by Salt)	200,000	—
Inventory	700,000	150,000
Plant Equipment (net)	600,000	300,000
Total Assets	$2,600,000	$700,000
Liabilities and Stockholders' Equity		
Accounts Payable	$ 400,000	$250,000
Note Payable (owed to Pepper)	—	200,000
Bonds Payable	800,000	—
Common Stock ($100 par)	600,000	100,000
Paid-in Capital in Excess of Par	350,000	40,000
Retained Earnings	450,000	110,000
Total Liabilities and Stockholders' Equity	$2,600,000	$700,000

Immediately after the acquisition, the balance sheet of Salt Corporation would not change because the cash is paid directly to the stockholders of Salt. In other words, because Pepper is purchasing the stock from the stockholders, not from Salt Corporation, the stock is still outstanding, with Pepper being the only stockholder. The balance sheet of Pepper would then reflect a decrease in cash of $250,000 and an increase in the corresponding investment in Salt.

Preparing a Consolidated Work Sheet

The consolidation is accounted for by setting up and completing a consolidated work sheet, as in Exhibit 15A–2. Note that the work sheet has five columns, two for the account balances of the two companies at the date of consolidation, two for the adjustment and elimination entries, and one for the consolidated balance sheet. The column for Pepper Corporation's accounts reflects the account balances immediately after the acquisition of the common stock of Salt Corporation.

EXHIBIT 15A–2

Pepper Corporation and Subsidiary

Consolidated Work Sheet as of December 31, 1983

Accounts	Pepper Corporation	Salt Corporation	Adjustments and Eliminations: Debits	Adjustments and Eliminations: Credits	Consolidated Balance Sheet
Assets					
Cash	200000	50000			250000
Accounts Receivable	650000	200000			850000
Note Receivable—Salt	200000			(1)200000	
Inventory	700000	150000			850000
Plant and Equipment	600000	300000			900000
Investment in Salt Corporation	250000			(2)250000	
Total Assets	2600000	700000			2850000
Liabilities and Stockholders' Equity					
Accounts Payable	400000	250000			650000
Note Payable—Pepper		200000	(1)200000		
Bonds Payable	800000				800000
Common Stock ($100 par)	600000	100000	(2)100000		600000
Paid-in Capital in Excess of Par	350000	40000	(2) 40000		350000
Retained Earnings	450000	110000	(2)110000		450000
Total Liabilities and Stockholders' Equity	2600000	700000	450000	450000	2850000

When the balance sheet accounts of the two companies are consolidated as a purchase, the individual asset and liability accounts are added together, except for items that are internal to the two companies, such as the $200,000 that Salt owed to Pepper. This is an intercompany transaction and requires an adjustment and elimination entry on the work sheet [entry (1)], as shown on the next page.

intercompany transaction *a transaction between a parent company and a subsidiary company*

Note Payable—Pepper	200,000	
Note Receivable—Salt		200,000

To eliminated Salt's obligation to Pepper.

Other types of intercompany transactions might involve one company selling inventory or equipment to the other.

A second type of adjustment and elimination entry is made to avoid a double counting of assets and equities [see entry (2)]. The entry involves the elimination of Pepper Corporation's Investment in Salt Corporation account against all the equity accounts of Salt Corporation. This is done because the asset account of the parent—Investment in Salt Corporation—and the equity accounts of the subsidiary both represent the net assets of the subsidiary, and these net assets are already included in the consolidated asset and liability accounts. To include these accounts as well as the net assets would result in a double counting. That is, if Investment in Salt Corporation and Salt's equity accounts were not eliminated, the consolidated entity would be overvalued. Elimination of these accounts is accomplished by the following entry.

Common Stock—Salt	100,000	
Paid-in Capital in Excess of Par—Salt	40,000	
Retained Earnings—Salt	110,000	
Investment in Salt Corporation		250,000

To eliminate the cost of Pepper Corporation's investment against Salt Corporation's equity accounts.

It might help you to understand the reason for these adjustment and elimination entries if you were to consider how the consolidated balance sheet would look without them.

Assets		Liabilities and Stockholders' Equity	
Cash	$ 250,000	Accounts Payable	$ 650,000
Accounts Receivable	850,000	Notes Payable—Pepper	200,000
Notes Receivable—Salt	200,000	Bonds Payable	800,000
Inventory	850,000	Common Stock—Pepper	600,000
Plant and Equipment (net)	900,000	Common Stock—Salt	100,000
Investment in Salt Corporation	250,000	Paid-in Capital in Excess of Par	390,000
		Retained Earnings	560,000
Total Assets	$3,300,000	Total Liabilities and Stockholders' Equity	$3,300,000

Clearly, this does not work. First, the same note (the Note Receivable—Salt and the Note Payable—Pepper) is counted as both an asset and a liability. Second, the purchase price of Salt Corporation (the amount in Investment in Salt Corporation) cannot be an asset of the consolidated statement since the net assets it represents are reflected individually in the balance sheet as the assets and liabilities of the subsidiary. Third, the stockholders' equity portion of Pepper Corporation already reflects the equity claim on Salt's assets. Including Salt's equity accounts would result in a double counting of the claims on those assets. It is also inappropriate to treat the subsidiary's stock as outstanding since it is now held by Pepper Corporation. Thus, the two Notes accounts, the Investment in Salt account, and all of Salt's subsidiary equity accounts (all stock accounts and Retained Earnings) must be eliminated on the consolidated work sheet in order to produce a consolidated balance sheet that fairly represents the two entities as a single economic unit.

Preparing a Consolidated Balance Sheet

After all necessary adjustment and elimination entries are made on the work sheet, all asset, liability, and equity accounts can be added across to the consolidated balance sheet columns to complete the work sheet. Bear in mind that the entries in the adjustment and elimination columns are *work sheet* entries only. They just serve to facilitate the elimination process; they are not recorded in the journals or accounts of either company. Only when an adjustment is made to correct an error on the books of one of the companies is an entry recorded in the company's accounts. The completed work sheet now serves as a basis for preparing the consolidated balance sheet of the parent company and its subsidiary, shown in Exhibit 15A-3. Note that the consolidated balance sheet shows the assets and liabilities of the two companies in combined form. The two Notes accounts have been eliminated, and so has the Investment in Subsidiary account on the parent's books. Also, the equity accounts are those of the parent company only. The subsidiary's stock is held within the consolidated entity as treasury stock.

EXHIBIT 15A-3

Pepper Corporation and Subsidiary
Consolidated Balance Sheet (Purchase Method)
as of December 31, 1983

Assets			**Liabilities and Stockholders' Equity**		
Current Assets:			*Current Liabilities:*		
Cash	$250,000		Accounts Payable	$650,000	
Accounts Receivable	850,000		*Long-Term Liabilities:*		
Inventory	850,000		Bonds Payable	800,000	
Total Current Assets		$1,950,000	Total Liabilities		$1,450,000
Long-Term Assets:			*Stockholders' Equity:*		
Plant and Equipment		900,000	Common Stock ($100 par)	$600,000	
			Paid-in Capital in Excess of Par	350,000	
			Retained Earnings	450,000	
			Total Stockholders' Equity		1,400,000
Total Assets		$2,850,000	Total Liabilities and Stockholders' Equity		$2,850,000

Consolidations Involving Payments over Book Value

The consolidated balance sheet in Exhibit 15A–3 involved a fairly straightforward combination of assets and liabilities because the purchase price paid by the parent was equal to the book value of the subsidiary's net assets. However, in many cases a company will pay more than the book value of the subsidiary.

To illustrate, we will assume that Pepper Corporation paid $300,000 cash for the common stock of Salt Corporation, even though the book value of the net assets (equity) of Salt Corporation amounted to $250,000 ($700,000 – $450,000). This $50,000 payment in excess of the book value of the net assets acquired must be accounted for as additional assets of the consolidated entity. The current theoretical assumption is that Pepper Corporation was willing to pay more than the book value of the net assets because specific assets of Salt Corporation were undervalued. For this example we will assume that the fair market value of the plant and equipment exceeds the net book value by $30,000. We will also assume that the fair market values of all other assets of Salt Corporation are equal to the book values. Based on these assumptions, there is $20,000 remaining excess cost ($50,000 – $30,000) to be accounted for. Because no other assets require adjustment to fair market value, the $20,000 must be attributed to an intangible asset called goodwill. Goodwill reflects the benefits the subsidiary enjoys in the form of good customer and employee relations, a reputation for product quality, and/or other intangible qualities that contribute to additional earnings. The excess cost can be accounted for as follows:

goodwill *an intangible asset showing that a business is worth more than the fair market value of its net assets because of strategic location, reputation, good customer relations, or similar factors; equal to the excess of cost over the fair market value of the net assets purchased*

Purchase Price	$300,000
Net Assets (Book Value) Acquired	250,000
Excess Cost	$ 50,000
Additional Fair Market Value of Plant and Equipment	30,000
Goodwill	$ 20,000

This excess payment must appear in the consolidated balance sheet. To include it, we insert in the adjustment and elimination columns debits of $30,000 for plant and equipment and $20,000 for goodwill. This brings the net assets up to the $300,000 paid for Salt Corporation. As before, the Investment in Salt Corporation account on Pepper Corporation's books and the equity accounts of Salt are eliminated. The result is the work sheet shown in Exhibit 15A–4. The consolidated balance sheet would show the account totals in the final column.

TO SUMMARIZE When one company acquires a controlling interest in another company (that is, acquires more than 50 percent of its stock) and the two companies have substantially similar business objectives, the financial statements of the companies are combined as consolidated statements. The acquiring company is called the parent company and the acquired company is called the subsidiary company. If the parent obtains the controlling interest by giving up cash or other assets in exchange for the common stock of the subsidiary, the combination is accounted for as a purchase. This means that the assets of the subsidiary are included in the consolidated balance sheet at their fair market values, and that any excess cost of acquisition over the fair market values of the subsidiary's assets is called goodwill. The key characteristics of a consolidated balance sheet for two companies, assuming that one has purchased 100 percent ownership of the other, are as follows:

EXHIBIT 15A-4

Pepper Corporation and Subsidiary
Consolidated Work Sheet as of December 31, 1983

Accounts	Pepper Corporation	Salt Corporation	Adjustments and Eliminations: Debits	Adjustments and Eliminations: Credits	Consolidated Balance Sheet
Assets					
Cash	150000	50000			200000
Accounts Receivable	650000	200000			850000
Note Receivable—Salt	200000			(1) 200000	
Inventory	700000	150000			850000
Plant and Equipment (net)	600000	300000	(2) 30000		930000
Goodwill			(2) 20000		20000
Investment in Salt Corporation	300000			(2) 300000	
Total Assets	2600000	700000			2850000
Liabilities and Stockholders' Equity					
Accounts Payable	400000	250000			650000
Note Payable—Pepper		200000	(1) 200000		
Bonds Payable	800000				800000
Common Stock ($100 par)	600000	100000	(2) 100000		600000
Paid-in Capital in Excess of Par	350000	40000	(2) 40000		350000
Retained Earnings	450000	110000	(2) 110000		450000
Total Liabilities and Stockholders' Equity	2600000	700000	500000	500000	2850000

1. Any amount paid in excess of the book value of the subsidiary's assets must be accounted for as additional assets of the subsidiary—either because the fair market value of its assets exceeds their book value, or because the subsidiary possesses the intangible asset, goodwill. The affected assets might be inventory, plant and equipment, or other assets whose book value is less than fair market value. Any excess cost that cannot be assigned to specific assets is used to create a goodwill account. Note that only the subsidiary's assets are adjusted to fair market value.

2. The common stock account is composed entirely of the outstanding stock of the parent company. From a consolidated statement point of view, the subsidiary stock is not outstanding, but is held within the consolidated entity as treasury stock.

3. The Retained Earnings account of the consolidated entity at the date of acquisition shows the retained earnings of the parent company only.

4. Assets and liabilities created in intercompany transactions are eliminated.

5. The Investment in Subsidiary asset account on the parent's books is eliminated against the Common Stock, Paid-in Capital in Excess of Par, and Retained Earnings accounts of the subsidiary, since including these accounts would duplicate the net assets and equity accounts in the consolidated balance sheet.

THE PURCHASE METHOD—CONSOLIDATED INCOME STATEMENTS

At the end of the consolidated entity's first year of operations, a consolidated income statement is prepared. To illustrate this process, we use the income statements shown in Exhibit 15A-5.

EXHIBIT 15A-5

Pepper and Salt Corporations
Condensed Income Statements
for the Year Ended December 31, 1984

	Pepper	Salt
Sales Revenue	$4,000,000	$1,200,000
Cost of Goods Sold	2,400,000	780,000
Gross Margin	$1,600,000	$ 420,000
Operating Expenses (including depreciation)	1,300,000	350,000
Income Before Taxes	$ 300,000	$ 70,000
Income Taxes	130,000	30,000
Net Income	$ 170,000	$ 40,000

If there are no intercompany transactions in the first year after Pepper acquires Salt, the combination of their income statements into a consolidated income statement is primarily a matter of combining the accounts on the two statements. However, if we return to our example in which Pepper paid $300,000 cash for Salt Corporation's stock, two adjustments will be necessary. First, additional depreciation was required during the year due to the write-up of plant and equipment by $30,000, and this depreciation must be included in the consolidated income statement for 1984. Second, the amortization of the goodwill of $20,000 must also be reflected there. The consolidated income statement of the two companies under the purchase method would be as shown in Exhibit 15A-6. This statement assumes that the increase in plant and equipment is written off over 5 years and that goodwill is amortized over 10 years. (APB Opinion No. 17 requires that the amortization of goodwill not exceed a period of 40 years.)

EXHIBIT 15A-6

Pepper Corporation and Subsidiary
Consolidated Income Statement
for the Year Ended December 31, 1984 (Purchase Method)

Sales Revenue		$5,200,000
Cost of Goods Sold		3,180,000
Gross Margin		$2,020,000
Operating Expenses Other than Extra Depreciation	$1,650,000	
Extra Depreciation Expense ($30,000 ÷ 5 years)	6,000	
Goodwill Amortization ($20,000 ÷ 10 years)	2,000	1,658,000
Income Before Taxes		$ 362,000
Income Taxes		160,000
Net Income		$ 202,000

In preparing this consolidated income statement, the revenues and cost of goods sold of the two companies were combined. Then, the additional depreciation on the increased value of plant and equipment and the amortization of goodwill were added to the companies' combined operating expenses. Finally, total expenses were deducted from gross margin to arrive at consolidated net income.

TO SUMMARIZE After a parent company acquires a controlling interest in a subsidiary, a consolidated income statement is prepared at the end of each year of operations. Under the purchase method, revenues and expenses on the two companies' income statements are combined, except that depreciation expense is increased for the write-up of depreciable assets to fair market value, and an amortization expense is established for the write-off of any goodwill created at the time the subsidiary was acquired.

THE POOLING-OF-INTERESTS METHOD—CONSOLIDATED BALANCE SHEETS

pooling-of-interests method *a method used to prepare consolidated financial statements when one company issues common stock to acquire at least 90 percent of the common stock of another company and when 11 other specific conditions are met*

Another technique for preparing consolidated financial statements is the pooling-of-interests method. For this method to be used, voting common stock of the acquiring company must be exchanged for at least 90 percent of the outstanding common stock of the acquired company or for its net assets. Pooling of interests involves an exchange, rather than a sale or purchase. The stockholders of the combining companies become owners of the consolidated entity; that is, they pool their interests and both companies continue as significant parts of the consolidated whole. Because net assets of the subsidiary have not been purchased, they need not be revalued and consolidation is a simple matter of adding the book values of the assets and equities of the combining companies.

The pooling-of-interests method is not as common as the purchase method, but it must be used when common stock is exchanged for at least 90 percent of the subsidiary's outstanding voting stock and when 11 other specific conditions are met. These conditions, which have been specified by accounting policy makers, involve such factors as the prior relationship of the combining companies, the timing and nature of the combination, and the absence of a plan to dispose of any major segment of either company after the combination takes place. It is beyond the scope of this text to discuss all of these technical requirements. The first condition—that common stock must be exchanged for at least 90 percent of the subsidiary's outstanding voting stock—is very significant, however, and will be discussed in this section.

To illustrate the pooling-of-interests method, we will assume that the shareholders of Salt Corporation give up all their common stock and receive Pepper Corporation's common stock in exchange. Prior to the acquisition, as you will recall, their condensed balance sheets appeared as shown in Exhibit 15A-7.

EXHIBIT 15A-7 **Pepper and Salt Corporations**
Condensed Balance Sheets as of December 31, 1983

Assets	**Pepper**	**Salt**
Cash	$ 450,000	$ 50,000
Accounts Receivable (net)	650,000	200,000
Note Receivable—Salt	200,000	—
Inventory	700,000	150,000
Plant Equipment (net)	600,000	300,000
Total Assets	$2,600,000	$700,000
Liabilities and Stockholders' Equity		
Accounts Payable	$ 400,000	$250,000
Note Payable—Pepper	—	200,000
Bonds Payable	800,000	—
Common Stock ($100 par)	600,000	100,000
Paid-in Capital in Excess of Par	350,000	40,000
Retained Earnings	450,000	110,000
Total Liabilities and Stockholders' Equity	$2,600,000	$700,000

Now assume that Pepper Corporation issues 1,000 shares of its $100-par-value common stock in exchange for all of Salt Corporation's outstanding common stock (1,000 shares). This means that the stockholders of Salt Corporation become stockholders of Pepper Corporation.

Under the pooling method, Pepper Corporation would record this exchange of 1,000 shares of its common stock for 1,000 shares of Salt Corporation common stock by the following entry.

Investment in Salt Corporation	250,000	
Common Stock ($100 par, 1,000 shares)		100,000
Paid-in Capital in Excess of Par		150,000

To acquire 100% of the common stock of Salt Corporation by issuing 1,000 shares of Pepper Corporation stock.

Note that Pepper's investment of $250,000 is equal to the book value of Salt's net assets ($700,000 − $450,000). Furthermore, Pepper's Paid-in Capital in Excess of Par account is not credited for the amount originally in Salt Corporation's Paid-in Capital in Excess of Par account ($40,000). Instead, it is adjusted up to balance the debits and credits of the elimination entry. Thus, it is debited for $150,000 to make up the difference between Pepper's investment ($250,000) and the par value of Salt Corporation's common stock ($100,000).

Immediately after the entry is made, the balance sheet of Pepper Corporation would be as follows:

Assets	
Cash	$ 450,000
Accounts Receivable (net)	650,000
Note Receivable–Salt	200,000
Inventory	700,000
Investment in Salt	250,000
Plant and Equipment	600,000
Total Assets	$2,850,000
Liabilities and Stockholders' Equity	
Accounts Payable	$ 400,000
Bonds Payable	800,000
Common Stock	700,000
Paid-in Capital in Excess of Par	500,000
Retained Earnings	450,000
Total Liabilities and Stockholders' Equity	$2,850,000

Note that Pepper's Common Stock and Paid-in Capital in Excess of Par have been increased (credited), whereas, for a purchase, Cash was decreased (credited).

The next section shows how to make elimination entries on the consolidated work sheet to account for Pepper and Salt's pooling of interests.

Preparing a Work Sheet and a Consolidated Balance Sheet

In preparing a consolidated balance sheet using the pooling-of-interests method, the assets and liabilities of the subsidiary are accounted for at their book values rather than at their fair market values, as was done with the purchase method. Since the investment is recorded at the total book value of the subsidiary's net assets (or equity), there is no excess cost and thus there are no asset values to write up or goodwill to record. Dealing with book values simplifies the consolidation process.

However, there are still two types of elimination entries to make: one to cancel intercompany debts, and one to cancel the parent company's investment account against the subsidiary's equity accounts. Exhibit 15A–8 shows the work sheet used in consolidating the two companies' balance sheets under the pooling method. Note that the Pepper Corporation accounts reflect the balances immediately after the issuing of its own common stock to acquire the common stock of Salt Corporation.

When the balance sheet accounts of the two companies are consolidated as a pooling of interests, the asset and liability accounts are added together. The intercompany note receivable and note payable are eliminated just as they are under the purchase method [entry (1) on the work sheet]. This avoids double counting of assets and liabilities. The Investment in Subsidiary account on the parent's books is also eliminated, but only against the Common Stock and Paid-in Capital in Excess of Par accounts on the subsidiary's books [see entry (2) on the work sheet]. This second elimination

EXHIBIT 15A-8

Pepper Corporation and Subsidiary

Consolidated Work Sheet as of December 31, 1983

Accounts	Pepper Corporation	Salt Corporation	Adjustments and Eliminations: Debits	Adjustments and Eliminations: Credits	Consolidated Balance Sheet
Assets					
Cash	450000	50000			500000
Accounts Receivable (net)	650000	200000			850000
Note Receivable—Salt	200000			(1) 200000	
Inventory	700000	150000			850000
Investment in Salt Corporation	250000			(2) 250000	
Plant and Equipment (net)	600000	300000			900000
Total Assets	2850000	700000			3100000
Liabilities and Stockholders' Equity					
Accounts Payable	400000	250000			650000
Note Payable—Pepper		200000	(1) 200000		
Bonds Payable	800000				800000
Common Stock ($100 par)	700000	100000	(2) 100000		700000
Paid-in Capital in Excess of Par	500000	40000	(2) 150000		390000
Retained Earnings	450000	110000			560000
Total Liabilities and Stockholders' Equity	2850000	700000	450000	450000	3100000

entry is different from that used under the purchase method because the retained earnings of the subsidiary are added to the retained earnings of the parent rather than being eliminated. This treatment of retained earnings is consistent with the pooling-of-interests philosophy that the combination of the two companies represents a continuation of both companies as significant parts of the consolidated whole. Observe the differences in the elimination entries under the two methods.

Pooling-of-Interests Method

Common Stock—Salt	100,000	
Paid-in Capital in Excess of Par	150,000	
Investment in Salt Corporation		250,000

Purchase Method

Common Stock—Salt	100,000	
Paid-in Capital in Excess of Par—Salt	40,000	
Retained Earnings—Salt	110,000	
Goodwill	20,000	
Plant and Equipment	30,000	
Investment in Salt Corporation		300,000

Under the pooling-of-interests method, the Investment in Salt Corporation is $50,000 less than the $300,000 it was under the purchase method. This is because under the purchase method, the company records the total amount paid in cash, that is, the fair market value of the subsidiary's net assets. The difference between fair market value and book value is recorded as an increase in the value of plant and equipment, for example, and, if necessary, as goodwill. With the pooling method, only the book value of the subsidiary's net assets is recorded, whether or not it is the same as the fair market value. Thus, although the company may issue common stock equal to the fair market value of the subsidiary's net assets, it records only the book value. Because the pooling method does not involve the revaluation of assets (which would be necessary if fair market value were recorded), there is no additional amortization or depreciation recorded on the consolidated income statement. As a result, net income under the pooling method is higher than it is under the purchase method.

With this last elimination entry, the work sheet is complete and will serve as a basis for preparing the consolidated balance sheet of the two companies, as shown in Exhibit 15A–9.

EXHIBIT 15A–9

Pepper Corporation and Subsidiary
Consolidated Balance Sheet
as of December 31, 1983
(Pooling-of-Interests Method)

Assets		
Current Assets:		
Cash	$500,000	
Accounts Receivable	850,000	
Inventory	850,000	
Total Current Assets		$2,200,000
Plant and Equipment		900,000
Total Assets		$3,100,000
Liabilities and Stockholders' Equity		
Current Liabilities:		
Accounts Payable		$ 650,000
Long-Term Liabilities:		
Bonds Payable		800,000
Total Liabilities		$1,450,000
Stockholders' Equity:		
Common Stock	$700,000	
Paid-in Capital in Excess of Par	390,000	
Retained Earnings	560,000	
Total Stockholders' Equity		1,650,000
Total Liabilities and Stockholders' Equity		$3,100,000

An Historical Note

The pooling-of-interests method was originally used in the early 1930s to account for a combination of similiar companies of like size, such as two public utilities, which would continue to operate after the consolidation as they did before. As the method became more popular, however, the criteria of like size and no basic change in operations began to be abandoned. In fact, during the 1960s, the pooling method came to be used in acquisitions of all sizes of companies and types of operations. This inappropriate application of the pooling philosophy led to the adoption of Opinion No. 16 (Business Combinations) by the Accounting Principles Board. APB 16 specifies the criteria that must be met in order for an acquisition to be treated as a pooling. Because many professionals are still uncomfortable with the accounting for business combinations, the Financial Accounting Standards Board is presently reconsidering the accounting for consolidations.

TO SUMMARIZE When one company (the parent) acquires controlling interest in another (the subsidiary) by issuing voting common stock in exchange for at least 90 percent of the outstanding voting stock of the subsidiary and when 11 other conditions are met, the acquisition can be accounted for using the pooling-of-interests method. The main characteristics of a consolidated balance sheet using the pooling-of-interests method are

1. The assets of the subsidiary are not written up to fair market value.
2. No amount is assigned to goodwill.
3. The common stock shown as outstanding on the consolidated balance sheet is the stock of the parent company, since the stock of the subsidiary is held within the consolidated entity. Remember that the parent had to issue more of its own stock in order to acquire the subsidiary's stock.
4. The retained earnings of the subsidiary are combined with the retained earnings of the parent, instead of being eliminated, as with the purchase method.
5. The intercompany receivables and payables are eliminated, and the Investment in Subsidiary account on the books of the parent company is eliminated against the Subsidiary's Common Stock and Paid-in Capital in Excess of Par accounts. Because the debits and credits of this elimination entry are usually not equal, the Paid-in Capital in Excess of Par is adjusted as necessary.

THE POOLING-OF-INTERESTS METHOD—CONSOLIDATED INCOME STATEMENTS

The process of consolidating the income statements of the two companies using pooling of interests is generally simpler than under the purchase method. Because there is no goodwill and because depreciable assets are not written up, the consolidated income statement is merely the sum of the two individual income statements.

To illustrate a consolidated income statement under pooling, we will again use the separate income statements for Pepper and Salt Corporations.

	Pepper	Salt
Sales Revenue	$4,000,000	$1,200,000
Cost of Goods Sold	2,400,000	780,000
Gross Margin	$1,600,000	$ 420,000
Operating Expenses	1,300,000	350,000
Income Before Taxes	$ 300,000	$ 70,000
Income Taxes	130,000	30,000
Net Income	$ 170,000	$ 40,000

Based on these income statements for the year 1984, the consolidated income statement under the pooling method would be as shown in Exhibit 15A-10. As you can see, this consolidated income statement results from simply combining the accounts of the two companies. The statement has been simplified by the assumption that there were no intercompany transactions involving inventories, operational assets, or securities. Such transactions are beyond the scope of this text.

EXHIBIT 15A-10 **Pepper Corporation and Subsidiary**
Consolidated Income Statement
for the year Ended December 31, 1984

Sales Revenue	$5,200,000
Cost of Goods Sold	3,180,000
Gross Margin	$2,020,000
Operating Expenses	1,650,000
Income Before Taxes	$ 370,000
Income Taxes	160,000
Net Income	$ 210,000

TO SUMMARIZE Under the pooling-of-interests method, income statements are consolidated by simply combining the balances in each account, assuming that there are no complicating factors.

DISCUSSION QUESTIONS

1 What is the overall purpose of consolidated financial statements?

2 What conditions must be met before the financial statements of an acquiring and an acquired company can be combined into consolidated financial statements?

3 What are the main conditions that determine whether consolidated financial statements are prepared under the purchase method or under the pooling-of-interests method?

4 What amount is recorded on the parent company's books for its investment in a subsidiary if the subsidiary is acquired (a) as a purchase and (b) as a pooling of interests?

5 What are the differences in the consolidated balance sheets under the purchase method and under the pooling-of-interests method?

6 What are the differences in the consolidated income statements under the purchase method and under the pooling-of-interests method?

7 In the consolidation process, why is the Investment in Subsidiary account on the parent's books offset against the equity accounts on the subsidiary's books?

8 Under the purchase method, if the cost of acquiring a subsidiary is greater than the book value of the subsidiary's assets, how is the excess cost accounted for?

9 What expenses would appear in a consolidated income statement under the purchase method that would not appear on a consolidated income statement under the pooling-of-interests method?

10 When a consolidated balance sheet is prepared, what disposition is made of the retained earnings of the subsidiary under (a) the purchase method and (b) the pooling-of-interests method?

EXERCISES

E15A-1 Recording an Investment

Proctor Company acquired 100 percent of the 4,000 shares ($10 par) of the voting common stock of Superior Corporation on January 2, 1983. Prepare the journal entry to record Proctor's investment in Superior under each of the following independent situations.

1. Proctor Company paid cash to Superior's shareholders at $28 per share. The acquisition was accounted for as a purchase.
2. Proctor issued 2,000 shares of its voting common stock in exchange for the 4,000 shares of Superior Corporation stock. The acquistion was accounted for as a pooling of interests. The fair market value of Proctor's stock at the time of the exchange was $60 per share ($40 par), and the book value of Superior's net assets was $107,000.

E15A-2 Elimination Entries

Able Company acquired 100 percent of the common stock of Easy Company when the stockholders' equity of Easy Company was as follows:

Common Stock ($100 par, 1,000 shares outstanding)	$100,000
Paid-in Capital in Excess of Par	20,000
Retained Earnings	50,000
Total Stockholders' Equity	$170,000

1. If Able Company purchased all of Easy Company's stock at $210 per share, give the elimination entry that would be made on the consolidated work sheet. Assume that the fair market values of Easy Company's assets are equal to their book values, except that land is undervalued by $25,000.
2. If Able Company acquired all of Easy Company's common stock by issuing its own common stock in exchange, what would the entry on the consolidated work sheet be under the pooling method? Assume that Able Company issued 500 shares of its voting common stock ($100 par) and recorded the investment in Easy Company at $170,000.

E15A-3 Elimination Entries

Just prior to acquisition by Parker Company, the balance sheet of Springer Company had the following balances.

Common Stock ($10 par, 10,000 shares)	$100,000
Paid-in Capital in Excess of Par	27,000
Retained Earnings	63,000
Total Stockholders' Equity	$190,000

Prepare the elimination entry on the consolidated work sheet if Parker Company purchased all the shares of Springer Company under each of the following independent situations.

1. Paid $19 per share. The fair market value of the net assets of Springer Company equaled the book value.
2. Paid $24 per share. The price paid was greater than the book value of Springer's net assets because land was undervalued by $50,000.
3. Paid $25 per share. Plant and equipment on the books of Springer Company was undervalued by $40,000. The fair market values of all other recorded assets, including land, of Springer Company were equal to their book values.

E15A-4 Accounting for Cost over Book Value with the Purchase Method

Referring to E15A-3, assume that Parker Company paid an excess of $70,000 over book value for its interest in Springer Company. Of the excess cost, $50,000 was assigned to depreciable equipment and $20,000 to goodwill. The equipment has a remaining life of 8 years and the goodwill is to be amortized over 10 years. (Straight-line methods are used for depreciation and amortization.) A full year's depreciation and amortization are taken in the year of acquisition. Under the purchase method, how much additional expense will be included in the consolidated income statement as a result of the excess cost paid for the Springer Company?

PROBLEMS

P15A-1 The Purchase Method

On January 1, 1984, Rouse Company acquired 100 percent of the common stock of Chope Company for a cash payment of $120,000. The balance sheets of the two companies just prior to the acquisition were as follows:

Assets	Rouse Company	Chope Company
Current Assets	$175,000	$ 70,000
Plant and Equipment	120,000	85,000
Land	50,000	20,000
Total Assets	$345,000	$175,000
Liabilities and Stockholders' Equity		
Current Liabilities	$ 90,000	$ 55,000
Common Stock ($100 par)	150,000	80,000
Paid-in Capital in Excess of Par	30,000	12,000
Retained Earnings	75,000	28,000
Total Liabilities and Stockholders' Equity	$345,000	$175,000

The fair market values of Chope Company's assets were equal to their book values.

Required:

1. Prepare the Rouse Company journal entry to account for the acquisition of Chope Company stock for $120,000 in cash.
2. Prepare the entry made on the consolidated work sheet to eliminate the appropriate asset and equity accounts.
3. Assume instead that Rouse Company acquired Chope Company's stock for a cash payment of $138,000. Also assume that the fair market value of Chope Company's land was $28,000, whereas the fair market values of all its other assets were equal to their book values. Prepare a consolidated work sheet as of January 1, 1984.

P15A-2 The Pooling-of-Interests Method

On April 1, 1984, Lee Corporation exchanged 7,000 shares of its $10-par-value common stock with a fair market value of $18 per share for all the common stock shares of Brite Corporation. As of March 31, 1984, the balance sheets of the two companies were as follows:

Assets	Lee Corporation	Brite Corporation
Current Assets	$ 75,000	$ 30,000
Property and Equipment	180,000	85,000
Land	65,000	15,000
Total Assets	$320,000	$130,000

Liabilities and Stockholders' Equity	Lee Corporation	Brite Corporation
Current Liabilities	$ 40,000	$ 20,000
Common Stock ($10 par)	200,000	60,000
Paid-in Capital in Excess of Par	25,000	10,000
Retained Earnings	55,000	40,000
Total Liabilities and Stockholders' Equity	$320,000	$130,000

On April 1, the fair market values of Brite Corporation's assets were equal to their book values, except that the land's fair market value was $25,000. The current assets on Lee Corporation's books included an account receivable of $12,000 from Brite Corporation. Likewise, the current liabilities on Brite Corporation's books include an account payable of $12,000 to Lee Corporation.

Required:

1. Prepare the entry in the books of Lee Corporation for the acquisition of Brite Corporation's common stock under the pooling-of-interests method.
2. Prepare a consolidated work sheet for the acquisition of Brite Corporation by Lee Corporation under the pooling-of-interests method.

P15A-3 The Purchase and Pooling-of-Interests Methods

The operating results of Hope Corporation and its wholly owned subsidiary, Lance Corporation, for the year ended December 31, 1984, are presented below.

	Hope Corporation	Lance Corporation
Sales Revenue	$600,000	$450,000
Cost of Goods Sold	410,000	320,000
Gross Margin	$190,000	$130,000
Selling and General Expense	110,000	75,000
Income Before Taxes	$ 80,000	$ 55,000
Income Taxes	17,000	11,000
Net Income	$ 63,000	$ 44,000

Required:

1. Prepare a consolidated income statement if the combination is accounted for as a purchase. When Hope Corporation acquired Lance on January 1, 1984, plant and equipment on Lance's books had a remaining life of 8 years and an excess of $20,000 of fair market value over book value. Consolidated goodwill amounted to $30,000. Goodwill is amortized over a 20-year period.
2. Assuming the same facts regarding the valuation of plant and equipment as in part (1) above, prepare a consolidated income statement if the combination is accounted for as a pooling of interests.

CHAPTER 16

Financial Statement Analysis

THIS CHAPTER EXPLAINS:

The reasons for financial statement analysis.

The basic techniques of financial statement analysis.

Analysis of operating performance, asset turnover, debt–equity management, and return on assets and equity.

Some limitations of financial statement analysis.

We have dealt with the way a firm collects and uses financial data in the preparation of the income statement, the balance sheet, and the statement of changes in financial position. These statements conveniently and succinctly summarize a firm's performance and its financial status at the end of each accounting period. Although they are historical in nature, the primary financial statements usually provide a good indication of what a firm's performance is likely to be during subsequent accounting periods. These clues may not be immediately evident, however. Interested users must analyze the statements carefully in order to obtain the particular information that suits their purposes.

Reasons for Financial Statement Analysis

There are several reasons why careful analysis of financial statements is necessary.

1. Financial statements are general-purpose statements. They are prepared for use by a variety of interested parties: stockholders, short- and long-term creditors, potential investors, government agencies, and management. These different users are involved in making different types of decisions, ranging from whether to make an investment (potential

owner), or whether opportunities exist for improving performance (manager), to whether the firm's activities require regulation (government agency). Each type of decision requires different information, and therefore a different analysis.

2. The relationships between key figures on the income statement, on the balance sheet, or on both, and the relationships between amounts on successive financial statements, are not obvious without analysis. Accordingly, knowledgeable users develop ratios and percentages that reflect meaningful relationships and that show trends from previous years.

3. Users of financial statements may be interested in seeing how well a company is doing in comparison to predetermined objective standards, other companies in the industry, or alternative opportunities for investment.

To a large extent, then, the amount of information one is able to draw from financial statements depends on the care and experience with which they are analyzed.

THE TYPE OF INFORMATION TO BE GAINED FROM FINANCIAL STATEMENT ANALYSIS

Most people who analyze financial statements are interested in making investment, credit, managerial, or regulatory decisions. What types of financial information do these different users need?

Investment and Credit Decisions

Owners and creditors of a company, and particularly potential owners and creditors, want to know what their return on investment is likely to be and what the chances are of achieving that return. The probability of achieving a certain return on an investment is referred to as the degree of risk, or uncertainty, involved. The amount of return to be expected and the degree of uncertainty that is acceptable are likely to be different for each type of user: stockholder, short-term creditor, or long-term creditor.

Stockholders can gain a return on investment both from dividends and from proceeds on the sale of stock at an increased price. They want to be able to predict a firm's future profits, because profitability is the best indicator of the ability to pay dividends and of the value the market is likely to place on the stock.

profitability *a company's ability to generate revenues in excess of the costs incurred in producing those revenues*

Short-term creditors, such as banks, are interested in a firm's ability to repay a loan promptly. Hence, the short-term cash-generating ability of a firm, its degree of liquidity, is important to these creditors.

liquidity *a company's ability to meet current obligations with cash or other assets that can be quickly converted to cash*

Long-term creditors, such as bondholders, would like to be able to predict a firm's ability to pay the interest obligation regularly and to repay the principal at maturity. Such payments are made over periods of years, so these creditors are interested in judging a firm's solvency, its long-run ability to pay debts.

solvency *a company's long-run ability to meet all financial obligations*

Managerial Decisions

The managers of a company have a responsibility to all other users of the financial statements (creditors, owners, government agencies, customers, suppliers, workers, and society in general). They must constantly monitor the firm's financial position and performance and take corrective action where necessary. Before they can take action, however, they must understand the company's major strengths and weaknesses. Financial statement analysis is one of the tools management uses for identifying problems having to do with operating efficiency and debt–equity management—problems that must be solved if a firm is to meet its short- and long-run profitability, liquidity, and solvency goals.

Regulatory Decisions

All firms are subject to some degree of government regulation. In discharging their oversight responsibilities, government agencies need to assess the operating results and financial status of companies under their jurisdiction. The Internal Revenue Service, for example, might want to determine whether related companies are avoiding income taxes by illegally shifting income. Or the IRS may make use of financial statement analysis to justify an assessment of taxes on the accumulated earnings of closely held corporations that forgo dividends in order to save income taxes for their high-tax-bracket owners. Similarly, the Federal Trade Commission and the Justice Department may use financial statement analysis to determine whether too much economic power is concentrated in too few companies in an industry. The Securities and Exchange Commission, in executing its enforcement powers with respect to new stock offerings and annual reporting, may use financial statement analysis to judge whether a company is misleading potential investors by not disclosing all relevant data in its financial statements.

TO SUMMARIZE Current and potential investors and creditors use financial statement analysis to help them judge the degree of profitability, liquidity, and solvency of a firm. Managers use statement analysis to identify problems having to do with operating efficiency and debt–equity management. Government agencies use financial statement analysis in various ways, depending on their jurisdiction.

Overview of Financial Statement Analysis

Financial statement analysis clearly has many applications for a variety of users. In the remainder of this chapter, we will describe some of the most useful techniques of analysis. The experienced user begins an analysis by identifying an objective (assessing profitability, liquidity, or solvency) and choosing the techniques that will accomplish the objective. Such a careful approach usually provides valuable information, but it does not answer all questions. Financial statement analysis has limitations that must be kept in mind, as will be explained later.

SOME BASIC TECHNIQUES

Four techniques are widely used in analyzing the financial statements of profit-oriented companies. They are

1. Ratio analysis: the appraisal of certain key relationships.
2. Vertical analysis: measuring relationships between items on a single year's income statement or balance sheet by expressing all items as percentages of net sales, or as percentages of total assets or of the total of liabilities and stockholders' equity.
3. Horizontal analysis: measuring changes in the same items on comparative statements over two or more years.
4. Common-size statements: income statements or balance sheets showing only the percentage relationships obtained by vertical analysis, with the dollar amounts omitted.

These techniques are sometimes described as alternative ways of assessing a company's status. A more logical approach is to consider each technique as an important part of a single, comprehensive analysis. This is the way financial statement analysis will be presented here. We will begin by presenting the four key relationships (ratios) for assessing a firm's profitability, liquidity, and solvency. Then, in a more detailed discussion of these assessment techniques, we will show how vertical and horizontal analyses and common-size statements are used along with more specific ratios to fill out the picture.

To illustrate the techniques, we will use hypothetical data from Marvel Company's financial statements for the calendar year ending December 31, 1984 and 1983, shown in Exhibits 16-1 and 16-2 (pages 560 and 561).

KEY RELATIONSHIPS

Four key relationships serve as a basis for assessing a firm's profitability, liquidity, and solvency.

1. $\dfrac{\text{net income (earnings)}}{\text{net sales}}$	a measure of operating performance for a period
2. $\dfrac{\text{net sales}}{\text{average total assets}}$	a measure of asset utilization
3. $\dfrac{\text{average total assets}}{\text{average stockholders' equity}}$	a measure of the management of debt and equity
4. $\dfrac{\text{net income (earnings)}}{\text{average stockholders' equity}}$	a measure of performance from a stockholder's viewpoint

The first ratio relates two income statement items, net income and net sales. It provides a measure of operating performance, and hence of profitability, for a period by showing the amount of earnings generated by each sales dollar.

The second ratio relates an income statement amount (net sales) to a balance sheet amount (total assets). Since the income statement covers a

EXHIBIT 16-1

Marvel Company
Income Statements
for the Years Ended December 31, 1984 and 1983

	1984	1983
Net Sales	$1,086,944	$988,417
Cost of Goods Sold	786,523	700,263
Gross Margin	$ 300,421	$288,154
Expenses:		
Selling and Administrative Expenses	$ 190,090	$172,661
Interest Expense	14,995	13,046
Total Expenses	$ 205,085	$185,707
Income Before Taxes	$ 95,336	$102,447
Income Taxes	54,961	50,197
Net Income from Operations	$ 40,375	$ 52,250
Extraordinary Gain (net of tax)	-0-	12,400
Net Income	$ 40,375	$ 64,650
Earnings per Share of Common Stock:		
Income Before Extraordinary Gain	$1.55	$2.01
Extraordinary Gain	—	0.48
Net Income	$1.55	$2.49

period of time and the balance sheet presents the financial position at a given moment in time, the relationship will not be entirely valid unless the balance sheet amount is revised to cover a period of time. This can be accomplished by using the average of the total assets for the period selected. (For example, to obtain the annual average, take the total assets at the beginning and end of each year, add them, and divide by two.) This second key ratio, which indicates how efficiently assets are being utilized, is often called the asset turnover ratio. The more efficiently assets are used, the more profitable a firm is and the more likely it is to be able to pay its obligations on a timely basis.

The third ratio relates two balance sheet amounts, and shows the degree to which debt and equity are used in financing the operations of a company. Average total assets divided by average stockholders' equity measures the firm's assets per dollar of its stockholders' equity. That is, the ratio shows the degree to which a firm is financing its total assets through the issuance of stock and the accumulation of past earnings. Since total assets minus total stockholders' equity is equal to total liabilities or debt, this ratio also may be used to analyze the amount of debt used during a period to maintain assets. The amount of debt a firm has obviously relates directly to the amount of liquid resources it needs to remain solvent. The debt-equity relationship also bears on profitability through the use of leveraging, which allows a company to earn for stockholders a rate of return higher than the cost of borrowed money. This concept was introduced in Chapter 12 and is also discussed later in this chapter.

EXHIBIT 16-2

Marvel Company
Balance Sheets
as of December 31, 1984 and 1983

Assets	**1984**	**1983**
Current Assets:		
Cash	$ 16,982	$ 9,020
Short-Term Securities	37,683	39,712
Accounts and Notes Receivable (net)	127,544	121,614
Inventory	195,512	173,999
Other Current Assets	9,499	7,634
Total Current Assets	$387,220	$351,979
Property, Plant, and Equipment (net)	406,599	395,098
Other Noncurrent Assets	28,571	40,801
Total Assets	$822,390	$787,878
Liabilities and Stockholders' Equity		
Current Liabilities:		
Notes Payable—Bank	$ 24,658	$ 22,576
Current Installments of Long-Term Debt	1,919	3,320
Accounts Payable and Notes Payable	78,967	69,475
Income Taxes Payable	15,090	14,656
Total Current Liabilities	$120,634	$110,027
Long-Term Debt	155,881	148,400
Deferred Income Taxes Payable	31,361	29,210
Stockholders' Equity (including Capital Stock and Retained Earnings)	514,514	500,241
Total Liabilities and Stockholders' Equity	$822,390	$787,878

The fourth ratio relates an income statement amount (net income) to an average of balance sheet amounts (average stockholders' equity). It is a measure of the productivity of a company in terms of current earnings and stockholders' investments plus accumulated earnings. That is, the ratio shows how much income was earned during the period per dollar of investment and accumulated earnings. The greater the return on stockholders' equity, the more profitable a firm is and the more likely it is to remain solvent. The fourth ratio, then, is an important indicator of a firm's overall performance.

If you think carefully about each of these ratios in terms of their components and their significance as indicators of profitability, liquidity, and solvency, you will notice that the first three can be chained together as a basis for explaining the fourth.

Operating Performance		**Asset Turnover**		**Debt-Equity Management**		**Return on Stockholders' Equity**
$\frac{\text{net income}}{\text{net sales}}$	×	$\frac{\text{net sales}}{\text{average total assets}}$	×	$\frac{\text{average total assets}}{\text{average stockholders' equity}}$	=	$\frac{\text{net income}}{\text{average stockholders' equity}}$

The return on stockholders' equity can be computed directly from the income statement and comparative balance sheets. However, to understand the factors that contribute to this measure of overall performance we must look again at each of the three areas of activity that influence it: operations, asset utilization, and management of debt and equity in financing operations.

To illustrate the relationships between these key ratios, Marvel Company's financial statements for 1984 and 1983 (Exhibits 16-1 and 16-2) were used in computing the following. Note that operating performance and return on stockholders' equity are usually expressed as percentages, whereas the asset turnover and the debt-equity management ratios are generally recorded as quotients.

	Operating Performance		Asset Turnover		Debt-Equity Management		Return on Stockholders' Equity
	net income / net sales	×	net sales / average total assets	×	average total assets / average stockholders' equity	=	net income / average stockholders' equity
1983:							
	$64,650 / $988,417	×	$988,417 / $764,306*	×	$764,306 / $477,210*	=	$64,650 / $477,210*
	6.54%	×	1.29 times	×	1.60 times	=	13.55%†
1984:							
	$40,375 / $1,086,944	×	$1,086,944 / $805,134*	×	$805,134 / $507,378*	=	$40,375 / $507,378*
	3.71%	×	1.35 times	×	1.59 times	=	7.96%

* These numbers are averages of beginning- and end-of-year balances. For average total assets, the beginning figure in 1983 was $740,734; for average stockholders' equity, the beginning figure in 1983 was $454,179.
† The factors may not multiply exactly to the products, due to rounding.

Analysis of Operating Performance

operating performance ratio *an overall measure of the efficiency of operations during a period; computed by dividing net income by net sales*

The ratio of net income to net sales is a measure of a firm's operating performance, or its profitability. For example, in 1984 Marvel Company earned for its stockholders approximately 3.71 cents on each net sales dollar. In 1983 the company had earned 6.54 cents per sales dollar on a smaller sales volume. The reasons for this decrease in profitability will be made clear in the following sections, as we analyze the elements that affect operating performance.

Comparing the current figure against previous years' ratios is one way of judging whether a particular ratio is satisfactory. However, such a comparison may not tell the whole story. The analyst should also compare the ratio against the company's expected operating performance ratio and against the operating performances of other companies in the same industry.

If the ratio is determined to be unsatisfactory, a company may improve it in one of two ways.

1. Increase net income and maintain the same level of sales revenue; that is, reduce costs without reducing sales revenue.
2. Maintain net income in spite of reduced revenues by eliminating the least profitable sales or products, in other words, by increasing the profit margin on each dollar of sales.

Two techniques used in assessing the likelihood of improving this ratio are vertical analysis of each year's income statement and horizontal analysis of the income statements of two or more periods. In addition, a common-size income statement may be prepared to highlight the proportionate changes indicated by vertical analysis.

INCOME STATEMENT VERTICAL ANALYSIS

vertical analysis of financial statements *a technique for analyzing the relationships between items on an income statement or balance sheet by expressing all items as percentages*

The vertical analysis of an income statement examines the relationship of each item to net sales. Generally, net sales is assigned 100 percent. This analysis reveals whether any particular revenue or expense item is out of line in its relationship to net sales. It also provides the analyst with clues as to the company's potential strengths and weaknesses in controlling costs and in achieving its profitability objectives. Exhibit 16-3 is a vertical analysis of the 1984 and 1983 income statements of Marvel Company. The percentages were obtained by dividing net sales into each item—for example, in 1984, $300,421 gross margin ÷ $1,086,944 net sales = 27.6%.

This vertical analysis reveals that Marvel's cost of goods sold was higher as a percentage of sales in 1984 than in 1983 (72.4 percent versus 70.8 percent). The combination of this increase and the lack of an extraordinary gain in 1984 were responsible for the significant drop in net income from 6.5 percent of sales to 3.7 percent of sales.

EXHIBIT 16-3

Marvel Company
Vertical Analysis of Income Statements
*for the Years Ended December 31, 1984 and 1983**

	1984		1983	
Net Sales	$1,086,944	100.0%	$988,417	100.0%
Cost of Goods Sold	786,523	72.4	700,263	70.8
Gross Margin	$ 300,421	27.6%	$288,154	29.2%
Expenses:				
Selling and Administrative Expenses	$ 190,090	17.5%	$172,661	17.5%
Interest Expense	14,995	1.4	13,046	1.3
Total Expenses	$ 205,085	18.9%	$185,707	18.8%
Income Before Taxes	$ 95,336	8.8%	$102,447	10.4%
Income Taxes	54,961	5.1	50,197	5.1
Net Income from Operations	$ 40,375	3.7%	$ 52,250	5.3%
Extraordinary Gain (net of tax)	—	—	12,400	1.3
Net Income	$ 40,375	3.7%	$ 64,650	6.5%

* The percentages may not add (or subtract) to the totals, due to rounding.

INCOME STATEMENT HORIZONTAL ANALYSIS

horizontal analysis of financial statements *a technique for analyzing the percentage change in individual income statement or balance sheet items from one year to the next*

In contrast to vertical analysis, which compares each income statement item with net sales for each year, horizontal analysis computes the percentage change in income statement items from one year to the next. This analysis thus enables the user to determine whether any particular item has changed in an unusual way in relation to the change in net sales from one period to the next. Exhibit 16-4 is a horizontal analysis of Marvel Company's 1984 and 1983 income statements. Note that the change for each item between 1983 and 1984 is shown on a dollar basis in column (3) and on a percentage basis in column (4). The percentages were determined by dividing the dollar increase or decrease in an account by the amount in the account during the base year.

EXHIBIT 16-4

Marvel Company
Horizontal Analysis of Income Statements
for the Years Ended December 31, 1984 and 1983

	(1) 1984	(2) 1983	(3) Dollar Change: (1) − (2)	(4) Percentage Change [(3) ÷ (2)] × 100%
Net Sales	$1,086,944	$988,417	+$98,527	+ 10.0
Cost of Goods Sold	786,523	700,263	+ 86,260	+ 12.3
Gross Margin	$ 300,421	$288,154	+$12,267	+ 4.3
Expenses:				
Selling and Administrative Expenses	$ 190,090	$172,661	+$17,429	+ 10.1
Interest Expense	14,995	13,046	+ 1,949	+ 14.9
Total Expenses	$ 205,085	$185,707	+$19,378	+ 10.4
Income Before Taxes	$ 95,336	$102,447	−$ 7,111	− 6.9
Income Taxes	54,961	50,197	+ 4,764	+ 9.5
Net Income from Operations	$ 40,375	$ 52,250	−$11,875	− 22.7
Extraordinary Gain (net of tax)	—	12,400	− 12,400	−100.0
Net Income	$ 40,375	$ 64,650	−$24,275	− 37.5

This horizontal analysis reveals that from 1983 to 1984 cost of goods sold increased by 12.3 percent ($86,260 ÷ $700,263) and the total of other expenses increased by 10.4 percent ($19,378 ÷ $185,707), whereas net sales increased by only 10.0 percent. These changes resulted in a 6.9 percent decrease in income before taxes. Despite lower earnings, taxes on income were higher in 1984, probably due to the timing of reporting certain revenue and expense items. In addition, there were no extraordinary gains in 1984. The overall effect of these changes was that net income in 1984 was 37.5 percent less than in 1983.

COMMON-SIZE INCOME STATEMENTS

common-size statement *an income statement or balance sheet showing only the percentage relationships obtained by vertical analysis; each item is expressed as a percentage of net sales, total assets, or total liabilities and stockholders' equity*

When a financial statement shows only the percentage relationships obtained by vertical analysis, a common-size statement has been prepared. For an income statement, this means that each item is expressed as a percentage of net sales. By omitting the dollar amounts shown on a vertical analysis, a common-size income statement highlights the changing proportions of revenues, expenses, and net income, making it easier for the analyst to compare several periods.

Besides being used to compare periods of a firm's operations, common-size income statements are well suited to comparisons between firms regardless of their relative size. Comparisons between companies in the same industry can draw attention to, and thus encourage investigation of, the variations in accounting practices and financial policies. For example, suppose the cost of goods sold percentages for two companies in the same industry are radically different. This might indicate that they are using different inventory costing alternatives or that one company is spending too much on inventory in relation to its net sales. The analyst would want to investigate the reasons for the variation.

A common-size income statement for Marvel Company is presented in Exhibit 16–5. This statement compares operating performance in 1984 and 1983.

Operating performance can be analyzed in a variety of other ways. For example, the current year's operating results (as reflected in the income statement) could be compared with the budgeted income statement for the period. Using several methods of analyzing operating performance will help management and others understand the company's operating strengths and weaknesses.

EXHIBIT 16–5

Marvel Company
Common-Size Income Statements
*for the Years Ended December 31, 1984 and 1983**

	1984	1983
Net Sales	100.0%	100.0%
Cost of Goods Sold	72.4	70.8
Gross Margin	27.6%	29.2%
Expenses:		
Selling and Administrative Expenses	17.5%	17.5%
Interest Expense	1.4	1.3
Total Expenses	18.9%	18.8%
Income Before Taxes	8.8%	10.4%
Income Taxes	5.1	5.1
Net Income from Operations	3.7%	5.3%
Extraordinary Gain (net of tax)	–	1.3
Net Income	3.7%	6.5%

* The percentages may not add to the totals, due to rounding.

TO SUMMARIZE The operating performance ratio is a measure of a firm's overall profitability. It is computed by dividing net sales into net income. To determine whether this ratio can be improved, a company can employ either of two techniques: vertical analysis of each year's income statement or horizontal analysis of the income statements of two or more periods. Common-size statements, which are derived from vertical analysis, show the percentage relationships of the individual items on a statement to the totals.

Analysis of Asset Turnover

asset turnover ratio *an overall measure of how effectively assets are used during a period; computed by dividing net sales by average total assets*

A measure of a company's efficiency in utilizing its resources is the asset turnover ratio; it is net sales divided by average total assets. This ratio shows the rate at which assets are "turned over." Stated in another way, it is a measure of the amount of sales revenue generated with each dollar of assets owned by the company. Marvel Company increased its asset turnover from 1.29 times in 1983 to 1.35 times in 1984.

$$\text{Asset turnover} = \frac{\text{net sales}}{\text{average total assets}}$$

$$1983 \quad \frac{\$988{,}417}{\$764{,}306} = 1.29$$

$$1984 \quad \frac{\$1{,}086{,}944}{\$805{,}134} = 1.35$$

As we noted earlier, in this ratio the numerator (sales) is an income statement amount that covers a period of time, whereas the denominator relates to a particular date. To develop a reliable ratio, the analyst must convert the denominator into a figure that reflects a period of time. This is accomplished by averaging total assets for the period. Thus, for Marvel Company in 1984, the beginning- and end-of-year balances for total assets would be added and divided by 2 [($822,390 + $787,878)/2 = $805,134]. If more precise results are desired, quarterly or monthly totals can be used in computing the average.

The asset turnover ratios for two years can be compared to indicate how well a company performed in the current year in relation to the previous year. Similarly, the ratio for the current year can be compared with the projected turnover, or with competitors' turnovers.

In order to improve its asset turnover, a company must analyze how well each of its major types of assets is being utilized. To do so, management uses vertical, horizontal, and ratio analysis, and common-size balance sheets.

BALANCE SHEET VERTICAL ANALYSIS

Vertical analysis of a balance sheet relates each account to total assets or to total liabilities and stockholders' equity, with each amount being expressed as a percentage of one of these larger categories. For example, cash would be expressed as a percentage of total assets, and accounts payable as a percentage of total liabilities and stockholders' equity. Exhibit 16-6 is a vertical analysis of the 1984 and 1983 balance sheets of Marvel Company.

As illustrated, there has been only a small increase in the percentage of current assets in relation to total assets, with a corresponding decrease in property, plant, and equipment and other assets. Thus, this vertical analysis does not reveal any significant shifts in the turnover of assets between the two years.

EXHIBIT 16-6

Marvel Company
Vertical Analysis of the Balance Sheets
*as of December 31, 1984 and 1983**

Assets	**1984**		**1983**	
Current Assets:				
Cash	$ 16,982	2.1%	$ 9,020	1.1%
Short-Term Securities	37,683	4.6	39,712	5.0
Accounts and Notes Receivable (net)	127,544	15.5	121,614	15.4
Inventory	195,512	23.8	173,999	22.1
Other Current Assets	9,499	1.2	7,634	1.0
Total Current Assets	$387,220	47.1%	$351,979	44.7%
Property, Plant, and Equipment (net)	406,599	49.4	395,098	50.1
Other Noncurrent Assets	28,571	3.5	40,801	5.2
Total Assets	$822,390	100.0%	$787,878	100.0%
Liabilities and Stockholders' Equity				
Current Liabilities:				
Notes Payable—Bank	$ 24,658	3.0%	$ 22,576	2.9%
Current Installments of Long-Term Debt	1,919	.2	3,320	.4
Accounts Payable and Notes Payable	78,967	9.6	69,475	8.8
Income Taxes Payable	15,090	1.8	14,656	1.9
Total Current Liabilities	$120,634	14.7%	$110,027	14.0%
Long-Term Debt	155,881	19.0	148,400	18.8
Deferred Income Taxes Payable	31,361	3.8	29,210	3.7
Stockholders' Equity	514,514	62.6	500,241	63.5
Total Liabilities and Stockholders' Equity	$822,390	100.0%	$787,878	100.0%

* The percentages may not add to the totals, due to rounding.

BALANCE SHEET HORIZONTAL ANALYSIS

Horizontal analysis of two or more balance sheets indicates the dollar and percentage changes from year to year for individual accounts. Exhibit 16-7 is a horizontal analysis of Marvel Company's 1984 and 1983 balance sheets.

The accounts that had the most significant changes (in terms of dollars *and* percentages) were Inventory, Other Noncurrent Assets, and Accounts Payable and Notes Payable. Major percentage changes also occurred in balance sheet items that were small in size, such as Cash, Other Current Assets, and Current Installments of Long-Term Debt. When balance sheet accounts change significantly, it usually means that management has revised aspects of its financial policy. In such cases, the statement user should seek additional information to explain these policy changes.

With horizontal analysis, it is important to recognize that a large percentage change in an item with a small absolute dollar amount (such as Current Installments of Long-Term Debt) is probably not a very significant change, not only because the dollar amount is small, but also because management may not have any immediate control over the item.

EXHIBIT 16-7

Marvel Company
Horizontal Analysis of the Balance Sheets
as of December 31, 1984 and 1983

Assets	1984	1983	Dollar Change	Percentage Change
Current Assets:				
Cash	$ 16,982	$ 9,020	$ 7,962	88.3
Short-Term Securities	37,683	39,712	(2,029)	(5.1)
Accounts and Notes Receivable (net)	127,544	121,614	5,930	4.9
Inventory	195,512	173,999	21,513	12.4
Other Current Assets	9,499	7,634	1,865	24.4
Total Current Assets	$387,220	$351,979	$35,241	10.0
Property, Plant, and Equipment (net)	406,599	395,098	11,501	2.9
Other Noncurrent Assets	28,571	40,801	(12,230)	(30.0)
Total Assets	$822,390	$787,878	$34,512	4.4
Liabilities and Stockholders' Equity				
Current Liabilities:				
Notes Payable—Bank	$ 24,658	$ 22,576	$ 2,082	9.2
Current Installments of Long-Term Debt	1,919	3,320	(1,401)	(42.2)
Accounts Payable and Notes Payable	78,967	69,475	9,492	13.7
Income Taxes Payable	15,090	14,656	434	3.0
Total Current Liabilities	$120,634	$110,027	$10,607	9.6
Long-Term Debt	155,881	148,400	7,481	5.0
Deferred Income Taxes Payable	31,361	29,210	2,151	7.4
Stockholders' Equity	514,514	500,241	14,273	2.9
Total Liabilties and Stockholders' Equity	$822,390	$787,878	$34,512	4.4

COMMON-SIZE BALANCE SHEETS

A common-size balance sheet shows percentage relationships of individual items to total assets or to total liabilities and stockholders' equity. For example, it shows the ratio of cash to total assets and the ratio of long-term debt to total liabilities and stockholders' equity. A common-size balance sheet thus focuses the reader's attention on: (1) the distribution of assets among current assets, property, plant, and equipment, and other assets; and (2) the distribution of liabilities and equities among current liabilities, long-term liabilities, and stockholders' equity.

Like a common-size income statement, a common-size balance sheet can be used to compare several periods of a firm's operations, thus revealing changing proportions of assets, liabilities, and equity. It can also be used to compare companies in the same industry.

BALANCE SHEET RATIO ANALYSIS

A number of ratios help explain why the asset turnover ratio changed as it did by indicating how well specific assets were utilized. These are the current ratio, the acid-test ratio, accounts receivable turnover, inventory turnover, working capital turnover, and property, plant, and equipment turnover. Each ratio is discussed separately and then related to the asset turnover ratio.

Current Ratio

As you know, working capital is the excess of total current assets over total current liabilities. The amount of the excess is a measure of liquidity and represents a margin of safety for meeting current liabilities. The relative margin of safety is usually expressed as the ratio of current assets to current liabilities, which is called the current ratio, or the working capital ratio.

current ratio (or working capital ratio) *a measure of liquidity that represents the margin of safety for meeting current liabilities; computed by dividing current assets by current liabilities*

The working capital totals and current ratios for Marvel Company for 1983 and 1984 are

	1984	1983
Current Assets	$387,220	$351,979
Current Liabilities	120,634	110,027
Working Capital	$266,586	$241,952
Current (Working Capital) Ratio	$\frac{\$387,220}{\$120,634} = 3.21$	$\frac{\$351,979}{\$110,027} = 3.20$

Working capital increased by $24,634 ($266,586 − $241,952) from 1983 to 1984, which represents a 0.01 change in the current ratio. At the end of 1984, the firm had $3.21 of current assets for every $1.00 of current liabilities.

A particular current ratio is considered high or low depending on the nature of the business involved. Many financial statement readers use 2:1 as an acceptable ratio of current assets to current liabilities. However, companies in different industries have different liquidity needs, and a 2:1 ratio may not be good for every type of business. Rule-of-thumb guidelines for any ratio are arbitrary and cannot be appropriate for all companies in all industries. The important thing is for the current ratio to be at the right level to meet the particular company's needs. If the ratio is too low, the company may not be sufficiently liquid to pay current liabilities or to take advantage of discounts for prompt payment. If it is too high, the company probably has too many assets tied up in working capital for its current level of activity and the excess assets are not earning an appropriate return.

Acid-Test Ratio

acid-test ratio (or quick ratio) *a measure of a firm's ability to meet current liabilities; more restrictive than the current ratio, it is computed by dividing net quick assets (all current assets, except inventories and prepaid expenses) by current liabilities*

The acid-test ratio (sometimes called the quick ratio) is calculated because the current ratio does not reflect the fact that a large portion of current assets, specifically inventory and prepaid assets, may not be very liquid and therefore not readily available for paying current liabilities.

The acid-test ratio is computed by dividing cash, marketable securities, and notes and accounts receivable by current liabilities. To illustrate, we will calculate the acid-test ratios for Marvel Company for 1983 and 1984 using information from Exhibits 16-1 and 16-2.

$$\text{Acid-test ratio} = \frac{\text{cash, short-term securities, notes and accounts receivable}}{\text{current liabilities}}$$

$$1983 \quad \frac{\$170{,}346}{\$110{,}027} = 1.55$$

$$1984 \quad \frac{\$182{,}209}{\$120{,}634} = 1.51$$

These figures show a slight drop in the acid-test ratio. For both years, liquid current assets are approximately one and one-half times as large as current liabilities. The size of this ratio will help users judge whether the firm is maintaining an efficient level of liquid assets to meet its current obligations.

Accounts Receivable Turnover

accounts receivable turnover *a measure used to determine a company's average collection period for receivables; computed by dividing net sales (or net credit sales) by average accounts receivable*

Accounts receivable turnover reflects a company's collection record. A trend toward a lower turnover could indicate a laxness in collection activity or a change in credit policy.

This ratio is computed by dividing net credit sales by average accounts receivable for a period. If net credit sales cannot be determined easily from the financial statements, then total sales are used as a substitute.

number of days' sales in receivables *a measure of the average number of days it takes to collect a credit sale; computed by dividing 365 days by the accounts receivable turnover*

Accounts receivable turnover is often more useful if dollar amounts are converted into the number of days of uncollected sales, which reflects the average time taken to collect a credit sale. The easiest way to compute the number of days' sales in receivables is to divide the number of days in the period by the accounts receivable turnover.

To illustrate the calculation of accounts receivable turnover and the number of days' sales in receivables, we will use the following data for Marvel Company.

	1984	1983
Net Credit Sales	$1,086,944	$988,417
Accounts Receivable (net):		
January 1	$ 121,614	$106,675
December 31	127,544	121,614
Total	$ 249,158	$228,289
Average (÷ 2)	$ 124,579	$114,145

$$\text{Accounts receivable turnover} = \frac{\text{net credit sales}}{\text{average accounts receivable}}$$

$$1983 \quad \frac{\$988{,}417}{\$114{,}145} = 8.66$$

$$1984 \quad \frac{\$1{,}086{,}944}{\$124{,}579} = 8.72$$

$$\text{Number of days' sales in receivables} = \frac{\text{number of days in a period}}{\text{accounts receivable turnover}}$$

$$1983 \quad \frac{365 \text{ days}^1}{8.66} = 42.1 \text{ days}$$

$$1984 \quad \frac{365 \text{ days}}{8.72} = 41.9 \text{ days}$$

Marvel Company increased its accounts receivable turnover from 8.66 times to 8.72 times between 1983 and 1984. This very small improvement in turnover reduced the number of days' sales in receivables from 42.1 to 41.9. An improvement in accounts receivable turnover and in the collection period means that less money is tied up in receivables, which, in turn, contributes to a higher asset turnover ratio. And as we have seen, Marvel's asset turnover increased from 1.29 times in 1983 to 1.35 times in 1984, showing a more efficient utilization of assets.

Inventory Turnover

inventory turnover *a measure of the efficiency with which inventory is managed; computed by dividing cost of goods sold by average inventory for a period*

Another influence on the asset turnover ratio is inventory turnover. This ratio, which is computed by dividing cost of goods sold for a period by the average inventory for the period, is useful in determining whether a company is managing its inventory efficiently. If the turnover is low, it means that the company is either overstocking or building up a stock of obsolete merchandise. Whichever the case, too high an inventory indicates that excess resources are being tied up in working capital instead of being used to earn a return for the company. If the turnover is too high, the company may lose sales because the goods are not in inventory when customers want them.

[1] In this chapter we assume 365 days in a year.

number of days' sales in inventory *an alternative measure of how well inventory is being managed; computed by dividing 365 days by the inventory turnover ratio*

Inventory turnover is often more meaningful if dollar amounts are converted into number of days' sales in inventory. This ratio indicates the average time it takes to dispose of inventory. It is computed by dividing the number of days in a period by the inventory turnover.

To illustrate the calculation of inventory turnover and the number of days' sales in inventory, we will use the following data from Marvel Company.

	1984	1983
Cost of Goods Sold	$786,523	$700,263
Inventories:		
January 1	$173,999	$167,286
December 31	195,512	173,999
Total	$369,511	$341,285
Average Inventory (÷ 2)	$184,756	$170,643

$$\text{Inventory turnover} = \frac{\text{cost of goods sold}}{\text{average inventory}}$$

$$1983 \quad \frac{\$700{,}263}{\$170{,}643} = 4.10$$

$$1984 \quad \frac{\$786{,}523}{\$184{,}756} = 4.26$$

$$\text{Number of days' sales in inventory} = \frac{\text{number of days in a period}}{\text{inventory turnover}}$$

$$1983 \quad \frac{365 \text{ days}}{4.10} = 89.0 \text{ days}$$

$$1984 \quad \frac{365 \text{ days}}{4.26} = 85.7 \text{ days}$$

Marvel Company increased its inventory turnover from 4.10 in 1983 to 4.26 in 1984. This had the effect of reducing the number of days' sales in inventory from 89.0 in 1983 to 85.7 in 1984. The improvement in inventory turnover, like the improvement in accounts receivable turnover, contributed to the improvement in Marvel's asset turnover ratio from 1983 to 1984.

working capital turnover *a measure of the amount of working capital used in generating the sales of a period; computed by dividing net sales by average working capital*

number of days' sales invested in working capital *an alternative measure of the amount of working capital used in generating the sales of a period; computed by dividing 365 days by the working capital turnover*

Working Capital Turnover

A more general ratio, which includes both accounts receivable turnover and inventory turnover in the sense that they both involve use of current assets, is working capital turnover. It is computed by dividing net sales by average working capital for a period, and it indicates the amount of working capital used in generating the sales of that period.

Like the other ratios we have discussed, this ratio may be more useful if dollar amounts are converted to number of days' sales invested in working capital. A decrease in number of days' sales invested in working capital would suggest an improvement in the utilization of current assets, which, in turn, would contribute to an improvement in the key ratio, the asset turnover ratio.

To illustrate the method of calculating working capital turnover and the number of days' sales invested in working capital, we will use the following data for Marvel Company.

	1984	1983
Net Sales	$1,086,944	$988,417
Working Capital:		
January 1	$ 241,952	$217,848
December 31	266,586	241,952
Total	$ 508,538	$459,800
Average (÷ 2)	$ 254,269	$229,900

$$\text{Working capital turnover} = \frac{\text{net sales}}{\text{average working capital}}$$

$$1983 \quad \frac{\$988{,}417}{\$229{,}900} = 4.30$$

$$1984 \quad \frac{\$1{,}086{,}944}{\$254{,}269} = 4.27$$

$$\text{Number of days' sales invested in working capital} = \frac{\text{number of days in a period}}{\text{working capital turnover}}$$

$$1983 \quad \frac{365 \text{ days}}{4.30} = 84.9 \text{ days}$$

$$1984 \quad \frac{365 \text{ days}}{4.27} = 85.5 \text{ days}$$

The working capital turnover for Marvel Company decreased very slightly from 1983 to 1984. This suggests that the small improvements in the accounts receivable and inventory turnovers were offset by larger investments in other current assets in relation to current liabilities. Marvel's overall improvement in asset turnover must therefore have been generated by an improvement in the turnover of property, plant, and equipment.

Property, Plant, and Equipment Turnover

property, plant, and equipment turnover *a measure of how well property, plant, and equipment are being utilized in generating a period's sales; computed by dividing net sales by average property, plant, and equipment*

Property, plant, and equipment turnover is computed by dividing net sales by property, plant, and equipment.[2] This ratio indicates how efficiently these assets are being utilized in generating sales volume.

[2] The ending amounts of property, plant, and equipment were used to calculate this ratio because the information to compute the average amount for property, plant, and equipment is not available for 1983. An average amount for the year is preferable unless there has been little change in the account during the year.

To illustrate, we will calculate Marvel's property, plant, and equipment turnover for 1983 and 1984, using information from Exhibits 16–1 and 16–2.

$$\text{Property, plant, and equipment turnover} = \frac{\text{net sales}}{\text{average net property, plant, and equipment}}$$

$$1983 \quad \frac{\$988{,}417}{\$395{,}098^2} = 2.50$$

$$1984 \quad \frac{\$1{,}086{,}944}{\$406{,}599^2} = 2.67$$

The increase in property, plant, and equipment turnover from 2.50 times in 1983 to 2.67 times in 1984 was a primary contributor to the increase in the asset turnover ratio from 1.29 times in 1983 to 1.35 times in 1984.

TO SUMMARIZE The asset turnover ratio is an important overall indicator of a company's efficiency in utilizing its assets. A number of ratios represent components of the asset turnover ratio: the current ratio, the acid-test ratio, accounts receivable turnover, inventory turnover, working capital turnover, and property, plant, and equipment turnover. Proper interpretation of these ratios not only helps managers determine how to improve asset turnover, but also enables investors and creditors to assess the profitability and liquidity of a company.

Analysis of Debt–Equity Management

debt–equity management ratio *a measure of the relative utilization of debt and equity; computed by dividing average total assets by average stockholders' equity*

The third key ratio, debt–equity management, indicates the extent to which debt and equity are used in financing a company's operations. It is computed by dividing average total assets by average stockholders' equity. The excess of average total assets over average stockholders' equity represents the average amount of debt outstanding during the year ($A - SE = L$).

The debt–equity management relationship is used in determining the margin of safety for creditors by identifying the extent to which a company is leveraging, or trading on, equity. Leveraging, as you recall, refers to the use of stockholders' equity as a base for borrowing money. If a company can use borrowed funds to earn more than the funds cost, the excess return accrues to the stockholders. Thus, leveraging benefits both the company, by increasing its assets, and the stockholders, by increasing earnings.

The amount of leveraging a company can employ is limited, however. Banks and other lending institutions will expect a company, especially a young company without much of a borrowing history, to have a satisfactory equity-to-debt ratio in order to be eligible for a loan. Also, interest on borrowed funds has to be paid before any dividends can be paid to stockholders. If income before the interest deduction is not large enough to cover the interest charge, then the stockholders will be deprived of dividends.

A prudent management tries to keep the amount of borrowed funds at such a level that the interest charges will be considerably less than the income before the interest deduction. The more stable a company's earnings, the greater the confidence with which management can determine the level of borrowed funds it can maintain without taking undue risks. A public utility, for example, can maintain a relatively large amount of debt because, as a quasi-monopoly, its earnings are relatively stable. An automobile manufacturing company, on the other hand, has large fluctuations in its earnings and so has to keep its debt small in relation to stockholders' equity. Otherwise, in a bad year the fixed interest charges may exceed earnings and cause a serious liquidity problem.

Although the ratio of average total assets to average stockholders' equity is the key measure of debt-equity management used in this chapter, analysts also use other ratios to complement and supplement this ratio. Some of these are

1. Long-term debt to total assets $= \dfrac{\text{long-term debt}}{\text{total assets}}$

   This ratio provides an indication of how much loss a corporation can suffer without any loss to creditors.

2. Times interest earned $= \dfrac{\text{income before interest and income taxes}}{\text{interest charges}}$

   This ratio indicates the company's margin above the fixed interest charges to be paid to creditors.

3. Long-term debt to stockholders' equity $= \dfrac{\text{long-term debt}}{\text{stockholders' equity}}$

   This ratio indicates the amount of funds supplied to a company by creditors as opposed to the amount provided by stockholders plus the accumulated earnings. Industry experience would dictate the maximum percentage of debt that would be reasonable.

These debt-equity management ratios are primarily measures of a firm's solvency. Thus, they indicate the degree of protection available to mortgage and bond holders, as well as the risk to common stockholders whose return becomes less certain as the proportion of debt increases.

To illustrate the calculations for these debt-equity management ratios, we will use data from Marvel's 1984 and 1983 financial statements (Exhibits 16-1 and 16-2).

	1984	1983
1. Long-term debt to total assets	$\dfrac{\$155{,}881}{\$822{,}390} = 18.95\%$	$\dfrac{\$148{,}400}{\$787{,}878} = 18.84\%$
2. Times interest earned	$\dfrac{\$110{,}331}{\$14{,}995} = 7.36$ times	$\dfrac{\$115{,}493}{\$13{,}046} = 8.85$ times
3. Long-term debt to stockholders' equity	$\dfrac{\$155{,}881}{\$514{,}514} = 30.30\%$	$\dfrac{\$148{,}400}{\$500{,}241} = 29.67\%$

As we showed on page 562, Marvel's ratio of average total assets to average stockholders' equity decreased from 1.60 times in 1983 to 1.59 times in 1984. This decrease, although slight, reflects a shift toward a greater use of leveraging and is confirmed by the trend in the debt-equity management ratios computed above. Note that the percentage of debt in Marvel Company's financial structure is not large. The margin of safety of earnings in 1984 was comfortable (interest is earned 7.36 times) and was clearly sufficient to cover any fixed interest charges, despite the fact that 1984 was not a good earnings year. Finally, note that the relationship of long-term debt to stockholders' equity is relatively unchanged.

TO SUMMARIZE The various debt-equity management ratios are generally consistent with each other and provide a picture of the amount of debt in relation to total assets and to stockholders' equity, and a measure of the extent of fixed interest charges relative to the earnings available to cover those charges.

Return on Assets and Stockholders' Equity

Each of the three key ratios—operating performance, asset turnover, and debt-equity management—gives an analyst important information about a company. However, as explained earlier, a view of a company's overall performance is provided only when the ratios are brought together. Thus, if the ratios for operating performance and asset turnover are chained together, the analyst can determine the return on total assets (or on total investment by creditors and stockholders). And if all the key ratios are chained together, the return on stockholders' equity can be computed.

RETURN ON TOTAL ASSETS

return on total assets ratio *a measure of operating performance and efficiency in utilizing assets; computed in its simplest form by dividing net income by average total assets*

The return on total assets ratio may be computed directly by dividing net income by average total assets. It may also be computed by chaining together the operating performance and asset turnover ratios.

Operating Performance	×	Asset Turnover	=	Return on Total Assets
$\frac{\text{net income}}{\text{net sales}}$	×	$\frac{\text{net sales}}{\text{average total assets}}$	=	$\frac{\text{net income}}{\text{average total assets}}$

To illustrate, we will calculate return on total assets for Marvel Company for 1983 and 1984 (again using Exhibits 16-1 and 16-2).

$$1983 \quad \frac{\$64{,}650}{\$988{,}417} \times \frac{\$988{,}417}{\$764{,}306} = \frac{\$64{,}650}{\$764{,}306}$$

$$6.54\% \times 1.29 \text{ times} = 8.44\%$$

$$1984 \quad \frac{\$40{,}375}{\$1{,}086{,}944} \times \frac{\$1{,}086{,}944}{\$805{,}134} = \frac{\$40{,}375}{\$805{,}134}$$

$$3.71\% \times 1.35 \text{ times} = 5.01\%$$

Another way of computing the return on total assets is to use income before taxes plus interest expense. Interest expense is added back to income because it is a payment for assets provided by creditors, and the numerator is supposed to reflect total return before any distributions to investors. Income before taxes is used because the interest expense reduced the amount of taxes paid; without interest expense, the taxes would be higher. Furthermore, any tax savings that result from interest expense have nothing to do with management's performance—which is what return on total assets is measuring. Thus, many financial analysts prefer to use this method because it more accurately reflects return to both creditors and investors.

To illustrate, in 1983, Marvel's income before taxes was $102,447 and its interest expense was $13,046, so the adjusted income figure would be $115,493; in 1984, income before taxes was $95,336 and interest expense was $14,995, which makes the adjusted income figure $110,331. Return on total assets is calculated as follows:

$$1983 \quad \frac{\$115{,}493}{\$988{,}417} \times \frac{\$988{,}417}{\$764{,}306} = 15.1\%$$

$$1984 \quad \frac{\$110{,}331}{\$1{,}086{,}944} \times \frac{\$1{,}086{,}944}{\$805{,}134} = 13.7\%$$

With either method of computing return on total assets, the chaining of the operating performance and asset turnover ratios reminds the analyst that the total return is a function of both controlling expenses and efficiently utilizing assets. To judge how satisfactory a return is, the analyst must compare it with the industry average and with the rate of return a company must earn to satisfy the demands of its owners and creditors. Return on total assets is thus a measure of a company's performance in meeting its responsibilities to its creditors and owners.

return on stockholders' equity *a measure of overall performance from a stockholder's viewpoint; includes management of operations, use of assets, and management of debt and equity, and is computed by dividing net income by average stockholders' equity*

RETURN ON STOCKHOLDERS' EQUITY

Return on stockholders' equity may be computed by chaining together the three key ratios: operating performance, asset turnover, and debt-equity management. To illustrate, we again present the calculation for Marvel Company in 1983 and 1984. Recall that return on stockholders' equity is a measure of a firm's overall performance.

	Operating Performance		Asset Turnover		Debt–Equity Management		Return on Stockholders' Equity*
	net income / net sales	×	net sales / average total assets	×	average total assets / average stockholders' equity	=	net income / average stockholders' equity
1983:							
	$64,650 / $988,417	×	$988,417 / $764,306	×	$764,306 / $477,210	=	$64,650 / $477,210
	6.54%	×	1.29 times	×	1.60 times	=	13.55%
1984:							
	$40,375 / $1,086,944	×	$1,086,944 / $805,134	×	$805,134 / $507,378	=	$40,375 / $507,378
	3.71%	×	1.35 times	×	1.59 times	=	7.96%

* The factors may not multiply exactly to the products, due to rounding.

Marvel's return on equity was lower in 1984 than in 1983, primarily because 1984 net income was only 3.71 percent of net sales, as compared with 6.54 percent in 1983.

Chaining the three key ratios is only one way of measuring the return to stockholders. Several others are useful. In this section, we will discuss four other commonly used methods: earnings per share, price-earnings ratio, dividend payout ratio, and book value per share.

EARNINGS PER SHARE

earnings per share (EPS) *the amount of net income (earnings) related to each share of stock; computed by dividing net income by the number of shares of common stock outstanding during the period*

Earnings per share (EPS) is used to measure earnings growth and earnings potential. If a company has a simple capital structure, with only common stock outstanding, earnings per share is computed by dividing net income by the average number of shares of common stock outstanding during the year. If the capital structure includes both preferred and common stock, the preferred dividend requirement must be subtracted from net income before earnings per share is computed.

For example, if total net income for the year is $130,000, and preferred stock is entitled to a current-dividend preference of $20,000, then earnings per share for common stock (assuming that 26,000 shares of common stock are outstanding) would be computed by dividing $110,000 of net income ($130,000 − $20,000) by 26,000 common shares to obtain earnings per common share of $4.23. To simplify our calculations, we will assume in the remainder of this section that the number of shares of common stock outstanding at the beginning of the year is the same as the number of shares outstanding at the end of the year—that is, no shares were issued or reacquired during the year.

To illustrate the computation for earnings per share, we will assume that Marvel Company's capital structure consists entirely of 26,000 shares of common stock. Earnings per share for 1983 and 1984 would be computed as follows:

$$\text{Earnings per share} = \frac{\text{net income}}{\text{(average) number of shares of common stock outstanding}}$$

1983 EPS—Net income from operations $= \dfrac{\$52{,}250}{26{,}000 \text{ shares}} = \$2.01$

EPS—Extraordinary gain $= \dfrac{\$12{,}400}{26{,}000 \text{ shares}} = \$0.48$

EPS—Net income $= \dfrac{\$64{,}650}{26{,}000 \text{ shares}} = \$2.49$

1984 EPS—Net income $= \dfrac{\$40{,}375}{26{,}000 \text{ shares}} = \$1.55$

Note that only one EPS number is needed for 1984 because there was no extraordinary gain. Earnings per share would be presented on the income statement in the following manner.

	1984	1983
Earnings per Share of Common Stock:		
Income Before Extraordinary Gain	$1.55	$2.01
Extraordinary Gain	—	0.48
Net Income	$1.55	$2.49

PRICE-EARNINGS RATIO

price-earnings (P/E) ratio *a measure of growth potential, earnings stability, and management capabilities; computed by dividing market price per share by earnings per share*

Financial analysts use the price-earnings (P/E) ratio in judging the potential value of a company's stock in relation to that of other companies. This is because the P/E ratios of a company over a period of years indicate the stability of its earnings, and are therefore assumed to reflect the capabilities of management and the growth potential of the company.

The ratio is computed by dividing the market price of a stock by its earnings per share. To illustrate, we will use the figures just calculated for Marvel Company. If the price of the stock was $18\frac{3}{8}$ ($18.375) when earnings were $1.55 per share, the stock would have a price-earnings ratio of 11.9.

$$\text{Price-earnings ratio} = \frac{\text{market price per share}}{\text{earnings per share}}$$

$$\frac{\$18.38}{\$1.55} = 11.9$$

A P/E ratio of 11.9 means that the stock is selling for 11.9 times annual earnings. To judge this ratio, the analyst will probably compare it with the price-earnings ratios for the stocks of Marvel's major competitors.

DIVIDEND PAYOUT RATIO

dividend payout ratio *a measure of earnings paid out in dividends; computed by dividing cash dividends by the net income available to each class of stock*

The dividend payout ratio indicates the percentage of earnings distributed to stockholders. It is computed by dividing cash dividends by the net income available to each class of stock.

To illustrate, we will assume that Marvel Company had the following dividend payout ratios on its common stock in 1983 and 1984.

$$\text{Dividend payout ratio} = \frac{\text{cash dividends}}{\text{net income available to common stockholders}}$$

$$1983 \quad \frac{\$26{,}000^*}{\$64{,}650} = 40\%$$

$$1984 \quad \frac{\$26{,}000^*}{\$40{,}375} = 64\%$$

The numerators suggest that the company has a policy of paying a stable dividend. It appears that in 1984 the board of directors, in keeping with a stable dividend policy, decided not to reduce dividends despite a poor earnings performance. This resulted in a much higher payout ratio than would have been appropriate for that year's net income.

If an investor is interested in buying stocks that will provide a significant annual cash return, the dividend payout ratio is an important piece of information. A "growth company" usually reinvests a large percentage of its earnings and pays little or nothing in dividends. A more stable, mature company, such as a public utility, is likely to pay out a high percentage of its earnings in dividends.

BOOK VALUE PER SHARE

book value per share *a measure of net worth; computed by dividing stockholders' equity for each class of stock by the number of shares outstanding for that class*

Book value per share is one measure of a company's net worth. Keep in mind that it usually will not reflect the fair market values of assets and liabilities, because balance sheets generally report only historical costs. Therefore, the book value concept must be used with care in assessing a firm's financial condition.

Book value per share is computed by dividing stockholders' equity by the number of shares outstanding at year-end. If the capital structure contains both preferred and common stock, a portion of stockholders' equity must be assigned to preferred stock before the balance can be used in computing book value per share of common stock. Note that book value per share uses number of shares outstanding at year-end rather than average number of shares, as EPS does. This is because book value is a measure of net assets per share as of a balance sheet date, not for a period of time.

* Assuming that there are 26,000 shares of common stock outstanding, the company paid dividends of $1.00 per share in both 1983 and 1984.

To illustrate the calculation of book value per share, we will now assume that Marvel Company's financial structure contains both preferred and common stock, and that some of its stock has been reacquired and placed in the treasury.

Marvel Company
Stockholders' Equity as of December 31, 1984

Preferred Stock (161 shares issued)		$ 16,100
Common Stock (26,000 shares issued)		26,000
Paid-in Capital in Excess of Par—Common Stock		47,067
Retained Earnings		434,642
Total		$523,809
Less Treasury Stock at Cost:		
Preferred Stock (43 shares reacquired)	$3,986	
Common Stock (193 shares reacquired)	5,309	9,295
Total Stockholders' Equity		$514,514

In computing book value per share, an analyst assigns to preferred stockholders the portion of stockholders' equity that represents the redemption value of the outstanding preferred shares, including any dividends in arrears. Assuming that there are no dividends in arrears on Marvel's preferred stock and that its redemption value is $102.75 per share ($12,125 ÷ 118*), the book value for preferred and common shares would be computed as follows:

Total Stockholders' Equity		$514,514
Less Portion of Equity Assigned to Preferred Stock:		
Outstanding Shares	118	
Redemption Value	×$102.75	12,125
Stockholders' Equity Applicable to Common Stock		$502,389

$$\text{Book value per share} = \frac{\text{stockholders' equity}}{\text{number of shares of stock outstanding}}$$

$$\text{Preferred stock} \quad \frac{\$12{,}125}{118} = \$102.75$$

$$\text{Common stock} \quad \frac{\$502{,}389}{25{,}807\dagger} = \$19.47$$

Care must be taken in assigning the appropriate portion of stockholders' equity to preferred stock. The amount assigned is not identical to the equity accounts that have the word "preferred" in their titles. Rather, preferred stock is assigned a portion of stockholders' equity based on the claims of preferred shareholders in liquidation, including any premium to be paid above par value and dividends in arrears on cumulative preferred stock. Thus, the stockholders' equity clearly assignable to preferred stock should

* 161 shares of preferred stock issued, less 43 shares in treasury.
† 26,000 shares of common stock issued, less 193 shares in treasury.

be used to compute the book value per share of preferred stock. The remainder should be assigned to common stock for the purpose of computing its book value per share.

Although book value per share often bears little resemblance to the actual market price of the stock, it may provide some useful information about a company's future. However, the other measures of overall performance—namely, return on stockholders' equity, earnings per share, dividend payout ratio, and price-earnings ratio—are better indicators of a company's expected performance.

Summary of Analysis of Financial Statements

Exhibit 16–8 summarizes the discussion of financial statement analysis by showing the relationships of the various subsidiary ratios to the four key ratios: operating performance, asset turnover, debt-equity management, and return on stockholders' equity. Always keep in mind, though, that other factors must be considered in analyzing a company, and be careful not to read too much into the numbers generated by these ratios.

Limitations of Financial Statement Analysis

Financial statement analysis serves an important function, but it must be used with care. Many people accept numbers computed by an expert without much question. Although ratios may be computed precisely, they are no better than the data on which they are based. Three areas of concern in computing ratios are (1) the use of estimates and judgments in measuring assets, liabilities, and income; (2) the fact that changing values and price levels frequently are not reflected in the financial statements; and (3) the fact that ratios are useful only when they can be related to comparable data, for example, industry statistics.

USE OF ESTIMATES

Estimates and judgments are used in allocating costs among periods—for example, in measuring depreciation, bad debts, warranty expenses, and prepaid expenses. The allocation judgments made by those who prepare the financial statements may result in different ratios. And, since ratios are meaningful only when they are compared, care must be taken that the ratios being compared have been computed in the same way, or at least that they can be translated into common terms. Many analysts attempt to recast statements in order to provide comparable data for financial statement analysis.

EXHIBIT 16-8 Summary of Financial Statement Analysis

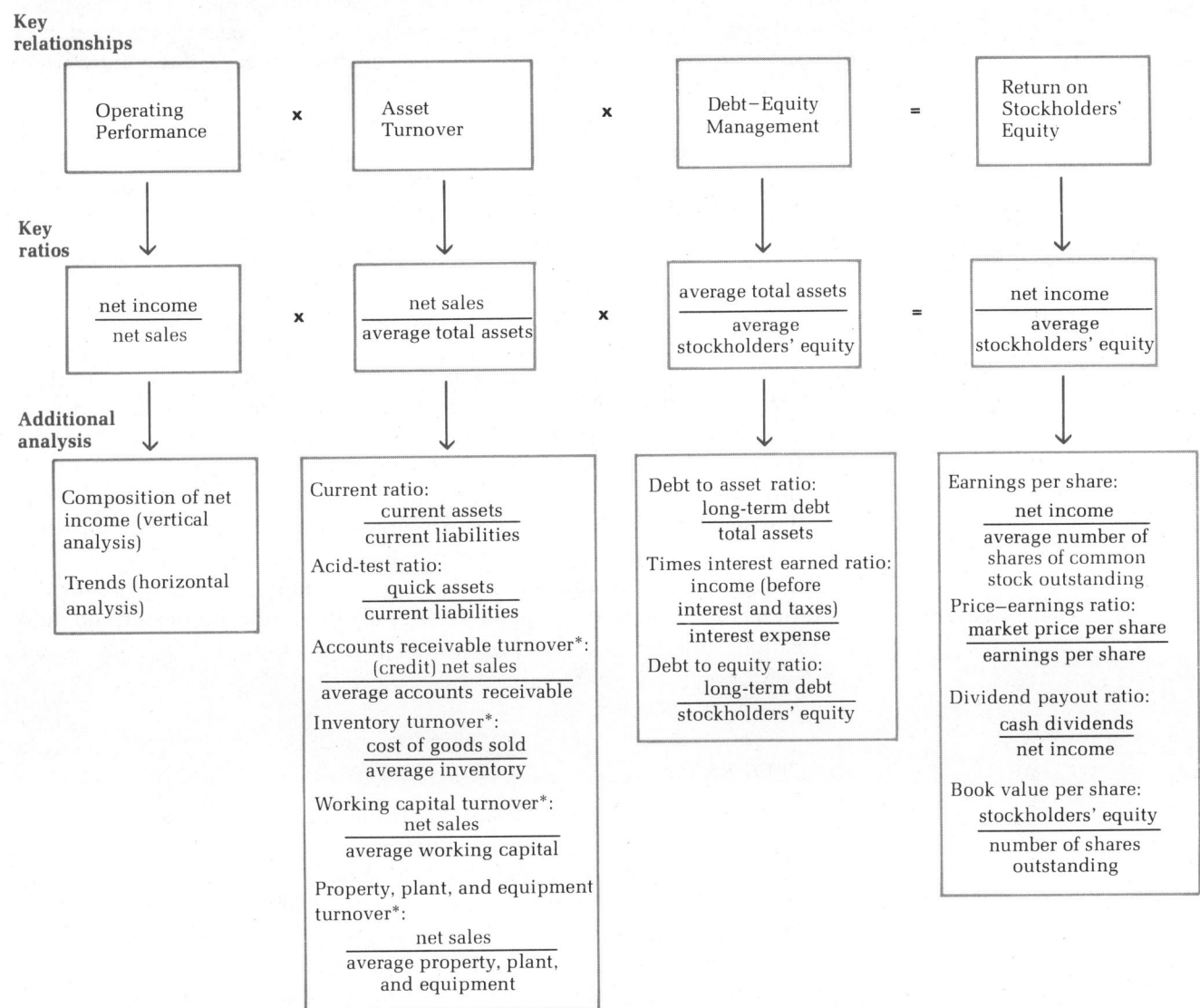

Key relationships	Operating Performance	×	Asset Turnover	×	Debt–Equity Management	=	Return on Stockholders' Equity
Key ratios	$\frac{\text{net income}}{\text{net sales}}$	×	$\frac{\text{net sales}}{\text{average total assets}}$	×	$\frac{\text{average total assets}}{\text{average stockholders' equity}}$	=	$\frac{\text{net income}}{\text{average stockholders' equity}}$
Additional analysis	Composition of net income (vertical analysis) Trends (horizontal analysis)		Current ratio: $\frac{\text{current assets}}{\text{current liabilities}}$ Acid-test ratio: $\frac{\text{quick assets}}{\text{current liabilities}}$ Accounts receivable turnover*: $\frac{\text{(credit) net sales}}{\text{average accounts receivable}}$ Inventory turnover*: $\frac{\text{cost of goods sold}}{\text{average inventory}}$ Working capital turnover*: $\frac{\text{net sales}}{\text{average working capital}}$ Property, plant, and equipment turnover*: $\frac{\text{net sales}}{\text{average property, plant, and equipment}}$		Debt to asset ratio: $\frac{\text{long-term debt}}{\text{total assets}}$ Times interest earned ratio: $\frac{\text{income (before interest and taxes)}}{\text{interest expense}}$ Debt to equity ratio: $\frac{\text{long-term debt}}{\text{stockholders' equity}}$		Earnings per share: $\frac{\text{net income}}{\text{average number of shares of common stock outstanding}}$ Price–earnings ratio: $\frac{\text{market price per share}}{\text{earnings per share}}$ Dividend payout ratio: $\frac{\text{cash dividends}}{\text{net income}}$ Book value per share: $\frac{\text{stockholders' equity}}{\text{number of shares outstanding}}$

* Can be converted to the number of days ratio by dividing the number of days in the period by the turnover rate.

CHANGES IN VALUES AND PRICE LEVELS

Financial statements are based on transactions that were recorded at cost when they were executed. Over time, gains and losses occur as the result of changes in values and changes in the purchasing power of the dollar. These changes in value and price level usually are not incorporated on a current basis into the primary financial statements and therefore may not be included in the analysis. The fact that unrealized gains and losses are not reflected is one reason that book value figures should be considered with care and in conjunction with other measurements.

RATIOS AS A BASIS FOR COMPARISON

Even if an analyst is able to overcome the measurement problems caused by estimates and value changes, there are pitfalls in the use of ratios. A ratio by itself is neither good nor bad. Before it can be judged, it must be compared with the ratios of other years or other companies, or with a predetermined standard. Comparisons with rule-of-thumb guidelines are usually not desirable. Furthermore, ratios may not provide a precise picture of the company's financial situation. More specific analysis may be required.

Financial statement analysis is an important tool in learning about the operations of a firm, but the process of analysis should be performed, and the results evaluated, with its limitations always in mind.

CHAPTER REVIEW

The information that financial statement analysis provides about a company's performance is not readily apparent from a quick reading of the statements themselves. Although the statements are historical in nature, they are often useful in predicting future performance. Investors and creditors use financial statement analysis in judging the degree of profitability, liquidity, and solvency of a firm. Management uses it in identifying problems and measuring performance related to operations, asset turnover, and debt–equity management. Regulators use financial statement analysis in assessing operating results and financial status as they relate to taxing income, measuring concentrations of economic power, and so forth.

Four techniques are commonly used in financial statement analysis: vertical analysis, horizontal analysis, common-size statements, and ratio analysis. The four key relationships (ratios) for assessing a firm's profitability, liquidity, and solvency are

Operating Performance		Asset Turnover		Debt–Equity Management		Return on Stockholders' Equity
$\frac{\text{net income}}{\text{net sales}}$	×	$\frac{\text{net sales}}{\text{average total assets}}$	×	$\frac{\text{average total assets}}{\text{average stockholders' equity}}$	=	$\frac{\text{net income}}{\text{average stockholders' equity}}$

As this equation shows, the ratios that measure operating performance, asset turnover, and debt–equity management can be chained together to compute the return on stockholders' equity (which defines overall performance). Use of this approach helps the analyst understand how much each aspect of a company's activity contributed to the overall result.

These basic ratios can be supplemented by vertical and horizontal analyses, by common-size statements, and by the computation of additional ratios. Vertical and horizontal analyses can be applied both to the income statement (to measure operating performance) and to the balance sheet (to measure asset turnover). Common-size statements show only the percentage relationships obtained by vertical analysis. The additional ratios for measuring asset turnover are the current (working capital) ratio, acid-test (quick) ratio, accounts receivable turnover, inventory turnover, working capital turnover, and property, plant, and equipment turnover. The additional ratios for measuring debt–equity management are the ratio of long-term debt to total assets, times interest earned, and the ratio of long-term debt to stockholders' equity. Additional ratios for measuring return on stockholders' equity include the return on total assets, earnings per share, price–earnings ratio, dividend payout ratio, and book value per share.

Management and outsiders should recognize that information generated through the use of financial statement analysis has limitations because: the underlying data are based on historical costs, estimates and judgments are used in allocating costs, accounting methods are not always comparable, and value and price-level changes may result in unrealized gains and losses that are not reflected in the financial statements.

KEY TERMS AND CONCEPTS

accounts receivable turnover (570)
acid-test ratio (or quick ratio) (570)
asset turnover ratio (566)
book value per share (580)
common-size statement (565)
current ratio (or working capital ratio) (569)
debt–equity management ratio (574)
dividend payout ratio (580)
earnings per share (EPS) (578)
horizontal analysis of financial statements (564)
inventory turnover (571)
liquidity (557)
number of days' sales in inventory (572)
number of days' sales in receivables (570)
number of days' sales invested in working capital (572)
operating performance ratio (562)
price–earnings (P/E) ratio (579)
profitability (557)
property, plant, and equipment turnover (573)
return on stockholders' equity (577)
return on total assets ratio (576)
solvency (557)
vertical analysis of financial statements (563)
working capital turnover (572)

REVIEW PROBLEM

Financial Statement Analysis

The comparative income statements and balance sheets for Collins Corporation for the years ending December 31, 1984 and 1983, are given below.

Collins Corporation
Income Statements
for the Years Ended December 31, 1984 and 1983

	1984	1983
Net Sales	$600,000	$575,000
Cost of Goods Sold	500,000	460,000
Gross Margin	$100,000	$115,000
Expenses:		
Selling and Administrative Expenses	$ 66,000	$ 60,000
Interest Expense	4,000	3,000
Total Expenses	$ 70,000	$ 63,000
Income Before Taxes	$ 30,000	$ 52,000
Income Taxes	12,000	21,000
Net Income	$ 18,000	$ 31,000

Earnings per share:
1984 $1.80
1983 $3.10

Collins Corporation
Balance Sheets
as of December 31, 1984 and 1983

Assets	1984	1983
Current Assets:		
Cash	$ 11,000	$ 13,000
Accounts Receivable (net)	92,000	77,000
Inventory	103,000	92,000
Prepaid Expenses	6,000	5,000
Total Current Assets	$212,000	$187,000
Property, Plant, and Equipment:		
Land and Building	$ 61,000	$ 59,000
Machinery and Equipment	172,000	156,000
Total Property, Plant, and Equipment	$233,000	$215,000
Less Accumulated Depreciation	113,000	102,000
Net Property, Plant, and Equipment	$120,000	$113,000
Other Assets	$ 8,000	$ 7,000
Total Assets	$340,000	$307,000

Liabilities and Stockholders' Equity		
Current Liabilities:		
Accounts Payable	$ 66,000	$ 55,000
Notes Payable	—	23,000
Dividends Payable	2,000	—
Income Taxes Payable	3,000	5,000
Total Current Liabilities	$ 71,000	$ 83,000
Long-Term Debt	75,000	42,000
Total Liabilities	$146,000	$125,000
Stockholders' Equity:		
Common Stock ($1 par)	$ 10,000	$ 10,000
Paid-in Capital in Excess of Par	16,000	16,000
Retained Earnings	168,000	156,000
Total Stockholders' Equity	$194,000	$182,000
Total Liabilities and Stockholders' Equity	$340,000	$307,000

Additional information:

Dividends Declared in 1984	$6,000
Market Price per Share, December 31, 1984	$14.50

Required:
Prepare a comprehensive financial statement analysis of Collins Corporation for 1984. Note that while financial statement analysts usually compare data from two or more years, we are more concerned with the methods of analysis than the results, so we will use only one year, 1984.

Solution

1. Key Relationships

As shown in Exhibit 16-9, the computation of the four key ratios for 1984 provides the analyst with an overall view of the company's performance and gives an indication of how well management performed with respect to operations, asset turnover, and debt-equity management.

2. Analysis of Operating Performance

   Operating performance is measured by means of vertical and horizontal analyses of the income statement, and by comparing two or more years of income statements on a percentage basis in the form of common-size statements.

   (a) Vertical analysis of the income statement: When the income statement is analyzed vertically, net sales is set at 100 percent, and each expense and net income are shown as percentages of net sales.

EXHIBIT 16-9 **Computation of Key Ratios**

Operating Performance		Asset Turnover		Debt-Equity Management		Return on Stockholders' Equity*
$\frac{\text{net income}}{\text{net sales}}$	×	$\frac{\text{net sales}}{\text{average total assets}}$	×	$\frac{\text{average total assets}}{\text{average stockholders' equity}}$	=	$\frac{\text{net income}}{\text{average stockholders' equity}}$
$\frac{\$18,000}{\$600,000}$	×	$\frac{\$600,000}{\$323,500}$	×	$\frac{\$323,500}{\$188,000}$	=	$\frac{\$18,000}{\$188,000}$
3.00%	×	1.85 times	×	1.72 times	=	9.57%

* The factors do not multiply to the product, due to rounding.

Collins Corporation
Vertical Analysis of Income Statement
for the Year Ended December 31, 1984

Net Sales	$600,000	100.0%
Cost of Goods Sold	500,000	83.3
Gross Margin	$100,000	16.7%
Expenses:		
Selling and Administrative Expenses	$ 66,000	11.0%
Interest Expense	4,000	0.7
Total Expenses	$ 70,000	11.7%
Income Before Taxes	$ 30,000	5.0%
Income Taxes	12,000	2.0
Net Income	$ 18,000	3.0%

(b) Horizontal analysis of the income statement: In horizontal analysis, the change in each income statement item from one period to the next is computed as a percentage increase or decrease using the earliest year as the base year. See Exhibit 16–10 below.

(c) Common-size statements: Common-size income statements for two or more years compared by vertical analysis on a percentage basis are shown below.

Collins Corporation
Common-Size Income Statements
*for the Years Ended December 31, 1984 and 1983**

	1984	1983
Net Sales	100.0%	100.0%
Cost of Goods Sold	83.3	80.0
Gross Margin	16.7%	20.0%
Expenses:		
Selling and Administrative Expenses	11.0%	10.4%
Interest Expense	0.7	0.5
Total Expenses	11.7%	11.0%
Income Before Taxes	5.0%	9.0%
Income Taxes	2.0	3.7
Net Income	3.0%	5.4%

* The percentages may not add to the totals, due to rounding.

EXHIBIT 16-10

Collins Corporation
Horizontal Analysis of Income Statements
for the Years Ended December 31, 1984 and 1983

	1984	1983	$ Change	% Change
Net Sales	$600,000	$575,000	+$25,000	+ 4.35
Cost of Goods Sold	500,000	460,000	+ 40,000	+ 8.70
Gross Margin	$100,000	$115,000	−$15,000	−13.04
Expenses:				
Selling and Administrative Expenses	$ 66,000	$ 60,000	+$ 6,000	+10.00
Interest Expense	4,000	3,000	+ 1,000	+33.33
Total Expenses	$ 70,000	$ 63,000	+$ 7,000	+11.1
Income Before Taxes	$ 30,000	$ 52,000	−$22,000	−42.31
Income Taxes	12,000	21,000	− 9,000	−42.86
Net Income	$ 18,000	$ 31,000	−$13,000	−41.94

3. Analysis of Asset Turnover

Asset turnover is analyzed by performing vertical and horizontal analyses of the balance sheets, preparing common-size comparative balance sheets, and computing some or all of the following: the asset turnover ratio and the ratios that together indicate efficient utilization of assets—current ratio, acid-test ratio, accounts receivable turnover, number of days' sales in receivables, inventory turnover, number of days' sales in inventory, working capital turnover, number of days invested in working capital, and property, plant, and equipment turnover.

(a) Vertical Analysis—Balance Sheet

Collins Corporation
Vertical Analysis of the Balance Sheet
*as of December 31, 1984**

Assets		
Current Assets:		
Cash	$ 11,000	3.2%
Accounts Receivable (net)	92,000	27.1
Inventory	103,000	30.3
Prepaid Expenses	6,000	1.8
Total Current Assets	$212,000	62.4%
Property, Plant, and Equipment:		
Land and Building	$ 61,000	17.9%
Machinery and Equipment	172,000	50.6
Total Property, Plant and Equipment	$233,000	68.5%
Less Accumulated Depreciation	113,000	33.2
Net Property, Plant, and Equipment	$120,000	35.3%
Other Assets	$ 8,000	2.4%
Total Assets	$340,000	100.0%
Liabilities and Stockholders' Equity		
Current Liabilities:		
Accounts Payable	$ 66,000	19.4%
Dividends Payable	2,000	0.6
Income Taxes Payable	3,000	0.9
Total Current Liabilities	$ 71,000	20.9%
Long-Term Debt	75,000	22.1
Total Liabilities	$146,000	42.9%
Stockholders' Equity	194,000	57.1
Total Liabilities and Stockholders' Equity	$340,000	100.0%

(b) Horizontal Analysis—Balance Sheet (See Exhibit 16-11).

(c) Common-Size Statements—Balance Sheets as of December 31, 1984 and 1983*

* The percentages may not add to the totals, due to rounding.

Collins Corporation
Common-Size Balance Sheets
as of December 31, 1984 and 1983

Assets	**1984**	**1983**
Current Assets:		
Cash	3.2%	4.2%
Accounts Receivable (net)	27.1	25.1
Inventory	30.3	30.0
Prepaid Expenses	1.8	1.6
Total Current Assets	62.4%	60.9%
Property, Plant, and Equipment:		
Land and Buildings	17.9%	19.2%
Machinery and Equipment	50.6	50.8
Total Property, Plant, and Equipment	68.5%	70.0%
Less Accumulated Depreciation	33.2	33.2
Net Property, Plant, and Equipment	35.3%	36.8%
Other Assets	2.4%	2.3%
Total Assets	100.0%	100.0%
Liabilities and Stockholders' Equity		
Current Liabilities:		
Accounts Payable	19.4%	17.9%
Notes Payable	—	7.5
Dividends Payable	0.6	—
Income Taxes Payable	0.9	1.6
Total Current Liabilities	20.9%	27.0%
Long-Term Debt	22.1	13.7
Total Liabilities	42.9%	40.7%
Stockholders' Equity	57.1	59.3
Total Liabilities and Stockholders' Equity	100.0%	100.0%

(d) Ratio Analysis—Asset Turnover

(1) Asset turnover ratio:

$$\frac{\text{net sales}}{\text{average total assets}} = \frac{\$600{,}000}{\dfrac{\$340{,}000 + \$307{,}000}{2}}$$

$$= \frac{\$600{,}000}{\$323{,}500} = 1.85:1$$

(2) Current ratio:

$$\frac{\text{current assets}}{\text{current liabilities}} = \frac{\$212{,}000}{\$71{,}000} = 2.99:1$$

(3) Acid-test ratio:

$$\frac{\text{cash, short-term securities, notes and accounts receivable (net)}}{\text{current liabilities}} = \frac{\$103{,}000}{\$71{,}000} = 1.45:1$$

EXHIBIT 16-11 Horizontal Analysis—Balance Sheet

Assets	**1984**	**1983**	**$ Change**	**% Change**
Current Assets:				
Cash	$ 11,000	$ 13,000	−$ 2,000	− 15.4
Accounts Receivable (net)	92,000	77,000	+ 15,000	+ 19.5
Inventory	103,000	92,000	+ 11,000	+ 12.0
Prepaid Expenses	6,000	5,000	+ 1,000	+ 20.0
Total Current Assets	$212,000	$187,000	+$25,000	+ 13.4
Property, Plant, and Equipment:				
Land and Building	$ 61,000	$ 59,000	+$ 2,000	+ 3.4
Machinery and Equipment	172,000	156,000	+ 16,000	+ 10.3
Total Property, Plant, and Equipment	$233,000	$215,000	+$18,000	+ 8.4
Less Accumulated Depreciation	113,000	102,000	+ 11,000	+ 10.8
Net Property, Plant, and Equipment	$120,000	$113,000	+$ 7,000	+ 6.2
Other Assets	$ 8,000	$ 7,000	+$ 1,000	+ 14.3
Total Assets	$340,000	$307,000	+$33,000	+ 10.7
Liabilities and Stockholders' Equity				
Current Liabilities:				
Accounts Payable	$ 66,000	$ 55,000	+$11,000	+ 20.0
Notes Payable	—	23,000	− 23,000	−100.0
Dividends Payable	2,000	—	+ 2,000	—
Income Taxes Payable	3,000	5,000	− 2,000	− 40.0
Total Current Liabilities	$ 71,000	$ 83,000	−$12,000	− 14.5
Long-Term Debt	75,000	42,000	+ 33,000	+ 78.6
Total Liabilities	$146,000	$125,000	+$21,000	+ 16.8
Stockholders' Equity	194,000	182,000	+ 12,000	+ 6.6
Total Liabilities and Stockholders' Equity	$340,000	$307,000	+$33,000	+ 10.7

(4) Accounts receivable turnover:

$$\frac{\text{net sales}}{\text{average accounts receivable}} = \frac{\$600{,}000}{\frac{\$92{,}000 + \$77{,}000}{2}} = \frac{\$600{,}000}{\$84{,}500} = 7.10 \text{ times}$$

(5) Number of days' sales in receivables:

$$\frac{365 \text{ days}}{\text{accounts receivable turnover}} = \frac{365}{7.10} = 51 \text{ days}$$

(6) Inventory turnover:

$$\frac{\text{cost of goods sold}}{\text{average inventory}} = \frac{\$500{,}000}{\frac{\$103{,}000 + \$92{,}000}{2}} = \frac{\$500{,}000}{\$97{,}500} = 5.13 \text{ times}$$

(7) Number of days' sales in inventory:

$$\frac{365 \text{ days}}{\text{inventory turnover}} = \frac{365}{5.13} = 71 \text{ days}$$

(8) Working capital turnover:

$$\frac{\text{net sales}}{\text{average working capital}} = \frac{\$600{,}000}{\frac{\$141{,}000 + \$104{,}000}{2}} = \frac{\$600{,}000}{\$122{,}500} = 4.90 \text{ times}$$

(9) Number of days' sales invested in working capital:

$$\frac{365 \text{ days}}{\text{working capital turnover}} = \frac{365}{4.90} = 74 \text{ days}$$

(10) Property, plant, and equipment turnover:

$$\frac{\text{net sales}}{\text{average net property, plant, and equipment}} = \frac{\$600{,}000}{\frac{\$120{,}000 + \$113{,}000}{2}} = \frac{\$600{,}000}{\$116{,}500} = 5.15 \text{ times}$$

4. Analysis of Debt–Equity Management

The management of debt and equity is measured by computing the following ratios: long-term debt to total assets, times interest earned, and long-term debt to stockholders' equity.

(a) Long-term debt to total assets:

$$\frac{\text{long-term debt}}{\text{total assets}} = \frac{\$75{,}000}{\$340{,}000} = 22.1\%$$

(b) Times interest earned:

$$\frac{\text{net income before interest and tax expense}}{\text{interest expense}} = \frac{\$30{,}000 + \$4{,}000}{\$4{,}000} = \frac{\$34{,}000}{\$4{,}000} = 8.5 \text{ times}$$

(c) Long-term debt to stockholders' equity:

$$\frac{\text{long-term debt}}{\text{stockholders' equity}} = \frac{\$75{,}000}{\$194{,}000} = 38.7\%$$

5. Analysis of Return on Stockholders' Equity

Return on stockholders' equity is a key measure of overall performance. Other measures of overall performance are return on total assets, earnings per share, price–earnings ratio, dividend payout ratio, and book value per share.

(a) Return on stockholders' equity:

$$\frac{\text{net income}}{\text{average stockholders' equity}} = \frac{\$18{,}000}{\frac{\$194{,}000 + \$182{,}000}{2}} = \frac{\$18{,}000}{\$188{,}000} = 9.6\%$$

(b) Return on total assets:

$$\frac{\text{net income}}{\text{average total assets}} = \frac{\$18{,}000}{\frac{\$340{,}000 + \$307{,}000}{2}} = \frac{\$18{,}000}{\$323{,}500} = 5.6\%$$

(c) Earnings per share:

$$\frac{\text{net income}}{\text{average number of shares of common stock outstanding}} = \frac{\$18{,}000}{\text{10,000 shares at \$1 par}} = \$1.80$$

(d) Price–earnings ratio:

$$\frac{\text{market price per share}}{\text{earnings per share}} = \frac{\$14.50}{\$1.80} = 8.1$$

(e) Dividend payout ratio:

$$\frac{\text{cash dividends}}{\text{net income}} = \frac{\$6{,}000}{\$18{,}000} = 33.3\%$$

(f) Book value per share:

$$\frac{\text{stockholders' equity}}{\text{number of shares outstanding}} = \frac{\$194{,}000}{\text{10,000 shares}} = \$19.40 \text{ per share}$$

DISCUSSION QUESTIONS

1 Why is financial statement analysis a desirable approach to studying financial statements?

2 How can the historical data reported by financial statements be used to make decisions affecting the future?

3 Who are the principal users of financial statements?

4 For what types of decisions is information from financial statements useful?

5 Identify and describe four common techniques of analyzing financial statements.

6 Identify the ratios used to measure operating performance, asset turnover, debt–equity management, and return on stockholders' equity.

7 What are the components of the asset turnover ratio and what does it measure?

8 Identify the components of the debt–equity management ratio. What does it measure?

9 What is the value of preparing a vertical analysis of an income statement?

10 What is the value of preparing a horizontal analysis of comparative income statements?

11 What types of financial statement analysis will help explain a trend in the asset turnover ratio?

12 Identify eight ratios that will help explain how efficiently assets were utilized during a given period.

13 Show how the current ratio is computed and explain its significance. What is considered to be an adequate current ratio?

14 Explain the different purposes of the current ratio and the acid-test ratio.

15 How is a firm's number of days' sales in receivables computed and what is its significance?

16 How is the inventory turnover ratio computed and what is its significance?

17 Explain the concept underlying property, plant, and equipment turnover.

18 What ratios might help explain changes over time in debt-equity management?

19 What is meant by the term "leveraging" and what is its relationship to the management of debt?

20 Identify two alternative methods of measuring return on stockholders' equity and indicate the relative significance of each.

21 Before financial statements can be analyzed, what steps should be taken to obtain comparability between years and among companies?

22 What are the limitations of financial statement analysis and how can these limitations be dealt with?

EXERCISES

E16-1 Bad Debt Write-off

North Corporation wrote off a $100 uncollectible account receivable against the $1,200 credit balance in Allowance for Doubtful Accounts. How would this write-off affect its current ratio?

E16-2 Accounts Receivable and Inventory Turnovers

Selected data for Delta Corporation are as follows:

Balance Sheet Data

	December 31	
	1984	**1983**
Accounts Receivable	$ 500,000	$ 470,000
Allowance for Doubtful Accounts	25,000	20,000
Net Accounts Receivable	$475,000	$450,000
Inventories at Cost	$600,000	$550,000

Income Statement Data

Net Credit Sales	$2,500,000	$2,200,000
Net Cash Sales	500,000	400,000
Net Sales	$3,000,000	$2,600,000
Cost of Goods Sold	$2,000,000	$1,800,000
Selling and General Expense	300,000	270,000
Other Expenses	50,000	30,000
Total Operating Expenses	$2,350,000	$2,100,000

What is the accounts receivable turnover for 1984? What is the inventory turnover for 1984?

E16-3 Inventory Turnover

On January 1, 1984, Lake Company's beginning inventory was $400,000. During 1984 Lake purchased $1,900,000 of additional inventory. On December 31 Lake's ending inventory was $500,000. What is the inventory turnover for 1984?

E16-4 Number of Times Bond Interest Was Earned

The following data were abstracted from the financial records of Gore Corporation for 1984.

Net Sales	$3,600,000
Bond Interest Expense	120,000
Income Tax Expense	600,000
Net Income	800,000

How many times was bond interest earned in 1984?

E16-5 The Effect of Transactions on the Current Ratio

Company B has a current ratio of 2:1. Describe the effect on the current ratio if the company

1. Receives a 5 percent stock dividend on one of its marketable securities.
2. Pays a large account payable that had been a current liability.
3. Borrows cash on a 6-month note.
4. Sells merchandise for more than cost and records the sale using the perpetual inventory method.

E16-6 Accounts Receivable and Inventory Turnovers

Assuming that a business year consists of 300 days, what are the number of business days' sales in average receivables and the number of business days' sales in average inventories for 1984, based on the following information?

Net Accounts Receivable at December 31, 1983	$ 900,000
Net Accounts Receivable at December 31, 1984	$1,000,000
Accounts Receivable Turnover	5 times
Inventory at December 31, 1983	$1,100,000
Inventory at December 31, 1984	$1,300,000
Inventory Turnover	5 times

E16-7 Acid-Test (Quick) Ratio

Information from River Company's balance sheet for December 31, 1984, is as follows:

Current Assets:	
Cash	$ 3,000,000
Marketable Securities (at cost, which approximates market value)	7,000,000
Accounts Receivable (net of Allowance for Doubtful Accounts)	100,000,000
Inventories (at lower of cost or market)	130,000,000
Prepaid Expenses	2,000,000
Total Current Assets	$242,000,000
Current Liabilities:	
Notes Payable	$ 4,000,000
Accounts Payable	40,000,000
Accrued Liabilities	30,000,000
Income Taxes Payable	1,000,000
Current Portion of Long-Term Debt	6,000,000
Total Current Liabilities	$ 81,000,000
Long-Term Debt	$180,000,000

What is the acid-test ratio?

E16-8 Dividends and the Current Ratio

1. Company A has a current ratio of 0.65:1. A cash dividend was declared last month but paid this month. What is the effect of this dividend payment on the current ratio and on working capital?

2. Company B has a current ratio of 1.60:1. An account was paid during this month. What is the effect of this payment on the current ratio and on working capital?

E16-9 Calculation of Key Ratios

Olympic Company's 1984 and 1983 financial statements are presented here in summary form.

Olympic Company
Income Statements
for the Years Ended December 31, 1984 and 1983

	1984	1983
Net Sales	$260,000	$220,000
Cost of Goods Sold	182,000	165,000
Gross Margin	$ 78,000	$ 55,000
Selling and Administrative Expenses	52,000	38,000
Income Before Taxes	$ 26,000	$ 17,000
Income Taxes	12,000	8,000
Net Income	$ 14,000	$ 9,000

Olympic Company
Balance Sheets (condensed)
as of December 31, 1984 and 1983

Assets	1984	1983
Current Assets	$30,000	$25,000
Property, Plant, and Equipment	40,000	28,000
Less Accumulated Depreciation	(6,000)	(4,000)
Other Assets	5,000	3,000
Total Assets	$69,000	$52,000
Liabilities and Stockholders' Equity		
Current Liabilities	$18,000	$14,000
Long-Term Liabilities	5,000	-0-
Capital Stock	25,000	25,000
Retained Earnings	21,000	13,000
Total Liabilities and Stockholders' Equity	$69,000	$52,000

Compute the following ratios for 1984.

1. Net income to net sales.
2. Asset turnover ratio.
3. Average total assets to average stockholders' equity.
4. Net income to average stockholders' equity.

E16-10 Common-Size Statements

On the basis of the information presented for Olympic Company in E16-9, prepare comparative common-size income statements for 1983 and 1984.

E16-11 The Current Ratio and Return on Total Assets

On the basis of the information presented for Olympic Company in E16-9, answer these questions.

1. How much was declared in dividends during 1984, in dollars and as a percentage of income?
2. What is the return on average total assets for 1984?
3. What was the current ratio in 1983 and in 1984?

E16-12 Asset Turnover Ratio and Inventory Turnover

The following information was taken from the 1984 and 1983 financial statements of Roberts Company.

	1984	1983
Net Sales	$288,000	$225,000
Cost of Goods Sold	190,000	172,000
Average Total Assets	180,000	150,000
Average Inventory	50,000	40,000
Average Accounts Receivable	20,000	15,000
Average Net Working Capital	75,000	60,000

1. Compute the asset turnover ratios for 1983 and 1984.
2. Compute the inventory turnover for 1983 and 1984.
3. Compute the number of days' sales in inventory for 1983 and 1984.
4. Did the company use more or less leverage in 1984 than in 1983?

E16–13 Accounts Receivable and Working Capital Turnovers

On the basis of the information presented for Roberts Company in E16–12:

1. Compute the accounts receivable turnover and the average number of days' sales in receivables for 1983 and 1984.
2. Compute the working capital turnovers for 1983 and 1984.
3. What effect did the changes in the inventory, accounts receivable, and working capital turnovers from 1983 to 1984 have on the total asset turnover from 1983 to 1984?

E16–14 Debt-Equity Management Ratios

The following information was taken from the 1984 and 1983 financial statements of King Company.

	1984	1983
Average Total Assets	$300,000	$260,000
Average Stockholders' Equity	200,000	180,000
Interest Expense	11,000	8,000
Net Income After Taxes	33,000	24,000
Tax Rate	40%	40%

1. Compute the key ratio of average total assets to average stockholders' equity for 1983 and 1984.
2. Compute the ratio of average debt to average stockholders' equity.
3. Compute the number of times interest was earned in 1983 and 1984.

E16–15 Book Value per Share

Georgia Corporation's stockholders' equity at June 30, 1984, consisted of the following.

Preferred Stock (10%, $50 par value, liquidating value $55 per share, 20,000 shares issued and outstanding)	$1,000,000
Common Stock ($10 par value, 500,000 shares authorized, 150,000 shares issued and outstanding)	1,500,000
Retained Earnings	500,000
Total Stockholders' Equity	$3,000,000

1. Compute the book value per share of the preferred stock, assuming that there are no dividends in arrears.
2. Compute the book value per share of the common stock. (Assume that common stock was the same at the beginning and end of the year.)

E16–16 The Price-Earnings Ratio

Information concerning Barnett Company's common stock is as follows:

	Per Share
Book Value at December 31, 1984	$12.00
Quoted Market Value on Stock Exchange on December 31, 1984	18.00
Earnings per Share for 1984	3.00
Par Value	2.00
Dividend Declared and Paid in 1984	1.00

What was the price-earnings ratio on common stock for 1984?

PROBLEMS

P16–1 Common-Size Income Statements

Following are income statements for Pinehurst and Myrtle Companies for the year ended 12/31/84.

	Pinehurst	Myrtle
Net Sales	$360,000	$500,000
Cost of Goods Sold:		
Beginning Inventory	$ 40,000	$ 80,000
Purchases (net)	290,000	320,000
Cost of Goods Available for Sale	$330,000	$400,000
Ending Inventory	60,000	60,000
Cost of Goods Sold	$270,000	$340,000
Gross Margin	$ 90,000	$160,000
Operating Expenses:		
Depreciation Expense	$ 6,000	$ 15,000
Salaries and Wages Expense	24,000	40,000
Other Expenses	12,000	30,000
Total Operating Expenses	$ 42,000	$ 85,000
Income Before Taxes	$ 48,000	$ 75,000
Income Taxes	18,000	35,000
Net Income	$ 30,000	$ 40,000

Required:

1. Prepare common-size income statements for the two companies.

2. **Interpretive Question** Comment on the significant differences between the two companies.

3. **Interpretive Question** How would your comparison of the two companies be affected if you knew that Pinehurst Company used the FIFO alternative of inventory costing and Myrtle Company used the LIFO alternative?

P16–2 Preparing Income Statements from Common-Size Statements

Bayard Company
Common-Size Income Statements
for the Years Ended December 31, 1983 and 1984

	1984	1983
Net Sales	100.0%	100.0%
Cost of Goods Sold	62.5	63.0
Gross Margin	37.5%	37.0%
Expenses:		
Selling and Administrative Expenses	23.4%	22.2%
Interest Expense	3.1	1.8
Total Expenses	26.5%	24.0%
Income Before Taxes	11.0%	13.0%
Income Taxes	5.5	6.5
Net Income from Operations	5.5%	6.5%

Assume that sales were $850,000 in 1984 and $675,000 in 1983.

Required:

Prepare income statements for the two years.

P16–3 Asset Turnover Ratios

Comparative balance sheets and income statements for Doner Company for the years 1984 and 1983 are as follows:

Doner Company
Balance Sheets as of December 31, 1984 and 1983

Assets	1984	1983
Current Assets:		
Cash	$ 20,000	$ 12,500
Marketable Securities	50,000	37,500
Accounts Receivable	175,000	150,000
Inventories	155,000	125,000
Total Current Assets	$ 400,000	$ 325,000
Investments	$ 150,000	$ 162,500
Property, Plant and Equipment	$1,000,000	$ 950,000
Less Accumulated Depreciation—Plant and Equipment	450,000	400,000
Total Property, Plant, and Equipment	$ 550,000	$ 550,000
Intangible Assets	$ 25,000	$ 12,500
Total Assets	$1,125,000	$1,050,000
Liabilities and Stockholders' Equity		
Current Liabilities:		
Accounts Payable	$ 62,500	$ 50,000
Notes Payable	125,000	100,000
Accrued Liabilities	100,000	75,000
Total Current Liabilities	$ 287,500	$ 225,000
Long-Term Debt:		
Bonds Payable	362,500	325,000
Total Liabilities	$ 650,000	$ 550,000
Stockholders' Equity:		
Common Stock (7,500 shares)	$ 75,000	$ 75,000
Paid-in Capital in Excess of Par	275,000	275,000
Retained Earnings	125,000	150,000
Total Stockholders' Equity	$ 475,000	$ 500,000
Total Liabilities and Stockholders' Equity	$1,125,000	$1,050,000

Doner Company
Income Statements
for the Years Ended December 31, 1984 and 1983

	1984	1983
Net Sales	$800,000	$675,000
Cost of Goods Sold	500,000	425,250
Gross Margin	$300,000	$249,750
Expenses:		
Selling and Administrative Expenses	$187,200	$149,850
Interest Expense	24,800	12,488
Total Expenses	$212,000	$162,338
Income Before Taxes	$ 88,000	$ 87,412
Income Taxes	44,000	43,706
Net Income	$ 44,000	$ 43,706

Required:
Using the foregoing balance sheets and income statements, calculate the following ratios for 1984.

1. The current ratio.
2. The acid-test ratio.
3. The accounts receivable turnover.
4. The inventory turnover.
5. The working capital turnover.
6. The property, plant, and equipment turnover.

P16–4 Debt-Equity Management Ratios

Refer to the financial statements in P16–3.

Required:
Calculate the following debt–equity management ratios for 1984.

1. Long-term debt to total assets.
2. Times interest earned.
3. Long-term debt to stockholders' equity.

P16–5 Return on Stockholders' Equity

Refer to the financial statements in P16–3.

Required:
Calculate the following ratios for 1984.

1. Return on total assets.
2. Return on stockholders' equity.
3. Earnings per share.
4. Book value per share (common).

P16–6 Unifying Problem: Key Ratios and Supplementary Ratios

The balance sheets and income statements of Britt Auto Supply Company for 1984 and 1983 are as follows:

Britt Auto Supply Company
Balance Sheets
as of December 31, 1984 and 1983

Assets	1984		1983	
Current Assets:				
Cash		$ 275		$ 450
Accounts Receivable		638		330
Inventories		907		660
Prepaid Insurance		1,620		1,590
Total Current Assets		$3,440		$3,030
Plant and Equipment	$2,350		$2,250	
Less Depreciation	910		780	
Total Property, Plant, and Equipment		1,440		1,470
Total Assets		$4,880		$4,500
Liabilities and Stockholders' Equity				
Current Liabilities:				
Accounts Payable	$ 666		$450	
Notes Payable	460		450	
Other Current Liabilities	210		210	
Total Current Liabilities	$1,336		$1,110	
Long-Term Debt	270		240	
Total Liabilities		$1,606		$1,350
Common Stock (par $10)	$1,000		$1,000	
Retained Earnings	2,274		2,150	
Total Stockholders' Equity		3,274		3,150
Total Liabilities and Stockholders' Equity		$4,880		$4,500

Additional information: Dividends paid in 1983—$50,000 (on 100,000 shares of common stock outstanding). Market price per share at December 31, 1983—$60.67 per share.

Britt Auto Supply Company
Income Statements
for the Years Ended December 31, 1984 and 1983
(in thousands)

	1984		1983	
Net Sales*		$8,746		$7,950
Cost of Goods Sold		6,258		5,600
Gross Margin		$2,488		$2,350
Expenses:				
Operating Expenses	$862		$635	
Depreciation Expense	130		120	
Interest Expense	148		145	
Total Expenses		1,140		900
Income Before Taxes		$1,348		$1,450
Income Taxes (50%)		674		725
Net Income		$ 674		$ 725

* Assume that all sales were made on credit.

Required:

1. Calculate the key ratios for measuring operating performance, asset turnover, and debt-equity management for 1984.
2. Using the ratios computed in item (1), assess the overall performance of the company from a stockholder's point of view.
3. Compute the following additional ratios to further analyze asset turnover, debt-equity management, and return on stockholders' equity.
   (a) current ratio.
   (b) quick ratio.
   (c) accounts receivable turnover.
   (d) number of days' sales in receivables.
   (e) inventory turnover.
   (f) numbers of days' sales in inventory.
   (g) working capital turnover.
   (h) property, plant, and equipment turnover.
   (i) long-term debt to total assets.
   (j) times interest earned.
   (k) long-term debt to stockholders' equity.
   (l) return on total assets.
   (m) earnings per share.
   (n) price-earnings ratio.
   (o) dividend payout ratio.
   (p) book value per share.
4. Classify each of the ratios listed in (3) above as to whether it is a measure of liquidity, solvency, or profitability.

P16-7 Vertical and Horizontal Analyses

Mr. Dills, manager of Milton's Pickle Company, is pleased to see a substantial increase in 1984 sales. However, he has asked you, as the company's financial analyst, to evaluate the effects of this increase in sales on company operations and earnings. Following are the company's income statements for 1984 and 1983.

Milton's Pickle Company
Income Statements
for the Years Ended December 31, 1984 and 1983

	1984	1983
Net Sales	$110,000	$80,000
Expenses:		
Cost of Goods Sold	$ 60,000	$48,000
Selling Expenses	22,000	16,000
General and Administrative Expenses	10,000	8,000
Interest Expense	2,000	2,000
Total Expenses	$ 94,000	$74,000
Income Before Taxes	$ 16,000	$ 6,000
Income Taxes (20%)	3,200	1,200
Net Income	$ 12,800	$ 4,800

Required:

1. Perform a vertical and a horizontal analysis of the company's income statement.
2. **Interpretive Question** Note any significant changes that should be brought to Mr. Dills' attention.

P16-8 Horizontal Analysis

On January 1, 1984, Z. N. Henry, sales manager for Petro-Chemical Products Corporation, decided to discontinue the 1983 discount policy of 2/10, n/30. He believed that the company's cash flow and sales levels would not be affected by eliminating the discount. Selected data for 1984 and 1983 are as follows:

	1984	1983
Net Sales	$1,310,000	$1,250,000
Cash on Hand	475,000	625,000
Average Accounts Receivable for the Year	89,726	41,200

Required:

1. Perform a horizontal analysis as a starting point for analyzing the effects of Mr. Henry's decision.
2. **Interpretive Question** Assume that all sales discounts in 1983 were taken by customers and that all sales were made on credit in both 1983 and 1984. What effect on accounts receivable can you see from discontinuing the discount policy? (Hint: What has happened to the turnover rate and the collection period?)
3. **Interpretive Question** Using the same assumptions as in (2), what was the effect of Mr. Henry's decision on net sales?

P16-9 Measuring and Judging Profitability

The controller of Bookstone Company selected the following data from the company's 1984 financial statements for further analysis.

Preferred Stock (par $100, 1,000 shares issued and outstanding, 7% cumulative dividend, no dividends in arrears)	$100,000
Common Stock (par $10, 40,000 shares issued and outstanding)	400,000
Retained Earnings at December 31, 1984	130,000
Net Income for 1984	79,000
Dividends Declared and Paid During 1984:	
Preferred	7,000
Common	40,000
Market Price per Share of Common Stock at December 31, 1984	$17\frac{1}{8}$

Required:

1. Compute the following amounts:
   (a) Book value per share for preferred and common stock.
   (b) Earnings per share for preferred and common stock.
   (c) Dividend payout ratio for common stock.
   (d) Return on common stockholders' equity.
   (e) Price-earnings ratio for common stock.

2. **Interpretive Question** What information would you like to have to judge whether the current market price of the stock represents a good buy?

P16-10 Selected Profitability Ratios

Following are selected financial data for Coast Rental Company for 1984 and some information about industry averages.

Financial Data for Coast Rental Company

Net Income		$ 164,000
Preferred Stock (6%, 5,500 shares at $100 par)		$ 550,000
Common Stock (25,000 shares at $1 par, market value $65/share)		25,000
Paid-in Capital in Excess of Par—Common Stock		400,000
Retained Earnings		468,750
Total		$1,443,750
Less Treasury Stock:		
Preferred (500 shares)	$45,000	
Common (1,000 shares)	20,000	65,000
Total Stockholders' Equity		$1,378,750

Additional information: Current year dividends on preferred stock—$20,000. Redemption value of preferred stock—$101.25 per share.

Industry Averages

Earnings per Share	$6.00
Price-Earnings Ratio	9.0
Return on Stockholders' Equity	15.0%

Required:

1. Calculate the earnings per share, the price-earnings ratio, book value per share, and the return on stockholders' equity ratio for Coast.

2. **Interpretive Question** Would you want to invest your money in the common stock of this company?

P16-11 Unifying Problem: Alternative Financing Plans

Pearl Company's balance sheet and additional information as of December 31, 1983, are presented here.

Pearl Company
Balance Sheet as of December 31, 1983

Assets	
Current Assets:	
Cash	$ 30,000
Accounts Receivable (net)	150,000
Notes Receivable	65,000
Inventories	245,000
Prepaid Expenses	10,000
Total Current Assets	$ 500,000
Property, Plant, and Equipment:	
Land	$ 20,000
Building (net)	155,000
Equipment (net)	325,000
Total Property, Plant, and Equipment	$ 500,000
Total Assets	$1,000,000
Liabilities and Stockholders' Equity	
Current Liabilities:	
Accounts Payable	$ 80,000
Income Taxes Payable	60,000
Accrued Liabilities	30,000
Total Current Liabilities	$ 170,000
Long-Term Note Payable (10%)	150,000
Total Liabilities	$ 320,000
Stockholders' Equity:	
Common Stock ($10 par)	$ 400,000
Retained Earnings	280,000
Total Stockholders' Equity	$ 680,000
Total Liabilities and Stockholders' Equity	$1,000,000

Additional information: Net income for 1983—$54,400. Effective tax rate—40%.

The company's board of directors is considering several alternative plans for expanding its operations. It has been estimated that an additional investment of $500,000 will make it possible to increase the volume of operations by 60 to 75 percent. The $500,000 would be used to expand the present building, buy additional equipment, and increase working capital. Of the $500,000 needed, $200,000 would be used to increase working capital.

The two most viable alternatives are

a. Sell $500,000 of 20-year bonds at an estimated interest rate of 9 percent.

b. Sell 15,625 shares of common stock at an estimated average price of $32 per share.

Required:

1. Assuming that one of these two alternatives was implemented in late 1983, prepare a balance sheet for each alternative as of December 31, 1983.

2. If net income before interest expense and income taxes was expected to be $190,000 for the year 1984, what would be the earnings per share for each alternative?

3. Compute the rate of return on stockholders' equity for 1984 under each alternative and compare these with the 1983 return. Assume that no dividends are paid in 1984.

4. Compute the debt–equity management ratio for each alternative and compare it with 1983.

5. **Interpretive Question** Which alternative would you recommend to the board of directors? Why?

CHAPTER 17

Financial Reporting for Nonprofit Organizations

THIS CHAPTER EXPLAINS:

- Differing characteristics of nonprofit organizations.
- Fund accounting.
- Accounting for the general fund.
- Key issues in nonprofit accounting.

nonprofit organization *an entity without a profit objective; oriented toward accomplishing nonprofit goals in an efficient and effective manner*

Most organizations sell products and provide services at prices that are expected to result in a reasonable return to owners, that is, to generate profits. This book is primarily concerned with financial reporting concepts and procedures for such profit-oriented organizations. However, nonprofit organizations—entities that have no profit objective but are oriented toward accomplishing service goals in an efficient and effective manner—have become a major factor in our economy. In fact, the nonprofit sector, which includes local, state, and federal governments as well as health care and educational institutions, accounts for approximately 25 percent of the national income.

Differences Between Nonprofit and Profit-Oriented Organizations

Accounting for a nonprofit organization is in many ways similar to accounting for a profit-oriented enterprise. The most basic and obvious similarity lies in the use of the double-entry system of accounts. Another similarity is that both systems follow the basic accounting cycle: analyzing transactions, journalizing and posting to general and subsidiary ledgers, summarizing ledger information, and preparing financial statements.

However, because nonprofit organizations have objectives that are different from those of profit-oriented entities, there are significant differences between the two types of accounting. First, the service objective—as opposed to the profit objective—means that there is less emphasis on the valuation of assets and on how much of an asset is consumed in providing service for a particular accounting period. As a result, the income statement is not applicable and the balance sheet does not serve the same purpose as it does for a profit-oriented enterprise. Furthermore, since it is difficult for a nonprofit organization to relate revenues and expenses to service output, dollar accountability is emphasized over efficient operations. Second, nonprofit organizations are quasi-public institutions. As such, they are subject to governmental regulation and must be concerned that they are using their resources in the manner and for the purpose stated in the law. The accounting records and financial statements of nonprofit organizations must therefore reflect the entity's compliance with legal requirements. Third, because of the legal provisions applying to nonprofit organizations and the diversity of government operations, it becomes necessary to use the technique of fund accounting, for which there is no counterpart in profit-oriented accounting.

In this chapter we describe nonprofit organizations in general and explain the basic principles of fund accounting as applied to the activities of governmental units.

Fund Accounting

In profit-oriented businesses, the unit accounted for is the total entity. All relevant economic events are recorded as a basis for developing financial statements for the entity as a whole, whether it is a proprietorship, a partnership, or a corporation. This orientation enables users of statements to judge the overall results of operations and the financial status of an entity.

In contrast, nonprofit accounting, especially accounting for governmental units, is usually organized and operated on a fund basis. The system is therefore referred to as fund accounting. A fund is a separate accounting entity within the governmental unit, with a self-balancing set of accounts that reflect only the activities of that entity. The set of accounts within a fund are self-balancing because they reflect all assets, liabilities, revenues, and expenses of the fund and also include an amount needed to bring the fund into balance. This fund balance serves the same purpose as the Retained Earnings account in bringing the equation A = L + OE into balance. Although the fund balance does not represent an ownership interest, it does reflect the amount of money available for the future use of the fund. A nonprofit organization is likely to have a number of funds, each of which carries on specific activities designed to achieve one of the objectives of the organization.

fund accounting *an accounting system that involves the use of a group of self-balancing accounts, called funds, for each activity of a nonprofit organization*

fund *a separate accounting entity that contains a self-balancing set of accounts reflecting only the activities of that entity*

TYPES OF FUNDS

A nonprofit organization will have the number and types of funds appropriate to its size and functions. The National Council on Governmental Accounting lists the following as funds used by various governmental units.

1. *General Fund.* Found in every governmental unit. It accounts for all resources that are not accounted for in a more specialized fund.
2. *Special Revenue Fund.* Accounts for revenues that are restricted for specified purposes, such as for recreation activities.
3. *Capital Projects Fund.* Accounts for financial resources segregated for use on major capital projects, such as acquiring a utility or building a new town hall.
4. *Special Assessment Fund.* Accounts for assessments levied to finance public improvements that will benefit the properties against which the assessments are levied.
5. *Debt Service Fund.* Accounts for the accumulation of resources that will pay the interest and principal on general long-term debts.
6. *Enterprise Fund.* Accounts for goods and services provided to the general public on a continuing basis when all or most of the costs involved are financed by charges to users; for example, a public utility operated by the governmental unit is financed by the users of the water, electricity, or other resources the utility provides.
7. *Internal Service Fund.* Accounts for the financing of goods and services provided by one department or agency to other departments or agencies of a governmental unit on a cost-reimbursement basis.
8. *Trust and Agency Funds.* Account for assets held by a governmental unit acting as a trustee or agent for individuals, private organizations, or other governmental units.

It is beyond the scope of this chapter to discuss the accounting procedures for each of these funds. We will restrict our attention to the general fund, which is common to all nonprofit organizations.

general fund *the primary fund of a nonprofit organization; it includes accounts for all transactions that do not fit into more specialized funds*

general fixed asset account group *a group of accounts used for recording the property, plant, and equipment of the general fund and certain other funds*

general long-term debt account group *a group of accounts used for recording long-term debt, such as bond issues, for the general fund and certain other funds*

THE GENERAL FUND

Virtually all nonprofit entities have a general fund, a catch-all set of accounts for transactions that do not fit any of the specific funds. Additional funds are established as needed. Thus, a governmental unit might maintain only a general fund or it might have all eight of the funds listed above.

The National Council on Governmental Accounting further recommends that two self-balancing groups of accounts be established—the general fixed asset account group and the general long-term debt account group. These two groups are used to account for fixed assets and long-term debt not assigned to other funds. For example, fixed assets acquired by the general fund are recorded as expenditures in the general fund, but it is only in the general fixed asset account group that such information as original cost and major improvements is recorded.

Accounting for the General Fund

Profit-oriented companies use budgets for planning and control purposes, but do not incorporate their budgets into the formal accounting system. Governmental units usually incorporate budgets into their formal accounting systems, partly as recognition that the adoption of the budget is a basic principle of governmental accounting and partly because the accounting system is expected to monitor revenues and to provide appropriate budgetary control over expenditures. The budget of a fund is initially an estimate of expected revenues and planned expenditures. Once the budget is approved, it becomes a formal measure of expected revenues and an authorization for expenditures. Each fund has a set of self-balancing budgetary accounts that constitute a formal record of the fund's financial plan.

budgetary accounts *a self-balancing set of accounts that constitute a formal record of a fund's financial plan*

To illustrate, we will assume that the general fund of the town of Merrimack has an approved budget for the fiscal year beginning July 1, 1983, in which revenues are estimated to be $465,000 ($425,000 from property taxes and $40,000 from licenses and fees) and authorized expenditures (called appropriations) are $460,000. The budget information would be recorded in the fund accounts as follows.

appropriations *formal authorizations to spend up to specified amounts in carrying out the objectives of a fund*

Estimated Revenues—Taxes	425,000	
Estimated Revenues—Licenses and Fees	40,000	
Appropriations		460,000
Fund Balance		5,000
To record the budget for the year.		

Several aspects of this entry are important to note. First, the budget accounts show only total estimated revenues and total expected expenditures; they do not identify specific costs. The budget accounts must be set out separately in the formal budget as the basis for comparing planned with actual costs. Second, the Appropriations account specifies the maximum amount of spending formally authorized during the period. Third, the excess of estimated revenues over appropriations constitutes the expected increase in the fund balance at the end of the accounting period.

Actual fund transactions—actual revenues and expenditures—are recorded in accounts separate from the budgetary accounts. These are called proprietary accounts. They are the subject of the next two sections.

proprietary accounts *separate fund accounts for recording actual transactions, that is, actual revenues and expenditures*

ACCOUNTING FOR REVENUES

For governmental units, the revenues of a general fund normally come from taxes, fees, and licenses. In the following example, we will assume that these are the sources of revenue for the general fund of the town of Merrimack.

To illustrate the recording of revenues, we will assume that property taxes in the amount of $434,000 are assessed by Merrimack. On an accrual basis, the property taxes would be recorded in the general fund at the time of assessment. At the same time, uncollectible taxes would be estimated and recorded in an Allowance for Uncollectible Taxes account. If uncollectible taxes are expected to amount to $4,000, the entry would be

Taxes Receivable	434,000	
Tax Revenues		430,000
Allowance for Uncollectible Taxes		4,000
To record the expected tax revenues.		

The asset account, Taxes Receivable, is reduced as the taxes are collected. Any taxes not received by the end of the fiscal year are transferred to Taxes Receivable—Delinquent. The summary entry to record the collection of $424,000 in taxes, the transfer of uncollected taxes to a delinquent account, and the transfer of the balance in Allowance for Doubtful Accounts to a deliquent account would be

Cash	424,000	
Allowance for Uncollectible Taxes	4,000	
Taxes Receivable—Delinquent	10,000	
Taxes Receivable		434,000
Allowance for Uncollectible Taxes—Delinquent		4,000
Collected taxes and transferred uncollected taxes to a delinquent account.		

Assuming that $5,000 of the delinquent taxes were later collected and that $3,000 were written off, the entries would be

Cash	5,000	
Taxes Receivable—Delinquent		5,000
Collected delinquent taxes.		
Allowance for Uncollectible Taxes—Delinquent	3,000	
Taxes Receivable—Delinquent		3,000
To write off delinquent taxes that are not collectible.		

After the above transactions are posted to the ledger accounts, the balances will be as shown below. Note that Merrimack still hopes to collect $2,000 of the delinquent taxes. If these remaining taxes are not collected within a predetermined period, they will be written off and transferred to the Allowance for Uncollectible Taxes—Delinquent account.

Taxes Receivable (Dr.)	Taxes Receivable (Cr.)	Tax Revenues (Dr.)	Tax Revenues (Cr.)	Allowance for Uncollectible Taxes (Dr.)	Allowance for Uncollectible Taxes (Cr.)
434,000	434,000		430,000	4,000	4,000

Cash

Debit	Credit
424,000	
5,000	
Bal. 429,000	

Taxes Receivable—Delinquent

Debit	Credit
10,000	5,000
	3,000
Bal. 2,000	

Allowance for Uncollectible Taxes—Delinquent

Debit	Credit
3,000	4,000
	1,000 . . . . Bal.

Other revenues, such as fees and licenses, are recorded on a cash basis; that is, they are recorded only when they are received. For example, if Merrimack collects $46,000 in licenses and fees, total actual revenues amount to $476,000 ($430,000 in tax revenues and $46,000 in licenses and fees). The entry to record the collection of these other revenues would be

Cash	46,000	
License and Fee Revenues		46,000
Collected revenues for licenses and fees.		

The budgeted revenues for the town of Merrimack were $465,000 and actual revenues are $476,000. Actual revenues are maintained in separate revenue accounts in order to distinguish them from budgeted revenues. The ledger accounts would be

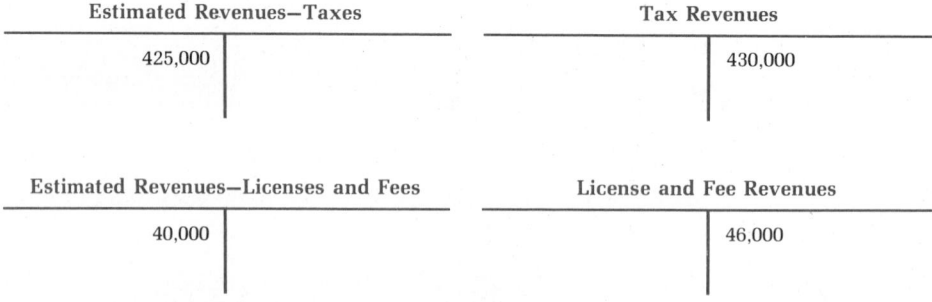

Estimated Revenues—Taxes

Debit	Credit
425,000	

Tax Revenues

Debit	Credit
	430,000

Estimated Revenues—Licenses and Fees

Debit	Credit
40,000	

License and Fee Revenues

Debit	Credit
	46,000

ACCOUNTING FOR ENCUMBRANCES AND EXPENDITURES

encumbrance *a formal record of commitments made now for expenditures to be made later; usually set up when a significant period of time is expected to elapse between the date of commitment and the time of the expenditure*

Reserve for Encumbrances *an account credited at the time a commitment is made for an expenditure*

The budget entry for Merrimack provided for authorized expenditures (appropriations) up to $460,000. To be certain that actual expenditures will not exceed authorized expenditures, and that the funds will be available when the goods or services are received, governmental units use an encumbrance, a formal record of the commitments made now for later expenditures. An Encumbrances account is used when a significant period is expected to elapse between the date of the commitment and the time of the expenditure, and, as an instrument of budgetary control, it is often used even when the elapsed time between the purchase order and payment date is short, say, a day or a week. The Encumbrances account and a related Reserve for Encumbrances account are opened as soon as orders are placed or contracts have been executed.

To illustrate, we will assume that on December 28, 1983, Merrimack orders a new fire truck at a cost of $30,000 and related equipment for $14,000. The truck is to be delivered in six months and the other equipment will arrive in about nine months. The entry to record this commitment would be

Encumbrances	44,000	
Reserve for Encumbrances		44,000
Ordered a fire truck and related equipment.		

When the fire truck is delivered six months later, with an invoice for $29,700, the entry to record its payment is

Expenditures	29,700	
Cash		29,700
Paid for fire truck.		

Once the fire truck has been paid for or the liability for it has been recorded, the $30,000 in the Encumbrances account is no longer necessary and must be reversed.

Reserve for Encumbrances	30,000	
Encumbrances		30,000
To reverse the encumbrance for the fire truck.		

Only the amount encumbered is reversed, whether the actual expenditure is more or less than this amount. An excess expenditure due to either an underestimated or an unforeseen expense is money spent that was never encumbered. If any encumbrance for a planned expenditure is not spent by the end of the fiscal year, the Reserve for Encumbrances account may remain open, if authorization is given. This account is then shown on the balance sheet of the general fund as a continuing commitment.

ACCOUNTING FOR RECURRING EXPENDITURES

Expenditures for such recurring items as salaries, interest, and supplies are not usually encumbered. A voucher (a signed document authorizing payment) is prepared and recorded in anticipation of payment in the near future. For example, if the normal expenditures for recurring items in June were expected to be $22,000, vouchers would be prepared and the entry to record their existence would be

Expenditures	22,000	
Vouchers Payable		22,000
To record the liability for June expenditures.		

If $13,000 of the vouchers were paid by June 30, the entry would be

Vouchers Payable	13,000	
Cash		13,000
Paid $13,000 of the June expenditure vouchers.		

The remaining vouchers usually will be paid early in the next month.

ACCOUNTING FOR TRANSFER PAYMENTS

transfer payment *a payment by one fund to another*

Another type of expenditure by the general fund is a transfer payment to another fund. To illustrate, we assume that the general fund of Merrimack provides $25,000 to the debt service fund so that it can pay principal and interest on general obligation bonds. The entries to record the obligation and the actual transfer of funds would be

Transfer to Debt Service Fund	25,000	
Due to Debt Service Fund		25,000
To record the obligation to transfer $25,000 to the debt service fund.		
Due to Debt Service Fund	25,000	
Cash		25,000
To record the transfer to the debt service fund.		

After the preceding expenditures, encumbrances, and transfer payments have been recorded, the General Ledger accounts for the fiscal year ended June 30, 1984, would be as follows (note that we have included the beginning balances for the Cash and Fund Balance accounts, as well as expenditures that were incurred in earlier months):

Cash

Debit	Credit
Beg. Bal. ... 28,000	365,300
424,000	29,700
5,000	13,000
46,000	25,000
Bal. 70,000	

Expenditures

Debit	Credit
Beg. Bal. .. 365,300	
29,700	
22,000	
Bal. 417,000	

Estimated Revenues—Taxes

Debit	Credit
425,000	

Estimated Revenues—Licenses and Fees

Debit	Credit
40,000	

Taxes Receivable—Delinquent

Debit	Credit
10,000	5,000
	3,000
Bal. 2,000	

Encumbrances

Debit	Credit
44,000	30,000
Bal. 14,000	

Transfer to Debt Service Fund	
25,000	

Due to Debt Service Fund	
25,000	25,000

Reserve for Encumbrances	
30,000	44,000
	14,000........ **Bal.**

Vouchers Payable	
13,000	22,000
	9,000 .... **Bal.**

Appropriations	
	460,000

Taxes Receivable	
434,000	434,000

Allowance for Uncollectible Taxes	
4,000	4,000

Allowance for Uncollectible Taxes—Delinquent	
3,000	4,000
	1,000........ **Bal.**

Tax Revenues	
	430,000

License and Fee Revenues	
	46,000

Fund Balance	
	28,000..... **Beg. Bal.**
	5,000
	33,000 .... **Bal.**

CLOSING THE GENERAL FUND ACCOUNTS

The closing process at the end of an accounting period is the same for a general fund as it is for a profit-oriented company. To illustrate, we will assume that the general fund has the following trial balance at the end of the fiscal year, June 30, 1984.

	Debits	Credits
Cash	$ 70,000	
Expenditures	417,000	
Estimated Revenues—Taxes	425,000	
Estimated Revenues—Licenses and Fees	40,000	
Taxes Receivable—Delinquent	2,000	
Encumbrances	14,000	
Transfer to Debt Service Fund	25,000	
Reserve for Encumbrances		$ 14,000
Vouchers Payable		9,000
Appropriations		460,000
Allowance for Uncollectible Taxes—Delinquent		1,000
Tax Revenues		430,000
License and Fee Revenues		46,000
Fund Balance		33,000
Totals	$993,000	$993,000

fund balance *the excess of a fund's assets over its liabilities and reserves; becomes the balancing account on the balance sheet of a nonprofit organization*

The accounts in the trial balance are of two types—permanent and temporary. The permanent accounts are balance sheet accounts, and they will remain open for future accounting periods. They include Cash, Taxes Receivable—Delinquent, Vouchers Payable, Reserve for Encumbrances, Allowance for Uncollectible Taxes—Delinquent, and Fund Balance. The temporary accounts appear on the statement of revenues and expenditures. These accounts are closed at the end of the accounting period, so that they have zero balances and can be used to accumulate revenue and expenditure information during the next accounting period. Note that Expenditures, Appropriations, and Encumbrances are control accounts; the details, which are in a subsidiary ledger, are shown in the formal statement of revenues and expenditures in Exhibit 17-1.

On the basis of the information in the trial balance, the entries to close the general fund's temporary accounts would be

Revenues—Taxes	430,000	
Revenues—Licenses and Fees	46,000	
Estimated Revenues—Taxes		425,000
Estimated Revenues—Licenses and Fees		40,000
Fund Balance		11,000
To close the revenue accounts.		
Appropriations	460,000	
Expenditures		417,000
Encumbrances		14,000
Transfer to Debt Service Fund		25,000
Fund Balance		4,000
To close the expenditure, encumbrance, and transfer accounts.		

As these closing entries show, actual revenues were greater than estimated revenues by $11,000, and expenditures, encumbrances, and transfers were less than appropriations by $4,000. Accordingly, during the year the fund's balance increased by $15,000 more than was planned.

Fund Balance, Beginning of Year		$28,000
Estimated Revenues in Excess of Estimated Appropriations		5,000
Fund Balance on Trial Balance		$33,000
Excess of Actual Revenues over Actual Expenditures, Encumbrances, and Transfers ($476,000 − $456,000)	$20,000	
Less Planned Excess	5,000	
Increase Above Plan		15,000
Fund Balance, End of Year		$48,000

We know that revenues were $476,000 and that total expenditures ($417,000), encumbrances ($14,000), and transfers ($25,000) were $456,000; so actual revenues exceeded expenditures, encumbrances, and transfers by $20,000. However, the planned excess of $5,000 must be deducted; otherwise, it would be counted twice. With this understanding of the change in fund balance and of the nature of the accounts in the trial balance, the financial statements for Merrimack can be prepared.

PREPARING THE FINANCIAL STATEMENTS

Three key financial statements would be prepared for the general fund at the end of the fiscal year: the statement of revenues and expenditures, the balance sheet, and the statement of changes in fund balance. Some nonprofit organizations also prepare a funds statement.

The Statement of Revenues and Expenditures

statement of revenues and expenditures *a formal statement prepared for a nonprofit organization; shows the relationship between actual revenues and expenditures, and may also include the budgeted amounts*

The statement of revenues and expenditures for a general fund shows the relationship between actual revenues and expenditures. In addition, it should have a column identifying budgeted revenues and appropriations so that readers can compare planned and actual results. Exhibit 17-1 is a statement of revenues and expenditures based on information in the trial balance presented earlier.

Note that the statement of revenues and expenditures indicates only the flow of funds and does not identify the causes of the differences between expected and actual results. In other words, it does not explain how efficient the revenue collection process was or how much benefit was realized from the expenditures. In order to measure whether the expenditures achieved adequate benefits, Merrimack would have to prepare a cost-benefit analysis, which is not easily accomplished because qualitative fac-

EXHIBIT 17-1

Town of Merrimack

Statement of Revenues and Expenditures—General Fund for the Fiscal Year Ended June 30, 1984

	Budgeted	Actual
Revenues:		
Taxes	$425,000	$430,000
Licenses and Fees	40,000	46,000
Total Revenues	$465,000	$476,000
	Appropriations*	**Actual Expenditures, Encumbrances, and Transfers***
Expenditures, Encumbrances, and Transfers:		
General Government	$178,000	$175,800
Police and Firefighter Services	85,000	90,000
Sanitation Services	108,000	106,700
Street Maintenance	54,000	47,000
Capital Expenditures	10,000	11,500
Debt Service	25,000	25,000
Total Expenditures and Transfers	$460,000	$456,000
Change in Fund Balance	$ 5,000	$ 20,000

* Until now, we have referred to these items in total only. To make the statement more realistic, we have included the specific elements that make up the totals. The specific elements include $14,000 of encumbrances not yet paid.

tors must be considered. Merrimack must also compare budgeted expenses with actual expenses on an accrual basis. Cost-benefit and expense-control analyses are appropriate subjects for a course in managerial accounting. At this point, it is sufficient to keep in mind that the usual operating statement of a nonprofit organization reflects resource flows and expenditure control, but it does not indicate how efficiently resources were used.

The Balance Sheet

The balance sheet for a general fund reflects the resources available to pay current vouchers and encumbrances as well as the amount in the fund balance available for appropriation in the coming period. The balance sheet for Merrimack, based on the trial balance prepared earlier, would be as shown in Exhibit 17-2.

EXHIBIT 17-2

Town of Merrimack

Balance Sheet—General Fund as of June 30, 1984

Assets		
Cash		$70,000
Taxes Receivable—Delinquent	$2,000	
Less Allowance for Uncollectible Taxes—Delinquent	1,000	1,000
Total Assets		$71,000
Liabilities, Encumbrances, and Fund Balance		
Vouchers Payable		$ 9,000
Reserve for Encumbrances		14,000
Fund Balance		48,000
Total Liabilities, Encumbrances, and Fund Balance		$71,000

Note that the fire truck acquired by Merrimack is not shown on the balance sheet of the general fund. The cost of the fire truck would be recorded as follows in the general fixed asset account group.

Fire Equipment	29,700	
Investment in General Assets—General Fund		29,700
Purchased a fire truck.		

As you will recall, the original purchase order for the fire truck was recorded as a debit to Encumbrances and a credit to Reserve for Encumbrances for $30,000. When the fire truck was delivered, this entry was reversed and another entry was made in the general fund—a debit to Expenditures and a credit to Cash for the $29,700 actually paid. Since the fire truck was recorded only as an expenditure in the general fund, the entry above to the general fixed asset account group was made to record the truck as an asset.

Similarly, the amount transferred from the general fund to cover debt service would be recorded in the debt service fund as follows.

Cash	25,000	
Transfer from General Fund		25,000
Transferred cash from the general fund for debt service.		

The fact that fixed assets are recorded in the general fixed asset account group and funds for debt service are transferred to a debt service fund illustrates the fragmented nature of fund accounting. Each fund has a separate set of self-balancing accounts. To get a clear picture of a governmental unit's entire operation, you should obtain a statement of revenues and expenditures, a balance sheet, and a combined statement of changes in fund balances, which includes all funds. This would allow you to view the general fund's financial statements in their proper perspective—as reflecting the general operations of a governmental unit, not its special activities.

The Statement of Changes in Fund Balance

statement of changes in fund balance *a formal statement prepared for a nonprofit organization; shows how the fund balance has changed from the beginning to the end of the period*

A statement of changes in fund balance serves the same function as the statement of changes in owners' equity (see page 44) for a profit-oriented business. It identifies the reasons for the difference between the beginning and ending fund balances. Exhibit 17-3 is a statement of changes in fund balance for Merrimack, based on data from the trial balance presented earlier.

EXHIBIT 17-3

Town of Merrimack

Statement of Changes in Fund Balance—General Fund for the Fiscal Year Ended June 30, 1984

Fund Balance, July 1, 1983		$28,000
Revenues	$476,000	
Expenditures and Encumbrances	456,000	
Excess of Revenues over Expenditures and Encumbrances		20,000
Fund Balance, June 30, 1984		$48,000

The budget for the fiscal year ending June 30, 1984, had projected an increase of $5,000 in the fund balance. That projected $5,000 increase would have been added to the $28,000 shown on the balance sheet at June 30, 1983, thus accounting for the $33,000 shown in the trial balance. The fund balance increased another $15,000 because actual revenues exceeded estimated revenues by $11,000 and actual expenditures and encumbrances were less than appropriations by $4,000. The general fund balance of $48,000 on June 30, 1984, reflects the amount that could be available for appropriations by the town governing board in the next fiscal year unless it is retained as a reserve.

TO SUMMARIZE Most nonprofit organizations use fund accounting, which is based on a group of self-balancing accounts for each entity within the organization. The general fund is the primary entity for all such organizations, although funds with narrower focuses also may be needed. Both budgetary expectations and actual transactions are recorded in the general fund accounts and are reflected in the three primary statements of the general fund of a nonprofit organization: the statement of revenues and expenditures, the balance sheet, and the statement of changes in fund balance.

The Current Environment of Nonprofit Accounting

Our discussion so far has probably given you the impression that accounting for nonprofit organizations is fairly routine, consistent, and relatively free of significant problems. Unfortunately, this is not the case. At the present time there is no uniform body of generally accepted accounting principles applicable to all nonprofit entities. Existing accounting principles have been developed according to the type of function (service) performed by the organization, such as health care, education, and municipal services. Thus, all hospitals follow the accounting guidelines developed by the American Hospital Association; colleges and universities base their accounting on principles laid down by the National Association of College and University Business Officers; and governmental units adhere to the principles of the National Council of Governmental Accounting and the Municipal Finance Officers' Association. At the same time, the American Institute of Certified Public Accountants (AICPA) has developed auditing guidelines (but not financial reporting principles) for hospitals, colleges and universities, governmental units, and other nonprofit organizations. In some states, financial accounting principles for governmental units are prescribed by statute.

Because nonprofit accounting principles have been based on the type of services performed, there has not been a unified and clearly defined set of objectives that apply to all nonprofit organizations. For example, it is not clear whether emphasis should be placed on service to clientele or on responsibilities to contributors (dollar accountability). Similarly, the uses for, and users of, nonprofit financial statements have not been well defined.

Recognizing these problems, the Financial Accounting Standards Board has taken a series of steps which could eventually lead to the establishment of uniform financial reporting standards for nonprofit organizations. First, it commissioned a "conceptual framework" research study to identify the key issues that face nonprofit accounting. Second, as part of its conceptual framework study, the FASB issued a Statement of Concepts that sets forth the objectives of financial reporting for nonprofit organizations. Third, the Financial Accounting Foundation, the governing body of the FASB, has approved the establishment of an accounting standards board that will define financial accounting and reporting standards for governmental units. Each of these steps will be discussed briefly.

KEY ISSUES IN NONPROFIT ACCOUNTING

The FASB's conceptual framework study identified 15 issues that should be resolved in order for uniform reporting standards to be developed. The following questions and partial answers cover the most significant issues.

1. Who are the primary users of financial information about nonprofit organizations?
Comment Identifying the users of financial information is a first step in determining the type of information needed. Five primary users were named: governing bodies, investors and creditors, resource providers, oversight bodies, and constituents.
2. What type of information is needed by users?
Comment Although the answer to this question depends on the decisions to be made, the FASB study suggests that the following information is most likely to be useful: financial viability, fiscal compliance (adherence to expenditure policies), managerial performance, and cost of services provided.
3. What types of financial statements would provide the most useful information about nonprofit organizations?
Comment To answer this question, a number of issues first need to be resolved. For example:
(a) Do users need a revenue and expenditure statement?
(b) Should encumbrances as well as expenditures be reported?
(c) Do users need an overall set of financial statements for the organization rather than separate financial statements for each fund?

Other questions raised by the FASB study include the following.

1. When should the depreciation of capital assets be recorded in the accounts of a nonprofit organization?
2. Should donated or contributed services be reported as expenses at their fair value?
3. How does the revenue recognition principle apply to nonrenewable operating inflows such as contracts and investment earnings?

These types of questions demonstrate that although accounting for certain types of nonprofit organizations (such as governmental units) is fairly standard, some fundamental issues need to be reexamined before additional generally accepted accounting principles can be established.

THE FASB'S STATEMENT OF CONCEPTS

In 1980, the FASB issued a Statement of Concepts that set forth seven objectives of the general-purpose external financial reports prepared by nonprofit organizations. The Statement specified that nonprofit financial reporting should present information that

1. Is useful to those who need to make rational decisions about the allocation of resources to a nonprofit organization.

2. Helps in assessing the services the organization provides, and its ability to continue to provide those services.

3. Helps in judging how managers of an organization have discharged their responsibilities.

4. Presents in detail the economic resources and obligations of an organization, and the effects of transactions, events, and circumstances on those resources.

5. Describes the performance of an organization during a period. This includes periodic measurement of the changes in net resources, along with information about the service efforts and accomplishments of the organization.

6. Shows how an organization obtains and spends its liquid resources; in other words, how it borrows and repays funds, and how other factors may affect its liquidity.

7. Is in a form that is easily understood.

This Statement of Concepts is a companion to an earlier statement that sets out the objectives of financial reporting by business enterprises. The two sets of objectives are designed to serve as the foundation for an integrated conceptual framework for financial accounting and reporting.

THE GOVERNMENTAL ACCOUNTING STANDARDS BOARD

The third step toward developing a uniform set of accounting standards for nonprofit organizations was the plan to establish a new five-member Governmental Accounting Standards Board (GASB), which will function similarly to, but separately from, the FASB. The GASB will have the authority to set financial accounting standards for all state and local governmental units except those that are similar to corresponding privately owned entities (for example, hospitals and utilities). The GASB and FASB will jointly issue standards for these entities.

Note that because the GASB will establish accounting standards only for state and local governmental units, until the FASB chooses to issue standards for other nonprofit organizations, these entities must continue to rely on their own associations for standards.

TO SUMMARIZE At the present time there is no body of generally accepted accounting principles for all nonprofit organizations. In an attempt to remedy this lack of uniformity, the FASB has commissioned a study of the key issues in nonprofit accounting, has set forth seven objectives for nonprofit organizations, and has approved the establishment of the GASB to prescribe financial accounting standards for most state and local governmental units. Key issues include identification of the users of the primary financial statements of nonprofit entities, the types of information needed by users, and the types of financial statements that would provide the most useful information. The GASB will base its standards on the FASB's 1980 Statement of Concepts, which sets out seven major objectives of general-purpose external financial reporting by nonprofit organizations.

CHAPTER REVIEW

A nonprofit organization is an entity that has no profit objective and that is oriented toward accomplishing its service goals in an efficient and effective manner. Accounting for nonprofit entities is similar in some ways to accounting for profit-oriented companies, but there are certain basic differences, such as the lack of a profit motive and the nonprofit organization's need to comply with legal restrictions regarding expenditures, that make significant differences in their accounting concepts and procedures necessary.

Financial reporting for nonprofit organizations is generally based on fund accounting. This means that a separate self-balancing set of accounts is created for each entity within the organization. A governmental unit may have as many as eight types of funds in addition to two account groups for fixed assets and long-term debt. The most commonly used fund is the general fund, which is used to collect information on all activities not recorded in the special-purpose funds.

The number of funds depends on the number of entities within the organization. The transactions of a particular activity are recorded in a designated fund; at the end of the accounting period these transactions are summarized for each fund in three primary financial statements: a statement of revenues and expenditures, a balance sheet, and a statement of changes in fund balance. In some cases, the statements for individual funds are aggregated into a statement for the organization as a whole.

The FASB has identified 15 key issues in nonprofit accounting. It has also issued a Statement of Concepts, which sets forth the major objectives for external financial reporting by nonprofit entities. Finally, the FASB has approved the establishment of the GASB to prescribe accounting standards for state and local governmental units.

KEY TERMS AND CONCEPTS

appropriations (602)
budgetary accounts (602)
encumbrance (604)
fund (600)
fund accounting (600)
fund balance (608)
general fixed asset account group (601)
general fund (601)
general long-term debt account group (601)
nonprofit organization (599)
proprietary accounts (602)
Reserve for Encumbrances (604)
statement of changes in fund balance (611)
statement of revenues and expenditures (609)
transfer payment (606)

REVIEW PROBLEM

Nonprofit Accounting

The general fund of the town of Myrtlewood has the following trial balance as of June 30, 1984.

Town of Myrtlewood
Trial Balance
as of June 30, 1984

	Debits	Credits
Cash	$ 100,000	
Expenditures	4,125,000	
Estimated Revenues	4,400,000	
Taxes Receivable	250,000	
Encumbrances	40,000	
Reserve for Encumbrances		$ 40,000
Vouchers Payable		120,000
Appropriations		4,200,000
Allowance for Uncollectible Taxes		25,000
Revenues		4,500,000
Fund Balance		30,000
Totals	$8,915,000	$8,915,000

Required:

1. Assuming that the fund balance as of July 1, 1983, was $(170,000) and that no budget revisions were made during the year, prepare the entry to record the budget.
2. Assuming that the encumbrances balance represents an order for a bus, prepare the entry to establish the Encumbrances account.
3. Prepare a statement of revenues and expenditures for the general fund for the year ended June 30, 1984.
4. Prepare a statement of changes in fund balance for the town of Myrtlewood for the year ended June 30, 1984.
5. Prepare a balance sheet for the town of Myrtlewood as of June 30, 1984.
6. Prepare the closing entries as of June 30, 1984.

Solution

1. In nonprofit accounting, the budget records are incorporated into the formal accounting system, as shown below.

Estimated Revenues	4,400,000	
Appropriations		4,200,000
Fund Balance		200,000

To record the budget for fiscal year 1983–1984.

[The $200,000 in the Fund Balance account is the difference between estimated revenues and appropriations. Note that the $(170,000) balance from 1983 is not included in the 1984 budget.]

2. An encumbrance is a formal record of a commitment made now for an expenditure to be made later.

Encumbrances	40,000	
Reserve for Encumbrances		40,000

Ordered a bus to be delivered in the next fiscal year.

3. A statement of revenues and expenditures shows the relationship of actual revenues and expenditures and also includes budgeted revenues and expenditures.

Town of Myrtlewood
Statement of Revenues and Expenditures—General Fund for the Fiscal Year Ended June 30, 1984

	Budgeted	Actual
Revenues	$4,400,000	$4,500,000
Appropriations	$4,200,000	
Expenditures		$4,125,000
Encumbrances		40,000
Totals	$4,200,000	$4,165,000
Change in Fund Balance	$ 200,000	$ 335,000

4. A statement of changes in fund balance explains the difference between the beginning and ending fund balances. It serves the same function as the statement of owners' equity does for a profit-oriented company.

Town of Myrtlewood
Statement of Changes in Fund Balance—General Fund for the Fiscal Year Ended June 30, 1984

Fund Balance, July 1, 1983		$(170,000)
Budget Adjustment:		
Estimated Revenues	$4,400,000	
Appropriations	4,200,000	
Expected Increase in Fund Balance		200,000
Fund Balance on Trial Balance		$ 30,000
Actual Operations:		
Revenues	$4,500,000	
Expenditures and Encumbrances	4,165,000	
Actual Increase in Fund Balance	$ 335,000	
Less Planned Increase	200,000	
Increase Above Plan		135,000
Fund Balance, June 30, 1984		$ 165,000

5. The balance sheet reflects the resources available to pay liabilities and encumbrances and the fund balance available for appropriation in the next fiscal period.

Town of Myrtlewood
Balance Sheet—General Fund
as of June 30, 1984

Assets		
Cash		$100,000
Taxes Receivable	$250,000	
Less Allowance for Uncollectible Taxes	25,000	225,000
Total Assets		$325,000
Liabilities, Encumbrances, and Fund Balance		
Vouchers Payable		$120,000
Reserve for Encumbrances		40,000
Fund Balance		165,000
Total Liabilities, Encumbrances, and Fund Balance		$325,000

6. The temporary accounts of a nonprofit organization are closed to the fund balance at the end of the accounting period so that they can be used to accumulate revenue and expenditure information in the next period.

Revenues	4,500,000	
Estimated Revenues		4,400,000
Fund Balance		100,000

To close the revenue accounts.

Appropriations	4,200,000	
Expenditures		4,125,000
Encumbrances		40,000
Fund Balance		35,000

To close the expenditure, encumbrance, and appropriations accounts.

DISCUSSION QUESTIONS

1 Distinguish between a nonprofit organization and a business enterprise.

2 Why is it difficult for accountants today to attest to the fair presentation of the financial statements of nonprofit organizations?

3 What is a fund? How many funds is a nonprofit organization likely to have?

4 How is budgetary information accounted for differently in a nonprofit organization as compared with a profit-oriented company?

5 What is the purpose of the Appropriations account in the general fund of a governmental unit?

6 If tax revenues of a municipality are not collected by the required due date, what journal entries are made to reflect delinquent taxes and uncollectible taxes?

7 What is an encumbrance system?

8 When is an Encumbrances account set up? What is the usual journal entry if $80,000 is encumbered to buy a piece of snow-clearing equipment for a municipality?

9 What happens to the Encumbrances account when an actual expenditure is made?

10 If an actual expenditure has not been made by the end of the accounting period, what disposition is made of the Encumbrances account and the Reserve for Encumbrances account?

11 Prepare typical entries to close the following general fund accounts: Estimated Revenues, Revenues, Appropriations, Expenditures, and Encumbrances. (Use x's for numbers.)

12 Identify and briefly describe the three primary financial statements prepared for the general fund of a governmental unit at the end of a fiscal year.

13 Do the financial statements of the general fund of a municipality reflect how efficiently resources were utilized? Explain.

14 What are the shortcomings of the general fund's financial statements in providing readers with a clear picture of the operations of a governmental unit?

15 What is the purpose of the statement of changes in fund balance?

16 Who are likely to be the primary users of the financial statements of (a) a governmental unit, (b) a college, (c) a revenue fund, and (d) a church?

17 Why would financial statement users want to know how much it costs for a nonprofit organization to provide its services?

18 Do users need an overall set of financial statements for nonprofit organizations or are separate statements for individual funds sufficient?

19 What type of information is most useful in assessing the performance of a nonprofit organization?

EXERCISES

E17-1 Budgetary Accounts and Proprietary Accounts

Identify the following accounts as budgetary accounts (B) or as proprietary accounts (P).

1. Appropriations
2. Fund Balance
3. Estimated Uncollectible Property Taxes
4. Encumbrances
5. Expenditures
6. Taxes Receivable
7. Estimated Revenues

E17-2 Recording the Budgetary Accounts

The annual budget of the general fund of a city shows estimated revenues of $950,000 and appropriations of $920,000. Prepare the journal entry to record this budgetary information in the fund accounts and reflect the excess estimated revenue.

E17-3 Recording an Encumbrance

Prepare the journal entry in the general fund to earmark $33,000 of the fund balance for goods ordered but not yet received.

E17-4 Relationships Among Accounts

For each situation below, describe in lay terms the action taken by a town board.

1. Appropriations exceed estimated revenues.
2. Actual expenses exceed estimated expenses.
3. Estimated revenues exceed appropriations.

E17-5 Paying Expenditures and Eliminating Encumbrances

Prepare the journal entries in the general fund to pay for the purchase of supplies costing $12,000 and to eliminate $13,000 previously established in an encumbrance account for these supplies.

E17-6 Closing Entries

The trial balance of the general fund of the town of Rio Hondo for the fiscal year ended June 30, 1984, follows. Prepare all entries necessary to close the temporary accounts.

	Debits	Credits
Cash	$ 60,000	
Expenditures	230,000	
Estimated Revenues	275,000	
Taxes Receivable	40,000	
Encumbrances	25,000	
Reserve for Encumbrances		$ 25,000
Vouchers Payable		8,000
Appropriations		260,000
Revenues		282,000
Fund Balance		55,000
Totals	$630,000	$630,000

E17-7 A Statement of Revenues and Expenditures

Refer to Rio Hondo's trial balance in E17-6 and prepare a statement of revenues and expenditures for the fiscal year ended June 30, 1984.

E17-8 A Balance Sheet

Refer to Rio Hondo's trial balance in E17-6 and prepare a balance sheet as of June 30, 1984.

E17-9 A Statement of Changes in Fund Balance

The fund balance in the general fund of the town of Rio Hondo was $40,000 on July 1, 1983. Prepare a statement of changes in fund balance for the fiscal year ending June 30, 1984, using appropriate information from the trial balance presented in E17-6.

E17-10 Journal Entries for a General Fund

Prepare journal entries for the following transactions of the general fund of the town of Belmont.

1. The budget is approved by the town council. Estimated revenues amount to $520,000 and estimated expenditures to $487,000.
2. Taxes of $475,000 are levied on property.
3. Miscellaneous license and fee revenues of $50,000 are collected.
4. Employee salaries of $35,000 are paid.
5. Two new police cars costing $12,000 each are ordered and encumbered.
6. An amount of $10,000 is transferred to the debt service fund to be used to meet the next principal and interest payment on the city's general debt.
7. The police cars are received. The actual cost of the two cars is $24,500. The invoice is paid.

PROBLEMS

P17-1 Recording Budget and Revenue Transactions

Required:

Prepare the General Journal entry that properly records each of the following events. (Omit explanations.)

1. The city of Salisbury adopted the following budget. Estimated revenues were $2,840,000; appropriations were $2,700,000.
2. A tax levy of $2,000,000 was recorded; it is estimated that 1 percent of the levy will be uncollectible.
3. $500,000 was collected in licenses and fees.
4. $1,975,000 was collected on the tax levy. Uncollected taxes were transferred to a delinquent account.

P17-2 Recording Expenditures

Required:

Prepare the General Journal entry that properly records each of the following events. (Omit explanations.)

1. A purchase order for $200,000 for a fleet of 25 police cars was issued.
2. Fifteen cars are received with an invoice for $123,000. The invoice was paid.
3. Salaries were $37,000. This item had not been encumbered.
4. A total of $35,900 was transferred to the debt service fund.

P17-3 General Fund Closing Entries

The following is a trial balance of a city's general fund.

	Debits	Credits
Cash	$ 33,500	
Taxes Receivable—Delinquent	2,500	
Allowance for Uncollectible Taxes—Delinquent		$ 500
Reserve for Encumbrances		7,000
Vouchers Payable		4,500
Fund Balance		16,500
Expenditures	208,500	
Estimated Revenues	232,500	
Encumbrances	7,000	
Transfer to Special Fund	12,500	
Appropriations		230,000
Revenues		238,000
Totals	$496,500	$496,500

Required:

Prepare all entries necessary to close the temporary accounts. (Omit explanations.)

P17-4 A Statement of Changes in Fund Balance

The following entry was made to record the budget of a general fund.

1/1/84	Estimated Revenues	500,000	
	Appropriations		490,000
	Fund Balance		10,000

Additional information:

Fund Balance, 1/1/84 (before above entry)	$ 16,000
Actual Revenues	480,000
Encumbrances	20,000
Expenditures	450,000

Required:

Prepare a statement of changes in fund balance.

P17-5 Unifying Problem: Adjusting and Closing Entries and Terminology

The controller of the municipality of Graymoor Junction developed the following trial balance for the general fund.

	Debits	Credits
Cash	$ 2,500	
Expenditures	79,500	
Estimated Revenues	129,600	
Taxes Receivable—Delinquent	65,400	
Transfer to Debt Service Fund	1,900	
Reserve for Encumbrances		$ 31,400
Vouchers Payable		7,800
Appropriations		124,000
Allowance for Uncollectible Taxes—Delinquent		13,000
Fund Balance		11,000
Revenues		123,100
Encumbrances	31,400	
Totals	$310,300	$310,300

She was about to close the temporary accounts when one of her assistants told her that a previously recalcitrant taxpayer had just paid $1,300 in taxes that had been written off. In addition, wages of $1,550 were still due the town manager.

Required:

1. Incorporate the above information in the trial balance. (Ignore payroll taxes.)
2. Prepare a combined journal entry to close the temporary accounts and explain why you are making it.
3. None of the town council members has a background in nonprofit accounting. Explain what each of the budgetary accounts is used for.

4. Explain the difference between actual revenues and estimated revenues.

P17-6 Unifying Problem: Assessment of Operational Efficiency

The Senate minority leader of Costa Linda has confronted the executive branch with comparative statements of revenues and expenditures for the National Water Authorities of Costa Linda and Sable Island. Sable Island is a neighboring country with a population, climate, and geography similar to Costa Linda's.

Water Authorities of Sable Island and Costa Linda
Comparative Statements of Revenues and Expenditures for the Fiscal Year Ended December 31, 1984 (in thousands)

	Costa Linda		Sable Island	
	Budgeted	Actual	Budgeted	Actual
Revenues:				
Commercial	$277	$274	$534	$510
Residential	568	575	213	292
Total Revenues	$845	$849	$747	$802
	Appropriations	Actual Expenditures and Transfers	Appropriations	Actual Expenditures and Transfers
Expenditures and Transfers:				
Administration	$114	$179	$166	$185
Maintenance	337	367	19	95
Supplies	97	99	424	415
Capital Improvements	212	215	138	23
Debt Service	85	85	-0-	2
Total Expenditures and Transfers	$845	$945	$747	$720
Change in Fund Balance	-0-	$(96)	-0-	$ 82

The senator made several charges based upon a comparison of the figures in these two statements.

a. Costa Linda citizens are paying too much for water.

b. Administration costs are higher in Costa Linda than they were expected to be.

c. Capital spending is too ambitious.

d. Maintenance costs are higher than they need to be.

e. Government inefficiency in Costa Linda has resulted in a heavy debt burden due to continued deficit spending.

Required:

1. The executive branch thought it had administered the water fund properly. Is it possible that the senator had arrived at inappropriate conclusions?
   (a) List the facts from the statements above that support the senator's criticisms.
   (b) What are some acceptable reasons for the differences between operations in Costa Linda and in Sable Island?

2. **Interpretive Question** Are lower capital and maintenance expenses always better? Explain.

3. **Interpretive Question** The senator implied that Sable Island has a better water authority than Costa Linda. Do you agree?

4. **Interpretive Question** The executive branch pointed out that fire insurance rates were lower in Costa Linda because there were more fire hydrants. Who benefits from the lower insurance? Is this relevant to the National Water Authority? Comment.

5. **Interpretive Question** Unemployment is lower in Costa Linda than in Sable Island because business taxes in Costa Linda are lower. Should this information be considered by the National Water Authority? Comment.

6. **Interpretive Question** When could deficit spending be considered similar to debt-funded capital expansion in a company operating for profit? Could there be other reasons for deficit spending?

P17-7 The Efficiency of Fund Raising

A recent college graduate decided to take a job as fund raiser for a nonprofit charitable organization. However, he found it difficult to choose between two charities, Alpha and Beta. To help in the decision, he thought he would look at how each charity spent its revenues. Alpha Charity sent him the following statement of revenues and expenditures for the previous fiscal year.

Alpha Charity
Statement of Revenues and Expenditures for the Fiscal Year Ended June 30, 1984

Revenues:	
Corporate Donations	$123,700
Individual Contributions	81,400
Total Revenues	$205,100
Expenditures and Transfers:	
Toxin Research	$ 11,900
Heart Disease Research	27,800
Cancer Research	28,900
Hematological Studies	24,600
Research on Children's Diseases	35,300
Birth Defects Research	10,600
Fund Raising	40,800
General Administration	36,400
Total Expenditures and Transfers	$216,300
Decrease in Fund Balance	($ 11,200)

Beta Charity sent him a brochure stating that its total revenues for the year ending December 31, 1984, were $163,123. The brochure also contained a diagram that showed how every dollar was spent during the preceding fiscal year.

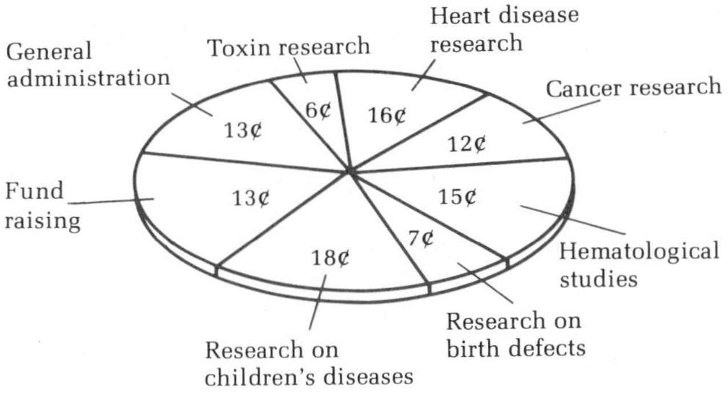

Required:

1. Prepare a statement of revenues and expenditures for Beta Charity. The increase in the fund balance was $16,167 (rounded to the nearest whole dollar).
2. Which charity spent less on fund raising in absolute terms? In relative terms?
3. **Interpretive Question** The fund raisers for Alpha Charity feel that the increased revenue is worth the extra amount spent for fund raising. What do you think?
4. **Interpretive Question** The management of Beta Charity is proud that it spends most of its revenues for charitable purposes. Do you think this pride is justified?
5. **Interpretive Question** Which charity would you want to work for? Why?

P17-8 A Statement of Changes in Financial Position

In 1984 the Museum of Modern Art bought several new paintings at a cost of $52,000. During the same period, some paintings that had been acquired for $64,300 were sold for $76,500. Negotiations with the Metropolitan Parks Authority have been completed and an unneeded portion of the museum's grounds has been sold for $18,800, representing a gain of $17,600 over the price paid in 1925 when the museum was first established. The museum retired $1,600 of long-term debt and issued $83,300 of notes due in the year 2000. (Financial statements appear in the right column.)

Required:

The museum's trustees have asked you to

1. Prepare a statement of changes in financial position using working capital as the concept of funds.
2. Prepare another statement of changes in financial position using cash as the concept of funds.
3. Comment on the similarities and differences between the statements.
4. Describe the museum's financial situation.

The Museum of Modern Art
Statement of Revenues and Expenditures
for the Year Ended December 31, 1984

Revenues:	
Gift Shop Sales	$ 18,700
Admissions	9,400
Gain on Sale of Land	17,600
Gain on Sale of Paintings	12,200
Donations and Membership Dues	64,800
Public Grants	55,300
Total Revenues	$178,000
Expenditures and Transfers:	
Cost of Gift Shop Goods Sold	$ 4,700
Salaries and Wages	106,600
Fuel Oil	33,200
Electricity	11,900
Janitorial Supplies	1,300
Fund Raising Expenses	32,600
Depreciation of Buildings and Physical Plant	9,400
Interest Expense	5,100
Other Expense Items	700
Total Expenditures and Transfers	$205,500
Decrease in Fund Balance	($ 27,500)

The Museum of Modern Art
Balance Sheets
as of December 31, 1984 and 1983

Assets	**1984**	**1983**
Cash	$ 75,500	$ 78,400
Long-Term Investments	36,900	36,900
Land	16,900	18,100
Buildings and Physical Plant	236,500	153,800
Less Accumulated Depreciation	(57,400)	(48,000)
Works of Art	331,900	344,200
Industrial Designs	5,300	5,300
Total Assets	$645,600	$588,700
Liabilities, Encumbrances, and Fund Balance		
Accounts Payable	$ 3,400	$ 3,100
Current Debt	11,800	10,800
Long-Term Debt	186,900	105,200
Memberships: Initial Contributions	31,900	30,500
Fund Balance (including Grants, Donations, and Membership Fees)	411,600	439,100
Total Liabilities, Encumbrances, and Fund Balance	$645,600	$588,700

P17–9 Unifying Problem: Understanding Financial Statement Relationships

The city of Lexington had some of its records destroyed in a fire. You have been asked to analyze the balance sheets of the current year (1984) and the previous year and to review the ledger account for the fund balance in order to answer certain questions.

City of Lexington
Comparative Balance Sheets—General Fund as of December 31, 1983 and 1984

	December 31, 1984	December 31, 1983
Cash	$ 81,000	$50,000
Taxes Receivable—Current	50,000	42,000
Allowance for Uncollectible Taxes—Current	(11,000)	(9,000)
Taxes Receivable—Delinquent	18,000	14,000
Allowance for Uncollectible Taxes—Delinquent	(7,000)	(8,000)
Total Assets	$131,000	$89,000
Accounts Payable	$ 21,000	$17,000
Reserve for Encumbrances	35,000	22,000
Fund Balance	75,000	50,000
Total Liabilities and Fund Balance	$131,000	$89,000

City of Lexington
Changes in Fund Balance

Balance, January 1, 1984	$50,000
Add: Excess of Estimated Revenues over Appropriations	8,000
Excess of Appropriations over Expenditures* and Encumbrances	10,000
Excess of Revenue over Estimated Revenue	7,000
Fund Balance, December 31, 1984	$75,000

* Amounted to $283,000 for 1984.

Required:

1. Determine the appropriations and total revenue for 1984.
2. Prepare the entry that was made to record the 1984 budget.
3. **Interpretive Question** Why are the budgets of governmental units included in the formal accounting system?

CHAPTER 18

Internal Control

THIS CHAPTER EXPLAINS:

The purpose of internal control.
The difference between administrative and accounting controls.
The characteristics of an effective system of internal control.
The effects of computers on internal control.

Roswell Steffen, chief teller at the Park Avenue branch of the Union Dime Savings Bank in New York City, earned a salary of $11,000. A quiet, modest man, he was well liked by his fellow workers and spent most evenings at home with his wife and two teen-age daughters in their $275-a-month garden apartment in New Jersey. An investigation by federal, state, and local authorities into a large-scale, illegal bookmaking operation revealed that Steffen had another side. He had been betting thousands of dollars a day on horse races and professional sports. Because of the size of the bets, the investigators consulted with officials of the Union Dime Bank, who conducted an extensive review of their records and found that Steffen had embezzled $1,500,000 over a 3- to 4-year period. Steffen, a compulsive gambler, admitted that he had lost the entire sum.

When asked how he had embezzled the money, Steffen explained that he had been given daily, unregulated access to the cash vault and that many of the tellers he supervised were inexperienced. As part of his supervisory duties he also had access to the computer terminals and the authority to modify the computerized data. This combination of circumstances allowed Steffen to take cash from deposits and manipulate computer inputs in order to conceal any shortages.

Steffen was not a computer "genius" and the mechanics of his crime were fairly simple. As the supervisor of tellers, he could override many of the basic controls on the bank's computerized accounting system. When a customer brought in a large deposit, Steffen would enter the amount in the customer's passbook. On the computer, however, he would record the deposit under the account number of a second passbook, which he later destroyed. Money was withdrawn periodically by Steffen from the second passbook account.

Steffen kept careful track of the fictitious deposits and constantly made corrections to juggle the more than fifty accounts he was manipulating. When this system became too complicated and time-consuming, he switched to 2-year certificates of deposit, which only required manipulation every 24 months. Occasionally, customers would discover an error in their accounts and march into the bank demanding a correction. The tellers would naturally refer these irate customers to Steffen, the chief teller, who would explain the difficulty as a computer error or a new teller's misposting. He would then make corrections, altering some other account to compensate for the "error."

These "errors" went undetected for almost four years because Steffen, who was not authorized to use the computer terminal except for administrative and clerical procedures, was in fact using it to enter transactions and manipulate the accounts so that they appeared to be correct. More important, Roswell Steffen was able to perpetrate this fraud because there was a serious breakdown of internal controls at the Union Dime Savings Bank.[1] Although the bank had most of the features of a good accounting system (sound reporting practices, timely data, and so on), it lacked strength in an essential area: internal control.

Chapter 9 briefly discussed the controls needed for cash and cash transactions. This chapter explains internal control in more detail. Because of the nature of the subject, information is presented here in a more conceptual and less procedural manner than in preceding chapters.

What Is Internal Control?

internal control *an organization's methods and procedures for safeguarding its assets, checking on the accuracy and reliability of its accounting data, promoting operational efficiency, and encouraging adherence to managerial policies*

The American Institute of Certified Public Accountants (AICPA) has defined internal control as "the plan of organization and all the coordinate methods and measures adopted within a business" to ensure that (1) its resources are protected against waste, fraud, inefficiency, and unauthorized use, (2) its accounting data are accurate and reliable, (3) its performance is evaluated periodically, and (4) its policies and procedures are followed.[2]

Although a good system of internal control would probably have prevented the fraud perpetrated by Roswell Steffen, fraud prevention is not its main purpose. The real purpose of internal control is to promote efficient operations. In fact, the concept of internal control is so basic that it affects every aspect of an organization, including the efficient acquisition, utilization, and conservation of all resources.

In a small coffee shop, for example, questions relating to internal control would include: Have the personnel been adequately trained? Is there a good refrigeration system to keep the food fresh? Do the waiters and waitresses

[1] Russell, Harold F., *Foozles and Frauds* (Altamonte Springs, Fla.: Institute of Internal Auditors), 1977.

[2] Statement on Auditing Standards No. 1, "Codification of Auditing Standards and Procedures" (American Institute of CPAs, 1973), Section 320.

have order booklets with serialized, preprinted numbers on them? Is there a cash register with an internal tape? Does the building have a fire sprinkler system? Is there good supervision of personnel? Are the duties of the cashier and of the waiters and waitresses adequately separated? Who makes the bank deposit of the day's receipts? Who has responsibility for the accounting records? In other words, internal control goes beyond the control of cash receipts and disbursements and the results of transactions as summarized in accounting reports; it extends to all phases of the operations of a business.

BASIC CATEGORIES: ADMINISTRATIVE AND ACCOUNTING CONTROLS

administrative controls *procedures that deal primarily with a company's operational efficiency and its employees' compliance with authorized policies and procedures*

Typically, there are two broad categories of internal control. Administrative controls deal primarily with operational efficiency and compliance with an organization's policies and procedures. Management establishes objectives and policies, and then sets up administrative control procedures to ensure that its objectives are being fulfilled.

A typical administrative control is the requirement that all new employees submit to a physical examination. Another might be the requirement that any capital expenditure exceeding $1,000 be approved by the controller. Still another is the design of security procedures to ensure that only certain authorized employees are allowed access to the computer. Other administrative controls are effected through the use of budgets, quality control reports, personnel evaluations, computer logs, statistical analyses, daily absentee records, market research, and periodic performance evaluations.

Thus, administrative controls are designed to achieve management's objectives. As such, they have little or no direct bearing on the accuracy and reliability of the financial statements and, therefore, are not of particular interest to the external auditor (that is, the independent certified public accountant). Because they deal primarily with operational efficiency and authorization, administrative controls are more the concern of the internal auditor, who is often a part of the management team.

accounting controls *the plan of organization and the procedures and records that are concerned with safeguarding a company's assets and assuring the reliability of the financial records*

In contrast, accounting controls "comprise the plan of organization and the procedures and records that are concerned with the safeguarding of assets and the reliability of financial records."[3] The separation of the custody of assets from the accounting for those assets is an example of an accounting control. Thus, the cashier receiving payments from customers should not also have the responsibility for recording those receipts in the journals. This fundamental control was violated in the case of Roswell Steffen, who not only had access to the cash vault but also to the computer terminals, where he was free to enter transactions and manipulate accounts. Another example is the separation of the authority to approve transactions from the custody of related assets. The person who authorizes the payment

[3] Statement on Auditing Standards No. 1, Section 320.28.

of a bill should not be the same person who signs the check that pays the bill. Obviously, that individual could authorize payments to himself or herself. Similarly, the person who distributes checks to employees should not have the authority to add new employees to the payroll, or to delete employees who have been terminated. Why? Because that person could then fire an employee and leave the person's name on the payroll, or hire a fictitious employee and pocket the checks. Still another example: It is not wise to allow programmers unrestricted access to the computer, because with such access they might be able to manipulate the computer programs for their own benefit.

Accounting controls are the direct concern of external auditors (CPAs), who seek assurance that a firm's accounting system is functioning properly. As a result, CPAs focus on a firm's ability to achieve the four basic categories of accounting control: authorization, recording, access to assets, and asset accountability. The objective for each category is explained briefly in Exhibit 18-1.

EXHIBIT 18-1 Internal Accounting Control Objectives

Control	Description
Authorization	Transactions are executed in accordance with management's general or specific instructions.
Recording	Transactions are recorded as necessary to (1) permit preparation of financial statements in conformity with generally accepted accounting principles or any other criteria applicable to such statements, . . . and (2) maintain accountability for assets.
Access to Assets	Access to assets is permitted only in accordance with management's authorization.
Asset Accountability	The record of assets is compared with the existing assets at reasonable intervals and appropriate action is taken with respect to any differences.*

* Exhibit 18-5 on page 635 provides more details on this important control.

Source: Statement on Auditing Standards No. 1, Sections 320.27-320.28

MANAGEMENT'S RESPONSIBILITY AND THE FOREIGN CORRUPT PRACTICES ACT

The independent auditor will always review a company's system of internal control to make sure that it meets the four objectives presented in Exhibit 18-1. However, management is directly responsible for establishing and maintaining that system. Until recently, management's responsibility to maintain an adequate internal accounting control system was only implied.

Foreign Corrupt Practices Act (FCPA) of 1977 *legislation that requires all companies registered with the Securities and Exchange Commission to keep accurate accounting records and maintain an adequate system of internal control*

There was no formal legal requirement. However, in the wake of illegal political campaign contributions, business frauds, and numerous illegal payments to foreign officials in exchange for business favors, Congress passed the Foreign Corrupt Practices Act (FCPA) of 1977. Portions of the FCPA were then incorporated by amendment into the Securities and Exchange Act of 1934. The result of this legislation is that all companies registered with the Securities and Exchange Commission (SEC) are required by law to keep records that represent the firm's transactions accurately and fairly. In addition, they must maintain systems of internal accounting control that meet the four objectives set forth in Exhibit 18-1.

Note that the law did not create any new responsibilities for management. However, it makes mandatory requirements that had been only implied previously. Some people have suggested new SEC regulations that would legally require a periodic review of internal controls by external auditors. Such regulations would require CPAs to report to management, the SEC, and the public on the internal control systems of the companies they audit and offer judgments as to whether or not the companies are in compliance with the law. For now, the SEC is merely encouraging rather than mandating such a review of internal control by external auditors.

COST-BENEFICIAL CONTROLS

cost-beneficial controls *controls that benefit a company to an extent that outweighs their costs*

In exercising its responsibility for maintaining adequate internal controls, management will want to be sure that the controls are cost beneficial. This means that the benefits must be greater than the costs. In designing a system that is cost beneficial, management evaluates a number of factors. Among them: the size and complexity of the business, the diversity of its operations, the degree of centralization of its financial and operating management, the types and values of its assets, its personnel policies, and even the prevailing political climate and the degree of economic stability. It would be ridiculous, for example, to hire armed guards for $10,000 a year to watch over a $500 petty-cash fund.

A company could install a system of internal controls that would prevent 99.9 percent of all errors in its accounting system, but it might not be cost beneficial. There is always some level of control that is adequate but not excessive, so management must weigh the potential benefits of having certain controls against the costs of providing them.

TO SUMMARIZE There are two broad categories of internal control. Administrative controls are measures used to promote operational efficiency and to encourage adherence to managerial policies. Accounting controls include the plan of organization and all other measures that a business uses to safeguard its resources, ensure that its accounting data are reliable, reduce irregularities, and detect errors. The Foreign Corrupt Practices Act and the related amendment to the Securities and Exchange Act of 1934 now require management to take the responsibility for maintaining good internal controls. Management will also want to confirm that these controls are cost beneficial.

Characteristics of an Effective System of Internal Control

There is no "perfect" system of internal control. Each organization is unique, which makes it literally impossible to install a system of internal control that is appropriate for all conditions and circumstances. We can, however, identify some general characteristics that, if implemented, would help a firm achieve the four basic objectives of internal control. The AICPA has suggested that a satisfactory system of internal control has the following characteristics.

1. A sound plan of organization, including appropriate segregation of functional responsibilities.
2. A system of authorization and recording that provides adequate accountability and control over assets, liabilities, revenues, and expenses.
3. Sound practices and procedures.
4. Competent and trustworthy personnel.

These characteristics are not separate and distinct. Considerable overlap exists, for example, between a system of authorization and recording and the sound practices that must be followed to ensure that authorization and recording are proper. In the same way, a sound plan of organization will be most effective where the company is staffed with competent and trustworthy personnel. In the following discussion of the four basic characteristics of internal control, you should keep in mind that each characteristic interconnects and overlaps with the others to form an efficient and effective total system.

PLAN OF ORGANIZATION

A sound plan of organization has two important characteristics: (1) well-defined lines of authority, and (2) segregation of functional responsibilities. The degree to which these characteristics are applied depends, of course, on a number of considerations, including the nature and size of the business, the style and philosophy of its management, the size and geographical distribution of its units, the variation in its product lines, and political and behavioral considerations. It is impossible, to use an extreme example, for the local Mom & Pop grocery store to have the same segregation of accounting duties as General Motors. A small business where members of the family share in the financial duties would not have the same type of organizational structure as a large corporation with well-defined lines of authority and segregation of responsibilities. A sound plan of organization depends on a number of internal and external factors, and any internal control system must be designed with these factors in mind.

Lines of Authority

Theoretically, only one person in a department should be responsible for each function, such as cash receipts, cash disbursements, purchasing, payroll preparation, or credit approval. It takes little imagination to envision the confusion that would result if a business gave every employee unlimited purchasing authority. There would be overstocking, duplication of orders, loss of quantity discounts, and tremendous waste. By designating responsibility for the purchasing function, or any other function, the organization runs more smoothly and control is maintained.

Normally, each company will have an organization chart that not only specifies the formal lines of authority but also indicates departmental responsibilities. Exhibit 18-2 on page 630 shows how the various functional areas of a typical organization might be separated, each with its respective lines of authority.

In addition to formal lines of authority, each organization will have an informal hierarchy that depends on the personalities of the individuals and on the group dynamics of the situation. These behavioral elements are beyond the scope of this text. However, they are important considerations and must be dealt with in managing an organization.

Segregation of Functional Responsibilities

A sound plan of organization should provide for the appropriate segregation of functional responsibilities. This means that no department should be responsible for handling *all* phases of a transaction. In some small businesses, of course, this segregation is not possible. However, there are three functions that should be performed by separate departments, or at least by different people.

1. *Authorization.* Authorizing and approving the execution of a transaction; for example, approving the sale of a building or land.
2. *Record Keeping.* Recording the transaction in the accounting journals.
3. *Custodial.* Having physical possession of or control over the assets involved in a transaction, including operational responsibility—for example, having the key to the safe in which cash or marketable securities are kept, or more generally, having control over the production function.

By separating the responsibilities for these duties, a company realizes the efficiency derived from specialization and also reduces the errors, both intentional and unintentional, that might otherwise occur.

Separating operational or custodial duties from record keeping helps ensure that reports are unbiased. For example, having the general accounting department prepare an analysis of accounts receivable for the credit manager helps ensure the objectivity and independence with which this information is compiled, and thereby enhances its usefulness. Separating the custody of assets from record keeping also protects against embezzlement and fraud. By giving custody of an asset to one person and control over the asset's records to another, a company reduces the risk that the asset will be used by an employee for personal gain. If Roswell Steffen, for example, had not had access to the record-keeping function, he would have had to conspire with the person in charge of the records in order to manipulate the customer deposits to his advantage. With these duties separated, the employee who has custody of an asset will be less inclined to steal.

EXHIBIT 18-2 Organization Chart

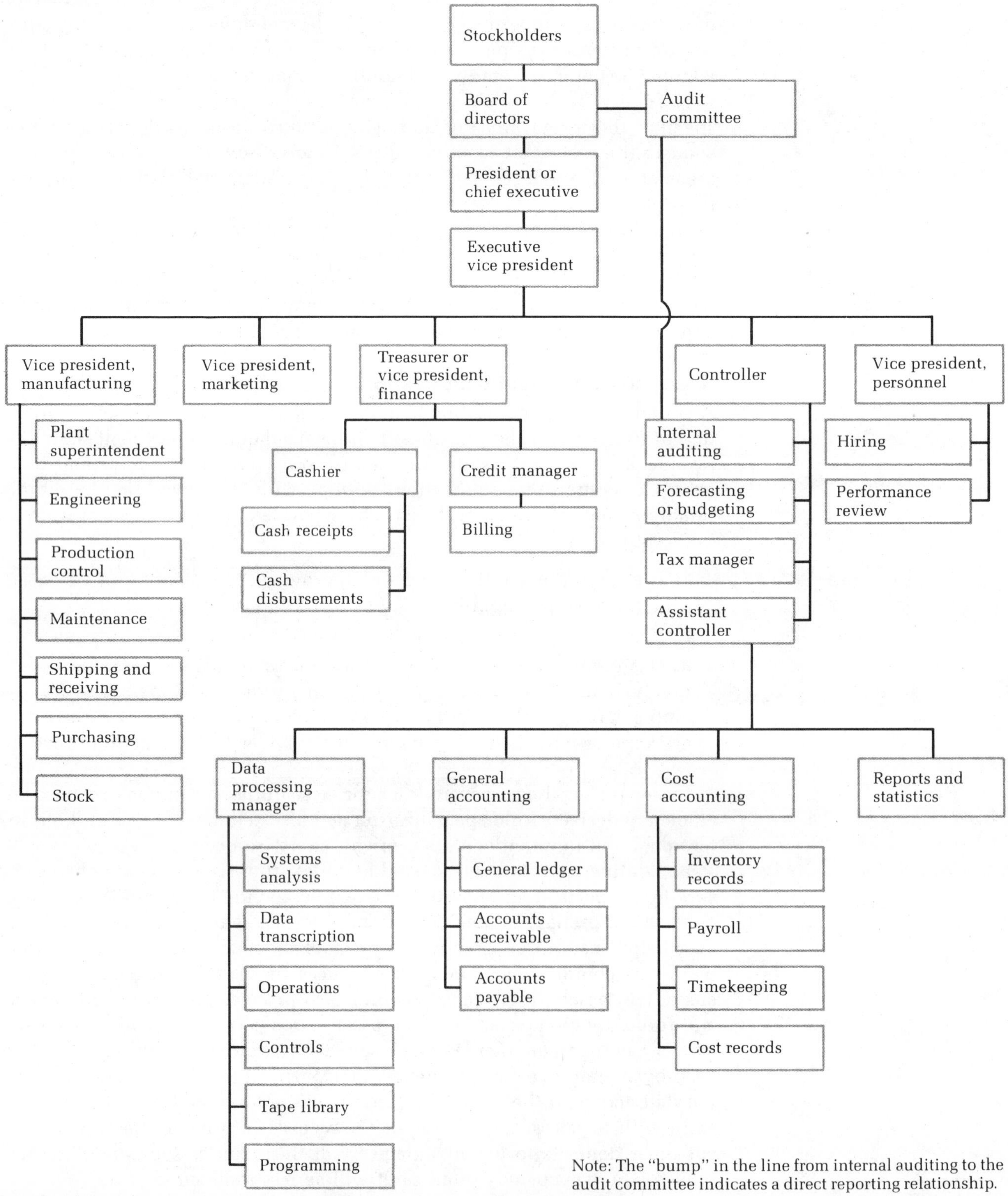

Note: The "bump" in the line from internal auditing to the audit committee indicates a direct reporting relationship.

Separating the custodial responsibility from the authorization and approval function also helps to prevent abuses. For example, a warehouse manager who has custody of scrap materials should not be able to authorize the sale of that scrap. Otherwise, the manager could authorize the sale of, say, 500 pounds of aluminum scrap, but actually sell 2,000 pounds and pocket the difference.

Exhibit 18–3 describes one internal control system—the segregation of duties related to cash receipts.

EXHIBIT 18–3 **Segregation of Duties Related to Cash Receipts**

In the presence of another employee, a mail clerk opens the day's mail and prepares a list of receipts in triplicate, including the name of the payer, the amount of each remittance, and whether it is cash or a check. The receipts are then totaled. This remittance list is given to a cash receipts clerk, who makes entries in the cash receipts journal, debiting Cash and crediting Accounts Receivable for each entry. Totals in the cash receipts journal must agree with the total on the remittance list.

An accounts receivable clerk also receives a copy of the remittance list. The clerk posts the individual accounts to the accounts receivable ledger, checking to be sure that the total agrees with the total cash receipts as reported by the mail clerk.

The mail clerk hand-carries the day's receipts to the cashier. The cashier counts the money and compares the total with the total on the remittance list. Assuming that the amounts agree, the cashier signs a copy of the remittance list and returns it to the mail clerk as a receipt. The cashier then prepares a deposit slip in duplicate and deposits the money in the bank. One copy of the deposit slip is kept by the cashier and one is given to a supervisor.

The supervisor compares the total on the remittance list with the total on the bank deposit slip (making certain that the bank has validated the deposit slip) to be sure that the day's receipts were actually deposited in the bank. The supervisor also periodically compares the totals in the cash receipts journal and the accounts receivable ledger to verify that the amounts are credited to the proper accounts.

This segregation of duties related to cash receipts ensures the integrity of the records and the control over cash. If the cashier were to pocket some of the receipts, the discrepancy would be discovered when the supervisor compared the remittance list with the deposit slip. Likewise, the mail clerk could steal receipts but it would be more difficult in the presence of another person. In addition, the clerk eventually would be caught when a customer complained that a payment had not been credited. Since the cash receipts clerk and accounts receivable clerk have no access to the cash, falsifying records would do them no good. And finally, the supervisor, who has control over the records, has no control over the cash. If two or more employees were in collusion to defraud, these controls would obviously break down. No controls can provide absolute protection against collusion.

SYSTEM OF AUTHORIZATION

A strong system of internal control requires proper authorization of every transaction. In the typical corporate organization, this authorization originates with the shareholders who elect a board of directors. It is then delegated from the board of directors to upper-level management and eventually throughout the organization. Whereas the board of directors and upper-level management possess a fairly general power of authorization, a clerk usually has limited authority. Thus, the board would authorize dividends, a general change in policies, or a merger, whereas a clerk would be restricted to the authorization of credit or a specific cash transaction.

Authorization, which enhances control by making individuals accountable for their actions, is closely tied to sound organizational policies. That is, if the methods of dealing with transactions are consistent with organizational policies, including proper lines of authority and segregation of duties, then the authorization of any transaction will be monitored and reviewed at various points in the operating cycle. For example, the approval of a cash disbursement for repair work requires several levels of authorization. Before the accounts payable clerk approves the disbursement, the work order should be checked to make sure that it was properly authorized. In addition, the work order should be reviewed to verify that the repair was completed satisfactorily. This overlapping process significantly strengthens the internal control system.

Adequate Documentation and Recording

A key to proper authorization is an adequate system of documentation and recording. As explained in Chapter 3, documents are the physical, objective evidence of accounting transactions. Their existence allows management to review any transaction for appropriate authorization. Documents are also the means by which information is communicated throughout an organization. In short, adequate documentation provides evidence that the recording, classifying, and summarizing functions are being performed properly.

A good system of documentation has several characteristics.

1. *Simplicity.* Documents should be as uncluttered as possible, so that they can be easily interpreted and understood.

2. *Multiple Use.* Documents should be designed with all possible uses in mind. There should be enough copies of a sales invoice, for example, so that it can be used for recording sales in the sales journal, for calculating commissions, for authorizing credit terms, for authorizing shipments, and as a back-up document for computing sales by sales representatives, territories, products, and other relevant categories.

3. *Good Design.* Forms should be designed with speed and efficiency in mind. The following are basic requirements: proper size for ease in filing and mailing, adequate room for handwritten notes, left-to-right and top-to-bottom design for ease in filling out, and the right grade, size, weight, and color of paper.

4. *Prenumbering.* Documents should be prenumbered. This facilitates identification of missing documents and filing of material for later reference.

5. *Timely Preparation.* Forms should be prepared as the transaction takes place in order to reduce the chance of unintentional error and/or manipulation. Computers can be used to speed up the preparation and processing of transactions.

The Chart of Accounts

chart of accounts *a systematic listing of all accounts used by a company*

A related but separate feature of sound documentation is a chart of accounts. As shown in Exhibit 18-4, this is a written classification of a company's accounts. Typically, the accounts are grouped by type in the order of

EXHIBIT 18-4 A Chart of Accounts for a Merchandising Business

Assets (100–199)

Current Assets (100–120):
101 Cash
102 Marketable Securities
103 Notes Receivable
105 Accounts Receivable
106 Allowance for Doubtful Accounts
107 Inventory
108 Supplies
109 Prepaid Rent
110 Prepaid Taxes
111 Prepaid Insurance

Investments (121–140):
131 Investment in Stock of X Co.

Property, Plant and Equipment (141–160):
141 Land
142 Buildings
143 Accumulated Depreciation—Buildings
144 Store Equipment
145 Accumulated Depreciation—Store Equipment
148 Office Furniture
149 Accumulated Depreciation—Office Furniture

Intangible Assets (161–180):
161 Patents
164 Goodwill

Other Assets (181–199)

Liabilities (200–299)

Current Liabilities (200–219):
201 Notes Payable
202 Accounts Payable
203 Salaries Payable
204 Interest Payable
205 Payroll Taxes Payable
206 Income Taxes Payable
219 Other Current Liabilities

Long-Term Liabilities (220–239):
222 Bonds Payable
223 Mortgage Payable

Stockholders' Equity (300–399)

301 Common Stock
302 Paid-in Capital in Excess of Par
330 Retained Earnings

Sales (400–499)

400 Sales Revenue
402 Sales Returns and Allowances
404 Sales Discounts
450 Purchases

Cost of Goods Sold (500)

Operating Expenses (501–599)

Selling Expenses (501–549):
501 Sales Salaries and Commissions
510 Freight-Out
520 Payroll Taxes
523 Utility Expense
524 Postage Expense
525 Travel Expense
528 Advertising Expense

General and Administrative Expenses (550–599):
551 Officers' Salaries
552 Office Salaries
553 Administrative Salaries
570 Payroll Taxes
571 Office Supplies Expense
573 Utility Expense
574 Postage Expense
575 Travel Expense
576 Depreciation Expense—Buildings
577 Depreciation Expense—Office Furniture
578 Office Equipment Rent Expense
579 Accounting and Legal Fees
581 Building Repair and Maintenance Expense
583 Doubtful Accounts Expense
584 Amortization of Goodwill
585 Amortization of Patents

Other Expenses (600–699)

601 Interest on Notes
602 Interest on Bonds
603 Interest on Mortgage

Other Income (700–799)

701 Interest Revenue
702 Revenue from Investments
704 Miscellaneous Income

their appearance on the financial statements and the other reports. Each group of accounts is assigned a sequence of numbers. The individual accounts are then given numbers, with gaps left in the sequence for accounts that may be added as the business grows.

The chart of accounts helps to organize the accounting records. In so doing, it contributes to the consistent reporting of similar transactions and to the proper presentation of information on a company's financial statements.

SOUND PROCEDURES

A well-designed system of internal control, complete with all the appropriate safeguards, will be ineffective unless the organization implements sound procedures. The strength of controls depends on the degree to which they are put into effect with proper procedures.

There is considerable overlap between this accounting characteristic and those just discussed: segregation of responsibilities, authorization, and proper documentation. However, sound procedures include several other elements, such as accounting and procedures manuals, physical safeguards, and internal auditing.

Accounting and Procedures Manuals

accounting manual *a document that lists all accounts and describes the proper bookkeeping for transactions likely to be processed through each account*

Large, complex organizations require a sophisticated accounting system. To ensure that the system is understood and properly used by all personnel, an accounting manual is created. Such a manual lists and describes each account and potential transaction and sets forth the proper bookkeeping procedures. Employees thus can check to be sure that they are handling transactions correctly. For example, suppose a clerk has to account for the purchase of $1,000 of cleaning solution. Should the amount be treated as an expense or as an asset? The answer can be found by looking in the accounting manual for a similar transaction.

procedures manual *a document that identifies the general policies of a company*

A procedures manual, which may be combined with the accounting manual, describes the general policies of a company. For example, it would describe the firm's credit policy and the policy on sales returns, as well as the reports to be prepared by each department. This manual would also include job descriptions that outline the duties, responsibilities, and authority of each position.

Physical Safeguards

Some of the most crucial policies and procedures involve the use of adequate physical safeguards to protect resources. For example, a bank would not allow significant amounts of money to be transported in an ordinary car. A company should not leave its valuable assets unprotected. Examples of physical security systems are fireproof vaults for the storage of classified information, currency, and marketable securities, and guards, fences, and remote control cameras for the protection of equipment, materials, and merchandise.

Records and documents are also important resources and must be protected. Recreating lost or destroyed records can be costly and time consuming. The high cost of back-up records (often on microfilm) is usually more than justified in protecting such valuable resources.

Internal Auditing

A major concern of management and auditors is how well the system of internal control is functioning. This brings us to the fourth basic objective of internal accounting control: "The record of assets is compared with the existing assets at reasonable intervals and appropriate action is taken with respect to any differences" (see Exhibits 18-1 and 18-5). In a large firm, operating results are generally being constantly monitored by a staff of internal auditors, as is the adherence of employees to management's policies. By reviewing the system of internal controls and making a periodic audit of operations, the internal audit department functions as an arm of management.

internal audit *an appraisal by internal accountants of employee performance and adherence to company policies, and an assessment of the reliability of the information system*

EXHIBIT 18-5 **Internal Auditing: Physical Comparison of Assets with Records**

Category	Description
Cash and Checking	Count petty cash and receive bank reconciliations regularly.
Accounts Receivable	Send audit letters to customers, asking them to confirm their accounts receivable balances.
Inventory	Perform periodic physical spot check counts in addition to the annual full count of inventory.
Long-Term Operational Assets	Count these assets and compare the result to the company's records.

An important characteristic of such a department, however, is its independence. To function properly, the internal audit staff should not be subordinate to any operating department; instead, it should report directly to top management. In most large companies the internal audit department is a functional part of the controller's office, but it reports directly to an audit committee composed of members of the board of directors who are not employees of the company (see Exhibit 18-2). This committee's responsibilities include nominating the independent auditors, reviewing their work, and acting as a liaison for the internal audit staff with the company's chief decision makers.

COMPETENT AND TRUSTWORTHY PERSONNEL

Having competent and trustworthy employees is the most important characteristic of a satisfactory system of internal control, yet it is the most difficult to evaluate. The best-structured system will fail if the company's employees are incompetent or dishonest. People are an organization's most important resource, and for this reason good personnel policies are essential in achieving a good system of internal control. Perhaps the most important areas to consider in ensuring that an organization has competent and trustworthy personnel are employee selection, employee training, employee supervision, performance review, and fidelity bonding.

Employee Selection

Prospective employees should be carefully screened. This process may include interviews, aptitude tests, background checks, and evaluation of references from past employers. Once the person's qualifications are confirmed, great care should be taken in matching jobs with talents. A disgruntled or frustrated employee can do considerable damage to an organization, and the selection process should be thorough enough to minimize this risk.

Employee Training

Programs for training employees should be designed to accelerate employee development and to increase the number of competent individuals available to assume the various levels of responsibility. In addition, employees should be trained to perform a variety of jobs, so that vacations and illnesses will not cause major disruptions in the company's operations. Such training procedures should also allow for the periodic rotation of assignments, a key element in internal control. Employees who know that someone else may soon be taking over their position usually perform better and are more conscientious in following the established policies and procedures. Rotation of employees also may reveal errors and irregularities that would otherwise go unnoticed.

In a parallel procedure, employees should be required to take vacations. This has the same effect as a periodic rotation of duties. Take the classic example of the bank clerk who had not taken a vacation in 20 years. Everyone thought that she was a most dedicated and efficient employee. An illness forced her to take a few weeks off and her work was performed by another clerk. As a result, it was discovered that for a number of years she had been embezzling large sums of money. She had been able to cover up the fraud only because she was always present. Rotation of employees and mandatory vacations would have prevented this fraud.

Employee Supervision and Performance Review

Even the most carefully selected and trained individuals need to have their work monitored. A qualified supervisor performs this role by assisting in the day-to-day activities and by conducting periodic performance reviews. These reviews, conducted at all levels of the organization, help identify both the strengths and the weaknesses of the employees' performance. A performance review also forces employees to account for the assets under their control. The system whereby employees are held directly responsible for the resources entrusted to their care is called "responsibility accounting."

Fidelity Bonding

fidelity bond *an insurance contract whereby a bonding company agrees to reimburse an employer for any theft, embezzlement, or fraud perpetrated by an employee covered by the bonding agreement*

Another important aspect of sound personnel policies and procedures is fidelity bonding. No system of internal control is foolproof, and losses can occur if employees who handle cash or other liquid assets are dishonest. As a result, employees in charge of easily converted assets may be bonded. A fidelity bond is simply an insurance contract whereby a bonding company agrees to reimburse the employer for any theft, embezzlement, or fraud perpetrated by an employee covered by the agreement. Its purpose is really twofold: (1) The company is insured against the misappropriation of assets by its employees, and (2) employees, realizing that the bonding companies generally prosecute to the fullest extent to recover losses, are more hesitant to commit dishonest acts.

TO SUMMARIZE An effective system of internal control must have a sound plan of organization, with clear lines of authority and adequate segregation of functional responsibilities. Its system of authorization and documentation must provide for accountability and control over resources. A chart of accounts is useful in this regard. In implementing sound procedures, companies use accounting and procedures manuals, establish physical safeguards over assets, and rely on internal auditors to monitor the practices being followed. Finally, a company must have competent and trustworthy personnel, developed by proper employee selection, employee training, and employee supervision and review. In addition, fidelity bonding helps protect against losses.

The Effects of Computers on Internal Control

Computers have contributed greatly to the speed and accuracy with which data are processed. And, because they reduce the amount of human intervention, they are consistently objective and reliable. When data are processed in accordance with the system's design and programs, very few mathematical or procedural errors will occur. Thus, computers tend to enhance the overall effectiveness and efficiency of accounting systems.

The elements of internal control discussed in this chapter apply equally to a computerized accounting system. Computer operators are usually bonded, duties are generally rotated and segregated where possible, and physical safeguards are maintained. In addition, computers are valuable assets that require environmental controls, such as sprinkler systems, climate control, guards or restricted access, and fireproof libraries.

For all its benefits, however, the computer can also be a source of problems in internal control, in the following ways.

1. Although the decrease in human involvement with the data will eliminate many mechanical and mathematical errors, it may also obscure errors that would otherwise be discovered in manual systems. For example, the receipt of two identical refunds from one company would be processed in the normal manner by a computer. A person, on the other hand, might become suspicious and, by checking into the matter, discover that a duplication had been made.
2. Because computer systems require such specialized skills, it may be difficult for a company to achieve the degree of segregation of duties necessary for sound internal control. For example, programmers in a small company may be asked to operate the computer system, making it possible for them to manipulate their own programs for personal benefit.
3. Data must be converted to tapes or disks, so errors may be introduced into the system during the data-conversion process.
4. Less documentary evidence usually remains after certain functions have been performed by the computer. This means that the internal controls that rely upon a review of documentation may be less meaningful. Computers may destroy or conceal much of the "audit trail."
5. Because management, and even auditors, may not thoroughly understand the computer, dishonest employees can take advantage of this ignorance. People can steal with the aid of a computer without actually having to carry away goods or cash.

Due to these factors, internal checks and controls must be adapted to and built into computer systems. Computer-based internal control systems are often complex and may be difficult for management and auditors to work with, but they are necessary in many companies.

CHAPTER REVIEW

Management needs assurance that a company's assets are being properly safeguarded, that reliable financial information is being generated, that operations are running efficiently, and that its policies and directives are being carried out. A good system of internal control helps provide this important assurance. The controls that are implemented to accomplish this goal should be cost beneficial; that is, the benefits of the controls should exceed the costs.

External auditors will want to make sure that a sound system of internal control exists in an organization. If controls are strong, then auditors can be more confident that the financial picture is accurate and reliable. If controls are weak, the external auditor will need to perform a much more detailed review.

Internal auditors are also concerned with the adequacy of internal controls. Where strong internal controls exist, the chances are greater that operations are functioning efficiently, that management's policies and procedures are being followed, and that assets are being properly protected.

Perhaps the best way to summarize the concepts discussed in this chapter is to use a checklist. Although the following questions are by no means all-inclusive, they do provide guidelines for evaluating a company's internal control system.

1. Does the organization have reliable and trustworthy personnel?
2. Is there adequate rotation of personnel, including mandatory vacations?
3. Are there adequate procedures for the physical protection of assets (that is, security systems, guards, safety deposit boxes, and so on)?
4. Are the controls cost beneficial?
5. Is the system of controls current?
6. Is there adequate separation of authority?
7. Has responsibility for various operations and functions been adequately defined?
8. Have company policies been put in writing and are these policies adhered to?
9. Are employees who work with highly liquid or sensitive assets bonded?
10. For a large firm, is there an adequate and independent internal audit department?
11. Are the accounting and record-keeping responsibilities adequately separated from the custodianship over the respective assets?
12. Is there a good system of employee selection? Of training? Of review and performance evaluation?
13. Are there adequate records and documentation?
14. Does a system of authorization and verification exist?
15. Does the organization have review procedures to evaluate efficiency as well as effectiveness?
16. Have controls been adapted to protect the organization that uses a sophisticated computer system?

KEY TERMS AND CONCEPTS

accounting controls (625)
accounting manual (634)
administrative controls (625)
chart of accounts (632)
cost-beneficial controls (627)
fidelity bond (637)
Foreign Corrupt Practices Act (FCPA) of 1977 (627)
internal audit (635)
internal control (624)
procedures manual (634)

REVIEW PROBLEM

Establishing Internal Control

Whett Paint Company has come to you for advice on setting up an internal control system. Several functions must be performed, but there are only three employees—Louise, Jane, and Denise. Each employee is qualified to handle any of the functions. Keeping in mind the characteristics of a good internal control system, assign the following tasks to the employees.

1. Maintaining the General Ledger.
2. Authorizing purchases of supplies and inventory.
3. Receiving cash payments.
4. Reconciling the bank statement.
5. Preparing checks.
6. Maintaining the perpetual inventory record.
7. Maintaining the accounts receivable and accounts payable records.
8. Safeguarding the stock certificates held for investment purposes.
9. Authorizing payment of invoices.
10. Verifying that proper quantities of supplies and inventory are received.

Solution

The functional responsibilities of authorizing, recording, and being custodian of assets should not be performed by the same person. Therefore, we will assign the authorizing responsibilities to Louise, the recording responsibilities to Jane, and the custodial responsibilities to Denise. Specific responsibilities are as follows.

Louise: Authorizing Responsibilities

2. Authorizing purchases of supplies and inventory.
4. Reconciling the bank statement.
9. Authorizing payment of invoices.

Jane: Recording Responsibilities

1. Maintaining the General Ledger.
6. Maintaining the perpetual inventory record.
7. Maintaining the accounts receivable and accounts payable records.

Denise: Custodial Responsibilities

3. Receiving cash payments.
5. Preparing checks.
8. Safeguarding stock certificates held for investment purposes.
10. Verifying that proper quantities of supplies and inventory are received.

DISCUSSION QUESTIONS

1 Why is internal control a critical element in accounting?

2 "Internal control refers only to measures taken to prevent fraud and embezzlement." Do you agree? Explain.

3 Distinguish between accounting and administrative controls.

4 List and discuss four objectives of internal accounting controls.

5 Who has primary responsibility for establishing and maintaining the internal control system within an organization? Discuss.

6 What is the significance of the Foreign Corrupt Practices Act of 1977 with respect to internal accounting controls?

7 Internal controls should be cost beneficial. Explain.

8 What are the principal characteristics of an effective system of internal control?

9 The general principle of adequate segregation of duties recognizes that three basic functions should be segregated by department, or at least be performed by separate people. What are those three functions? Why is it important to separate them?

10 Adequately segregating functions and responsibilities provides several benefits. What are they?

11 A good system of internal control includes proper documentation, which has several desirable characteristics. Discuss each.

12 "The internal audit department in a large corporation should always report to the treasurer or to the vice president of production." Do you agree? Explain.

13 With respect to internal control, identify the three most important areas to consider in evaluating a firm's personnel.

14 A fidelity bond protects a business from losses by dishonest employees in more than one way. Explain.

15 Computerized accounting systems have had a tremendous impact upon internal accounting controls. Although they increase the speed and accuracy of data processing and enhance the overall efficiency of the accounting information system, computers also have some negative effects upon internal control. Discuss.

EXERCISES

E18–1 Purposes of Internal Control

People often feel that the main purpose of internal accounting control is to prevent fraud, or at least to make it easier to detect. Other purposes of internal control are often overlooked. What other specific purposes does a system of internal control accomplish? Discuss.

E18–2 Administrative and Accounting Controls

Classify each of the following as either an administrative or an accounting control.

1. Potential employees are required to have a complete physical examination.
2. A computer is used to store payroll records and prepare paychecks.
3. The cashier has no access to the accounting journals.
4. The computer programmer does not operate the computer.
5. A record of employee absences is kept.
6. A study is conducted to determine the amount of time required to make one unit of product.
7. The bank statement is reconciled by someone who neither handles the cash nor maintains the accounting records.
8. A feasibility study is conducted before a new computer system is implemented.
9. An independent CPA audits the company records annually.
10. Company procedures and policies are put in writing and made available to employees.

E18–3 The Auditor's Review of Internal Control

A CPA typically reviews a client's system of internal accounting control to ascertain the reliability of the client's records. The CPA then plans the audit on the basis of this review of the internal control system. Explain why this procedure is followed.

E18–4 Internal Accounting Control Objectives

For each of the following, list the objective of the internal control procedure.

1. An annual physical inventory is taken, although the perpetual inventory method is used by the company.
2. The purchasing department must approve all machine repairs.
3. Only the cashier is authorized to make disbursements from the petty-cash fund.
4. A prenumbered receipt is prepared in duplicate for each cash payment received from a customer.
5. All supplies must be purchased through the purchasing department.
6. The petty-cash fund is audited by the company's internal auditor at irregular, unannounced intervals.
7. All cash disbursements are made by check.
8. All proposed acquisitions of heavy machinery must be approved by the operations vice president.

E18–5 Cost-Beneficial Systems

Sharpshooter Gun Company has grown dramatically in recent years. As a result, its labor force has increased from 100 to 175 workers. The payroll officer, Monica Bradley, cannot handle the increased workload. Obviously, something must be done, or the employees will not receive their checks on time. The company has two alternatives: It either can hire an assistant to work with Monica, or it can install a small computer to perform some of the routine tasks. Before making its decision, what factors must Sharpshooter's management consider?

E18–6 Separation of Duties

The city of Westchester can afford to hire only one employee to give out parking tickets. This employee is also responsible for collecting fines and money from parking meters, as well as for keeping records for all monies collected.

1. What are the internal control weaknesses of this arrangement?
2. If two employees are available, what arrangements might be made for better control?

E18–7 Internal Control of Assets and Records

For each of the following assets or records, give an example of a physical safeguard.

1. A raw materials inventory.
2. Marketable securities.
3. An inventory of small, expensive electronic components.
4. Perishable goods.
5. Petty cash.
6. Cash received through the mail.
7. Cash received by clerks in a retail operation.
8. Magnetic tapes with accounts receivable information stored on them.

9. Scrap aluminum or other metals used in making a product.
10. Office supplies.

E18–8 Reasons for Internal Control

Discuss the reasons for each of the following control procedures.

1. Before the treasurer of Kane Candy Company signs disbursement checks, she reviews the supporting data. Afterwards, the supporting data are returned to the accounting department, and the checks are mailed by the treasurer's secretary.
2. Each clerk in a department store has a separate cash drawer and does not have access to the cash drawers of other clerks.
3. The ticket-taker at Nemrow Theatre is required to tear each admission ticket in half. He drops half in a box, and presents the stub to the patron.
4. At Lewis Widget Company four copies of each purchase order are prepared. The fourth and final copy is sent to the receiving department. The form is designed in such a way that the quantity ordered does not appear on the fourth copy.
5. Volunteers who solicit contributions for a local charity are required to issue a receipt for any cash contributions. The receipt book is serially prenumbered and has a single carbon copy for each receipt.
6. Richard Jones, the cashier for Allen & Allen Manufacturing Company, is required to keep copies of all voided (invalidated) receipts.

E18–9 The Accounting Manual and the Chart of Accounts

You have been hired to audit Silverman Pest Control Company, which performs exterminating services in sixteen cities of the Southwest. You notice that the company has no accounting manual or chart of accounts. When you mention this to the manager, he responds that such documents would not be helpful in his business. Respond to this comment.

E18–10 The Audit Committee

Sally Meldrum, the major stockholder of Meldrum Corporation, has decided that the corporation needs an internal audit committee. She proposes a five-member committee composed of herself, the manager of the accounts receivable department, the head cashier, the manager of the sales department, and the chief computer operator. You, as the independent external auditor, must advise her on the formation of this committee. What would you recommend?

E18–11 Employee Fraud

I. B. Hall was a respected and competent employee of Highwater Sales, Inc. He had shown exceptional devotion and had been rewarded with increased responsibility. Hall never took a vacation and had held his current position for over 10 years. President Dan Barnez was shocked, therefore, when he discovered that Hall had embezzled approximately $200,000 over the past decade. Hall was able to steal the money because he had access to the sales journal and to cash receipts. Thus, he would not record some invoices in the sales journal, and would pocket the respective amounts. What major weaknesses of internal control allowed this fraud to go undetected?

E18–12 Responsibility Accounting

Under a system of responsibility accounting, individuals are held accountable for the assets and resources placed in their care. Refer to Exhibit 18–2 and match the following activities with the appropriate position of responsibility (for example, review of operations is performed by an internal auditor).

1. Care of raw materials.
2. Signing checks.
3. Authorization for purchasing raw materials.
4. Care of a petty-cash fund.
5. Supervision of workers.
6. Care of plant machinery.
7. Design of an internal control system.

E18–13 Internal Control for a Small Business

Most small businesses do not have a staff of internal auditors. Instead, the internal audit functions are performed by managers or owners. Suggest and discuss several internal audit steps that an owner or manager might perform to ensure that the company's policies and procedures are being carried out.

PROBLEMS

P18–1 Control of Cash Receipts

Helpful Charities, Inc. solicits contributions and then distributes the monies to a number of local nonprofit and charitable organizations. The officers and directors are local clergymen, bankers, lawyers, and doctors, all leaders of the community. A clerk and a cashier constitute the only full-time salaried employees. The records of Helpful Charities are limited to a cash receipts journal and a checkbook, which is used to maintain a record of all disbursements.

Volunteers from other organizations solicit contributions during fund-raising campaigns. The volunteers are not assigned any specific areas and tend to solicit primarily from friends, relatives, neighbors, and other acquaintances. Helpful Charities is constantly seeking new volunteers from among church groups, business and professional organizations, local PTAs, and other community groups.

Typically, contributions are collected in the form of cash and checks. The solicitors collect the donations, fill out receipts, and give them to the donors. They then complete the accompanying stub, noting the donor's name, address, and the amount of the contribution. There are no carbon copies of the receipts and no system for accounting for every receipt. Periodically, the volunteers submit the stubs and the contributions to the cashier at Helpful Charities, who then deposits the money. Donors may also mail their contributions directly to the cashier.

Required:

Discuss the procedures that should be implemented by Helpful Charities, Inc. to improve internal control over donations. Specifically, discuss what controls would ensure that all monies collected by the solicitors are turned over to the cashier. *(AICPA adapted)*

P18–2 Internal Control Techniques

A company's overall internal control system is strengthened by each control procedure that is well thought out. Thus, printing checks on special paper so that amounts cannot be erased without detection is one safeguard against theft. And a voucher system that provides for all invoices to be properly authorized, checked for accuracy, and recorded before being paid reduces the likelihood that an invoice will be misplaced, a discount lost, or that improper or unauthorized disbursements will be made.

Required:

Discuss the purposes of the following procedures and explain how each helps strengthen internal control.

1. Fidelity bonding of employees.
2. Budgeting for capital expenditures (such as the purchase of land).
3. Listing of remittances (cash received) when the mail is first opened.
4. Maintaining a ledger for plant and equipment purchases and depreciation expenses.

(AICPA adapted)

P18–3 Unifying Problem: Design of Internal Control and Separation of Responsibilities

Svendsen Drug Company has come to your accounting firm with the following problem. Its three employees—Norm Svendsen (the owner's son), Craig Spackman, and Dale Johnson—must perform all the following functions.

a. Receive and deposit all cash receipts.
b. Reconcile the bank account.
c. Prepare checks and the accompanying voucher documents for signature.
d. Maintain a General Ledger.
e. Maintain an accounts payable ledger.
f. Maintain an accounts receivable ledger.
g. Maintain a cash disbursements journal.
h. Issue credits for all returns and allowances.

You are told that all three employees are capable of performing any of these tasks and that they will have no other duties.

Required:

1. Assign the functions to the three employees in such a manner as to ensure the highest degree of internal control. Assume that, except for the routine jobs of bank reconciliation and the issuance of credits, all jobs require an equal amount of time and labor.
2. List at least four specific combinations of these functions that would be unsatisfactory.

P18–4 Examination of an Internal Control System

Assume that you are a member of the internal audit staff of Valdez Company. The controller asks that you review the company's cash payroll system.

Required:

What questions might you ask as you review the system of internal control relative to payroll procedures? Include questions having to do with each of the following categories.

1. Reliable personnel.
2. Separation of responsibilities.
3. Supervision.
4. Responsibility.
5. Document control.
6. Bonding, vacations, and rotation of employees.
7. Independent checks.
8. Physical safeguards.

(AICPA adapted)

P18–5 Improvement in an Internal Control System

The town of Oak Park operates a private parking lot near the railroad station for the benefit of town residents. The guard on duty issues annual prenumbered parking stickers to commuters who submit an application form and show evidence of residency. The sticker is affixed to the auto and allows the resident to park for up to 12 hours at a price of 50 cents per 3-hour period. Applications are maintained in the guard's office at the lot. The guard checks to see that only residents are using the lot and that no resident has parked without paying the required meter fee.

Once a week the guard, who has a master key for all meters, empties the meters and places the coins in a locked steel box. The guard delivers the box to the town hall, where it is opened, and the coins are manually counted by a storage department clerk who records the transaction on a "Weekly Cash Report." This report is sent to the town accounting department and the cash is placed in a safe in the storage department. The cash is picked up the next day by the town's treasurer, who manually recounts the cash, prepares a bank deposit slip, and delivers the deposit to the bank. The deposit slip, authenticated by the bank teller, is sent to the accounting department where it is filed with the Weekly Cash Report.

Required:

Describe weaknesses in the existing system of internal control over the parking lot cash receipts, and recommend one or more improvements for each weakness. *(AICPA adapted)*

Organize your answer sheet as follows:

Weakness	Recommended Improvement(s)

P18–6 Unifying Problem: Control Procedures for Hiring Personnel and for Payroll

Comiski Manufacturing Company employs about fifty production workers and has the following hiring practices and payroll procedures.

The factory foreman interviews applicants and either hires or rejects them. When hired, a person fills out a W-4 form (an Employee's Withholding Exemption Certificate) and gives it to the foreman. The foreman writes the hourly rate of pay for the new employee in a corner of the W-4 form and then gives the form to a payroll clerk as notice that the worker has been employed. The foreman verbally advises the payroll department of any hourly rate adjustments.

A supply of blank time cards is kept in a box near the entrance to the factory. The workers each take a time card on Monday morning, fill in their names, and then keep the card for a week, during which time they note in pencil their daily arrival and departure times. At the end of the week the workers drop the time cards in another box, which is also near the entrance to the factory.

The completed time cards are taken from the box on Monday morning by a payroll clerk. Two payroll clerks divide the cards alphabetically between them, one taking A to L and the other M to Z. Each clerk is responsible for his or her section of the payroll. The clerk computes the gross pay, deductions, and net pay; posts the amounts to the employee's earnings records; and prepares and numbers the payroll checks. Employees are automatically removed from the payroll when they fail to turn in a time card.

The payroll checks are signed by the chief accountant and given to the foreman. The foreman distributes the checks and arranges for the delivery of checks to workers who are absent. The payroll bank account is reconciled by the chief accountant, who also prepares the company's various quarterly and annual payroll tax reports.

Required:

List your suggestions for improving Comiski Manufacturing Company's system of internal control for hiring practices and payroll procedures.

(AICPA adapted)

P18–7 Unifying Problem: Deficiencies in Internal Control

The cashier of Mira Vista Company is custodian of the petty-cash fund. At the beginning of July he intercepted a $500 check from customer A and deposited it in a bank account that was part of the company petty-cash fund. He then wrote himself a $500 check from the petty-cash fund, which he cashed. At the end of the month, while processing the monthly statements to customers, he changed the statement to Customer A, showing that A had received credit for the $500 check. Ten days later he made an entry in the cash receipts journal that purported to record receipt of a remittance of $500 from

Customer A. Thus, he restored A's account to its proper balance, but overstated cash in the bank. He covered the overstatement by omitting two checks, worth a total of $500, from the list of outstanding checks in the bank reconciliation.

Required:

Discuss briefly what you regard as the more important deficiencies in Mira Vista Company's system of internal control. Include what you consider to be a proper remedy for each deficiency. *(AICPA adapted)*

PART II

MANAGERIAL ACCOUNTING

SECTION 5

The Fundamentals of Managerial Accounting

CHAPTER 19

An Overview of Managerial Accounting

THIS CHAPTER EXPLAINS:

Differences between managerial and financial accounting.
The managerial decision-making process.
The functions of managerial accounting.
The functions of the accounting information system.
How the accounting information system is organized within companies.

external users *investors, creditors, analysts, and other groups interested in the financial affairs of a company but not involved in its day-to-day activities*

internal users *the managers who are responsible for making the day-to-day decisions that lead an organization to its profit and service goals*

financial accounting *the area of accounting concerned with measuring and reporting, on a periodic basis, the financial status and operating results of organizations to interested parties*

managerial accounting *the area of accounting concerned with assisting managers in decision making, specifically with planning, budgeting, controlling costs, generating revenues, and evaluating performance*

Accounting was defined in Chapter 1 as a service activity designed to accumulate, measure, and communicate economic information about organizations. That information is then used by individuals and groups—called external and internal users—as the basis for making economic decisions.

The major external users, as you recall, are investors, creditors, financial analysts, and other interested groups not involved in the day-to-day activities of a business. The primary internal users are a company's management, the people responsible for making long-run planning decisions, day-to-day operating decisions, and certain short-run nonroutine operating decisions. For example, managers use accounting information in deciding what products to manufacture, what prices to charge, how to market those products, and which costs need to be controlled in order to meet the profit and service objectives of a firm. Accounting data also enable a company to meet the requirements of government agencies, such as the Internal Revenue Service and the Securities and Exchange Commission. In brief, accounting provides management with information that is essential for planning, budgeting, cost determination and control, performance evaluation, and similar activities.

In Part I we concentrated on financial accounting—reporting information for use primarily by external decision makers. In Part II we will focus on managerial accounting—reporting information for use by managerial decision makers. The emphasis continues to be on profit-oriented organizations, including manufacturing, merchandising, and service firms.

We begin this chapter by comparing managerial and financial accounting in greater depth than we have done previously. We next outline the major steps in the decision-making process and discuss the functions of managerial accounting and the accounting information system. We conclude by showing how the accounting information system is typically organized within companies.

Managerial Accounting Versus Financial Accounting

A major difference between managerial and financial accounting has to do with the ability of internal users to acquire information beyond that required by generally accepted accounting principles. Managers must constantly make decisions on a variety of matters, and their position within the company enables them to obtain the information upon which these decisions are based. For example, in deciding on the advertising budget for a given product, a manager can obtain information about the product's prior sales, its profit potential at various sales levels, and its profitability in comparison to other company products. This sort of specific and detailed information is not available to external users, who must rely primarily on the data contained in the financial statements.

A related difference involves the kinds of decisions made by internal and external users. Investors and creditors, the primary external users, have essentially one decision to make—whether to buy or sell stock, or whether to loan money. The information relevant to these decisions is contained in the published financial statements. Managers have a broad range of decisions to make, some of which require very different kinds of information. Thus, managerial accounting is oriented toward providing the information for a wide variety of decisions, whereas financial accounting focuses on the general-purpose needs of investors and creditors.

Although these are the two major differences between managerial and financial accounting, other distinctions exist. Because financial accounting is based on historical costs, it has tended to have a retrospective orientation, as opposed to the prospective, or forward-looking, orientation of managerial accounting. This difference is becoming less noticeable, however, because financial accounting is becoming less retrospective, with greater emphasis on such topics as future cash flows and current values.

A fourth difference exists in the level of aggregation of data. As our advertising example indicates, managerial accounting must provide internal users with information about individual products or about groups of employees or subdivisions of a company, whereas financial accounting is primarily concerned with the company as a whole. Although for external financial reporting many companies are now required to provide supplemental information about departments or other segments, this information is still in far less detail than that available to managers.

A fifth difference is that plans, expectations, and forecasts are usually available only to managers. Companies are reluctant to provide this kind of information to external users for a number of reasons, including the possible loss of confidence in management on the part of stockholders if forecasts prove to be inaccurate, and the loss of tactical advantages if competitors learn of the company's plans. Today, there is less of this kind of secrecy; in some cases standard-setting bodies (such as the FASB) recommend that companies provide forecasts with the financial statements in order to meet the full-disclosure standard.

A final difference between managerial and financial accounting is that while external users receive primarily financial information (which is quantified in numbers), managerial accountants have access to qualitative information as well. Managerial accountants recognize that financial data may be only partial evidence and that qualitative factors may be even more important in making specific decisions. For example, it may be more economical to locate a plant in city X than in city Y, but the plant may still be located in Y if the executives prefer to live in that city. Similarly, two employees may be equally capable in a technical sense, but the employee judged as having the better attitude and an ability to get along with people is the one who will be promoted. External users must also evaluate qualitative factors, such as management's ability to increase the company's profitability. However, external users generally do not have access to as much qualitative information.

TO SUMMARIZE There are several differences between managerial and financial accounting. These differences have to do with (1) the manager's much greater access to specific and detailed information; (2) the greater variety and scope of the decisions to be made by managers; (3) the orientation—whether prospective or retrospective; (4) the level of aggregation of the data; (5) the availability of plans, expectations, and forecasts; and (6) the availability of, and need for, qualitative information. The first two distinctions continue to be the most significant.

The Managerial Decision-Making Process

Management is, in effect, a decision-making process. Managers must answer such questions as: What product(s) should the company manufacture and sell? Should each element of the product be manufactured or should some materials be purchased from outside suppliers? Should funds be obtained from earnings, borrowing, issuing stock, or some combination of sources? In answering these types of questions, effective managers generally follow a well-defined set of procedures.

STEPS IN THE DECISION-MAKING PROCESS

In general, making a business decision involves the following steps.

1. Recognizing a current opportunity or problem.
2. Defining the opportunity or problem.
3. Identifying reasonable alternative courses of action.
4. Gathering and analyzing information about these alternatives.
5. Selecting the best alternative.

6. Implementing a plan of action.
7. Monitoring the results to keep performance in line with plans.
8. Taking corrective action when necessary.

cost-benefit analysis
techniques for selecting the alternative that provides the greatest benefit at the lowest cost

These steps are diagrammed in Exhibit 19-1. In selecting the best alternative (step 5), management should always consider the costs and the benefits of each alternative. Cost-benefit analysis underlies most decisions made by managers. Although future costs and benefits are often difficult to estimate, the underlying philosophy of cost-benefit analysis is that the net benefits—that is, the potential benefits of the alternative selected minus its costs—should be greater than they would be for any alternative.

EXHIBIT 19-1 **The Managerial Decision-Making Process**

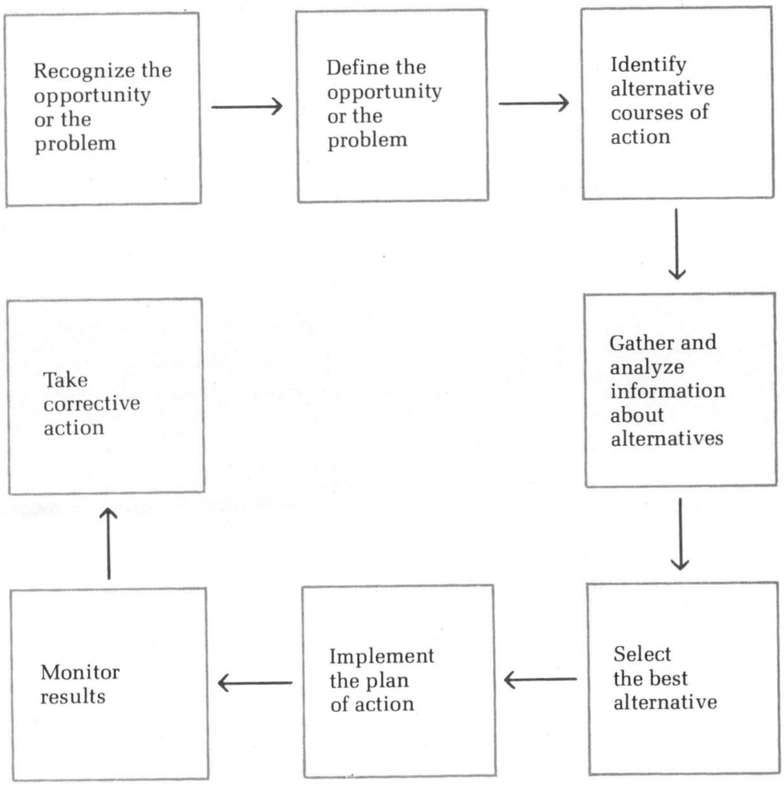

INFORMATION FOR DECISION MAKING

Effective decisions depend to a great extent on the reliability and the relevance of the information provided. This information comes from many sources. It may be routinely supplied by data generated by accountants or it may require a search from sources both inside and outside the company. Managers often look to various specialists—accountants, economists, engineers, and so forth—to supply the information.

Economists, for example, may provide data related to national output, employment, inflation, and other economic conditions. Such economic indicators are used in making long-range planning decisions when the historical data generated by the financial accounting system must be adjusted to reflect current economic conditions. The rapidity of change also makes economic data useful for many short-run planning decisions, such as those involved in preparing the next period's operating budget.

Specialists in marketing provide information that is helpful in choosing a product line, selecting geographic areas for special sales concentration, identifying appropriate channels of distribution, and selecting effective ways of promoting products. Finance specialists provide the data used in deciding, for example, whether to borrow, and if so, when and how to borrow. Engineers provide information about production methods, materials to use, labor skills required, and quality standards. And finally, accountants are responsible for providing the financial information on which so many managerial decisions depend.

The Functions of Managerial Accounting

Internal decision making may be divided into three functions:

1. Planning: a systematic program for accomplishing certain goals.
2. Control: methods employed to bring operating results into line with expected (planned) results.
3. Performance evaluation: methods of testing whether goals have been reached.

budget *an itemized summary of probable revenues and expenditures for a given period, which shows how an entity is expected to acquire and use its resources during that time*

For each of these functions a budget plays an important role. A budget is an itemized summary of anticipated revenues and expenses; it shows how a firm is expected to acquire and use its resources. It is usually expressed in monetary terms and covers a specified period of time. The nature of the budget and the time period covered are different for planning, control, and performance evaluation. The following sections identify the types of budgets applicable to each function and explain why accurate and timely accounting information is critical.

PLANNING

planning *the process of selecting objectives and determining the means to attain them*

Planning is the process of making decisions about future operations. A company's resources must be used efficiently to achieve the goals established by management. There are two basic types of planning:

1. Long-run planning.
2. Short-run planning, which includes
   (a) Short-run operating decisions.
   (b) Short-run nonroutine operating decisions.

long-run planning *the process of establishing goals that extend 3 to 5 years into the future; involves decisions about products, labor, facilities, and financial resources*

capital budgeting *systematic planning for long-term investment decisions*

short-run planning *the process of making decisions about current operations and those of the immediate future; includes day-to-day and nonroutine operating decisions*

operating budget *an itemized summary of immediate goals for sales, production, expenses, costs, and the availability of cash*

nonroutine operating decisions *managerial decisions that require more extensive analysis than day-to-day decisions but less than capital budgeting decisions*

Long-run planning involves making decisions about company goals that extend several years into the future—usually three to five years but sometimes longer. This includes decisions about products, labor requirements, productive facilities, and financial resources.

One significant aspect of long-run planning is capital budgeting, planning for the purchase and use of major assets to help the company meet its long-range goals. Capital budgeting procedures are discussed in Chapter 28.

Short-run planning is divided into two categories on the basis of frequency and type of decision. Some decisions have to do with operations in the current accounting period and may be made as often as daily or weekly. Such decisions are characterized by their regularity and frequency and are referred to as short-run operating decisions.

The short-run plan for operations is generally expressed in the form of an operating budget, which identifies the expected inflows of revenues and outflows of costs, based on an assumed level of production for a period. In most companies the operating budget is prepared on an annual basis and is then broken down into budgets for shorter periods, usually months. Prepared from information generated by accountants and by specialists in marketing, sales, finance, and production, the operating budget is communicated throughout the organization and is an essential tool in helping management control operations and measure performance. The operating budget is discussed in Chapter 24.

The second category of short-run planning has to do with nonroutine operating decisions. These decisions require more analysis than short-run operating decisions but less than capital budgeting decisions. The key question in capital budgeting usually is: What additional major assets, such as plant and equipment, are needed to meet the company's long-run goals? Nonroutine operating decisions, on the other hand, involve the question: What is the best use of existing resources? Typical nonroutine decisions include whether to add or drop a product or department, whether to make or buy a component, whether to sell a product before or after additional processing, and what prices to charge for products. In order to make these decisions—that is, to choose a course of action from among the available alternatives—management prepares budgets that compare the costs of the alternatives being considered. Nonroutine operating decisions are discussed in Chapter 27.

CONTROLLING OPERATIONS AND EVALUATING PERFORMANCE

standard *a quantitative measure of the expected level of performance*

performance control report *a comparison of actual and planned results, in which significant variances are identified*

Short-run plans are generally translated into an operating budget, which provides a standard of attainment. Thus, the budget is a quantitative measure of the expected level of performance. At the end of an operating period (a month, a year, or however often management feels is appropriate), a performance control report is prepared. This report compares actual operating results with the budget and identifies significant differences. Using the control report as a guideline, management is able to evaluate and eventually control operations.

management by exception *the process of comparing planned and actual results to identify significant variations that call for action by management*

Following the principle of management by exception, management attempts to learn the reasons for any significant variations between budgeted and actual costs and revenues. Steps can then be taken to correct the weaknesses or to modify the budget to reflect more realistic expectations. For example, suppose that a performance control report shows that the labor costs to manufacture a product have exceeded expectations. Management should determine whether the increased costs were due to higher labor rates, to the fact that employees were wasting time, or to some other cause. If higher labor rates were involved, management's decision would probably be to modify the budget, since the excess costs may be unavoidable. If time was being wasted, management might revise work schedules to reduce inefficiencies. The performance control report thus helps management to maintain efficiency levels and thereby to attain its short- and long-run objectives.

While helping managers to keep operations in line with expectations, a control report also enables higher-level managers to evaluate the performance of subordinates. The criteria used will depend on the extent of the manager's responsibilities. Companies that are decentralized, delegating many decisions to lower-level managers, rely heavily on performance control reports. This area of managerial accounting is discussed further in Chapter 26.

TO SUMMARIZE Accountants provide data to assist managers in making planning, control, and performance evaluation decisions. Planning is the process of making decisions about future operations. Long-run planning involves major decisions about the manufacture, use, and acquisition of products and resources over a period of several years. Short-run planning involves decisions about day-to-day operations, as well as nonroutine decisions. Control involves setting standards to reflect expected performance. The standards are used to prepare the operating budget; actual results are then compared with the budget; and, where possible, corrective action is taken to bring actual results into line with expectations. Standards are also used by managers to evaluate the performance of subordinates. A performance control report facilitates this process.

The Functions of an Accounting Information System

accounting information system *the methods by which the data derived from recorded transactions are collected, processed, and reported in order to provide the financial information needed by a firm*

Ideally, every company should have an accounting information system that provides relevant and timely information for a variety of purposes. In serving such purposes, accounting information systems generally evolve through a series of stages related to the size of the company and the needs of management. At each stage the information system might have a different primary orientation, as in the following sequence.

1. Income tax planning and return preparation.
2. External financial reporting.
3. Internal planning and control.

Note that these stages are cumulative. Although planning and control are the focus of an accounting system at stage 3, for example, the system is also generating data for external financial reports and income taxes. A brief look at these stages shows how the accounting system may serve different needs at different periods in a company's development.

INCOME TAX PLANNING AND RETURN PREPARATION

Small, closely held service or merchandising firms usually do not provide reports to outsiders. Financial data are collected primarily to meet the annual requirements for filing income tax returns. The thrust of the information system, therefore, is to ensure that the firm's tax obligations are computed accurately and that they are the least amount allowed by the law. The types of information needed are discussed in Chapter 29.

EXTERNAL FINANCIAL REPORTING

Service, merchandising, and manufacturing firms may be required, or may find it desirable, to supply creditors and stockholders with financial statements. These external reports allow interested groups to see how efficiently and profitably management is operating the company. Although the orientation of the information system is toward providing these reports, the data generated will be modified as needed to meet income tax planning and reporting objectives. At this stage, the necessary data for internal decision making are likely to be developed on an *ad hoc* basis.

INTERNAL PLANNING AND CONTROL

Financial reporting and income tax return preparation involve relatively uniform procedures and are mandatory as well, whereas managerial accounting techniques for internal decision making are often unique to each organization and are optional. For this reason managerial accounting information systems are usually put into effect later in a company's development. Many large companies have highly sophisticated information systems that provide data for the planning and control functions of management. At year-end these information systems also supply all the figures needed to meet external reporting requirements on the basis of generally accepted accounting principles.

The Organizational Setting for an Information System

A fully developed accounting system should generate data for all information needs. This requires a careful structuring of the accounting and information-processing functions within an organization.

Exhibit 19-2 shows how an accounting information system typically fits into a company's organizational structure. The chief financial officer of a company is usually the vice president of finance. Two key individuals reporting to that officer are the treasurer and the controller. (Note that in small companies one person may perform all three functions.) The treasurer is generally responsible for making financial contacts outside the firm, and for making sure that an adequate amount of cash is available for operations and capital acquisitions. The treasurer is also usually responsible for granting credit, collecting receivables, maintaining good banking relationships, dealing with stockholders, and managing the cash, working capital, and insurance requirements of a company. The controller is the chief officer responsible for all the accounting functions of a firm. These include internal

EXHIBIT 19-2 **An Accounting Information System Within a Typical Organizational Hierarchy**

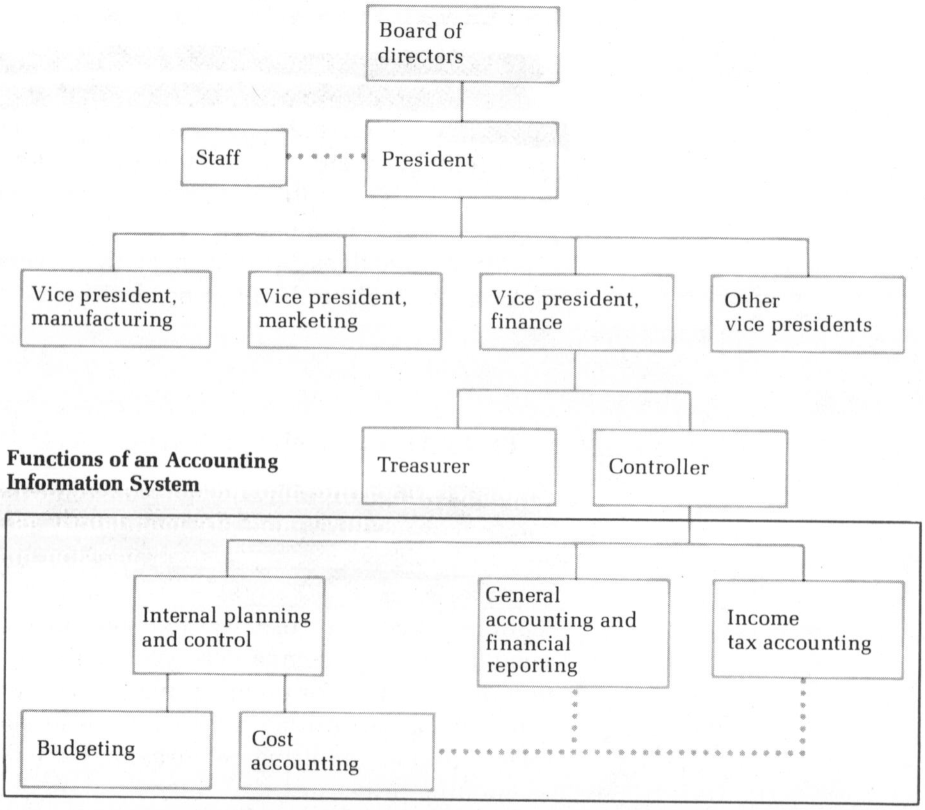

planning and control, general accounting and financial reporting, income tax accounting, and cost accounting.

Internal planning and control involve the preparation of operating and capital expenditure budgets and related analyses that assist management in planning and controlling the activities of a firm. General accounting typically covers accounting for payrolls, accounts receivable, accounts payable, and other items in the General Ledger, as well as financial statement preparation. Income tax accounting refers to the preparation of tax returns and the planning of transactions that may have a significant tax impact.

income tax accounting *the preparation of income tax returns and the planning of transactions that have a significant tax impact*

cost accounting *the process of accumulating actual cost data to be used in controlling costs, in preparing external financial reports and tax returns, and in making planning and control decisions*

Another significant function shown in Exhibit 19-2 is cost accounting. It deserves special attention, for it is important to all three of the accounting functions just described and therefore to both managerial and financial accounting. In a comparison of actual data with planned data to identify variances from expected results, budgeting provides the planned data and cost accounting provides the actual data. Management uses these comparisons to decide how to bring inadequate revenues and excess costs back into line. The data also reveal how well the managers responsible for the specified revenues and costs are performing.

Cost accounting is particularly important in manufacturing firms because managers need to keep track of quantities and costs as the product flows through a complex process: from raw materials inventories through work-in-process and finished goods to cost of goods sold (see Chapter 23). Furthermore, managers must determine what wages have been earned and where the wage costs should be assigned.

As an integral part of financial, income tax, and managerial accounting, the cost accounting system should provide sufficient information to track the flow of costs to an extent that is consistent with generally accepted accounting principles. These principles specify what costs must be included in a company's inventories and cost of goods sold. Similarly, the income tax laws specify how costs must be accumulated and reported in computing taxable income. In some cases, the requirements for preparing external financial reports and tax returns are the same; in other cases, they are not. The information system must be able to generate data for both sets of requirements.

You can now recognize that cost accounting is an important link between the various accounting functions. That is, cost accounting provides data for planning and control, for external reporting, and for income tax accounting. At the same time, cost accounting is only one of several elements in the larger function of managerial accounting. The broader category—managerial accounting—encompasses all parts of the accounting information system, and combines them to meet the needs of a company's management in making business decisions.

TO SUMMARIZE Accounting information systems provide data for a variety of purposes. Such systems often evolve in stages, satisfying needs for (1) income tax planning and return preparation, (2) external financial reporting, and (3) internal planning and control. In a typical company, the controller is responsible for the accounting information system, which generates data for internal planning and control, financial reporting, and income tax accounting. Cost accounting provides data for all three functions.

CHAPTER REVIEW

Managerial accounting may be distinguished from financial accounting primarily on the basis of the managers' much greater access to company information and the larger variety and scope of the decisions they are required to make. Because of the changing nature of financial accounting requirements, other differences are not as pronounced today, though they still exist. Examples include the level of aggregation of data, the orientation of information (prospective versus retrospective), and the access to qualitative information and to company forecasts and plans.

Management is a decision-making process that involves problem identification, analysis of alternative solutions, and selection of the most appropriate course of action. Accountants and other specialists assist managers in making decisions by providing relevant and timely information.

Managerial accounting provides information for planning, control, and performance evaluation. Planning for future operations may be long- or short-run. Long-run planning is most often associated with capital budgeting. Short-run planning includes both operational budgeting and the making of nonroutine decisions. Control involves comparing actual results with established standards of attainment and investigating and correcting exceptions. Performance control reports are used in evaluating the performance of managers and their subordinates.

Accounting systems serve various purposes, including internal planning and control, external financial reporting, and tax planning and preparation. The controller is generally responsible for the accounting information system and the functions it serves. Cost accounting is crucial to all the functions of managerial accounting.

KEY TERMS AND CONCEPTS

accounting information system (656)
budget (654)
capital budgeting (655)
cost accounting (659)
cost-benefit analysis (653)
external users (650)
financial accounting (650)
income tax accounting (659)
internal users (650)
long-run planning (655)
management by exception (656)
managerial accounting (650)
nonroutine operating decisions (655)
operating budget (655)
performance control report (655)
planning (654)
short-run planning (655)
standard (655)

DISCUSSION QUESTIONS

1 Why is external financial reporting based on generally accepted accounting principles?

2 Distinguish between financial and managerial accounting.

3 Of what significance are qualitative factors in the managerial decision-making process?

4 Discuss the steps in the decision-making process.

5 What role does the accountant perform in management's decision-making process?

6 What types of specialists provide data for management's decisions?

7 What are the primary functions of the managerial accountant?

8 Distinguish between short-run and long-run planning.

9 Compare the focuses of cost control and performance evaluation.

10 What is a standard? Briefly, why is it important in controlling operations and measuring performance?

11 What is a budget and how is it related to a standard?

12 Describe the evolution of an accounting information system.

13 What accounting functions are frequently the responsibility of the vice president of finance?

14 Explain how cost accounting contributes to cost control and performance evaluation, as well as to financial reporting.

EXERCISES

E19–1 Financial and Managerial Accounting

A friend who is thinking about majoring in accounting has asked you to distinguish between financial accounting and managerial accounting. What will you say?

E19–2 Characteristics of Accounting Reports

For each of the following, note whether it is characteristic of financial accounting reports, managerial accounting reports, or both.

1. They are used primarily by creditors, investors, and suppliers.
2. They aid management in identifying problems.
3. They are based on generally accepted accounting principles.
4. Historical costs have been a primary focus.
5. They provide much of the quantitative information for decision making by management.
6. They measure performance and isolate differences between planned and actual results.
7. Current and future values are required in some cases.
8. They are timely and are prepared for very specific uses.

E19–3 Functions of Managerial Accountants

A local business club has asked you to write a paragraph or two on the primary functions of managerial accountants. Prepare a response.

E19–4 Planning

For each of the following, indicate whether the situation appears to require a routine operating decision (ROD), a nonroutine operating decision (NOD), or a long-term investment decision (LTI).

1. Deciding the price for a product.
2. Deciding whether employees should work an overtime shift the next day.
3. Deciding whether to drop a product line.
4. Deciding whether to discard leftover scraps of raw material or use the scraps to produce another item for sale.
5. Deciding whether to obtain a large computer for an accounting system.
6. Deciding whether to accept a special order from a customer.

E19–5 Performance Reports

You are employed as a production manager in a small company that manufactures vacuum tubes. The president asks you to suggest some means of measuring your performance so that your qualifications for a raise, a bonus, or a promotion to a better position can be determined. What recommendations would you make to give the president a more objective basis for measuring the performance of managers?

E19–6 Organization Chart

Following is a list of positions at Corona Manufacturing Corporation.

Board of directors
President
Vice president, production
Vice president, marketing
Vice president, finance
Salespeople
Controller
Internal auditor
Manager of external financial reporting
Manager of internal accounting
Chief accountant
Director of quality control
Director of market research
Treasurer
Director of production planning
Assembly-line manager
Manager of cash planning and investments
Regional sales directors

1. Prepare an organization chart. (Note that several alternative charts could exist.)

2. **Interpretive Question** Examine your organization chart. Can you suggest any reasons for the independence of the different departments? Why should the treasurer be accountable to the vice president of finance instead of reporting directly to the president?

E19–7 Controlling Operations

You have just established a company to produce artificial flowers. What kind of information would you want to have? Where you know the name of a report, identify it as such.

E19–8 Variance Analysis

"We thought our materials costs would be $75,000, but they turned out to be $83,000!" What are some potential reasons for this difference between the expected costs and actual costs for materials?

E19–9 Variance Calculations

A manufacturer of calculators compiled the following data for each carton containing 1,000 units of its cheapest model.

Actual Cost to Make	$6,000
Expected Cost to Make	5,500
Retail List Price (at $9.95)	9,950
Amount of Plastic Expected to Be Used	100 pounds
Amount of Plastic Used This Period	120 pounds
Actual Price per Pound of Plastic	$8.25
Expected Price per Pound of Plastic	8.00

Why did the actual cost to make 1,000 calculators exceed the expected cost? Give two reasons.

CHAPTER 20

Cost Concepts and Classifications

THIS CHAPTER EXPLAINS: Cost concepts and classifications for financial reporting, cost control, planning, and choosing among alternatives.

In Chapter 19 we learned that internal decision making may be divided into three categories: planning, control, and performance evaluation. The information needs associated with these three functions are not always the same. A fully developed accounting system should provide relevant and timely information for these functions as well as for external reporting. The controller's department is generally responsible for developing and maintaining the accounting information system that provides this information. In providing cost data, the controller and his staff should keep in mind a fundamental principle of managerial accounting: that different cost data are needed for different purposes. In order to provide the appropriate cost data for each function, accountants have developed a variety of cost concepts and classifications.

This chapter is a brief introduction to these concepts and classifications and their uses. Exhibit 20–1 identifies the concepts that will be considered here and in later chapters. Note that the table lists major cost concepts for the areas of financial reporting, cost control, planning, and choosing among alternatives. Financial reporting is included because the managerial accounting system must generate data for financial statement preparation. Cost control and planning are included for obvious reasons; they are two functions of managerial accounting. Choosing among alternatives is not so obvious. However, if you refer back to Chapter 19, you will see that this category describes the process of making nonroutine decisions, a special type of planning. Performance evaluation, the third major function of managerial accounting, has been omitted because it does not involve any special cost terms. Performance evaluation compares actual costs with budgeted costs (calculated at the planning stage) and assesses how well employees and managers met expectations.

EXHIBIT 20-1 Cost Concepts and Classifications

Purpose for Which the Data Will Be Used	Major Cost Concepts
Financial reporting	Product costs and period expenses Manufacturing costs and nonmanufacturing expenses Direct and indirect product costs Absorption and variable costing
Cost control	Responsibility centers Traceable and nontraceable costs Controllable and noncontrollable costs Fixed and variable costs
Planning	Estimated and actual costs Standard costs
Choosing among alternatives	Differential costs Sunk costs Opportunity costs

Cost Concepts and Classifications for Financial Reporting

product cost *any cost associated with and assigned to a product*

period expense *an expenditure that cannot be associated with or assigned to a product and so is reported as an expense in the period in which it is incurred*

For financial reporting purposes, costs are usually classified as product costs or period expenses. A product cost is the cost associated with and assigned to a product. This means that for as long as the product is held by the firm, this cost is shown on the balance sheet as an asset called inventory. When the product is sold, the cost of that product is transferred from the balance sheet to Cost of Goods Sold on the income statement. A product cost, therefore, becomes an expense (Cost of Goods Sold) in the period in which the product is sold, and its cost is then matched against the revenue derived from its sale.

A period expense is an expenditure that is not assigned to a product. Instead, it is associated with the accounting period in which it is incurred and is reported as an expense on that period's income statement. For example, the salaries of personnel in administration, sales, advertising, planning, accounting, finance, and legal services are all period expenses.

The concepts of product costs and period expenses apply to all kinds of firms—service, merchandising, and manufacturing—as you will see in the following sections. Note that the income statements and balance sheets used throughout the discussion are sometimes incomplete; they are intended only to illustrate the concepts being presented.

PRODUCT COSTS AND PERIOD EXPENSES IN A SERVICE FIRM

Service firms sell a variety of professional and/or technical services. A professional firm of doctors provides medical services. A management consulting firm provides advice about management problems. A CPA firm offers auditing, accounting, tax planning, and tax return preparation services.

The income statement of a service company is usually composed of revenues and operating expenses, as shown in Exhibit 20-2. Because a service firm does not sell a product, it generally has no product costs to classify as assets in an Inventory account. Thus, the expenditures that contribute directly to the firm's revenues are treated as expenses of the period in which they are incurred.

EXHIBIT 20-2

ABC Service Company
Income Statement
for the Year Ended December 31, 1984

	Revenues from Services		$140,000
	Operating Expenses:		
Expenses of the period	Rent Expense	$ 8,000	
	Utilities Expense	10,000	
	Wages Expense	80,000	
	Depreciation Expense	20,000	
	Selling Expense	15,000	133,000
	Income Before Taxes		$ 7,000

As the partial balance sheet in Exhibit 20-3 indicates, other expenditures may be classified initially as assets, which will be expensed on the income statement as the assets are used in later periods. These are usually referred to as prepaid expenses (such as insurance paid in advance). For example, the cost of office supplies is shown on the balance sheet as an asset until the supplies are used. When used, their cost is a period expense that will be listed on the income statement.

EXHIBIT 20-3

ABC Service Company
Balance Sheet (Partial) as of December 31, 1984

	Current Assets:	
No product costs; hence, no inventories	Cash	$12,000
	Accounts Receivable	18,500
	Marketable Securities	15,200
	Prepaid Expenses	3,800
	Office Supplies on Hand	1,500
	Total Current Assets	$51,000

PRODUCT COSTS AND PERIOD EXPENSES IN A MERCHANDISING FIRM

A merchandising firm buys products and sells them to its customers. For example, the bread, milk, and fruit you buy from the local grocer have been purchased, in turn, from various suppliers. In a merchandising firm, certain costs are considered to be directly related to the product, and hence are called product costs. Typically, these include the invoice cost of the product plus the freight, insurance, and handling costs—all the costs incurred in providing the goods for sale. Until the product is sold to customers, these costs are classified as product costs and are included as Merchandise Inventory on the balance sheet. When the product is sold, the costs are transferred to the income statement as Cost of Goods Sold.

A merchandising firm also has period expenses, that is, expenditures associated more with the period in which they are incurred than with the flow of the product from purchase through sale. Examples of period expenses are selling and administrative expenses—such as sales and administrative salaries and advertising, depreciation (other than factory), utilities, rent, repairs, and warehousing costs. Thus, the cost of repairing a store's cash register is an expense that was incurred to keep the business operating in a particular period and is therefore a period expense.

The accountant in a merchandising firm must separate product costs from period expenses. Product costs are shown either as Merchandise Inventory on the balance sheet (for products not sold) or as Cost of Goods Sold on the income statement (for products sold in that period). By contrast, period expenses are always shown as selling or administrative expenses on the income statement. The separation of product costs and period expenses for a merchandising firm is illustrated in Exhibits 20-4 and 20-5, an income statement and a partial balance sheet for Regal Ballpoint Pen Company.

Thus far, we have seen that service firms incur period expenses for the most part, whereas merchandising firms will always have both product costs and period expenses.

EXHIBIT 20-4

Regal Ballpoint Pen Company
Income Statement
for the Year Ended December 31, 1984

	Revenues		$175,000
	Cost of Goods Sold:		
To calculate product costs (for goods sold)	Beginning Inventory	$ 12,000	
	Net Purchases	100,000	
	Goods Available for Sale	$112,000	
	Ending Inventory	8,000	
Product costs (for goods sold) →	Cost of Goods Sold		104,000
	Gross Margin		$ 71,000
	Operating Expenses:		
Period expenses	Selling Expenses	$ 15,000	
	Administrative Expenses	12,000	27,000
	Income Before Taxes		$ 44,000

EXHIBIT 20–5

Regal Ballpoint Pen Company
Balance Sheet (Partial) as of December 31, 1984

	Current Assets:	
	Cash	$25,000
	Accounts Receivable	60,000
Product costs (for unsold goods) ··········>	Merchandise Inventory	8,000
	Prepaid Expenses	5,000
	Total Current Assets	$98,000

PRODUCT COSTS AND PERIOD EXPENSES IN A MANUFACTURING FIRM

A manufacturing company buys raw materials and converts them to finished goods through the use of equipment and labor. The manufactured goods are then sold through the company's marketing organization. For example, bread is produced by a company that purchases flour and other ingredients from millers and other manufacturers.

A manufacturing firm generally has a more complex cost structure than do merchandising or service firms. This is because its activities include not only the buying, selling, and administrative functions, but also a production function, which frequently involves complex cost accumulation and control activities. Thus, to measure income and account for inventories properly in a manufacturing firm, expenditures first must be classified as manufacturing costs or nonmanufacturing expenses.

Manufacturing Costs Versus Nonmanufacturing Expenses

manufacturing costs *costs incurred in the manufacturing process to bring a product to completion; include direct-materials, direct-labor, and manufacturing overhead costs; treated as product costs*

Manufacturing costs are those costs incurred in bringing a product to completed form, ready for sale. They include direct materials, direct labor, and manufacturing overhead (which will be discussed later). All of these are product costs. The cost of packaging the product may or may not be included as a manufacturing cost. (For financial reporting and income tax purposes, all manufacturing costs are included as product costs. We will see in Chapter 23 that, for purposes of managerial decision making, other ways of treating certain manufacturing costs are often useful.)

nonmanufacturing expenses *expenditures not closely associated with the preparation of a product; includes selling and administrative expenses; treated as period expenses*

Nonmanufacturing expenses are all expenditures not closely related to the preparation of the product. They include all selling and administrative expenses. Nonmanufacturing expenses are considered period expenses.

Direct Versus Indirect Manufacturing Costs

Manufacturing costs may be classified as direct or indirect. Direct materials and direct labor are direct costs, whereas manufacturing overhead is an indirect cost. Exhibit 20–6 shows this relationship. When applied to materials and labor, the word "direct" means that the cost of these items—the price of raw materials and the payments to production workers—are specifically identifiable with the product. Thus, the costs of materials that become part of the product are direct-materials costs. The wages of laborers who work directly on the product are direct-labor costs. All other costs associated with the manufacturing process are classified as indirect costs and are

direct-materials costs *the costs of materials that become part of a manufactured product*

direct-labor costs *the costs of labor directly associated with a manufactured product*

EXHIBIT 20-6 **Direct Versus Indirect Manufacturing Costs**

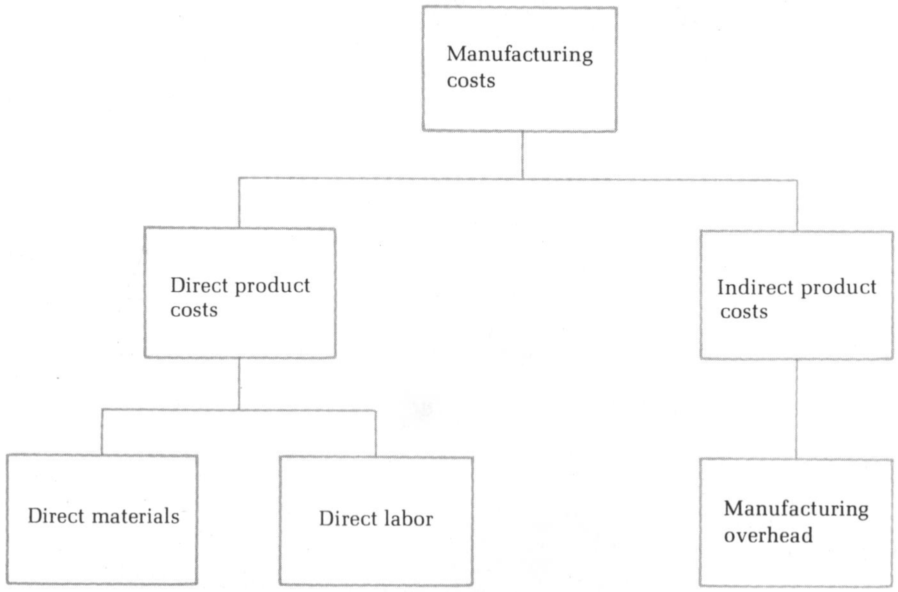

manufacturing overhead *manufacturing costs that are not directly assigned to the manufacture of a specific product*

called manufacturing overhead. Included in this category are indirect labor, indirect materials, depreciation, utilities, rent, insurance, and other similar factory costs. We now examine these three types of manufacturing costs in more detail.

Direct-Materials Costs This category includes the costs of materials that become a part of a finished product and are directly traceable to that product. In the production of shoes, for example, direct materials might consist of cowhide, rubber (for soles), and laces.

Some materials costs that are identifiable with the product are not classified as direct-materials costs because they cannot be efficiently identified and recorded. For example, glue and thread are clearly part of a shoe. However, they are used in such small quantities for any one pair of shoes that it would not be efficient to classify and record them as direct materials. Thus, they are usually classified as indirect materials.

Direct-Labor Costs This category includes the salaries and wages of individuals who work directly on a particular product. For example, the employees who operate the machines and the assembly-line workers who put the components together to form a completed product are considered direct labor.

indirect-materials costs *material costs that are included as manufacturing overhead and assigned to products on some reasonable allocation basis*

Manufacturing Overhead Costs All manufacturing costs that are not classified as direct materials and direct labor are included in manufacturing overhead. Indirect materials, indirect labor, rent, utilities, insurance, depreciation, and other factory costs fall into this category. Indirect materials are all materials that cannot be easily and economically traced to a product. For example, manufacturing supplies (oil, grease, paper towels) and uniforms for indirect laborers are classified as indirect materials. Indirect labor would include all labor costs that cannot be directly traced to the product or are too costly to trace—such as the wages of maintenance people, janitors, supervisors, factory cost accountants, guards, engineers, and others who are an important part of the production operation but who do not work directly on a product.

indirect-labor costs *labor costs that are included as manufacturing overhead and assigned to products on some reasonable allocation basis*

The classification of labor costs as direct or indirect is a complex issue because some of these costs are difficult to classify—for example, overtime pay, idle time, and fringe benefits. In most firms, overtime and idle time are classified as indirect labor and treated as part of manufacturing overhead. In some firms, fringe benefits are also treated as indirect labor. In others, the fringe benefits provided to direct laborers are treated as direct labor and those of indirect laborers as indirect labor.

The Accumulation of Product Costs

As we have mentioned, direct materials, direct labor, and overhead costs are all manufacturing costs. All manufacturing costs are treated as product costs if the company uses an absorption costing approach. This approach is required for financial reporting and for income taxes. Another approach to product costing is variable costing, which is particularly useful for managerial decision making. Under variable costing all manufacturing costs except fixed overhead costs are treated as product costs; fixed overhead is accounted for as a period expense. Chapter 23 deals with how manufacturing costs are assigned to products under both absorption costing and variable costing. A brief overview of absorption costing is presented here. A discussion of variable costing is postponed until you have an understanding of manufacturing costs under absorption costing.

absorption costing *an approach to product costing that assigns all fixed and variable manufacturing costs to the units produced*

variable costing *an approach to product costing that assigns only variable costs as product costs and treats fixed overhead costs as period expenses*

work-in-process *partially manufactured products; includes all manufacturing costs assigned to products that are in process but have not been completed*

Exhibit 20-7 is a diagram of the production process with absorption costing. Note that direct materials, direct labor, and manufacturing overhead costs are transferred to a Work-in-Process account. Then, when the

EXHIBIT 20-7 The Accumulation of Product Costs (Absorption Costing)

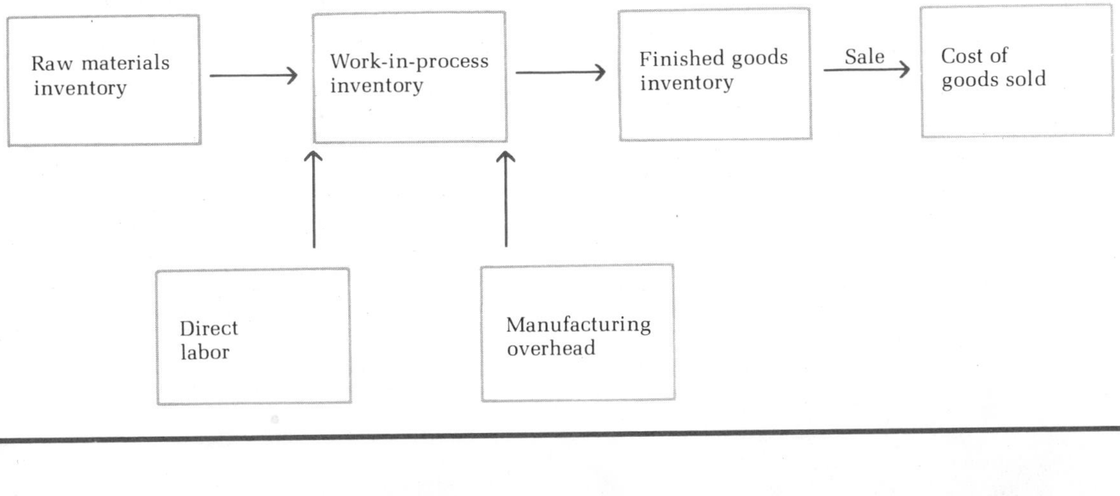

finished goods *manufactured products ready for sale; includes all manufacturing costs assigned to products that have been completed but not yet sold*

goods are completed, costs are transferred to Finished Goods. Thus, a manufacturing firm has three different inventory accounts on its balance sheet: Raw Materials, Work-in-Process, and Finished Goods. Finally, when finished goods are sold, their costs are transferred to Cost of Goods Sold on the income statement. Exhibits 20-8 and 20-9 show how Cost of Goods Sold is

EXHIBIT 20-8

Ajax Soap Company
Income Statement
for the Year Ended December 31, 1984

	Sales Revenue		$380,000
	Cost of Goods Sold:		
Product costs	Beginning Finished Goods Inventory	$ 40,000	
	Cost of Goods Manufactured (Exhibit 20-9)	203,000	
	Finished Goods Available for Sale	$243,000	
	Ending Finished Goods Inventory	33,000	
	Cost of Goods Sold		210,000
	Gross Margin		$170,000
	Less Operating Expenses:		
Period expenses	Selling Expenses	$ 44,000	
	Administrative Expenses	31,000	
	Total Operating Expenses		75,000
	Income Before Taxes		$ 95,000

EXHIBIT 20-9

Ajax Soap Company
Cost of Goods Manufactured Schedule
for the Year Ended December 31, 1984

Direct Materials Used		$ 42,000
Direct Labor		86,000
Manufacturing Overhead:		
Indirect Materials	$ 8,000	
Indirect Labor	18,000	
Utilities—Factory	4,800	
Insurance—Factory	3,600	
Rent—Factory	15,000	
Depreciation—Factory	20,600	
Property Taxes—Factory	14,000	84,000
Total Manufacturing Costs Added This Period		$212,000
Add Work-in-Process, January 1		43,000
Total Manufacturing Costs		$255,000
Less Work-in-Process, December 31		52,000
Cost of Goods Manufactured (transferred to Finished Goods)		$203,000

computed on a manufacturing company's income statement. Readers are referred to Chapter 7 for a review of various cost flow alternatives, such as FIFO and LIFO; these will affect the Inventory balances, Cost of Goods Manufactured, and Cost of Goods Sold.

cost of goods manufactured schedule *a summary of the costs of manufacturing products during a period; includes beginning work-in-process inventory plus manufacturing costs during the period minus ending work-in-process inventory*

The cost of goods manufactured on the income statement can be explained by a cost of goods manufactured schedule, as illustrated in Exhibit 20-9. This schedule computes cost of goods manufactured during the period by combining beginning work-in-process inventory (costs from the previous period for products not yet completed) with total manufacturing costs added this period, and then subtracting ending work-in-process inventory.

Referring again to the income statement in Exhibit 20-8, we see that cost of goods manufactured (completed) in a period is added to beginning finished goods inventory. Then, when cost of goods sold is transferred out of finished goods, the balance represents the ending inventory that will appear as a current asset on the balance sheet. In fact, as shown in Exhibit 20-10, all three categories of manufacturing inventories—raw materials, work-in-process, and finished goods—are included as current assets on the balance sheet.

EXHIBIT 20-10

Ajax Soap Company

Balance Sheet (Partial) as of December 31, 1984

	Current Assets:		
	Cash		$ 27,000
	Accounts Receivable		83,000
	Inventories:		
Product costs	Raw Materials	$29,000	
Product costs	Work-in-Process	52,000	
Product costs	Finished Goods	33,000	114,000
	Prepaid Expenses		12,000
	Total Current Assets		$236,000

TO SUMMARIZE In financial reporting, product costs are costs associated with and assigned to a product, and carried on the balance sheet as inventory until the product is sold. Period expenses are costs that are associated with a particular accounting period and that go directly to the income statement. Service firms usually have only period expenses. Merchandising and manufacturing firms have product costs as well. There are three types of manufacturing costs: direct materials, direct labor, and manufacturing overhead. The first two are usually direct product costs; the last is an indirect product cost. All manufacturing costs are product costs under an absorption costing approach (used for financial reporting and income taxes). Under variable costing (used for managerial decision making), manufacturing costs except for fixed overhead are treated as product costs. Under absorption costing, product costs flow from a Work-in-Process inventory account to Finished Goods when products are completed and then to Cost of Goods Sold when products are sold. Calculating the cost of goods sold for a manufacturing firm involves the preparation of a cost of goods manufactured schedule.

Concepts and Classifications for Cost Control

Costs are classified for external financial reporting on the basis of generally accepted accounting principles to assure users that the financial statements are presented in a uniform and consistent manner. In keeping with the fundamental principle of managerial accounting—that different cost data are needed for different purposes—costs need to be collected and classified in other ways so that managers can perform their internal functions of planning, control, and performance evaluation. In the remainder of this chapter we discuss cost concepts and classifications for these managerial functions. Note throughout that the concepts are generally applicable to service, merchandising, and manufacturing firms.

In Chapter 19 we discussed the managerial functions of planning and control in the sequence in which they occur. In this chapter, control is discussed first in order to introduce at the outset the concepts of responsibility centers and cost variability. We begin with some basic definitions.

RESPONSIBILITY CENTERS

The term "control" implies that individual managers have enough information about and influence over the organizational units under their authority to take responsibility for their functioning effectively. The term "cost control" relates to a manager's ability to keep the unit's costs within a range of acceptability.

responsibility center *an organizational unit in which the manager has control over and is held accountable for performance*

Cost control is facilitated by the establishment of responsibility centers, clearly identifiable organizational units involving operations for which performance is to be measured. In a merchandising firm, two such centers would be the sales and accounting departments. A manufacturing firm would probably recognize responsibility centers for such functions as production, marketing, and administration. The number of such centers depends on the size and the needs of a company.

Costs can be classified and accumulated in a number of ways, depending on the degree of control desired. A fundamental principle is that costs are controlled by people. Thus, to achieve cost control, it is necessary for a company to adopt certain essential policies. It must

1. Establish responsibility centers.
2. Identify for each responsibility center a manager who is responsible for authorizing and controlling the costs.
3. Accumulate costs in the responsibility centers.
4. Make certain that managers are aware of the way costs behave in their responsibility centers.
5. Compare actual costs with expected costs.
6. Provide performance control reports to the manager of each responsibility center.
7. Require that any significant deviations from expected costs be investigated.

8. Take corrective action when needed.

Because they are independent units of activity, responsibility centers provide a way for management to identify costs and assign responsibility for them. The important cost concepts in this process are

1. Traceable and nontraceable costs.
2. Controllable and noncontrollable costs.
3. Fixed and variable costs.

TRACEABLE VERSUS NONTRACEABLE COSTS

traceable costs *costs that are directly associated with and assigned to specific responsibility centers*

A traceable cost[1] is one that can be identified with a particular responsibility center. Suppose, for example, that a group of machines, located in a room that has its own meter to measure electricity, is designated as a responsibility center. The center's traceable costs would include materials (direct and indirect), labor (direct and indirect), electricity, depreciation on the machines, and other manufacturing overhead costs associated with that responsibility center. A cost is traceable to a responsibility center if it is clearly identifiable with the center.

nontraceable costs *costs that are not directly identified with the responsibility centers to which they are assigned*

Costs that are not directly identified with the responsibility centers to which they are assigned are nontraceable costs. To the extent that these costs are incurred because of the activity in a responsibility center, they are usually allocated on the basis of such factors as units of production, square footage, or number of employees. For example, a portion of the cost of insuring the building might be allocated to a group of machines designated as a responsibility center. The allocation of insurance would be based on some measure such as the fair market value of the machines or the square footage of the room in which the machines are located. These allocated insurance costs are treated as nontraceable costs to the responsibility center.

Nontraceable costs often cannot be controlled by a responsibility center's manager. To illustrate, if heat for the factory building is allocated among responsibility centers on the basis of square feet of floor space, the manager of the machine room has little or no control over the cost of this overhead item. He or she did not authorize the heat and generally cannot change the amount allocated to the responsibility center. These nontraceable costs are controllable by managers of other responsibility centers—for example, heat might be controlled by the administrative department.

The distinction between traceable and nontraceable costs is made so that management can more accurately assign responsibility in accounting for the various costs. Only traceable costs are candidates for control by a particular responsibility center manager. Nontraceable costs are controllable in other centers. This is true for all types of organizations—service, merchandising, or manufacturing.

[1] Many textbooks use the terms direct and indirect instead of traceable and nontraceable. We chose the latter so as not to confuse these terms with direct and indirect product costs.

CONTROLLABLE VERSUS NONCONTROLLABLE COSTS

controllable costs *costs that are incurred in a responsibility center and that are the direct responsibility of the manager of the center*

noncontrollable costs *costs that are assigned to a responsibility center but that are only indirectly the responsibility of the manager of that center, because they are under the control of another center manager*

Even traceable costs are not always subject to control by responsibility center managers. Thus, an important cost concept is the classification of traceable costs as controllable or noncontrollable.

To illustrate a traceable noncontrollable cost, suppose that a machining department is a responsibility center. The cost of repairing the machines would be treated as a traceable cost, but the maintenance department, another cost center, would actually make the repairs and control the efficiency of this work. Thus, cost control in this case would be the direct responsibility of the maintenance department manager. In other words, the repair costs would be traceable costs in the machining department and controllable costs in the maintenance department. Similarly, although warehouse labor and building depreciation are both traceable costs to a warehousing cost center, the manager can only authorize a change in the amount of labor employed. He has no control over the depreciation cost. Exhibit 20-11 shows the relationship of costs in a responsibility center.

The distinction between controllable and noncontrollable costs is made so that responsibility center managers can quickly spot controllable costs that are excessive. The control report may list all of the traceable (and even

EXHIBIT 20-11 **Responsibility Center Costs**

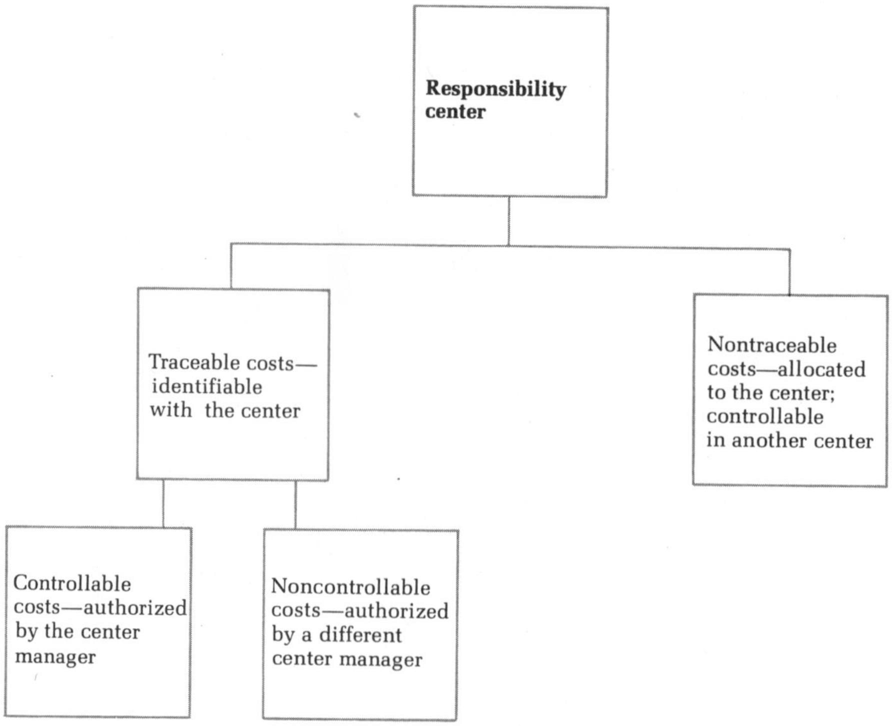

nontraceable) costs of that center, but the controllable costs are usually segregated, as these are the manager's prime responsibility.

FIXED VERSUS VARIABLE COSTS

To control a cost, a manager must understand how it behaves under varying circumstances. Cost behavior usually refers to how a cost changes in relation to varying levels of activity. The measure of activity might be units produced, direct-labor hours, machine hours, or number of employees. As the activity level changes, a cost may change proportionately or disproportionately to the change in activity, or it may not change at all. These three types of cost behaviors are the topic of Chapter 21; here we present a brief overview of the costs that vary proportionately with changes in the volume of activity (variable costs) and the costs that do not change when volume changes (fixed costs).

variable costs *costs that change in total proportionately with changes in activity level*

A variable cost changes in terms of total dollars spent at different levels of activity. For example, if a pound of direct materials costs $3 and 2 pounds are used to produce each unit, the total material cost to produce 800 units is $4,800 ($3 × 2 pounds × 800 units), and the total cost to produce 1,500 units is $9,000 ($3 × 2 pounds × 1,500 units). The variable costs increase in total as the number of units produced increases. Note in the following schedule that the variable cost *per unit* stays the same at the various activity levels.

Units Produced	Variable Cost per Unit*	Total Variable Cost
800	$6	$4,800
1,000	6	6,000
1,200	6	7,200
1,500	6	9,000

* $3 per pound of material; 2 pounds of material per unit.

fixed costs *costs that do not vary in total with changes in activity level*

Fixed costs do not vary in total as production varies. For example, depreciation on a building would be a fixed cost because its amount does not change when the number of units produced changes. The annual plant depreciation will be the same, say $12,000, whether one unit or 1,000 units are produced.

TO SUMMARIZE In cost control, traceable costs are clearly identifiable with a responsibility center. Nontraceable costs cannot be identified with the particular responsibility centers to which they have been assigned but must be allocated on some equitable basis. Traceable costs can be categorized into controllable and noncontrollable costs. Managers of responsibility centers both authorize and monitor controllable costs. Noncontrollable costs are usually authorized by other center managers. Costs can be controlled only when their behavior is understood. Costs that are constant per unit produced and thus change proportionately in total with variations in production volume are variable costs. Costs that do not change in total with production volume changes are fixed costs.

Cost Concepts for Planning

Planning involves setting goals for future operations. It can be for the long run or the short run, and it is performed at several levels of management. Planning should not be confused with control: Planning sets the goals, whereas control tests whether those goals have been reached and, if necessary, takes corrective action to bring operating results into line with planned (expected) results. Cost concepts related to planning are estimated costs or standard costs versus actual costs.

ESTIMATED VERSUS ACTUAL COSTS

A plan usually consists of detailed estimates of expected revenues, costs, and profits. These estimates are used to (1) quantify the operating plan for the next accounting period, and (2) help management control operations by providing expected results that can be compared with actual results. The process of estimating and analyzing revenues, costs, and profits is called budgeting. There are several different types of budgets; the most comprehensive is the master budget, an integrated summary of a company's goals for the next accounting period. It includes specific budgets for responsibility centers, as well as a projected balance sheet, income statement, funds statement, and a cash receipts and expenditures budget for the firm as a whole. The master budget is described in Chapter 24.

STANDARD COSTS

Costs used in preparing budgets may be either estimated costs or standard costs. An estimated cost is based on an analysis of actual costs incurred in prior periods and would be applied when a company has not conducted the necessary studies to develop standard costs.

standard costs *systematically determined estimates of the expected cost of a unit of output; they include the anticipated costs of materials, labor, and overhead for a given level of activity*

A standard cost is a systematically determined cost estimate, often based on engineering analyses. Used extensively for planning, control, and performance evaluation, standard costs specify, for example, how much material should be used to make a product, how much labor should be required to perform a particular task, and what quantities of electricity, supplies, and other overhead items should be necessary for a particular purpose. When standard costs are developed, management is able to set more realistic goals for the next period, and also to establish more effective cost-control programs. This is possible because a comparison of actual results with a standard provides more detailed and more dependable indications of why the variations from budget occurred.

To illustrate how standard costing works, we will assume the following situation. Alpha Company has determined that it should take 40 pounds of material to make a product. Since the material sells for $1.00 per pound, total materials costs for the product should be $40. In manufacturing the product, however, the company actually spends $39.60 on materials. Why did actual costs differ from standard costs by $0.40? In analyzing the difference, management uncovered two reasons. First, to produce each unit, 44 pounds of material were used, a variance of 4 pounds of material from the standard amount, or $4 per unit of product. Second, the price actually paid for the material was $0.90 per pound, a 10-cent variance from the standard price, or $4.40 per unit of product (44 pounds × $0.10). Thus, the $39.60 was accounted for as follows:

Standard Cost (40 pounds × $1.00/pound)	$40.00
Materials Variance—Extra Pounds of Material at Standard Cost (4 pounds × $1.00)	4.00
Price Variance—Savings per Pound ($0.10 × 44 pounds)	(4.40)
Total Cost	$39.60

As this example indicates, knowing the variances between actual and standard costs alerts management to potential problems and allows a company to take corrective action. In this case, the use of standards may have identified a critical trouble area. Whereas the total favorable variance of $0.40 per unit of product may seem insignificant, the use of 4 extra pounds of material per unit may be a serious problem. The extra materials usage could be caused by careless employees, obsolete machines, poor material quality, or employee fraud. Without using standards, management would not have recognized the problem because the favorable purchase price variance for this period concealed the 10 percent overuse of materials. This process is an example of management by exception, because it directs the manager's attention to the costs that are most out of line with expectations.

TO SUMMARIZE As used in planning, estimated costs form the basis of budgets and thus serve as benchmarks against which actual costs can be compared. Standard costs are systematically determined cost estimates. Comparisons between actual costs and standard costs suggest the reasons for variations from budget.

Cost Concepts for Choosing Among Alternatives

A large part of a manager's job is making decisions. The decisions may be routine (made regularly) or nonroutine (made only occasionally). Routine decisions usually involve the cost concepts already discussed, such as direct and indirect costs, controllable and noncontrollable costs, fixed and variable costs, and standard costs and budgets. They include such decisions as how many of each unit are to be produced in a certain week, and whether to have employees work overtime or to hire additional employees. Nonroutine decisions involve longer time periods. They relate to such questions as whether certain products should be added to or dropped from the product line, whether equipment should be purchased or rented, whether components should be produced internally or bought from other companies, what prices should be charged for products, and how products should be sold.

Frequently, a number of factors must be considered before a nonroutine decision can be made. For example, although the monthly rental fees for a machine over its useful life may exceed its purchase price, the purchase price must be paid immediately whereas rental payments are spread over a number of years. When the rental payments are discounted to their present value to account for the time value of money, the purchase price may be higher than the rental payments.

Three cost concepts that can help management in making nonroutine decisions are differential costs, sunk costs, and opportunity costs.

DIFFERENTIAL COSTS

differential (or incremental) costs *costs that are not the same for the alternatives being considered*

In making a nonroutine decision, management usually considers alternatives that involve some identical costs as well as some costs that are different. The costs that are different for each of the alternatives are differential, or incremental, costs. Since only differential costs are relevant to making a decision, the costs that are the same for all of the viable alternatives can be ignored.

To illustrate the use of differential costs in making nonroutine decisions, we assume that a management consulting firm provides a pension advisory service to clients at a rate of $75 per hour. The rate is computed as follows:

Consultant Labor per Hour	$40
Other Variable Costs	4
Indirect Overhead (fixed)	16*
Total Cost per Hour	$60
Billing Rate per Hour	$75

* $16 at 1,000 hours' capacity.

A potential client would like to establish a pension plan but cannot afford the $75 hourly rate. Instead, the potential client offers to pay $50 per hour for an estimated 100 hours. Should the consulting firm accept the job on these terms?

Assume that the consulting firm has a capacity of 1,000 hours per month and that it will be operating at 90 percent of capacity (900 hours) if the new client is not accepted. A full analysis of the revenues and costs under the two alternatives suggests that the new client should be accepted.

	Without New Client		With New Client	
Revenues (hours × billing rate)	(900 × $75)	$67,500	(900 × $75)	$67,500
			(100 × $50)	5,000
				$72,500
Variable Costs:				
Direct Labor (hours × labor rate)	(900 × $40)	$36,000	(1,000 × $40)	$40,000
Other Variable Costs (hours × variable costs)	(900 × $4)	3,600	(1,000 × $4)	4,000
Fixed Costs:				
Overhead		16,000		16,000
Total Costs		$55,600		$60,000
Income Before Taxes		$11,900		$12,500

Clearly, the consulting firm has a $600 increase in pretax profits if it accepts this client. Note that the overhead costs remain the same whether the firm bills out 900 or 1,000 hours during the month. This is so because the overhead in this case is a fixed cost. Such a detailed analysis is unnecessary, however. An analysis of only the differential revenues and costs will give the same result.

Differential Revenues (100 hours at $50)	$5,000
Differential Costs:	
Consulting Labor (100 hours × $40)	$4,000
Other Variable Costs (100 hours × $4)	400
Total Differential Costs	$4,400
Incremental Profit	$600

The differential revenues of $5,000 are $600 greater than the differential costs of $4,400. Therefore, from a financial perspective the new client's business should be accepted. Since the overhead costs will be incurred regardless of whether the new client is accepted, they are common to both alternatives and can be ignored in making the analysis. (One of the assumptions involved in accepting this client is that the price differential will not affect the prices charged to other clients. If prices to some other clients have to be reduced when they learn of the lower rates for the new client, the differential revenues would need to be reduced by the lost revenues from other clients.)

SUNK COSTS

sunk costs *costs that have already been incurred and cannot be changed by current or future decisions*

A sunk cost is a cost that has already been incurred because of past decisions. It cannot be changed or avoided by current or future decisions. Hence, a sunk cost is the same for all alternatives and can be ignored in making a decision.

To illustrate a sunk cost, we assume that a company is trying to decide whether to shut down a department. One of the machines in the department has a book value of $8,000 (original cost, $20,000; accumulated depreciation, $12,000) and no salvage value. The $8,000 book value is a sunk cost. It will be written off as a loss if the department is dropped or as a depreciation expense if the department is continued. Thus, the sunk cost of $8,000, which is common to both alternatives, should be ignored.

OPPORTUNITY COSTS

opportunity cost *the amount of money that could be earned by putting financial resources to the best alternative use compared with the one being considered*

When a manager decides to follow a particular course of action by committing resources to achieve an economic gain, the opportunity to commit those same resources to another course of action is lost. The net economic benefit that would have been derived from the next best alternative course of action is the opportunity cost of selecting the preferred course of action. The term "opportunity cost" comes from economics, where the cost of a course of action is measured by the benefit given up in not following the next best alternative. An opportunity cost is not a cash outlay, so it is not included in the accounting records. It is, however, an imputed cost that managers must consider in order to make a fair comparison of available alternatives.

Opportunity costs exist whenever choices are made between alternatives. For example, the opportunity cost of money invested in plant or equipment might be the dividend or interest revenue that would have been earned had the money been invested in stocks, bonds, savings accounts, or other such alternatives. Similarly, the opportunity cost of space used for a snack bar in a department store is the net revenue that would have been gained from selling another product in that space or leasing the space to another company.

To illustrate the concept of opportunity cost, we assume that a stationery-store owner has earned $14,000 per year for the past several years. The income is computed as follows:

Sales Revenue	$72,000
Cost of Goods Sold	42,000
Gross Margin	$30,000
Less Operating Expenses (excluding owner's salary)	16,000
Net Income	$14,000

The owner has an opportunity to sell the store for $75,000. If she chooses not to sell the business, she may be ignoring opportunity costs. That is, she may be ignoring the benefits she would gain in salary by taking a job as a manager in another store and in interest or dividends by putting her $75,000 into securities or other investments. Suppose that the owner could earn $10,000 a year as a manager and could invest the $75,000 selling price to yield an annual return of 12 percent. The following calculations present the owner's alternatives.

Earnings from Stationery Store		$14,000
Less Opportunity Costs:		
Manager's Salary	$10,000	
Return on Securities ($75,000 × 0.12)	9,000	19,000
Opportunity Loss if Store Is Not Sold		$(5,000)

From a financial point of view, the owner should sell the store; she would earn $5,000 more each year if she managed another store and invested her money in securities.

As you will recall from Chapter 19, however, decisions should not be made only on the basis of monetary benefits. Nonmonetary factors should be considered as well. In this case, the manager may get more satisfaction from being her own boss than from working for someone else. She may also think that the store's potential is greater than recent results have indicated. In any case, an understanding of the opportunity costs, as well as the nonmonetary factors, will help her make a more intelligent decision about alternative courses of action.

TO SUMMARIZE In choosing among alternatives, one must consider the various costs involved. Differential costs include only the amounts that differ for each of the alternatives. They highlight the relevant financial factors involved in a decision. A sunk cost is one already incurred due to past decisions. Because sunk costs cannot be changed or avoided, they do not affect a decision and thus can be ignored. An opportunity cost is the net economic benefit that would have been derived from the next best alternative course of action. Although opportunity costs do not represent actual cash outlays, they should be considered whenever a financial decision is made.

CHAPTER REVIEW

Accountants provide data to help management with external reporting, cost control, planning (including choosing among alternatives), and performance evaluation. A number of cost concepts have been developed for the first three categories to ensure that the data are relevant and timely. The fourth area—performance evaluation—has no special cost concepts associated with it. Instead, it makes use of the results obtained during the planning stage.

For financial reporting, costs are classified as product costs or period expenses, as manufacturing costs or nonmanufacturing expenses, and as direct or indirect costs. Service firms generally have only period expenses, whereas merchandising and manufacturing firms have both product costs and period expenses. Product costs of a manufacturing firm are classified as direct (direct materials and direct labor) and indirect (manufacturing overhead). What constitutes product costs depends on whether the company is using absorption costing or variable costing. Under either of these costing methods the product costs are recorded in a Work-in-Process Inventory account during production and are transferred to Finished Goods Inventory when production is completed. When products are sold, their product costs are transferred from Finished Goods Inventory on the balance sheet to Cost of Goods Sold on the income statement. Selling and administrative expenses are period expenses and are treated as operating expenses on the income statement. In a manufacturing firm, manufacturing costs are summarized in a cost of goods manufactured schedule, which reflects the flow of costs into and out of the Work-in-Process Inventory account.

The concepts developed by accountants for cost control include traceable and nontraceable costs, controllable and noncontrollable costs, and fixed and variable costs. Traceable costs can be identified with particular responsibility centers, whereas nontraceable costs must be allocated to responsibility centers on some equitable basis. Traceable costs may be controllable or noncontrollable. Although all costs are controllable at some level of management, responsibility center managers can control only the costs they can authorize. Costs cannot be controlled effectively unless their behavior is known. Costs are therefore classified as variable or fixed on the basis of whether they change in total in relation to variations in the volume of activity.

Cost concepts for planning are estimated costs and standard costs. Estimated costs are usually based on past actual costs and are used in preparing a budget, which provides a basis for comparison with actual costs. Standard costs are established with considerable precision, often through engineering analysis. Standard costs are useful in identifying the causes of variances between expected and actual results. The process of identifying and analyzing variances that need management's attention is referred to as management by exception.

Three cost concepts used in choosing among alternatives are differential (or incremental) costs, sunk costs, and opportunity costs. Differential costs can be used to simplify the decision-making process because they include only the costs that are not common to all the alternatives being considered. Sunk costs need to be identified so that they can be excluded from the decision-making process; these costs are unchanging and identical for all alternatives. Opportunity costs do not represent actual cash outlays, but they must be identified and measured because a particular course of action can be more realistically judged by comparing its benefits with the benefits given up by not following an alternative course of action.

Overview of the Remaining Managerial Accounting Chapters

Chapters 19 and 20 have introduced some of the basic concepts and terms of managerial accounting. Chapters 21 through 29 provide in-depth coverage. Before you study these chapters, we suggest that you obtain a clearer perspective of what is to come by reading the short introductions in italic type at the beginning of each chapter and relating them to the following discussion.

Managerial accounting provides information to internal decision makers for their use in planning, controlling, and evaluating performance. The costs and other quantitative data required for these functions come from the accounting information system, for which a variety of cost concepts and classifications have been developed.

In order to use these concepts properly, the accountant must first understand which data are appropriate for the decision being made. For example, does the decision call for total costs or incremental costs? Actual costs or standard costs? Is there any opportunity cost that must be considered? For many decisions it is important to know the way costs behave as volume changes. Chapter 21 discusses cost behavior patterns and the techniques used to analyze them. Given an understanding of these patterns, cost-volume-profit analysis can be used to determine break-even points and target net income levels. Chapter 22, which covers cost–volume–profit analysis, is thus an application of the knowledge of cost behavior patterns. The information that results from this analysis is useful in controlling costs and in planning for costs in subsequent periods.

Chapter 23 describes the way costs are classified for manufacturing firms and explains the cost accumulation methods under both variable and absorption costing, the two approaches to accounting for manufacturing costs.

In planning future operations, budgets are an important tool of management. The type of budget needed depends on the nature of the planning: strategic, long-term asset investment, or operations. Chapter 24 puts the budgeting process into perspective with special emphasis on the master budget and its network of detailed budgets, which are used in planning operations for the coming year. The concept of a flexible budget is introduced in this chapter.

Standard costs and flexible budgets are used in controlling costs in a manufacturing firm. To develop standard costs and flexible budgets, the accountant must have knowledge of the company's cost behavior patterns and the traceability and controllability of its costs. These concepts are explained in Chapter 25. Once standard costs and flexible budgets are understood, they can be used to study the cost control and decision-making problems described in Chapter 26. In this chapter, we discuss the three types of responsibility centers and explore the problems of measuring performance and setting transfer prices for transactions between responsibility centers.

Managers must not only plan for and control regular operations, but they must also make periodic decisions that are not of a routine nature. These nonroutine decisions include whether to buy or make a component, whether to add or drop a product or department, whether to process a product further or sell it as is, how to use existing resources to the best profit advantage, and what prices to set for products. This type of decision requires an understanding of such cost concepts as differential costs, sunk costs, and opportunity costs. Qualitative factors must also be taken into account; in fact, they may be considered more significant than the cost data when a final decision is made. All of these considerations are explained in Chapter 27.

Chapter 28 explores the systematic planning that must be done for long-term investments in assets. The emphasis in this chapter is on capital budgeting techniques and sensitivity analysis. The qualitative factors that may affect a capital budgeting decision are also discussed.

The managerial accountant must be aware of the impact of income taxes on business decisions. Chapter 29 explores this subject, including the tax effects of investments in current and long-term assets. Decisions regarding inventory methods, depreciation methods, and methods of acquiring, using, and disposing of assets all have income tax implications that must be kept in mind by business executives.

As you begin to study each chapter, try to view it in its overall relationship to managerial accounting. This approach will enhance your understanding of the subject by prompting you to keep in mind how individual concepts fit into the total picture.

KEY TERMS AND CONCEPTS

absorption costing (669)
controllable costs (674)
cost of goods manufactured schedule (671)
differential (or incremental) costs (678)
direct-labor costs (667)
direct-materials costs (667)
finished goods (670)
fixed costs (675)
indirect-labor costs (669)
indirect-materials costs (668)
manufacturing costs (667)
manufacturing overhead (668)
noncontrollable costs (674)
nonmanufacturing expenses (667)
nontraceable costs (673)
opportunity cost (679)
period expense (664)
product cost (664)
responsibility center (672)
standard costs (676)
sunk costs (679)
traceable costs (673)
variable costing (669)
variable costs (675)
work-in-process (669)

REVIEW PROBLEM

Cost of Goods Manufactured

Holland Manufacturing Company collected the following data for the month of October 1984 for one of its production units.

Raw Materials:	
Beginning Inventory	$20,000
Purchases (net)	80,000
Ending Inventory	14,000
Direct Labor:	
Direct-Labor Costs Incurred (4,000 hours at $5/hour)	$20,000
Manufacturing Overhead:	
Indirect Materials	$14,000
Indirect Labor	11,000
Depreciation—Plant and Equipment	20,000
Supplies	1,000
Property Taxes—Factory	6,000
Insurance—Factory	800
Other Factory Expenses	9,200
Work-in-Process:	
Beginning Inventory	$28,000
Ending Inventory	40,000
Finished Goods:	
Beginning Inventory	$50,000
Ending Inventory	42,000

Required:

Given this information, compute the cost of goods manufactured.

Solution

The cost of goods manufactured is equal to the dollar amount of goods transferred out of the Work-in-Process Inventory account. It is computed by adding raw materials, direct labor, and manufacturing overhead to beginning Work-in-Process and then subtracting ending Work-in-Process.

Holland Manufacturing Company
Cost of Goods Manufactured Schedule
for the Month Ended October 31, 1984

Raw Materials Used:		
Beginning Inventory	$ 20,000	
Purchases (net)	80,000	
Cost of Raw Materials Available	$100,000	
Ending Inventory	16,000	
Direct Materials Used		$ 84,000
Direct Labor (4,000 hours × $5)		20,000
Manufacturing Overhead:		
Indirect Materials	$ 14,000	
Indirect Labor	11,000	
Depreciation—Plant and Equipment	20,000	
Supplies	1,000	
Property Taxes—Factory	6,000	
Insurance—Factory	800	
Other Factory Expenses	9,200	
Total Manufacturing Overhead		62,000
Total Manufacturing Costs Added This Period		$166,000
Add Beginning Work-in-Process		28,000
		$194,000
Less Ending Work-in-Process		40,000
Cost of Goods Manufactured		$154,000

DISCUSSION QUESTIONS

1 Distinguish between a product cost and a period expense.

2 Give examples of product costs and period expenses in service, merchandising, and manufacturing firms.

3 Distinguish between direct and indirect product costs in a manufacturing firm.

4 Define and describe direct-materials and direct-labor costs in a manufacturing firm.

5 Give at least three examples of manufacturing overhead costs.

6 What costs are included in (a) manufacturing costs, (b) the cost of goods manufactured, and (c) the cost of goods sold, all under absorption costing?

7 What is a responsibility center? Explain its function in the cost-control process.

8 Distinguish between direct product costs and traceable responsibility center costs.

9 What is the reason for the distinction between traceable and nontraceable costs?

10 What is a controllable cost? Who is responsible for controlling allocated costs?

11 Are the noncontrollable costs of a specific responsibility center ever controllable? Explain.

12 What is a fixed cost? Explain why a cost may still be called fixed if it decreases from $5 to $4 per unit of product over the normal range of activity.

13 What is a variable cost? Explain why a cost is called variable if it remains the same per unit of product over the normal range of activity.

14 Distinguish between planning and control.

15 What is the role of the budget in planning and control?

16 What is a standard cost? What purpose does it serve?

17 What is a differential cost? Why is this concept important?

18 What is a sunk cost? Why is this concept important?

19 What is an opportunity cost? Identify some opportunity costs in business situations.

20 Why is an understanding of cost behavior important in the planning and control processes?

EXERCISES

E20–1 Cost of Goods Sold

All American, Inc. is a merchandising firm that sells sporting goods. Its beginning-of-the-year inventory cost $83,000. During the year, the company purchased an additional $149,000 of sporting goods. Through a physical count of inventory at the end of the year, the ending inventory was determined to be $52,000. Determine All American's cost of goods sold for the year.

E20–2 Cost of Goods Manufactured

Compute the cost of goods manufactured from the following data.

Direct Materials Used	$21,000
Direct Labor	44,000
Depreciation—Factory	10,000
Factory Insurance	3,000
Factory Maintenance	18,000
Indirect Labor	15,000
Indirect Materials	2,000
Advertising Expense	12,000
Work-in-Process, January 1	25,000
Work-in-Process, December 31	32,000

E20–3 Cost of Goods Manufactured and Sold

During 1984, Hosler Corporation purchased direct materials for $140,000. Direct-labor costs incurred were $180,000 and manufacturing overhead amounted to $130,000. Inventories at the beginning and end of the year were as follows:

Inventories	January 1, 1984	December 31, 1984
Direct (Raw) Materials	$30,000	$27,000
Work-in-Process	60,000	48,000
Finished Goods	38,000	44,000

Compute the following for 1984.

1. The cost of goods manufactured.
2. The cost of goods sold.

E20–4 Classification of Costs

For each of the following, indicate whether it is a product cost or a period expense.

1. Raw materials used in production.
2. A personnel manager's salary.
3. Assembly-line workers' wages.

4. The cost incurred to move the product from the manufacturing floor to the inventory warehouse.
5. Training costs for newly hired salespersons.
6. Insurance costs on the warehouse.
7. Supplies used in the executive offices.
8. Property taxes on office buildings.
9. Depreciation on factory buildings.

E20–5 Fixed Costs Versus Variable Costs

Classify each of the following as either a fixed cost or a variable cost. As you classify the costs, consider the behavior over a range of activity. Fixed costs will not change as the volume of production changes.

1. Fuel used to run machines.
2. Overtime wages for production workers.
3. Taxes on plant equipment.
4. Materials-handling costs (moving materials within the plant).
5. Research and development costs.
6. Property insurance.
7. Indirect materials.
8. Executives' salaries.
9. Straight-line depreciation.
10. Direct labor.
11. Direct materials.
12. Supplies used by production workers.

E20–6 Examples of Cost Concepts

Thomas Hart has invented a part for an automobile engine that is expected to increase gas mileage by 1 mile per gallon. He has patented the device and plans to make and sell it himself. Materials will cost $3 per part, and labor for part-time help will cost about $2 per part. Hart intends to do most of the work himself and will quit his regular job, where he now makes $800 per month. He has rented a building for $200 a month and can use some secondhand tools that he owns, which originally cost $175. The replacement cost of the tools is $400. Hart intends to pay a sales agent $2 for each part sold. If Hart decides not to undertake the manufacturing himself, he can have the device made by another company for $8 per part. Classify the above costs as

1. Sunk costs.
2. Fixed costs.
3. Direct-materials costs.
4. Direct-labor costs.
5. Period expenses.
6. Manufacturing overhead costs.
7. Product costs.
8. Opportunity costs.
9. Differential costs.
10. Variable costs.

E20–7 Allocating Costs to Responsibility Centers

Concannon Inc. has three responsibility centers—production, marketing, and administration. All three centers are located in one factory, which has only one electric meter. During the year, electricity costs of $24,000 were incurred by Concannon. Other data are shown in the following table.

	Production	Marketing	Administration
Space Occupied (sq. ft.)	15,000	2,000	3,000
Number of Employees	200	100	100

1. Allocate the total electricity costs to each responsibility center on the basis of: (a) square feet of space occupied, and (b) number of employees.
2. Why would the company allocate these costs?

E20–8 Cost Variances

California Company produces a variety of saws for both commercial and residential use. The manufacture of one large commercial saw should have required 70 pounds of metal costing $12 per pound. Actual production, however, required 73 pounds of metal, for which the purchasing department paid $12.50 a pound.

1. What is the materials variance in pounds and dollars?
2. What is the price variance per pound and in total?
3. What is the total difference (variance) between expected and actual materials costs?
4. What benefit might a company receive from calculating variances similar to those in (1), (2), and (3)?

E20–9 Differential Costs

Montana Mining Company is considering the replacement of one of its old machines. The following data have been provided.

New Machine	
Purchase Price	$24,000
Expected Useful Life	3 years
Disposal Value in 3 Years	-0-
Annual Variable Costs to Operate the Machine	$23,000
Annual Fixed Costs to Operate the Machine	$12,000
Annual Revenue from Sales	$60,000

Old Machine	
Original Cost	$20,000
Present Book Value	$6,000
Remaining Useful Life	3 years
Disposal Value Now	-0-
Disposal Value in 3 Years	-0-
Annual Variable Costs to Operate the Machine	$30,000
Annual Fixed Costs to Operate the Machine	$12,000
Annual Revenue from Sales	$60,000

1. Identify the differential costs relevant to this nonroutine decision. Ignoring the time value of money, what is the net differential cost?

2. Would your analysis result in a different answer if you considered all costs?

E20–10 Differential Costs

Refer to E20–9, and assume that the old machine presently has a disposal value of $5,000.

1. Does this change the decision about acquiring the new machine?

2. How is the $5,000 selling price of the old machine used in deciding whether the new machine should be acquired?

E20–11 Classification of Decisions

Indicate how each of the following decisions should be classified: short-run operating decision (OD), short-run nonroutine decision (NRD), or long-run decision (LRD).

1. The board of aldermen of a municipality is considering whether to change the zoning ordinance for a street from single-family dwellings to business operations.

2. The price of corn has increased substantially in the past year. A hog farmer is considering whether to raise sheep instead of hogs.

3. A company plant has some temporary idle capacity. The plant manager is considering whether to start making some components of its products, rather than continuing to purchase them.

4. The direct-materials variance was significantly unfavorable for the month of July. The production department manager is considering what action to take to get materials usage under control.

5. The local United Fund is having a meeting to allocate its funds to charitable and civic agencies for the next year. The board is considering whether any funds should be allocated to a new agency created to operate a blood bank.

6. The vice president of marketing has just analyzed the sales volume of three products for the past period and noted that one of the products had a decline in volume. He is considering whether to increase the advertising budget for this product.

E20–12 Assignment of Costs

Beringer Company manufactures several sizes of television tubes, including Nos. 18 and 24. During one week in August, an assembly-line worker spent 28 hours on No. 18 tubes and 16 hours on No. 24 tubes. The total of 44 hours worked represents 40 hours of regular time and 4 hours of overtime. The worker is paid $12.00 per hour for regular time and time and a half for overtime.

1. What portion of the week's labor cost of this assembly-line worker should be assigned to each tube, if the overtime was necessary because of additional product demand for tube No. 24?

2. How would the assembly-line worker's labor cost be assigned if the overtime was necessary because the previous week there was a shortage of raw materials used in all the television tubes produced?

PROBLEMS

P20–1 Cost of Goods Manufactured and Sold

Computer Manufacturing Company collected the following data for the month of June for one of its production centers.

Raw Materials:	
Beginning Inventory	$10,000
Purchases (net)	40,000
Ending Inventory	14,000
Direct Labor:	
Direct-Labor Costs Incurred (8,000 hours at $4.50 per hour)	36,000
Manufacturing Overhead:	
Indirect Materials	7,000
Indirect Labor	5,500
Depreciation—Plant and Equipment	12,000
Supplies	1,000
Property Taxes—Factory	3,000
Insurance—Factory	500
Other Factory Expenses	8,000
Work-in-Process:	
Beginning Inventory	30,000
Ending Inventory	32,000
Finished Goods:	
Beginning Inventory	43,000
Ending Inventory	39,000

Required:

1. Compute the cost of goods manufactured.

2. Compute the cost of goods sold.

3. Using T-accounts, show the flow of costs to Cost of Goods Sold.

4. **Interpretive Question** Explain how direct labor and indirect labor are distinguished and why it is necessary to make a distinction.

P20-2 Standard Cost Variances

Chateau Company uses standard costs. A raw material called Homme is used to produce the product Caron. Information about the purchase and use of Homme for September is as follows:

Standard Unit Price	$3.00
Actual Purchase Price per Unit	$3.10
Actual Materials Purchased	4,500 units
Actual Materials Used	4,200 units
Standard Materials Allowed for Production of Caron	4,000 units

Required:

1. What is the materials quantity variance in dollars for Homme for September?
2. Compute the excess of total cost incurred over the total standard cost of the purchased quantity.
3. **Interpretive Question** What is the purpose of standard costs?

P20-3 Application of Cost Concepts

Carolyn Company manufactures soap and cosmetics. The manager of one of the responsibility centers furnished the following information regarding costs in her center for the month of April.

Raw Materials Used	$20,000
Direct Labor	35,000
Depreciation—Machinery	4,000
Repairs to Machinery	12,000
Indirect Labor	6,000
Indirect Materials	1,000
Taxes (allocated on floor space)	1,800
Rent (allocated on floor space)	2,400
Insurance (allocated on value of machinery)	300
Interest Expense	4,000
Selling and Administrative Expenses	15,000

Required:

Using the above costs, compute the total dollar amounts that are

1. Direct manufacturing costs.
2. Traceable to the responsibility center.
3. Total manufacturing costs.
4. Period expenses.
5. Manufacturing overhead costs.

P20-4 Fixed and Variable Costs

Peter Smith has accepted a job as a traveling salesman for the Yellow Pencil Company, starting January 2, 1984. The company expects Smith to use his own car, for which he will be reimbursed at the rate of 24 cents per mile. The rate was based on the cost to Smith of operating his car for 12,000 miles in the previous year.

Gasoline, Oil, Tires, and Repairs	$ 850
Insurance	390
Licenses and Inspections	40
Depreciation ($8,000/5 years)	1,600
Total Cost	$2,880
Cost per Mile ($2,880/12,000)	$ 0.24

During his first year as a salesman for the company, Smith expects to drive his car 15,000 miles on business and 5,000 for personal use.

Required:

1. Which operating costs are fixed and which are variable?
2. What is the expected total cost of driving 20,000 miles in 1984?
3. What is the estimated cost per mile in 1984?
4. Why is the estimated cost per mile lower in 1984 than in the previous year?
5. **Interpretive Question** Should Smith consider any other factors before agreeing to use his own car at a reimbursement rate of 24 cents per mile?

P20-5 Unifying Problem: Sunk Costs, Differential Costs, and Opportunity Costs

Robert Martin estimates that it cost him 30 cents per mile to operate his large, gas-guzzling car in making deliveries for his pizza business. The computation is as follows:

Gas, Oil, Tires, and Repairs	$ 900
Insurance	350
Licenses and Inspections	50
Depreciation ($8,500/5 years)	1,700
Total Cost	$ 3,000
Miles Driven	10,000
Cost per Mile ($3,000/10,000)	$ 0.30

He is trying to decide whether to sell the car and contract for a commercial delivery service at the rate of 28 cents per mile. His car is 4 years old and has an estimated cash resale value of $700.

Required:

1. What is the car's book value at the beginning of the 5th year, assuming straight-line depreciation?
2. What is the amount of sunk cost that Martin can ignore in deciding whether to sell the car?
3. What is Martin's opportunity cost of operating his own automobile in the business this next year?
4. If Martin were to ask you whether he should continue to use his own car or sell it and hire the commercial

delivery service, what would your advice be? Prepare a cost comparison that shows how you reached your decision.

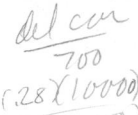

5. If Martin has the car inspected, buys a license, and obtains insurance coverage for the 5th year, how should he compute the cost per mile of using the car for a business trip?

6. If another merchant rides with Martin on a buying trip and agrees to pay half the actual cost, how much should the merchant pay per mile?

P20-6 Unifying Problem: Cost Classifications, Cost Flow, and the Income Statement

In the absence of the regular bookkeeper, a temporary employee prepared the following income statement for the Meridian Company for March 1984.

The Meridian Company
Income Statement
for the Month Ended March 31, 1984

Sales Revenue (8,000 units at $17)		$136,000
Cost of Goods Manufactured:		
Direct Materials	$40,000	
Direct Labor	35,000	
Manufacturing Overhead	15,000	
Total	$90,000	
Finished Goods Inventory, March 31	14,400*	
Cost of Goods Sold		75,600
Gross Margin		$ 60,400
Selling and Administrative Expenses		44,000
Net Income		$ 16,400

* 2,000 units at $7.20 each.

The president of the company was expecting a larger profit, so he asks you to check the income statement to determine if it was properly prepared. Your examination of the accounting records generates the following additional information:

a. There was no beginning inventory of finished goods.

b. There was no beginning or ending inventory of work-in-process.

c. The selling and administrative expenses included the following factory costs: heat, light, and power, $1,500; salary of factory manager, $5,000; taxes on factory building and equipment, $1,200; and depreciation on factory building and equipment, $4,300.

Required:

1. Prepare the income statement on the basis of generally accepted accounting principles.

2. **Interpretive Question** Should all manufacturing costs be classified as product costs for both external financial reporting and internal decision making? Why?

P20-7 Unifying Problem: Cost of Goods Manufactured and Sold, and the Income Statement

Required:

Following are hypothetical income statements for four manufacturing firms. Supply the missing data on each income statement to review your understanding of the determination of cost of goods manufactured, cost of goods sold, and net income.

	A	B	C	D
Sales Revenue	$40	$?	$50	$?
Direct Materials	$?	$ 6	$ 5	$ 4
Direct Labor	3	?	5	4
Manufacturing Overhead	3	7	?	3
Total Manufacturing Costs	$ 8	$20	$12	$?
Beginning Work-in-Process Inventory	4	6	?	5
Ending Work-in-Process Inventory	?	8	6	5
Cost of Goods Manufactured	$10	$?	$ 8	$?
Beginning Finished Goods Inventory	?	8	10	10
Ending Finished Goods Inventory	4	?	5	4
Cost of Goods Sold	$16	$20	$?	$?
Gross Margin	$?	$30	$?	$20
Selling Expenses	2	?	4	3
Administrative Expenses	2	6	4	?
Net Income Before Taxes	$20	$22	$?	$10

P20-8 Unifying Problem: Differential Costs and Sunk Costs

Keepin' Kool Company manufactures 40,000 refrigerators a year. The company presently makes the motors for its refrigerators. Another company has offered to supply the motors for the 40,000 refrigerators at a total cost of $700,000. The costs for Keepin' Kool to produce 40,000 motors are

Direct Costs:	
Direct Materials	$340,000
Direct Labor	230,000
Manufacturing Overhead:	
Variable Costs	115,000
Fixed Costs	80,000
Total Manufacturing Costs	$765,000

If Keepin' Kool were to buy rather than make the motors, the company could rent the space presently used for production to another company for $40,000 a year. The equipment used by Keepin' Kool to manufacture the motors has a book value of $160,000. The equipment cannot be used by Keepin' Kool for any other purposes and, because of its unique characteristics, cannot be sold.

Required:

1. Determine whether Keepin' Kool should buy the motors or continue to make them.
2. **Interpretive Question** Explain the distinction between differential costs and variable costs.

P20-9 Cost Classifications

The president of Pacific Ballbearing Company, a small manufacturing company, recently returned from a seminar on managerial accounting and cost concepts. He has asked you to classify the company's costs as listed below.

The president is interested in several cost classifications. All the costs should be classified as either fixed (F) or variable (V). Manufacturing costs should be further classified as either direct (D) or indirect (ID). Nonmanufacturing expenses should be classified as selling (S) or administrative (A).

1. Sales commissions.
2. Factory utilities.
3. Straight-line depreciation on an office building.
4. Fringe benefits for factory workers.
5. The sales manager's salary.
6. Overtime wages for the drilling machine operator.
7. Paint for the finished product.
8. Nuts and bolts for an automobile.
9. Company picnic costs.
10. Office secretarial salaries.
11. Paper used in the office.
12. The salary for the supervisor of production control.
13. The financial vice president's salary.
14. Depreciation (based on miles driven) on sales cars.
15. Research and development costs.
16. Accounting department costs.
17. Advertising costs.
18. Lubricants for machines.
19. Fire insurance for the factory.
20. Products given away by sales representatives.
21. Public accounting fees.

Required:

Prepare your answer using the following format. Two examples have been provided.

Cost	Cost Behavior	Manufacturing (Product Costs)	Nonmanufacturing (Period Expenses)
Direct Materials .	V	D	
General Office Supplies	V		A

P20-10 Allocating Overhead Costs for a Pricing Decision

Firestone Manufacturing Company produces two products and, as a basis for setting their prices, has accumulated the following information.

	Product R	Product S
Units to Be Produced	6,000	12,000
Expected Costs per Unit:		
Direct Materials	$3	$5
Direct Labor ($3 per hour)	6	9
Variable Overhead	4	9

Additional information: Firestone's fixed overhead is $200,000 and it uses a 30% markup on total costs for pricing.

Required:

1. If the fixed overhead costs are allocated to the two products based on the number of direct-labor hours used in manufacturing each item, what should the selling price be for each product?
2. **Interpretive Question** Why would the fixed overhead allocation be based on the number of direct-labor hours? Can you think of any alternative ways of allocating the fixed overhead costs?

P20-11 Understanding Cost Relationships

The following information was taken from the accounts of Spring Manufacturing Company for the years ending December 31, 1985 and 1984.

	1985	1984
Raw Materials Inventory	$125,000	$141,000
Work-in-Process Inventory	168,000	187,000
Finished Goods Inventory	210,000	168,000
Accrued Factory Payroll	8,000	12,000
Prepaid Factory Supplies	4,500	6,000
Unpaid Factory Supplies Received ..	3,000	5,000
Factory Supplies Inventory	15,000	12,000

The income statement for the year 1985 included the following amounts:

Raw Materials Used	$565,000
Cost of Goods Sold	877,000
Factory Labor Used	329,000
Factory Supplies Used	17,000

Required:

Compute the following amounts:

1. Raw materials purchased in 1985.
2. Cost of goods manufactured in 1985.
3. Factory labor paid in 1985.
4. Factory supplies paid in 1985.

CHAPTER 21

36,000 / 36,000 + 1080000

Cost Behavior Patterns

THIS CHAPTER EXPLAINS: The behavior of variable, fixed, and semivariable costs.
The high-low and scattergraph methods of analyzing semivariable costs.
The contribution-margin income statement.

In Chapter 20, the different types of costs were identified. In this chapter, we discuss the behavior of these costs—that is, whether and how they change in response to changes in operating level or volume of activity. This analysis provides guidelines for predicting the effect of an operating decision on future profitability. These profitability guidelines can then be used to plan organizational activities and to guide and evaluate the performance of employees.

Because an understanding of cost behavior patterns is so important to good decision making, this entire chapter is devoted to a discussion of these patterns and the techniques for analyzing them. Our discussion is divided into three parts: (1) an overview of cost behavior patterns, (2) methods of analyzing semivariable costs, and (3) a description of the contribution-margin income statement.

Types of Cost Behavior Patterns

Knowledge of cost behavior patterns is necessary for management to properly perform its planning and control functions. For example, if a company forecasts sales of 2,000 additional units during the next year, it must be able to predict how much costs will increase with the additional production. Similarly, management cannot attempt to control costs if it does not know which costs will react to changes in activity level.

Activity level is measured in terms of what is called the activity base. Since most businesses either produce or sell goods, the number of units produced or sold is a common activity base. Other measures of activity might include the number of: direct-labor hours worked, machine hours used, letters typed by a secretary, meals served, or miles driven.

There are three common cost behavior patterns: variable, fixed, and semivariable. A cost is classified into one of these categories by the way it reacts to changes in activity level. Costs that change in total in proportion to changes in activity level are called variable costs. Those that do not change in total are called fixed costs. A cost is classified as variable only if it changes in relation to the specified activity base. If it does not change in relation to that activity base, it is fixed. Semivariable, or mixed, costs contain both variable and fixed components.

VARIABLE COSTS

variable costs *costs that vary in total proportionately with changes in activity level, within the relevant range*

Variable costs change in total in proportion to changes in the activity level of a firm. Examples are the costs of direct materials, which change with the number of units produced, and sales commissions, which change with sales volume. An automobile manufacturer might have many such variable costs. If engines, tires, axles, and steering wheels were purchased from suppliers, their costs would be variable because the total cost of steering wheels, for example, would vary proportionately with the number of cars produced.[1] If no cars are produced, there are no tire or axle costs. On the other hand, if 1,000 cars are manufactured during a period, the total cost for axles, tires, and other purchased parts is 1,000 times the unit cost of each of these items. As more cars are produced, the total cost of each item increases. The unit cost, however, remains constant regardless of the level of production, at least within a certain range of activity.

This relationship between total variable costs and level of activity is shown graphically in Exhibit 21-1, which relates the number of cars produced to the total cost of steering wheels used in production.

In addition to sales commissions and materials, many other costs (such as labor) could also have a variable cost behavior pattern. For example, if it takes 4 hours of labor to assemble a frame and each hour costs $12, then $48 per frame would be variable and the total labor cost would be $48 times the number of frames produced.

FIXED COSTS

fixed costs *costs that do not vary in total with changes in activity level, at least within a relevant range*

relevant range *the range of operating level, or volume of activity, over which the relationship between total costs and activity level is approximately linear*

Fixed costs remain constant in total regardless of activity level, at least within a certain range of activity—the relevant range. Examples are property taxes, insurance, executives' salaries, plant depreciation, and rent. Because total fixed costs remain constant as production increases, the fixed cost per unit decreases. This is in contrast to variable costs, where cost per unit remains constant through changes in level of activity.

Exhibit 21-2(a) shows the relationship between an automobile manufacturer's fixed property tax expense and the total number of cars produced. Exhibit 21-2(b) then illustrates how that total property tax cost breaks down on a per-car basis.

[1] This example assumes no quantity discounts or other factors that increase or decrease the cost per unit.

EXHIBIT 21-1 **An Example of Variable Costs**

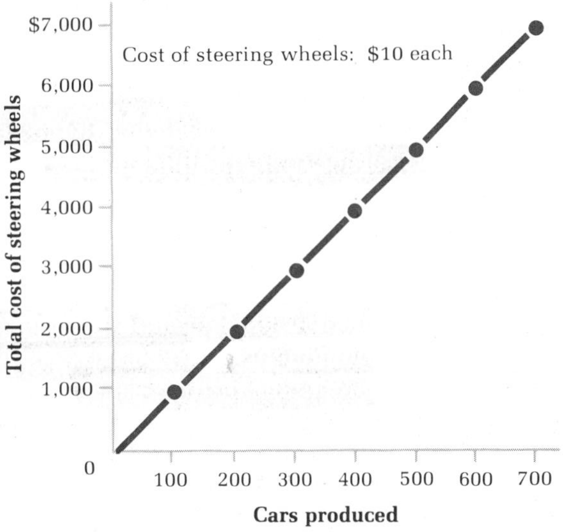

EXHIBIT 21-2 **An Example of Fixed Costs**

(a) Total Property Tax: $10,000

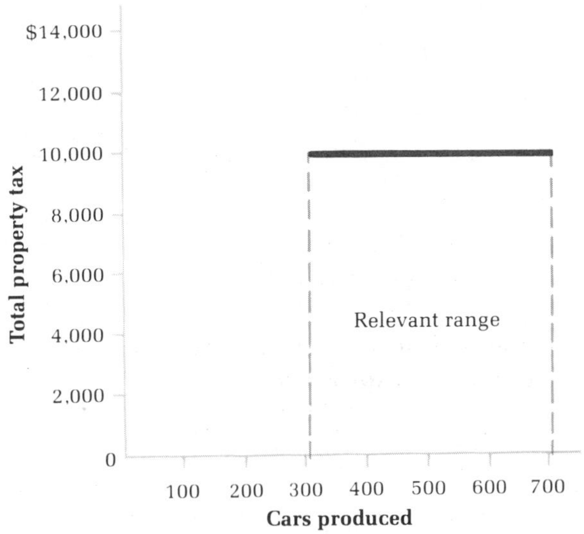

(b) Per-Car Fixed Property Tax

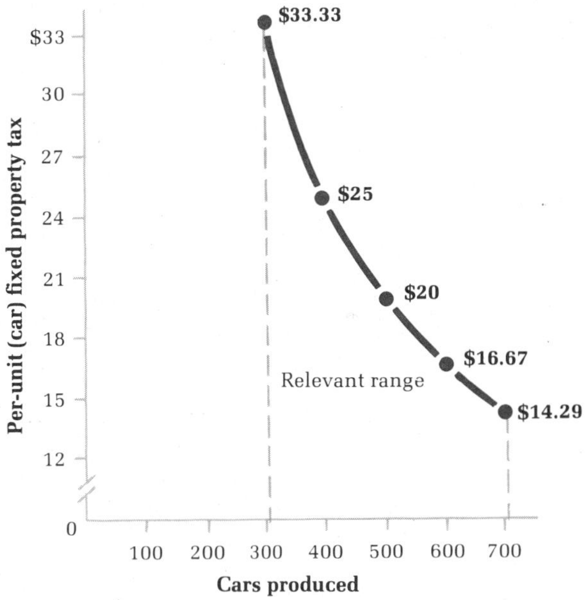

As the charts in Exhibit 21-2 show, total fixed costs do not change over the relevant range of activity, regardless of whether 300 or 700 cars are produced. The per-unit fixed cost, on the other hand, drops considerably as production increases. If just 300 cars are manufactured, each car must bear a burden of $33.33 ($10,000 divided by 300) for property taxes. With 700 cars, however, the burden is only $14.29 ($10,000 divided by 700) per car. Certainly, then, the higher the fixed costs, the more a company must produce in order to be profitable.

SEMIVARIABLE, OR MIXED, COSTS

semivariable (mixed) costs *costs that contain both variable and fixed cost components*

Semivariable, or mixed, costs are costs that contain both variable and fixed components. An example is rent that includes a fixed rental fee plus a percentage of total sales. Thus, the rental terms for an automobile dealer's showroom might include a flat payment of $400 per month plus 2 percent of each month's sales. The 2 percent of sales would be the variable portion, and the $400 would be the fixed cost. The total rent, therefore, would be considered a semivariable, or mixed, cost and would be diagrammed as shown in Exhibit 21-3.

Exhibit 21-3 shows that the cost of renting the showroom increases as sales increase. The total rent is $400 when there are no sales, $800 when sales are $20,000 [$400 + 0.02($20,000)], and $1,200 when sales are $40,000 [$400 + 0.02($40,000)].

EXHIBIT 21-3 **An Example of Semivariable, or Mixed, Costs**

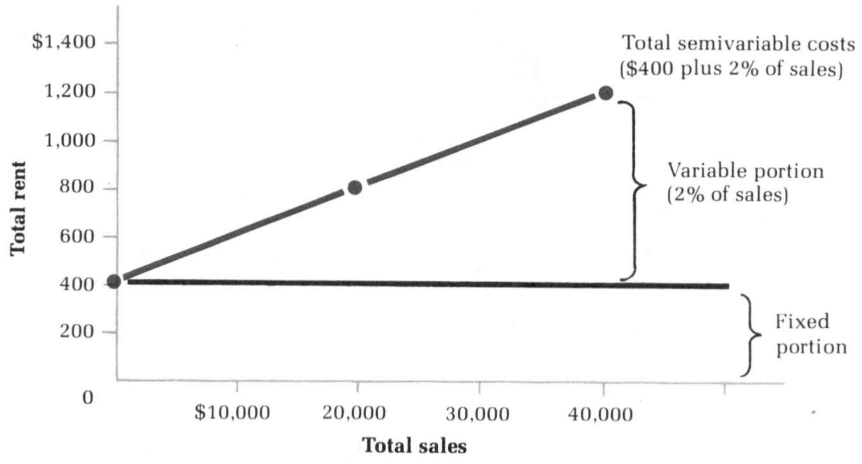

ISSUES RELATED TO FIXED AND VARIABLE COST BEHAVIOR PATTERNS

For good profit planning and decision making, all costs should be classified as either fixed or variable. It is often difficult, however, to identify how much of a semivariable cost is variable and how much is fixed. For example, although overhead costs often vary in total, they rarely change in exact proportion to changes in activity level. We will consider several methods of analyzing these semivariable costs, but first we should clarify the following issues related to fixed and variable costs: (1) the relevant-range phenomenon, (2) the trend toward fixed costs, (3) discretionary versus committed fixed costs, and (4) the linearity assumption.

The Relevant-Range Phenomenon

Thus far, we have classified costs that change in total in proportion to changes in the volume of activity as variable costs and costs that do not change in total, regardless of activity level, as fixed costs. In practice, these kinds of relationships are usually only appropriate for certain ranges of production. If significant increases or decreases in production take place, variable- or fixed-cost relationships will probably change. For example, if an automobile manufacturer has to reduce substantially the number of automobiles produced, the company might close various plants, lay off executives, or take other drastic measures to reduce fixed costs such as depreciation, rent, and executives' salaries. In addition, changes in other factors, such as overtime work and bulk-purchase discounts, may subject even the variable costs to significant fluctuation. That is why we say that fixed and variable costs are applicable only to relevant ranges, as shown in Exhibit 21–4.

EXHIBIT 21–4 The Concept of Relevant Range

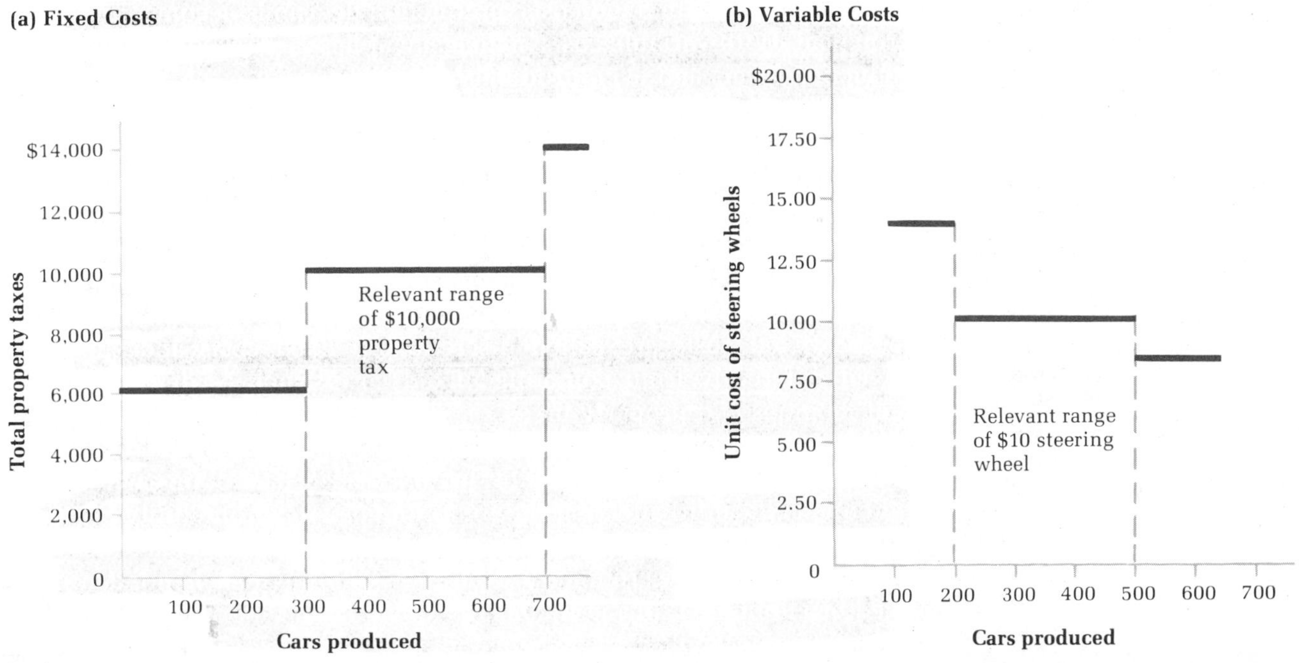

Exhibit 21–4(a) shows that the $10,000 fixed cost for property taxes is only applicable to production levels ranging from 300 to 700 cars per period. If less than 300 cars are produced, property taxes can be reduced to $6,000—by selling some of the production facilities, for example. If more than 700 cars are produced, property taxes will increase to $14,000 (because a new plant will have to be acquired). In Exhibit 21–4(b), a $10 steering wheel is only relevant to production ranging from 200 to 500 cars per period. If less than 200 cars are made, the cost of steering wheels is higher than $10, probably because the firm cannot take advantage of quantity discounts. On the other hand, if more than 500 cars are produced, the cost of each steering wheel is less than $10, either because larger quantity discounts can be obtained from the supplier or because the company can make its own steering wheels.

The Trend Toward Fixed Costs

As a result of several developments over the past few decades, more and more variable costs have been converted to fixed costs. Probably the most significant development is the increase in automation. As each manual-type job is replaced by a machine, costs change from variable labor costs to fixed depreciation and rental charges. In addition, automation tends to increase the need for executives and administrators, which tends to raise fixed costs.

A second major development that has contributed to this change in cost behavior patterns is the increased bargaining power of labor unions. Unions have been able to obtain for their members job-security guarantees that prevent management from laying off and rehiring employees as needed for production. This has meant that management now must deal with a constant minimum number of employees, regardless of production level. The result is a labor cost that is more fixed than variable.

This greater burden of fixed costs has a significant effect on the decision-making process. With fixed costs, production decisions become much more permanent. With variable costs, management has more flexibility to change production levels and even products.

Discretionary Versus Committed Fixed Costs

There are other circumstances in which costs that are not by nature fixed in behavior can become fixed, usually by management's initiative. For example, the management of an automobile manufacturing company might decide to spend a fixed amount on advertising, research and development, and employee training regardless of production level or sales volume. These types of fixed costs are called discretionary fixed costs and should be viewed differently from committed fixed costs, such as depreciation on plant facilities and property taxes.

discretionary fixed costs *fixed costs that are less permanent than committed fixed costs*

committed fixed costs *fixed costs that management cannot readily change*

The major difference between discretionary and committed fixed costs relates to their permanence. Committed fixed costs cannot be easily altered without significantly affecting the long-run goals or profitability of a firm. Certainly, the decision to reduce depreciation by selling a plant has long-run consequences. Discretionary fixed costs, on the other hand, can be reduced or eliminated during financially difficult times. Consider how these concepts would apply to a personal situation. Over your lifetime you will probably commit yourself to various fixed expenditures. Some of the more common ones are monthly payments on a house or a car and monthly contributions to a savings plan. Your house and car payments cannot be reduced without seriously impairing your long-run goals and so are like committed fixed costs. On the other hand, your monthly savings contribution can be temporarily terminated during periods of low income or high spending, and so it is more like a discretionary fixed cost.

The Linearity Assumption

linearity assumption *the assumption that total variable costs rise at a rate directly proportionate with activity level throughout the relevant range*

curvilinear costs *variable costs that do not vary in direct proportion to changes in activity level but at decreasing or increasing rates due to economies of scale, productivity changes, and so on*

Our explanation of variable cost behavior patterns has assumed that all variable costs have a linear relationship to the volume of activity—that is, when the level of production rises, total variable costs rise at a directly proportionate rate. This linearity assumption does not apply to all situations, however. In fact, nonlinear, or curvilinear, relationships are more common. For example, the economies of scale that result from worker familiarity, quantity discounts, and the like make the variable costs involved in the production of automobiles curvilinear. That is, the variable costs per car decrease as the number of cars produced increases.

The linear approach, although it may only approximate the actual situation, simplifies the calculations, and its use can be justified over a reasonably small relevant range. This is because the relationship between total variable costs and activity level tends to be nearly linear within small ranges. Exhibit 21-5(b) shows how the curvilinear, or real, cost relationship is approximated by linear segments within relevant ranges.

EXHIBIT 21-5 **Linear and Curvilinear Variable Costs**

(a) Linear Costs

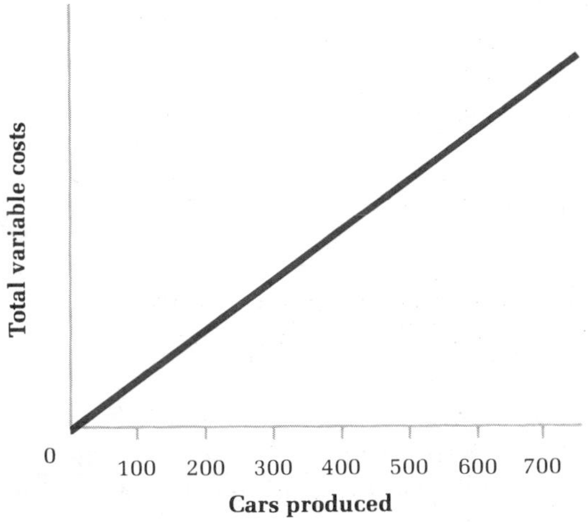

(b) Nonlinear, or Curvilinear, Costs

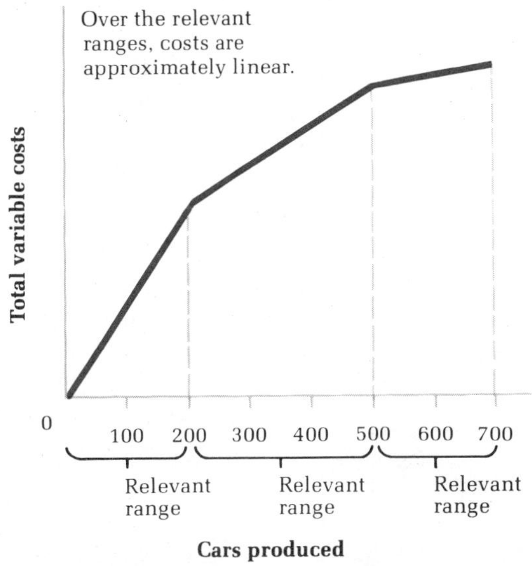

TO SUMMARIZE There are three common cost behavior patterns: variable, fixed, and semivariable (or mixed). Variable costs change in total in proportion to changes in the volume of activity. Fixed costs do not change in total over the relevant range. Semivariable costs are a combination of variable and fixed costs. These cost patterns are useful in predicting future costs. However, in using these patterns, relevant ranges should be kept in mind. Because of such factors as automation and the bargaining power of unions, many costs that were once variable are now fixed. Fixed costs of this kind, which cannot be altered without significantly affecting long-run goals, are referred to as committed fixed costs. Fixed costs that can be reduced or eliminated are called discretionary fixed costs. Although many variable costs really have a curvilinear relationship as the volume of activity varies, an assumption of linearity is justified within certain relevant ranges.

Analysis of Semivariable Costs

As noted earlier, a semivariable, or mixed, cost is one that exhibits both fixed and variable cost behavior patterns. Usually, the fixed portion represents the cost necessary to have a service (such as a telephone) or a facility (such as a building) available, and the variable portion covers its actual use. Recall the example of the automobile showroom's rental cost, part of it a flat monthly fee and part a percentage of sales. Other common semivariable costs are leases, electricity, repairs, heat, telephone, maintenance, and other overhead costs.

One way of separating fixed and variable cost components is to analyze each invoice according to the two classifications. For example, the monthly service charge on a telephone bill would be classified as a fixed cost and any long-distance charges as variable costs. This approach would be time-consuming, however, and would probably cost more than it is worth (that is, it would not be cost-beneficial). Therefore, semivariable costs are usually classified on the basis of past activity. That is, the sizes of the fixed and variable components are estimated for each level of activity based on prior analysis.

There are several methods of separating aggregate semivariable costs into their fixed and variable components. In this chapter we concentrate on two: the scattergraph, or visual-fit, method; and the high–low method. A third method, least squares, is covered in the chapter Supplement.

scattergraph, or visual-fit, method *a method of segregating the fixed and variable components of a cost by plotting on a graph total costs at several activity levels and drawing a regression line through the points*

regression line *on a scattergraph, the straight line that most closely expresses the relationship between the variables*

THE SCATTERGRAPH, OR VISUAL-FIT, METHOD

Probably the simplest method of segregating semivariable costs into their variable and fixed components is the scattergraph, or visual-fit, method. The total semivariable costs for each level of activity are plotted on a graph and a straight line (called the regression line) is visually fitted through the points. The fixed portion of the semivariable cost is estimated to be the amount on the cost (vertical) axis at the point where it is intercepted by the regression line. The variable rate is equal to the slope of the regression line.

To illustrate the scattergraph method, we will assume the following electricity costs for an automobile manufacturer. In the analysis and calculations that follow, all costs are assumed to fall within the relevant range of activity.

Month	Total Electricity Cost	Direct-Labor Hours Worked
January	$ 70,000	7,000
February	60,000	6,000
March	100,000	12,000
April	80,000	6,000
May	120,000	18,000
June	110,000	14,000

Exhibit 21-6 is the scattergraph on which these costs and hours have been plotted. It appears that the total fixed cost for electricity is about $40,000 per month, which is where the regression line intersects the cost axis. The variable cost rate is approximately $4.44 per direct-labor hour, which is the slope of the regression line. The slope of $4.44 is derived by dividing the change in electricity cost by the change in direct-labor hours. For example, when direct-labor hours change from 0 to 18,000, total electricity costs increase from approximately $40,000 to $120,000, or by $80,000. When 18,000 hours are divided into the increase of $80,000, the result is a change of approximately $4.44 per hour.

EXHIBIT 21-6 **Total Electricity Costs**

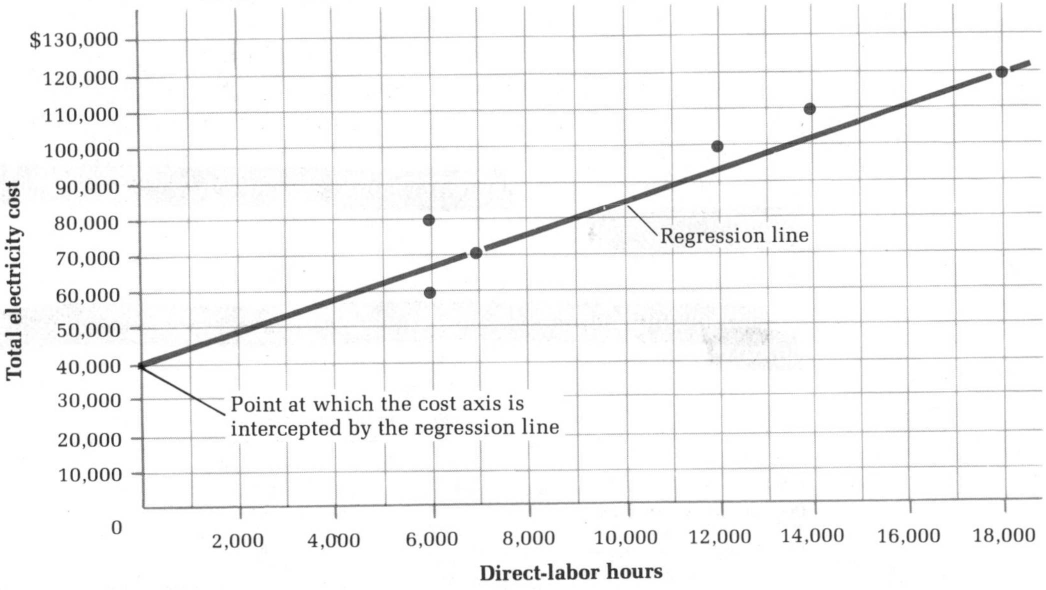

Although the scattergraph provides only estimates of the fixed and variable portions of semivariable costs, it can be an extremely useful tool. For instance, it shows at a glance any trends and abrupt changes in cost behavior patterns. It is also a means of checking whether costs are rising at a directly proportionate rate. As such, it can be used as a preliminary step to more sophisticated methods. Note that instead of electricity cost, any other semivariable cost could have been used, such as rent, telephone, or repairs. Also, the activity, instead of being direct-labor hours, could have been number of units produced, total sales, or machine-hours worked, just as long as the activity selected provided a basis upon which to segregate fixed and variable costs.

THE HIGH-LOW METHOD

high-low method *a method of segregating the fixed and variable components of a semivariable cost by analyzing the costs at the high and the low activity levels within a relevant range*

The second approach is the high-low method, which analyzes semivariable costs on the basis of total costs incurred at both the high and the low levels of activity. Fixed costs are assumed to be the portion of total costs that remains constant at both the high and low levels of activity. The variable cost is the portion that changes as activity levels change.

To illustrate this method, we refer again to the list of electricity costs of the automobile manufacturer.

Month	Total Electricity Cost	Direct-Labor Hours Worked
January	$ 70,000	7,000
February	60,000	6,000
March	100,000	12,000
April	80,000	6,000
May	120,000	18,000
June	110,000	14,000

Although these two columns of figures do not show trends as clearly as the scattergraph does, they do suggest that as the activity level (direct-labor hours) increases, total electricity costs increase. Given this relationship, the high-low method can be used to determine the fixed and variable portions of the electricity cost. The first step is to identify the highest and lowest activity levels—18,000 hours in May and 6,000 hours in February (or April). These two months also represent the highest and lowest levels of electricity costs, or $120,000 and $60,000, respectively.

The second step is to determine the differences between the high and low points.

	Total Electricity Cost	Direct-Labor Hours
High point (May)	$120,000	18,000
Low point (February)	60,000	6,000
Difference	$ 60,000	12,000

The third step is to calculate the variable cost rate. The formula is the same as the one used to compute the slope of the regression line in the scattergraph method. The results are different, of course, because in one case we are using an average change estimated by considering all the points, whereas in the other case we are using an average change estimated more roughly with only the high and low points.

$$\text{variable cost rate} = \frac{\text{change in cost}}{\text{change in activity}} = \frac{\$60{,}000}{12{,}000} = \$5 \text{ per direct-labor hour}$$

The fourth step is to determine fixed costs based on the variable cost rate ($5, in this case). The formula for this computation is

$$\text{fixed costs} = \text{total costs} - \text{variable costs}$$

At the high level, the calculation would be

$$X = \$120{,}000 - (18{,}000 \times \$5)$$
$$X = \$120{,}000 - \$90{,}000$$
$$X = \$30{,}000$$

At the low level of activity, it would be

$$X = \$60{,}000 - (6{,}000 \times \$5)$$
$$X = \$60{,}000 - \$30{,}000$$
$$X = \$30{,}000$$

In both cases, within the relevant range the variable portion of the total electricity cost is $5 per direct-labor hour and the fixed portion is $30,000 per month. This means that $30,000 is the amount the company pays each month just to have electricity available, and $5 is the average additional electricity cost for each hour of direct labor worked.

A COMPARISON OF THE SCATTERGRAPH AND HIGH-LOW METHODS

As we have illustrated, the scattergraph and high-low methods may produce quite different results.

Method	Variable Cost	Fixed Cost
Scattergraph	$4.44	$40,000
High-low	5.00	30,000

The scattergraph method takes more of the data into account and is therefore likely to be more accurate. The adequacy of the high-low method results can be examined by plotting the data on a scattergraph to see if the high and low points are representative of the costs incurred at all levels of activity. For example, if you examine the regression line in the scattergraph of Exhibit 21-6, you will notice that the low point lies below the line, indicating that, in this case, a straight line drawn through the high and the low points would not be precisely representative of the six data points plotted. Nevertheless, both methods can be used to predict future costs. If, for example, management wanted to know how much electricity would cost next month with 10,000 direct-labor hours budgeted, you would make one of the following calculations.

Method	Formula	Estimated Cost
Scattergraph	$40,000 + 10,000($4.44)	$84,400
High-low	$30,000 + 10,000($5.00)	$80,000

TO SUMMARIZE Two common techniques for analyzing semivariable, or mixed, costs are the scattergraph and the high-low methods. The first consists of visually fitting a straight line (the regression line) through points plotted on a graph, then noting where the line intercepts the cost axis (the fixed cost) and calculating the slope of the line (the variable cost rate). In the second method, the high and the low levels of activity are used to calculate first a variable rate and then the fixed cost. Both methods involve estimates and can be subject to error if they are not used with caution.

The Contribution-Margin Income Statement

Cost behavior patterns are applicable to many of the concepts discussed later (particularly in Chapter 22). To illustrate one example of their use and to serve as a bridge between this chapter and the next, here we describe the contribution-margin income statement—and then briefly show how contribution margins are used to compute break-even points.

functional income statement *an income statement that segregates all costs by use; it shows revenues less cost of goods sold (gross margin) less selling and administrative expenses*

contribution-margin income statement *an income statement that separates costs according to their behavior patterns; it shows revenues less variable costs (contribution margin) less fixed costs*

The classified income statement discussed in Chapter 6 follows a functional approach; that is, it groups costs according to their use. Thus, all production costs (whether fixed or variable) form a section (cost of goods sold), and selling and administrative expenses (whether fixed or variable) form a separate section. This approach is useful for financial reporting purposes; it provides outside readers with information about a company's progress and about which functional areas are being emphasized. For management's use in the decision-making process, however, an income statement that follows a cost behavior approach, often referred to as a contribution-margin income statement, is more valuable. (Exhibit 21-7 contrasts "contribution-margin" and "functional" income statements. The figures shown are arbitrary and bear no relation to other examples in this

EXHIBIT 21-7

Comparative Income Statements

Contribution-Margin Approach

Sales Revenue (1,000 units at $100 each)		$100,000
Variable Expenses:		
Variable Cost of Goods Sold (1,000 units at $40 each)	$40,000	
Variable Selling Expenses (1,000 units at $5 each)	5,000	
Variable General and Administrative Expenses (1,000 units at $4 each)	4,000	
Total Variable Expenses		(49,000)
Contribution Margin		$ 51,000
Fixed Expenses:		
Fixed Cost of Goods Sold	$10,000	
Fixed Selling Expenses	10,000	
Fixed General and Administrative Expenses	16,000	
Total Fixed Expenses		(36,000)
Net Income		$ 15,000

Functional Approach

Sales Revenue (1,000 units at $100 each)			$100,000
*Cost of Goods Sold:**			
Fixed Expenses	$10,000		
Variable Expenses	40,000		
Total Cost of Goods Sold			(50,000)
Gross Margin			$ 50,000
Less Operating Expenses:			
Selling Expenses:*			
Fixed Selling Expenses	$10,000		
Variable Selling Expenses	5,000		
Total Selling Expenses		$15,000	
General and Administrative Expenses:*			
Fixed General and Administrative Expenses	$16,000		
Variable General and Administrative Expenses	4,000		
Total General and Administrative Expenses		20,000	
Total Operating Expenses			(35,000)
Net Income			$ 15,000

* On a typical "functional" income statement, the fixed and variable portions of these expenses would not be identified and labeled. They are segregated here to highlight differences between the two types of income statements.

contribution margin *the difference between total revenues and total variable costs; it is the portion of sales revenue available to cover fixed costs*

chapter.) The term contribution margin is used to denote the margin, or amount of revenue, left to cover fixed costs after variable costs have been deducted from sales. It is based on the following relationships.

  Sales Revenue
− Variable Costs
= Contribution Margin
− Fixed Costs
= Net Income

break-even point *the amount of sales revenue or the number of units sold at which total costs equal total revenues: the point at which there is no profit or loss*

Given a knowledge of sales revenue, variable costs, and fixed costs, a company can utilize the contribution-margin approach to approximate its break-even point and its expected profit at various levels of sales and production.

As an illustration of how management might use a contribution-margin income statement, note in Exhibit 21–7 that the total fixed expenses are \$36,000. Since the company has a unit contribution margin of \$51 (\$51,000/1,000 units), it must sell approximately 706 units, or \$36,000/\$51, to cover the fixed costs and thus to break even for the period.

Stated another way, the break-even point for either a company or a product is the point at which total sales revenue is equal to total fixed costs plus total variable costs. Algebraically, the break-even point is the level of sales where

$$\text{sales revenue} = \text{fixed costs} + \text{variable costs}$$

In Exhibit 21–7, revenues were 1,000 units at \$100 each, total fixed costs were \$36,000, and total variable costs were \$49,000, or \$49 per unit (\$49,000 ÷ 1,000 units). The break-even point in number of units (x) is computed as follows:

$$\$100x = \$36{,}000 + \$49x$$
$$\$51x = \$36{,}000$$
$$x = 706 \text{ units}$$

Knowing the break-even level of operations is useful because it helps management determine what appropriate selling prices and production volumes are, how much to spend on discretionary fixed costs, whether to promote or drop a product, and so on.

Although break-even analysis is discussed at length in Chapter 22, one final example may help you to understand this concept. Suppose a company has two divisions, each of which makes a single product: Division A makes product alpha and division B makes product beta. The following revenue and cost data are applicable.

	Division A	Division B
Selling Price of Product	\$ 26	\$ 22
Total Annual Fixed Costs	70,840	32,000
Per-Unit Variable Cost	4	12

Division A is highly automated, which accounts for the larger fixed costs. Division B is primarily manual and thus has relatively few fixed costs.

Given these cost and revenue structures, the respective break-even points for divisions A and B are

Division A	**Division B**
\$26x = \$70,840 + \$4x	\$22x = \$32,000 + \$12x
\$22x = \$70,840	\$10x = \$32,000
x = 3,220 units	x = 3,200 units

In this example, division B has a lower break-even point than division A. However, soon after its break-even point has been realized, division A will become more profitable because of its higher contribution margin (\$22 versus \$10). For example, if each division sells 4,000 units of its product, division A's profits would be \$17,160 compared with \$8,000 for division B, as shown below.

Division A

\$26(4,000 units) = \$70,840 + \$4(4,000 units) + profit

\$22(4,000 units) = \$70,840 + profit

\$88,000 = \$70,840 + profit

\$17,160 = profit

or

\$22 contribution margin
× 780 units (4,000 − 3,220)
\$17,160

Division B

\$22(4,000 units) = \$32,000 + \$12(4,000 units) + profit

\$10(4,000 units) = \$32,000 + profit

\$40,000 = \$32,000 + profit

\$8,000 = profit

or

\$10 contribution margin
× 800 units (4,000 − 3,200)
\$8,000

TO SUMMARIZE Once costs are divided into their fixed and variable components, they can be used in decision making. One use of cost behavior patterns is the contribution-margin income statement. Sales revenue minus variable costs equals contribution margin, and contribution margin minus fixed costs equals net income. The unit contribution margin (or the unit sales revenue minus the unit variable cost) and total fixed costs are used to calculate the number of units a company must sell to break even for a period.

CHAPTER REVIEW

All costs can be classified by their behavior patterns. Costs that vary in total in proportion to changes in the volume of activity are variable costs. Costs that do not change in total with changes in activity level, within a relevant range, are fixed costs. Costs that contain both fixed and variable components are semivariable, or mixed, costs.

Before semivariable costs can be analyzed and used in decision making, they must be divided into their fixed and variable components. The scattergraph and the high-low methods may be used to analyze semivariable costs.

The first method involves visually plotting a straight line through points on a graph of cost data at various activity levels; in the second, the variable rate and total fixed costs are calculated on the basis of the costs associated with the highest and lowest levels of activity.

A contribution-margin income statement classifies costs by behavior and is more useful for many management decisions than a functional income statement. It shows that sales revenue minus variable costs equals contribution margin, and that contribution margin minus fixed costs equals net income. At the break-even point, total sales equal total fixed costs plus variable costs.

KEY TERMS AND CONCEPTS

break-even point (704)
committed fixed costs (696)
contribution margin (704)
contribution-margin income statement (702)
curvilinear costs (697)
discretionary fixed costs (696)
fixed costs (692)
functional income statement (702)
high-low method (700)
least squares method (714)
linearity assumption (697)
regression line (698)
relevant range (692)
scattergraph, or visual-fit, method (698)
semivariable (mixed) costs (694)
variable costs (692)

REVIEW PROBLEM

Variable and Fixed Costs and the Break-Even Point

Fujimoto Corporation makes bathtubs and toilets. During 1984, Fujimoto accumulated the following summary information about its two products.

	Bathtubs	Toilets
Selling Price	$130	$65
Number of Units Sold	14,000	9,000

	Bathtubs Units	Bathtubs Costs	Toilets Units	Toilets Costs
Jan.	1,200	$ 112,000	800	$ 39,600
Feb.	900	91,000	600	30,000
Mar.	800	76,400	450	25,800
Apr.	1,400	124,800	900	36,900
May	950	92,650	1,000	47,000
June	1,600	146,800	1,200	57,300
July	1,400	134,600	1,300	60,600
Aug.	1,700	154,500	650	32,195
Sept.	1,550	140,200	850	44,250
Oct.	1,500	134,500	500	27,000
Nov.	600	62,500	350	20,700
Dec.	400	44,000	400	22,000
Totals		$1,313,950		$443,345

Required:

1. Use the high-low method to estimate the variable and fixed production costs of bathtubs and toilets.
2. If all selling costs are fixed and they total $200,000 for bathtubs and $80,000 for toilets, prepare a contribution-margin income statement for each product at sales of 10,000 bathtubs and 10,000 toilets.
3. Compute break-even points for bathtubs and toilets.

Solution

1. Variable and Fixed Costs

The high-low method involves finding the variable and fixed costs at the high and low levels of production. In this case:

	Bathtubs	Toilets
High-Production Month	1,700 (Aug.)	1,300 (July)
Low-Production Month	400 (Dec.)	350 (Nov.)
Difference	1,300	950
Total Production Costs of High Month	$154,500	$60,600
Total Production Costs of Low Month	44,000	20,700
Difference	$110,500	$39,900

Once the differences are known, the change in units (production) is divided into the change in costs to determine variable cost per unit.

$$\frac{\text{change in cost}}{\text{change in units}} = \text{variable cost per unit}$$

$$\text{Bathtubs} \quad \frac{\$110{,}500}{1{,}300} = \$85$$

$$\text{Toilets} \quad \frac{\$39{,}900}{950} = \$42$$

Since total variable costs equal unit variable cost times number of units produced, and total costs equal total variable costs plus total fixed costs, fixed costs can now be calculated.

total costs − (variable cost per unit)(number of units) = total fixed costs

	Bathtubs
High Production Level	$154,500 − $85(1,700) = X
	$154,500 − $144,500 = X
	X = $10,000
Low Production Level	$44,000 − $85(400) = X
	$44,000 − $34,000 = X
	X = $10,000

	Toilets
High Production Level	$60,600 − $42(1,300) = X
	$60,600 − $54,600 = X
	X = $6,000
Low Production Level	$20,700 − $42(350) = X
	$20,700 − $14,700 = X
	X = $6,000

Thus, we have the following.

	Bathtubs	Toilets
Variable Cost per Unit	$ 85	$ 42
Total Fixed Costs	10,000	6,000

2. Contribution-Margin Income Statements

Fujimoto Corporation
Contribution-Margin Income Statements
for the Year Ended December 31, 1984

	Bathtubs	Toilets
Sales Revenue (at 10,000 units)	$1,300,000	$650,000
Variable Cost of Goods Sold*	(850,000)	(420,000)
Contribution Margin	$ 450,000	$230,000
Fixed Cost of Goods Sold	(10,000)	(6,000)
Fixed Selling Costs	(200,000)	(80,000)
Net Income	$ 240,000	$144,000

* $85 for bathtubs; $42 for toilets.

3. Break-Even Points

The break-even point is the level of sales where total revenues are equal to total fixed costs plus total variable costs.

Bathtubs

total revenues	= total fixed costs + total variable costs
$130 (# bathtubs)	= $10,000 + $85 (# bathtubs)
($130 − $85)(# bathtubs)	= $10,000
$45 (# bathtubs)	= $10,000
(# bathtubs)	= $10,000/$45
break-even	= 223 bathtubs

Toilets

total revenues	= total fixed costs + total variable costs
$65 (# toilets)	= $6,000 + $42 (# toilets)
($65 − $42)(# toilets)	= $6,000
$23 (# toilets)	= $6,000
(# toilets)	= $6,000/$23
break-even	= 261 toilets

In this company fixed costs are very low for both bathtubs and toilets, so the break-even points are low. Break-even points decrease if either total fixed costs decrease or the unit contribution margin increases.

DISCUSSION QUESTIONS

1 What are some examples of variable costs?

2 What are some examples of fixed costs?

3 Why must all semivariable costs be segregated into their fixed and variable components for analysis?

4 Why is the relevant-range concept important?

5 What factors seem to have caused the shift from variable to fixed cost patterns?

6 Which category of fixed costs—discretionary or committed—is management most likely to reduce during a recessionary period? Why?

7 What is the major limitation of the high–low method of analyzing semivariable costs?

8 What is the major weakness of the scattergraph, or visual-fit, method of analyzing semivariable costs?

9 Why is it important to know the contribution margin of a product?

10 How is the break-even point determined?

11 Which do you think would be higher: the level of activity needed by a service firm to break even or the level needed by a manufacturing firm?

12 If all other factors remain constant, how would a decrease in fixed costs affect profitability?

13 If all other factors remain constant, how would an increase in the variable cost rate affect profitability?

14 If each dollar of advertising spent yielded the same number of new customers, would a company be more inclined to advertise its high-contribution-margin products or its low-contribution-margin products?

EXERCISES

NOTE: Several of the exercises and problems that follow the Supplement to this chapter on least squares analysis provide additional use of the scattergraph and high–low methods.

E21-1 Fixed and Variable Costs over the Relevant Range

Miner Corporation manufactures plastic garbage cans. In a typical year, the firm produces between 20,000 and 25,000 cans. At this level of production fixed costs are $10,000 and variable costs are $2 per can. If the level of production were to drop below 20,000 cans, total fixed costs would be reduced by $5,000. If production were to exceed 25,000 units, fixed costs would increase to $20,000. At all levels, variable costs would remain at $2 per can.

1. Graph the cost of producing cans, with cost as the vertical axis and production output as the horizontal axis.

2. Indicate on the graph the relevant range of the $10,000 in fixed costs and explain its significance.

3. What would total production costs be if 23,000 cans were produced?

4. If the company could sell for $3 per can all the cans it could produce, would it be better to produce and sell 35,000 garbage cans or 25,000 garbage cans?

E21-2 Analysis of Semivariable Costs

Given the following scattergraph, how would you segregate the fixed and variable cost components of the monthly utility costs?

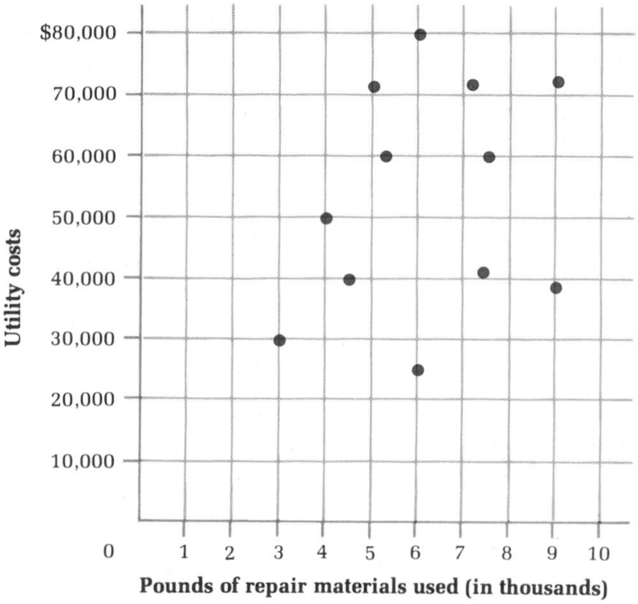

E21-3 Fixed Costs—The Relevant Range

Higgins Company manufactures airplanes. The following schedule shows total fixed costs at various levels of airplane production.

Units Produced	Total Fixed Costs
0–200	$200,000
201–500	300,000
501–800	400,000

1. What is the fixed cost per unit when 50 airplanes are produced?
2. What is the fixed cost per unit when 250 airplanes are produced?
3. What is the fixed cost per unit when 800 airplanes are produced?
4. Plot total and per-unit fixed costs on graphs similar to those in Exhibit 21-2.

E21-4 The Scattergraph Method of Analyzing Semivariable Costs

Whirlee Company makes windmills. The company has the following total costs at the given levels of windmill production.

Units Produced	Total Cost
20	$16,000
30	20,000
40	24,000
50	28,000
60	34,000
70	38,000

1. Use the scattergraph method to estimate the fixed and variable elements of Whirlee's total costs.
2. Compute the total cost of making 100 windmills, assuming that total fixed costs are $10,000 and that the variable cost rate computed in part (1) does not change.

E21-5 The Scattergraph Method of Analyzing Semivariable Costs

Given the following semivariable costs at various levels of production, complete the requirements below.

Month	Units Produced	Semivariable Costs
January	2	$13.75
February	3	16.50
March	1	11.00
April	5	22.00
May	2	13.75

1. Plot the information on a scattergraph and visually fit a straight line through the points.
2. Based on your graph, estimate the monthly fixed cost and the variable cost per unit produced.
3. Compute the total cost of producing 20 units in a month, assuming that the same relevant range applies.
4. Why is it so important to be able to determine the components of a semivariable cost?

E21-6 The High-Low Method of Analyzing Semivariable Costs

Bluewater Corporation makes boats and has the following costs at the given levels of production.

Units Produced	Total Cost
200	$200,000
250	225,000
300	250,000
350	275,000
400	300,000
450	325,000

1. Use the high-low method to compute the variable and fixed elements of Bluewater's total costs.
2. Compute the total cost of making 600 boats, assuming that total fixed costs and the variable cost rate do not change.

E21-7 The High-Low Method of Analyzing Semivariable Costs

The *Bicknell Daily Herald* has determined that the annual printing of 500,000 newspapers costs 9 cents a copy. If production were to be increased to 750,000 copies per year, the per-unit cost would drop to 7 cents a copy.

1. Determine the total fixed and variable costs of printing at a production rate of 500,000 copies per year.
2. What is the variable rate at the 500,000-copy level of production?
3. What would be the total cost of producing 600,000 copies?

E21-8 The Contribution-Margin Income Statement

Kunzler Company manufactures dolls. Using the following data, prepare contribution-margin income statements at activity levels of 20,000 and 30,000 dolls.

Sales Revenue	$10 per doll
Fixed Selling Expenses	$40,000
Variable Selling Expenses	$2 per doll
Fixed Manufacturing Costs	$50,000
Variable Manufacturing Costs	$3.00 per doll

E21-9 The Contribution-Margin Income Statement

The data below apply to Hansen Company for 1984.

Sales Revenue (10 units at $25 each)	$250
Variable Selling Expenses	45
Variable Administrative Expenses	25
Fixed Selling Expenses	30
Fixed Administrative Expenses	15
Direct Labor	50
Direct Materials	60
Fixed Manufacturing Overhead	5
Variable Manufacturing Overhead	3

1. Prepare a contribution-margin income statement. Assume that there were no beginning or ending inventories in 1984.

2. How much would this company have lost if only five units had been sold during 1984?

E21–10 Analysis of the Contribution Margin

Dr. Marriott and Dr. Lopez, owners of the Basin Clinic, have $150,000 of fixed costs per year. They receive 20,000 visits from patients in a year. They charge each patient an average of $20 per visit and have variable costs averaging $2 per visit (needles, medicines, and so on).

1. What is the contribution margin per patient?
2. What is the total contribution margin per year?
3. What is the total pretax profit for a year?
4. Drs. Marriott and Lopez can ask another doctor to join them at a salary of $100,000 per year. If this new doctor will see 5,000 patients per year, should he or she be hired? (Assume that no additional fixed costs will be incurred.)

E21–11 Analysis of a Contribution-Margin Income Statement

Find the unknowns in the following three cases.

	Case I	Case II	Case III
Sales Revenue	$100,000	$120,000	$(7) ?
Direct Materials } Cost of	$ 25,000	$(4) ?	$10,000
Direct Labor } Goods Sold	(1) ?	30,000	10,000
Variable Selling and Administrative Expenses	7,000	(5) ?	5,000
Contribution Margin	$(2) ?	$ 40,000	$(8) ?
Gross Margin	40,000	60,000	20,000
Fixed Selling and Administrative Expenses*	11,000	20,000	(9) ?
Rent Expense	(3) ?	10,000	1,000
Depreciation Expense	10,000	5,000	4,000
Net Income	$ 8,000	$(6) ?	$ -0-

* Except rent and depreciation.

E21–12 Analysis of Fixed and Variable Costs

Little John Company and Big John Company both make rocking chairs. They have the same production capacity, but Little John is more automated and unionized than Big John. At an output of 1,000 chairs per year, the two companies have the following costs.

	Little John	Big John
Fixed Costs	$40,000	$20,000
Variable Costs at $10 per Chair	10,000	
Variable Costs at $30 per Chair		30,000
Total Cost	$50,000	$50,000
Unit Cost (÷ 1,000)	$ 50	$ 50

Assuming that both companies sell chairs for $70 each and that there are no other costs or expenses for the two firms, complete the following.

1. Which company will lose the most money if production and sales fall to 500 chairs per year?
2. How much would each company lose at production and sales levels of 500 chairs per year?
3. How much would each company make at production and sales levels of 2,000 chairs per year?

E21–13 Graphing Revenues and Fixed, Variable, and Total Costs

Cavenaugh Company manufactures chocolate candy. Its manufacturing costs are as follows:

Annual Fixed Costs	$10,000
Variable Costs	$2 per box of candy

1. Plot variable costs, fixed costs, and total costs on a graph for activity levels of 0 to 30,000 boxes of candy.
2. Plot a revenue line on the graph, assuming that Cavenaugh sells the chocolates for $5 a box.
3. Determine the break-even point in number of boxes of candy sold.

PROBLEMS

P21-1 Graphing and Analyzing Fixed and Variable Costs

Denver Corporation makes automobile batteries. During 1984 it had the following costs and revenues.

Fixed Manufacturing Costs	$20,000
Variable Manufacturing Costs per Battery	22
Fixed Selling and Administrative Expenses	5,000
Variable Selling and Administrative Expenses per Battery	8
Sales Price per Battery	50

Required:

1. Plot the above data on a graph and label (a) fixed costs, (b) variable costs, (c) total costs, (d) revenues, and (e) the break-even point.
2. Compute the break-even point in number of batteries sold.
3. Compute the break-even point in total sales revenue.

P21-2 The High-Low and Scattergraph Methods of Analysis

Morrell and Company, manufacturer of surfboards, has kept records of semivariable overhead expenses for the past 8 months, along with corresponding production levels.

Month	Units Produced	Overhead Costs
January	4,000	$2,500
February	3,000	1,700
March	5,000	3,200
April	5,500	3,000
May	7,000	4,100
June	2,600	2,300
July	2,000	1,500
August	6,000	2,700

Required:

1. Estimate the total monthly fixed overhead cost and the variable cost per unit using the
   (a) High-low method.
   (b) Scattergraph method.
2. **Interpretive Question** Which method is more accurate? Why?

P21-3 The High-Low and Scattergraph Methods of Analysis

Harvey Company makes bed linens. During the first 6 months of 1984, it had the following production costs.

Month	Units Produced	Total Cost
January	10,000	$34,000
February	20,000	50,000
March	15,000	45,000
April	8,000	26,000
May	17,000	47,000
June	12,000	37,000

Required:

1. Use the high-low method to compute the monthly fixed cost and the variable cost per unit produced.
2. Plot the costs on a scattergraph.
3. **Interpretive Question** Based on your scattergraph, do you think the fixed costs and variable rate determined in part (1) are accurate? Why?

P21-4 The Contribution-Margin Income Statement

Early in 1985, Dunlop Company (a retailing firm) sent the following income statement to its stockholders.

Dunlop Company
Income Statement
for the Year Ended December 31, 1984

Sales Revenue (1,000 units)	$60,000	
Less Cost of Goods Sold (variable)	40,000	
Gross Margin		$20,000
Less Operating Expenses:		
Selling	$ 6,000	
Administrative	4,000	
Depreciation (fixed)	1,000	
Insurance (fixed)	50	
Utilities ($20 fixed and $30 variable)	50	(11,100)
Net Income		$ 8,900

Required:

1. Prepare a contribution-margin income statement. (Assume that the fixed components of the selling and administrative expenses are $3,000 and $2,000, respectively.)
2. How many units must Dunlop sell to break even?
3. **Interpretive Question** Why is a contribution-margin income statement helpful to management?

P21-5 The Functional and Contribution-Margin Income Statements

Wayne Boat Company is a retail outlet for customized speedboats. The average cost to the company of a boat is $12,500. Wayne includes a markup of 30 percent of cost in the sales price. In 1984, Wayne sold 33 boats and finished the year with the same amount of inventory it had at the beginning of the year. Additional operating costs for the year were as follows:

Selling Expenses:	
Advertising (fixed)	$ 500 per month
Commissions (semivariable)	4,500 per month plus 2% of sales
Depreciation (fixed)	300 per month
Utilities (fixed)	150 per month
Freight on Delivery (variable)	100 per boat
Administrative Expenses:	
Salaries (fixed)	$4,000 per month
Depreciation (fixed)	300 per month
Utilities (fixed)	150 per month
Clerical (variable)	25 per sale

Required:

1. Prepare a traditional income statement using the functional approach.

2. Prepare an income statement using the contribution-margin format.

3. **Interpretive Question** Which statement is more useful for decision making? Why?

P21-6 The Contribution-Margin and Functional Income Statements

The following information is available for Carl Rae Company for 1984.

Sales Revenue (at $20 per unit)	$151,200
Fixed Manufacturing Costs	24,000
Variable Manufacturing Costs (at $8 per unit)	60,480
Fixed Selling Expenses	70,000
Variable Selling Expenses (at $2 per unit)	15,120

Required:

1. Prepare a contribution-margin income statement.

2. Prepare a functional income statement.

3. Calculate the number of units sold.

4. Calculate the contribution margin per unit.

5. Calculate the number of units that must be sold to break even.

6. Calculate markup as a percentage of manufacturing costs.

7. **Interpretive Question** Why is a knowledge of the contribution margin more useful than a knowledge of the markup per unit when management has to make a decision about profitability?

P21-7 The Contribution-Margin Income Statement and Break-Even Calculations

Fowler Widget Corporation pays its sales personnel a 20 percent commission on each sale made. Fowler's other costs and expenses are as follows:

Rent	$ 1,500 per month
Administrative Salaries	40,000 per year
Total Production Costs	53,000 in 1985 50,000 in 1984

During 1984 and 1985, Fowler's production totaled 1,400 units ($140,000) and 1,500 units ($150,000), respectively.

Required:

1. Assuming that miscellaneous overhead includes both fixed and variable components, prepare a contribution-margin income statement for 1985.

2. Compute Fowler's break-even point in total units and total dollars.

3. Compute Fowler's break-even point in units, assuming that the company decided to pay sales personnel fixed salaries totaling $30,000 per year instead of a 20 percent commission.

4. **Interpretive Question** If Fowler expects sales to increase, which method of paying sales personnel would be more profitable—a fixed salary of $30,000 or a 20 percent commission?

P21-8 Unifying Problem: The High-Low Method and the Contribution-Margin Income Statement

Kenny's Shoe Company has determined that the number of pairs of shoes made and the total manufacturing costs for the past 6 months were as follows:

Month	Pairs Produced	Manufacturing Costs
July	2,000	$ 8,000
August	4,000	11,000
September	3,000	10,500
October	5,000	14,000
November	2,500	9,200
December	6,000	15,000

Required:

1. Use the high-low method to determine Kenny's fixed and variable manufacturing costs.

2. Assume that all of Kenny's sales personnel work on a commission basis and receive $2 for every pair of shoes sold. Shoes sell for $10 a pair. If there are no additional administrative or selling expenses in the company, how many pairs of shoes must Kenny's sell during a year to break even?

3. Prepare a contribution-margin income statement, assuming that Kenny's sells 10,000 pairs of shoes a year at $10 per pair.

P21-9 Unifying Problem: The High–Low Method, Contribution Margins, and Analysis

Fuji Corporation publishes two major magazines: *Star Life* and *Weekly News*. During 1984, *Star Life* sold 3 million copies at $1.00 each, and *Weekly News* sold 2.1 million copies at $1.10 each. Fuji accumulated the following cost information.

	Star Life		Weekly News	
Month	**Copies Produced**	**Manu-facturing Cost**	**Copies Produced**	**Manu-facturing Cost**
January . . .	400,000	$170,000	300,000	$170,000
February .	300,000	150,000	150,000	105,000
March	400,000	180,000	130,000	100,000
April	200,000	120,000	120,000	90,000
May	250,000	140,000	200,000	130,000
June	200,000	125,000	250,000	150,000
July	240,000	130,000	150,000	110,000
August . . .	200,000	130,000	200,000	135,000
September	180,000	110,000	150,000	105,000
October . .	230,000	130,000	150,000	108,000
November	200,000	125,000	150,000	115,000
December .	200,000	126,000	150,000	112,500

Required:

1. Use the high–low method to estimate the variable and fixed manufacturing costs of each magazine. (Round per-unit variable costs to three decimal places.)
2. If all selling expenses are fixed and they total $500,000 for *Star Life* and $400,000 for *Weekly News*, prepare contribution-margin income statements for the two magazines at sales of 3 million copies each.
3. Which magazine is more profitable at sales of 2 million copies?
4. **Interpretive Question** If the same total dollar amount spent on either magazine will result in the same number of new subscriptions, which magazine should be advertised?

SUPPLEMENT

Least Squares Analysis

least squares method *a method of segregating the fixed and variable portions of a semivariable cost; the regression line, a line of averages, is statistically fitted through all cost points so that the sum of the squared errors of the costs predicted by the line is minimized*

The least squares method is probably the most accurate method of determinining the fixed and variable portions of a semivariable cost. Like the scattergraph, the least squares method fits a straight line through all points on a graph. However, instead of visually fitting the regression line through the cost points, it uses statistical analysis to guarantee that the line is the best possible fit for the points.

The formula for the least squares method is based on the equation for a straight line.

$$Y = a + bX$$

In this equation, Y represents the total predicted cost; a represents the intercept and, if in the relevant range, the fixed cost; b represents the variable rate or the slope of the line; and X represents the activity level. Using cost and activity level data, this method involves the use of simultaneous equations to find the values of a and b. Once computed, these values can be combined with the projected activity level, X, to predict total future costs, Y. For example, if the values of a and b were computed to be $200 and $5, respectively, for an estimated activity level of 100 direct-labor hours, we would find that

$$\begin{aligned} \text{total predicted cost} &= \$200 + \$5(100 \text{ hours}) \\ &= \$200 + \$500 \\ &= \$700 \end{aligned}$$

Obviously, since the regression line is a line of averages, actual total costs for 100 direct-labor hours might be somewhat different from the predicted cost of $700. The method of least squares, however, attempts to minimize the squared differences between predicted and actual costs. Once a regression line has been fitted to historical data, the fixed and variable costs represented by the line can be used to predict the level of future costs.

In calculating the estimates of a (the fixed portion) and b (the slope, or variable rate), the following two simultaneous equations are used.

$$(1)\ \Sigma XY = a\Sigma X + b\Sigma X^2$$

$$(2)\ \Sigma Y = na + b\Sigma X$$

where

a = fixed cost

b = variable cost

n = number of observations

Σ = summation sign (which means the sum of all available historical data)

X = activity level, or independent variable

Y = total (predicted) semivariable cost, or dependent variable

The method of least squares is most easily performed with calculators or computers. By use of a standard computer program, large amounts of data can be analyzed very quickly. Indeed, one way to pursue this discussion would be to describe and interpret the typical output from a computerized application of least squares analysis. Instead, we will work through a very simple example, so that you can understand how least squares compares with the methods discussed previously.

To illustrate the concept of least squares, we return again to the electricity cost data used in the chapter to describe the scattergraph and high–low methods. (Note that the data are given for only 6 months; thus, the resulting regression equation will be less accurate than it would be with more data.)

Month	Total Electricity Cost	Total Direct-Labor Hours
January	$ 70,000	7,000
February	60,000	6,000
March	100,000	12,000
April	80,000	6,000
May	120,000	18,000
June	110,000	14,000

The first step is to compute the product of X and Y and the square of the X's and then add each column of variables.

X	Y	XY	X^2
7,000	$ 70,000	$ 490,000,000	49,000,000
6,000	60,000	360,000,000	36,000,000
12,000	100,000	1,200,000,000	144,000,000
6,000	80,000	480,000,000	36,000,000
18,000	120,000	2,160,000,000	324,000,000
14,000	110,000	1,540,000,000	196,000,000
63,000	$540,000	$6,230,000,000	785,000,000

Next, these amounts would be substituted into the two simultaneous equations.

(1) $(\Sigma XY = a\Sigma X + b\Sigma X^2)$
$\$6{,}230{,}000{,}000 = 63{,}000a + 785{,}000{,}000b$

(2) $(\Sigma Y = na + b\Sigma X)$
$\$540{,}000 = 6a + 63{,}000b$

When solving two simultaneous equations, you must eliminate one of the unknowns, either a or b in this case. In our example, you can accomplish this most easily by multiplying the second equation by 10,500 (63,000 ÷ 6) and then subtracting the second equation from the first. These calculations are

Equation (1): $\$6{,}230{,}000{,}000 = 63{,}000a + 785{,}000{,}000b$

Multiply equation (2) by 10,500:
$\$5{,}670{,}000{,}000 = 63{,}000a + 661{,}500{,}000b$

Subtract equation (2) from (1): $\$560{,}000{,}000 = 123{,}500{,}000b$
$b = \$4.534$

Now, by substituting \$4.534 for b in equation (2), the value of a can be determined.

$$\$540{,}000 = 6a = 63{,}000\ (\$4.534)$$
$$6a = \$254{,}358$$
$$a = \$42{,}393$$

Therefore, assuming no relevant-range constraints, the fixed electricity cost per month is \$42,393 and the variable cost is \$4.534 per direct-labor hour. These estimates of fixed and variable costs ensure that the regression line has been fitted to the points as closely as possible.

The method of least squares is essentially equivalent to simple regression analysis, which is taught in most elementary statistics courses and is programmed into many hand calculators.

As the following table shows, the least squares method provides predictions that are quite close to those derived using the scattergraph and high-low methods.

Method	**Formula**	**Estimated Cost**
Scattergraph	\$40,000 + 10,000 (\$4.44)	\$84,400
High-low	\$30,000 + 10,000 (\$5.00)	\$80,000
Least squares	\$42,393 + 10,000 (\$4.534)	\$87,733

DISCUSSION QUESTIONS, EXERCISES, AND PROBLEMS

Discussion Questions

15 How does the method of least squares differ from the scattergraph method?

16 Would the solution to a least squares equation ever be inappropriate for predicting future costs? If so, when?

Exercises

E21-14 Semivariable Costs—Least Squares Analysis

San Juan Corporation makes waterbeds. During the past 6 months, its production levels for waterbeds and costs were as follows:

Month	Units Produced	Total Cost
July	600	$120,000
August	500	110,000
September	800	145,000
October	700	132,000
November	900	154,000
December	600	115,000

1. Use the least squares method to calculate the fixed and variable elements of San Juan's total costs.
2. Assuming that cost relationships do not change, what would be the total cost of producing 1,000 waterbeds in a month?

E21-15 Semivariable Costs—Least Squares Analysis

Given the following semivariable costs at various levels of production, complete the requirements below.

Month	Units Produced	Semivariable Costs
January	2	$15
February	3	18
March	1	11
April	5	22
May	2	13

1. Using the method of least squares, calculate the monthly fixed and variable components of semivariable costs.
2. Using these estimates, compute the total cost of producing four units in a month.
3. Describe a major advantage and a major disadvantage of the least squares method.

Problems

P21-10 Least Squares Analysis

Arnold Company, manufacturer of motorcycles, has kept detailed records of semivariable overhead expenses for the last 8 months. These overhead expenses appear below, along with corresponding production levels.

Month	Motorcycles Produced	Overhead Costs
1	2,000	$2,500
2	1,500	1,700
3	2,500	3,200
4	2,750	3,000
5	3,500	4,100
6	1,300	2,300
7	1,000	1,500
8	3,000	2,700

Required:
Use the least squares method to calculate total monthly fixed costs and variable costs per unit.

P21-11 Least Squares Analysis of Selling Expenses

During the first 6 months of 1984, White Corporation had the following sales revenue and selling expenses.

Month	Total Sales Revenue (in thousands)	Total Selling Expenses (in thousands)
January	$ 25	$ 9
February	20	8
March	30	10
April	40	12
May	40	12
June	50	14
Totals	$205	$65

Required:
1. Use the least squares method to compute the variable and fixed portions of the selling expenses.
2. What would the total amount of selling expenses be for July if total sales for that month were $60,000? (Assume that $60,000 falls within the relevant range.)
3. What would the total amount of selling expenses be if there were no sales? [Assume that total fixed costs and the variable cost rate calculated in part (1) are appropriate.]

P21-12 The High-Low Method and Least Squares Analysis

Sherwood Corporation makes aluminum fishing boats. During the first 7 months of 1984, its manufacturing costs were as follows:

Month	Units Produced	Manufacturing Costs (in hundreds)
January	20	$60
February	18	55
March	15	51
April	24	68
May	30	79
June	14	48
July	10	41

Required:

1. Use the least squares method to determine Sherwood's total fixed and variable manufacturing costs.
2. Use the high-low method to determine Sherwood's total fixed and variable manufacturing costs.
3. **Interpretive Question** Does it appear that the costs associated with the high and low levels of production are representative of all costs?

P21-13 The Scattergraph and Least Squares Methods

Mary Company, producer of concrete, found that its total repair costs were related to the amount of direct materials used in production. In order to analyze the extent of the relationship, the company plotted on the following graph the repair costs and direct materials used for the period January through July.

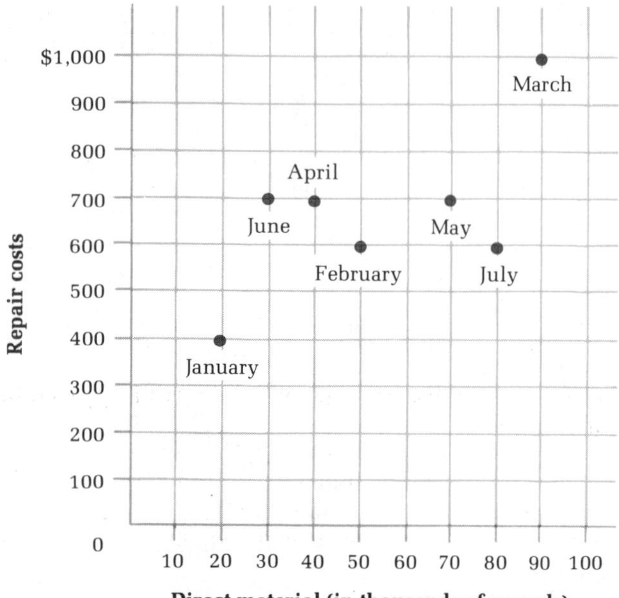

Required:

1. What does the point plotted for June mean?
2. Visually fit a line through the points and determine the fixed and variable components of the monthly repair costs.
3. Use the least squares method to compute the fixed and variable components of the monthly repair costs.
4. **Interpretive Question** Which method would you recommend? Why?

P21-14 The High-Low Method, Least Squares Analysis, and the Contribution-Margin Rate

Mingo Enterprises produces two different kinds of hairdryers. Pertinent information for each dryer is shown below.

	Model A	Model B
Sales Price per Unit	$15.00	$20.00
Variable Costs and Expenses per Unit:		
Materials	2.50	3.00
Labor	5.50	8.00
Selling	4.00	5.00

In addition, the following information concerning overhead costs is available.

	Overhead Costs	
Units Produced	Model A	Model B
5,000	$11,000	$15,000
4,500	10,700	14,400
4,000	10,500	13,900
3,500	10,100	13,100
3,000	9,800	12,400
2,500	9,400	11,600
2,000	9,000	10,100

Required:

1. Use the high-low method to determine which model has the higher contribution margin.
2. Use the least squares method to determine which model has the higher contribution margin.
3. Assuming that model A requires 1.5 machine hours to produce and that model B requires 2 hours to produce, which model should Mingo produce if it is already at full capacity and can sell what it can make?

CHAPTER 22

THIS CHAPTER EXPLAINS:

Three methods of computing break-even points: the contribution-margin, equation, and graphical approaches.

The calculation of target net income.

The changes that occur in C–V–P variables and the effect of these changes on a company's profitability.

The assumptions of C–V–P analysis.

break-even point *the amount of sales or the number of units sold at which total costs equal total revenues: the point at which there is no profit or loss*

cost-volume-profit (C–V–P) analysis *techniques for determining how changes in costs and volume affect the profitability of an organization*

In the last chapter we analyzed costs in terms of their behavior patterns: fixed, variable, and semivariable. We then used those behavior patterns to determine contribution margins and eventually break-even points. Here we will discuss how the analysis of cost behavior patterns allows managers to understand the effects that changes in costs, volumes, and revenues will have on profits. The techniques for studying these relationships are collectively referred to as cost-volume-profit (C–V–P) analysis. They can be used in making decisions about selling prices, production volume, levels of discretionary fixed costs, and so on.

Methods of Cost–Volume–Profit Analysis

There are three common and related ways to perform cost-volume-profit analysis: (1) the contribution-margin approach, (2) the equation approach, and (3) the graphical approach. We will introduce all three techniques, illustrating how each can help management understand how profits change in response to changes in variable costs, fixed costs, sales volume, and the mix of products sold.

THE CONTRIBUTION-MARGIN APPROACH

contribution margin *the difference between total revenues and total variable costs; the portion of sales revenue available to cover fixed costs*

In Chapter 21, we defined the contribution margin as the amount of sales revenue that can be applied to cover fixed costs and provide a profit after variable costs have been deducted from sales revenue. Contribution margin is one of the most important managerial accounting concepts you will study. A great many operating decisions are made on the basis of how contribution margins will be affected. For example, a company may decide to advertise one product more than others because it has a higher contribution margin.

To illustrate the concept of contribution margin, we will use income statement data for Lang Corporation, a small producer of home video games.

Lang Corporation
Contribution Margin Income Statement
for the Month Ended November 30, 1984

	Total	Per Unit
Sales Revenue (1,000 games)	$200,000	$200
Less Variable Costs	110,000	110
Contribution Margin	$ 90,000	$ 90
Less Fixed Costs	63,000	
Net Income	$ 27,000	

per-unit contribution margin *the excess of the sales price of one unit over its variable costs*

As this income statement shows, for internal decision making Lang Corporation computes its contribution margin on a per-unit and total dollar basis. During November, Lang's per-unit contribution margin is $90 and the total contribution margin at a sales volume of 1,000 video games is $90,000.

Computing the break-even sales volume is easy once the unit contribution margin is known. As was illustrated in the last chapter, the break-even point is the amount of sales revenue or the number of units sold at which total costs equal total revenues. The break-even point is equal to the total fixed costs ($63,000) divided by the per-unit contribution margin ($90), or $63,000/$90 = 700 units. In other words, every unit sold adds $90 to the total contribution margin, until Lang Company breaks even at a sales level of 700 video games.

	Total	Per Unit
Sales Revenue (700 games)	$140,000	$200
Less Variable Costs	77,000	110
Contribution Margin	$ 63,000	$ 90
Less Fixed Costs	63,000	
Net Income	$ -0-	

Assuming that fixed costs remain constant, when Lang Company reaches its break-even point the net income will increase by $90 for every additional video game sold. If 701 video games are sold, net income will be $90. If 900 video games are sold, net income will be 200 (900 − 700) times the $90 contribution margin, or $18,000. We can check these figures with the calculations shown on the next page.

	At 701 Units		At 900 Units	
	Total	Per Unit	Total	Per Unit
Sales Revenue	$140,200	$200	$180,000	$200
Less Variable Costs ..	77,110	110	99,000	110
Contribution Margin .	$ 63,090	$ 90	$ 81,000	$ 90
Less Fixed Costs	63,000		63,000	
Net Income	$ 90		$ 18,000	

On the basis of these calculations, we can see that when the break-even point is attained, net income increases by the per-unit contribution margin for each additional unit sold. It is not necessary for a company to prepare a series of income statements to know what the net income will be at various sales volumes. Rather, management can simply multiply the expected excess of units sold over the break-even point by the per-unit contribution margin to identify the expected profit at any level of sales.

The Contribution-Margin Ratio

contribution-margin ratio *the percentage of sales revenue left after variable costs are deducted*

The contribution margin may be expressed on a percentage basis as well as a per-unit or total dollar basis. Knowing the contribution-margin ratio, which is the percentage of sales revenue left after variable costs are deducted, management can compare the profitability of various products. For example, if product A has a 45 percent contribution margin and product B's margin is only 30 percent, the company should emphasize product A, assuming that other factors are equal.

To illustrate the calculation of contribution-margin ratios, we refer again to the Lang Corporation example. If 1,000 games are expected to be sold, the ratio would be computed as follows:

	Total	Per Unit	Percentage
Sales Revenue (1,000 games)	$200,000	$200	100%
Less Variable Costs	110,000	110	55%
Contribution Margin	$ 90,000	$ 90	45%
Less Fixed Costs	63,000		
Net Income	$ 27,000		

The contribution-margin ratio is 45 percent of sales revenue, which means that for every $1.00 increase in sales revenue, the contribution margin increases by 45 percent of $1.00, or $0.45. If fixed costs are already covered, net income will also increase by $0.45 for every $1.00 increase in sales.

With contribution-margin ratios, it is easy to analyze the impact of future changes in sales on net income. For example, if Lang's management estimates that sales will increase by $20,000, it can apply the contribution-margin ratio of 45 percent and estimate that net income will increase by $9,000 ($20,000 × 0.45). The higher the contribution-margin ratio, the larger the share of each additional dollar of sales that will go toward covering fixed costs and increasing net income.

Variable Costs Versus Fixed Costs

Contribution margins highlight the different effects that variable and fixed costs have on profitability. That is, they help answer such questions as "Is it better to have high variable costs and low fixed costs, or vice versa?" and "Should a company seek a cost structure that emphasizes fixed costs or variable costs?" To answer these questions we will use the following two examples.

	Company A			Company B		
	Total	Per Unit	Percentage	Total	Per Unit	Percentage
Sales Revenue (1,000 units) . . .	$100,000	$100	100%	$100,000	$100	100%
Less Variable Costs	50,000	50	50%	20,000	20	20%
Contribution Margin	$ 50,000	$ 50	50%	$ 80,000	$ 80	80%
Less Fixed Costs	30,000			60,000		
Net Income	$ 20,000			$ 20,000		

As these examples show, the two companies have the same net income at sales of 1,000 units. However, this is the only level of sales at which net income will be equal. For every unit sold over 1,000 units, Company A's net income will increase by only $50 (the per-unit contribution margin), whereas Company B's net income will increase by $80. For sales under 1,000 units, Company A's net income decreases by only $50 per unit whereas Company B's decreases by $80.

The above example indicates that there is no simple answer to the question about which type of cost structure is best. Each company is different, so several factors must be considered: whether sales are expected to increase or decrease from the current level, how stable sales volumes are, and whether management is willing to take risks. In our example, if sales are expected to stay above 1,000 units in the future, Company B's cost structure is better; if sales are expected to decrease, Company A has the better cost structure. Certainly, low fixed costs and high variable costs (Company A's cost structure) is a much more conservative cost structure than low variable costs and high fixed costs (Company B's cost structure). Thus, if management is not willing to take risks, it will want its costs to be variable rather than fixed, whenever possible. In our example, Company A will experience much narrower swings in net income than will Company B. Company B will be more profitable in good times but will have higher losses in bad times.

TO SUMMARIZE The contribution margin is the amount of sales revenue left to cover fixed costs and provide a profit after variable costs have been deducted from sales. The contribution margin can be expressed in total, on a per-unit basis, or on a percentage basis. When fixed costs remain constant and the break-even point has been reached, net income increases by the amount of the per-unit contribution margin for every additional unit sold. The break-even point (expressed in units) is equal to total fixed costs divided by the per-unit contribution margin. A company with a low level of variable costs and high fixed costs will have much wider swings in net income in response to changes in sales volume than will a company with a high level of variable costs and low fixed costs. Thus, a conservative cost structure is one with high variable costs and low fixed costs, and a risky cost structure is one with high fixed costs and low variable costs.

THE EQUATION APPROACH

As discussed in Chapter 21, the break-even point in equation form is the level of sales where

revenues = variable costs + fixed costs

A firm's profit, then, is equal to the excess of revenues over variable and fixed costs, or

profit = revenues − (variable costs + fixed costs)

To illustrate the use of these two equations, we will return to the Lang Corporation example. Remember that Lang Corporation sells its video games for $200, incurs a variable cost of $110 per game, and has fixed costs totaling $63,000. If x is the number of games that needs to be sold to break even, the equation is

$$\begin{aligned} \text{revenues} &= \text{variable costs} + \text{fixed costs} \\ \$200x &= \$110x + \$63{,}000 \\ \$90x &= \$63{,}000 \\ x &= 700 \end{aligned}$$

Like the contribution-margin approach, the equation approach shows that Lang Corporation will break even after selling 700 video games. When the break-even point in units sold is known, the break-even point in sales dollars can be computed. This is done by multiplying the number of units sold times the per-unit sales price. At sales of 700 units (the break-even point), total dollar sales are $140,000 (700 × $200).

Given the break-even point, we can now use the equation to compute profits. The equation shows that total profits at sales of 1,000 games are $27,000, the same amount that was derived using the contribution-margin approach.

$$\begin{aligned} \text{profits} &= \text{revenues} - (\text{variable costs} + \text{fixed costs}) \\ &= \$200(1{,}000 \text{ games}) - [\$110(1{,}000 \text{ games}) + \$63{,}000] \\ &= \$200{,}000 - (\$110{,}000 + \$63{,}000) \\ &= \$27{,}000 \end{aligned}$$

THE GRAPHICAL APPROACH

Cost-volume-profit relationships can also be expressed in graphical form. In fact, the graphical format may be the most useful because it allows managers to examine cost and revenue data over a range of activity rather than at a single volume.

EXHIBIT 22-1 A Cost-Volume-Profit Graph

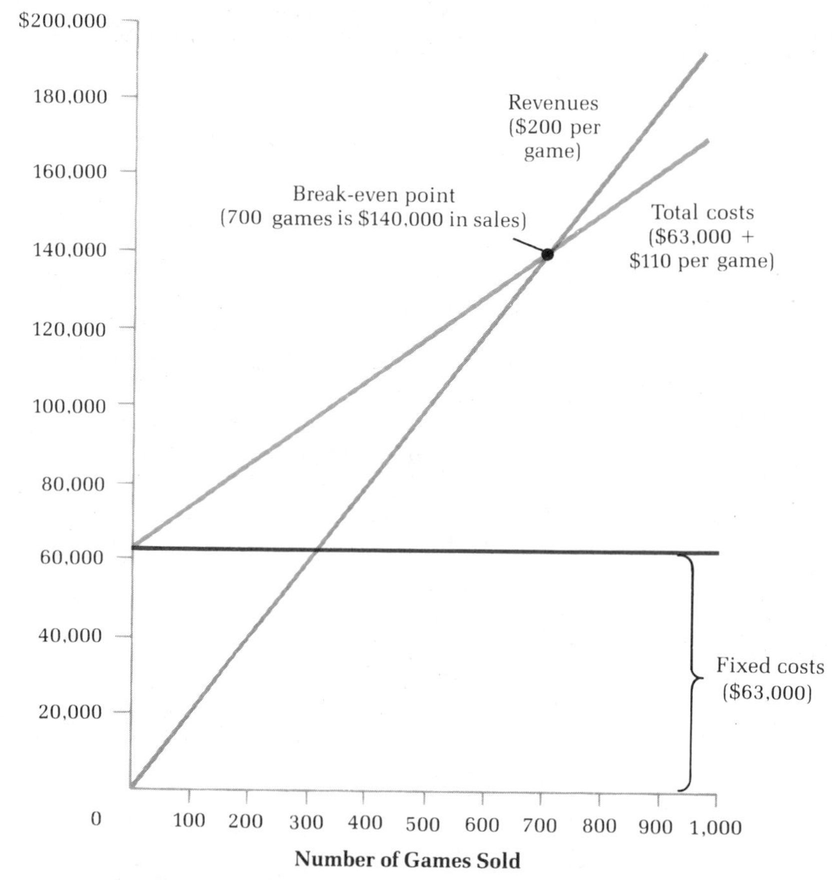

Graphical C-V-P analysis usually involves preparing a graph on which volume or activity level is shown on the horizontal axis and total dollars of sales or costs are shown on the vertical axis. Lines are then drawn representing total fixed costs, total costs, and total revenues. Exhibit 22-1 is a cost-volume-profit graph for Lang Corporation's video games.

The graph shows that total fixed costs are $63,000. (We are assuming that fixed costs do not change with volume changes between 0 and 1,000 games.) Total costs are $74,000 at 100 games [$63,000 + ($110 × 100 games)], $85,000 at 200 games [$63,000 + ($110 × 200 games)], $96,000 at 300 games [$63,000 + ($110 × 300 games)], and so on. Total revenues are $20,000 at 100 games ($200 × 100 games), $40,000 at 200 games, $60,000 at 300 games, and so on. The break-even point is 700 games, the point at which total revenues equal total costs.

As shown in Exhibit 22-2, the graphical format can also be used to isolate such items of interest as total variable costs, total fixed costs, the area in which losses occur, the area in which profits will be realized, and the break-even point.

EXHIBIT 22-2 **Cost-Volume-Profit Graphs**

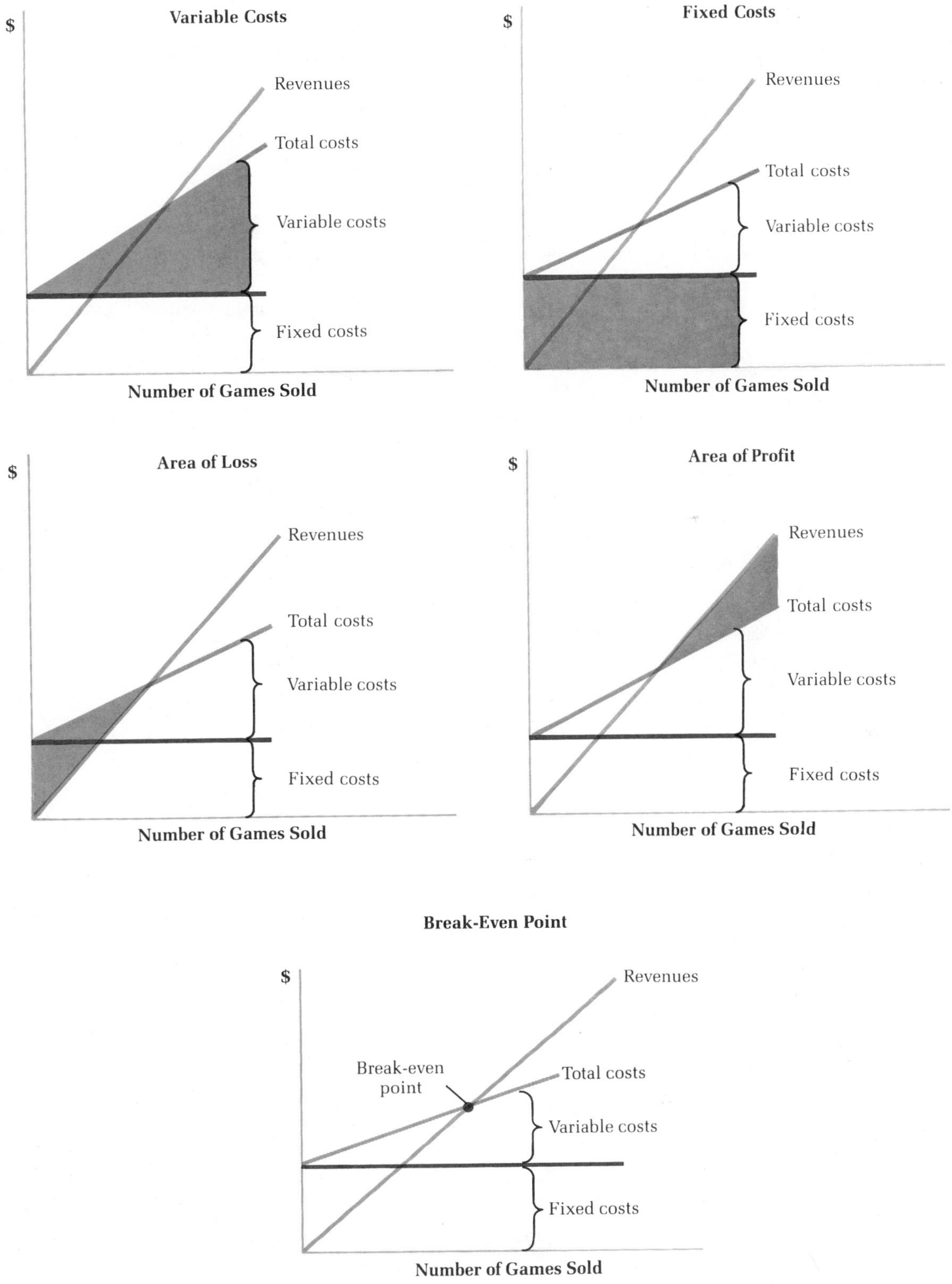

As you can see, cost–volume–profit graphs can be very useful. Because they illustrate a wide range of activity, management can quickly determine how much profit or loss will be realized at various levels of sales.

An Alternative Graphical Approach

The C–V–P graph we have discussed is the one used by most companies. Two other graphical formats are also used in C–V–P analyses. The first of these reverses the order of fixed and variable costs, placing fixed costs above variable costs. When this approach is used, the "revenues" and "total cost" lines are the same as those shown in Exhibit 22–1, but variable costs occupy the lower portion of the graph and fixed costs comprise the upper. This allows us to show the contribution margin on the graph. Exhibit 22–3 is prepared in this way.

In Exhibit 22–3, the contribution margin is depicted as the difference between the variable-cost line and the revenues line. The break-even point occurs where revenues intersect fixed costs and the contribution margin is exactly equal to total fixed costs (700 games). Sales beyond the break-even point result in a profit; sales below 700 games result in a loss.

EXHIBIT 22–3 A Cost–Volume–Profit Graph (Alternative Approach)

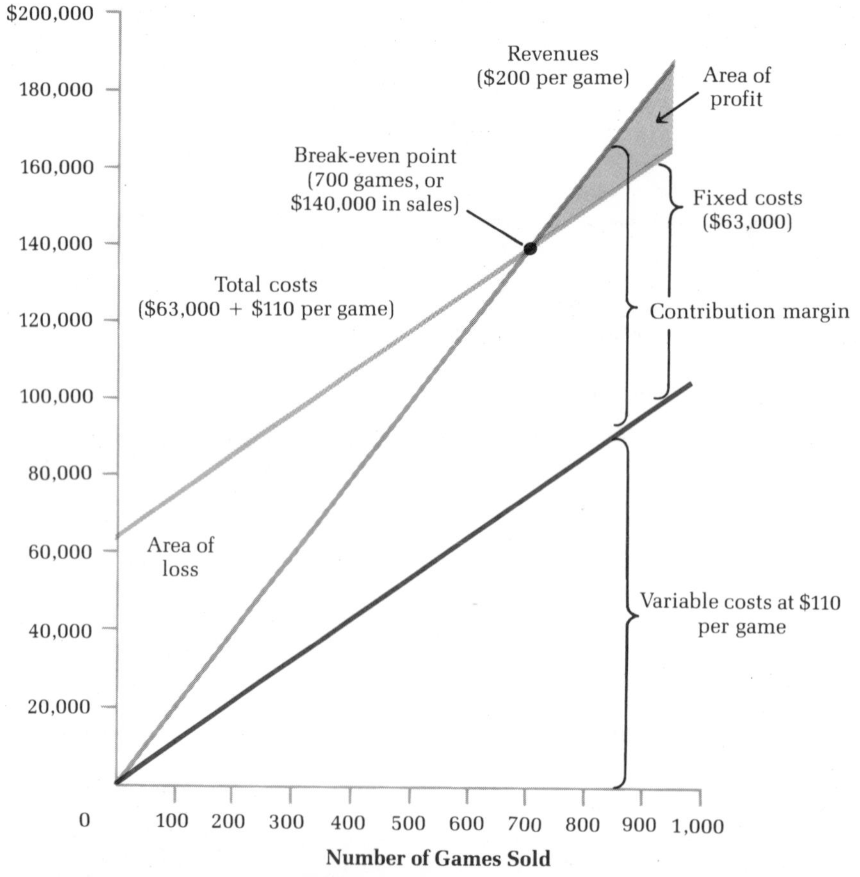

The Profit Graph

profit graph *a graph that shows how profits vary with changes in volume*

A third graphical approach is the profit graph, which plots only profits and losses and omits costs and revenues. Exhibit 22-4 shows a profit graph for Lang Corporation.

Notice that the horizontal axis of the profit graph is the same as those of the previous graphs. The vertical axis represents profits and it includes negative numbers to represent losses. As long as the contribution margin is positive, the maximum amount of losses that can occur is at a zero level of sales. With no sales, total losses will be $63,000, the amount of the fixed costs. With the axes properly labeled, the profit line is drawn as follows:

1. Locate the total fixed costs on the vertical axis at zero sales volume (in this case, − $63,000).
2. Locate the points of profit or loss at other levels of activity. For example, at sales of 700 games, profits are zero [$140,000 − ($63,000 + $77,000)]. At sales of 1,000 games, profits are $27,000 [$200,000 − ($63,000 + $110,000)].
3. After two or three profit or loss points have been identified, draw a line through the points back to the vertical axis.

Because of its simplicity, the profit graph is widely used for making comparisons of competing projects. It has the disadvantage, however, that it does not show how costs vary with changes in sales volume.

EXHIBIT 22-4 **A Profit Graph**

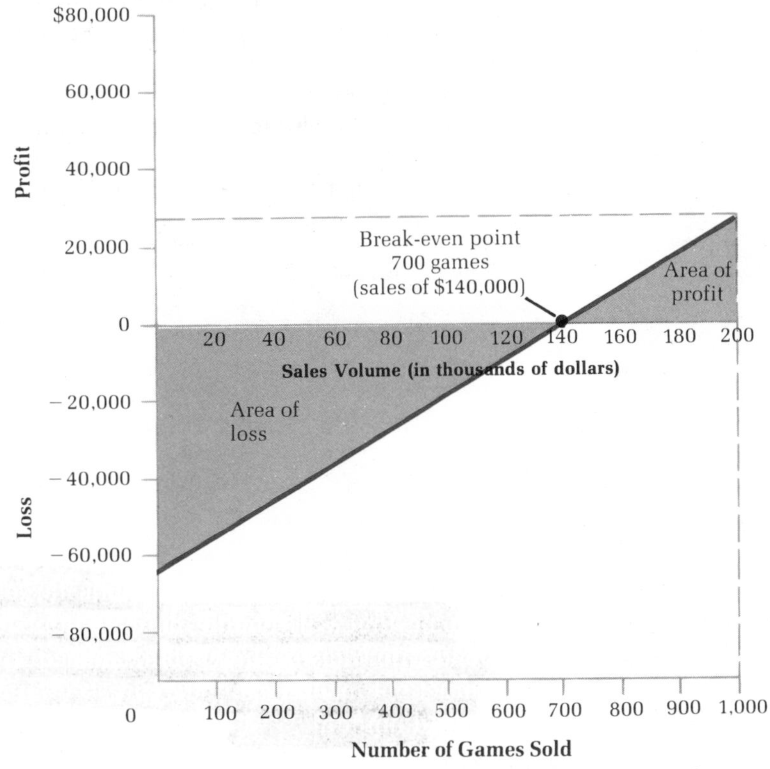

A COMPARISON OF THE THREE C–V–P APPROACHES

The three C–V–P approaches (contribution margin, equation, and graphical) are really just alternative representations of the same calculations. In fact, as the following break-even analysis shows, the contribution margin is derived in a step of the equation approach: In Step 2 below, "revenues − variable costs" equals the contribution margin, which at the break-even point equals the fixed costs.

Break-Even Formula	Lang Company Example
1. revenues = fixed costs + variable costs	1. \$200x = \$63,000 + \$110x
2. revenues − variable costs = fixed costs	2. \$90x = \$63,000
3. $\dfrac{\text{fixed costs}}{\text{total revenues} - \text{variable costs}}$ = break-even point	3. $x = \dfrac{\$63{,}000}{\$90} = 700$ units

Because the three approaches are similar, you may use whichever one appeals to you. We personally prefer the equation approach for making computations (because it is more precise), but we like graphs to illustrate and clarify certain concepts. Therefore, with the exception of the first illustration in the next section, we will use the equation approach in the remainder of this chapter.

TO SUMMARIZE In addition to the contribution-margin approach, cost–volume–profit analysis can be performed by using either equations or graphs. Using equations, the break-even point occurs where revenues = fixed costs + variable costs. Profit is equal to the excess of revenues over total costs. The graphical approaches can be useful because they highlight cost–volume–profit relationships over wide ranges of activity. The most common graphical approach involves plotting fixed costs as a horizontal line with variable costs above fixed costs. An alternative approach highlighting the contribution margin involves plotting fixed costs on top of variable costs. A profit graph is much simpler, but it does not show how costs vary with changes in sales volume. The C–V–P approaches are all based on the same calculations.

Target Net Income

target net income *a profit level desired by management*

Once a break-even point is determined, management often wants to know how many units must be sold or how much service must be performed to reach a target net income.[1] This target usually represents an amount of income that will enable management to reach its objectives—paying dividends, purchasing new plant and equipment, or paying off existing loans. Target net income can be expressed either as a percentage of revenues or as a fixed amount.

[1] In this chapter we are using net income to mean pretax income.

From the Lang Corporation example, we know that the company will break even after selling 700 video games a month. How many games must Lang sell to earn a monthly profit of $36,000? As the following analyses show, all three C-V-P approaches reveal that 1,100 games must be sold.

The Contribution-Margin Approach

Number of games needed to break even	700
Additional games needed to earn $36,000 profit:	
$\frac{\text{desired profit}}{\text{unit contribution margin}} = \frac{\$36{,}000}{\$90} = 400$	400
Total games needed	1,100

or

$$\frac{\text{fixed costs} + \text{desired profit}}{\text{unit contribution margin}} = \frac{\$63{,}000 + \$36{,}000}{\$90} = 1{,}100 \text{ games}$$

The Equation Approach

$$\text{revenues} = \text{fixed costs} + \text{variable costs} + \text{desired profit}$$
$$\$200x = \$63{,}000 + 110x + \$36{,}000$$
$$\$90x = \$99{,}000$$
$$x = 1{,}100 \text{ games}$$

The Graphical Approach

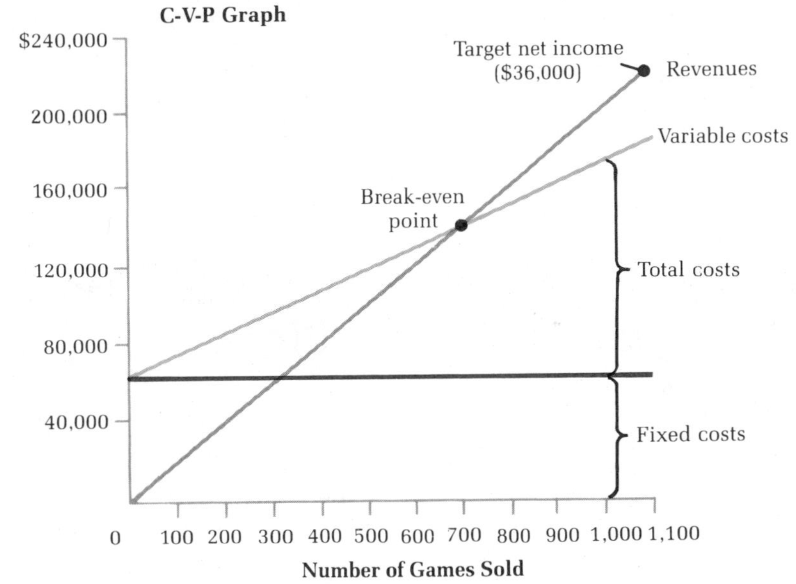

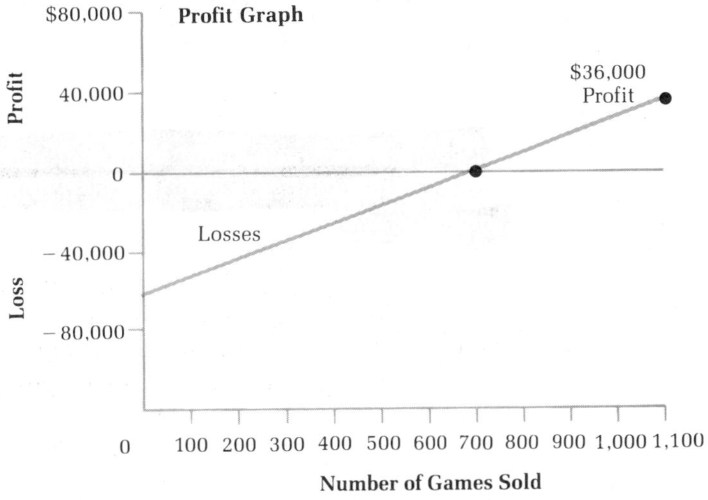

return on sales revenue *a measure of operating performance; computed by dividing net income by total sales revenue*

A fixed dollar amount of profit, such as the $36,000 that would be earned by selling 1,100 video games, is probably the most useful goal for many companies. However, because investors often evaluate companies partially on the basis of their return on sales revenue (or simply "return on sales"), management may want to earn a certain percentage return as opposed to a fixed amount of income. For example, if a company decided to try for a 20 percent return on sales, the computation would be

$$\begin{aligned}
\text{desired profit} &= \text{desired rate of return} \times \text{revenues} \\
\text{revenues} &= \text{fixed costs} + \text{variable costs} + \text{desired profit} \\
\$200x &= \$63{,}000 + \$110x + 20\%(\$200x) \\
\$200x &= \$63{,}000 + \$110x + \$40x \\
\$200x - \$110x - \$40x &= \$63{,}000 \\
\$50x &= \$63{,}000 \\
x &= 1{,}260 \text{ games}
\end{aligned}$$

The 20 percent return on revenues would be earned after selling 1,260 video games. For comparison purposes, the target net incomes of $36,000 and 20 percent of revenues have been plotted in Exhibit 22-5.

The Effect of Changes in Costs, Prices, and Volume on Profitability

The basic techniques of C-V-P analysis—break-even and target net income calculations—are used almost daily by management in making business decisions. Managers must be adept at evaluating the effects on profitability of the five most common changes in C-V-P variables: (1) the level of fixed costs, (2) the level of variable costs, (3) the sales price, (4) the sales volume, or number of units sold, and (5) combinations of these variables.

CHANGES IN FIXED COSTS

If all other factors remain constant, an increase in fixed costs always increases the number of units needed both to break even and to reach a target net income. To illustrate, we will assume that Lang Corporation's fixed costs increase from $63,000 to $81,000. The increase in fixed costs could be caused by the building of a new plant, an increase in management's salaries, or a number of other factors. The new break-even point is computed as follows:

$$\begin{aligned}
\$200x &= \$110x + \$81{,}000 \\
\$90x &= \$81{,}000 \\
x &= 900
\end{aligned}$$

EXHIBIT 22-5 **Target Net Incomes**

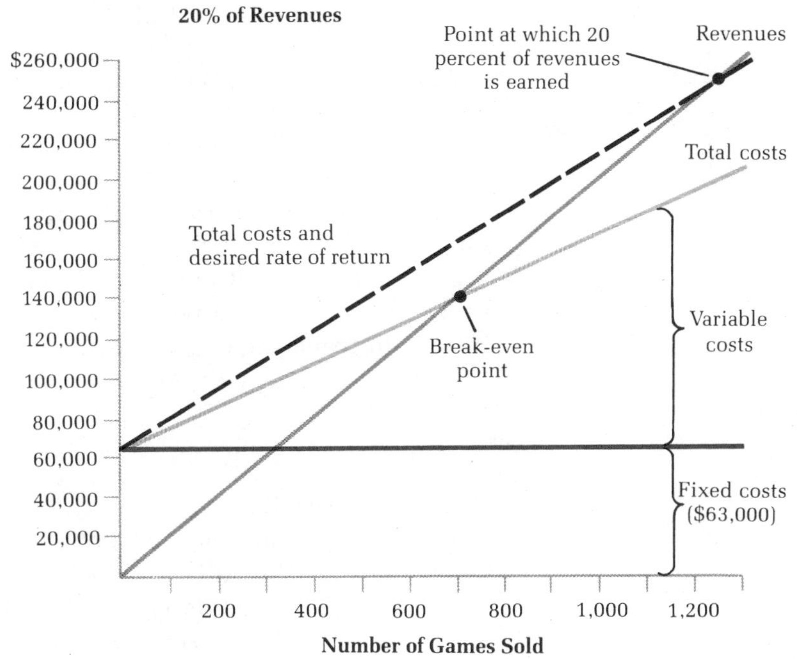

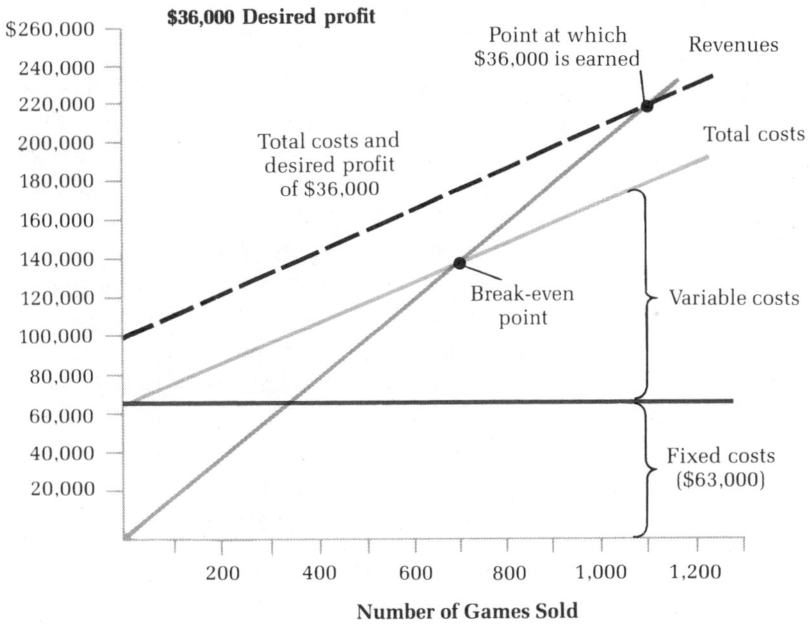

Because of the added fixed costs, the break-even point increases from 700 to 900 video games. In order to earn the targeted $36,000, Lang must now sell 1,300 video games instead of 1,100.

$$\begin{aligned} \$200x &= \$110x + \$81{,}000 + \$36{,}000 \\ \$90x &= \$117{,}000 \\ x &= 1{,}300 \text{ video games} \end{aligned}$$

The computations are quite simple. In fact, you may have found them unnecessary, realizing that if the fixed costs increase by $18,000 ($81,000 − $63,000) and the unit contribution margin is $90 per game, 200 additional games ($18,000 ÷ $90) will have to be sold in order to break even (700 + 200), or to reach the target net income (1,100 + 200).

CHANGES IN VARIABLE COSTS

Like an increase in fixed costs, an increase in variable costs also increases the number of units needed both to break even and to reach target net income levels, when all other factors remain constant.

Suppose that variable costs increased from $110 per game to $130 per game because of increased wages for factory personnel, increased costs of direct materials, or other factors. With this increase, the break-even point and the target net income would be calculated as follows (assuming that fixed costs are again $63,000 and rounding to the nearest dollar).

Break-even point:

$$\begin{aligned} \$200x &= \$130x + \$63{,}000 \\ \$70x &= \$63{,}000 \\ x &= 900 \text{ games} \end{aligned}$$

Target net income of $36,000:

$$\begin{aligned} \$200x &= \$130x + \$63{,}000 + \$36{,}000 \\ \$70x &= \$99{,}000 \\ x &= 1{,}414 \text{ games} \end{aligned}$$

The increase in variable costs reduces the unit contribution margin (from $90 to $70), which means that more games must be sold to break even and to maintain the same profit level. With a unit contribution margin of $90 the company could make a $36,000 profit after selling 1,100 games; with a unit contribution margin of only $70, an additional 314 (1,414 − 1,100) games must be sold to earn a $36,000 profit.

CHANGES IN THE SALES PRICE

If all other variables remain constant, an increase in the sales price decreases the sales volume needed to break even, and hence to reach a target net income. This is because an increase in price increases the unit contribution margin per video game and decreases the number of games that must be sold to earn the same amount of profit.

To illustrate, we will assume that the demand for video games is overwhelming and that the company cannot produce games fast enough. To reduce the demand, or at least to increase profits, a decision is made to increase the price from $200 to $230 per game. As a result of the price increase, the number of games that must be sold to break even and reach target net income decreases (assume fixed costs of $63,000 and variable costs of $110 per game).

Break-even point:
$230x = $110x + $63,000
$120x = $63,000
x = 525 games

Target net income of $36,000:
$230x = $110x + $63,000 + $36,000
$120x = $99,000
x = 825 games

With this price increase of $20 per game, the new break-even point is 525 games and the new target net income level is 825 games. Obviously, a decrease in the price would have the opposite effect: it would increase the number of units needed both to break even and to reach the target net income.

Thus, an increase in sales price increases the contribution margin, which reduces the number of games required to break even. A decrease in sales price decreases the contribution margin, which increases the number of games required to break even.

CHANGES IN THE SALES VOLUME

As you probably have noticed, the sales volume (the number of games to be sold) for both the break-even point and the target net income has changed with each change in one of the other variables. When other variables remain constant, an increase in the sales volume will result in an increase in income. Very simply, the more games sold, the higher the profit. The degree of change in profits resulting from volume changes depends on the size of the unit contribution margin. When the unit contribution margin is high, a slight change in volume results in a dramatic change in profit. With a lower unit contribution margin, the change in profit is less.

SIMULTANEOUS CHANGES IN SEVERAL VARIABLES

Thus far, we have examined changes in only one variable at a time. Individual changes are quite rare, however; more often, several variables, all affecting profits, change at the same time. Such simultaneous changes can be entered into the calculations quite easily, as we will show with the Lang Corporation example. Let us recap the data.

Initial Example		**Later Changes**
Sales Price per Game	$200	$230 (to decrease demand or increase profits)
Variable Costs per Game	$110	$130 (because of increased wages or direct-materials costs)
Fixed Costs	$63,000	$81,000 (because of new plant costs or administrative salary increases)

If all three variables were to change simultaneously, the computation for break-even point and target net income level would be as shown on the next page.

	Initial Data	Revised Data
Break-even point	$\$200x = \$110x + \$63{,}000$	$\$230x = \$130x + \$81{,}000$
	$\$200x - \$110x = \$63{,}000$	$\$230x - \$130x = \$81{,}000$
	$\$90x = \$63{,}000$	$\$100x = \$81{,}000$
	$x = 700$ games	$x = 810$ games
Target net income	$\$200x = \$110x + \$63{,}000 + \$36{,}000$	$\$230x = \$130x + \$81{,}000 + \$36{,}000$
	$\$200x - \$110x = \$63{,}000 + \$36{,}000$	$\$230x - \$130x = \$81{,}000 + \$36{,}000$
	$\$90x = \$99{,}000$	$\$100x = \$127{,}000$
	$x = 1{,}100$ games	$x = 1{,}270$ games

TO SUMMARIZE The calculations of break-even points and target net income levels are basic applications of C–V–P analysis. They show the effects of changes in costs, revenues, and volume on profits.

Assumptions of Cost–Volume–Profit Analysis

C–V–P analysis is an extremely useful tool for assisting management in making short-term revenue and cost decisions. There are, however, some limiting assumptions of C–V–P analysis that must not be overlooked.

THE SALES MIX ASSUMPTION

sales mix *the relative proportion of total units sold (or total sales dollars) that is represented by each of a company's products*

An unstated assumption made in the preceding analysis is that the sales mix of a company's products does not change. The sales mix is the proportion of the total units sold (or the total dollar sales) represented by each of a company's products. To avoid complications involving sales mix, we used a company that sold only one product. If Lang had sold two or more products, we would simply have assumed that each product's percentage of the company's total sales remained constant. To illustrate how a change in sales mix can affect a company's break-even point, we will now assume that Lang Corporation sells three different video games. Following are the monthly revenues and costs for each type of game.

	Game A		Game B		Game C		Total	
	Amount	Percent	Amount	Percent	Amount	Percent	Amount	Percent
Sales Revenue	$25,000	100%	$45,000	100%	$30,000	100%	$100,000	100%
Less Variable Costs	20,000	80	30,000	$66\frac{2}{3}$	21,000	70	71,000	71
Contribution Margin	$ 5,000	20%	$15,000	$33\frac{1}{3}$%	$ 9,000	30%	$ 29,000	29%
Sales Mix	25%		45%		30%		100%	

Total sales are $100,000, which in this example includes $25,000 in sales of Game A, $45,000 of Game B, and $30,000 of Game C. Therefore, the sales mix is 25 percent Game A, 45 percent Game B, and 30 percent Game C, for a total of 100 percent. If this company had fixed costs of $17,400, the break-even point in sales dollars would be

$$\frac{\text{fixed costs}}{\text{average contribution-margin ratio}} = \frac{\$17{,}400}{0.29} = \$60{,}000$$

The 29 percent average contribution-margin ratio is determined by subtracting variable costs of $71,000 from total sales of $100,000. Obviously, $60,000 is the break-even point only if the sales mix does not change.

To illustrate how the break-even point can change if the sales mix changes, assume that the total sales revenue and the sales prices of each game remain the same but that the sales mix changes as follows:

	Game A		Game B		Game C		Total	
	Amount	Percent	Amount	Percent	Amount	Percent	Amount	Percent
Sales Revenue	$50,000	100%	$30,000	100%	$20,000	100%	$100,000	100%
Less Variable Costs	40,000	80	20,000	66⅔	14,000	70	74,000	74
Contribution Margin	$10,000	20%	$10,000	33⅓%	$ 6,000	30%	$ 26,000	26%
Sales Mix	50%		30%		20%		100%	

In this example, the contribution-margin ratio for each game remains the same, but the sales mix changes. Game A now comprises 50 percent of total sales instead of 25 percent. Since Game A has a lower contribution-margin ratio than games B and C, the total contribution-margin ratio decreases from 29 percent to 26 percent. Accordingly, the break-even point increases to $66,923 (rounded off to the nearest dollar), as shown below.

$$\frac{\text{fixed costs}}{\text{average contribution-margin ratio}} = \frac{\$17{,}400}{0.26} = \$66{,}923$$

As you can see, a sensible profit-maximizing strategy for management would be to maintain as large a contribution margin as possible on all products and then emphasize the products with the largest contribution margins. The remaining chapters of this text discuss procedures management can use to control costs, and hence maintain high contribution margins. The second part of this strategy—emphasizing the products with the highest contribution margins—is a marketing function. Lang Corporation, for example, should promote Game B more aggressively than Game A. Other factors being equal, a company should spend more advertising dollars and pay higher sales commissions on its higher-contribution-margin products. In fact, instead of paying commissions based on total sales, a good strategy would be to base salespeople's commissions on the contribution margins generated. This way, the mix of products that maximizes the sales staff's commissions will be the mix that provides the company with the greatest profit.

OTHER ASSUMPTIONS

In addition to assuming that the sales mix remains constant, C–V–P analysis is based on two other vital assumptions. They are

1. That the behavior of revenues and costs is linear and does not change throughout the relevant range. For this assumption to be true, the sales prices of the products must remain constant, the unit variable costs of the products cannot change, and the fixed costs must remain level. If changes in volumes trigger changes in costs or revenues—such as worker-productivity variations, quantity discounts, and changes in sales prices—this assumption is not valid.
2. That all costs can be accurately divided into fixed and variable categories. As we discussed in Chapter 21, semivariable costs must be separated into their fixed and variable components before meaningful analysis can take place.

TO SUMMARIZE C–V–P analysis is based on three critical assumptions: (1) that the sales mix does not change, (2) that the behavior of revenues and costs is linear throughout the relevant range, and (3) that all costs can be categorized as either fixed or variable. Other things being equal, in order to maximize profits management should put greater emphasis on the sale of products with higher contribution-margin ratios.

CHAPTER REVIEW

C–V–P analysis helps management understand how profits change in relation to changes in sales volume, fixed costs, variable costs, and sales revenue. Three common methods of C–V–P analysis are (1) contribution margins, (2) the break-even and target net income equations, and (3) graphical analysis. Although all three are variations of the same calculations, each approach has its advantages. The graphical approach allows the simultaneous analysis of several different activity levels.

Among other things, C–V–P analysis is used to compute break-even points and target net income levels. The equation approach is especially useful in assessing how profits change when costs or revenues change.

Three limiting assumptions of C–V–P analysis are (1) that the sales mix is constant, (2) that cost and revenue behavior patterns are linear and remain constant over the relevant range, and (3) that all costs can be categorized as either fixed or variable. When sales volumes are relatively stable, management should always emphasize the products with the highest contribution-margin ratios.

KEY TERMS AND CONCEPTS

break-even point (719)
contribution margin (720)
contribution-margin ratio (721)
cost-volume-profit (C-V-P) analysis (719)
per-unit contribution margin (720)
profit graph (727)
return on sales revenue (730)
sales mix (734)
target net income (728)

REVIEW PROBLEM

The Effect of Changes in Costs, Prices, and Volume on Profitability

McGraw Company has budgeted the following data for the coming year.

Sales Volume	100,000 units
Sales Price	$2.50 per unit
Variable Costs	$1.30 per unit
Fixed Costs	$60,000

Required:

1. Determine McGraw's expected net income.
2. Compute what the net income would be under each of the following independent assumptions.
   (a) The sales volume increases by 20 percent.
   (b) The sales price decreases by 20 percent.
   (c) Variable costs increase by 20 percent.
   (d) Fixed costs decrease by 20 percent.

Solution

1. (Units sold × sales price) = (units sold × variable unit cost) + fixed costs + profit

$$100{,}000(\$2.50) = 100{,}000(\$1.30) + \$60{,}000 + x$$
$$\$250{,}000 = \$130{,}000 + \$60{,}000 + x$$
$$\$250{,}000 = \$190{,}000 + x$$
$$x = \$60{,}000$$

This answer can be validated by dividing fixed costs by the per-unit contribution margin to find the break-even point, and then multiplying the excess units to be sold over the break-even point by the per-unit contribution margin.

$$\frac{\$60{,}000 \text{ (fixed costs)}}{\$1.20 \text{ (per-unit contribution margin)}} = \begin{matrix}50{,}000 \text{ units}\\ \text{(break-even point)}\end{matrix}$$

Units Sold	100,000
Less Break-Even Point (units)	50,000
Excess	50,000
Times per-Unit Contribution Margin	×$1.20
Expected Profit	$60,000

2(a) The Sales Volume Increases by 20 Percent

$$[100{,}000 + 0.20\,(100{,}000)]\,\$2.50 = [100{,}000 + 0.20(100{,}000)] \times (\$1.30) + \$60{,}000 + x$$
$$(120{,}000)\,\$2.50 = (120{,}000)\,\$1.30 + \$60{,}000 + x$$
$$\$300{,}000 = \$156{,}000 + \$60{,}000 + x$$
$$\$300{,}000 = \$216{,}000 + x$$
$$x = \$84{,}000$$

In this case, the contribution margin does not change. Therefore, the answer can be validated by multiplying the units to be sold in excess of the break-even point by the per-unit contribution margin of $1.20 to find the expected profit.

Units Sold	120,000
Less Break-Even Point (units)	50,000
Excess	70,000
Times per-Unit Contribution Margin	×$1.20
Expected Profit	$84,000

2(b) The Sales Price Decreases by 20 Percent

$$100{,}000[\$2.50 - 0.20(\$2.50)] = 100{,}000(\$1.30) + \$60{,}000 + x$$
$$100{,}000(\$2.00) = \$130{,}000 + \$60{,}000 + x$$
$$\$200{,}000 = \$190{,}000 + x$$
$$x = \$10{,}000$$

In this case, the contribution margin changes. Therefore, the answer can be validated by dividing fixed costs by the new per-unit contribution margin of $0.70 ($2.00 − $1.30) to find the new break-even point, and then multiplying the units to be sold in excess of the break-even point by the new per-unit contribution margin.

$$\frac{\$60{,}000 \text{ (fixed costs)}}{\$0.70 \text{ (new per-unit contribution margin)}} = 85{,}714 \text{ units (new break-even point)}$$

Units Sold	100,000
Less Break-Even Point (units)	85,714
Excess	14,286
Times per-Unit Contribution Margin	×$0.70
Expected Profit	$10,000

2(c) Variable Costs Increase by 20 Percent

$$\begin{aligned} 100{,}000(\$2.50) &= 100{,}000[\$1.30 + 0.20(\$1.30)] + \$60{,}000 + x \\ \$250{,}000 &= 100{,}000\ (\$1.56) + \$60{,}000 + x \\ \$250{,}000 &= \$156{,}000 + \$60{,}000 + x \\ \$250{,}000 &= \$216{,}000 + x \\ x &= \$34{,}000 \end{aligned}$$

In this case, the contribution margin changes. Therefore, the answer can be validated by dividing fixed costs by the new per-unit contribution margin of $0.94 ($2.50 − $1.56) to find the new break-even point, and then multiplying the units to be sold in excess of the break-even point by the new per-unit contribution margin.

$$\frac{\$60{,}000 \text{ (fixed costs)}}{\$0.94 \text{ (new per-unit contribution margin)}} = 63{,}830 \text{ units (new break-even point)}$$

Units Sold	100,000
Less Break-Even Point (units)	63,830
Excess	36,170
Times per-Unit Contribution Margin	×$0.94
Expected Profit	$34,000

2(d) Fixed Costs Decrease by 20 Percent

$$\begin{aligned} 100{,}000(\$2.50) &= 100{,}000(\$1.30) + [\$60{,}000 - 0.20(\$60{,}000)] + x \\ \$250{,}000 &= \$130{,}000 + (\$60{,}000 - \$12{,}000) + x \\ \$250{,}000 &= \$130{,}000 + \$48{,}000 + x \\ \$250{,}000 &= \$178{,}000 + x \\ x &= \$72{,}000 \end{aligned}$$

In this case, the contribution margin does not change, but fixed costs and hence the break-even point do. Therefore, the answer can be validated by dividing the old per-unit contribution margin of $1.20 into the new fixed costs to find the break-even point, and then multiplying the units to be sold in excess of the break-even point by the per-unit contribution margin.

$$\frac{\$48{,}000 \text{ (fixed costs)}}{\$1.20 \text{ (per-unit contribution margin)}} = 40{,}000 \text{ units (new break-even point)}$$

Units Sold	100,000
Less Break-Even Point (units)	40,000
Excess	60,000
Times per-Unit Contribution Margin	×$1.20
Expected Profit	$72,000

DISCUSSION QUESTIONS

1 Why is it important for managers to know the contribution margin of their products?

2 How much will profits increase for every unit sold over the break-even point?

3 Company A has high fixed costs and low variable costs. Company B has high variable costs and low fixed costs. Which company will lose the most money during recessionary periods, when both companies' sales are below their break-even points?

4 Referring to Question 3, which company will make more profit during good times, when both companies' sales are above their break-even points?

5 What is the major advantage of the graphical form of C-V-P analysis?

6 What is the equation for computing the break-even point?

7 When other factors are constant, what is the effect on profits of an increase in fixed costs?

8 When other factors are constant, what is the effect on profits of a decrease in variable costs?

9 What is the result of dividing total fixed costs by the unit contribution margin?

10 What effect is a change in the sales mix likely to have on a firm's overall contribution-margin ratio?

EXERCISES

E22–1 Contribution-Margin Analysis

Graceland Company is a manufacturer of alarm clocks. The following information pertains to Graceland's 1984 sales.

Sales Price per Unit	$ 15
Variable Costs per Unit	11
Total Fixed Costs	300,000

1. Determine Graceland Company's unit contribution margin.
2. Using the contribution-margin approach, compute
   (a) The break-even point in sales dollars and units.
   (b) The sales volume (in dollars and units) needed to generate an income of $50,000.
3. Using the equation approach of C–V–P analysis, compute
   (a) The break-even point in sales dollars and units.
   (b) The sales volume (in dollars and units) needed to generate a 20 percent return on sales.

E22–2 Contribution-Margin Ratios

Phatt Company had a break-even sales volume of $150,000 per month. Because of a $10,000-per-month increase in fixed costs, the break-even sales volume increased to $180,000 per month.

Based on the above information, compute
1. The contribution-margin ratio.
2. The total variable costs.
3. The total fixed costs.

E22–3 Contribution-Margin Analysis

Compute the missing amounts for the following independent cases. (Assume zero beginning and ending inventories.)

	Case I	Case II	Case III
Sales Volume (units)	15,000	(5)____	10,000
Sales Price per Unit	$5	$4	(9)$____
Variable Costs (total)	(1)$____	$50,000	25,000
Contribution Margin (total)	(2) ____	(6)____	15,000
Contribution Margin per Unit	$2	$1.50	(10)____
Fixed Costs (total)	(3) ____	(7)____	(11)____
Fixed Costs per Unit	(4) ____	$1.00	(12)____
Net Income	10,000	(8)____	10,000

E22–4 Contribution-Margin Analysis

Filo Company manufactures products X, Y, and Z. The following information relates to the three products.

	Product X	Product Y	Product Z
Sales Volume (in units)	50,000	25,000	10,000
Sales Revenue	$150,000	$125,000	$100,000
Variable Costs	100,000	85,000	70,000
Fixed Costs	30,000	30,000	30,000

1. At the current level of sales, which product provides the most profit?
2. With each additional unit of sales, which product provides the least contribution to profit?
3. If you could sell only 5,000 units but all 5,000 could be either product X, Y, or Z, which would you sell?
4. If you could sell only 50,000 units but all 50,000 could be either product X, Y, or Z, which would you sell?
5. If you had $5,000 for advertising and each dollar of advertising resulted in a one-unit increase in sales volume, which product would you advertise?

E22–5 The Break-Even Point—Graphical Analysis

Using the following graph, complete the requirements.

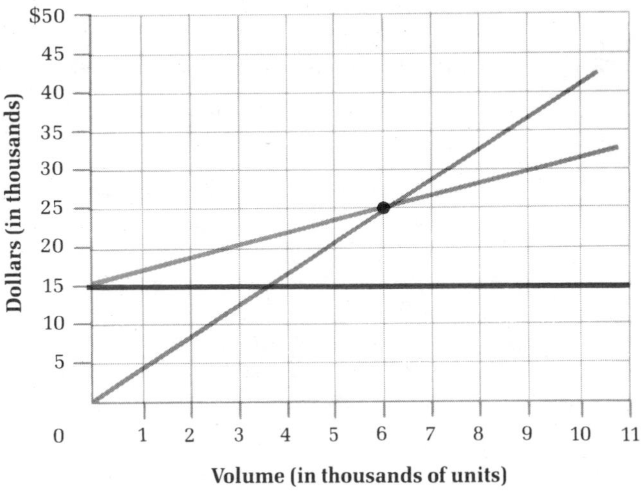

1. Redraw the graph and identify fixed costs, variable costs, revenues, the total-cost line, and the break-even point.
2. Determine the break-even point in both sales dollars and volume.
3. Suppose that as a manager you forecast sales volume at 7,000 units. At this level of sales, what would your total fixed costs, variable costs, and profit (or loss) be?
4. At a sales volume of 2,000 units, what would the level of fixed costs, variable costs, and profit (or loss) be?

E22-6 C-V-P Graphical Analysis

Using the following graph, complete the requirements.

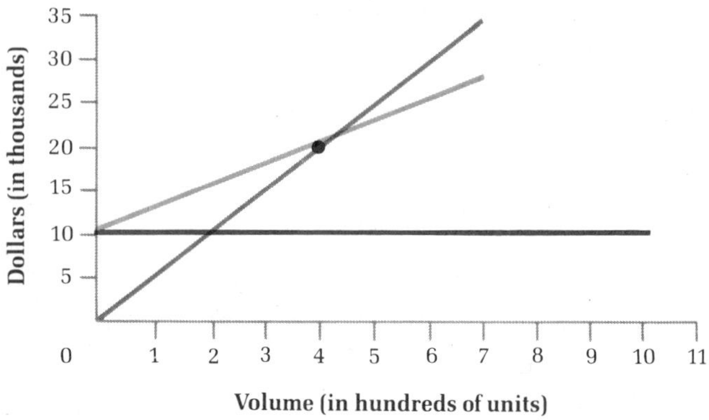

1. Determine the following.
(a) The break-even point in sales dollars and volume.
(b) The sales price per unit.
(c) The variable cost per unit.
(d) The unit contribution margin.
(e) Total fixed costs.
(f) Total variable costs at the break-even point.
2. What volume of sales must the company generate in order to reach a target net income of $7,500?

E22-7 The Break-Even Point—Graphical Analysis

Using the following graph, answer the questions.

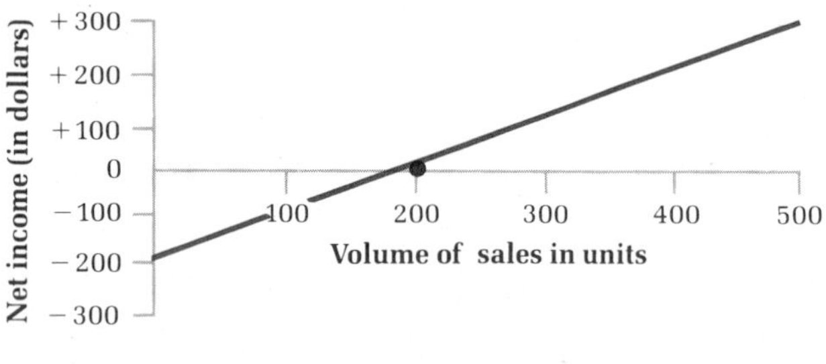

1. What is the break-even point in sales volume (in units)?
2. Approximately what volume of sales (in units) must this company have to generate an income of $300?
3. How much are the fixed costs?

E22-8 The Break-Even Point and Target Net Income

Brown Company manufactures and sells one product for $20 per unit. The unit contribution margin is 40 percent of the sales price, and fixed costs total $80,000.
1. Using the equation approach to determine the break-even point, compute
(a) The break-even point in sales dollars and units.
(b) The sales volume (in units) needed to generate a profit of $20,000.
(c) The break-even point (in units) if variable costs increase to 80 percent of the sales price and fixed costs increase to $100,000.
2. Using the per-unit contribution margins, recalculate items 1(a), 1(b), and 1(c).

E22-9 The Break-Even Point—Variable and Fixed Costs

The following information is available for Walker Furniture Company.

Average Sales Price per Unit	$ 150
Variable Cost per Unit	110
Total Fixed Manufacturing Costs	25,000

Joe Walker, president of Walker Furniture, is trying to decide whether he should buy a new lathe. The lathe would increase fixed costs by $15,000, but variable costs would decrease by $10 per unit.
1. Based on a break-even analysis, what recommendation would you give Mr. Walker?
2. Assuming that Walker has a target net income of $40,000, what would you recommend?
3. At what level of sales (in units) would Mr. Walker make the same profit with or without the new lathe?

E22-10 C-V-P Analysis—Target Net Income

Benson Products, Inc. estimates 1984 costs to be as follows:

Direct Materials	$4 per unit
Direct Labor	$7 per unit
Overhead	$2 per unit
Selling and Administrative Expenses	$50,000

1. Assuming that Benson will sell 40,000 units, what sales price per unit will be needed to achieve a $60,000 profit?
2. Assuming that Benson decides to sell its product for $16 per unit, determine the break-even sales volume in dollars and units.
3. Assuming that Benson decides to sell its product for $16 per unit, determine the number of units it must sell to generate a $50,000 profit.

E22-11 C-V-P Analysis—Changes in Variables

Chalmere Company estimates that next year's results will be

Sales Revenue (150,000 units)	$1,125,000
Less Variable Costs	(600,000)
Less Fixed Costs	(400,000)
Net Income	$ 125,000

Recompute net income, assuming each of the following independent conditions.

1. A 10 percent increase in the contribution margin.
2. A 6 percent increase in the sales volume.
3. A 6 percent decrease in the sales volume.
4. A 6 percent increase in variable costs per unit.
5. A 7 percent decrease in fixed costs.
6. A 7 percent increase in fixed costs.
7. A 7 percent increase in the sales volume and a 5 percent increase in fixed costs.

E22-12 C-V-P Analysis

Carson's Trading Post is a tourist stop in a resort community. Kim Carson, the owner of the shop, sells authentic animal skins for an average price of $30 per skin. Kim buys the skins from a supplier for an average cost of $21. In addition, he has selling expenses of $3 per skin. Kim rents the building for $300 per month, and pays one employee a fixed salary of $500 per month.

1. Determine the number of skins Kim must sell to break even.
2. Determine the number of skins Kim must sell to generate an income of $1,000 per month.
3. Assume that Kim can produce and sell his own skins at a total variable cost of $16 per skin, but that he would need to hire one additional employee at a monthly salary of $600.
   (a) Determine the number of skins Kim must sell to break even.
   (b) Determine the number of skins Kim must sell to generate an income of $1,000 per month.

E22-13 C-V-P Analysis—Change in Variables

Westborough Corporation is in the business of selling electronic games. Its three salesmen are currently being paid fixed salaries of $30,000 each. The sales manager has suggested that it might be more profitable to pay the salesmen on a straight commission basis. He has suggested a commission of 15 percent of sales. Current data for Westborough Corporation are as follows:

Sales Volume	15,000 units
Sales Price	$40 per unit
Variable Costs	$29 per unit
Fixed Costs	$140,000

1. Assuming that Westborough Corporation has a target net income of $50,000 for next year, which alternative is more attractive?
2. The sales manager believes that by switching to a commission basis, sales will increase 20 percent. If this is the case, which alternative is more attractive? (Assume that sales are expected to remain at 15,000 units under the fixed salary alternative.)

E22-14 Sales Mix

Hamilton Distributors sells products X and Y. Because of the nature of the products, Hamilton sells two units of product X for each unit of product Y. Relevant information about the products is as follows:

	X	Y
Sales Price per Unit	$20	$30
Variable Cost per Unit	16	24

1. Assuming that Hamilton's fixed costs total $140,000, compute Hamilton's break-even point in sales dollars and units of products X and Y.
2. Assuming that Hamilton sells two units of product Y for each unit of product X, and fixed costs remain at $140,000, compute Hamilton's break-even point in sales dollars and units of products X and Y.
3. Explain any differences in your answers to items (1) and (2).

E22-15 Sales Mix

Sherwood Ice Cream Company produces and sells ice cream in three sizes: quart, half-gallon, and gallon. Relevant information for each of the sizes is as follows:

	Quart	Half-Gallon	Gallon
Sales Price	$1.00	$1.75	$3.00
Less Variable Cost	.80	1.30	2.05
Unit Contribution Margin	$0.20	$0.45	$0.95
Sales Mix (% of sales)	15%	60%	25%

Sherwood anticipates sales of $500,000 and fixed costs of $120,000 in 1984.

1. Determine the break-even sales volume in dollars and units for 1984.
2. Determine Sherwood's 1984 projected net income.
3. Assume that Sherwood's sales mix changes to 10 percent quarts, 35 percent half-gallons, and 55 percent gallons. Determine Sherwood's break-even sales volume in dollars and units.

PROBLEMS

P22–1 Contribution-Margin Analysis—Changes in Variables

Phillips Corporation is a producer of hand-held electronic games. Its 1984 income statement was as follows.

Phillips Corporation
Contribution-Margin Income Statement
for the Year Ended December 31, 1984

	Total	Per Unit
Sales Revenue (150,000 games)	$5,250,000	$35
Less Variable Expenses	3,750,000	25
Contribution Margin	$1,500,000	$10
Less Fixed Expenses	900,000	
Net Income	$ 600,000	

In preparing its budget for 1985, Phillips Corporation is evaluating the effects of changes in costs, prices, and volume on net income.

Required:
Evaluate the following independent cases, and determine Phillips Corporation's 1985 budgeted net income or loss in each case (assume that 1984 figures apply unless stated otherwise).
1. Fixed costs increase by $150,000.
2. Fixed costs decrease by $100,000.
3. Variable costs increase by $3 per unit.
4. Variable costs decrease by $4 per unit.
5. The sales price increases by $5 per unit.
6. The sales price decreases by $5 per unit.
7. The sales volume increases by 25,000 units.
8. The sales volume decreases by 15,000 units.
9. The sales price decreases by $4 per unit, the volume increases by 40,000 units, and variable selling expenses decrease by $2.50 per unit.
10. Fixed costs decrease by $100,000 and variable selling costs increase by $4 per unit.
11. The sales volume increases by 30,000 units, with a decrease in sales price of $2 per unit. Variable costs drop by $1.50 per unit and fixed costs increase by $50,000.

P22–2 Break-Even Analysis

Cindy Clark has paid $150 to rent a carnival booth for four days. She has to decide whether to sell donuts or popcorn. Donuts cost $1.20 per dozen and can be sold for $2.40 per dozen. Popcorn will require a $75 rental fee for the popcorn maker and $0.05 for the popcorn, butter, salt, and bag necessary to make a bag of popcorn, which could sell for $0.30.

Required:
1. Compute the break-even point in dozens of donuts if Cindy decides to sell donuts exclusively, and the break-even point in bags of popcorn if she decides to sell popcorn exclusively.
2. Cindy estimates that she can sell either 50 donuts or 30 bags of popcorn every hour the carnival is open (10 hours a day for four days). Which product should she sell?
3. Cindy can sell back to the baker at half cost any donuts she fails to sell at the carnival. Unused popcorn must be thrown away. If Cindy sells only 80 percent of her original estimate, which product should she sell? (Assume that she bought or produced just enough to satisfy the demands she originally estimated.)

P22–3 The Break-Even Point and the Target Net Income

Jones Boat Company is a retail outlet for customized speedboats. The boats are purchased by Jones for an average cost of $12,500. Jones adds 30 percent to this cost to arrive at the sales price. In 1984, Jones sold 33 boats and finished the year with an inventory equal to the inventory at the beginning of the year. Additional operating expenses for the year are identified below.

Selling Expenses:	
Advertising (fixed)	$ 500 per month
Commissions	4,500 per month fixed cost plus 2 percent of sales variable cost
Depreciation (fixed)	300 per month
Utilities (fixed)	150 per month
Freight on Delivery (variable)	100 per boat
Administrative Expenses:	
Salaries (fixed)	$4,000 per month
Depreciation (fixed)	300 per month
Utilities (fixed)	150 per month
Clerical (variable)	25 per sale

Required:
1. Calculate the break-even point in number of boats sold.
2. If Jones wishes to generate a profit of $50,000, how many boats must he sell in a year?
3. Should Jones continue in business if he thinks the most he can sell is an average of 35 boats per year? How much would the company make (or lose) given a sales volume of 35 boats per year?
4. If a sales level of 35 units per year were achieved, by what amount must (a) fixed costs and (b) variable costs be reduced or increased in order to break even? (Assume that all other variables remained unchanged.)

P22-4 C-V-P Analysis—Return on Sales

The federal government recently placed a ceiling on the selling price of sheet metal produced by GSM Company. In 1984, GSM was limited to charging a price that would earn a 20 percent return on gross sales. On the basis of this restriction, GSM had the following results for 1984.

Sales Revenue (1,150,000 feet at $2 per foot)		$2,300,000
Variable Costs (1,150,000 feet × $1.40)	$1,610,000	
Fixed Costs	230,000	1,840,000
Net Income		$ 460,000

In 1985, GSM predicted that the sales volume would decrease to 900,000 feet of sheet metal. With this level of sales, however, the company anticipated no changes in the levels of fixed and variable costs.

Required:

1. Determine GSM's net income for 1985 if all forecasts are realized. Compute both the dollar amount of profit and the percentage return on sales.
2. GSM plans to petition the government for a price increase so that the 1984 rate of return on sales (20 percent) can be maintained. What sales price should the company request based on 1985 projections? (Round to the nearest cent.)
3. How much profit (in dollars) will GSM earn in 1985 if this sales price [as determined in question (2)] is approved?
4. **Interpretive Question** What other factors must be considered by GSM and the government?

P22-5 The Income Statement and Break-Even Analysis

Ipsen Company records the following costs associated with the production and sale of a steel slingshot.

Selling Expenses:	
Fixed	$6,500
Variable	$0.50 per unit sold
Administrative Expenses:	
Fixed	$4,500
Variable	$0.25 per unit sold
Manufacturing Costs:	
Fixed	$15,500
Variable	$7.50 per unit produced

Assume that in 1984 the beginning and ending inventories were the same. Also assume that 1984 sales were 11,000 units at $11.50 per slingshot.

Required:

1. Prepare a contribution-margin income statement.
2. Determine the break-even point in sales volume.
3. **Interpretive Question** Ms. Ipsen believes that sales volume could be improved by 20 percent if an additional commission of $0.50 per unit were paid to the salespeople. She also believes, however, that the same percentage increase could be achieved through an additional $3,000 investment in advertising. Which action, if either, should Ms. Ipsen take? Why?

P22-6 Unifying Problem: C-V-P Analysis and Changes in Variables

The 1984 budgeted income statement for R. J. Gilson, Inc. was as follows:

R. J. Gilson, Inc.
Budgeted Income Statement
for the Year Ended December 31, 1984

Sales Revenue (5,000 units)	$800,000
Less Variable Costs:	
Production	(350,000)
Selling	(100,000)
Administrative	(100,000)
Contribution Margin	$250,000
Less Fixed Costs	(200,000)
Net Income	$ 50,000

The Board of Directors, upon reviewing the budget, determined that some changes would need to be made to increase the 1984 projected net income.

Required:

1. Calculate the break-even point in sales dollars and units.
2. Assuming that you are assigned the task of determining the best method to maximize R. J. Gilson's 1984 profits, evaluate the following independent proposals and determine the net income or loss and the break-even sales volume under each.
   (a) The sales manager has told you that a shift in selling expenses to a straight commission basis will increase variable selling expenses by $10 per unit, and decrease fixed costs by $60,000. He also believes that this will cause a 10 percent increase in sales volume.
   (b) The marketing manager believes that by spending an additional $50,000 in advertising expense, sales volume will increase 15 percent. (Advertising expense is a fixed cost.)
   (c) The marketing manager believes that a 10 percent reduction in sales price will lead to a 20 percent increase in sales volume.
   (d) The production manager has informed you that the production equipment is becoming obsolete. She feels that a $100,000-per-year increase in capital investment will reduce variable production costs by 20 percent.

(e) In conferring with the marketing, sales, and production managers, you feel that by changing to the straight commission basis [as in item (a)], decreasing advertising expense by $30,000, and reducing the sales price by 5 percent, you can increase sales volume by 30 percent.

P22-7 C-V-P Analysis—Changes in Variables

Jensen Manufacturing Company produces electric carving knives. The firm has not been as profitable as expected in the past three years. As a result, there is excess capacity that could be used to produce an additional 10,000 knives per year. However, any production above that amount would require a capital investment of $50,000. Operating results for the previous year appear below. Assume that there is never any ending inventory.

Sales Revenue (125,000 knives × $8)		$1,000,000
Variable Costs (125,000 knives × $5)	$ 625,000	
Fixed Costs	350,000	975,000
Net Income		$ 25,000

Required:

Respond to the following independent proposals and support your recommendations.

1. The production manager believes that profits could be increased through the purchase of more automated production machinery, which costs $100,000 and could reduce the variable costs by $0.75 a knife. Is he correct if sales are to remain at 125,000 knives annually?
2. The sales manager believes that a 5 percent discount on the sales price would increase the sales volume to 135,000 units annually. If he is correct, would this action increase or decrease profits?
3. Would the implementation of both proposals be worthwhile?
4. The sales manager believes that an increase in sales commissions could improve the sales volume. In particular, he suggests that an increase of $0.50 a knife would increase the volume to 30 percent. If he is correct, would this action increase profits?
5. The accountant suggests another alternative: Reduce administrative salaries by $10,000 so that prices can be reduced by $0.10 per unit. She believes that this action would increase the volume to 130,000 units annually. If she is correct, would this action increase profits?
6. The corporate executives finally decide to spend an additional $30,000 in advertising to bring the sales volume up to 135,000 units. If the increased advertising could bring in these extra sales, is this a good decision?

P22-8 Unifying Problem—Contribution Margins and C-V-P Analysis

Cromartie Craft produces two models of cabinets. Demand for either model is sufficient to allow Cromartie to produce at full capacity (7,000 direct-labor hours). Factory overhead totals $210,000, one-half of which is fixed. Other information for the two models follows.

	Model X		Model Y	
Sales Price		$360		$250
Unit Costs:				
Materials (variable)	$ 50		$ 35	
Labor (variable)	150		100	
Overhead (applied at a rate of $30 per direct-labor hour)	90		60	
Selling Expenses (variable)	30		25	
Total Costs per Unit		320		220
Profit per Unit		$ 40		$ 30
Direct-Labor Hours Required		3		2

Required:

1. Assuming that Cromartie will produce only one model, which model is more profitable to produce? Why?
2. Assuming that Cromartie has additional fixed expenses of $70,000, how many units of the more profitable model must it produce to break even?
3. What will Cromartie's profit or loss be if only Model X is produced? If only Model Y is produced?

P22-9 Graphical Analysis of C-V-P Relationships

Make six copies of the following graph and label them (a), (b), (c), (d), (e), and (f). (Each graph is to represent an independent situation.)

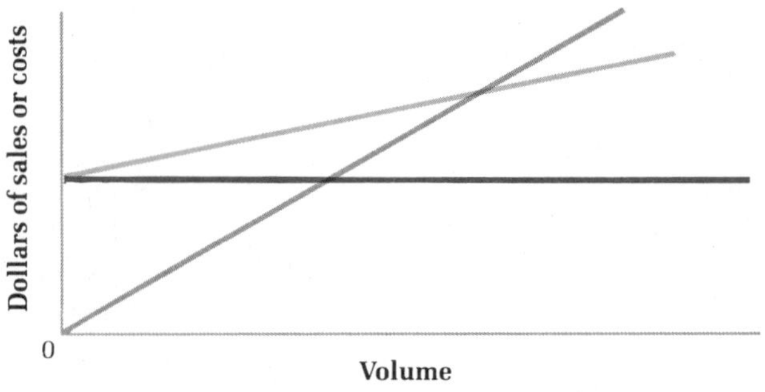

Required:

1. On each of the six graphs, label the lines as either total fixed costs, total costs, or total sales. Also identify and label the break-even point.

2. On each of the six graphs, draw (as a dotted line) the change caused by the appropriate one of the following events. Indicate the new break-even point in each case, and show the change (increase or decrease) in the new volume required to break even.
   (a) An increase in the unit sales price.
   (b) A decrease in the unit sales price.
   (c) An increase in unit variable costs.
   (d) A decrease in unit variable costs.
   (e) An increase in fixed costs.
   (f) A decrease in fixed costs.

P22–10 Sales Mix

Bell Corporation produces and sells three types of calculators. Selected information about the calculators is as follows:

	Model		
	B-10	**B-20**	**B-30**
Sales Prices	$25.00	$50.00	$90.00
Variable Costs:			
Production	17.50	30.00	49.50
Sales Commissions	2.50	5.00	9.00

Bell Corporation's fixed expenses are $5,000 per month.

Sales volumes for the months of September and October 1984 are as follows:

	B-10	B-20	B-30	Total
September	500	350	150	1000
October	300	300	400	1000
Totals	800	650	550	2000

Required:

1. Prepare contribution-margin income statements for Bell Corporation for September and October. Arrange the income statements as follows:

Model							
B-10		**B-20**		**B-30**		**Total**	
Amount	%	Amount	%	Amount	%	Amount	%

(Fixed expenses need not be allocated among the models.)

2. Why has net income changed when the total number of units sold has remained constant? Explain.
3. Calculate Bell Corporation's break-even point in units and sales dollars for September and October.
4. If Bell Corporation has an unlimited demand for its calculators and it can produce an additional $10,000 worth of calculators per month, which should it produce? Why?

CHAPTER 23

Cost Accumulation for Manufacturing Firms

THIS CHAPTER EXPLAINS:

Approaches to product costing in manufacturing firms.
The method of job-order costing.
The method of process costing.

product costing *the assignment of manufacturing costs to products in order to determine the cost of finished goods*

For a merchandising company, the cost of a product consists mainly of the amount paid to a supplier. In a manufacturing firm, however, the cost of a product is determined by adding direct materials, direct labor, and overhead—the three types of manufacturing costs. This chapter examines product costing, the methods of assigning costs to manufactured products. By necessity, the chapter is procedural and is oriented toward cost accounting.

There are at least two reasons why product costs must be determined on an accurate and timely basis: (1) product cost data are used for daily operating decisions, and (2) product costs are necessary for financial reporting. Obviously, a product cannot be priced intelligently if manufacturing costs are not known. Similarly, management may use its knowledge of product costs to make such decisions as what commissions to pay salespeople, and whether to expand or contract production of an item.

With regard to financial reporting, income can be correctly determined only if product costs are accurately identified. This is because product costs provide the basic data for assessing the beginning and ending inventory costs that are used to calculate cost of sales, and hence to measure income.

An Overview of Product Costing Methods

absorption costing *a product costing approach that assigns all fixed and variable manufacturing costs to the units produced*

There are two basic approaches to product costing: absorption costing and variable costing. The absorption costing approach, which is required for financial reporting and income tax purposes, includes both fixed and variable manufacturing costs as product costs, whereas the variable costing

variable costing *a product costing approach that assigns only variable costs as product costs and treats fixed overhead costs as period expenses*

approach includes only variable costs (fixed overhead costs are expensed in the period incurred). Since the variable costing method is more useful for decision-making purposes, it is emphasized in this chapter and in the remainder of the text.

With either approach, there are two principal methods of accumulating and assigning costs: job-order costing and process costing. Both methods are averaging processes whereby unit costs are computed by dividing the total number of units produced (the denominator) into the total manufacturing cost (the numerator). The difference between the two methods lies in how the pool of manufacturing costs is assigned to units. Job-order costing is most often used for tracing the costs of custom-ordered products (such as wedding announcements or, on a larger scale, commercial buildings). Process costing is usually reserved for averaging the costs of basically identical products, such as bricks, flour, or gasoline.

JOB-ORDER COSTING

job-order costing *a method of product costing whereby each job, product, or batch of products is costed separately*

Job-order costing is used by firms in which each product, job, or batch of products is costed separately. For example, a custom furniture manufacturer would want to accumulate the costs of each sofa, table, and chair separately so that appropriate prices can be charged. Similarly, a builder must know how much lumber, brick, concrete, labor, and so on, were used in building each house. Because each job requires different amounts of materials, labor, and overhead, building costs cannot be allocated equally to all the houses under construction as they would be in a company making identical products.

PROCESS COSTING

process costing *a method of product costing whereby costs are accumulated by process or work centers and averaged over all products manufactured in those centers.*

To use process costing, a firm must manufacture products that pass through a series of uniform steps. Thus, process costing is especially useful in mass-production industries—for example, the rubber, lumber, brick, textile, milling and flour, food-processing, and gasoline industries. When the units are indistinguishable, the product costs are determined by dividing the total manufacturing costs by the number of units produced. The cost of all units is then the same.

TO SUMMARIZE Absorption costing, which includes both fixed and variable costs in the cost of a product, is required for income tax and financial reporting purposes. Variable costing, which includes only variable costs as product costs, is more useful for internal decision making. With either approach, there are two ways of accumulating and assigning costs: job-order and process costing. With job-order costing, each product is costed separately because of its uniqueness. With process costing, which is applied to mass-produced, identical products, the products are costed together.

The Method of Job-Order Costing

Firms that use job-order costing must have an accurate means of accumulating materials, labor, and overhead costs for each job. In this section, we introduce the job cost sheet that is used in this process. We then examine the ways in which costs are assigned to products.

THE JOB COST SHEET

job cost sheet *a document prepared for each manufacturing job that is job-order costed; it contains a summary of direct-materials, direct-labor, and overhead costs*

The job cost sheet is the basic document for keeping track of costs in a job-order costing system. Each job has a separate sheet, which summarizes all materials, labor, and overhead costs assigned to that job. Exhibit 23–1 is the completed job sheet for a mahogany table manufactured by Broyman Furniture Company for a particular customer, Marlin Dockweiler. It shows that the production of the table is a custom job requiring two operations: machining (cutting and preparing the mahogany) and finishing (assembling and staining the table).

Job cost sheets are prepared by a firm's accounting department upon notification that a sales order has been received and that the production departments have started work (as evidenced by a production order). Production (in this case, machining and finishing) begins only after the sales department has confirmed in writing that the price, shipment date, quantity, and other terms have been agreed to by the customer.

Exhibit 23–1 shows that the mahogany table cost $314.50 to make. This amount includes $135 of materials (documented on materials requisition forms 872, 876, and 877), $134 of direct labor (identified on time tickets 25, 61, and 75), and $45.50 of overhead (which includes heat, light, depreciation on plant and machinery, and so on). The job cost sheet also indicates that the direct-labor hourly wage rate was $10 per hour in machining and $12 per hour in finishing, and that the overhead rate was $4 per direct-labor hour in machining and $3 per direct-labor hour in finishing. The higher overhead rate in the machining department was probably caused by the larger amount of equipment needed for this process. The wage rate in the finishing department was probably higher because more experienced and skilled workers were used.

Although the job cost sheet is started when production begins, it cannot be completed until the accounting department receives all the relevant materials requisition forms and time tickets from the production departments.

ACCOUNTING FOR DIRECT-MATERIALS COSTS

To illustrate the accounting for direct-materials costs, we will assume that Broyman purchased a supply of mahogany and placed it in a materials storeroom. The entry to record this purchase would be as shown on page 750.

EXHIBIT 23-1 **A Job Cost Sheet**

Broyman Furniture Company

Job Cost Sheet

52
Job order number

Product was made for stock ___ Yes _X_ No

Product was specially ordered _X_ Yes ___ No

Customer name Marlin Dockweiler

Mahogany Table 4'×8'

Date started January 3,1984 Date completed January 6,1984

Machining department

Materials			Direct labor			Manufacturing overhead		
Date	Requisition number	Amount	Time ticket number	Hours	Amount	Hours	Rate	Amount
1/3/84	872	$100.00	25	8	$80	8	$4 per direct-labor hour	$32

Finishing department

Materials			Direct labor			Manufacturing overhead		
Date	Requisition number	Amount	Work ticket number	Hours	Amount	Hours	Rate	Amount
1/6/84	876	$30.00	61	3	$36	4.5	$3 per direct-labor hour	$13.50
1/6/84	877	5.00	75	1.5	18			
		$35.00		4.5	$54			

Cost summary

	Machining	**Finishing**	**Total**
Materials	$100.00	$35.00	$135.00
Labor	80.00	54.00	134.00
Overhead	32.00	13.50	45.50
Total Cost	$212.00	$102.50	$314.50
Unit Cost			$314.50

Raw Materials Inventory	50,000	
Accounts Payable (or Cash)		50,000
Purchased 25,000 board feet of mahogany at $2.00 per foot.		

materials requisition form *a document used to request raw materials from the storeroom*

At the appropriate time, the machining department would send to the storeroom a materials requisition form, identifying the quantity and type of materials needed (see Exhibit 23-2).

EXHIBIT 23-2 **A Materials Requisition Form**

Requisition number 872
Job number 52

Department Machining
Date January 3, 1984
Authorized by J.S.

Description	Quantity	Unit cost	Amount
50 board feet of mahogany	1	$2.00 per foot*	$100.00*

* Added by the accounting department.

The materials requisition form is a source document, meaning that it serves as the basis for entries in the accounting records. Thus, the storeroom manager would send this form to the accounting department, where the unit cost would be filled in and the total cost calculated. The accountants would then make the following entry to record the transfer of mahogany from storage to machining.

Work-in-Process Inventory	100	
Raw Materials Inventory		100
Issued 50 board feet of mahogany to production.		

indirect-materials costs *materials costs that are not assigned directly to specific products but are instead included as manufacturing overhead and assigned to products on some reasonable allocation basis*

The 50 board feet of mahogany were used directly in the manufacture of the table, and the cost should be assigned to the Dockweiler job. Other materials and supplies—relatively inexpensive items such as glue, nails, and varnish—are also used in production. These materials would also be ordered from the storeroom by using a materials requisition form. It is not cost-beneficial, however, to trace such miscellaneous items to a particular job, so these indirect-materials costs are usually charged to manufacturing overhead. The following entry records the requisitioning of such materials by the machining department.

Manufacturing Overhead	xxx	
Raw Materials Inventory (or Supplies on Hand)		xxx
Issued miscellaneous supplies to the machining department.		

The materials requisition form provides a convenient way of charging materials and supplies to the various departments. The departments then assign them to specific products either as direct materials or as manufacturing overhead. At the end of a period, the amount of materials and supplies that remain unused and on hand would be shown on the balance sheet as Raw Materials Inventory and Supplies on Hand.

ACCOUNTING FOR DIRECT-LABOR COSTS

time ticket *a record of each production employee's hour-by-hour activities, kept so that labor costs can be assigned to the proper jobs or products*

The method of charging direct-labor costs to production jobs is similar to that for direct-materials costs. As employees work on specific jobs, they record their hourly activities on time tickets, like the one shown in Exhibit 23-3. This time ticket shows that employee no. 641 (each employee would be assigned a number) worked on the mahogany table for 8 hours on January 3, 1984. Since only one employee prepared the table, the total direct-labor cost of machining was $80 ($10 per hour × 8 hours).

EXHIBIT 23-3 A Time Ticket

Employee no. 641 Date January 3, 1984 Job no. 52

Work performed Sizing & Cutting Hourly rate $10 Dept. Machining

Time started 8:00 a.m. Total amount $80

Time stopped 5:00 p.m. Number of units completed 1

Type of job Mahogany Table for Dockweiler

Time ticket number 25

Most jobs, however, involve several employees. At the end of a job, all the time tickets are completed and sent to the accounting department. There, the total labor cost of the job is calculated and entered on the job cost sheet. The entry to record the direct-labor cost is (ignoring payroll withholdings) shown on the next page.

Work-in-Process Inventory	80	
Wages Payable		80
To record the machining department's payroll costs on job order number 52.		

indirect-labor costs *labor costs that are not directly assigned to specific products but instead are included as part of manufacturing overhead and assigned to products on some reasonable allocation basis*

Like materials costs, labor costs can be either direct or indirect. Direct-labor costs have already been discussed. Indirect-labor costs include the wages of employees who perform functions not related to a specific job, such as maintenance and cleaning. These employees may still complete time tickets but their salaries will become a part of the indirect-labor costs that are assigned to manufacturing overhead. The entry to record indirect-labor costs would be

Manufacturing Overhead	xxx	
Wages Payable		xxx
To record indirect-labor costs as overhead.		

ACCOUNTING FOR MANUFACTURING OVERHEAD

manufacturing overhead *production costs that are not directly assigned to the manufacture of a specific product*

Manufacturing overhead is the third type of product cost. Like direct materials and direct labor, it is an important element in determining the unit cost of a product. But unlike direct materials and direct labor, which can be readily assigned to specific jobs or products, overhead costs are difficult to trace directly to the production of a single item. In fact, by definition, overhead costs benefit all the products made in a department or company.

Overhead is a broad category and includes such items as the nuts, bolts, and screws used in fixing the machines, as well as other factory costs, such as depreciation, insurance, repairs, and the salary of the plant manager. In many cases, the overhead costs are fixed; that is, they do not vary with changes in the volume of production over the relevant range. Other overhead costs are variable or semivariable. Because production output is not known until the end of the period, any attempt to assign overhead costs to products before the end of the period requires estimation. The error that can result from such estimates is one reason that variable costing, which treats fixed overhead as a period expense, is better for decision making. As indicated previously, however, both the IRS and generally accepted accounting principles require the use of absorption costing, which includes fixed overhead costs as product costs.

The following example illustrating how overhead is assigned to products highlights the difference between variable and absorption costing. Mayberry Company prints stationery, name cards, and wedding announcements. The stationery sells for $20 a box. The variable costs of a box of stationery are

Direct Materials (paper)	$3
Direct Labor ($\frac{1}{3}$ hour at $6 per hour)	2
Variable Overhead (ink, indirect labor, and other indirect materials: $6 hour × $\frac{1}{3}$ hour)	2
Total Variable Costs	$7

In addition, Mayberry has the following annual fixed overhead costs.

Rent	$3,600
Insurance	700
Depreciation on Equipment	500
Total Fixed Overhead Costs	$4,800

During 1984 Mayberry produced 1,200 boxes of stationery and sold 1,000 boxes. Management estimated at the beginning of 1984 a production volume of 1,200 boxes of stationery. Thus, for GAAP and IRS purposes, $4 of fixed overhead was allocated to each box of stationery ($4,800 ÷ 1,200 estimated boxes). The net income (from stationery only) that the variable and absorption methods produce is calculated in Exhibit 23-4. (Note that the example assumes no beginning inventory, and selling and administrative expenses of $4,000.) The two methods produce net incomes that differ by $800 because 200 more units were produced during the period than were sold. Absorption costing gives the higher net income because fixed overhead is included in the cost of the product, and therefore $4 times 200 units, or a total of $800, of fixed overhead remains in inventory rather than being subtracted from gross margin. The net effect is the expensing of $4,800 of fixed overhead under variable costing and only $4,000 under absorption costing.

EXHIBIT 23-4 Variable Costing Versus Absorption Costing—Mayberry Company (Stationery Only)

	Variable Costing			Absorption Costing		
Sales Revenue (1,000 boxes at $20)			$20,000			$20,000
Cost of Goods Sold:						
Beginning Inventory		$ -0-			$ -0-	
Manufacturing Costs (1,200 boxes)						
Direct Materials ($3 per box)	$3,600			$3,600		
Direct Labor ($2 per box)	2,400			2,400		
Variable Overhead ($2 per box)	2,400			2,400		
Fixed Overhead ($4 per box)	-0-			4,800		
Total Manufacturing Costs Added to Inventory		8,400*			13,200†	
Cost of Goods Available for Sale		$8,400			$13,200	
Less Ending Inventory (200 boxes)		1,400*			2,200†	
Cost of Goods Sold			7,000			11,000
Gross Margin			$13,000			$ 9,000
Less Fixed Manufacturing Costs			4,800			-0-
Less Selling and Administrative Expenses			4,000			4,000
Net Income			$ 4,200			$ 5,000

* This may be calculated by multiplying the number of boxes by a unit cost of $7 ($3 + $2 + $2).

† This may be calculated by multiplying the number of boxes by a unit cost of $11 ($3 + $2 + $2 + $4).

Clearly, if all units produced had been sold during the period, there would be no difference in net income. When more units are produced than sold, net income is higher under absorption costing. Net income under variable costing is always tied to sales volume and cannot be increased or decreased by varying production levels.

From a decision-making point of view, variable costing makes more sense. Certainly, a method that shows an increase in net income merely because of a spurt in production cannot be used effectively to reward performance, assess contribution margins, make investment decisions, or plan for the future. Supporters of variable costing further argue that fixed overhead costs should not be included as part of inventory because they are more closely related to production capacity than to the manufacture of specific units. Supporters of absorption costing contend that inventories should carry a fixed-cost component because both fixed and variable costs are necessary to produce goods, regardless of the differences in their cost behavior patterns. Because we are more concerned here about product costing for planning, control, and performance evaluation than we are with product costing for financial reporting, we will use variable costing in the remaining sections of the chapter.

Estimating Variable Overhead

In the Mayberry Company example, variable overhead costs were $2 per box. However, $2 is not a precise accounting of the actual amount of variable overhead spent on each box of stationery. Rather, it is an "allocated" amount based on an estimate of overhead costs for a certain period or a certain number of jobs. Allocation of overhead involves the following steps.

1. Choose a base for allocating overhead to each job. In the Mayberry example, the number of boxes of stationery was used as the allocation base. Other common bases include the number of direct-labor hours worked, the amount of direct materials used, and the number of such units as miles driven, meals served, or letters typed.
2. Estimate the total variable overhead costs for the period.
3. Divide the estimated total variable overhead costs (step 2) by the expected total base units (step 1) to determine an overhead application rate.
4. Multiply the overhead application rate by the actual number of base units for each project or job to determine how much variable overhead should be applied to each project or job.

overhead application rate *a rate at which estimated variable overhead costs are assigned to products throughout the year; equals total estimated variable overhead costs divided by a suitable allocation base, such as number of units produced, direct-labor hours, direct materials used, or direct-labor costs*

variable overhead *the overhead costs assigned to products (included in work-in-process) on the basis of a predetermined application rate*

The equation that results from the first three of these steps is

$$\frac{\text{estimated total variable overhead costs}}{\begin{array}{c}\text{estimated total units}\\ \text{(direct-labor hours, direct materials,}\\ \text{direct-labor costs, or another base)}\end{array}} = \begin{array}{l}\text{variable overhead}\\ \text{application rate}\end{array}$$

Note that the numerator represents estimated variable overhead costs, because actual overhead costs will not be known until year-end. The variable overhead rate is then applied to jobs as they are completed throughout the year. Since actual and estimated overhead costs are rarely the same, at the end of a year any differences between them must be properly accounted for. The method of handling these differences is discussed later in the chapter.

To illustrate the process of allocating variable overhead costs to products, we will assume that Mayberry Company anticipated the following variable overhead costs during 1984.

Indirect Materials	$4,000
Indirect Labor	5,000
Repairs	2,000
Maintenance	1,000
	$12,000

These variable overhead costs must be allocated to the various jobs on some equitable basis, such as number of direct-labor hours worked. For example, if we assume that Mayberry has only one production employee who works fifty 40-hour weeks per year, the number of direct-labor hours is 2,000.

Using this base of 2,000 hours, we would calculate a predetermined variable overhead rate as follows:

$$\frac{\text{total estimated costs (\$12,000)}}{\text{number of direct-labor hours (2,000)}} = \begin{array}{l}\text{\$6 per direct-labor hour} \\ \text{(variable overhead} \\ \text{application rate)}\end{array}$$

Because it takes only one-third of a direct-labor hour to print a box of stationery, $2 of variable overhead is assigned to each box. Since 1,200 boxes of stationery were printed during 1984, $2,400 (1,200 × $2) of variable overhead is assigned to stationery and the remaining $9,600 ($12,000 − $2,400) must be allocated to the other products: name cards and wedding announcements.

Accounting for Variable Overhead

Accounting for variable overhead costs (as well as fixed overhead costs under an absorption costing system) requires keeping track of both actual costs incurred and overhead applied to products or jobs. To illustrate, we will assume that during March, Mayberry's actual variable overhead costs included $300 of indirect labor, $400 of indirect materials, and $200 of repairs. As the actual costs were incurred, they were debited to a Manufacturing Overhead account as follows:

Manufacturing Overhead	900	
Cash (or Repairs)		200
Wages Payable		300
Raw Materials Inventory		400
Incurred overhead costs of $900 in March.		

Recall that a manufacturing firm always has three different types of inventory: (1) raw materials, which have not yet been used in production; (2) work-in-process; and (3) finished goods.

Throughout the year, similar entries were made as overhead costs were incurred. At the end of the year, Manufacturing Overhead had debit entries for the total amount of actual overhead costs. Whereas actual overhead costs were entered on the debit side of Manufacturing Overhead, estimated costs were entered on the credit side as jobs were completed. These latter costs were based on the overhead application rate of $6 per direct-labor hour. Thus, if a job had been completed in 2 hours, the estimated overhead entry would have been

Work-in-Process Inventory	12	
Manufacturing Overhead		12
Applied variable overhead to a 2-hour stationery job (2 × $6).		

The Manufacturing Overhead account, therefore, has numerous debit and credit entries throughout the year, as Exhibit 23-5 shows.

At the end of the year, Manufacturing Overhead has a debit balance if actual overhead exceeds the estimate, a credit balance if the estimate exceeds actual overhead, or a zero balance if debits and credits are equal (which is unlikely).

EXHIBIT 23-5 **Actual Versus Estimated Overhead**

Manufacturing Overhead	
Actual overhead costs are entered as debits on a regular basis as they are incurred. →	← Estimated overhead costs are entered as credits as production takes place; costs are applied on the basis of the variable overhead application rate.

COMPUTING THE TOTAL UNIT COST

As jobs are completed, the products are transferred from manufacturing to finished goods. The transfer is then entered in the accounting records. With arbitrary numbers, the entry would be

Finished Goods Inventory	8,000	
Work-in-Process Inventory		8,000
To record the completion of goods.		

With the completion of finished goods, the unit cost of the product can be computed. This is accomplished by adding the materials, labor, and overhead costs that were entered on the job cost sheet and dividing the total by the number of units produced. Of course, if only one unit is produced, the unit cost is simply the total. The job cost sheet is then sent to the finished goods inventory file and the unit-cost data are used in pricing the product, making contribution-margin decisions, and rewarding performance.

DETERMINING COST OF GOODS SOLD

As products are sold, the unit cost is used to transfer the cost of finished goods to the Cost of Goods Sold account. For example, recall the mahogany table that cost $314.50 to make. The entry to record its cost at the time of sale would be

Cost of Goods Sold	314.50	
Finished Goods Inventory		314.50
To record the cost of goods sold of a table.		

With the entry transferring costs from Finished Goods Inventory to Cost of Goods Sold, costs have been traced all the way through the production cycle and onto the income statement. Indeed, two major tasks have been accomplished: (1) The total cost of producing an item has been summarized on the job cost sheet, and (2) the proper entries have been made to account for production costs. These entries are necessary so that at any point in time the correct amount of net income and the financial position of a company can be reported.

The flow of documents through a manufacturing firm is summarized in Exhibit 23-6, and the flow of costs through a firm is charted in Exhibit 23-7.

EXHIBIT 23-6 The Flow of Documents in a Job-Order Costing System

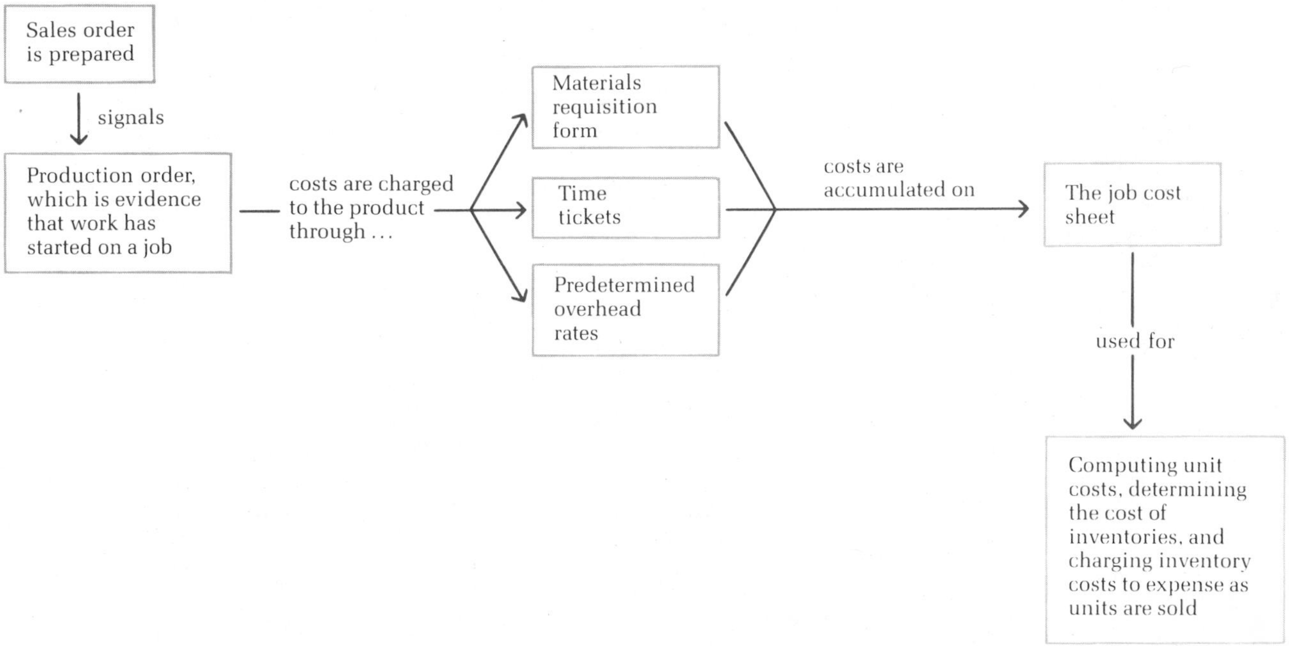

EXHIBIT 23-7 A Summary of Cost Flows

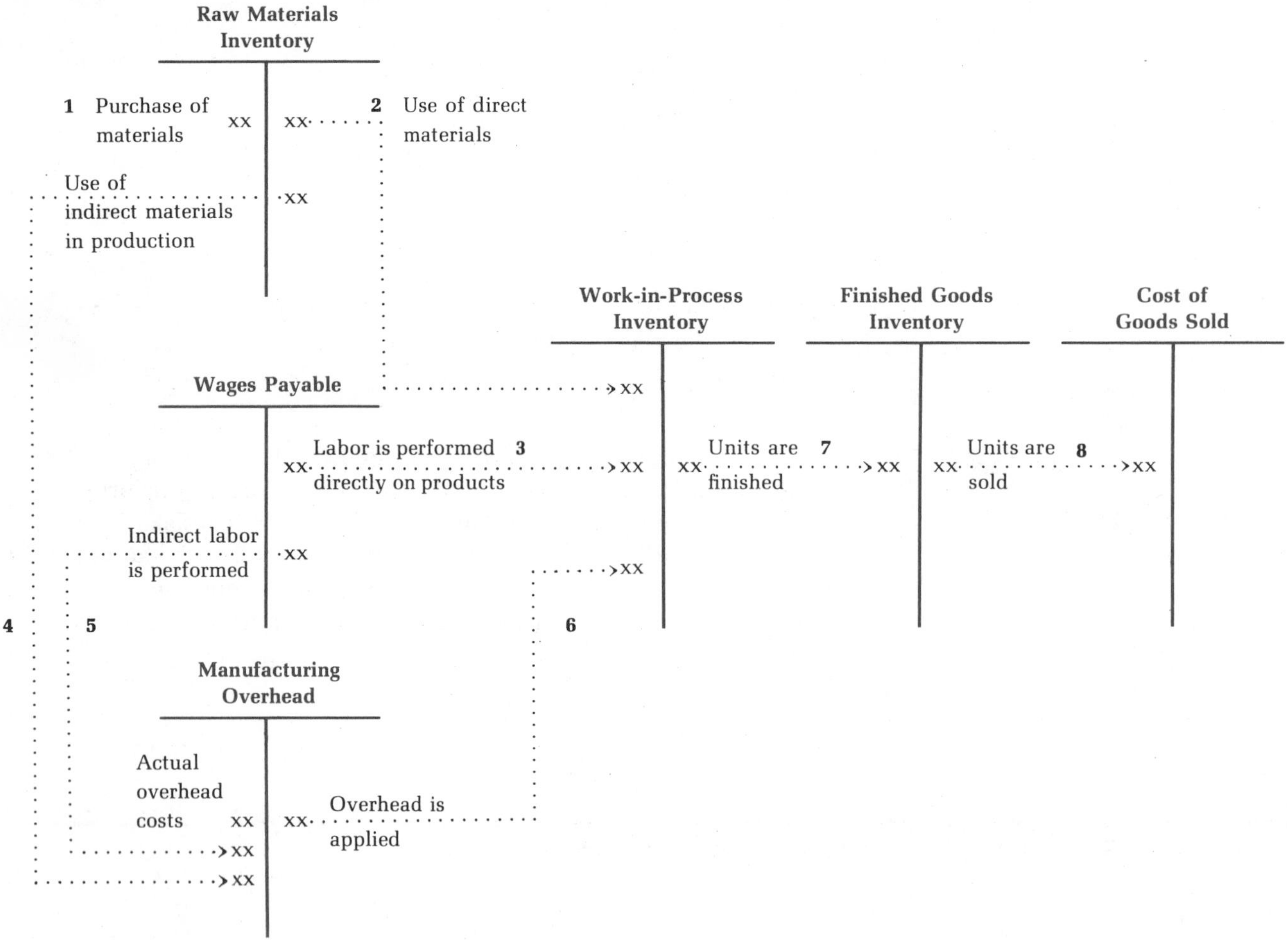

Journal Entries for Manufacturing Firms:

		Debit	Credit
1	Raw Materials Inventory	xx	
	Accounts Payable (or Cash)		xx
	Purchased raw materials.		
2	Work-in-Process Inventory	xx	
	Raw Materials Inventory		xx
	Used direct materials in production.		
3	Work-in-Process Inventory	xx	
	Wages Payable (or Cash)		xx
	Incurred direct-labor costs.		
4	Manufacturing Overhead	xx	
	Raw Materials Inventory		xx
	Used indirect materials in production.		
5	Manufacturing Overhead	xx	
	Wages Payable		xx
	Incurred indirect-labor costs.		
6	Work-in-Process Inventory	xx	
	Manufacturing Overhead		xx
	Applied variable overhead to production.		
7	Finished Goods Inventory	xx	
	Work-in-Process Inventory		xx
	Completed production of certain jobs.		
8	Cost of Goods Sold	xx	
	Finished Goods Inventory		xx
	Sold certain finished goods.		

TO SUMMARIZE When the job-order costing method is used, all direct-labor, direct-materials, and overhead costs are accumulated on a job cost sheet. These data are used in computing the estimated unit cost of a product. This cost is an estimate because variable overhead cannot be determined exactly until the accounting period is completed. As inventory is produced and sold, costs are transferred from Work-in-Process Inventory to Finished Goods Inventory and then to Cost of Goods Sold.

THE COST OF GOODS MANUFACTURED SCHEDULE

cost of goods manufactured schedule *a schedule supporting the income statement; summarizes the total cost of goods manufactured during a period, including materials, labor, and overhead costs*

The job cost sheet summarizes the costs of a specific product or job. However, management also needs to know the total cost of all goods manufactured during a period. For this reason, a cost of goods manufactured schedule, like the one in Exhibit 23-8 or the one on page 670 in Chapter 20, is usually prepared. (The numbers in Exhibit 23-8 are arbitrary and do not relate to prior examples in this chapter.) Note that a cost of goods manufactured schedule does not provide new information; it merely recaps and summarizes the data that were recorded in the journal entries.

Exhibit 23-8 shows that the total cost of goods manufactured ($436,800) is $80,000 less than total manufacturing costs ($516,800). This difference is due to the fact that work-in-process inventory increased by $80,000 during the

EXHIBIT 23-8

Howard Company
Cost of Goods Manufactured Schedule
for the Year Ended December 31, 1984

Direct Materials:		
Raw Materials Inventory, January 1	$ 70,000	
Add Raw Materials Purchased	280,000	
Total Raw Materials Available	$350,000	
Less Raw Materials Inventory, December 31	60,000	
Total Direct Materials Used in Production		$290,000
Direct Labor		165,000
Actual Variable Manufacturing Overhead:		
Indirect Labor	$ 14,300	
Indirect Materials	35,000	
Utilities	3,500	
Custodial Salaries	12,000	
Total Overhead Costs	$ 64,800	
Less Underapplied Overhead	3,000	
Overhead Applied to Work-in-Process		61,800
Total Manufacturing Costs		$516,800
Add Beginning Work-in-Process		110,000
		$626,800
Less Ending Work-in-Process		190,000
Total Cost of Goods Manufactured		$436,800

year. Notice also that an underapplied overhead of $3,000 has been subtracted from actual overhead costs. (Underapplied overhead is the amount by which actual overhead costs exceeded estimated overhead costs.) This deduction is necessary because an estimated variable overhead of only $61,800 was applied to work-in-process inventory and only those costs actually charged to products during the period are shown on this schedule. The cost of goods manufactured schedule represents a summary of costs flowing through the Work-in-Process account during a period, and therefore must exclude all overhead costs that were incurred but not applied to production. These will be disposed of by adding them directly to cost of goods sold or by allocating them among cost of goods sold, work-in-process, and ending inventory, as described in the next section.

Knowing the total cost of goods manufactured makes it easy to determine the total cost of goods sold. To illustrate, we again consider the information in Exhibit 23–8, which is used in the cost of goods sold calculation along with the beginning and ending finished goods inventories.

Beginning Finished Goods Inventory	$ 60,000
Add Cost of Goods Manufactured	436,800
Cost of Goods Available for Sale	$496,800
Less Ending Finished Goods Inventory	80,000
Cost of Goods Sold	$416,800

The total cost of goods sold ($416,800) is then subtracted from net sales on the income statement to arrive at gross margin. As you can see, a careful assignment of costs is important in measuring income. Errors in accounting for raw materials inventory, direct labor, overhead, work-in-process inventory, or finished goods inventory can significantly affect the accuracy of the net income a firm reports.

Disposition of Over- and Underapplied Overhead

underapplied overhead *the excess of actual overhead costs over the applied overhead costs for a period*

overapplied overhead *the excess of applied overhead (based on a predetermined application rate) over the actual overhead costs for a period*

We have noted several times that the variable overhead charged to products is based on a predetermined, estimated application rate, and that the amount of overhead applied may therefore be higher or lower than the actual overhead for a period. If total actual overhead exceeds the amount applied, overhead is said to be underapplied. If applied overhead exceeds actual costs, overhead is overapplied. There are two methods of treating over- and underapplied overhead.

1. Closing over- or underapplied overhead directly to Cost of Goods Sold.
2. Apportioning over- or underapplied overhead among Work-in-Process Inventory, Finished Goods Inventory, and Cost of Goods Sold on the basis of the ending balances in these accounts.

Of the two methods, the first is easier and more commonly used. It requires only a single entry to correct the amount of overhead.

In the Howard Company example (Exhibit 23-8), overhead was underapplied by $3,000. The entry to close this underapplied overhead to Cost of Goods Sold would be

Cost of Goods Sold	3,000	
Manufacturing Overhead		3,000

To recognize the excess of actual overhead costs over the applied overhead for 1984.

With this entry, Cost of Goods Sold for Howard Company increases to $419,800, as shown below:

Original Cost of Goods Sold (page 760)	$416,800
Add Underapplied Overhead	3,000
Cost of Goods Sold	$419,800

The second alternative, which allocates over- and underapplied overhead to Work-in-Process Inventory, Finished Goods Inventory, and Cost of Goods Sold, is more accurate because, theoretically, any difference between applied and actual overhead should be allocated proportionately to all items in production during the period. This includes those produced and sold, those produced and not sold, and those still being produced. If the estimate had been accurate, overhead costs would have been allocated proportionately to all products. It follows that those products actually sold should not be burdened with, or relieved of, the entire amount of the estimation error. However, because this alternative requires calculations and several journal entries, it is rarely used in practice and we will not illustrate it here. Most accountants believe that this more accurate recording is not worth the extra effort required.

The Method of Process Costing

As we have explained, process costing is appropriate for assigning costs to manufactured products that pass through a series of continuous and homogeneous processes—for example, bricks, lumber, paint, soft drinks, and newspapers. For process costing to be appropriate, two general conditions must exist.

1. The activity performed in each process center must be performed uniformly on all units.
2. The units produced as a result of passing through the process centers must be basically the same.

STEPS IN PROCESS COSTING

A firm whose products and processes meet the above conditions would employ process costing and would use five steps. The steps are outlined briefly here and explained in the following sections.

1. Identify the process centers. For example, a lumber manufacturer might have two process centers—sawing and planing.
2. Accumulate all the materials costs and the processing (labor and overhead) costs for each process center for each period of time.
3. Compute the productive output of each process center for the period.
4. Divide the total materials costs and the total processing costs for each center (step 2) by the period's output (step 3) to determine a unit cost in the process center.
5. Accumulate the unit costs of all processes to determine the total cost of each unit produced.

Identify Process Centers and Accumulate Costs

The first two steps are to identify the process centers and accumulate all materials and processing costs. The process centers are simply the various locations in a factory where work is performed directly on goods produced. Once these centers are identified, the total materials, labor, and overhead costs of a given process can be accumulated. Exhibit 23-9 shows how products and costs move through process centers.

EXHIBIT 23-9 **The Flow of Products and Costs Through Process Centers**

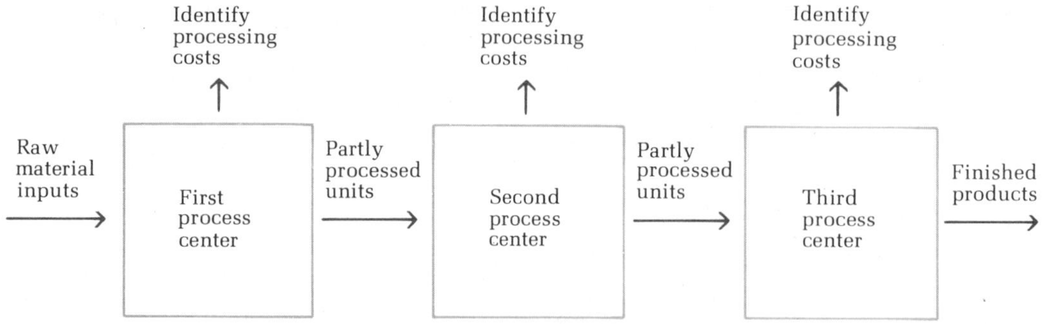

Measure Productive Output

Step 3—determining the total number of units produced—is somewhat more difficult than it may seem. A process center deals with a single continuous production process. When machines are shut down at the end of a period, not all units will have been completed. In fact, units are usually in process both at the beginning and at the end of a period. Were it not for these beginning and ending work-in-process inventories, the number of units completed could be determined merely by counting all units passing through a process center.

equivalent units of production *a concept used in a process costing system to measure accurately the productive output for a period; equals the sum of all units completed during a period plus the number of completed units equivalent to the work performed on the ending inventory less the number of completed units equivalent to the work performed on the beginning inventory in the prior period*

Because of these work-in-process (WIP) inventories, a concept known as the equivalent units of production is used. Essentially, equivalent units of production is a measure of the amount of work performed during a period. When a processing center has ending work-in-process inventories, part of the center's costs relate to the partially completed units in the ending inventory. These partially completed units will have to be converted to equivalent units and considered together with the fully completed units in measuring the period's output. For example, if at the end of the period, 100 units are 40 percent complete, the number of equivalent units in ending inventory would be 40. These 40 equivalent units of production would be added to the fully completed units as a step in computing the total output for the period.

By the same reasoning, beginning inventory must also be converted to equivalent units of production. However, the equivalent units in beginning inventory would relate to work performed in the prior period and so would be deducted from the completed units of the current period. For example, if beginning inventory consisted of 120 units that were 30 percent complete, 36 (120 units × 0.30) equivalent units would have already been completed before processing in the current period began. These 36 equivalent units would be deducted from the current period's final completed output to determine the period's actual output.

To illustrate the computation of a period's output in equivalent units, we will assume that the following data apply to production in the refining department of ABC Company.

Work-in-Process, January 1, 1984	1,000 units, 40% complete
Units Finished in 1984	4,000 units
Work-in-Process, December 31, 1984	800 units, 60% complete

Equivalent units would be computed as follows:

4,000	completed
480	ending inventory (800 × 0.60)
(400)	beginning inventory (1,000 × 0.40)
4,080	total equivalent units

The amount of work performed on the beginning WIP inventory last period is subtracted from the units completed this period because we want a measure of the productive output (activity) performed in this period only. Failure to deduct the prior period's work on these units would result in double counting.

This example was quite simple. In real situations, materials are not usually put into production at the same rate and time as labor and other processing costs are incurred. In many cases, all materials are placed in production at the beginning of the process. Because of these variations in the timing of materials and processing costs, these two categories of costs are usually analyzed separately. In such an analysis, processing costs, the combined costs of labor and manufacturing overhead, are sometimes referred to as conversion costs.

conversion costs *the costs of converting raw materials to finished products; include direct-labor and manufacturing overhead costs*

To illustrate the calculation of equivalent units in a more realistic situation, we will assume that Allied Cement Company has two process centers—mixing and bagging—and that the following activity occurred in the mixing process center during 1984. Note that materials are assumed to be fully completed when they reach the mixing center.

	Materials		Processing (Conversion)	
	Pounds	Percentage Completed	Pounds	Percentage Completed
Beginning WIP Inventory	800	100%	800	30%
Units Started in Production	10,000	—	10,000	—
Ending WIP Inventory	600	100%	600	20%
Units Completed During the Year and Transferred to Bagging	10,200	—	10,200	—

Equivalent units for the period are calculated as follows:

	Materials	Processing
Add:		
(a) Units Completed and Transferred to Bagging	10,200	10,200
(b) Equivalent Units in Ending WIP Inventory:		
(600 × 1.00)	600	—
(600 × 0.20)	—	120
Deduct:		
(c) Equivalent Units in Beginning WIP Inventory:		
(800 × 1.00)	(800)	—
(800 × 0.30)	—	(240)
Total Equivalent Units	10,000	10,080

In this example, the number of equivalent units in processing is less than the actual number of units completed and sent to bagging. This difference occurred because the beginning work-in-process inventory was larger and further along in production than the ending work-in-process inventory. The number of equivalent units can be greater than, equal to, or less than the actual number of units completed.

Compute the Total Unit Cost

The final two steps, which involve computing the total unit cost, are straightforward. In step 4, materials and processing costs are divided by the number of equivalent units. In step 5, unit costs in all process centers are added.

To illustrate, we will assume that total costs of mixing the cement were $4,000 for materials and $6,048 for processing. Thus, the unit costs of mixing would be

Materials:	$4,000 ÷ 10,000 equivalent units =	$0.40 per pound
Processing:	$6,048 ÷ 10,080 equivalent units =	$0.60 per pound
	Total:	$1.00 per pound

This $1.00 would then be added to the unit costs in the bagging department to arrive at the total cost per pound of cement produced.

TO SUMMARIZE Process costing involves five steps: (1) identifying process centers, (2) accumulating the materials costs and the processing costs, (3) calculating the equivalent units produced in each process center, (4) dividing the materials and processing costs by the number of equivalent units, and (5) adding the unit costs in all process centers to determine the total unit cost.

THE FLOW OF UNITS AND COSTS BETWEEN PROCESS CENTERS

Until now, we have focused on individual process centers. That is, we have calculated unit costs and equivalent units for specific cost centers, paying no attention to how these costs flow from center to center. In this section, we explain the flow of units and costs from center to center, as well as some of the problems that companies encounter in transferring these costs and units.

To illustrate the flow of costs between process centers, we will assume that Spencer Chocolate Company requires three processes to make chocolate bars: (1) mixing—combining chocolate, milk, sugar, and other ingredients; (2) cooking—boiling the chocolate in large vats; and (3) packaging—molding the chocolate into appropriate shapes and packaging it for sale to candy stores throughout the world. For March 1984, Spencer's accounting records revealed the following information, which will form the basis of our study of the flow of units and costs.

	Mixing		Cooking		Packaging	
	Pounds	Percentage Completed	Pounds	Percentage Completed	Pounds	Percentage Completed
Beginning WIP Inventory	2,000	30%	4,000	40%	3,000	60%
Units Started in Production	12,000	—	11,000	—	13,000	—
Ending WIP Inventory	3,000	70%	2,000	30%	2,000	40%
Units Completed and Transferred	11,000	—	13,000	—	14,000	—

In addition, the total costs for the mixing department in March were $43,750 and the total costs from the previous month of beginning WIP inventory were $1,800.

The Flow of Units Between Process Centers

production report *a document used for transferring units and/or costs from one process center to another*

Process costing, as you will recall, is an averaging procedure whereby all costs are equitably allocated to all units produced. It is vital, therefore, that all units be accurately accounted for. Such an accurate accounting is accomplished by means of a production report, which is a record of all units worked on during a period by the various process centers. Exhibit 23-10 shows a unit production report for Spencer Chocolate Company for March 1984.

EXHIBIT 23-10 **Spencer Chocolate Company**
Unit Production Report for March 1984 (in Pounds)

	Mixing	Cooking	Packaging
Units to Be Accounted for:			
Beginning Inventory	2,000	4,000	3,000
Units Started in Production	12,000	11,000	13,000
Total Units Available	14,000	15,000	16,000
Units Accounted for as Follows:			
Transferred Out During the Period (total available minus ending inventory)	11,000	13,000	14,000
Ending Inventory	3,000	2,000	2,000
Total Units Accounted for	14,000	15,000	16,000
Equivalent Units of Production:			
Units Transferred Out During the Period	11,000	13,000	14,000
Add Equivalent Units of Ending Inventory:			
3,000 pounds × 0.70	2,100	–	–
2,000 pounds × 0.30	–	600	–
2,000 pounds × 0.40	–	–	800
	13,100	13,600	14,800
Deduct Equivalent Units of Beginning Inventory:			
2,000 pounds × 0.30	(600)	–	–
4,000 pounds × 0.40	–	(1,600)	–
3,000 pounds × 0.60	–	–	(1,800)
Output for the Period in Equivalent Units of Production	12,500	12,000	13,000

You will note that the units started in production in the cooking and packaging departments are those units that were transferred out of the mixing and cooking departments, respectively. This production report has been kept simple: Materials and processing costs in each department have not been separated; rather, in this example it has been assumed that materials and processing costs are added at exactly the same time and in proportionate amounts.

The Flow of Costs Between Process Centers

If the costs of producing units remained constant from period to period, transferring them between departments would be simple. You would merely divide the total costs incurred in each process center during a period by the total number of equivalent units for that center, and add all these per-unit costs together to calculate the total per-unit cost of the completed product. You would not need to assume a given cost flow pattern, such as FIFO, LIFO, or weighted average. However, in most environments, inflation and other factors change costs so that they rarely remain constant from period to period. As a result, the materials in, say, the beginning work-in-process inventory usually have a different unit cost than do the materials in the current work-in-process inventory or in ending inventory. For this reason, some cost flow alternative usually must be used. In this chapter, we will illustrate both FIFO and weighted-average cost flows.

FIFO (first-in, first-out) *an inventory cost flow whereby the first goods purchased are assumed to be the first goods sold; the ending inventory consists of the most recently purchased goods*

FIFO Cost Flows As you will recall, in a merchandising firm FIFO means that the first goods in are the first goods sold. In a manufacturing firm, where items pass through several stages of production, this cost flow alternative is applied to each processing center. That is, the cost of the first goods into the department are assumed to be the costs of the goods transferred to the next department. This is an important point because costs may change from one period to the next. Thus, with a FIFO cost flow, the units from the beginning work-in-process inventory are transferred to the next department at the prior period's costs ($1,800 in our example) plus the costs incurred this period to complete the beginning inventory. All units started and completed during the current period are transferred at the current period's costs. To illustrate, we will again consider the data for Spencer Chocolate Company's mixing department. You will note that the units (in number of pounds) are the same as before and that materials and processing costs have been combined again.

	Pounds	Percentage Completed
Beginning WIP Inventory	2,000	30%
Units Started in Production	12,000	–
Ending WIP Inventory	3,000	70%
Units Completed During the Period and Transferred to Cooking	11,000	–

Given these data, the unit cost for the current period can be determined by dividing the total costs of the mixing department during this period ($43,750) by the equivalent units produced by the mixing department (12,500, from Exhibit 12–10) as follows:

$$\frac{\text{total mixing department costs during this period}}{\text{equivalent units}} = \frac{\$43{,}750}{12{,}500} = \$3.50$$

This calculation shows that the unit cost in the mixing department for the current period is $3.50. Now, if a FIFO cost flow is assumed, the 11,000 pounds that were transferred to cooking must be divided into two segments: beginning inventory (2,000 pounds) and inventory started and completed during the current period (9,000 pounds). The two segments would be costed as follows:

Cost of Beginning Inventory	$ 1,800
Cost Required to Complete the Units in Beginning Inventory (2,000 lbs. × 0.70 × $3.50)	4,900
Costs Required to Complete the Units Started and Completed During the Period (9,000 lbs. × $3.50)	31,500
Total Cost of All Units Transferred Out During the Period	$38,200

We now add this cost information for the mixing department to the unit production report that was illustrated in Exhibit 23-10. The result is Exhibit 23-11, a production report showing cost accounting under the FIFO alternative. Note that the cost of the ending inventory is based on the current period's cost per equivalent unit.

EXHIBIT 23-11

Spencer Chocolate Company
Production Report for the Mixing Department —FIFO Cost Flow

Units to Be Accounted for:	
Beginning Inventory (30% complete)	2,000
Units Started in Production	12,000
Total Units Available	14,000
Units Accounted for as Follows:	
Transferred Out During the Period	11,000
Ending Inventory (70% complete)	3,000
Total Units Accounted for	14,000
Costs to Be Accounted for:	
Beginning Inventory	$ 1,800
Added During This Period	43,750
Total Costs	$45,550
Costs Accounted for as Follows:	
Transferred Out During the Period	$38,200
Ending Inventory (2,100 equivalent units × $3.50)	7,350
Total Costs Accounted for	$45,550

weighted average *a periodic inventory cost flow alternative whereby the cost of goods sold and the ending inventory are determined by using a weighted-average cost of all merchandise available for sale during the period*

Weighted-Average Cost Flows When the much simpler weighted-average cost flow alternative is used, no attempt is made to differentiate between costs incurred in the prior period and those of this period. Instead, all costs (including those of beginning inventory and those incurred during the current period) are added and allocated to all units equally. In addition, units in beginning inventory are treated as if *they were started and completed during the current period*. Thus, work performed in the prior period is not subtracted when computing the current period's output or equivalent units.

To illustrate, we will again consider the data for Spencer Chocolate Company's mixing department. Exhibit 23-12 shows the equivalent units and unit costs using the weighted-average method. As shown, the per-pound cost of chocolate in the mixing department is determined as follows:

$$\frac{\text{cost of beginning inventory} + \text{costs added during the period}}{\text{units transferred out} + \text{equivalent units of ending inventory}}$$

$$= \frac{\$1{,}800 + \$43{,}750}{11{,}000 + 2{,}100} = \frac{\$45{,}550}{13{,}100 \text{ pounds}} = \$3.477 \text{ per pound}$$

EXHIBIT 23-12 *Unit Cost Using the Weighted-Average Method*

Costs to Be Accounted for:	
Cost of Beginning Inventory	$ 1,800
Costs Added by the Mixing Department	43,750
Total Cost	$45,550
Equivalent Units:	
Units Transferred Out	11,000
Add Equivalent Units—Ending Inventory	2,100
	13,100
Computation of Unit Cost:	
Total Cost	$45,550
Equivalent Units	13,100
Unit Cost ($45,550 ÷ 13,100)	$3.477

The $3.477-per-pound figure is then used to cost all the chocolate mixed during March, whether it was in beginning inventory or started during the month. This includes chocolate transferred to cooking as well as the equivalent units of ending inventory in mixing. The unit cost in the mixing department for the next period would then be the average of the remaining ending inventory costs and those costs incurred during the next period. Thus, in every department a new average must be calculated each period. A production report that summarizes these costs is shown in Exhibit 23-13. The $7,303 of costs in ending inventory becomes the cost of beginning inventory in the next period's calculation.

EXHIBIT 23-13 **Spencer Chocolate Company**
Production Report for Mixing Department
—Weighted-Average Cost Flow

Costs to Be Accounted for:	
Costs in Beginning Inventory	$ 1,800
Costs Added During the Period	43,750
	$45,550
Costs Accounted for as Follows:	
Costs Transferred to Cooking ($3.477 × 11,000)	$38,247
Costs in Ending Inventory ($3.477 × 3,000 × 0.70)	7,303*
	$45,550

* Rounded.

TO SUMMARIZE With process costing, both units and costs must be transferred from center to center until the final unit cost is accumulated at the end of the production process. The production report provides a convenient method of accounting for the flow of units between process centers. Several cost flow alternatives could be used to account for the flow of costs between process centers. With the FIFO cost flow alternative, units in beginning inventory are transferred at a figure that includes both the prior period's and the current period's costs. All other units completed during the current period are transferred at the current period costs. With the weighted-average method, costs of the beginning inventory are simply added to costs incurred during the current period and units in beginning inventory are not deducted when computing the period's output in equivalent units.

Classifying Overhead Costs

Manufacturing overhead includes all manufacturing costs except direct materials and direct labor. For example, indirect materials, indirect labor, factory depreciation, maintenance, and repairs, factory utilities, taxes on factory equipment, and factory supplies are all manufacturing overhead costs. These costs may be treated as product costs or period expenses, depending on whether absorption or variable costing is used. Under absorption costing, all manufacturing overhead costs, fixed and variable, are product costs. In fact, for absorption costing, the distinction between fixed and variable costs is unnecessary. Under variable costing, overhead costs must be separated into their fixed and variable elements; this is because variable manufacturing overhead costs are treated as product costs and fixed manufacturing overhead costs are treated as period expenses.

Both absorption and variable costing are important concepts. Absorption costing is required by generally accepted accounting principles and by the Internal Revenue Service for income tax purposes, whereas variable costing is more useful to management for planning, control, and performance evaluation. For these key aspects of managerial accounting, then, you must understand the function for which the manufacturing overhead costs will be used before they can be properly classified as product costs or period expenses.

CHAPTER REVIEW

There are two basic approaches to product costing: absorption and variable costing. Absorption costing, which includes both fixed and variable overhead as product costs, is required by both the IRS and GAAP. Variable costing, which includes only variable overhead as a product cost, is more useful for internal decision-making purposes.

With either approach, there are two principal methods of accumulating and assigning costs: job-order and process costing. Job-order costing is used for costing products that are custom ordered or in firms where different types of products are made with the same equipment. Process costing is appropriate for firms in which identical products are mass-produced by passing them through a series of uniform production steps or processes. The goal of either cost-accumulation method (job-order or process costing) is the same: to generate unit inventory data for planning, control, and financial reporting purposes.

The job cost sheet is the primary document in a job-order costing system. It is here that materials, labor, and overhead costs are recorded and unit costs are determined. As supporting documents to the job cost sheet, materials requisition forms are prepared for materials put into production and time tickets are prepared to account for the direct-labor hours spent on each job. When materials are purchased by a manufacturing firm, their costs are entered into a Raw Materials Inventory account. As materials are used, costs are removed from this account and debited to Work-in-Process Inventory. Similarly, direct-labor or overhead costs are entered in the Work-in-Process Inventory account. As units are completed, they are transferred from Work-in-Process Inventory to Finished Goods Inventory. When sold, they are transferred to Cost of Goods Sold.

Whereas direct-materials and direct-labor costs assigned to products are actual costs, overhead is assigned to products on the basis of some predetermined application rate. Expected overhead costs for a period are estimated at the beginning of the period so that products can be costed as they are produced. This estimated overhead is credited to the Manufacturing Overhead account. Then, as actual overhead costs are incurred, they are debited to Manufacturing Overhead. The Manufacturing Overhead account is thus a clearing account. At the end of the year, under- and overapplications of overhead costs are closed directly to Cost of Goods Sold or allocated among Cost of Goods Sold, Finished Goods Inventory, and Work-in-Process Inventory. The cost of goods manufactured schedule, which supports the income statement for a manufacturing firm, shows total manufacturing costs actually charged to products during a period.

There are five steps in the process costing approach: (1) identifying process centers, (2) accumulating materials and processing costs, (3) calculating the productive output (equivalent units) of each process center during the period, (4) dividing total materials and processing costs by the number of equivalent units produced, and (5) accumulating the unit costs of each process to determine the total cost of each unit produced. The first four steps are concerned with accumulating costs and the fifth with transferring costs from one center to another.

A production report provides unit-cost data, which in turn are used to cost inventory transfers from one center to the next and to cost the ending work-in-process inventory of each center. If costs remained constant from period to period, this transfer would be relatively simple. Because costs usually are not stable, a cost flow pattern must be assumed. The most common cost flow alternatives are FIFO and weighted average.

In addition to product costs, a firm usually has selling and administrative expenses. These nonmanufacturing costs are treated as period expenses.

KEY TERMS AND CONCEPTS

absorption costing (746)
conversion costs (763)
cost of goods manufactured schedule (759)
equivalent units of production (763)
FIFO (first-in, first-out) (767)
indirect-labor costs (752)
indirect-materials costs (750)
job cost sheet (748)
job-order costing (747)
manufacturing overhead (752)
materials requisition form (750)
overapplied overhead (760)
overhead application rate (754)
process costing (747)
product costing (746)
production report (765)
time ticket (751)
underapplied overhead (760)
variable costing (747)
variable overhead (754)
weighted average (768)

REVIEW PROBLEM

Job-Order Costing

Required:

1. Prepare journal entries for the following 1984 transactions of Reynolds Manufacturing Company. Assume that overhead costs are applied on the basis of direct-materials cost. The 1984 predictions for these costs are

Direct-Materials Cost	$300,000
Manufacturing Overhead	111,000

(Round entries to the nearest dollar.)

(a) Raw materials purchased for cash, $500,000.
(b) Raw materials issued to production (80 percent for direct use, 20 percent for indirect purposes), $400,000.
(c) Direct-labor costs, $250,000.
(d) Indirect-labor costs, $40,000.
(e) Administrative and sales salaries, $70,000 and $60,000, respectively.
(f) Manufacturing overhead costs incurred are: utilities, $9,000; plant depreciation, $18,000; supplies, $8,000; cash paid for miscellaneous overhead items, $6,000. (Assume that all are product costs.)
(g) Manufacturing equipment depreciation, $6,000.
(h) Overhead is applied.
(i) Factory foreman's salary, $30,000. (Assume that this is a product cost.)
(j) Sixty-five percent of existing work-in-process is transferred to finished goods. (Beginning WIP inventory was $13,000.)
(k) Ninety percent of finished goods are sold. (Assume no beginning or ending inventories; sales are marked up 50 percent of cost.)
(l) Over- or underapplied overhead is closed to cost of goods sold.

2. Assuming a beginning raw materials inventory balance of $20,000, a beginning work-in-process inventory of $13,000, and no beginning finished goods inventory, prepare a cost of goods manufactured schedule for Reynolds Manufacturing Company.

Solution

1. Journal Entries

a	Raw Materials Inventory	500,000	
	Cash		500,000
	Purchased raw materials inventory.		
b	Manufacturing Overhead	80,000	
	Work-in-Process Inventory	320,000	
	Raw Materials Inventory		400,000
	Used raw materials in production.		

(In this case, 20 percent is debited to Manufacturing Overhead because indirect materials is an overhead item. Manufacturing Overhead is debited for actual overhead expenditures and credited for overhead applications.)

c	Work-in-Process Inventory	250,000	
	Wages Payable (or Cash)		250,000
	Incurred direct-labor costs.		
d	Manufacturing Overhead	40,000	
	Wages Payable (or Cash)		40,000
	Incurred indirect-labor costs.		
e	Salaries Expense—Sales	70,000	
	Salaries Expense— Administrative	60,000	
	Wages Payable (or Cash)		130,000
	Incurred sales and administrative salary expenses.		

f	Manufacturing Overhead	41,000	
	Utilities Payable (or Cash)		9,000
	Accumulated Depreciation—Plant		18,000
	Supplies		8,000
	Cash		6,000
	Incurred overhead costs.		

(The actual overhead expenditures are debited to the overhead account.)

g	Manufacturing Overhead	6,000	
	Accumulated Depreciation—Equipment		6,000
	To depreciate equipment and apply it to manufacturing overhead.		
h	Work-in-Process Inventory	118,400	
	Manufacturing Overhead		118,400
	Applied overhead to work-in-process inventory.		

[The application rate is equal to estimated total manufacturing overhead divided by estimated direct-materials costs ($111,000 ÷ $300,000), or 37 percent of direct-materials costs. In this case, $118,400 ($320,000 × 0.37) is applied, because direct-materials costs were $320,000 ($400,000 × 0.80).]

i	Manufacturing Overhead	30,000	
	Wages Payable		30,000
	Incurred salary expense for factory foreman.		
j	Finished Goods Inventory	455,910	
	Work-in-Process Inventory		455,910
	Transferred 65% of work-in-process inventory to finished goods inventory.		

The amount transferred is determined as follows.

Work-in-Process Inventory

Debit		Credit
Beg. Bal.	13,000	
b	320,000	
c	250,000	
h	118,400	
	701,400	
	× 0.65	
	455,910	

k	Accounts Receivable	615,479	
	Sales Revenue		615,479
	Cost of Goods Sold	410,319	
	Finished Goods Inventory		410,319
	Sold 90% of finished goods inventory.		

[Since finished goods inventory is $455,910 (entry **j**), cost of goods sold is 90 percent of $455,910, or $410,319. Since finished goods inventory is marked up 50 percent, sales revenue is 150 percent of $410,319, or $615,479.]

l	Cost of Goods Sold	78,600	
	Manufacturing Overhead		78,600
	Closed underapplied overhead.		

The amount of underapplied overhead is determined as follows.

Manufacturing Overhead

Debit		Credit	
b	80,000	118,400	h
d	40,000		
f	41,000		
g	6,000		
i	30,000		
Bal.	78,600		

2. The Cost of Goods Manufactured Schedule

The easiest way to prepare a cost of goods manufactured schedule is first to post the journal entries to T-accounts and then to transfer the balances to the schedule. The necessary T-accounts follow.

Cash

Debit	Credit	
	500,000	a
	6,000	f

Accounts Receivable

Debit		Credit
k	615,479	

Raw Materials Inventory

Debit		Credit	
Beg. Bal.	20,000	400,000	b
a	500,000		
Bal.	120,000		

Work-in-Process Inventory

Debit		Credit	
Beg. Bal.	13,000	455,910	j
b	320,000		
c	250,000		
h	118,400		
Bal.	245,490		

Finished Goods Inventory

Debit		Credit	
j	455,910	410,319	k
Bal.	45,591		

Supplies

Debit	Credit	
	8,000	f

Accumulated Depreciation—Plant

	18,000 . . . f

Accumulated Depreciation—Equipment

	6,000 . . . . g

Wages Payable

	250,000 . . c
	40,000 . . d
	130,000 . . e
	30,000 . . i

Utilities Payable

	9,000 . . . . f

Sales Revenue

	615,478.50 k

Cost of Goods Sold

k . . . 410,319	
l . . . 78,600	

Salaries Expense—Sales

e 60,000	

Salaries Expense—Administrative

e 70,000	

Manufacturing Overhead

b 80,000	118,400 . . h
d 40,000	78,600 . . l
f 41,000	
g 6,000	
i 30,000	

Reynolds Manufacturing Company
Cost of Goods Manufactured Schedule
for the Year Ended December 31, 1984

Direct Materials:		
Raw Materials Inventory January 1, 1984	$ 20,000	
Add Raw Materials Purchases	420,000*	
Total Raw Materials Available	$440,000	
Less Raw Materials Inventory, December 31, 1984	120,000	
Total Direct Materials Used in Production		$320,000
Direct Labor		250,000
Manufacturing Overhead:		
Indirect Materials	$ 80,000	
Indirect Labor	40,000	
Utilities	9,000	
Plant Depreciation	18,000	
Maintenance	8,000	
Miscellaneous Overhead	6,000	
Depreciation—Equipment	6,000	
Foreman's Salary	30,000	
Total Manufacturing Overhead	$197,000	
Less Underapplied Overhead	78,600	118,400
Total Manufacturing Costs		$688,400
Add Beginning Work-in-Process Inventory		13,000
		$701,400
Less Ending Work-in-Process Inventory		245,490
Total Cost of Goods Manufactured		$455,910

* Represents only direct materials ($500,000 − $80,000); indirect materials are in overhead.

DISCUSSION QUESTIONS

1 Which costs are usually included as product costs in a manufacturing company for financial reporting purposes?

2 Why should a firm know how much it costs to manufacture its products?

3 What is the major difference between variable and absorption costing?

4 What is the major difference between job-order and process costing?

5 What is the difference between direct materials and indirect materials and between direct labor and indirect labor?

6 Why are actual overhead costs not assigned directly to products as incurred?

7 What are some common bases for applying overhead costs to products?

8 Why is Manufacturing Overhead referred to as a "clearing account"?

9 What are the three common types of inventory usually associated with a manufacturing firm?

10 How does a firm dispose of over- and underapplied overhead costs?

11 What two conditions are necessary for process costing to be appropriate?

12 Why is it necessary to determine equivalent units of production when using a process costing system?

13 In a process costing system why is a cost flow alternative (such as FIFO or weighted average) necessary?

14 Is depreciation a product cost or a period expense?

EXERCISES

E23–1 Accounting for Manufacturing Transactions—Journal Entries

Zula Company uses a job-order costing system. Following is a partial list of the accounts that appear in the company's General Ledger.

Cash
Manufacturing Overhead
Sales Revenue
Cost of Goods Sold
Sales Expense
Administrative Expense
Accounts Receivable
Commissions Payable

Prepare a T-account for each of the above and post each transaction below in the appropriate T-account. For example:

1. Goods previously purchased on account were paid for in cash, $500.

Cash		Accounts Payable	
	500 1	1........ 500	

2. Raw materials were purchased for $1,000 on account.
3. Direct-labor costs of $2,000 were recorded.
4. Raw materials costing $800 were issued directly to production.
5. Depreciation of $1,500 on manufacturing equipment was recorded. (Assume that this is a product cost.)
6. Property taxes payable of $1,600 were accrued, half to manufacturing and half to administration.
7. Overhead costs of $300 were applied to a job in process.
8. Materials previously purchased on account were paid for in cash, $1,000.
9. Sales commissions of $240 were accrued.
10. Goods costing $1,700 were transferred from work-in-process to finished goods.
11. Finished goods costing $1,300 were sold for $2,100 on credit, and the cost of goods sold was recorded.
12. Underapplied overhead of $80 was charged to the Cost of Goods Sold account.

E23–2 Job Cost Sheets and Other Documentation

McMahan Manufacturing Company uses a job-order costing system. For job #131, the production manager requisitioned $400 of materials and used 15 hours of direct labor at $7.00 an hour. Overhead is applied on the basis of direct-labor hours. At the beginning of the year, $300,000 of overhead costs were estimated for the year, with 100,000 direct-labor hours forecast.

1. Prepare the cost summary section of a job cost sheet for job #131.
2. What accounting forms would be used as source documents for the direct-materials and direct-labor costs? Explain their use in the accounting system.

E23–3 Applying Manufacturing Overhead

Brandon Corporation has four independent manufacturing divisions. The following data apply to the divisions for the year ended December 31, 1984.

	A	B	C	D
Direct-Materials Costs	$130,000	$130,000	$75,000	$65,000
Direct-Labor Hours	30,000	24,000	16,000	14,000
Direct-Labor Costs	$120,000	$ 72,000	$80,000	$42,000
Actual Manufacturing Overhead	$120,000	$120,000	$19,000	$16,500
Machine Hours Worked	15,000	12,000	10,000	8,000
Variable Overhead Rate	100% of direct-labor costs	60% of direct-materials costs	$1.20 per direct-labor hour	$2 per machine hour
Number of Units Produced	100,000	2,000	15,000	5,000

1. For each of the four divisions, calculate:
   (a) Applied overhead.
   (b) Over- or underapplied overhead.
   (c) Cost of goods manufactured, assuming no work-in-process inventories.
   (d) Average cost per unit produced.
2. How would you recommend that the over- or underapplied overhead be disposed of in each division? Why?

E23–4 Applying Manufacturing Overhead

Merrimac Corporation uses a job-order costing system. Thus, management must establish a predetermined rate for applying manufacturing overhead. During the past 3 years, the following data have been accumulated.

	1983	1984	1985
Direct-Labor Hours	40,000	48,000	60,000
Machine Hours	80,000	60,000	40,000
Direct-Materials Costs	$300,000	$290,000	$310,000
Actual Manufacturing Overhead	$ 60,000	$ 45,000	$ 30,000

1. What would the overhead application rate be for each of the 3 years, if based on: (a) direct-labor hours, (b) machine hours, (c) direct-materials costs? (No under- or overapplied overhead should remain in any of the 3 years.)

2. Which basis would you recommend be used in the future for applying manufacturing overhead? Why?

E23–5 Applying Manufacturing Overhead

Mercy Company has four manufacturing subsidiaries: A, B, C, and D. Each subsidiary keeps a separate set of accounting records. Manufacturing cost forecasts for 1984 for each subsidiary are

	Subsidiaries			
	A	B	C	D
Materials to Be Used (pounds) .	75,000	60,000	40,000	52,500
Direct-Labor Hours	50,000	37,500	20,000	35,000
Direct-Labor Costs	$10,000	$5,000	$ 2,500	$ 5,000
Machine Hours ..	25,000	20,000	12,500	37,500
Manufacturing Overhead	$25,000	$30,000	$10,000	$35,000

The variable overhead application rates for each subsidiary are based on the following.

A: Machine hours
B: Direct-labor costs
C: Materials used
D: Direct-labor hours

1. Compute the predetermined overhead rate to be used in 1984 by each subsidiary.

2. If subsidiary B actually had $6,000 of direct-labor costs and $34,000 of manufacturing overhead, will overhead be over- or underapplied and by how much?

3. If subisidiary C used 66,000 pounds of materials in 1984, what would be the applied overhead?

4. Identify the two most commonly used methods of disposing of under- or overapplied overhead. What is the major advantage of each method?

E23–6 Work-in-Process Analysis

Jill Fotten, an independent auditor, is currently auditing the Work-in-Process account of a client who uses a job-order costing system. Jill has forgotten the basic cost accounting concepts and asks for your assistance. Identify the four types of transactions or events that affect the Work-in-Process Inventory account. Prepare and explain a sample journal entry for each type of transaction.

E23–7 Analyzing Manufacturing Costs and Preparing a Cost of Goods Manufactured Schedule

The following T-accounts represent inventory costs as of December 31, 1985.

Raw Materials Inventory

	Debit	Credit
Bal. 12/31/84	32,000	100,000
	104,000	
Bal. 12/31/85	36,000	

Work-in-Process Inventory

	Debit	Credit
Bal. 12/31/84	50,000	500,000
	100,000	
	124,000	
	280,000	
Bal. 12/31/85	54,000	

Finished Goods Inventory

	Debit	Credit
Bal. 12/31/84	132,000	584,000
	500,000	
Bal. 12/31/85	48,000	

Manufacturing Overhead

Debit	Credit
26,000	124,000
24,000	
28,000	
52,000	

1. Determine direct-labor costs for 1985.
2. Compute cost of goods manufactured for 1985.
3. Determine cost of goods sold for 1985.

4. Compute over- or underapplied overhead for 1985.
5. Determine actual indirect manufacturing costs for 1985.
6. Prepare a cost of goods manufactured schedule for 1985.

E23-8 The Cost of Goods Manufactured and Sold

Jackson Corporation has maintained the following job cost information for 1984.

Beginning Inventories:	
Raw Materials	$ 50,000
Work-in-Process	86,000
Finished Goods	52,000
Ending Inventories:	
Raw Materials	32,000
Work-in-Process	82,000
Finished Goods	86,000
Variable Manufacturing Costs and Related Data:	
Raw (Direct) Materials Purchased	266,000
Direct Labor	316,000
Indirect Labor	50,000
Utilities	6,000
Indirect Materials	100,000
Overapplied Overhead Costs	6,000
Sales and Administrative Expenses:	
Utilities Expense	6,000
Salaries Expense	150,000
Depreciation Expense	14,000
Income Tax Expense	8,000

1. Prepare a cost of goods manufactured schedule for 1984.
2. Calculate cost of goods sold, assuming that the differences between applied and actual overhead costs are closed directly to cost of goods sold each year.

E23-9 Equivalent Units of Production—Process Costing

P. L. Larsen Chair Company makes rocking chairs. The company has two process centers, assembly and painting. During 1984 the following activities took place.

Assembly Department

	Materials		Processing	
	Chairs	**Percentage Completed**	**Chairs**	**Percentage Completed**
Beginning Inventory	30	100%	30	30
New Chairs Put in Process	600		600	
Ending Inventory	50	100%	50	70

Painting Department

	Materials		Processing	
	Chairs	**Percentage Completed**	**Chairs**	**Percentage Completed**
Begininng Inventory	15	100%	15	40
Chairs Transferred from Assembly to Painting	?		?	
Ending Inventory	25		25	60

1. How many chairs were transferred from assembly to painting? From painting to finished goods?
2. Compute the output for both materials and processing for 1984 (in equivalent units) for both the assembly and painting process centers.

E23-10 Equivalent Units and Unit Costs—Process Costing

Chatterton Corporation began producing "quick-stick glue" in April 1984. The manufacturing process involves only one step and in April the costs were $8,000 for materials and $6,688 for processing. During the month, 6,400 pounds of materials were placed in production. At the end of April, 800 pounds of materials were still being processed and were 60 percent complete. Assume that all materials are added at the beginning of the production process.

1. Compute the number of equivalent units of output for April.
2. Determine the total costs of inventory in process at the end of April and the total goods transferred to finished goods inventory.

E23-11 FIFO Cost Flow—Process Costing

The cleaning division of Brian Grain Company had the following data for January 1984.

	Tons	Percentage Completed	Total Costs
Beginning WIP Inventory	8,000	40%	$ 7,200
Units Started in Production	48,000	—	177,600
Ending WIP Inventory	12,000	60%	
Units Completed During the Month and Transferred to Packing	44,000	—	

1. Compute the per-ton cost of grain processed by the cleaning department this period.

2. Using the FIFO cost flow alternative, compute the cost of the 44,000 tons of grain that were transferred to the packing division.
3. Compute the cost of the ending inventory.

E23–12 FIFO Cost Flow—Process Costing

Exploratory Oil Company has three process centers: drilling, processing, and distributing. During September 1984, the processing department had the following operating data:

	Barrels	Percentage Completed	Total Costs
Beginning WIP Inventory	2,000	60%	$ 4,000
Units Started in Production	23,000	–	73,000
Ending WIP Inventory	3,000	30%	
Units Completed During the Month and Transferred to Distributing	22,000	–	

Assuming a FIFO flow of costs, compute:
1. The output for September in equivalent units of production.
2. The cost per barrel of oil in the process center.
3. The ending costs that are not transferred to the distributing center.

E23–13 Weighted-Average Cost Flow—Process Costing

Refer to E23–12. Assuming a weighted-average flow of costs, compute
1. The cost per barrel of oil in the process center.
2. The ending amount of costs that are not transferred to the distributing center.
3. The cost of all oil transferred to distributing.

E23–14 Variable Versus Absorption Costing

Springville Manufacturing Company makes automobiles. The cost of assembling an automobile during 1984 is estimated to be

Direct Materials	$4,400
Direct Labor (100 hours at $20 per hour)	2,000
Variable Overhead (estimated to be $8 per direct-labor hour)	800
Fixed Overhead (estimated to be $12 per direct-labor hour)	1,200
	$8,400

How much higher (lower) would absorption costing net income be than variable costing net income if
1. There were 100 more cars on hand at the end of 1984 than there were at the beginning of 1984? Why?
2. There were 50 fewer cars on hand at the end of 1984 than there were at the beginning of 1984? Why?
3. The number of cars on hand at the beginning and end of 1984 was the same?

E23–15 Variable Versus Absorption Costing

1. Use the following data to compute operating income under both absorption and variable costing methods.

Sales: 2,000 units at $10 each
Beginning inventory: 100 units at $6 each (including $2 of fixed overhead)
Production during current period: 1,400 units
Direct-materials costs: $2,800
Direct-labor costs: $2,100
Variable overhead costs: $700
Fixed overhead costs: $2,800
Selling and administrative expenses: $3,000

2. What causes the difference between the two net income numbers?

PROBLEMS

P23–1 Job-Order Costing—Journal Entries

Following are 1984 transactions for Jumbo Manufacturing Company. Assume that the company has no beginning work-in-process inventory.

1. Jumbo purchased $400,000 of raw materials, paying 10 percent down, with the remainder to be paid in 10 days.
2. $240,000 of materials were requisitioned by the production manager (90 percent for direct use and the remainder for indirect purposes).
3. The liability incurred in part (1) was paid in full.
4. Twenty-four thousand hours of direct labor and 2,000 hours of indirect labor were incurred. (Assume an average hourly wage rate of $9.00 for both direct and indirect labor.)

5. The following salaries were paid.

Factory supervisor (a product cost)	$70,000
Administration executives	$60,000
Sales personnel	$80,000

6. Rent and utilities for the building were $20,000 and $6,000, respectively. Three-fourths of these expenses are applicable to manufacturing, and the remainder to administration.

7. Depreciation on factory equipment was $10,000.

8. Advertising costs for the year totaled $15,000.

9. Overhead is applied at a rate of $5.80 per direct-labor hour. (Over- or underapplied overhead is closed directly to Cost of Goods Sold.)

10. All but $24,000 of the work-in-process was completed and transferred to finished goods.

11. The sales price of finished goods that were sold was 130 percent of manufacturing costs. Assume that all finished goods were sold.

Required:
Prepare journal entries for the transactions above.

P23-2 Cost of Goods Manufactured and Sold Schedules

Each month, the president of Maxim Corporation requires the controller to prepare cost of goods manufactured and cost of goods sold schedules. Maxim uses a job-order costing system. Overhead is applied at the rate of 40 percent of direct-labor costs. On January 1, 1984, the corporation had the following General Ledger account balances.

Raw Materials Inventory	$30,000
Work-in-Process Inventory	70,000
Finished Goods Inventory	44,000

The following are summaries of all of the transactions that affected manufacturing costs during the month of January.

a.	Raw materials purchased	$450,000
b.	Raw materials issued to production	460,000
c.	Direct-labor costs (24,000 hours)	230,000
d.	Actual manufacturing overhead	96,000
e.	Work-in-process transferred to finished goods	800,000
f.	Finished goods inventory, January 31, 1984	60,000

Required:

1. Prepare a cost of goods manufactured schedule.
2. Prepare a cost of goods sold schedule, assuming that any under- or overapplied overhead is closed directly to cost of goods sold.
3. **Interpretive Question** What would the effect on cost of goods sold have been if the underapplied overhead had been allocated to work-in-process inventory, finished goods inventory, and cost of goods sold?

P23-3 Manufacturing Costs—Job-Order Costing

The following data apply to Avondet and Adams Companies.

	Avondet	Adams
Raw Materials Inventory, December 31, 1984	(1)$____	$4,000
Raw Materials Purchased	21,000	(4) ____
Raw Materials Inventory, December 31, 1985	6,000	3,000
Manufacturing Overhead (actual)	8,000	(5) ____
Manufacturing Overhead (applied)	(2) ____	16,000
Selling and Administrative Expenses	14,000	25,000
Work-in-Process Inventory, December 31, 1984	(3) ____	20,000
Work-in-Process Inventory, December 31, 1985	16,000	22,000
Direct Materials Used in Production	15,000	(6) ____
Direct-Labor Costs	25,000	30,000
Cost of Goods Manufactured	49,000	55,000
Overapplied (or Underapplied) Overhead	(2,000)	4,000

Required:
Fill in the unknowns for the two cases. (Hint: Indirect materials are not used in either company.)

P23-4 Unifying Problem: Job-Order Costing and Overhead Costs

Mikelos Manufacturing Company applies overhead on the basis of direct-materials costs. The 1984 estimates were

Direct-Materials Costs	$500,000
Manufacturing Overhead	150,000

Following are the 1984 transactions of Mikelos Manufacturing Company.

a. Raw materials purchased on account, $660,000.

b. Raw materials issued to production, 90 percent for direct use, and 10 percent for indirect use, for a total of $300,000.

c. Direct-labor costs, $440,000.

d. Indirect-labor costs, $60,000.

e. Administrative and sales salaries, $110,000 and $70,000, respectively.

f. Utilities, $15,000; plant depreciation, $30,000; maintenance, $10,000; miscellaneous overhead, $4,000. (These costs are allocated on the basis of plant floor space—administrative facilities, 500 square feet; manufacturing, 2,500 square feet; sales facilities, 1,000 square feet.)

g. Manufacturing equipment depreciation, $9,000.

h. Additional raw materials issued to production for direct use, $250,000.

i. Overhead is applied.

j. Accrued factory foreman's salary, $44,000.

k. Ninety percent of existing work-in-process is transferred to finished goods. (Work-in-process beginning inventory was $30,000.)

l. All finished goods are sold. (Assume no beginning or ending inventories. Sales are marked up 50 percent of cost.)

m. Over- or underapplied overhead is closed to Cost of Goods Sold.

Required:

1. Prepare a journal entry for each of the transactions above. (Assume that fixed overhead is a product cost.)

2. Assuming that the following are the beginning inventory amounts, prepare a cost of goods manufactured schedule for 1984 for Mikelos Manufacturing Company.

Raw Materials	$40,000
Work-in-Process	30,000
Finished Goods	-0-

3. **Interpretive Question** Comparing actual overhead with estimates for 1984, what would you recommend that Mikelos Company estimate for overhead costs in 1985?

P23-5 Applying Manufacturing Overhead

Kenworthy Manufacturing Company made the following estimates at the beginning of the year.

	Department G	Department H
Direct-Labor Costs	$219,000	$166,980
Factory Overhead	$ 86,700	$153,340
Machine Hours	17,000	12,500
Direct-Labor Hours	30,000	22,000

Overhead is applied on the basis of machine hours in department G and on the basis of direct-labor hours in department H. During 1984, the following two jobs were completed.

	Job #29	
	Department G	Department H
Materials Used	$16,000	$ 9,200
Direct-Labor Costs	$18,250	$14,420
Direct-Labor Hours	2,500	1,900
Machine Hours	1,410	1,080

	Job #30	
	Department G	Department H
Materials Used	$17,500	$ 8,100
Direct-Labor Costs	$19,710	$13,920
Direct-Labor Hours	2,700	1,800
Machine Hours	1,530	1,020

Required:

1. Determine the overhead application rate for each department.

2. Determine the amount of overhead to be charged to each job.

3. Determine the total cost of each job.

4. Given that the actual overhead costs for the year in departments G and H were $88,200 and $152,500, respectively, that the actual machine hours in department G were 18,100, and that the direct-labor hours in department H were 21,600, compute the amount of over- or underapplied overhead.

P23-6 Preparing a Production Report—Process Costing

Milburn Company uses three process centers to manufacture bread. The following data pertaining to May 1984 are available.

	Units	Percentage Completed
Process 1:		
Beginning Inventory	2,000	30%
Ending Inventory	1,500	50%
Units Started in Production	21,000	
Process 2:		
Beginning Inventory	3,000	20%
Ending Inventory	4,000	30%
Process 3:		
Beginning Inventory	4,000	50%
Ending Inventory	3,000	60%

Units of production begin in process 1 and flow through processes 2 and 3 before entering finished goods.

Required:

1. Prepare a production report for May 1984 for Milburn Company, showing the units available for production in each process, the ultimate accounting for these units, and the output for each process in equivalent units of production.

2. Given the following May production costs, determine the per-unit cost of production for each process.

	Costs
Process 1	$5,629
Process 2	844
Process 3	852

3. **Interpretive Question** Why is the number of equivalent units produced in process 1 greater than the number of units started in production?

P23–7 Equivalent Units and Weighted-Average Cost Flow—Process Costing

Barnum Manufacturing Company has two process centers—manufacturing and assembly. The data that follow show the production and cost results for the assembly division for June 1984.

Production Data:	
Units in Process, June 1, 1984 (materials 50 percent complete, processing 40 percent complete)	500
Units Started in Production	2,500
Units in Process, June 31, 1984 (materials 100 percent complete, processing 60 percent complete)	700
Cost Data:	
Units in Process, June 1, 1984:	
Materials	$ 3,000
Processing	6,400
Materials Used in June	27,500
Processing for June	73,080
Total	$109,980

Required:

1. Determine the weighted-average output measure to be used.
2. Assuming a weighted-average cost flow, determine the cost of goods transferred to finished goods.
3. Assuming a weighted-average cost flow, determine the cost of goods in ending inventory.
4. Prepare a schedule that shows how the $109,980 is accounted for by combining the costs accumulated in parts (2) and (3).

P23–8 FIFO Cost Flow—Process Costing

The assembly department of E&G Electronics Company reported the following data for June 1984.

	Units	Costs
Beginning Inventory (60 percent complete)	2,000	
Units Transferred from Prior Department	15,000	
Ending Inventory (50 percent complete)	3,000	
Cost of Beginning Inventory (materials $12,000, processing $12,000)		$ 24,000
Cost of Materials Used in the Assembly Department		75,000
Processing Costs for June in the Assembly Department		114,400
Total Cost		$213,400

(Note: Materials used in the assembly department are added at the beginning of the assembly process.)

Required:

1. Compute the number of units transferred to the next department.
2. Compute the unit cost and equivalent units for the assembly department.
3. Assuming a FIFO cost flow, compute the cost of goods transferred to the next department.
4. Compute the cost of the ending inventory.
5. Prepare a schedule that shows how total costs are accounted for in the assembly department.

P23–9 Unifying Problem: Process Costing

The Work-in-Process Inventory account for the mashing process of Rita Company appears below.

Work-in-Process—Mashing

Beginning Inventory, January 1, 1984 (3,000 pounds, 40 percent complete)	$ 9,000
Direct-Materials Costs (100,000 pounds)	80,000
Direct-Labor Costs	120,000
Overhead	35,000
Total	$244,000
Completed and Transferred to Next Process	?
Ending Inventory, January 31, 1984 (5,000 pounds, 80 percent complete)	?

The cost per pound of materials in beginning inventory is 75 cents. All materials are added at the beginning of the process (the 40 percent refers to processing) and Rita Company uses the weighted-average cost flow alternative in its computations.

Required:

1. Determine the number of pounds transferred to the next process.
2. Determine January output to be used in weighted-average cost computations.

2162

P23–10 Variable and Absorption Costing

Mitsuzuki Company makes snowmobiles. During the first 11 months of 1984, the company had the following results.

Sales Revenue (200 at $1,500 each)		$300,000
Cost of Goods Sold:		
Beginning Inventory (40 at $1,000, including $700 of fixed expenses)	$ 40,000	
Manufacturing Costs (210 at $1,000, including $700 of fixed expenses)	210,000	
Goods Available for Sale	$250,000	
Ending Inventory (50 at $1,000)	50,000	
Cost of Goods Sold		200,000
Gross Margin		$100,000
Selling and Administrative Expenses ($5,000 per month)		55,000
Net Income		$ 45,000

The company expects to sell an additional 40 units during December. Production capacity is 80 snowmobiles per month and the firm should never make less than 15 in order to maintain a stable work force. (Actual factory overhead for 1984 is $147,000 but it is applied at the rate of $700 per snowmobile.)

Required:

1. How many units should the workers produce in order to maximize net income (under an absorption costing system)? How much is net income at this level of production?

2. What would absorption costing net income be if only 15 units were produced?

3. How much would variable costing net income be during 1984 at production levels of 80 and 15 units?

4. **Interpretive Question** If your bonus were tied to net income, which method would you prefer?

SECTION 6

Managerial Accounting for Planning, Control, and Performance Evaluation

CHAPTER 24

Operations Budgeting: Short-Term Planning

THIS CHAPTER EXPLAINS:

Types of budgets and their characteristics.
The advantages of budgeting.
The evolution of budgeting within a firm.
The master budget, including: sales forecasts, production budgets, selling and administrative expense budgets, cash budgets, and budgeted financial statements.

strategic planning *broad, long-range planning usually conducted by top management*

capital budgeting *the systematic planning for long-term capital investments*

operations budgeting *the setting of immediate goals for sales, production, expenses, and the availability of cash*

One of the most important areas of managerial responsibility is the planning of future operations. Planning is the formulation of a program for the accomplishment of a goal, and in business this involves the evaluation of a great many factors in an attempt to reach appropriate decisions. Business planning is usually one of three types. At the uppermost level is strategic planning, which leads to the making of decisions that affect a company's long-run operations. Management at this top level decides such issues as which products or services to produce or offer, which market segments to seek, where to locate production and marketing facilities, and how to obtain adequate financing.

The second type of planning is capital budgeting, which leads to the making of decisions that will help a firm achieve the objectives outlined by top management at the strategic-planning level. Here, management decides, for example, whether to build one large production facility or several smaller ones.

The third and most specific level of planning is operations budgeting, the setting of sales, production, expense, and cash plans for the immediate period. Management at this level makes decisions that affect the day-to-day operations of the company. With an operations budget, for example, management can predict when excess cash will be on hand and when cash will have to be obtained by short-term borrowing.

This chapter focuses on operations budgeting only. Chapter 28 deals with capital budgeting, and strategic planning is usually considered in a later course.

An Overview of Budgeting

budget *an itemized summary of probable revenues and expenditures for a given period, which shows how an entity is expected to acquire and use its resources during that time*

A budget is a quantitative expression of a plan of action that shows how a firm will acquire and use its resources over some specified period of time. Budgets may be prepared for the firm as a whole or for its various segments. Individuals, of course, can also prepare budgets that project their personal sources and uses of cash. For example, if Al Somers earns $2,000 a month, he might prepare the following personal budget.

Gross Salary		$2,000
Withholdings:		
Federal Income Taxes	$300	
State Income Taxes	100	
FICA Taxes	120	
Other Withholdings	180	(700)
Net Take-Home Pay		$1,300
Fixed Expenses:		
House Mortgage Expense	$550	
Car Payment	250	
Insurance Expense	150	(950)
Net Disposable Income		$ 350
Utilities Expense	$150	
Food Expense	200	
Clothing Expense	100	
Entertainment Expense	100	
Miscellaneous Expenses	200	750
Net Surplus (or Deficit)		$ (400)

This budget contains the important warning that spending is expected to exceed earnings. The commitment of $950 to fixed expenses leaves only $350 to cover all the necessary expenditures for utilities, food, clothing, and such. Since Al cannot cover these expenditures on his net disposable income of $350 a month, he must revise his plans, perhaps by asking for a raise, getting a second job or a new job that pays more, obtaining a loan, or decreasing his spending.

ADVANTAGES OF BUDGETING

The preceding example shows the obvious advantage of a personal budget: It forces the individual to plan. In an organization, budgets have at least six major purposes.

1. *Planning.* The preparation of a budget forces managers to consider explicitly where the firm is going and how it is going to get there. It forces them to formalize their planning efforts.
2. *Performance measurement (evaluation).* Budgets provide quantitative measurements of expectations and objectives. These objectives later serve as benchmarks against which the performance of executives and others in a firm can be evaluated.

3. *Coordination.* Budgets help management to coordinate the activities of a business's segments. By coordinating and integrating the goals of each subunit, management helps ensure that its efforts to meet the overall objectives of the firm will be realized.

4. *Motivation.* Budgets help motivate employees to perform. When employees know that their performance will be measured against a budget, they try to accomplish the things necessary to meet that budget.

5. *Communication.* Budgets enhance communication between the various management levels of a business, helping managers plan activities so that bottlenecks are avoided, and, in general, assisting in the smooth functioning of a business enterprise. Budgets relay top management's expectations and show each subunit how it fits into the overall plan of action.

6. *Authorization.* Once budgets are approved by top management, they provide authorization for spending, investing, producing, and borrowing by lower-level managers and employees.

THE EVOLUTION OF BUDGETING WITHIN A FIRM

The six purposes of budgeting are closely interrelated, as indicated by the following description of the stages through which budgeting typically evolves. The first stage is represented by the new, small business in which there is no budgeting or record keeping because the owners do not understand their importance. They have no specific plans when they open for business beyond the general notion, say, of running a restaurant, and they evaluate their performance over past periods by counting the money in their pockets.

Even these "seat-of-the-pants" businesses soon develop a need for records. One of the main incentives for keeping records is the need to comply with the regulations of the Internal Revenue Service. And some companies start to keep records because they have other needs—to obtain a bank loan, for example—that force them to measure how well they have performed. The second stage of budgeting and record keeping, then, is to measure revenues and expenses for the past period and to assess past profits. This quantitative measure of historical performance usually satisfies the IRS, and even many banks, but it does not provide much help in the areas of planning, performance evaluation, coordination, motivation, communication, and authorization.

Because such measures of historical performance do not provide many of the benefits of a formal plan, most firms soon begin to budget. Thus, budgets usually evolve because firms grow tired of fighting one crisis after another (such as cash shortages) and of coping with the inefficiencies that result from a lack of planning. Typically, a firm develops its first budget by forecasting expected revenues or sales, then budgeting production costs and other expenses, and finally projecting net income. These estimated expense and profitability levels are the plans on which work schedules are based and against which performance is evaluated.

To illustrate basic budgeting procedures, we will assume that El Greco Art Company estimates revenues for the coming year at $100,000, and accordingly budgets merchandise costs of $60,000 and other expenses of $20,000. El Greco could then prepare the following budget, in which total revenues, costs, and expenses are estimated, but possible changes in the level of operations are not considered (called a static budget).

static budgeting *financial planning that establishes specified amounts of revenues, costs, and expenses that do not vary with activity level*

Sales Revenue	$100,000
Cost of Sales	60,000
Gross Margin	$ 40,000
Expenses	20,000
Net Income	$ 20,000

In this example, budgeted net income is $20,000. Actual net income, however, usually differs from the budgeted amount in either or both of two ways: (1) revenues are higher or lower than estimated, and (2) costs and expenses per dollar of revenue are higher or lower than estimated.

Static budgeting helps a firm to plan, motivate employees, communicate actions, and coordinate and authorize activities. However, it has its drawbacks with respect to performance evaluation. For example, suppose that El Greco's actual cost of sales was $50,000, instead of $60,000. Since actual costs were less than the amount budgeted, it seems reasonable to suppose that profits will be up and that the employees responsible for cost of sales did a good job. But that, of course, depends on whether sales actually were $100,000. If they were and if the cost of sales was $50,000, profits obviously would be higher than projected. However, if actual sales were only $80,000 and the cost of sales was $50,000, then profits would be down and the cost of sales, even though it was lower than the budgeted dollar amount, would represent approximately 63 percent of revenues ($50,000/$80,000), instead of the 60 percent ($60,000/$100,000) budgeted. Thus, before cost performance can be evaluated, the actual level of operations must be known.

flexible budgeting *financial planning in which revenues and costs are projected in relation to varying activity levels*

The type of budgeting that takes into account the level of operations is called flexible budgeting, and it is particularly useful for performance evaluation. In essence, flexible budgeting says, "You tell me what your level of operations was and I'll tell you what your costs (and profits) should have been." This is different from static budgeting, which says, "These were your projected revenues, expenses, and costs, and since your actual costs (or revenues or expenses) were less (or more) than planned, you performed well (or poorly)." Static budgeting is the focus of this chapter; flexible budgeting is discussed in Chapter 25.

budget committee *a management group responsible for establishing budgeting policy and for coordinating the preparation of budgets*

Budgeting is such an important activity that the top executives of most companies participate in the budgeting process. Large firms usually establish a budget committee, which includes among its members the vice presidents of sales, production, purchasing, and finance, and the controller or chief financial officer. These executives independently coordinate the preparation of a detailed budget in their areas of responsibility, and then together oversee the preparation of a comprehensive budget for the firm.

Budgets can be prepared for any period of time. However, they usually cover one year because that is the common planning horizon for most firms. Once established, annual budgets are not immutable. In fact, they are usually broken down into quarterly or monthly budgets that are updated as new information becomes available. In many firms, as each month or quarter expires, a new month or quarter is added; the result is the availability of a continuously updated budget. Certainly, a budget need not be completely realized to be valuable. Such a budget will still be useful in activity coordination, performance measurement, motivation, communication, and authorization.

TO SUMMARIZE A budget is a quantitative expression of a plan of action. Budgets can assist management in six ways: (1) planning, (2) measuring performance, (3) coordinating activities, (4) motivating employees, (5) communicating activities and plans, and (6) authorizing actions. There are four stages in the evolution of budgeting and record keeping within many firms, although the first stage is quite rare: (1) no budgeting and little, if any, record keeping, (2) measuring historical performance, (3) static budgeting, and (4) flexible budgeting. The normal budgeting period is 1 year.

The Master Budget

master budget *a network of many separate schedules and budgets that together provide an overall financial plan for the coming period*

Each year, most firms prepare a master budget, an integrated group of detailed budgets that covers a specific time period. The master budget begins with a forecast of sales or revenues, is followed by detailed budgets for the production, selling, and administrative activities, and culminates in a set of budgeted (or pro forma) financial statements. The flow of the preparation of the individual budgets within this master network is shown in Exhibit 24–1 for a manufacturing firm. Notice that the final items are the budgeted financial statements. Review this exhibit carefully because we will follow these schedules in sequence in the remainder of this chapter.

To help explain these budgeting steps, a single integrated example is used throughout the chapter: Fish Creek Boat Company, which produces fishing boats. The boats are made of fiberglass and wood and are available in 12- and 15-foot sizes. The discussion that follows may seem mechanical, but you should keep in mind that this formalized budgeting activity forces management to make many important decisions that guide a company toward its goals. For example, decisions regarding production scheduling, pricing, borrowing, investing, and research and development need to be made before the budget can be completed.

variable costing *an approach to product costing that assigns only variable costs as product costs and treats fixed overhead costs as period expenses; differs from absorption costing, where fixed overhead costs are included in the cost of inventory*

The following information is available to management as it begins to prepare the 1985 master budget. Note that Fish Creek Boat Company uses variable costing and that the budgets are prepared for a 1-year period—although in most companies some of these budgets are updated at least quarterly, and often monthly.

Information Item 1. *Basic Cost Figures:*

Wood	$1 per board foot
Fiberglass	$0.50 per square foot
Direct Labor	$7 per hour
Variable Overhead	Applied on the basis of $6 per direct-labor hour

EXHIBIT 24-1 **The Master Budget**

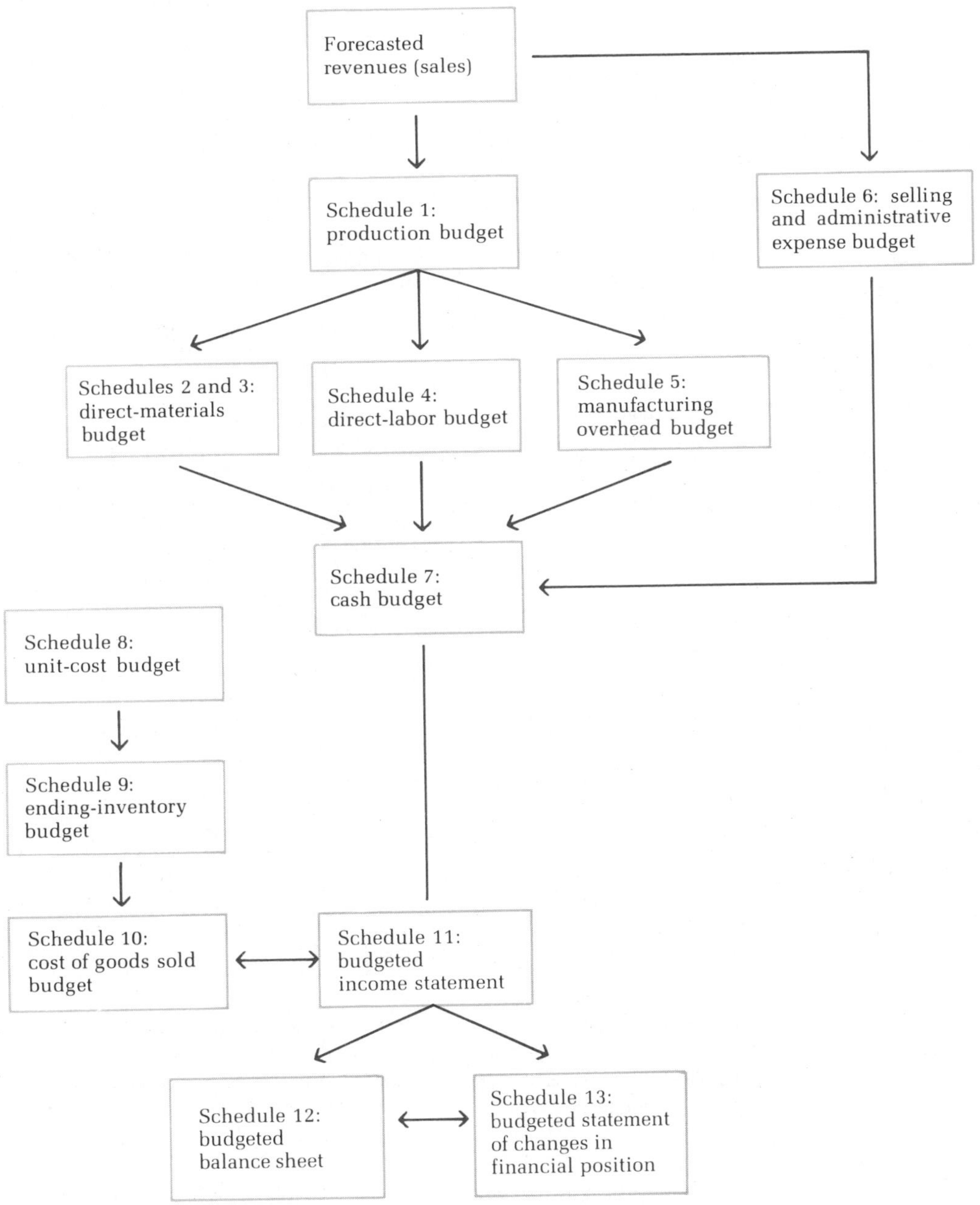

Information Item 2. *Materials and Labor Requirements per Type of Boat:*

	12-Foot Boat	15-Foot Boat
Wood	70 board feet	100 board feet
Fiberglass	50 square feet	65 square feet
Direct Labor	8 hours	10 hours

Information Item 3. *Balance Sheet for the Year Just Ended:*

Fish Creek Boat Manufacturing Company
Balance Sheet as of December 31, 1984

Assets

Current Assets:			
Cash		$ 15,000	
Accounts Receivable		20,000	
Direct Materials		1,800	
Finished Goods		9,000	$ 45,800
Property, Plant, and Equipment:			
Land		$ 22,000	
Building and Equipment	$150,000		
Less Accumulated Depreciation	(12,000)	138,000	160,000
Total Assets			$205,800

Liabilities and Stockholders' Equity

Current Liabilities:		
Accounts Payable	$ 9,000	
Income Taxes Payable	21,000	$ 30,000
Stockholders' Equity:		
Common Stock, $5 Par Value, 20,000 Shares Outstanding	$100,000	
Paid-in Capital in Excess of Par—Common Stock	25,000	
Retained Earnings	50,800	175,800
Total Liabilities and Stockholders' Equity		$205,800

Information Item 4. *Budgeted Cash Flows:**

	Quarter				
	1	2	3	4	Total
Collections from Customers	$35,000	$30,000	$38,000	$47,000	$150,000
Payments:					
Materials	10,000	8,000	6,000	7,000	31,000
Payroll	10,000	8,000	6,000	12,000	36,000
Other Costs and Expenses	8,000	10,000	6,000	6,000	30,000
Equipment Purchase	—	15,000	—	—	15,000
Income Taxes	21,000	—	—	—	21,000
Dividends	—	3,000	—	3,000	6,000

* These data would usually be derived from the other schedules. They have been included in this format to simplify the illustration.

Information Item 5. *Additional Information for 1985:*

	12-Foot Boats	15-Foot Boats
Expected Sales	100 boats	120 boats
Selling Price per Boat	$600	$800
Desired Ending Inventory (finished boats)	20 boats	22 boats
Beginning Inventory (finished boats)	18 boats	26 boats

Desired Direct-Materials Ending Inventory—Wood	1,200 board feet
Desired Direct-Materials Ending Inventory—Fiberglass	1,000 square feet
Beginning Direct-Materials Inventory—Wood	1,400 board feet
Beginning Direct-Materials Inventory—Fiberglass	800 square feet

Information Item 6. *Budgeted Overhead and Selling and Administrative Expenses for 1985:*

	Overhead		Selling and Administrative Expenses	
	Variable	**Fixed**	**Variable**	**Fixed**
Indirect-Materials Costs	$ 2,000			
Indirect-Labor Costs	3,000			
Other Payroll Costs	4,856			
Utilities Expense	2,000			
Property Taxes		$ 700		
Insurance Expense		600		
Depreciation Expense—Plant		2,000		
Supervision Expense		2,628		
Advertising Expense				$ 8,000
Sales Commissions Expense			$16,000	
Depreciation Expense—Office Building				4,000
Executives' Salaries Expense				22,000
Delivery Costs			5,000	
Miscellaneous Expenses				1,000
Totals	$11,856	$5,928	$21,000	$35,000

Information Item 7. *Cash Balance:*

The company wishes to have a $14,000 cash balance at the end of each quarter. Since it has a $100,000 line of credit with Wayne County National Bank, it can readily borrow up to $100,000 at any time. Assume that borrowing must take place in multiples of $1,000, that interest on all money borrowed is 16 percent per year, and that interest is paid for a full quarter in both the quarter in which the money is borrowed and the quarter in which it is repaid. In other words, money is assumed always to be borrowed on the first day of a quarter and repaid on the last day of a quarter.

SALES FORECAST

sales (revenues) forecast *the expected level of sales during the budget period*

The first step in developing a master budget is to prepare a sales (revenues) forecast. This is not called a "sales budget" because management cannot control sales to the same extent that it controls production and other activities. Sales are as much a function of external variables, such as customer tastes and economic conditions, as they are of management's ability to provide the goods for sale. The sales forecast is the cornerstone of the entire master budget. If it is accurate, costs can be budgeted accurately. If it is inaccurate, budgeted costs will probably differ considerably from actual results.

It is often difficult to forecast sales. A reliable sales estimate can make the difference between a profitable and an unprofitable operation, however, so many companies invest a substantial amount of effort in estimating sales.

Managers use a variety of forecasting methods. At the simplest level, they gather the opinions of executives, salespeople, and others, and try to achieve a consensus. On a more sophisticated basis, they use computer models, statistical programs, and quantitative techniques. No matter what methods are used, however, virtually all forecasts take into consideration such factors as past sales, economic and industry-wide conditions and outlook, price changes, advertising levels, the size of the sales force, social conditions, competition, and production capacity.

Fish Creek Boat Company has projected 1985 sales to be 100 12-foot boats and 120 15-foot boats. At the anticipated sales prices, this translates to $156,000 in revenues ($60,000 for the 12-foot boats at $600 each and $96,000 for the 15-foot boats at $800 each).

PRODUCTION BUDGET

production budget *a schedule of production requirements for the budget period*

Once sales have been forecast, the desired amount of ending inventory must be determined. Factors to be considered are: how long it takes to obtain new supplies, how long it takes to make a boat, and the amount of expected sales for the period. Given the desired level of ending inventory, production can be budgeted. Usually, the desired ending inventory for any period is expressed as a percentage of the following period's expected sales volume. The production budget (Schedule 1), which is always expressed in terms of units produced (in this case, boats), is the focal point from which all other cost budgets flow. Proper production and ending inventory budgets ensure that management will have enough boats on hand to meet customer demand but not so many that unnecessary expenses will be incurred due to excessive inventory. Firms that can maintain appropriate levels of production and inventory enjoy satisfied customers and low inventory investments and storage costs; they also avoid the high cost of crash production efforts.

The production budget for Fish Creek Boat Company is shown below.

Schedule 1
Production Budget—1985

	Number of 12-Foot Boats	Number of 15-Foot Boats
Expected Sales (Information Item 5)	100	120
Add Desired Ending Inventory of Finished Boats (Information Item 5)	20	22
Total Number of Boats Needed	120	142
Less Beginning Inventory of Finished Boats (Information Item 5)	18	26
Budgeted Production	102	116

direct-materials usage budget *a schedule of direct materials to be used in production during the budget period*

direct-materials purchases budget *a schedule of direct materials to be purchased during the budget period*

Direct-Materials Budgets

Following the preparation of an overall production budget, management then begins work on the detailed budgets. Usually, the first two of these are the direct-materials usage and direct-materials purchases budgets (Schedules 2 and 3). These budgets help management schedule purchases from suppliers. For Fish Creek Boat Company, they are as follows:

Schedule 2
Direct-Materials Usage Budget—1985

Direct Materials	Production Requirements: 12-Foot Boats (102 boats)	Production Requirements: 15-Foot Boats (116 boats)	Total Usage	Unit Cost of Materials*	Cost of Materials Used
Wood (70 board feet per 12-foot boat and 100 board feet per 15-foot boat) (Information Item 2)	7,140 board feet	11,600 board feet	18,740 board feet	$1.00/board foot	$18,740
Fiberglass (50 square feet per 12-foot boat and 65 square feet per 15-foot boat) (Information Item 2)	5,100 square feet	7,540 square feet	12,640 square feet	$0.50/square foot	$ 6,320
					$25,060

* Information Item 1.

Schedule 3
Direct-Materials Purchases Budget—1985

	Wood (board feet)	Fiberglass (square feet)	Total Cost of Materials to Be Purchased
Desired Ending Direct-Materials Inventory (Information Item 5)	1,200	1,000	
Direct Materials Needed for Production (see Schedule 2)	18,740	12,640	
Total Direct Materials Needed	19,940	13,640	
Less Beginning Direct-Materials Inventory (Information Item 5)	1,400	800	
Direct Materials to Be Purchased	18,540	12,840	
Unit Cost (Information Item 1)	×$1.00	×$0.50	
Direct-Materials Purchases Cost	$18,540	$6,420	$24,960

Like the production budget, these budgets depend on the desired level of ending inventory. In this case, it is the inventory of raw materials, not finished goods. Maintaining appropriate inventory levels is important. If management does not maintain sufficient inventory levels, costly work stoppages can occur; if inventories are excessive, inventory investment and storage costs may be unduly high.

direct-labor budget *a schedule of direct-labor requirements for the budget period*

Direct-Labor Budget

The third detailed production budget is the direct-labor budget (Schedule 4). Management must plan so that sufficient, but not excessive, labor is always available. Otherwise, the company is likely to suffer the high cost of frequent hirings, firings, layoffs, and overtime work. Probably even more important than the high cost of employee turnover, however, is the feeling of demoralization among employees that such events can cause. If employees lack security, they usually behave in ways that maximize their own personal short-run benefits—for example, they may slow down production, thus creating the need for overtime work.

The direct-labor budget for Fish Creek Boat Company is

Schedule 4
Direct-Labor Budget—1985

	Number of Boats to Be Produced	Direct-Labor Hours per Unit*	Total Hours	Cost per Hour†	Total Direct-Labor Cost
12-Foot Boats	102	8	816	$7	$5,712
15-Foot Boats	116	10	1,160	$7	8,120
			1,976		$13,832

* Information Item 2.
† Information Item 1.

As noted earlier, the other production budgets are usually prepared on an annual basis. However, because labor is costly, the direct-labor budget is often revised on a quarter-by-quarter, month-by-month, or even week-by-week basis.

Manufacturing Overhead Budget

manufacturing overhead budget *a schedule of production costs other than those for direct labor and direct materials*

The manufacturing overhead budget (Schedule 5) includes all production costs other than those for direct materials and direct labor. The total amount of manufacturing overhead budgeted will depend to some extent on the overhead cost behavior pattern of the company. If most overhead costs are fixed, budgeted overhead will not change much in response to expected changes in production. If the majority of overhead costs are variable, anticipated changes in production can drastically alter the manufacturing overhead budget.

The manufacturing overhead budget for Fish Creek Boat Company is shown below.

Schedule 5
Manufacturing Overhead Budget—1985
(based on 1,976 hours; see Schedule 4)

Variable Overhead (Information Item 6):		
Indirect-Materials Costs	$2,000	
Indirect-Labor Costs	3,000	
Other Payroll Costs	4,856	
Utilities Expense	2,000	
Total Variable Overhead		$11,856
Fixed Overhead (Information Item 6):		
Property Tax Expense	$ 700	
Insurance Expense	600	
Depreciation Expense—Plant	2,000	
Supervision Expense	2,628	
Total Fixed Overhead		5,928
Total Manufacturing Overhead		$17,784

Since Fish Creek uses variable costing for planning purposes, only variable manufacturing overhead is included in the cost of products. Fixed manufacturing overhead costs are taken directly to the income statement, where they are treated as period expenses. The variable overhead application rate is $6 per direct-labor hour; it was calculated by dividing total variable costs ($11,856) by the total number of direct-labor hours (1,976).

SELLING AND ADMINISTRATIVE EXPENSE BUDGET

selling and administrative expense budget *a schedule of all nonproduction spending that will occur during the budget period*

The selling and administrative expense budget (Schedule 6) includes planned expenditures for all areas other than production. The costs of the paper clips, paper, and pencils used by the office staff, the salaries of the sales manager and company president, and the depreciation of office buildings all belong in this category. Because this budget covers several areas, it is usually quite large and may be supported by individual budgets for specific items.

The selling and administrative expense budget for Fish Creek is

Schedule 6

Selling and Administrative Expense Budget—1985

Variable Expenses (Information Item 6):		
Delivery Costs	$ 5,000	
Sales Commission Expense	16,000	
Total Variable Expenses		$21,000
Fixed Expenses (Information Item 6):		
Executives' Salaries Expense	$22,000	
Depreciation Expense—Office Building	4,000	
Advertising Expense	8,000	
Miscellaneous Expenses	1,000	
Total Fixed Expenses		35,000
Total Selling and Administrative Expenses		$56,000

CASH BUDGET

cash budget *a schedule of expected cash receipts and disbursements during the budget period*

The cash budget (Schedule 7 on page 800), which shows expected cash receipts and disbursements during a period, summarizes much of the information discussed thus far. Most firms prepare a month-by-month, or even a week-by-week, cash budget. (Because of space limitations, however, the cash budget for Fish Creek is divided into quarters.)

A detailed cash budget will point out when a company has excess cash and when it has to borrow funds. This allows a firm to earn maximum interest on excess funds and avoid the costs of unnecessary borrowing. The cash budget is probably the most important budget a company will prepare.

Typically, a cash budget is divided into four sections:

1. Cash receipts.
2. Cash disbursements.
3. Cash excess or deficiency.
4. Financing.

The cash receipts section summarizes all cash expected to come into the business during the budget period. Because companies generally extend credit to their customers, a significant portion of their sales are originally recorded as accounts receivable. The collection of accounts receivable is thus a major source of cash and its timing is an important consideration in preparing a cash budget.

To illustrate how the collection of accounts receivable is budgeted, we will assume that Fish Creek's sales during the last 2 months of 1984 and its estimated sales for the first quarter of 1985 are as follows:

	November 1984	December 1984	January 1985	February 1985	March 1985
Sales Revenue . .	$30,000	$20,000	$5,000	$8,000	$12,000

On the basis of past experience, the company estimates that 30 percent of credit sales are collected during the month of sale, 50 percent during the month following the sale, and the remaining 20 percent in the second month following the sale. Budgeted collections for the first quarter of 1985 can be calculated as follows:

		Collection Month					
Sales Month	**Sales**	**January**		**February**		**March**	
November	$30,000	$ 6,000	(20%)				
December	20,000	10,000	(50%)	$4,000	(20%)		
January	5,000	1,500	(30%)	2,500	(50%)	$1,000	(20%)
February	8,000			2,400	(30%)	4,000	(50%)
March	12,000					3,600	(30%)
Totals	$75,000	$17,500		$8,900		$8,600	

This analysis shows that the accounts receivable balance at December 31, 1984, should have been $20,000 (20 percent of November's sales plus 70 percent of December's sales) and that total collections during the first quarter of 1985 are budgeted to be $35,000 ($17,500 + $8,900 + $8,600). In this example, we have assumed that all proceeds from credit sales are eventually collected. Usually, however, there are a few customers who never pay and these uncollectible accounts must be considered when analyzing estimated cash collections from accounts receivable.

The cash disbursements section summarizes all expected cash outlays by a firm during the budget period. These include payments of accounts payable, payroll, other costs and expenses, capital improvements, and dividends. Note that in order to compute cash disbursements for "other costs and expenses," depreciation and other noncash items must *not* be included.

The section related to cash excess or deficiency merely reports the difference between budgeted cash receipts and disbursements. With a prospective excess of cash, management should look for the most attractive short-term investments. A deficiency obviously means that additional short-term funds will be needed.

The financing section analyzes the timing and amounts of all projected borrowings and repayments during the period. It also estimates the amount of interest to be paid on borrowed funds. By accurately projecting these amounts and events, firms can give banks and other lending institutions advance notice of their needs. Banks appreciate and sometimes insist on this. Because money has a time value, management always walks a tightrope between having too much or too little cash on hand.

Exhibit 24-2 shows how a typical company's cash balance and requirements fluctuate constantly. Most of this fluctuation is due to the varying amounts of raw materials and finished goods that are needed in the different seasons of the year. A prosperous firm could, if it desired, maintain enough cash on hand so that short-term borrowing would never be necessary. But such a policy might not be cost-beneficial. Long-term investments in productive assets usually earn considerably more than short-term cash investments, so firms are generally better off maintaining lower cash balances, keeping as much capital as possible "at work" in the company's productive assets and borrowing from time to time for short periods. For this reason, most companies obtain a line of credit from banks.

EXHIBIT 24-2 A Typical Relationship Between Cash Balance and Cash Needs

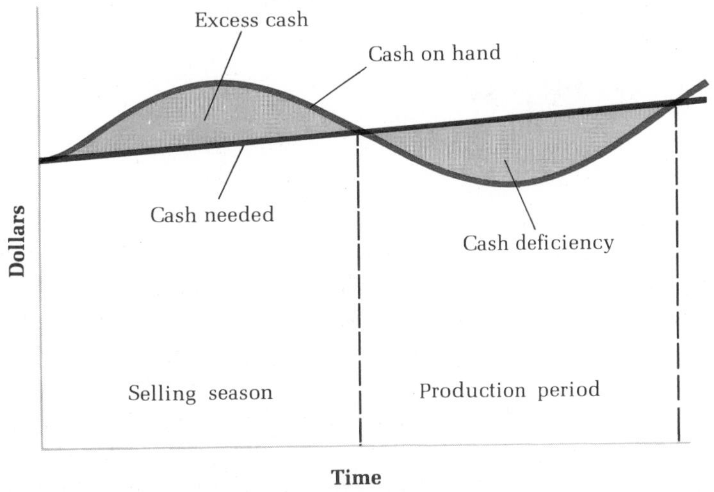

The quarterly cash budgets for Fish Creek Boat Company for 1985 appear below.

Schedule 7
Cash Budgets—1985

	Analysis by Quarter 1	2	3	4	Analysis for the Total Year
Cash Balance, Beginning	$ 15,000*	$ 14,000	$ 14,000	$ 14,040	$ 15,000*
Add Collections from Customers (Information Item 4)	35,000	30,000	38,000	47,000	150,000
(1) Total Available Before Financing	$ 50,000	$ 44,000	$ 52,000	$ 61,040	$165,000
Less Disbursements (Information Item 4)					
For Materials	$ 10,000	$ 8,000	$ 6,000	$ 7,000	$ 31,000
For Payroll	10,000	8,000	6,000	12,000	36,000
For Other Costs and Expenses	8,000	10,000	6,000	6,000	30,000
For Income Tax	21,000	—	—	—	21,000
For Equipment Purchase	—	15,000	—	—	15,000
For Dividends	—	3,000	—	3,000	6,000
(2) Total Disbursements	$ 49,000	$ 44,000	$ 18,000	$ 28,000	$139,000
Minimum Cash Balance Desired (Information Item 7)	14,000	14,000	14,000	14,000	14,000
Total Cash Needed	$ 63,000	$ 58,000	$ 32,000	$ 42,000	$153,000
Excess (or Deficiency of) Cash Available (or Needed) Before Financing	$(13,000)	$(14,000)	$ 20,000	$ 19,040	$ 12,000
Financing:					
Borrowings	$ 13,000	$ 14,000	—	—	$ 27,000
Repayments	—	—	$(18,000)	$ (9,000)	(27,000)
Interest (at 16%)	—	—	(1,960)[a]	(1,080)[b]	(3,040)
(3) Total Effect of Financing	$ 13,000	$ 14,000	$(19,960)	$(10,080)	$ (3,040)
(4) Ending Cash Balance (1 − 2 + 3)	$ 14,000	$ 14,000	$ 14,040	$ 22,960	$ 22,960

* Information Item 3.

[a] $13,000 × 0.16 × 3/4 = $1,560
$5,000 × 0.16 × 1/2 = 400
$1,960

[b] $9,000 × 0.16 × 3/4 = $1,080

This cash budget assumes that when cash is needed during a period, it is borrowed at the beginning of the period and repaid at the end. It also assumes that loans are repaid on a first-in, first-out basis, and that interest is paid only when the principal is repaid. Of the $18,000 budgeted to be repaid in the third quarter (*a*), $13,000 has been outstanding for three quarters and $5,000 has been outstanding for two quarters. The $9,000 repaid in the fourth quarter (*b*) had been outstanding for three quarters. Also note that the entries in the total year column do not always equal the sum of the four quarters because the beginning cash balance and the minimum cash balance desired are the same for the year as they are for the first quarter.

UNIT-COST, ENDING INVENTORY, AND COST OF GOODS SOLD BUDGETS

Before the budgeted financial statements can be prepared, three additional supporting budgets must be completed: (1) the unit-cost budget (Schedule 8), (2) the ending inventory budget (Schedule 9), and (3) the cost of goods sold budget (Schedule 10).

Unit-Cost Budget

unit-cost budget *an estimation of the total direct materials, direct labor, and overhead costs required to make one unit of a product*

The unit-cost budget identifies the cost of each item to be produced. When the unit cost is known, it can be multiplied by the number of units sold and by the number on hand to determine the cost of goods sold and the ending inventory. The unit-cost budget for Fish Creek Company would be prepared as follows:

Schedule 8
Unit-Cost Budget—1985

		12-Foot Boats		15-Foot Boats	
	Input Cost*	Required Inputs†	Amount per Boat	Units†	Amount per Boat
Wood	$1.00/board foot	70 board feet	$70.00	100 board feet	$100.00
Fiberglass	$0.50/square foot	50 square feet	25.00	65 square feet	32.50
Direct Labor	$7.00/hour	8 hours	56.00	10 hours	70.00
Variable Factory Overhead	$6.00/hour	8 hours	48.00	10 hours	60.00
Total Unit Cost			$199.00		$262.50

* Information Item 1.
† Information Item 2.

Ending Inventory Budget

The unit costs of the two boats are multiplied by the number of boats expected to be in ending inventory to obtain the total cost of finished goods in the ending inventory budget. In the case of Fish Creek, there are two ending inventories—finished goods and direct materials—that will have to be computed and added together. (We are assuming that there are no ending work-in-process inventories.)

Schedule 9
Ending Inventory Budget as of December 31, 1985

Units (Information Item 5)	Cost	Total Costs	
Direct Materials:			
Wood, 1,200 Board Feet	$1.00/board foot	$1,200	
Fiberglass, 1,000 Square Feet	$0.50/square foot	500	
Total Direct Materials			$ 1,700
Finished Goods:			
12-Foot Boats, 20 (Schedule 8)	$199.00	$3,980	
15-Foot Boats, 22 (Schedule 8)	262.50	5,775	
Total Finished Goods			9,755
Total Ending Inventory			$11,455

Cost of Goods Sold Budget

Following in sequence, the expected inventory cost is used to compute the cost of goods sold budget. For Fish Creek, this calculation is

Schedule 10

Variable Cost of Goods Sold Budget as of December 31, 1985

	Total Costs	
Beginning Finished Goods Inventory		$9,000
Add Variable Cost of Goods Manufactured:		
Direct Materials Used (Schedule 2)	$25,060	
Direct Labor (Schedule 4)	13,832	
Variable Manufacturing Overhead (Schedule 5)	11,856	
Total Variable Manufacturing Costs		50,748
Variable Cost of Goods Available for Sale		$59,748
Less Ending Finished Goods Inventory (Schedule 9)		9,755
Total Variable Cost of Goods Sold		$49,993

Thus far, ten schedules have been described. Together these schedules provide the data needed for preparing the budgeted financial statements. Beginning with the production budget, which depends on the sales forecast, many of these schedules are based on information from preceding schedules. Thus, they should be prepared in sequence.

PREPARING THE BUDGETED INCOME STATEMENT

The budgeted income statement (sometimes called a pro forma income statement) projects profits for the coming period and therefore is valuable to management in making key decisions. Such questions as how big a dividend to pay, whether or not to invest in a new plant, and how strenuously to bargain with unions are usually decided on the basis of projected and actual profits. Fish Creek's budgeted income statement is

Schedule 11

Budgeted Income Statement for the Year Ended December 31, 1985

Sales Revenue (see page 794)		$156,000
Less Variable Expenses:		
Variable Cost of Goods Sold (Schedule 10)	$49,993	
Variable Selling and Administrative Expenses (Schedule 6)	21,000	70,993
Contribution Margin		$ 85,007
Less Fixed Expenses:		
Manufacturing Overhead (Schedule 5)	$ 5,928	
Selling and Administrative Expenses (Schedule 6)	35,000	40,928
Net Operating Income		$ 44,079
Less Interest Expense (Schedule 7)		3,040
Income Before Taxes		$ 41,039
Income Taxes (estimated)		20,000
Net Income		$ 21,039

Note that this income statement has been prepared on a contribution-margin basis. As we explained in Chapter 21, this type of income statement is useful for decision-making purposes because it allows management to assess the different levels of profits resulting from changes in costs and revenue.

THE BUDGETED BALANCE SHEET AND STATEMENT OF CHANGES IN FINANCIAL POSITION

The final two items to be projected are the balance sheet and the statement of changes in financial position. These statements are presented in Schedules 12 and 13.

Schedule 12

Budgeted Balance Sheet as of December 31, 1985

Assets		
Current Assets:		
Cash (from Schedule 7)	$ 22,960	
Accounts Receivable (Note 1)	26,000	
Direct Materials (from Schedule 9)	1,700	
Finished Goods (from Schedule 9)	9,755	$ 60,415
Long-Term Operational Assets:		
Land (beginning balance from Information Item 3)	$ 22,000	
Building and Equipment (Note 2)	165,000	
Less Accumulated Depreciation (Note 3)	(18,000)	169,000
Total Assets		$229,415

Liabilities and Stockholders' Equity		
Current Liabilities:		
Accounts Payable (Note 4)	$ 18,576	
Income Taxes Payable (Note 5)	20,000	$ 38,576
Stockholders' Equity:		
Common Stock, $5 Par, 20,000 Shares Outstanding (Information Item 3)	$100,000	
Paid-in Capital in Excess of Par—Common Stock (Information Item 3)	25,000	
Retained Earnings (Note 6)	65,839	190,839
Total Liabilities and Stockholders' Equity		$229,415

Notes:

1. *Accounts Receivable:*

beginning balance	+ sales	− collections	= ending balance
(Information Item 3)	(Schedule 11)	(Schedule 7)	
$20,000	+ $156,000	− $150,000	= $26,000

2. *Building and Equipment:*

beginning balance	+ equipment purchase	= ending balance
(Information Item 3)	(Schedule 7)	
$150,000	+ $15,000	= $165,000

3. *Accumulated Depreciation:*

beginning balance	+ plant overhead	+ selling and administrative expenses	= ending balance
(Information Item 3)	(Schedule 5)	(Schedule 6)	
$12,000	+ $2,000	+ 4,000	= $18,000

4. *Accounts Payable:*

beginning balance	+ direct materials purchased	+ direct labor	+ manufacturing overhead (less depreciation)
(Information Item 3)	(Schedule 3)	(Schedule 4)	(Schedule 5)
$9,000	+ $24,960	+ $13,832	+ $15,784 ($17,784 − $2,000)

+ selling and administrative expenses (less depreciation)	− amount paid for materials	− amount paid for payroll
(Schedule 6)	(Schedule 7)	(Schedule 7)
+ $52,000 ($56,000 − $4,000)	− $31,000	− $36,000

− amount paid for other costs and expenses	= ending balance
(Schedule 7)	
− $30,000	= $18,576

5. *Income Taxes Payable:*

beginning balance	+ estimated taxes	− payment	= ending balance
(Information Item 3)	(Schedule 11)	(Schedule 7)	
$21,000	+ $20,000	− $21,000	= $20,000

6. *Retained Earnings:*

beginning balance	+ net income	− dividends	= ending balance
(Information Item 3)	(Schedule 11)	(Schedule 7)	
$50,800	+ $21,039	− $6,000	= $65,839

Schedule 13
Budgeted Statement of Changes in Financial Position
for the Year Ended December 31, 1985 (Cash Basis)

Sources of Cash		
Operations:		
Net Income (Schedule 11)		$21,039
Add: Depreciation (Schedules 5 and 6)	$ 6,000	
Increase in Accounts Payable*	9,576	
Decrease in Direct Materials*	100	15,676
Subtract: Increase in Accounts Receivable*	$ (6,000)	
Increase in Finished Goods*	(755)	
Decrease in Income Taxes Payable*	(1,000)	(7,755)
Total Cash from Operations		$28,960
Borrowings (Schedule 7)		27,000
Total Sources of Cash		$55,960
Uses of Cash		
Payment of Dividends (Schedule 7)		$ 6,000
Purchase of Equipment (Schedule 7)		15,000
Repayment of Loans (Schedule 7)		27,000
Net Increase in Cash		7,960
Total Uses of Cash		$55,960

* From a comparison of the 1984 actual and 1985 projected balance sheets (Info. Item 3 and Schedule 12).

The master budget is now complete. It is ready for use in planning, measuring performance, motivating employees, communicating information, and coordinating and authorizing activities. The decisions to be made on the basis of this budget depend on the answers to such questions as:

1. Is a net income of $21,039 adequate? If not, how can it be increased?
2. Is the projected increase in cash sufficient to meet the firm's goals?
3. How does the expected financial position at the end of the year fit with long-range objectives and goals?
4. Are there sufficient liquid assets to purchase needed assets?
5. How should management be rewarded if these budgets are met?
6. Who should be responsible for meeting production and cost goals?

These are only a few of the questions that management needs to answer. However, they should give you a sense of the master budget's usefulness. In fact, it is hard to imagine how a company could be profitable in the long run without such planning.

Several areas of budgeting were not dealt with in this chapter. For example, how do budgets affect employees? Exactly how does management arrive at budget figures? How are other types of budgets, such as flexible budgets, prepared? Some of these topics are discussed in later chapters, and others are left to more advanced courses. But once you have mastered the concepts and procedures covered here, you are well on your way to understanding one of the most important tools of managerial accounting.

CHAPTER REVIEW

There are three types of business planning: (1) broad strategic planning, (2) capital budgeting, and (3) operations budgeting. Plans made at each level have different uses and cover different time periods. However, when used together these plans help management prepare for the future, measure performance, coordinate events, motivate employees, and communicate and authorize activities. Budgets often evolve as growing firms pass through four stages. First, the company may have no budget or measure of historical performance. Second, there is record keeping but still no budget. At more advanced stages there is static budgeting and finally there is flexible budgeting.

A master budget is an integrated network of several detailed budgets: revenues (which is a forecast rather than a budget), production, direct materials, direct labor, manufacturing overhead, selling and administrative expenses, cash, unit costs, ending inventory, cost of goods sold, income statement, balance sheet, and statement of changes in financial position. Together these budgets provide management with a master plan of action for the coming year.

KEY TERMS AND CONCEPTS

budget (787)
budget committee (789)
capital budgeting (786)
cash budget (797)
direct-labor budget (795)
direct-materials purchases budget (795)
direct-materials usage budget (795)
flexible budgeting (789)
manufacturing overhead budget (796)
master budget (790)
operations budgeting (786)
production budget (794)
sales (revenues) forecast (793)
selling and administrative expense budget (797)
static budgeting (789)
strategic planning (786)
unit-cost budget (801)
variable costing (790)

REVIEW PROBLEM

The Sales Forecast and the Cash Collection, Production, Direct-Materials, and Direct-Labor Budgets

The following information is available for Frontier Company.

Expected Sales (units):	
March	900
April	1,050
May	1,300
Selling Price per Unit	$12
Accounts Receivable Balance, March 1	$4,000
Desired Finished Goods Inventory, May 31 (units)	240
Beginning Finished Goods Inventory, March 1 (units)	270
Direct Materials Needed per Unit	11 feet
Desired Direct-Materials Inventory, May 31	2,800 feet
Beginning Direct-Materials Inventory, March 1	2,700 feet
Total Direct-Labor Time per Finished Unit	3 hours
Direct-Materials Cost per Foot	$0.60
Direct-Labor Cost per Hour	$8

Additional information:

a. 70 percent of a month's sales is collected by the month's end; the remaining 30 percent is collected in the following month.

b. The desired ending finished goods inventory every month is 30 percent of the next month's sales.

c. The desired ending direct-materials inventory every month is 20 percent of the next month's production needs.

Required:

1. Prepare a sales forecast for March, April, and May (in dollars).
2. Prepare a cash collection budget for March, April, and May (in dollars).
3. Prepare production budgets for March, April, and May (in dollars).
4. Prepare direct-materials usage budgets for March, April, and May (in dollars).
5. Prepare direct-materials purchase budgets for March, April, and May (in dollars).
6. Prepare direct-labor budgets for March, April, and May (in dollars).

Solution

Most of these budgets are quite simple. In this solution, we merely present them.

1. Sales Forecasts

	March	April	May
Expected Sales (units)	900	1,050	1,300
Selling Price per Unit	× $12	× $12	× $12
	$10,800	$12,600	$15,600

2. Cash Collection Budget

	March	April	May
From Accounts Receivable	$ 4,000	–	–
From March's Sales (70%, 30%)	7,560	$ 3,240	–
From April's Sales (70%, 30%)	–	8,820	$ 3,780
From May's Sales (70%)	–	–	10,920
Totals	$11,560	$12,060	$14,700

3. Production Budgets

	March	April	May
Expected Sales (units)	900	1,050	1,300
Add Desired Ending Inventory (30% of next month's sales)	315	390	240 (given)
Total Needed	1,215	1,440	1,540
Less Beginning Inventory	(270) (given)	(315)	(390)
Budgeted Production	945	1,125	1,150

4. Direct-Materials Usage Budgets

	March	April	May
Units to Be Produced	945	1,125	1,150
Direct Materials Needed per Unit	× 11 feet	× 11 feet	× 11 feet
Total Production Needs	10,395 feet	12,375 feet	12,650 feet
Cost per Foot of Materials	×$0.60	×$0.60	×$0.60
Cost of Materials Used	$ 6,237	$ 7,425	$ 7,590

5. Direct-Materials Purchases Budgets

	March	April	May
Desired Ending Direct-Materials Inventory (20% of next month's production needs)	2,475	2,530	2,800 (given)
Feet Needed for Product	10,395	12,375	12,650
Total Feet Needed	12,870	14,905	15,450
Less Beginning Inventory	(2,700) (given)	(2,475)	(2,530)
Direct Materials to Be Purchased	10,170	12,430	12,920
Cost per Foot	×$0.60	×$0.60	×$0.60
Direct-Materials Purchase Cost	$ 6,102	$ 7,458	$ 7,752

6. Direct-Labor Budgets

	March	April	May
Units to Be Produced	945	1,125	1,150
Direct-Labor Hours per Unit (given)	× 3	× 3	× 3
Total Hours Needed	2,835	3,375	3,450
Cost per Hour	× $8	× $8	× $8
Direct-Labor Cost	$22,680	$27,000	$27,600

DISCUSSION QUESTIONS

1 What are the advantages of budgeting?

2 How are strategic planning, capital budgeting, and operations budgeting different?

3 What are four typical stages in the evolution of budgeting and record keeping in a firm?

4 What is the major weakness of static budgeting?

5 Why are budgets usually prepared for 1 year?

6 Why must sales be forecast rather than budgeted?

7 Why does the accuracy of the entire master budget depend on a reliable sales forecast?

8 Identify the sequence of schedules used in preparing a master budget.

9 Describe the four sections of a cash budget.

10 How does management use the operations budget?

EXERCISES

E24-1 Personal Budgeting

Jeri Jackson works as an interior decorator for Worldwide Furniture Corporation. Her annual salary is $30,000. Of that amount, 15 percent is withheld for federal income taxes, 5 percent for state taxes, 6 percent for FICA taxes, and 2 percent as a contribution to United Way. Another 5 percent is deposited directly into a company credit union for savings. Jeri has four monthly payments: $125 for her car, $80 for furniture, $450 for rent, and $75 to repay college loans. Jeri's other monthly expenses will be approximately:

Food Expense	$200
Clothing Expense	100
Entertainment Expense	125
Utilities Expense	80
Gas and Maintenance Expenses on Car	70
Miscellaneous Expenses	200
Total	$775

Prepare both a monthly and an annual budget for Jeri that identifies gross pay, net take-home pay, net disposable income, and net surplus or deficit.

E24-2 Personal Budgeting

Mickey Williams recently was graduated from college and started working for Dudley Corporation at a salary of $30,000 per year. In anticipation of his high salary, he purchased a new $14,000 automobile, and will pay for it at a rate of $350 per month, including interest, for 4 years. He also rented a townhouse for $400 a month and bought some furniture on time for $200 a month. In addition, Mickey figures that his other monthly expenses will be

Food Expense	$200
Clothing Expense	100
Entertainment Expense	250
Insurance Expense	80
Gas and Other Car Expenses	120
Utilities Expense	100

1. On the assumption that Mickey also pays income and FICA taxes of 20 and 6 percent, respectively, prepare his monthly budget.

2. Mickey plans to get married soon and have a family, so he intends to save enough money for a down-

payment on a house. If a $15,000 down-payment is needed, how long will it take to save the needed amount? (Ignore interest on savings, and assume that Mickey does not have any savings at the present time.)

E24-3 Production Budgeting

Brinkerhoff Electric makes and sells two kinds of radios—an AM-FM radio and an AM radio. The sales forecasts for these radios for the next 4 months are as follows:

	AM-FM Radios	AM Radios
January	70	30
February	78	39
March	66	27
April	90	45
Totals	304	141

At present (December 31), Brinkerhoff has 40 AM-FM radios and 20 AM radios in stock. Past experience has shown that Brinkerhoff must maintain an inventory equal to two-thirds of the next month's sales.

How many radios of each type must be produced during January, February, and March in order to meet sales and inventory demands?

E24-4 Production Budgeting

E-Z Rest Furniture Company makes and sells two products: rocking chairs and recliners. The sales forecasts for these chairs for the next 4 months are as follows:

	Rocking Chairs	Recliners
March	80	60
April	70	50
May	100	76
June	110	80
Totals	360	266

On March 1, E-Z has a stock of 40 completed rocking chairs and 30 recliners. Past experience indicates that E-Z must maintain an inventory equal to one-half of the next month's sales.

How many rocking chairs and recliners must be produced during March, April, and May in order to meet sales and inventory demands?

E24-5 Direct-Materials Usage and Purchases Budgeting

Little Children's Wheel Store assembles and sells tricycles and bicycles. The frames are purchased from one supplier and the wheels from another. The following materials are required.

Bicycles	Tricycles
One 22-inch frame, $25	One 12-inch frame, $10
Two 22-inch wheels, $8 each	Two 4-inch wheels, $5 each
	One 12-inch wheel, $4

Management anticipates that 50 bicycles and 60 tricycles will be assembled during January 1985. On December 31, 1984, the following assembly parts are on hand.

22-inch frames—12
22-inch wheels—20
12-inch frames— 8
4-inch wheels—24
12-inch wheels—10

Also, management decides that, beginning in January, the inventory of parts on hand at the end of each month should be sufficient to make 10 bicycles and 10 tricycles.

Prepare direct-materials usage and direct-materials purchases budgets for January.

E24-6 Direct-Materials Usage and Purchases Budgeting

E-M Candy Company makes and sells two kinds of candy: chocolate almond bars and coconut bars. E-M buys the ingredients from a supplier on the East Coast. For each type of candy, the following ingredients are needed to make a box of 24 candy bars.

	Chocolate Almond Bars	Coconut Bars
Chocolate	$1\frac{1}{2}$ pounds at $2.00/pound	1 pound at $2.00/pound
Almonds	1 pound at $4.00/pound	
Coconut		$1\frac{1}{4}$ pounds at $1.50/pound
Sugar	2 pounds at $0.20/pound	$1\frac{3}{4}$ pounds at $0.20/pound

Management expects that 600 boxes of chocolate almond bars and 500 boxes of coconut bars will be produced during February 1984. On January 31, the following ingredients are on hand.

Chocolate	160 pounds
Almonds	45 pounds
Coconut	60 pounds
Sugar	800 pounds

Also, management decides that, beginning in February, the inventory of ingredients on hand at the end of each month should be as follows:

Chocolate	200 pounds
Almonds	50 pounds
Coconut	50 pounds
Sugar	1,000 pounds

Prepare direct-materials usage and direct-materials purchases budgets for February.

E24–7 Direct-Labor Budgeting

Frozen Dessert Company makes three desserts: ice cream, frozen yogurt, and pudding. The production budget for the next 3 months for each type of dessert is

	Ice Cream (gallons)	Yogurt (pints)	Pudding (12-ounce cans)
January	3,000	5,400	3,600
February	2,700	6,000	6,600
March	3,600	6,600	3,800

From past experience, Frozen's management knows that it takes 20 minutes of direct labor to make a gallon of ice cream, 5 minutes to make a pint of yogurt, and 6 minutes to make a can of pudding. Frozen's direct-labor employees are paid $5 per hour.

Prepare a direct-labor budget for each of the 3 months in both hours and costs.

E24–8 Direct-Labor Budgeting

As indicated in E24–6, E-M Candy Company makes and sells two kinds of candy: chocolate almond bars and coconut bars. The production budget for the next 3 months for each of the bars is as follows:

	Boxes of Chocolate Almond Bars	Boxes of Coconut Bars
April	700	600
May	800	650
June	1,000	750

From past experience, E-M's management knows that it takes approximately 20 minutes to make a box of chocolate almond bars and 30 minutes to make a box of coconut bars. E-M pays its direct-labor employees $8 per hour.

Prepare a direct-labor budget for each of the 3 months in both hours and costs.

E24–9 Cash Budgeting—Hospital

The management of Chicago Memorial Hospital needs to prepare a cash budget for July 1984. The following information is available.

a. The cash balance on July 1, 1984, is $236,000.

b. Actual services performed during May and June and projected services for July are

	May	June	July
Cash Services (bills paid by individuals as they leave the hospital)	$110,000	$ 90,000	$120,000
Credit Services (bills paid by insurance companies and Medicare)	900,000	1,000,000	875,000

Credit sales are collected over a 2-month period with 60 percent collected during the month the service is performed and 40 percent in the following month.

c. Hospital personnel plan to purchase $80,000 of supplies during July on account. Accounts payable are usually paid one-half in the month of purchase and one-half in the following month. The Accounts Payable balance on July 1, 1984, is $35,000.

d. Salaries and wages paid during July will be approximately $600,000. (Ignore income and other tax withholdings.)

e. Depreciation on the hospital and equipment for July will be $100,000.

f. A short-term bank loan of $80,000 (including interest) will be repaid in July.

g. All other cash expenses for July will total $56,000.

Prepare the hospital's July cash budget.

E24–10 Cash Budgeting

Beachcraft, Inc. buys automobile parts from various manufacturers and sells them to retail stores. Management is presently trying to prepare a cash budget for August and has the following information available.

a. The cash balance on August 1 is $45,000.

b. Actual sales for June and July and projected sales for August are as follows:

	June	July	August
Cash Sales	$ 30,000	$ 45,000	$ 60,000
Credit Sales	100,000	120,000	130,000

Credit sales are collected 70 percent during the month of sale, 20 percent in the month following the sale, and 10 percent in the second month following the sale.

c. Beachcraft's actual purchases for June and July and its projected purchases for August are as follows:

	June	July	August
Cash Purchases	$10,000	$20,000	$25,000
Credit Purchases	40,000	50,000	60,000

All accounts payable are paid in the month following the purchase.

d. Total administrative and selling expenses (including $14,000 depreciation) for August are expected to be $92,000.

e. Beachcraft expects to pay a $26,000 dividend to stockholders and to purchase, for cash, a $35,000 piece of land during August.

f. Cash on hand should never drop below $40,000.

Prepare Beachcraft's August cash budget, assuming that the company borrows any amounts needed to meet its minimum desired balance.

E24-11 Computation of Unit Costs

Dunn Garage Door Company makes two types of garage doors: aluminum and wood. During the past several years, management has kept accurate records of costs and resource requirements and has determined that the following is needed to make the garage doors.

Wood Door	Production Requirements	Unit Cost
Wood	200 board feet	$ 0.40
Paint	2 gallons	10.00
Direct Labor	6 hours	9.00
Variable Factory Overhead	6 hours	3.00

Aluminum Door	Production Requirements	Unit Cost
Aluminum	40 pounds	$ 2.00
Paint	$1\frac{1}{2}$ gallons	10.00
Direct Labor	12 hours	9.00
Variable Factory Overhead	12 hours	3.00

Compute the total unit costs of the wood and aluminum garage doors.

E24-12 Computation of Unit Costs

As indicated in E24-6, E-M Candy Company makes and sells two kinds of candy bars: chocolate almond and coconut bars. During the past several years, the company has kept accurate records of costs and resource requirements and has determined that the following is needed to make the candy bars.

One Box of 24 Chocolate Almond Bars	Cost
Chocolate ($1\frac{1}{2}$ pounds)	$2.00/pound
Almonds (1 pound)	4.00/pound
Sugar (2 pounds)	0.20/pound
Direct labor (20 minutes)	6.00/hour
Variable manufacturing overhead (20 minutes)	4.00/direct-labor hour

One Box of 24 Coconut Bars	Cost
Chocolate (1 pound)	$2.00/pound
Coconut ($1\frac{1}{4}$ pounds)	1.50/pound
Sugar ($1\frac{3}{4}$ pounds)	0.20/pound
Direct labor (30 minutes)	6.00/hour
Variable manufacturing overhead (30 minutes)	4.00/direct-labor hour

1. Compute the unit cost of making a box of each type of candy bar.

2. If management wants to mark up each box of candy 50 percent to cover other costs and earn a profit, how much should be charged for a box of each type of candy bar?

E24-13 The Budgeted Statement of Changes in Financial Position

The accountants at Lavelle's Sports Equipment Company are presently preparing the budgeted statement of changes in financial position for August. In getting ready to prepare the statement, they have the following information available.

Dividends to Be Paid in August	$ 8,000
Bonds to Be Issued in August	50,000
Equipment to Be Sold in August	16,000
Repayment of Short-Term Loans in August	24,000
Depreciation Expense During August	4,000
Expected August Net Income	17,000
Expected Changes in Current Assets and Liabilities During August:	
Accounts Receivable Increase	4,000
Accounts Payable Decrease	3,000
Increase in Inventory	2,000
Decrease in Income Taxes Payable	12,000

Prepare Lavelle's budgeted statement of changes in financial position using the cash concept of funds.

E24-14 The Budgeted Statement of Changes in Financial Position

The accountants at Edwards Department Store are preparing the budgeted statement of changes in financial position for 1985. The following information is available.

Expected Net Income	$60,000
Dividends to Be Paid	20,000
Equipment to Be Purchased	35,000
Expected Short-Term Borrowing	10,000
Expected Long-Term Borrowing	25,000
Expected Depreciation Expense for 1985	11,000
Expected Issuance of Common Stock	80,000
Expected Purchase of a New Plant	62,000
Expected Changes in Current Assets and Liabilities During 1985:	
Increase in Accounts Receivable	800
Increase in Accounts Payable	1,200
Increase in Inventory	2,000
Decrease in Income Taxes Payable	2,400

Prepare the budgeted statement of changes in financial position using the cash concept of funds for Edwards Department Store.

E24–15 The Budgeted Income Statement

Orsen Company has asked you to prepare the budgeted income statement for the coming year. The following information is available.

Expected Sales Revenue	$700,000
Manufacturing Costs:	
Variable Cost of Goods Sold	318,000
Fixed Overhead	62,000
Selling Expenses:	
Variable Expenses	90,000
Fixed Expenses	42,000
Administrative Expenses:	
Variable Expenses	17,000
Fixed Expenses	70,000
Other:	
Interest Expense	28,000
Income Tax Rate	30%

Prepare a budgeted contribution-margin income statement for Orsen Company.

PROBLEMS

P24–1 Production and Direct-Materials Budgets

Zilmer Manufacturing Company makes two products: widgets and gidgets. The following information is available on August 1.

a. Direct materials needed to make a widget: six units of X, three units of Y.

Direct materials needed to make a gidget: two units of X, six units of Y.

b. Number of units available at beginning of August:

Direct Material X	66 units
Direct Material Y	32 units
Finished Widgets	8
Finished Gidgets	12

c. Expected sales during August:

Widgets	80
Gidgets	90

d. Desired levels of ending inventory:

Direct Material X	60 units
Direct Material Y	30 units
Widgets	10
Gidgets	12

e. Cost of direct materials:

Direct Material X	$2 per unit
Direct Material Y	$3 per unit

Required:
Prepare a production budget, a direct-materials usage budget, and a direct-materials purchases budget for Zilmer Company for the month of August.

P24–2 Production and Direct-Materials Budgets

Christiansen Furniture Company makes two products: bookshelves and rocking chairs. The following information is available for November.

a. Production requirements:

	Bookshelf	Rocking Chair
Materials Needed:		
Wood	100 board feet at $0.70/foot	90 board feet at $0.70/foot
Stain	2 gallons at $8/gallon	3 gallons at $8/gallon
Bolts, Nuts, etc.	1 dozen at $2/dozen	1½ dozen at $2/dozen
Direct Labor	12 hours at $9/hour	10 hours at $9/hour
Variable Factory Overhead	12 hours at $3/direct-labor hour	10 hours at $3/direct-labor hour

b. Desired levels of ending inventory:

Wood	1,000 board feet
Stain	10 gallons
Bolts, Nuts, etc.	8 dozen
Finished Bookshelves	3
Finished Rocking Chairs	4

c. Beginning inventory:

Wood	1,100 board feet
Stain	9 gallons
Bolts, Nuts, etc.	7 dozen
Finished Bookshelves	4
Finished Rocking Chairs	5

d. Expected sales during November:

Bookshelves	25
Rocking Chairs	35

Required:

1. Prepare production, direct-materials usage, and direct-materials purchases budgets for Christiansen Furniture Company for November.
2. Given the anticipated production levels, how many full-time production employees must Christiansen have so that no overtime will be needed if each production employee works 160 hours per month? (Assume that there is no wasted time by employees.)
3. Assume that the company has three full-time production employees. If overtime pay is $1\frac{1}{2}$ times as much as regular pay and if the extra one-time cost of hiring a new person is $600, would it be less expensive to have the three employees work overtime or to hire a new employee?
4. **Interpretive Question** What other factors should be considered in deciding whether to hire a new employee or have current employees work overtime?

P24-3 Cash Budgeting

Wendy Walkinshaw, owner of W & W Department Store, is negotiating a $50,000, 15 percent, 4-month loan from the Wayne County National Bank, effective October 1, 1984. The bank loan officer has requested that W & W prepare a cash budget for each of the next 4 months as evidence of its ability to repay the loan. The following information is available for W & W Department Store as of September 30, 1984.

Cash on Hand	$ 5,000
Accounts Receivable	60,000
Inventory	34,000
Accounts Payable	90,000

The accounts payable are all to be paid in October. Sales for October and sales forecast for the next few months are: October—$90,000; November—$150,000; December—$200,000; January—$100,000; February—$50,000. Collections on sales are usually made at the rate of 20 percent in the month of sale, 60 percent during the month following the sale, and 18 percent in the second month after the sale. Two percent of accounts receivable are written off as uncollectible. Forty thousand dollars of the $60,000 of accounts receivable on hand at September 30 will be collected in October, and $20,000 will be collected in November. Cost of Goods Sold is 60 percent of sales, with all purchases paid for in the month following purchase. Ending Inventory should always equal the cost of the goods that will be sold during the next month. Operating expenses are $10,000 a month plus 5 percent of sales, all paid in the month following their incurrence.

Required:

Prepare a cash budget showing receipts and disbursements for October, November, December, and January. Also prepare supporting schedules for cash collections, purchases, and operating expenses.

P24-4 Cash Budgeting

Englewood Outdoors is a sporting goods store. The following data are available for use in preparing its forecast of cash needs for June.

a. Current assets (May 31):

Cash	$24,000
Inventory	13,500
Accounts Receivable	30,000
Property, Plant, and Equipment	80,000
Accounts Payable (for merchandise purchases only)	14,250
Recent and Estimated Future Sales:	
May	50,000
June	45,000
July	55,000

b. Sales are made 60 percent on credit and 40 percent for cash. All credit sales are collected in the month following the sales.

c. Englewood's June expenses are estimated to be

Salaries and Wages Expense	20% of sales
Rent Expense	4% of sales
All Other Cash Expenses	6% of sales
Depreciation Expense	$600
Gross Margin	40% of sales

d. Englewood buys all of its sporting goods inventory from stores on the West Coast and wants to maintain an inventory level equal to one-half of the next month's sales. Payments for merchandise are made 50 percent during the month of purchase and 50 percent in the next month.

e. Other cash expenditures planned for June are
  (1) The purchase of $10,000 of furniture.
  (2) The payment of $5,000 of dividends.

f. Englewood desires to maintain a minimum cash balance of $22,000. The store has an arrangement with a local bank whereby it can borrow money in multiples of $1,000. Interest is charged on all loans at an annual rate of 10 percent and is assessed for a full quarter both in the quarter in which the money is borrowed and in the quarter in which the money is repaid. Interest is paid when the loan is repaid.

Required:
Prepare Englewood's cash budget for June.

P24-5 Cash Budgeting

LeAnn Manufacturing Company makes wax for furniture and floors. As part of overall planning, a cash budget is prepared by quarters each year. You have been asked to assist in preparing the cash budget for the fourth quarter of the company's fiscal year. The following information is available.

a. Sales:

Third quarter (actual)	$200,000
Fourth quarter (expected)	150,000

All sales are made on account with 80 percent collected in the quarter in which the sales are made and 20 percent collected during the following quarter.

b. Merchandise purchases are scheduled as follows:

Third quarter (actual)	$80,000
Fourth quarter (expected)	90,000

Merchandise is purchased on account and is paid for at the rate of 70 percent in the quarter of purchase and 30 percent in the following quarter.

c. Direct-labor and factory overhead costs (including $6,000 of depreciation) are expected to be $45,000 and $16,000, respectively, during the fourth quarter.

d. Selling and administrative expenses are expected to total $24,000 during the fourth quarter, including $2,000 of depreciation.

e. Plans have been made to purchase, for cash, $15,000 of equipment during the fourth quarter.

f. The cash balance at the beginning of the quarter is $16,000. The company can borrow money in $1,000 multiples at 12 percent interest from a local bank. The bank assesses interest for full quarters, both for the quarter in which the money is borrowed and for the quarter in which it is repaid. All interest is paid at the time of note repayment. LeAnn ran short of cash during the third quarter and had to borrow $8,000 from the bank. LeAnn wishes to maintain a minimum cash balance of $16,000.

Required:
Prepare a schedule showing the cash budget and financing needs of LeAnn Manufacturing Company for the fourth quarter.

P24-6 Unit-Cost, Ending Inventory, and Cost of Goods Sold Budgets

As indicated in P24-2, Christiansen Furniture Company makes two products: bookshelves and rocking chairs. The following information is available for September.

a. Production requirements:

	Bookshelves	Rocking Chairs
Materials Needed:		
Wood	100 board feet at $0.70/foot	90 board feet at $0.70/foot
Stain	2 gallons at $8/gallon	3 gallons at $8/gallon
Bolts, Nuts, etc.	1 dozen at $2/dozen	$1\frac{1}{2}$ dozen at $2/dozen
Direct Labor	12 hours at $9/hour	10 hours at $9/hour
Variable Factory Overhead	12 hours at $3/direct-labor hour	10 hours at $3/direct-labor hour

b. Desired levels of inventories:

	Beginning	Ending
Wood	1,100 board feet	1,000 board feet
Stain	9 gallons	10 gallons
Bolts, Nuts, etc.	7 dozen	8 dozen
Finished Bookshelves	4	3
Finished Rocking Chairs	5	4

c. Total resources used for production during September:

Direct Materials	$5,172
Direct Labor	5,652
Variable Manufacturing Overhead	1,884

Required:
1. Prepare unit-cost, ending inventory, and cost of goods sold budgets for Christiansen Manufacturing Company for September. (Assume that the beginning finished goods inventory has the same unit cost as the ending finished goods inventory and that there is no work-in-process inventory.)
2. If, at the current level of production, fixed overhead costs are $6 per unit, how much higher or lower would cost of goods sold be under the absorption costing approach?
3. **Interpretive Question** Which costing approach (variable or absorption) is better for evaluating performance? Explain.

P24-7 The Budgeted Income Statement and Balance Sheet

Young International makes hair dryers. During the past few days, its accountants have been preparing the master budget for the coming year, 1985. To date, they have gathered the following projected data.

Sales Revenue (at $20 per unit)	$245,000
Variable Selling Expenses	15,000
Variable Administrative Expenses	35,000
Interest Expense (not included in selling and administrative expenses)	1,500
Cost of Goods Sold (includes only variable costs)	90,000
Ending Cash Balance	26,500
Ending Accounts Receivable Balance	41,000
Ending Balance in Land Account	21,000
Ending Balance in Buildings Account	62,000
Ending Balance in Equipment Account	21,000
Ending Accumulated Depreciation on Buildings	41,000
Ending Accumulated Depreciation on Equipment	8,000
Ending Direct-Materials Inventory	14,000
Ending Finished Goods Inventory	22,000
Ending Accounts Payable Balance	6,000
Ending Common Stock Balance	28,000
Retained Earnings Balance, 1/1/85	56,000
Balance in Paid-in Capital in Excess of Par Account	20,000
Fixed Selling Expenses	20,000
Fixed Administrative Expenses	25,000
Fixed Manufacturing Overhead	10,000
Income Tax Rate	30%

Required:

1. Prepare a projected income statement (contribution-margin approach) and balance sheet for the coming year. Any income taxes owed on the coming year's net income will be paid in the following year.
2. By approximately how much would Young's profits increase if another 3,000 units were produced and sold for $20 each?

P24-8 The Budgeted Income Statement and Balance Sheet—Service Industry

William Scott Company is a small engineering corporation that surveys land for development. The company has grown rapidly over the past few years, and management has to decide whether new engineers should be hired and new offices opened. In order to assess future growth, the company's accountant has gathered budgeted information for the coming year, 1984.

Ending Balance in Common Stock Account	$ 32,000
Beginning Retained Earnings Balance	26,000
Ending Accounts Payable Balance	4,000
Ending Balance in the Equipment Account	106,000
Ending Balance in the Accumulated Depreciation Account	16,000
Accounts Receivable Balance	$ 13,000
Ending Cash Balance	12,000
Interest Expense	2,000
Salary Expense	70,000
Other Expenses (including depreciation)	25,000
Service Revenue	200,000
Income Tax Rate	25%

Income taxes due on the coming year's net income will be paid during 1985. Dividends of $50,000 are to be declared and paid during 1984.

Required:

1. Prepare a budgeted income statement and a budgeted balance sheet for 1984, from which the company president can make expansion decisions.
2. **Interpretive Question** On the basis of this information, is the company very profitable? How should this level of profits affect its expansion plans?

P24-9 The Budgeted Balance Sheet (Including Supporting Schedules)

The following balance sheet is available for Rowe Company at December 31, 1984.

Rowe Company
Balance Sheet as of December 31, 1984

Assets		
Current Assets:		
Cash	$ 15,000	
Accounts Receivable	40,000	
Inventory	31,250	
Total Current Assets		$ 86,250
Property, Plant, and Equipment:		
Land	$ 45,000	
Building and Equipment	160,000	
Less Accumulated Depreciation	(40,000)	
Total Property, Plant, and Equipment		165,000
Total Assets		$251,250
Liabilities and Stockholders' Equity		
Liabilities:		
Accounts Payable	$ 55,000	
Long-Term Notes Payable (12%)	50,000	
Total Liabilities		$105,000
Stockholders' Equity:		
Common Stock (5,000 shares at $20)	$100,000	
Retained Earnings	46,250	
Total Stockholders' Equity		146,250
Total Liabilities and Stockholders' Equity		$251,250

In light of the economy and the company's financial position, Rowe Company has made the following predictions for 1985.

a. Sales will be $250,000, or $62,500 per quarter.

b. Cost of goods sold averages 50 percent of sales with purchases being paid for in the quarter following purchase.

c. The ending inventory each quarter should equal the next quarter's sales.

d. Current accounts payable will be paid in the first quarter of 1985.

e. Rowe requires a cash balance of $15,000 at the end of each quarter.

f. If financing is needed, it will be secured and repaid in increments of $1,000 with 10 percent interest paid on the unpaid balance. Interest is paid both in the quarter the money is borrowed and in the quarter it is repaid.

g. Sales during the first quarter of 1986 are expected to be $65,000.

h. Operating expenses will total 30 percent of sales plus $5,000 each quarter; these expenses are paid in the quarter incurred.

i. Dividends of $0.50 per share will be paid in the second and fourth quarters.

j. One year's interest plus a $10,000 principal payment are due on the long-term note in the fourth quarter.

k. All receivables on hand at December 31, 1984, will be collected during the first quarter of 1985.

l. All sales are credit sales that are collected at the rate of 40 percent during the quarter of the sale and 60 percent during the following quarter.

m. The interest rate on the long-term note receivable is 12 percent.

n. The building and equipment are being depreciated on a straight-line basis over 20 years with no estimated salvage value.

Required:

Prepare the budgeted balance sheet as of December 31, 1985. (Hint: You will need to prepare several supporting schedules, including a purchases schedule, an operating expense schedule, a cash collection schedule, and a cash budget for each of the four quarters.)

P24–10 Unifying Problem: Sales, Cash Collections, Production, Direct-Materials Usage, Direct-Materials Purchases, and Direct-Labor Budgets

The following information is available for Dawson Company.

Expected Sales in Units:	
January	600
February	700
March	900
Selling Price per Unit	$10
January 1 Accounts Receivable Balance	$2,000
Desired Finished Goods Inventory, March 31	190
Beginning Finished Goods Inventory, January 1	150
Direct Materials Needed per Unit	8 pounds
Desired Direct-Materials Inventory, March 31	600 pounds
Beginning Direct-Materials Inventory, January 1	400 pounds
Total Direct-Labor Time per Finished Product	2 hours
Direct-Materials Cost per Pound	$0.50
Direct-Labor Cost per Hour	$6

Additional Information:

a. 60 percent of a month's sales is collected by month-end; the remaining 40 percent is collected in the month following.

b. The desired finished goods inventory every month is 20 percent of the next month's sales.

c. The desired direct-materials inventory every month is 10 percent of the next month's production needs.

Required:

1. Prepare a sales forecast for January, February, and March (in dollars).
2. Prepare a cash collection budget for January, February, and March (in dollars). Assume that all sales are on credit.
3. Prepare production budgets for January, February, and March (in units).
4. Prepare direct-materials usage budgets for January, February, and March (in dollars).
5. Prepare direct-materials purchases budgets for January, February, and March (in dollars).
6. Prepare direct-labor budgets for January, February, and March (in dollars).

P24–11 Unifying Problem: The Budgeted Income Statement, Balance Sheet, and Statement of Changes in Financial Position

Merriweather Corporation makes trailers for trucks. During the past few days, the company's accountants have been preparing the master budget for 1985. To date they have gathered the following projected data.

Sales Revenue	$9,000,000
Variable Selling Expenses	400,000
Variable Administrative Expenses	600,000
Interest Expense	60,000

Cost of Goods Sold (variable costs only)	5,000,000
Fixed Manufacturing Expenses	700,000
Fixed Administrative Expenses	440,000
Fixed Selling Expenses	300,000
Cash Balance at December 31, 1985	400,000
Accounts Receivable Balance at December 31, 1985	150,000
Balance in Land Account at December 31, 1985	373,000
Balance in Buildings Account at December 31, 1985	450,000
Balance in Equipment Account at December 31, 1985	320,000
Balance in Accumulated Depreciation on Equipment Account at December 31, 1985	80,000
Balance in Accumulated Depreciation on Buildings Account at December 31, 1985	80,000
Direct-Materials Inventory Balance at December 31, 1985	95,000
Finished Goods Inventory Balance at December 31, 1985	105,000
Accounts Payable Balance at December 31, 1985	93,000
Common Stock Balance at December 31, 1985	600,000
Retained Earnings Balance at January 1, 1985	350,000
Balance in Paid-in Capital in Excess of Par Account	40,000
Balance in Income Taxes Payable Account	200,000
Dividends to Be Declared and Paid During 1985	600,000
Income Tax Rate	30%

In addition, last year's balance sheet was as follows:

Merriweather Corporation
Balance Sheet as of December 31, 1984

Assets		
Cash		$ 80,000
Accounts Receivable		130,000
Direct-Materials Inventory		80,000
Finished Goods Inventory		110,000
Land		300,000
Buildings	$400,000	
Less Accumulated Depreciation	(40,000)	360,000
Equipment	$290,000	
Less Accumulated Depreciation	(60,000)	230,000
Total Assets		$1,290,000
Liabilities and Stockholders' Equity		
Liabilities:		
Accounts Payable	$ 75,000	
Income Taxes Payable	225,000	
Total Liabilities		$ 300,000
Stockholders' Equity:		
Common Stock	$600,000	
Paid-in Capital in Excess of Par–Common Stock	40,000	
Retained Earnings	350,000	
Total Stockholders' Equity		$ 990,000
Total Liabilities and Stockholders' Equity		$1,290,000

Required:

1. Prepare a budgeted income statement for 1985 (contribution-margin approach).
2. Prepare a budgeted balance sheet as of December 31, 1985.
3. Prepare a budgeted statement of changes in financial position for 1985 using the cash concept of funds.

CHAPTER 25

Using Standard Costs for Control and Performance Evaluation

THIS CHAPTER EXPLAINS:

The concepts of standard costs and variances.
How standard costs are determined.
Methods of computing variances.
Analysis and control of materials costs, labor costs, and manufacturing overhead costs.
Analysis and investigation of variances.
Advantages and disadvantages of a standard cost system.

In previous chapters we have discussed a variety of techniques that management uses to measure performance and make operating decisions. These techniques include job-order and process costing, operations budgeting, contribution-margin income statements, and break-even analysis—all of which involve the use of actual historical costs. For controlling operations and evaluating performance, however, standard costs, which are systematically predetermined costs, are often more appropriate.

A Framework for Standard Costs

Historical costs are the actual costs incurred in manufacturing a product. When one period's historical costs are compared with a prior period's, management can see whether costs have increased or decreased. However, the prior period may not be a useful guide for judging the results of the later period's operating decisions. For example, the cost of materials may have decreased from one period to the next, but the prior period's cost may have been too high to begin with.

Standard costs, on the other hand, are management's realistic assessment of what costs should be. They are thus more useful for planning and controlling costs for repetitive activities, such as production, shipping, and routine office jobs. When current actual costs are compared with standard costs (rather than with historical costs), an important new approach to control and performance evaluation becomes possible.

The Concepts of Standard Cost and Variances

standard *a quantitative measure of the expected level of performance*

standard costs *systematically predetermined estimates of the costs required to produce a unit of output; they include the anticipated costs of materials, labor, and overhead for a given level of activity*

The idea of a standard cost is derived from the concept of a standard, which is an established measure of comparison. Standards serve as a basis for determining the quality of actual results. For example, in golf, each hole has a designated par, which represents the standard number of strokes for that hole. To say that you shot a hole in four strokes means little unless you know what par is for that hole. Thus, a standard is a guide for judging how well a particular activity is performed. In a manufacturing company, the measure of comparison by which an actual cost is judged to be high, low, or reasonable is the standard cost, which is usually determined on the basis of experience and careful analysis. In general, standards can be set for two components of a cost—price and quantity. The standard quantity is multiplied by the standard price to arrive at the standard dollar cost, which defines the total amount of cost that should have been incurred for that particular resource.

COMPUTING VARIANCES

variance *any deviation from standard*

Once a standard cost is known, a manager can compare it with the actual cost and note any difference, or variance. Since a standard cost has a price (or rate) component and a quantity component, the comparison can result in two variances: a price (or rate) variance and a quantity (or usage) variance. These variances are usually computed for materials and labor, and often for manufacturing overhead.

To illustrate, we assume the following costs of meat for 200 hamburgers.

Standard cost:	50 pounds of hamburger × $1.10 per pound =	$55.00
Actual cost:	48 pounds of hamburger × $1.20 per pound =	57.60
	Total variance:	$ 2.60

The quantity variance is the difference between the standard 50 pounds and the actual 48 pounds multiplied by the standard price: (50 − 48) × $1.10 = $2.20. The price variance is the difference between the actual and standard price per pound ($1.20 − $1.10) multiplied by the actual quantity used (48 pounds), which equals $4.80. Because less hamburger was used than the standard called for, the quantity variance is favorable. The price variance is unfavorable because the actual price per pound was higher than the standard. The net unfavorable variance of $2.60 is the combination of the favorable quantity variance and the unfavorable price variance. To better understand how this combination works, you might think of unfavorable as meaning "minus" and favorable as meaning "plus."

Quantity variance	$2.20 F
Price variance	−4.80 U
Net variance	$2.60 U

(Note that in this chapter and in subsequent chapters we label a favorable variance with an "F" and an unfavorable variance with a "U.")

The most difficult problem in computing variances is remembering which price is multiplied by the difference in quantity to get the quantity variance and which quantity is multiplied by the difference in price to get the price variance. The diagram labeled Method 1 in Exhibit 25-1 helps some students remember how each variance is computed. Other students prefer the diagram labeled Method 2 in the Exhibit. We suggest that you use one of these approaches on a regular basis. Note that the difference in quantity is multiplied by the standard price so that the quantity variance will not be influenced by price changes. The difference in price is multiplied by the actual quantity in order to determine the total effect of the price change on the cost of the resources acquired or used.

EXHIBIT 25-1 **Computing Variances**

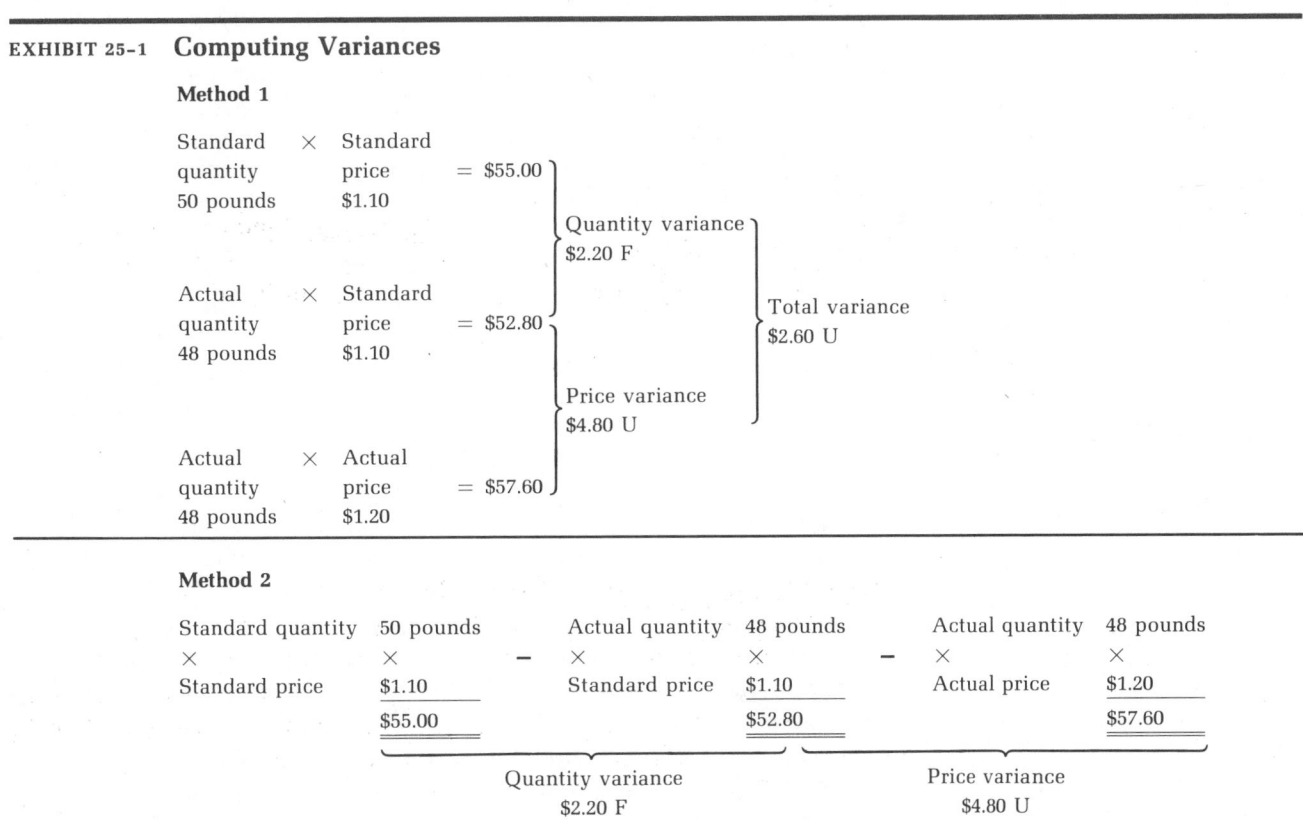

Method 1

Standard quantity 50 pounds	×	Standard price $1.10	= $55.00	
			Quantity variance $2.20 F	
Actual quantity 48 pounds	×	Standard price $1.10	= $52.80	Total variance $2.60 U
			Price variance $4.80 U	
Actual quantity 48 pounds	×	Actual price $1.20	= $57.60	

Method 2

Standard quantity × Standard price	50 pounds × $1.10	−	Actual quantity × Standard price	48 pounds × $1.10	−	Actual quantity × Actual price	48 pounds × $1.20
	$55.00			$52.80			$57.60

Quantity variance $2.20 F

Price variance $4.80 U

Total variance $2.60 U

STANDARD COSTS AND CONTROL

Variances provide management with information for controlling costs and evaluating performance. However, the presence of a variance does not automatically mean that corrective action is necessary. A manager uses judgment in deciding when a variance is large enough to warrant making changes in the operating process. In addition, company guidelines may specify when an actual cost is considered significantly out of line with the standard cost.

Herein lies the essence of control through the use of standard costs. Managers use standard costs as guidelines in establishing operating procedures. As a result, most variances will be small. This allows a manager to concentrate on the large variances—to determine why they occurred and to take action to keep them from recurring. This strategy of dealing with significant variations from standard is commonly referred to as management by exception; it is a fundamental concept in operating a standard cost system.

management by exception *the strategy of focusing attention on the actual costs that vary significantly from standard costs*

TO SUMMARIZE Management employs a variety of methods to measure performance and to provide a reliable base on which to make operating decisions. An important technique is the use of standard costs to plan, measure, and evaluate performance. Standards are guides for judging how well an activity is performed. A standard cost based on experience and careful analysis, rather than an estimate based primarily on the prior period's results, establishes a level of performance that management can rely upon to meet profit objectives in a competitive environment. The difference between the standard cost and the actual cost is called a variance. Management follows a strategy of concentrating on the significant variances (management by exception) as an effective way of improving future performance.

Types of Standards

The golf analogy can be used again in explaining alternative standards for measuring and evaluating performance. When golfers compare their scores with par, they are evaluating performance against an ideal standard. That is, par is the score a golfer should achieve if every shot were played in the desired manner. This standard is beyond the capabilities of most golfers, so a handicapping system has been established. A handicap is computed by taking 96 percent of the difference between (1) the average of the 10 best scores the golfer has had in the last 20 18-hole rounds played and (2) the course rating, that is, par over the 18 holes. [Suppose, for example, that the average of a golfer's 10 best scores is 98 and that the course rating is 70; the golfer's handicap would be $(98 - 70) \times 0.96 \cong 27$.] When added to par, this handicap provides an attainable standard, one the golfer can achieve by playing at his or her best. But it is not as demanding as the "ideal" standard of par.

ideal standard *a guide for judging actual performance based on very efficient productivity*

attainable standard *a guide for judging actual performance based on efficient, but not perfect, productivity*

Now suppose that even the attainable standard based on the handicapping system is still out of reach on a particular day. The golfer can apply an even less rigorous standard by comparing today's score with his or her average score for the last 20 games, or for some designated period of time. This is referred to as an historical standard, a measure of current performance in relation to general past performance, including both good and bad performances.

historical standard *a guide for judging actual performance based on the average productivity of recent periods*

These concepts of ideal, attainable, and historical standards can be applied in the setting of price and quantity standards in any economic activity. A key question is: Which standard should be used to measure performance? If an ideal standard could hardly ever, and perhaps never, be achieved, it would tend to discourage even the most highly motivated workers. A standard beyond the normal capabilities of the workers is also beyond a manager's scope in taking corrective action.

On the other hand, an historical standard may not be demanding enough. It may reflect past inefficiencies that management is trying to eliminate. Thus, it may not motivate workers to strive for greater efficiency.

As you can see, both ideal and historical standards have basic weaknesses. An attainable standard is more realistic. As a standard, it is neither too high nor too low to be useful to management in planning and controlling each responsibility center's activities. For example, it allows for normal inefficiencies, such as coffee breaks, machinery repairs, and setup time, but it does alert management to significant, but avoidable, inefficiencies that would show up as a variance from standard. It also alerts management to an unusual favorable variance that may imply the need for an adjustment of the standard. The use of attainable standards makes the concept of management by exception operationally effective because significant variances should signal problems that management will want to address.

Developing Attainable Standards

Assuming that a firm wants to use attainable standard costs, how are they determined? The process of setting standards may be expensive and time-consuming, and it frequently involves trial and error. Standard setting is something like gazing into a crystal ball, in that it specifies what costs should be under conditions that will prevail during a subsequent period. The process requires the cooperative effort of many people in an organization, including accountants, industrial engineers, purchasing agents, and the managers of the departments to be judged. These individuals may also have roles to play in the use of standards.

The accountant has an important role in developing standards because he or she is in a good position to determine how past costs have changed at various volume levels. This is not an easy task. Changes in methods of production, technology, worker efficiency, and plant layout, for example, can affect the behavior of costs. Before they can serve as standard costs, past costs often have to be adjusted to take such changes in operating conditions into account. These changes may occur gradually and may not be easily perceptible; hence, it is difficult for the accountant to identify the cost characteristics that will be useful in setting standards for the future.

Engineers are involved in setting standard costs because of their knowledge of the most efficient way of performing each task in relation to the existing technology of the operation. This knowledge is based on time and motion studies of workers' performance and on analyses of such matters as the most efficient ways of using raw materials. The engineering staff is also responsible for establishing an effective maintenance program, which can influence materials, labor, and overhead standards.

Managers who will be judged by the standards should be involved in the standard-setting process, because they are more likely to be motivated to meet the standards if they have participated in setting them and have accepted them. And, of course, the participation of such managers also makes effective use of their experience and judgment.

TO SUMMARIZE There are three types of standards: ideal, historical, and attainable. For a manufacturing firm, attainable standards are more appropriate than either ideal or historical standards. Attainable standards aid management in planning, since it is reasonable to expect that budgets based on them will be met. They are also most likely to motivate employees to perform at their highest level, since they represent goals that are within reach but that require a high degree of efficiency to achieve.

The standard-setting process is a combination of engineering estimates, managerial judgments, and accountants' analyses of recent cost behavior. The initial standards will probably be "rough," but they can be refined through experience to become an effective guideline for controlling costs.

A Standard Cost System

standard cost system *a product costing system in which standard costs are used instead of actual costs*

A standard cost system might be defined as a cost-accumulation system based on the product costs that should have been incurred rather than those that actually were incurred. The purpose of the standard cost system, of course, is to assist management in planning, control, and performance evaluation through the process of comparing actual costs with standard costs and isolating the variances, some of which will need attention. The steps in the establishment and operation of a standard cost system are to

1. Develop standard costs.
2. Prepare budgets based on standard costs.
3. Collect actual costs.
4. Compare actual and budgeted costs to identify variances.
5. Report operating results, including variances, to the managers of responsibility centers.
   (a) Analyze the causes of significant controllable variances.
   (b) Take action to eliminate the significant variances.
6. Journalize actual costs and standard costs, and record the variances.

These steps describe a typical standard cost system. You can find some or all of these elements in most organizations, but you will not find all elements in all firms. For example, an automobile repair shop might have standard labor hours for the most frequently performed jobs, a restaurant might have standard quantities of food for each serving, or a bank or insurance company might have standard labor hours for routine clerical functions. You are most likely to find an extensive standard cost system in a manufacturing firm, which usually will have standard costs for materials, labor, and manufacturing overhead. These standard costs would be reported on cost cards like the one shown for Kemper Manufacturing Company in Exhibit 25-2.

EXHIBIT 25-2 **Kemper Manufacturing Company**
Standard Cost Card—Manufacturing Division

	Standard Quantity	Standard Price or Rate	Standard Cost
Direct Materials	2 pounds	$ 2.00	$ 4.00
Direct Labor	2 hours	6.00	12.00
Variable Overhead	2 hours	12.75	25.50
Total Standard Cost per Unit			$41.50

standard cost card *an itemization of the components of the standard cost of a product*

The standard cost card for Kemper Manufacturing Company presents standard variable costs only. This is consistent with the use of variable costing, which is especially valuable to managers in the decision-making process.

The standard cost card shows the predetermined variable cost of one unit of a product, assuming that production is performed in an efficient manner. These unit standard costs will be built into a flexible budget, which will include the total expected costs for the expected volume of production. The variable budget for Kemper's manufacturing division for August 1984, based on the standard cost card in Exhibit 25-2 and assuming production of 4,000 units, would be

	Budgeted Production Capacity and Standard Costs	Budgeted Costs
Direct Materials	4,000 × $ 4.00	$ 16,000
Direct Labor	4,000 × 12.00	48,000
Variable Overhead	4,000 × 25.50	102,000
Total Budget for Variable Manufacturing Costs		$166,000

This budget establishes Kemper's expected variable costs for 4,000 units of production. It also highlights the difference between a standard cost and a budgeted cost. A standard cost is a per-unit figure, whereas a budgeted cost is the total cost of producing a designated number of units. Although the terms are often used interchangeably, it is more accurate to distinguish the unit concept of a standard from the total concept of a budget amount.

Given this background information about standard costs and their relationship to budgets, you are now ready to learn how standard costs are used for analyzing materials, labor, and variable overhead costs. Our discussion will include the calculation of appropriate variances, use of those variances for control and performance evaluation, and accounting for the flow of costs.

Analysis and Control of Materials and Labor Costs

The analysis of overhead cost variances is somewhat different from that of materials and labor variances, so overhead will be discussed separately. In this section we compare Kemper's budgeted figures with actual results to determine materials and labor variances.

MATERIALS VARIANCES

As explained earlier, for each standard cost there is a price, or rate, variance and a quantity, or usage, variance. To illustrate the computation of the price and quantity variances for direct materials, we will assume the following actual results for Kemper's manufacturing division.

Direct Materials Purchased	10,000 pounds at $2.15
Direct Materials Used	8,300 pounds
Units Produced	4,000

Keep in mind throughout the following discussion that the standard cost card specifies that materials should cost $2 for each pound.

The Materials Price Variance

materials price variance *the extent to which the actual price varies from the standard price for the quantity of materials purchased or used; computed by multiplying the difference between the actual and standard prices by the quantity purchased or used*

The materials price variance reflects the extent to which the actual price varies from the standard price for the quantity of materials purchased or used. It is computed by multiplying the difference between the actual and the standard prices by the quantity purchased or used. The price variance can be computed either when materials are purchased or when they are put into production.

When is the best time to determine the materials price variance—on purchase or use? The purchasing department would find this information useful when the materials are purchased. Without it, the purchasing manager will not know whether corrective action is needed. If the price variance is not useful for controlling the purchasing function—for example, because prices are controlled in another responsibility center—this variance should be computed when the materials are transferred to production. Regardless of when price variances are computed, they should be kept separate from quantity variances.

Assuming that standard costs are introduced when the materials are purchased, the price variance would be computed as shown here.

Materials Price Variance (Based on Quantity Purchased)

Actual Price of Direct Materials	$2.15
Standard Price of Direct Materials	2.00
Difference	$0.15 U
Quantity Purchased	× 10,000
Total Price Variance (Unfavorable)	$1,500 U

This variance indicates that the company spent $1,500 more than the standard for raw materials. The buyer responsible for these purchases should be able to explain the variance, even though he or she may not be responsible for its occurrence. This may be the case, for example, when prices change after the standard is set. Or the production manager might unexpectedly run out of materials and order a small quantity on a rush basis, which usually raises the price of the materials as well as the cost of shipping. The key point is that the cause of any significant variance must be explained and steps taken to prevent such variances in the future.

Now assume that the materials price variance is computed at the time the materials are transferred to Work-in-Process Inventory. If 8,300 pounds were used in production, the variance would be based on that amount rather than on the 10,000 pounds purchased: ($2.15 − $2.00) $0.15 U × 8,300 pounds = $1,245 U. In this case an unfavorable variance of $1,245 would result, as shown.

Materials Price Variance (Based on Quantity Transferred to Production)

Actual Price of Direct Materials	$2.15
Standard Price of Direct Materials	2.00
Difference	$0.15 U
Quantity Transferred to Production	× 8,300
Total Price Variance (Unfavorable)	$1,245 U

The Materials Quantity Variance

For its manufacturing division, Kemper budgeted 8,000 pounds of raw material to produce 4,000 units. Actual usage amounted to 8,300 pounds. On the basis of this information, the computation of the materials quantity (usage) variance would be

materials quantity (usage) variance *the extent to which the actual quantity of materials varies from the standard quantity; computed by multiplying the difference between the actual quantity and the standard quantity of materials used by the standard price*

Materials Quantity Variance

Actual Usage of Direct Materials	8,300 pounds
Standard Usage (2 pounds × 4,000) of Direct Materials	8,000 pounds
Difference	300 pounds U
Standard Price	× $2.00
Total Quantity Variance	$600 U

The company used 300 more pounds of material than expected. This information would be communicated to the production manager, perhaps as shown in Exhibit 25-3.

EXHIBIT 25-3

Kemper Manufacturing Company
Manufacturing Division Report of Materials Quantity Variance for the Month Ended August 31, 1984

Item	Actual Quantity	Standard Quantity	Standard Price	Actual Quantity × Standard Price	Budgeted Cost	Materials Quantity Variance
Raw Materials	8,300	8,000	$2.00	$16,600	$16,000	$600 U

Just as the purchasing manager must explain significant price variances, the production manager must analyze significant quantity variances to determine their cause. Any one of several factors may contribute to an unfavorable quantity variance. For example, the quality of the material may not be satisfactory, the workers handling the material may be inexperienced, or the machines through which the material passes may need repair. If the material is of inferior quality, the purchasing manager rather than the production manager may be responsible for the variance. Again, the important point is that the cause of a significant variance should be determined and actions taken to prevent its recurrence.

Accounting for Materials Variances

If the materials price variance is isolated when the materials are purchased and the materials quantity variance is determined when the materials are used in production, Kemper would make the following journal entries.

Raw Materials Inventory (10,000 lbs. at $2.00)	20,000	
Materials Price Variance [($2.15 − $2.00) × 10,000 lbs.]	1,500	
Cash (or Accounts Payable) ($2.15 × 10,000 lbs.)		21,500
Purchased 10,000 pounds of raw materials at $2.15 per pound and put them in inventory at the standard price of $2.00 per pound.		
Work-in-Process Inventory (8,000 lbs. at $2.00)	16,000	
Materials Quantity Variance [(8,300 − 8,000) lbs. at $2.00]	600	
Raw Materials Inventory (8,300 lbs. at $2.00)		16,600
To transfer 8,300 pounds of materials out of inventory and record standard usage of 8,000 pounds of material to produce 4,000 units of output.		

As shown above, the Materials Price Variance and Materials Quantity Variance accounts are debited when the variances are unfavorable; they are credited when the variances are favorable. An unfavorable variance can be thought of as an expense; a favorable variance can be considered miscellaneous income. Note that the $16,000 debit to Work-in-Process Inventory is the budgeted cost for the 4,000 units (8,000 pounds of standard materials × $2.00 standard price). The excess actual costs are now in the variance accounts, which are usually transferred to the Income Summary account and show up on the income statement as expenses (if unfavorable) or as miscellaneous income (if favorable). Work-in-Process Inventory and Finished

Goods Inventory will include only the standard costs of materials times the standard quantities of materials needed for the production achieved.

LABOR VARIANCES

A labor rate variance and a labor efficiency variance are usually computed for manufacturing labor when a standard cost system is being used. These variances are computed in a manner similar to calculation of the materials price and quantity variances.

The Labor Rate Variance

labor rate variance *the extent to which the actual labor rate varies from the standard rate for the quantity of labor used; computed by multiplying the difference between the actual rate and the standard rate by the quantity of labor used*

A labor rate variance is a price variance. It shows the difference between actual wage rates and standard wage rates. For Kemper's manufacturing division, the standard cost per unit for direct labor was 2 hours at $6 per hour, and the budget for August based on 4,000 units of production was $48,000 (2 × $6 × 4,000 units). Actual labor used during the month was 8,352 hours at $6.20 per hour. On the basis of this information, there was an unfavorable labor rate variance of approximately $1,670, computed as follows:

Labor Rate Variance

Actual Direct-Labor Rate	$6.20	or	8,352 Hours × $6.20 (rounded)	$51,782
Standard Direct-Labor Rate	6.00		8,352 Hours × $6.00	50,112
Difference	0.20 U		Labor Rate Variance (rounded)	$ 1,670 U
Actual Hours Worked	× 8,352			
Labor Rate Variance (rounded)	$1,670 U			

As this variance indicates, $1,670 more than the standard amount for the actual number of hours used was spent for direct labor because actual labor rates were higher than standard rates. The company's guidelines would determine whether the variance should be investigated. Depending on the firm's hiring policies and the degree of authority given to operating managers in setting wage rates and assigning workers to particular jobs, the managers may or may not be responsible for this labor rate variance.

The Labor Efficiency Variance

labor efficiency variance *the extent to which the actual labor used varies from the standard quantity; computed by multiplying the difference between the actual quantity and the standard quantity of labor by the standard rate*

The labor efficiency variance is a quantity variance. It measures the cost (or benefit) of using labor for more (or fewer) hours than prescribed by the standard. The labor efficiency variance is computed in the same manner as the materials quantity variance, as illustrated in the following schedule for Kemper's manufacturing division.

Labor Efficiency Variance

Actual Direct-Labor Hours	8,352	or	8,352 Hours × $6.00	$50,112
Standard Direct-Labor Hours (2 hours × 4,000 units)	8,000		8,000 Hours × $6.00	48,000
Difference	352 U		Labor Efficiency Variance	$ 2,112 U
Standard Rate	× $6.00			
Labor Efficiency Variance	$2,112 U			

The manufacturing division used 352 more direct-labor hours than standard, which caused an unfavorable efficiency variance of $2,112. The manager would learn this information from a report like the one in Exhibit 25-4.

EXHIBIT 25-4

Kemper Manufacturing Company
Manufacturing Division Report of Labor Efficiency Variance
for the Month Ended August 31, 1984

Actual Hours Worked	Standard Hours	Standard Rate	Actual Hours × Standard Rate	Budgeted Cost	Labor Efficiency Variance
8,352	8,000	$6.00	$50,112	$48,000	$2,112 U

Labor efficiency is one of the most important manufacturing variances. It reflects the effective utilization of a department's work force, which is one of the manager's major responsibilities. The manager of such a department may not receive a similar report for a labor rate variance, because those variances are more likely to be controlled by personnel managers than by production managers.

Accounting for Labor Variances

The labor costs and variances for Kemper's manufacturing division can be accounted for in a single journal entry, since the labor rate and labor efficiency variances are both computed for a given period of time or for a given amount of production.

Work-in-Process Inventory (8,000 hours × $6.00)	48,000	
Labor Rate Variance [($6.20 − $6.00) × 8,352 hours]	1,670	
Labor Efficiency Variance [(8,352 − 8,000) hours × $6.00] . .	2,112	
Accrued Payroll (8,352 hours × $6.20)		51,782

To charge Work-in-Process Inventory for standard labor hours at the standard wage rate to produce 4,000 units of output, and to set up unfavorable labor rate and efficiency variances to reflect the use of 352 hours above standard at an average wage rate of $0.20 above standard.

As with the materials variances, the unfavorable labor variances, which reflect the actual labor cost over the budgeted labor cost, will be closed to the Income Summary Account. Work-in-Process Inventory will reflect only the budgeted labor cost for 4,000 units of product.

TO SUMMARIZE The difference between actual and standard costs of materials for a given production volume may be separated into a materials price variance and a materials quantity variance. The materials price variance can be computed when the materials are purchased or when they are issued to production. The managers responsible for the variances must determine their causes and take action if the variances are outside an acceptable range.

The labor rate variance is the difference between the actual and standard rates multiplied by the actual hours worked. The labor efficiency variance is the difference between actual and standard hours multiplied by the standard wage rate. Labor efficiency variances are usually controllable by manufacturing division managers. Labor rate variances are usually controllable in the personnel department.

The materials variances (price and quantity) and the labor variances (rate and efficiency) are recorded in individual accounts when the materials are acquired or used and when the labor is used. Work-in-Process Inventory reflects only budgeted materials and labor costs.

Measuring, Controlling, and Reporting Manufacturing Overhead Costs

Overhead is the third type of manufacturing cost that should be controlled and accounted for. It includes such costs as indirect materials, indirect labor, utilities, repairs and maintenance, insurance, taxes, and depreciation. As you learned in Chapter 21, some of these costs are fixed and some are variable. In a standard cost system, a firm may use either the absorption costing or the variable costing approach to account for fixed and variable overhead costs. When a firm uses absorption costing (which is required for financial reporting and income tax determination), both fixed and variable overhead costs are treated as product costs. This means that they are included with materials and labor as inventory costs until the product is sold. With variable costing, only variable overhead is included as a product cost; fixed overhead costs are treated as period expenses. Because variable costing is more useful for internal decision making (see Chapter 23), we will use it in our discussion of both overhead cost control and accounting for overhead costs.

MEASURING AND CONTROLLING OVERHEAD COSTS

Like materials and labor, overhead is measured and controlled by establishing standard costs, preparing a budget of planned costs, measuring and analyzing variances from budget, and reporting the variance results to managers so they can take any necessary corrective action. Since overhead costs are more complex than direct materials and labor, the control process can be understood more easily if we break it into three stages.

Stage 1 Before the Accounting Period Starts (Planning Stage)

1. Identify each overhead cost as fixed, variable, or semivariable. Then separate the semivariable costs into their fixed and variable elements.
2. Establish the standard costs for each variable overhead cost item.
3. Prepare an operating budget.

Stage 2 During the Accounting Period (Operating Stage)

4. Collect actual variable overhead costs.

5. Apply budgeted variable costs to Work-in-Process Inventory and transfer them to Finished Goods Inventory and Cost of Goods Sold.

Stage 3 After the End of the Accounting Period (Control Stage)

6. Compare actual variable costs with budgeted variable costs and compute any variances.

7. Analyze major variances in order to isolate the causes as a basis for taking any necessary corrective action.

Each of these stages requires further explanation to demonstrate how variable overhead costs are controlled and accounted for.

The Planning Stage

The first step in controlling overhead costs is to study the behavior of each overhead item in order to identify whether its cost is fixed, variable, or semivariable. Then, segregate the semivariable costs into their fixed and variable elements. Since we are using the variable costing approach, which treats fixed costs as period expenses, we will not include fixed costs in our calculations. (For a discussion of techniques for controlling fixed costs, you may refer to advanced managerial accounting texts.)

The second step is to develop for each variable overhead cost a standard cost that will reflect how much the overhead cost will change as the number of units of production (output) changes. Remember that variable costs change in total in proportion to some measure of activity, such as the number of units manufactured, the number of labor or machine hours, or the amount of labor dollars. For both direct materials and direct labor, the units of materials (for example, pounds) and labor (for example, hours) vary directly with the units manufactured. One additional unit of product requires a specific number of pounds of material and hours of labor. No such direct relationship exists between manufacturing overhead costs and specific units of product. In addition, the cost per unit of product of each overhead item, such as pounds of indirect material, kilowatts of electricity, hours of indirect labor, or machine hours for maintenance, usually does not justify an individual measure of its use.

For overhead costs, therefore, accountants must select an activity measure that they believe will reasonably reflect the variation in the overhead costs in relation to the units of output. The activity measure can be an output measure (the units of output) or an input measure (direct-labor hours, machine hours, or direct-labor dollars). Performance can be measured more accurately if we use a standard input measure rather than an output measure. This is because a standard input measure is not affected by the inefficiencies that actual output and input measures may be subject to. It is also better to use a physical input measure (labor hours or machine hours) than a dollar input measure (labor dollars), in order to keep the activity measure free of price or rate changes. In general, the activity measure chosen should be one that is not governed by any factors other than the volume of production. If standard direct-labor hours or standard machine hours are used, the activity measure will only be affected by the volume of output and not by price or rate changes or inefficiencies in the use of the actual physical inputs. In our subsequent discussion, the activity base we will use for setting standard variable overhead costs will be standard direct-labor hours.

To illustrate, we assume that the indirect labor in a manufacturing department is a variable cost that is expected to be $3,700 for a particular month during which 10,000 direct-labor hours are to be worked. The standard cost for indirect labor would be $0.37 per standard direct-labor hour ($3,700 ÷ 10,000 expected direct-labor hours). Such a standard cost per direct-labor hour would be developed for each variable cost item.

After the standard costs are established, they serve as a basis for preparing an operating budget (step 3) for the coming accounting period at the expected level of activity (that is, for the expected number of direct-labor hours). As you learned in Chapter 24, a budget at only one level of activity is a static budget. It is not of much help in controlling overhead costs or evaluating performance if the actual level of activity is different from the level used to prepare the budget. A budget that takes into account various possible levels of operations is called a flexible budget. In a flexible budget, total variable costs are calculated for several activity levels within a realistic range. Managers can then be held responsible for the costs that should have been incurred at the level of activity achieved. The flexible budget is thus a key tool in determining whether costs are within control for the output achieved—a significant criterion for evaluating a manager's performance.

flexible budgeting *financial planning in which revenues and costs are projected in relation to varying activity levels*

To illustrate the development of a flexible budget to control variable overhead costs, we will assume that after a careful study of overhead cost behavior patterns, Kemper Company developed the following information for its manufacturing division.

Budgeted Annual Variable Overhead Costs	$144,000
Budgeted Annual Production	48,000 units
Budgeted Direct-Labor Hours at the Normal Activity Level (2 labor hours per unit of production)	96,000 hours

Using these annual production and cost projections, the standard variable overhead rate per direct-labor hour would be

$144,000/96,000 hours = $1.50

In determining the annual overhead rate presented above, the accounting department of Kemper Company would have studied the cost behavior patterns of individual overhead cost elements over the relevant range of activity and would have used this information to compute standard variable overhead rates for each cost element. Let us assume that the study of cost behavior patterns for the manufacturing division of Kemper Company produced the following rates for the individual overhead costs.

Overhead Cost Element	Standard Variable Overhead Costs per Direct-Labor Hour
Indirect Materials—Supplies	$0.45
Indirect Labor—Other	0.37
Heat, Light, and Power	0.19
Maintenance and Repairs	0.49
Total	$1.50

Based on these standard variable overhead costs, a flexible budget can be prepared at the beginning of the production period for a number of activity levels.

For the month of May 1985, Kemper's manufacturing division expects to use 8,000 direct-labor hours (96,000 ÷ 12) to produce 4,000 units (48,000 ÷ 12), but asks the accounting department to prepare a flexible budget showing variable overhead costs for 7,600, 8,000, and 8,400 direct-labor hours. Exhibit 25-5 illustrates the May flexible budget.

EXHIBIT 25-5

Kemper Corporation
Manufacturing Division's Flexible Budget
for the Month Ended May 31, 1985

Variable Overhead Costs	Standard Variable Overhead Costs per Direct-Labor Hour	Direct-Labor Hours 7,600	8,000	8,400
Indirect Materials—Supplies	$0.45	$ 3,420*	$ 3,600*	$ 3,780*
Indirect Labor—Other	0.37	2,812	2,960	3,108
Heat, Light, and Power	0.19	1,444	1,520	1,596
Maintenance and Repairs	0.49	3,724	3,920	4,116
Total Variable Costs	$1.50	$11,400	$12,000	$12,600

* ($0.45 × 7,600 = $3,420; $0.45 × 8,000 = $3,600; $0.45 × 8,400 = $3,780)

TO SUMMARIZE When a standard cost system is used, the control of overhead costs involves three stages: Planning (the analysis of cost behavior patterns, the establishment of standard variable costs, and the preparation of an operating budget), operating (collecting actual variable overhead costs and accounting for the flow of budgeted variable overhead costs), and control (isolating variances and analyzing them as a basis for taking any necessary corrective action). When the variable costing approach is used, the first step in the planning stage is to identify all variable overhead costs for analysis (fixed overhead costs are accounted for as period expenses). In developing standard costs for variable overhead cost items, a physical input measure, such as standard direct-labor hours, is a desirable measure of activity that will not cause overhead costs to vary except in relation to the actual volume of production (units of output). The standard cost for each overhead item is used to prepare a flexible (variable) overhead cost budget at the expected level of activity (that is, for the expected direct-labor hours) and at other levels within the relevant production range. A flexible budget is particularly useful in determining whether costs are within control and in evaluating the performance of managers.

The Operating Stage

During the accounting period, the actual overhead costs will be incurred, collected, and recorded in the accounts. In a standard cost system, however, actual costs do not become the product costs; they are simply collected for comparison with the budgeted costs. The budgeted variable overhead costs become the product costs; that is, they are applied to Work-in-Process Inventory and flow through Finished Goods Inventory to Cost of Goods Sold. These budgeted variable overhead costs are based on the standard variable cost rates used in preparing the flexible budget. In the case of Kemper's manufacturing division, the rate used was $1.50 per direct-labor hour.

To illustrate the accounting for actual and budgeted variable overhead costs based on Kemper's flexible budget for May, we assume that the company's actual production for the month was 3,800 units and that it took 7,800 direct-labor hours to achieve this production. The actual results, including the total variable overhead costs incurred, are summarized as follows:

Units Produced	3,800
Direct-Labor Hours Used	7,800
Standard Direct-Labor Hours for Units Produced (2 hours × 3,800 units)	7,600
Actual Variable Overhead Costs Incurred:	
Indirect Materials—Supplies	$3,370
Indirect Labor—Other	2,900
Heat, Light, and Power	1,500
Maintenance and Repairs	4,200

Usually, actual overhead costs are recorded in the individual accounts, while budgeted costs are applied to Work-in-Process Inventory in total at regular intervals throughout the month. To simplify our example, we record all costs at the end of the period. The summary journal entries for recording Kemper's actual variable overhead costs in individual accounts and transferring them to Variable Manufacturing Overhead, the control account, would be

Indirect Materials—Supplies	3,370	
Indirect Labor—Other	2,900	
Heat, Light, and Power	1,500	
Maintenance and Repairs	4,200	
Various Payables (or Cash)		11,970
To record actual variable overhead costs incurred.		
Variable Manufacturing Overhead	11,970	
Indirect Materials—Supplies		3,370
Indirect Labor—Other		2,900
Heat, Light, and Power		1,500
Maintenance and Repairs		4,200
To transfer variable overhead costs to the control account for manufacturing overhead.		

On the basis of 7,600 standard direct-labor hours to produce an actual output of 3,800 units, total variable overhead would be applied (debited) to

Work-in-Process Inventory for $11,400 (7,600 hours × $1.50 per hour), as follows:

Work-in-Process Inventory	11,400	
Variable Manufacturing Overhead		11,400

To apply budgeted variable overhead costs to Work-in-Process (7,600 standard hours × $1.50 = $11,400).

Remember that under the variable costing approach the fixed overhead costs are expensed each period and do not become part of product costs.

After these entries are posted, the T-accounts for Variable Manufacturing Overhead and Work-in-Process Inventory would be

Variable Manufacturing Overhead

Debit	Credit
Actual Cost 11,970	11,400 ..... **Applied Cost**
Bal. 570	

Work-in-Process Inventory

Debit	Credit
From Manufacturing Overhead 11,400	

As this example shows, actual variable overhead costs are debited to Variable Manufacturing Overhead, whereas budgeted variable overhead costs are credited to Variable Manufacturing Overhead and debited to Work-in-Process Inventory. When the goods in work-in-process are completed, the budgeted overhead cost for the completed units will be transferred to Finished Goods Inventory, and then to Cost of Goods Sold when the units are sold. The debit balance ($570) in Variable Manufacturing Overhead is the total variable overhead variance. This variance will be analyzed when we discuss stage 3, the cost-control and performance measurement stage.

total variable overhead variance *the extent to which actual overhead varies from the amount included in work-in-process inventory; the difference between actual and applied overhead*

TO SUMMARIZE The second stage in the process of controlling overhead costs is the operating stage, during which actual variable overhead costs are collected and recorded in individual overhead accounts, and budgeted costs, which become the product inventory costs and eventually flow to Cost of Goods Sold, are also recorded. The total of actual costs is transferred to the debit side of the Variable Manufacturing Overhead account. This account is credited for the total amount of variable overhead applied to Work-in-Process Inventory. The amount applied is a standard measure of activity (such as standard direct-labor hours for the units produced) multiplied by the standard variable overhead rate. The debit to Work-in-Process Inventory thus represents the budgeted variable overhead that should have been incurred for the production of that period. When the units being produced are completed, the budgeted overhead cost for them will be transferred from Work-in-Process Inventory to Finished Goods Inventory, and eventually to Cost of Goods Sold when the products are sold. The difference between the debit to Variable Manufacturing Overhead for actual variable overhead costs and the credit to that account for budgeted variable overhead applied to Work-in-Process Inventory is the total variable overhead variance.

The Control Stage

After the end of the accounting period, when the actual level of production is known, the actual variable overhead costs can be compared with the budgeted variable overhead costs for the activity level achieved. The variances are computed and reported to the responsibility center managers.

In our example, the actual production of Kemper Company's manufacturing division for May was 3,800 units, for which 7,800 actual direct-labor hours were used. However, the standard direct labor allowed for 3,800 units is only 7,600 direct-labor hours. Therefore, if we compare actual variable overhead costs with the flexible budget for 3,800 units or 7,600 standard direct-labor hours (both bases will result in the same budget), we generate one variance, which we have already referred to as the total variance. This total variance is $570 U. Since this total variance does not tell us which cost elements of overhead caused the unfavorable results, we must break it down by comparing the flexible budget for each cost element with the actual costs. A cost analysis report prepared using 3,800 units or 7,600 standard direct-labor hours might look as shown in Exhibit 25-6.

EXHIBIT 25-6

Kemper Corporation
Manufacturing Division's Cost Analysis Report
for the Month Ended May 31, 1985

Budgeted Production (in units)	4,000
Actual Production (in units)	3,800
Standard Direct-Labor Hours	7,600
Actual Direct-Labor Hours	7,800

	Standard Variable Overhead Costs				
	Per Unit	Per DLH*	Flexible Budget: 3,800 Units or 7,600 DLH	Actual Variable Overhead Costs	Total Variance
Indirect Materials—Supplies	$0.90†	$0.45	$ 3,420	$ 3,370	$ 50 F
Indirect Labor—Other	0.74	0.37	2,812	2,900	88 U
Heat, Light, and Power	0.38	0.19	1,444	1,500	56 U
Maintenance and Repairs	0.98	0.49	3,724	4,200	476 U
Totals	$3.00	$1.50	$11,400	$11,970	$570 U

* Direct-labor hour.

† ($3,420 ÷ 3,800 units)

Although the report in Exhibit 25-6 shows which specific costs were above and below budget and by how much, it does not explain why, and management needs this information in order to attempt to eliminate the unfavorable variances in the future. It is beyond the scope of this text to explain in detail the causes of these variances, but a preliminary explanation can be found by breaking the total variance for each overhead cost item into a spending variance and an efficiency variance. These variances are determined by preparing a flexible budget at two levels: at the 7,600 standard direct-labor hours for the production achieved, and at the 7,800 actual direct-labor hours used. The May cost analysis report for Kemper's manufacturing division, using both activity levels, would be as shown in Exhibit 25-7.

EXHIBIT 25-7

Kemper Corporation
Manufacturing Division's Cost Analysis Report
for the Month Ended May 31, 1985

Budgeted Production (in units)	4,000
Actual Production (in units)	3,800
Standard Direct-Labor Hours	7,600
Actual Direct-Labor Hours	7,800

	Standard Variable Overhead Costs per DLH	Actual Variable Overhead Costs	Flexible Budget at Actual DLH (7,800)	Flexible Budget at Standard DLH (7,600)	Variances Spending	Variances Efficiency
Indirect Materials—Supplies	$0.45	$ 3,370	$ 3,510	$ 3,420	$140 F	$ 90 U
Indirect Labor—Other	0.37	2,900	2,886	2,812	14 U	74 U
Heat, Light, and Power	0.19	1,500	1,482	1,444	18 U	38 U
Maintenance and Repairs	0.49	4,200	3,822	3,724	378 U	98 U
Totals	$1.50	$11,970	$11,700	$11,400	$270 U	$300 U

Spending variance $270 U   Efficiency variance $300 U

Total variance $570 U

This report shows that the total variable overhead variance of $570 U can be separated into a $270 U spending variance and a $300 U efficiency variance. The report also shows the spending and efficiency variances for each variable overhead cost. These individual variances will be analyzed by the division manager and others to determine whether any costs can be reduced in the next period. A brief discussion of the nature of spending variances and efficiency variances will help explain how such an analysis can contribute to cost control.

variable overhead spending variance *the difference between actual manufacturing overhead incurred and the budgeted overhead for the actual activity level*

THE VARIABLE OVERHEAD SPENDING VARIANCE

The variable overhead spending variance is the difference between the actual variable overhead costs incurred ($11,970 in total) and the amount that should have been incurred at the actual activity level of the manufacturing division ($11,700 in total: 7,800 direct-labor hours × $1.50). As Exhibit 25-7 has illustrated, this variance can be computed for each overhead cost item.

For a further analysis of its causes, the spending variance for each variable overhead cost can be separated into a price dimension and a quantity dimension, just as we have done with the variances for direct materials and direct labor. The spending variance would be unfavorable, for example, if the *price* paid for indirect materials or the rate paid for indirect laborers was greater than the price or rate included in the flexible budget. Similarly, if the *amount* of indirect materials or indirect labor used was greater than the amount incorporated into the flexible budget, the spending variance would be unfavorable. The same price and quantity variances would apply to heat, light, and power, and to maintenance and repairs as well. Thus, the spending variance is a reflection of both price (or rate) and quantity (or usage) factors.

The spending variance provides an opportunity for control over individual overhead items by highlighting the differences between the budgeted amounts and the actual costs incurred. In order to exercise control over the individual items, each variance must be analyzed to identify the reasons for the price and/or usage differences. Managers are more likely to have control over the usage of a particular overhead item than over its price or rate.

THE VARIABLE OVERHEAD EFFICIENCY VARIANCE

variable overhead efficiency variance *the difference between overhead costs budgeted at actual hours and overhead costs budgeted at standard hours*

The $300 unfavorable variable overhead efficiency variance is the standard variable overhead rate times the difference between the standard and actual activity levels ($1.50 × 200 direct-labor hours). When direct-labor hours are used as the basis for assigning overhead, the efficiency variance indicates the number of dollars saved (or spent) as a result of using fewer (or more) actual direct-labor hours than the standard number of hours for the actual output. As you will recall, the same relationship was used in computing the direct-labor efficiency variance. The difference between the two calculations is in the rates used (labor in the first case and overhead in the second). The reason for computing the two efficiency variances is to show that inefficient use of labor not only causes variances in labor costs but also in overhead. If you use more direct-labor hours than you should, more overhead is applied to the product; if you control labor, you control overhead.

To illustrate, since Kemper's direct-labor efficiency variance was unfavorable (see page 827), the variable overhead efficiency variance also was unfavorable. If the direct-labor variance had been favorable, the overhead efficiency variance would, of course, have been favorable. The manager who is responsible for the control of direct-labor hours is the person who should be held responsible for an unfavorable overhead efficiency variance, since the variance is a measure of the efficiency with which direct labor is used. Thus, the overhead efficiency variance is really an additional aspect of the labor efficiency variance.

TO SUMMARIZE The third stage in monitoring and accounting for overhead costs occurs after the end of the accounting period and is referred to as the control stage. The actual units of production, the actual variable overhead costs, and the actual volume of activity are now known. The actual variable overhead cost for each element can be compared with its budgeted cost (using a flexible budget) for the production achieved. The difference between each actual overhead cost and its budgeted cost is the variance. These individual variances and the total variance can each be segregated into two variances: spending and efficiency. The overhead spending variance measures the difference between the variable overhead costs actually incurred and the amount that should have been incurred at the actual activity level. The overhead efficiency variance is the difference between budgeted variable overhead at the actual and standard activity levels. Because the spending variance highlights the differences between actual costs incurred and budgeted amounts for individual overhead items, it is generally the most useful for control purposes.

A SUMMARY OF VARIABLE OVERHEAD COSTS AND VARIANCES

Now that we have computed the two variable overhead variances, it might help you to understand how they relate to actual and budgeted variable overhead costs by studying Exhibits 25-8 and 25-9.

As Exhibit 25-8 shows, comparing actual variable overhead with budgeted variable overhead using actual direct-labor hours gives the spending variance. Reference to Exhibit 25-7 will remind you that the total spending

EXHIBIT 25-8 A Schematic Comparison of Actual and Budgeted Overhead Costs

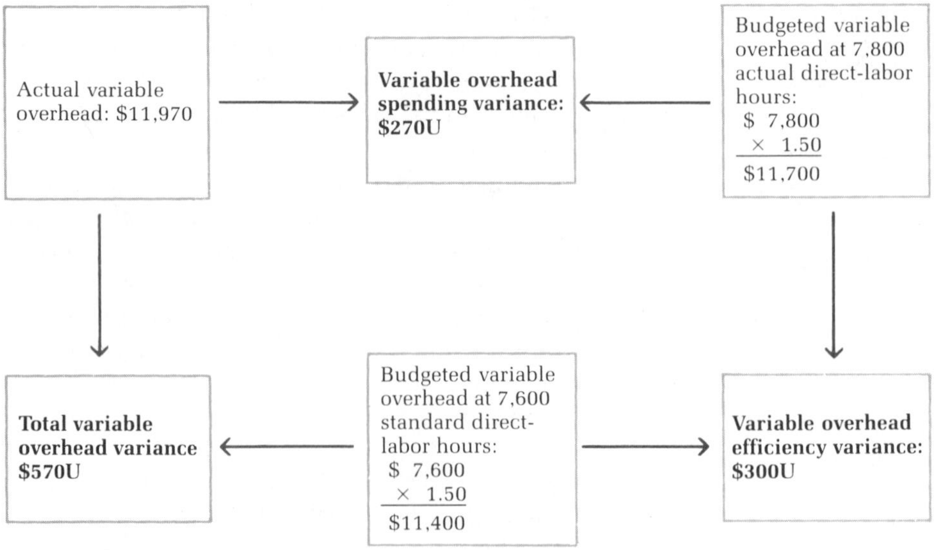

EXHIBIT 25-9 **A Graphical Comparison of Actual and Budgeted Overhead Costs**

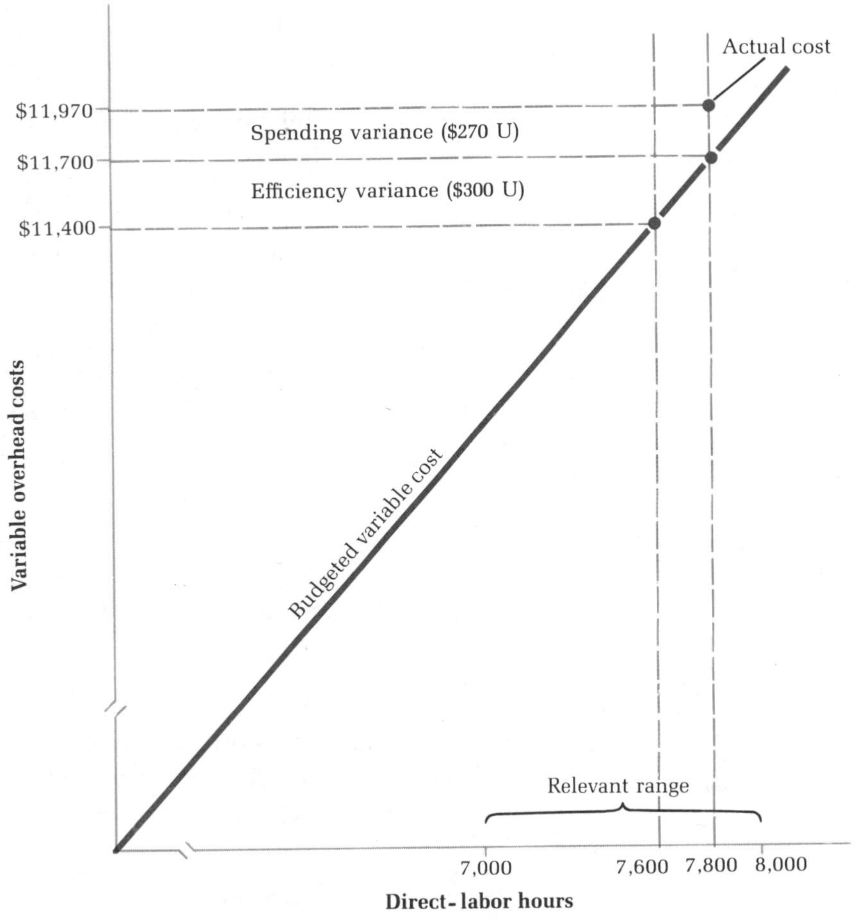

variance can be explained by comparing actual costs with budgeted costs for individual overhead items. Comparing budgeted overhead at actual hours with budgeted overhead at standard hours provides the overhead efficiency variance. It is the difference between actual direct-labor hours and standard direct-labor hours multiplied by the variable overhead rate [(7,800 hours − 7,600 hours) × $1.50].

In Exhibit 25-9 the budgeted variable overhead cost line has a slope that corresponds to $1.50 in variable cost for each standard direct-labor hour of activity; hence, the variable overhead cost line is at $11,400 for 7,600 standard direct-labor hours and is at $11,700 at 7,800 actual direct-labor hours. The difference in these two costs is represented in the exhibit as the unfavorable efficiency variance of $300. The difference between the budgeted variable overhead cost at actual direct-labor hours and the actual variable overhead cost represents the spending variance. The 7,600 standard direct-labor hours for the production achieved and the 7,800 actual direct-labor hours used both fall within the relevant range over which the variable costs are expected to be linear in behavior.

ACCOUNTING FOR OVERHEAD VARIANCES

In recording variable overhead costs during the accounting period (stage 2), actual costs are debited to Variable Manufacturing Overhead and standard variable overhead costs applied to Work-in-Process Inventory are credited to Variable Manufacturing Overhead. This account contains the following summary entries for Kemper's manufacturing division for the month of May.

Variable Manufacturing Overhead

Actual Cost 11,970	11,400 .... **Applied Cost**

After the spending and efficiency variances are determined at the end of the accounting period, they are recorded in individual variance accounts with the offsetting debit or credit recorded in Variable Manufacturing Overhead. The result should be a zero balance in Variable Manufacturing Overhead.

The unfavorable spending variance of $270 for Kemper's manufacuring division in May represents an additional expense, which is usually charged against revenues for the current period. The entry in the General Journal to record the spending variance would be

Variable Overhead Spending Variance	270	
Variable Manufacturing Overhead		270
To record the spending variance for the manufacturing division for May.		

This entry would be reflected in the accounts as follows:

Variable Manufacturing Overhead

Actual Cost	*Applied Cost*
11,970	11,400
	270

Variable Overhead Spending Variance

270	

If the spending variance had been favorable, there would have been a credit balance in Variable Manufacturing Overhead, thus requiring an entry opposite to the one above.

The unfavorable efficiency variance also represents an expense. The entry in the General Journal to record the efficiency variance would be

Variable Overhead Efficiency Variance	300	
Variable Manufacturing Overhead		300
To record the efficiency variance for the manufacturing division for May.		

This entry would be reflected in the accounts as follows:

Variable Manufacturing Overhead		Variable Overhead Efficiency Variance	
Actual Cost	*Applied Cost*	300	
11,970	11,400		
	270		
	300		

Analysis and Investigation of Variances

At the beginning of this chapter, we mentioned that when standard costs are carefully determined, most variances will be within an expected range of deviation and will not need to be investigated. Only the significant deviations will require management's attention, as is consistent with the concept of management by exception.

A key question remains: Which variances are to be considered significant? In general, the answer might be to inquire into the causes of those variances for which corrective action will lead to the largest savings in costs. As a practical matter, however, it is not always easy for a manager to judge where the cost savings might be the greatest. Hence, guidelines for action are frequently established. Such guidelines may include some or all of the following.

1. *Size.* Investigate any variance that differs from a budgeted cost by a specified dollar amount or from a standard cost by a given percentage. For example, investigate any variance that exceeds $1,000, or 5 percent of standard cost.
2. *Frequency of Occurrence.* Investigate any variance that is consistently above or below standard. It may well be that the standard is out of date or is being disregarded.
3. *Controllability.* Separate costs into those that are controllable by the manager of the responsibility center and those that are not. The manager would be expected to investigate any sizable variances within his or her control, but not other variances, although their existence should be recognized. Examples of variances not within the manager's control would be those caused by increases in utility rates, changes in property tax rates, wage increases from union contract negotiations, and changes in insurance rates or coverage.

4. *Impact on Long-Run Profitability.* Carefully monitor the costs that are most critical to the profitability of an enterprise over time. An important example is maintenance costs. If a manager runs a favorable maintenance variance regularly, it may be an indication that necessary maintenance is being postponed, which could have a serious long-run impact on profits. That is, machinery and equipment might break down more often than they should or wear out sooner than expected. The size guidelines may be smaller for investigating variances of critical cost items.

These guidelines are based primarily on management's judgment. A more scientific approach involves the use of statistical techniques. Although it is beyond the scope of this text to discuss these techniques in depth, in general they attempt to identify the variances that are significant, and not due to random causes, such as a fire in a plant. In one approach, the actual cost data are statistically sampled and the samples are plotted on a control chart. The chart shows upper and lower limits of acceptable deviation from the budgeted amount. Costs that fall outside the acceptable limits are considered material exceptions requiring investigation. Exhibit 25-10 is a simple illustration of a possible control chart for an overhead cost. The limits can be set as wide or as narrow as appears desirable, depending on how critical the cost item is in relation to the long-run profitability of the firm.

EXHIBIT 25-10 **A Control Chart for Overhead Cost**

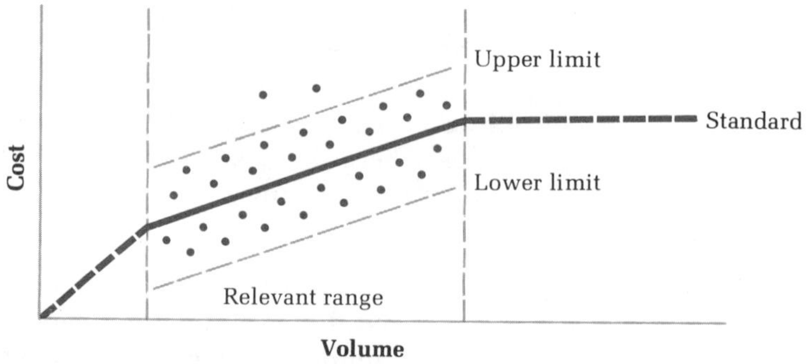

As Exhibit 25-10 indicates, a manager is expected to investigate both favorable and unfavorable variances that are outside acceptable limits. Obviously, unfavorable variances are undesirable and should be corrected. Favorable variances may be just as undesirable if a manager is not incurring costs for items that are essential to long-run profitability, such as maintenance costs. Such factors are likely to affect the quality of the product and eventually cause a drop in sales. Although the immediate cost savings may improve short-run profits, they may be made at the expense of larger long-run profits. Of course, it is also possible that a large favorable variance is due to a standard that is too low.

Evaluation of a Standard Cost System

A standard cost system has some obvious advantages as well as some disadvantages. First, the advantages include the following.

1. A standard cost system helps to identify and control problem areas; this leads to increased efficiency and economy of operation.
2. Standard costs serve as a guide for expected performance and therefore are a major asset in future planning.
3. Standard costs provide a basis for measuring the performance of each manager of a responsibility center. They are integral to responsibility accounting (see Chapter 26).
4. The development of standard costs requires an analysis of cost behavior, including a determination of the fixed and variable components of overhead costs. When cost behaviors have been identified, flexible budgets can be prepared and then used to control overhead costs.
5. A standard cost system is simpler to operate than an historical cost system. The cost flows are recorded at standard and inventories can be maintained in quantities only, to be multiplied by the standard cost when a dollar figure is needed.
6. The setting of standard costs requires a careful analysis of operations. Such an analysis can lead to efficiences and economies even before the standard cost system is fully operative.
7. A standard cost system is compatible with the principle of management by exception, which contributes to the effective utilization of management's time and effort.

The disadvantages include the following.

1. A standard cost system is expensive and time-consuming to develop.
2. Standard costs are of limited usefulness for custom operations.
3. It is easy to misinterpret the causes of a variance because so many factors are involved.
4. Standard costs must be changed as conditions change—for example, as the product, the materials, or the production methods change. Sometimes these changes occur so quickly that standards become out of date before management realizes it.
5. Labor tends to view measures of efficiency with mistrust. Responsibility may be erroneously assigned for significant variances, leading to morale problems.
6. The setting of standards is not an exact science. Standards are reported as specific figures but are treated by managers as ranges of acceptable performance. Random fluctuations are to be expected, but often are hard to distinguish from causal fluctuations.

Although the disadvantages noted here are real and should not be minimized, standard cost systems are generally cost-beneficial and are therefore widely used.

CHAPTER REVIEW

Standard costs and flexible budgets are important tools for planning and control in a manufacturing operation. A cost standard is a basis for judging the degree to which a manager's actual performance is consistent with planned performance for a period. A number of different standards can be used: ideal, attainable, or historical. Attainable standards generate the most desirable attitudes in employees, encourage efficiency, and make the concept of management by exception operationally effective.

Direct materials and direct labor are controlled by generating two variances for each of these costs—a price, or rate, variance and a quantity, or usage, variance. The materials variances are frequently referred to as a materials price variance and a materials quantity variance. The labor variances are usually called a rate variance and an efficiency variance. The price or rate variance is the difference between the standard price or rate and the actual price or rate multiplied by the actual quantity. A quantity or efficiency variance is the difference between the standard and actual quantities multiplied by the standard price or rate.

The control of overhead costs involves establishing standard costs (which are always unit costs), preparing a budget for planned costs, measuring and analyzing variances from standard, and reporting the results to managers, so that they can take corrective action when necessary. These activities occur in three stages—the planning stage (which occurs before the accounting period starts), the operating stage (which occurs during the accounting period), and the control stage (which occurs after the operating results for the period are known).

Standards are set and a flexible budget is prepared during the planning stage. Actual variable overhead costs are collected and budgeted variable overhead is applied to Work-in-Process Inventory during the operating stage. Actual costs are compared with budgeted costs and variances are investigated after the end of the accounting period.

Variable overhead costs are accounted for as product costs in a variable costing system. In setting standards for variable overhead items, the activity base selected is usually a standard input measure such as direct-labor hours or machine hours. The flexible budget costs are derived from the standard cost card, which usually identifies costs on a per-unit of standard input. In comparing actual variable overhead costs with budgeted variable overhead costs, two overhead variances are usually computed—spending and efficiency. The budgeted cost of each variable overhead item for the actual level of activity is compared with the actual cost to determine the spending variance. The efficiency variance is computed by multiplying the difference between actual input and standard input for the output achieved by the standard variable overhead rate. The efficiency variance reflects the extra overhead spent (or the amount of overhead saved) because the actual input (direct-labor hours) was greater (or smaller) than the standard input. The overhead efficiency variance will vary in the same direction (favorable or unfavorable) as the direct-labor efficiency variance if direct labor is the measure of activity used.

Guidelines are often established to help determine when a variance from standard should be investigated. These guidelines include the size of variance, its frequency of occurrence, its controllability, and the likely impact of the variance on long-run profitability. Another approach is to plot samples of actual cost data on a control chart and then identify variances that fall outside acceptable deviations.

A standard cost system has both advantages and disadvantages. The former include identification of problem areas, the desirable effect of analyzing costs into their fixed and variable components, use of the concept of management by exception, and simplification of the record-keeping process. Among the disadvantages are the expense and time involved in developing standards, the difficulty of interpreting the variances, labor's mistrust of efficiency measures, and the problem of keeping standards current as conditions change.

KEY TERMS AND CONCEPTS

attainable standard (820)
flexible budgeting (831)
historical standard (821)
ideal standard (820)
labor efficiency variance (827)
labor rate variance (827)
management by exception (820)
materials price variance (824)
materials quantity (usage) variance (825)
standard (818)
standard cost card (823)
standard costs (818)
standard cost system (822)
total variable overhead variance (834)
variable overhead efficiency variance (837)
variable overhead spending variance (836)
variance (818)

REVIEW PROBLEM

Manufacturing Overhead Variances

The standard cost sheet of Kendra Box Company shows the following unit costs for direct materials and direct labor for each box made.

Direct Materials (4 board feet of lumber at $2)	$ 8
Direct Labor (2 standard hours at $6)	12
Total Standard Cost per Unit (excluding overhead)	$20

The flexible budget shows the following monthly manufacturing overhead costs at several production levels.

Percent of Standard Capacity	80%	90%	100%
Expected Number of Boxes	20,000	22,500	25,000
Expected Direct-Labor Hours	40,000	45,000	50,000
Variable Manufacturing Overhead Costs	$80,000	$90,000	$100,000

The company normally produces at 100 percent of capacity. During the month of October, 20,000 boxes were produced at the following costs.

Lumber Purchased (100,000 feet at $2.20)	$220,000
Lumber Used (83,000 feet at $2.10)	174,300
Direct Labor (39,600 hours at $6.05)	239,580
Variable Manufacturing Overhead Costs	83,000

Required:

1. Compute the materials and labor variances.
2. Compute the manufacturing overhead cost rate for variable costs (a) per box and (b) per direct-labor hour.
3. Compute the variable manufacturing overhead variances for October for spending and efficiency.

Solution

1. Materials and Labor Variances

Materials Variances

The price variance is computed when the lumber is purchased, and the quantity variance is computed when the lumber is used.

Materials Price Variance:

Purchase Price per Foot for 100,000 Feet	$2.20
Standard Price per Foot	−2.00
Difference	$0.20 U
Feet of Lumber Purchased	×100,000
Total Price Variance	$20,000 U

Materials Quantity Variance:

Actual Lumber Used	83,000 feet
Standard Lumber Required (20,000 boxes × 4 feet)	−80,000 feet
Difference	3,000 feet U
Standard Cost per Foot	×$2
Total Quantity Variance	$6,000 U

Labor Variances

The labor rate and labor efficiency variances are both based on direct-labor hours used; thus, they are computed at the same point in time.

Total Direct-Labor Variance:

Actual Direct-Labor Cost (39,600 hours at $6.05)	$239,580
Standard Direct-Labor Cost (20,000 boxes × 2 hours = 40,000 hours × $6.00)	240,000
Total Direct-Labor Variance	$ 420 F

Labor Rate Variance:

Actual Rate	$6.05
Standard Rate	−6.00
Difference	$0.05 U
Actual Hours	×39,600
Total Labor Rate Variance	$1,980 U

Labor Efficiency Variance:

Actual Direct-Labor Hours	39,600
Standard Direct-Labor Hours	40,000
Difference	400 F
Standard Direct-Labor Rate	× $6
Total Labor Efficiency Variance	$2,400 F

2. Manufacturing Overhead Cost Rates

		Cost per Unit	Cost per Hour
Flexible Budget at Normal Capacity:			
Boxes Produced per Month	25,000		
Labor Hours per Month	50,000		
Variable Manufacturing Overhead Costs	$100,000	$4.00	$2.00

3. Manufacturing Overhead Variances

The diagram below shows the computation of the overhead spending and efficiency variances. The overhead efficiency variance also can be computed by multiplying the difference between actual labor hours and standard labor hours by the variable overhead cost rate per hour (39,600 − 40,000 = 400 F; 400 F × $2.00 = $800 F).

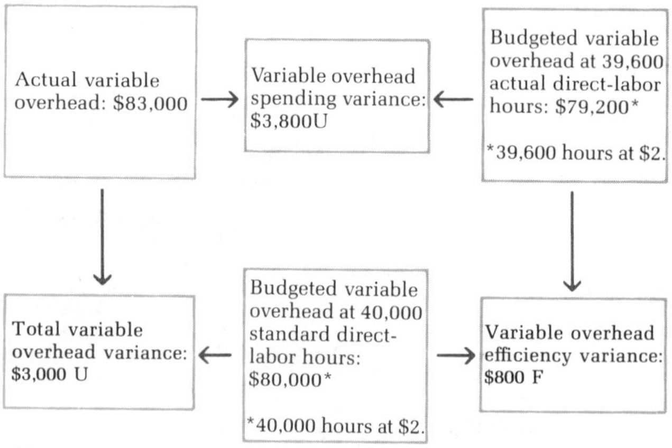

Spending Variance	$3,800 U
Efficiency Variance	800 F
Total Overhead Variance	$3,000 U

DISCUSSION QUESTIONS

1 Distinguish among ideal, attainable, and historical standards. Which of these types of standards is most desirable for a manufacturing firm, and why?

2 Why is it difficult to develop effective cost standards?

3 What is a standard cost?

4 What is the purpose of a standard cost system?

5 What are the steps in establishing and operating a standard cost system?

6 Who is responsible for the development of the standards to be used in a standard cost system?

7 What is the relationship of a standard cost system to the principle of management by exception?

8 What is a variance from standard?

9 Why are the direct-materials and direct-labor costs divided into a price, or rate, variance and a quantity, or efficiency, variance?

10 Who is usually responsible for each of the following variances?
- (a) Materials price variance.
- (b) Materials quantity variance.
- (c) Labor rate variance.
- (d) Labor efficiency variance.

11 What is the relationship of a flexible budget to a standard cost system?

12 What are some desirable characteristics to keep in mind in selecting an activity measure that will reflect variable manufacturing overhead costs?

13 What is a variable overhead spending variance? What does it indicate about overhead costs?

14 What is a variable overhead efficiency variance? How does it relate to the labor efficiency variance?

15 What is the relationship of the overhead rate used to apply overhead costs to Work-in-Process Inventory and the overhead rate used in a flexible budget?

16 When is a variance significant enough to be investigated?

17 What are the major advantages and disadvantages of a standard cost system?

EXERCISES

E25-1 Materials Price Variance

Colt Manufacturing Company has just adopted a standard cost system. You have been asked to analyze the materials purchases and usage for the month of August to determine the materials price variance to be recorded at the end of the month. During August, 5,000 gallons of a chemical were purchased at $3.20 per gallon. Only 4,200 gallons were used. The standard price per gallon is $3.15. Compute the following variances.

1. The materials price variance if the chemical is carried in inventory at the standard price.
2. The materials price variance if the chemical is carried in inventory at actual price and is charged to Work-in-Process at the standard price.

E25-2 Materials and Labor Variances

The standard cost card for Vogue Machinery Company shows the following costs for producing one of its machines.

Direct materials:	400 pounds at $8 = $3,200
Direct labor:	150 hours at $15 = $2,250

During April, four machines were built, with actual costs as follows:

Materials purchased:	2,000 pounds at $8.20 = $16,400
Materials used:	1,700 pounds
Direct labor incurred:	625 hours at $14.80 = $9,250

1. Compute the following variances:
   - (a) Materials price variance (assuming that raw materials inventory is carried at standard cost).
   - (b) Materials quantity variance.
   - (c) Labor rate variance.
   - (d) Labor efficiency variance.
2. Record the standard materials and labor costs in Work-in-Process Inventory and set up the variances in separate accounts.

E25-3 Variable Manufacturing Overhead Spending and Efficiency Variances

Chateau Company manufactures one product. The standard capacity is 20,000 units per month. Manufacturing overhead costs are budgeted on the basis of direct-labor hours. At standard capacity, the monthly variable overhead budget would be $50,000 at 2 direct-labor hours per unit. During February, 18,000 units of product were manufactured, and $46,000 of variable manufacturing overhead was incurred. Actual direct-labor hours were 35,000.

Compute the manufacturing overhead spending and efficiency variances.

E25-4 Materials Variance

Mr. Hoffman, the production manager, has received a report showing a $15,500 unfavorable total materials variance. He knows that production used 10,000 pounds less than the budgeted amount for raw materials. Mr. Hoffman also knows that the standard price for raw materials was determined to be 80 cents per pound.

What was the actual cost of raw materials used during the period if the budgeted amount was estimated to be 500,000 pounds?

E25-5 Direct Materials Purchased and Used

Mary Clarke is concerned about her performance as a recently employed purchasing agent. The accounting department has provided her with the following data for the month of August.

Units produced:	2,000
Materials used:	1,078 tons
Materials purchased:	1,400 tons at $43 per ton

The standard materials usage set by management for one unit of product is half a ton of materials per unit, at $45 per ton. Her performance report shows the following variances.

Used (1,078 tons − 1,000 tons standard) × $45 per ton	$3,510 U
Purchased ($45 per ton standard − $43 per ton actual) × 1,400 tons	2,800 F
	$ 710 U

If you were Mary Clarke, how would you explain this report, which indicates a $710 unfavorable variance?

E25-6 Responsibility for Labor Costs

Raymond Stone, just graduated from business school, has taken a job with Farben Corporation as production manager. His job is to see that production is efficient. After his first month, he is given this memo.

Performance Report

Ray Stone:	$8,100 Unfavorable

Given the following data, what justification would you give if you were in his position, keeping in mind that Stone is not responsible for hiring, firing, and wage rates?

Units Produced:
750 units

Direct Labor Used:

Manufacturing:	7,600 hours at $5.00
Assembly:	2,050 hours at $4.00

Standard Direct-Labor Hours per Unit:

Manufacturing:	10 hours at $4.00
Assembly:	3 hours at $3.60

E25-7 Responsibility for Labor Rates

In E25-6, what is theoretically wrong with the conclusion that Ray Stone is not responsible for labor rates?

E25-8 Materials and Labor Variances

Given the information below, calculate the materials price and quantity variances and labor rate and efficiency variances. Note that the materials price variance is recognized at the time of purchase.

Materials (actual):
Purchases of raw material *A*: 1,300 pounds × $5.25
Purchases of raw material *B*: 750 pounds × $2.50
Used 900 pounds of raw material *A*
Used 525 pounds of raw material *B*

Direct Labor (actual):

Manufacturing:	1,050 hours × $4.90
Assembly:	450 hours × $2.50

Standard Costs per Unit:

Material *A*: 2 pounds × $5.20/pound	$10.40
Material *B*: 1 pound × $2.60/pound	2.60
Direct labor—manufacturing: 2 hours × $4.00	8.00
Direct labor—assembly: 1 hour × $3.00	3.00
Standard cost per unit	$24.00

Units Made:
500 units

E25–9 Materials and Labor Variances

Compute the missing amounts.

Actual materials	2,000 tons
Actual hours used	1,500 hours
1. Standard materials for output (tons)	______
2. Standard hours for output	______
3. Actual cost per ton of material	______
Standard cost per ton of material	$4.00
Actual cost per direct-labor hour	$4.00
4. Standard cost per direct-labor hour	______
Total labor variance	$1,625 U
Total materials variance	$ 400 F
5. Direct-materials price variance	______
Direct-materials quantity variance	$ 0
Direct-labor rate variance	$ 750 U
6. Direct-labor efficiency variance	______

E25–10 Variable Overhead Variances

Engraph Manufacturing Company uses standard direct-labor hours as a basis for charging variable overhead to Work-in-Process Inventory. The following data are given.

Data for August:	
Budgeted units	9,000
Budgeted hours	36,000
Actual variable manufacturing overhead	$ 217,000
Actual units produced	8,000
Actual direct-labor hours	33,000

Variable Manufacturing Overhead Data (Annual):	
Estimated variable cost	$2,560,000
Estimated direct-labor hours	400,000
Estimated units	100,000

1. Find the variable overhead rate applied to Work-in-Process Inventory per direct-labor hour.
2. Determine the variable overhead spending variance for August.
3. Determine the variable overhead efficiency variance for August.
4. Prepare the General Journal entry to transfer standard variable overhead cost to Work-in-Process Inventory and record the variances.

E25–11 Graphical Presentation of Variable Overhead Costs

Reed Paint Company's budgeted variable manufacturing overhead costs at a normal monthly volume of 5,000 gallons of paint (10,000 direct-labor hours) are

Variable overhead per direct-labor hour	$ 8
Variable overhead per gallon	16

During October the company produced 4,500 gallons of paint and incurred variable overhead costs of $75,000. Actual direct-labor hours were 9,300.

Draw a graph showing the relationship of actual overhead, budgeted overhead at actual hours, and budgeted overhead at standard hours. Identify the spending and efficiency variances.

PROBLEMS

P25–1 Materials Price and Quantity Variances

John North, production manager, has just received a report stating that the total materials variance for last month was $3,000 unfavorable. However, he is not sure whether the production foremen are overdrawing from inventory or the purchasing department has been unable to acquire materials at reasonable prices. The information he needs is contained in the following report.

Standard production	150,000 units
Actual production	146,000 units
Standard materials per unit	2 pounds
Materials used in March	300,000 pounds
Standard price for materials	$1.50/pound
Actual price for materials	$1.47/pound

Required:

1. Compute the materials price and quantity variances for the month.
2. **Interpretive Question** What was the cause of the unfavorable variance and what recommendation would you make to Mr. North?

P25–2 Labor Variances

During the year, Thompson Plastics was in negotiation with the local union over wages. A settlement was finally reached and the average wage per hour was increased to $3.28. Production fell to 145,000 units, and 220,000 hours were incurred. Standard production has been set at 150,000 units; 1.5 hours of labor were expected to produce one unit at a standard labor cost of $4.875 per unit.

Required:

1. Calculate the labor variances at Thompson Plastics.
2. **Interpretive Question** Are these variances significant?

P25–3 Variable Manufacturing Overhead Spending and Efficiency Variances

The following production and budget information was presented for Clemmons Corporation.

Standard production	150,000 units
Actual production	145,000 units
Actual variable overhead	$175,000
Variable overhead applied	$0.80/hour
Actual direct-labor hours	220,000 hours
Standard hours per unit produced	1.5 hours

Required:

1. Calculate the variable overhead spending and efficiency variances for Clemmons Corporation.
2. **Interpretive Question** Explain how the spending variance is used to control overhead cost.
3. **Interpretive Question** How can the efficiency variance be used to control overhead cost?

P25–4 Labor Variances

Required:
Compute the missing amounts.

Total labor variance	$ 47,500 U
Labor efficiency variance	42,500 U
Actual labor hours incurred	110,000
1. Standard labor hours allowed	________
Units produced	50,000
Standard hours allowed per unit	2
Total actual labor costs	$467,500
2. Actual labor cost per hour	________
3. Actual labor cost per unit	________
4. Labor rate variance	________
5. Standard labor cost per hour	________
6. Standard labor cost per unit	________

P25–5 Employee Morale and Production Efficiency

Linton Fabrics is a nonunion textile firm. Employee morale and production efficiency have dropped in the last few weeks, causing management some concern. Also, quality control problems have resulted in a 10 percent increase in rejects in the last two weeks. The following information may help management identify the causes of current problems.

Employee Production Efficiency Report (in percentages)

Employee	Wk 14	Wk 15	Wk 16	Wk 17	Wk 18	Wk 19	Wk 20
Baker	96	100	86	93	91	89	85
Johnson	101	97	89	90	93	91	87
Becker	105	109	93	96	95	92	90
Howard	99	98	88	93	97	94	88
Kettle	92	93	81	85	90	91	90

Additional information:

a. Standards for measuring worker efficiency were raised at the start of week 16.

b. Linton Fabrics changed its source of supply for raw materials in week 15.

Required:

1. From the Production Efficiency Report can you identify trends in the efficiency of individual workers? Which ones might have low morale?
2. **Interpretive Question** What clues to the causes of the diminishing efficiency and quality can you draw from the information given?

P25–6 Unifying Problem: Materials, Labor, and Variable Overhead Variances

The following information was accumulated by the cost accounting department of F. B. Harding Corporation for June 1982.

a. Standard variable costs per unit of finished product:
   (1) Raw materials: 2 pounds at $2.50/pound
   (2) Direct labor: 1 hour at $3.00/hour
   (3) Variable overhead: $2 applied on the basis of direct-labor hours

b. Actual costs, inputs, and outputs:
   (1) Units produced: 10,000
   (2) Raw materials used: 20,150 pounds
   (3) Purchase price of raw materials: $2.48/pound
   (4) Labor hours incurred: 10,800 hours
   (5) Average labor rate: $3.10
   (6) Actual variable overhead: $20,000

Required:

1. Compute the standard variable cost and total variable costs for the units produced by F. B. Harding Corporation.
2. What is the variance between total standard variable costs and actual costs?
3. Compute the materials price and quantity variances. Are these variances favorable or unfavorable?
4. Compute the labor rate and efficiency variances. Are they favorable or unfavorable?

5. Journalize the transfer of materials and labor to Work-in-Process Inventory at standard cost and recognize the variances.

6. What is the total variable overhead variance?

P25-7 Variable Overhead Variances

Gunther Tile Company attempts to control manufacturing overhead costs through the use of a flexible budget. Standards were set by studying historical overhead cost data and are given below. Actual total overhead costs for each month of the third quarter are also given.

Standards:
Variable overhead: $1.70 per direct-labor hour

Months	Direct-Labor Hours	Total Variable Overhead Costs (Actual)
June	50,000	$150,000
July	60,000	$185,000
August	40,000	$ 90,000

Required:

1. Compute the variable overhead spending variance for each month.

2. **Interpretive Question** Give several reasons why the overhead variances for all three months might be unfavorable.

P25-8 Journal Entries for Variable Manufacturing Overhead

Actual variable overhead costs incurred by Fox Radio, Inc. for 1984 totaled $165,000. This included indirect labor, repairs, and utilities. The variable overhead rate to be applied on standard direct-labor hours is $15.75 per hour. The company produced 19,000 units in 1984. The standard for each unit was one-half hour of direct labor. Actual direct-labor hours incurred were 9,800.

Required:

1. Make the journal entry to record actual overhead costs in a lump sum.

2. Make the journal entry to apply manufacturing overhead to Work-in-Process Inventory.

3. What is the amount of the total variable overhead variance? Is it favorable or unfavorable?

P25-9 Unifying Problem: Variance Analysis

Kinder Manufacturing Company produces high-quality men's pajamas for several large retail stores. The standard variable cost card for each dozen pairs of pajamas is as follows:

Standard Volume:	
Direct materials: 30 yards at $0.80	$24.00
Direct labor: 4 hours at $5.00	20.00
Manufacturing Overhead:	
Variable cost: 40 percent of direct-labor cost	8.00
Total Variable Costs	$52.00

During the month of September, the company filled three orders of pajamas at the following costs.

Order	Number of Dozens	Materials Used (Yards)	Labor Hours
8	400	12,200	1,500
9	900	26,750	3,750
10	500	15,450	2,140
	1,800	54,400	7,390

The following additional information involving materials, labor, and variable overhead costs was supplied by the accounting department.

a. Purchases of material during the month amounted to 60,000 yards at 82 cents per yard.

b. Total direct-labor cost for the month was $37,689.

c. Total variable overhead cost for September amounted to $14,000.

Required:

1. Compute the materials price variance for September. (Materials are carried in Raw Materials Inventory at standard.)

2. Compute the materials quantity variance for September by order and in total.

3. Compute the labor rate variance for September.

4. Compute the labor efficiency variance for September by order and in total.

5. Compute the variable overhead spending and efficiency variances.

6. Prepare journal entries to record the purchase of materials and the flow of costs through Work-in-Process Inventory to Cost of Goods Sold.

P25-10 Unifying Problem: Determining How Variances Are Computed

RFA Company uses a standard cost system in its accounting for the manufacturing costs of its only product. The standard cost card for a normal capacity of 5,000 direct-labor hours per month is as follows:

Direct materials: 3 pounds at $4	= $12
Direct labor: 1 hour at $6	= 6
Variable factory overhead:	
1 hour at $3	= 3
Total variable cost per unit	$21

During April of its first year of operation, the company completed 4,400 units and had the following variances.

Materials price variance	$ 700 F
Materials quantity variance	3,200 U
Labor rate variance	900 U
Labor efficiency variance	600 U
Variable overhead spending variance	1,500 F
Variable overhead efficiency variance	300 U

There was no work-in-process inventory at the beginning or end of April.

Required:

Compute the following amounts.

1. What is the total standard variable cost of producing 4,400 units of product?
2. The total overhead budget for the number of units produced.
3. The actual overhead incurred in April.
4. The amount of material, labor, and overhead debited to Work-in-Process during April.
5. Pounds of materials used in production.
6. The actual hours of labor used in production.
7. The actual price per pound of materials.
8. The actual labor rate per hour.
9. Total variable manufacturing costs in April.

P25–11 Unifying Problem: Flexible Budget, Variances, Cost Flows

Redbud Corporation uses a standard cost system with standard materials and labor costs per unit produced as follows:

Materials:	20 pounds at $2	= $40
Labor:	5 hours at $4	= $20

Variable manufacturing overhead is applied to Work-in-Process Inventory on the basis of standard direct-labor hours, using overhead rates established at the beginning of the year. The variable overhead budget for the year based on a projected 120,000 direct-labor hours is $150,000.

The normal level of activity for May is 9,000 direct-labor hours. The actual operating results for May were as follows:

Variable overhead	$10,200
Level of operation achieved—standard direct-labor hours	7,500
Actual units produced	1,500
Actual materials costs (31,000 pounds)	$63,550
Actual labor costs (7,400 hours)	$31,080

Required:

1. Prepare the flexible budget for the actual level of activity in May.
2. Compute the variances for materials, labor, and variable overhead.
3. Set up T-accounts and show the flow of costs to Finished Goods.

CHAPTER 26

Managing Decentralized Operations

THIS CHAPTER EXPLAINS:

Decentralization: its benefits and costs.

Responsibility centers and responsibility accounting.

The return-on-total-assets and residual income methods for measuring performance.

Transfer pricing.

Service-cost allocation.

A company can be thought of as a group of individuals working toward common goals. In earlier chapters we examined techniques that are useful in identifying and reaching these goals: budgeting, cost–volume–profit relationships, cost accumulation, and variance analysis. In this chapter we take a broader view and address such questions as

1. *What is the best compromise for a company to make between a decentralized operation, in which the responsibility for decision making is spread among managers at lower organizational levels, and a centralized operation, in which top management makes all decisions?*
2. *What are the benefits and drawbacks of decentralization?*
3. *What are some key areas to monitor in order to be sure that decisions prompted by internal competition—that is, competition between units of a decentralized firm—are not in conflict with the overall best interests of the company?*

Obviously, finding answers to such questions is extremely important for all companies, because organizations that can make better and faster decisions will operate more efficiently and will have a competitive edge in the marketplace. These companies are potentially more profitable than their less efficient counterparts. And, as higher profits are realized and reinvested in productive assets, the gap between the more and the less efficient firms may widen until, ultimately, only the firms that operate with optimal decision-making capability will survive.

Decentralization and Responsibility Centers

When a business is first established, it is not uncommon for one person to oversee a number of different activities within the organization. For example, a sole proprietor may handle sales, production, engineering, personnel, and even accounting. As the business grows, responsibility for these activities will be assigned to different individuals, and eventually to different groups, divisions, or even companies. Most large corporations have many subsidiary companies, divisions, units, and even subunits, like those depicted in Exhibit 26-1.

The organization chart for International Manufacturing Corporation (IMC) in Exhibit 26-1 shows three operating companies: Acme Computer, Edison Automobile, and Jennifer Cosmetics. Although each of these companies has several divisions and subunits, only a few of those of Edison Automobile are shown. Edison has three geographical bases: the United States, the Far East, and Europe. The making and selling of automobiles in the Far East division requires sales, production, engineering and planning, accounting, and personnel departments. The production function is separated into the manufacturing of motors, the assembling of automobiles, and the painting of finished cars. Assume that Edison's other geographical divisions have similar subdivisions.

Given this organization chart, how much autonomy should the executives of each division be granted by corporate management? If each company (Acme, Edison, and Jennifer) has its own president, vice presidents, and other officers, should these executives be allowed to operate independently of one another? If Acme, for example, is the most profitable company, should it be given more operating capital than Edison and Jennifer, or less? Should a decision for Acme to expand into microcomputers be made by Acme's executives or by IMC's corporate officers? Within Edison Automobile, how much autonomy should each of the geographical offices have? Should a decision to double the advertising budget or offer consumer rebates in the Far East division be made by the chief officer of that division, by the top management of Edison Automobile, or by the president of IMC?

Questions such as these are difficult to answer. In fact, it would probably be difficult to find two companies that would answer all of them the same way. It might be argued that all major decisions should be made by top management at IMC, that only they have an overview of the entire company and the capability, as a result, of making the best decisions. An organization based upon such a management philosophy would be centralized. With centralization, questions such as whether or not to offer rebates in the Far East division of Edison Automobile must be answered by IMC's top executives.

centralization *an organizational philosophy in which top management makes most of the major decisions for the entire company rather than delegating them to managers at lower levels*

decentralization *an organizational philosophy in which managers at all levels have the authority to make decisions concerning the operations for which they are responsible*

The opposing point of view is that a decentralized organization is best, that managers at all levels should have the authority to make decisions concerning the operations for which they are responsible. According to this point of view, subunit managers are closer to the problem and so can make quicker and more informed decisions. Regarding the question of rebates, for example, the best policy would be for the operating manager of the Far East

EXHIBIT 26-1 **An Organization Chart**

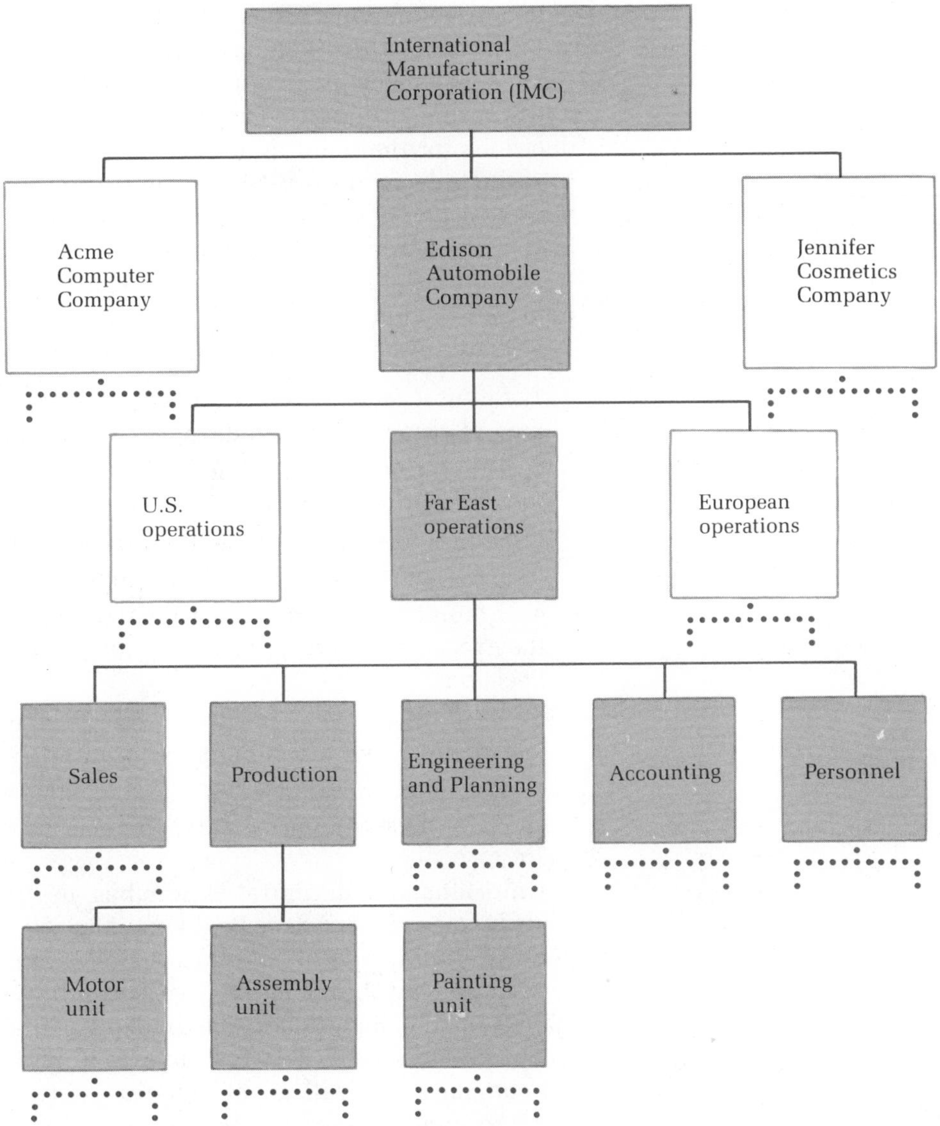

division to decide whether or not to offer them. Likewise, the manager of the motor unit should decide where to buy engine parts, and the manager of painting should have sole responsibility for the type and quantity of paint purchased. These managers would also be held responsible for the consequences of their decisions.

As we shall see, decentralization and centralization really represent two ends of a continuum. In practice, there are few, if any, firms that are completely centralized or decentralized. It therefore makes more sense to speak about the degree of centralization or decentralization.

BENEFITS AND COSTS OF DECENTRALIZATION

When and to what degree should a company decentralize? Clearly, a large company employing thousands of people in several geographic locations could not remain completely centralized, with top management making all the decisions. The president of IMC would not know enough about the costs and varieties of paint in Japan or have enough time to make all operating decisions for the painting unit of the Far East division of Edison Automobile. Such decisions must be made by someone in the Far East division. A view that favors decentralization would delegate such decisions to a manager in the painting unit; while a point-of-view more inclined towards centralization would consider someone at a higher level, say the chief operating officer of the Far East division, to be more appropriate.

Decentralization has a number of advantages.

1. Subunit managers have more information about matters within their area of responsibility than higher-level management has.
2. Subunit managers are in a better position to see current problems and to react quickly to local situations.
3. Higher-level management can spend more time on broader policy issues because the burden of daily decision making is distributed.
4. Subunit managers have a greater incentive to perform well because they receive the credit or blame for performance that results from their decisions.
5. Employees have greater incentives because there are more positions of leadership when a company is decentralized.
6. Managers and officers can be evaluated more easily because their responsibilities are more clearly defined.

Unfortunately, decentralization has its drawbacks as well. Decisions made by managers of decentralized units are sometimes not consistent with the overall objectives of the firm. For example, the assembly division of a company might find it less expensive to buy parts from an outside source than from the manufacturing division of the company. Such a decision would be more profitable for the assembly division, but it might decrease the company's overall profit. For this and other reasons, most companies resort to some compromise between the two extremes of centralization and decentralization. That is, they try to find the level of decentralization that will enable them to reach their overall objectives most efficiently.

RESPONSIBILITY ACCOUNTING

responsibility center *an organizational unit in which the manager has control over and is held accountable for performance*

The organization chart in Exhibit 26-1 is hypothetical. However, it provides a useful picture of the kinds of responsibility centers that exist within most companies. In our example, the president of IMC is responsible for the entire organization and should be held accountable for the company's overall successes and failures. At lower levels, the chief executive officer of Edison Automobile Company, the manager of Edison's operations in the United States, the vice president in charge of production in Edison's Far

East division, and the foreman of the assembly unit would be held responsible for operations within their respective units.

responsibility accounting *a system of evaluating performance; responsibility center managers are held accountable for the costs, revenues, assets, or other elements assigned to their centers*

cost center *an organizational unit in which a manager has control over and is held accountable for costs*

profit center *an organizational unit in which a manager has responsibility for both costs and revenues*

This notion of assigning responsibility for controlling costs or generating revenues to individuals at various levels is referred to as responsibility accounting. Wherever costs, revenues, or profits are accumulated and measured, a responsibility center can exist. Even a single machine can be a center, with its operator responsible for its costs.

There are three basic types of responsibility centers: cost, profit, and investment. As the name implies, a cost center is any organizational unit in which the manager has control over the costs incurred. Because a cost center does not generate revenues, the manager has no responsibility for revenues or investments. A profit center, however, does generate revenues, so the manager has responsibility for both costs and revenues. Thus, a machine could be designated as a cost center but not a profit center because it incurs costs but does not generate revenues. Profit centers are usually found at higher levels in an organization than are cost centers. In IMC, the different geographical regions (U.S., Far East, and European) of Edison Automobile would probably be profit centers.

investment center *an organizational unit in which a manager has responsibility for costs, revenues, and investments*

In an investment center, a manager is responsible for costs, revenues, and investments. He or she is therefore accountable for the level of investment in assets and liabilities that is necessary to generate the costs and revenues. Investment centers are usually found at relatively high levels in organizations. The different companies in IMC (Acme Computer, Edison Automobile, and Jennifer Cosmetics) would probably be investment centers.

We should emphasize that responsibility center managers sometimes do not have control over all the costs or revenues generated by their centers. For example, the manager of the motor unit may be held responsible for labor costs but may not be able to control them completely because employee wages are determined by a union scale. Similarly, a production manager usually has no control over utility rates and depreciation charges on equipment or buildings. Care should be taken to design performance reports so that managers will be held responsible for only the costs, revenues, and investments under their control.

Reporting in a Decentralized Operation

Regardless of the degree of autonomy given managers at various operating levels, reports need to flow up the organization so that top management can know what is going on in all subunits. Such reports serve as a basis for rewarding and motivating employees and providing feedback to management. Exhibit 26-2 illustrates the kind of responsibility accounting that a company might use. You will note in this exhibit that reports start at the bottom and work upward, with each manager receiving information on his or her own performance as well as on the performance of other managers at lower levels.

exception report *a report that compares actual and budgeted performance and points out the variables, or exceptions, between the two*

The report shown in Exhibit 26-2 is an exception report, which means that only variances from or exceptions to the budget are highlighted. Management can examine the exceptions or variances and see immediately where corrective action needs to be taken. In a decentralized operation, management would use this type of report to gain feedback on how lower-level managers are performing, to reward past performance, and to set in-

EXHIBIT 26-2

IMC Corporation

Responsibility Accounting for Edison Automobile Company

President, Edison Automobile	**Responsibility Centers**	**Budget**	**Actual**	**Variance**
The president receives from each geographical area of operations a report summarizing its performance. The president can see where corrective action needs to be made by tracing the variances downward to their sources.	U.S.	x	x	x
	Far East	$58,000	$65,000	$7,000 U
	European	x	x	x

Manager, Far East Operations	**Responsibility Centers**	**Budget**	**Actual**	**Variance**
The manager of Far East operations receives a report from each department head. These reports are then summarized and passed on to the president of Edison Automobile.	Sales	x	x	x
	Production	$21,000	$23,000	$2,000 U
	Engineering and Planning	x	x	x
	Accounting	x	x	x
	Personnel	x	x	x
		$58,000	$65,000	$7,000 U

Production Supervisor	**Responsibility Centers**	**Budget**	**Actual**	**Variance**
The production supervisor receives from each unit a report summarizing its performance. These reports are combined on the production supervisor's report and sent up to the next level, the manager of Far East operations.	Motor Unit	$ 9,000	$10,200	$1,200 U
	Assembly Unit	x	x	x
	Painting Unit	x	x	x
		$21,000	$23,000	$2,000 U

Motor Unit Supervisor	**Variable Costs of the Motor Unit**	**Budget**	**Actual**	**Variance**
The supervisor of each unit receives a performance report on his or her center of responsibility. The totals from these reports are then communicated to the production supervisor, the next level of responsibility.	Direct Materials	$2,000	$ 2,500	$ 500 U
	Direct Labor	6,000	6,400	400 U
	Manufacturing Overhead	1,000	1,300	300 U
		$9,000	$10,200	$1,200 U

* U means unfavorable.

centives for future performance. In a centralized operation, this report would provide information to top management so that more informed decisions could be made.

TO SUMMARIZE Centralization and decentralization are opposite ends of the continuum between top management making all decisions and the delegation of decision-making authority throughout the company to those most immediately involved. Because decentralization has many advantages, most companies are decentralized to some extent, and are divided into fairly independent responsibility centers. There are three types of responsibility centers: cost, profit, and investment. Managers of responsibility centers usually have control over and are held accountable for the performance of the center. Regardless of the degree of decentralization, almost all companies use performance reports that show variances from budgeted amounts for each division, department, and unit. These reports pass upward through an organization so that supervisors and managers at all levels can assess the performance of the units serving under them.

Measuring Performance in an Investment Center

Almost by definition, decentralization means that a company is made up of a number of relatively independent units. Managers of these units have the freedom to make most of their own decisions. With this freedom comes the responsibility for that unit's performance in relation to all other units. Since companies have only limited resources, assets are allocated to divisions on the basis of performance. The responsibility centers that perform better are viewed more favorably by top management and are usually given preference with respect to additional investment capital and promotion of managers.

In order for higher-level management to determine how much of the company's assets each responsibility center should receive, there must be some objective means of measuring performance. There are several techniques available. For example, as discussed in Chapter 25, a comparison of actual costs to standard costs provides a measure of performance in a cost center. For a profit center, contribution-margin income statements, when compared with budgets, show how well sales and cost objectives have been met (see Chapter 21). Investment centers are evaluated not only by means of contribution-margin income statements but also by the rate of return they are able to earn on invested assets.

contribution margin *the difference between total revenues and total variable costs; it is the portion of sales revenue available to cover fixed costs*

RETURN ON TOTAL ASSETS AS A MEASURE OF PERFORMANCE

As you may recall from Chapter 16, the return on total assets [sometimes called the rate of return or the return on investment (ROI)] is a measure of how much has been earned on an investment. It is equal to net income (or net operating income) divided by average total assets. For example, if you earned $1,000 interest on $10,000 deposited in a savings account for 1 year, your return on total assets would be $1,000/$10,000, or 10 percent.

return on total assets *a measure of operating performance and efficiency in utilizing assets; computed in its simplest form by dividing net income by average total assets*

An investment center can improve its return on total assets in one of two ways: (1) it can increase its operating performance ratio (net income divided by net sales), or (2) it can increase its asset turnover ratio (net sales divided by average total assets). A center with major assets—for example, a steel plant with large plant and equipment needs—will have a slow asset turnover and will therefore have to rely primarily on the first method to increase its return. A center with few assets, such as a cosmetics company, has the potential for a rapid asset turnover and could use the second method, or a combination of the two. Although Jennifer Cosmetics Company might make only 1 or 2 cents profit per dollar of product sold, its asset turnover of 15 to

operating performance ratio *an overall measure of the efficiency of operations during a period; computed by dividing net income by net sales*

asset turnover ratio *an overall measure of how effectively assets are used during a period; computed by dividing net sales by average total assets*

20 times a year makes its return on total assets much higher than 1 or 2 percent. The relationships between operating performance and asset turnover can be stated as follows:

$$\text{operating performance} \times \text{asset turnover} = \text{return on total assets}$$

$$\frac{\text{net income}}{\text{net sales}} \times \frac{\text{net sales}}{\text{average total assets}} = \frac{\text{net income}}{\text{average total assets}}$$

Because operating performance and asset turnover are influenced by three factors (net income, net sales, and average total assets), and because net income tends to rise and fall with sales, return on total assets can be increased by increasing net income or net sales or by decreasing total assets. Jennifer Cosmetics might reduce expenses and thus increase income by using less expensive packaging materials; sales might be increased by a better advertising program; and the level of assets could be lowered by reducing inventory or eliminating nonproductive assets, such as little-used machines or excess plant space.

To illustrate the three ways of increasing return on total assets, we will assume that Alberta Company has net sales of \$100,000, net income of \$10,000, and average total assets of \$50,000. The return on total assets is

$$\frac{\$10{,}000}{\$100{,}000} \times \frac{\$100{,}000}{\$50{,}000} =$$

$$10\% \times 2 = 20\%$$

The following illustrations show how each of the three alternatives increases the return on total assets.

1. Increase return by reducing expenses, so that net income becomes \$14,000:

$$\frac{\$14{,}000}{\$100{,}000} \times \frac{\$100{,}000}{\$50{,}000} =$$

$$14\% \times 2 = 28\%$$

2. Increase return by increasing net sales to \$120,000 (profits increase proportionately):

$$\frac{\$12{,}000}{\$120{,}000} \times \frac{\$120{,}000}{\$50{,}000} =$$

$$10\% \times 2.4 = 24\%$$

3. Increase return by reducing average total assets to \$40,000:

$$\frac{\$10{,}000}{\$100{,}000} \times \frac{\$100{,}000}{\$40{,}000} =$$

$$10\% \times 2.5 = 25\%$$

In calculating return on total assets we could have eliminated the net sales figures because they cancel each other out, making return on total assets equal to net income divided by average total assets. However, the inclusion of sales draws attention to two extremely important concepts: (1) Return on total assets is a function of both operating performance *and* asset turnover; and (2) by increasing sales, profits can be increased. For example, a grocery store that turns its assets (mostly inventory) over 20 times a year needs to make only 1 cent on each dollar of sales to have the same return as a clothing store that makes 20 cents on each dollar of sales but only turns its inventory over once a year.

Although return on total assets is a very effective way of evaluating managers of investment centers, it has its drawbacks. For example, because management knows that net income can be increased in a period of constant sales by reducing expenses, critical expenditures such as the repair and maintenance of machinery may be neglected. Disregarding necessary repairs and maintenance may lead to expensive replacement of assets in the future. In addition, overemphasizing the return-on-total-assets ratio may lead to the use of inferior materials, the making of sales decisions that are inappropriate for the long run, the nonreplacement of critical assets, and frequent hirings and firings of employees just to make the ratio look good. In fact, a manager in a strategic position could maintain a high return on total assets while allowing net income, net sales, and operating assets to be reduced significantly. As the following analysis shows, the return-on-total-assets ratio is just as high with small asset, sales, and income levels as it is with high asset, sales, and income levels.

	High Asset, Sales, and Income Levels	Low Asset, Sales, and Income Levels
Net Sales	$100,000	$10,000
Net Income	10,000	1,000
Total Assets	50,000	5,000
Return on Total Assets	$\frac{\$10,000}{\$100,000} \times \frac{\$100,000}{\$50,000} = 20\%$	$\frac{\$1,000}{\$10,000} \times \frac{\$10,000}{\$5,000} = 20\%$

RESIDUAL INCOME AS A MEASURE OF PERFORMANCE

residual income *the amount of net income an investment center is able to earn above a specified minimum rate of return on total assets*

Although the return-on-total-assets approach is widely practiced, some companies measure the performance of investment centers by using residual income. Residual income is the amount of net income an investment center is able to earn above a certain minimum rate of return on total assets. Using this approach, investment centers are encouraged to maximize their residual income, not their absolute return on total assets. Exhibit 26-3 compares the residual income and return-on-total-assets approaches.

Exhibit 26-3 assumes that the company's minimum accepted rate of return on total assets is 15 percent. Subtracting the 15 percent return, or $15,000, from net income of $25,000 gives a residual income of $10,000.

EXHIBIT 26-3 A Comparison of Return on Total Assets and Residual Income

	Return on Total Assets	Residual Income
Average Total Assets	$100,000	$100,000
Net Income	$ 25,000	$ 25,000
Return on Total Assets	25%	
Minimum Accepted Rate of Return on Total Assets (15%)		$ 15,000
Residual Income		$ 10,000

The advantage of residual income is that it encourages managers to make as much profit as possible rather than merely achieving a certain return on assets. Because residual income emphasizes the level of profits, its use often means that managers make investment decisions that would be avoided if performance were measured by return on total assets.

To illustrate, we assume that the division for which data were given in Exhibit 26-3 has an opportunity to invest $40,000 in a new project that will generate a return of 20 percent, or $8,000 per year. Suppose also that the company wants to invest only in projects that will return more than 15 percent. A manager being evaluated on return on total assets would probably reject this investment opportunity because, as the following analysis shows, it would reduce the overall return ratio from 25 percent to 23.5 percent.

	Without the New Investment	New Investment	Total
Average Total Assets	$100,000	$40,000	$140,000
Net Income	25,000	8,000	33,000
Return on Total Assets	25%	20%	23.6%

On the other hand, a manager being evaluated on a residual income basis (with a minimum rate of return of 15 percent) would probably be quite enthusiastic about the project because it increases residual income from $10,000 to $12,000. The fact that return on total assets would be lower is not important because performance in this case is being measured on the basis of residual income.

	Without the New Investment	New Investment	Total
Average Total Assets	$100,000	$40,000	$140,000
Net Income	$ 25,000	$ 8,000	$ 33,000
Minimum Rate of Return (15%)	15,000	6,000*	21,000
Residual Income	$ 10,000	$ 2,000	$ 12,000

* $40,000 × 0.15 = $6,000

Obviously, the company as a whole would benefit if the investment were made. However, whether or not the investment should actually be made depends on what other alternatives are or will be available. A manager being evaluated on return on total assets might wait for a more attractive investment opportunity. If no other opportunity arises, the company loses. On the other hand, a manager whose performance is being judged on the residual income approach might apply all available resources to this investment and then not be able to take advantage of a better opportunity later on.

TO SUMMARIZE The performance of an investment center may be measured by return on total assets or by residual income. Return on total assets is equal to net income divided by average total assets. It can be improved by increasing operating performance and/or asset turnover. These goals can be accomplished by: (1) increasing net income by reducing expenses, (2) increasing net sales (assuming that profits increase at least proportionately as a result), or (3) reducing the level of asset investments. Because residual income emphasizes the magnitude of net income over a certain minimum level of return, it often encourages managers to accept projects they would decline if they were evaluated solely on a return-on-total-assets basis.

Coordination of Goals in a Decentralized Firm

Because responsibility centers are often ranked and rewarded on the basis of performance, unit managers may be prompted to compete with one another as though they were operating separate businesses. Certain aspects of this competition can create problems for the company as a whole.

To illustrate, we will consider a company with two divisions—manufacturing (A) and home construction (B). Division A makes several products, one of which (a window frame) is used by the home construction division. These frames are made for $30 each and sold to division B for $50. Another company sells similar window frames for $40 each, and the home construction division, in order to reduce its costs, would like to buy its frames from this outside source. Although the price from the other company is lower ($40 versus $50), the cost to the company as a whole is higher ($40 versus $30). So, although buying outside would make the home construction division look better, this would not be in keeping with the company's overall goal of maximizing profits. (In this example, we are assuming that there is no outside market for window frames at $50 and that there are no other equally profitable products for the manufacturing division to produce and sell. If there were, the home construction division should, of course, buy its frames from the outside source for $40 each and the manufacturing division should sell its frames for $50 each or produce the other more profitable products.) Because of such situations, top-level management tries to establish criteria that will diminish conflict between the goals of the responsibility centers and those of the firm as a whole. Two areas that often need close monitoring are transfer pricing and the allocation of service costs.

TRANSFER PRICING

transfer price *the monetary value assigned to goods and services exchanged between units of an organization*

Goods and services are often exchanged among various profit and investment centers within a company. When these goods are exchanged, what transfer price should be charged for internal reporting purposes? If the price is too high, the buying division will be encouraged to look elsewhere for the product. If the price is too low, the supplying division will want to sell elsewhere. Because both the buying and selling divisions are evaluated on the basis of their respective profits, some equitable price must be found that will satisfy both managers and yet maximize the profits of the organization as a whole.

Some of the transfer prices a company may consider using are

1. A price based on the total variable and fixed costs incurred in making the product (total cost).
2. A price based on the total variable costs incurred in making the product.
3. The price for which the product could be sold on the outside market (market price).
4. A negotiated price.

Total-Cost Transfer Prices

total cost *all the direct and allocated costs of a product; the total variable and fixed costs incurred in making the product or providing the service*

Transferring goods at total cost is a common practice in business. Companies argue that the availability of the total-cost figures makes them easily understood and convenient. There are, however, two serious drawbacks to using total cost as a transfer price. First, the only divisions that show any profits are those that make the final sales to outside parties. The supplying divisions record no profits on intracompany sales, so rate of return on total assets and residual income are not appropriate performance measures for these divisions.

Second, total-cost transfer prices create no incentives for supplying divisions to hold down their costs or to operate efficiently. Since the division managers know that all costs will be passed on to another division, they may be less vigilant about eliminating wastefulness and inefficiency. It is the buying division that may be burdened with such inefficiencies. Because of this weakness, many companies have found that using total costs leads to higher expenses, disagreements among divisions, and sometimes pressure from buying divisions to purchase from outside suppliers. This problem is especially severe when a supplying division sells both to outsiders and to other divisions within the company. Since the total-cost approach allows all costs to be transferred to other departments, employees often try to burden the products transferred within the company with inefficiencies and overhead costs so that products they sell to outside markets will be highly profitable.

Despite these drawbacks, total-cost transfer prices continue to be widely used, simply because they are readily available. Companies using this approach can minimize problems by using standard costs rather than actual costs, so that inefficiencies and waste cannot be transferred from one department to another.

Variable-Cost-Based Transfer Prices

variable cost *cost that varies in total proportionately with changes in activity level within the relevant range*

The use of variable cost as the basis for a transfer price does not solve either of the problems associated with total cost. Inefficiencies can still be passed along, and only the divisions selling to outsiders will have profits. On the other hand, when variable costs are used as the basis for transfer prices, maximum utilization of total corporate facilities is ensured over the short run. This is because fixed costs do not change in the short run, so any use of facilities that creates revenues in excess of variable costs will be accepted. For example, if a supplying division has already covered fixed costs but has excess capacity, it could readily supply another division's order at any price that exceeds variable costs.

The danger with using variable costs as the basis for transfer prices is that these prices are good only for the short run. If a project extends beyond the estimated time period, fixed costs, which are not accounted for in the transfer price, may increase. If fixed costs are covered by other production jobs, however, the variable cost of completing an additional job is the price at which the supplying division is theoretically indifferent about using its facilities to produce the item. Any price above variable cost encourages acceptance by the supplying division; any price below variable cost discourages acceptance.

Market-Based Transfer Prices

market price *the price at which goods are exchanged in arm's-length transactions in the marketplace*

Most managers agree that where possible, market price is probably the best transfer price to use. Market prices make the supplying division indifferent as to whether it sells outside or inside the firm, and likewise make the buying division indifferent as to whether it buys outside or inside. Most important, market prices allow companies to use profit-based measures to evaluate divisional performance. Thus, each division is encouraged to act as if it were a separate company. Such actions soon lead to the kind of competitive market conditions that promote good-faith bargaining, production efficiency, and objective decision making. Market-based transfer prices work better in a decentralized company than in a centralized one because managers have the autonomy to act independently of each other.

Negotiated Transfer Prices

Sometimes an outside market either does not exist or is not a viable alternative. In such cases, management may choose to allow the parties involved to negotiate a transfer price rather than use a cost-based approach. A negotiated price is never lower than the variable cost and should never be higher than the market price, if one exists. Negotiated prices are usually affected by whether or not fixed costs have already been covered, whether or not the supplying division is operating at full capacity, and how strong the relative bargaining powers of the supplying and buying divisions are.

An Analysis of Alternative Transfer Prices

Each of the transfer prices we have discussed has advantages and disadvantages. Because use of the market price benefits both parties, most accountants would argue that it should be used whenever possible. When no outside market exists (as might be the case with components, for example) and the supplying division has excess capacity, any price over variable cost will be to the supplying division's benefit. If, however, the supplying division has no excess capacity, a negotiated price above the total cost is probably the best solution.

To illustrate the applicability of these various transfer prices, we will refer again to division A's window frames, which division B uses in constructing houses. Assume that division A operated at capacity and had the following data for last year.

	Sales to Outsiders	**Sales to Division B**	**Total**
Sales Revenue (10,000* frames at $50 each)	$300,000	$200,000	$500,000
Variable Costs ($30 per frame)	180,000	120,000	300,000
Contribution Margin	$120,000	$ 80,000	$200,000
Fixed Costs			100,000
Net Income			$100,000

* 6,000 frames sold to outsiders; 4,000 frames sold to division B.

Division A sold the 4,000 frames to division B at the market price of $50 each. If division B decides that it can afford to pay only $31 per frame, or just over the variable cost, should division A continue to sell to division B? Division A's decision will depend on whether or not the additional 4,000 frames can be sold to outside customers. If they can, division A will not want to sell to division B. If no outside customers exist, division A would be better off selling to division B because

1. Fixed costs are already covered by outside sales.
2. The $31 offered exceeds the variable cost of $30.
3. Division A has excess capacity and is capable of making these additional 4,000 frames.

The additional profit that results from this decision is shown in the following comparison.

	Division A Does Not Sell to Division B		**Division A Sells to Division B at $31**
Sales Revenue (6,000 frames)	$300,000	Sales Revenue (10,000 frames)	$424,000*
Variable Costs (at $30)	180,000	Variable Costs (at $30)	300,000
Contribution Margin	$120,000	Contribution Margin	$124,000
Fixed Costs	100,000	Fixed Costs	100,000
Net Income	$ 20,000	Net Income	$ 24,000

* 6,000 at $50; 4,000 at $31.

Although division A's income is increased by selling the frames to division B for $31, the increment is not very much ($4,000). In fact, division A's manager may decide that the small increase is not worth the extra effort.

As an alternative, division A's manager would prefer a price that is equal to the total variable and fixed costs incurred in making the product—that is, the total cost. At a production level of 10,000 frames, this price is

Total Variable Costs (at $30)	$300,000
Total Fixed Costs	100,000
Total Costs	$400,000
Price per Unit ($400,000/10,000 frames)	$40

At $40, the cost of each frame sold to division B bears its share of fixed as well as variable costs. Division A's net income would then be $60,000, as shown below.

	Division A Sells to Division B at $40 (Total Cost)
Sales Revenue	$460,000*
Variable Costs (at $30)	300,000
Contribution Margin	$160,000
Fixed Costs	100,000
Net Income	$ 60,000

* 6,000 at $50; 4,000 at $40.

At $60,000 net income, division A's manager may still think the price is too low or division B's manager may now think the price is too high. The fourth alternative, then, is to let the two managers negotiate a mutually acceptable price. The negotiated price will most likely fall between the market price of $50 (the upper limit) and the variable cost of $30 (the lower limit).

Exhibit 26-4 shows transfer-price guidelines that would result in agreement among this firm's managers. Keep in mind though that every situation must be analyzed and that the impact of the various transfer prices on a company's goals, on the incentives of managers, and on the autonomy of divisions must be studied. In such analyses, the following rule should always be considered. The minimum transfer price should be the sum of (1) the outlay costs incurred to the point of transfer (if fixed costs are already covered, outlay cost is equal to variable cost), and (2) the opportunity cost to the firm as a whole. The opportunity cost is the profit given up if goods are transferred internally.

outlay cost *the actual cash outflow directly associated with the production and transfer of a product or service; in transfer pricing, if fixed costs are covered, outlay cost equals the total of the variable costs incurred in making the product or providing the service; if fixed costs have not been covered by outside sales, outlay cost equals total cost*

opportunity cost *the amount of money that could be earned by putting financial resources to their best alternative use compared with the one being considered*

EXHIBIT 26-4 **Guidelines for Transfer Pricing**

Condition	Price When Excess Capacity Exists	Price When No Excess Capacity Exists
Outside market exists	Market price	Market price
No outside market exists	Anything over variable cost, or a negotiated price	Anything over total cost, or a negotiated price

Applying this rule to our window-frame example, we can determine minimum transfer prices as follows.

Minimum Transfer Price	=	Outlay Cost	+	Opportunity Cost	=	Total
Excess capacity, no outside market	=	$30	+	probably 0	=	$30
Excess capacity, outside market	=	$30	+	$20 ($50 market price − $30 variable cost)	=	$50
No excess capacity, no outside market	=	$40*	+	probably 0	=	$40
No excess capacity, outside market	=	$40*	+	$10 ($50 market price − $40 outlay cost)	=	$50

* This price assumes a production volume of 10,000 units and thus includes variable costs of $30 and fixed costs of $10 per unit ($100,000/10,000 units).

SERVICE-COST ALLOCATION

service costs *operating costs of service departments that are usually allocated to production departments*

service department *an organizational unit that does not directly produce goods but instead serves other departments*

Another potential source of disharmony among subunits in decentralized firms is the allocation of service costs to departments or profit centers. Most businesses have departments that do not produce goods but rather service other departments. Examples are data processing, accounting, planning, personnel, and cafeteria and medical facilities. Service departments carry out essential auxiliary services for an organization, and their costs must be covered by the producing departments. Allocation of these costs may be based on any number of factors—for example, revenues, usage, number of employees, or hours worked.

There are several reasons for allocating service department costs to production departments.

1. Allocation helps in costing the product because service department costs should be viewed as part of a product's cost.
2. Allocation helps production departments realize the cost of the services received.
3. Allocation usually results in a more equitable distribution of services between production departments.

allocation of service costs *the assigning of service costs to various production centers, usually on the basis of benefits received by those centers*

To illustrate the allocation of service costs, we will use sales revenue and number of employees as bases. Assume that Palmer Company has four divisions: home products, commercial, manufacturing, and the cafeteria. During 1984, the four divisions had the following operating data.

	Home Products	Commercial	Manufacturing	Cafeteria
Sales Revenue	$600,000	$400,000	$200,000	$35,000
Variable Costs	320,000	200,000	80,000	60,000
Fixed Costs	180,000	120,000	60,000	75,000
Number of Employees	70	60	20	30

If cafeteria losses [\$35,000 − (\$60,000 + \$75,000) = (\$100,000)] are allocated on the basis of sales revenue, the three producing divisions would bear the following cafeteria costs.

Home Products	Commercial	Manufacturing
$\frac{\$600,000}{\$1,200,000^*} \times (\$100,000) = (\$50,000)$	$\frac{\$400,000}{\$1,200,000} \times (\$100,000) = (\$33,000)$	$\frac{\$200,000}{\$1,200,000} \times (\$100,000) = (\$16,667)$

* \$600,000 + \$400,000 + \$200,000

On the other hand, if cafeteria losses are allocated on the basis of number of employees in each producing division, the allocation of the cafeteria's net service costs would be

Home Products	Commercial	Manufacturing
$\frac{70}{150^*} \times (\$100,000) = (\$46,667)$	$\frac{60}{150} \times (\$100,000) = (\$40,000)$	$\frac{20}{150} \times (\$100,000) = (\$13,333)$

* 70 + 60 + 20

In this case, both home products and manufacturing would argue for an allocation based on number of employees, whereas the commercial division would want cafeteria losses allocated on the basis of total sales revenue.

Because allocated service costs reduce a production department's return on total assets, there is an incentive to avoid using these services when they are allocated on the basis of number of employees or other such measures. Therefore, management must consider several issues before deciding how to allocate service costs. For example

1. What is the most equitable basis for allocating service costs to the various profit and investment centers? Traditionally, distribution has been based on the benefits received by the various departments. Examples of service-cost allocation bases are shown below.

Service Department	Basis for Service-Cost Allocation
Cafeteria	Number of employees in each division
Accounting	Hours worked in each division
Building and utility costs	Square footage of each division
Data processing	Usage by each division
Personnel	Number of employees in each division

2. Should all service costs be allocated? Perhaps the costs of services that top management requires all departments to use should not be allocated at all. Examples are internal auditing and personnel training. Since charging on the basis of usage often discourages use, some other arrangement, such as a flat fee, should be established if allocation is considered necessary.

3. Should actual or standard service costs be allocated? If actual costs are allocated, production departments may be burdened with the inefficiencies of the service departments. Because of this potential inequity, standard costs, adjusted for the actual level of activity, are usually used. Remaining costs created by inefficiencies are the responsibility of the service departments.

In general, although it may be necessary to allocate service costs, firms must do so carefully. Otherwise, profit center managers, in trying to keep their rates of return high, may be inclined to make decisions that are not in the overall best interest of the company.

TO SUMMARIZE Because the performance of responsibility centers is measured on the basis of minimizing costs and maximizing profitability within the center, managers may be motivated to operate in ways that reduce the overall profits of a decentralized firm. Two principal areas where this kind of goal confusion can arise are the choosing of equitable and efficient transfer prices and the proper allocation of service costs. Whenever possible, the market price should be used as the transfer price. Service costs should be allocated to producing departments as equitably as possible, and in a way that does not discourage use of essential services.

CHAPTER REVIEW

As firms grow in size and complexity, it becomes important to divide activities and responsibilities in a way that ensures continued success. Most large firms divide responsibilities by function, region, product, and division. Some firms are decentralized, which means that managers at various levels are relatively free to make their own decisions; other firms are primarily centralized, meaning that top management makes most of the decisions. Decentralization has several benefits; for example, it fosters the making of more timely decisions and it permits better performance evaluation.

In a decentralized operation, responsibility for controlling costs or generating revenue is assigned to individuals at various levels; this is the concept of responsibility accounting. There are three types of responsibility centers: cost, profit, and investment. Although a cost center can be found anywhere in an organization, profit and investment centers are usually found at relatively high levels of management.

Companies use performance reports that move upward through an organization to provide feedback to higher-level managers. Managers of responsibility centers are usually held accountable for the success of their particular centers. The most common measures of success are actual costs versus standard costs in a cost center, contribution margin in a profit center, and rate of return on total assets or residual income in an investment center. Return on total assets is a function of operating performance and asset turnover, which are affected by three factors: net income, net sales, and average total assets. Any of these factors can be modified to increase or decrease the rate of return. Residual income encourages the maximization of income above a specified minimum rate of return.

Evaluating responsibility centers on the basis of performance in reducing costs and increasing profitability sometimes creates intense competition between units. Because of this, a manager may make a decision that increases the center's profitability at the expense of the total organization. In an attempt to eliminate such consequences, management establishes criteria designed to promote agreement on goals. Two areas that need close monitoring are transfer pricing and the allocation of service costs to production centers. Transfer prices are the prices charged by profit and investment centers when they sell goods and services to one another. There are four common transfer prices: total cost, variable-cost-based, market price, and a negotiated price. The costs of operating service departments should be allocated in a way that does not lead to inappropriate decisions by profit- and investment-center managers.

KEY TERMS AND CONCEPTS

allocation of service costs (868)
asset turnover ratio (859)
centralization (854)
contribution margin (859)
cost center (857)
decentralization (854)
exception report (857)
investment center (857)
market price (865)
operating performance ratio (859)
opportunity cost (867)
outlay cost (867)
profit center (857)
residual income (861)
responsibility accounting (857)
responsibility center (856)
return on total assets (859)
service costs (868)
service department (868)
total cost (864)
transfer price (864)
variable cost (865)

REVIEW PROBLEM

Cost Allocation and Rate of Return on Total Assets

Kunzler Corporation has three divisions: a restaurant, a hotel, and a data processing center. The data processing division services the other two divisions; the restaurant and the hotel are separate investment centers. The following operating data are available for 1984.

	Restaurant	Hotel	Data Processing
Net Sales Revenue	$1,800,000	$2,100,000	–
Fixed Costs	1,100,000	1,200,000	$ 90,000
Variable Costs	300,000	400,000	22,000
Average Total Assets	1,200,000	1,500,000	200,000
Number of Data Processing Terminals	11	14	4

Required:

1. If data processing costs are not allocated, what are the rates of return on total assets in the restaurant and hotel divisions?
2. If data processing costs are allocated to the restaurant and the hotel on the basis of number of terminals, how much of the data processing costs will each division bear?
3. Recompute the return on total assets for the restaurant and the hotel, assuming the allocation scheme of item (2).

Solution

1. The rate of return on total assets is calculated as shown on the next page.

$$\frac{\text{net income}}{\text{net sales}} \times \frac{\text{net sales}}{\text{average total assets}}$$

$$\text{restaurant} = \frac{\$400{,}000^*}{\$1{,}800{,}000} \times \frac{\$1{,}800{,}000}{\$1{,}200{,}000} = 33\%$$

$$\text{hotel} = \frac{\$500{,}000^\dagger}{\$2{,}100{,}000} \times \frac{\$2{,}100{,}000}{\$1{,}500{,}000} = 33\%$$

* $1,800,000 − ($1,100,000 + $300,000)
† $2,100,000 − ($1,200,000 + $400,000)

2. Data processing costs are $112,000 ($90,000 + $22,000). If these costs are allocated on the basis of the number of terminals, the results are

$$\text{restaurant} = \frac{11}{25} \times (\$112{,}000) = (\$49{,}280)$$

$$\text{hotel} = \frac{14}{25} \times (\$112{,}000) = (\$62{,}720)$$

In this case, the hotel division bears more data processing costs because it has more terminals.

3. Before computing the return on total assets, the new incomes must be calculated.

	Restaurant	**Hotel**
Sales Revenue	$1,800,000	$2,100,000
Fixed Costs	(1,100,000)	(1,200,000)
Variable Costs	(300,000)	(400,000)
Allocated Costs from Data Processing	(49,280)	(62,720)
Net Income	$ 350,720	$ 437,280

$$\text{restaurant} = \frac{\$350{,}720}{\$1{,}800{,}000} \times \frac{\$1{,}800{,}000}{\$1{,}200{,}000} = 29.23\%$$

$$\text{hotel} = \frac{\$437{,}280}{\$2{,}100{,}000} \times \frac{\$2{,}100{,}000}{.\$1{,}500{,}000} = 29.15\%$$

It is easy to see why production divisions do not want service costs to be allocated. In both divisions, returns were reduced by approximately 4 percent (33 percent − 29 percent). If the managers of these divisions are rewarded on the basis of rate of return, they may resent having to pay for data processing. In fact, they might demand that the terminals be taken out of their divisions. The behavioral problems that can result from cost allocation are significant.

DISCUSSION QUESTIONS

1 What are the advantages of decentralization?

2 What is the major disadvantage of decentralization?

3 What are the differences between cost, profit, and investment centers?

4 Are all costs in a responsibility center controllable by that center's manager? Explain.

5 How is the performance of responsibility centers evaluated?

6 How can the manager of an investment center increase the rate of return on total assets?

7 What is the major disadvantage of using the rate of return on total assets to evaluate the performance of investment centers?

8 What is the major advantage of using residual income to evaluate the performance of investment centers?

9 What is the major disadvantage of using residual income to evaluate the performance of investment centers?

10 Describe a decision made by a profit-center manager that would benefit the center but not the organization as a whole.

11 When should the market price be used as a transfer price?

12 What are the major disadvantages of using total cost as a transfer price?

13 What is the rationale for allocating service department costs to production departments?

14 Should standard or actual service costs be allocated to production departments? Why?

15 When might a company not want to allocate service costs on the basis of usage?

EXERCISES

E26–1 Rate of Return on Total Assets

Compute the missing data in the following table.

	Division X	Division Y	Division Z
Sales Revenue (net)	$600,000	$500,000	$?
Net Income	30,000	25,000	?
Average Total Assets	?	100,000	200,000
Operating Performance Ratio	?	?	10%
Asset Turnover Ratio	?	?	4 times
Return on Total Assets	12%	?	?

E26–2 Rate of Return on Total Assets

Worldwide Trade Corporation has two divisions: the Far East division and the America division. Following are their operating data for 1984.

	Far East Division	America Division
Sales Revenue	$100,000	$100,000
Net Income	8,000	7,000
Average Total Assets	50,000	40,000
Stockholders' Equity	24,000	16,000
Long-Term Debt	23,000	20,000

1. Calculate the rate of return on total assets for each division.
2. On the basis of this return, which division appears to have the better performance? Why?

E26–3 Rate of Return on Total Assets

During 1984, the North and South divisions of Mayberry Company reported the following.

	North Division	South Division
Return on Total Assets	21%	15%
Operating Performance Ratio	6%	5%
Net Sales Revenue	$60,000	$80,000
Net Operating Assets	30,000	20,000

1. What was each division's asset turnover ratio in 1984?
2. What operating performance ratio would each division need in order to generate a return on total assets of 25 percent?

E26–4 Rate of Return on Total Assets

The following information for 1984 applies to the two sales divisions of Crosgrove Enterprises.

	Division A	Division B
Average Inventory	$33,333	$37,500
Operating Performance	12%	16%
Net Income	$12,000	$10,000

1. Calculate each division's net sales revenue.
2. Calculate each division's asset turnover ratio.
3. Which division has the better performance for the period?

E26–5 Evaluating Performance with Contribution Margins

Damond Corporation has three divisions: North, East, and West. During 1984, the three divisions had the following operating data.

	North	East	West
Revenues (at $10 per unit)	$100,000	$150,000	$200,000
Fixed Costs:			
Costs Unique to the Division	30,000	61,000	70,000
Costs Allocated by Corporate Headquarters	20,000	30,000	40,000
Variable Costs	$6/unit	$6/unit	$4/unit

Damond's management is concerned because the company is losing money. They ask you to

1. Calculate each division's net income.
2. Calculate each division's contribution margin and the contribution each makes to overall company profits.
3. Determine, on the basis of these calculations, which division(s) (if any) should be discontinued. (Assume that the 1984 performance is indicative of all future years, and ignore all nonfinancial factors.)

E26–6 Contribution-Margin Analysis

El Pico Company has two divisions: Maya and Aztec. During 1984, the two divisions had the following operating data.

	Maya Division	Aztec Division
Sales Revenue	$100,000	$120,000
Fixed Costs:		
Costs Unique to the Division	50,000	45,000
Costs Allocated by Corporate Headquarters	11,000	10,000
Variable Costs	$4/unit	$4/unit
Sales Price of Division's Product	$10/unit	$8/unit

1. Compute each division's net income.
2. Compute each division's contribution margin and the contribution each makes to overall company profits.
3. Based on the above financial information only, should either division be discontinued? Why?

E26–7 Measuring Performance: Residual Income and Rate of Return on Total Assets

In 1984, the speaker division of Phillips Corporation, which has average total assets of $250,000, generated a net income of $55,000, or 8 percent of sales. The operating results are expected to be the same in 1985. In early 1985, the speaker division receives a proposal for a $50,000 investment that would generate an additional $10,000 of income per year.

1. Phillips Corporation measures the performance of its divisions by using the residual income approach, with a minimum accepted rate of return of 16 percent. Should the manager of the speaker division make the investment?
2. Would your answer to item (1) be any different if Phillips Corporation used the return-on-total-assets approach to evaluate the performance of its various divisions? Why?

E26–8 Measuring Performance: Residual Income and Rate of Return on Total Assets

Southwick Corporation recently received three investment proposals. Details of the proposals appear below.

	Proposals 1	2	3
Required Investment	$80,000	$50,000	$65,000
Annual Return	13,000	9,000	9,500

Southwick Corporation uses the residual income method to evaluate all investment proposals. Its minimum rate of return is 15 percent.

1. As president of Southwick Corporation, which of the investments, if any, would you make? Why?
2. Assuming that Southwick Corporation uses the return-on-total-assets approach to evaluate investment proposals, which investments, if any, would you make? (Southwick Corporation's current return on total assets is 20 percent.)

E26–9 Measuring Performance: Residual Income and Rate of Return on Total Assets

The printing division of Gateway Corporation had income of $550,000 and average total assets of $3,000,000 in 1984. The figures are expected to be similar in 1985. The manager of the printing division has an opportunity to purchase a new high-speed printing press for $250,000. In evaluating the investment, the manager concludes that the new press would increase annual net income by $44,000.

1. Calculate the current return on total assets and the expected return on the proposed investment.
2. Calculate the printing division's current residual income and the expected residual income on the proposed investment. (Assume that the division's minimum accepted rate of return is 17 percent.)
3. Should the high-speed press be purchased
   (a) If the division uses the return-on-total-assets method?
   (b) If the division uses the residual income method?

E26–10 Transfer Pricing When an Outside Market Exists

The sawmill division of Davidson Company makes lumber for building houses. The construction division builds prefabricated modular homes and usually buys its lumber from the sawmill division at a price of $100 per 1,000 board feet. The manager of the construction division recently found an outside supplier that will furnish lumber at $85 per 1,000 board feet; now the construction manager is demanding that the sawmill division meet this price. The sawmill division's sales and costs are as follows:

	To the Construction Division	To Outside Customers
Sales Revenue:		
1,000,000 board feet	$100,000	
500,000 board feet		$50,000
Variable Costs	45,000	22,500
Contribution Margin	$ 55,000	$27,500
Fixed Costs	40,000	20,000
Net Income	$ 15,000	$ 7,500

Assume that you are the manager of the sawmill division.

1. What are the total costs (at the present level of sales) per 1,000 board feet of lumber?

2. Would you meet the price of $85 per 1,000 board feet being offered by the outside supplier?

3. If you were the company president, would you require the sawmill division to meet the $85 price?

E26–11 Transfer Pricing When No Outside Market Exists

Morocco Company, which makes paper supplies, has two divisions: manufacturing and printing. The manufacturing division makes paper products from wood pulp, and the printing division uses these products to make stationery and other paper supplies. During 1984, the manufacturing division produced 5,000 pads of paper at a cost of $2 per pad (there are no fixed costs), which the printing division further processed at an additional cost of 10 cents per pad and sold for $3 per pad. Given these costs and the sales price, answer the following questions (assume that there is no outside market for the manufacturing division's output).

1. At what minimum price could manufacturing sell to the printing division and not suffer a loss?

2. What is the maximum price the printing division could pay and not suffer a loss?

3. What negotiated price would allow both divisions to have the same percentage of net income?

4. At a negotiated transfer price of $2.40, what is each division's percentage return on its total costs?

E26–12 Transfer Pricing

The semiconductor division of Reynolds Corporation sells the semiconductors it produces at a price of $20 per unit. Budgeted operating data for the division appear below.

Sales Revenue (25,000 units)	$500,000
Variable Costs	200,000
Contribution Margin	$300,000
Fixed Costs	140,000
Net Income	$160,000

Reynolds Corporation has just opened a new home computer division. This new division would like to purchase 10,000 units per year from the semiconductor division. The semiconductor division has a capacity of 40,000 units per year.

1. What transfer price should be charged to the home computer division? Why?

2. If an outside market did exist for the additional 10,000 units of semiconductors, what transfer price should be charged to the home computer division? Why?

3. If variable costs of $1.50 per unit were attributable to direct selling expenses, would your answers to items (1) and (2) differ?

E26–13 Allocation of Service Costs

Tobler Company has four divisions: radio, transmitter, television, and a cafeteria. During 1984, the four divisions had the following operating data.

	Radio	Transmitter	Television	Cafeteria
Sales Revenue	$500,000	$300,000	$200,000	–
Variable Costs	200,000	100,000	150,000	$40,000
Fixed Costs	60,000	80,000	20,000	80,000
Number of Employees	60	50	40	25

1. How much of the cafeteria costs should each of the other divisions bear if the costs are allocated on the basis of
   (a) The number of employees in each producing division?
   (b) The total revenues of each division?

2. As the radio division manager, which of the two allocation schemes would you prefer? Which would you prefer if you were the television division manager?

E26–14 Allocating Budgeted and Actual Costs

Handy Company has three divisions: painting, processing, and personnel. The following are their operating data for 1984.

	Painting Division	Processing Division	Personnel Division
Sales Revenue	$100,000	$80,000	–
Expenses–Actual	80,000	63,000	$14,000
Expenses–Budgeted	80,000	63,000	12,000
Total Assets	50,000	50,000	5,000
Number of Employees	10	6	1

1. If the actual expenses of the personnel division are allocated on the basis of the number of employees in each of the producing divisions, how much should be borne by the painting and the processing divisions?

2. If the budgeted expenses of the personnel division are allocated on the basis of the number of employees, how much should each division bear?

3. What are the returns on total assets for the painting and processing divisions if
   (a) Actual service costs are allocated?
   (b) Budgeted service costs are allocated?

4. Which is a more equitable allocation basis–actual or budgeted costs? Why?

E26-15 Allocation of Costs: Two Service Departments

Livingston Company has four departments: books, magazines, accounting, and administration. All operating expenses of the two service departments are allocated to the production departments. The company uses a sequential allocation plan, beginning with the allocation of administration costs to the other three departments, followed by the allocation of accounting costs to the two production departments. The following data are available for Livingston Company's 1984 fiscal year.

	Books	Magazines	Accounting	Administration
Sales Revenue . .	$500,000	$350,000	–	–
Variable Costs	250,000	200,000	$50,000	$20,000
Fixed Costs .	125,000	50,000	50,000	55,000
Number of Employees	60	25	5	10

All administration costs are allocated according to the number of employees in each department, and accounting costs are allocated on the basis of departmental revenues.

Given the above, allocate all administration and accounting costs, and determine net income for the book and magazine departments.

PROBLEMS

P26-1 Rate of Return on Total Assets and Contribution-Margin Analysis

Electronic Data Corporation has three divisions: computer, calculator, and typewriter. During 1984, these divisions had the following operating data.

	Computer	Calculator	Typewriter
Sales Revenue	$100,000	$150,000	$200,000
Variable Costs	50,000	90,000	135,000
Fixed Costs	45,000	56,000	53,000
Average Total Assets . . .	50,000	38,000	120,000

Required:

1. Compute the contribution margin for each division.
2. Compute the net income for each division.
3. Compute the return on total assets for each division.
4. Which division had the highest operating performance ratio?

5. **Interpretive Question** Which division had the best performance in 1984? Why?

P26-2 Rate of Return on Total Assets and Residual Income

Required:
Compute the missing data in the following table:

	Division W	Division X	Division Y	Division Z
Net Sales Revenue	$100,000	$300,000	(9)$?	$850,000
Net Income	(1) ?	$ 90,000	(10)$?	(13)$?
Average Total Assets	$ 85,000	(5)$?	$550,000	(14)$?
Operating Performance Ratio	15%	(6) ?	6%	(15) ?
Asset Turnover Ratio	(2) ?	0.75 times	(11) ?	4.0 times
Return on Total Assets	(3) ?	(7) ?	(12) ?	21%
Minimum Accepted Rate of Return	13%	(8) ?	15%	12%
Residual Income .	(4)$?	$ 12,000	$ 17,500	(16)$?

P26-3 Rate of Return on Total Assets and Residual Income

Pacific Corporation has a number of autonomous divisions. Its real estate division has recently received a number of investment proposals.

a. A new office building would cost $450,000 and would generate yearly net income of $80,000.

b. A new computer would cost $350,000 and would reduce bookkeeping and clerical costs by $50,000 annually.

c. A new apartment house would cost $900,000 and would generate yearly net income of $150,000.

The real estate division currently has average total assets of $1,800,000 and net income of $350,000.

Required:

1. Assuming that the performance of the manager of the real estate division is evaluated on the basis of the division's return on total assets, evaluate each of the independent proposals and determine whether it should be accepted or rejected.

2. Assuming that the manager's performance is evaluated on a residual income basis, determine whether each of the proposals should be accepted or rejected. (The division's minimum accepted rate of return is 15 percent.)

P26–4 Rate of Return on Total Assets and Residual Income

The manager of the manufacturing division of Lafayette Company is evaluated on a residual income basis. He is currently in the process of evaluating three investment proposals. The independent proposals are

a. Pay $500,000 for a new machine that will increase production substantially. This will result in an increased income of $80,000 annually.

b. Pay $350,000 for a new machine that will reduce labor costs by $70,000 annually.

c. Pay $800,000 for a new machine that will increase annual net income by $115,000.

The manufacturing division currently has average total assets of $1,200,000 and net income of $200,000. Its minimum accepted rate of return is 15 percent.

Required:

1. Evaluate the three investment proposals independently, and determine whether they should be accepted or rejected.

2. Assuming that the division manager is evaluated on the basis of the division's return on total assets, determine whether each of the proposals should be accepted or rejected.

3. **Interpretive Question** Is the residual income approach a better measure of performance than the return-on-total-assets approach? Explain.

P26–5 Rate of Return on Total Assets and Residual Income

Albertson Furniture Company is a retailer of home furnishings. It currently has stores in three cities—San Francisco, Los Angeles, and Phoenix. Operating data for the three stores in 1984 were as follows:

	San Francisco	Los Angeles	Phoenix
Sales Revenue	$1,500,000	$1,900,000	$1,800,000
Variable Costs	900,000	1,200,000	1,200,000
Fixed Costs	300,000	350,000	250,000
Average Total Assets	1,800,000	2,500,000	1,300,000

Required:

1. Compute the net income for each store.

2. Compute the operating performance ratio for each store.

3. Compute the asset turnover for each store.

4. Compute the return on total assets for each store.

5. Compute the residual income for each store. (The minimum accepted rate of return for the stores are: San Francisco, 15 percent; Los Angeles, 13 percent; and Phoenix, 18 percent.)

P26–6 Transfer Pricing

Jolly Red Tomato Company has two divisions: farming and canning. The farming division grows the tomatoes at a cost of $4 per bushel and sells them to outside customers and to the canning division for $6.50 per bushel. The canning division processes and cans the tomatoes at an incremental cost of $1 per bushel, and then sells them for $0.50 per can. At the present time, one bushel will make 20 cans of processed tomatoes.

Required:

1. Compute each division's percentage return on its cost.

2. **Interpretive Question** The canning division has found an outside supplier that sells tomatoes for $5 a bushel. Would it be wise for the farming division to lower its price to $5? Explain.

3. Compute a negotiated transfer price that would allow the same percentage of net income for each division.

4. What are the two divisions' operating performance ratios with the transfer price calculated above?

P26–7 Transfer Pricing

Hall Enterprises has two divisions: picture tubes and televisions. The picture tube division has always supplied its picture tubes to the television division at a price of $90 per unit. The television division recently found an outside corporation that would supply picture tubes at a cost of $75 per unit. As the television division wishes to maximize its own profits as well as the profits of Hall Enterprises as a whole, it is seeking a more favorable and competitive transfer price from the picture tube division. The picture tube division is currently producing at its capacity of 10,000 units per year. Its variable costs are $50 per unit and it has fixed costs of $200,000 per year.

Required:

1. Assuming that the picture tube division could sell its entire yearly output to outside corporations at its current price of $90 per unit, what transfer price should it charge the television division in order to maximize the net income of Hall Enterprises? Why?
2. If the picture tube division were only able to sell 5,000 units per year to outside television manufacturers at its current price of $90 per unit, what transfer price should it charge the television division to maximize the income of Hall Enterprises? Why?
3. Discuss the advantages and disadvantages of giving the two divisional managers complete autonomy in negotiating transfer prices between the divisions.

P26-8 Unifying Problem: Rate of Return on Total Assets and Cost Allocations

Mesa Corporation, maker of fine sweets, has four divisions: nuts, candy, gum, and the cafeteria. During 1984, the four divisions had the following operating data.

	Nuts	Candy	Gum	Cafeteria
Net Income (assumes no allocation)	$200,000	$150,000	$ 260,000	–
Sales Revenue	900,000	800,000	1,200,000	–
Average Total Assets	400,000	350,000	700,000	$ 80,000
Operating Expenses	700,000	650,000	940,000	182,000
Number of Employees	90	40	10	13

Required:

1. Compute the return on total assets for the producing divisions, assuming that no cafeteria expenses are allocated to the three producing divisions.
2. Compute the amount of cafeteria expenses that would be allocated to the three producing divisions on the basis of the number of employees.
3. Compute the resulting return on total assets for the producing divisions.
4. **Interpretive Question** If you were the manager of the nuts division, how would you feel about the arrangement for allocating cafeteria costs described in (2) above?

P26-9 Unifying Problem: Rate of Return on Total Assets and Cost Allocations

J. R. Holliday Corporation manufactures television sets. The corporation has six departments. Their 1984 operating results are listed below.

	Manufacturing	Packaging	Sales
Sales Revenue	$1,485,000	$2,070,000	$2,475,000
Transfer Costs	–	1,485,000	2,070,000
Variable Costs of the Department	945,000	270,000	135,000
Fixed Costs	300,000	150,000	105,000
Average Total Assets	550,000	300,000	25,000
Number of Employees	42	12	7

	Accounting	Administration	Cafeteria
Sales Revenue	–	–	–
Transfer Costs	–	–	–
Variable Costs of the Department	$ 5,000	–	$40,000
Fixed Costs	130,000	$190,000	15,000
Average Total Assets	30,000	45,000	50,000
Number of Employees	6	8	5

During 1984, 4,500 television sets were produced and sold by J. R. Holliday Corporation. The costs of the three service departments (cafeteria, administration, and accounting) are allocated to the three producing departments.

Required:

1. Determine the pre-allocation return on total assets for each of the producing departments.
2. Allocate all service department costs in the following sequence:
   (a) Cafeteria costs—by number of employees.
   (b) Administration costs—by number of employees.
   (c) Accounting costs—by total departmental costs (including transfer costs) before any allocations.
3. Determine the return on total assets for each producing department after the allocation of service department costs. Also calculate the return on total assets for J. R. Holliday Corporation as a whole.
4. **Interpretive Question** Assuming the Holliday Corporation rates its producing departments by their return on total assets, do you feel that the current transfer prices are satisfactory to the managers of all departments?

P26–10 Unifying Problem: Transfer Prices, Cost Allocations, and Rate of Return on Total Assets

J. C. Willey Corporation has three departments: production, sales, and the cafeteria. The production department makes fire-fighting trucks, which are sold by the sales department, and the cafeteria services these two departments. The following operating data are available for 1984.

	Production	Sales	Cafeteria
Sales Revenue	$1,200,000*	$1,500,000	$12,000
Fixed Costs	600,000	180,000	15,000
Variable Costs	400,000	1,200,000†	21,000
Operating Assets	800,000	400,000	15,000
Number of Employees	8	22	10

* Ten trucks at $120,000 each.
† The cost of the trucks from the production department.

Required:

1. If cafeteria costs are not allocated, what are the returns on total assets for the production and sales departments?
2. At a transfer price of $113,800 per truck and assuming no allocation of the cafeteria's costs, what is each department's operating performance ratio? (Transfer prices are used for performance measurement only.)
3. If cafeteria losses are allocated to production and sales on the basis of the number of employees, how much of the costs will each department bear?
4. Recompute the return on total assets for the two departments, assuming the allocation scheme described in (3) above. (Assume a transfer price of $120,000 per truck.)
5. **Interpretive Question** What are the behavioral and managerial problems associated with allocating service costs to production divisions?

SECTION 7

Managerial Accounting for Decision Making

CHAPTER 27

Nonroutine Operating Decisions

THIS CHAPTER EXPLAINS:

The types of information needed for making nonroutine operating decisions.

How to analyze nonroutine operating decisions, including whether to make or buy a component, whether to drop or add a product, whether to process a product further or sell it as is, how to select the best use of existing resources, and how to set normal and special-order selling prices.

The variety of decisions made by managers can be divided into three broad categories, as we have mentioned in earlier chapters. By far the most numerous are routine decisions that are made on a daily basis and deal primarily with the short run. At the other extreme are capital investment decisions that are made much less frequently and involve the commitment of large amounts of resources for substantial periods of time. In between these extremes are nonroutine operating decisions, which require more careful analysis than routine decisions but are usually less complicated than capital investment decisions.

This chapter describes nonroutine operating decisions that involve revenues and expenses. The next chapter deals with nonroutine decisions that also involve investments—that is, capital investment decisions.

Some Typical Nonroutine Operating Decisions

Some of the most common nonroutine decisions that involve revenues and expenses but not significant investments are

1. Whether to make or buy a component.
2. Whether to add or drop a product or a line of products.
3. Whether to continue processing a product or to sell it as is.

4. How to use existing resources to the best profit advantage.
5. What prices to set for products.

Although every situation is unique, certain principles and approaches apply to all such decisions. Here, an accountant's role is primarily to provide revenue and cost information that will help managers to make decisions that will result in the best short-term utilization of available resources.

The Nature of the Information Needed

Suppose that a manager is thinking of replacing several workers with a new machine. In order to make an intelligent decision, the manager needs to know the costs and probable consequences of each alternative—that is, of buying the machine and of keeping the workers. The extent to which the relevant information may be quantified, or expressed in numbers, is also pertinent to the decision. A manager should always be careful to think through the degree to which the numbers provided are relevant, and to give equal consideration to any qualitative factors involved.

THE DEGREE OF QUANTIFICATION

Some aspects of most business alternatives can be described quantitatively. Other considerations, however, are qualitative and cannot be measured precisely. For example, an accountant can calculate the reduction in hours of labor and wages if the company buys a new machine; but how the union will respond to the purchase is another matter—and impossible to measure with numbers.

In making a decision, a manager must weigh the quantitative factors along with qualitative ones and determine their relative importance. In our example, although the machine might provide cost savings, a manager may reject or defer the purchase plan for fear that employee resentment would cause severe morale problems, with the likelihood of decreased productivity.

Since the accountant's primary function is to accumulate quantitative information, the rest of this chapter is devoted to this aspect of nonroutine operating decisions.

DETERMINING WHICH COSTS ARE RELEVANT

total cost *all the direct and allocated costs of a product; the total of the variable and fixed costs incurred in making the product or providing the service*

In accumulating quantitative information for decision making, the accountant's most difficult task is to determine which information is relevant. You are already familiar with the principle that different costs are needed for different purposes. Thus, total cost—all variable and fixed costs—is used for measuring inventories and cost of goods sold under generally accepted accounting principles. On the other hand, two other cost concepts may apply

differential costs *costs that are not the same for the alternatives being considered*

sunk costs *costs that have been incurred and that cannot be changed by current or future decisions*

to nonroutine operating decisions: differential costs and sunk costs. Differential costs are current or future costs that are different for each alternative under consideration. Costs that are the same for the various alternatives can be ignored in making the decision. Sunk costs are past costs that cannot be changed, and so are not relevant in the decision-making process.

In thinking about decisions involving two or more alternatives, you should be careful to distinguish between differential costs and variable costs. Variable costs are the costs that change as the level of activity changes. Differential costs refer to the total of all costs that distinguish one alternative from the other. For example, if a company needs to decide how many units to produce within a relevant range (the range over which fixed costs do not change), then the variable costs for each production level will be the only differential costs. If the production levels are not within the same relevant range, then the differential costs will include the changing fixed costs as well as the variable costs. In addition, many decisions involve alternatives for which the level of activity does not change. In such cases, the differential costs may be other combinations of variable and/or fixed costs.

To illustrate the relevance of these cost concepts to a decision, we assume that A. B. Hall Company is thinking of purchasing a delivery truck with an estimated useful life of 5 years. Following are the costs of acquiring and operating such a truck.

Costs		
Original Cost		$10,000
Variable Costs per Mile:		
Gasoline and Oil	$0.25	
Repairs and Maintenance	0.03	
Tires	0.02	
Total Variable Costs per Mile		$0.30
Fixed Costs per Year:		
Insurance	$ 500	
Licenses	110	
Depreciation Expense ($10,000/5 years)	2,000	
Total Fixed Costs		$2,610

These variable and fixed operating costs are incurred each year the truck is used. However, they are not all relevant to every decision made about the truck. For the following decisions, we identify the differential costs and the sunk costs, and explain the reason for the classifications.

Decision 1

Should the truck be purchased?

Differential costs: All variable costs (30 cents per mile driven) and all fixed costs ($2,610 per year).

Sunk costs: None.

Comment: All costs are relevant because the truck has not yet been purchased and all costs can be avoided by an alternative decision.

Decision 2

The truck has been owned and used for 2 years but has not been licensed or insured for the current (3rd) year. Should it be licensed and insured or should some other means of transportation be used?

Differential costs:	All variable costs (30 cents per mile driven) and some fixed costs (insurance, $500; licenses, $110).
Sunk costs:	Remaining book value of the truck, $6,000 (at the beginning of the year).
Comment:	As soon as the truck is purchased, its cost becomes a sunk cost. During its estimated life, its remaining book value is a sunk cost. For simplicity, assume that the truck has no resale value. The company must absorb the cost of the truck either by using the truck (and depreciating its cost each year) or by writing off the entire cost. All costs except the depreciation expense and the remaining book value are, therefore, differential and relevant to the decision to license and insure the truck for use.

Decision 3

The truck has been owned and used for 2 years and has been licensed and insured for the current year. Should the truck be used for transporting inventory this year? Should other means be arranged?

Differential costs:	All variable costs (30 cents per mile driven) and no fixed costs.
Sunk costs:	Insurance, $500; licenses, $110; remaining book value, $6,000 (at the beginning of the year).
Comment:	If insurance and license fees are not refundable, these are sunk costs. The depreciation expense for the year and the remaining book value are also sunk costs. That is, the firm must absorb these costs, either by using the truck or by writing them off if the truck is disposed of.

Analysis of these three decisions should help you understand how differential costs are determined and why past costs are usually not considered relevant in making a decision. When they are sunk costs, they have nothing to do with the future. The three decisions also illustrate that variable costs are usually differential.

TOTAL COSTS AND DIFFERENTIAL COSTS

In order to judge which of two alternatives costs less, an accountant may use either the total-cost approach or the differential-cost approach. With the total-cost approach, all costs (both differential and sunk) are identified and assigned to each alternative. Unless qualitative factors alter the picture, a manager will select the alternative with the lowest total cost. The differential-cost approach deals only with differential costs; in other words, it disregards sunk costs and other costs that are the same for the alternatives being considered.

To illustrate the total-cost approach, we will assume that A. B. Hall Company has another decision to make about its truck.

Decision 4

The truck has been owned for 4 years, but it has not yet been licensed or insured for the current (5th) year. Should the truck be used for the last year of its economic life or should it be traded for a new truck?

Pertinent information is in the following table.

	Old Truck	New Truck
Original Cost	$10,000	$12,500
Current Book Value	2,000	
Current Resale Value	1,700	
Resale Value at End of Year	-0-	10,000
Variable Operating Costs	$0.30 per mile	$0.27 per mile
Annual Fixed Costs:		
Insurance	$ 500	$ 550
Licenses	110	110
Depreciation Expense	2,000	2,500
Estimated Mileage per Year	50,000	50,000

On the basis of this information, the total cost of operating the old truck and the total cost of operating the new truck are shown in Exhibit 27-1.

Note that the total cost of operating the old truck includes the yearly $2,000 depreciation expense. If the new truck is bought, this $2,000 book value of the old truck must still be written off. Thus, the $2,000 is a sunk cost and is the same under both alternatives, so it is not relevant to the decision at hand. The current resale value of the old truck, however, is a reduction in cost that will occur only if the new truck is purchased.

EXHIBIT 27-1 **Total-Cost Analysis for the Current Year: Operating the Old Truck Versus Selling It and Buying a New Truck**

Total Costs	Old Truck		New Truck
Variable Costs:			
$0.30 × 50,000 miles	$15,000		
$0.27 × 50,000 miles			$13,500
Fixed Costs:			
Insurance	500		550
Licenses	110		110
Depreciation Expense	2,000		2,500
Book Value of Old Truck to Be Written Off			2,000
Resale Value of Old Truck	-0-		(1,700)
Total Cost of Operation	$17,610		$16,960
Difference		$650	

Three observations should be made about the total-cost approach to analyzing alternatives. First, it highlights the more attractive alternative in terms of cost only. In our example, the data appear to favor buying a new truck. However, this requires an investment of additional funds, which forces a consideration of other factors. Since these factors are covered in the next chapter, we have tried to keep our example simple by assuming a fair market value of $10,000 for the new truck at the end of 1 year. This means that the new truck's annual depreciation expense of $2,500 is equal to the difference between its original cost and its resale value after 1 year. Had the drop in value been greater than the depreciation expense, the excess would have been an additional cost of using the new truck during its first year.

qualitative considerations *factors that affect a decision but that are not subject to measurement in dollar terms*

A second observation is that certain qualitative considerations may override the apparent cost advantage of buying the new truck. For example, the company may find that it can achieve the same savings but with less trouble by hiring an outside firm to ship its product.

Third, the total-cost approach is time-consuming because it involves differential costs as well as costs that are the same for all alternatives under consideration. With the differential-cost approach, only costs that are different need to be accumulated and analyzed. Thus, the costs of licensing both trucks and the $2,000 book value of the old truck to be depreciated or written off would not be considered. Exhibit 27-2 is a list of differential costs taken from Exhibit 27-1.

EXHIBIT 27-2 **Differential-Cost Analysis for the Current Year: Operating the Old Truck Versus Selling It and Buying a New Truck**

Differential Costs	Old Truck	New Truck
Variable Costs	$15,000	$13,500
Insurance	500	550
Depreciation Expense		2,500
Resale Value of Old Truck		(1,700)
Total Differential Costs	$15,500	$14,850
Difference	$650	

Although the differential-cost approach does not produce the same comparative costs as the total-cost approach, it does not alter the relative attractiveness of the alternatives. Both the total-cost and differential-cost analyses show a savings of $650 if the new truck is purchased.

CHOOSING BETWEEN A TOTAL-COST AND A DIFFERENTIAL-COST APPROACH

Since both the total-cost and differential-cost approaches produce the same numerical answer, how does an accountant decide which to use? The answer depends on the circumstances. Assuming that differential costs can easily be identified, the differential-cost approach is usually preferable because it takes less time and reduces the chance of error in the calculation: The fewer costs there are, the less likely it will be that some data will be handled incorrectly. However, a manager may ask to see the total cost of each alternative if he is worried that some relevant costs are more likely to be overlooked with the differential-cost approach.

PRECISION VERSUS RELEVANCE IN THE COLLECTION OF COST DATA

Accountants sometimes must sacrifice cost precision for relevance. Most information collected for financial reporting purposes is historical in nature. Therefore, even if accurate, these past costs may be of little use in the decision-making process. Future costs, though they are only estimates, are often more relevant to decision making. For example, A. B. Hall Company had to decide whether to purchase a new truck before the old truck had worn out. The decision had to be made on the basis of estimates of the new truck's variable cost of operation (which included an estimate of the decline in its value over the year), of the annual mileage, and of the current resale value of the old truck. All these costs were relevant to the decision, but they could not be determined with complete precision.

Basically, then, an important principle of cost use is that it is often necessary to accept less precision for relevance. Managers and accountants need to guard against the use of information simply because it is available. However, they also should strive to make the information used as accurate as possible.

TO SUMMARIZE In making nonroutine operating decisions, managers and accountants must first have a good understanding of which costs are relevant. There are two approaches to analyzing alternatives: total cost and differential cost. With the total-cost approach, all costs—including sunk costs—are accumulated. The differential-cost approach excludes sunk costs and deals only with costs that are not the same for the alternatives being considered. Once the quantitative analysis has been completed, qualitative factors must be considered. Only then can the least-cost alternative be accepted or rejected.

Whether to Make or Buy a Component

If a product consists of a number of parts, management must decide for each component whether to make it or to purchase it from an outside supplier. Over time and based on a consideration of the relevant quantitative and qualitative factors, management develops a long-run policy regarding the use of its facilities to produce components for its products.

The fact that a long-run policy has been established does not mean that the issue is closed. For example, if a firm has idle facilities, management may wish to find a use for those facilities. One possibility is to use the idle capacity in manufacturing components that are normally purchased.

Whether this decision is wise depends not only on the cost considerations, but also on a number of qualitative factors, such as the likely effect on the regular source of supply, the company's ability to produce a high-quality component, and management's interest in keeping workers on the payroll. Thus, even though a firm has a long-run policy of purchasing some components and producing others, certain situations may require decisions that alter that policy.

Assuming that the qualitative factors favor the use of idle facilities in producing the part, what costs are relevant to a make-or-buy decision? In general, the purchase cost and all other costs that can be avoided if the part is purchased are differential costs. Any cost that will be incurred whether the part is purchased or manufactured is not a differential cost and is irrelevant.

To illustrate how the relevant costs in such a decision are identified, we will assume that Ritter Manufacturing Company has excess capacity, which could be used in producing wheel bearings. The accounting department has compiled the following total-cost figures for producing the bearings.

	Costs per Unit	Costs for 1,000 Units
Direct Materials	$ 3.00	$ 3,000
Direct Labor	8.00	8,000
Variable Overhead	4.00	4,000
Fixed Overhead, Direct	2.50	2,500*
Fixed Overhead, Indirect	5.00	5,000†
Total Costs	$22.50	$22,500

* $1,500 of this cost will be avoided if the part is purchased.
† None of the indirect fixed costs will change if the part is purchased.

The company has been buying this bearing from a regular supplier in 1,000-unit quantities at a price of $19 per unit. Should Ritter make or buy the bearings? To answer this question, management must identify the differential costs of each alternative, taking into account any additional resources that may be needed, as well as alternative uses for the idle facilities. Two possible situations are presented here.

SITUATION 1

The idle facilities have no alternative uses.

opportunity cost *the amount of money that could be earned by putting financial resources to their best alternative use compared with the one being considered*

If the idle facilities do not have any practical alternative use, the opportunity cost is zero. With no opportunity cost, the differential costs would be the costs strictly associated with purchasing (for instance, the purchase price) and with manufacturing (direct labor, materials, and so on).

Upon referring to the schedule of costs compiled by the accounting department, you will note that there are two types of irrelevant costs: $1,000 of direct fixed costs that will be incurred whether the part is made or purchased, and indirect fixed costs. The costs of the two alternatives can be presented on a total-cost or a differential-cost basis, as shown in Exhibit

EXHIBIT 27-3 **Analyses of the Costs of Using Idle Facilities (Situation 1)**

	Total-Cost Analysis		Differential-Cost Analysis	
	Buy	Make	Buy	Make
Purchase Cost	$19,000		$19,000	
Direct Materials		$ 3,000		$ 3,000
Direct Labor		8,000		8,000
Variable Overhead		4,000		4,000
Fixed Overhead:				
Direct	1,000	2,500		1,500
Indirect	5,000	5,000		
Total Cost	$25,000	$22,500	$19,000	$16,500
Differences	$2,500		$2,500	

27-3. Although each analysis produces different total costs, both demonstrate that the firm would save $2,500 per 1,000 units ($2.50 per unit) by making the component rather than buying it. The company's final decision would depend, of course, on whether there were negative qualitative factors that would, in the opinion of management, more than offset the $2.50 unit-cost advantage of making the part.

SITUATION 2

The facilities can be rented during the time they are likely to be idle for an incremental net cash inflow of $3,000. Management estimates that, if the facilities are not rented, 1,000 wheel bearings could be manufactured during this time.

incremental net cash inflows *the additional cash generated, as the result of a decision, after all expenses have been deducted; equal to incremental revenues less incremental costs*

incremental revenues *the additional cash generated as the result of a decision*

incremental costs *the additional costs incurred as the result of a decision*

If the only feasible alternative use of the idle facilities will generate incremental net cash inflows (incremental revenues less incremental costs) of $3,000, then the opportunity cost of producing the component will be $3,000, or $3 per unit ($3,000 ÷ 1,000 units). This opportunity cost is an important consideration in the firm's decision to buy or make the part, as shown in Exhibit 27-4. When the opportunity cost is considered, the unit cost of producing the part is 50 cents more than the cost of buying it. Unless there are qualitative factors that override this incremental cost, Ritter should buy the bearing and rent the idle facilities. Remember, the essence of the make-or-buy problem is management's desire to achieve the best utilization of existing facilities in the short run.

Because opportunity costs do not represent actual transactions, they are not recorded in the accounts. However, they are always significant in the decision-making process, since each decision has at least one alternative. Thus, opportunity costs provide a good illustration of why a manager cannot rely solely on the data collected for external financial reports.

EXHIBIT 27-4 **The Effect of an Opportunity Cost on the Analyses (Situation 2)**

	Full-Cost Analysis		Differential-Cost Analysis	
	Buy	Make	Buy	Make
Purchase Cost	$19,000		$19,000	
Direct Material		$ 3,000		$ 3,000
Direct Labor		8,000		8,000
Variable Overhead		4,000		4,000
Fixed Overhead:				
Direct	1,000	2,500		1,500
Indirect	5,000	5,000		
Opportunity Cost, Rental		3,000		3,000
Total Costs	$25,000	$25,500	$19,000	$19,500
Differences	$500		$500	

TO SUMMARIZE In choosing whether to make or buy a component, management must compare the differential costs of making the part, including the opportunity cost of alternative uses of the facilities, with the cost of purchasing the part. Qualitative factors must also be considered, since they may be significant enough to reverse a decision based only on quantitative considerations.

Whether to Drop or Add a Product or a Line of Products

When a product or a market segment (several related products) is losing money, management must decide whether to drop it. Similarly, management must decide when the addition of new products or segments would increase the firm's profits. Such decisions are particularly difficult because the differential costs are not easy to identify and this can lead to analyses based on invalid assumptions, as the following example demonstrates.

Augusta Wholesale Company is thinking of dropping its line of dairy products. The question of the line's value arose because of the July financial results for the company's three divisions.

	Groceries	Drugs	Dairy Products	Totals
Sales Revenue	$250,000	$90,000	$60,000	$400,000
Cost of Goods Sold	170,000	40,000	30,000	240,000
Gross Margin	$ 80,000	$50,000	$30,000	$160,000
Operating Expenses	55,000	30,000	35,000	120,000
Net Income (or Loss)	$ 25,000	$20,000	$ (5,000)	$ 40,000

If the dairy products line is dropped, it seems reasonable to assume that the company's profits will increase by $5,000 as shown here.

	Groceries	Drugs	Totals
Sales Revenue	$250,000	$90,000	$340,000
Cost of Goods Sold	170,000	40,000	210,000
Gross Margin	$ 80,000	$50,000	$130,000
Operating Expenses	55,000	30,000	85,000
Net Income	$ 25,000	$20,000	$ 45,000

This analysis is based on three assumptions.

1. That all the costs shown are differential and therefore relevant to the decision. In other words, there are no joint costs (costs that are common to two or more products or responsibility centers).
2. That the sales of the other lines will not be affected by dropping dairy products.
3. That no qualitative factors have a bearing on the decision.

Before dropping the dairy products line, the company's general manager should check the validity of these assumptions. For simplicity, suppose that assumptions 2 and 3 are valid, and that only assumption 1 needs checking. First, the accounting department must separate the total costs of each division into variable costs, direct fixed costs, and indirect fixed costs, which must be allocated among the divisions. With this new information, the modified report for July might be

	Groceries	Drugs	Dairy Products	Totals
Sales Revenue	$250,000	$90,000	$60,000	$400,000
Variable Costs	190,000	50,000	40,000	280,000
Contribution Margin	$ 60,000	$40,000	$20,000	$120,000
Direct Fixed Costs	20,000	15,000	18,000*	53,000
Contribution to Indirect Fixed Costs	$ 40,000	$25,000	$ 2,000	$ 67,000
Indirect Fixed Costs (allocated on the basis of space used)	15,000	5,000	7,000	27,000
Net Income	$ 25,000	$20,000	$(5,000)	$ 40,000

Only $6,000 of this cost is avoidable if the dairy products line is dropped.

The manager will then analyze the dairy line's contribution to the overall profit of the company in order to determine which costs are avoidable if the line is dropped. The modified report answers this question in part, but not entirely. The variable costs are clearly avoidable since they vary directly with volume. However, indirect fixed costs will be incurred whether or not dairy products are sold. As such, they are not avoidable and will have to be allocated to the remaining divisions if the dairy products line is dropped. The direct fixed costs may or may not be avoidable. For example, depreciation on fixtures or equipment that cannot be used elsewhere or disposed of would be a sunk cost and would be unavoidable.

Assuming that $6,000 of the direct fixed costs of the dairy products line is avoidable, total avoidable costs if the dairy products line is dropped are $46,000 ($6,000 + $40,000 of variable costs). In subtracting this amount from expected dairy products revenues of $60,000, we see that the dairy products line is contributing $14,000 toward covering unavoidable fixed costs, as the following schedule shows.

Sales Revenue		$60,000
Less Differential Costs:		
Variable Costs	$40,000	
Avoidable Direct Fixed Costs	6,000	46,000
Contribution to Cover Unavoidable Direct Fixed Costs and Indirect Fixed Costs		$14,000

By covering $14,000 of indirect and unavoidable fixed costs, the dairy products line is really contributing $14,000 to the company's overall profits. If the dairy products line is dropped, profits will decrease by $14,000 because the sunk portion of the direct fixed costs ($12,000) and all of the allocated indirect fixed costs assigned to dairy products ($7,000) will have to be reassigned to the other product lines. To illustrate this potential decline in profits, the following schedule reassigns the dairy line's unavoidable fixed costs to groceries and drugs.

	Groceries	Drugs	Totals
Sales Revenue	$250,000	$90,000	$340,000
Variable Costs	190,000	50,000	240,000
Contribution Margin	$ 60,000	$40,000	$100,000
Direct Fixed Costs	26,000*	21,000*	47,000
Contribution to Indirect Fixed Costs	$ 34,000	$19,000	$ 53,000
Indirect Fixed Costs	18,500†	8,500†	27,000
Net Income	$ 15,500	$10,500	$ 26,000

* $12,000 of direct fixed costs (sunk costs) attributable to dairy products have been assigned equally to drugs and groceries.

† $7,000 of indirect fixed costs attributable to dairy products have been assigned equally to drugs and groceries.

Although the original report suggested that profits would increase by $5,000 if the dairy products line were dropped, total profits would actually decrease by $14,000 ($40,000 − $26,000). The reason is that the dairy products line is generating revenues that are $14,000 greater than differential costs (variable costs and avoidable fixed costs). This analysis suggests that the dairy products line should not be dropped—unless it can be replaced by another line of products that will contribute more than $14,000 to cover unavoidable fixed costs.

TO SUMMARIZE A product or a market segment should not be dropped unless (1) it does not make a contribution toward covering unavoidable fixed costs, or (2) an alternative product or line of products can be added that will contribute more toward covering any unavoidable fixed costs.

Whether to Process a Product Further or to Sell It As Is

joint manufacturing process *using a single material input to produce more than one product*

joint product costs *all costs incurred before different products are split for separate processing*

In some companies, all of the products evolve out of a joint manufacturing process. Gasoline, oil, and kerosene, for example, are all produced in refining crude oil; various cuts of beef are provided in butchering a steer; and different qualities and types of lumber are available from timber. When this is the case, management must decide whether a particular product from the joint manufacturing process should be sold as it is or processed further at additional cost with the expectation of obtaining a higher price.

In choosing the best time to stop processing a product, management basically compares the incremental costs that would be incurred from further processing with the incremental revenues. If the incremental revenues are greater than the incremental costs, net income is increased and additional processing is worthwhile (unless qualitative factors dictate otherwise). If the incremental revenues are less than the incremental costs, the product should probably be sold without further processing. The costs that a firm incurs before the point at which the different products are split for separate processing are called joint product costs. They are incurred whether the separate products are sold at the point of split or are processed further. Thus, they are not relevant to a choice between the two alternatives.

To illustrate the decision-making process related to further processing, we will assume that Royal Chemical Company derives two products, Boron and Kapon, from a product called Royal. Royal cannot be sold independently, but both Boron and Kapon can be, either at the point of split or after further processing. The cost of producing 75,000 gallons of Royal is $300,000 up to the point of split. Royal is then separated into 40,000 gallons of Boron and 30,000 of Kapon. The remaining 5,000 gallons are lost in the process of separation. The selling prices of Boron and Kapon at the point of split, the costs of processing them further, and the selling prices after this further processing are estimated by the accounting department to be

	Gallons	Net Selling Price per Gallon at Split	Additional Processing Costs	Net Selling Price per Gallon After Processing
Boron	40,000	$7.00	$80,000	$10.00
Kapon	30,000	5.00	90,000	7.50

To help management decide whether to sell Boron and Kapon at the point of split or to process them further, the following analysis would be prepared.

Product: Boron

Sales Revenue After Further Processing (40,000 gallons at $10)	$400,000
Sales Revenue at Point of Split (40,000 gallons at $7)	280,000
Incremental Revenue from Further Processing	$120,000
Incremental Processing Costs	80,000
Incremental Profit from Further Processing	$ 40,000

Product: Kapon

Sales Revenue After Further Processing (30,000 gallons at $7.50)	$225,000
Sales Revenue at Point of Split (30,000 gallons at $5)	150,000
Incremental Revenue from Further Processing	$ 75,000
Incremental Processing Costs	90,000
Incremental Loss from Further Processing	$(15,000)

This analysis shows that further processing of Boron will contribute an additional $40,000 to net income because the additional revenues generated exceed the additional processing costs by $40,000. On the other hand, further processing of Kapon will reduce net income by $15,000 because the additional processing costs are larger than the additional revenues by that amount. Therefore, Kapon should be sold at the point of split.

Another type of analysis assumes that the sales revenue at the point of split is the opportunity cost of further processing. Thus, the sales revenue forgone (opportunity cost) is added to the cost of further processing and the total is compared with the sales revenue after further processing to determine whether further processing is warranted. As the following calculation shows, the decision should be the same as before: Sell Kapon at the point of split and Boron after further processing.

	Boron	Kapon
Sales Revenue at Point of Split (revenue forgone)	$280,000	$150,000
Additional Processing Costs	80,000	90,000
Total Relevant Costs	$360,000	$240,000
Sales Revenue After Additional Processing	400,000	225,000
Gain or Loss from Additional Processing	$ 40,000	$(15,000)

This calculation illustrates that decisions concerning further processing involve opportunity costs, which may or may not be stated explicitly. The schedule in Exhibit 27-5 identifies the best choice.

Selling both products after further processing increases net income by $25,000, but the best choice is to sell Kapon at the point of split and to process Boron further before it is sold. Note that the joint processing costs were not considered in the earlier analyses of the individual products since they are sunk costs. In the analysis of the alternative treatments of Boron and Kapon, however, the joint costs were included simply to illustrate the

EXHIBIT 27-5 A Comparison of Alternatives: Selling After Joint Processing or After Further Processing

	Sell Both Products at Split	Sell Both Products After Further Processing	Sell Kapon at Split and Process Boron Further
Sales Revenue:			
Boron	$280,000	$400,000	$400,000
Kapon	150,000	225,000	150,000
Total Sales Revenue	$430,000	$625,000	$550,000
Joint Product Costs	$300,000	$300,000	$300,000
Further Processing Costs	-0-	170,000	80,000
Total Costs	$300,000	$470,000	$380,000
Net Income	$130,000	$155,000	$170,000

total-cost approach. But they are not really necessary since the difference in net income is the same whether or not the $300,000 of joint costs are included.

In deciding whether to sell products at the point of split or after further processing, management must consider more than the financial advantages and disadvantages of each course of action. Qualitative factors must also be taken into account. For example, management will need to consider the hiring or firing of employees and customers' demands for particular products.

TO SUMMARIZE The analysis of situations involving the processing of products that were derived from a joint process is an example of incremental cost analysis. Joint costs prior to the point of split are sunk costs, which can be ignored in deciding whether products should be sold at the point of split or processed further. Only the incremental revenues and costs after the point of split are relevant to the decision.

Selecting the Best Uses of Existing Resources

When a firm that produces more than one product is operating at or near capacity, management has to answer the question: Should the sales staff try to sell all products to an equal extent? A related question is: Should all orders be accepted regardless of the product? In other words, management must decide how much of each product to sell in order to maximize net income. A firm will normally maximize net income by focusing on the products that contribute the most toward covering fixed costs and providing

critical resource factor *in the manufacturing process, the element that determines operating capacity by its availability*

profit in relation to the critical resource factor. This factor refers to the resource that determines operating capacity by its availability. For instance, if machine hours are the most critical resource, then a company should concentrate on the product for which revenues exceed variable costs by the highest margin per machine hour. Other critical resources might be labor hours, floor space, or special raw materials.

To illustrate, we assume that Condor Manufacturing Company makes brass bowls and trays and is operating at capacity. The company can sell as many bowls and trays as it can produce, but its capacity, at least in the short run, is limited by the availability of skilled direct labor. The revenue and cost data for bowls and trays are

	Bowls	Trays
Selling Price	$10	$16
Variable Costs	6	8
Contribution Margin per Unit	$ 4	$ 8
Percentage Contribution (Contribution Margin ÷ Selling Price)	40%	50%

On the basis of this limited information, it would appear that trays are more profitable than bowls. The sale of one tray will contribute $8 toward fixed costs, whereas the sale of one bowl will contribute only $4.

Before the company can decide whether or not to emphasize trays, however, management must consider the extent to which each product uses the critical resource, skilled-labor hours. If Condor can produce $2\frac{1}{2}$ bowls per hour and only 1 tray per hour, then the sale of bowls will make a greater total contribution to profits than the sale of trays, as shown by the following schedule.

	Bowls	Trays
Contribution Margin per Unit	$ 4	$ 8
Units Produced per Hour	× $2\frac{1}{2}$	× 1
Contribution Margin per Hour	$ 10	$ 8
Number of Hours Available	×8,000	×8,000
Total Contribution–8,000 Hours	$80,000	$64,000

Management can reach the same conclusion if it reverses the calculation—that is, if it begins by multiplying the number of hours available by the units produced per hour. Thus, the maximum number of trays or bowls that could be produced with 8,000 skilled-labor hours is

	Bowls	Trays
Available Labor Hours	8,000	8,000
Units Produced per Hour	× $2\frac{1}{2}$	× 1
Maximum Units of Production	20,000	8,000
Contribution Margin per Unit of Product	× $4	× $8
Total Maximum Contribution	$80,000	$64,000

Even though trays have a higher contribution margin per unit of product ($8 versus $4), bowls have a higher contribution margin per skilled-labor hour ($10 versus $8), which is the critical variable. The management of Condor Company should produce bowls rather than trays, assuming that the company's only critical resource is skilled labor.

However, what if the demand for bowls is limited? In that case, the company should manufacture as many bowls as it can sell and use the balance of the critical resource for producing trays. To illustrate, we assume that the market demand for bowls is 15,000 units. Since it takes only 6,000 skilled-labor hours to make that many bowls (15,000 units ÷ $2\frac{1}{2}$ units/hour = 6,000 hours), 2,000 skilled-labor hours are available to make trays. This means that 2,000 trays can be produced. The combined sales of bowls and trays will contribute $76,000 to cover fixed costs and provide a profit ($4,000 less than the production of bowls alone), as shown here.

	Bowls	Trays
Units Produced:		
Bowls (6,000 hours × $2\frac{1}{2}$)	15,000	
Trays (2,000 hours × 1)		2,000
Contribution Margin per Unit	× $4	× $8
Contribution Margin	$60,000	$16,000
Total Contribution Margin of Bowls and Trays	$76,000	

Note that the foregoing analyses dealt with only two constraints: skilled labor and product demand. If a firm is further limited by other factors—such as machine capacity—management generally has to use the quantitative technique of linear programming to help decide which and how many products to produce and sell. You can learn about this technique in advanced accounting courses. Regardless of the number of constraints, though, the essence of the decision is, once again, to achieve the best short-run utilization of available resources.

TO SUMMARIZE In deciding which product to manufacture, management should choose the item that provides the greatest contribution margin per unit of the most critical resource.

Setting Selling Prices

Pricing a product is partly a matter of guesswork because managers rarely know with any precision how price affects demand—for example, how many more units could be sold if the price were to be lowered by a certain amount. In addition, factors other than price affect the sale of a product; costs are subject to change; and other variables can alter pricing considerations.

The pricing process is further complicated by the fact that there are several broad categories of pricing decisions and the same cost information is not appropriate to all of them. Two primary categories are the normal pricing of products and the pricing of a special order. Other pricing categories, including the pricing of new products, are covered in advanced accounting and marketing texts.

special order *an order that may be priced below the normal price in order to utilize excess capacity and thereby contribute to company profits*

NORMAL PRICING OF PRODUCTS

The price normally charged for a product must be high enough to cover all costs—including production, marketing, and administrative costs—and still provide a reasonable return on the owners' investment. Therefore, all costs—variable as well as a fair share of fixed costs—are relevant to the pricing decision. In some cases, however, the final price may be set somewhat above or below the price suggested by total cost plus a reasonable return. This occurs when pricing decisions are based primarily on supply and demand, competition, and other market factors. For example, textbook prices are strictly competitive. Whether it costs $100,000 or $250,000 to produce a textbook, its price has to be close to that of the nearest competitors.

In supplying cost data to aid management in normal pricing decisions, accountants may present costs by function (manufacturing, selling, administrative) or by behavior (fixed or variable). To illustrate the two approaches, we assume that Apco Electronics is pricing a calculator. The relevant costs for each approach are as follows:

By Function

Direct Materials	$ 6
Direct Labor	8
Manufacturing Overhead (200% × number of direct-labor hours)	16
Total Manufacturing Cost	$30
Markup to Cover Selling and Administrative Expenses and Provide a Reasonable Return on Investment (0.40 × selling price)	20
Estimated Normal Selling Price	$50

By Cost Behavior

Direct Materials	$ 6
Direct Labor	8
Variable Manufacturing Overhead	7
Variable Selling and Administrative Overhead Expenses	4
Total Variable Costs	$25
Markup to Cover Fixed Costs and Provide a Reasonable Return on Investment (0.50 × selling price)	25
Estimated Normal Selling Price	$50

The markups used in these two approaches are based on the selling price. Since it is customary for marketing people to base markups on selling price, it is desirable for accountants to compile data using the same base. How do we calculate the markup as a percentage of the selling price before that price is known? If the markup is to be 40 percent of the selling price, as in our first example, the total manufacturing cost must be 60 percent of the selling price. So we simply divide the manufacturing cost by 60 percent to get the selling price ($30 ÷ 0.60 = $50). Then the selling price minus the manufacturing cost is the markup ($50 − $30 = $20).

If costs are assembled by function, the markup must be large enough to cover all selling and administrative costs and provide a reasonable return on investment. If costs are assembled by their behavioral characteristics, the markup must be large enough to cover all fixed costs and generate a reasonable return on investment. Of the two approaches, the cost behavior approach is the more practical one. Because it provides insights into the behavior of costs and their relationship to volume and profits, it is applicable to both normal pricing and special orders.

PRICING SPECIAL ORDERS

Managers frequently have to decide whether to reduce the price of a product to obtain an order that otherwise would be lost to the competition. Typical situations involving a possible price reduction are

1. A manufacturer sells products under its own brand name, as well as to retail chain stores for sale under the chain's brand name.
2. A firm, such as a building contractor or an equipment manufacturer, sells its products or services in a competitive bidding situation.
3. A firm sells a product under distress conditions, for instance, when there has been a sharp decline in demand for its products because of a new product offered by a competitor.
4. A firm has excess capacity and would like to increase its profits through better utilization of its resources. Management believes that a price reduction would stimulate demand enough to make full use of the idle capacity.
5. A product has a significant sales potential with a firm's foreign customers, whose market demands lower prices than those in the United States.

In these situations, there is an implication that a firm has unused capacity that can be utilized to fill the special order. In pricing such orders, management must adhere to a basic principle: As long as the price charged is greater than the incremental costs of manufacturing the product, a firm will increase its overall profits by the excess of the revenues over these incremental costs. Management must therefore know the incremental costs. This information will indicate the price at which the special order will begin to contribute to the firm's profits.

To illustrate, we will assume that Apco Electronics, which usually sells hand calculators for $19, receives an order from a large department store chain for 10,000 calculators at a price of $13 each. The calculators are to be sold under the store's brand name. Apco currently has excess capacity that could be used in producing enough calculators to fill the order. Should the company accept the order?

The answer to this question does not, of course, depend on cost and price factors alone. An obvious consideration, for example, would be whether the order would result in a significant loss of sales of the company's own brand of calculators.

The decision could also depend on how the cost information is presented. If the accounting department presents the data on a total-cost basis, categorizing costs by function, the manager might erroneously reject the order on the assumption that the firm would lose money, as the following calculations suggest.

Special Order for Calculators

Sales Price		$ 13
Manufacturing Costs:		
Direct Materials	$3	
Direct Labor	4	
Manufacturing Overhead	9	
Total Manufacturing Costs		16
Loss per Unit		$ 3
Number of Units in Order		× 10,000
Expected Loss Exclusive of Marketing and Administrative Expenses		$ 30,000

It is not unusual for managers to base decisions on total-cost information because the data are readily available, having been collected in order to prepare the annual financial statements. Unfortunately, such information may lead management to the wrong conclusion—in this case, to reject the order.

The contribution-margin approach to product pricing, on the other hand, takes cost behavior into account. Thus, if the accounting department presents the cost data on an incremental cost basis, the calculation is as follows:

Special Order for Calculators

Sales Price		$ 13
Variable Costs:		
Direct Materials	$3	
Direct Labor	4	
Variable Manufacturing Overhead	3	
Variable Marketing and Administrative Expenses	1	
Total Variable Costs		11
Contribution Margin to Cover Fixed Costs and Provide a Profit		$ 2
Number of Units in Order		× 10,000
Expected Contribution to Fixed Costs and Profit if Order Is Accepted		$ 20,000

This analysis clearly suggests that management should accept the order. The contribution-margin approach provides not only the relevant costs, but also a price floor (the total incremental costs of $11) below which management should probably not accept the order. As long as the price exceeds total incremental costs, the firm will increase its profits by accepting the order. This analysis assumes that fixed costs will not change, that the company has no better alternative uses for its excess capacity, and that special sales by the chain will have no adverse effect on Apco's normal sales. However, what if regular customers hear about this special order and insist on lower prices, thus disrupting the normal pricing structure? This and other qualitative factors must be considered.

A manager must also consider whether acceptance of such an order would be a violation of the Robinson–Patman Act. This legislation, enacted in 1936, prohibits firms from quoting different prices to competing customers for the same goods unless differences in price can be attributed to differences in cost. In the case of Apco Electronics, the sale is probably legal because the calculators are to be sold under the store's brand name, and the store will assume all advertising costs.

The contribution-margin approach to pricing can also be used in explaining why theater tickets are less expensive for matinees than for evening performances, why airline economy fares are less expensive than regular tourist-class fares, and why it is cheaper to make telephone calls at night and on weekends than on weekdays. If there is excess capacity that can be used to provide a service or make a product that will generate more revenue than the incremental cost of providing the service or making the product, then the firm will increase its profits by the amount of the contribution margin.

A few words of caution are in order when making these types of decisions. First, absolutely all incremental costs must be identified or the analysis may lead to an erroneous decision. Second, a company must not accept too many orders that cover only variable costs or it will not be able to cover its fixed costs. This could happen if a manager making normal pricing decisions were to base them on total variable costs rather than on total cost.

TO SUMMARIZE For normal pricing of products, management should use the total-cost approach, which prevents the deterioration of a firm's long-run pricing structure. For special-order pricing decisions, the contribution-margin approach is more appropriate. If the contribution approach is used for normal pricing, the markup should be high enough to cover total fixed costs and provide a reasonable return on investment.

CHAPTER REVIEW

Nonroutine operating decisions involve the best uses of existing resources in order to maximize profits. Examples include (1) whether to make or buy a component, (2) whether to drop or add a product or line of products, (3) whether to sell a product at the point of split from a joint process or to process it further, (4) how best to utilize an existing resource that limits production, and (5) what price to set on regular products and on special orders. These decisions require consideration of both quantitative and qualitative information.

The relevant cost and revenue data for decision making are not always generated by the firm's information system. For instance, opportunity costs are not recorded in the accounts and many costs will not have been characterized as fixed or variable. In addition, the information system usually collects historical data for the purpose of preparing the annual financial statements. Since historical costs are usually sunk costs, they often are not relevant to decisions about the future.

Whether a cost is considered in a given situation depends on what approach is used. If the analysis of alternatives is based on total costs, all future costs, including opportunity costs, are relevant. If the analysis is based on differential costs, only those future costs, including opportunity costs, that will differ among the alternatives are relevant costs.

Cost and revenue information helps management decide which of the alternatives will maximize profits in the short run. However, managers must also be aware of qualitative factors—the events or elements that may affect the choice but that are not subject to measurement. If qualitative factors dictate against a particular alternative, then that alternative may be rejected, even though the quantitative analysis suggests that it will make the greatest short-run contribution to profit.

KEY TERMS AND CONCEPTS

critical resource factor (897)
differential costs (884)
incremental costs (890)
incremental net cash inflows (890)
incremental revenues (890)
joint manufacturing process (894)
joint product costs (894)
opportunity cost (889)
qualitative considerations (887)
special order (899)
sunk costs (884)
total cost (883)

REVIEW PROBLEM

A Nonroutine Decision: Whether to Make or Buy a Part

Ajax Manufacturing Company makes lawn mowers. It has been buying a component from a regular supplier for $11.50 per unit. Since Ajax has been operating recently at less than full capacity, the president is considering whether to make the part rather than purchase it. The estimated total cost of making the part under the company's absorption costing system is $14.40, computed as follows:

Direct Materials	$ 3.20
Direct Labor	5.60
Manufacturing Overhead (100% of direct-labor cost)	5.60
Estimated Total Cost to Make	$14.40

Variable overhead costs are estimated to be 40 percent of direct-labor costs.

Solution

Unless qualitative factors override the cost estimates, Ajax should make the part rather than purchase it from an outside supplier. The decision will be the same whether the calculations are based on differential costs only or on total costs.

Differential-Cost Analysis

	Cost to Make	Cost to Buy
Purchase Price		$11.50
Direct Materials	$ 3.20	
Direct Labor	5.60	
Variable Manufacturing Overhead (40% of direct-labor cost)	2.24	
Differential Cost to Make the Part	$11.04	
Differential Cost to Buy the Part		$11.50
Cost Savings by Making the Part	$ 0.46	

Total-Cost Analysis

	Cost to Make	Cost to Buy
Purchase Price		$11.50
Direct Materials	$ 3.20	
Direct Labor	5.60	
Variable Manufacturing Overhead	2.24	
Fixed Manufacturing Overhead	3.36	3.36
Total Cost to Make	$14.40	
Total Cost to Buy		$14.86

The fixed manufacturing overhead cost applies to both making and buying the part under the total-cost analysis, since these costs will be incurred whichever alternative is selected.

DISCUSSION QUESTIONS

1 Most accounting systems are designed to collect financial information for the purpose of preparing financial statements. What problems does this create for an accountant who is asked to compile relevant data for use by managers making nonroutine decisions? Explain.

2 What is a differential cost? Give an example of how differential costs are used by managers making nonroutine decisions.

3 What is a sunk cost? Why are sunk costs irrelevant in nonroutine decision making?

4 In deciding whether to replace an old asset with a new one, which of the following are differential revenues and costs?

(a) The cost of the new equipment.
(b) The resale value of the old equipment.
(c) The resale value of the new equipment.
(d) The book value of the old equipment.
(e) The operating costs of the new equipment.

5 Distinguish between the total-cost approach and the differential-cost approach to analyzing data for nonroutine decisions.

6 What is the major limitation of using the total-cost approach to analyze data for nonroutine decisions?

7 Why must business decisions be based on qualitative, as well as quantitative, information? Explain.

8 Distinguish between the relevance and the accuracy of a cost. Why is the distinction important?

9 Explain what costs are generally relevant to make-or-buy decisions.

10 What is an opportunity cost? Give an example.

11 Explain why opportunity costs are not included in the accounting records.

12 What is an incremental cost? Give an example of how incremental costs are used by management in making nonroutine decisions.

13 Distinguish between incremental costs and differential costs.

14 Distinguish between variable costs and differential costs. Why is the distinction important?

15 What determines whether a product should be sold at the point of split from a joint process or processed further? (Assume that the decision is to be based solely on quantitative information.)

16 Why is the contribution margin per unit of a critical resource more important than the contribution margin per unit of product in deciding which products to produce and sell?

17 Identify four types of resources that could be limiting factors in selecting which products to make and sell.

18 The contribution-margin approach is most useful for setting prices on special orders. Explain.

19 Can a fixed cost be relevant to a decision? Explain.

20 If total manufacturing costs, including fixed overhead, are larger than the price offered by a purchaser for a special order, the order should not be accepted because the profits of the company will be adversely affected. Do you agree? Explain. (Ignore qualitative factors.)

21 What is the significance of idle capacity in determining the price of a special order?

EXERCISES

E27-1 Classifying Decisions

For each situation below, indicate whether the decision appears to be a routine operating decision (ROD), a nonroutine operating decision (NOD), or a long-run investment decision (LRI).

1. Echo Corporation is deciding whether to make a part for a new product or to buy the part from another company.
2. Xalo Company produces three products. The production manager needs to prepare a weekly schedule in order to determine how much of each product to manufacture on each machine.
3. Bloch Company is considering investing in a new production plant in Mexico.
4. Ace Company is considering discontinuing production of marked playing cards.
5. The inventory manager of Pronto Company is determining how much raw material to order next month.
6. Montco, Inc. has received a special order to produce 10,000 units of its best-selling product but the purchase price is less than the normal selling price.

E27-2 Qualitative Factors

Cane Chair Company manufactures wooden chairs. In producing the chairs, a great deal of scrap wood is created. The company presently uses the wood as fuel in a factory furnace. However, it has the opportunity to send the scrap wood to a subcontractor, which would turn it into pressed board that can be used to produce small end tables as a new product.

Identify any qualitative factors that Cane Chair might want to consider in deciding how to use the scrap wood.

E27-3 Relevant Costs

E. Z. Dozit Company provides janitorial services for office buildings. Last year the firm acquired a cleaning machine for $100,000. The firm expected to use the machine for 5 years. However, this year a new, more efficient machine has been introduced on the market. The accountant for E. Z. Dozit has determined that the annual total operating costs for the old machine were $240,000. The annual operating costs for the new machine would be $200,000 and the purchase price is $130,000. The president of E. Z. Dozit feels the company should not buy the new machine. He points out that the operating costs of $200,000 and the purchase price of $130,000 for the new machine, plus the original cost of the old machine of $100,000, are greater than the operating costs for the old machine.

1. Do you agree with the president?
2. What type of cost is the $100,000 purchase price of the old machine?

E27-4 Make-or-Buy Decisions

Clarke Company needs 40,000 miniature engines to complete its toy fire trucks. The relevant costs of making and buying the part are as follows:

Cost to Make the Part:		
Direct Materials	$ 5	
Direct Labor	10	
Variable Overhead	7	
Fixed Overhead	8	$30.00
Cost to Buy the Part from Another Company:		$28.80

If Clarke Company buys rather than makes the part, some of the facilities still cannot be used in another manufacturing activity. Twenty-five percent of the fixed overhead costs will still be incurred regardless of which decision is made.

Identify the differential costs of making the part as a basis for deciding whether to make or buy it.

E27-5 Make-or-Buy Decisions

Reece Company has been manufacturing 8,000 units of part X for its products. The unit cost for the part is as follows:

Direct Materials	$ 3
Direct Labor	8
Variable Overhead	4
Applied Fixed Overhead	6
Total	$21

A supplier has offered to sell 8,000 units of part X to Reece for $18 each. If the part is purchased, Reece can use the facilities to manufacture another product, which would generate a contribution margin of $4,000. Seventy-five percent of the fixed overhead costs will still be incurred even if the part is purchased.

Compute the net differential cost to Reece in deciding whether to make or buy the part.

E27-6 Dropping a Product Line

Murray, Inc. manufactures skis, ski boots, and ski poles for downhill skiing. The company is thinking of dropping ski poles as a product line. The following report was prepared by the accounting department.

	Skis	Ski Boots	Ski Poles	Total
Sales Revenues	$480,000	$210,000	$50,000	$740,000
Variable Costs	370,000	140,000	24,000	534,000
Contribution Margin	$110,000	$ 70,000	$26,000	$206,000
Direct Fixed Costs	40,000	20,000	27,000*	87,000
Contribution to Indirect Fixed Costs	$ 70,000	$ 50,000	$(1,000)	$119,000
Indirect Fixed Costs†	35,000	20,000	5,000	60,000
Net Income	$ 35,000	$ 30,000	$(6,000)	$ 59,000

* These are sunk costs and are unavoidable even if the product line is dropped.
† Allocated on the basis of direct-labor hours.

Should the ski-pole line be dropped? Why or why not?

E27-7 Dropping a Product Line

Refer to E27-6. Assume the same facts except that all of the direct fixed costs of making ski poles could be avoided if the line were dropped.

Should Murray, Inc. drop the ski-pole line? Why or why not?

E27-8 Adding a New Product

Morgan Corporation is thinking of adding a new product line. Marketing surveys indicate that sales of the product would be 200,000 units. Each unit sells for $4. Variable costs would be $2.80 per unit, direct fixed costs would be $120,000, and $90,000 of the company's indirect fixed costs would be allocated to the new product. The company does not expect the new product to affect the sales of its other products.

Should Morgan Corporation add the new product? Why or why not?

E27-9 Incremental Processing Costs and Revenues

Fancy Paints Company has been known for years for its two excellent interior wall paints: Nice & Smooth and Rich & Thick. The company has discovered that by processing Rich & Thick further it could produce a slightly different paint.

Nice & Smooth and Rich & Thick are produced jointly at a cost of $160,000, which is allocated equally between them. If Rich & Thick were processed further, its selling price would increase by $2.25 per unit and the additional cost per unit would be $1.80.

1. On the basis of the information given (and disregarding qualitative factors), should the company process Rich & Thick further? Do you have enough information to make a recommendation? Explain.
2. Is the joint cost of $160,000 relevant to this decision? Why or why not?

E27-10 Contribution Margin per Unit of a Critical Resource

Round Ball Company produces two products: soccer balls and volleyballs. Both products are extremely popular and the company can sell as many as it can produce. Round Ball, however, can produce only a limited number of balls because only 12,000 direct-labor hours are available. It takes 2 hours of direct labor to produce a soccer ball and 1.5 hours to produce a volleyball. The selling price of a soccer ball is $34 and the variable costs are $20. The selling price of a volleyball is $26, with variable costs of $14.

Should Round Ball Company produce and market soccer balls or volleyballs?

E27-11 Contribution Margin per Unit of a Critical Resource

Communications, Inc. is planning production for the next year. The company produces both walkie-talkies and CB radios. Sales for each product are estimated to exceed production capacity, which is limited because of a special metal used in both walkie-talkies and CBs. The contribution margin for walkie-talkies is $10 per set and for CBs is $8 per set. Two sets of walkie-talkies can be produced with 1 pound of the special metal, whereas three CBs can be produced with 1 pound of the metal. Communications, Inc. has 20,000 pounds of the metal available for this year's production.

Which product should Communications, Inc. produce? Why?

E27-12 Contribution Margin per Unit of a Critical Resource

Stearns, Inc. manufactures three super-sports-hero dolls: Super Dunk, Pete Tulip, and Zonk. Production, however, is limited by the skilled labor necessary to produce these unique dolls. Data on each of the dolls are as follows:

	Super Dunk	Pete Tulip	Zonk
Contribution Margin per Doll	$6	$4	$5
Dolls Produced per Hour	20	28	25
Expected Total Market Volume (units)	20,000	9,000	100,000

Total skilled-labor hours available: 4,500 hours.

Assuming that there are no relevant qualitative factors, how many dolls of each type should be produced by Stearns, Inc.?

E27-13 Critical Resource Constraints

Whiz Kids manufactures two computer games. Far Out is a quiz game about astronomy and Dynamite is a mystery game. The company has a limited supply of skilled labor and also has been able to obtain only a limited amount of "chips," a necessary part in the production process.

Information on each product is as follows:

	Far Out	Dynamite
Contribution Margin per Unit	$4	$3
Units Produced per Hour	2	3
Units Produced per 100 Chips	80	60

Anticipated sales exceed capacity for both products.
Total labor hours available: 9,000 hours.
Total chips available: 30,000 chips.

1. Identify the scarce resource under which Whiz Kids must operate.
2. Which product should be produced?

E27-14 Pricing Regular Products

Personal Care, Inc. is considering what price to charge for Sparkle, a toothpaste. The accountant has been asked to prepare an estimated normal selling price based on the costs. Costs of producing one tube of Sparkle are 20 cents for direct materials, 10 cents for direct labor, 20 cents for variable manufacturing overhead, and 10 cents for variable selling and administrative overhead. Total direct fixed costs are $10,000. The company estimates that a markup of 40 percent of the selling price is necessary to cover fixed costs and provide a reasonable return on investment.

1. Calculate the estimated normal selling price.
2. Would you recommend that the company obtain any other information before establishing a sales price?

E27–15 Special-Order Pricing

You are the controller for Moore Shoe Company. The company has excess shoes, which it has not been able to market through its own distribution outlets. The president is negotiating with a large department store chain to sell Moore's shoes in order to utilize excess capacity. He has asked you to estimate the minimum selling price below which Moore should not accept an order from the retail chain.

Cost information per pair of shoes is

Direct Materials	$8
Direct Labor	5
Manufacturing Overhead:	
Variable	3
Fixed	2
Selling and Administrative:	
Variable	1
Fixed	3

The fixed costs are the same whether or not the order is accepted.

1. What is the minimum selling price the company should accept based solely on cost information (not considering qualitative factors)?
2. Assume that the president agrees to sell 20,000 pairs at a price of $19 per pair. What would the expected increase in profit be?

PROBLEMS

P27–1 Make-or-Buy Decisions

Moline Company manufactures several toy products. One is a large plastic truck, which requires a plastic truck body, two metal axles, and four rubber wheels. Moline presently manufactures all the parts and assembles them into a finished product.

Another toy company has offered to sell the parts to Moline at $1.70 per truck if 20,000 or more parts are purchased each year, and at $2 per truck if less than 20,000 parts are purchased. Moline is considering this offer. The space used in producing the parts could be used for a new toy, which is scheduled to begin production next year. If Moline continues to produce the parts for the plastic truck, the company will have to lease space from another company in an adjacent building to produce the new toy. The yearly lease (rent) would be $8,000 per year.

Other information related to each truck is

	Produce Parts	Assemble Truck	Totals
Direct Materials	$1.10	$0.20	$1.30
Direct Labor	0.30	0.20	0.50
Variable Overhead	0.20	0.15	0.35
Fixed Overhead	0.20	0.40	0.60
Total Manufacturing Costs	$1.80	$0.95	$2.75

The marketing department has estimated that sales for the plastic truck will be approximately 16,000 units per year for the next 3 years.

Required:

1. Describe Moline Company's two alternatives for this decision.
2. What costs are relevant to the decision?
3. Which alternative should Moline Company select?
4. What would be the best decision had Moline planned to purchase the parts and leave the space idle?
5. **Interpretive Question** What are some of the qualitative factors that Moline Company might consider in making the decision?

P27–2 Unifying Problem: Make-or-Buy Decisions (Differential Costs, Sunk Costs, Opportunity Costs)

Zero Corporation manufactures freezers for residential use. The company is planning to produce a new freezer suitable for apartments. These smaller freezers require a component that Zero Corporation can either make itself or buy from a subcontractor. The subcontractor will sell the part for $46. The costs for making 12,000 units of the part are as follows:

Direct Materials	$20 per unit
Direct Labor	$15 per unit
Variable Overhead	$10 per unit
Fixed Overhead	$40,000*

* The $40,000 fixed overhead includes $24,000 of indirect fixed costs allocated to the part and $16,000 for a production manager.

If the part is produced, Zero Corporation will use an idle machine it already owns. If the part is bought, the company plans to rent the machine and the factory space to another company for $8,000 and $14,000, respectively, a year.

Zero expects that, if the part is produced, the company will be able to schedule production so that no warehouse space will be needed. However, if the part is bought, Zero will need to use warehouse space for which it will have to pay $2,000 a year in rent.

Required:

1. Identify any opportunity costs relevant to the decision to make or buy the component.
2. Determine the differential costs of making the product.
3. Determine the differential costs of buying the product.
4. Would you recommend that Zero make or buy the component? Why? What qualitative considerations should be part of this decision?

P27-3 Special-Order Pricing

Sound Company manufactures portable radios. R. H. Gamble, a large retail merchandiser, wants to buy 200,000 radios from Sound Company for $12 each. The radio would carry Gamble's name and would be sold in its stores.

Sound Company normally sells 420,000 radios a year at $16 each; its production capacity is 540,000 units a year. Cost information for the radios is as follows:

Production Costs:	
Variable Production Costs	$7
Fixed Overhead ($2,100,000 ÷ 420,000 units)	5
Selling and Administrative Expenses:	
Variable	1
Fixed ($420,000 ÷ 420,000 units)	1

The $1 variable selling and administrative expenses would not be applicable to the radios ordered by R. H. Gamble, since that is one large order. R. H. Gamble has indicated that the company is not interested in signing a contract for less than 200,000 radios.

Required:

1. Identify any opportunity costs that Sound Company should consider when making the decision.
2. Determine whether Sound Company should accept R. H. Gamble's offer.

P27-4 Choosing Between Two Machines

Quick Burger is thinking of making the hamburger rolls for its chain of fast-food restaurants. Two machines, A and B, are being considered for purchase. The company now purchases the rolls from an outside supplier for 12 cents each. The cost information for producing the rolls would be

	Machine A	Machine B
Variable Costs per Roll	$0.08	$0.07
Fixed Costs—Annual Operating Costs	$1,750	$ 2,500
Initial Cost of Machine	$5,000	$12,000
Salvage Value at End of 5 Years	-0-	$ 4,000
Estimated Life of Machine	5 years	5 years

Required:

1. At a sales volume of 300,000 rolls per year, which of these alternatives is better—buying the rolls or using machine A or machine B? (Ignore the time value of money and assume straight-line depreciation.)
2. At what level of production would you be indifferent between machine A and machine B? Which machine is preferable if production exceeds this volume?

P27-5 Adding and Dropping Product Lines

Brent Manufacturing Company has been producing three products: A, B, and C. Now that the plant has been shifted to an assembly-line operation, a fourth product, D, has been added. Each product has its own assembly-line operation producing 10,000 units. Total fixed costs of $23,000 are divided proportionately based on the space allocated to each assembly line. Other pertinent information is given below.

	A	B	C	D
Selling Price per Unit	$3.00	$2.50	$2.70	$1.50
Variable Cost per Unit	$2.00	$1.80	$1.80	$1.30
Number of Square Feet	800	600	500	400

Required:

1. Prepare a schedule that shows net income for each product line.
2. Would total company income increase if product D were dropped? Why or why not?
3. If you could double the production of A, B, or C in place of having D, which would you choose?

P27-6 Discontinuing a Product Line

Execudesk Company presently sells three products: desk calendars, pen sets, and paper-clip holders. The company is thinking of discontinuing the production and sales of paper-clip holders. However, because many customers buy the products as a set, Execudesk estimates that the sales of the other two products will decrease by 20 percent if the paper-clip holders are discontinued.

Current data on each of the three products are provided below.

	Desk Calendars	Pen Sets	Paper-Clip Holders	Totals
Units	40,000	20,000	12,000	
Sales Revenue	$280,000	$240,000	$24,000	$544,000
Variable Costs	$160,000	$160,000	$26,000	$346,000
Direct Fixed Costs	$ 40,000	$ 20,000	$ 5,000*	$ 65,000
Indirect Fixed Costs	$ 30,000	$ 40,000	$ 6,000	$ 76,000

* No direct fixed costs are avoidable if the product line is dropped.

Required:

1. What is the contribution of the paper-clip holders to covering fixed costs?
2. Would you recommend dropping the paper-clip-holder product line? Why or why not?

P27-7 Shutting Down or Continuing Operations

Conestoga Campground is open year round. However, 80 percent of its revenues are generated from May through October. Since only 20 percent of the revenues are generated from November to April, the campground is considering closing during those months. The yearly revenues and cost information expected by Conestoga for next year if the campground does not close are

Camping Fees	$1,800,000
Variable Costs	990,000
Fixed Costs ($40,000 per month)	480,000

The cost to close the campground at the end of October would be $20,000, and the cost to reopen in May would be $50,000. If the campground is closed, the total fixed costs are only $25,000 per month rather than the $40,000 per month when the campground is open.

Required:

Determine if Conestoga Campground should close from November to April or remain open for the entire year.

P27-8 Determining Production with a Critical Resource Limitation

A company is examining two of its products, X-121 and Y-707. The following information is being reviewed.

	X-121	Y-707
Unit Selling Price	$28.50	$21.00
Materials Required per Unit	$ 3.00	$ 1.50
Direct Labor Required per Unit	$ 2.50	$ 1.25
Overhead (variable) per Unit	$ 0.50	$ 1.00
Production Time per Unit (in hours)	1.5	1

Required:

1. Which item should the company manufacture if there is no constraint on hours of production?
2. If full production capacity is 1,500 hours, and if the company can sell all the units it makes, which item should it manufacture? Why?

P27-9 Production and Advertising

Martin Company manufactures only two products—a battery charger and a testing machine for automobile engines. An average of 30,000 chargers and 50,000 testers are sold each year. This year, the company can afford only $60,000 for advertising the products, which is just enough to advertise one product effectively. The marketing manager expects that the sales of chargers will increase by 20 percent if they are advertised, and that the sales of testers will increase by 10 percent if they are advertised.

The following information about the two products has been provided by the accountant.

	Charger	Tester
Selling Price per Unit	$70	$90
Variable Cost per Unit	$30	$40
Fixed Cost per Unit	$30	$40
Production Time per Unit (in hours)	2	4

Required:

1. If Martin had an unlimited number of labor hours, would you recommend that it advertise either of its products? If yes, which one and why?
2. Assume that Martin has a capacity of 260,000 labor hours. Would you still advertise? If so, which product would you advertise?

P27-10 Incremental Processing Costs and Revenues

NBD Company manufactures three items—Nian, Bian, and Dian—which are used in the production of fabrics. Each item can be sold at the point that all three split from the joint production process, or they can be processed further. Presently, Nian and Bian are processed past the point of split. The joint cost of producing the three items to the point of split is $450,000. The costs past the point of split are variable and can be traced to each product. The $450,000 joint costs are allocated to each product equally.

The following information is available.

	No. of Gallons Produced	Selling Price per Gallon at Point of Split	Additional Processing Costs	Selling Price per Gallon After Processing
Nian	100,000	$10	$120,000	$12
Bian	40,000	9	90,000	11
Dian	60,000	11	?	13

Required:

1. Do you agree with NBD's present strategy of selling Nian and Bian after the two products have been processed further? Why?
2. What maximum additional processing costs could be incurred to process Dian further and still leave a profit?

P27–11 Determining Production with a Critical Resource Limitation

Cates Corporation produces three sizes of television sets: 10-inch screen, 19-inch screen, and 24-inch screen. The revenues and costs per unit for each size are as follows:

	Screen Size		
	10-inch	19-inch	24-inch
Selling Price	$195	$325	$450
Variable Costs:			
Direct Materials	$ 55	$100	$126
Direct Labor	80	120	180
Variable Overhead	40	60	90
Total Variable Costs	$175	$270	$396
Contribution Margin	$ 20	$ 45	$ 54
Units Ordered for Next Week	200	150	75

The company has a constraint on the amount of skilled labor available to produce television sets. Direct laborers are paid $8 per hour. The total amount of labor time available for the next week's production is 2,700 hours.

Required:

If the company has more orders each week than it can fill, which size or sizes of television sets should be produced and sold first to maximize the company's profit?

CHAPTER 28

Capital Budgeting

THIS CHAPTER EXPLAINS:

The concepts that underlie capital budgeting.

The major capital budgeting techniques: the payback method, the unadjusted rate of return method, the net present value method, and the internal rate of return method.

Sensitivity analysis: assessing the potential effects of uncertainty in capital budgeting.

How to use capital budgeting techniques in ranking projects.

The need for evaluating qualitative factors in capital budgeting decisions.

Some people seem incapable of planning effectively. They move from one emergency to another, never stopping to consider future needs. As a result, minor problems often turn into major ones.

Unfortunately, some businesses are operated in a similar manner. To keep production going, a foreman will repair, at considerable cost, an old, obsolete machine that will probably have to be replaced in 6 months. Management will add a new product that improves current earnings but loses money in the long run. A company will purchase a component that it could have manufactured more economically. Many such instances of poor planning could be cited, but these make the essential point: Proper planning and careful consideration of investment alternatives—particularly those that involve large outlays and the potential for a significant long-run effect on profitability—are essential if management's goals are to be reached.

capital budgeting *systematic planning for long-term investment decisions*

In this chapter we examine capital budgeting, the systematic planning for long-term investment decisions. Note that while long-term investments are generally defined to include the purchase of stocks and bonds as well as operational assets such as land, buildings, and equipment, in capital budgeting the term "investment" refers to the purchase of operational assets only.

To assist management in making long-term investment decisions, several techniques have been developed, the most widely used of which are dis-

cussed in this chapter. The focus is on the methods that take into account the time value of money: the net present value method and the internal rate of return method. But first we must introduce some basic concepts.

The Conceptual Basis of Capital Budgeting

capital *the total amount of money or other resources owned or used to acquire future income or benefits*

return of investment *a return to an investor of only the principal amount of money invested*

return on investment *a return to an investor of earnings on money invested*

The term capital may be defined broadly as any form of material wealth. As used in business, it is more specifically defined as the total amount of money or other resources owned or used by an individual or a company to acquire future income or benefit.

Thus, capital is something to be invested with the expectation that it will be recovered along with a profit, and capital budgeting is the planning for that investment. From a quantitative viewpoint, the success of an investment depends on the amount of future net cash inflows (or future cash savings) in relation to the cost (current cash outlays) of the investment. Ignoring the time value of money for the moment, if a company invests $10,000 and receives only $10,000 in the future, there has only been a return of investment. However, if $15,000 is received in future, there is not only a return of the original investment, but also a return on investment of $5,000. Other things being equal, investors seek to maximize their return on investments—that is, to receive the greatest future benefits for the least cost.

CAPITAL BUDGETING AND PROFITABILITY

Three aspects of capital budgeting make it critical to long-run profitability:

1. Decisions to invest in such assets as land, buildings, and equipment usually require large outlays of capital. Unless a reasonable return is received on such significant investments, the overall profitability of a firm will suffer dramatically.
2. Long-term investments, by definition, extend over several years. Thus, poor capital budgeting that results in a bad investment decision is likely to have an adverse effect on earnings over a long period.
3. Long-term investments in land, buildings, and specialized equipment are much less liquid than other investments. Investments in stocks and bonds, for example, can usually be terminated by sale through regularly established markets at almost any time.

WHEN SHOULD CAPITAL BUDGETING BE USED?

Clearly, all long-term investment decisions are important. The larger the investment, however, the more critical is the budget for that expenditure. And the longer the time period, the more difficult it is to assess future outcomes and to plan accordingly. Given these characteristics of investment decisions, the following are typical situations that lend themselves to analysis with capital budgeting techniques.

1. A student intends to save enough money to buy a car. Should the car be new or used?
2. A machine breaks down. Should the manager have the machine repaired or replaced?
3. If it is decided to replace the machine, should machine A, B, or C be purchased?
4. Should a company add to its manufacturing facility or build a new, larger factory?
5. Should a young married couple borrow money in order to buy a house, or should they rent an apartment?

screening *determining whether a capital investment meets a minimum standard of acceptability*

ranking *the ordering of acceptable investment alternatives from most to least desirable*

Situations such as these require careful consideration of all factors, qualitative as well as quantitative. Capital budgeting analysis can help by answering two basic questions. First, does the investment make sense; does it meet with a minimum standard of acceptability? This is the screening function of capital budgeting. Second, is an investment the best among the acceptable alternatives? We find this out by ranking the alternatives. Before we discuss the screening and ranking of investment alternatives, we will briefly remind you about the time value of money.

THE TIME VALUE OF MONEY

Like other commodities, money has value because it is a scarce resource. Therefore, a payment is generally required for its use. This payment is called interest or, when deducted or paid in advance, discount. Because the time value of money is widely recognized, few people today would consider hiding money in a mattress or otherwise keeping large amounts of it idle; they realize that there is a significant opportunity cost in doing so. Money left idle will not earn interest, nor will it earn the potentially higher returns that can be obtained from investments in corporate stocks and bonds or real estate, for example.

Since money has value over time, the timing of expected cash flows is important in investment decisions. This is the essence of capital budgeting—comparing the cost of an investment with the expected future net cash inflows in order to decide whether, given the risks and available alternatives, the project should be undertaken. An investment made today, however, will not generate cash inflows until the future, either periodically over a number of years or in a lump sum several years hence. Thus, for the comparison of cash flows to be accurate, all amounts should be stated at their value at one point in time, generally the present; this means that all future cash flows should be discounted to their present values.

Remember also that when prices are rising, the purchasing power of the dollar declines with time. Consequently, the inflation rate must also be taken into account in determining the rate at which future amounts should be discounted. We will return later to the problem of finding a correct discount rate.

In the balance of this chapter we will assume that you understand the concept of present value and the underlying notion of the time value of money. To refresh your memory, you might want to review Chapter 11.

DISCOUNTING CASH FLOWS

Because of the time value of money, a difference in the timing of cash flows can make one investment more attractive than another, even if both involve the same total amount of money. To illustrate, we assume that project A will produce $100,000 at the end of one year and that project B will return $50,000 at the end of each year for two years. Both projects will generate a total of $100,000. However, by using present value tables[1] and assuming a discount rate of 10 percent, you will see that the discounted cash flow from project A is $90,909 and that the flow from project B is $86,775. If all other factors—that is, the qualitative considerations—are the same, an investor would be $4,134 better off by investing in project A.

Project A

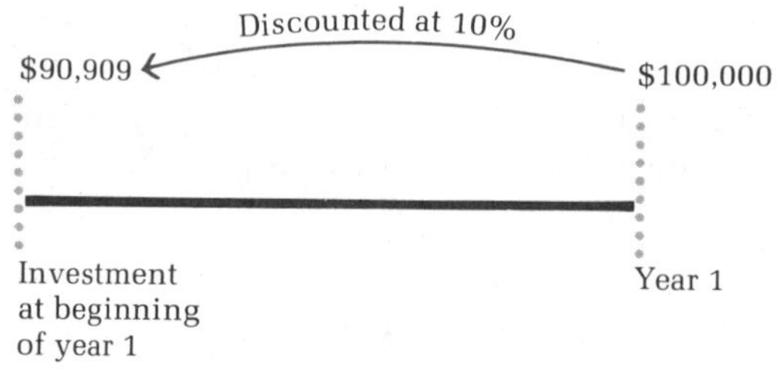

Project B

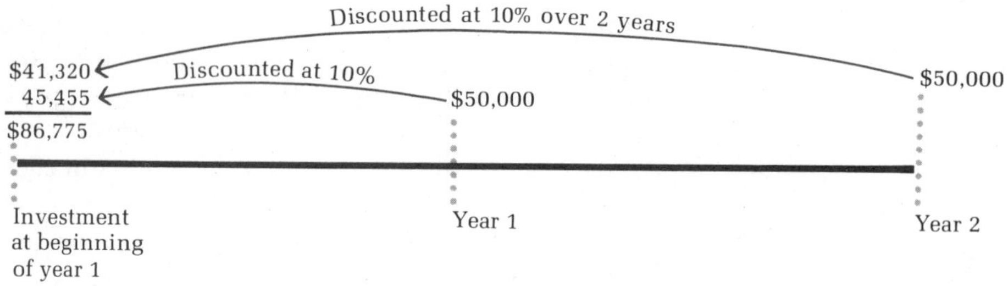

As this analysis shows, discounted cash flows reflect the time value of money and so should be used in capital budgeting. The determination of net income in accordance with GAAP is based, as you know, on accrual concepts that recognize income when it is earned, not when cash is actually received. Thus, accounting net income ignores the time value of money. For short-run investments, this approach does not affect the results materially. However, it would be very misleading for long-term investments.

In order to be able to compare cash outflows and inflows, you should have a solid understanding of the discounting of cash flows. The following sections provide some definitions and examples.

[1] The tables for present values appear on page 395. You might want to review this page, since you will be referring to it throughout the chapter.

Cash Outflows

cash outflows *the initial cost and other expected outlays associated with an investment*

Cash outflows include the initial cost of an investment plus any other expected future cash outlays associated with the investment. For example, suppose that a company purchases a drill press for $8,000 cash less a trade-in allowance of $500 for its old press. With maintenance expenses of $400 at the end of each year for the 5-year life of the press, and assuming a 12 percent discount rate, the present value of the cash outflows for the investment would be

	Time Period	Cash Flows	Present Value Factor	Present Value of Cash Flows
Initial Cash Outlay . .	Today	$7,500	1.0000	$7,500
Future Cash Outlays .	Years 1–5	400	3.6048*	1,442
Total Present Value of Cash Outflows				$8,942

* From Table II–5 years at 12 percent.

The $7,500 is invested immediately, so it is already stated at its present value. The $400 series of equal payments (an annuity) is to be extended over 5 years, so it has to be discounted to its present value equivalent.

Maintenance expense is only one category of future cash outflows. Another is factory overhead costs, such as heat, electricity, and rent, that may be incurred as a consequence of an investment. Income taxes, which are considered in Chapter 29, are still another category—although a tax credit that favors an investment would be considered a cash inflow. In brief, all current or expected cash outlays (expressed in terms of present values) should be considered as cash outflows in evaluating investments.

Note that some expenses, although they are deducted from revenues in arriving at accounting net income, do not involve actual cash disbursements, and so should not be considered outflows in capital budgeting. It would obviously be wrong, for example, to include depreciation expenses as outflows.

Cash Inflows

cash inflows *any current or expected revenues or savings directly associated with an investment*

Cash inflows include all current and expected future revenues or savings directly associated with an investment. For example, rent receipts, installment payments, and other revenues represent cash inflows. Returning to our earlier example, we now assume that the drill press is expected to generate annual revenues of $2,500 for 5 years, after which it can be sold as scrap for $750. The present value of the cash inflows for the investment would be

	Time Period	Cash Flows	Present Value Factor	Present Value of Cash Flows
Revenues	Years 1–5	$2,500	3.6048*	$9,012
Salvage Value	Year 5	750	0.5674†	426
Total Present Value of Cash Inflows				$9,438

* From Table II–5 years at 12 percent.
† From Table I–5 years at 12 percent.

These revenues may be shown "net"—that is, reduced by any direct expenses, such as those for maintenance or materials and supplies. Thus, the net annual cash inflow from the drill press would be $2,100 per year ($2,500 − $400 maintenance expense).

Less obvious cash inflows are represented by the present value of the savings to be derived from an investment that reduces costs. In brief, the present value of all cash that is likely to be received or saved as a result of an investment should be included as cash inflow.

TO SUMMARIZE Certain long-term investment decisions require significant capital outlays. Proper planning for these decisions is critical to long-run profitability. Capital budgeting techniques are designed to help in analyzing the quantitative factors relating to these decisions. Essentially, capital budgeting involves a comparison of the current and expected cash outflows and inflows in order to decide whether, given the risks and available alternatives, an investment should be made. To make comparisons more meaningful, all future cash flows should be discounted to the present. Qualitative as well as quantitative factors should always be considered in reaching long-term investment decisions.

Undiscounted Capital Budgeting Techniques

The four most commonly used capital budgeting techniques are (1) the payback method, (2) the unadjusted rate of return method, (3) the net present value method, and (4) the internal rate of return method. We will discuss the first two methods in this section, and the latter two in the next section.

We have chosen the sequence of our discussion to parallel the pattern of most companies as they grow larger and become more sophisticated in the way they make investment decisions. That is, companies generally first use the payback method or the unadjusted rate of return method, because these techniques are relatively simple. They both have a serious weakness, however, in that they ignore the time value of money. As a result, most companies eventually turn either to net present value or to internal rate of return, which are more theoretically correct approaches to capital budgeting. The last two techniques are referred to as discounted cash flow methods because they use a discount rate in comparing the cash flows of investments.

discounted cash flow methods *capital budgeting techniques that take into account the time value of money by comparing discounted cash flows*

THE PAYBACK METHOD

payback method *a capital budgeting technique that determines the amount of time it takes the net cash inflows of an investment to repay the cost*

The payback method is widely used in business because it is simple to apply and it provides a preliminary screening of investment opportunities. Basically, this method is used to determine the length of time it will take the net cash inflows of an investment to equal the outlay. Assuming that the payback period is to be computed in years (any time frame can be applied), the formula for a project's payback period is

$$\frac{\text{investment cost}}{\text{annual net cash inflows}} = \text{payback period}$$

To illustrate the payback method, we will consider Susan Armstrong's decision to purchase a typewriter in order to type essays and term papers for other students. For this kind of work she needs a reasonably good typewriter, which will cost \$500. She can borrow the \$500 from her father, who requires no interest but needs to be repaid at the end of 6 months. Susan expects to make \$100 per month after paying for supplies and other related expenses. The payback period may be computed as follows:

\$500/\$100 = 5 months

Since Susan would generate sufficient cash to recover the investment in 5 months, she could repay her father within the agreed period of time.

This is one of the strengths of the payback method: It can be used to determine whether an investment fits within an acceptable period for the use of funds. For example, a company's cash position may lead it to establish a rule of thumb that no investment with a payback period exceeding, say, 3 years will be accepted. In such a situation, a manager may be obliged to select an investment with a slightly lower rate of return but a shorter payback period than an alternative.

The payback method does, however, have several weaknesses. One is that it measures the time needed to recover the initial outlay, but not the investment's profitability. Investments obviously are made in order to earn an acceptable return, not just to recover their cost. In our example, Susan is not only interested in recovering the \$500 in the shortest time possible. Her purpose in buying the typewriter is to earn some extra money. Assuming that the typewriter will last for more than 5 months, Susan not only will recover her investment but will also generate subsequent earnings. Although the payback method may provide some clues about the advisability of investments, it does not measure profitability directly.

To clarify this last point and show why the payback method must be used with care, we consider a manager's decision to purchase one of two machines. Machine A costs \$5,500 and is expected to generate \$1,000 of net cash inflows annually. Machine B costs \$3,500 and will produce \$800 of net cash inflows per year. The payback period for machine A is 5.5 years (\$5,500 ÷ \$1,000); for machine B, the period is 4.4 years (\$3,500 ÷ \$800). Other things being equal, the payback method would indicate that the manager should purchase machine B because it would result in a shorter payback period. That is, its original cost would be recovered in a shorter time. However, if machine B were expected to last less than 4.4 years, such an investment would be unwise. The machine would not last long enough to recover its original cost, let alone generate any earnings.

Now suppose that both machines were estimated to have a 7-year life. Which machine would be the better investment? What if the estimated lifetimes of both machines were more than 10 years? To answer these questions, we would have to use one of the discounted cash flow methods in conjunction with the payback method.

This example highlights the other major weakness of the payback method: that it does not take into account the time value of money. As a result, incorrect investment decisions may result unless the payback period is relatively short.

THE UNADJUSTED RATE OF RETURN METHOD

unadjusted rate of return method *a capital budgeting technique in which a rate of return is calculated by dividing the average annual net income a project will add by the initial investment cost*

Another commonly used capital budgeting technique is the unadjusted rate of return method. Also referred to as the simple rate of return or the accounting rate of return method, it is computed as follows:

$$\frac{\text{increase in future average annual net income}}{\text{initial investment cost}} = \text{unadjusted rate of return}$$

To illustrate the unadjusted rate of return method, we will consider the following situation. ABC Corporation manufactures cans for fruits, vegetables, and other farm produce. Management wants to add a new, larger can size to the product line in order to take advantage of a potential demand for food storage items in the western states. This new can is expected to increase the company's annual net income by an average of $30,000 a year for 10 years. The additional machinery needed to manufacture the can will cost $215,000. The expected return on the investment is

$30,000/$215,000 = 14 percent (rounded)

Unlike the payback method, the unadjusted rate of return method attempts to measure the profitability of an investment. A company compares the unadjusted rate of return with a preselected rate that it considers acceptable. Management invests only in projects with rates of return that are equal to or greater than the established standard. Thus, if ABC's standard acceptance rate is less than or equal to 14 percent, the project would be acceptable.

The main weakness of the unadjusted rate of return method is that, like the payback method, it does not consider the time value of money. The computation uses average future net income rather than expected future earnings discounted to the present. A second problem is that this method counts the initial investment cost twice. This occurs because depreciation is a component in the computation of the average net income added by a project.

The problem of double counting can be eliminated by using refined models of the unadjusted rate of return method.[2] The more serious problem—the omission of the time value of money—cannot be corrected. And since this omission can produce misleading results and incorrect long-term investment decisions, the unadjusted rate of return method must be used with extreme care.

[2] For example, the weighted-average investment over the life of the asset can be substituted for the initial investment.

TO SUMMARIZE The payback method measures the time required to recover the initial cost of an investment from future net cash inflows (investment cost divided by annual net cash inflows). It may be useful as a preliminary screen of investment projects. The unadjusted rate of return method provides a measure of the profitability of an investment (future average increases in annual net income divided by the cost of the investment). If the resulting return is greater than the company's minimum standard of acceptability, the project is acceptable quantitatively. Because the payback and the unadjusted rate of return methods do not consider the time value of money, they should be used only in conjunction with one of the discounted cash flow methods.

Discounted Cash Flow Methods

There are two capital budgeting techniques that do recognize the time value of money—the net present value method and the internal rate of return method. Both methods apply discounted cash flow principles in determining whether an investment is acceptable.

THE NET PRESENT VALUE METHOD

net present value method *a capital budgeting technique that uses discounted cash flows to compare the present values of an investment's expected cash inflows and outflows*

The net present value method compares all expected cash inflows associated with an investment with the current and future cash outflows. All cash flows are discounted to their present values, giving recognition to the time value of money. For this reason, the net present value method is superior to both the payback method and the unadjusted rate of return method and has gained in popularity, especially in recent years.

In general, the net present value method involves the following three steps.

Step 1. Using a predetermined interest rate or discount factor, compute the present values of all the expected cash inflows and outflows of an investment. (Note that most present value tables assume end-of-year inflows and outflows.)

Step 2. Subtract the total present value of the cash outflows from the total present value of the cash inflows. The difference is the investment's net present value.

net present value *the difference between the present values of an investment's expected cash inflows and outflows*

Step 3. If the net present value of the investment is positive, or at least zero, the project is acceptable from a quantitative standpoint.

The following case illustrates the net present value method. The traffic manager of Altameda Brush Company is thinking of replacing an old truck before it begins to need major repairs. The company has limited funds and cannot spend more than $6,000, so the manager is considering a small, foreign-made pickup truck that is presently selling for that amount. The truck would save the company $2,000 a year in gas and other expenses. It has an estimated life of 4 years and an expected salvage value of $800. The company uses a 12 percent discount rate. What is this investment's net present value? Should the truck be purchased?

Step 1 of the net present value method is to use the predetermined discount rate to state all cash flows at their present values.

Cash inflows:

annual cash savings	× discount factor		= present value	
$2,000	×	3.0373*	=	$6,075
salvage value	× discount factor		= present value	
$800	×	0.6355†	=	$508

Cash outflows:

initial cost	× discount factor		= present value	
$6,000	×	1.0000	=	$6,000

* From Table II—4 years at 12 percent.
† From Table I—4 years at 12 percent.

Step 2 is to compute the net present value, that is, the difference between the present value of cash inflows and outflows.

Present value of inflows:	
Cash savings	$6,075
Salvage value	508
Total	$6,583
Less present value of outflows:	
Cost of truck	6,000
Net present value	$ 583

Step 2 shows that investing in the truck would produce a positive net present value. In other words, there would be a savings if the expected cash inflows and outflows were discounted at the 12 percent rate required by the company. Thus, from a quantitative standpoint, it seems that the truck should be purchased. Exhibit 28-1 is a tabular illustration of the process just described.

Before the company decides whether to purchase the truck, however, management must consider other factors. For example, a policy of support for U.S. car manufacturers or a lack of particular safety features on the pickup might dictate a different course of action. Qualitative factors are discussed in greater detail at the end of the chapter.

Least-Cost Decisions

The net present value method generally assumes that an investment of funds must be justified by the cash savings or increased revenues it creates. Sometimes, however, funds must be used to purchase assets regardless of whether they can be justified financially. Such situations arise, for example, when (1) government regulations require a firm to purchase safety or pollu-

EXHIBIT 28-1 **Computing Net Present Value**

	Present Time	Year 1	Year 2	Year 3	Year 4
Cost	$6,000				
Savings		$2,000	$2,000	$2,000	$2,000
Salvage Value					800

	Time Period	Cash Flows	Present Value Factor	Present Value of Cash Flows
Present Value of Cash Inflows:				
Savings	Years 1–4	$2,000	3.0373*	$6,075
Salvage Value	Year 4	800	0.6355†	508††
				$6,583
Present Value of Cash Outflows	Today	(6,000)	1.0000	(6,000)
Net Present Value				$ 583

* From Table II—4 years at 12 percent.
† From Table I—4 years at 12 percent.
†† Rounded to the nearest dollar.

tion-control equipment, (2) personnel contracts stipulate the establishment of retirement funds, or (3) a company is required to invest in cafeteria or recreational facilities to comply with a labor union contract, or because management is persuaded that morale considerations warrant it.

least-cost decision *a decision to undertake the project with the smallest negative net present value*

Such situations may seem to be beyond help from capital budgeting. However, the net present value method may assist managers in making a least-cost decision—a decision that satisfies certain requirements at the lowest possible cost to the firm. The two major differences between least-cost and all other capital budgeting decisions are

1. Least-cost decisions are limited to alternatives that fulfill certain imposed requirements.
2. Neither alternative selection may produce a positive net present value.

To illustrate, we will assume that Johnson Paper Mill has been told by the Environmental Protection Agency to install a pollution-control device. One alternative would cost $1,000,000 immediately but would not add to operating costs. It would last for 10 years. A second alternative is a device that costs $200,000 immediately but would add $125,000 to annual operating costs. Like the first device, it would last 10 years. Which device should be purchased? The firm uses a 12 percent discount rate.

The first alternative involves no future cash inflows or outflows. Its outlay cost in net present value terms is its initial cash outlay of $1,000,000. The second alternative has an initial cost of $200,000 plus future cash outflows of $125,000 per year for the next 10 years. Therefore, its outlay cost in net present value terms would be as shown on the next page.

annual cash outflows	×	discount value	=	present value
$125,000	×	5.6502*	=	$706,275
Initial cost				200,000
Outlay cost at net present value				$906,275

* From Table II—10 years at 12 percent.

If the company had a choice between installing and not installing, neither alternative would be acceptable because both net present values are negative. However, one of the alternatives must be accepted. Since a cost of $906,275 is better than a cost of $1,000,000, the second alternative should be chosen to keep costs to a minimum.

TO SUMMARIZE The net present value method is a capital budgeting technique that takes into consideration the time value of money by discounting future cash flows to their present values. By comparing the discounted net cash inflows and outflows, this method derives a net present value figure. If the net present value is zero or positive, the project is acceptable from a quantitative standpoint. The discount rate used is the minimum rate of interest that a company will accept. The net present value method may also be used in making least-cost decisions.

THE INTERNAL RATE OF RETURN METHOD

internal rate of return method *a capital budgeting technique that uses discounted cash flows to find the "true" discount rate of an investment; this true rate produces a net present value of zero*

The internal rate of return method, also known as the time-adjusted rate of return method or the discounted rate of return method, is similar to the net present value approach in that it emphasizes the profitability of investments and takes into account the time value of money. As a discounted cash flow method, it is superior to either the payback method or the unadjusted rate of return method. Because the calculation involves discounting by "trial and error" when uneven cash flows exist, some accountants consider the internal rate of return method more tedious than the net present value method. Some managers, however, prefer to analyze investment alternatives in terms of comparative rates of return rather than net present values.

internal rate of return *the "true" discount rate that will produce a net present value of zero when applied to the cash flows of an investment*

The internal rate of return is defined as the "true" discount rate that an investment yields. Stated differently, the internal rate of return is the discount rate that yields a net present value of zero when applied to the cash flows of an investment—both inflows and outflows.

To help you understand this concept, we will again refer to Altameda Brush Company's plan to purchase a new truck. For the purposes of this explanation, however, we will ignore the truck's salvage value; later we will show how to incorporate salvage value into the calculation. Like the net present value approach, the internal rate of return method involves three steps:

Step 1. Calculate the present value factor with the following formula.

$$\frac{\text{investment cost}}{\text{annual net cash inflows}} = \text{present value factor}$$

$$\$6{,}000/\$2{,}000 = 3.0000$$

Note that this is also the formula for calculating the payback period.

Step 2. In Present Value Table II, find the applicable row for the life of the investment. By moving across the table, you can find the present value factor closest to the number derived in step 1. In our example, the investment's life is known to be 4 years, so find row 4 and move across the row until you come to the factor 3.0373. This is the factor for 12 percent. The next factor, 2.9137, represents 14 percent. Since the factor 3.0000 is between these two numbers, the truck project yields between 12 and 14 percent.

interpolation *a method of determining the internal rate of return when the factor for that rate lies between the factors given in the present value table*

Step 3. Use interpolation to find the exact internal rate of return. Interpolation is most easily visualized by setting up a table as follows:

		Present Value Factors	
	Rate of Return (Discount Rate)	High and True Factors	High and Low Factors
High Factor*	12%	3.0373	3.0373
True Factor		3.0000	
Low Factor	14%		2.9137
Differences	2%	0.0373	0.1236

* Note that the high factor is associated with the low rate, and that the low factor is associated with the high rate.

The number 0.0373 is the difference between the high factor and the true factor determined in step 1. The number 0.1236 is the difference between the high factor and the low factor. Two percent is the difference between the discount rates for the high and the low factors. To find the exact rate of return in this example, you would make the following calculation.

$$0.12 + (0.02 \times 0.0373/0.1236) = 0.1260$$

$$\text{internal rate of return} = 12.6 \text{ percent}$$

What we are doing is adding the proportion 0.0373/0.1236 of the 2 percent difference to the low rate to get the true rate. The result, 12.6 percent, means that if the annual savings of $2,000 were discounted at 12.6 percent, the net present value of the investment would be zero.

The purpose of interpolation is to determine the "true" rate of interest indicated by the present value factor. Although the factor's true rate of interest is fairly easy to estimate, interpolation produces a more precise rate. Of course, if you have access to an annuity table with factors for numerous interest rates, interpolation may not be necessary.

Using the Internal Rate of Return

hurdle rate *the minimum rate of return that an investment must provide in order to be acceptable*

To determine the value of an investment, management must compare the project's internal rate of return with the company's standard discount rate, often called the hurdle rate, or the rate that must be cleared for a project to be accepted. If the internal rate is higher than or equal to the company's hurdle rate, the project is acceptable. If the internal rate is lower than the hurdle rate, the project is usually rejected. As with any of the capital budgeting techniques, even if the investment is acceptable from an internal rate of return standpoint, qualitative factors must still be considered before a final decision can be made.

The Problem of Uneven Cash Flows

In the truck example, annual cash flows were the same because salvage value was ignored. However, when salvage value is considered, the investment will have uneven cash flows. When this occurs, an annuity table cannot be used. Each cash flow has to be discounted back at an assumed rate until the net present value of all the cash flows discounted at this rate approximates zero. The rate that results after a trial-and-error process is the internal rate of return. A simplified example of this method is shown on pages 927 and 928. Although this can be a tedious procedure, it is facilitated by using computers or calculators.

Approximating the Internal Rate of Return

payback reciprocal method *a capital budgeting technique in which the reciprocal of the payback period is used in computing an investment's approximate internal rate of return*

When an investment has (1) a useful life that is at least twice as long as the payback period, and (2) relatively uniform annual cash inflows over its life, the reciprocal of the payback method provides an approximation of the internal rate of return. The payback reciprocal method has the advantage of being a simple procedure that does not require the use of present value tables. It has the disadvantage of producing a figure that only approximates the true internal rate of return. The payback reciprocal is computed as follows.

$$\frac{\text{annual net cash inflows}}{\text{initial investment cost}} = \text{payback reciprocal}$$

To illustrate the payback reciprocal method, we will assume that Miller's Manufacturing Company has decided to purchase a new widget maker. The machine costs $8,384 and will last for 10 years. Management expects the machine to save the company $2,000 a year over its useful life. The first step is to compute the payback period.

$$\$8{,}384/\$2{,}000 = 4.192 \text{ years}$$

Since the machine's useful life is more than twice the payback period and the annual cash inflows are uniform over the life of the investment, the payback reciprocal method may be used to approximate the internal rate of return.

$$\$2{,}000/\$8{,}384 = 23.9 \text{ percent}$$

If you examine the 10-year row in Table II, you will see that the factor 4.1925, which is the present value factor for this investment as well as the payback period, appears in the 20 percent column. Therefore, the true internal rate of return for the project is 20 percent. As the example illustrates, the payback reciprocal only approximates the internal rate of return. In this case, there is an error of almost 4 percent. As long as management recognizes the limitations of the method, the payback reciprocal can save considerable time in screening investment alternatives. However, the payback reciprocal should not be considered a substitute for the internal rate of return method.

TO SUMMARIZE The internal rate of return is a capital budgeting technique that utilizes the discounted cash flow method. It derives the "true" rate of return for an investment by comparing the cost of the project with the amounts to be returned. This produces a present value factor that is associated with the internal rate of return for the project. Often, the rate must be derived by interpolation and, if uneven cash flows are involved, by trial and error. Under some circumstances, the payback reciprocal can be used to approximate the internal rate of return on an investment.

FINDING THE PROPER DISCOUNT RATE

Net present value and internal rate of return are both discounted cash flow methods. The former uses a standard discount rate to restate all cash flows in terms of present values, and then makes comparisons. The latter method calculates the investment's "true" discount rate of return and compares it with the firm's hurdle rate. Thus, an appropriate standard discount rate is extremely important in capital budgeting. How is this rate determined? Two methods are commonly used to determine a discount rate: the cost of capital rate and an intuitive rate.

The Cost of Capital Rate

cost of capital *the weighted-average cost of a firm's debt and equity capital; equals the rate of return that a company must earn in order to satisfy the demands of its owners and creditors*

The most theoretically correct discount rate is a rate equal to a business entity's cost of capital. The cost of capital is basically a weighted average of the cost of a firm's debt capital (primarily bank loans and bonds) and its equity capital (primarily common and preferred stock and retained earnings). These costs are measured in terms of interest payments, bond amortization, dividend payments, and the opportunity cost of retained earnings. In essence, then, the cost of capital is the rate a company must earn in order to satisfy its owners and creditors.

The computation of the cost of a capital is complex and beyond the scope of this book. However, the following example should help you understand the concept. Assume that 30 percent of a company's total capital is debt, 20 percent is equity from the issuance of stock, and 50 percent is equity from retained earnings. Upon analysis, the company has determined that the cost of its debt capital is 10 percent, and the cost of its equity capital is 16 percent from stock and 22 percent from retained earnings. The firm's cost of capital would be determined as shown on the next page.

Type	Cost of Capital		Weight		Weighted-Average Cost of Capital
Debt (bonds)	10%	×	30%	=	3.0%
Equity (stocks)	16%	×	20%	=	3.2%
Equity (retained earnings)	22%	×	50%	=	11.0%
Total Cost of Capital			100%		17.2%

The weighting procedure may seem fairly simple. However, as you will learn in more advanced courses, it is not so easy to calculate the costs of the different types of capital. This is because the necessary information is often not readily available or absolutely verifiable. For example, debt costs must be adjusted to an after-tax basis and equity costs include some subjective elements, such as the opportunity cost of retained earnings. Although you now have a general understanding of the cost of capital, you will need further explanation in order to use this concept.

The Intuitive Rate

Another method of determining a capital budgeting discount rate is through an intuitive process. This procedure is obviously less exact than the cost of capital method, but it does offer a practical alternative, one that is commonly used in business.

Management begins by choosing a rate that it intuitively feels is correct. The rate may then be altered depending on whether it helps management select reasonable projects. If too many projects are accepted that are not fulfilling the goals of management, the rate is raised. If too few projects are accepted, the rate is lowered.

A COMPARATIVE EXAMPLE

To solidify your understanding of the capital budgeting techniques introduced in this chapter, we present the example of Gas Stop, a small service station that sells gasoline on a self-service basis as its only source of revenue. Since one wall of the enclosed station area is vacant, the manager has decided to install one or two fast-food machines. A sales representative has suggested that a freezer for ice cream and other dairy items would do well. The freezer would cost $42,045. It has an estimated useful life of 10 years, with an expected salvage value of $4,000. The sales representative is confident that the freezer will generate revenues of $15,000 a year on goods that cost $7,600. The freezer will need $8,000 of servicing during its fifth year of operation. The increase in Gas Stop's average yearly net income if the freezer is purchased is estimated to be $3,500. Note that the difference between annual net cash inflow of $7,400 ($15,000 − $7,600) and the estimated average net income of $3,500 is due to changes in various income statement items. For example, if the freezer is depreciated on a straight-line basis, the annual expense would be $3,804, which is deducted from gross margin ($7,400) in calculating net income.

The manager of the station has come to you for advice, indicating that the firm's hurdle rate is 12 percent, Gas Stop's estimated cost of capital. Compute the payback period, the unadjusted rate of return, the net present value of the project, and the internal rate of return. (Because the income tax effects of the discounted cash flow methods used in capital budgeting are not covered until the next chapter, we can keep the present example fairly simple.) Then give your recommendations. Note that companies generally do not analyze an investment with all of these techniques. They are all used here for illustrative purposes.

1. *Payback period:*

$$\frac{\$50{,}045 \text{ (total investment cost)*}}{\$7{,}400 \text{ (annual net cash inflows)}} = 6.76 \text{ years}$$

* $42,045 initial investment + $8,000 servicing cost after 5 years.

Note that the salvage value and the increase in future average annual net income are not considered here.

2. *Unadjusted rate of return:*

$$\frac{\$3{,}500 \text{ (increase in future average annual net income)}}{\$42{,}045 \text{ (initial investment cost)}} = 8.3 \text{ percent}$$

3. *Net present value:*

	Time Period	Cash Flows	Present Value Factor	Present Value of Cash Flows
Present Value of Cash Inflows:				
Net Revenues ($15,000 − $7,600) . .	Years 1–10	$ 7,400	5.6502*	$41,811
Salvage Value	Year 10	4,000	0.3220†	1,288
Total Cash Inflows				$43,099
Present Value of Cash Outflows:				
Initial Cost	Today	$42,045	1.0000	$42,045
Servicing Cost	Year 5	8,000	0.5674††	4,539
Total Cash Outflows				$46,584
Net Present Value . . .				$(3,485)

* From Table II—10 years at 12 percent.
† From Table I—10 years at 12 percent.
†† From Table I—5 years at 12 percent.

4. *Internal rate of return:*

Since the cash flows are uneven due to the servicing cost and the salvage value, a trial-and-error process is required in computing the internal rate of return. From the net present value method, we can see that the 12 percent rate is too high. However, if the rate is close enough to 12 percent, perhaps other factors, such as the probability that the additional customers attracted by the freezer items will also buy gas, might make the project acceptable. A 10 percent rate is selected for trial, and the net present value at that rate is calculated.

	Time Period	Cash Flows	Present Value Factor	Present Value of Cash Flows
Present Value of Cash Inflows:				
Net Revenues ($15,000 − $7,600) . .	Years 1–10	$ 7,400	6.1446*	$45,470
Salvage Value	Year 10	4,000	0.3855†	1,542
Total Cash Inflows				$47,012
Present Value of Cash Outflows:				
Initial Cost	Today	$42,045	1.0000	$42,045
Servicing Cost	Year 5	8,000	0.6209††	4,967
Total Cash Outflows				$47,012
Net Present Value . . .				$ -0-

* From Table II—10 years at 10 percent.
† From Table I—10 years at 10 percent.
†† From Table I—5 years at 10 percent.

At 10 percent, the net present value is zero. Therefore, 10 percent is the internal rate of return.

Conclusion

On the basis of the foregoing information, you should recommend rejection. The payback period is well within the life of the investment; however, it is not short enough to warrant any special consideration. The unadjusted rate of return is only 8.3 percent, and the internal, or adjusted, rate of return of 10 percent is well under Gas Stop's hurdle rate, which means that the project's net present value is negative. Therefore, unless qualitative factors are introduced that outweigh the quantitative results, the manager should look for an opportunity that is more attractive financially.

Dealing with Uncertainty in Capital Budgeting

sensitivity analysis *a method of assessing the reasonableness of a decision that was based upon estimates; involves calculating how far reality can differ from an estimate without invalidating the decision*

Throughout this chapter, we have applied capital budgeting techniques as though the future were certain. That is, we have assumed perfect knowledge of expected cash flows, the useful lives of assets, salvage values, and so forth. Actually, the future is almost always uncertain and the applicable numbers are estimates. By using "sensitivity analysis," we can evaluate, at least to some extent, the degree to which an error in a particular estimate is likely to invalidate the decision reached. Essentially, sensitivity analysis is a method of examining the effect of changes in an estimate on the results of the calculations. We use sensitivity analysis to determine whether the conclusions will still seem reasonable under modified circumstances.

To illustrate this approach, we will consider the following situation. An asset can be purchased for $100,000; it is expected to provide $20,000 of annual net cash inflows. It has a 10-year life and an expected disposal value of $10,000. The hurdle rate is 8 percent. We can use either of the discounted cash flow techniques to assess this investment opportunity. For illustrative purposes, we use both.

Net present value method:

Discounted Expected Cash Inflows ($20,000 × 6.7101)	$134,202
Discounted Disposal Value ($10,000 × 0.4632)	4,632
Net Cash Inflows	$138,834
Net Cash Outflows	100,000
Net Present Value	$ 38,834

Internal rate of return method:

$$\frac{\text{investment } (\$100{,}000 - \$4{,}632)}{\text{annual net cash inflows}} = \frac{\$95{,}368}{\$20{,}000} = 4.7684 \text{ present value factor}$$

For 10 years the internal rate of return is between 16 and 20 percent.

The net present value is greater than zero and the internal rate of return is between 16 and 20 percent, which is considerably more than the minimum acceptable rate of 8 percent. Therefore, from a quantitative standpoint, we should accept this investment opportunity. But what about the uncertainties? What if $20,000 is not received each year? What if the asset does not last 10 years? What if the disposal value is less than $10,000? Sensitivity analysis enables us to evaluate the potential effect of each of these uncertainties.

IF EXPECTED CASH FLOWS ARE UNCERTAIN

To assess the amount of error we can tolerate in expected cash flows, we need to determine the break-even amount of net cash flow—that is, the annual cash flow that would earn the minimum rate of 8 percent. We accomplish this by determining the discounted net cost of the investment and dividing that amount by the present value factor for the minimum acceptable interest rate (8 percent) for 10 years.

Computations:

Initial Cost	$100,000
Discounted Disposal Value	4,632
Net Cost of Investment	$ 95,368

$95,368 ÷ 6.7101 (present value factor at 8 percent) = $14,213 cash flow return in order to break even.

We could then assess how likely it is that this project will generate annual cash flows of at least $14,213. Any amount above that, of course, would be acceptable with an 8 percent hurdle rate.

IF THE USEFUL LIFE IS UNCERTAIN

To assess the amount of error we can tolerate in the estimate that the asset will have a useful life of 10 years, we take the discounted net cost of the investment and divide it by the expected cash flows. This produces a present value factor of 4.7684. Looking under 8 percent interest in Table II, we find that this factor falls between 6 and 7 years. Thus, assuming that the $20,000 estimate of cash inflows is reliable, the asset does not have to last a full 10 years for the investment to be acceptable. In fact, only 7 years are necessary.

Computations:

$$\frac{\text{net cost of investment}}{\text{annual net cash inflows}} = \frac{\$95{,}368}{\$20{,}000}$$

$$= 4.7684 \text{ at 8 percent}$$

$$= \text{between 6 and 7 years of useful life in order to break even}$$

IF THE DISPOSAL VALUE IS UNCERTAIN

Usually, the disposal value is an insignificant factor in the investment decision. However, to see if it would make a difference in the acceptability of a project, we can assume it is zero. In our example, if the asset has a zero disposal value, the investment cost of $100,000 divided by $20,000 annual net cash inflows equals a 5.00 present value factor. For an assumed 10-year life, the return is between 15 and 16 percent, which is clearly acceptable according to our 8 percent hurdle rate.

Computations:

$$\frac{\text{initial investment cost}}{\text{annual net cash inflows}} = \frac{\$100{,}000}{\$20{,}000}$$

$$= 5.00 \text{ for 10 years}$$

$$= \text{between 15 and 16 percent return}$$

TO SUMMARIZE Capital budgeting decisions always involve estimates of future amounts, and estimates involve uncertainty. To evaluate the potential effects of this uncertainty, we can use sensitivity analysis, which shows how far reality can deviate from the estimate without invalidating the investment decision.

Capital Rationing

Thus far, we have dealt exclusively with the screening function of capital budgeting—that is, determining whether an investment meets a minimum standard of acceptability. In many cases, however, a company has not one but several investment opportunities, all of which offer returns in excess of the company's hurdle rate. Since a company's resources are limited, some projects should be given priority. The ranking function of capital budgeting enables management to select the most profitable investments first. Naturally, projects should not be ranked until after the screening process is completed.

capital rationing *allocating resources among ranked acceptable investments*

The objective of ranking is to help a company use its limited resources to the best advantage by investing only in the projects that offer the highest return. The process of allocating resources based on the ranking of projects is called capital rationing. Either the internal rate of return or the net present value method may be used in ranking investments.

RANKING BY THE INTERNAL RATE OF RETURN METHOD

If the internal rate of return method is used, investments are ranked in the order of their internal rate of return, from highest to lowest. This method is simple, requires no additional computations, and is widely used.

To illustrate the process, we will assume the following situation. Sunshine Candy Company wants to invest in at least three new projects. Management requires a minimum return of 15 percent on its investments. The following projects are possibilities.

Project	Expected Rate of Return	Screening Decision	Ranking Decision
A	10%	Reject	–
B	18%	Accept	3
C	12%	Reject	–
D	22%	Accept	1
E	20%	Accept	2
F	16%	Accept	4

From a quantitative standpoint, the projects should be screened and ranked as shown. Resources would be allocated to project D first, then to projects E, B, and F, respectively.

RANKING BY THE NET PRESENT VALUE METHOD

If the net present value method is used for ranking investments, additional computations are necessary because the net present value of one investment usually cannot be directly compared with that of another. Only projects that require the same amount of investment are comparable. For example,

profitability index *the present value of net cash inflows divided by the cost of an investment*

you cannot readily compare an investment of $10,000 that produces a $2,000 net present value (project A) with a $20,000 investment that also results in a $2,000 net present value (project B), although project A certainly seems more desirable. To rank such projects, we need to compute a profitability index as follows:

$$\frac{\text{present value of net cash inflows}}{\text{investment cost}} = \text{profitability index}$$

Projects can then be ranked from highest to lowest in terms of their respective profitability indexes. The project with the highest profitability index will obviously be undertaken first; other projects will be undertaken depending on the amount of resources available for investment.

To illustrate the ranking of projects using the net present value method, we will use the example in the preceding paragraph.

	Project A	Project B
Present Value of Net Cash Inflows	$12,000 (*a*)	$22,000 (*a*)
Investment Cost	10,000 (*b*)	20,000 (*b*)
Net Present Value	$ 2,000	$ 2,000
Profitability Index ($a \div b$)	1.20	1.10
Rank Order	1	2

Note that the profitability index must be 1.0 or greater for a project to be acceptable; this means that the net present value is at least zero.

Exhibit 28-2 summarizes the rules for making screening and ranking decisions using the net present value (with the profitability index) and the internal rate of return methods. Note that each technique leads management to the same screening decision. However, the methods may produce different rankings. In selecting between the two for the purposes of ranking, the profitability index is more reliable than the internal rate of return method; it always selects the most profitable alternative.

EXHIBIT 28-2 Capital Budgeting Decision Rules

	Decision Rules	
Selected Capital Budgeting Techniques	**Screening**	**Ranking**
Net present value method (NPV), using the profitability index (PI)	If PI > 1, invest PI = 1, indifferent PI < 1, don't invest	For two projects, *a* and *b*: If $PI_a > PI_b$, pick *a*, etc.
Internal rate of return (IRR)	If IRR > CC,* invest IRR = CC, indifferent IRR < CC, don't invest	For two projects, *a* and *b*: If $IRR_a > IRR_b$, *pick a*, etc.

* CC = cost of capital, or hurdle rate.

Qualitative Factors in Investment Decisions

In explaining the fundamental concepts of capital budgeting, we have focused on the quantitative aspects of analyzing investment alternatives. However, a discussion of capital budgeting is incomplete without at least mentioning the factors that cannot be reduced to numbers. These qualitative factors are often of overriding importance.

Consider, for example, consumer safety. In a lawsuit, a major U.S. automobile manufacturer was cited for producing cars that were not as safe as they should have been. The company was essentially accused of comparing the present value of the legal and other costs that might result from the unsafe condition of the cars with the cash savings from manufacturing the cars more cheaply, and of choosing the less expensive route. The question was then posed: What is the worth of a life? This situation provides a dramatic illustration of the need to include qualitative factors in capital budgeting.

Qualitative factors may include such matters as: (1) government regulations, (2) pollution control and environmental protection, (3) worker safety, (4) company image and prestige, (5) preferences of owners and management, and (6) the general welfare of the community in which the company operates. Many more examples could be mentioned, but the point is that numbers alone do not control the investment decisions of a good manager.

CHAPTER REVIEW

The systematic planning for long-term investments is known as capital budgeting. Long-term investments are usually large and represent commitments that are difficult to change, so capital budgeting is crucial to the long-run profitability of a company.

Several capital budgeting techniques have been developed to assist in this decision-making process. The payback and unadjusted rate of return methods are commonly used in business because they are simple to apply. However, they generally should be used together with the discounted cash flow methods—net present value and internal rate of return—which are more correct because they take into consideration inflation and the time value of money.

The net present value method uses a predetermined discount rate to state all the cash flows of an investment in present value terms. This rate is generally based on a company's cost of capital or on a discount rate derived from an intuitive process. The cash inflows and outflows are then compared, and if the result is positive, or at least zero, the project is acceptable.

The internal rate of return method determines the "true" rate of return on an investment. This is the discount rate at which a project would have a net present value of zero. The internal rate is compared with the company's hurdle or minimum acceptance rate. If the internal rate is higher than or equal to the hurdle rate, the project is acceptable from a quantitative standpoint.

Sensitivity analysis is used to assess the potential effect of uncertainty in regard to capital budgeting. It enables management to examine how the results of the calculations would vary if certain estimates were to change, and thereby to gauge how reasonable the conclusion is.

Capital budgeting deals with both the screening and the ranking of projects. Investments must first be screened to determine which are acceptable. They must then be ranked to ensure that a company's limited funds are invested in the projects that will earn the greatest rate of return and otherwise best further the company's overall objectives.

Qualitative factors, such as consumer and worker safety, are important considerations in capital budgeting and may override conclusions suggested by quantitative data.

KEY TERMS AND CONCEPTS

capital (912)
capital budgeting (911)
capital rationing (931)
cash inflows (915)
cash outflows (915)
cost of capital (925)
discounted cash flow methods (916)
hurdle rate (923)
internal rate of return (922)
internal rate of return method (922)
interpolation (923)
least-cost decision (921)
net present value (919)
net present value method (919)
payback method (916)
payback reciprocal method (924)
profitability index (932)
ranking (913)
return of investment (912)
return on investment (912)
screening (913)
sensitivity analysis (928)
unadjusted rate of return method (918)

REVIEW PROBLEM

Capital Budgeting

Clark Company has an opportunity to make an investment that will yield $1,000 net cash inflow per year for the next 10 years. The investment will cost $6,000 and will increase the future average annual net income by $800. Compute the following.

1. The payback period.
2. The unadjusted rate of return.
3. The net present value (use a 10 percent discount rate).
4. The internal rate of return (the hurdle rate is 10 percent).

Solution

1. To compute the payback period, divide the investment cost by the annual net cash inflows.

$$\frac{\text{investment cost}}{\text{annual net cash inflows}} = \frac{\$6{,}000}{\$1{,}000} = 6 \text{ years}$$

2. To compute the unadjusted rate of return, divide the increase in future average annual net income by the initial investment.

$$\frac{\text{increase in future average annual net income}}{\text{initial investment cost}} = \frac{\$800}{\$6{,}000} = 13.3 \text{ percent}$$

3. To compute the net present value, first state in present value terms all expected cash outflows and inflows.

present value of 10 annual payments of $1,000 discounted at 10 percent	=	$6,144.60
present value of payment of $6,000 now	=	6,000.00
net present value of project (present value of cash inflows minus present value of cash outflows)	=	$ 144.60

Since this investment's net present value is greater than zero, it is acceptable from a quantitative standpoint.

4. To compute the internal rate of return, first compute the present value factor, as follows:

$$\frac{\text{investment cost}}{\text{annual net cash inflows}} = \frac{\$6{,}000}{\$1{,}000} = 6.0000$$

Next, use this present value factor to find the investment's internal rate of return in a present value table. Using Table II, find the row for 10 years, the life of the investment. Move across the row until you find the present value factor closest to 6.0000, which is 6.1446. This is the factor for 10 percent. Since 6.0000 is between 6.1446 and 5.6502, the investment's internal rate of return is between 10 and 12 percent. We next use interpolation to find a more exact internal rate of return.

	Rate of Return	Present Value Factors	
High Factor	10%	6.1446	6.1446
True Factor		6.0000	
Low Factor	12%		5.6502
Differences	2%	0.1446	0.4944

The number 0.1446 is the difference between the high factor and the true factor. The number 0.4944 is the difference between the high factor and the low factor. The difference between the high rate and the low rate is 2 percent. The proportion 0.1446/0.4944 of this 2 percent difference must be added to the low rate to give the true internal rate of return.

$$\text{true internal rate of return} = 0.10 + (0.1446/0.4944 \times 0.02) = 10.58 \text{ percent}$$

This internal rate of return is next compared with the hurdle rate. Since it is greater, the investment is acceptable quantitatively. Note that this is the same screening decision we reached upon calculating the net present value.

DISCUSSION QUESTIONS

1 Define capital budgeting. Give two examples of long-term investment decisions that require capital budgeting.

2 Why do long-term investment decisions have such a significant effect on the profitability of a company?

3 Distinguish between the screening and ranking functions of capital budgeting.

4 Why is the time value of money so important in investment decisions?

5 If the time value of money is so important, why isn't the timing of cash flows emphasized in the accounting cycle?

6 How are depreciation expenses treated when the discounted cash flow methods are used? Why?

7 How are cost savings and increased revenues related in capital budgeting?

8 Identify four capital budgeting methods and explain why some are better than others.

9 Why is the payback method inferior to the discounted cash flow methods? Under what conditions will the payback method be helpful?

10 What is the major weakness of the unadjusted rate of return method?

11 Does a net present value of zero indicate that a project should be rejected? Explain.

12 As the desired rate of return increases, does the net present value of a project increase? Explain.

13 Under what circumstances might a project with a negative net present value be accepted?

14 What discount rate yields a net present value of zero? How is it determined?

15 What is a company's hurdle rate? How is it used?

16 What rate does the payback reciprocal approximate and how can this information be useful?

17 How can we deal with some of the uncertainties involved in capital budgeting?

18 Of what value is a profitability index in capital budgeting?

19 Identify several qualitative factors that may have an effect on investment decisions. Why are they important?

EXERCISES

NOTE: Unless otherwise indicated, the exercises and problems assume that all payments and rents are made or received at the end of the year.

E28–1 Present Values

Consider each part independently.

1. Chris would like to move his auto repair shop to a downtown location in order to attract more customers. What is the maximum Chris should pay to buy a building at the new location, assuming that the company needs to earn 12 percent? The new building will last 40 years. He estimates that moving to the new location will result in a $10,000 increase in annual income.
2. If Nancy Meadows buys a new small automobile that costs $8,000 and provides annual gasoline savings of $655, how long must she own the car before the savings justify its cost? Assume a cost of capital of 8 percent.

E28–2 Time Value of Money

Your late uncle left you $180,000. The executor of the estate has asked if you would rather receive the full amount now or $20,000 a year for the next 40 years.

Which of these options would you take assuming that your desired rate of return is

1. 10 percent?
2. 12 percent?

E28–3 Payback Method

The manager of Dry Well Company must choose between two investments. Project A costs $50,000 and promises cash savings of $10,000 a year over a useful life of 10 years. Project B costs $60,000 and the estimated cash savings are $11,000 per year over a useful life of 11 years. Using the payback method, determine which project the manager should choose.

E28–4 Unadjusted Rate of Return Method

Marble Shop, a marble distributor, is thinking of adding a new processor. A marketing firm has estimated that the new machine could increase revenues by $30,000 a year for the next 5 years. The expenses directly relating to the machine total $60,000 ($12,000 × 5 years). The initial purchase cost would be $80,000. What is the unadjusted rate of return?

E28–5 Net Present Value Method

Royal Broom Company is thinking of purchasing a new automatic straw-binding machine. The company president, Karla Royal, has determined that such a machine would save the company $10,000 per year in labor costs. The machine would cost $46,500 and would have a useful life of 10 years and a scrap value of $500. The machine would require servicing after 5 years at a cost of $1,000. Royal uses a discount rate of 16 percent. Compute the net present value. From a quantitative standpoint, should the machine be purchased?

E28–6 Least-Cost Decision

The local fire department has determined that Backrest Mattress Company is not in full compliance with local fire regulations. To comply, Backrest has two alternatives: It may install an automatic sprinkler system or it may hire a fire safety expert to make weekly fire safety checks. The automatic sprinkler system will cost $100,000, including installation charges, and will last for 10 years. It will have no salvage value. The entire system is virtually maintenance-free. The fire safety expert's fee is $12,000 per year. Which alternative should Backrest Company choose? Why? The cost of capital is 10 percent.

E28–7 Internal Rate of Return

Joe Alston, the president of Nutty Corporation, is trying to decide whether he should buy a new nut-cracking machine. The machine will increase cash inflows $5,000 a year for 5 years. It will cost $18,000 and there will be no salvage value. What is the internal rate of return?

E28–8 Internal Rate of Return

You have been offered the opportunity to purchase a franchise of Uncle Scrooge's Christmas Candy Stores. You will have to pay $155,625 for the initial investment in the store and its equipment, plus $30,000 per year for the lease payments and the franchise fee. The franchise contract obligates you for 10 years. Operating costs for each year will be $125,000 and the expected revenue is $180,000 a year. Your hurdle rate is 10 percent. Does this investment yield a satisfactory rate of return?

E28–9 Cost of Capital

CP Corporation has 10,000 shares of $10-par-value common stock outstanding. Shareholders expect to receive annual dividends of $2 per share. In addition, the corporation has issued $100,000 of 10 percent bonds. The corporation has also accumulated $50,000 in earnings that have been retained in the company. If this cash were deposited in money market certificates, it would earn 12 percent interest. Using the weighting procedure discussed in the chapter, calculate CP Corporation's cost of capital. (Ignore taxes in calculating the cost of debt.)

E28-10 Screening Function

Your company's cost of capital has been determined to be 12 percent. Several investment alternatives are being considered and the discounted cash flows have given the following results.

Net present value:

1. A new machine was analyzed and a net present value of zero resulted.
2. A new product line was analyzed and a net present value of −$60 resulted.
3. An investment was being considered. The analysis yielded a net present value of $250.

Internal rate of return:

1. A plant expansion project promised a yield of 12 percent.
2. An investment in additional transport trucks would yield an internal rate of return of 10 percent.
3. The addition of another assembly line would add cash flows that would give an internal rate of return of 16 percent.

Determine which projects should be accepted as investment opportunities and which should be rejected.

E28-11 Using the Payback Reciprocal to Estimate the Internal Rate of Return

The manager of Quick Freeze Ice Cream is thinking of buying a new soft ice cream machine. The machine will cost $13,500 and will last 10 years. Soft ice cream sales are expected to generate $3,000 in income per year. Using the payback reciprocal method, approximate the internal rate of return. What is the "true" internal rate of return from Table II?

E28-12 Sensitivity Analysis

You have accumulated $10,500 in a savings account that pays 10 percent interest. You are offered the opportunity to buy 30 ounces of gold at $350 per ounce. The price of gold is expected to rise to $700 per ounce by the end of 10 years. You realize, however, that this is only an estimate. Before you buy the gold, you would like to know how much room for error there is in the estimate. To what price would gold have to rise in order to earn a 10 percent return? (Note that the future value factor for $10,500 at 10 percent at the end of 10 years is 2.5937.)

E28-13 Choosing Among Alternatives

Josh wants to buy a boat but is short of cash. Two alternatives are available: He can accept $2,000 per year from his brother for partial ownership in the boat, or he can earn money by renting the boat to others. Rental income would be $2,500 per year. Under either alternative, the boat will last 8 years. If Josh rents the boat out, he will have to pay $3,000 to overhaul the engine at the end of the fourth year. Which alternative should Josh select, assuming that the cost of capital is 12 percent and that only quantitative considerations are involved?

E28-14 Profitability Index

Boston Company is trying to determine the relative profitability of two alternative investments. Investment A requires an initial cash outlay of $10,000 and has a net present value of $500. Investment B requires an initial cash outlay of $2,000 and has a net present value of $150. Compute the profitability index of each investment. Which alternative is more profitable?

E28-15 Qualitative Considerations

Good Deal Department Store has been plagued with shoplifting. The president, W. Marcus Wilson, has suggested that the store hire a security force to "frisk" all customers as they leave the store. It is estimated that annual shoplifting losses are $100,000. Expenses associated with the security force are estimated to be $50,000 annually. Before Mr. Wilson makes his final decision, what other factors must he consider?

PROBLEMS

P28-1 Capital Budgeting Methods

Griff's Landscaping contemplates purchasing a new ditch-digging machine that promises savings of $5,600 per year for 10 years. The machine costs $21,970, and no salvage value is expected. The company's cost of capital is 12 percent.

Required:

For this investment, compute

1. The payback period.
2. The unadjusted rate of return.
3. The net present value.
4. The payback reciprocal.
5. The internal rate of return.

P28-2 Net Present Value Method—Uneven Cash Flows

Fred's Garbage and Junk needs to buy a car smasher. The machine would add the following revenues to the business over the next 3 years.

Year 1 Cash savings = $30,000
Year 2 Cash savings plus additional scrap sales = $40,000
Year 3 Cash savings plus additional scrap sales = $55,000

The initial cost of the machine is $100,000. At the end of 3 years its salvage value is estimated at $20,000. The firm has a cost of capital of 12 percent.

Required:

Using the net present value method, determine whether the company should purchase the machine.

P28-3 Unifying Problem: Internal Rate of Return and the Hurdle Rate

Robert Behrman has the opportunity to invest in a timber forest. He would have to invest $100,000. Revenues of $20,000 per year are projected for 20 years. However, these revenues will not be earned for 5 years because the timber must be seasoned before cutting and selling can begin. Mr. Behrman's hurdle rate is 10 percent.

Required:

1. Calculate the internal rate of return and determine whether or not Mr. Behrman should make the investment.
2. If Mr. Behrman has to borrow the $100,000 necessary for the investment from his bank at 12 percent interest, should he make the investment?
3. **Interpretive Question** Why is it important for Mr. Behrman to determine his cost of capital before making this investment decision?

P28-4 Net Present Value Used to Rank Alternatives

Pepperoni Pizza Company has to choose a new delivery car from among three alternatives. Assume that gasoline costs $1.30 per gallon and that the firm's cost of capital is 12 percent. The car will be driven 12,000 miles per year.

	Car 1	Car 2	Car 3
Cost	$12,000	$4,000	$8,000
Mileage per gallon	40	8	12
Useful life	5 years	5 years	5 years
Salvage value	$2,000	$500	$1,000

Required:

1. Which car should the company purchase?
2. How would your answer change if the price of gasoline were $2 per gallon?

P28-5 Lease-or-Buy Decision

A small sales company is committed to supplying three sales representatives with new cars. The company has two alternatives. It can either buy the three cars and sell them after 2 years, or it can lease the cars for 2 years. The company uses a 16 percent discount rate. The information for each alternative is as follows:

Alternative 1: Buy

Cost	$30,000
Annual service costs	3,000
Anticipated repairs during the 1st year	700
Anticipated repairs during the 2nd year	1,500
Salvage value at the end of 2 years	10,000

Alternative 2: Lease

To lease the cars, the company would simply pay $16,000 a year for the 2 years.

Required:

Determine the better alternative.

P28-6 Rent-or-Purchase Decision

As one aspect of its business, Custom Dredging Company currently rents a ditch-digging machine for an average of $46.50 per job. A used machine is available for

$995 but would cost $498 to repair. The machine, if purchased, would cost $800 a year to maintain and in 2 years would need a new chain costing $394. The used digger has a useful life of 4 years with no salvage value.

Required:
If the company averages 30 jobs a year and has a cost of capital of 10 percent, which alternative is more profitable?

P28-7 Payback, Net Present Value, and Internal Rate of Return Methods

Clifton Company is thinking of purchasing a new cigar-wrapping machine at a cost of $370,000. The machine should save the company approximately $70,000 in operating costs per year over its estimated useful life of 10 years. The salvage value at the end of 10 years is expected to be $15,000.

Required:
1. What is the machine's payback period?
2. Compute the net present value of the machine if the cost of capital is 12 percent.
3. What is the expected internal rate of return for this machine?

P28-8 Unifying Problem: Sell-or-Rent Decision

Sam Corning has inherited an apartment complex. He is now faced with the decision of whether to sell or to rent the property. A real estate adviser believes that Sam should rent the property because he could receive $65,000 per year for 10 years and then could sell the property for $400,000. A development company has offered Sam $350,000 down and promises to pay $50,000 per year for the next 15 years. The land has a remaining mortgage of $130,000. If Sam sells the complex, he will have to pay that sum now. If he rents the property, he will have to pay $20,000 per year for 10 years. The cost of capital is 16 percent.

Required:
1. Calculate the net present value of each alternative.
2. **Interpretive Question** Discuss the qualitative factors that might affect the decision to sell or rent.

P28-9 Unifying Problem: Net Present Value and Internal Rate of Return Methods

Shirley Cross, an investment analyst, wants to know if her investments during the past 4 years have earned at least a 12 percent return. Four years ago, she had the following investments.

a. She purchased a small building for $50,000 and rented space in it. She received rental income of $8,000 for each of the 4 years and then sold the building this year for $55,000.

b. She purchased a small refreshment stand near the city park for $25,000. Annual income from the stand was $5,000 per year for each of the 4 years. She sold the stand for $20,000 this year.

c. She purchased an antique car for $5,000 four years ago. She sold it this year to a collector for $7,000.

Required:
1. Using the net present value method, determine whether or not each investment earned at least 12 percent.
2. Did the investments as a whole earn at least 12 percent? Explain.

P28-10 Unifying Problem: Payback, Internal Rate of Return, and Payback Reciprocal Methods

The management of Dave's Fix-It Shop is thinking of buying a new drill press to aid in adapting parts for different machines. The press is expected to save Dave $8,000 per year in costs. However, Dave has an old punch machine that isn't worth anything on the market and that will probably last indefinitely. The new press will last 12 years and will cost $41,595.

Required:
1. Compute the payback period of the new machine.
2. Compute the internal rate of return.
3. Compute the payback reciprocal and determine if it is close to the internal rate of return.
4. **Interpretive Queston** What uncertainties are involved in this decision? Discuss how they might be dealt with.
5. **Interpretive Question** Explain the relationship between the payback reciprocal and the internal rate of return.

P28-11 Unifying Problem: Comparing the Internal Rate of Return and the Net Present Value Methods

Peggy Carlson has to choose between two investment opportunities. Investment A requires an immediate cash outlay of $100,000 and provides income of $20,000 per year for 10 years. Investment B requires an immediate cash outlay of $1,000 and generates income of $350 per year for 5 years.

Required:
1. Using a cost of capital of 12 percent, calculate the net present value of each investment and determine which one Mrs. Carlson should select.

2. Calculate the internal rate of return on each investment. On the basis of this method, which opportunity should she select?

3. **Interpretive Question** How do you account for the difference in rankings? Under the circumstances, which method would you rely on for your decision?

P28-12 Unifying Problem: Capital Rationing Using the Payback and Net Present Value Methods

Money-Wise Company is trying to decide which of five investment opportunities it should undertake. The company's cost of capital is 16 percent. Due to a cash shortage, the company has a policy that it will not undertake any investment unless it has a payback period of less than 3 years. The company is unwilling to undertake more than two investment projects. The following data apply to the alternatives.

Investment	Initial Cost	Expected Returns
A	$100,000	$30,000 per year for 5 years
B	50,000	25,000 per year for 6 years
C	30,000	8,000 per year for 10 years
D	20,000	7,000 per year for 6 years
E	10,000	3,500 per year for 3 years

Required:

1. Using the payback method, screen out any investment projects that fail to meet the company's payback period requirement.

2. Using the net present value method, determine which of the remaining projects the company should undertake, keeping in mind the capital rationing constraint.

3. **Interpretive Question** What advantages do you see in using the payback method together with other capital budgeting methods?

P28-13 Payback Reciprocal Method

J. Walter Wheelwright is considering investing in a coin-operated laundromat. He can buy a small laundromat for $10,000. Expected revenues after expenses for maintenance and cleaning are $2,500 per year for the next 10 years. At the end of 10 years the machines will have a total scrap value of $500.

Required:

1. Use the payback reciprocal to estimate the internal rate of return.

2. **Interpretive Question** Under what circumstances would you recommend using the payback reciprocal method?

CHAPTER 29

The Impact of Income Taxes on Business Decisions

THIS CHAPTER EXPLAINS:

- Basic tax terminology.
- The tax treatment of each of the three forms of business organization.
- Tax-planning guidelines.
- Capital gains and ordinary income.
- The tax effects of investments in current and operational assets.
- Tax considerations in capital budgeting.

The federal tax rate for corporate taxable income of more than $100,000 is 46 percent. This means that for every dollar of ordinary income above $100,000 earned by a corporation, the federal government takes 46 cents. Many states also levy a corporate income tax. Obviously, taxes are an important consideration in business decisions. If management plans wisely and takes taxes into account when making business decisions, the company's effective tax rate usually can be reduced.

In this chapter we examine some of the major provisions of the federal income tax law and the related tax-planning opportunities that give managers some flexibility and allow them to make decisions that will lessen the company's tax liability. In fact, managers are expected to use whatever legitimate means are available to avoid, reduce, or postpone taxes. Although many of the tax-planning opportunities presented here are applicable to all types of businesses, we focus on those most appropriate for corporations, and restrict the discussion to federal income taxes unless otherwise noted.

As you read this chapter, bear in mind that this introduction to income taxes is limited by three factors. First, although the basic principles should have relevance for years to come, tax laws change frequently and often dramatically, as they did in 1981; these changes may have an important effect on a company's strategies for limiting taxes. Second, the basic principles are generalizations and may not apply equally well to all situations. Third, the illustrations presented here are far from exhaustive; they provide only a sampling of the possible tax situations.

Income Taxation: An Overview

The first federal income taxes on corporations in the United States were levied by Congress in 1908, although similar taxes had been established by the states during the previous century, and before that by the colonies. Then, as now, basing taxes on income seemed to be the fairest way to tap a company's ability to provide financial support for government functions. Today, the federal income tax has such a large impact on corporations and is so complex that very few business decisions should be made without first considering their income tax consequences.

BASIC CORPORATE TAX TERMINOLOGY

The subject of income taxes brings with it a whole new vocabulary. This section will serve as a brief introduction, beginning with an overview of the general process for computing a tax liability and concluding with a discussion of key concepts.

The income tax law outlines the following five-step procedure for calculating a tax liability. (Exhibit 29-1 presents the steps graphically.)

gross income *the taxable portion of a company's gross receipts, less the cost of sales*

exclusions *gross receipts that are not subject to tax and are not included in gross income, such as interest on state and local government bonds*

deductions *business expenses or losses that are subtracted from gross income in computing taxable income*

business expenses *expenses that have been paid or incurred in the course of business, and that are ordinary, necessary, and reasonable in amount*

taxable income *the income remaining after all exclusions and deductions have been subtracted from gross margin*

1. Determine gross income. This includes all taxable receipts, most of which are sales, less the cost of sales. Also included are certain other cash receipts such as rents, property received for services rendered (at fair market value), and gains on sales of operational assets. An example of a nontaxable receipt, or exclusion, is interest income on state and local government bonds.
2. Determine the expenses to be deducted from gross income. These deductions include all business expenses that are ordinary and necessary, reasonable in amount, and paid or incurred. Deductions should not always be equated with "expenses" in the accounting sense, for a number of reasons, including the following. First, the tax law allows a more rapid write-off of the cost of depreciable assets, such as automobiles, machinery, equipment, and buildings. For financial reporting, however, these long-lived assets must be written off over their useful lives. Second, accounting principles usually stipulate that expenses are recorded on an accrual basis, whereas in certain cases an expense is not deductible for tax purposes until it is paid; an example is an expenditure in connection with a product warranty. Third, expenses related to tax-exempt income are not considered deductions for tax purposes. Note also that the tax law imposes some limitations on the amount deductible for certain expenses, such as for charitable contributions.
3. Subtract the total deductions from gross income to arrive at the tax base, or taxable income. Taxable income is generally not the same as accounting income before federal income taxes because many of the tax rules for measuring revenues and expenses are different from generally accepted accounting principles.

EXHIBIT 29-1 Steps for Calculating the Federal Income Tax Liability of a Corporation

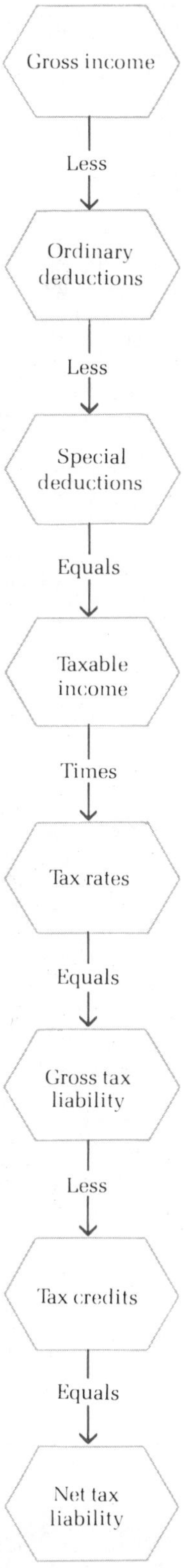

Net receipts or sales less cost of sales; dividends received, including nontaxable portion; interest income on U.S. obligations (including government bonds); other interest income, excluding nontaxable interest; gross rents and royalties; capital gain net income; other income, such as lease income.

Salaries and wages, repairs, bad debts, rent, taxes (other than federal income tax), interest expense, contributions (limited), amortization, depreciation, depletion, advertising, contributions to employee pension and profit-sharing plans (limited), and other "ordinary" expenses.

85 percent of dividends received from a domestic corporation subject to federal income tax.

Note that taxable income is generally not the same as net income for financial reporting purposes, because many income tax regulations are different from generally accepted accounting principles.

The present corporation income tax rate on ordinary taxable income is: 15 percent on the first $25,000 of taxable income, 18 percent on the next $25,000 of taxable income, 30 percent on the next $25,000 of taxable income, 40 percent on the next $25,000 of taxable income, and 46 percent on taxable income over $100,000.

This is the amount a corporation would pay if there were no special tax credits.

Special tax credits include the foreign tax credit, the investment tax credit (ITC), and the targeted jobs credit.

All corporations must make installment payments of their estimated net tax liability for the coming year if the amount is expected to be $40 or more. The date the corporation can reasonably expect its tax to be $40 determines the number of installments, due dates, and amounts.

gross tax liability *the amount of tax computed by multiplying the tax base (taxable income) by the appropriate tax rates*

4. Multiply the increments of taxable income by the appropriate tax rates to arrive at the gross tax liability. The tax rates are percentages that increase with the level of taxable income. Each successive $25,000 increment of income up to $100,000 is taxed at a higher rate; any amount over $100,000 is taxed at 46 percent.

net tax liability *the amount of tax computed by subtracting tax credits from the gross tax liability*

tax credit *a direct reduction in the tax liability, usually granted to encourage certain classes of taxpayers to take a particular action*

5. Where applicable, reduce the gross tax liability by tax credits to arrive at the net tax liability. A tax credit is a benefit granted to taxpayers; it directly reduces the gross tax liability. For example, a business taxpayer may be entitled to an investment tax credit, which reduces the gross tax liability by up to 10 percent of the cost of certain machinery and equipment purchased and used in a tax year. Note that since a tax credit is a direct reduction in the tax liability, its tax impact is greater than that of a deduction. If a corporation is in the 46 percent tax bracket, a $100 deduction will reduce the tax liability by $46, but a $100 tax credit will reduce the tax liability by $100.

The following example should help clarify the procedure for calculating the tax liability of a corporation.

Gross Margin per Books		$180,000	
Less Exclusion—Interest Earned on Local Government Bonds		(11,500)	
Equals	Gross income	$168,500	
Less Total Operating Expenses and Provisions for Local Income Taxes		(100,000)	Ordinary deductions
Less Deduction for Dividends Received (0.85 × $10,000)		(8,500)	Special deductions
Equals	Taxable income	$ 60,000	
Tax Calculations:			
Tax rates: 0.15 × $25,000 = $3,750			
0.18 × 25,000 = 4,500			
0.30 × 10,000 = 3,000		$ 11,250	Gross tax liability
Less Investment Tax Credit		(1,650)	Tax credits
Equals	Net tax liability	$ 9,600	

In the above illustration, the company's effective tax rate is only 12 percent, calculated as follows:

$$\frac{\text{net tax liability}}{\text{net book income (\$180,000 − \$100,000)}} = \frac{\$\ 9,600}{\$80,000} = 12\%$$

Taxable income was only $60,000 [as opposed to the $80,000 net book income ($180,000 − $100,000)] because, in addition to the ordinary deductions, there was an exclusion of $11,500 of tax-exempt interest on local government bonds and a special deduction of $8,500 for dividends received. The gross tax liability of $11,250 was reduced by a $1,650 investment tax credit. The highest tax rate was 30 percent, but the average tax rate on taxable income was only 18.75 percent ($11,250 ÷ $60,000).

SOME CONSIDERATIONS IN CALCULATING TAXABLE INCOME

The first two steps in computing a tax liability are to determine gross income and deductible expenses. Since gross income for income tax purposes may not be the same as gross margin and since not all accounting expenses are deductible for income tax purposes (or some may be deductible in another period), these steps require calculations different from those used to prepare financial statements. The following considerations are involved.

The Realization Principle

Gross income includes all taxable receipts (exclusions are nontaxable receipts). However, amounts received are not considered gross income until they are realized. Realization, you will recall, means that a transaction has taken place in which assets have been given up in exchange for the cash and/or other assets received. A realization may also occur when an exchange of property is determined to be a taxable transaction. For example, if an operational asset (land, building, or equipment) is exchanged for inventory, the fair market value of the operational asset would be realized.

Cash- Versus Accrual-Basis Accounting

constructive receipt rule *the idea that cash has been received when a taxpayer can exercise control over it, whether or not the cash has been physically received*

Identification of gross income also depends on the accounting system used—cash or accrual. On a cash basis, gross income is the amount received; on an accrual basis, it is the amount earned, regardless of when it is received. Note that "receipt of cash" is defined rather precisely for income tax purposes. That is, the tax law employs the constructive receipt rule, which states that cash is considered to have been received when a taxpayer can exercise control over it, whether or not the cash has actually been received. For example, interest deposited by a bank in a cash-basis taxpayer's savings account before year-end is considered to be gross income in the year of deposit, even if the taxpayer does not withdraw it until the next year.

As you know, the timing of a business expense as a deduction follows the same pattern. With a cash-basis system, an expense is recognized and deducted when it is paid. On an accrual basis, an expense is recognized when it is incurred, which may be before or after the period in which it is paid. In an accrual-based system, for example, employees' wages are expenses in the period they are earned, regardless of when they are paid. Likewise, an insurance premium paid in advance is an expense over the duration of the periods in which the policy provides protection.

The government allows companies to use either cash- or accrual-basis accounting, except in cases where inventories are a significant factor in the measurement of income. Then, accrual-basis accounting must be used for purchases and sales. The reasons for this policy are probably apparent to you. Suppose that Ernie's Machine Company is in its first year of operation.

During the year, management pays cash for 100 widgets at $10 each. By the end of the first year Ernie's has sold 90 widgets and has 10 in inventory. On a cash basis, the company would show revenues for the 90 widgets sold and expenses for the 100 widgets purchased; income therefore would be understated by $100 (10 widgets × $10), which is significant in this case. The ending inventory of 10 units would have a zero cost. Since it is misleading to match expenses for 100 widgets with revenues for 90 widgets, Ernie's should use accrual-basis accounting, which matches expenses for 90 widgets with revenues for 90 widgets. This more appropriately measures income for the period and automatically provides for an ending inventory of 10 units at $10 each. In this example, accrual-basis accounting is appropriate for financial reporting purposes, as well as being required for income tax purposes.

Deductions for Expenses and Losses

As we have indicated, not all expenses are deductible for corporate federal income tax purposes. Expenses that are directly related to the operation of a company are deductible from gross income if they are ordinary and necessary, reasonable in amount, and paid or incurred. Certain types of losses, such as the sale or exchange of assets at a loss, bad-debt losses, and casualty losses, are another category of deductible expenses. Losses from the sale or exchange of assets held purely for personal use are not deductible.

TO SUMMARIZE A corporation's gross income is its taxable receipts (exclusions are nontaxable receipts) less the cost of sales. Business deductions and any special deductions are subtracted from gross income to arrive at taxable income. The tax rate increases with the level of taxable income to $100,000, and stays at 46 percent thereafter. The increments of taxable income multiplied by the appropriate tax rates give the gross tax liability, from which tax credits are subtracted to determine the net tax liability. The time of recognition of gross income and expenses depends on whether the cash or accrual basis is used. A company can choose either method, except that the accrual basis must be used for purchases and sales when inventories are a significant factor in computing income.

How Each Form of Business Is Taxed

As we have explained in Chapters 13 and 14, the three basic types of business organizations—proprietorships, partnerships, and corporations—are treated differently from a tax point of view. In fact, the income tax consequences to the company and its owners are usually a key consideration in selecting which type of organization a new business is to be. Of course, other factors, such as the desire for limited liability and the ability to raise capital, are essential considerations as well.

HOW PROPRIETORSHIPS ARE TAXED

conduit principle *the idea that all income earned by an entity must be passed through to the owners and reported on their individual tax returns; applicable to proprietorships, partnerships, and, in a modified form, to Subchapter S corporations*

Because a proprietorship is not considered a legal entity separate from its owner, it is taxed under the conduit principle. This means that all income earned by the proprietorship is reported on the owner's personal income tax return. The owner lists the revenues and expenses of the business on Schedule C of his or her personal tax return. The income reported on this schedule is added to any other income the proprietor may have outside the company and taxed as personal income, whether or not any of the income was withdrawn from the business for personal use. Since the owner of the proprietorship is not considered an employee of the business, his or her salary cannot be deducted from gross income on Schedule C.

Besides having to report all business income as personal income, owners of proprietorships are considered to be self-employed and so cannot take advantage of tax-free fringe benefits such as group life insurance, medical expense reimbursement, certain death benefits to surviving relatives, and stock option plans—all of which can be made available to employees of corporations. However, a self-employed proprietor now has the opportunity to create a pension plan in the form of a Keogh Plan. Basically, the law provides for self-employed individuals to contribute to a retirement plan up to 15 percent of their earned income, or $15,000 per year, whichever is less, and to deduct this amount from their gross income. A minimum contribution of up to $750 can be made and deducted regardless of the 15 percent limitation, provided the contribution does not exceed the individual's earned income.

Keogh Plan *a pension plan for a self-employed individual taxpayer who has earned income; the annual contribution is limited to 15 percent of earned income, but it is not to exceed $15,000*

The primary advantage of a proprietorship is its ease of formation and the fact that its income is taxed only to the owner; the proprietorship is not taxed as a separate legal entity as well. This avoids the double taxation that occurs with corporations, when income is taxed to the corporation and then that portion of it paid out in dividends is again taxed as income to the shareholders.

HOW PARTNERSHIPS ARE TAXED

Like a proprietorship, a partnership is taxed under the conduit principle. Each partner's personal tax return includes that person's share of partnership income. Unlike a proprietorship, a partnership is required to file a separate annual tax return. However, since the partnership is not required to pay a tax on its income, this return is for information purposes only.

The partnership return includes a Schedule K, which shows the breakdown of income, expenses, and credits by type: ordinary income, capital gains and losses, dividends from domestic corporations, charitable contributions, investment credit, and tax-preference income. These items are divided among the partners and are reported on a Schedule K-1 for each partner. Individuals then report the items in appropriate categories on their personal tax returns. The entire partnership income is taxed to the partners regardless of whether it is left in the business or distributed to the partners.

Like a proprietorship, the primary advantages of a partnership are the ease of formation and the avoidance of double taxation.

HOW CORPORATIONS ARE TAXED

The tax law recognizes three types of corporations: regular corporations, Subchapter S corporations, and tax-exempt corporations.

Regular Corporations

A regular corporation is a legal entity separate from its owners and, as such, is required to file its own tax return and pay its own taxes. Because dividend payments to stockholders are not allowable deductions for federal income tax purposes, corporate taxes are calculated on income before dividend distributions. As a result, earnings are taxed at the corporate level, and distributed earnings (dividends) are taxable income to stockholders. In other words, dividends are taxed twice, first as corporate income and again as dividend income to the stockholder. To limit the amount of double taxation, the government allows the individual taxpayer to exclude from income the first $100 of dividends received each year.

This double taxation of a portion of earnings is a characteristic of the corporate form of business that makes it less attractive than proprietorships or partnerships. However, corporations also provide important tax advantages. For example, owner–managers are considered employees and so their salaries are deductions from the corporation's gross income. In addition, owner–managers may receive tax-free fringe benefits that are not available to proprietors and partners.

In general, the key advantages of the corporate form of organization are the tax advantages of fringe benefits and such nontax benefits as limited liability, ease of raising capital, and ease of ownership transfer.

Subchapter S Corporations

Subchapter S corporation *a domestic corporation that is recognized as a regular corporation under state law, but is granted special status for federal income tax purposes*

A Subchapter S corporation is a regular corporation in all respects, except for its special tax status. None of the income of a Subchapter S corporation is taxed to the corporation; instead, it is passed through to the individual stockholders on a per-share, per-day basis and in the same manner that the conduit principle is applied to proprietorships and partnerships. Thus, the owners of such a corporation have the advantage of limited liability while avoiding the problem of double taxation. If the owners are also employees, they receive many of the tax-free fringe benefits mentioned earlier, such as life insurance and medical insurance. However, their pension and profit-sharing benefits are limited to plans that are no better than the retirement plans available to proprietorships and partnerships.

To initially qualify as a Subchapter S corporation, a company must meet the following requirements.

1. It must be a domestic corporation.
2. It can have only one class of stock outstanding
3. It cannot have more than 35 stockholders. Note that spouses are considered to be one stockholder, without regard to the manner in which the stock is held.
4. All stockholders must be U.S. citizens or resident aliens.

5. The corporation must elect to be taxed as a Subchapter S corporation. The election can be made any time during the preceding year or on or before the 15th of the third month of the current year.

Subchapter S status may be terminated automatically or voluntarily. Automatic termination will occur for any of the following reasons.

1. The corporation violates one of the requirements for being a Subchapter S corporation. If the termination is inadvertent, however, the company may appeal to the IRS to have its termination revoked.
2. The corporation has more than 25 percent of its gross receipts in the form of passive income (such as dividends, interest, or rent) for three consecutive years *and* has accumulated profits at the end of each of those three years. If, however, the shareholders report all the taxable income of the corporation on their individual tax returns and if the corporation pays out profits above taxable income as dividends, then the existence of excess passive income will not terminate the election.

Note that automatic termination is effective on the date the corporation ceases to qualify for Subchapter S status.

A corporation may terminate its Subchapter S status voluntarily if over one-half the stockholders consent. For termination to be effective at the beginning of the tax year, consent must be made by the 15th day of the third month of the current tax year. Otherwise, the termination is effective on the date chosen for cessation of Subchapter S status.

One of the most important benefits of the Subchapter S corporation is that operating losses are passed through to the stockholders, thus offsetting other types of personal income and reducing the stockholders' tax liability. Often, when a company is established, it elects to be taxed as a Subchapter S corporation in its formative years, when losses are likely. This reduces the financial burden on those who have invested in the new venture, because their personal taxes due to income from other sources will be diminished by their share of the fledgling corporation's losses. As profits are realized, the company may decide to terminate its Subchapter S status.

Tax-Exempt Corporations

tax-exempt corporation *a legal entity chartered by a state for scientific, religious, educational, charitable, or other purposes deemed beneficial to society*

Corporations that are formed for scientific, religious, educational, charitable, or other socially beneficial purposes are eligible for tax-exempt status if they meet certain conditions. In general, they must be operated for the benefit of society and no part of their net income may accrue to the benefit of an individual. In Chapter 17, we explained the basic concepts and procedures of financial reporting for nonprofit organizations, including tax-exempt corporations.

CHOOSING THE FORM OF ORGANIZATION

A number of factors must be considered when individuals are choosing the form of organization that will minimize the business entity's income taxes and best meet its objectives. Some factors are listed on the next page.

Nontax Factors:

1. Ease of raising new capital.
2. Extent of owners' liability.
3. Transferability of ownership.

Tax Factors:

1. Availability of tax-free fringe benefits.
2. Ease of disposing of the business. The tax effect of selling shares of corporate stock is different from that of selling an interest in a proprietorship or partnership.
3. Disposition of net operating losses. Net operating losses pass through to the owners of proprietorships, partnerships, and Subchapter S corporations. They do not pass through in regular corporations.
4. Disposition of certain kinds of income, such as long-term gains. In a partnership, for example, capital gains pass through to the owners who are taxed on them at the lower capital gains rates. In regular corporations, capital gains become part of corporate income and are taxed at capital gains rates; the portion that may be passed on to owners as dividends is then taxed again as ordinary income, not as capital gains. (We discuss capital gains income in more detail later in this chapter.)

TO SUMMARIZE The IRS recognizes three forms of business organizations: proprietorships, partnerships, and corporations (regular, Subchapter S, and tax-exempt). Tax planning when selecting the form of organization attempts to minimize taxes for the company, the owners, and the employees (including owner–employees). Several tax factors, including the availability of tax-free fringe benefits, and nontax factors, such as the extent of the owners' liability, should be considered in determining the form of organization.

Tax-Planning Guidelines

Tax consequences continue to be an important consideration after a business has been established. To the extent that management has some control over the timing of a tax liability, its objective is to pay the least amount of tax at the latest possible time. In essence, management should take advantage of all legal approaches to avoiding a tax and, if the tax cannot be avoided, then all legal means should be used to postpone its payment as long as possible. Judge Learned Hand expressed it well: "Nobody owes any duty to pay more than the law demands. . . ."

To accomplish the "least and latest" objective, management should follow a number of tax-planning guidelines in executing transactions that may have tax consequences.

1. *Know the tax law.* Only through knowledge of the law can management take advantage of its favorable provisions. If a company cannot

afford a full-time tax adviser, management should ask a CPA or a tax lawyer for advice on special transactions and for help in preparing the tax returns.

2. *Plan transactions to minimize the tax effect.* The tax impact of a transaction is often determined by how it is executed, because the method chosen may dictate when or how the transaction will be reported. For example, if a used operational asset is sold and a new operational asset of like kind is purchased, the gain or loss is included in income in the year of sale. However, if the old asset is traded for a similar asset, some or all of the gain or loss may be postponed to future years.

3. *Keep adequate records.* Adequate records are necessary to justify the deduction of legitimate expenses and the exclusion of receipts that are not taxable. They not only provide proof that the expense was incurred, but also ensure that the taxpayer does not overlook deductible expenses.

Capital Gains and Ordinary Income

capital gain *the excess of proceeds over costs from the sale of a capital asset, as defined by the Internal Revenue Code*

A business entity's income is taxed either at regular rates as ordinary income or at special lower rates as a capital gain. Because of these differences, management should plan its investments so that, whenever possible, capital gains tax rates will apply. Generally, income from the sale of an asset is classified as a capital gain and taxed at a maximum rate of 28 percent if the following conditions are met.[1]

1. The asset disposed of was a capital asset.
2. The asset was held for longer than 1 year.
3. The asset was sold or exchanged.

capital assets *all investments in securities; used for income tax purposes*

Capital assets are all assets except real and depreciable property used in a business (land and buildings), accounts and notes receivable, inventories, and certain other assets. In a positive sense, capital assets are primarily investment assets (stocks, bonds, and real estate held for personal or investment purposes).

Section 1231 *a provision in the tax law that allows businesses to report the following as capital gains: real and depreciable property that is used in the business for more than 12 months and then is sold, exchanged, or involuntarily converted, and whose selling price exceeds its original cost*

Section 1231 of the tax law provides an exception to this restriction by allowing businesses to treat gains on the sale of certain business property as capital gains. Generally, the law permits capital gains treatment for business property that meets the following conditions. It must be

1. Land, buildings, and depreciable property used in a business.
2. Held for more than 1 year.
3. Sold, exchanged, or involuntarily converted.
4. Disposed of at a gain.

[1] A corporation may elect to have all of its gains from the sale or exchange of capital assets held for more than 1 year taxed at the normal corporate rates or at a 28 percent rate. Individuals may deduct 60 percent of the gain from the sale or exchange of such assets. The treatment of capital losses is also significantly different.

Before Section 1231 can be applied, any gain on depreciable, personal[2] property must be treated as ordinary income to the extent of the cost recovered or the depreciation taken ("recaptured"). To illustrate, we will assume the following data.

Sales Price (Machine)		$80,000
Original Cost	$60,000	
Accumulated Depreciation	35,000	
Remaining Book Value		25,000
Gain on Sale		$55,000
Depreciation to Date		35,000
Remaining Section 1231 Gain		$20,000

Based on these data, $20,000 is treated as a capital gain and $35,000 as ordinary income. Note that since the capital gain is only the portion of the total gain that exceeds the accumulated depreciation, there can be a Section 1231 gain only when the selling price exceeds the original cost.

The application of Section 1231 suggests the possibility of tax-planning opportunities. If the combined result of all similar transactions that qualify for Section 1231 is a net gain, the gain is taxed as a capital gain. If the result is a net loss, the loss is treated as a deduction from ordinary income. Suppose, for example, that a firm expects one of its investment transactions to result in a loss and another in a gain. In order to meet the "least and latest" tax objective, management would probably want to execute these transactions in different years. A loss reported by itself in one year would be an ordinary loss and a gain reported by itself in another year would be a capital gain (over and above the depreciation taken). If the two transactions were executed in the same year, the ordinary loss would offset the capital gain in whole or in part and so would minimize the tax benefit of the gain.

Investments in Current Assets

We have discussed investments in capital assets such as stocks, bonds, and real estate. But investments in two types of current assets—accounts receivable and inventories—also have significant tax ramifications. The existence of alternative methods of accounting for accounts receivable and inventories suggests that careful tax planning is needed.

TAX CONSIDERATIONS IN ACCOUNTING FOR ACCOUNTS RECEIVABLE

The main tax question concerning accounts receivable is determining how and when to recognize losses from bad debts. For tax purposes, a company generally has a choice of using the direct write-off method or the allowance method. Under the direct write-off method, accounts receivable that are

[2] Personal refers to all depreciable business property other than buildings and their structural components.

determined not to be collectible are written off at the time they become uncollectible. No special attempt is made to estimate the amount of bad debts that may result from credit sales, as is required for financial reporting. Thus, costs and revenues are not closely matched nor is the bad debt written off in the earliest possible period.

Under the allowance method, however, an estimate of the dollar amount of accounts receivable expected to be uncollectible is made at the end of each year. That amount is an expense of the period, even though the specific bad debts cannot be identified at that time. The allowance method thus provides a better matching of costs with revenues, as well as an expense deduction at an earlier date. Although the direct write-off method is simpler to administer, it is not consistent with the principle of paying the least tax at the latest time.

TAX CONSIDERATIONS IN ACCOUNTING FOR INVENTORIES

For the first period in which inventories become a material factor in the determination of net income, the taxpayer is permitted to select among a number of inventory costing alternatives (see Chapter 7): FIFO, LIFO, weighted average, and specific identification.

Once an inventory costing alternative has been selected and used, however, the taxpayer must stay with that alternative until the Internal Revenue Service grants permission to make a change.

If LIFO is used in calculating income taxes, it must also be used for financial reporting. If another alternative is chosen for income taxes, the taxpayer is free to use any alternative for financial reporting.

Choosing an inventory alternative is a form of tax planning because each alternative has a different impact on the income tax liability of a firm. FIFO and LIFO generally produce the highest and the lowest taxable income, whereas the weighted-average alternative usually results in a taxable income figure somewhere in between. Whether FIFO or LIFO will result in the lowest or highest taxable income depends on the pattern of replacement prices over a period of time. During periods of rising prices, LIFO will result in the lowest taxable income. During periods of falling prices, FIFO will produce the lowest taxable income.

The following example presents the effects of FIFO, LIFO, and weighted average on taxable income.

	Units	Unit Cost	Total Cost
Facts: Beginning Inventory	10	$10	$100
Purchases (in chronological order)	10	$ 11	$110
	10	12	120
	10	13	130
	10	14	140
Total Purchases	40	$12.50	$500
Inventory Available for Sale	50	$12	$600

Ending Inventory: 10 units
Selling Price per Unit: $18

	FIFO		LIFO		Weighted Average	
Sales Revenue (40 × $18)		$720		$720		$720
Cost of Goods Sold:						
Cost of Goods Available for Sale	$600		$600		$600	
Less Ending Inventory:						
FIFO (10 at $14)	140					
LIFO (10 at $10)			100			
Weighted Average (10 at $12)					120	
Cost of Goods Sold		460		500		480
Gross Margin		$260		$220		$240

As you can see, LIFO shows the lowest gross margin and income during a period of rising prices, FIFO the highest, and weighted-average falls between FIFO and LIFO. Again, this pattern is reversed when costs are falling.

For the best tax situation, a company should switch from FIFO to LIFO only when prices are at a low point and are expected to rise. A substantial number of companies shifted to LIFO in 1976, for example, when the United States was in an economic recession. Despite the potential savings, some companies chose not to make the shift because they would be required to use LIFO for financial reporting as well. This would result in the reporting of lower earnings, and hence lower earnings per share.

If prices rise for one or more periods and then fall to their original level in subsequent periods, FIFO and LIFO will result in the same total taxable income over the entire span of time, assuming that unit sales are the same each year. For example, if prices rise in 1985 and 1986, LIFO will produce the lowest taxable income and FIFO the highest. If prices fall in 1987 and 1988, FIFO will produce the lowest income and LIFO the highest. Over the 4-year period, the total taxable income will be the same under either method, if 1988 prices return to their 1985 level and if unit sales are the same each year. Note, however, that the taxpayer using LIFO will be better off than the one using FIFO because the former paid lower taxes in the earlier years and thus had use of the tax savings during that time.

Two other observations are significant regarding the choice of an inventory costing alternative. First, if prices rise because of inflation and do not return to earlier levels, the firm using LIFO will pay less in total taxes over a long period of time. Second, if prices fluctuate without any identifiable pattern of increases or decreases, the weighted-average alternative may be the most useful one for smoothing out the price fluctuations.

TO SUMMARIZE To meet the "least and latest" objective, companies should follow basic tax guidelines: Know the tax law, plan transactions to minimize the tax effect, and keep adequate records. Investments in capital assets, accounts receivable, and inventories have significant tax ramifications. Income from the sale of capital assets is taxed at the lower capital gains rates. Through the application of Section 1231, income from the sales of certain business property may also be taxed as capital gains. The major tax consideration for accounts receivable is whether to use the direct write-off or the allowance method of accounting for bad-debt losses. The allowance method not only is required for financial reporting purposes, but also is usually consistent with the goal of paying the least tax at the latest possible time. The choice of an inventory costing alternative primarily affects the timing of income taxes. When prices are rising, LIFO produces the lowest income and the lowest tax. When prices are falling, FIFO produces the lowest income and lowest tax.

Investments in Long-Term Operational Assets

A company's income tax liability is affected by the way long-term operational assets are acquired, depreciated, and disposed of. Operational assets, as you recall, include such resources as plant and equipment, land, patents, and goodwill. In this section, we focus on the tax effects resulting from various methods of acquiring long-term operational assets, of calculating depreciation, and of disposing of these assets.

TAX EFFECTS OF WAYS OF ACQUIRING LONG-TERM OPERATIONAL ASSETS

Operational assets may be acquired directly by paying cash, by issuing securities, by leasing, or by construction. Or they may be acquired indirectly by buying the stock of a corporation. Each of these types of transactions has a different tax effect.

Acquisition by Purchase

investment tax credit *a direct reduction in a business's tax liability by a designated percentage of the cost of a tangible personal business property in the year it is put in use*

tangible, personal, depreciable business property *property that is used in a business and is not considered to be real estate*

recovery period *the time period designated by Congress for depreciating business assets*

When an operational asset is acquired by paying cash, two important tax-related questions are: (1) What should be included in the cost of the asset? (2) Does the asset qualify for an investment tax credit? In principle, the cost of the asset should include all costs incurred to prepare the asset for its intended use—for example, the invoice price, sales tax, freight, installation, and start-up costs. The total of these costs is the cost recovery base used for depreciating the asset. To qualify for the investment tax credit in a particular year the asset generally must be tangible, personal, depreciable business property that has been put into use in that tax year. The percentage of the credit depends on (1) the designated cost recovery period for the asset, and (2) whether the cost recovery base is reduced by one-half the investment credit. For example, a $10,000 light truck has a 3-year cost recovery period and therefore would be entitled to a 6 percent credit if the cost recovery base used for depreciation were reduced to $9,700 [$10,000 − ($10,000 × 0.06 × ½)]. If the asset's recovery base is not reduced, the investment credit percentage is reduced to 4 percent. For assets with 5- and 10-year recovery periods, the credit is 10 percent if the base is reduced and 8 percent if the base is not reduced. In the case of the light truck, management would have to decide whether to take a $600 investment tax credit (0.06 × $10,000), in preference to a $400 credit (0.04 × $10,000), even though the depreciation of the truck's cost over its 3-year accelerated recovery period would thereby be reduced by $300—from $10,000 to $9,700. The decision will depend on the present value of the net tax effect of the two alternatives.

The investment tax credit percentage is based on the specified recovery period for the asset, regardless of the life assumed by the taxpayer in depreciating the asset. The credit provides a direct reduction in tax liability by the appropriate percent of the cost of a qualifying asset in the year it is put into service. Note that the credit is for the year the asset is put into service, regardless of when it is purchased or paid for. Only $125,000 of *used* property is eligible for the credit in any one year; there are also certain factors that limit the total amount of investment credit in any one year. A credit not used in a particular year because of this limitation may be carried back 3 years and forward 15 years; that is, it may be applied to the 3 years preceding the year the asset was put in service, or to the 15 years following that date. If the asset is not held as long as originally planned, any excess credit taken for the years of the asset's use must be repaid as additional tax in the year the asset is disposed of. This is referred to as investment credit recapture and is an important consideration in the managerial decision-making process.

The purpose of the investment tax credit is to stimulate economic activity, promoting the purchase of eligible assets by reducing their cost. The availability of the investment tax credit provides management with some tax-planning alternatives. For example:

1. Management must decide when to put the asset to use. Since the taxpayer is eligible to take the investment tax credit in the year the asset is put in service, maximum benefit would be achieved by buying and using an asset before the end of a current tax year rather than waiting until after the beginning of the next tax year. Thus, the company would be partially reimbursed for the investment sooner.
2. Where applicable, management must decide whether to purchase and put into use eligible used property that is worth more than $125,000. Since a greater credit will be earned if less than $125,000 of used property is put into use in any one year, the purchase of used property should be spread over several years if it exceeds $125,000.
3. Because buildings and most of their structural components are not eligible for a tax credit, management must decide whether a new asset can be installed in such a way as to be considered tangible personal property rather than part of a building. The use of movable partitions in place of stationary interior walls is an example.
4. Management must decide whether to reduce the cost recovery base or take a reduced investment tax credit. If the present value of the net tax effect of the two alternatives is about the same, taking a reduced investment credit will be a simpler way of accounting for the asset's cost recovery.

Acquisition by Issuing Securities

Assets acquired by issuing stocks or bonds are usually major assets, such as a building or another company. When such assets are acquired, a key question is: At what cost should the asset be recorded? Generally, the asset should be recorded at its fair market value or at the fair market value of the securities traded for the asset. The fair market value assigned to the asset would then be used as the basis for calculating depreciation if the asset is a depreciable asset—and for determining the investment credit if the asset qualifies.

Acquisition by Leasing

A company may choose to lease assets rather than buy them, possibly because the company does not want its capital tied up in operational assets. Leasing may have important tax ramifications as well. For example, the rental payment for the use of leased land is a deductible expense, whereas land that is owned cannot be depreciated for tax purposes. In addition, leased property may qualify for the investment tax credit, which may be taken by the lessor or passed through to the lessee. Usually, the disposition of the investment credit is an important factor in determining the rent on the property. If the lessor takes the credit, the rent will probably be lower than if the credit is passed on.

The tax situation is somewhat different for a lease arrangement that is in substance an installment purchase of an asset. With this type of lease arrangement, at the end of the lease term title may pass to the lessee without any payment beyond the final period's rent. Or, the lessee may have the option to buy the asset for substantially less than its estimated fair market value. In such cases, the lease payments cannot be treated as rental expense. Instead, the asset must be recorded in the company's books at its fair market value with a related liability shown for the future rental payments. This provides an annual tax deduction for the depreciation of the asset and for the interest on the installment loan. Usually, the sum of the depreciation and interest expenses will be larger in the early years of the lease than the rental payment, and smaller in the later years, as Exhibit 29-2 indicates.

EXHIBIT 29-2 A Lease as an Installment Purchase

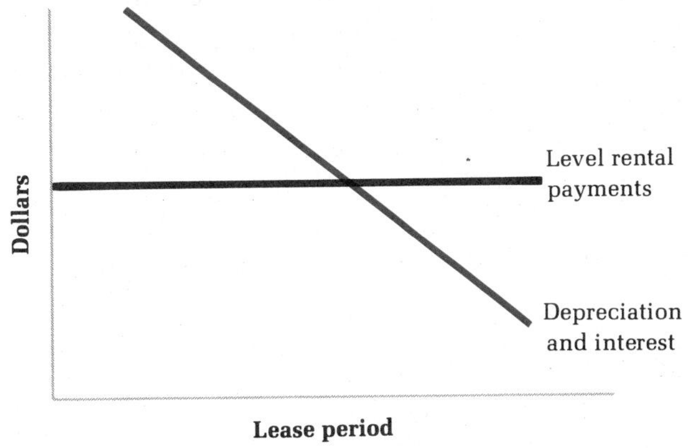

Acquisition by Construction

When a company constructs its own assets, such as a building, the primary tax consideration is: Which costs must be recorded as part of the building and which can be written off as an expense immediately? For instance, should interest expense and the property taxes incurred during the construction period be allocated to the building cost, as generally accepted accounting principles suggest, or can they be deducted as normal operating expenses? Likewise, must overhead costs be allocated to the construction activity or can they be assigned to work-in-process as costs of producing goods for sale? In general, when an asset is constructed, costs such as these may be expensed as they occur rather than after the building is completed as part of its annual depreciation expense. This approach of taking expense deductions at the earliest possible time is usually consistent with the overall tax-planning objective of paying the least tax at the latest time. One drawback to immediate expensing is that such costs are not available for the investment tax credit.

TAX EFFECTS OF WAYS OF DEPRECIATING LONG-TERM OPERATIONAL ASSETS

accelerated cost recovery system (ACRS) *IRS regulations that allocate the cost of an asset according to predefined recovery percentages*

The primary tax consequence of using an operational asset is the amount of depreciation expense the taxpayer is allowed to deduct. In Chapter 10 we described several methods of calculating depreciation for financial reporting purposes. We also introduced the accelerated cost recovery system (ACRS), the depreciation system recently established by Congress for income tax purposes. As you may recall, ACRS is a plan for allocating the cost of an asset according to predefined percentages based on the recovery period for each type of asset. For most corporations, depreciable assets fall into one of three classes: 3-year property (automobiles, light trucks, special tools), 5-year property (most machinery, equipment, and furniture), or 15-year property (buildings and other depreciable real property).

The class to which an asset is assigned is, in fact, its cost recovery period. For each class, there is an accelerated depreciation schedule. Exhibit 29–3 shows schedules for recovering the costs of 3-year and 5-year tangible personal property put into service anytime after 1980. These schedules apply whether the property is new or used. If a company does not elect to use the established recovery period, it can recover the cost of the asset on a straight-line basis over one of the designated optional recovery periods. For

EXHIBIT 29–3 **Accelerated Recovery Tables for 3- and 5-Year Personal Property**

	Property Class	
Recovery Year	3-Year	5-Year
1	25%	15%
2	38	22
3	37	21
4	—	21
5	—	21

example, the cost of a 3-year property may be recovered over a period of 3, 5, or 12 years; a 5-year property may be recovered over a period of 5, 12, or 25 years. Generally, straight-line depreciation should be used if the company's tax rate is less than 46 percent.

The IRS recovery percentages reflect use of the 150 percent declining-balance method with a change to the straight-line method at the optimal point, that is, when the deduction under the straight-line method becomes greater than the deduction under the declining-balance method. The percentage for the first year assumes that the asset was put into service at midyear, regardless of when it was acquired. (This half-year convention must be used even if the straight-line method is selected.) The company multiplies this percentage by the undepreciated cost of the asset (ignoring salvage value) to determine the amount of depreciation for the first year. In each subsequent year, the undepreciated cost is multiplied by the percentage for that year to determine the year's depreciation deduction.

To illustrate the ACRS rules for tangible personal property, we will assume that a company paid $12,000 for a new machine with a cost recovery period of 5 years. Although the machine has a salvage value of $2,000, this amount is ignored for the purpose of these calculations. The depreciation expense each year under the ACRS and under the optional straight-line method would be as follows:

	Accelerated Cost Recovery*		
Year	**Percentage**	**Amount**	**Straight-Line ($12,000 ÷ 5 years)**
1	15%	$ 1,800	$ 1,200
2	22	2,640	2,400
3	21	2,520	2,400
4	21	2,520	2,400
5	21	2,520	2,400
6	—	—	1,200
		$12,000	$12,000

* Assumes that the firm elected a reduced investment tax credit—8% instead of 10%.

Whereas the recovery percentages for 3-year and 5-year properties are based on the 150 percent declining-balance method, the percentages for 15-year real property are based on the 175 percent declining-balance method with a switch to the straight-line method at the optimal time. Exhibit 29-4 on the next page shows the percentages for most real property.

The rate schedule a company will use for a particular asset depends on the month the real property was placed in service. For example, if the property was placed in service in April of the first tax year, the undepreciated cost of the asset would be multiplied by 9 percent to compute the first year's depreciation deduction. In the second year, the undepreciated cost would be multiplied by 11 percent as selected from the April column of Exhibit 19-4 for year 2. If the company does not wish to use the schedule shown in Exhibit 19-4, it may apply the straight-line method for optional recovery periods of 15, 35, or 45 years.

EXHIBIT 29-4 Accelerated Cost Recovery Percentages for Real Property Other than Low-Income Housing

Recovery Year	Month Put into Service											
	Jan.	Feb.	Mar.	Apr.	May	Jun.	Jul.	Aug.	Sept.	Oct.	Nov.	Dec.
1	12%	11%	10%	9%	8%	7%	6%	5%	4%	3%	2%	1%
2	10	10	11	11	11	11	11	11	11	11	11	12
3	9	9	9	9	10	10	10	10	10	10	10	10
4	8	8	8	8	8	8	9	9	9	9	9	9
5	7	7	7	7	7	7	8	8	8	8	8	8
6	6	6	6	6	7	7	7	7	7	7	7	7
7	6	6	6	6	6	6	6	6	6	6	6	6
8	6	6	6	6	6	6	5	6	6	6	6	6
9	6	6	6	6	5	6	5	5	5	6	6	6
10	5	6	5	6	5	5	5	5	5	5	6	5
11	5	5	5	5	5	5	5	5	5	5	5	5
12	5	5	5	5	5	5	5	5	5	5	5	5
13	5	5	5	5	5	5	5	5	5	5	5	5
14	5	5	5	5	5	5	5	5	5	5	5	5
15	5	5	5	5	5	5	5	5	5	5	5	5
16	—	—	1	1	2	2	3	3	4	4	4	5

Selecting the Cost Recovery Period for an Asset

In choosing a cost recovery period for depreciable assets, the taxpayer has two options: (1) to select the appropriate accelerated cost recovery percentages, or (2) to select an optional recovery period and use straight-line depreciation. The taxpayer's choice will depend on the type of asset and the taxpayer's expected income. If a taxpayer is already in the 46 percent corporate tax bracket, the company should select the method and period that provides the maximum depreciation deduction at the earliest time. Thus, the taxpayer would select the accelerated cost recovery method rather than an optional straight-line method. One of the optional straight-line periods should be selected if the taxpayer is paying less than 46 percent in taxes and does not expect to reach the 46 percent bracket until a later year.

With ACRS, taxpayers are likely to use a more rapid recovery period for income tax purposes than would be allowed for financial reporting. Whatever period and method is used for tax purposes, the taxpayer must use the same method throughout the life of the asset unless the Commissioner of Internal Revenue gives permission to change the method. It should be noted that the investment tax credit percentage under ACRS is determined by the cost recovery period designated for the asset and is not affected by the selection of a longer optional recovery period. For example, since light trucks are in the 3-year class, the eligible investment credit is 6 percent (or 4 percent if the cost recovery base is not reduced), regardless of whether the taxpayer chooses an optional cost recovery period of 5 years or 12 years.

Election to Expense Certain Business Assets

If certain qualifications are met, business taxpayers can elect to take an expense deduction for the cost of tangible personal business property instead of treating the cost as a capital expenditure. To qualify for the expense deduction, the property must be eligible for the investment tax credit; that is, it must be tangible personal property purchased for use in a trade or business. If the expense deduction is taken, the amount that can be expensed is $5,000 in 1983, $7,500 in 1984 and 1985, and $10,000 in 1986 and thereafter. However, if the expense deduction is taken, the investment tax credit is not allowed on the amount expensed. Generally, the taxpayer will benefit from expensing up to $10,000 since it provides an earlier deduction. On the other hand, the benefit is tempered by the fact that the amount expensed does not qualify for the investment tax credit.

TAX EFFECTS OF WAYS OF DISPOSING OF LONG-TERM OPERATIONAL ASSETS

Most operational assets are eventually used up, either through natural wear or obsolescence, or as a result of an untimely event, such as a fire. When the asset is no longer economically useful, it must be disposed of, either by sale for cash, by exchange for another asset, by installment sale, by involuntary conversion, or by abandonment.

Disposal by Sale for Cash

When an operational asset is sold for cash in an arm's-length transaction, a gain or loss is recorded for the difference between the selling price and the book value at the time of sale. If an asset has been held for 1 year or less, the gain on the sale is considered to be ordinary income. If an asset has been held for more than a year, the income from its sale is ordinary income to the extent of depreciation recapture, as discussed earlier, and any remaining gain is a Section 1231 gain eligible for treatment as a long-term capital gain.

Disposal by Exchange

For financial reporting purposes, when independent parties (buyers and sellers) exchange similar assets, both gains and losses are usually recognized on the company's books. For income tax purposes, however, the exchange of similar assets is treated as a continuation of the original transaction and is therefore considered to be a nontaxable exchange. Thus, if a taxpayer expects to have a gain on the disposal of an asset, the gain can be postponed for tax purposes by exchanging the asset for a similar one. If the taxpayer expects to incur a loss on the disposal of the asset, the loss can be deducted only if the asset is sold (rather than exchanged) and a replacement asset is purchased.

If, on the other hand, the assets are not alike, the exchange transaction is considered a taxable exchange. In that case, the IRS requires that the gain or loss be recognized in the year of the exchange, just as it is for financial reporting purposes.

Disposal by Installment Sale

installment sale *a transaction that involves a down-payment and a series of payments over a period of 2 or more years*

If the contract of sale for real estate or tangible personal business property involves payments spread over 2 or more years, the gain may be reported as the cash is collected in the year of sale and/or in years subsequent to the year of sale. The gain reported each year is treated as ordinary income to the extent of depreciation recapture and the balance is treated as a possible capital gain. The installment sale rules permit the taxpayer to postpone reporting a gain from the year of sale to the year of cash collection.

Disposal by Involuntary Conversion

involuntary conversion *a transaction in which an asset is destroyed (for example, by fire or storm), stolen, or taken by a government agency through condemnation proceedings*

An asset is involuntarily converted when it is damaged beyond use or destroyed due to fire, storm, shipwreck, or other casualty; or if it is stolen; or if it is surrendered as a result of condemnation proceedings by the federal, state, or local government. A loss due to an involuntary conversion is either an ordinary loss or a capital loss in the year incurred. The type of loss depends on the type of involuntary conversion and on the amount of the loss in relation to other involuntary conversions by the same taxpayer.

It would seem that irreparable damage to an asset would always result in a loss. However, sometimes there is a gain, as, for example, when the insurance proceeds are greater than the asset's book value. If there is a gain, the taxpayer can elect to report it in the year it occurs or to postpone all or a portion of the gain by adjusting the basis[3] of the replacement asset acquired. This election to postpone the gain is allowed only if the converted asset is replaced with a like asset within 2 calendar years after the year in which any proceeds from the conversion are received. The total gain is postponed only if the cost of the new asset equals or exceeds the proceeds received from the old asset. A gain must be recognized to the extent that the cost of the new asset is less than the proceeds from the converted asset, but no more than the original total gain need be recognized. For example, assume that a company's warehouse, which originally cost $180,000 and has a current book value of $108,000, was destroyed by fire. The company collected $120,000 in insurance proceeds and built a smaller warehouse at a cost of $100,000. The company would recognize a gain as follows:

Insurance Proceeds	$120,000
Less Book Value of Warehouse	108,000
Actual Accounting Gain	$ 12,000

Insurance Proceeds	$120,000
Cost of New Warehouse	100,000
Insurance Proceeds Not Reinvested	$ 20,000
Gain Recognized (the lesser of actual gain or proceeds not reinvested)	12,000
Return of Investment	$ 8,000

[3] Basis refers to the valuation amount of the asset. For new assets, it is the cost. For used assets, it is generally the book value.

Disposal by Abandonment

If an asset has no value at the end of its economic life, or if the cost of disposal will exceed the fair market value, a taxpayer may choose to abandon the asset and write off the remaining book value as an ordinary loss. The taxpayer has control over the timing of the loss deduction by choosing when to abandon the asset.

TO SUMMARIZE A taxpayer has a variety of tax-planning opportunities with respect to the purchase, use, and disposal of long-term operational assets. The timing and method of executing a transaction can affect when a gain is reported and whether it is considered ordinary income or a capital gain.

When an asset is acquired by purchase, it may qualify for an investment tax credit. When an asset is acquired by issuing securities, it should generally be recorded at fair market value as a basis for determining depreciation. If an asset is leased, the lessee may deduct the rent as an expense; if the lease arrangement is an installment purchase, the lessee is allowed to take depreciation on the asset under ACRS or the optional straight-line method. When a company constructs its own building, it should determine which costs should be included as part of the building and which costs can be written off immediately as normal operating expenses.

For income tax purposes, a company may elect to use the accelerated cost recovery system (ACRS) or straight-line depreciation with an optional recovery period to depreciate its assets. ACRS is an IRS plan for allocating the cost of an asset according to predefined recovery percentages.

An asset can be exchanged or sold, depending on whether it is more desirable to postpone the gain or to deduct the loss. A gain from an involuntary conversion can be reported or postponed, depending on which approach is most advantageous to the taxpayer.

Income Tax Considerations in Capital Budgeting

Thus far, we have separately considered the tax effects of different ways of acquiring, depreciating, and disposing of long-term operational assets. We now combine these decisions using the concepts and terminology of Chapter 28 (capital budgeting) to show the effect that income taxes can have on investment decisions.

capital budgeting *systematic planning for long-term investment decisions*

net present value *the difference between the present values of an investment's expected cash inflows and outflows*

Capital budgeting, as you recall, is the systematic planning for long-term investments in plant and equipment. You will also remember that an investment is acceptable from a quantitative standpoint if the net present value of the cash flows is zero or positive, given a desired rate of return. The discount rate used to compute the net present value is generally based on the company's cost of capital, which is usually the minimum rate of return a company must earn to satisfy its owners and creditors.

To simplify your introduction to capital budgeting, we did not consider the income tax effects of investment decisions. For example, as explained earlier, an investment may allow a company to take an investment tax credit and/or expense deductions for repairs and depreciation. Similarly, the resulting income from operations and the gain on the eventual sale of an asset are affected by taxes. Such tax effects can be so significant that they can change the net present value of the cash flows from positive to negative, or vice versa.

To illustrate these income tax effects, we will use the Gas Stop example from Chapter 28 (page 926). Recall that the gas station owner was thinking of installing a freezer for ice cream and other dairy products. The cost of the freezer was $42,045; it was expected to have a salvage value of $4,000 at the end of its 10-year useful life and to generate revenues of $15,000 per year on goods that cost $7,600. Thus, the cash inflow was expected to be $7,400 per year ($15,000 − $7,600). At the end of the fifth year, the freezer would need $8,000 of repairs and servicing. Based on this information, Gas Stop's management decided not to buy the freezer because, at a hurdle rate of 12 percent, the net present value was negative. Furthermore, the internal rate of return was only 10 percent.

In making this decision, management neglected to consider the income tax effects. Here we will incorporate the tax effects of the investment, based on the following initial assumptions: (1) Gas Stop is a small corporation that is taxed at 30 percent, and (2) the hurdle rate is an after-tax rate. Assumption (2) means that the calculation of cost of capital reflects the after-tax cost of interest expense, which is a deduction in computing a corporation's tax liability.

To compute the present values of the cash inflows and outflows, we must first convert them to after-tax amounts. This conversion is accomplished as follows:

1. Income on the freezer before taxes was $7,400 ($15,000 revenues − $7,600 cost of goods sold). At a 30 percent tax rate, after-tax cash flow (income) is $5,180 ($7,400 × 0.30 = $2,220; $7,400 − $2,220 = $5,180). In other words, the company keeps 70 percent of the net revenues from the freezer ($7,400 × 0.70 = $5,180).

2. The income tax law allows a company to reduce its income tax liability by either 8 or 10 percent of the cost of tangible personal property with a cost recovery period of 5 or more years. If Gas Stop elects a depreciation deduction on the full cost of the asset ($42,045), the company would be entitled to an investment tax credit of $3,364 (the $42,045 purchase cost × 0.08).

3. Although the freezer has an estimated life of 10 years, the accelerated cost recovery system would allow Gas Stop to write the freezer off over a 5-year period on an accelerated basis or over 5 or more years on a straight-line basis. We will assume that Gas Stop elects the optional straight-line recovery method over a 5-year period. The cost recovery each year on this basis will be $8,409 ($42,045 ÷ 5 years)*. At a 30 percent rate, a cost recovery deduction of $8,409 will save the company $2,523 in income taxes each year ($8,409 × 0.30 = $2,523).

4. Under ACRS the entire cost of the freezer will have been written off as a tax deduction in the first 5 years of its life. If the freezer is sold at the

* This is a simplifying assumption. Actual depreciation in the first and sixth years is only $4,205 because the company is allowed to take depreciation on only a half year in the year of purchase.

end of 10 years at its $4,000 estimated salvage value, there will be a $4,000 gain on the sale. This gain will be taxable as ordinary income at 30 percent, so the after-tax cash inflow will be only $2,800 ($4,000 × 0.70).

5. The estimated repairs and servicing cost of $8,000 at the end of year 5 is an expense deduction from the company's income for that year. Therefore, the net cost to the company of this expense is only $5,600 ($8,000 × 0.70).

These adjusted cash flows can now be used to compute the net present value of the cash inflows and outflows that would result if the freezer were purchased. The present values of these cash flows are presented in Exhibit 29-5 at three different hurdle rates: 8, 10, and 12 percent.

EXHIBIT 29-5

Gas Stop Company

Net Present Value of Cash Inflows and Outflows (30% Tax Rate)

			8%		10%		12%	
Type of Cash Flow	**Period**	**After-Tax Cash Flow**	**Present Value**	**Amount***	**Present Value**	**Amount***	**Present Value**	**Amount***
Revenue less cost of goods sold (net of tax): ($15,000 − $7,600) × 0.70	Years 1–10	$ 5,180	6.7101	$34,758	6.1446	$31,829	5.6502	$29,268
Investment tax credit (0.08 × $42,045)	End of Year 1	3,364	0.9259†	3,115	0.9091	3,058	0.8929	3,004
ACRS [($42,045 ÷ 5) × 0.30]	Years 1–5	2,523	3.9927	10,074	3.7908	9,564	3.6048	9,095
Salvage value ($4,000 × 0.70)	End of Year 10	2,800	0.4632	1,297	0.3855	1,079	0.3220	902
Total Cash Inflows				$49,244		$45,530		$42,269
Initial Freezer Cost	Today	42,045	1.0000	$42,045	1.0000	$42,045	1.0000	$42,045
Repairs and Servicing Cost ($8,000 × 0.70)	End of Year 5	5,600	0.6806	3,811	0.6209	3,477	0.5674	3,177
Total Cash Outflows				$45,856		$45,522		$45,222
Excess Cash Inflow (Outflow)				$ 3,388		$ 8		($ 2,953)

* After-tax cash flow × present value.

† Note that this is the present value of the cash flow discounted for 1 year.

Three different rates are used to illustrate that the net present value decreases as the hurdle rate increases from 8 to 12 percent. In other words, as the internal rate of return increases, the present value of the cash inflows decreases in relation to the present value of the cash outflows, eventually changing the net present value from positive to negative. The point at which

EXHIBIT 29-6

Gas Stop Company
Net Present Value of Cash Inflows and Outflows (40% Tax Rate)

			8%		10%		12%	
Type of Cash Flow	**Period**	**After-Tax Cash Flow**	**Present Value**	**Amount***	**Present Value**	**Amount***	**Present Value**	**Amount***
Revenue less cost of goods sold (net of tax): ($15,000 − $7,600) × 0.60	Years 1–10	$ 4,440	6.7101	$29,793	6.1446	$27,282	5.6502	$25,087
Investment tax credit (0.08 × $42,045)	End of Year 1	3,364	0.9259†	3,115	0.9091	3,058	0.8929	3,004
ACRS [($42,045 ÷ 5) × 0.40]	Years 1–5	3,364	3.9927	13,431	3.7908	12,752	3.6048	12,127
Salvage value ($4,000 × 0.60)	End of Year 10	2,400	0.4632	1,112	0.3855	925	0.3220	773
Total Cash Inflows				$47,451		$44,017		$40,991
Initial Freezer Cost	Today	42,045	1.0000	$42,045	1.0000	$42,045	1.0000	$42,045
Repairs and Servicing Cost ($8,000 × 0.60)	End of Year 5	4,800	0.6806	3,267	0.6209	2,980	0.5674	2,724
Total Cash Outflows				$45,312		$45,025		$44,769
Excess Cash Inflow (Outflow)				$ 2,139		$(1,008)		($ 3,778)

* After-tax cash flow × present value.

† Note that this is the present value of the cash flow discounted for 1 year.

the present values of the inflows and outflows are equal reflects the expected internal rate of return. If the expected return is less than the company's hurdle rate, it is unlikely that the company will acquire the asset, unless there are compensating qualitative factors.

Exhibit 29-5 shows that at a tax rate of 30 percent, the internal rate of return remains at 10 percent, the same as it was without considering the income tax effects. This is to be expected since the tax rate is relatively low. If, however, the tax rate were 40 percent, which is more likely, the internal rate of return would decrease from 10 percent to approximately 9 percent, as shown in Exhibit 29-6. The return decreases because the negative effect of the tax expense on gross margin (revenues less cost of goods sold) is greater than the positive effect of the tax savings from the depreciation tax deduction. The change in rate has no effect on the amount of the investment tax credit and little effect on the salvage value and the repair costs. Thus, the increased tax rate reduces the internal rate of return, which makes it less likely that the expected rate of return will exceed the company's hurdle rate.

These exhibits also demonstrate why Congress uses such techniques as accelerated depreciation and the investment tax credit to stimulate the economy. If a depreciation method that provided larger depreciation deductions in the early years of the freezer's life had been used, and if Congress had continued to allow a 10 percent investment tax credit without reducing the asset's cost base for depreciation, the internal rate of return would have been higher than 10 percent at the 30 percent tax rate and higher than 9 percent at the 40 percent tax rate. Thus, these specific tax benefits tend to increase the internal rate of return.

You should remember that when the net present value at a selected hurdle rate is at or near zero, the important qualitative factors not incorporated into the calculations of net present value will be the primary determinants of whether the asset is acquired.

TO SUMMARIZE The quantitative analysis for making long-term investment decisions for property, plant, and equipment is called capital budgeting. If no qualitative factors affect the decision, such an investment will be made if the present value of the cash inflows is equal to, or greater than, the present value of the cash outflows. The cash inflows and outflows must be converted to after-tax amounts before the present values are computed in order to obtain a realistic measure of net present value. Cash inflows and outflows are converted to after-tax amounts by including such factors as the investment tax credit, the accelerated cost recovery system, the gain on disposal, and the cash operating revenues and expenses.

CHAPTER REVIEW

Tax consequences are an important consideration in selecting the form of a business organization. Proprietorships and partnerships are not taxed as separate entities; their income is taxed to the proprietor or to the partners under the conduit principle. Because corporations are separate legal entities, corporate earnings are taxed to the corporation and then the distributed portion of the earnings is taxed as dividends to the stockholders. However, income from Subchapter S corporations, whether distributed or not, is taxed to stockholders only. Both regular corporations and Subchapter S corporations can provide special tax benefits to employees in the form of tax-free fringe benefits that are not available to the owners of partnerships or proprietorships.

The basic objective of tax planning is to pay the least amount of tax at the latest possible time. Three important tax guidelines that will help management meet this objective are: (1) knowing the law, (2) planning transactions to minimize the tax effect, and (3) keeping good records.

The manner in which a transaction is executed and accounted for may determine whether income is to be reported as ordinary income or as a capital gain, and when that income is to be reported. The methods selected for measuring bad-debt losses and the cost of inventory will influence the amount of profit reported and taxes paid in any one year. The way in which the acquisition of a long-term operational asset is recorded will affect the amount and timing of expenses to be charged for the purchase of the asset. Similarly, the depreciation method and recovery period selected to measure the use of an operational asset will determine the timing of the write-off of the asset's cost to expense. And finally, the method of disposing of an operational asset will be a factor in the timing of the recognition of the gain or loss.

The tax effects of investment decisions are an important consideration in capital budgeting analyses. The cash inflows and outflows must be converted to after-tax amounts before the present values are computed in order to obtain a realistic measure of net present value. This means that the taxes on the additional income to be derived from the investment and on the gain from the asset's disposal, as well as the tax reductions due to repairs and servicing expenses, investment tax credits, and ACRS deductions, must be included in the calculations.

KEY TERMS AND CONCEPTS

accelerated cost recovery system (ACRS) (958)
business expenses (942)
capital assets (951)
capital budgeting (963)
capital gain (951)
conduit principle (947)
constructive receipt rule (945)
deductions (942)
exclusions (942)
gross income (942)
gross tax liability (944)
installment sale (962)
investment tax credit (955)
involuntary conversion (962)
Keogh Plan (947)
net present value (963)
net tax liability (944)
recovery period (955)
Section 1231 (951)
Subchapter S corporation (948)
tangible, personal, depreciable business property (955)
taxable income (942)
tax credit (944)
tax-exempt corporation (949)

REVIEW PROBLEM

Computing Tax Liability

Arce Corporation collected the following revenue, expense, and other related tax information for computing its annual tax return.

Gross Receipts from Services	$280,000
Excludable Income (tax-exempt interest)	5,000
Gain on the Sale of Machinery (total depreciation taken, $15,000)	8,000
Section 1231 Gain on Condemnation of Land	15,000
Ordinary Business Expenses	150,000
Investment Tax Credit	3,500
Taxes Paid During the Year on Estimated Income	40,000

Required:
Compute Arce Corporation's tax liability for the year.

Solution

Gross Receipts from Services		$280,000
Gain on Sale of Machinery (ordinary income as depreciation is recaptured)		8,000
		$288,000
Less Ordinary Business Expenses		150,000
Ordinary Taxable Income		$138,000
Tax on Ordinary Income of $138,000:		
15% × $25,000	$ 3,750	
18% × $25,000	4,500	
30% × $25,000	7,500	
40% × $25,000	10,000	
46% × $38,000	17,480	$ 43,230
Tax on Section 1231 Gain on Land (28% × $15,000)		4,200
Gross Tax Liability		$ 47,430
Less Investment Tax Credit		3,500
Net Tax Liability		$ 43,930
Less Taxes Paid in Advance		40,000
Tax Due		$ 3,930

DISCUSSION QUESTIONS

1 Distinguish between the following terms as they are used for tax purposes.
  (a) Gross receipts and gross income.
  (b) Exclusions and deductions.
  (c) Deductions and credits.

2 What characteristics of a business expense would allow it to be a deduction in the determination of taxable income?

3 Distinguish between revenues per the income statement and gross income per the tax return.

4 What is meant by the constructive receipt rule in measuring taxable income?

5 What are the two major categories of income with respect to the determination of tax rates? Give the rates currently applicable to corporations.

6 What types of losses are deductible for tax purposes?

7 From a tax point of view, what are the three types of corporations?

8 Describe the philosophy of the conduit principle as it relates to the taxation of proprietorships, partnerships, and Subchapter S corporations.

9 What are the key tax and nontax factors to consider in choosing the appropriate form of business organization?

10 What is the objective of following good tax-planning guidelines?

11 What are three tax-planning guidelines?

12 Why is it important to keep good records as a basis for preparing a tax return?

13 What is a capital asset as defined by the tax laws, and how are capital gains and losses taxed to corporations?

14 Describe the two acceptable methods of accounting for bad debts for tax purposes.

15 In a period of rising prices, which inventory valuation alternative will result in the lowest taxable income for a business? Why?

16 What effect does the investment tax credit have on the decision to acquire a depreciable asset?

17 Under the accelerated cost recovery system, what is the recovery period for each of the following assets?
  (a) Furniture.
  (b) Automobiles.
  (c) Machinery.
  (d) Buildings.

18 Under ACRS, what are the optional straight-line recovery periods for 3-, 5-, and 15-year properties?

19 What factors should the taxpayer consider in choosing between accelerated and straight-line depreciation for an asset?

20 If an asset, such as a light truck, has a 3-year recovery period, can the taxpayer choose a 5-year straight-line recovery period and elect a 10 percent investment tax credit? Explain.

21 Explain the tax effects of the choice between selling an old asset and buying a new one versus trading an old asset for a new one.

22 What effect do the investment tax credit and depreciation expense have on the calculation of the rate of return on a new investment?

EXERCISES

E29-1 Computation of Tax Liability

Evergreen Corporation files its tax return on a calendar year basis. Its gross revenues for 1983 were $180,000 and its deductible business expenses were $120,000. Compute the corporation's tax liability for 1983 using the tax rates in Exhibit 29-1 on page 943.

E29-2 Individual Income—The Subchapter S Corporation

A Subchapter S corporation reported taxable income of $75,000 on its 1983 calendar year tax return. During 1983 and prior to March 15, 1984, the corporation had distributed $40,000 in dividends to its stockholders. If the corporation has five stockholders, each owning 20 percent, how much income must each stockholder report on his or her 1983 individual income tax return?

E29-3 Deductible Losses

James Gregory operates a plumbing business as sole proprietor. During the calendar year 1983 one of the trucks used in his business was involved in a wreck and was totally demolished. The truck had a book value of $1,800 at the time of the accident. Gregory collected $1,300 in insurance and immediately purchased a new truck for $7,000. Gregory also owned a sailboat, which he sailed occasionally on weekends. He decided that he did not get to use it often enough so he sold it during 1983. The boat originally cost $3,300 and he sold it for $2,000. How much is Gregory's deductible loss for 1983 in connection with the truck and the sailboat?

E29–4 Bad-Debt Expense

Roberts Corporation uses the allowance method of accounting for bad debts for financial reporting and the direct write-off method for tax purposes. In 1983 the corporation added $4,800 to Allowance for Doubtful Accounts and wrote off $6,000 of uncollectible accounts receivable. Allowance for Doubtful Accounts had a balance of $1,500 on January 1, 1983.

1. What is the bad-debt deduction allowed on the corporation's 1983 tax return?

2. What is the balance in Allowance for Doubtful Accounts on December 31, 1983, for financial reporting purposes?

3. Which method of accounting for bad debts is more consistent with the tax-planning objective of paying the least tax at the latest possible time? Why?

E29–5 A Taxable Gain

During 1981, Fowler Corporation sold some machinery that was no longer needed in its business. The selling price was $18,000. The machinery had been purchased several years ago for $42,000 and its book value at the date of sale was $12,000. How much is the gain on the sale and what type of gain is it?.

E29–6 ACRS—Accelerated and Straight-Line

On October 10 of the current year, Rogers Company purchased a new machine for $30,000. The machine had a useful life of 10 years and a salvage value of $3,000. Compute the depreciation expense for the year under ACRS on both an accelerated and a 5-year straight-line basis. Assume that there is no reduction in the cost recovery base from taking an investment tax credit.

E29–7 A Casualty Loss

Regal Manufacturing Company used a special furnace in its cooking process. Due to an unexpected defect, the furnace exploded and was destroyed. The book value of the furnace was $8,000. Insurance proceeds amounted to $11,000 and a new furnace was purchased for $15,000.

1. What was the taxable gain or loss on the old furnace?

2. If the accumulated depreciation on the old furnace amounted to $5,000, how would the gain be recognized as income?

3. What would be the basis of the new asset for tax purposes?

E29–8 Partners' Shares of Profits

Roger Redding and Beth Hasler formed a partnership to operate a flower center in the local mall. For the calendar year 1983, the net income of the partnership amounted to $40,000. If Roger and Beth share profits and losses on a 60/40 percent basis, what amount would each report as income for the year 1983, if Roger withdraws $500 per month and Beth withdraws $300 per month for each month during 1983?

E29–9 Depreciation Expense Under ACRS

On July 1, 1984, Chris Company paid $12,000 for a new light truck to be used to deliver merchandise to customers. The truck has a useful life of 6 years with no salvage value. If the company uses ACRS, how much is the total depreciation deduction for 1984 on an accelerated basis? What amount of investment tax credit is the company entitled to on this asset?

E29–10 Calculating ACRS Depreciation Expense for Alternative Recovery Periods

Steven Mills acquired a textile machine in early January at a cost of $42,000. The machine is expected to have a useful life of 10 years with a salvage value of $2,000. How much depreciation expense is allowable in the calendar year of acquisition under ACRS using each of the following: (1) an accelerated basis, and (2) a straight-line basis for 5, 12, and 25 years? Assume that a reduced percentage is taken as an investment tax credit.

E29–11 A Gain on Involuntary Conversion

Green Chemical Company purchased land and a building on July 1, 1984. The land cost $50,000 and the building cost $360,000. The building had a useful life of 30 years. On December 30, 1984, the building was completely destroyed by fire. The insurance proceeds amounted to $375,000. If the cost of the building was recovered on an accelerated basis under ACRS, what was the gain from the involuntary conversion of the building?

E29–12 The Basis of Replacing Property from Involuntary Conversion

Refer to E29–11 and assume that Green Chemical Company elects to postpone the gain on the conversion of the building destroyed by fire. If Green purchases a new building (within 2 years) for $400,000, what is its depreciation basis for tax purposes?

E29–13 Capital Budgeting

Palmer Corporation is thinking of purchasing a new piece of equipment. The equipment will cost $135,600 and is expected to have a life of 5 years. The gross cash flow savings is estimated to be $50,000 per year. The company elects to take a reduced investment tax credit (assume immediate realization) and will depreciate the full cost of the asset for tax purposes under ACRS on a 5-year straight-line basis. The company is in the 40 percent tax bracket. What is the after-tax cash flow savings on the asset? What is the after-tax return on investment that will equate the present value of the savings with the net outlay cost?

PROBLEMS

P29-1 Inventory Valuation Alternatives

For 1984, its second year of operation, Richard Company had revenues of $300,000 from the sale of 600 mopeds at an average price of $500 per unit. Inventories and purchases of mopeds for the year were as follows:

Beginning inventory:	60 units at $300
Purchases—January 1984:	130 units at 300
March 1984:	150 units at 310
July 1984:	140 units at 315
October 1984:	170 units at 320
Ending inventory:	50 units

Required:

1. Compute the cost of goods sold and the total cost of the ending inventory using the FIFO, LIFO, and weighted-average inventory alternatives. (Round the weighted-average figures to two decimal places.)
2. Which alternative shows the highest profit in a period of rising prices?
3. **Interpretive Question** If a company has been using the FIFO inventory alternative, when should it consider converting to LIFO in order to get the most benefit from the tax laws?

P29-2 Unifying Problem: Depreciation Expense and the Investment Tax Credit

On April 2, 1984, Rolex Company purchased a heavy-duty truck for $12,000. The truck has an 8-year useful life and a $2,000 salvage value. The company plans to take maximum advantage of the tax law in computing depreciation and using the investment tax credit.

Required:

1. Using a full-cost base, what is the maximum depreciation deduction allowed in the year of acquisition?
2. If the truck was purchased for cash, how much of the initial outlay was recovered in the form of tax savings in the first year by means of the maximum depreciation deduction and a reduced investment tax credit? (Assume an effective tax rate of 40 percent.)

P29-3 Unifying Problem: Partnerships and Subchapter S Corporations

Marjorie Habstrum is a partner in a venture that reports net income of $60,000 for the current taxable year. Her share is 25 percent. Her withdrawals from the partnership during the year were $15,000.

Required:

1. In preparing her income tax return for the year, what amount is Marjorie required to report as income from the partnership?
2. **Interpretive Question** What are the income tax advantages of a Subchapter S corporation over a partnership? What are the disadvantages?

P29-4 The Subchapter S Corporation

Marlboro Corporation was organized on January 2, 1983, as a Subchapter S corporation. Its taxable income for calendar year 1984 was $24,000 and its dividends distributed to stockholders in the same year were $20,000, as shown below. Its taxable income in 1983 had been $18,000, of which $15,000 had been distributed to its stockholders. The corporation made the following distributions during 1984 and early 1985.

March 1, 1984	$ 3,000
June 15, 1984	11,000
November 10, 1984	6,000
March 15, 1985	2,000

Required:

How will these distributions be treated by shareholders on their 1984 income tax returns?

P29-5 The Investment Tax Credit

Rio Trucking Company acquired the following assets in 1983. All of the assets except the used equipment were placed in service in 1983. The used equipment was first plaçed in service in 1984.

Asset	Estimated Useful Life	Cost	Salvage Value
Heavy-Duty Truck (new)	10	$14,000	$2,000
Heavy-Duty Truck (used)	5	9,000	1,000
Light Truck (used)	2	4,000	500
Equipment (new) .	7	10,000	1,200
Equipment (used) .	4	3,000	500
Building (new)* ...	25	60,000	4,000

* Acquired and put into use on October 10, 1983.

Required:

1. Compute the amount of the investment tax credit for which the company is eligible in 1983.
2. **Interpretive Question** What effect does the investment tax credit have on management's decisions about replacing assets?

P29–6 Unifying Problem: Depreciation and Salvage Value

Required:

1. Refer to the information about Rio Trucking Company in P29–5. For each asset listed, what is the maximum percentage of the cost recovered in the year of acquisition (assuming the company takes a reduced investment tax credit)?
2. For each asset listed, how much salvage value must be taken into account in computing the tax deduction for depreciation?
3. **Interpretive Question** Explain the advantage to a taxpayer of being allowed to ignore the salvage value in computing the depreciation deduction.

P29–7 A Gain on the Sale of Machinery

On December 1, 1984, Parker Company sold a machine for $8,000 that it had purchased in 1974 for $27,000. Depreciation expense from the date of purchase to the date of sale amounted to $24,000.

Required:

1. What is the amount of gain on the sale?
2. How is the gain reported for tax purposes?
3. **Interpretive Question** If the company had preferred to postpone the gain, how should the asset have been disposed of?

P29–8 Unifying Problem: Expense Election, Regular Depreciation, and the Investment Tax Credit

Circle Corporation acquired a machine on January 3, 1983, for $60,000. Assume that the machine has a life of 8 years and no salvage value. The company has an effective tax rate of 40 percent.

Required:

1. What is the maximum tax saving in 1983 if the corporation uses the maximum expense election allowed, uses ACRS on an accelerated basis, and takes a reduced investment tax credit?
2. If the company elects to use straight-line depreciation and the life of the machine is listed as 8 years, what are the optional lives it can elect for depreciation without expecting any dispute from the Internal Revenue Service?
3. **Interpretive Question** Under what circumstances would it be to the company's advantage not to take the expense election and not to use accelerated depreciation?

P29–9 Partnership Income

X, Y, and Z are partners in Letters Company. They share profits in the ratio of 6:3:1, respectively. This past year, the partnership income totaled $92,000; X withdrew $20,000, Y withdrew $10,000, and Z withdrew no funds during the year.

Required:

What taxable incomes will the partners be required to report on their individual tax returns?

P29–10 Inventory Valuation Alternatives

Cream Typewriter Company was established this year. Management has asked you to determine which inventory system would result in the lowest taxable income: LIFO, FIFO, or weighted average.

Purchases during the year:	20 typewriters at $385 =	$ 7,700
	42 typewriters at $375 =	15,750
	49 typewriters at 370 =	18,130
	63 typewriters at 365 =	22,995
	12 typewriters at 395 =	4,740
Total purchases:	186 typewriters	$69,315
Ending inventory:	29 typewriters	
Average selling price: $450		

Required:

1. Assuming no other receipts, what is the gross income using each of the three inventory alternatives? (Round the weighted-average figure to two decimal places.)

2. **Interpretive Question** If a company has been using the LIFO inventory alternative during a period of rising prices, what will be the effect on the company's profits in a year in which the ending inventory is substantially less than the beginning inventory?

3. **Interpretive Question** Under what circumstances would the weighted-average inventory alternative be more desirable than either LIFO or FIFO?

P29–11 ACRS Depreciation for Buildings

On August 10, 1984, Holmes Corporation acquired land and a building for $600,000. The portion of the cost assignable to the land was $40,000.

Required:

1. What is the maximum depreciation Holmes Corporation is entitled to for each of the years 1984, 1985, and 1986?
2. Is the company entitled to an investment tax credit in 1984? Why?
3. Is the company entitled to elect an expense deduction in 1984? Why?
4. **Interpretive Question** Ordinarily the cost of land is not eligible for a depreciation expense deduction. Are there any circumstances when the cost of land is deductible for income tax purposes? Explain.

P29–12 Capital Budgeting

Bancroft Manufacturing Company is trying to decide whether to purchase new equipment to perform operations currently being performed on less efficient equipment. The purchase price is $72,000 delivered and installed. The company elects an 8 percent investment tax credit to be realized at the end of year 1. A company engineer estimates that the new equipment will save $14,000 in labor and other direct costs annually. The new equipment will have an economic life of 10 years and zero salvage value at the end of the 10 years. The equipment will be depreciated at full cost under ACRS for income tax purposes on a 5-year straight-line basis. The existing equipment has a book value of $10,000, a remaining economic life of 5 years, and can be disposed of now for $2,000. A loss on the sale would be an ordinary loss at the end of this tax year. The company's average tax rate is 40 percent and its after-tax cost of capital is 16 percent.

Required:

1. Should the new equipment be purchased?
2. What would the decision be if the cost of capital had been 14 percent?
3. **Interpretive Question** Assuming that the net present value of an investment in new equipment is so small that you are indifferent as to whether to make the purchase or keep the old equipment, what other factors would you consider in making the decision?

EPILOGUE

Throughout this book we have tried to show the relationship of accounting to business and to society in general. As a product of its environment, accounting is continually changing, although sometimes not as rapidly as many people in business and government would like. In this epilogue on the current environment of accounting, we begin by describing the organizations that influence accounting and conclude by noting some of the challenges facing the profession.

Organizations That Influence Accounting Practice

Various groups have been influential in the development of accounting practices. Among the most prominent are the American Accounting Association (AAA), the American Institute of Certified Public Accountants (AICPA), the Financial Accounting Standards Board (FASB), the Financial Executives' Institute (FEI), the National Association of Accountants (NAA), and the Securities and Exchange Commission (SEC).

AAA

The American Accounting Association has more than 15,000 members; one-third of them are educators and most of the others work for large industrial and CPA firms. Although accounting professors constitute less than half of the membership, they control the organization through an elected, nonpaid executive committee and an extensive volunteer committee system. The AAA emphasizes educational developments and research.

The Accounting Review, which the AAA publishes quarterly, is considered one of the major academic journals in accounting.

AICPA

More than 185,000 CPAs belong to the American Institute of Certified Public Accountants. Established in 1887, the AICPA is the major organization for the development of the auditing procedures used by CPA firms. Although CPAs are licensed by individual states, there is close cooperation between the states and the AICPA, which biannually makes available to each state a national, uniform CPA examination. An individual must pass this exam as well as meet state licensing requirements in order to become a certified public accountant, or CPA, and qualify for membership in the AICPA.

The *Journal of Accountancy* is published monthly by the AICPA. This magazine is designed to help CPAs keep abreast of current developments in accounting.

FASB

As we explained in Chapter 1 and its Supplement, the Financial Accounting Standards Board is responsible for establishing generally accepted accounting principles. It has jurisdiction over both the private sector and the nonprofit area.

FEI

The Financial Executives' Institute, formerly known as the Controllers' Institute, is a national organization comprised of financial executives of large corporations. Its members include treasurers, controllers, financial vice presidents, and others who hold important positions in the financial community. The FEI has been involved in sponsoring research projects on a wide variety of important business topics.

The Financial Executive is published monthly by the FEI. This magazine contains articles on financial management as well as on technical accounting topics.

NAA

The National Association of Accountants is the largest accounting group in the United States. Most of its members are engaged in managerial accounting. Consequently, the NAA is concerned primarily with such issues as budgeting, cost accounting, and information systems. Research sponsored by the NAA has traditionally dealt with the uses of accounting data within business organizations, although several recent studies have addressed external reporting considerations as well.

The NAA's monthly publication is *Management Accounting*, which focuses on issues related to the accountant's role in the decision-making process and the specific functions of planning and control.

SEC

With the possible exception of the FASB, the Securities and Exchange Commission has the greatest influence on accounting principles and practices. The SEC was created in 1934 and administers both the 1933 and the 1934 Securities and Exchange Acts. It is a quasi-judicial, quasi-legislative governmental body that regulates the issuance and trading of corporate securities and attempts to ensure full and fair disclosure to the public of all material facts concerning those securities. In order to perform its "watchdog" role, the SEC was given statutory power to prescribe accounting principles and reporting practices. Except in a few instances, the SEC has not exercised that power, but relies instead on the FASB and the AICPA. Nevertheless, the direct and subtle pressure of the SEC has significantly influenced existing accounting practices.[1]

Challenges Facing the Profession

Accounting is faced with many complex challenges. Among the most important are the challenges faced by individual accountants as increasing numbers of them assume leadership roles in businesses and nonprofit organizations. Accountants are no longer thought of simply as suppliers of financial data; they are also asked to interpret the data and to assist directly in the decision-making process. Accountants are becoming a part of the management team charged with making the decisions needed to accomplish organizational objectives. The profession must ask itself: Is the training provided in colleges and universities adequate to prepare students to take on these greater responsibilities?

The continuing development of generally accepted accounting principles provides another important challenge for the profession. As explained in Chapter 1, this task was assumed by a committee of the AICPA—the Accounting Principles Board (APB)—in 1959. Later, in 1973, the responsibility for establishing accounting principles was given to the FASB, an independent body. Some of the same criticisms leveled at the APB are now being directed toward the FASB. Congressional hearings in 1977, for example, criticized the FASB for allowing so many alternative accounting principles to exist. However, as the FASB explains, it is extremely difficult to establish generally accepted accounting principles that are sufficiently flexible to allow for the complexity of U.S business and yet uniform enough to provide comparability for investors and other users of accounting data.

Still other challenges are facing the accounting profession. For example, what modifications are needed in accounting to keep pace with new technological developments, such as electronic funds transfers and microcomputers? Should auditors be expected to detect fraud? What is the auditor's responsibility in terms of illegal payments made by the company being

[1] For an expanded discussion of the nature and workings of the SEC, see K. Fred Skousen, *An Introduction to the SEC*, 3rd ed. (Cincinnati: South-Western Publishing Co., 1983).

audited? What are the limits of an accountant's legal liability? Should accounting continue to be based on transactions recorded at historical costs, or should some other method of valuation be used in the primary financial statements? Should we account for inflation and, if so, how?

For the accounting profession, the next several years are of particular significance. This is especially true with respect to potential governmental influence on accounting. During the mid-1970s, the late Senator Lee Metcalf conducted an extensive study of the "Accounting Establishment." The resulting staff report contained several serious allegations. In essence, the report said that the accounting profession lacks independence, that it is self-serving and not in the public interest and therefore contributes to certain social ills, such as the misallocation of resources, fraud, and illegal payments. The problem, according to Metcalf's staff, is that the so-called "Big 8" public accounting firms control the AICPA, and indirectly the FASB, which sets flexible accounting and auditing standards. This, in turn, helps the clients of the large accounting firms—and these are, of course, the major corporations in the United States. The report further suggested that the SEC, by delegating its standard-setting authority to the FASB, was failing to protect the public and to fulfill its congressional mandate, and so was condoning this "conspiracy" within the accounting profession. Metcalf's staff concluded that the only way of improving accounting practices would be for the government to set the standards and thus regulate the profession.

It is an understatement to say that Metcalf's report created considerable excitement within the accounting profession as well as the business community. Eventually, Senate committee hearings were held and a final report was issued in November 1977.[2] This report concluded that improvements were needed in the accounting profession, but that self-reform, not governmental regulation, was the appropriate action for the present time. If the accounting profession, working with the SEC, was unwilling or unable to make needed changes, the report continued, then additional congressional action was likely to be forthcoming.

During the late 1970s, Representative John E. Moss also conducted an investigation of the accounting profession. However, Representative Moss went further than Senator Metcalf and introduced a bill, the Public Accounting Regulatory Act, which called for the establishment of a governmental organization to regulate the accounting profession. This regulatory agency would monitor the activities of the accounting firms that furnish audit reports and documents that are filed by companies in registering with the SEC. Fortunately, in our opinion, this bill was not passed by the 95th Congress. However, it may have set a precedent for future legislation.

Partly because of these pressures and partly because of a self-determined need, the accounting profession has conducted its own studies, which will greatly influence the future development of generally accepted accounting principles. As a result of one of these studies, the FASB was made completely independent of the AICPA, and an SEC Practices Division of the AICPA was established. Public accounting firms that have clients who re-

[2] *Improving the Accountability of Publicly Owned Corporations and Their Auditors* (Washington, D.C.: Government Printing Office, 1977).

port to the SEC belong to this division. These CPA firms are required to submit to an annual "peer review," an appraisal by another firm to ensure a high quality of practice. A Public Oversight Board for the accounting profession was also established.

In another study, the responsibilities of auditors were outlined. Several recommendations of this study—for example, the establishment of a full-time audit committee as a means of improving the process of setting auditing standards—have been implemented.

These and other efforts by the profession have helped accounting to grow and develop. Problems that seemed troublesome in the past have now been solved. Progress is being made. However, new problems arise to take the place of old ones. Finding solutions to these new problems presents a continuing challenge. It will take the combined efforts of a great many accountants, working through and with all the organizations mentioned here, including perhaps the Congress, to ensure that future accounting principles and practices will be founded in good accounting theory, and that they will meet the demands of the various users of accounting information.

SUPPLEMENT A

Present and Future Value Tables

Table I The Present Value of $1 Due in *n* Periods

Period	1%	2%	3%	4%	5%	6%	7%	8%	9%	10%	12%	14%	15%	16%	18%	20%	24%	28%	32%	36%
1	.9901	.9804	.9709	.9615	.9524	.9434	.9346	.9259	.9174	.9091	.8929	.8772	.8696	.8621	.8475	.8333	.8065	.7813	.7576	.7353
2	.9803	.9612	.9426	.9246	.9070	.8900	.8734	.8573	.8417	.8264	.7972	.7695	.7561	.7432	.7182	.6944	.6504	.6104	.5739	.5407
3	.9706	.9423	.9151	.8890	.8638	.8396	.8163	.7938	.7722	.7513	.7118	.6750	.6575	.6407	.6086	.5787	.5245	.4768	.4348	.3975
4	.9610	.9238	.8885	.8548	.8227	.7921	.7629	.7350	.7084	.6830	.6355	.5921	.5718	.5523	.5158	.4823	.4230	.3725	.3294	.2923
5	.9515	.9057	.8626	.8219	.7835	.7473	.7130	.6806	.6499	.6209	.5574	.5194	.4972	.4761	.4371	.4019	.3411	.2910	.2495	.2149
6	.9420	.8880	.8375	.7903	.7462	.7050	.6663	.6302	.5963	.5645	.5066	.4556	.4323	.4104	.3704	.3349	.2751	.2274	.1890	.1580
7	.9327	.8706	.8131	.7599	.7107	.6651	.6227	.5835	.5470	.5132	.4523	.3996	.3759	.3538	.3139	.2791	.2218	.1776	.1432	.1162
8	.9235	.8535	.7894	.7307	.6768	.6274	.5820	.5403	.5019	.4665	.4039	.3506	.3269	.3050	.2660	.2326	.1789	.1388	.1085	.0854
9	.9143	.8368	.7664	.7026	.6446	.5919	.5439	.5002	.4604	.4241	.3606	.3075	.2843	.2630	.2255	.1938	.1443	.1084	.0822	.0628
10	.9053	.8203	.7441	.6756	.6139	.5584	.5083	.4632	.4224	.3855	.3220	.2697	.2472	.2267	.1911	.1615	.1164	.0847	.0623	.0462
11	.8963	.8043	.7224	.6496	.5847	.5268	.4751	.4289	.3875	.3505	.2875	.2366	.2149	.1954	.1619	.1346	.0938	.0662	.0472	.0340
12	.8874	.7885	.7014	.6246	.5568	.4970	.4440	.3971	.3555	.3186	.2567	.2076	.1869	.1685	.1372	.1122	.0757	.0517	.0357	.0250
13	.8787	.7730	.6810	.6006	.5303	.4688	.4150	.3677	.3262	.2897	.2292	.1821	.1625	.1452	.1163	.0935	.0610	.0404	.0271	.0184
14	.8700	.7579	.6611	.5775	.5051	.4423	.3878	.3405	.2992	.2633	.2046	.1597	.1413	.1252	.0985	.0779	.0492	.0316	.0205	.0135
15	.8613	.7430	.6419	.5553	.4810	.4173	.3624	.3152	.2745	.2394	.1827	.1401	.1229	.1079	.0835	.0649	.0397	.0247	.0155	.0099
16	.8528	.7284	.6232	.5339	.4581	.3936	.3387	.2919	.2519	.2176	.1631	.1229	.1069	.0930	.0708	.0541	.0320	.0193	.0118	.0073
17	.8444	.7142	.6050	.5134	.4363	.3714	.3166	.2703	.2311	.1978	.1456	.1078	.0929	.0802	.0600	.0451	.0258	.0150	.0089	.0054
18	.8360	.7002	.5874	.4936	.4155	.3503	.2959	.2502	.2120	.1799	.1300	.0946	.0808	.0691	.0508	.0376	.0208	.0118	.0068	.0039
19	.8277	.6864	.5703	.4746	.3957	.3305	.2765	.2317	.1945	.1635	.1161	.0829	.0703	.0596	.0431	.0313	.0168	.0092	.0051	.0029
20	.8195	.6730	.5537	.4564	.3769	.3118	.2584	.2145	.1784	.1486	.1037	.0728	.0611	.0514	.0365	.0261	.0135	.0072	.0039	.0021
25	.7798	.6095	.4476	.3751	.2953	.2330	.1842	.1460	.1160	.0923	.0588	.0378	.0304	.0245	.0160	.0105	.0046	.0021	.0010	.0005
30	.7419	.5521	.4120	.3083	.2314	.1741	.1314	.0994	.0754	.0573	.0334	.0196	.0151	.0116	.0070	.0042	.0016	.0006	.0002	.0001
40	.6717	.4529	.3066	.2083	.1420	.0972	.0668	.0460	.0318	.0221	.0107	.0053	.0037	.0026	.0013	.0007	.0002	.0001	†	†
50	.6080	.3715	.2281	.1407	.0872	.0543	.0339	.0213	.0134	.0085	.0035	.0014	.0009	.0006	.0003	.0001	†	†	†	†
60	.5504	.3048	.1697	.0951	.0535	.0303	.0173	.0099	.0057	.0033	.0011	.0004	.0002	.0001	†	†	†	†	†	†

† The value of 0 to four decimal places.

Table II The Present Value of an Annuity of $1 per Period

Number of payments	1%	2%	3%	4%	5%	6%	7%	8%	9%	10%	12%	14%	15%	16%	18%	20%	24%	32%
1	0.9901	0.9804	0.9709	0.9615	0.9524	0.9434	0.9346	0.9259	0.9174	0.9091	0.8929	0.8772	0.8596	0.8621	0.8475	0.8333	0.8065	0.7576
2	1.9704	1.9416	1.9135	1.8861	1.8594	1.8334	1.8080	1.7833	1.7591	1.7355	1.6901	1.6467	1.6257	1.6052	1.5656	1.5278	1.4568	1.3315
3	2.9410	2.8839	2.8286	2.7751	2.7232	2.6730	2.6243	2.5771	2.5313	2.4869	2.4018	2.3216	2.2832	2.2459	2.1743	2.1065	1.9813	1.7663
4	3.9820	3.8077	3.7171	3.6299	3.5460	3.4651	3.3872	3.3121	3.2397	3.1699	3.0373	2.9137	2.8550	2.7982	2.6901	2.5887	2.4043	2.0957
5	4.8884	4.7135	4.5797	4.4518	4.3295	4.2124	4.1002	3.9927	3.8897	3.7908	3.6048	3.4331	3.3522	3.2743	3.1272	2.9906	2.7454	2.3452
6	5.7985	5.6014	5.4172	5.2421	5.0757	4.9173	4.7665	4.6229	4.4859	4.3553	4.1114	3.8887	3.7845	3.6847	3.4976	3.3255	3.0205	2.5342
7	6.7282	6.4720	6.2303	6.0021	5.7864	5.5824	5.3893	5.2064	5.0330	4.8684	4.5638	4.2883	4.1604	4.0386	3.8115	3.6046	3.2423	2.6775
8	7.6517	7.3255	7.0197	6.7327	6.4632	6.2098	5.9713	5.7466	5.5348	5.3349	4.9676	4.6389	4.4873	4.3436	4.0776	3.8372	3.4212	2.7860
9	8.5660	8.1622	7.7861	7.4353	7.1078	6.8017	6.5152	6.2469	5.9952	5.7590	5.3282	4.9464	4.7716	4.6065	4,3030	4.0310	3.5665	2.8651
10	9.4713	8.9826	8.5302	8.1109	7.7217	7.3601	7.0236	6.7101	6.4177	6.1446	5.6502	5.2161	5.0188	4.8332	4.4941	4.1925	3.6819	2.9304
11	10.3676	9.7868	9.2526	8.7605	8.3064	7.8869	7.4987	7.1390	6.8052	6.4951	5.9377	5.4527	5.2337	5.0286	4.6560	4.3271	3.7757	2.9776
12	11.2551	10.5733	9.9540	9.3851	8.8633	8.3838	7.9427	7.5361	7.1607	6.8137	6.1944	5.6603	5.4206	5.1971	4.7932	4.4392	3.8514	3.0133
13	12.1337	11.3484	10.6350	9.9856	9.3936	8.8527	8.3577	7.9038	7.4869	7.1034	6.4235	5.8424	5.5831	5.3423	4.9095	4.5327	3.9124	3.0404
14	13.0037	12.1062	11.2961	10.5631	9.8986	9.2950	8.7455	8.2442	7.7862	7.3667	6.6282	6.0021	5.7245	5.4675	5.0081	4.6106	3.3616	3.0609
15	13.8651	12.8493	11.9379	11.1184	10.3797	9.7122	9.1079	8.5595	8.0607	7.6061	6.8109	6.1422	5.8474	5.5755	5.0916	4.6755	4.0013	3.0764
16	14.7179	13.5777	12.5611	11.6523	10.8378	10.1059	9,4466	8.8514	8.3126	7.8237	6.9740	6.2651	5.9542	5.6685	5.1624	4.7296	4.0333	3.0882
17	15.5623	14.2919	13.1661	12.1657	11.2741	10.4773	9.7632	9.1216	8.5436	8.0216	7.1196	6.3729	6.0472	5.7487	5.2223	4.7746	4.0591	3.0971
18	16.3983	14.9920	13.7535	12.6593	11.6896	10.8276	10.0591	9.3719	8.7556	8.2014	7.2497	6.4674	6.1280	5.8178	5.2732	4.8122	4.0799	3.1039
19	17.2260	15.6785	14.3238	13.1339	12.0853	11.1581	10.3356	9.6036	8.9501	8.3649	7.3658	6.5504	6.1982	5.8775	5.3162	4.8435	4.0967	3.1090
20	18.0456	16.3514	14.8775	13.5903	12.4622	11.4699	10.5940	9.8181	9.1285	8.5136	7.4694	6.6231	6.2593	5.9288	5.3527	4.8696	4.1103	3.1129
25	22.0232	19.5235	17.4131	15.6221	14.0939	12.7834	11.6536	10.6748	9.8226	9.0770	7.8431	6.8729	6.4641	6.0971	5.4669	4.9476	4.1474	3.1200
30	25.8077	22.3965	19.6004	17.2920	15.3725	13.7648	12,4090	11.2578	10.2737	9.4269	8.0552	7.0027	6.5660	6.1772	5.5168	4.9789	4.1601	3.1242
40	32.8347	27.3555	23.1148	19.7928	17.1591	15.0463	13.3317	11.9246	10.7574	9.7791	8.2438	7.1050	6.6418	6.2335	5.5482	4.9966	4.1659	3.1250
50	39.1961	31.4236	25.7298	21.4822	18.2559	15.7619	13.8007	12.2335	10.9617	9.9148	8.3045	7.1327	6.6605	6.2463	5.5641	4.9995	4.1666	3.1250
60	44.9550	34.7609	27.6756	22.6235	18.9293	16.1614	14.0392	12.3766	11.0480	9.9672	8.3240	7.1401	6.6651	6.2482	5.5553	4.9999	4.1667	3.1250

Following are the tables for the future value of $1 and the future value of an annuity of $1. Although these are not used in the text, we have included them for those who might wish to cover future values in class.

Table III Amount of $1 Due in n Periods

Period	1%	2%	3%	4%	5%	6%	7%	8%	9%	10%	12%	14%	15%	16%	18%	20%	24%	32%
1	1.0100	1.0200	1.0300	1.0400	1.0500	1.0600	1.0700	1.0800	1.0900	1.1000	1.1200	1.1400	1.1500	1.1600	1.1800	1.2000	1.2400	1.3200
2	1.0201	1.0404	1.0609	1.0816	1.1025	1.1236	1.1449	1.1664	1.1881	1.2100	1.2544	1.2996	1.3225	1.3456	1.3924	1.4400	1.5376	1.7424
3	1.0303	1.0612	1.0927	1.1249	1.1576	1.1910	1.2250	1.2597	1.2950	1.3310	1.4049	1.4815	1.5209	1.5609	1.6430	1.7280	1.9066	2.3000
4	1.0406	1.0824	1.1255	1.1699	1.2155	1.2625	1.3108	1.3605	1.4116	1.4641	1.5735	1.6890	1.7490	1.8106	1.9388	2.0736	2.3642	3.0360
5	1.0510	1.1041	1.1593	1.2167	1.2763	1.3382	1.4026	1.4693	1.5386	1.6105	1.7623	1.9254	2.0114	2.1003	2.2878	2.4883	2.9316	4.0075
6	1.0615	1.1262	1.1941	1.2653	1.3401	1.4185	1.5007	1.5869	1.6771	1.7716	1.9738	2.1950	2.3131	2.4364	2.6996	2.9860	3.3652	5.2899
7	1.0721	1.1487	1.2299	1.3159	1.4071	1.5036	1.6058	1.7138	1.8280	1.9487	2.2107	2.5023	2.6600	2.8262	3.1855	3.5832	4.5077	6.9826
8	1.0829	1.1717	1.2668	1.3686	1.4775	1.5938	1.7182	1.8509	1.9926	2.1436	2.4760	2.8526	3.0590	3.2784	3.7589	4.2998	5.5895	9.2170
9	1.0937	1.1951	1.3048	1.4233	1.5513	1.6895	1.8385	1.9990	2.1719	2.3579	2.7731	3.2519	3.5179	3.8030	4.4355	5.1598	6.9310	12.166
10	1.1046	1.2190	1.3439	1.4802	1.6289	1.7908	1.9672	2.1589	2.3674	2.5937	3.1058	3.7072	4.0456	4.4114	5.2338	6.1917	8.5944	16.059
11	1.1157	1.2434	1.3842	1.5395	1.7103	1.8983	2.1049	2.3316	2.5804	2.8531	3.4785	4.2262	4.6524	5.1173	6.1759	7.4031	10.657	21.198
12	1.1268	1.2682	1.4258	1.6010	1.7959	2.0122	2.2522	2.5182	2.8127	3.1384	3.8960	4.8179	5.3502	5.9360	7.2876	8.9161	13.214	27.982
13	1.1381	1.2936	1.4685	1.6651	1.8856	2.1329	2.4098	2.7196	3.0658	3.4523	4.3635	5.4924	6.1528	6.8858	8.5994	10.699	16.386	36.937
14	1.1495	1.3195	1.5126	1.7317	1.9799	2.2609	2.5785	2.9372	3.3417	3.7975	4.8871	6.2613	7.0757	7.9875	10.147	12.839	20.319	48.756
15	1.1610	1.3459	1.5580	1.8009	2.0789	2.3966	2.7590	3.1722	3.6425	4.1772	5.4736	7.1379	8.1371	9.2655	11.973	15.407	25.195	64.358
16	1.1726	1.3728	1.6047	1.8730	2.1829	2.5404	2.9522	3.4259	3.9703	4.5950	6.1304	8.1372	9.3576	10.748	14.129	18.488	31.242	84.953
17	1.1843	1.4002	1.6528	1.9479	2.2920	2.6928	3.1588	3.7000	4.3276	5.0545	6.8660	9.2765	10.761	12.467	16.672	22.186	38.740	112.13
18	1.1961	1.4282	1.7024	2.0258	2.4066	2.8543	3.3799	3.9960	4.7171	5.5599	7.6900	10.575	12.375	14.462	19.673	26.623	48.038	148.02
19	1.2081	1.4568	1.7535	2.1068	2.5270	3.0256	3.6165	4.3157	5.1417	6.1159	8.6128	12.055	14.231	16.776	23.214	31.948	59.567	195.39
20	1.2202	1.4859	1.8061	2.1911	2.6533	3.2071	3.8697	4.6610	5.6044	6.7275	9.6463	13.743	16.366	19.460	27.393	38.337	73.864	257.91
30	1.3478	1.8114	2.4273	3.2434	4.3219	5.7435	7.6123	10.062	13.267	17.449	29.959	50.950	66.211	85.849	143.37	237.37	634.81	4142.0
40	1.4889	2.2080	3.2620	4.8010	7.0400	10.285	14.974	21.724	31.409	45.259	93.050	188.88	267.86	378.72	750.37	1469.7	5455.9	66520.
50	1.6446	2.6916	4.3839	7.1067	11.467	18.420	29.457	46.901	74.357	117.39	289.00	700.23	1083.6	1670.7	3927.3	9100.4	46890.	†
60	1.8167	3.2810	5.8916	10.519	18.679	32.987	57.946	101.25	176.03	304.48	897.59	2595.9	4383.9	7370.1	20555.	56347.	†	†

† Values in excess of 100,000.

Table IV Amount of an Annuity of $1 per Period

Number of Periods	1%	2%	3%	4%	5%	6%	7%	8%	9%	10%	12%	14%	15%	16%	18%	20%	24%	32%
1	1.0000	1.0000	1.0000	1.0000	1.0000	1.0000	1.0000	1.0000	1.0000	1.0000	1.0000	1.0000	1.0000	1.0000	1.0000	1.0000	1.0000	1.0000
2	2.0100	2.0200	2.0300	2.0400	2.0500	2.0600	2.0700	2.0800	2.0900	2.1000	2.1200	2.1400	2.1500	2.1600	2.1800	2.2000	2.2400	2.3200
3	3.0301	3.0604	3.0909	3.1216	3.1525	3.1836	3.2149	3.2464	3.2781	3.3100	3.3744	3.4396	3.4725	3.5056	3.5724	3.6400	3.7776	4.0624
4	4.0604	4.1216	4.1836	4.2465	4.3101	4.3746	4.4399	4.5061	4.5731	4.6410	4.7793	4.9211	4.9934	5.0665	5.2154	5.3680	5.6842	6.3624
5	5.1010	5.2040	5.3091	5.4163	5.5256	5.6371	5.7507	5.8666	5.9847	6.1051	6.3528	6.6101	6.7424	6.8771	7.1542	7.4416	8.0484	9.3983
6	6.1520	6.3081	6.4684	6.6330	6.8019	6.9753	7.1533	7.3359	7.5233	7.7156	8.1152	8.5355	8.7537	8.9775	9.4420	9.9299	10.980	13.405
7	7.2135	7.4343	7.6625	7.8983	8.1420	8.3938	8.6540	8.9228	9.2004	9.4872	10.089	10.730	11.066	11.413	12.141	12.915	14.615	18.695
8	8.2857	8.5830	8.8923	9.2142	9.5491	9.8975	10.259	10.636	11.028	11.435	12.299	13.232	13.726	14.240	15.327	16.499	19.122	25.678
9	9.3685	9.7546	10.159	10.582	11.026	11.491	11.978	12.487	13.021	13.579	14.775	16.085	16.785	17.518	19.085	20.798	24.712	34.895
10	10.462	10.949	11.463	12.006	12.577	13.180	13.816	14.486	15.192	15.937	17.548	19.337	20.303	21.321	23.521	25.958	31.643	47.061
11	11.566	12.168	12.807	13.486	14.206	14.971	15.783	16.645	17.560	18.531	20.654	23.044	24.349	25.732	28.755	32.150	40.237	63.121
12	12.682	13.412	14.192	15.025	15.917	16.869	17.888	18.977	20.140	21.384	24.133	27.270	29.001	30.850	34.931	39.580	50.894	84.320
13	13.809	14.680	15.617	16.626	17.713	18.882	20.140	21.495	22.953	24.522	28.029	32.088	34.351	36.786	42.218	48.496	64.109	112.30
14	14.947	15.973	17.086	18.291	19.598	21.015	22.550	24.214	26.019	27.975	32.392	37.581	40.504	43.672	50.818	59.195	80.496	149.23
15	16.096	17.293	18.598	20.023	21.578	23.276	25.129	27.152	29.360	31.772	37.279	43.842	47.580	51.659	60.965	72.035	100.81	197.99
16	17.257	18.639	20.156	21.824	23.657	25.672	27.888	30.324	33.003	35.949	42.753	50.980	55.717	60.925	72.939	87.442	126.01	262.35
17	18.430	20.012	21.761	23.697	25.840	28.212	30.840	33.750	36.973	40.544	48.883	59.117	65.075	71.673	87.068	105.93	157.25	347.30
18	19.614	21.412	23.414	25.645	28.132	30.905	33.999	37.450	41.301	45.599	55.749	68.394	75.836	84.140	103.74	128.11	195.99	459.44
19	20.810	22.840	25.116	27.671	30.539	33.760	37.379	41.446	46.018	51.159	63.439	78.969	88.211	98.603	123.41	154.74	244.03	607.47
20	22.019	24.297	26.870	29.778	33.066	36.785	40.995	45.762	51.160	57.275	72.052	91.024	102.44	115.37	146.62	186.68	303.60	802.86
30	34.784	40.568	47.575	56.084	66.438	79.058	94.460	113.28	136.30	164.49	241.33	356.78	434.74	530.31	790.94	1181.8	2640.9	12940.
40	48.886	60.402	75.401	95.025	120.79	154.76	199.63	259.05	337.88	442.59	767.09	1342.0	1779.0	2360.7	4163.2	7343.8	22728.	†
50	64.463	84.579	112.79	152.66	209.34	290.33	406.52	573.76	815.08	1163.9	2400.0	4994.5	7217.7	10435.	21813.	45497.	†	†
60	81.669	114.05	163.05	237.99	353.58	533.12	813.52	1253.2	1944.7	3034.8	7471.6	18535.	29219.	46057.	†	†	†	†

† Values in excess of 100,000.

SUPPLEMENT B

The Financial Statements of International Business Machines (IBM) Corporation

Most large corporations issue an annual report to stockholders. The report includes the primary financial statements, along with notes to the statements (which are an integral part of the statements), supporting schedules, and management's analysis of operations and expectations for the future. Following are the financial statements and related material from the 1981 Annual Report of IBM. Frequent reference to this supplement as you study the text will help to illustrate and clarify the concepts and procedures discussed in the chapters.

Report of Management

Responsibility for the integrity and objectivity of the financial information presented in this Annual Report rests with IBM management. The accompanying financial statements have been prepared in conformity with generally accepted accounting principles, applying certain estimates and judgments as required.

IBM maintains an effective system of internal accounting control. It consists, in part, of organizational arrangements with clearly defined lines of responsibility and delegation of authority. We believe this system provides reasonable assurance that transactions are executed in accordance with management authorization, and that they are appropriately recorded, in order to permit preparation of financial statements in conformity with generally accepted accounting principles and to adequately safeguard, verify and maintain accountability of assets. An important element of the system is an on-going internal audit program.

To assure the effective administration of internal control, we carefully select and train our employees, develop and disseminate written policies and procedures, provide appropriate communication channels, and foster an environment conducive to the effective functioning of controls. We continue to believe that it is essential for the company to conduct its business affairs in accordance with the highest ethical standards, as set forth in the IBM Business Conduct Guidelines. These guidelines, translated into numerous languages, are distributed to employees throughout the world, and reemphasized through internal programs to assure that they are understood and followed.

Price Waterhouse, independent accountants, are retained to examine IBM's financial statements. Their accompanying report is based on an examination conducted in accordance with generally accepted auditing standards, including a review of internal accounting controls and tests of accounting procedures and records.

The Audit Committee of the Board of Directors is composed solely of outside directors, and is responsible for recommending to the Board the independent accounting firm to be retained for the coming year, subject to stockholder approval. The Audit Committee meets periodically and privately with the independent accountants, with our internal auditors, as well as with IBM management, to review accounting, auditing, internal accounting controls and financial reporting matters.

John R. Opel
President and Chief Executive Officer

Dean P. Phypers
Senior Vice President, Finance & Planning

Report of Independent Accountants

To the Stockholders
and Board of Directors of International
Business Machines Corporation

In our opinion, the accompanying consolidated financial statements, appearing on pages 22, 24, 26 and 28 through 37, present fairly the financial position of International Business Machines Corporation and its subsidiary companies at December 31, 1981 and 1980, and the results of their operations and changes in funds for the years 1981, 1980 and 1979, in conformity with generally accepted accounting principles consistently applied. Also, in our opinion, the Five-Year Comparison of Selected Financial Data for 1977 through 1981 presents fairly the financial information included therein. Our examinations of these statements were made in accordance with generally accepted auditing standards and accordingly included such tests of the accounting records and such other auditing procedures as we considered necessary in the circumstances.

Price Waterhouse

January 26, 1982
New York, N.Y.

Price Waterhouse

gross income *receipts from the sale of products and services and the rentals of products and equipment*

cost of sales, rentals, and services *the costs incurred during the period to produce the merchandise sold, maintain rental equipment, and provide services, exclusive of selling, developmental, engineering, and general and administrative expenses; equal to beginning inventory plus cost of goods manufactured less ending inventory*

gross margin (not shown on IBM statement) *revenues minus cost of sales, rentals, and services; indicates the amount of revenues left to contribute to paying expenses; for IBM, it is (in millions)* $17,054 [$29,070 − ($5,321 + $4,152 + $2,543)]

interest expense *interest paid for use of money borrowed from a bank or other lending institution*

net earnings (income) *a measure of the overall performance of a business entity; equal to revenues plus gains minus expenses and losses for the period*

earnings per share *net earnings divided by the average number of shares of stock outstanding during the period; stated as a per-share amount so that shareholders can easily determine their individual portion of total net earnings for a year*

International Business Machines Corporation
and Subsidiary Companies

Consolidated Statement of Earnings
for the year ended December 31:

	1981		1980		1979	
(Dollars in millions except per share amounts)						
Gross Income:						
Sales	$ 12,901		$ 10,919		$ 9,473	
Rentals	10,839		10,869		10,069	
Services	5,330		4,425		3,321	
		$ 29,070		$ 26,213		$ 22,863
Cost of sales	5,321		4,197		3,267	
Cost of rentals	4,152		3,771		3,491	
Cost of services	2,543		2,181		1,655	
Selling, development and engineering, and general and administrative expenses	11,027		10,324		9,205	
Interest expense	407		273		141	
		23,450		20,746		17,759
		5,620		5,467		5,104
Other income, principally interest		368		430		449
Earnings before income taxes		5,988		5,897		5,553
Provision for U.S. Federal and non-U.S. income taxes		2,680		2,335		2,542
Net Earnings		$ 3,308		$ 3,562		$ 3,011
Per share		$ 5.63		$ 6.10		$ 5.16

Average number of shares outstanding:
1981–587,803,373
1980–583,516,764
1979–583,373,269

The notes on pages 29 through 36 are an integral part of this statement.

22 *IBM 1981 Annual Report*

Management Discussion

Results of Operations

Advances in technology continued at a rapid pace, resulting in the delivery to users of greater productivity at lower cost. This trend has led to substantial expansion of the customer base, with many new users finding utility in IBM information processing products. High levels of orders and product shipments, and expanding services continued worldwide in 1981 in spite of a general downturn in the economy.

Total gross income increased 10.9% over 1980. Gross income from U.S. operations was $15,088 million, an increase of 21.4% over 1980. Gross income from non-U.S. operations amounted to $13,982 million. This increase of only 1.4% resulted principally from the effects of the strengthening U.S. dollar. Net earnings before income taxes increased 1.5% over 1980. After providing for income taxes, net earnings for the year were down $254 million from 1980, a decrease of 7.1%.

Sales of data processing equipment were $9,449 million, an increase of 23.9% over 1980. Although there were substantial new rental machine installations during the year, as well as selective price increases, worldwide data processing rental income remained flat. U.S. data processing equipment rentals increased by 12.6%, while non-U.S. rentals showed a period-to-period decline. The high level of sales of installed rental equipment in recent periods and the translation effect of a stronger U.S. dollar held down rental income growth. Gross income from maintenance, program products, and other support services continued strong throughout the business, showing an increase of 20.4% over 1980.

Gross income and earnings from office products reflected the general weakness in the economy, as well as the shift of word processing workload from stand-alone products to new higher-function products and systems.

The rapid fall of major foreign currencies against the U.S. dollar in late 1980 and in 1981 was unprecedented in recent times (graphs illustrating these relationships appear on page 31). While a strong dollar may benefit the United States economy in many ways, the abruptness and magnitude of these currency changes had an adverse effect on IBM's consolidated financial results. Had currency rates remained constant year-to-year, and if the effects of currency rate changes on business volumes, pricing and other operating decisions were disregarded, it is estimated that consolidated gross income for 1981 would have been over $2 billion greater, and net earnings over $600 million greater.

Gross profit margins on both sales and rentals have been eroded by high front-end costs of new products, changing product mix, and major expenditures for productive capacity. In addition, the strong surge in U.S. currency has significantly affected period-to-period margin comparisons. For example, non-U.S. gross income from rentals was adversely affected by the current exchange rates, but with no favorable impact on depreciation costs which are translated at historical exchange rates. Overall margins have also been impacted by the faster growth of lower margin service activities, such as maintenance and support services. The margins on these services are improving.

The strengthened U.S. dollar had a beneficial effect on selling, development, engineering and general and administrative expense by reducing the non-U.S. component of these expenses when translated into dollars.

The company recorded exchange gains in 1981 of $94 million. These gains resulted primarily from the translation of assets and liabilities recorded or denominated in currencies other than the U.S. dollar. This compares with an exchange gain of $24 million for 1980. Such gains are principally unrealized.

The consolidated effective income tax rate in 1981 was 44.8%, compared to 39.6% in 1980. The variance reflects higher effective tax rates on non-U.S. earnings which resulted primarily from the impact of currency translation, and from adjustments made in 1980 for prior period tax liabilities. The 1981 effective tax rate is more in line with rates in recent years preceding 1980.

The company's goals are to continue to be the high-quality, low-cost producer; to accelerate real growth and achieve greater financial returns. Through substantial investments in research and development, in high-technology manufacturing processes and equipment, and through effective cost and expense controls, IBM intends to achieve these objectives and continue to offer new products to our customers at lower cost for similar or improved function. New methods of marketing and maintenance have been initiated. Quality programs are expected to yield significant cost savings from more reliable products that require less service support.

The substantial investment in additional capacity and the development of new channels of distribution, have positioned the company to more efficiently supply the requirements of its rapidly growing customer base. Economic uncertainty will likely persist. Sharp changes in foreign currency rates may again have short-term effects. But the increasing demand for IBM products and services, and the productivity they deliver, should assure a long-range trend of steady and sustained real growth in business volumes and financial performance.

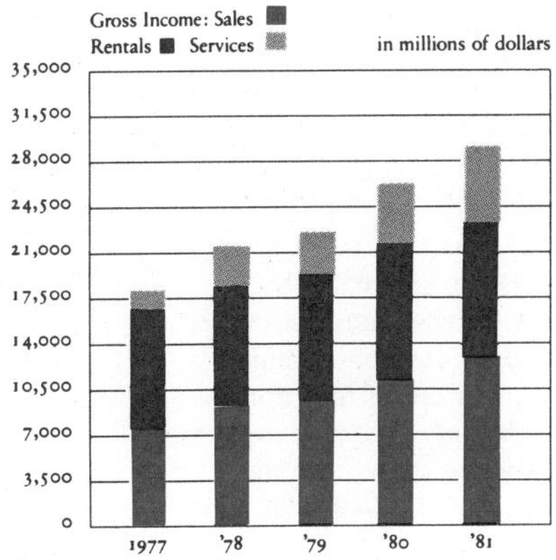

International Business Machines Corporation and Subsidiary Companies

Consolidated Statement of Financial Position at December 31:

	1981		1980	
	(Dollars in millions)			
Assets				
Current Assets:				
Cash	$ 454		$ 281	
Marketable securities, at lower of cost or market	1,575		1,831	
Notes and accounts receivable–trade, less allowance: 1981, $187; 1980, $195	4,382		4,562	
Other accounts receivable	410		315	
Inventories	2,805		2,293	
Prepaid expenses	677		643	
		$ 10,303		$ 9,925
Rental Machines and Parts	17,241		15,352	
Less: Accumulated depreciation	7,651		6,969	
		9,590		8,383
Plant and Other Property	12,895		11,018	
Less: Accumulated depreciation	5,207		4,384	
		7,688		6,634
Deferred Charges and Other Assets		2,005		1,761
		$ 29,586		$ 26,703
Liabilities and Stockholders' Equity				
Current Liabilities:				
Taxes	$ 2,412		$ 2,369	
Loans payable	773		591	
Accounts payable	872		721	
Compensation and benefits	1,556		1,404	
Deferred income	389		305	
Other accrued expenses and liabilities	1,318		1,136	
		$ 7,320		$ 6,526
Deferred Investment Tax Credits		252		182
Reserves for Employees' Indemnities and Retirement Plans		1,184		1,443
Long-Term Debt		2,669		2,099
Stockholders' Equity:				
Capital stock, par value $1.25 per share. Shares authorized, 650,000,000. Issued: 1981–592,293,624; 1980–584,262,074	4,389		3,992	
Retained earnings	13,772		12,491	
	18,161		16,483	
Less: Treasury stock, at cost 1980–455,242 shares	—		30	
		18,161		16,453
		$ 29,586		$ 26,703

The notes on pages 29 through 36 are an integral part of this statement.

24 *IBM 1981 Annual Report*

current assets *cash and other assets that may reasonably be expected to be converted to cash within one year or during the normal operating cycle*

accumulated depreciation *the total amount of depreciation expense recorded on the rental machines and parts and on plant and other property since the items were acquired*

deferred charges and other assets *deferred charges represent long-term prepayments for assets that will benefit the company over several years in the future; "other assets" may represent intangible assets that have material value to the company*

current liabilities *debts or other obligations that will be paid with current assets or otherwise discharged within one year; deferred income is income previously received that will be earned during the current period*

deferred investment tax credits *investment tax credit rules stipulate a maximum investment credit that may be taken in any one year; amounts over the maximum are deferred (postponed) until subsequent years*

reserves for employees' indemnities and retirement plan *obligations arising from pension and other contractual agreements for future payments to employees*

stockholders' equity (owners' equity) *the ownership interest in an enterprise's assets; equals net assets (total assets minus total liabilities) and is comprised of two elements, contributed capital and retained earnings*

treasury stock *issued stock that has subsequently been reacquired by the corporation*

Management Discussion

Financial Condition

The company has increased its investment substantially over the past several years to take advantage of expanding market opportunities. In the last three years, IBM's investments in capital assets and research and development have totalled $24 billion. Capital expenditures in 1981 amounted to $6.8 billion, of which one-third was invested in plant and equipment, with the remainder in rental machines. In addition, the company invested $1.6 billion in research and development in 1981.

Although funds for IBM's expansion continue to be generated principally from operations, the investment in rental machines, plant and equipment, and inventory required additional external sources of capital during 1981. Management initiated a variety of actions to maintain a strong capital structure while obtaining funds at relatively low cost. New long-term borrowings consisted primarily of $360 million of Eurodollar notes and a $168 million Swiss franc loan. The company established the IBM Credit Corporation as a wholly owned subsidiary to finance customer installment payment agreements; it raised funds through the employee stock purchase plan by using authorized unissued stock and discontinuing the purchase of treasury shares; it entered into agreements with several companies to purchase their unutilized tax credits and related deductions under the provisions of the Economic Recovery Tax Act of 1981; and it negotiated currency swap agreements with the World Bank, which effectively eliminated the foreign exchange risk associated with the $254 million German mark and $112 million Swiss franc loans undertaken in 1980.

Despite periodic shortages of capital, high interest rates, and dramatic shifts in currency exchange rates, IBM has been able to utilize its high credit rating and acquire appropriate levels of financing through worldwide sources. IBM has frequently borrowed in currencies other than the U.S. dollar. While there are risks associated with foreign currency obligations, there are also clear advantages. Interest rates are often much lower than comparable dollar loans, and the exchange loss risk associated with repayment is minimized by the availability of foreign source income in most major countries. Consequently, the company has considerable financing flexibility in many different currencies throughout the world. In addition, IBM has approximately $3.2 billion of unused lines of credit, mostly short-term.

Mindful of the high cost of borrowing and the long lead-time before technological investments yield payback, management has placed increased emphasis on the effective employment of assets. Internal measurements on managerial performance emphasize return on invested capital, inventory turnover, cash flow, payback and other indices of asset management.

Large capital investments are expected to exert pressure on operational cash flow. The ability to assess the resulting funding requirements is complicated by uncertain economic conditions, particularly inflation, volatile interest rates, and foreign currency fluctuations. In addition, cash flows are substantially affected by the customer's largely unpredictable decision to purchase or lease equipment. In this environment, the company's ability to generate or obtain cash on a timely basis is of primary importance. IBM's strong balance sheet position and high credit rating allow management to consider a full range of financing options for future capital needs. The choices will ultimately depend upon the prevailing financial market and economic conditions.

To set forth cash flow information more clearly, IBM's financial statements now include a Statement of Funds Flow, which replaces the Statement of Changes in Financial Position. Years 1980 and 1979 have also been restated. The Statement of Funds Flow depicts the sources of cash and cash equivalents, how they were used, and how much remains available.

Management feels certain that growth prospects for IBM's business will remain strong. National policies regarding tax relief, capital formation, and deregulation are likely to have substantial positive effects on industry in general. Internal and external forecasts point to continuing high demand for information products, and IBM is confident that it has the resources and the people to meet the challenges of the changing marketplace.

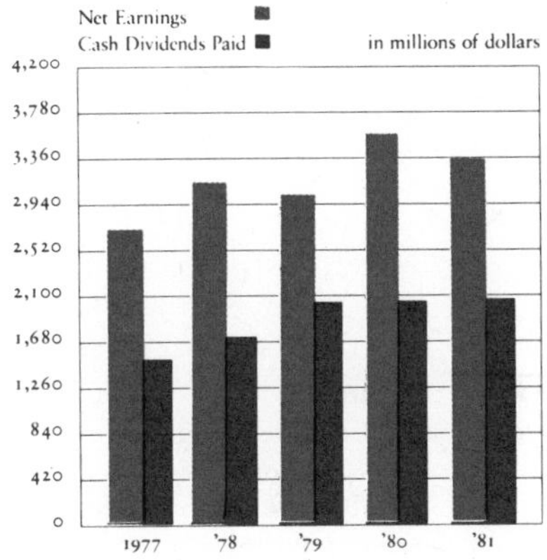

funds statement *the primary financial statement that shows an entity's major sources and uses of financial resources (funds) during a period; IBM defines funds as cash and marketable securities, other companies may define funds as cash or working capital*

capital expenditures *expenditures that are recorded as assets because they are expected to benefit more than the current period; for IBM, they include expenditures for rental equipment, plant, and other property*

employee stock plans *the rights of certain employees, under fixed conditions of price, time, and amount, to acquire shares of the corporation's capital stock*

International Business Machines Corporation and Subsidiary Companies

Consolidated Statement of Funds Flow for the year ended December 31:

	1981		1980		1979	
	(Dollars in millions)					
Funds (Cash and Marketable Securities) at January 1		$ 2,112		$ 3,771		$ 4,030
Provided from Operations:						
Sources:						
Net earnings	$ 3,308		$ 3,562		$ 3,011	
Depreciation charged to costs and expenses	2,899		2,362		1,970	
Depreciation of manufacturing facilities capitalized in rental machines	430		397		351	
Net book value of rental machines and other property retired or sold	1,255		1,009		779	
Other	(189)		90		353	
	7,703		7,420		6,464	
Uses:						
Investment in rental machines	4,610		4,334		4,212	
Investment in plant and other property	2,235		2,258		1,779	
	6,845		6,592		5,991	
Increase in deferred charges and other assets	244		275		338	
Net change in working capital (excluding cash, marketable securities, loans payable and dividend payable)	(151)		310		343	
	6,938		7,177		6,672	
Net provided from operations		765		243		(208)
Provided from External Financing:						
Net change in long-term debt	570		510		1,304	
Net change in loans payable	182		(342)		691	
Net provided from external financing		752		168		1,995
Provided from (used for) Employee Stock Plans		423		(62)		(38)
		4,052		4,120		5,779
Less: Cash Dividends Paid		2,023		2,008		2,008
Funds (Cash and Marketable Securities) at December 31		$ 2,029		$ 2,112		$ 3,771

The notes on pages 29 through 36 are an integral part of this statement.

26 *IBM 1981 Annual Report*

Summary of Sources of Funds (in millions)

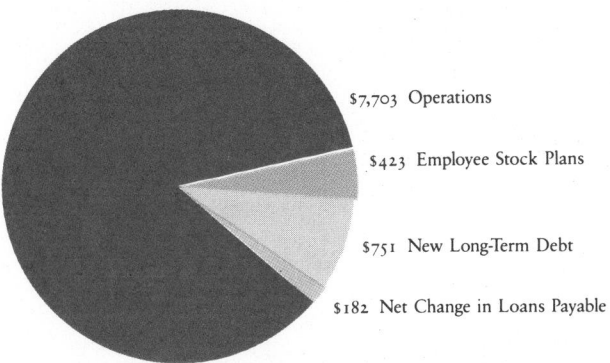

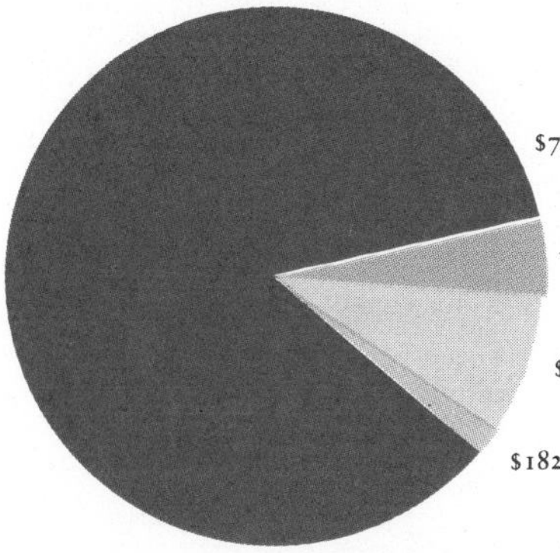

Summary of Uses of Funds (in millions)

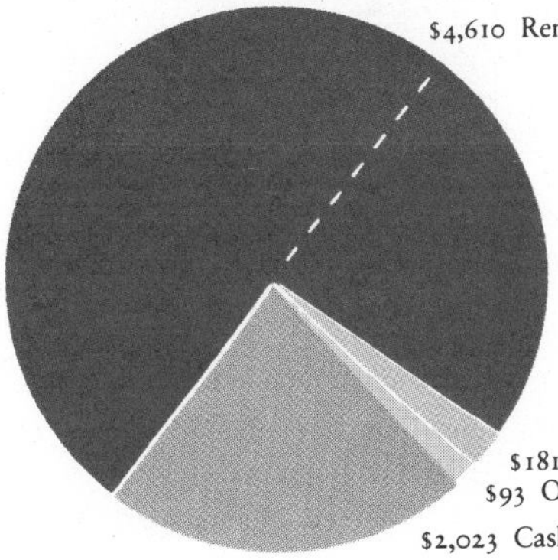

Capital Expenditures

During 1981, IBM's growing business, together with the company's need to replace obsolete equipment, required a worldwide investment of $6,845 million, including $4,610 million for rental machines.

Retirements, covering obsolete and dismantled equipment, as well as rental machines sold that previously were under lease to customers, amounted to $3,079 million in 1981, including $2,721 million of rental machines. These retirements were charged against amounts provided out of prior and current years' earnings, or against cost of sales.

The major IBM facilities that were completed or under construction throughout the world in 1981 are listed below.

Completed	Purpose	Sq. Ft. (in thousands)
†Rochester, Minnesota	*Mfg. & Dev.*	699
†Burlington, Vermont	*Mfg. & Dev.*	482*
†Boeblingen, Germany	*Mfg.*	457*
†Austin, Texas	*Mfg. & Dev.*	410*
†Vimercate, Italy	*Mfg.*	342
Santa Palomba, Italy	*Mfg.*	303
†Raleigh, North Carolina	*Mfg. & Dev.*	287*
†Manassas, Virginia	*Mfg. & Dev.*	247
†Mainz, Germany	*Mfg.*	232*
†Endicott, New York	*Mfg.*	224
†Boca Raton, Florida	*Mfg. & Dev.*	202*
†Essonnes, France	*Mfg.*	167
Charlotte, North Carolina	*Mfg. & Dev.*	158
†Hannover, Germany	*Mfg.*	153
†Yasu, Japan	*Mfg.*	150

Under Construction		
New York, New York	*Mktg.*	1031
†San Jose, California	*Mfg. & Dev.*	926
†Charlotte, North Carolina	*Mfg. & Dev.*	714
Kawasaki, Japan	*Mktg.*	440
†Manassas, Virginia	*Mfg. & Dev.*	425
Milan, Italy	*Distr. Center*	424
†Portsmouth, England	*Adm.*	365
Buenos Aires, Argentina	*Mktg.*	347
St. Louis, Missouri	*Mktg.*	308
London, England	*Mktg.*	300
†Toronto, Canada	*Mfg.*	277
Stuttgart, Germany	*Adm. & Mktg.*	276
†Greenock, Scotland	*Mfg.*	266
Herrenberg, Germany	*Mktg.*	225
†Jarfalla, Sweden	*Mfg.*	219
†Boca Raton, Florida	*Mfg.*	188
†Austin, Texas	*Mfg. & Dev.*	186
†Burlington, Vermont	*Mfg. & Dev.*	145
†Endicott, New York	*Mfg.*	116

† Additions to existing facilities.
* Excludes square footage completed in years 1979 and/or 1980.

statement of stockholders' equity *a financial statement showing the significant changes in a company's equity accounts during the year*

International Business Machines Corporation and Subsidiary Companies

Consolidated Statement of Stockholders' Equity for the year ended December 31:

	Capital Stock	Retained Earnings	Treasury Stock	Total
	(Dollars in millions)			
1979				
Stockholders' Equity, January 1, 1979	$ 3,942	$ 9,576	$ (24)	$ 13,494
Net earnings		3,011		3,011
Cash dividends declared		(1,506)		(1,506)
Capital stock issued under employee plans (391,300 shares)	24			24
Purchases (6,357,500 shares) and sales (6,319,289 shares) of treasury stock under employee plan–net		(69)	(1)	(70)
Tax reductions applicable to stock related to employee plans	8			8
Stockholders' Equity, December 31, 1979	3,974	11,012	(25)	14,961
1980				
Net earnings		3,562		3,562
Cash dividends declared		(2,008)		(2,008)
Capital stock issued under employee plans (288,816 shares)	16			16
Purchases (7,674,300 shares) and sales (7,597,773 shares) of treasury stock under employee plan–net		(75)	(5)	(80)
Tax reductions applicable to stock related to employee plans	2			2
Stockholders' Equity, December 31, 1980	3,992	12,491	(30)	16,453
1981				
Net earnings		3,308		3,308
Cash dividends declared		(2,023)		(2,023)
Capital stock issued under employee plans (8,031,550 shares)	394			394
Sales (455,242 shares) of treasury stock under employee plan		(4)	30	26
Tax reductions applicable to stock related to employee plans	3			3
Stockholders' Equity, December 31, 1981	$ 4,389	$ 13,772	$ —	$ 18,161

The notes on pages 29 through 36 are an integral part of this statement.

28 *IBM 1981 Annual Report*

International Business Machines Corporation
and Subsidiary Companies

Notes to Consolidated Financial Statements:

Significant Accounting Policies

Principles of Consolidation:

The consolidated financial statements include the accounts of International Business Machines Corporation and its U.S. and non-U.S. subsidiary companies, other than IBM Credit Corporation, a wholly owned financing subsidiary. The equity method is used to account for the investment in IBM Credit Corporation and for investments in joint ventures and affiliated companies in which IBM has 50% or less ownership.

Translation of Non-U.S. Currency Amounts:

Assets and liabilities denominated in currencies other than U.S. dollars are translated to U.S. dollars at year-end exchange rates, except that inventories and plant, rental machines and other property are translated at approximate rates prevailing when acquired. Income and expense items are translated at average rates of exchange prevailing during the year, except that inventories charged to cost of sales and depreciation are translated at historical rates. Exchange gains and losses are included in earnings currently.

Gross Income:

Gross income is recognized from sales when the product is shipped or in certain cases upon customer acceptance, from rentals in the month in which they accrue, and from services over the contractual period or as the services are performed. Rental plans include maintenance service and contain discontinuance and purchase option provisions. Rental terms are predominantly monthly or for a two-year period, with some covering periods up to five years.

Depreciation:

Rental machines, plant and other property are carried at cost and depreciated over their estimated useful lives. Depreciation of rental machines is computed using the sum-of-the-years digits method. Depreciation of plant and other property is computed using either accelerated methods or the straight-line method.

Retirement Plans:

Current service costs are accrued currently. Prior service costs resulting from improvements in the plans are amortized generally over 10 years.

Selling Expenses:

Selling expenses are charged against income as they are incurred.

Income Taxes:

Income tax expense is based on reported earnings before income taxes. It thus includes the effects of timing differences between reported and taxable earnings that arise because certain transactions are included in taxable earnings in other years. Investment tax credits are deferred and amortized as a reduction of income tax expense over the average useful life of the applicable classes of property. Purchased tax credits and deductions are offset against the purchase cost.

Inventories:

Raw materials, operating supplies, finished goods and work in process applicable to equipment sales are included in inventories at the lower of average cost or market. Work in process applicable to equipment rentals is similarly valued and included in rental machines and parts.

Non-U.S. Operations		1981	1980	1979
			(Dollars in millions)	
At end of year:	Net assets employed			
	Current assets	$ 5,430	$ 5,547	$ 5,826
	Current liabilities	4,102	3,911	3,608
	Working capital	1,328	1,636	2,218
	Plant, rental machines and other property, net	7,633	6,823	5,477
	Deferred charges and other assets	894	971	839
		9,855	9,430	8,534
	Reserves for employees' indemnities and retirement plans	1,184	1,443	1,395
	Long-term debt	496	437	294
		1,680	1,880	1,689
	Net assets employed	$ 8,175	$ 7,550	$ 6,845
	Number of employees	149,794	146,973	146,800
For the year:	Gross income from sales, rentals and services	$ 13,982	$ 13,787	$ 12,244
	Earnings before income taxes	$ 2,392	$ 2,946	$ 2,731
	Provision for U.S. Federal and non-U.S. income taxes	1,153	1,044†	1,304
	Net earnings	$ 1,239	$ 1,902	$ 1,427
	Capital expenditures	$ 3,274	$ 3,367	$ 2,800

† See Taxes on page 32.

Shipments of data processing equipment in non-U.S. operations continued at high levels and strong growth rates in 1981. Despite this strong performance, non-U.S. financial results were affected even more than U.S. operations by inflation and other factors. Adding to these conditions was the severe impact of the stronger U.S. dollar. The Management Discussion on page 23 refers to this effect in greater detail. The graphs on the following page further illustrate the decline in value, in relation to the dollar, of the five major foreign currencies in which IBM conducts most of its non-U.S. business.

Undistributed earnings of non-U.S. subsidiaries included in consolidated retained earnings amounted to $6,428 million at December 31, 1981, $6,108 million at December 31, 1980, and $5,529 million at December 31, 1979. These earnings are indefinitely reinvested in non-U.S. operations. Accordingly, no provision has been made for taxes that might be payable upon remittance of such earnings.

Foreign Currency Valued in U.S. Dollars

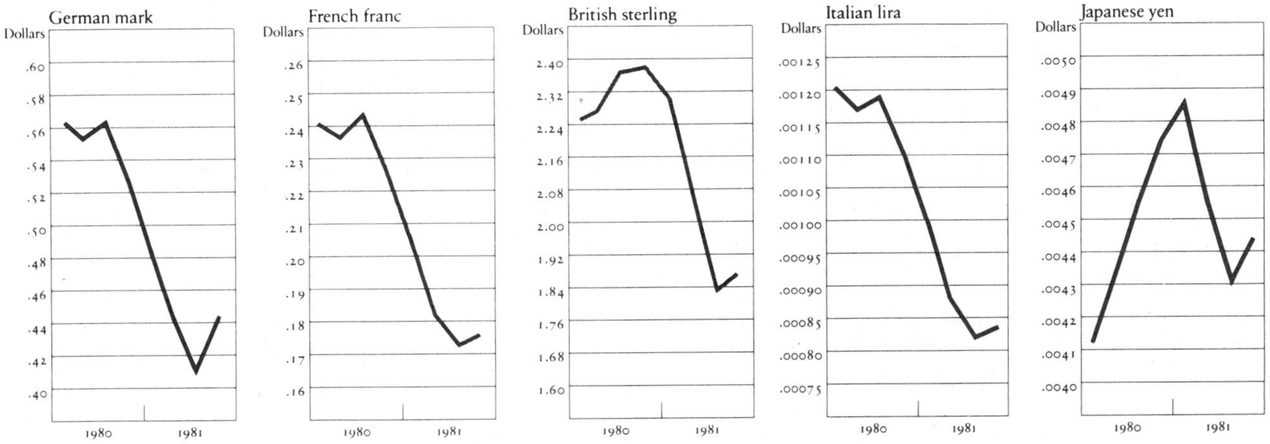

Inventories

	December 31, 1981	December 31, 1980
	(Dollars in millions)	
Finished goods	$ 547	$ 524
Work in process	1,999	1,518
Raw materials and operating supplies	259	251
Total	$ 2,805	$ 2,293

Rental Machines and Parts

Rental machines and parts are comprised of capitalized machines, rental machine work in process and field service parts. Rental machines include machines installed with IBM in the amount of $2,318 million and $1,886 million at December 31, 1981 and 1980, respectively, with accumulated depreciation of $1,696 million and $1,396 million. Rental machine work in process and field service parts totaled $3,806 million and $3,595 million at December 31, 1981 and 1980.

Plant and Other Property

	December 31, 1981	December 31, 1980
	(Dollars in millions)	
Land and land improvements	$ 653	$ 623
Buildings	5,123	4,351
Factory, laboratory and office equipment	7,119	6,044
	12,895	11,018
Less: Accumulated depreciation	5,207	4,384
Total	$ 7,688	$ 6,634

Taxes	1981	1980	1979
		(Dollars in millions)	
Earnings before U.S. Federal and non-U.S. income taxes:			
U.S. operations	$ 3,596	$ 2,951	$ 2,822
Non-U.S. operations	2,392	2,946	2,731
	$ 5,988	$ 5,897	$ 5,553
Provision for U.S. Federal and non-U.S. income taxes:			
U.S. operations	$ 1,527	$ 1,291	$ 1,238
Non-U.S. operations	1,153	1,044	1,304
	2,680	2,335	2,542
Real estate, personal property, state and local franchise (including state income taxes of $200 million in 1981, $138 million in 1980, and $127 million in 1979), social security and other taxes	1,587	1,480	1,315
Total	$ 4,267	$ 3,815	$ 3,857
The components of the provision for U.S. Federal and non-U.S. income taxes are as follows:			
U.S.:			
Current	$ 994	$ 776	$ 914
Net tax effects of timing differences	49	(34)	86
Net deferred investment tax credits	70	42	30
	1,113	784	1,030
Non-U.S.:			
Current	1,464	1,546	1,575
Net tax effects of timing differences	103	5	(63)
	1,567	1,551	1,512
Total provision	$ 2,680	$ 2,335	$ 2,542

The consolidated effective U.S. Federal and non-U.S. income tax rate was 44.8% in 1981, 39.6% in 1980 and 45.8% in 1979. In 1980, the lower effective tax rate on earnings of non-U.S. operations accounts for 5.3 percentage points of the difference between the effective rate and the U.S. statutory rate of 46.0%.

The consolidated tax provision for 1980 includes the effect of a reduction of prior periods income tax liabilities of $224 million (38¢ per share), resulting from changes in tax laws and other adjustments of prior years income tax expenses. Of this amount, $207 million relates to non-U.S. operations.

Long-Term Debt

	December 31, 1981	December 31, 1980
	(Dollars in millions)	
U.S. Operations:		
9½% notes due 1986	$ 500	$ 500
9⅜% debentures due 2004 (with sinking fund payments 1985-2003)	500	500
10.80% notes due 1983-1986	300	300
Other (average interest rate at December 31, 1981, in parentheses) payable in:		
U.S. dollars, due 1984-2001 (13.2 %)	416	—
Swiss francs, due 1986-1987 (6.4%)	262	112
German marks, due 1985-1988 (10.1%)	199	254
	2,177	1,666
Non-U.S. Operations:		
Various obligations (average interest rate at December 31, 1981, in parentheses) payable in:		
U.S. dollars, due 1983-1992 (14.5%)	182	150
French francs, due 1983-1991 (12.4%)	170	178
Other currencies, due 1983-2011 (16.8%)	144	109
	496	437
	2,673	2,103
Less: Unamortized discount, related principally to the 9½% notes and 9⅜% debentures	4	4
Total	$ 2,669	$ 2,099

Annual maturity and sinking fund requirements in millions of dollars on long-term debt outstanding at December 31, 1981, are as follows: 1983, $158; 1984, $289; 1985, $290; 1986, $928; 1987, $269; 1988 and beyond, $739.

Interest Cost

Interest on borrowings amounted to $480 million in 1981, $325 million in 1980 and $141 million in 1979. Of these amounts, $73 million in 1981 and $52 million in 1980 were included in the cost of buildings under construction, resulting in a net earnings increase of $39 million and $31 million, respectively. Prior to 1980, all interest was charged against income as incurred.

Lines of Credit

At December 31, 1981, the company had unused lines of credit available with a number of U.S. banks. These lines of credit permit the company to borrow up to an aggregate of $2,000 million outstanding at any time, at interest rates not to exceed the banks' prime rate. Included in these lines of credit is $1,875 million, which is shared with the IBM Credit Corporation. In addition, a number of non-U.S. subsidiaries had available unused lines of credit of approximately $1,200 million. Interest rates on borrowings would vary from country to country depending on local market conditions. About $160 million of such unused lines require the payment of commitment fees, which generally range from ¼% to ½%.

IBM Credit Corporation

IBM Credit Corporation, a wholly owned unconsolidated subsidiary, finances installment payment agreements relating to sales by IBM of its products in the United States. Its operations commenced as of May 1, 1981. IBM's investment in the IBM Credit Corporation is accounted for by the equity method, and IBM Credit Corporation earnings are included in other income in IBM's consolidated statement of earnings. IBM has agreed to cause the IBM Credit Corporation to have a positive net worth at all times. IBM Credit Corporation has $205 million of lines of credit available, in addition to those shared with the IBM Corporation.

The following information has been summarized from the financial statements of the IBM Credit Corporation. Additional information is available in its 1981 Annual Report. Copies may be obtained by writing to: IBM Credit Corporation, 1200 High Ridge Road, Stamford, Connecticut 06904.

Earnings for the period May 1, 1981 to December 31, 1981	(Dollars in thousands)
Finance and other income	$ 49,212
Expenses	34,270
Provision for income taxes	5,075
Net earnings	$ 9,867

Financial position at December 31, 1981	
Assets:	
Cash and cash equivalents	$ 532
Installment payment agreement receivables–net	689,553
Deferred charges and other assets	1,644
Total Assets	$ 691,729
Liabilities and Stockholder's Equity:	
Commercial paper	$ 318,426
Due to IBM Corporation	97,162
Taxes and other accruals	9,036
Long-term debt	162,238
Stockholder's equity	104,867
Total Liabilities and Stockholder's Equity	$ 691,729

Research and Development

Research and development expenses amounted to $1,612 million in 1981, $1,520 million in 1980 and $1,360 million in 1979.

Retirement Plans

The company and its U.S. subsidiaries have trusteed, noncontributory retirement plans, for which accrued costs are funded, covering substantially all regular and part-time employees. At December 31, 1981, there were 13,538 individuals receiving benefits under the plans. Most subsidiaries outside the United States have retirement plans under which funds are deposited with trustees, annuities are purchased under group contracts, or reserves are provided.

The cost of all plans for 1981, 1980 and 1979 was $1,060 million, $1,109 million and $971 million respectively. Unfunded or unaccrued prior service costs under all plans amounted to $516 million at December 31, 1981, and $821 million at December 31, 1980. Updating of the actuarial assumptions, including the assumed investment rate of return, used to value the U.S. retirement plans had the effect of reducing unfunded prior service costs in 1981 by approximately $185 million. However, the effect of such changes on the pension cost for 1981 was not material.

The following table compares estimated benefits and net assets for U.S. retirement plans calculated as prescribed by the Financial Accounting Standards Board. The assumed rate of return used in determining the actuarial present value of accumulated benefits was 5½ percent for 1981 and 4¾ percent for 1980.

At December 31	1981	1980
	(Dollars in millions)	
Actuarial present value of accumulated benefits:		
Vested	$ 5,158	$ 5,166
Nonvested	232	168
	$ 5,390	$ 5,334
Net assets available for benefits	$ 6,155	$ 5,712

At December 31, 1981 and at December 31, 1980 the market value of fund assets and reserves of non-U.S. plans exceeded or approximated the present value of vested benefits computed in the usual actuarial manner.

Stock Purchase Plan

In April, 1981, stockholders approved a new five-year Employees Stock Purchase Plan, effective July 1, 1981, which authorizes up to 40 million shares of capital stock for the Plan. Employees who are not participants in a stock option plan may purchase IBM's capital stock through payroll deductions of up to 10% of their compensation. The price an employee pays for a share of stock is 85% of the average market price on the date the employee has accumulated enough money to buy a share.

Under the 1981 Plan and its predecessor 1976 Plan, employees purchased 8,284,857 shares during the year, including 455,242 treasury shares, for which $408 million was paid to IBM. At December 31, 1981, 35,839,693 reserved unissued shares remain available for purchase under the 1981 Employees Stock Purchase Plan.

Stock Option Plans

The stock option plans provide for granting officers and other key employees options to purchase IBM's capital stock at 100% of the market price on the day of grant. Options have a maximum duration of 10 years and may be exercised in four annual installments, commencing one year from date of grant.

The following table summarizes stock option transactions during 1981:

	Number of Shares	
	Under Option	Available for Option
Balance at January 1, 1981	12,942,483	2,327,095
Options granted	2,377,223	(2,377,223)
Options terminated	(339,446)	160,944
Options exercised	(95,251)	—
Balance at December 31, 1981	14,885,009	110,816
Exercisable at December 31, 1981	10,284,165	

IBM received $5.2 million for the 95,251 shares purchased during 1981. The 14,885,009 shares under option at December 31, 1981, are at option prices ranging from $41.60 to $85.40 per share.

Litigation

In January, 1982, the Department of Justice agreed to a dismissal of the civil antitrust action it had commenced against IBM in 1969.

In December, 1980, the Commission of the European Communities filed a "statement of objections" seeking modification of certain IBM business practices in the Common Market area. The Commission may also seek to impose fines. Most of the practices to which the Commission has objected have been held to be legitimate competition in the United States. IBM has denied the charges in this proceeding and is defending its position.

Geographic Area and Industry Segment Information

Financial information by geographic area and industry segment for the years 1981, 1980 and 1979 is summarized below to provide a better understanding of IBM's operations. Material interdependencies and overlaps exist among IBM's operating units and, therefore, the information may not be indicative of the financial results of, or investments in, the reported areas and segments were they independent organizations.

Geographic Areas	1981	1980	1979
		(Dollars in millions)	
United States			
Gross income–Customers	$ 15,088	$ 12,426	$ 10,619
Interarea transfers	1,857	1,615	1,101
Total	$ 16,945	$ 14,041	$ 11,720
Net earnings	2,094	1,725	1,612
Assets at December 31	16,022	13,737	12,631
Europe/Middle East/Africa			
Gross income–Customers	$ 9,312	$ 9,932	$ 8,837
Interarea transfers	383	491	531
Total	$ 9,695	$ 10,423	$ 9,368
Net earnings	758	1,511	1,082
Assets at December 31	9,499	9,573	8,987
Americas/Far East			
Gross income–Customers	$ 4,670	$ 3,855	$ 3,407
Interarea transfers	659	450	410
Total	$ 5,329	$ 4,305	$ 3,817
Net earnings	470	398	355
Assets at December 31	4,650	3,975	3,358
Eliminations			
Gross income	$ (2,899)	$ (2,556)	$ (2,042)
Net earnings	(14)	(72)	(38)
Assets	(585)	(582)	(446)
Consolidated			
Gross income	$ 29,070	$ 26,213	$ 22,863
Net earnings	$ 3,308	$ 3,562	$ 3,011
Assets at December 31	$ 29,586	$ 26,703	$ 24,530

In the Europe/Middle East/Africa area, European operations accounted for approximately 95% of gross income in 1981, 1980 and 1979.

Net earnings in 1980 include the effect of a reduction of prior periods tax liabilities of $17 million in the United States, $187 million in Europe/Middle East/Africa, and $20 million in Americas/Far East.

Interarea transfers, consisting principally of completed machines, sub-assemblies and parts, are priced at cost plus an appropriate service charge, applied consistently throughout the world. The cost and service charges that relate to asset transfers are capitalized and depreciated or amortized by the importing area. Interarea accounts receivable, the unamortized portion of service charges, and the net change during the year in unamortized service charges, have been eliminated in consolidation.

Industry Segments	1981	1980	1979
		(Dollars in millions)	
Information-Handling Business:			
Data Processing			
Gross income—Customers	$ 24,073	$21,367	$18,338
Operating income	5,832	5,330	4,737
Assets at December 31	23,846	21,088	17,373
Depreciation expense	2,576	2,061	1,683
Capital expenditures	6,094	6,027	5,359
Office Products			
Gross income—Customers	4,219	4,135	3,849
Operating income	263	479	566
Assets at December 31	3,495	3,377	3,316
Depreciation expense	306	287	275
Capital expenditures	714	537	608
Federal Systems			
Gross income—Customers	719	647	612
Operating income	56	37	35
Assets at December 31	436	371	329
Depreciation expense	16	13	11
Capital expenditures	37	27	23
Other Business			
Gross income—Customers	59	64	64
Operating income	2	3	6
Assets at December 31	32	36	39
Depreciation expense	1	1	1
Capital expenditures	—	1	1
Consolidated			
Gross income—Customers	$ 29,070	$26,213	$22,863
Operating income	$ 6,153	$ 5,849	$ 5,344
General corporate and interest expense	(533)	(382)	(240)
Other income, principally interest	368	430	449
Earnings before income taxes	$ 5,988	$ 5,897	$ 5,553
Assets identified to segments	$ 27,809	$24,872	$21,057
Assets not identified to segments, including marketable securities	1,777	1,831	3,473
Total assets at December 31	$ 29,586	$26,703	$24,530
Depreciation expense	$ 2,899	$ 2,362	$ 1,970
Capital expenditures	$ 6,845	$ 6,592	$ 5,991

IBM's operations, with very minor exceptions, are in the field of information-handling systems, equipment and services. However, for purposes of segment reporting, IBM's information-handling business has been reported as three segments:

Data Processing—consists of information-handling products and services such as data processing machines and systems, computer programming, systems engineering, education and related services and supplies for commercial and government customers.

Office Products—consists of information-handling products, systems and services such as electric and electronic typewriters, magnetic media typewriters and systems, information processors, document printers, copiers, and related supplies and services for commercial and government customers.

Federal Systems—consists of specialized information-handling products and services for United States space, defense and other agencies and, in some instances, other customers.

Other Business consists of educational, training and testing materials and services for school, home and industrial use.

Intersegment transfers of products and services similar to those offered to unaffiliated customers are not material.

Gross Income by Segment ††

	1981	1980	1979
		(Dollars in millions)	
Data Processing segment:			
Equipment			
Sales	$ 9,449	$ 7,627	$ 6,335
Rentals	9,660	9,591	8,846
	19,109	17,218	15,181
Maintenance contracts, program products, parts and supplies			
Sales	458	411	385
Rentals	24	25	24
Services	4,482	3,713	2,748
	4,964	4,149	3,157
	24,073	21,367	18,338
Office Products segment:			
Sales	2,245	2,183	2,084
Rentals	1,155	1,253	1,199
Services	819	699	566
	4,219	4,135	3,849
All other segments:			
Sales	749	698	669
Services	29	13	7
	778	711	676
Total	$ 29,070	$ 26,213	$ 22,863

††This information should be read in conjunction with the Industry Segments notes on pages 35 and 36. Gross income from rentals includes maintenance service on rented equipment. Gross income from services consists of maintenance service on sold equipment, program products and other services.

Five-Year Comparison of Selected Financial Data

		1981	1980	1979	1978	1977
			(Dollars in millions except per share amounts)			
For the year:	Gross income from sales, rentals and services	$ 29,070	$ 26,213	$ 22,863	$ 21,076	$ 18,133
	Net earnings	3,308	3,562	3,011	3,111	2,719
	Per share †	5.63	6.10	5.16	5.32	4.58
	Cash dividends paid	2,023	2,008	2,008	1,685	1,488
	Per share †	3.44	3.44	3.44	2.88	2.50
	Investment in plant, rental machines and other property	6,845	6,592	5,991	4,046	3,395
	Return on stockholders' equity	19.1%	22.7%	21.2%	23.8%	21.4%
At end of year:	Total assets	$ 29,586	$ 26,703	$ 24,530	$ 20,771	$ 18,978
	Net investment in plant, rental machines and other property	17,278	15,017	12,193	9,302	7,889
	Working capital	2,983	3,399	4,406	4,511	4,864
	Long-term debt	2,669	2,099	1,589	285	256
	Stockholders' equity	18,161	16,453	14,961	13,494	12,618

†Adjusted for 1979 stock split.

Supplemental Financial Information

Information on Effects of Changing Prices

Sustained high inflation has eroded industry's ability to fund the replacement and expansion of productive capacity. Under conventional accounting principles, financial statements are prepared on the basis of historical costs, i.e. the actual dollars exchanged at the time of the transaction. Financial statements prepared in this manner, however, do not adequately reflect the decline in the purchasing power of those dollars and the subsequent effect on cash flows required for future replacement of capital assets.

In an attempt to measure the effects of inflation, the Financial Accounting Standards Board prescribed two methods for experimentation. The Current Cost Method uses estimated changes in specific prices to restate the value of inventories, rental machines, plants and other property. Such estimates are based upon latest production costs, published price indices, current suppliers' prices, and appraised valuations, and represent year-end costs, or costs in effect at date of sale, to attain the same functional service potential as embodied in the company's existing assets. The Constant Dollar Method restates these assets, both U.S. and non-U.S., simply by factoring the increase in the rate of general inflation, as measured by the U.S. Consumer Price Index for all Urban Consumers (CPI-U).

The Current Cost Method better measures the impact of inflation on IBM because it reflects the positive effects of technological and other productivity improvements. It also recognizes changes in vendor prices caused by supply and demand and other factors which cause the specific prices of IBM's vendor purchases to fluctuate differently than price changes resulting solely from general inflation.

Comparison of Selected Financial Data Adjusted for Changes in Specific Prices (Current Cost)

	As Reported in Financial Statements	Restated in Average 1981 Dollars		
	1981	1981	1980	1979
		(Dollars in millions except per share amounts)		
Gross income from sales, rentals and services	$ 29,070	$ 29,070	$ 28,932	$ 28,647
Cost of sales, rentals and services	12,016	11,964	11,449	10,717
Expenses and other income	11,066	11,185	11,377	11,268
Provision for U.S. Federal and non-U.S. income taxes	2,680	2,680	2,577	3,185
Net earnings	$ 3,308	$ 3,241	$ 3,529	$ 3,477
Earnings per share	$ 5.63	$ 5.51	$ 6.05	$ 5.96
Stockholders' equity (net assets)	$ 18,161	$ 19,749	$ 20,193	$ 20,827
Loss from decline in purchasing power of net monetary assets		$ 62	$ 301	$ 570
Increase in general price level of inventories, rental machines and plant and other property		$ 1,982	$ 2,350	$ 2,302
Increase (decrease) in specific prices (Current Cost)		(212)	504	840
Excess of increase in general price level over increase (decrease) in specific prices		$ 2,194	$ 1,846	$ 1,462

Experimentation with the Constant Dollar Method as described above, has proven to have little or no application to IBM's business. Under this method, IBM's 1981 restated earnings would be $1,899 million and stockholders' equity $21,694 million.

Using the Current Cost Method the company's 1981 financial results, when adjusted for changing prices, show a decline of $67 million from reported net earnings and an increase in stockholders' equity of $1,588 million. The estimated current cost of acquiring existing plants and other property is $2,239 million greater than the depreciated acquisition costs; the current production costs of rental machines are $665 million less, and inventories $49 million less. The above changes in cost represent the additional cash investment the company would have to expend at current prices to acquire the same service potential of existing assets. The additional depreciation in 1981 on these restated assets would have been $215 million. Other costs would have been reduced by $148 million. Therefore, had the company made this added investment, the 1981 earnings would have been $67 million less.

Productivity improvements from technological advances continued to partially offset inflationary pressures and are reflected in the lower estimated current costs of inventories and rental machines.

In addition, the difference between the amounts reported in the financial statements and the restated amounts using current costs is significantly influenced by changes in currency exchange rates. The Current Cost Method prescribes that non-U.S. inventories, rental machines and plant and other property, as well as the related depreciation expense and other costs, be translated into U.S. dollars using current exchange rates. In preparing consolidated financial statements, the company uses historical exchange rates to translate these assets and the related depreciation expense and other costs. The use of different translation measurements, therefore, has a significant effect on the comparability of data reported in the financial statements and the information prepared using current costs.

When a company retains monetary assets or liabilities such as cash or debt, gains and losses in purchasing power occur during periods of inflation. IBM's net monetary asset position resulted in a significantly reduced purchasing power loss in 1981, reflecting increased debt and cash outlays made for productive capacity and rental machines.

Although inflation-adjusted information is an imprecise estimate, it nevertheless serves to emphasize the debilitating effects of inflation. It points out the importance of bringing inflation under control and the need for further public policy initiatives to encourage capital investment.

Five-Year Comparison of Selected Financial Data Adjusted for General Inflation (Constant Dollar)

The amounts shown below for the years 1977 to 1980 have been converted into the equivalent purchasing power of 1981 dollars by applying to the amounts reported the rate of changes in the average CPI-U from that year to year 1981.

	1981	1980	1979	1978	1977
	(Dollars in millions except per share amounts)				
Gross income from sales, rentals and services	$ 29,070	$ 28,932	$ 28,647	$ 29,381	$ 27,214
Cash dividends paid per share†	$ 3.44	$ 3.80	$ 4.31	$ 4.01	$ 3.75
Market price per share† (at December 31)	$ 56.88	$ 74.92	$ 80.67	$ 104.04	$ 102.63
Average Consumer Price Index for all Urban Consumers (1967=100.0)	272.4	246.8	217.4	195.4	181.5

The actual market price of IBM stock on the New York Stock Exchange composite tape at December 31, for years 1977 to 1981 (adjusted for stock split) was $68.38, $74.63, $64.38, $67.88 and $56.88 respectively.
† Adjusted for 1979 stock split.

Selected Quarterly Data

1981	Gross Income	Gross Profit	Net Earnings	Per Share Earnings	Per Share Dividends	Stock Prices High	Stock Prices Low
	(Dollars in millions except per share and stock prices)						
First Quarter	$ 6,461	$ 3,900	$ 730	$ 1.25	$ .86	$ 71.50	$ 60.25
Second Quarter	6,895	4,047	804	1.37	.86	63.38	55.13
Third Quarter	6,721	3,875	693	1.18	.86	58.88	52.25
Fourth Quarter	8,993	5,232	1,081	1.83	.86	57.63	48.38
Total	$ 29,070	$ 17,054	$ 3,308	$ 5.63	$ 3.44		
1980							
First Quarter	$ 5,748	$ 3,611	$ 681	$1.17	$ .86	$72.00	$51.38
Second Quarter	6,181	3,813	764	1.31	.86	60.38	50.38
Third Quarter	6,479	3,981	884†	1.51†	.86	69.13	58.38
Fourth Quarter	7,805	4,659	1,233†	2.11†	.86	72.75	63.25
Total	$26,213	$16,064	$3,562	$6.10	$3.44		

† Includes the effect, $70 million (12¢ per share), and $154 million (26¢ per share) in the third and fourth quarters respectively, of reductions in income tax expense applicable to prior years.

There were 742,162 stockholders of record at December 31, 1981. During 1981, stockholders received $2,023 million in cash dividends. The regular quarterly cash dividend payable March 10, 1982, will be at the rate of $.86 per share. This dividend will be IBM's 268th consecutive quarterly cash dividend.

The stock prices reflect the high and low prices for IBM's capital stock on the New York Stock Exchange composite tape for the last two years.

GLOSSARY

A

absorption costing: A product costing approach that assigns all fixed and variable manufacturing costs to the units produced; also called full costing; *compare* variable costing. (669, 746)

accelerated cost recovery system (ACRS): IRS regulations that allocate the cost of an asset according to predefined recovery percentages. (344, 958)

account: An accounting record in which the results of similar transactions are accumulated; shows increases, decreases, and a balance. (61)

accounting: A service activity designed to accumulate, measure, and communicate financial information about organizations for decision-making purposes. (17)

accounting concepts and assumptions: Fundamental ideas that provide the foundation upon which the principles and procedures of accounting theory rest. (22)

accounting controls: The plan of organization and the procedures and records that are concerned with safeguarding a company's assets and assuring the reliability of the financial records. (625)

accounting cycle: In the accounting process, the sequence of procedures that includes analyzing business documents, journalizing, posting, determining account balances and preparing a trial balance and work sheet, journalizing and posting adjusting entries, preparing financial statements, closing nominal accounts, balancing the accounts, and preparing a post-closing trial balance. Interpretation of reports, while not usually considered a routine step in the accounting cycle, is a vital function of accountants. (60)

accounting equation: An algebraic equation that expresses the relationship between assets (resources), liabilities (obligations), and owners' equity (net equity, or the residual interest in a business after all liabilities have been met): Assets = Liabilities + Owners' Equity. (21)

accounting information system: A subset of the managerial information system; the system whereby the financial data derived from recorded transactions are collected, processed, and reported in order to provide the financial information needed by a firm. (56, 656)

accounting manual: A document that lists all accounts and describes the proper bookkeeping for transactions likely to be processed through each account. (634)

accounting model: The basic accounting concepts and assumptions that determine the manner of recording, measuring, and reporting an entity's transactions. (18)

accounting principles: Broad guidelines that identify the procedures to be used in specific accounting situations. (23)

Accounting Principles Board (APB): The organization established by the AICPA in 1959 to set standards for financial accounting and reporting. (24)

accounting procedures: Specific rules or methods for applying accounting principles. (23)

accounting process: The means of transforming economic data into accounting reports that can be interpreted and used in decision making; often used interchangeably with accounting cycle. (54)

account payable: Money owed to creditors. (306)

account receivable: Money due from rendering services or selling merchandise on credit; a current asset. (206, 301)

accounts receivable turnover: A measure used to determine a company's average collection period for receivables; computed by dividing net sales (or net credit sales) by average accounts receivable. (570)

accrual-basis accounting: A system of accounting in which revenues and expenses are recorded as they are earned and incurred, not necessarily when cash is received or paid; *compare* cash-basis accounting. (107)

accrual-basis historical cost method: An income measurement method in which income is defined as revenues earned minus expenses incurred during a period, without regard to changes in the values of assets or liabilities or in the general price level. (201)

accrued liability: An obligation for benefits received but not yet paid for. (307)

accumulated depreciation: The total amount of depreciation expense that has been recorded on an asset since it was originally purchased; a contra account deducted from the original cost of an asset on the balance sheet. (138, 278, 337)

acid-test ratio (or quick ratio): A measure of the liquidity of a business; equal to cash plus short-term investments and receivables divided by current liabilities. (312, 570)

adjusting entries: Entries required at the end of each accounting period to recognize, on an accrual basis, revenues and expenses for the period and to report proper amounts for asset, liability, and owners' equity accounts. (109)

administrative controls: Procedures that deal primarily with a company's operational efficiency and its employees' compliance with authorized policies and procedures. (625)

aging accounts receivable: The process of categorizing each account receivable by the number of days it has been outstanding. (212)

all-financial-resources concept: A concept used in preparing a funds statement that reflects all financing and investing activities for a period as sources and uses of funds, whether or not they increase or decrease cash or working capital. (499)

allocation of service costs: The assignment of service costs to various production centers, usually on the basis of benefits received by those centers. (868)

Allowance for Doubtful Accounts: A contra account, deducted from Accounts Receivable, that shows the estimated losses from uncollectible accounts. (210)

allowance method: The recording of estimated losses due to uncollectible accounts as expenses during the period in which the sale occurred; *compare* direct write-off method. (209)

American Accounting Association (AAA): The national organization representing accounting educators and practitioners; it serves as a forum for the expression of accounting ideas and encourages research. (24)

American Institute of CPAs (AICPA): The national organization representing certified public accountants (CPAs) in the United States. (24)

amortization: The process of cost allocation that assigns the original cost of an intangible asset to the periods benefited. (352)

amortization of bonds: The systematic writing off of a bond discount or premium over the life of the bond. (383)

annuity: A series of equal amounts to be received or paid at the end of equal time periods. (378)

appropriations: In nonprofit accounting, formal authorizations to spend up to specified amounts in carrying out the objectives of a fund. (602)

arm's-length transactions: Business dealings between independent and rational parties who are looking out for their own interests. (20)

articles of incorporation: *See* charter.

articulation: The idea that financial statements tie together, that operating statement items (for example, net income) explain or reconcile changes in major balance sheet categories (for example, retained earnings). (42)

asset approach: An accounting method whereby prepaid expenses are originally debited to an asset account; a year-end adjustment is required to record the asset value used up as an expense of the period and to adjust the related asset account to its proper balance; *compare* expense approach. (118)

assets: Economic resources that are owned or controlled by an enterprise as a result of past transactions or events, and that are expected to have future economic benefits (service potential). (35)

asset turnover ratio: An overall measure of how effectively assets are used during a period; computed by dividing net sales by average total assets. (566, 859)

attainable standard: A guide for judging actual performance based on efficient, but not perfect, productivity. (820)

audit report: A statement issued by an independent certified public accountant that expresses an opinion about the company's adherence to generally accepted accounting principles. (45)

authorized stock: The amount and type of stock that may be issued by a company, as specified in its articles of incorporation. (428)

automated accounting system: A system in which most of the data processing is performed by machines instead of people. (56)

B

bad debt: An uncollectible account receivable. (209)

balance sheet (statement of financial position): The primary financial statement that shows the financial resources of an enterprise at a particular date and the claims against those resources, and therefore the relationships of assets, liabilities, and owners' equity. (38, 270)

bank reconciliation: The process of systematically comparing the cash balance as reported by the bank with the cash balance on the company's books, and explaining any differences. (299)

board of directors: Individuals elected by the shareholders to govern a corporation. (426)

bond: A certificate of debt issued by a company or government agency guaranteeing a stated rate of interest and payment of the original investment by a specified date; usually issued in units of $1,000. (374)

bond discount: The difference between the face value and the sales price when bonds are sold below their face value. (376, 404)

bond indenture: A contract between a bond issuer and a bond purchaser that specifies the terms of the bond. (375)

bond maturity date: The date at which the bond principal becomes payable. (375)

bond maturity value: *See* face value of a bond.

bond premium: The difference between the face value and the sales price when bonds are sold above their face value. (376, 406)

bond principal: *See* face value of a bond.

book value (or carrying value): The net amount shown in the accounts for an asset, liability, or owners' equity item. (278, 337)

book value of accounts receivable: The net amount that would be received if all receivables considered collectible were collected; equal to total accounts receivable less the allowance for doubtful accounts; also called net realizable value. (210)

book value per share: A measure of net worth; computed by dividing stockholders' equity for each class of stock by the number of shares outstanding for that class. (580)

break-even point: The amount of sales revenue or the number of units sold at which total costs equal total revenues; the point at which there is no profit or loss. (704, 719)

budget: An itemized summary of probable revenues and expenditures for a given period, which shows how an entity is expected to acquire and use its resources during that time. (654, 787)

budgetary accounts: In nonprofit accounting, a self-balancing set of accounts that constitute a formal record of a fund's financial plan. (602)

budget committee: A management group responsible for establishing budgeting policy and for coordinating preparation of the budgets. (789)

business documents: Records of transactions used as the basis for recording accounting entries; includes invoices, check stubs, receipts, and similar business papers. (65)

business enterprise: An organization with a profit objective that derives its earnings by providing goods or services. (16)

business expenses: Expenses that have been paid or incurred in the course of business, and that are ordinary, necessary, and reasonable in amount. (942)

C

calendar year: An entity's reporting year, covering twelve months and ending on December 31. (106)

callable bonds: Bonds for which the issuer reserves the right to retire the obligation before its maturity date. (375)

capital: The total amount of money or other resources owned or used to acquire future income or benefits. (912)

Capital account: An account in which a proprietor's or partner's interest in a firm is recorded; it is increased by owner investments and net income and decreased by owner withdrawals and net losses. (459)

capital assets: All investments in securities; used for income tax purposes. (951)

capital budgeting: Systematic planning for long-term investment decisions. (655, 786, 911, 963)

capital expenditure: An expenditure that is recorded as an asset because it is expected to benefit more than the current period. (346)

capital gain: The excess of proceeds over costs from the sale of a capital asset, as defined by the Internal Revenue Code. (951)

capitalization: The recording of an expenditure expected to benefit more than the current period as an asset. (415)

capital rationing: Allocating resources among ranked acceptable investments. (931)

capital stock: The portion of owners' equity contributed by investors (the owners) through the issuance of stock; the general term applied to all shares of ownership in a corporation. (39, 428)

cash-basis accounting: A system of accounting in which transactions are recorded, and revenues and expenses are recognized, only when cash is received or paid. (107)

cash-basis method: An income measurement method in which income is defined as cash receipts less cash disbursements during an accounting period. (200)

cash budget: A schedule of expected cash receipts and disbursements during the period. (797)

cash concept of funds: A concept used in preparing a funds statement that reflects transactions in which cash is either received or paid. (499)

cash discount: *See* sales discount.

cash dividend: A cash distribution of earnings to shareholders. (435)

cash flow: The receipt of cash in the form of dividends or interest, and from the proceeds upon liquidation of an investment or repayment of a loan principal. (33)

cash inflows: Any current or expected revenues directly associated with an investment. (915)

cash outflows: The initial cost and other expected outlays associated with an investment. (915)

Cash Over and Short: An account used to record overages and shortages in petty cash. (296)

centralization: An organizational philosophy in which top management makes most of the major decisions for the entire company rather than delegating them to managers at lower levels; *compare* decentralization. (854)

certified public accountant (CPA): A special designation given to an accountant who has passed a national uniform examination and has met other certifying requirements; CPA certificates are issued and monitored by state boards of accountancy or similar agencies. (45)

charter (articles of incorporation): A document issued by a state that gives legal status to a corporation and details its specific rights, including the authority to issue a certain maximum number of shares of stock. (426)

chart of accounts: A systematic listing of all accounts used by a company. (76, 632)

classified balance sheet: A balance sheet on which assets, liabilities, and owners' equity are subdivided by age, use, and source. (39, 275)

clearing account: A temporary account, such as Income Summary, used to collect a group of costs and/or revenues so as to simplify the transfer of the balance to another account (or accounts). (146)

closing entries: Entries that reduce all nominal, or temporary, accounts to a zero balance at the end of each accounting period, transferring their pre-closing balances to permanent, balance sheet accounts. (144)

committed fixed costs: Fixed costs that management cannot readily change. (696)

common-size statement: An income statement or balance sheet showing only the percentage relationships obtained by vertical analysis; each item is expressed as a percentage of net sales, total assets, or total liabilities and stockholders' equity. (565)

common stock: The class of stock most frequently issued by corporations; it usually confers a voting right in the corporation; its dividend and liquidation rights generally come second to those of preferred stock. (428)

compounding period: The period of time for which interest is calculated. (378)

compound interest: Interest calculated on the principal amount plus any previously earned interest.

compound journal entry: A journal entry that involves more than one debit or more than one credit, or both. (70)

computerized accounting system: A system in which most of the data processing is performed by computers. (56)

conduit principle: The idea that all income earned by an entity must be passed through to the owners and reported on their individual tax returns; applicable to proprietorships, partnerships, and, in a modified form, to Subchapter S corporations. (947)

consignee: A vendor who sells merchandise owned by another party, known as the consignor, usually on a commission basis. (241)

consignment: An arrangement whereby merchandise owned by one party (the consignor) is sold by another party (the consignee), usually on a commission basis. (241)

consignor: The owner of merchandise to be sold by someone else, known as the consignee. (241)

consolidated financial statements: Statements that show the operating results and financial position of two or more legally separate but affiliated companies as if they were one economic entity. (370, 538)

consolidation: The combining of two or more companies into a new corporation, with the original companies going out of existence. (539)

constant-dollar method: An income measurement method in which income is defined as revenues less expenses as adjusted by a general (economy-wide) price index, plus any purchasing power gains or losses due to changes in the general price level; also called the general price-level-adjusted historical cost method. (202, 273)

constructive receipt rule: The idea that cash has been received when a taxpayer can exercise control over it, whether or not the cash has been physically received. (945)

contingent liability: A potential obligation, dependent upon the occurrence of future events. (311)

contra account: An account that is offset or deducted from another account. (207)

contributed capital: That portion of owners' equity contributed by investors (the owners) through the issuance of stock. (280, 427)

contribution margin: The difference between total revenues and total variable costs; it is the portion of sales revenue available to cover fixed costs. (704, 720, 859)

contribution-margin income statement: An income statement that separates costs according to their behavior patterns; it shows revenues less variable costs (contribution margin) less fixed costs. (702)

contribution-margin ratio: The percentage of sales revenue left after variable costs are deducted. (721)

control account: A summary account in the General Ledger that is supported by detailed individual accounts in a subsidiary ledger. (93)

controllable costs: Costs that are incurred in a responsibility center and that are the direct responsibility of a manager of the center. (674)

conversion costs: The costs of converting raw materials to finished products; include direct labor and manufacturing overhead costs. (763)

convertible bonds: Bonds that can be traded for or converted to capital stock after a specified period of time. (375)

corporation: A legal entity chartered by a state, with ownership represented by transferable shares of stock. (19, 426)

cost accounting: The process of accumulating actual cost data to be used in controlling costs, in preparing external financial reports and tax returns, and in making planning and control decisions. (659)

cost-beneficial controls: Controls that benefit a company to an extent that outweighs their costs. (627)

cost-benefit analysis: Techniques for selecting an alternative that provides the greatest benefit at the lowest cost. (653)

cost center: An organizational unit in which a manager has control over and is held accountable for costs; *compare* profit center and investment center. (857)

cost method of accounting for investments in stocks: Accounting for an investment in another company where less than 20 percent of the outstanding voting stock is owned, by recording the initial acquisition at cost and recognizing dividends as revenue earned; *compare* equity method. (371)

cost of capital: The weighted-average cost of a firm's debt and equity capital; equals the rate of return that a company must earn to satisfy the demands of its owners and creditors. (925)

cost of goods manufactured schedule: A schedule supporting the income statement; summarizes the cost of goods manufactured during a period, including materials, labor, and overhead costs; beginning work-in-process inventory plus manufacturing costs during the period minus ending work-in-process inventory. (671, 759)

cost of goods sold: The expense incurred to purchase raw materials and manufacture the products sold during a period, or to purchase the merchandise sold during this period; equal to beginning inventory plus cost of goods purchased or manufactured less ending inventory. (72, 214)

cost-volume-profit (C-V-P) analysis: Techniques for determining how changes in costs and volume affect the profitability of an organization. (719)

coupon bonds: Bonds for which owners receive periodic interest payments by clipping a coupon from the bond and sending it to the issuer as evidence of ownership. (375)

credit: An entry on the right side of an account. (62)

critical resource factor: In the manufacturing process, the element that determines operating capacity by its availability. (897)

cumulative-dividend preference: The right of preferred shareholders to receive current dividends plus all dividends in arrears before common shareholders receive any dividends. (438)

current assets: Cash and other assets that may reasonably be expected to be converted to cash within one year or during the normal operating cycle. (276, 293)

current-dividend preference: The right of preferred shareholders to receive current dividends before common shareholders receive dividends. (437)

current liabilities: Debts or other obligations that will be paid with current assets or otherwise discharged within one year or the normal operating cycle. (279, 306)

current ratio (or working capital ratio): A measure of the liquidity of a business; equal to current assets divided by current liabilities. (279, 311, 569)

current-value method: The income measurement method in which income is defined as the excess of revenues over expenses plus the net increases or decreases in the values of specific assets and liabilities during a period. (204)

current values: The amounts that assets or liabilities are presently worth in the marketplace; generally equal to the replacement costs, net realizable values, or net present values of items. (274)

curvilinear costs: Variable costs that do not vary in direct proportion to changes in activity level but at decreasing or increasing rates due to economies of scale, productivity increases, and so on. The rate of change in these costs varies as activity levels change, creating a nonlinear relationship. (697)

D

data: Inputs to the accounting process that are derived from transactions. (55)

date of record: The date selected by a corporation's board of directors on which the shareholders of record are identified as those who will receive dividends. (436)

debentures: Bonds for which no collateral has been pledged; also called unsecured bonds. (375)

debit: An entry on the left side of an account. (62)

debt–equity management ratio: A measure of the relative utilization of debt and equity; computed by dividing average total assets by average stockholders' equity. (574)

debt financing: Raising money, or capital, by borrowing; *compare* equity financing. (396)

decentralization: An organizational philosophy in which managers at all levels have authority to make decisions concerning the operations for which they are responsible; *compare* centralization. (854)

declaration date: The date on which a corporation's board of directors formally decides to pay a dividend to shareholders. (435)

declining-balance depreciation methods: Accelerated depreciation methods in which an asset's book value is multiplied by a constant depreciation rate (such as double the straight-line percentage, in the case of double-declining-balance). (340)

deductions: Business expenses or losses that are subtracted from gross income in computing taxable income. (942)

deferred income taxes: The difference between income tax expense, calculated as a function of accounting income based on generally accepted accounting principles, and current taxes payable, calculated as a function of taxable income based on the Internal Revenue Service and other tax codes. (413)

depletion: The process of cost allocation that assigns the original cost of a natural resource to the periods benefited. (351)

depreciation: The process of cost allocation that assigns the original cost of plant and equipment to the periods benefited. (138, 278, 335)

differential (or incremental) costs: Costs that are not the same for the alternatives being considered. (678, 884)

direct-labor budget: A schedule of direct-labor requirements for the budget period. (795)

direct-labor costs: The costs of labor directly associated with a manufactured product. (667)

direct-materials costs: The costs of materials that become part of a manufactured product. (667)

direct-materials purchases budget: A schedule of direct materials to be purchased during the budget period. (795)

direct-materials usage budget: A schedule of direct materials to be used in production during the budget period. (795)

direct write-off method: The recording of actual losses from uncollectible accounts as expenses during the period in which accounts receivable are determined to be uncollectible; *compare* allowance method. (209)

discount: The amount charged by a bank when a note receivable is sold, or discounted; calculated as maturity value times discount rate times discount period. (303)

discounted cash flow methods: Capital budgeting techniques that take into account the time value of money by comparing discounted cash flows; *see also* net present value method and internal rate of return method. (916)

discounting a note receivable: The process of the payee's selling notes to a financial institution for less than the maturity value. (303)

discount period: The time between the date a note is issued or sold to a financial institution and its maturity date. (303)

discount rate: The interest rate charged by a financial institution for buying a note receivable. (303)

discretionary fixed costs: Fixed costs that are less permanent than committed fixed costs. (696)

distributions to owners: Decreases in a company's net assets, resulting from the transfer of assets to owners, or the transfer of liabilities from the owners to the entity. (36)

dividend payout ratio: A measure of earnings paid out in dividends; computed by dividing cash dividends by the net income available to each class of stock. (580)

dividends: The periodic distribution of earnings in the form of cash, stock, or other property to the owners (stockholders) of a corporation. (33, 435)

dividends in arrears: Missed dividends for past years that preferred shareholders have a right to receive under the cumulative-dividend preference when dividends are declared. (438)

double-entry accounting: A system of recording transactions in a way that maintains the equality of the accounting equation. (22)

Doubtful Accounts Expense: An account that represents the portion of the current period's receivables that are estimated to become uncollectible. (210)

drawings: Distributions to the owner(s) of a proprietorship or partnership; similar to dividends for a corporation. (148)

Drawings account: A temporary account in which the owners' withdrawals of cash or other assets from proprietorships or partnerships are recorded. (459)

E

earnings (or loss) per share (EPS): The amount of net income (earnings) related to each share of stock; computed by dividing net income by the number of shares of common stock outstanding during the period. (41, 224, 578)

earnings potential: The ability of a company to generate positive future net cash flows from operations. (33)

economic income: The maximum amount a person or firm can consume during an accounting period and still be as well off at the end of the period as at the beginning. (199)

effective-interest amortization: A method of systematically writing off a bond premium or discount, taking into consideration the time value of money and resulting in an equal rate of amortization for each period; *compare* straight-line interest amortization. (384, 404)

effective (or yield) rate of interest: The actual interest rate earned or paid on a bond investment; takes into account the interest earned by buying at a discount or the interest lost by paying a premium. (379, 405)

encumbrance: In nonprofit accounting, a formal record for commitments made now for expenditures to be made later; usually set up when a significant period of time is expected to elapse between the date of commitment and the time of the expenditure. (604)

entity: An organizational unit (a person, partnership, or corporation) for which accounting records are kept and about which accounting reports are prepared. (18)

equity financing: Raising money, or capital, by issuing stock or otherwise receiving contributions from owners; *compare* debt financing. (396)

equity method of accounting for investments in stocks: Accounting for an investment in another company where significant influence can be imposed (presumed to exist when 20 to 50 percent of the outstanding voting stock is owned), by recording the initial acquisition at cost and recognizing (1) dividends as a return of investment and (2) its share of earnings as revenue that increases the value of the investment; *compare* cost method. (372)

equivalent units of production: A concept used in a process costing system to measure accurately the productive output for a period; equals the sum of all units completed during a period plus the number of completed units equivalent to the work performed on the ending inventory less the number of completed units equivalent to the work performed on the beginning inventory in the prior period. (763)

exception report: A report that compares actual and budgeted performance and points out the variances, or exceptions, between the two. (857)

exclusions: Gross receipts that are not subject to tax and are not included in gross income, such as interest on state and local government bonds. (942)

expense approach: An accounting procedure whereby prepaid expenses are originally debited to an expense account, even though future benefits exist; a year-end adjustment is required to bring the expense account to its proper balance and to establish a companion asset account equal to the remaining future benefits; *compare* asset approach. (118)

expenses: Costs of assets used up or additional liabilities incurred in the normal course of business to generate revenues. (37, 64, 200)

external users: Investors, creditors, analysts, and other groups interested in the financial affairs of a company but who are not involved in managing its day-to-day activities. (650)

extraordinary items: Special nonoperating gains and losses that are unusual in nature, infrequent in occurrence, and material in amount. (224)

F

face (maturity) value of a bond: *See* principal of a bond.

fair market value: The amount that would be paid or received for an asset in an arm's-length transaction. (334)

FICA: *See* social security taxes.

fidelity bond: An insurance contract whereby a bonding company agrees to reimburse an employer for any theft, embezzlement, or fraud perpetrated by an employee covered by the bonding agreement. (637)

FIFO (first-in, first-out): An inventory cost flow whereby the first goods purchased are assumed to be the first goods sold, so that the ending inventory consists of the most recently purchased goods. (244, 767)

financial accounting: The area of accounting concerned with measuring and reporting, on a periodic basis, the financial status and operating results of organizations to interested external parties; *compare* managerial accounting. (17, 650)

Financial Accounting Standards Board (FASB): The private organization responsible for establishing the standards for financial accounting and reporting in the United States. (25)

finished goods: Manufactured products ready for sale; includes all manufacturing costs assigned to products that have been completed but not yet sold. (242, 670)

fiscal year: An entity's reporting year, covering a 12-month accounting period. (106)

fixed costs: Costs that do not vary in total with changes in activity level, at least within a relevant range; *compare* variable costs. (675, 692)

flexible budgeting: Financial planning in which revenues and costs are projected in relation to varying activity levels. (789, 831)

FOB (free-on-board) destination: Business term meaning that the seller of merchandise bears the shipping costs and maintains ownership until the merchandise is delivered to the buyer. (242)

FOB (free-on-board) shipping point: Business term meaning that the buyer of merchandise bears the shipping costs and acquires ownership at the point of shipment. (242)

Foreign Corrupt Practices Act (FCPA) of 1977: Legislation that requires all companies registered with the Securities and Exchange Commission to keep accurate accounting records and maintain an adequate system of internal control. (627)

franchise: An exclusive right to sell a product or offer a service in a certain geographical area. (279, 353)

Freight-In: An account used to record the costs of transporting into a firm all purchased merchandise or materials intended for sale; added to Purchases in calculating cost of goods sold. (218)

functional income statement: An income statement that segregates all costs by use; it shows revenues less cost of goods sold (gross margin) less selling and administrative expenses. (702)

fund: In nonprofit accounting, a separate accounting entity that contains a self-balancing set of accounts reflecting only the activities of that entity. (600)

fund accounting: An accounting system that involves the use of a group of self-balancing accounts, called funds, for each activity of a nonprofit organization. (600)

fund balance: The excess of a fund's assets over its liabilities and reserves; becomes the balancing account on the balance sheet of a nonprofit organization. (608)

funds: The financial resources that flow into and out of a company; usually defined as working capital or cash. (499)

G

gains (or losses): Net increases (or decreases) in an entity's resources derived from peripheral activities or associated with nonrecurring, unusual events and circumstances. (37)

general fixed asset account group: A group of accounts used for recording the property, plant, and equipment of the general fund and certain other funds in a nonprofit organization. (601)

general fund: The primary fund of a nonprofit organization; it includes accounts for all transactions that do not fit into more specialized funds. (601)

general long-term debt account group: A group of accounts used for recording long-term debt, such as bond issues, for the general fund and certain other funds in a nonprofit organization. (601)

generally accepted accounting principles (GAAP): Authoritative guidelines that define accounting practice at a particular time. (24)

general price level: An index of the overall market value of a group of goods or services at a point in time. (202)

general-purpose (or primary) financial statements: The financial statements intended for general use by a variety of external groups; include the income statement, the balance sheet, and the funds statement. (33)

going concern: The idea that an accounting entity will have a continuing existence for the foreseeable future. (21)

goodwill: An intangible asset showing that a business is worth more than the fair market value of its net assets because of strategic location, reputation, good customer relations, or similar factors; equal to the excess of cost over the fair market value of the net assets purchased. (354, 470, 544)

gross income: The taxable portion of a company's gross receipts, less the cost of sales. (942)

gross margin: The excess of net sales revenues over the cost of goods sold. (41, 239)

gross margin method: A procedure for estimating the dollar amount of ending inventory; the historical relationship of cost of goods sold to sales revenue is used in computing ending inventory; *compare* retail inventory method. (254)

gross tax liability: The amount of tax computed by multiplying the tax base (taxable income) by the appropriate tax rates. (944)

H

high–low method: A method of segregating the fixed and variable components of a semivariable cost by analyzing the costs at the high and the low activity levels within a relevant range. (700)

historical costs: The acquisition costs of assets; equal to current values at the dates of acquisition.

historical standard: A guide for judging actual performance based on the average productivity of recent periods. (821)

horizontal analysis of financial statements: A technique for analyzing the percentage change in individual income statement or balance sheet items from one year to the next. (564)

hurdle rate: The minimum rate of return that an investment must provide in order to be acceptable. (923)

I

ideal standard: A guide for judging actual performance based on very efficient productivity. (820)

imprest petty-cash fund: A petty-cash fund in which all expenditures are documented by vouchers and vendors' receipts or invoices; the total of the vouchers and cash in the fund should equal the established balance. (295)

income statement (statement of earnings): The primary financial statement that summarizes the revenues generated, the expenses incurred, and any gains or losses of an entity during a period of time. (40)

Income Summary: A clearing account used to close all revenues and expenses at the end of an accounting period; the preclosing balance of the Income Summary account represents the operating results (income or loss) of a given accounting period. (146)

income tax accounting: the preparation of income tax returns and the planning of transactions that have a significant tax impact. (659)

incremental costs: The additional costs incurred as the result of a decision. (890)

incremental net cash inflows: The additional cash generated, as the result of a decision, after all expenses have been deducted; equal to incremental revenues less incremental costs. (890)

incremental revenues: The additional cash generated as the result of a decision. (890)

indirect-labor costs: Labor costs that are not directly assigned to specific products but instead are included as manufacturing overhead and assigned to products on some reasonable allocation basis. (669, 752)

indirect-materials costs: Materials costs that are not assigned directly to specific products but are instead included as manufacturing overhead and assigned to products on some reasonable allocation basis. (668, 750)

inflation: An increase in the general price level of goods and services; alternatively, a decrease in the purchasing power of the dollar. (201)

information: Data organized by the accounting process. (55)

installment sale: A transaction that usually involves a down-payment and a series of payments over a period of 2 or more years. (962)

intangible assets: Long-lived assets that do not have physical substance and are not held for sale. (278, 352)

intercompany transaction: A transaction between a parent company and a subsidiary company. (541)

interest: The amount charged for using money. (301, 375)

interest rate: The cost of using money, expressed as an annual percentage. (301)

internal audit: An appraisal by internal accountants of employee performance and adherence to company policies, and an assessment of the reliability of the information system. (635)

internal control: An organization's methods and procedures for safeguarding assets, checking on the accuracy and reliability of its accounting data, and promoting operational efficiency and adherence to managerial policies. (59, 624)

internal rate of return: The "true" discount rate that will produce a net present value of zero when applied to the cash flows of an investment. (922)

internal rate of return method: A capital budgeting technique that uses discounted cash flows to find the "true" discount rate of an investment; this true rate produces a net present value of zero. (922)

internal users: The managers of a company who are responsible for making the day-to-day decisions that lead an organization to its profit and service goals. (650)

interpolation: A method of determining the internal rate of return when the factor for that rate lies between the factors given in the present value tables. (923)

inventory: Goods held for sale to customers; refers to both the number of units involved and the dollar amount of inventory. (137, 200)

inventory cutoff: The determination of which items should be included in the year-end inventory balance. (238)

inventory turnover: A measure of the efficiency with which inventory is managed; computed by dividing cost of goods sold by average inventory for a period. (571)

investment: An expenditure to acquire assets that are expected to produce future earnings. (365)

investment center: An organizational unit in which a manager has responsibility for costs, revenues, and investments; *compare* cost center and profit center. (857)

investments by owners: Increases in a company's net assets, resulting from the transfer of resources from an investor to the enterprise in return for a part ownership in the entity. (36)

investment tax credit: A direct reduction in a business's tax liability by an appropriate percentage of the cost of a tangible personal business property in the year it is put in use. (955)

involuntary conversion: A transaction in which an asset is destroyed (for example, by fire or storm), stolen, or taken by a government agency through condemnation proceedings. (962)

J

job cost sheet: A document prepared for each specific manufacturing job that is job-order costed; it contains a summary of direct-materials, direct-labor, and overhead costs. (748)

job-order costing: A method of product costing whereby each job, product, or batch of products is costed separately; *compare* process costing. (747)

joint manufacturing process: Using a single material input to produce more than one product. (894)

joint product costs: All costs incurred before different products are split for separate processing. (894)

journal: An accounting record in which transactions are first entered; provides a chronological record of all business activities. (67)

journal entry: A recording of a transaction where debits equal credits; usually includes a date and an explanation of the transaction. (67)

K

Keogh Plan: A pension plan for a self-employed individual taxpayer who has earned income; the annual contribution is limited to 15 percent of earned income, but it is not to exceed $15,000. (947)

L

labor efficiency variance: In a standard cost system, the extent to which the actual labor used varies from the standard quantity; computed by multiplying the difference between the actual and the standard quantities of labor by the standard rate. (827)

labor rate variance: In a standard cost system, the extent to which the actual labor rate varies from the standard rate for the quantity of labor used; computed by multiplying the difference between the actual and the standard rates by the quantity of labor used. (827)

lapping: A procedure used to conceal the theft of cash by crediting the payment from one customer to another customer's account on a delayed basis. (294)

lease: A contract whereby the lessee (user) agrees to pay periodic payments (rents) to the lessor (owner) for the use of an asset. (414)

lease obligations: The net present value of all future lease payments discounted at an appropriate rate of interest. (415)

least-cost decision: A decision to undertake the project with the smallest negative net present value. (921)

least squares method: A method of segregating the fixed and variable portions of a semivariable cost; the regression line, a line of averages, is statistically fitted through all cost points so that the sum of the squared errors of the costs predicted by the line is minimized. (714)

ledger: A book of accounts in which data from transactions recorded in journals are posted and thereby classified and summarized. (75)

legal capital: The amount of contributed capital not available for dividends as restricted by state law for the protection of creditors; usually equal to the par or stated value or the contributed amount of outstanding capital stock. (429)

lessee: An entity that agrees to pay periodic rents for the use of leased property. (414)

lessor: A renter or owner of leased property. (414)

leveraging: The use of borrowed money to finance a business when the net interest rate of the borrowed funds is less than the company's earnings rate. (397)

liabilities: Obligations of an enterprise to pay cash or other economic resources in return for past or current benefits; they represent claims against assets. (35)

liability approach: An accounting procedure whereby unearned revenues are originally credited to a liability account; a year-end adjustment is required to record the revenues earned during that period and to reduce the companion liability account; *compare* revenue approach. (114)

LIFO (last-in, first-out): An inventory cost flow whereby the last goods purchased are assumed to be the first goods sold, so that the ending inventory consists of the first goods purchased. (245)

limited liability: The legal protection given stockholders whereby they are responsible for the debts and obligations of a corporation only to the extent of their capital contribution. (426)

linearity assumption: The assumption that total variable costs rise at a rate directly proportionate with activity level throughout the relevant range. (697)

line of credit: An arrangement whereby a bank agrees to loan an amount of money (up to a certain limit) on demand for short periods of time, usually less than a year. (366)

liquidating dividend: Distributions of a firm's assets to its shareholders when a corporation is permanently reducing its operations or going out of business. (435)

liquidation: The process of dissolving a partnership by selling the assets, paying the debts, and distributing the remaining equity to the owners. (478)

liquidity: A company's ability to meet current obligations with cash or with other assets that can be quickly converted to cash. (33, 293, 557)

long-run planning: The process of establishing goals that extend three to five years into the future; involves decisions about products, manpower, facilities, and financial resources. (655)

long-term investments: Expenditures for nonoperational assets that a business intends to hold for more than a year or the normal operating cycle. (278, 370)

long-term liabilities: Debts or other obligations that will not be paid for or otherwise discharged within one year or the normal operating cycle. (279)

long-term operational assets: Long-lived assets acquired for use in the business rather than for resale; includes (1) property, plant, and equipment; (2) natural resources; and (3) intangible assets. (332)

lower-of-cost-or-market (LCM) rule: A basis for valuing certain assets at the lower or original cost or market value (current replacement cost), provided that the replacement cost is not higher than net realizable value minus normal profit. (253, 368)

M

maker: A person (entity) who signs a note to borrow money and who assumes responsibility to pay the note at maturity. (301)

management: Individuals who are responsible for overseeing the day-to-day operations of a business and who are the "internal" users of accounting information. (17)

management by exception: The process of comparing planned and actual results to identify significant variations that call for action by management. (656)

managerial accounting: The area of accounting concerned with assisting managers in decision making, specifically with planning, budgeting, controlling costs, evaluating performance, and generating revenues. (17, 650)

managerial information system: The system whereby all information used by management is collected, processed, and reported. (56)

manufacturing costs: Costs incurred in the manufacturing process to bring a product to completion; include direct-materials, direct-labor, and manufacturing overhead costs; treated as product costs. (667)

manufacturing overhead: Production costs that are not directly assigned to a specific product. (668, 752)

manufacturing overhead budget: A schedule of production costs other than those for direct labor and direct materials. (796)

market price: The price at which goods are exchanged in arm's-length transactions in the marketplace. (865)

marketable securities: See short-term investments.

market rate of interest: The prevailing interest rate in the marketplace for certain categories and grades of securities. (376)

master budget: A network of many separate schedules and budgets, which together provide an overall financial plan for the coming period. (790)

matching principle: The idea that all costs and expenses incurred in generating revenues must be recognized in the same reporting period as the related revenues. (107, 209)

materials price variance: In a standard cost system, the extent to which the actual price varies from the standard price for the quantity of materials purchased or used; computed by multiplying the difference between the actual and standard prices by the quantity used. (824)

materials quantity (usage) variance: In a standard cost system, the extent to which the actual quantity of materials used varies from the standard quantity; computed by multiplying the difference between the actual quantity and the standard quantity of materials used or purchased by the standard price or rate. (825)

materials requisition form: A document used to request raw materials from the storeroom. (750)

maturity date: The date on which a note or other obligation becomes due. (264)

maturity value: The amount of an obligation to be collected or paid at maturity date; equal to principal plus any interest. (265)

merger: The acquisition of one company by another company, whereby the companies combine as one legal entity, with the acquired company going out of existence. (539)

minority interest: The interest owned in a subsidiary by stockholders other than those of the parent company; occurs when the acquiring company has less than a 100 percent ownership interest. (539)

mixed costs: *See* semivariable costs.

monetary items: Those assets and liabilities that command a fixed amount of future dollars (determined by nature or contract) in the marketplace. (273)

money measurement: The idea that money, as the common medium of exchange, is the accounting unit of measurement, and that only economic activities measurable in monetary terms are included in the accounting model. (21)

mortgage amortization schedule: A schedule that shows the breakdown between interest and principal for each payment over the life of a mortgage. (411)

mortgage payable: A written promise to pay a stated amount of money at one or more specified future dates; a mortgage is secured by the pledging of certain assets—usually, real estate—as collateral. (411)

moving average: A perpetual inventory cost flow alternative whereby the cost of goods sold and the ending inventory are determined by using a weighted-average cost of all merchandise on hand after each purchase. (250)

mutual agency: The right of all partners in a partnership to act as agents for the partnership, with the authority to bind it to business agreements. (460)

N

natural resources: Assets, such as minerals, oil, timber, and gravel, that are extracted or otherwise depleted. (351)

net assets: Total assets minus total liabilities; equal to owners' equity. (35, 61)

net income (earnings): A measure of the overall performance of a business entity; equal to revenues plus gains minus expenses and losses for the period. (37, 239)

net present value: The difference between the present values of an investment's expected cash inflows and outflows. (919, 963)

net present value method: A capital budgeting technique that uses discounted cash flows to compare the present values of an investment's expected cash inflows and outflows. (919, 963)

net proceeds: The difference between maturity value and discount when a note receivable is discounted. (303)

net realizable value: The selling price of an item less reasonable selling costs. (252)

net tax liability: The amount of tax computed by subtracting tax credits from the gross tax liability. (944)

nominal accounts: Accounts that are closed to a zero balance at the end of each accounting period; temporary accounts that generally appear on the income statement. (144)

noncontrollable costs: Costs that are assigned to a responsibility center but that are only indirectly the responsibility of the manager of that center, because they are under the control of another center manager. (674)

noncurrent accounts: All operational asset, long-term investment, long-term liability, and owners' equity accounts; all accounts except for working-capital accounts. (504)

nonexpendable fund: In not-for-profit accounting, a fund in which the capital resources must be preserved. (494)

nonmanufacturing expenses: Expenditures not closely associated with the preparation of a product; include selling and administrative expenses; treated as period expenses. (667)

nonmonetary items: Those assets and equities that are not fixed in the amount of future dollars they can command and hence fluctuate in value according to their demand in the marketplace. (273)

nonprofit organization: An entity without a profit objective, oriented toward accomplishing nonprofit goals in an efficient and effective manner. (16, 599)

nonroutine operating decisions: Managerial decisions that require more extensive analysis than day-to-day decisions but less than capital budgeting decisions. (655)

nontraceable costs: Costs that are not directly identified with the responsibility centers to which they are assigned. (673)

no-par stock: Stock that does not have a par value printed on the face of the stock certificate. (429)

note payable: A debt owed to a creditor, evidenced by an unconditional written promise to pay a sum of money on or before a specified future date and signed by the maker. (306, 398)

note receivable: A claim against a debtor, evidenced by an unconditional written promise to pay a certain sum of money on or before a specified future date. (276, 301)

notes to financial statements: Explanatory information considered an integral part of the primary financial statements. (44)

NSF (Not Sufficient Funds) check: A check that is not honored by a bank because of insufficient cash in the customer's account. (297)

number of days' sales in inventory: An alternative measure of how well inventory is being managed; computed by dividing 365 days by the inventory turnover ratio. (572)

number of days' sales in receivables: A measure of the average number of days it takes to collect a credit sale; computed by dividing 365 days by the accounts receivable turnover. (570)

number of days' sales invested in working capital: An alternative measure of the amount of working capital used in generating the sales of a period; computed by dividing 365 days by the working capital turnover. (572)

O

operating budget: An itemized summary of immediate goals for sales, production, expenses, costs, and the availability of cash. (655)

operating cycle: The general pattern of business activity whereby cash and other resources are converted to inventory and operational assets and eventually to products or services that can be sold for cash and other resources. (271)

operating expenses: Costs incurred in the course of the day-to-day, operating cycle, activities of a firm.

operating income: A measure of the profitability of a business from normal operations; equals revenues minus operating expenses. (38)

operating performance ratio: An overall measure of the efficiency of operations during a period; computed by dividing net income by net sales. (562, 859)

operations budgeting: The setting of immediate goals for sales, production, expenses, and the availability of cash. (786)

opportunity cost: The amount of money that could be earned by putting financial resources to the best alternative use compared with the one being considered. (679, 867)

outlay cost: The actual cash outflow directly associated with the production and transfer of a product or service; in transfer pricing, if fixed costs are covered, outlay cost equals the total of the variable costs incurred in making the product or providing the service; if fixed costs have not been covered by outside sales, outlay cost equals total cost. (867)

outstanding stock: Issued stock that is still being held by investors. (428)

overapplied overhead: The excess of applied overhead (based on a predetermined application rate) over the actual overhead costs for a period. (760)

overhead application rate: A rate at which estimated overhead costs are assigned to products throughout the year; equals total estimated overhead costs divided by a suitable allocation base, such as number of units produced, direct-labor hours, direct materials used, or direct-labor costs. (754)

owners' equity (stockholders' equity): The ownership interest in the assets of an enterprise; equals net assets (total assets minus total liabilities). (35)

P

parent company: A company that owns or maintains control over other companies, known as subsidiaries, which are themselves separate legal entities; control generally refers to ownership of 50 percent or more of the stock of another company. (370, 538)

participating-dividend preference: The right of preferred shareholders to receive equal distributions of dividends on a proportionate basis with common shareholders. (438)

partnership: An unincorporated business owned by two or more individuals or entities. (19, 457)

partnership agreement: A legal agreement between partners; it usually specifies the capital contributions to be made by each partner, the ratios in which partnership earnings will be distributed, the management responsibilities of partners, and the partners' rights to transfer or sell their individual interests. (457)

par value (or face value): The nominal value printed on the face of a bond or share of stock. (280, 402)

par-value stock: Stock that has a nominal value assigned to it in the corporation's charter and printed on the face of each share of stock. (428)

patent: An exclusive right granted for up to 17 years by the federal government to an inventor to manufacture and sell an invention. (279, 353)

payback method: A capital budgeting technique that determines the amount of time it takes the net cash inflows of an investment to repay the cost. (916)

payback reciprocal method: A capital budgeting technique in which the reciprocal of the payback period is used in computing an investment's approximate internal rate of return. (924)

payee: The person (entity) to whom payment on a note is to be made. (301)

payment date: The date on which a corporation pays dividends to its shareholders. (436)

performance control reports: A comparison of actual and planned results, in which significant variances are identified. (655)

period expense: An expenditure that cannot be associated with or assigned to a product and so is reported as an expense in the period in which it is incurred; *compare* product cost. (664)

periodic inventory method: A system of recording inventory in which cost of goods sold is determined and inventory is adjusted at the end of the accounting period, not when merchandise is purchased or sold. (217)

permanent accounts: *See* real accounts.

perpetual inventory method: A system of recording inventory in which detailed records of the number of units and the cost of each purchase and sales transaction are prepared throughout the accounting period. (214)

per-unit contribution margin: The excess of the sales price of one unit over its variable costs. (720)

petty-cash fund: A small amount of cash kept on hand for making miscellaneous payments. (295)

planning: The process of selecting objectives and determining the means to attain them. (654)

pooling of interests: The acquisition of one company by another, whereby the acquiring company issues voting stock to the acquired company's shareholders in exchange for at least 90 percent of the acquired company's outstanding voting stock and 11 other conditions are met. (539)

pooling-of-interests method: A method used to prepare consolidated financial statements when one company issues common stock to acquire at least 90 percent of the common stock of another company and when 11 other specific conditions are met. (547)

post-closing trial balance: A listing of all real account balances after the closing process has been completed; provides a means of testing whether debits equal credits for all real accounts prior to beginning a new accounting cycle. (149)

posting: The process of classifying and grouping similar transactions in common accounts by transferring amounts from the journal to the ledger. (75)

preferred stock: A class of stock issued by corporations; it usually confers dividend and liquidation rights that take precedence over those of common stock. (428)

premium on stock: The excess of the issuance (market) price of stock over its par or stated value. (429)

prepaid expenses: Payments made in advance for items normally charged to expense. (117, 277, 305)

present value: The value today of an amount to be received or paid in the future; the future amount must be discounted at a specified rate of interest. (398)

present value of an annuity of \$1: The value today of a series of equally spaced payments of \$1 to be made or received in the future, given a specified interest, or discount, rate. (378)

present value of \$1: The value today of \$1 to be received at some future date, given a specified interest rate. (377)

price–earnings (P/E) ratio: A measure of growth potential, earnings stability, and management capabilities; computed by dividing market price per share by earnings per share. (579)

principal (face value, maturity value) of a bond: The amount that will be paid on a bond at the maturity date. (375)

principal on a note: The face amount of a note; the amount (excluding interest) that the maker agrees to pay the payee. (301)

prior-period adjustments: Adjustments made directly to Retained Earnings in order to correct errors in the financial statements of prior periods. (442)

procedures manual: A document that identifies the general policies of a company. (634)

process costing: A method of product costing whereby costs are accumulated by process or work centers and averaged over all products manufactured in those centers; *compare* job-order costing. (746)

product cost: Any cost associated with and assigned to a product; *compare* period expense. (664)

product costing: The assignment of manufacturing costs to products in order to determine the cost of finished goods; *see also* absorption, job-order, process, and variable costing. (747)

production budget: A schedule of production requirements of the budget period. (794)

production report: A document used for transferring units and/or costs from one process center to another. (765)

profitability: A company's ability to generate revenues in excess of the costs incurred in producing those revenues. (34, 557)

profitability index: The present value of net cash inflows divided by the cost of an investment. (932)

profit center: An organizational unit in which a manager has responsibility for both costs and revenues; *compare* cost center and investment center. (857)

profit graph: A graph that shows how profits vary with changes in volume. (727)

property dividend: The distribution to shareholders of assets other than cash or stock. (435)

property, plant, and equipment: Tangible, long-lived assets acquired for use in the business rather than for resale. (278, 333)

property, plant, and equipment turnover: A measure of how well property, plant, and equipment are being utilized in generating a period's sales; computed by dividing net sales by average property, plant, and equipment. (573)

proprietary accounts: In nonprofit accounting, separate fund accounts for recording actual transactions, that is, actual revenues and expenditures. (602)

proprietorship: An unincorporated business owned by one person. (19, 457)

pro rata: A term describing an allocation that is based on a proportionate distribution of the total. (435)

purchase: The acquisition of one company by another, whereby the acquiring company exchanges cash or other assets for more than 50 percent of the acquired company's outstanding voting stock. (539)

purchase discount: A reduction in the purchase price, allowed if payment is made within a specified period. (218)

purchase method: A method used to prepare consolidated financial statements when one company has acquired a controlling interest in another company with similar activities by exchanging cash or other assets for more than 50 percent of the acquired company's outstanding voting stock. (540)

Purchase Returns and Allowances: A contra-purchases account in which the returns of or allowances for previously purchased merchandise are recorded. (218)

Purchases: An account in which all inventory purchases are recorded; used with the periodic inventory method. (217)

Q

qualitative considerations: Factors that affect a decision but that are not subject to measurement in dollar terms. (887)

R

ranking: The ordering of acceptable investment alternatives from most to least desirable. (913)

raw materials: Goods purchased for use in manufacturing products. (242)

real accounts: Accounts that are not closed to a zero balance at the end of each accounting period; permanent accounts appearing on the balance sheet. (144)

receivables: Claims for money, goods, or services. (300)

recourse: The right to seek payment on a discounted note from the payee if the maker defaults. (304)

recovery period: The time period designated by Congress for depreciating business assets. (955)

registered bonds: Bonds for which the names and addresses of the bondholders are kept on file by the issuing company. (375)

regression line: On a scattergraph, the straight line that most closely expresses the relationship between the variables. (698)

relevant range: The range of operating level, or volume of activity, over which the relationship between total costs and activity level is approximately linear. (692)

Reserve for Encumbrances: In nonprofit accounting, an account credited at the time a commitment is made for an expenditure. (604)

residual income: The amount of net income an investment center is able to earn above a specified minimum rate of return on total assets. (861)

residual value: *See* salvage value.

responsibility accounting: A system of evaluating performance whereby responsibility center managers are held accountable for the costs, revenues, assets, or other elements assigned to their centers. (857)

responsibility center: An organizational unit in which the manager has control over and is held accountable for performance; *see also* cost center, investment center, profit center. (672, 856)

retail inventory method: A procedure for estimating the dollar amount of ending inventory; the ending inventory at retail prices is converted to a cost basis by using a ratio of the cost and the retail prices of goods available for sale; *compare* gross margin method. (255)

retained earnings: The accumulated portion of owners' equity that has been earned and retained from profitable operations and not paid out in dividends or restricted for some other use; equal to owners' equity less contributed capital. (39, 280)

return of investment: Return to an investor of only the principal amount of money invested. (912)

return on investment: Return to an investor of earnings on money invested. (912)

return on sales revenue: A measure of operating performance; computed by dividing net income by total sales revenue. (730)

return on stockholders' equity: A measure of overall performance from a stockholder's viewpoint; includes management of operations, use of assets, and management of debt and equity, and is computed by dividing net income by average stockholders' equity. (577)

return on total assets ratio: A measure of operating performance and efficiency in utilizing assets; computed in its simplest form by dividing net income by average total assets. (576, 859)

revenue approach: An accounting procedure whereby unearned revenues are originally credited to a revenue account, even though the amount is not yet earned; a year-end adjustment is required to reduce the revenue to that actually earned during the period and to establish a corresponding liability for the amount not earned at year-end; *compare* liability approach. (113)

revenue recognition principle: The idea that revenues should be recorded when (1) the earnings process has been substantially completed, and (2) an exchange has taken place. (107)

revenues: Resource increases from the sale of goods or services derived primarily from the normal operations of an enterprise. (36, 64, 205)

reversing entry: A journal entry made at the beginning of a year that exactly reverses an adjusting entry made at the end of the previous year. (170)

S

sales discount: A reduction in the sales price, allowed if payment is received within a specified period; also called cash discount. (207)

sales mix: The relative proportion of total units sold (or total sales dollars) that is represented by each of a company's products. (734)

Sales Returns and Allowances: A contra-revenue account in which the returns of or allowance for the reduction in price of merchandise previously sold are recorded. (208)

sales (revenues) forecast: The expected level of sales during the budget period. (643, 793)

salvage value: Estimated value or actual price of an asset at the conclusion of its useful life, net of disposal costs; sometimes called residual value. (335)

scattergraph, or visual fit, method: A method of segregating the fixed and variable components of a cost by plotting on a graph total costs at several activity levels and drawing a regression line through the points. (698)

screening: Determining whether an investment meets a minimum standard of acceptability. (913)

Section 1231: A provision in the tax law that allows businesses to report the following as capital gains: real and depreciable property that has been used in the business for more than 12 months and then sold, exchanged, or involuntarily converted, and whose selling price exceeds its original cost. (951)

secured bonds: Bonds for which assets have been pledged in order to guarantee repayment. (375)

Securities and Exchange Commission (SEC): The government body responsible for regulating the financial reporting practices of most publicly owned corporations in connection with the buying and selling of stocks and bonds. (24)

selling and administrative expense budget: A schedule of all nonproduction spending that will occur during the budget period. (797)

semivariable (mixed) costs: Costs that contain both variable and fixed cost components. (694)

sensitivity analysis: A method of assessing the reasonableness of a decision that was based upon estimates; involves calculating how far reality can differ from an estimate without invalidating the decision. (928)

serial bonds: Bonds that mature in a series of installments at specified future dates. (375)

service costs: Operating costs of service departments that are usually allocated to production departments. (868)

service department: An organizational unit that does not directly produce goods but instead serves other departments. (868)

short-run planning: The process of making decisions about current operations and those of the immediate future; includes day-to-day and nonroutine operating decisions. (655)

short-term investments: Expenditures for nonoperational assets that a business enterprise intends to hold only for a short period of time, usually less than a year; also called marketable securities. (276, 367)

simple interest: Interest calculated only on the principal amount each period.

social security (FICA) taxes: Federal Insurance Contributions Act taxes imposed on employee and employer; used mainly to provide retirement benefits. (308)

solvency: A company's long-run ability to meet all financial obligations. (34, 557)

special journals: Books of original entry for recording similar transactions that occur frequently. (92)

special order: An order that may be priced below the normal price in order to utilize excess capacity and thereby contribute to company profits. (899)

specific identification: A method of valuing inventory and determining cost of goods sold, whereby the actual costs of specific inventory items are assigned to them. (246)

standard: A quantitative measure of the expected level of performance. (655, 818)

standard cost card: An itemization of the components of the standard cost of a product. (823)

standard costs: Systematically predetermined estimates of the expected costs of a unit of output; they include the anticipated costs of materials, labor, and overhead for a given level of activity. (676, 818)

standard cost system: A product costing system in which standard costs are used instead of actual costs. (822)

stated (or nominal) rate of interest: The interest rate printed on a bond; used to determine how much cash will be paid or received each period as bond interest. (379)

stated value: The nominal value assigned to no-par stock by the board of directors of a corporation. (429)

statement of changes in financial position (funds statement): The primary financial statement that shows an entity's major sources and uses of financial resources (funds) during a period. (41, 497)

statement of changes in fund balance: A formal statement prepared for a nonprofit organization; shows how the fund balance has changed from the beginning to the end of the period. (611)

statement of changes in owners' equity: A report that shows the total changes in owners' equity (including retained earnings) during a period of time. (43)

statement of partners' capital: A partnership report that reconciles the balances in the partners' equity accounts from year to year; similar to a statement of changes in retained earnings for a corporation. (463)

statement of retained earnings: A report that shows the changes in retained earnings during a period of time. (42, 443)

statement of revenues and expenditures: A formal statement prepared for a nonprofit organization; shows the relationship between actual revenues and expenditures, and may also include the budgeted amounts. (609)

static budgeting: Financial planning that establishes specified amounts of revenues, costs, and expenses that do not vary with activity level. (668, 789)

stock certificate: A document issued by a corporation to a shareholder evidencing ownership in the corporation. (426)

stock dividend: A pro rata distribution of additional shares of stock to shareholders. (435)

stockholders' equity: The ownership interest in an enterprise's assets; equals net assets (total assets minus total liabilities). (280)

stockholders (shareholders): Individuals or organizations that own a portion (shares of stock) of a corporation. (19, 426)

stock split: A reduction in the par or stated value of stock and a proportionate increase in the number of shares outstanding. (441)

straight-line depreciation method: The depreciation method in which the cost of an asset is allocated equally over the periods of the asset's estimated useful life. (336)

straight-line interest amortization: A method of systematically writing off a bond premium or discount in equal amounts each period until maturity; *compare* effective-interest amortization. (383, 404)

strategic planning: Broad, long-range planning usually conducted by top management. (786)

Subchapter S corporation: A domestic corporation legally organized in such a way that income or loss is passed through to individual shareholders without being taxed at the corporate level. (426, 948)

subsidiary company: A company owned or controlled by another company, known as the parent company. (370, 538)

subsidiary ledger: A grouping of individual accounts that in total equal the balance of a control account in the General Ledger. (93)

sum-of-the-years'-digits (SYD) depreciation method: The accelerated depreciation method in which a declining depreciation rate is multiplied by a constant balance (cost minus salvage value). (338)

sunk costs: Costs that have been incurred and that cannot be changed by current or future decisions. (679, 884)

supplies: Materials used in a business that do not generally become part of the sales product and were not purchased to be resold to customers. (137)

T

T-account: A simplified depiction of an account in the form of a letter T, showing debits on the left and credits on the right. (62)

tangible, personal, depreciable business property: Property that is used in a business and that is not considered to be real estate. (955)

target net income: A profit level desired by management. (728)

taxable income: The income remaining after all exclusions and deductions have been subtracted from gross margin. (942)

tax credit: A direct reduction in the tax liability, usually granted to encourage certain classes of taxpayers to take a particular action. (944)

tax-exempt corporation: A legal entity chartered by a state for scientific, religious, educational, charitable, or other purposes deemed beneficial to society. (949)

temporary accounts: *See* nominal accounts.

term bonds: Bonds that mature in one lump sum at a specified future date. (370)

time-period assumption (periodicity concept): The idea that the life of a business is divided into distinct and relatively short time periods so that accounting information can be timely. (106)

time ticket: A record of each production employee's hour-by-hour activities, kept so that labor costs can be assigned to the proper jobs or products. (751)

total cost: All the direct and allocated costs of a product; the total of the variable and fixed costs incurred in making the product or providing the service. (864, 883)

total variable overhead variance: The extent to which actual overhead varies from the amount included in work-in-process inventory; the difference between actual and applied overhead. (834)

traceable costs: Costs that are directly associated with and assigned to specific responsibility centers. (673)

transaction analysis: The procedures for analyzing, recording, summarizing, and reporting transactions of an entity. (54)

transactions: Exchanges of goods or services between entities (whether individuals, businesses, or other organizations), as well as other events having an economic impact on a business. (20)

transfer payment: In nonprofit accounting, a payment by one fund to another. (606)

transfer price: The monetary value assigned to goods and services exchanged between units of an organization. (864)

treasury stock: Issued stock that has subsequently been reacquired by the corporation. (428)

trial balance: A listing of all account balances; provides a means of testing whether debits equal credits for the total of all accounts. (78, 133)

U

unadjusted rate of return method: A capital budgeting technique in which a rate of return is calculated by dividing the average annual net income a project will add by the initial investment cost. (918)

underapplied overhead: The excess of actual overhead costs over the applied overhead costs for a period. (760)

unearned revenues (or advances from customers): Amounts received before they have been earned. (113, 309)

unit cost budget: An estimation of the total direct-materials, direct-labor, and overhead costs required to make one unit of a product. (801)

units-of-production depreciation method: The depreciation method in which the cost of an asset is allocated to each period on the basis of the productive output of the asset during the period. (337)

unlimited liability: The lack of a ceiling on the amount of liability a proprietor or partner must assume, meaning that if business assets are not sufficient to settle creditor claims, the personal assets of the proprietor or partners can be used to settle the claims. (458)

unrecorded expenses and accrued liabilities: Expenses not previously recognized, and companion payable accounts, that are incurred during a period but have not been paid for by the end of that period. (111)

unrecorded revenues and accrued assets: Revenues not previously recognized, and companion receivable accounts, that are earned during a period but have not been received by the end of that period. (110)

unsecured bonds: *See* debentures.

V

variable costing: A product costing approach that assigns only variable costs as product costs and treats fixed overhead costs as period expenses. *See also* absorption costing. (669, 747, 790)

variable costs: Costs that vary in total proportionately with changes in activity level within the relevant range; *compare* fixed costs. (675, 692, 865)

variable overhead: The overhead costs assigned to products (included in work-in-process) on the basis of a predetermined application rate. (754)

variable overhead efficiency variance: The difference between overhead costs budgeted at actual hours and overhead costs budgeted at standard hours. (837)

variable overhead spending variance: The difference between actual manufacturing overhead incurred and the budgeted overhead for the actual activity level. (836)

variance: Any deviation from the standard. (666, 818)

vertical analysis of financial statements: A technique for analyzing the relationships between items on an income statement or balance sheet by expressing all items as percentages. (563)

W

weighted average: A periodic inventory cost flow alternative whereby the cost of goods sold and the ending inventory are determined to be a weighted-average cost of all merchandise available for sale during the period. (246, 768)

working capital: The funds available to finance current operations; equal to current assets minus current liabilities. (279, 292, 502)

working-capital concept of funds: A concept used in preparing a funds statement that reflects transactions in which current assets or current liabilities are either increased or decreased. (499)

working capital turnover: A measure of the amount of working capital used in generating the sales of a period; computed by dividing net sales by average working capital. (572)

work-in-process: Partially completed units in production. (242, 669)

work sheet: Columnar schedule used to summarize accounting data. (132)

INDEX

B

D

J

K

L

Q

R

T

U

V

W

P15-1 Total uses of working capital, $40,000
P15-2 No key figure
P15-3 Total uses of cash, $47,000
P15-4 Increase in working capital, $320,500
P15-5 Net decrease in working capital, $736
P15-6 (1) Net increase in working capital, $442
P15-7 Total working capital from operations, $153
P15-8 Total cash from operations, $40,300
P15-9 (3) Increase in working capital, $1,248
P15-10 (1) Total sources of cash, $2,058
P15-11 (4) Cash from operations, $119,000

E16-2 Accounts receivable turnover, 5.41 times
E16-3 Inventory turnover, 4 times
E16-4 Times interest earned, 12.67 times
E16-5 (2) Increase
E16-6 Number of days' sales in inventory, 60
E16-7 Acid-test ratio, 1.36 to 1
E16-8 (2) Increase in current ratio
E16-9 (4) Net income/average stockholders' equity, 33.33%
E16-11 (2) Return on average total assets, 23.1%
E16-12 (1) Asset turnover ratio (1984), 1.6 times
E16-13 (2) Working capital turnover (1984), 3.84 times
E16-14 (1) Debt-equity management ratio (1984), 1.5 times
E16-15 (2) Book value per share (common stock), $12.67
E16-16 Price-earnings ratio, 6 to 1
P16-1 Net income—Pinehurst, 8.3%; Myrtle, 8.0%
P16-2 Net income (1984), $46,750
P16-3 (3) Accounts receivable turnover, 4.92 times.
P16-4 (2) Times interest earned, 4.55 times
P16-5 (3) Earnings per share, $5.87
P16-6 (3o) Dividend-payout ratio, 7.4%
P16-7 No key figure
P16-8 (2) Accounts receivable collection period (1984), 25 days
P16-9 (1d) Return on common stockholders' equity, 13.6%
P16-10 Price-earnings ratio, 10.8 times
P16-11 (3) Return on stockholders' equity: (change 1) 10.3%; (change 2) 8.2%; (change 3) 8%

E17-7 Excess of revenues over expenditures and encumbrances, $27,000
E17-8 Fund balance, June 30, 1984, $100,000
E17-9 Total assets, $67,000
P17-1 No key figure
P17-2 No key figure
P17-3 No key figure
P17-4 End-of-year fund balance, $26,000
P17-5 No key figure
P17-6 No key figure
P17-7 No key figure
P17-8 (1) Decrease in working capital from operations, $47,900; (2) Decrease in cash from operations, $47,600
P17-9 Appropriations, $328,000; total revenues, $343,000

Chapter 18 No key figures

Chapter 19 No key figures

E20-1 Cost of goods sold, $180,000
E20-2 Cost of goods manufactured, $106,000
E20-3 Cost of goods sold, $459,000
E20-7 By space: production, $18,000; marketing, $2,400; administration, $3,600
E20-8 (1) Materials variance, $36 U; (2) price variance, $36.50 U
E20-9 Net differential cost, $3,000
E20-10 (1) Benefit to buy, $2,000
E20-12 (1) Labor cost, Tube #24: $216
P20-1 (1) Cost of goods manufactured, $107,000
P20-2 (1) Materials quantity variance, $600 U
P20-3 (2) Traceable costs, $78,000
P20-4 (3) Estimated cost per mile, $0.17235
P20-5 (4) Cost per mile, $0.20
P20-6 (1) Net income, $16,400
P20-7 C: Net income before taxes, $29
P20-8 (1) Buy; save $25,000
P20-9 No key figure
P20-10 (1) Selling prices: product R, $34.23; product S, $42.90
P20-11 Factory supplies paid in 1985, $20,500

E21-1 (3) Profit, $15,000
E21-3 (3) $500 per unit
E21-4 (2) Total costs, $50,000
E21-5 (2) Per-unit variable cost, $2.75
E21-6 (2) Total costs, $400,000
E21-7 (3) Total costs, $48,000
E21-8 At 30,000 dolls, net income = $60,000
E21-9 (1) Net income, $17
E21-10 (4) $90,000 additional contribution margin
E21-11 (9) Contribution margin, $10,000
E21-12 (13) Little John net income, $80,000
E21-13 (3) Number of boxes, 3,333 1/3
E21-14 (2) Total costs, $166,560
E21-15 (2) $19.69
P21-1 (3) $62,500
P21-2 (2) $0.50 variable cost per unit
P21-3 (1) Fixed costs, $10,000
P21-4 (1) Net income, $8,900
P21-5 (1) Net loss, $9,900
P21-6 (5) Break-even point, 9,400 units
P21-7 (2) Break-even point, $132,000
P21-8 (3) Net income, $58,000
P21-9 (1) Fixed costs, $36,800
P21-10 Fixed costs, $760
P21-11 (2) b = $0.20
P21-12 (2) Fixed costs, $2,200
P21-13 (3) Fixed costs per month, $400
P21-14 (2) Fixed costs, $7,479

E22-1 (3) Break-even point, 75,000 units
E22-2 (2) Total variable costs, $120,000
E22-3 Case I, fixed costs per unit, $1.33
E22-4 (3) Net loss product Y, $22,000
E22-5 (4) Loss of $10,000
E22-6 (2) 700 units
E22-7 (3) $200
E22-8 (1c) 25,000 units
E22-9 (3) Net income with lathe, $35,000
E22-10 (3) 33,333 units
E22-11 (2) Net income, $156,500
E22-12 (3) Unit contribution margin, $14
E22-13 (1) Fixed costs, $50,000
E22-14 (3) Difference in break even, 1,250 units
E22-15 (2) Net income, $11,725
P22-1 (9) Net income, $715,000
P22-2 (3) Loss on donuts, $10
P22-3 (2) Number of boats, 52
P22-4 (1) Net income, $310,000
P22-5 (2) Break even, 8,154 slingshots
P22-6 (2e) Net income, $807,576
P22-7 (5) Additional profits, $12,000
P22-8 (3) Model Y profits, $35,000
P22-9 No key figure
P22-10 (2) Break-even point, $17,422

E23-2 (1) Total cost, $550
E23-3 (1) Cost of goods manufactured in B, $280,000
E23-4 (1c) 1983 overhead application rate, 20%
E23-5 (3) Applied overhead, $16,500
E23-7 (2) Cost of goods manufactured, $500,000
E23-8 (1) Cost of goods manufactured, $766,000
E23-9 (1) Completed units transferred to finished goods, 570
E23-10 (2) Cost of goods transferred, $13,160
E23-11 (3) Cost of ending inventory, $26,640
E23-12 (2) $3.3641
E23-13 (3) Total cost of oil transferred, $73,973
E23-14 (3) Incomes could be the same
E23-15 (1) Difference in net income, $800
P23-1 Entry 11, underapplied overhead, $2,300
P23-2 (2) Cost of goods sold, $788,000
P23-3 (6) Work-in-Process Inventory, ending balance, $23,000
P23-4 (2) Cost of goods manufactured, $1,031,400
P23-5 (4) Overapplied overhead, $2,162
P23-6 (1) Process 2 output in equivalent units, 21,100